OVERSIZE 971.0049 M389u 1982

Marunchak, Mykhailo H.,
1914-

The Ukrainian Canadians

Rochester Public Library

General Pulaski
Community Library
1151 Hudson Avenue
Rochester, N.Y. 14621-3598

JAN 1 3 1993

THE UKRAINIAN CANADIANS:
A HISTORY

ІСТОРІЯ
УКРАЇНЦІВ КАНАДИ

L'HISTOIRE

DES UKRAINIENS-CANADIENS

Par

MICHAEL H. MARUNCHAK

Winnipeg   1982   Ottawa

L'ACADÈMIE UKRAINIENNE
DES ARTS ET SCIENCES (UVAN)
AU CANADA

THE UKRAINIAN CANADIANS:
A HISTORY

by

MICHAEL H. MARUNCHAK

Winnipeg   1982   Ottawa

UKRAINIAN ACADEMY
OF ARTS AND SCIENCES (UVAN)
IN CANADA

Copyright, Canada, 1970,
by the author.

Second Edition
Supplemented and reprinted
with corrections, 1982

Canadian Cataloguing in Publication Data

FC106-U5M3   1982
FI035-U5M3   1982
971.00491791   C83-090006-3

Printed by Friesen Printers, Altona, Manitoba

THIS WORK HAS BEEN PUBLISHED WITH
THE ASSISTANCE OF A GRANT FROM THE
UKRAINIAN CANADIAN FOUNDATION OF
TARAS SHEVCHENKO AND SUBSIDIZED BY
THE DEPARTMENT OF MULTICULTURALISM
IN OTTAWA

FOREWORD
To the First Edition

It would be difficult to find another study which covers more ground. It is undoubtedly the most detailed description of the religious, social, economic and political development of the Ukrainian ethnic group (in 1961 the fourth largest ethnic group in Canada). Dr. Marunchak is one of the main contributors in the study of Ukrainians in Canada as the formidable list of his historical books testifies. All of his works however have been published in the Ukrainian language and therefore are not easily accessible to other than Ukrainian historians and readers. The present study was also originally written in Ukrainian and later translated into English.[1]

The Author was born October 4, 1914 in the village of Dalesheva in the district of Horodenka, Galicia, then part of the Austro-Hungarian Empire (later Western Ukraine), son of Hryhoriy and Maria Marunchak. He attended primary school in his native village and secondary school (classic gymnasium "Ridna Shkola" of Taras Shevchenko) in the city of Horodenka. On graduation he became a law student at the University of Lviv. The Second World War interrupted his studies and nearly ruined his life. However he managed to complete his studies later at the University of Prague, Czechoslovakia, obtained his LL.D. and also attended social science and history courses at the Ukrainian Free University in Prague.

The years of his youth coincided with the most turbulent years which shook not only his native land but the whole of the civilized world as well. His participation in political events began when he was only sixteen years old. Polish authorities arrested him, together with other students, during the notorius "pacification" of 1930. "The bloody *pacification* lasted from September 16 to November 30, 1930, during which over 700 villages were terrorized. Men and women were dragged from their homes and beaten with clubs...[2]

He was again arrested by the Polish police at the beginning of the Second World War for participation in the Ukrainian independence movement but was liberated by his compatriots who assisted him to escape and to go into hiding. The German Gestapo caught up with him again in 1942 and he spent three years in the concentration camps of Theresienstadt, Auschwitz, Mauthausen, Melk and Ebensee to be released with the advent of the Allied Army after Hitler's defeat. For the next few years he shared the lot of displaced persons and took a lively part in the life of the Ukrainian community in Germany. He served as President of the League of Ukrainian Political Prisoners in Europe, and refused the Soviet invitation to displaced persons "to return to the homeland". He chose freedom, emigrating to Canada instead. On arrival in Canada he immediately joined the long established Ukrainian community. Having acquired a fair command of the English language he entered the Social Work Department of the University of Manitoba and on completion of his studies became a Social Worker. During the last fifteen years he was employed as School Social Worker in the system of the Child Guidance Clinic of Greater Winnipeg. At the same time he became deeply interested in the history of Ukrainian settlement in Canada, in the history of the growth and development of their social and religious life, cultural-educational work, and in the pioneer settlers themselves. His literary and academic achievements merited him membership in the Ukrainian Shevchenko Scientific Society and Fellowship in the Ukrainian Free Academy of Sciences in Canada. He was made Member of the Presidium of the Academy and Chairman of its Historical Section. In 1961 he became the recipient of the Shevchenko Medal from the Ukrainian Canadian Committee and in 1967 the recipient of the Canadian Centennial Medal. The Ukrainian Canadian Committee appointed Dr. Marunchak Chairman of its Political Commission which position he held for ten years until three years ago.

The list of his historical studies is formidable indeed. They cover thousands of pages and deal with the whole period of Ukrainian immigration to Canada. They are based on contemporary documentary material, on researches conducted in places of original settlements, on memoirs and personal interviews, and are thus a most valuable source of information for historians of the Canadian West.

The present study, "The Ukrainian Canadians: A History" doubtless will be read with appreciation not only by scholars in the Slavic field but by the general public as well. It is a complete account of all aspects of the Ukrainian ethnic group in Canada, from its very beginnings to the present time. It covers full 732 pages of text and with bibliography and additions reaches 800 pages.

A brief survey of topics dealt with in the study will give a picture of the scope covered.

The study is divided into three main sections corresponding to the three phases of Ukrainian immigration to Canada. Each section contains a number of chapters dealing with various topics. The first section bears the title "First Era — Pioneer Era" and starts with the description of social and political factors conducive to emigration. It stresses the important role played by Dr. Josef Oleskow (Osyp Oleskiw), the "Promoter of Mass Movement of Ukrainian Settlers to Canada", and is followed by the description of the immigration movement from its very beginnings to the outbreak of the First World War in 1914. The author describes the geographic distribution of Ukrainian settlements established during the pioneer era, recounts the difficulties encountered by the newcomers in a strange land and dwells more amply on the "First Steps" in Canada. He further discusses religious and educational problems which to the pioneer settlers were of paramount importance, describes the establishment of public schools in rural districts settled by Ukrainians, the founding of private schools and students' institutes (bursas) to enable the sons and daughters of pioneer settlers to proceed to towns to continue their studies in high schools, normal colleges and universities. The chapter on "Cultural and Educational Work" describes these activities according to provinces. Of particular interest is the chapter "The Press". Precisely and meticulously prepared, supplies an excellent description of the beginnings of the "written word". During the early period of immigration, up to 1903, the American weekly "Svoboda" (Liberty), served the pioneer settlers as the only medium of printed communication. The paper carried regularly a Canadian section for that purpose. In 1903 this task was taken over by the first Ukrainian language newspaper to be published in Canada, the Canadian Farmer. With the growth of the numbers of settlers this also increased the number of publications which gave birth to the "Literature of the Pioneers" described in the following chapter.

The second section of the study, "The Second Era — Era of Developmental Processes" covers the between the wars period. It is equally divided into a number of chapters, starting with an introduction and continuing with the description of the founding of numerous social, political and economic organizations, such as the Ukrainian Self-Reliance League of Canada, Ukrainian Catholic Brotherhood, Ukrainian National Federation, Ukrainian Labour and Farmers' Temple Association, United Hetman Organization and many others. The chapter on "Churches and Religious Orders" is followed by the very well prepared chapter on "The Press" and literary activities of the group.

The third section is entitled "The Third Era — Era of Consummation". It starts a preceding section, with an introduction which is followed by the description of "Ukrainian War Efforts during World War II". The chapter deals also with the post-World-War-Two immigration, the "Social Structure of Third Immigration" and its distribution in Canada. The author dwells on the achievements of the Ukrainian ethnic group during the decades of their sojourn in Canada, and points to their integration into Canadian life. A separate chapter deals with the "Church Life", its component parts, the Ukrainian Catholic Church, the Ukrainian Greek Orthodox Church, the Ukrainian Evangelical Alliance and the Ukrainian Evangelical Baptist Alliance. Of particular interest is the description of the emergence of new organizations and societies, such as the Ukrainian Canadian Veterans' Association composed of Ukrainian Branches of the Royal Canadian Legion; the Ukrainian Canadian Council of Learned Societies, Ukrainian Free Academy of Sciences in Canada, Ukrainian Shevchenko Society, Ukrainian Canadian Research Foundation and many others. Of great importance was the bringing together of existing organizations to form a unified overall body, the Ukrainian Canadian Committee. The teaching of "Ukrainian Language in Public Schools and Universities" is the subject of a separate chapter, it also deals with the description of existing private schools in all parts of Canada. The chapter on "The Press" has such sub-headings as: Weeklies, Toronto and the East, Winnipeg and the West, Catholic Press, Orthodox Press, Protestant or Evangelical Press. It ends with the author's description of the "Characteristics of the Press". There is also a chapter on "Radio, Television and Film" and in conclusion the author's observation on "Horizontal and Vertical Integration" of the Ukrainian society, its activities on the political arena, in the Provincial Legislative Assemblies, in the Federal House of Commons and the Senate. The study concludes with the description of the "Ideological Principles in the Ukrainian Canadian History" and the aspirations of Ukrainian Canadians.

Dr. M. H. Marunchak's study "The Ukrainian Canadians: A History" deserves to be put on the shelves of all Universities and Public Libraries as a valuable contribution to the history of Canada in general, and as a reference book on the Ukrainian ethnic group.

Of particular interest are the numerous (and rare) photos of persons mentioned in the study, pictures of pioneer settlements, churches and photographic reproductions of the front pages of newspapers published in the pioneer era, most of these not seen by students of Ukrainian press.

V. J. KAYE.
Ottawa, Ontario

Footnotes on next page.

¹Some of Dr. M. H. Marunchak's Historical Studies:

Studii do istorii ukrainciv Kanady / Studies in the History of Ukrainians in Canada — Published by the Ukrainian Free Academy of Sciences in Canada, in five Volumes:
  Volume I. Shotlandski poselenci ta ukrainska hromada v Point Douglas / The Selkirk Settlers and the Ukrainian Community in Point Douglas. Winnipeg: 1964-1965. Pp. 255. Text in Ukrainian, Acknowledgements and Preface by Senator Paul Yuzyk in English.
  Volume II. Istoria suspilno-kulturnoho rostu ukrainciv Manitoby. Pionerska doba / History of Socio-Cultural Development of Ukrainians in Manitoba. Pioneer Era. Winnipeg: 1966-1967. Pp. 544. Text in Ukrainian, Preface by Dr. M. I. Mandryka and the Foreword by the Author in English.
  Volume III. Istoria presy, literatury i druku pionerskoi doby / The Press, Literature, and Publication in the Pioneer Era. Winnipeg: 1968-1969. Pp.284. Text in Ukrainian, Introduction by Prof. J. B. Rudnyckyj in English. (Second Edition in 1969).
  Volume IV. Narysy, statti, eseyi do Pionerskoi doby / Sketches, Articles, Essays to the Pioneers' Era. Winnipeg: 1970-1972. Pp. 311. Text in Ukrainian, Introduction by Dr. M. I. Mandryka in English.
  Volume V. Rozvidky ta dokumenty do Mizhvoiennoi doby / Essays and Documents to the Interwar Era. Winnipeg: 1973-1980. Pp. 299. Text in Ukrainian, documents in English. Introduction by Dr. M. Ewanchuk in English.
  Istoria Ukrainciw Kanady. Tom I / The Ukrainian Canadians — A History. Volume I. Published by the Ukrainian Free Academy of Sciences in Canada: Winnipeg 1969. Pp. 467. Text in Ukrainian.
  Istoria Ukrainciv Kanady. Tom II / The Ukrainian Canadians — A History. Volume II. Published by the Ukrainian Free Academy of Sciences in Canada: Winnipeg 1974. Pp. 512. Text in Ukrainian.
  Petro-Hawrysychyn — pioneer-budivnychyi Shashkevychivskoi dilnyci. Point Douglas u Winnipegu / Petro Hawrysyshyn — Pioneer Builder of Shashkevych Centre (Point Douglas) in Winnipeg. Ukrainian Canadian Pioneer's Library. Winnipeg: 1962-1963. Pp. 110. Text in Ukrainian, Editor's Note by Prof. J. B. Rudnyckyj in English.
  V zustrichi z ukrainskymy pioneramy Alberty / Among Ukrainian Pioneers in Alberta. General Library "UKT": Winnipeg 1964. Pp. 88. Text in Ukrainian, introductory note in English.
  Kanadiyska Terebovla / Canadian Terebowla (Trembowla). The Site of the First Ukrainian Church Service. General Library "UKT" Winnipeg 1964. Pp. 40. Text in Ukrainian, Introduction by the Publishers in English.
  Ukrainci v SSSR poza kordonamy URSR / Ukrainians in USSR Beyond the Borders of Ukrainian SSR. Published by Ukrainian Free Academy of Sciences in Canada, Winnipeg: 1974- . Pp. 248. Text in Ukrainian.
  Ukrainci v Rumunii, Checho — Slovachchyni, Polshchi, Yugoslavii / Ukrainians in Rumania, Czechoslovakia, Poland, Jugoslavia. Published by the General Library, Winnipeg: 1969. Pp. 68. Text in Ukrainian.
  Zmahannia za nezalezhnist Ukrainskoi Cerkvy v Kanadi / Struggle for the Self-rule of the Ukrainian Church in Canada. Published by Sts. Volodymyr and Olha Cathedral in Winnipeg 1966-1967. Pp. 99. Text in Ukrainian.
  Do orthanizaciynykh prochatkiw Ukrainskoi Katolyckoi Cerkvy v Kanadi i ZSA / Organizational Beginnings of the Ukrainian Catholic Church in Canada and U.S.A. Published by the Council of Ukrainian Organizations for the Patriarchate of the Ukrainian Catholic Church, 1978. Pp. 31. Text in Ukrainian.
  On the 80th Anniversary of Fr. Nestor Dmytriw's Sojourn in Canada. Published by the Ukrainian National Association in U.S.A. Canada, 1977. Pp. 20 Tabloid. Text in Ukrainian and English.
  Istoria kolonizacii Ukrainy / History of Colonization of Ukraine, condenced lectures read at the Ukrainian Catholic University at Rome. Rome: Ukrainian Catholic University of St. Clement, 1975. Pp. 20. Mimeographed Edition with added maps.

²Yaremko, Michael. **Galicia-Halychyna.** From Separation to Unity. Shevchenko Scientific Society. Toronto-New York-Paris: 1967. P. 241.

PUBLISHER'S INTRODUCTION
To the Second Edition

With great satisfaction we present to the readers this second, revised, supplemented and up-dated edition comprising the research studies by Dr. Michael Marunchak: "The Ukrainian Canadians: A History." It encompasses the complete history of the 90 year settlement of Ukrainians in Canada from 1891-1981.

This history represents the growth and development of the Ukrainian Canadian community in all aspects of life. It comprises cultural, educational, professional life, economics, political and church activities and others. This is a history of achievements in the fields of arts, research, humanities and science. This is also a constant struggle for the preservation and enhancement of cultural values of the nation. It is indeed, a daily strife for cultural existence, a strife of the community for its identity and a place in multicultural Canada.

The first edition of this history appeared in 1970 and received high evaluation from the professional literary critics. Reviews were printed in daily papers and journals, (Winnipeg Free Press, Winnipeg Tribune, Edmonton Journal, Ottawa Citizen, Slavic Revue) as well as in most of the Ukrainian newspapers in diaspora. An anglophone critic expressed himself in the following words about this first edition.

"Ukrainian Canadians, thanks to the research of Dr. Marunchak now have one of the most substantial histories of any Canadian ethnic groups. Indeed, only the French and Scots have histories that match Marunchak's work, in size. This solid volume may be accurately described as encyclopedic in scope and it is for this reason perhaps the single most useful book on the half million Ukrainian Canadian community."

This new edition of history is far more extensive. It comprises the 90 year existence of the Ukrainian Canadian community. To the 1970 edition there is added the succeeding ten years which the author call the *"Decade of Multiculturalism"* that began in 1971 when this basic principle of *Canadian Multiculturalism* was finally announced in Parliament and approved by political parties. This added chapter contains close to two hundred pages of research work dealing with our present era.

The author also enlarged indexes, especially the subject index, which enables the reader to easily find the required material in this approximately 1000 page book. New research sources were supplemented, particularly in this decade. Inevitable errors that had crept into the first edition were corrected. The enlarged chapter is enriched by historical pictures of the 1970's. For those who financially supported the high cost of publication, a separate pamphlet has been prepared with an appreciation of their contribution and generosity. The publishers provided an artistically designed book cover by the late renowned cartoonist Peter Kuch.

The book reviewer quoted earlier ends his evaluation with the following statement:

"In conclusion it might be said that: *"The Ukrainian Canadians: A History"*, by Michael Marunchak is a great achievement for one scholar to research and for an ethnic community to produce. Intelligent Ukrainian Canadians who realize that knowledge of the record of the past contributes to a knowledge of the present will want to have this book in their library. This history is highly recommended for every university, college and library in Canada."*

These well-earned recommendations about the first edition may also apply to the revised edition which comprises a fuller and more proficient appearance. It is worthwhile to add: This book should be found on bookshelves of homes so that the young Canadian generation which suffers from a lack of basic sources about their past have a reliable source of information. From this book they will get knowledge about their cultural heritage and appreciation of the hard work put in by their ancestors who, so gloriously, helped to build Canada into a mighty nation of the future. This book is an excellent source of information for every reader and especially for the student of history.

**Forum,* A Ukrainian Review, Scranton, U.S.A., Fall 1971, Andrew Gregorovich, Scarborough and Erindale College Libraries, University of Toronto.

ACKNOWLEDGEMENTS
To the First Edition

There is nothing more pleasant for the author, at the conclusion of his work, than to express his indebtedness and deepest gratitude to all those who, either through words or deeds, have so graciously infused themselves into this worthwhile project.

This history book, which we are now placing into the hands of our readers, began to form itself during the life span of those Ukrainian pioneers who still remember very clearly the first far off beginnings, closely entwined with the lives of the Ukrainian settlers in Canada.

It is only fitting and proper to mention here such outstanding pioneer figures as Vasyl and Ivan Romaniuk, P. Svarich, T. Tomashevsky, Maria Tanchak, N. V. Bachynsky, T. Bodnar, J. Hrushovy, D. Lobay and others. These and others like them form the advancing phalanx of those deserving souls through whose numerous correspondence and personal talks the author was supplied with the needed information for his work and their sincere encouragements helped to set the favourable climate for the writing mood. Following in the footsteps of the above individuals, and others not here recalled, a second generation came to fill the breach in the never-ending march of history. Here we take pride to single out such illustrious names as Rev. D. Popovych, OSBM., M. Pohorecky, W. Kossar, W. Kochan, S. Wolynec and others who, while recognizing the great value of the role that history plays in the life of its people, also look upon it as a true mirror which clearly reveals the hidden psychological processes that take place in the unifying force of the nation.

Tied closely to this work was the help rendered by such rugged individuals and highly rated historians as Senator Paul Yuzyk and Dr. V. J. Kaye. Not only do they merit sincere appreciation for their professional evaluation and advice but they also have earned a well-deserving "thank you" from the author on whose behalf they submitted an unconditional recommendation to the Centennial Commission in Ottawa.

The author of this book has been singularly fortunate in having had, at his advice, a long array of generous individuals who hastened to his aid by opening up their rich archives for his benefit, and others who have sent in numerous publications consisting of books, journals, documents, pictures and other printed and written material. Here we take time to list a few names of the owners whose collections have been of greatest service to the author. These include W. Mihaychuk, K. S. Prodan, J. J. Ruryk, D. Gerych, A. Kurdydyk, D. M. Elcheshen, P. J. Lazarowich, M. Petrowsky, M. H. Boykowich, M. Chypchar, S. F. Porayko, S. Pawluk, M. Boychuk, A. Gregorovich, D. Fodchuk and from the United States of America — J. Panchuk and T. Hrycyk.

A separate recognition of valuable services given towards the completion of this all-encompassing volume is reserved for the following: M. Luchkovich, W. Mihaychuk, O. E. Miles Malycky, S. Urchak, A. J. Yaremovich, M. H. Hykawy, A. Zaharychuk, D. Stasiuk, M. Petrowsky, H. Hawryluk,

M. Paley, and especially for the untiring labour of V. Barabash who devoted a great deal of time and effort to expidite preparation of material for the publishers.

We are greatly indebted to Wm. J. Prochuk and M. A. Negrich who expertly handled the technical side of the script and the final editing of the completed work.

In the department of photography the assignment was capably carried out by A. Kuziw who in addition also assisted in safeguarding the valuable collection of cuts and photography.

The key to this history book lies wrapped in its diverse and abundant index. Here again a great amount of labour was expended by V. Barabash and A. Kuziw in order to scan and record, in detail, every single page.

Undoubtedly the greatest boost toward the printing of this history book was provided first, by the Canadian Centennial Commission and later on by the Ukrainian Canadian Foundation of Taras Shevchenko and the Ukrainian Free Academy of Sciences. To these Foundations and to all other benefactors, both named and unnamed, who in larger or smaller degree helped us with the work of this publication the author extends his deepest gratitude.

And finally — the responsibility for the contents of this volume, both, its good points and shortcomings, rests exclusively upon the shoulders of the author.

ACKNOWLEDGEMENTS
Second Edition

A number of people contributed to this edition. The author is especially indebted to those who contributed with their essays on special topics: I. Keywan, P. Savaryn, Y. Sokolyk, Z. Hrycenko-Luhovy, B. Stebelsky, Y. Stefanyk.

Special thanks go to those who supplied indispensable and needed material Stefania Yurkiwsky, G. Zerebecky, V. Balan, St. Groch, B. Bilash, E. Roslycky, I. Bodnarchuk, W. Didiuk, W. Makar, Y. Temnyk, M. Shebets, L. Fil, M. Figol, V. Pedenko, Maria Doliszny, St. Haras, A. Wach, Vera Buchynsky, M. Chomiak, M. Gawa, Rev. T. Minenko and Rev. J. Iwaskiw.

Immensely grateful to V. Barabash, J. D. Bzowy, G. Hnatiuk, who handled the technical side of the manuscript and expedited preparation of material for the publisher.

The author acknowledges with gratitude also the voluntary contributions made by such individuals as Halia B. Charney, Anne Smigel, Michael Negrich, Olenka Negrych, Christine Krucko, Lew Kurdydyk.

Special thanks are directed to A. J. Yaremovich and Vera Birakowska-Marchuk for their final linguistic touch to the manuscript.

Especially and profoundly grateful to those who helped financially to carry burden of the publication and especially to the noble pioneer Domka Babij of Toronto. The names of other founders and donors are in a special booklet attached to this volume.

The cooperation of all is gratefully acknowledged.

THE FIRST ERA

PIONEER ERA

EXPLANATORY NOTE

There is no uniform system of transliteration of surnames. The spelling used is that adopted by each of the individuals mentioned. The reader will find, e.g., "Yuriy" appears as Yuri, Yurey, Jurij; "Yaroslav" as Jaroslaw, Yaroslaw; "Vasyl" as Wasyl; "Volodymyr" as Wolodymyr, Volodimir; "Boris" as Borys; "Mariyka" as Marika; "Lesia" as Lesya; "Mykhaylo" as Mykhailo, etc. The author preferred legal transliteration rather than literary uniformity.

Transliteration of place names and surnames from Ukraine are rendered in generally accepted transliteration. Where quotations are used the original spelling of names was retained, often differing from the accepted version.

In some cases where two versions appear, preference was given to the first version or the one which index indicates.

The words Galician, Bukovinian, Ruthenian, which in the early period of Ukrainian immigration were generally used instead of the proper designation "Ukrainian", have been retained in quotations from documents or contemporary writings.

SOCIAL AND POLITICAL FACTORS IN UKRAINIAN IMMIGRATION TO CANADA

In order to totally merge oneself in the history of the Ukrainian Canadians, their arrival into this country, and the further growth and progress of this country's new community, as well as to understand the processes involved in this development, it would be worthwhile to explore the pages of history of their forebears and, at least in general terms become informed of the political and social factors which gave rise to the mass immigration of these people not only to Canada but to other countries as well.

History is quite cognizant of the emigration of various peoples. To the most ancient emigrations can be added the wanderings and settlement of the Jewish people in Egypt and the subsequent return to their former homeland. We know of the peregrination of the Greeks and their settlement on the Aegean Islands and contiguous territories. We, too, have read of the Phoenicians wanderings and how a whole people in total made settlements elsewhere. To such a category can be added the Hungarians, the Tartars and the Bulgarians and others. With the discovery of America, hundreds of thousands of alien peoples from Europe resettled on this continent and in South America. Leading this movement were the Anglo-Saxons, Romanic and German peoples, and later on, the Slavs: Czechs, Poles, Slovaks, Russians, Serbs, Croats and Ukrainians.

Every exodus and resettlement of the people can be explained by some basic reason. Frequently the intolerant behaviour of the superimposed races or even of separate classes, was the cause of mass resettlements. Those denominations which settled on the North American continent, such as the Quakers, Mennonites, Hutterites, Dukhobors, can here serve as classic examples of emigrations. More frequent causes of emigration were socio-economic and political factors, particularly, colonial exploitation over subjugated peoples. The Irish, the Poles, the Czechs and the Slovaks, may be regarded as a case in point. The Ukrainians also appear to fit the general category. The social and political oppressions which arose in Ukraine during several centuries resulted in the fact that the husbandmen of the land, known universally as the "Bread Basket of Europe", were being compelled by force of circumstances to abandon their native land and "leave home into the unknown" in the words of the poet. It is quite evident that the social and political pressures must have left their mark on those who fled from them and sought better economic and political accord.

How was it then that this 45,000,000 Ukrainian nation had found itself in such unfortunate circumstances?

Ukrainian history dates back to the end of the 8th Century. In 988 this nation had accepted Christianity from the East. The capital of this state was Kiev, an eminently cultured city, situated far inland in Eastern Europe. The Polish historian Zakrzewski wrote that Kiev, in the 11-12 centuries, was for the Ukrainian cities at that time what Rome was in its time for the Germanic tribes. The Kievan state, which bore the name Rus, lasted until the 13th century. The Mongolian invasion of Genghis Khan from Asia dealt a devastating blow to Kievan Rus in 1239, from which it took a long time to recover.

More meaningful was the case, at this time, of the Western-Ukrainian lands: Galicia, Volyn and Sub-Carpathia. Soon after the fall of the Kievan state the Ukrainian people not only had to contend with the Asiatic nomads but also to defend themselves against pressure from monarchical Poland in the West; and on the North they had to ward off the Muscovite aggression. This was a new power which grew up behind the back of the Kievan State. All the same, when later on there appeared on the scene the Lithuanian-Rus Princedom, the dominating culture of that State was the Kievan Rus culture. This fact spoke eloquently for the high level of culture during that ancient period. The Polish aristocracy cleverly took advantage of the vacuum left in Southern Ukraine as a result of the Tartar invasions, gradually taking possession of these devastated lands. The Ukrainian Cossack State, with an elected Hetman as its head, which represented the Kievan State in the 15th-16th centuries, strongly objected to this state of affairs. This resistance took on large scale proportions during the rule of Bohdan Khmelnytsky who organized a mass military crusade against the Polish king, inflicting heavy losses upon the Polish armies in 1648. But now with three fronts lined up against him he was forced to relinquish one of them, signing a peace treaty with the northern enemy, Moscow, in 1654 in the city Pereyeslav. This was the beginning of Khmelnytsky's downfall.

Moscow, the other party to the treaty, took advantage of it by waiting for an opportunity to double-cross the Ukrainians; and so in 1667 Moscow agreed with Poland whereby the Western Ukrainian lands would be given over to the dictatorship of Poland while the Eastern Ukrainian territories were retained by Moscow. The Ukrainians naturally did not agree with such a situation, and so the following years were noted for the fierce struggle of the Ukrainians for their independence.

The crowning military opposition against the imperialistic policy of Moscow was the battle of Poltava in 1709 when the Hetman of Ukraine, Ivan Mazepa, in alliance with the Swedish king Charles XII, conducted the whole military campaign in defence of Ukrainian liberty. The unsuccessful battle of Poltava was but the forerunner of further Muscovite inroads in the direction of the complete liquidation of Ukrainian rights and liberties. In 1745 the Hetmanic system was abolished. In 1775 the Zaporozhian Sitch was liquidated as the last bastion of Ukrainian liberties. While Moscow was establishing political control and russification in Ukraine, Poland was erecting serfdom and polonization in Western Ukrainian lands. The XVIII century was marked by the failure of Ukrainian efforts and the ultimate enslavement of its people, both politically and socially. Half of the cultivated lands came into the hands of the great landlords. In both occupations serfdom was established. The peasants were obligated to work several days of each week as the landlord's portion. They were not allowed without the permission of the "pan " (lord) to transfer to another place. In order to keep the people in ignorance, there was no stress on education, but instead distilleries and taverns were established in the villages. The peasants drank themselves out of their last coin or product and so this made them further dependent on their masters, the landlords and the innkeepers. The landlords had the right to appoint the clergy to administrative posts as well as to the parishes. Often the owner of these "rights" sold them to the inn-keepers. It often happened that social differentiation took place along the lines of national appurtenance.

The landlords on Western Ukrainian lands were for the most part Poles, and on Eastern Ukrainian lands they were Russians. Trade and commerce passed into Jewish hands while most of the Ukrainians were peasants. All this did not exclude the exceptions. Simultaneously with social pressure, there was also a national and political suppression. In the western lands which came into Polish possession, this pressure was exercised by degrees until in 1772 these territories by the partition of Poland were taken over by Austrian rule. Historians claim that it is by reason of the lack of sound social basis in monarchical Poland that brought about the collapse of the state, and that the partitions of Poland took place almost without any armed opposition. The large masses of the enslaved Polish and Ukrainian people did not wish to take part in the defence of a country where exploitation by man over man existed for centuries. The transfer of Ukrainian lands under the rule of Austria in 1772 in no way had changed the social dependence of the wide classes of the peasantry upon the great Polish landlords. When the "Springtime of the Nations" had come to Europe, only then was serfdom liquidated in Galicia and Bukovina. The condition of social enslavement on the eastern lands was annulled in 1861, but political conditions were not changed. Almost simultaneously with the social enslavement under the Tsarist rule, were the pressures on the intellectual circles to wipe out the Ukrainian language off the face of the earth. The Russian Minister of Interior, Valuev, publicly proclaimed: "There is not, there never was, there never will be a Ukrainian language".

Thirteen years later by an "Ukase" (edict) from Moscow all publications in the Ukrainian language were banned. Later on the pressures under Tsarist rule were somewhat relaxed, and under Austrian rule they also were eased in the national-cultural field. By degrees, cultural and then political resurrection of the people took place. The banner year of this revival was in 1848. The current romanticism and the "Springtime of the Nations" drew the attention of the peoples to the ordinary man, his feelings and rights, and finally to the whole nation. The despotic tsarist regime likewise could not oppose these currents. But these changes came about slowly. They cost the Ukrainians jail terms, and often, bloody sacrifices. The struggle for better conditions was opposed by the big landlords who with the abolition of serfdom lost a gratuitous labor, political influence and prestige. Although the peasantry slowly recovered its influence over the local administration and rid itself of serfdom, it could not, however, improve its material position. The wide expanses of land were still left in the hands of the big land owners, while the peasants continued to live on dwarfed economies. Half of the land which belonged to the peasants on western Ukrainian territories, were economies of less than two hectares. Only 17% of the economies were self-sufficient and their size varied from 5-10 hectares. The matter appeared somewhat better in eastern Ukrainian lands. The agrarian question seemed most tragic in Sub-Carpathia. Count Schoenborn held in his own possession 20% of the land, and a large part was held by the Hungarian barons. Therefore very little was left for the peasants. For the most part there were small economies. In 1873 according to statistics, there were 59,453 economies in Sub-Carpathia with shares of up to 2.85 hectares; 85% of the village population were occupied in the village economy; and in industry and transport the percentage was only 9.6%.

It is particularly in social and political pressures that one must seek the reasons for Ukrainian emigration. It is self-evident that the small landholders, as well as the average land owners, sought additional income in order to survive. It was not only because of the dearth of land that the people felt the pinch,—heavy taxes, high prices for industrial products such as clothing and farm machinery, were additional causes. In proportion to all this, farm production was low and was usually bought up by the traders at low prices. This is a typical picture in the economy of agricultural countries.

When the curtain of enslavement was finally drawn up and people began to think and feel that the state become the protector of their inerests, they began to seek methods whereby, through organized force, they could build a favorable political system. Thus began the fierce struggle for the rights of the people, and emigration was the demonstrative-passible manifestation of this struggle.

In the first half of the 19th century there were two notable emigrations from Ukraine. From Galicia there emigrated a large group of Ukrainians to Bachka under Hungarian rule, and at present Yugoslavia. From the eastern lands, a considerable portion of the population resettled in Asia, firstly in "Zeleny Klyn" (Green Wedge), not far from the Pacific Ocean, and then further into Siberia. This settlement, for the most part, was taken advantage of by the Ukrainians who were under Muscovite rule. The Ukrainians who were under Austro-Hungarian rule, that is, from Galicia and Bukovina, profited the most from seasonal earnings, especially from work in Prussia, France, and Hungary. But this, however, did not completely solve the earning necessities of the peasantry. The eyes of the peasants were turned westward, to North America, to which the settlers from western Europe flocked by the thousands. The eastern Europeans did not have the same rights as their western neighbours.

But the time came when the situation also changed, and improved, for the peoples of eastern Europe. The United States of North America facilitated the entry of eastern Europeans somewhat earlier than Canada. When emigration to the United States began in the late 1800's, particularly to solve the labor shortage in the coal-mines of Pennsylvania, Ukrainians from Sub-Carpathia took advantage of the opportunity offered. According to the estimate of some statisticians during the fifty years of emigration (1870-1920) from Sub-Carpathia alone, over 430,000 of the population left the country. This was more or less the same number of persons as remained at home. "The desire to emigrate became an epidemic", wrote the bishop of Mukachiv to the premier at Budapest. "The population by the hundreds have left their villages behind them, selling their houses, also their movables and real estate property at any price in order to raise money for the fares for their families" [1]. During the 8-year period (1900-1907) the emigration to the U.S.A. and Canada rose to 81,409 persons [2]. The picture was similar in Galicia, which, during the period of increased emigration to Canada, was composed of 83% of rural population, the majority of them working on meagre and non-profitable farms. The statistical table of 1902 speaks eloquently of this Galician situation:

---

[1] State Archives of Sub-Carpathian region, p. 151, op. 2.
[2] Educational Anthology of "Prosvita", yearly XIII-XIV. Uzhorod, 1938, pp. 25-26.

Measure of land in hectares	Number of economies	on a % basis	Amount of land in thousands of hectares	
To 2	278,991	42.7	371.4	7.2
2.5	242,727	37.2	035.4	20.0
5-10	44,843	14.6	866.8	16.7
10,100	31,848	4.9	820.963	15.83
over 100	3,895	0.6	2089.0	40.3

The economy of Bukovina was even less advanced. At the end of the last century the population numbered over 800,000, 90% of which was engaged in agriculture. According to established data, 16% of the population did not even own a furrow of land, 42% of the farms were composed of no more than 3 hectares of land apiece, while 26,000 economies lived on leased land [3].

Incidents took place where the villagers made combined pleas to the administration to allow them to emigrate because the economic circumstances were of such a nature that there was a constant threat of starvation. The period 1899-1900 already numbers thousands of emigrants; even in the first decade of the past century there emigrated to the U.S.A., and more so to Canada, 34,000 persons [4]. It is interesting to note that all the governmental statistics of Austro-Hungary inform us that besides official data registered by the government there were many emigrants who left the country without registering. In other words, they left secretly. There was a stiff sentence for illegal emigration. These rigid demands applied foremostly on territories that owed allegiance to Hungary, namely, Sub-Carpathia. During one year alone 115 persons were sentenced in the Uhochansky Komitat (District); in the Berezhky, 502; in the Marmarosky, 79, in the Uzansky, 984 [5]. In order to discourage this mass emigration and suppress the movement, the official factors gravely decided to approach the problem as if it were "an emigration epidemic". Discussions and conferences took place in Chernivtsi, the capital of Bukovina. The regional administration factors of the territory, following a consultation in the spring of 1901 officially certified that, "emigration is a symptom of a sick condition which depends upon the premise that the wide classes of the Ukrainian population under the circumstances of their dwarfed economies are unable to safeguard their existence" [6].

This conference, as well as the others, did not mention the political pressures which were an additional misfortune of the population that not only yearned for economic prosperity but national and social liberty. In answer to this Ivan Franko, spiritual leader of the wide Ukrainian masses of that time, wrote addressing the current powers that be: "If, Sirs, you do not desire emigration to America (e.g., the U.S.A. and Canada), as well as South America, please apply yourself... to the betterment of peasantry's economic and social situation" [7].

---

[3] Wiadomosci statystyczne o stosunkach krajowych, T. XX, 3. II, Lwów 1908, t. 5, pp. 72-73.
[4] Protokole der Auswanderungs-Konferenzen, p. 31.
[5] Educational Anthology of "Prosvita" Society, yearly XIII-XIV, Uzhorod, p. 30.
[6] State Archives Chernivtsi Region.
[7] The Writings of Ivan Franko, V. VII, Lviv, 1914, p. 107.

While western Ukrainian lands under Austro-Hungarian rule, namely Galicia, Bukovina and Sub-Carpathia, gave thousands of immigrants to Canada, the U.S.A., Brazil and Argentina before the first world war, notably few Ukrainians emigrated for permanent settlement in the aforementioned countries from territories under the rule of the Russian Empire. On the basis of statistical estimates of Ukrainian emigration, one can deduce that 97% of the emigrants originated in western lands under Austro-Hungary, and only 3% in eastern Ukrainian lands under Russian occupation. The reasons for emigration in eastern Ukraine are almost identical with those from western Ukrainian lands. The landowners, the big lords in their eastern expanses, acquired into their own hands over sixteen million hectares of land, while the 3,100,000 economies comprised only 25½ million hectares of land. The average economy had little more than 6/10, but there were hundreds of thousands of economies which had 1/6 or 2/6 of the so called "desiatyna" [8].

Besides these economic factors, there were intolerable ones about which the Ukrainian Soviet researcher A. M. Shlepakov relates: "The emigration of the peasantry to America took place from Ukrainian territory, which was then a part of the Russian framework. This process took on the same characteristic marks as in Galicia and Bukovina and Sub-Carpathia" [9]. Elsewhere the same author writes: "Generally known was the spectacle of political injustices of the laboring masses, and the various manifestations of national pressure in the field of educational and cultural activity" [10].

It is essential to answer the question why so few Ukrainians from Ukrainian lands under Russia emigrated for settlement beyond the sea, when factors of a special social and political nature were the same in Austria and Hungary. The first basic reason was the rigid determination of the Russian Government not to allow any of its citizens to emigrate beyond the borders of the Empire since it planned to settle Siberia, with its wide expanses remaining uninhabited. In the years 1906-1912 almost a million Ukrainian peasants migrated to Siberia. A. M. Shlepakov writes: "The resettlement took place under frightful circumstances. The prospective settlers were deprived of the essential inventory and machinery. Furthermore they were unable to secure possession of their land portions, and so they were compelled to return. In 1911, 70% of these settlers returned to Ukraine" [11].

In order to prevent the peasants from emigrating beyond the sea, the Tsarist Regime made stringent changes in the passport formalities, prolonging the matter so as to discourage those anxious to emigrate. But in spite of these difficulties there were some hardy and courageous individuals who succeeded in leaving the country so as to secure a better life for themselves and their immediate families.

From both Ukrainian territories, Austro-Hungary and Russia, mass emigration to North America began in huge proportions in the last decade of the past century. The corner stone of Ukrainian Immigration to Canada was laid in 1891.

---

[8] Desiatyna—measure of land—2.70 acres.
[9] A. M. Schlepakov, Ukrainian Workers Emigation to U.S.A. and Canada, Publishing House of the Ukrainian Academy of Sciences U.S.S.R., Kiev, 1960 p. 42.
[10] Ibid. p. 43.
[11] Ibid, p. 43.

THE BEGINNING OF UKRAINIAN IMMIGRATION AND THE YEAR 1891

People in general, love legends, although legends cannot always be equated with the truth. Such a legend has been spun around the arrival in Canada of the "two first" Ukrainian settlers, namely, Wasyl Elyniak and Ivan Pylypiw.

For a long time the Ukrainian community in Canada sought a corner stone of its history in this country. The most proper source of information might be found in the Department of Immigration. Thus the St. Raphael's Association in Winnipeg, in conjunction with CPR Colonization Department, in order to establish the date of the arrival of the first Ukrainians in Canada, started a correspondence with the Department of Immigration [1].

On July 11, 1933 the Department of Immigration acknowledged that on the files of the Steamship "Oregon" were the names of the two Ukrainians, e.g., "W. Ililik" and "I. Pylypiwski", who, on September 7th, 1891, arrived from Port Quebec to Montreal. The steamship left Europe at the harbor of Hamburg, leaving Liverpool on the 28th of August, 1891. The Department of Immigration also informed that in the month of September of that year other Ukrainians had also arrived, since in the files of other steamships there were also Ukrainian names. This information from the Department of Immigration sufficed for accepting this date as the date of the arrival of the first Ukrainians to Canada. It was certified that W. Ililik was the misspelled name of Wasyl Elyniak, and that I. Pylypiwski was the name of Ivan Pylypiw. At the time of the correspondence apropos of this matter, they were both still alive, boasting of many grandchildren and great-grandchildren and their large families. They both came from the village of Nebyliv, District of Kalush, spending some time in the province of Manitoba, in which they even had their homesteads, ultimately resettling themselves at Edna-Star and Chipman, Alberta. Ivan Pylypiw was so taken up with Canada that at the end of 1892 he returned home in order to bring his wife and children back with him, as well as the wife and children of W. Elyniak. While he was there he started to agitate among his compatriots to follow him to Canada. For this action he was given a month's jail sentence. The District Court of Stanislawiw (now Ivano-Frankiwsk) regarded his action illegal. The laws, and still more, the politics of Austria, aimed at preventing the source of cheap labor to gravitate towards Canada. The freedom of Canada, as well as the $10 homesteads, about which Ivan Pylypiw spoke so glowingly aroused the latent ambitions even in those who were frightened by the police. Even while Ivan was being questioned about his comments on the liberty and wealth of Canada, there were groups of his fellow-villagers who were recruited earlier by Pylypiw into emigrating to the "Free Lands" of Canada as was then the vogue of expression in relation to this "strange, rich and alluring country" beyond the sea. This group, which passed into history as the "Nebyliv Group", comprised 33 persons with as many fami-

---

[1] I. Bobersky: "How the First Two Ukrainians came to Canada in the year 1891".—Canadian Farmer Calendar, pp. 122-138, 1937, and Memoirs of W. Elyniak —"He came in the year 1891", Written up by the Almanac "Leader", 1933, pp. 31-34.

lies: [2]) Anton Paish, and six children; Mykola Tychkovsky and 5 children; Dmytro Wiznovich and two children; Michael Eleniak and 3 children; Wasyl Jaciw and wife; Joseph Paish, bachelor; Michael and Yawdocha Romaniuk and four children. They entered Canada at the Port of Quebec in 1892, that is, nine months after the entry of W. Elyniak and I. Pylypiw into Canada. All members of this group, some sooner and others later, settled in Alberta in the Beaver Lowland, the Edna-Star locality, in the years 1892 and 1894 and later. It can be certainly considered that this was the first Ukrainian group settlement in Canada. The Nebylovites originated the first great Ukrainian settlement which today encompasses and embraces a rectangular expanse 100 miles in length and 70 miles in width.

In this area there was a whole series of localities settled in large measure almost solely by Ukrainians, such as Lamont, Chipman, Mundare, Vegreville, Krakiw, Wostok, Derwent, Hilliard, Two Hills, New Kiev, Myrnam, and finally the locality itself, as the first one in this area which later had its name changed to Star, and many others. The Nebylite group in the Beaver Lowland became eventually associated with Ivan Pylypiw, who after the sentence served upon him, left to Canada permanently with his whole family.

The imprisonment of Ivan Pylypiw had its own results. It somewhat cooled the impulsive dispositions of the villagers to cross the ocean into Canada, but news of Canada's liberty and her great free expanses spread from village to village. This inspired not only those to think who actually wanted to emigrate but also those who at first were opposed to the emigration.

In the reminiscences of Wasyl Elyniak and Ivan Pylypiw, written up by Professor Ivan Bobersky, are pictured the onerous beginnings of the first years in Canada. There were many such scenes in later memoirs, published in various books and newspapers, covering social, religious, political and cultural conflicts in the new land and the difficulties in the adaptation of the settlers to life in Canada about which other pages will relate. Here we wish to note that there were some alleviations in this regard, since the Ukrainians were not the first who came to Canada from Ukraine. The cultural co-relation at first played a great role. In the Great Central Plain the Ukrainians in Canada met their own countrymen of other nationalities. In this category were the Mennonites who began to settle in Canada since 1874, coming over in large groups; and then there were the Jews who, too, arrived from the eastern lands of Tsarist Russia to escape persecution at the hands of that regime, the victims of discrimination as a result of government-inspired pogroms [3]). The first transport of Jews arrived from Ukraine in 1882, and later on in 1892, 1903 and 1908. Both of those national groups spoke Ukrainian, and they were drawn to the Ukrainians by a common fate and misfortune of social and national pressure, as was brought to light by historical researches; along with the Mennonites some Ukrainians even came from the eastern lands, who under cover of belonging to the Mennonites were able to avoid political persecution at the hands of the Tsarist police. We are speaking here about such legendary persons as M. Neli-

---

[2]) M. H. Marunchak: "Among Ukrainian Pioneers of Alberta", Winnipeg, General Library, UKT, 1964, pp. 13-15.
[3]) Arthur Chiel: "The Jews of Manitoba", Winnipeg, 1961.

THE BEGINNING OF UKRAINIAN IMMIGRATION... 25

dov [4]), Wasyl Kotsur and his wife Anna, who came to Canada in 1888 and settled in the German Colony of Landetz, N. Koroluk and others. It appears that the first Ukrainian settlers co-existed closely with the German colonists from western Ukraine and that amongst them Ivan Pylypiw and Wasyl Elyniak found their close friends even from their youthful years. At Gretna, Bruderheim and Altona and other Mennonite colonies our first Ukrainian settlers found not only opportunities for work, but also friendly advice in a language understandable to themselves.

In this manner social and cultural ties were tightened with the Ukrainians in the new territory on which the Ukrainians were already an original minority, by means of cultural communication. And further the Mennonites called one of their colonies after the historical name of "Chortitz", one of the islands on the Dnieper where the Zaporozhian Sitch (Seech) was organized, which was the symbol of the great liberty of the Ukrainian people.

Furthermore, researches of a historical character indicate that some Ukrainians came to Canada long before the arrival of those who arrived with the Mennonites. In 1813 there came to Canada a military group which fought on the side of England from 1801 on various fronts. This group was properly called the "De Meurons", or else the "De Watteville" soldiers. The soldiers remained in military activities in eastern Canada, and 1817 a part of them arrived with the expedition of Lord Selkirk to the valley of the Red River. The Polish historian Mieczyslaw Haiman, who had access to the archives of the Ministry of Defence in London [5]) asserts that there were some Ukrainians among the "De Watteville" Regiment, although in the Lord Selkirk Papers [6]) they are mentioned as Poles. This was a mistake because the commander of the "De Meurons" group was Koloszinski, who looked upon himself as a Pole. In the archives of the "De Watteville" Regiment were such names as Wasyl Leschuk, Ivan Bilan, Ivan Boyko, while in the Lord Selkirk group were Peter Komdrowsky, Andrew Yankowsky from Tarnopol, and others. Some of them accounted for and others not accounted for, indicate unmistakably their Ukrainian origin. It is interesting to note that the name Koloszinski in the Papers ends in "ski" [7]), while others end in "sky". This indicated the national variety of the soldiers. Without doubt four Slavic nationalities were represented here. Besides Poles there were Ukrainians, Czecho-Slovaks, and also Russians. It can be clearly proved that this variety of the Slavic group was already established in Canada at the beginning of the 19th century.

In his researches, undertaken in the Archives of Ukraine and elucidated in the work: "Ukrainian Labor emigration to the U.S.A. and Canada", A. M. Shlepakov points to yet another category of Ukrainians who stayed on Canadian terrain up to the arrival of W. Elyniak and Ivan Pylypiw. These were various Tsarist missions to Canada, in which there, too, were Ukrainians. It would be of interest at this point to mention the role of Peter Poletica who distinguished himself in the diplomatic ties of Russia with

---

[4]) "Among Ukrainian Pioneers of Alberta", pp. 16-18.
[5]) War Office, London, England: W. O. 25/679, Register, Various Descriptions and Session Book Watteville Rgt. etc.
[6]) Lord Selkirk Papers, Volume XV, pp. 5237-5238, and pp. 2282 and 2289.
[7]) M. H. Marunchak: "Studies in the History of Ukrainians in Canada", V. I. pp. 14-16.

the American Continent, and who delineated the boundary line between Alaska and Canada [8]).

In order to exhaust finally the topic of the so-called "pre-historical" ties of the Ukrainians with the country of Canada, it would be in place to mention something about the version of Father Ahapiy Honcharenko from the U.S.A., former editor of the "Alaska Herald" and the originator of the theory that the Ukrainians arrived on American soil and thus by the same token on Canadian territory, at the end of the 18th century, when Tsarist Russia completely destroyed the liberties of Ukraine, demolishing Sitch (Seech) and destroying any opposition to Tsarist occupation by exile to Siberia. Some of these political exiles may have reached Kamchatka, then Alaska, and from there Canada and the U.S.A. This theory has been rather meagerly researched but it is not deprived of practical thought and historical consideration. Long years of the editorial labor of A. Honcharenko in defence of Alaska and American democracy earned a measure of credibility for this theory. It is thus a great pity that he did not supply sufficient ground on which to base this theory and follow it up with sound historical arguments. A. Honcharenko frequently speaks of a "Pacific Ukraine", and in the Archives his visiting card was preserved with the same name on it.

The history of the Ukrainians in Canada notes with certainty some data concerning the fellow settlers who entered Canada from the U.S.A. These latter Ukrainians started to settle considerably earlier than 1891. It is most likely that from this source there arrived a number of families who settled in Winnipeg and were members of the Immaculate Conception Church on Austin Street. The parochial birth certificate list of this Church, which dates from the year 1883, contains many Ukrainian names such as Mychajlo Koleshar, 1884; Maria Bubnyk, 1886; Anna Chapets from Biely Potok (white stream), 1887; Anton, Susana and Teresa Carstiak from the same locality, 1888. We also found the certificates of such names as Andrij Kopys, Joseph Piliak, Michael Sycora, E. Kravchenko, and later on A. Maluta, Ivan Slota, Anna Chopyk, Maria Shpak and many others. But all of them in later history and religious conflict were lost in the general confusion, and there were some who even left Canada completely.

A similar group of the same origin was established at Lethbridge in the coal-mine region, but this unfortunately was a transitory element of wage-earners that did not want to stay put in one place nor try to create any lasting values in its surroundings and environment.

Notwithstanding the considerable data which were here introduced to the Ukrainians on Canadian territory before the arrival of Wasyl Elyniak and Ivan Pylypiw, the Ukrainian Community of Canadian and Ukrainian historiography have accepted the year 1891 as the first solid corner stone of its history in this country. The quesion arises as to what arguments prevailed regarding the basis of this decision. The answer may be supplied as follows:

With 1891 the mass immigration began, and with it too, begins the connective history of the Ukrainian, sociologically integrated entity. In the footsteps of W. Elyniak and I. Pylypiw others followed in turn, and in the short course of time colonies were being formed, with an intimately de-

---

[8]) M. Huculak, Ph.D.: A Ukrainian, Pierre De Poletica, co-author of the Canadian-Alaskan Boundaries, Vancouver — Toronto, 1967.

lineated sketch (tracery) of Ukrainian culture. This was not clearly manifested in the material and social-cultural life of the new immigrants of other days—those fore-runners of W. Elyniak and I. Pylypiw—whose memory was dissolved in history, with hardly any trace being left behind them.

Entirely different were the dies cast during this second period of attempt, following the year of 1891. In all the activities of communal life a new history was being recorded, which we rightfully name as the Ukrainian Canadian history and which simultaneously forms a distinctive chapter in the comprehensive and total composition of the great Canadian epos. In this same multi-sided epos we can clearly see the Ukrainian Canadians busily engaged in taming the widely stretching prairies of the west; in the building of railroad networks and country highways; in the development of new settlements and the formation of organizations of communal life. They become creators of a new religio-church oriented life and builders of the cultural-educational centres. They help to organize the political aspect of life—sending their representative members to provincial legislatures and Dominion Parliament. They organize publishing houses and create inspiring literature and works of art. In all branches of community activity, in Canada, we may clearly detect the spiritual and cultural outline of this new identity that is so prominently displayed in the mosaic structure of Canada.

And although Ukrainian historiographers are mostly engaged in recording this Ukrainian connective contribution to the developmental growth of Canada, they do not forget about the fore-runners of W. Elyniak and I. Pylypiw who, at other times and climes were- like those ever-returning swallows—the harbingers of Spring—constantly predicting the mass migration of their own countrymen.

DR. O. OLESKIW, PROMOTER OF MASS MOVEMENT OF UKRAINIAN SETTLERS TO CANADA

The emigration to Canada, started by W. Elyniak and I. Pylypiw of the village of Nebyliw, in 1891, did not at once expand into any great proportions. There were some important reasons for this. I. Pylypiw was punished for his agitation favoring departure to Canada and the people were afraid even to talk about Canada louder than a whisper. Besides, the Austrian official agencies, particularly the owners of large estates, that is the village great proprietors, continued spreading fearful propaganda against Canada. They frightened the people with very severe cold in winter and frosts in summer, with the infertile wasteland and lack of protection of settlers by the government and many other bugaboos.

Concerning the leadership of the Ukrainian people, there were also divided ideas about resettlement and emigration. Its conservative circles upheld the advice that only seasonal emigration would be beneficial for the people, considering the point that massive and permanent emigration would leave a void in the national substance and would be very detrimental to national economy because the emigrants would sell their land to anybody, that is, not necessarily to their countrymen thereby national possession of land would diminish to the disadvantage of Ukrainian community.

Let us take into consideration that at that time, both in Galicia and Bukovina, there raged, both a national and social struggle between Ukrainians on the one side and landowners, tenants and liquor retailers-inn-keepers on the other. These categories of persons, especially, had the greatest means with which to buy the land from those leaving their homes for a strange country beyond the sea. As a result of their considerations, the conservative circles were decidedly opposed to any emigration. Of a different opinion was the so-called radical party of which the indisputable authority among the common people was, poet, writer, also scholar and publicist, Ivan Franko.

The radical circles strongly advocated the necessity of emigration for Ukrainian peasantry, because the overpopulation in Galicia and Bukovina was so critical on the small pieces of land that it threatened aggravated suffering from hunger. This party was also against the transfer of villagers' lands into other than Ukrainian ownership. Therefore they planned an organized procedure which should create people's savings banks and co-operatives serving the villagers with long-term loans and thus prevent the land from falling into the hands of unscrupulous speculators, and which should only go to the ownership of those who worked on this land.

The general idea of the radical party was to support an organized emigration and stop those various steamship agents and speculators taking advantage of the illiterate people. The reason for this argument was further strengthened, at that time, by the frenzied propaganda of the Brazilian cotton and coffee plantation owners who had their paid solicitors organizing for them cheap central European labor. We must remember the year 1888, when the most inhuman and brutal slavery of Negroes was abolished in Brazil. As soon as the abolition of serfdom was proclaimed, Negroes deserted their masters, the plantation owners. The result was that plantation properties, being neglected, were losing out completely. Then the plantation owners, in desperation, began organizing the recruitment of European whites whom they treated about the same way as they had treated the black slaves. They paid for the passage from Europe to Brazil and let the laborers avail themselves of what food and clothing, as promised by the plantation agents, was supplied by the plantation owners. But their charge for these supplies was so high that no worker could ever hope to gain his economic independence. And what was worse, the plantation masters frequently had the new workers committed nightly to the old slave lockups, to hold them down and prevent their escape from intolerable forced labor.

In Europe, people did not know the reverse side of this "promised and shiny Brazilian medal", because the plantation pitchmen had assured the villagers of free transportation, good food and the best wages. Their disappointments came far too late when there was no return.

This Brazilian fever captured the imagination of the Ukrainians who then lived under Austrian rule, reaching considerable proportions. Thousands of single and married men with their families started to escape to the sea ports of Western Europe. They thought they had a great chance. And they didn't have to sell their lands and homes, or worry about transportation costs. However something had to be done to stop this unfortunate mass exodus and save the poor people from their folly and consequent bondage. This noble deed and duty was done by the central society "Prosvita" which had many affiliations in almost every village.

This edifying work was undertaken by Dr. O. (Joseph) Oleskiw (also written Oleskow) who was then one of the prominent members of "Prosvita" and also professor of teachers' seminary in Lviv, (then called Lemberg, in German-Austrian). Hastily he wrote a 38 page pamphlet entitled "About Free Lands" published at the expense of "Prosvita" in July, 1895. Its subtitles speak for themselves as to its contents. Answering his own question: "Will our native land sustain us?" in the following chapters, Dr. Joseph Oleskiw convincingly demonstrated that if the people had to leave their native land, definitely they "should not emigrate to Brazil". In his last chapter his reply to, "then whither shall we migrate?" was very definit . Naming different countries, Dr. Joseph Oleskiw designated Canada and assigned this country the most space in his brochure, emphasizing that Canada was the most suitable for colonization by his countrymen, the Ukrainians from Galicia and Bukovina. He was their Moses of a sort, leading them to a promised land. Moreover, in his booklet he assured them that he personally would visit Canada accompanied by two villagers to look over and check the practical conditions in Canada for settlement and, particularly the opportunities for employment and wages, and to investigate the quality and suitability of the territory for husbandry and agriculture where Ukrainians could settle and help themselves mutually and not become a burden to the state.

The question of emigration to Canada or U.S.A., Dr. Oleskiw resolved in one paragraph; however, he considered that the purpose of emigration to U.S.A. should be temporary and job-seeking, whereas emigrants to Canada should be real settlers and aim for steady occupation on their farms, creating social life "supported by their own colonies" (page 36).

Dr. Oleskiw assured the readers of his book that after his return from Canada he will write a second informative booklet and that the first batch of colonists should start for Canada in the early spring in the year of 1896 (page 37).

The author of "About Free Lands" lived up to his promise. The booklet had hardly reached the many readers when he and a villager named, Ivan Dorundiak, from Kolomyja district, departed for Canada, as official Ukrainian representatives, to confer with the Canadian Government on the question of Ukrainian group settlements in this country so that the newly started immigration in colonies would not devolve into wild desertions of homesteads for the pursuit of happiness in the wide world. Those who initiated the idea of "settlements by colonies", so called by the press at the time, earnestly wished the emigration to be "healthy and sensible" (page 36).

When Dr. Oleskiw was preparing to leave for Canada, his name was not entirely unknown to Canadian officials. Beginning March 16, 1895, he had corresponded with the Department of the Interior in Ottawa. In a communication of that date he had explained to the Canadian Government the social and political situation in Galicia and the desire of Ukrainian emigrants to settle in Canada and he also reported his readiness to come to Canada to get acquainted with the industry of the country, requesting the Canadian Government to give him detailed data about Canada in the field of statistics and geography.

The correspondence between Dr. Joseph Oleskiw and the Canadian Government was conducted with the aid of High Commisioner in London, Sir Charles Tupper, subsequently premier of Canada. The initial correspondence with the Canadian officials limited itself exclusively to information about Ukrainians in Galicia and Bukovina, their social conditions, about the role of the Association of "Prosvita", the cultural-educational institution, whose membership numbered approximately 12,000 and supporting Dr. Oleskiw's efforts to promote Ukrainian emigration to Canada, and simultaneously conducting vigorous propaganda against their emigrating to Brazil.

Meanwhile, Canadian officials endeavored to receive proper information as to who Dr. Joseph Oleskiw really was, who took the cause of his countrymen's emigration to Canada so seriously upon himself. In due time the High Commmissioner in London informed the officials in Ottawa that Dr. Oleskiw was Ukrainian, (in official language the term used was "Ruthene") that he was of Greek Catholic denomination, that he was a professor at the Teachers' Seminary in Lemberg at approximately $1000.00 yearly salary; he was 34 years old, married, was the owner of farm property near Ternopol (Galicia) which was valued at 12,000 florins, and which was free and clear. Dr. Oleskiw's reputation was good among his countrymen: he had written a great deal about emigration and he was very much opposed to Ukrainian emigration to Brazil [1]).

As we see it, the official information was sound and accurate. The correspondence between Dr. Oleskiw and the Canadian officials began in the

---

[1]) The Public Archives, Ottawa, Oles. /22312, May 13, 1895, John Dyke, Agent, Liverpool to J. G. Colmer, London.—We are citing from Dr. J. Kaye's book, "Early Ukrainian Settlements in Canada 1895-1900, Dr. Josef Oleskow's role in the Settlement of the Canadian Northwest".

German language, but later Dr. Oleskiw wrote his letters in English.

Dr. Oleskiw, with I. Dorundiak, left Lviv (Galicia) 25th of July, 1895 and on the 29th of July he conferred with the Canadian High Commissioner in London. The delegation arrived at the Canadian port of Montreal on the 12th of August. After a brief visit in Ottawa, they started out West to inspect the country. They had received free transportation tickets, and from Winnipeg had the official assistance in the person of Hugo Carstens who was the immigration officer and German interpreter in the Dominion Land Office in Winnipeg.

Beginning at Ottawa, Dr. Oleskiw had a series of official conversations. In the capital city he was received by the acting deputy of the minister and superintendent of immigration John Hall, with whom Dr. Oleskiw left a memorandum pertaining to immigration of Ukrainians into Canada, because of the Minister's absence at the time. In Winnipeg he had an important conference with the Dominion Lands Commissioner, H. H. Smith, and more discussions in Edmonton with the Minister of the Interior Affairs of Canada, T. Mayne Daly.

Minister Daly, already being acquainted with the contents of Dr. Oleskiw's memorandum, helped the delegation to concentrate their discussions on the four basic questions: Position of the Canadian Governmment in respect to the proposed immigration; the role of the transportation companies in organizing immigration and their drawback in that respect; the financial condition of the Ukrainian immigrant, his agricultural possibility, and the attitude of the Austrian government regarding the emigration, which at that time, was inimical.

The official correspondence shows that all those interested were favorably impressed by Dr. Oleskiw's businesslike approach to the indicated problems. His plans were envisaged on realistic principles and practical solutions. He particularly requested that each homesteader should be assisted by a government grant in the sum of $60.00, but that this sum should not go directly into the settler's pocket; it would be paid into settler's community funds which would take care of mutual community needs and purchases of agricultural implements, in that way avoiding the intervention of agents-speculators. These settlers' community partnerships would also take care of marketing the farm products, and helping to form community dairies, granaries and elevators.

Again Dr. Oleskiw assured the government officials that he will direct all his endeavors to organize a fellowship of emigration, in the capital of Galicia, which will take care of a well planned emigration and also endeavor to obtain from Austrian officials the necessary legalization of such fellowship with official authority; that this fellowship or society should have the necessary finances to be able to conduct proper educational propaganda re emigration. Dr. Oleskiw had presented the Canadian Government with a request for the same government allowance to steamship agencies since 1882, viz. $5.00 per adult. For publicity purposes he proposed a separate sum.

Dr. Oleskiw's propositions were neither rejected nor accepted; however, promises were made they would be investigated by proper authorities in due time. Nonetheless, the Ukrainian delegation returned to Lviv with great plans and high hopes. An intensive correspondence with the Canadian Government, and planning in Lviv, continued. There, many consultations were held and articles and appeals, concerning emigration to Canada, were published. In the meantime Canadian administration, under Sir MacKenzie Bowell, underwent an important change due to the resignations of several ministers, which made it difficult, if not impossible, to carry out any extended plans concerning immigration, especially if they demanded any changes in the budget or additional spending. Finally MacKenzie Bowell resigned. The new premier, Sir Charles Tupper, had formed a new cabinet, leaving out minister Th. M. Daly who was very positively oriented towards Oleskiw's propositions.

There followed also a change in the position of High Comissioner in London. The new minister of the interior, Sir Hugh John MacDonald had no time to be bothered by Dr. Joseph Oleskiw's plans because Tupper's conservative party was defeated in July, 1896 by the new liberal party with Sir Wilfred Laurier as premier of the Dominion of Canada. This change was followed by a shifting of the key officials in the ministries which worsened the situation for a realization of Dr. Oleskiw's plans. In fact, as it was later revealed, they were temporarily forgotten.

But Dr. Oleskiw's position remained unchanged. As soon as he returned to Lviv, and this was the middle of October the same year, he called a conference, within a month, of the leading representatives of the Ukrainian national movement, for a common consultation on the subject of how to help the Ukrainian peasant-farmer and worker to emigrate to Canada. This representative conference was held in the spacious hall of the National Home, (Narodny Dim) in Lviv. From the report as it was published in "Dilo" at that time, the leading Ukrainian daily newspaper, and later appearing in United States of America, reprinted by "Svoboda", the then only Ukrainian weekly published on the American continent [2]) — we learn that the more progressive younger generation took an active part in the discussions at the conference which the older generation failed to attend. Regardless of the different opinions, the conference performed its duty successfully.

It is interesting, that besides the radical circles, the progressive elements, the so-called "nationals" (narodovtsi), has taken an active part in the discussions on the floor of this important meeting. From outside the city of Lviv prominent personages came to the conference: the lawyer from Zolochiv, Longinus Rozankovsky; poet Pavlo Dumka, from Kupchyntsi; later, a member of the Provincial Parliament (Soym); statesman Ivan Radulak from Hlushkiv; parliamentary councillor Teophil Okunewsky, from Horodenka; and other city and village community leaders—Mychaylo Lavryshko, Ivan Hoshovatiuk, and Petro Rybitsky; also from Pokuttia came Cyril Genik-Berezovsky, teacher from Bereziv. And from Berezhany came lawyer and writer Andriy Chaykovsky; from Kupchyntsi, hospodar Stepan Harmatiy; from Potutory Father Ivan Maschak. From the city of Lviv came among others, Ivan Franko, lawyer Mykola Shukhevych, lawyer Andriy Kos, member of parliament in Vienna in later years; and Vyacheslav Budzynovsky, writer and editor of the weekly "Hromadsky Holos" (Community Voice) which very actively supported emigration to Canada.

After hearing Dr. Oleskiw's report on his trip to Canada, the conference resolved unanimously to apply itself to practical solutions of the emigration problems. "It is impossible to wait any longer", it was written in the report

---

[2]) "Svoboda", Weekly, No. 46, 1895.

of the meeting, "and look on indifferently, when our people in desparation, because of their poverty, sell their households to Jewish tavern-keepers for half the real value and being baited and lured by the paid native and foreign agents they crowd blindly into Brazilian Hell at so much per head" [3].

This was the voice, the cry of despair, because it was confirmed by those present who knew the facts, that on the trips across the sea, the emigrants are badly treated, with the humiliation far below human dignity and were made victims of "merciless extortions perpetrated by greedy leeches".

This Lemberg conference restored to life the Emigration Relief Committee, to continue the work started by Dr. Joseph Oleskiw. The chairman of this committee was the well-known economist and cooperator, Mykola Nahirny, the founder of "National Commerce" (Narodna Torhovla). Other members of this committee were, above named Vyacheslav Budzynovsky, Joseph Markiv, the editor of newspaper "Halychanyn", Kost Levytsky—advocate-parliamentarian at Vienna and Lviv, also president of Ukrainian members of parliament and premier of the Western Ukrainian Republic in 1918-1919; also advocate Longinus Rozankovsky and Fathers: M. Kachala from Ternopol, M. Hirniak and Alexander Stefanovych from Lviv.

The conference also decided to plan the establishment of a credit institution which would, in the future, attend to the buying of land from those leaving for Canada and in this way prevent the sale of properties to other than Ukrainian hands. Indeed, such an institution became a reality under the name "The Protection of Land". Further, Dr. Oleskiw even made requests to Canadian and British financial institutions for convenient credits for the purpose. Above all, Dr. Oleskiw became the prime mover and the soul of all this carefully planned task. He continued corresponding with the Canadian Government authorities and also with those interested in emigration; through the press he informed them of the currently related events. He was in continuous contact with the Ukrainian spokesman in U.S.A. with whom he also planned a practical solution of settlement in Canada.

First of all, he kept the promise he gave his people, to write another brochure about Canada titled "About Emigration" published by "The Society of Kachkovsky" in Lviv in the month of December, 1895. A pertinent question came up. Why Dr. Oleskiw, a reliable Ukrainian patriot and philantropist, had his brochure published by a Russophile society? But it must be remembered that this society at that time enjoyed quite a lot of support and also had great influence over the masses, particularly in Lemkiwschyna and Carpathian Ukraine. To save the innocent from extortion and needless suffering he decided to collaborate with adherents of Russophilism so that in this manner he would aid the Ukrainian villagers. Moreover, he also wrote, not too well-known to the general public, a brochure in the Polish language about emigration, titled "Rolnictwo za Okeanem a Przesiedlna Emigracja" which appeared in the year 1896. He strove most earnestly to have the truth about Canada disseminated among the greatest numbers.

Oleskiw's booklet, "About Emigration" was, and it still is, of double significance to the history of Canadians of Ukrainian origin. It had served as an advanced mobilizing factor for the settling of Ukrainians in Canada,

---

[3] "Svoboda", Nr. 1-2, January, 1896.

at the time of its appearance, and for the present, this booklet still remains a number one source material which tells us how Ukrainian settlers were assigned to various Canadian settlements in the year 1895.

The weekly newspaper "Canadian Farmer" (published in Winnipeg) had this booklet reprinted on its pages in 1927, renaming its title "The Description of Canada From Before Thirty Two Years". This booklet is a bibliographical rarity, numbering 72 pages. In its introduction there is the description of the voyage, both by train and steamship. Next is the chapter, "The Arrival in Canada" as it begins for the immigrant at the harbors of Halifax and Quebec. The latter port was closed because of ice in the winter time. The settlers travelled on hard maple seats in special coaches bearing the sign, "Colonists". The immigrants benefited by the reduced railroad rates. As Dr. Oleskiw travelled the long hundreds of miles of wilderness and uninhabited prairies, he visualized how the product of this great land would support the lives of hundreds of thousands of his people, as they developed boundless resources with unlimited possibilities and opportunities!

In his notebook he wrote that Canadian soil and climate in many respects proved to be akin to those in Ukraine, though, with minor differences, according to the zones and latitudes? He also extended an accurate description of a Canadian settler's imagination of the fabulous 160-acre homestead which was one quarter of a Canadian square mile, equivalent to 133 Austrian morgs [4]) of land! Fantastic! So much of this dear and precious, God's holy earth, available to the eager homesteader for only $10.00! But he also felt anxious and disturbed by the speculation in land, knowing that bankers, railroad companies and other speculators were picking up the better and choicer tracts for re-sale, the profits of which would have to come from the poorest homesteaders.

With his whole heart and soul Dr. Oleskiw loved the Canadian prairies. The undulating and boundless prairies impressed him deeply. They enchanted him. He called them The Great and Wondrous North West. He crossed and recrossed them, riding the iron horse and behind the real horse team in a lumber wagon. On these open wide spaces he met the first Ukrainian settlers.

First of all, he visited a group of Ukrainian settlers in Winnipeg where he met some citizens who later played an important role in organizing the Ukrainian community, either in a religious endeavor or social-educational. The author-promoter mentions talking with Vasyl Jatsiv, Yurko Panischak, Hnat Dmytryshyn, Ivan Barsky, Luka Kulchycky, Dmytro Vydymovych and Yurko Roshko.

"For the colonist", says the author, "the proper stopping places were the immigration shelters (halls, buildings) where his future action and destiny were decided upon". These decisions the immigrants could make themselves in 1895. After 1895 the situation changed by which the immigrant lost his right of choice when the immigration agents made their decisions quite often against the wishes of the immigrants.

As usual the women stayed at the "immigration home" while the men travelled on free railroad tickets looking for suitable homesteads in various country locations. Oleskiw's reports point out that most of those who decided to remain in Winnipeg came from the village of Nebyliw. In the

---

[4]) One morg equals two hectares, and one hectar equals 100 acres.

Manitoba Mennnonite colony at Gretna, Oleskiw heard of a herdsman, a "cowboy-lemko", who had taken care of cattle belonging to a whole German colony. He was the first Nebyliw man in Canada working for the Mennonites, and his name was Wasyl Elyniak. Oleskiw tells us how hospitably and kindly the Mennonites and other German colonists treated him and his fellow traveller, I. Dorundiak. Besides Gretna, they visited German colonies of Josefsberg, Neudorf and Assiniboia. At Grenfell near Neudorf a colony of over a dozen Ukrainian families had just opened up, where the oldest settler was Ilko Pylypiw who, according to Oleskiw and Dorundiak, had left the old country in 1891 and that was before Wasyl Elyniak and Ivan Pylypiw. Here settlers, Fedir Ilkiw, Tymko Pylypiw, Pavlo Shymko and a few others had already settled on their homesteads.

Stony Plains, a colony near Edmonton, consisting of some 70 German families from Galicia, impressed the Ukrainian travelling delegation the most. And near it was a smaller colony of Ukrainians from the village of Nebyliw. The one nearest this German colony, Antin Paich, settled on his homestead and farther to the east, in the vicinity of Beaver Hills, the following settlers made their new homes: Andriy Paich, Stepan Chychak, Mychaylo, Mykola and Fedir Melnyk . Vasyl Feniak, Iwan Pylypiw, Mychaylo Pulyshiy, Mykola Tychkovsky, Petro and Matviy Melnyk from Perehinsko, and Mychaylo and Iwan Dubrowsky from near Sambor.

Oleskiw in his brochure was never too liberal in praising his countrymen, but at the end of it, he points to the fact that the Ukrainian's first dwellings were better built than those of their Anglo-Saxon new compatriots. One of his countrymen even had the roof of his house shingled with real cedar shingles! Oleskiw was not only an optimist but also a realist, when he maintained that his "Israelites", once they were freed from the Galician house of bondage and got across the deep-wide sea, would attain prosperity in Canada, their promised land, after a few years of honest toil.

From Dr. Joseph Oleskiw's written account we learn that on the whole, Ukrainian colonies were small in number and quite primitive. At that time there were only three well established Ukrainian centres: Winnipeg, Manitoba; Grenfell, Saskatchewan and Beaver Hills-Edna in Alberta. There is no mention in his accounts of any church activity or cultural-educational endeavor among them. Considering the difficulties they had in shaping their own domestic needs, they hardly had any time or energy left for the above mentioned type of activity.

Oleskiw's booklets, "About Free Lands" and "About Emigration" had given the Ukrainian village people, struggling to make a scant living under the Austrian regime, just what they needed—a true guidebook to resettlement in the free land, Canada. The ones still with us tell us what they heard from their fathers, that Dr. Oleskiw's booklets had a healthy and mobilizing effect; they cured many who had the Brazilian fever to go to Brazil, "the country where everything was supposed to have been for nothing and free". They also opened the eyes of many to see a hopeful future in Canada. These booklets were most popular with those who were looking for a better life beyond their unfortunate fatherland, ruled by foreign stepfathers, speculators and usurers.

In the meantime The Emigration Relief Committee made ready the first transport of Ukrainian settlers to Canada. The helmsman of this important action was none other than the well-known and tireless promoter, Dr.

Oleskiw. By the end of March, 1896, the register of the first transport was ready and by the last date of the next month, this group, which numbered 107 persons under the guardianship of Dr. Oleskiw's brother, Volodymyr, embarked for Canada. These first 107 steamboat passengers disembarked at the port of Quebec, April the 30th, 1896, and they started the massive, continuous influx of Ukrainian immigration to Canada which had only been interrupted by the First World War. This first transport, almost entirely, was settled in the Edna, Alberta, region and there began their new colony which they named "Ruska Svoboda" (Ruthenian Freedom).

THE YEAR 1896

While planning the settlements for Ukrainians in Canada, Dr. Joseph Oleskiw, had in mind not only material well-being for the immigrants, although that was his foremost consideration in his scheme of action, but he and his committee had also taken into their deliberation and attention the higher level for the settlers—the spiritual and cultural aspects and needs which, under favorable Canadian environment, began immediately to unfold and grow. Soon after the first transport left for Canada, Dr. Oleskiw wrote to the Canadian Government officials about the urgent need of clergymen for the Ukrainian settlers.

No doubt that even at the time of his visit to Canada Dr. Oleskiw had discussed the religious question with the first settlers, and this question had been also taken up with the Canadian Immigration authorities. As documented by later correspondence, this discussion had been printed in the weekly "Svoboda" (Freedom) published in U.S.A., and that Dr. Oleskiw felt embittered about the Roman Catholics in Winnipeg having a different view on this question because they considered themselves the only ones called to administer to Greek Catholics in Canada. Dr. Oleskiw and the Relief Committee in Lviv made earnest efforts in beseeching proper clerical officialdom to allow clergymen of the same denomination as that of the emigrants, to emigrate with them to Canada, to satisfy the settlers' spiritual needs and be their advisers and leaders in the newly founded colonies. They knew that those emigrating to Canada were mainly peasants (villagers) and the presence of a man of God among them would solve many problems not only spiritual but cultural-educational. No wonder, the initiators of the massive settlements in Canada tried solving these problems at their origin. His efforts, however, were fruitless at the beginning.

In his letter of May 16, 1896, Dr. Oleskiw wrote to Ottawa, stating that the settlers of Greek Catholic Church (Ukrainian Catholic Church) ritual, who had just settled in North West territory in the vicinity of Edna, in Neudorf near Grenfell, and certain localities in Manitoba, have no way to satisfy their spiritual needs, because up to this time there was not even one priest of their ritual (Greek Catholic Church). Simultaneously, Dr. Oleskiw proposed Rev. Father Ostap Nyzankiwsky for the first Ukrainian priest, who was a celebrated composer at Lviv, and was also interested in emigration to Canada. The Canadian Government, not having funds for such purposes, passed the case to the Roman Catholic hierarchy at Winnipeg which chose to take a negative stand in this request, probably because Father Ostap was married and Roman Catholics did not recognize married priesthood in Canada. Anyway, the Ukrainian settlers did not get their priest in 1896.

But the insistent Dr. Joseph Oleskiw remembered that when he visited the U.S.A. for the purpose of discussing emigration with such personalities as Father Iwan Kostankevich and Father Nestor Dmytriw of Mount Carmel, who, besides their priesthood duties, took part as leaders in community life and edited the newspaper "Svoboda" and that they concurred in his ideas and sympathized with Ukrainian settlers' problems in Canada. So he asked Father Dmytriw to offer them his helping hand in their religious needs. Hence the beginning of assistance of "Ukrainian shepherds of the soul" came from U.S.A. and their care of the settlers' religious requirements continued in Canada until a larger mission of Ukrainian priesthood arrived from the old country to attend regularly to spiritual needs of Ukrainian Catholics living in Canada. This guardianship from U.S.A. eventually ended in 1912 with the arrival of the first Ukrainian Bishop Nykyta Budka, to Canada.

Thanks to Dr. Oleskiw's efforts, Rev. Father Dmytriw came to Canada the following year (1897) and left his imprint of spiritual devotion to his calling and unselfish service to God and the new Canadian settlers. In addition to religious questions Dr. Oleskiw was taking keen interest in school matters and public instruction problems that seemed to arise out of the new fertile Canadian soil before his eyes as he mentally viewed those boundless undulating prairies and roadless swamps and impenetrable, pristine forests. In his correspondence with immigration authorities and also from his publications and comments in the press, he promulgated and defended the idea that the future of Canada lay in cultural diversity of diverse nationalities, that these nationalities as inhabitants-citizens of Canada shall create an original Canadian society, but different from homogeneous European societies—nations. He emphasized the necessity of healthy adaptation and intelligent application of economic and civilized requirements of the new country.

As we noted, the year 1896 and the efforts of Dr. Oleskiw prepared the way to cultural development and growth of Ukrainians of Canada. As if to confirm the benefits resulting from Dr. Oleskiw's efforts, public voices were heard from the settlers themselves, who with sincerity and certain sentiment, expressed their grievious yearning for religious practice and services. For example, we quote the voice of Anton Savka, one of the leaders of the newly founded colony, "Ruska Svoboda", in Alberta (later named "Vostok"), which was printed in "Svoboda", U.S.A. Upon being informed their priest could not come, he wrote to "Svoboda": "Our grief is beyond belief that we have to stay yet for some time like orphans without church service and without a minister. We would be able to build a chapel of some kind and a manse for our priest; otherwise, we will do the best we can, all winter long without church consolation and learning. Our children grow healthy but for learning there's so little chance" [5].

Other transport arrivals which followed in the year 1896, in the majority, stayed in Manitoba. One of the larger groups which sailed on steamship "Sicilia" arrived at Winnipeg, July 1896, whose monitor was Cyril (Karl) Genik, and, somewhat later, the first Ukrainian official in the civil service system in Canada. After a short lodging in the Immigration House and some searching as to where would be the best place to settle down in Manitoba, everybody in this group decided to go to Stuartburn and its environs

---

[5] "Svoboda", September 10, 1896.

and there build a colony and name it "Rus". Twenty seven families and some single men arrived August 11, 1896, riding in lumber wagons and walking 18 miles east of Dominion City, blazing a trail, starting from scratch the forming of a large colony of Ukrainians, and in subsequent years expanding it to the now well-known places, Gardenton, Tolstoi (formerly Oleskiw), Shevchenko, (now Vita), Rosa, Senkiw, Arbakka, Caliento, Sundown, Sandylands and Sirko.

The next group gave a start to another string of Ukrainian colonies. Under the leadership of Vasyl Ksionzyk this group was directed towards Dauphin Lake region, starting there a new colony and naming it "Trembowla" (Terebowla), now named Valley River.

The following year, around this colony, there grew new ones: Sifton, Kosiw, Keld, Volkivtsi (Mink River), Kolomyja (Venlaw), Dnipro (Drifting River). The Ukrainians were settling together not only in large groups, although to begin with, this was their basic way of settling in Canada; they also settled separately by individual families. In a letter dated August 18, 1896, the Dominion Lands Office informed Dr. Oleskiw about smaller settlements of Ukrainians in Manitoba, and the above mentioned few in Alberta. Sixteen families homesteaded free homesteads at Beausejour and Brokenhad east of Winnipeg. There were three families at St. Andrew and three more at Springfield near Winnipeg. And twenty families bought two acres each from Roman Catholic diocese in Saint Norbert. Not all of those twenty families could pay for the land and take possession of it right then, for lack of money the which they would earn as hired helpers.

According to the bureau of statistics in Winnipeg, at the end of the year 1896, the total number of Ukrainian immigrants arriving in Canada had reached, that first year, around one thousand. This presented an imposing figure compared to the number arriving prior to 1896. But this was only the beginning of a much greater flow of settlers yet to arrive. Soon after the arrival church congregations were created and social-cultural activities were taking shape.

For six full years Dr. Joseph Oleskiw nursed these settlements and he strengthened them with the steady flow of new settlers. Even when others quit, he did not give up his work. In 1900 the government transferred him from Lviv to Sokal to serve in the latter city as a director of another seminary where it was difficult for him to take care of immigration affairs. And ironically, an unexpected illness struck him and he died in 1903, in the forty-third year of his life. He did not live to see the luxuriant, social-cultural, economic-industrial bloom in the lives of those thousands whom he had prepared and guided on their way to Canada. There was no Ukrainian weekly in Canada at the time of his death to write his biography and obituary. Only at a later date, when Ukrainian press came into being, occasionally at historical festivals, some one of his countrymen would mention his name as that of a man of achievement and great vision of a better future. They referred to him as Ukrainian Moses, others wrote that he was their father.

Not all of Dr. Oleskiw's contemporaries understood him, but the history of Ukrainians of Canada, in the perspective of their 90th anniversary, writes his name as that of a man of achievement and great vision of a better future, of a dedicated humanist and philanthropist, an unquestionable patriot who laid solid and wide foundations for the growth of the Ukrainian community in Canada. He became a part of the history of Ukrainians of Canada, as the first helmsman who marked their course for centuries to come.

NESTOR DMYTRIW ON THE FIRST UKRAINIAN SETTLEMENTS

A detailed description about the beginnings of Ukrainian settlements in Canada is preserved in the pamphlet, "Recollections of My Travels", by Rev. N. Dmytriw, titled "Canadian Rus" (Roos) [1]. As we know it, in the early spring of 1897 Rev. Dmytriw, answering the request of Dr. Joseph Oleskiw, had come from U.S.A. to Canada before Easter Holidays to pay a visit to the principal Ukrainian colonies and together with the settlers to celebrate the "Resurrection", which in the Ukrainian tradition has a greater significance than Christmas. According to Rev. Dmytriw's records, there were 15 families, together with children, 78 persons, settled at that time, in the colony named Trembowla (Terebowla), the oldest Ukrainian settlement in the vicinity of Dauphin. These were mainly the immigrant settlers from counties: Borshchiw, Chortkiw, Buchach and Terebowla. Because most of the settlers came from Terebowla, they named their new place of abode, "Terebowla".

For the 15 homesteads these settlers had among them: 5 oxen, 2 cows, 2 calves and one wagon. Almost all men from this new settlement, soon after their arrival, went seeking harvest work in the vicinity of Brandon, so they could earn some money for provisions for the coming hard winter. The season they arrived in did not allow them to cultivate their own fields and gardens. Wasyl Ksionzyk (Ksionsek) was the head man of the colony. In a short time he became a "land-guide" for the Immigration authorities and was in close contact wih Dr. Joseph Oleskiw.

There were 45 families, 175 people in all [2], who came and named their new abode "Rus" (Roos) which, they soon found out, had the original name of Stuartburn (Post Office). Most of them arrived here in the month of September, others later in autumn, and some even during the winter of 1896 and 1897. Most of these people came from counties like Zalischyky, Borshchiw, Kolomyja, Towmach and also from Bukovina. The leading group in "Rus" colony were settlers from Kolomyja county, whence also came Cyril Genik, who by the end of 1896 had been employed by the Immigration bureau in Winnipeg as an official translator and interpreter. After Genik's departure, P. Maykowsky became leader of the information centre. The first Bukovinian in Canada, Vasyl Zahara, came to Stuartburn in September, 1896. This colony was somewhat better off, for the new settlers had ample chances to get harvest work in the neighborhood States of Minnesota and North Dakota. The distance to the city of Winnipeg was not too great. "Snakeroot" digging was quite an industry and a big help for Stuartburn pioneers. A good number of them not only traded snakeroots for sugar and flour but paid for their wagons, plows, cows, shirts and shoes.

Stuartburn colony, Ukrainianized to an almost unrecognized form of "Shtombur", was somewhat better off economically than Terebowla. Stuartburnites were luckier because they settled on their homesteads one month earlier than Terebowlians and therefore their colony was given a title as the first Ukrainian colony in Manitoba.

But according to Rev. N. Dmytriw's memoirs, Winnipeg's Ukrainian

---

[1] Nestor Dmytriw, "Kanadiyska Rus": "Podorozni Spomyny", Mt. Carmel, U.S.A., 1897.
[2] Ibid. p. 27.

population numbered about two hundred. Rev. N. Dmytriw had them divided into two categories. Some of them spent their winter in the Immigration Hall, aiming to depart to their homesteads in Manitoba with the arrival of spring. Ohers negotiated for their homesites in the city. And still others had no desire to go to far off homesteads, preferring to stay in the city of Winnipeg, seeking available employment.

The most populous and the oldest Ukrainian colony in Canada, was Edna or Beaver Creek, later renamed Star. The Ukrainians called it Nebyliw Colony, which was started by immigrants from the village of Nebyliw (in old Galicia), County of Kalush, with Mykola Tychkowsky, the earliest homesteader. There were 75 families [3] already settled there in Townships and Ranges: 55-18, 56-18, 56-19, 56-20, 57-18, 57-20, comprising an area of 12 sq. miles. As we mentioned before, this area was settled by the first transport sent out by Dr. Joseph Oleskiw selected for the most part from the County Borshchiw. This settlement was exemplary in several respects; it had the nicest household establishments with wide stretches of plowed land and fields of growing grain which made a favorable impression on visitors. And Antin Sawka had the honor of being the leading man in this settlement. Having acquired a secondary school education he had already organized an elementary school and was an inspiration in the religious and educational life of the colony.

Near Edna-Star, a short distance from Fort Saskatchewan, there also lived a few Ukrainian families in Township 55, Range 21, on Sections 36 and 28 [4]. They were the homesteaders, Antin Paish, from Nebyliw, the first one of them, and Mykhaylo Prokopchak, who was considered by some old-timers, to have been the first Lemko [5] in Canada.

In the year of 1896, eleven Ukrainian families formed an isolated colony at Rabbit Lake, near present day Rabbit Hill [6] from Yaroslav County, mostly from villages of Vysotske, Vetlyn and Lazy. This region had been formerly settled by Mennonites from Ukraine and some of their farms had been bought by Ukrainian settlers. Some of those farms were sold for $700.00 and some for even more. This indicates that some Ukrainian settlers were coming to Canada with considerable cash, for those years. Teodor Fur was the leader of this colony.

In this pamphlet, Rev. Nestor Dmytriw, mentions also such colonies (in Manitoba) as Gonor, Broken Head, Beausejour, Tyndall, Cromwell. From other reliable sources of information we know that in those days there were Ukrainian settlers at St. Norbert and Springfield, Manitoba. The Grenfell, Saskatchewan settlement deserves particular mention, where Fedir Pylypiw was the leading farmer and community organizer, and where also were settled some families that came with Mennonites from Ukraine as mentioned by Ivan Bodrug, prominent public leader of the pioneer days, in his memoirs [7]. He calls them sectarians who came with Germans from Galicia. Some of them took their homesteads around Rosthern.

From Rev. Nestor Dmytriw's account and other researches, we find that Ukrainian colonists directed their steps towards Western Canada's homesteads, that is, agriculture was their basic aim and occupation.

---

[3] Ibid, p. 36.
[4] Ibid. pp. 36 & 46.
[5] A native of the most westerly region of Western Ukraine territory.
[6] "Kanadiyska Rus", pp. 36 & 46.
[7] Memoirs of pastor Ivan Bodrug, "History of Reformation among Ukrainians", 1903-1913, p. 35 of his manuscript.

THE YEARS OF INTENSIVE IMMIGRATION
1897 — 1914

As we see from the preceding section of this history, the year 1896 stands out as a turning point of the Ukrainian immigration to Canada. Nevertheless, it was just a modest beginning. A massive influx of immigrants increased its dimensions in 1897 and fluctuated with small dips and rises until the outbreak of the First World War. In the last chapter of his booklet, "Podorozni Spomyny", Rev. N. Dmytriw writes that in the early part of May 1897, when he returned to Winnipeg from Alberta colonies, he found there the first transport of Ukrainians who arrived from Galicia and Bukovina, numbering 1081 persons, making up 400 families. The next day, 116 families left for Terebowla colony, officially marked as Lake Dauphin; 60 families departed to Alberta, to Edna-Star region, some to Stuartburn, Manitoba, and others to different, less known places in Manitoba.

During the month of June 1897, a small group of Ukrainian settlers came into Interlake District and took their homesteads in Rockwood Municipality, starting a new Ukrainian colony in Manitoba. This group, consisting of 11 families, formed the nucleus for Pleasant Home settlement. A few years later this colony numbered several thousand people. Besides Pleasant Home there grew other Ukrainian centers in the neighborhood of Gimli, such as Dnister, Foley, Winnipeg Beach, and further west, Komarno, Malonton, and to the north, Rembrandt, Jaroslaw, Zbaraz, Fisher Branch, Okno, Chatfield, Poplarfield. In a short time, Ukrainian settlers occupied the Municipality of Kreuzburg, Chatfield, renamed Fishers, Bifrost, Gimli and South of Lake Winnipeg, St. Andrew.

By the end of June 1897, another big transport of immigrants arrived at Winnipeg. Like the preceding one it was divided into several groups. Some of the immigrants were settled at Lake Dauphin, some were sent to Stuartburn, and 587 persons went to Assiniboine which is now the Province of Saskatchewan. At Saltcoats this group was divided again: 142 persons remained there and 440 persons were transferred to Yorkton, where after a short interval, they settled in Townships 28, 29, 30—Ranges 2 and 3, West of Second Meridian, which opened up Crooked Lakes district, laying the foundation for a large, new colony in Saskatchewan. The first one at Pheasant Forks (Grenfell) had not grown to any appreciable number. The colony north of Yorkton was called "New Yaroslaw" (at present Rural Municipality of Sliding Hills), was settled by 96 families, from the very beginning, and in a month 14 more families arrived there. Among this group of families there were some from U.S.A. who came here as a result of steady and persuasive propaganda by American "Svoboda" extolling the boundless prairie benefits in the Canadian North West. Among these families from U.S.A. are noted: Alexander Varkholyk, Ivan Khokholak, Roman Slezin, Sylvester Palachek, Andriy Yurchyk. A. Zylych arrived at Virden, Manitoba, and Theo. Wachna at Stuartburn, Manitoba, both from U.S.A.

For Saskatchewan colonization this was quite a beginning. As a result of continuous drought in the former years, Saskatchewan was losing its population that began arriving there in the years of 1800, mainly from Great

Britain and U.S.A. Climatic conditions and beginners' hardships were the causes for homesteaders abandoning their grants and going to look for better environment. The superintendent of Mounted Police, Perry, had reported, in the year of 1895, that some districts, already well enough settled, were almost totally deserted. Some districts had only two or three homesteaders left [1].

As disclosed by the early history of Saskatchewan, there were considerable difficulties in trying to people this great space of land. It is understandable why the Immigration Officials in Winnipeg were unusually glad when they could place there an important number of Ukrainian families as permanent settlers-farmers. In 1897, when of the total of 186 families settled in Saskatchewan, 51 remained in Beaver Hills, 110 in Crooked Lakes (Novy Yaroslaw) and 21 families in Saltcoats. Saltcoats, as a first colony, that was being born during June, 1897, regrettably was not successful because newcomers were not too eager to go to places not settled by their countrymen. Besides, when they learned that those who came there earlier were leaving their homesteads, they felt justified in their reluctance. To send out the first group of immigrants to Saskatchewan, Immigration Officials tried to use forceful persuasion and even unreliable information. Such tactics produced negative effects, setting the people against going there. It so happened, that those sent to Saltcoats did not want to stay there, which brought on serious arguments between the settlers and the Immigration Officials. But bad feelings were soon nullified and Saltcoats gradually developed.

It came to somewhat greater complications the next year, when Immigration Officials started to settle Fish Creek, Saskatchewan, not informing the settlers where they were being shipped, and under pretext that they were going to Edmonton. Only on their way, at Saskatoon, they learned that they were assigned to Fish Creek which they did not like, and of the 59 families only 12 homesteaded in Township 41, Range 1. Thirty families insisted, and departed for Alberta and 17 families returned to Sifton district in Manitoba.

As a result of such complications, the commissioner of Immigration at Winnipeg, B. F. McCreary, proposed to the Deputy Minister of Interior Affairs, James Smart, that he compel the settlers to go where they were told by the Government. Mr. McCreary wrote: "Now, there is no doubt some change has got to be made in the way of these people. They cannot be allowed to come here and select for themselves where they are going; there must be some means of compelling them to go where Government Agents select" [2].

Despite the fact that McCreary's order was not officially confirmed, investigation shows that Immigration Officials and lesser agents practiced coercion, more or less, upon settlers in subsequent years. And the settlers protested that, since they were asked to come by the Immigration agents, they should therefore be allowed to have a free choice [3].

Saskatchewan settlement had met with many difficulties, especially at Fish Creek, where in June, 1898, 21 families took their various homesteads, and a few days after their arrival—this was the 13th of June—the district was hit by frost, heavy enough to form ice ¾ inch on water standing outdoors.

---

[1] V. J. Kaye, Early Ukrainian Settlement in Canada 1895-1900, p. 181.
[2] May 25, 1898, Public Archives, Department of the Interior (Immigration).
[3] Early Ukrainian Settlements in Canada, 1895-1900, by Vladimir Kaye, p. 281.

THE YEARS OF INTENSIVE IMMIGRATION 1897—1914

No doubt this could not have been favorably accepted even by the most stalwart of those who intended to stay. Next day 35 members of this colony started out on their way to look for more favorable climatic conditions. Immigration Officials at Winnipeg used various means and pains to repair this passing crisis when evidence disclosed that in this place and instance children slept on bare ground without any covers or blankets [4]. Then the authorities acceded to immigrants' necessities and even tried to extend them mediocre financial assistance. In due time Fish Creek crisis was alleviated and Ukrainian settlers, after initial hard knocks, gradually developed their colony so that by the end of 1898 it equalled Rosthern, numbering about 1000 souls, and Immigration correspondence, five months after the arrival of the first groups, has the following to record: "These people have done remarkably well, and very permanently settled in good substantial houses, many of which are a credit to these people. They have made great progress for their time of stay and their improvements are more permanent than those of any other colony of their nationality hitherto established by the Department. The evidence of the people in the district goes to prove almost unanimously that they are desirable settlers" [5].

The districts of Yorkton and Saltcoats, Saskatchewan, were demonstrating healthy development when Immigration authorities reported that in February, 1901, there was, in those two districts, a Ukrainian population of 4500, and only in less than two years.

But Manitoba was leading in Ukrainian population which fact may be credited in considerable degree, to the efforts of Cyril Genik, who at that time served as Immigration Official at Winnipeg and, possessing a publicist ability, he wrote many articles which were printed in "Svoboda", U.S.A. advocating immigration to Manitoba. His unqualified praise and recommendation of Manitoba brought out a re-action resulting in polemics between Cyril Genik and Rev. Damascin Polivka who used to travel up and down in Manitoba, 1899, and had his own adverse opinions about the lands settled and owned by Ukrainian homesteaders. The controversy was carried on the pages of "Svoboda" in the year of 1890. Having the benefit of time perspective, it may be said that Rev. D. Polivka's observations were quite fair. But at the time when emigration fever in old Ukrainian villages was growing from year to year to intensified restlessness and with the immigrants arriving in Canada and wishing to settle near their relatives or countrymen, the demand for homesteads increased. The result was that people settled on poorer, sub-marginal, sandy or stony lands. Being excited and bewildered by the new world, the beginners were poor judges of the quality of soil. There was little time to make experiments. In haste and anxiety, they settled on the swampy and stony parts of the Interlake region. And when this region had no more homesteads and Stuartburn and Lake Dauphin homesteads were also all pre-empted, those who wished to stay in Manitoba turned to the infertile, and unsuitable land for agriculture, in the region south of the Riding Mountains, in the vicinity of Shoal Lake which the pioneers Ukrainianized to "Shoylyk". In the early spring of 1899 a Ukrainian group began to settle along the south slope of Riding Mountains,

---

[4] Report by W. F. McCreary to James Smart, Ottawa, June 21, 1898, Department of the Interior.
[5] Report by C. W. Speers to the Superintendent of Immigration in Ottawa, see "Early Ukrainian Settlements in Canada, 1895" by V. J. Kaye, p. 310.

where during the next few years, some three thousand of them settled in the environs, which at present bear such names as Olga, Seech, Zaporozhe, Ruska Rava, Mohyly, Chmelnytsky, Ruthenia, Dolyny, Horod, Ozerna, and further in the vicinity of Menzie, Sandy Lake and Elphinstone. This area, in length is over 80 miles and in width from 20 to 40 miles, branches out, reaching almost Lake Manitoba with localities like Alonsa, Kellwood, Glenella. These homesteads were of secondary quality.

The first transport for "Shoylyk" arrived in May and was accommodated in two immigrant centers, Selkirk and Winnipeg. Here it may be proper to state that, when the influx of immigrants increased, the Immigration Officials opened one more immigration center in Selkirk, twenty five miles north east of Winnipeg, in the old railroad roundhouse at East Selkirk [6]. Also they expanded the Winnipeg Immigration Building, and the overflow found shelter in the old Dufferin schoolhouse, at Logan and Salter Street. The overflow from those three buildings was sent to Shoal Lake district. That transport is memorable, not only for initiating a large new Ukrainian colony in Manitoba, but more so because its members lived through some shocking experiences and dire tragedies in their new demesne. In addition to their steamboat and railroad hardships, long waiting at immigration centers and the lack of proper food from which the children suffered most, especially infants, they contracted an infectious disease. The disease struck the group on their way to Shoal Lake. During this trip three children died. When this group of about 400 souls reached the last railroad station, Strathclair, it was necessary for the families to be put up in farm barns. The Anglo-Saxon dwellers of Strathclair met the strangers from Galicia with animosity which increased considerably when they found out that the disease among Galician children was spreading. They demanded an immediate departure of the newcomers. After three days in Strathclair the immigrants were made to leave for their designated farmsteads, which were farther north and closer to the hills. There was no help and the children were dying at Strathclair. Twelve of them were buried along the railroad. As misfortune would have it, the day the wagons pulled out in the northerly direction, it rained hard, and the temperature dropped to below freezing and the rain changed to snow. On the shore of Lake Patterson, twenty miles north of Shoal Lake, tents were pitched on wet and cold ground. Consequently, in two weeks 40 more children and two grown ups died [7]. At the site where those tents stood, today stands a monument erected there by the Ukrainian community in the year 1941, commemorating the fiftieth anniversary of the Ukrainian Settlers in Canada.

The following groups, coming later to settle this colony, were more fortunate. They did not have to live through any exceptional tragedies. They gradually established themselves on their own farmsteads. Despite the fact that the soil they cultivated was not best suited for agriculture, they, by their diligence and thrift, made notable progress. Dominion Colonization Agent Speers, in his report in the year of 1900, wrote to Deputy Minister of the Interior thus: "This colony is in a very satisfactory condition. These people have good gardens; they have also improved their dwellings; they have purchased a great number of cattle... They stretch their colony over

---

[6] M. H. Marunchak: "Petro Hawrysyshyn" — Winnipeg, 1962-1963, p. 14.
[7] Studies in the History of Ukrainians in Canada, Vol. II, chapter "Tragic Days", p. 273.

thirty miles of country, commencing at Township 19, Range 21, north and westward to Townships 21, 26, and have settled at the base of the Mountains, outside the permanent timber reserve. I consider that this colony has made rapid progress since its establishment... They are good customers for a large amount of our manufactured products... They also purchase large quantities of clothing and other commodities.

At all other portions of this country, where these settlers are placed, they seem to be getting along nicely, they are healthy, contented and doing well".

Studying the correspondence of the Immigration Department which at that time was under the jurisdiction of the Ministry of the Interior Affairs, especially the one which is so minutely reprinted in the work of Vladimir Kaye, "Early Ukrainian Settlers in Canada, 1895-1900", we generally find unusually favourable opinions about the first Ukrainian settlers. But the best opinion of its development was received by the first colony of Edna-Star. As early as 1898 there were two schools going strong, one in Limestone Lake and another in Beaver Creek. At that time two churches were also being built—thus proving that the new settlers had discarded their individual-husbandry chores and troubles and had taken up their duties as socio-cultural workers. Already at that time, they sought means to satisfy their educational and spiritual needs. They sought for a bilingual teacher so that their children would be taught in their native language. Particularly, the Immigration reports speak very well of the economic conditions of this colony, indicating that the settlers were not only producers but also consumers: "The merchants speak highly of them, stating that they are honest. And men who were against them and their coming here are now catering for their trade. Thus it will be observed that they are honest and industrious and are not only producers but are also great consumers of our manufactured products as well. About 350 of these people have been employed on the railway. They have earned a great deal of money. They have all been self-sustaining. None wanting any support, no destitution and the majority of them very comfortably off" [8].

We venture to say that this progress of Edna-Star colony as compared with other Ukrainian colonies, no doubt, can be attributed to the longer duration of its development and also to the better quality of land taken by the settlers in Townships and Ranges as follows: Town. 46, R. 17; Town. 47, R. 15 & 16; Town. 48, R. 16; Town. 50, R. 16; Town. 51, R. 15, 16, 17; Town. 52, R. 16, 17; Town. 53, R. 15, 16, 17, 18; Town. 54, R. 15, 16, 17, 18, 19; Town. 55, R. 14, 16, 17, 18, 19, 21; Town. 56, R. 15, 16, 17, 18, 19, 20, 21; Town. 57, R. 14, 15, 16, 17, 18, 19, 20, 21; Town. 58, R. 15, 16, 17, 18, 23, 24; Town. 59, R. 15, 17.

West of Edmonton, Townships 26 and 27, Ranges 48 and 49 received ample quota of Ukrainian settlers where, according to school board reports, they had two school districts in which students made great progress in acquiring an education.

The progress and success made by the Ukrainian settlers in Canada, was an encouragement for those back in the old country, who were very much excited and interested in the life of their native brethren who went across the ocean to wondrous Canada. In thousands of letters, full of words of

---

[8] C. W. Speers, Winnipeg to Frank Pedley, Ottawa, Dec. 13, 1898. Public Archives, Reports 70396.

praise, mailed from Canada to the natives of Ukraine, the free land and free country were emphasized. Those letters put the special emigration agents out of their nefarious business. It was not necessary for them to agitate and recruit new emigrant settlers any more. However, this praise, by acquaintances and relatives, quite often overstated the prosperity of the country and exaggerated their own acquisitions, causing in due time, some disappointments. For that reason there appeared Cyril Genik's published articles in the press, admonishing his countrymen—for he was their leader —guardian-adviser, such was their opinion of him—to tell the truth in their letters, " to stop and think, if and whom to advise to come to them in Canada from native country" [9]. Great effort was required for a family to get re-established on a new land in a strange country, particularly for those who had small children and as statistics show, there were many. Advice was given for the heads of families to come first alone, to select a homestead and then bring the family.

As we now know, the Ukrainian settlers have made progress, but behind it have been hiding long and often painful personal and family dramas, particularly when families became separated for years at a stretch. We read about them in tens and many hundreds of the pioneers' reminiscences scattered in newspapers, almanacs and various publications. But despite all that, the immigration increased from year to year. The best proof of this, are figures which we transcribe from official statistics of the first four years of massive immigration of Ukrainians to Canada, the years of 1897-1900 [10].

Year	Total figure of immigrants	Immigrants from Galicia
1897	21,717	4,999
1898	31,900	5,509
1899	44,543	7,276
1900	41,681	6,618

A slight drop in immigration of 1900 may be explained by crop failure due to drought. Generally speaking, low economic levels always influenced the influx of immigrants. Similar situation repeated itself the following year, but from then on immigration increased. Comparing the quoted figures of the Ukrainian immigrant influx in the last four years of the past century with the preceding four years, viz. 1893-1896, when the number of Ukrainian settlers reached 2,634, that is, in only one year, 1897, it was greater than in the four preceding years. As statistics indicate Ukrainian immigration increased every year thus: in 1893—254; in 1894—616; in 1895 —489; and in 1896—1275. By the official figures of Canadian immigration, overall arrivals of immigrants to Canada in these years diminished: In the year 1893, 29,633 immigrants arrived in Canada. The following year only 20,829; in 1895, 18,790 and in 1896, 16,835 immigrants. This points to stronger evidence that the mass movement of Ukrainian immigration had begun as a result of Dr. Joseph Oleskiw's efforts. Cyril Genik who prepared the statistics up to 1900, informs us that by that time Canada received 27,036 Ukrainian immigrants from Galicia and Bukovina and of that num-

---

[9] "Svoboda", April 10, 1901.
[10] Commissioner of Immigration, Winnipeg, to the Secretary, Department of the Interior, Ottawa, Feb. 1, 1901, Public Archives, Vol. 139859.

PIONEER ERA — ILLUSTRATIONS

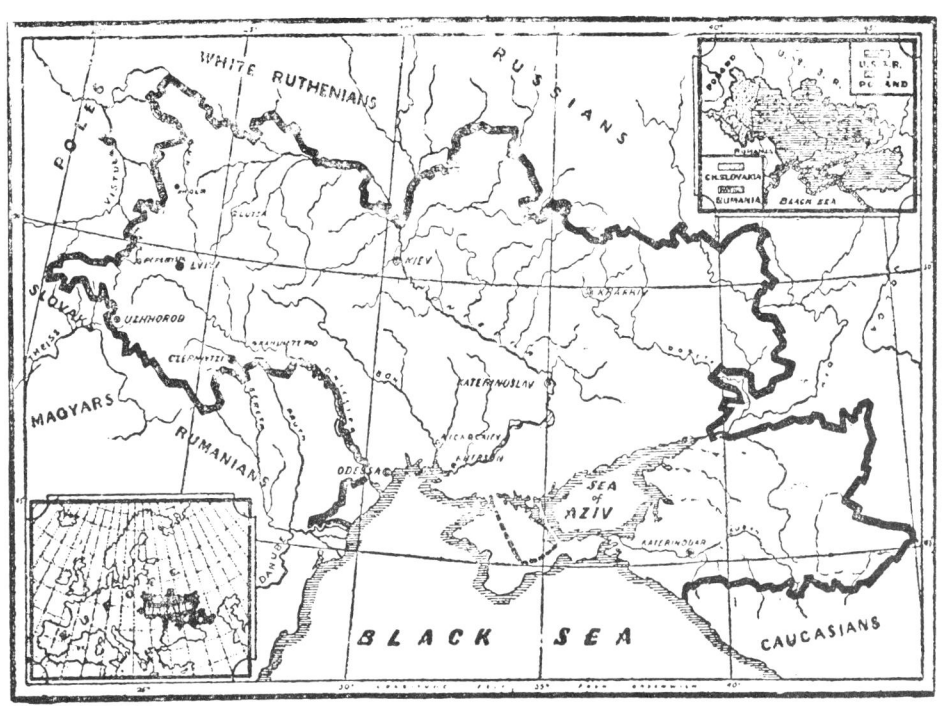

From cultivated farms of the Ukraine to virgin prairie homesteads and wilderness.

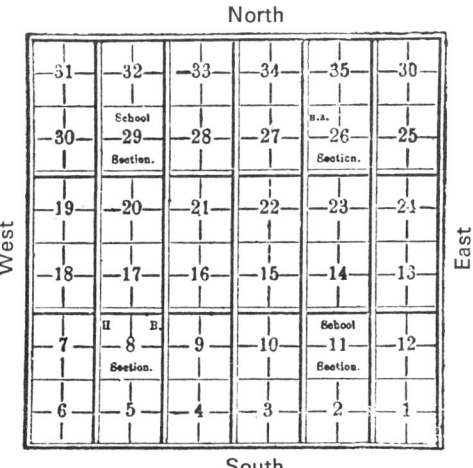

Above: Map of Ukraine.   Underneath: Map of Canadian township.

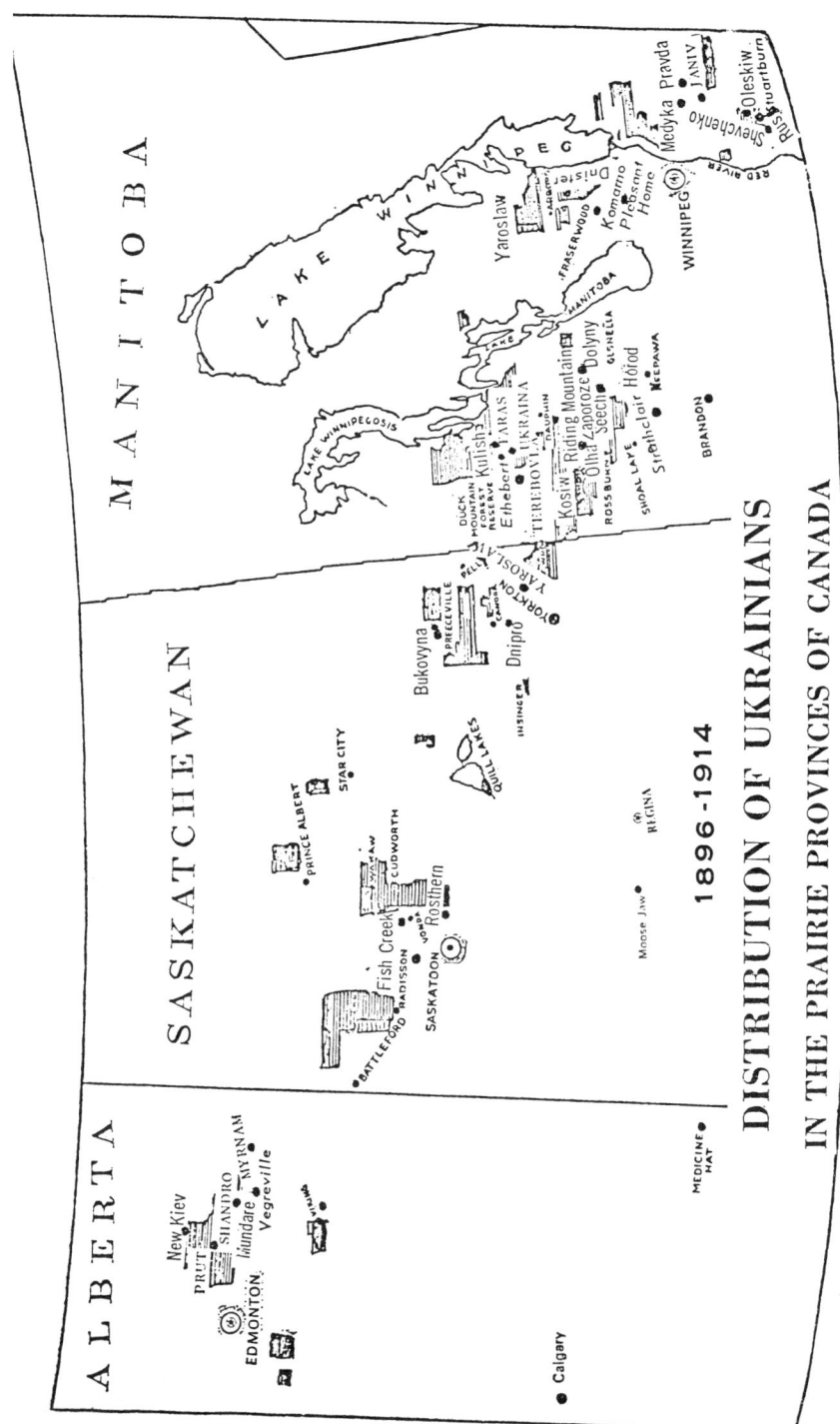

PIONEER ERA — ILLUSTRATIONS 49

Examples of first pioneer architecture: mud-hut, farm-house, church (Volkivtsi, 1899), school (Drifting River, 1899)

The land and woods had to be cleared before a house coud be built on the prairies. Women always gave a helping hand

PIONEER ERA — ILLUSTRATIONS 51

Women worked beside the homes, while the men worked on the construction of roads

Above: Road construction at Keld, Manitoba
Below: Railway construction in British Columbia

Grist mill and oven on the prairies—fundamental means of supporting the family

Oxen, cows and horses were not only essential in developing the homesteads but also the farmer's prestige

PIONEER ERA — ILLUSTRATIONS

Typical national clothing of the first settlers

Above: Pioneer families from Pokuttia, Halychyna
Below: Woman's light and heavy sheepskin coats from Bukovina

Women's costumes worn on Easter at Arbakka, Manitoba, 1912

Hucul costumes

Trisagion—symbol of unity and ritual solemnity; farmers of Podillia

PIONEER ERA — ILLUSTRATIONS

Variety of women's colored costumes

Above: Girls' costumes
Below: Women's costumes

Two memorable events in every family—wedding and funeral

Above: Pioneer wedding with violin and cymbal
Below: Parastas beside the grave

PIONEER ERA — ILLUSTRATIONS

**FIRST UKRAINIANS TO EMIGRATE
WHO LEFT INDELIBLE MARK IN THE NEW COUNTRY**

Wasyl Elyniak

Iwan Pylypiw

Wasyl Zahara and his wife Wasylyna

UKRAINIAN SETTLERS IN THE FIRST UKRAINIAN COLONY IN MANITOBA — STUARTBURN

Iwan and Wasylyna Mihaychuk

Iwan and Anna Sokolyk

Matwiy and Oksana Probizansky

Wasyl and Mariya Tanchak

Mariya Kohut

PIONEER ERA — ILLUSTRATIONS 59

**THOSE WHO LEFT THEIR IMPRINT ON THE CULTURAL LIFE
OF THE UKRAINIAN PIONEER IN CANADA**

Dr. Joseph Oleskiw

Rev. Nestor Dmytriw

Kyrylo (Cyril) Genik

Pioneer Tekla Ksionzyk — Stanko shows the author the location of the first Ukrainian High Mass in Canada — Terebowla (called Trembowla) and today Valley River, Manitoba

Memorial of the Ukrainian pioneers in the Interlake District, Pleasant Home, Manitoba

PIONEER ERA — ILLUSTRATIONS 61

Memorial of the 42 victims of the pioneer hardships —
Patterson Lake (north of Oakburn, Manitoba

The site of the encampment of the original settlers,
Patterson Lake, where 42 children and adults perished.

The first Basilian Fathers' chapel, Mundare, Alta., still preserved as a witness of the pioneer era.

The Federal Government to commemorate the first Ukrainian settlers in Alberta erected a model of a settler's home in Elk Island Park (near Edmonton).

THE YEARS OF INTENSIVE IMMIGRATION 1897—1914

ber Manitoba alone received 12,536 settlers. Dauphin district, with places like Sifton and Ethelbert, received 5,000; south of the Riding Mountains— Shoal Lake, 1200; Interlake region, 1,400; Stuartburn and vicinity, 3,000; Poplar Park, 36; St. Norbert, 100; Gonor, 3,000; Whitemouth 2,000; Cooks Creek 2,000; Broken Head 600... All these are round figures. A somewhat higher number was assigned to North West Territories, where at that time figures showed: Edna-Star and surrounding settlements of Edmonton had 9,000; Fish Creek and Rosthern 1,000; Yorkton and Saltcoats 4,500; total of 14,500. It is necessary to consider that Galician Poles were counted as registered by confused agents and officials, as Galician Ukrainians. But by official statistics there were no more than 10% of Poles in Galicia.

Some refute these data, (creating ethnological confusion) saying that all Catholics in Galicia who were not of Eastern Church ritual, were considered as Poles. Although on the other hand, a great majority of Roman-Catholic Galicians felt they were Ukrainians. However, if this observation is given consideration, then the total figures of Galician Poles would drop to 5%. But even accepting the maximum figure of 10% of Poles, we still would have 24,333 Ukrainians in Canada by the end of 1900. The records show 38,435 souls of Galicians and Bukovinians. By 1902 there were 18,954 persons in Manitoba and 19,471 in North West Territories, which is today's Saskatchewan and Alberta. Ukrainian immigration gradually increased in the next few years as is seen from additional study of statistics. According to Cyril Genik's memoranda [11]), as this versatile individual had firsthand information about the Ukrainian settlements, the Edna-Star colony alone had settled about 2,500 families; 2,000 families lived in this one solid colony and 500 families lived scattered over the surrounding townships. Its population was estimated then at 16,000, averaging six and one half members to a family, with over four children in each. They were young families, their ages between 30 and 40 years, their energies and life expectancies the greatest, assuring a steady progress of new generations. Obviously, they were a very important asset in the national economy of Canada.

The migration of Ukrainian immigrants to Canada continued during the ensuing years. In the year of 1907 alone it came to 21,000 Ruthenians, Bukovinians and Galicians. The impetus of the immigration waves did not abate until the outbreak of First World War in 1914, which interrupted it for some six long years and by doing so it formed one separate rounded period of history of Ukrainians in Canada. In this period, according to Department of Immigration data, no less than 170,000 Galicians, Bukovinians and Ruthenians entered Canada, not counting those Ukrainians that were written up after the name of the country from which they emigrated, such as Austrians and Russians, often too, as Poles, Hungarians and even Rumanians. A pertinent question that arises when it comes to Ukrainian nationality is where lies the cause of the chaotic denomination of this nationality, prior to First World War? It is necessary to answer this question in order to faciliate our readers' understanding of this problem as it appears in our subsequent chapters of this history. This confusion derives, to a greater degree, from the Anglo-Saxon idea of identifying people's nationality with the name of the state from which they come. This school holds that

---

[11]) Memorandum to the Commissioner of Immigration in Ottawa submitted by the Office of the Commissioner of Immigration in Winnipeg. Prepared by Cyril Genik.

if one comes from France, he is French; if he is from Germany, he is German, etc. By such reasoning, the Immigration officials put down the Ukrainians who came from Austria, as Austrians; those from Russia, as Russians; and the ones who were under Hungarian rule, as Hungarians etc. There were protests among the more knowledgeable Ukrainians who would rather have themselves signed by the name of their province—those who came from Galicia, as Galicians and those who had forsaken Bukovina, as Bukovinians. And the small percentage of Polish people from Galicia also called themselves Galicians. Hence the name "Galician" covered two nationalities, the Ukrainian and Polish. There were instances of many Germans from Galicia, calling themselves Galicians. But most Ukrainians wished to be signed up by their real nationality and at that time they were called Ruthenian or Rusyn. The meaning of Rusyn was translated into English as Ruthenian or Ruthenean and they are old historic names for "Ukraina" and "Ukraine". These latter names began to be used in the first decade of this century to take the place of "Rusyn' and "Rusky", used earlier. As we see it, the lack of delineation or differentiation between national and state extraction in the West and also political dramatic situation of the Ukrainian people at the time, created a series of notions as to the true recognition of Ukrainian nationality in Canada. This complication began to get clarified in Canadian statistics only after the First World War, although in some cases, it still exists today, as the press and publicists writing about Ukrainians and Ukraine, often use the terms "Russian" and "Russia" which do not correspond with the true state of things. These writers and editors name other nationalities from Soviet Union the same way. Often newspapermen's nomenclature infiltrates science, which then suffers from inaccuracy. Of necessity we adapt these reflections to the statistics of Ukrainian settlers in Canada, prior to First World War, in which, by reason of different confused thinking, we have not got an accurate data on Ukrainian people in Canadian census and immigration statistics. But despite all obscurities and great difficulties, it is possible to establish approximate figures which we employ in outlining our position from the beginning of emigration in this pioneering period that ended with an approximate total of 170,000—180,000 Ukrainians arriving in Canada during the early pioneer era. The so-called exceeded figure of 170,000 Ukrainians who came to Canada prior to World War one, is also accepted by Charles H. Young in his work, "The Ukrainian Canadians, A study in Assimilation", who is very careful in the use of statistical data. Mr. Young's data are accepted as sufficiently valid, therefore, 200,000 Ukrainians in Canada before the First World War is the figure nearer the truth.

More accurate data are given by William Darcovich and Paul Yuzyk in their Statistical Compendium. According their research 171,500 Ukrainians arrived to Canada before the First World War.*

---

*Statistical Compendium on the Ukrainians in Canada, Part I, 1977, Page 9.

GEOGRAPHIC DISTRIBUTION OF UKRAINIAN SETTLEMENTS IN PIONEER DAYS

Inaccurate as the statistics may be, there is ample proof, nevertheless, that Ukrainian immigrants first of all populated the three Western Provinces, Manitoba, Saskatchewan and Alberta. They settled in blocks or groups along forest-prairie stretches of lands in Manitoba and parts in Saskatchewan and Alberta. Starting in the easternmost Manitoba, they founded such colonies as Sirko, Arbakka, Shevchenko (Szewczenko) (Vita), Oleskiw (Tolstoi), Gardenton, Stuartburn, Caliento, Sundown, Rosa and Senkiw; and more colonies in the Interlake Region—Pleasant Home, Foley, Winnipeg Beach, Gimli, Dnister, Jaroslaw, Frazerwood, Fisher Branch, Poplarfield; Winnipegosis at the southern tip of Lake Winnipegosis; south of Dauphin Lake, Glenella, Mountain Road, Kelwood; and south of Riding Mountains, grew colonies—Olga, Mohyla, Ruthenia, Seech, Oakburn, Sandy Lake, Ozerna, Dolyny, Rossburn and Roblin; north of Riding Mountains, in the Dauphin Lake area, Terebowla (Valley River) made a start and then Sifton, Kosiw, Kolomyja (Venlaw), Ethelbert, Garland, Fork River, Dnipro (Fishing River), Ukraina. These settlements are separated from Ukrainian colonies in Saskatchewan by the Duck Mountain Forest Reserve. On the Saskatchewan side, a similar block of colonies were created—Wroxton, Calder, Yorkton, Canora, Preeceville, Insinger, Prince Albert, Wakaw, Rosthern, Cudworth, Vonda; farther across Redberry settlement, Radison, Krydor and Hafford. This tract continues into the Province of Alberta right into greater Vegreville area which embraces the territory 100 miles long and 70 miles wide, where again we have a string of Ukrainian colonies—Star, Lamont, Chipman, Krakiw, Ruska Svoboda (Vostok), Derwent, Hillard, Two Hills, Novy Kiev, Myrnam and Vegreville itself—as a capital of this, almost thoroughly Ukrainian region. There were official and unofficial warnings and stipulations regarding Ukrainian block settlements in the prairie provinces, but Charles H. Young says in his book "The Ukrainian Canadians" [1]: "Ukrainians have simply done what the Scotch did before them in Breton, Picton, Glengary, etc., the French in Quebec and Acadia and the English in the Barr Colony under the leadership of Bishop Lloyd".

Often the settlers of these different towns and places named them after the place names of their origin, viz. Kolomyja (Venlaw) and Kosiw were settled by immigrants from villages of Bereziv, Kolomyja County; Alvena and Hafford people from Horodenka; Lemberg and Keld from the village of Hleshchava, Terebowla County; colony Sokal, settlers from Sokal, Ukraine; colony Theodore—from villages of Doroshivtsi and Pohorylivtsi, etc. [2]. Because of the strong feeling of national origin, homesteads unfit for farming were pre-empted and settled. Though such poor lands required a lot of hard work, living close together with relatives, gave the newcomers a sense of security and assistance in case of family misfortune and sickness. The old country-people will stand by, ready to help. From these moral

---

[1] Charles H. Young, The Ukrainian Canadians, Toronto, 1931, p. 77.
[2] M. H. Marunchak, Canadian Terebowla (Trembowla) 1966, p. 37.

deductions flowed practical and mutual assistance in daily life, in the building of living quarters and farm barns, the improvement of land, procurement of provisions, clothing and other necessities, not excluding financial aid and household service. There were instances in the new settlements of communal gardens supplying all members of the colony with vegetables. Kosiw and Keld were the classical example of this enterprise in Manitoba. The seed for these gardens was brought from Ukraine [3]. Also we have spoken of tradition from oldtimers that they used community stoves and outdoor ovens and common utensils and oxen owned in common. Lastly, they themselves were united by common cultural acquisitions—speech, religion, customs, tradition, songs, experience of the past and present hardships—common lot was binding all of them into one family. The pioneers have given us written reminiscences and verbally transmitted stories of the pioneer life and of the unusually good family feeling and neighbourly atmosphere among all settlers in all colonies. When we read about the Orthodox and Catholic church members forming common parochial committees, then we admit that this was the summit of ecumenical tolerance and self-comprehension (example, Stuartburn [4]). In their commonly organized living those Ukrainian Canadian pioneers found their dignity and strength; and this feeling of partnership and togetherness reflected in each of their steps. Hence the creation of the so-called block settlements.

Their inadequacy, want and insecurity in the new surroundings, strengthened their community solidarity and responsibility. We find that pioneer reminiscences contain many notes expressing high sentiment of common national roots among Ukrainian settlers, although they came from different provinces, cities and villages, divided by various occupational authorities. In initial pioneer struggles and hardships their individual considerations quite often were set aside in favor of public duty and community needs. Being in a homogeneous state had its influence on their further social and cultural growth, which will be dealt with in another chapter.

That the reader might have a clearer picture of the distribution of Ukrainians in the provinces prior to the First World War, we follow the statistics, inaccurate as they are, and transcribe the data from the 1911 census of population in Canada. In doing so, we consider such names of Ukrainians, at that time, as Bukovinians, Galicians and Ruthenians, not including such names as Austrians, Russians, Hungarians and others who named the country from which they emigrated for the census taker as their nationality and which was so registered. Their number percentage-wise was important enough. We leave them out simply because their inclusion would complicate the picture already muddled enough. The statistics below we accept as original average arithmetic with certain possible digressions: [5]

---

[3] M. H. Marunchak, Studies in the History of Ukrainians in Canada, V. II, page 129.
[4] Ibid. pp. 29 and 56.
[5] "Rozselennia Ukraintsiv Kanady", I. Tesla, Almanac Golden Jubilee, Winnipeg, 1957, p. 66.

GEOGRAPHIC DISTRIBUTION... 67

	Bukovinians Male	Bukovinians Female	Galicians Male	Galicians Female	Ruthenians Male	Ruthenians Female	All Ukrainians	% male
Nova Scotia	2	..	206	83	1	..	292	95:5
Prince Edward Island	4	..	..	..	..	..	4	100.0
New Brunswick	16	1	1	..	..	..	18	94.4
Quebec	193	17	211	80	33	9	453	76.6
Ontario	162	15	1186	113	1191	412	3078	82.5
Manitoba	320	184	7235	5721	9250	7974	30684	54.8
Alberta	1732	1578	6066	3901	2309	1998	17583	57.5
Saskatchewan	3106	2638	5775	4029	3549	3179	22276	55.6
British Columbia	82	9	497	54	33	7	682	89.7
Canada	5514	4446	21177	13981	16366	13479	74572	57.7

From the above statistics, we see that about 94% of all Ukrainian emigration in the pioneer period was concentrated in the three prairie provinces among which Manitoba had the lead. We find that Manitoba had then 3/7 of all Ukrainian population in Canada. The Province of Saskatchewan held the second place; Alberta, the third place. Outside the prairie provinces, Ukrainians settled also in Ontario, British Columbia, Quebec and Nova Scotia. The new population in these four provinces differed notably from the prairie settlers. The Ukrainian colonies on the prairies were agricultural and therefore permanently rooted in the soil, while those in Ontario or British Columbia consisted of industrial laborers who were usually transients drifting from place to place, seeking better working conditions. They were mostly men whose women remained in the old country until their husbands earned enough money to send for the whole family for a permanent residence in the new country,—for example, Ontario had 82.5% men and 17.5% women of Ukrainian immigrant population. These statistics show also that there was a very small percentage of complete families in cities and also that often whole families, as they earned sufficient money, moved West to the prairies where they acquired their homesteads and became independent husbandry men. The love of the land drew Ukrainian settlers to the Canadian West, to the promised land, as the pioneers tell us. Due to the feeling of their cultural belonging and householder security, they acquired significant energy for their future development. In proportion to settlers in the prairie provinces, Ukrainians constituted 6.8% of Manitoba population in 1901; 4.7% in Alberta and 4.5% in Saskatchewan. Concerning electoral divisions, the largest concentrations of Ukrainians were: Dauphin, Manitoba, 6,722; Selkirk, Manitoba (Interlake Area), 8,217; and Marquette (south of Riding Mountains) 4,372 voters. In electoral division of MacKenzie, in Saskatchewan, there were 10,662 souls.

Simultaneously with homestead settlements, urban centers of Western Canada were receiving their share of Ukrainian people. They pushed forward into streets and blocks, city after city, as is shown by statistics in the year 1911: Winnipeg embraced 3,519 people; Saskatoon received 3,004; Prince Albert placed 1,536; as Edmonton had 1,588 and Strathcona, 1,692. This shows us that Edmonton-Strathcona formed a community, reaching 3,280 and was already at that time a notable rival to Ukrainian Winnipeg in Western Canada.

Besides the above named block or compact order of colonies, there was a string of smaller, separate ones, scattered in all three provinces; for instance, in northern Manitoba, in Winnipegosis and vicinity; in Saskatchewan, south of Saskatoon around Moose Jaw and Regina and in Alberta, in places like Lethbridge, Medicine Hat, Calgary, etc. We also have a string of colonies of other nationalities, forming in the midst of Ukrainian block colonies in the prairie provinces and often the Ukrainians came and joined the other nationalities that had settled there before them. They were Anglo-Saxon, French, Scandinavian, German . To fill out the mosaic of these settlements, Hungarian, Rumanian, Polish and also Dukhobor colonies are worthy of mention.

CANADIAN WEST AT THE END OF 19th CENTURY

The Canadian official census of 1891, that is the time when Ukrainian immigrants began to arrive in Canada, shows the Canadian population to be 4,833,000, of which only 152,506 persons were settled in Manitoba and less than 100,000 in North West Territories, which is today Saskatchewan and Alberta. This unusually unpretentious figure of the population was losing itself in proportion to hundreds of thousands of square miles of land in the present prairie provinces: Manitoba and Alberta that together contained 753,497 square miles.

As we know, Saskatchewan and Alberta were a part of the territory administered at that time directly by the Ottawa Government through its appointees in Regina. The North-West Territories, as they were then officially named, remained almost unknown geographically—immense and unutilized reserves of forests and fertile soil, untouched by man's plow, that could feed and take good care of thousands upon thousands of land hungry Europeans. But as we had noted previously, the immigration into Canada decreased. The Anglo-Saxon settlers who homesteaded in the North West Territories in 1880's, especially in Saskatchewan, as a result of pioneer hardships, cold long winters, droughts and crop failures, were abandoning their homesteads, departing East to milder climate and a more civilized world. Canadian West, instead of gaining population by way of immigration and natural growth, began to lose even the people that had been there earlier, and new blood came very slow.

The settlers from British Isles and Scandinavian countries did not seem to make very great progress in the Canadian West, although they were substantially financed by the government. Being used to more orderly, civilized and cultural life, they did not wish to invest much exertion in the West because in other parts of Canada, particularly in the East, they always could find better and easier living among their country people. Those who came from U.S.A. often returned home when their adventures and hopes turned sour and getting-rich-quick failed to materialize. Of the 1,376 homestead grants issued them in 1874, only 463 remained occupied. But, for only about 20 years of colonizing, that is from 1870 to 1890, when Ukrainians began to settle Western Provinces—Manitoba, Saskatchewan and Alberta—the combined population reached 251,473 persons. The majority of them made Manitoba their choice. Besides Anglo-Saxons, Mennonites who came from Ukraine in 1874, and also Icelanders, founded their first colonies in Manitoba (1876); somewhat later came Germans and Hungarians. A few years later (1886) Baron Hirsch led a campaign for settling Jews in Saskatchewan. But regardless of all the effort put forth, in the overall summary, only minimal movement resulted. For instance, in 1896, only 902 candidates reported and almost half of them abandoned their farming, due to very difficult conditions.

To show graphically how the prairie provinces stood as regards population at that time, we offer the statistics of the contemporary urban centers which during the years of 1891, 1901, 1906 were insignificant or did not exist at all.

Place	1891	1901	1906
Winnipeg	25,638	42,340	90,153
Brandon	3,778	5,620	10,408
Neepawa	774	1,418	1,895
Selkirk	950	2,188	2,700
Killarney		585	1,117
Souris		839	1,413
Dauphin		1,135	1,670
Calgary	3,876	4,382	13,573
Edmonton		4,176	14,088
Regina		2,249	6,169
Moose Jaw		1,558	6,249
Weyburn		113	996
Wetaskiwin		550	1,652
Cardston		639	1,001
Indian Head		768	1,545
Raymond			1,568
Vermillion			623
Moosomin		863	1,152
Saskatoon		113	3,011
Rosthern		413	918
Yorkton		700	1,368

Somewhat different conditions were found in British Columbia which numbered 98,173 inhabitants in 1891; 178,657 in 1901; and 392,480 in 1911. The growth of this province was significantly boosted by the growth of the three prairie provinces.

The last decade of the 19th century was marked by the first serious crisis in the Dominion Government, since Confederation. In this decade Canada had prime ministers: Sir J. A. MacDonald finished his term of office in parliament in 1891 and after him, passed, in their turns, the governments of Sir John Abbott, Sir John Thompson, Sir MacKenzie Bowell, Sir Charles Tupper. All of them held the premier's office between 1891 and 1896, which was only five years. Such frequent changes in the premiership position did not help in far-reaching government planning. As the premiers changed so did their different ministers and with them also the directors or heads of different departments. With the departure of department leaders, departed also into oblivion the plans of their departments. And before the new ministers planned something new or confirmed the plans of their predecessors, a great deal of time elapsed and by then they were followed by new leaders to repeat the same procedure when another set of ministers were appointed. Such was the case with the immigration plans of these changing governments. Under Sir MacKenzie Bowell, the minister of the Department of Interior Affairs, Sir Mayne Daly, prepared great immigration plans and discussed them with Dr. Joseph Oleskiw about immigration concerning Ukrainians. But when T. M. Bowell and T. M. Daly were ousted from their posts, the case was shelved for two long years. Only under Sir Wilfred Laurier and the stability of his administration for a full 15 years, was there a wider planning and realization of the sound government plans for the development of Canada and greater colonization of Western Provinces assured. Considering the boundless empty spaces of the Great North West, and planning realistically, Laurier appointed just the right young man for the task. He was Clifford Sifton, thirty five years of age and a lawyer, who had already been attorney general during the years of 1891-1906, and who had also served as minister of education in the Provincial Government of Manitoba. Clifford Sifton entered federal politics as a member of Parliament from Brandon constituency in 1896. Premier Laurier observed C. Sifton's unusual abilities and gave him the portfolio of minister of the Department of Interior Affairs and General Superintendent of Indian Affairs. The Minister of the Department of Interior Affairs, in those days, was also the Minister of Immigration, a separate department in his ministry. Clifford Sifton held this post for ten years and during his administration (1896-1905) he devoted his energy and abilities to the colonization of Western Canada, creating a very important chapter in the history of Ukrainians of Canada.

Some researchers of Canadian history name Clifford Sifton as a great friend and benefactor of Ukrainians upon whom he bestowed great favors and sympathies. They affirm that he was the one who had given their immigration its massive beginning. These statements are far from being true. The initial plans and experiments to settle Ukrainians in Canada were made in the year of 1895, when John Hall held the position of Superintendent of Immigration, and T. Mayne Daly was Minister of the Interior Affairs; that is, they were both members of the conservative government headed by Sir MacKenzie Bowell. They were the ones who, together with Dr. Joseph Oleskiw, originated and elaborated the plans for settling the Canadian West, of which there are preserved several memoranda composed by Dr. Joseph Oleskiw. Sir Charles Tupper, one of the fathers of Confederation, played an important role as mediator between Dr. Joseph Oleskiw and the Government of Canada in 1895. Sir Charles Tupper, at that time, held the post of High Commissioner in London. The first group transports arrived in Canada in the spring and summer of 1896, when Sir Charles Tupper was the premier of Canada. In May, 1896, he resigned his position of High Commissioner in London and assumed the position of Prime Minister which he held for only three months and after him came Sir Wilfred Laurier. It was then, that is, in the autumn of 1896, that Clifford Sifton took the helm of Immigration Department. Prior to his administration there were established the following Ukrainian colonies: Stuartburn, Terebowla, Ruska Svoboda, Edna, Brokenhead and others, which resulted from the endeavours of the immigration policies of Sir Wilfred Laurier's and Clifford Sifton's predecessors. To Clifford Sifton belongs praiseworthy acknowledgement for his constructive plans of the settlements in the "wild west;" for his clear vision of its development and knowing how to stand up in defence of the policies of those settlers for whose benefit his great predecessor had done so much. Clifford Sifton had strong support in Sir Wilfred's government. T. M. Daly lived through the regimes of two premiers (Sir J. Thompson's and Sir T. M. Bowell's) but he could not find a common ground on which to stand with the third one, Sir Charles Tupper; he did not even get into his cabinet. Clifford Sifton had not only vision, but aggressiveness, too. As soon as he acquainted himself with Dr. Oleskiw's immigration plans, he appointed him his unofficial Canadian representative in Galicia and tried to support his active service by moral and financial means. In taking over the Department of Interior Affairs, Clifford Sifton's important steps, in improving and enlarging the immigration to Western Canada, were based on his convincing view, which he defended at every step, — that Slavs, viz. "East-European people were just as good settlers as those from Western Europe or the Anglo-Saxons, themselves", for that matter. Moreover, Sifton considered that the East-European element, especially Ukrainians, who were then popularly called Galicians, were more suitable to settle in Western Canada than people from Western Europe. He perceived their worthiness in their particular attachment to, and love for, the soil which the Ukrainians had cherished from generation to generation and passed it on from grandfather to son and grandson. Their aptitude and endurance at work and their patience and forbearance in carrying on against odds and heavy burdens,—these were additional attributes of the Ukrainian settler, which Mr. Sifton valued highly. One more value which Clifford Sifton appreciated, were the large families of the Ukrainians, and the industry and diligence of Ukrainian women Mr. Sifton often noted: "I think a stalwart peasant in a sheepskin coat, born on the soil, whose forefathers have been farmers for ten generations, with a stout wife and half a dozen children, is a very desirable settler".

To endow the immigration machinery with greater flexibility and more efficient operation, Clifford Sifton re-organized the Department of Immigration. He established a position for an Inspector of Canadian Agents in Europe with the main office in London. In other words, Clifford Sifton transferred the Immigration Affairs of Canada from the High Commissioner in London to a man whose exclusive duty was to attend to, and direct those affairs. This function he assigned to an experienced official of the Immigration Department, V. T. P. Preston.

V. T. P. Preston's job was to spread effective propaganda in Europe in favor of emigration to Canada. He went to Galicia twice to confer with Dr. Joseph Oleskiw. Hundreds of thousands of pamphlets were distributed in Galicia, Bukovina and beyond the Carpathian Mountains, under Austrian regime, with such eloquent titles as: "Free land is waiting for you", "Live and work for yourself and your family", "Canada will give you land", "Be your own master husbandman", "Take care of your children's future", "The wondrous Canadian West", "The country called Canada", "Live in Canada", and others.

Circulars were sent out in different languages, but most of them in Ukrainian. And it was soon proved that "men in sheepskin coats" as Ukrainians were then disparingly referred to, could withstand the most tiring toil and the severest cold of winter. Clifford Sifton's theory justified itself hundredfold. Alberta and Saskatchewan population had risen considerably.

When the question of "settlers in sheepskin coats" became also political party's walking cane in election propaganda, Clifford Sifton's opponents dubbed the Ukrainians with one more undeserved epithet, "Sifton's pets", to which Mr. Sifton answered in his well-expressed comment:

"I am not much inclined to granting immigrants special favours. The only time that I remember where this class of immigrants got any assistance was when a number of their poor people got stranded in the immigration sheds at Winnipeg. We sent them east of the Red River, towards the border of fair land and gave them flour and bacon *as a loan,* every cent of which was paid back, which I imagine is one of the few instances where a government loan was ever fully repaid".

The above quotation shows that Sir Clifford Sifton was not an altruist at all in his dealings with Ukrainian settlers in Canada. They were based on cold economic calculations. However, Ukrainian pioneer reminiscences about those who took advantage of the temporary government help as mentioned by Clifford Sifton, do not mention the "bacon" which was supposed to have been given to the settlers as a temporary loan. They well remember the flour, popularly branded with big XXXX in red, on white 98 lb. cotton sacks (the lowest priced kind of flour) and potatoes and sometime sugar. The fact is that all temporary aid in the first winter in Canada was later paid back in full. No special government privileges whatever were received by Ukrainian immigrants. The pioneers mention cases where immigrants were refusing these loans. They would rather go hungry for a while than incur debt against their homesteads. Clifford Sifton, no doubt, saw these thrifty qualities of Ukrainian peasants and therefore again, in another instance, said this about them:

"If one should examine twenty people who turn up at Hamburg to emigrate, he might find one escaped murderer, three or four wasters and never-do-wells, some very poor shopkeepers, artisans or labourers, and there might be one or two stout, hard peasants in sheepskin coats. Obviously the peasants are the men who are wanted here".

Political wrangles and party accusations against Sifton's immigration policy concerning "Galician settlers", did not stop Clifford Sifton from coming to an agreement with the North Atlantic Trading Co., in 1899, about recruiting Ukrainians and other eastern peasants as settlers for Canada. This company was getting five dollars for each head of the family and two dollars for other family members. This was quite an encouragement for the above mentioned company and its agents in recruiting more settlers. This agreement was renewed in 1904.

But the best propaganda in Canada's favor is gleaned from the letters of the first settlers who already had their homesteads and those who came after. Those letters to relatives in Ukraine, bragged about the 160 acres for only $10.00, the freedom in Canada, the many great chances of building up this country, about bilingual schools, and their own individual, social and cultural gain and growth. It was the best living propaganda of greater power than the two or five dollar commission per person. And thousands of Ukrainian settlers began to arrive in Canada. Upon perceiving this, Clifford Sifton cancelled the per capita commission with the North Atlantic Trading Company. In line with his preparations in Europe, Clifford Sifton made changes in the immigraton set-up. He appointed James A. Smart, his long time friend, who was also his colleague in Manitoba parliament, as his deputy minister. J. A. Smart was correctly informed about the Canadian West and shared the opinions of his chief about the adaptability of Ukrainian immigrants. Simultaneously with this nomination, Frank

---

[6]) Bilingual Schools—it means here—English and Ukrainian Schools.

Pedley was chosen as Superintendent of Immigration, who was a devotee of Sifton's policy in Winnipeg, the main center for the West and its colonization. Also a bureau of Commissioner of Immigration was created, with William Forsythe McCreary at its helm, who was also mayor of Winnipeg in 1897. In Manitoba, Saskatchewan and Alberta, immigration shelters were constructed to alleviate transport and sojourn difficulties of immigrants in the first days after their arrival in Canada.

Despite all the invectives cast upon Clifford Sifton's head concerning the "Galician settlers", the immigration machine worked efficiently. In the wild spaces where formerly stretched an endless terrain for hunters and adventure seekers, sprung up mud huts, followed by comfortable dwellings, and cultivated farms in the new settlers' colonies. These grew each year, the trails widened, then came well-beaten highways and the railroads began to cut through the terrain of prairie provinces and the Canadian West started to live the life of the whole of Canada, making this once wild country a civilized part of Canadian national organism. Clifford Sifton's immigration policy drew to Canada from year-to-year, 30 to 40 thousands new immigrants, among whom Ukrainians occupied an important place. From U.S.A. alone, in 1898-1904, 168,684 settlers came and from British Isles 148,642. The population in the prairie provinces increased, for in 1906 it already numbered 900,000. In that year Clifford Sifton departed from Wilfred Laurier's government. Although the administration of immigration changed hands somewhat earlier, yet once directed, the immigration stream flowed on in the same direction and with the same intensity.

Only the First World War interrupted the historic pace which Clifford Sifton began so successfully. He had grasped the fundamental idea of his predecessor, Minister T. M. Daly and that great inspirator of this whole idea, Dr. Joseph Oleskiw, who together with Clifford Sifton formed the great trinity of the development of Canada's West. As the two first men departed into the shadow of history, Clifford Sifton was left to become a prominent promoter and a fine architect of the prairie provinces. During his ministry two new provinces—Saskatchewan and Alberta—joined the Confederation of Canada and became a living fabric with broad perspectives of the young sovereign country. These two new provinces straightened out the state organism of Canada, drawing to its pulse and heart the most remotely placed, in the west, British Columbia. So began to be written a new page in the story of the great and united Canada. To recognize and ascribe to Clifford Sifton the value of his personal efforts in this imposing country, is not to obscure the desserts and merits of all those nameless and despised "Galicians" who applied their sinewed and calloused hands, healthy brains and warm hearts to this great development under very difficult conditions and yet had to live in the shadow of contempt and insults from their fellow Canadians.

WELCOME NEWCOMERS AND RACIAL PREJUDICE

As we already know, Ukrainians entered the pages of the Canadian English language press and got introduced to Canadian community as "Galicians" and "Bukovinians". This came about only when the massive immigration began in 1896. At first, there appeared only short and inconspicuous notes of information about Galicians and Bukovinians, a little about their past, that they come from Austria and what different denominations existed among them, etc. Dr. Joseph Oleskiw wrote an explanatory article which was printed in the Winnipeg Free Press. These were scanty and elemental news about people who began to arrive in Canada in great numbers and about whom Canadian public in general literally knew nothing.

The attitude of the English press towards Ukrainians began to take its form only in 1897. In September of that year "The Daily Nor-Wester" in Winnipeg which continued the policy of its incomparable predecessor "Nor-Wester" had supported the resolution of the Rosedale Municipal council against the settling of "destitute immigrants on timber lands around the Riding Mountains in the Municipality of Rosedale, Manitoba".

"The Daily Nor-Wester" commented on this resolution in a lengthy editorial which is important to be quoted for history's sake, because on its premises rested the basic opinions of the English-speaking public for years to come. The following is "The Daily Nor-Wester's" editorial:

"The protest against destitute settlers relate in particular to certain of Mr. Sifton's Galician paupers whom the immigration officers have located in Rosedale Municipality. The protest of the council is quite justified. The dumping down of these filthy, penniless and ignorant foreigners into progressive and intelligent communities is a serious hardship to such a community. These people have not sufficient capital to carry them through the winter... They also bring with them disease in almost every consignment, cases of scarlet fever, measles or some other contagious malady are discovered, and their dirty habits render the stamping out of infection among them a very difficult matter. They will be the means of spreading these diseases among the settlers into whose midst they are intruded. A few of the families will constitute a permanent menace to the public health of the neighborhood... Being poor and unprogressive... They will retard instead of promote the progress of the municipality. They will increase the cost of running the schools; for, under the new school law, where there are 10 Galician children, the school District must employ a teacher who can teach in their language... They are not people who will mix socially with the English speaking population... The difficulty is greatly increased when people of alien race and religion come in and take up the lands which would otherwise be taken up by settlers who would contribute to the support of an existing place of worship. By their unintelligent methods of farming they will lower the reputation of the products of the community... and their farms will be centres from which weeds and animal diseases will be disseminated in the fields and herds of their neighbors...".

These and similar abusive slander the editor-in-chief concluded with the following assertions:

"It cannot be too emphatically repeated that the people of Manitoba want no such "Settlers" as these "Galicians". "At this point, it is in line to remember what this newspaper on December 23, 1896, under the title "Undesirable Immigrants", wrote that "The southern Slavs are probably the least promising of all the material that could be selected for nation building".

A few days after the appearance of the "Nor-Wester's" pasquinade, Rev. Nestor Dmytriw had his explanatory reply printed in the Winnipeg Free Press. As the first Ukrainian priest in Canada, he travelled around Ukrainian colonies rendering spiritual services to the new settlers and simultaneously working as an immigration official for the Winnipeg bureau. In his answer, Rev. N. Dmytriw pointed to the fact that his people were struggling with great difficulties of moral and material order as new settlers-beginners. He gave data about their pioneer farming, their industry and well managed homesteads; how they in five years had achieved rewarding results on Canadian farms. Nevertheless, those calumnies, once broadcast, spread very fast. As misfortune would have it, only one year after this general attack by the chauvinistic element, what happened in Stuartburn, an almost thoroughly Ukrainian settlement, started press virulence going stronger than ever, because a Ukrainian family got murdered by two local settlers. The killers were sentenced to be hanged. One of them was mentally ill. The press, still hostile to Sifton's immigration efforts, renewed its attacks with big, black headlines: "Galician Murderers", "Galicians Will Hang". Without exception the write-ups aimed to stir up racial hatred, implying tha Galicians were not only "dirty" but very "murderous", too. Next year, this unfortunate story was topped by New York's "dreadful news", that "an invasion of 50,000 Galicians threatened Canada", not the United States, because U.S. "won't have those most undesirable class of settlers". This was meant to warn the citizen voters against Sifton and the "rotten liberals". In connection with this news, "Toronto Mail" continued its severe criticism. How inimical newspaper atmosphere and moral pressure at that time against Galicians was, can be judged by the fact that the immigration official did not announce in the press about the death of about forty Ukrainian children who died during three long weeks in the ill-fated transport to Strathclair-Patterson under frightfully unhygienic and climatic conditions, and this news was seemingly withheld for the reason of "not wishing to worsen the already bad news about Galicians".

With such situations and conditions haunting our memories, it is a pleasure to note objective voices reversing the tone, for the benefit of the helpless immigrants of those days. In a number of these voices we include the Winnipeg Free Press, saying, May 13, 1899: "Any man, no matter what his nationality, so long as he desires to earn an honest living and is willing to till the soil, is a welcome addition to this western country, and his arrival is a national blessing".

Finally "Toronto Mail" mustered enough courage to take on an objective journalistic attitude towards Galicians. To gather an accurate report of the situation in colonies settled by Galicians and Bukovinians, a correspondent of this Toronto newspaper visited a number of settlements in Manitoba and Saskatchewan, in 1898, and prepared a lengthy account for his daily paper. This account, to some extent, is an historic document, for as an eye witness he straightened out a long string of accusations against Galician immigrants. And he brought out credible data about achievements of these settlers in their first years of sojourn in Canada. This report is more meaningful because of its appearance in a strong Conservative daily newspaper, which had sharply criticised Clifford Sifton's policies. We quote: "A great deal of prejudice has been excited against the Galicians, partly through the effort of ignorant writers, who have but made a superficial study of them, perhaps not even that, but got their opinions second hand, partly also through the deliberate misrepresentation of party organs whose aim in all things it to score against the government and whose hope in this particular case is to discredit the Immigration Department. We carry our politics so far in this country that everything is discussed with the view to making party capital; the truth being such an exceedingly minor consideration that it is more often than not left out of the account. The prejudice has been confirmed and aggravated in many instances by our observation of them as they arrive in the country uncouthly clad and tired, dirty, and dejected after a journey of six or seven thousand miles. They are srange to our eyes and far from pleasing, and we go away with a deepened prejudice. Those who see more of them, and see them from week to week and month to month, know how diligently and resolutely they apply themselves to the task of establishing themselves in their new homes, and then they have a different opinion. They are said and popularly supposed to be dirty. There is no class of immigrants more clean in their personal habits than the Galicians. They have a mania for bathing. This statement will probably incite a sneer. It is safe to say that the average Galician family on the prairie, within reasonable reach of a river or with reasonable means of convenience, bathes oftener than the sneerer does. Very likely all Galicians are not clean; certainly Anglo-Saxons are not. They come poor, it is said. They do, for the most part, but poverty is neither a crime nor a sin, and if a misfortune, it is the one that afflicts a great many more than Galicians. Many of those who today sneer at them probably came to this country as they are, and for the same purpose, to better their fortunes. What matter their poverty if they have the aptitude and the spirit to get on? They have good, comfortable houses, commodious stables and nearly all have horses, cattle, poultry, and good supply of farm implements".

"We have been accustomed to praising Icelanders for the splendid progress they have made; they must not be too cast down if they find the palm wrested from them by these industrious Slavs, who seem to have an extraordinary knack of getting on, when blessed, to bear in mind, and that is that Galician immigration was inaugurated by a conservative government. Then years hence, they will be glad to recall this and take credit for it, if the promise of today is realized; but at present it is convenient to ignore it, as they think that in the Galicians they have the weapon with which to beat the government of the day" [1].

The next one in line came the C.P.R. president, W. Van Horn, who got up to defend Galicians. He deposed a public declaration about them, saying that they had paid the Canadian Pacific Railroad every cent they owed for their transportation to Canada. Following Van Horn, came the immigration summaries from Commissioner Spears that spoke plainly about the progress of those rejected by chauvinistic elements, as if they were the last trash of society. Commissioner Spears also confirmed that Ukrainians paid

---

[1] Winnipeg Free Press, Nov. 22, 1898, page 1, reprint from Toronto Mail.

back every penny contracted for government help, such as flour, potatoes and other food products. And thus was started the slow progress of explanation from objectively thinking citizens who could see a good colonizing element in the new settlers of Ukrainian extraction. These were Clifford Sifton's principles and sentiments.

A general opinion about Ukrainians being good quality settlers was slow in coming. The nail for the casket lid of chauvinistic feeling against Ukrainians was driven in by Sir R. L. Borden as late as 1906. This respectable politician refuted it with the following declaration: "In the year 1903 and again in 1904 I said to this House that I was subject to some prejudice against these people, but I had gone to the West and I was glad to see that my original fears were proved to be entirely wrong as the Ukrainians had made good settlers".

The indisputable fact remains that there were long years of discrimination against Ukrainians in Canada, but they, with great stoicism, tolerated it individually and collectively, and simply ignored undeserved calumniation. Denying his personal "ego" the Ukrainian settler worked out his own destiny, building up his husbandry in step with the social life in different aspects. With his blistered and calloused hands and in a copious rain of sweat, often at the cost of his health and life, the Ukrainian carried on and gained some prestige due him.

Quoting John W. Dafoe's book, "Clifford Sifton in Relation to his Times", we repeat the following words: "The impression that Mr. Sifton's immigration policies flooded the West with unassimilable Slavs still lingers as an echo from those days of bitter controversy".

FIRST STEPS IN HOMELAND AND CANADA

In order to get to Canada from Europe the emigrant had to buy steamship and railroad tickets that would cost an average of $85.00 for the adults and half that price for children up to ten years of age. To scrape together a sum of nearly $300.00 for a family of four was quite an undertaking. In addition to this an extra sum of $25.00 had to be on hand to show the Canadian authorities at the port of entry, plus the expense money to pay for food and other essentials during the land and ocean passage. Those who were leaving Europe had to sell their land and property—providing they had enough of it—to pay for their transportation, and thus for them the problem would be solved. The land was usually sold to the richer farmers and inn-keepers. In the eyes of the community this was an act of unpatriotic gesture, as the land and estates passed into an outsider's hands, the hands of other nationalities. Those leaving the country also had to consider an interim course of borrowing a certain amount of cash, usually from credit unions, but more often from inn-keepers and money-lending-sharks who made fortunes on these deals—usually at 12 percent interest from the borrowed sum—to be paid first, which was considered an act of favor on their part. Estates were sacrificed to these vulture-like brokers and even the property of relatives and friends was often used as the medium of security for the borrowed cash. In the beginning it was easy to sell property as those who wished to emigrate were very few. But following 1895, when emigration to Canada and U.S.A. was greatly increased, the opportunities for disposing of land and estate were getting fewer all the time. The land value started to go down and the credit went up accordingly. A timely and redeeming idea came from Dr. O. Oleskiw, who formalized a plan of long term land credits agency for the purpose of buying up these mortgaged lands from the emigrants. Unfortunately, the planned credit union did not have much to show for its efforts, as Dr. Oleskiw's attempts to borrow money in England and Canada for this purpose was only partially successful. So it was no wonder that the emigrants, who were leaving the old country, had not sufficient funds to take care of their needs. Official researches, dealing with emigration to U.S.A. reveal that Ukrainians from Galicia (Western Ukraine) had only an average of $12.86 per person when those of other nationalities could each show $21.57 [1]).

An interesting research study, dealing with the above matter, was made by Dr. J. S. Woodsworth, who on the basis of questionnaire, covering 832 families, was able to verify that 50% of the immigrants who settled in Canada had no capital whatsoever, and 42% had less han $500.00 and only 8% had over $500.00. It must be noted that the transports of immigrants handled by Dr. O. Oleskiw were in better financial circumstances than those who travelled on their own. To this event Dr. V. J. Kaye, in his very comprehensive study about "The Early Ukrainian Settlers in Canada 1895-1900", [2]) draws our attention.

---

[1]) Immigration Commission, Washington, 1911.
[2]) Published for the "Ukrainian Canadian Research Foundation" by University of Toronto Press, 1964.

When first the flow of mass emigration to Canada began it was difficult to keep control of the records regarding the many thousands that were involved. For a short while such a control did exist in the hands of a special emigration committee that was established by Dr. O. Oleskiw in Lviv. This committee, sad to relate, did not live long, but still it had a moral background—in its brief role of a faithful informing agency—in telling us about the emigrants leaving for Canada. Be it to his credit that Dr. O. Oleskiw performed this useful function without any financial reward, not having any funds from either the Canadian government or from his fellow countrymen. This committee differed from similar committees of other nationalities— English, Swedish, Dutch, Norwegian, German and others, for they had their government representatives to back them up and to advise them as well as to help them financially with transportation and with credit loans for making a start on the farms. The stateless Jewish emigrants were well looked after by the rich Baron Hirsh. On the other hand, from the financial point of view, the Ukrainian immigrant-settler had to depend entirely on his own brain and brawn. Very often when he could not bring his family with him, due to lack of sufficient transportation funds, he came out by himself. Mother and children were left back at home to look after their little estates while the father went out alone, for a year or more, to earn enough money with which to buy the passage ticket for his family.

"Galicians and Bukovinians threw themselves into hard work", wrote a chronicler of those days. "This was of great help, both in the development of farm life and for the old country as well. Money was earned and sent to the old country to pay for the previously incurred debts as well as to finance the bringing of their families to Canada" [3].

The lone immigrants coming to Canada, without their families very often experienced a kind of a personal shock which had psychological effects. Many who were deprived of family life and separated from their loved ones over a long period of time often ended up in misunderstanding and family tragedies. Many times a family would pull its resources together to finance passage to Canada for one or more of their "braver" members, with the idea that they in turn would help to bring others to the new country. On this score the statistics of Ukrainian immigration show a much larger percentage of men over women. This one sided balance may best be observed in industrial centres, where male single wage earners saved their money in order to pay for the transportation of their families to Canada, while on the farms males and females were more equally divided. So the portion of the Anglo press that was bitterly opposed to C. Sifton's immigration policy and was strongly against Ukrainian immigration to Canada, was correct on one single point, when it stated that: "The Galicians are penniless farmers whom we may rightly compare, in regard to financial matters, with the Irish immigrants of 1850, who came to Canada without any financial reserves". But the rich treasures of the soul and character which these same Galician farmers brought with them were of greater value than the mere and miserable $25.00 that was required as a necessary password to allow their entrance into Canada. It wasn't their fault that they did not have the $25.00. The guilt belonged to them who had misruled their country and brought it to such a sorry state of affairs that its sons and daughters were

---

[3] "Western Canada", Winnipeg, 1907, p. 8.

compelled to abandon it and go out into the world to seek a better future for themselves and their children in a strange world.

The difficulty involved in paying for the "shifcard" (steamship ticket) — as it was then popularly called—was only the beginning of that heavy burden which all Ukrainian immigrants had to bear and live with during the early stage. It is hard to imagine now what went on in the life of a human being that grew up in such closely knit surroundings, without ever going any farther than twenty kilometers from the village and then suddenly to tear oneself away from wife, children and family and leave for unknown shores.

Pioneers in their memoirs and recollections describe that this leave-taking from the old country was almost like saying the final "good-bye to this world—I may never return". To these psychological upheavals were added further material difficulties and the lowering of morale. Days of long voyage lay ahead. Very fortunate indeed were those who could cross the European continent without any long waiting for their health or passport clearance. Those who were detained at ports of departure were often at the mercy of clever fortune hunters, manipulators of phoney tickets and fake money changers, or those who made false promises of speeding up the passage to the other side. Very often when these emigrants reached Canada they did not have a cent to their name. One of the first immigrants showed the author of this volume an old cent, saying: "See this memento of the year 1897. It was all I had left from the $225.00 that remained after I had paid for my steamship and railroad tickets to Canada. On the way to Hamburg, and during my stay in that city, I was thoroughly bilked of all my money by the clever "agent-advisers" and when I arrived in Halifax this one cent was all that I had left. This is an expensive souvenir, and I will pass it on to my offspring as being all I have to show for my long years of toil on a five morg piece of land in the old country".

The boat trip was filled with untoward adventures, bitter experiences and at times even tragedies. It is not any news to say that many immigrants travelled to Canada on freight and cattle steamers. Usually from North American continent cattle, grain and other cargo were shipped to Europe and on the return trips these were loaded with emigrants—the would-be-citizens—for Canada and U.S.A. It was a lucky emigrant who could book his passage on a boat that had not been used for carrying pigs and cattle; but such occasions were very rare, indeed. This matter of having people travel on cattle boats, considered from hygienic point of view, was finally thrashed out in Canadian Parliament and we take time to quote a fragment from the discussion on this subject:

"As regards the cleanliness of the Dukhobors and Galicians, I would point out they had just left a vessel on which they had been two or three weeks crossing the sea and if the honorable members of the Commons could see the condition in which the holds of such vessels are kept—vessels that have brought cattle across and returned with immigrants—they would realize how difficult it was for these people to have any regard for cleanliness" [4].

On the pages of the military journal "Good News" of Nov. 20, 1913, a mention is made of the boat "Vulturno" that was sunk because, as this journal stated, it was an old tub, used only for transporting "the world's miserables",—the Galician emigrants. Pages were written about the loss

---

[4] Sessional Papers, 1901, Vol. 1, page 2900.

of "Titanic" but nothing was said about "Volturno"—for who could ever care about these "nonentities".

In Canadian ports of entry every immigrant had to pass the so-called medical examination and documentary control. During this visit he received "Inspection Card for Immigration Officer at port of arrival in Canada".

In addition to the medical and civic headings on these cards there was another one relating to money matters, which read: "Inland Exchange Order". Here had to be declared how much money each immigrant brought with him to Canada. The last heading was for "Vaccination Protected". It was signed by the ship's doctor. For immigrant's identification the card had spaces marked for—name and surname of the immigrant, name of the boat he came on, name of the country he came from, the European port of departure and the date of his arrival at Canadian port. On the opposite side of this card was this notice: "This card has to be preserved for a period of three years. It must be presented to the authorities at their request". This information was printed in twelve languages: English, Czech, Russian, Ukrainian, German, French, Dutch, Hungarian, Swedish, Polish, Italian and Hebrew. Although the Ukrainian language was fourth on the list still the information was printed in such a garbled gibberish that even a Ukrainian could not understand it. The Latin alphabet was used and here is a prime sample of it: "Ruthenian. Cro kampky mreda mpu poku sobamu. Tllpeda so nokazamu upragnekam npabume pens bch hure, hanoru zasthagotoml, moro". If you my dear reader, can make this out in Ukrainian, then you are a genius [5]).

The boat trip was not the end of it. Several full days of railroad travel still awaited the "pleasure" of the immigrant. The trains had special cars marked: "Colonist Cars". No soft seats for you here—just the bare boards. No eating facilities whatsoever, and cars were locked and sealed while on the move and were only opened up at larger stations. During the stopover one could buy some food—especially milk for the children—but you had to pay five times the value of the food, compared with regular prices. As a rule most trains were heading in the direction of Winnipeg, for that city was the colonization centre for western Canada. The next immigration centre was Strathcona —Edmonton. The last named point was assigned for Alberta which was only a stopping place and not a distributing centre. The arrival of new transports to Winnipeg was for its citizens something of a sensational event. Friends and relatives would hasten to meet and talk with those whom they had not seen for many years or go there out of mere curiosity. To some these were "extra-ordinary people,—as was written by one of the first pioneer poets in 1900. The "extraordinary" title stemmed from the fact that the new candidates for Canadian citizens, having spent three or four weeks on the road, arrived unshaved, besmeared, ill-clothed and half starving. They came with hope in their hearts, believing that their long, lean and harsh journey has ended and that the wide Canadian prairie will receive them as its own children and take them into its fold. But these were but the illusions for the time being—the dreams had to be lived and proved. Without these dreams the Ukrainian settler could never have had the strength to live through what the future had in store. But there were

---

5) A copy of the above mentioned document is preserved in the archives of the author. It was dated June 23, 1910.

also other unsavory elements that came to meet the new immigrants at the trains. These were the immigration hyenas who made their living off the poor and not very well oriented souls. These parasites sold worthless shabby clothes, and not much better food, and sold land and property around Winnipeg that often did not even exist on the map. In the contemporary press we often meet loud warnings about the vultures of that kind.

In Winnipeg the immigrants stayed over for a while in the immigration building until such time as the formalities were completed as to the final destination and homestead dispositions. This intervening period usually lasted two or more weeks. As a rule, women and children remained in the immigration building and men would go out to stake their homesteads. With them would go an immigration agent to show where the land was and what homesteads to choose. One had to have a certain affinity for the soil to be able to evaluate its fertility and to know what homestead held the best prospect. As a rule the settler took what the agent showed, reserving only for himself the right to choose as to who his neighbor should be—usually one with family ties or a friend. When the final settlement had been arranged the new immigrant would return to pick up his wife and children and go back to the newly chosen homestead.

All transportation was handled by the railroads. Often one had to travel by wagon twenty or thirty miles from the railroad stop, to where the homesteads were. These wagon trips sometimes took several days to complete because there were no roads. Trails had to be cut and cleared. Men and women too, would arm themselves with axes to hew their way through trees and brush before a wagon could make its way. The axe was the first and most useful tool and implement on the farm. Having arrived on their homestead the family would pitch its tent, as a temporary abode, until the homesteads were properly surveyed and allocated. To own a homestead you had to pay ten dollars. As a receipt the immigrant-homesteader received a temporary so-called "Interim Homestead Receipt" on the title of which could be seen a somewhat more assuring inscription: "Dominion Lands". This receipt had the name and surname of the homesteader, description of the homestead and, farther on, the given number of section, township and range.

On the basis of "Dominion Lands Act", the homestead could be acquired when the would-be owner had lived on it for a period of twelve months and had, during that time, put into cultivation 30 acres of land. One could take possession of the homestead after living on it for only six months, but the procedure had to be repeated every year for a total period of three years. If at the end of five years the owner had not applied for a patent, as required by the Act, then he could lose the right of ownership. All these requirements were clearly stated on the documents. For those who did not know the English language this information had no practical meaning. For the grownups who had the necessary ten dollars it wasn't at all difficult to get the homestead. The whole country was divided into townships of 36 square mile areas. The townships were subdivided into sections and those in turn were parcelled into quarters. Each quarter was half a mile long and the same in width. These quarters of 160 acres each, were the apportioned homesteads for each settler. Usually the even numbered sections belonged to the government and the odd numbered ones were at the disposition of the railroad companies. This plan was agreed upon between the railroads and the government. This privilege, enjoyed by the railway companies was usually in those districts that were already served—or in the process of building—by the railroads. In addition to the above arrangement every 8th and 26th section belonged to the Hudson Bay Co. and every 11th and 29th was reserved for the schools. From this allocation plan it will be seen that every township of land could accommodate 65 farmers.

The dividing lines between each section went straight and parallel to each other. These were wide enough for the roads that were to be built by the immigrants themselves. But no one even thought about the roads in those days. The first duty of every homesteader was to slap-bang together any kind of a hut with the roof over it, and then move his family from the tent into it. The huts were very primitive. Usually they consisted of dug-outs, framed over with the network of rafters and covered, in turn, with sods. Ledges, in sod, were cut inside the huts to serve as seats, shelves and other purposes. A thick layer of hay or swamp reeds took the place of the beds and on these the whole family slept—in corduroy fashion. If the summer happened to be a dry one such aboriginal huts served their purpose well. But it was otherwise, in the wet weather. The rain-soaked earth would practically dissolve and the inside of the hut would be turned into a mud-hole. In the course of time the homesteaders exchanged their temporary huts for a more substantial house consisting usually of two rooms and a porch. The houses were built on the old country style from logs, or heavy slabs with the empty spaces between logs filled with a special kind of brown clay mixed with hay—to give it the adhesive quality—and the walls made finally attractive by a generous application of white limestone trimmed with blue, and the roofs covered with a thatch. They were quite picturesque in appearance. All this, as we have said, took time and willing energy.

The Ukrainian settler, having built his house, spent very little time living in it. He had to leave his house, wife and children and go out to earn enough, as it was fondly said, to pay for the doors and windows for that same house. There were things needed with which to furnish this new built home—benches, tables, chairs and beds, in one word, all that was necessary to transform the house into a home. And all this had to be paid for with the hard earned dollars, with the only aid of his ten fingers and a will to make good. Those same two hands and the ardent desire to strive for a better tomorrow, were the faithful companions of his hopes and the main driving force during his pioneer days. There were a few fortunate ones who could buy all the necessary furnishings for the house and even farm equipment, with the money brought from the old country, but these were few and far between, when compared with the overwhelming majority who, by their own hard earnings, were able to set themselves up, in Canada, on their own feet.

Women and children who were left behind in the huts, did not lead an idle life. They prepared the wood to build the house, as well as barn and granary. The logs had to be hewed on two sides to make an even wall and hauled into place. The stones had to be brought in for the foundations and other chores had to be taken care of. When the head of the family returned with his first earning the building of house began. This was a great event when the foundation was laid for a large "fit for a human being" house—

later to be completed with doors and windows. Not too soon would this house see a wooden floor. Besides the building of a house, a source of nourishment for the family, especially for the children, had to be acquired, which was none other than the cow—the first animal to fulfill the homesteader's dreams. Before all this was realized many weeks and months had come and gone. Lonely and meagre was the life of the mother and children, while the father was far away working in harvest fields, on railroads or engaged at some other work. Berries and wild game were the main source of food for the family. The berries were often picked and carried on foot for many miles, to be sold in nearest towns. With the money so earned, sugar, flour, fat and sometimes even articles of clothing were bought. The biggest profits were made from digging and selling the so-called "Seneca Roots", or "Seneca Snake Roots" and sometimes also called Polygia Seneca, while the Ukrainians called them by the simple name of "snake roots". As we know, in some districts like "Shtomboor" (Stuartburn) the "snake roots' provided the main source of living—the basis of their economic life. Before anything could be planted in the fields, and almost as soon as the snow had gone, the seneca roots could be located and dug up. This work was mostly done by women, but even children did not shirk in their duty to supplement the family budget. All pitched in to dig the roots, dry them out in the sun and take them to the town markets. Many families were fed and clothed by this means and even other household needs were met through the sale of this humble root. Many budget necessities were satisfied by means of working in the woods—either on one's own homestead or on company lands. Trees were cut into cordwood and hauled away, to be sold in towns. Those who had no oxen of their own, made deals with their neighbors who possessed these useful animals. Some districts, like Teulon in Manitoba, were over-loaded with wood fuel. The earnings from this back-breaking work were not very large. One cord of wood was priced at 40 cents and sometimes a little more. This amount would barely cover the going wages of the average homesteader-farmer, but one had to work to pay for implements—the plow, harrows, and binder—whose prices were high.

To possess one's own shotgun in those days meant not only to have protection for the family living in the bush, but it also enabled the homesteader to hunt for game, especially for the wild ducks and rabbits. The first supplied the meat and feathers for the pillows and the rabbits provided skins for clothing. Hunting in pioneer days was not so much for pleasure as for necessity. It proved to be the necessary means of preventing the family from going hungry [6].

The hardest of all to live through, for the settlers, was the first winter on the farm. Canadian winters are much harsher than those in Ukraine. Lack of well insulated houses, warm clothing and sufficient food took heavy toll of the immigrants' health. The old story was repeated over and over again: the father of the family would leave for work not only somewhere far away to other parts of Canada but quite often, to U.S.A.—especially those who lived near the American border. Mothers with children would stay at home to share the last of what was left of flour, to count the dwindling stock of potatoes and to wait hopefully for the return of the breadwinner. Life's

---

[6] From protocols and information pamphlets of Wasyl Mihaychuk, from Pontiac, U.S.A., in the archives of the author.

misery would take its toll and it is not to be wondered that the returning father could hardly recognize the faces of his half-starved family, and overwhelmed by his grief at the sight of his loved ones. It is true that when the Immigration Authorities heard about this starvation of the first Ukrainian colonies, as in Stuartburn, Lake Dauphin, Saltcoats and others, they sent their agents to look over and appraise this state of affairs. The needy families were supplied with bagfuls of flour and potatoes. For receiving this government aid a "lien note" was slapped immediately upon each homestead stating that the given aid had to be repaid. Not much of a help this was, in the long run, but for the time being it saved the people from immediate starvation. This government aid stirred a hornet's nest in the chauvinistic press. Authors of the emotion-filled protesting articles advised the government that all those immigrants, requiring outside help, should be shipped back—post haste—to where they came from. But the statesmanly mind of Clifford Sifton knew very well that these were only temporary difficulties in the life of immigrant pioneers. As soon as the snow melted and work began, every cent of the provided aid was paid for, and no loss of any kind was realized by the state [7]).

In those first difficult beginnings the most helpless victims were the children. The ocean passage on unsanitary boats, the ride on the sealed trains and long stay in the immigration buildings and crowded tents, tended to undermine the health of these youthful human creatures. Their death was a common occurrence. Not only did they die during the long voyage by boats but there were even incidents of children dying on trains; but most of all in tents, at the immigration stations. Shocking scenes are described by those who witnessed the tragic death of children at Patterson Lake, north of Oakburn [8]).

Not only were these appalling incidents due to the inadequate transportation facilities and the harshness of Canadian climate, but they were also the result of a lack of sufficient nourishment. Pioneer cemeteries of Manitoba, Saskatchewan and Alberta are filled with little graves of Ukrainian children who died unnecessarily before their time. In many of these places where the immigrants settled, it took sometimes as long as two full days to return with a doctor or medical supplies. With husbands many miles away at work, the wives, very often, had to go through the child-birth process without any outside medical care whatsoever and so, naturally the results were often shocking to relate.

One of the pioneers who witnessed the tragic days by Patterson Lake, spoke the truth when he said that the homesteaders of that district paid very dearly for their homesteads. When we see the numerous children's graves around Dauphin or Vegreville a question could be asked if the Patterson Lake district alone knew the secret of the children's tragedy. How many memories of individual and family pain and grief were blown away into forgetfulness by the unrelenting winds of the prairies! But Ukrainian immigrants did not quail. With admirable patience and stoic courage they lived through the physical and moral blows of fate. They worked hard on their homesteads and with the dedicated labor of their hands they cleared the wilds of brush and stones and made it into a promised land. Money

---

[7]) "Studies in the History of Ukrainians in Canada" Vol. II, p. 85.
[8]) "The tragic days and unbroken faith", 4th chapter of "Studies in the History of Ukrainians in Canada", Vol. II.

was scarce, the strange and alien neighbors looked upon them askance and to add to their further misery, their farms were in poor shape. In a separate chapter we spoke that, prior to the coming of Ukrainian immigrants to prairie provinces, an effort had been made to settle the wide stretches of land in Saskatchewan but unfortunately a great number of these first homesteaders capitulated very soon. In 1872 the soldiers of the Wolseley expedition took into their possession a large number of homesteads in Stuartburn district of Manitoba, but these were soon abandoned as the land was unfit for cultivation. Similar stories were repeated in other districts in the West, where much hard work had to be done but the dividends were few. Although in the "Sessional Papers" we read that the "Galician prefers to get on land where there is scrub or timber, with which to build his small house and provide himself with fuel" [9] it may be truthfully stated that though they did not favor the turfy or sandy and gravelly soil they still were ignorant of the fact that the lands which they were choosing were only useless left-overs and totally unfit for growing grain or other type of farming.

The land was measured with straight lines from east to west and north to south and as it was surveyed it was at the same time allotted by turns. The new settlers wanted to be close to their countrymen, especially to those who had some experience of farming in the new country. Under the influence of these specific conditions the immigrants settled upon any available quarter section irrespective of whether these homesteads were fit for cultivation. No one took the least notice of this matter. It was accepted as a necessary situation about which Charles H. Young writes in these words:

"So the Ukrainians finally settled in the different parts of the west, handicapped at times by the want of funds to the point of destitution and starvation and limited in their choice of land to the accessible districts, which had been either abandoned or avoided by the earlier immigrants" [10].

Dr. A. J. Hunter who lived in the Interlake District of Manitoba for about 40 years, wrote an interesting booklet about his life among the Ukrainians that had settled in this region in the earlier history of Western Canada. One of the chapters of this work is titled "Unwise Settlement", in which we read:

"Some of the land in our part of the Country was excellent and there were a few really successful farmers, other districts were rocky or swampy, or both, and some parts were almost a desert" [11].

When the question of the profits from land that had been settled by Ukrainians, became later a public question and especially, when a series of research studies were made as for example Dr. J. S. Woodsworth's study of 1917, or Charles H. Young's study from before the thirties, and when these same studies verified the fact about the hopeless farming situations in some of the settled districts, then an effort was made to place all the blame and responsibility on the shoulders of those who selected their own homesteads. However, the very objective observer, in his own appraisal of these matters, Charles H. Young, has this to say: "Granting some responsibility of the Ukrainians in this connection, a study of the situation leads one neverthe-

---

[9] "Sessional Papers", 1901, Vol. I, p. 2900.
[10] Charles H. Young, "The Ukrainian Canadians", p. 57.
[11] A Friendly Adventure, The Story of the United Church Mission—among new Canadians at Teulon, Manitoba, Toronto 1939.

less to the conclusion that the subsequent fiasco in land settlement was due to a lack of provision on the part of the governmental authorities" [12]).

Charles Young who shared Dr. J. S. Woodsworth's and Dr. A. J. Hunter's ideas, maintained that: "There is no doubt that much of the submarginal lands in Eastern and Northern Manitoba, for instance, should never have been opened for settlement. That it was opened up, and this with the cognizance of the officials who were perfectly aware of the nature of the land, is unfortunately too true" [13]).

It is understandable to surmise that the immigration authorities were not always totally informed as to the real value of the land or the clarity of the complete situation at any given point.

The unwise selection of land for the settlement purposes, on the part of the government, cost the Ukrainian settlers additional and unnecessary efforts. What effect this had on the further development and progress of the Ukrainians in Canada, in general, and on the success of the settlements themselves in particular, will be revealed further in other chapters of this work.

A great difficulty for the Ukrainian settlers in Canada, at the beginning was the lack of knowledge of the official language of his country. In other parts of this history we pointed out examples of an unintelligible inscription on official documents which even a highly educated person could not decipher. True enough, at a later date, the official government pamphlets and notices were printed in clear Ukrainian language. One such example was a pamphlet printed in Ukrainian, called: "Battle with prairie fires". At the expense of the Department of State, a short history of "Western Canada" was printed in Ukrainian—which was truly a concise history of what the Ukrainians had achieved in Canada. (1907) [14]). The provincial governments of Manitoba, Saskatchewan and Alberta also published, for Ukrainian settlers, official documents and papers in Ukrainian, such as—Workmen's Compensation Act 1910, "the Liquor Act laws" (The Liquor Act of 1915), the "information pertaining to the organization of school districts" printed by the Department of Education of Saskatchewan, the School Acts of Manitoba, Saskatchewan and Alberta, and many others. All this published material also appeared in English and in French. We have not made any mention here of the many official municipal notices and documents in which Ukrainian was used as an official language, along with the English, as for example in Ethelbert, Stuartburn, Dauphin and other districts. Lack of knowledge of the English language was not the exclusive privilege of Ukrainians alone. The "Census of Prairie Provinces", from the year 1916, under the title, "Inability to speak English" informs us that: "Of the total population of 1,240,374, ten years of age or over, 102,425 or 8.3 percent reported themselves as being unable to speak English. Of the number unable to speak English, Manitoba had 37,504 persons including 3,620 French, 3,416 Germans, 9121 Austro-Hungarians, 2,830 Poles, 4,154 Russians, 5,256 Ukrainians and 1,507 Dutch. Most of the latter were returned as Germans in 1911; Saskatchewan had 40,126 persons, including 2,753 French, 6,736 Germans, 14,304 Austro-Hungarians, 1,256 Poles, 5,065 Russians and 1,590 Ukrainians. Alberta had 24,795 persons, including 1,589 French, 6,935

---

[12]) Charles H. Young, "The Ukrainian Canadians", p. 57.
[13]) Ibid. p. 57.
[14]) Unique Editions—Author's Archives.

Austro-Hungarians, 794 Poles, 1,800 Russians and 2,108 Ukrainians [15]).

It must be noted that the government acts, printed in the Ukrainian or other languages, were not issued on account of the language problem only. It was also an expression of democratic principles and a show of respect in its multilingual citizens, an assurance that they could communicate, with the government, in their own mother tongue. Of great help to the first Ukrainian pioneers—in their language communication with the surrounding community—were the former fellow countrymen from Ukraine, namely: the Jews, Germans and Mennonites. Some of them had been settled in Canada ten or more years ahead of the Ukrainians. These nationalities provided the trading element among the new settlers. But the traders got a much better deal by enriching themselves at the expense of immigrants whose knowledge of the prices and business know-how was almost nil.

Lack of material necessities of life, the arrogance of strange neighbors and the poor condition of farm lands—especially in Manitoba, stood like the Chinese Wall before the eyes of the first settlers in Canada. Long struggles lay ahead in every phase of life before one could arrive on a higher ground of cultural growth and by his day to day progress prove himself worthy to stand—shoulder to shoulder—with other fellow Canadians. All the farm work was still performed mostly by women and children, even until such times as when small profits were already being realized from the products of the soil. But these profits were very meagre.

"All that most of these people could afford to buy in the early years", wrote Dr. A. Hunter, "were a few sacks of flour, a little sugar and tea, overalls, and a few odds and ends... Many of them would handle no more than two hundred dollars of money in one year, some much less, and there were taxes to pay, for schools and roads, for everything was new and everything had to be paid for" [16]).

Earnings in prairie provinces were small. All the three provinces were agricultural—through and through—with very few industrial plants. The threshing season was too short to allow for any bigger wages and opportunities for work in the cities of the west were not any better. The settlers in Alberta had a slightly better chance to work in coal mines and lumber camps in the neighboring province of British Columbia where the mining industry was going ahead with a fast tempo. Somewhat in a much poorer situation were the Ukrainian settlers in Manitoba. Their only source of wage-earning came from building railroads. "Canadian Pacific", "Canadian Northern" and "Grand Trunk Pacific" were in the midst of building their railroad networks throughout Western Canada. At the beginning of this century Canada could boast of 7,000 miles of railroads. "Canadian Pacific" had its network of branches between Winnipeg, Portage La Prairie and Brandon; "Canadian Northern" was reaching toward Pacific Ocean and the "Great Northern", which was extending its line northward from U.S.A. and was now pushing its way to Winnipeg, with plans to go farther on in the direction of Portage La Prairie, Brandon and the distant West, was the fourth such railroad line in Manitoba. Railroad development, in the key province, was a real blessing for all who wanted to work. Ukrainian settlers proved to be the inexhaustible source of human energy in the building and

---

[15] Census of Prairie Provinces Population and Agriculture, Manitoba, Saskatchewan and Alberta in 1916, Ottawa, 1918, p. XXXII.
[16] "The Early Adventure", Chapter 2, in "The Edge of Poverty", p. 61.

FIRST STEPS IN HOMELAND AND CANADA

development of railroad networks in Western Canada. Manitoba was not the only province covered with a network of railways. Saskatchewan too was making its progress with the Canadian Northern building its roads in Prince Albert region and extending it in the direction of Edmonton. In Alberta, the Canadian Pacific spread its roads between Calgary and Edmonton, through Lacombe, Wetaskiwin and eastward. Great Northern was completing its line from U.S.A. north into Alberta. Everywhere you looked the railroads were being built. According to the summary of an unknown chronicler, something like 10,000 Ukrainians were busy building railroads during 1906-1907 [17]. Statistics show that about every second Ukrainian father was at one time or another working on a railroad. Earnings were not very large but just the same an average worker made between $30.00 and $50.00 a month—the pay being $1.25 per day, although 50 cents a day was deducted for board and room.

Railroad companies took advantage of the fact that there was a plentiful supply of eager workers on hand. Besides that, there was the advantage of living quarters. True enough these quarters consisted mostly of barracks and the food was nothing to brag about, but the money-needing settlers, wishing to earn enough to help them in the betterment of their home surroundings were willing to accept any terms. This was true at least, in the beginning. Later on strikes came in and with them the easement of conditions. Companies demanded that labourers should work even during the church holidays. Ukrainians made their request for payless holidays during the Christmas and New Year days. The companies fired them [18].

A rigid "unwritten" pioneer code was the order of those days. It always protected the employer and the boss—that meant those who were in power. Unions were unheard of and any striving action in that direction was out of the question. Ely Culbertson, an author of memoirs "Strange Lives of One Man" wrote about the work of Ukrainian laborers on "extra gangs" in the Canadian Rockies:

"The construction of the Grand Trunk Pacific was a tremendous undertaking. Over terrific mountain passes a series of working camps was strung along, at intervals of ten or fifteen miles. The common labourers were for the most part Ukrainians. These naive, trustful bearded giants worked like elephants, laughed like children and asked no questions. They were shamelessly exploited. At that time the labour laws in Canada and America, especially for immmigrants, were made chiefly for the benefit of the contractors. The country had to be built and built quickly".

Ely Culbertson presents quite a revealing expose about Ukrainian laborers in workcamps, saying:

"The lowliest of labourers got three dollars a day, a bunk with a vermin infected blanket and pillow and free grub. But the food doled out in meagre rations was barely edible. In my commissary the labourers could buy bacon, flour and canned goods of tolerable quality, but for prices that New York night clubs would be ashamed to ask. Those who didn't like it could get out (at their own expense) for there was a never ending stream of new serfs".

Strength and desire to work and to adapt themselves to the new way of

---
[17] "Western Canada", p. 8.
[18] "Petro Hawrysyshyn", chapter "First Christmas in Canada", p. 18.

life there was plenty of—and that was very good. Of "buts" and "may be's" or any other "ameliorating conditions" there were none. The labourers worked 10 hours a day and the so-called "holiday" came only when the work ended or heavy winter arrived. Then the toiler-settlers would hurry home to their families. From the nearest railroad points, with sacks loaded with sugar, tea, coffee, new shoes and clothing for the wife and children they would carry their valuable "burden" to their homes. This was then a big holiday—a day of rejoicing—for him and the loved ones whom he had not seen for months. Similar stories could be told about those working in the coal mines at Frank, Lethbridge, Nanaimo, Belleview, Fernie, Hosmer and other places. In somewhat even less hopeful circumstances were cast the lives of those labourers who toiled in lumber camps. These had no homesteads, farms or families to go to and were destined to spend their winters, in the cities, in utter loneliness.

The lonely life of labourers, in woods and at work on "extra gangs" and in the coal mines, followed them later into the cities as well. In most cases these were young men who were seeking recreation and diversion in their own social circles. Starved for many months for social life, they threw themselves eagerly into the whirl of gay life, including excessive drinking. This was a natural reaction after the harsh treatment they had received from their labour overseers and their dreary working surroundings. It wasn't so easy to find work in the cities. The oldsters—those in the know—would often speak about some immigrant who would arrive and worry anxiously about obtaining any kind of work, wasting their time and hopefully waiting at the labour bureau's door. The policeman hounded him in his steps and sometimes even the firehose sprayed him—when too many of his kind gathered in one spot. The immigrant, dissappointed, disillusioned and indignantly treated by others, once he obtained some kind of work threw his whole being into it. And when he heard the thunder-crashing sound of "hareeyaap" (hurry up) he would harness up and put to use the last ounce of his energy, so as not to be "fired by the boss". When the work ended and he managed to save a few cents and reach the city he did not know what to do with himself. And so he turned to drinking. "Good luck" once —twice—and so the time went. A few hours and glasses later there would be brawling and fighting sprees, often ending in court-trials and in jails. Such behaviour was not the one to elicit good opinion on the part of his own countrymen or fellow Canadians. But just as soon as the social-cultural life of Ukrainian Canadians developed in the cities, the boisterous life of these carousing "jacks" (a derisive name, and all-inclusive, for Jack or John taken as a group) came to an end. They were absorbed by the dramatic and cultural activities of different drama leagues and cultural centres. The hardest period of all was that created by strikes and work lay-offs. There was no such thing as social welfare in those days to take care of you when the pockets were almost empty. For the familied ones, returning to the farms, enough bread could always be found—and even something to go with the bread—and some work around the house. A different situation faced those who had no families. An aimless wandering awaited them, in hopeful search of work. Still during the winter months the kind-hearted countrymen, living on farms, never refused to give refuge to those who were homeless and without families. There are several model examples of how the jobless Ukrainians helped themselves, collectively, during the slack periods. One such related incident took place in Edmonton in 1901. During a C.P.R. strike, when labourers asked for a raise in wages from the then in existence pay of $1.25 per day to $1.50, for each day's work, many were left without any employment. Hunger and cold were staring everybody in the face. One of the Ukrainian strike leaders presented to a group of striking labourers, his idea of building, on the site where the present Macdonald Hotel stands in Edmonton, which was then an empty piece of property, some cave dwellings in the banks overlooking Saskatchewan river, popularly named as "Galician Hotel". Here was situated an organized workingmen's village complex whose members went out to work on lawns, dig ditches and sweep the city streets. The profits made were equally divided amongst them all and the money so earned paid for running a community kitchen where all were fed and even some funds were left over for "rainy days". As soon as the C.P.R. strike was over the "Galician Hotel" was "out and over" too [19].

Examples of such mutual self-help were many. The former denizens of Vasylkivci village in Western Ukraine during the jobless period decided to settle themselves on a farm near Gimli in Manitoba and managed to live most economically for nearly a year, until the short-work depression was over. Here was at work not only the instinct of self-preservation but also the moral expression of national-collective responsibility. In many cities Ukrainian community kitchens were opened where free meals were served to the jobless. The most popular one was in connection with the St. Vladimir's and Olga parish in Winnipeg. Similar community kitchens existed in Edmonton, Montreal, Toronto and other cities. Not only was the group settlement spirit at work but also group care and responsibility as well.

---

[19] M. H. Marunchak, Among Ukrainian Pioneers of Alberta, Winnipeg: General Library UKT, 1964, pp. 40-41.

HOMESTEADERS AND LABOURERS

What spiritual nourishment could be found in woods and wilds of Canada to feed the hearts and souls of the people who came from the picturesque villages of Ukraine, where there was to be heard the magic sound of the hauntingly beautiful national songs; where the colorful costumes charmed the beholder's eyes; where the age-old symbolical rituals, customs and traditions were passed from generation to generation; where the whole nation bathed itself in the glowing memory of its glorious past; where through numerous centuries the spirit of freedom reigned; where no one willingly would bend his neck before the oppressor's whip but bravely fight for freedom's cause? What were their innermost thoughts when they had to leave their native land—the fabulous land of their ancestors? What contrast would they find in the new world—these up-rooted wanderers, who were obliged to sever, perhaps for ever, their spiritual cord!

Instead of fertile fields and paved highways there was thick growth of tamarac and scrubby trees, through which one had to cut his way in order to reach his neighbors. Instead of the prim flower beds there were the boggy swamps, most unattractive and overgrown with scrawny tough willows and reeds, swamps that had to be drained and cleared. Instead of an inviting and cultured Ukrainian village all one could find was the widely spreading kingdom of the western wilderness. Nothing else was left for choosing but to make and take the nearest step, along with a fortified decision and strong desire to transform these barren prairies and primeval forests into cultured villages and flourishing gardens. With zeal and dedication the Ukrainian pioneers began to build their future. But to be able to work with dedicated zeal they first had to fall in love with the woods and the prairies—to feel affection for them—for the sake of a brighter future, for themselves and their children. Not in vain were these words put into song:

"We toiled and we suffered.
That better times should come—that others may prosper".

Truthfully said, the work burgeoned into life on the prairies of Western Canada. And it was a life of struggle and suffering, which the present generation cannot even imagine. To take even a small glimpse into the heroic past of the pioneer era that Ukrainian settlers had to go through it would be only necessary to hear the stories of the eye-witnesses to these events. Much material has been preserved in articles printed in Ukrainian and English press. In their harsh struggles the Ukrainian pioneers were still able to keep a vision of a better world. This same vision lulled them into a restful sleep and awakened them again into a new tomorrow. The hard labor evolved its own unyielding determination. Most difficult it was for the newcomers to forget their loved ones left behind—fathers, mothers, sisters, brothers, friends. The lonely life on lonely prairies brought about a strong nostalgia, the yearning pains, the longing for the past—the days of youth—for the sun-drenched days and magic nights of native land. Only tears could relieve this pain of the heart. The sentimental Ukrainian soul was weighted with grief in living through his family separation and felt deeply this contrasting reality of fate. The grey haired pioneers describe, with pardonable emotion, their mothers' weeping by day and night. When asked about the why of it they would only give such meaningless answers: "O it's just nothing so". No doubt they gave this "a-no-answer" reply so as not to add more to the children's grief and to better adapt themselves to the Canadian way of life. But weeping was the means with which to make a break-through and pierce the stark reality. It had to stop—this was no place for it. It could only be used as a boundary line, in its outer form, between the world of yesterday and the new and unknown world so promisingly rich in expectations and full of bright hopes.

The work was geared to a high tempo—on farms, highways and on railroads. There were no idlers. Even the pre-school youngsters picked the small stones left over on fields, by the pre-historic glaciers that once had moved their icy weight down the wide prairies of Western Canada. The older and the stronger members of the family struggled with bigger stones and hurled them into the swamps or used them to build the new roads. As time went on it wasn't convenient to walk the narrow paths, cut through the woods, or follow the far stretched Indian trails. The farmers bought oxen and wagons, and these needed the wider travelling lanes. After a while, thanks to a great deal of hand-blistering toil, not only were there to be seen new little homes showing their unique shapes and colors on the horizon—and differing somewhat from those of other neighbors—but all around them little green fields of wheat and other grains, were adding their contribution to the colorful landscape. This was a reminder for the new settlers of their own little, picturesque fields they left behind in their homeland, with this one difference: their small and newly cultivated fields, here, were but the forerunners of larger ones to come. Here they were living on the edge of virgin land that seemingly stretched into infinity, awaiting muscle and plow to be transformed into a promised land—the land flowing with milk and honey. Here was a renewal of hope that helped to encourage the new immigrants in Canada to forge their way ahead. Even their fellow Canadians, of different nationalities, could not help but detect this new revelation of Ukrainian national identity. One of the school inspectors from the Department of Education of Manitoba, writing about the Ukrainian colonies in that province, said: [1])

"I drive from Ethelbert across to Sifton, through the heart of Galician settlements. I was impressed with prosperous appearance of most of the farms. The country is flat and uninviting—once the ridge upon which Ethelbert is situated is left—but in spite of the apparently unfertile nature of the soil, the little homesteads are surrounded by patches of wheat, rye and hemp and invariably a good vegetable garden. Most of the houses are small but with their thatched roofs and heavy overhanging eaves, on plastered walls, they are quite picturesque. I saw some quite large houses too".

Similar public attestations to the Ukrainian prowess in farming and other occupations were also voiced in Saskatchewan and Alberta where of course, there were better lands for cultivation. Every passing year, in these Ukrainian settlements, could record fresh progress in newly plowed fields and recently put up buildings. On a material plane, great achievements were to be noted, thanks to the concerted labor of the whole families.

---

[1]) Report of the Department of Education for 1900, pp. 31-32.

Ukrainian pioneers were not only adept in turning over the sod of the wild prairie. Even in the dim beginning they had already displayed their business and professional abilities, in places where there existed economic necessity and business opportunity. The settlers needed plows, harrows, shovels, axes, knives and household utensils. Trading centres, in prairie provinces, were too far away to run to for a rake or a hoe, to re-tire the wagon or make repairs on plow and harrows. These needs had to be taken care of right in the colonies. This led to the building of blacksmith shops and all broken scraps of iron were turned into many useful and badly needed articles on the farms. The pioneers relate of how the railway tracks, then being built, became the source of raw material for the blacksmith.

The blacksmith shops were also used for farmers' gathering points where they came not only to have their plowshares "honed" but also to discuss about their problems and every day affairs. Whilst husbands were whiling their time away in blacksmith shops, the wives were busy, hunting for the pottery maker. Whoever heard of gas or electric stoves in those days or even of metal pots and pans. The earthenware was then in style for the Ukrainian farmers who did their cooking and baking in large baked-clay ovens—inside the house during the winter and outside in the summer. Precisely made for these clay ovens were the ideal home-made earthenware pots. To cook in these pots and to maintain an even temperature in those clay ovens, was an art in itself. The making of pottery was highly developed in the ancestral homeland of the pioneer settlers and the ceramic art was on the highest plane. The pottery-making tradition found its way into Canada. All that was necessary was a suitable clay in any district—and there the art of pottery would flourish. The centre of pottery-making industry in Manitoba was Sifton which supplied earthenware products not only for the settlers in Manitoba but also for those living beyond. Petro Kowalsky was one of the more outstanding potters and Antin Serafin his nearest competitor. Another such clay-pounding pioneer, whose handiwork would have made the heart of Omar Khayyam (Persian poet) beat faster in his grave and whose pottery was known for miles around Rossburn in Manitoba, was Alexander Sulima (later changed to Slym).

One of the more important articles in the business of farming was the "zhorna" (millstone) for grinding wheat and other grains and which acted as a miniature indoor flour mill for the settler's needs. It was constructed somewhat on the principle of flour mill mechanics. Two flat, round stones and a handle turned by hand, would tear and powder the grain to change it into flour. With zhorna in the house you had a fair supply of flour and granulated buckwheat in your pantry and that was no mean achievement or addition to the food stock of the Ukrainian pioneer. The millstone for the zhorna had to be of a special kind and one had to know how to shape it and encase it before it could be put to its proletarian use. Without this knowledge you would only have a heap of ruins to show for your good effort. The pioneers fondly relate that where these zhorna first appeared, never once would they stop turning and grinding. Neighbors from near and far would actually stand in line waiting to have their turn at the zhorna. As a rule no charge was made. All this was free—hard work and all.

A separate and unique farm "factory" and one that was widely sought for by the housewives, was the hand made and operated "oliynia", the oil pressing machine for squeezing cooking oil out of flax and hemp seeds.

For the purpose of making grits out of wheat, barley or buckwheat, a special type of contraption called "stoopa", had to be constructed for dehusking the different grains that were used for making grits. All these unique and useful household factories in miniature were hand-made by the pioneers and proved to be invaluable and irreplaceable during those early days. Take away the potter's wheel, the zhorna, the oliynia and the erstwhile smithy and it becomes doubtful if the Ukrainian settler would have managed to take the next and further step—on the farming plane—to build his own flour mills, farm implements and other necessary equipment, to the extent that would enable him to rise to a higher level of civilization. It would be an incomplete story, while describing this phase of pioneer days, if we did not mention the weaving looms on which the Ukrainian pioneer women wove their own scarves, aprons, shawls and other articles of clothing. A start was also made to produce ordinary white linen cloth, for undergarments and other useful purposes, but this branch of weaving could not compete, for very long, with factory-made cotton and so the attempt was dropped. But the woven woollen products and the art of making them, lasted for a long time, no doubt due not only to the practical use of it but also on account of its beautiful craft-work.

Hand in hand with this diminutive and home-made-craft industry small merchandising business followed, as a matter of course. Towards the end of the last century in every newly settled Ukrainian colony could be seen an oblong and shed-like building with the sign "General Store" boldly lettered on its front. Here one could buy sugar, salt, kerosene (coal-oil), matches, flints for the lighters and flintstones to sharpen the scythes, high boots and shoes—all the most necessary and utilitarian articles to be used on the farm.

There isn't any doubt that Ukrainian pioneers were making great progress on the material plane. Agrarian, industrial and commercial activities resolved their own problems almost in unison, and practically at the same time. For even here, each one had to await its turn—as was dictated by the stern decree of stark necessity. But still, when the settlers found themselves in the midst of harsh circumstances, they did not flinch nor break down in their spirit, as had been done by their predecessors during those other years of trials. On the contrary, with heads held high, they marched ahead to plant the first seeds of civilization on their newly projected farms. This onward drive toward a brighter future, must be attributed not only to the strengh and determination of their wills but also to their inherent character, that was passed on to them from their fathers and ancestors. And this was only a single page from the history of activities in the life of Ukrainian pioneers in Canada—their own characteristic reply to the challenge flung at them, by the forces of bare necessity. This indomitable determination, and strong will, showed itself at work in drying out the marshes and transforming the stony, scrubby lands into green harvest fields. A few figures of statistics would present a far better picture than a thousand words. True enough, this is not to be so easily accomplished, for in the statistics on farming the hardest ones to find are those dealing with any ethnic group in Canada and even more so concerning the Ukrainian pioneers, especially when we take into consideration their many former homelands. But fortunately, even under those difficult circumstances, we are still able to find some fragments of information on which to build a few historical deductions.

In 1898, Rev. Pavlo Tymkevych, the second in line for the title of Ukrainian pioneering priests in Canada who had visited the then existing Ukrainian colonies, made a summary of his journey in an article, "How many farmers in Canada" [2]. In it he says that there were something like 10,000 Ukrainian settlers, comprising 2,000 families. Five hundred of these families, according to Rev. P. Tymkevych, were engaged directly in homestead farming, having sufficient funds, which at that time necessitated a more or less specified sum of $250.00. Three fourths of the settlers were lacking that sum. They were lucky to have enough to see them through the long winter—says this pioneer missionary.

In the midst of all these conditions stood the question of wages. No great wages were paid to men in those days. For a whole season of hard work a man made no more than $50.00. In the economic set-up of the settlers even youngsters, especially young girls, played an important role in supplementing the family budget. They would bring in $20.00 to $30.00, for a season's work. But not all went to work, nor did they all bring in the wages. By the law of averages we could say that 1,000 men would bring in $50.000.00 to be put into farming development. These were minimal earnings but the settlers were satisfied even with these small profits, remembering their miserable lives in Galicia where no one would dare to dream, in comparison, of such high wages. From Rev. P. Tymkevych's reports we can see that in the beginning, the pioneering days of Ukrainian settlers revolved themselves a great deal around the question of wages. Profits from agricultural industry were not realized until two or three years later—when the moneyless farmer had managed to pay for his plow, harrows, oxen, harness etc.

From the numerous pioneer memoirs and from the press articles of that time we glean many tributes paid to Ukrainian women, who in many cases, as we have formerly stated took care of the farms. They cut and up-rooted the trees, picked roots and stones, plowed, dug and hoed—in one word, they transformed the brushwood and the prairie into a fertile grain-growing soil. Thousands of acres were prepared for planting, by these steadfast and heroic women. When in 1881 Manitoba had only 51,300 acres under cultivation, by 1902 there was the staggering total of 3,189,000 acres under cultivation and in 1903, 3,757,000 acres were seeded, including 2,443,000 put into wheat [3]. Included in these thousands and millions of cultivated acres was a fair share of the back-breaking labour contributed by the Ukrainian pioneer women.

With the cultivation of land came also the raising of cattle, and the statistical chart, presented here, speaks for itself:

	1881	1902	1906
Horses	16,730	182,649	340,000
Cattle	60,281	369,850	600,000
Sheep	6,073	42,000	60,000
Hogs	17,358	145,650	200,827

---

[2] "Svoboda", No. 44, Nov. 3, 1898.
[3] "Western Canada": Brief explanation about its wealth and land, 1907, p. 18.

Exceptionally imposing figures may be found in an article printed in 1912 entitled: "Canadian Ruthenians in the limelight of official statistics" [4]. In it we read that there were 52,000 persons of Ukrainian descent engaged in farming industry in Manitoba, 60,000 in Saskatchewan and 50,000 in Alberta. In 1912 there were some 70,000 individual Ukrainian farms listed in Western Canada. The largest number consisted of a minimum quarter section of land. If we accept the general sum of $15,00 per acre, which was then the going price, we could then conclude that the land of the pioneers alone was worth $184,000,000. When we add to this sum the value of farm machinery, stock and poultry, plus the buildings which would be around $120.00 per each farm, then we will have an additional sum of $92,000,000. This will show us that the minimal value of Ukrainian farming industry—including land, buildings, stock and equipment—amounted to a grand total of $270,000,000, in the year of 1912 [5]. If we go further and add to the above the wealth of all Ukrainian laborers at that time it would raise still higher the complete total. Of course this last estimate would be very difficult to conduct because, as we have already mentioned, this particular phase of Ukrainian activity was very fluid—many pioneers being both farmers and wage-earning labourers. Generally speaking it is assumed that about 20 per cent of the pioneers were in the labouring class. These were in most cases seasonal workers, as well as labourers, in such manufacturing cities as Hamilton, Toronto, Quebec, Montreal and others. Many Ukrainians worked in the coal mines of British Columbia, Alberta, Ontario and Nova Scotia and in the logging and lumbering industry in Saskatchewan and Ontario, not to mention the building of the railroads and the digging of ditches for city waterworks. In fact, wherever there was work to be done that required energy, perseverance and the tolerance of its humble state, there you would find a Ukrainian labourer, conscientiously performing his daily task. In 1912 one could earn from four to six dollars a day in the coal mines and about forty-five dollars per month in the lumber camps. The least paid work of all was in the harvest fields, which netted from $3.00 to $3.50 for a 16 hour day. It is no secret, as we have stated before, that labourers were unmercifully exploited, especially in lumber camps, where very often the contractors would wind up their work and leave without ever paying the back-wages to their labourers. Many industries were not covered by unions nor subject to any labour code and these would shamelessly take advantage of the workers, by prolonging the hours of work over the agreed time or paying less than what the labourer earned. But in spite of all these hardships all were reasonably happy to earn a living and to have the assurance of at least an immediate security. With this was also tied the worker's dream of owning his own homestead, of bringing his loved ones from the old country and living a peaceful family life.

In the long run the Ukrainian pioneers were not satisfied with just a mere existence. They filled their every-day life with their inborn spirituality. They yearned to lead the kind of a life they led in their homeland—in Ukraine, according to the customs and traditions of their fathers, to preserve

---

[4] "New Country", No. 28 & 29, 1912.
[5] These are not officially verified figures, but it gives us a general picture about the value of agriculture of the Ukrainian pioneers. For the exact and correct answers we may have to reduce these figures by 10-15 percent, due to the fact that the figures given for "Galicians" also included some Poles.

their language, their literature and to cultivate their beautiful native art. They desired to teach the young generation not only the language of their newly acquired country but also the meaning of their own; to communicate to them the glorious past history of the land of their fathers, to find the means of producing, on paper the printed word, to publish a paper, a book, that would bind them together and bring them closer to the other Ukrainian colonies scattered throughout Canada. In their own villages back home from whence they came, there were churches, schools and social, cultural and educational organizations. Only in the most backward villages was there a lack of these. But here, in Canada, they wished to have them all. They wanted to display it for themselves and for their new and friendly environment, for they knew with an innate self-assurance, that the strength of a nation lies in its organized life and in its culture. Hardly had the first mud-huts been demolished and the new foundations laid for a more modern habitation, when the Ukrainian pioneers began to worry about their educational and cultural life. The first expression of this concern was the concept of their relationship to God and church. Even as their forefathers had been, from immemorial times, a God-fearing people, so now their descendants, the new settlers, were likewise highly religious. In their attitude toward God there also lay their daily philosophy of life and the greatest need of their soul found its satisfaction in attending church on Sundays and holidays. Children were born and many of them died, but the Christian way of life ordains that the first ones be baptized and consecrated for living, and those last ones mentioned, be given a Christian burial. The Sunday sermon of the priest was the spiritual food and comfort for their souls—especially for those who had been working hard for months, without even a glimpse of the cultured and civilized world. And so it was understandably enough, that a strong voice arose among the people, saying that the spiritual need of having priests and churches had now become a prime necessity.

THE RELIGIOUS QUESTION

The religious question, for the Ukrainian settlers, was the key question on the spiritual plane. Viewed properly through the transparent prism of this one problematical question all other questions would be solved. The total philosophy of the settlers was centered in their faith in God and the paved road leading to it was that centuries-old and gradually developed, specifically Ukrainian church ritual, with which were also bound ancient customs and traditions. No wonder the settlers had such a high respect for their church and its rituals. What pangs of grief and longing for "their own" they must have felt in their hearts, what hounds of spiritual hunger must have been gnawing at their souls during the years they had to wait before they could see and hear their own priests and join their hearts with theirs in sacred rituals and ceremonies. To all this must be added the fact that, in their actual church rituals, the Ukrainians made no distinction—both the Catholics and the Orthodox, acknowledged the Byzantine rite, but better known as the Eastern rite which had behind it a well-established and typically Ukrainian colorful history and identity. On the organizational plane the Ukrainian Catholics adhered to Rome, while Ukrainian Orthodox, as the unwilling victims of circumstances had to pay their allegiance to the Russian Orthodox Church. Ukrainian Catholics came mostly from Galicia and Carpatho-Ukraine, while the Orthodox came from Bukovina and Eastern Ukraine. There were also among the settlers a small number of Ukrainian Roman-Catholics and likewise a small number of Baptists, but these were generally lost in the huge sea of the Greek-Catholics and Greek-Orthodox.

In the early beginnings the matter of spiritual care, for the Ukrainian Catholic settlers on the jurisdictional level, had not been settled with the church officials in Rome. Ukrainian bishops from Lviv and Peremyshl sent the priests to North America at their own discretion. Later on, this non-authoritative vacuum was administered from the Metropolitan seat in Lviv, where Cardinal Sembratovych was in charge. The Holy Congregation for the Propagation of Faith, in Rome, which had a direct authority over missionary fields in North America, issued, on April 1, 1897, church regulations that would allow Ukrainian priests in America to perform their religious services. In other words, by these two above mentioned regulations, the then existing status quo was legalized but at the same time it also placed those Ukrainian priests who were already working on American territory under the jurisdiction of Roman Catholic bishops. This brought on a state of conflict between Ukrainian priests and Roman Catholic bishops, for in the existing history of the Eastern church there was a canonical law, stating that the priests of the Eastern Rite were under the jurisdiction of their own rite and superior authority. This conflict sharpened itself even more when it was revealed that the Roman Catholic bishops, especially those on U.S.A. territory, did not show much respect, either to the Byzantine rite or to its adherents. This misunderstanding often stemmed from the ignorance of ritual practices.

As we have already mentioned before, the first Ukrainian priest to visit

Ukrainian settlers in Canada was Rev. Nestor Dmytriw. His visit to Canada was the result of Dr. O. Oleskiw's efforts who already in 1896 kept contact with Ukrainian priests in U.S.A. and made mutual plans on the best way to bring spiritual care and comfort to the Ukrainian settlers in Canada. And although Dr. O. Oleskiw himself held a most liberal opinion, he still had a high respect for the role played by the church, among the Ukrainian settlers in Canada. We already know about his efforts in Lviv, to bring Ukrainian priests into Canada. When Dr. O. Oleskiw began his discussions with Rev. N. Dmytriw, the latter was then a parish priest and editor of the newspaper "Svoboda" in Mount Carmel, Pennsylvania—which was the first Ukrainian weekly newspaper on the North American continent.

Rev. N. Dmytriw was well aware of the spiritual needs of Ukrainian settlers as many of them subscribed to "Svoboda" and sent articles about their "good times" in the new country. They very often pleaded with Rev. N. Dmytriw to send some priests to Canada. But this was not so easily done. Ukrainian priests in the old country, whether Catholic or Orthodox, were as a rule married. The Roman Catholic clergy on the North American continent, were vehemently opposed to having any Ukrainian married priests in North America, fearing it would arouse indignation and ill-feeling among their priesthood with which conclusion the Roman Church authorities readily concurred. The result of this was that only unmarried clergy were allowed to work in U.S.A., and this same rule was applied later to Canada. But the number of such priests was very small and comprised mostly of monks and widowers. This led to a great shortage of Ukrainian priests in U.S.A. In "Svoboda" Rev. N. Dmytriw devoted much space and attention to the needs of Ukrainians in Canada and so instead of sending some other priest he decided to come himself.

On April 4h of 1897 he paid his visit to the Ukrainian settlers in Canada. When he arrived on that same date in Winnipeg he found a pleasant surprise awaiting him in the form of jurisdictional documents from Metropolitan Sembratowych of Lviv. Receiving this document from a Ukrainian Prelate and having been a witness to the constant struggle of the Ukrainian Greek-Catholic clergy and parishes with the Irish Roman-Catholic bishops for the independence of the Greek-Catholic Church from the influence of U.S.A. Roman-Catholicism, as well as taking into consideration the desire of the Greek-Catholics to have their own Ukrainian hierarchy and a separate Greek Catholic Church in America, Rev. N. Dmytriw was amply justified, both in his religious and political arguments, to bring out into the light of day the basic need for an independent (non-American Roman-Catholic influence) Ukrainian Greek-Catholic Church.

Rev. N. Dmytriw began his spiritual work right in Winnipeg, holding religious services and giving confessions and holy communions in the immigration building. Later on, he travelled to Terebowla, now Valley River. It was there that he celebrated the first Ukrainian High Mass on Canadian soil. A week after that he came to Stuartburn and from there to Edna-Star in Alberta. Following his first visit to Canada during April and May in 1897, Rev. N. Dmytriw returned to Canada again, in the same year, with the purpose of organizing Ukrainian Catholic Church in Canada.

Everywhere that Rev. N. Dmytriw went he organized church parishes. This was true of Stuartburn on August 1, of 1897, and on August 8 of the same year in Terebowla. On the 12th of September, 1897, Rev. N. Dmytriw, in Terebowla, the first Ukrainian Catholic Church in Canada—actually a small chapel to hold a few people—and on the 26th of September, 1897 he founded the church parish in Edna-Star district of Alberta. In this same district, and through Rev. N. Dmytriw's initiative efforts, the first large Ukrainian Church in Canada, was built. In all the larger Ukrainian settlements visited by Rev. N. Dmytriw, the now famous "Crosses of Freedom" were built, in memory of Ukrainians' arrival to Canada—the land of liberty. This had a great moral effect upon the newcomers, for it helped to strengthen the grateful feeling of Ukrainian settlers toward their new country in which they had found religious and political freedom. Such crosses were put up on April 12th, 1897, in Terebowla [1]), Edna-Star and Stuartburn. When we take into consideration that Rev. N. Dmytriw served not only for the Catholics, but also for the Ukrainians of Bukovina, it will show that he was the first Ukrainian priest in whom the modern ecumenical spirit matured, 60 years sooner than it was talked about in the western church circles, and which was only recently formalized at the Second Ecumenical Congress in the Vatican. That this was not a baseless assumption we now quote M. Stechishin, one of the ideologists of organized Ukrainianism in Canada, who, in writing about that first pioneer ecumenism, in 1922, makes the following statement:

"There was a time, which many of us still remember, when Ukrainians in Canada did not have any discriminative differences amongst them... were not split into parties, and even lived in agreement in their religious adherence, although some were Catholics and others Orthodox...

Today we still may see churches that were built by the mutual efforts of the Uniates from Galicia and the Orthodox from Bukovina; all of them, evidently lived through those trying processes, some of which found their way to the Privy Council in London, and yet in spite of that they stand as monuments to remind us of the primal harmony that existed among the first Ukrainian settlers in Canada, even in the religious affairs" [2]).

While living in Canada, Rev. O. Dmytriw was working for a while in the immigration bureau in Winnipeg. This helped him greatly in his religious field as he travelled widely through the western provinces, the cost of which would not have been possible to meet otherwise. The Ukrainian settlers could not have helped him for they were very poor themselves. The mass inflow of Ukrainian immigrants in 1898 completely absorbed all of Rev. Nestor Dmytriw's energy in the immigration bureau. In the winter of the same year he left Canada for U.S.A. never to return.

During his nearly two years of sojourn in Canada, Rev. N. Dmytriw left behind him lasting footprints in the organizing field of the Ukranian Catholic Church in Canada. He met the Roman Catholic hierarchy eye-to-eye, and revealed to them most clearly his own and the general national stand, regarding the over-all relationship between the Roman Catholic Church— and its hierarchy — and the newly organized "Ruthenian Greek Catholic Church." In his frank discussion with Bishop Legale which took place in St. Albert, Alberta, he boldly declared that in accordance with the canonical law there was to be in Canada an independent Ukrainian Catholic Church,

---

[1]) "Cross of Freedom" in Terebowla was designated as a "Centennial Project" during the restoration and dedication, that took place on July 30, 1966.
[2]) Myroslav Stechishin: "Self-Reliance League in Canada, Principles and Programs", p. 12, Chapter "Political Combinations", Winnipeg, 1928.

governed by its own bishop and subordinated to Lviv-Rome. In other words it would be equal with the Roman Catholic Church [3]). Along this same "straight-shooting" line followed the other priests who came after Rev. N. Dmytriw. While he was living in Canada Rev. N. Dmytriw wrote interesting reports, which have become a rich source of material for the studies of Ukrainian life in Canada during the pioneer era [4]).

The contemporary Ukrainian press of those days, both Canadian and American, was full of letters and convincing articles, voicing the urgent need for Ukrainian priests in Canada. Interesting enough all the requests asked for the married priests—"the kind we had in the old country"—stated the pioneers. Without any doubt, the sentiment of custom and ritual played an important role here. Letters and pleas were directed toward the Lviv hierarchy. The Edna-Star colony of Alberta sent an official letter in 1898 to Cardinal S. Sembratovych of Lviv [5]) with a request not only for the services of a priest but for material aid as well. Their last request was based on the fact that the Russian Orthodox Mission in U.S.A. began its advancing attack upon Ukrainian Catholic Church in Canada, especially in Alberta, and that it had large aid to back it up in this move. It may be worth mentioning that the membership of the Russian Orthodox Mission also included some Ukrainian Orthodox people as well (there had not been any separation of the Russian Orthodox and Ukrainian Orthodox Church at that time yet), and this aided the work of the Russian Mission among the Ukrainian Catholics. One of these was Rev. Ivan Malarevsky of Minneapolis, (1897-1898) who served in those days the Ukrainian Orthodox parish in Stuartburn (today's Gardenton) and others. He was the first Ukrainian Orthodox priest in Canada.

The Edna-Star letter no doubt had one good result, for it brought a second priest to Canada, the Rev. Pavlo Tymkevych. As soon as he began his work in Edna-Star he met not only the Russian Mission opposition but also the ire of the Roman Catholic Church authority who were endeavouring to bring the Ukrainian church in Edna under their jurisdiction. The parish and the priest took a determined stand against two onslaughts. During his priesthood days in Edna, Rev. P. Tymkevych not only looked after the spiritual needs of the settlers and the church but he also took time to organize the educational and cultural life in this district, and the result of this was that he cultural centre called "Prosvita"[6]), and the first of its kind in Canada, was built here. This was the first Ukrainian cultural-educational association in this country. It was located in the home of Alexander Karpets and in its first year of existence it could already boast of an 80 volume library. For those, now long departed days, this was some achievement. Along with the religious life there also flourished the cultural-educational orientation. Rev. P. Tymkevych, in addition to the above mentioned various activities, tried to establish an evening school for girls, who were working in Edmonton, but had to abandon his plans and leave for U.S.A.—as the Ukrainian pioneers were too poor to support a priest during those lean years.

---

[3]) "Studies in the History of Ukrainians in Canada", Vol. II, pp. 375-376.
[4]) For more information about the work along this line see the separate chapter, "Ukrainian Literature in Canada".
[5]) Text of this letter and the appeal in "Svoboda", dated 24. II. 1898.
[6]) "Svoboda", August 4, 1898.

Following the departure of Rev. N. Dmytriw and Rev. P. Tymkevych from Canada nearly a year passed before another priest came to this country, in the person' of Rev. Damaskyn Polivka of the Basilian Fathers. He was to have officiated at the blessing of a church in Edna but had been detained for a while in Winnipeg where he celebrated the first Ukrainian High Mass for the Ukrainian settlers, in the Roman Catholic Church of the Holy Ghost. People were highly enthused and would not let him leave for the West. There were several Ukrainian colonies around Winnipeg, which were comprised of about 150 families, and this convinced him to make his permanent home here and pay periodical visits to other colonies farther in the west. It was then that the first Ukrainian parish in Winnipeg was organized. This organizational step led to a conflict with the Roman Catholic Church of the Holy Ghost, which had been given the authority by Bishop Langevin, to look after the spiritual care of Ukrainians. In this conflict Bishop Langevin took the side of the Holy Ghost Church. The newly opened parish, which later took on the name of "Ruthenian Greek-Catholic Church of St. Nicholas", continued its religious duties against the wishes of the bishop. Disillusioned by the intrigues of the local Roman Catholic clergy, Rev. D. Polivka, after paying his farewell visits to all the colonies surrounding Winnipeg, left for U.S.A. in December of the same year.

The fourth Ukrainian priest in Canada was Rev. Ivan Zaklynsky, who arrived in July of 1900, and remained here for a longer period of time. By this time there were six somewhat prosperous parishes with their own churches. These were in Winnipeg, Gonor, Stuartburn and Sifton in Manitoba and Edna-Star and Rabbit Hills in Alberta. All of these churches were blessed by Rev. I. Zaklynsky. His longest stay was in Edna-Star district but when open hostilities arose, leading to the split of the parish into two segments—Catholic and Orthodox—Rev. I. Zaklynsky left for the East and remained for the most part in Manitoba. In Edna both sides to the dispute took this matter to court where it dragged on for a long time. Similar court cases took place in other parts of Canada—thus, wasting a great deal of national wealth and energy.

The onslaught of the Russian Orthodox Mission upon Ukrainian Catholics, that was first initiated by the two clergymen, W. Alexandrow and D. Kamyenyew during their Whit Sunday services on the farm of Kost Nemirsky in Vostok in 1897, also caused great alarm among the Roman Catholic hierarchy, which was empowered by the Vatican to look after the Greek-Catholics. In 1898, Bishop Albert Pascal of Prince Albert made a hurried trip to Vienna, Lviv and Rome to plead with the state and church authorities for aid in bringing Ukrainian clergy to Canada. In this, he was aided by the Abbot of Oblate Fathers in Belgium, P. Lelouge. Two years later, on a similar mission to Europe, went the Vicar-General of St. Albert, the well known in Canadian church history Father A. Lacombe, who, having an extensive experience in pioneer missionary work, suggested the idea that Ukrainians should have their own bishop. This bright thought of Father Lacombe about a Ukrainian bishop in Canada did not meet with much approval from Bishop Langevin [7]), at first. In the meantime, Rev. P. Tymkevych and Rev. D. Polivka presented their reports to their hierarchies in

---

[7]) According to Dr. M. Kazymyra's research in his book: "Ukrainian Hierarchs..." in Almanac of the Golden Jubilee—1905-1955, Winnipeg, p. 36.

Galicia, about the crying need of Ukrainian priests in Canada. The whole matter revolved around the scarcity of celibate priests, in view of the fact that the idea of married clergy for Canada was frowned upon by the Roman Catholic church. There was another difficulty, too: the Ukrainian Catholic priests did not wish to be subordinated to the Roman Catholic hierarchy and demanded the right to be subservient to their own hierarchy in Lviv, with which there was also tied the question of the deeding of church wealth and property.

To analyze this matter on the spot the then head of the Ukrainian Catholic Church, Metropolitan Andrey Shepticky, not having received from "Propaganda Fide" the permission to leave for Canada, sent his fully empowered representative in the person of Rev. Wasyl Zholdak who arrived in Winnipeg at the end of 1901. For it was here that religious contentions between the Greek and Roman Catholics were at their highest point, wherein the bishop of St. Boniface refused to give his recognition to the Ukrainian parish. Father Zholdak found himself between the hammer and the anvil. The Roman Catholic hierarchy with a fresh memory of the Edna-Star dispute in Alberta, made its sharp demand that all the Ukrainian churches and property be transferred under the jurisdicion of the Roman Catholic corporation, to which the Ukrainian parishes were most strongly opposed. In the vanguard of this struggle was the Winnipeg parish. Ukrainians, in general, believed that this capitulation to the Roman Catholic demand, amounted not only to the resignation from their church rights but also a national betrayal as well. The zest for this drive on the Roman Catholic side was supplied by the several Polish priests of Roman Catholic allegiance —like the two Kulawy Brothers in Winnipeg and Rev. F. Olszewski in Alberta— who went so far as to try to convert the Ukrainian settlers to Roman Catholic religion and to undermine the settlers' confidence in their own religion by belittling and slandering the Ukrainian Catholic priests in Canada. This led to the rejuvenation of the old sentiments left over from the previous fierce religious warfare that went on for years between Ukrainian and Polish people in the old country.

The enmity continued from year to year. The Ukrainian parishes, in order to free themselves from the domination of Latin hierarchy, chose to place themselves under the jurisdiction of the Association of the Ruthenian Church Parishes of U.S.A. and Canada. The first of the Ukrainian churches to make this decision, were Sifton and Fishing River, to which were added later Ethelbert, Terebowla (Valley River) and Winnipeg. Having made his tour of Manitoba, Saskatchewan and Alberta, Rev. W. Zholdak left for Lviv in the spring of 1902, with a valid report. Along with him went Father Jean of Oblate order, as a representative of Bishop Legal. Half a year later, in October of 1902, Rev. W. Zholdak returned to Canada but this time with three more missionary priests of the Basilian Order, the Rev. S. Dydyk, A. Strotsky and P. Filas, with the last one mentioned being in charge. Along with this first mission came also four Sister Servants of Mary Immaculate, namely, Sisters Ambrosia Lenkevych, Isydora Shypovska, Emilia Klapoushok and Taida Vrublevska. These Basilian fathers and Sister Servants took steps to establish the two Ukrainian religious orders in Canada that were to play important roles in future history. To the assistance of these three missionary priests of those momentous years, four other Basilian Fathers—Matey Hura and Navkraty Kryzhanovsky, in 1903, and

Atanazy Fylypiw and Ivan Tymochko, in 1904—came to Canada.

The work of this first steady-abiding mission, differed basically from the work of the previous priests, whose stay in Canada was mostly of a temporary nature. In addition to this, none of the former priests received any assistance, with the exception of Rev. D. Polivka, who obtained a small aid from "Propaganda fide". All of them were forced, sooner or later, to leave Canada. The Basilian mission in Canada had the backing of their homeland religious order and a good support from the Lviv Metropolitan. The financial situation in Canada was also greatly improved, as the settlers began to stand solidly on their feet.

The arrival of the Basilian Mission also helped to mellow the menacing mood in the Greek and Roman Catholic religious camp. The first group of Basilian fathers worked in Alberta and Saskatchewan and Rev. M. Hura and Rev. N. Kryzhanovsky in Manitoba. Rev. W. Zholdak, whom Archbishop Langevin appointed as the administrator of the Greek Catholic Church, was also stationed in Manitoba. It appeared that the mutual relationships had been finally normalized. But the situation became complicated somewhat when on the 25th of February, 1903, Joseph Bernier MLA, made an announcement in the Manitoba legislature about which the "Tribune" printed the following report:

"Mr. Joseph Bernier from the Archbishop of St. Boniface, praying for an act to amend chapter 23 of 38 Vic. conveying properties of the Greek Ruthenian Church in communion with Rome, into the control of the Church of Rome".

This report stirred the hornets' nest among the Ukrainian settlers for the petition of the fully-accredited Roman archbishop, was contending that the Roman Catholic hierarchy had the right to control the wealth of the Greek Catholic communities. Such a precedence, once having been established in Manitoba, could become legal practice in other parts of the west— particularly in Alberta and Saskatchewan. The instinctive sensitiveness of Ukrainians towards the Roman Catholics, now became even more pronounced. Massive protests were sent to Ottawa and passions rose high between the two religious denominations. This turn of events somewhat complicated the work of the Basilian priests who were subject to the authority of the Roman Catholic Church in Canada, but still refused to sign over their church property to that institution but were handing it over to their own religious order. Archbishop Langevin's decisive action helped to prepare andvantageous political field for the harvesting work of Bishop Serafym (real name: Stefan Ustvolsky) who in the spring of that same year (1903) began to carry on the work of the so-called "Greek Independent Church" in Canada.

Ustvolsky came to Winnipeg from New York, U.S.A. and in agreement with the Presbyterian Church and its supporters led the campaign for the establishment of an Independent Ukrainian Church. Seeing the need for more clergymen he began to ordain into the ministry of the church some of the more intellectual people, as for instance the "diaky" (church cantors or deacons), for these were already acquainted with the church services and rituals. In no time at all, Bishop Serafym had produced more than half a hundred of these newest church neophytes. In towns and villages, many parishes of "Greek Independent Church" were being organized. This was its official name but it was popularly known as "Ruthenian (Ukrainian)

Independent Church" and also as "Independent Orthodox Church". At the head of its organizing apparatus stood Ivan Bodrug, a teacher from Sifton and Ivan Negrych, also a teacher from Terebowla, who in 1898 were already taking their theological training at the Manitoba College, in Winnipeg. Both of them were ordained by Bishop Serafym and together with the officials of the Manitoba College, including its head, Dr. William Patrick, they formalized the new statute of the Greek Independent Church. Right from the start this newly formed church took an unfriendly stand towards the "uniates" and "tsarophiles" [8]) and set itself up as champion and brightest aureola of the independent Ukrainian church and its policy in Canada. The concept of independence in religious matters became very attractive in the early days of this church and so it was no surprise that it gained many adherents. It gained the support of many leading figures of the contemporary community activities. A the head of this elite group were: Kyrylo Genik, Petro Svarich, Toma Tomashevsky, Panteleymon Bozyk, W. Novak, D. Lazaruk, P. Hryhorchuk, I. Zelenetsky, P. Rudyk, D. Yaremiy, Leon Boykowich, Wasyl Vivchar, I. Drohomiretsky and others. Very soon a consistorium was formed composed of the following clergy: Ivan Danylchuk, Teodor Stefanyk, Hawrylo Tymchuk, Oleksa Bachynsky, Julian Bohonko and Ivan Negrych. The consistorium was formed on the advice of Bishop Serafym and officially formalized on the 27th of July, 1903. Six months later, on the 26th and 27th of January, 1904, a religious convention (called "sobor") of this church took place in Winnipeg. The sobor, which selected a new consistorium, was held in Taras Shevchenko Hall which was the only cultural and educational centre in Winnipeg at that time. This strengthened even further the convictions of the masses that the newly created church stood on solid national and independent principles.

The Independent Greek Church became an important factor in the lives of the Ukrainians in Canada. In Manitoba alone it organized tens of community centres. As many more were organized in Saskatchewan and Alberta.

In later years, for the sake of a more practical way of organizing, the prairie provinces were divided into three regional districts, one for each province. Each district had its own administrative apparatus that was in charge of organizing church activities. This rapid growth of the Independent Greek Church, greatly alarmed the Roman Catholic hierarchy of western Canada. As a result of this, Archbishop A. Langevin [9]) made a hurried trip to Europe, paying visits to Vienna and Rome where he clarified the Ukrainian church question. While in Venna he presented a special memorial to the Emperor of Austria, regarding this same matter, with a request for financial aid for the building of Ukrainian churches and schools in Canada. Extra emphasis was stressed by Archbishop Langevin for the need of qualified teachers from the old country for, as he mentioned in his memorial—there were about 4,000 Ukrainian children in Western Canada that did not have the benefit of a school. After his return from Rome, Archbishop Langevin aided financially in the building of the so-called "Big"

---

[8]) The "uniates" were those Ukrainian Catholics who declared their allegiance to Rome. The name was derived from the first word in "union with Rome, the tsarophiles (tsaroslavni) were those Orthodox Ukrainians who gave their allegiance to the "Russian Orthodox Mission in U.S.A."

[9]) Vienna in those days was considered to be a great Catholic Centre and a protectorate over those Catholics who went from Galicia to Canada.

church in Winnipeg and at the same time assistance came from the Roman Catholics in St. Albert, towards the building of a church in Edmonton, a matter which had been discussed by the Ukrainians since the year of 1903. Thus could be clearly discerned two powerful church agencies supporting the Ukrainian church affairs. On one side, we have the direct influence of the Presbyterians upon the Independent Greek Church who paid regular pensions to the clergy of this church. On the other side stood the Roman Catholic hierarchy which supported the Basilian order in the developmental growth of the Greek Catholic Church. In addition to this, the Roman Catholic hierarchy called for volunteers among their priests who would be willing—with Rome's approval—to be trained for celebrating church liturgy according to the Eastern (Byzantine) rite and carry on their priestly duties among Ukrainian Catholics. From that time on there were such dedicated re-ordained priests working among Ukrainians, as the Redemptorist Fathers A. Delaere, H. Boels, N. M. Decamp and K. Tacher and of the secular priests—A. Sabourin (1907) and others.

Many Ukrainians were worried by this help coming from the Presbyterians and the Roman Catholics, fearing that all this financial aid may have an undesirable influence upon the self-governing rights, as well as the traditionally religious rites, of the two Ukrainian churches. Some strong convictions were being formed that Ukrainians should build and develop their own kind of church and religious life, free from any outside intereference and to ask Rome to allow the Greek-Catholic Church in Canada to be either under the jurisdiction of the Metropolitan in Lviv, or else have their own bishop in Canada, not subject to the Roman Catholic hierarchy in this country. When in 1908 the Ukrainian Catholics in U.S.A. got their own bishop in the person of Soter Ortynsky, the eyes of the national-independent movement of the Ukrainians in Canada were all turned in that direction. What's more, in the summer of 1907 Rev. Mykola Strutynsky, and close collaborator of Bishop Ortynsky arrived in Winnipeg and took charge of the so-called "Small Church" of St. Vladimir and Olha which had been carrying on a political opposition to the other so-called "Big Church" in charge of the Basilian Fathers who accepted, without any reservations, the authority of the Roman Catholic hierarchy. Father M. Strutynsky made several trips through Manitoba and Saskatchewan in his organizing work and also carried on a campaign among Ukrainian Catholic parishes to bring them under Bishop Ortynsky's jurisdiction in U.S.A. His policy received the support of the larger parishes in Manitoba and Saskatchewan, like Stuartburn, Gimli (Dnister), Sifton, Terebowla, Ethelbert, Gonor, Brandon, Portage la Prairie and others. In this way was formalized the third group of the church known as "Nationally-Catholic-Independent" under the leadership of the parish of St. Vladimir and Olga, in Winnipeg. The support for this movement also came, though somewhat later, from the so-called "Committee for the defence of our people and our Greek-Catholic Church in America", located in Philadelphia, which began to propagate the complete separation of the Greek-Catholic Church in Canada from the domination by its sister church and hierarchy, the Roman Catholic. It is believed that Bishop Ortynsky gave his silent blessing to this committee's work but just as silently withdrew his influence when the apostolic delegate to Canada intervened into this delicate and controversial affair. The committee carried on its war for a little while longer before it silently folded up. But no such silent folding up came from the many parishes in Canada, who doggedly demanded the total independence for their own Ukrainian hierarchy. The strength of this national-independent movement of the Greek-Catholic Church grew still more when in December of 1907, an open split developed in the "Independent Greek Church" in which the so-called progressive elements took the lead and were clamoring loudly about the need of breaking away from the worn out ritual traditions of the Greek-Catholic and Greek-Orhodox Churches [10]). Such policy drove away hundreds of the faithful from its church and almost all of them threw their support behind the national-independent movement of the Catholics whose strength grew to the extent that they collected petitions, demanding Ukrainian hierarchy for the Greek-Catholic Church in Canada. The crown of this action was the public manifestation of the Ukrainians in Winnipeg on August 28, 1910. Speakers at this manifestation demanded that married clergy be allowed to come to Canada and in addition to have their own bishop, and that the Greek-Catholic Church be completely independent from Roman Catholic hierarchy. Those taking part, declared their loyalty to the Ukrainian Greek-Catholic hierarchy in the old country, and stressed particularly their fidelity and respect for Metropolitan Andrey Shepticky who was then on his way to attend Eucharistic Congress in Montreal. All speeches at this great gathering turned into one simple socio-national plea to the Metropolitan and Roman Catholic capital for the creation of a Ukrainian Catholic ecclesiastical province in Canada. The contemporary Anglo press in its commentaries supported these Ukrainian pleas that had been initiated and strongly backed by the parish of St. Vladimir and Olga and its parish priest, Rev. E. Krasicky.

Metropolitan Shepticky, taking advantage of his short stay in Montreal, made his visitation tour to all the Ukrainian churches and parishes in Canada. Between Winnipeg and Vancouver especially, he paid numerous visits to different communities in order to acquaint himself with the needs and desires of Ukrainian Catholics, and met with many Ukrainian delegates to discuss the problems of their local church affairs. Metropolitan Shepticky's arrival in Canada and his many visitations to Ukrainian communties was the answer to their pleadings and the culminating point of the ardent desires of the Ukrainian Catholics in Canada. It is worth our mentioning that a year before Metropolitan's visit to this country the apostolic delegate to Canada, S. Sbaretti, presented a well documented brief on the condition of the Ukrainian Catholic Church affairs in Canada at the first Canadian Sobor that was held in the city of Quebec. This widely circulated brief was prepared by the Redemptorist Father, Rev. A. Delaere, at the request of D. Sbaretti, and was titled, "The Memorial in regard to Ukrainians of north-western Canada". In addition to Rev. A. Delaere's signature to this brief, it was also signed by Rev. A. Fylypiw, on behalf of Basilian Fathers and by Rev. A. Sabourin representing the secular priests. This was the first such document from Canadian priesthood in support of the appointment of a Ukrainian bishop for Canada and which also had the full support of the former Roman Catholic priests who had now be reordained into Ukrainian Byzantine rite.

Rev. H. P. Boels, with the help of Rev. Dr. A. E. Burke, head of the

---

[10]) As is well known the religious rites in both churches are the same.

"Association (Society) for the advancement of Catholic Church in Canada", carried on a similar action.

Returning to Lviv, Metropolitan A. Shepticky prepared, without delay, an appeal to all the Roman Catholic bishops in Canada, entitled: "Address on the Ruthenian Question to Their Lordships the Archbishops and Bishops of Canada".

Metropolitan was truly able to grasp the whole situation and assay the feelings and desires of Ukrainians in Canada, weighing them correctly on the basis of religious, political and legal matters, and backed by the statistical figures for, according to the report of the presented memorial, only one Greek Catholic church had been signed over to the Latin bishops' corporation. The next in order, ten churches were incorporated with the Basilian Order and another ten churches were simply referred to as Greek-Catholic Parishes, while an overwhelming number of seventy-two churches were un-assigned (undesignated)—and awaiting Ukrainian bishop. These arguments and figures alone, were convincing enough, for those who were interested in the problems of Ukrainian Catholic parishes, that a Ukrainian bishop for the Ukrainian settlers in Canada was of prime importance. The result of this was that the Roman Catholic bishops—Archbishop Langevin, Bishop E. Legal of St. Albert and Bishop A. Pascal of Prince Albert—by means of a special declaration-letter, dated July 28, 1911, informed the apostolic delegate in Ottawa that all the Roman Catholic bishops of North-western Canada are favourably disposed toward the idea of appointing a separate ecclesiastical province for the Ukrainians in Canada. At the same time, they declared themselves to be in favor of giving full support to the bishop of the newly created ecclesiastical province.

Through this declaration, the status of the Ukrainian Catholics in Canada became clarified. In 1912 the Apostolic See formed a separate ecclesiastical province for the Greek-Catholic Church in Canada and Rev. Nykyta Budka, the prefect of the Theological Seminary of Lviv, was appointed as its first bishop, arriving in Canada December 6, 1912, to take over his duties as the head of the Greek-Catholic Church. Ukrainians greeted his arrival with great enthusiasm, remembering also the fact that he had been the founder of the emigrant "St. Raphael's Association" in Lviv, and the help received from it by the immigration in Canada. This Association had been publishing its monthly journal "The Emigrant", as well as almanacs, pamphlets and circulars, full of information for those who had left or were planning to leave the old country.

To show respect and gratitude for those who strove on behalf of Ukrainian Church in Canada, Bishop Budka elevated the St. Vladimir and Olga parish to the rank and dignity of: "Pro-cathedral of the Ukrainian Greek-Catholic Church". Both religious Orders, the Basilian and the Redemptorist Fathers as well as the Sister Servants acknowledged the Bishop's jurisdiction over them, although they had been, up till then, under the Roman Catholic hierarchy's jurisdiction.

When Bishop N. Budka first came to Canada there were 17 missionary priests working in the religious field. These were: the five Basilian Fathers —M. Hura, N. Kryzhanovsky, S. Dydyk, A. Fylypiw and W. Ladyka; four Redemptorist Fathers—A. Delaere, H. Boels, H. M. Decamp and K. Tacher. Of the secular priests there were: E. Krasicky, E. Andruchowych, Dr. K. Yermy, I. Zhuravetsky, K. Rozdolsky, M. Kinash, W. Wynarsky and S.

Fedorenko. Of the French priests who turned to Ukrainian rite there were: Father—J. Jean, A. Sabourin, J. Gagnon and D. Clavellaux. Together with his secretary, Rev. I. Bala, who accompanied Bishop Budka to Canada, there were thirteen secular priests. There were also eight Sister Servants who were to look after schools and orphan homes. An apostolic Missionary School was established in Sifton with Rev. A. Sabourin in charge and a day school at St. Nicholas, Winnipeg, which had been built by Archbishop Langevin in 1911, with Sister Servants in charge. Two other schools run by Sister Servants were established in Mundare and Edmonton. In addition to this, "Canadian Ruthenian", the official organ of Ukrainian Catholic Church, was being published in Winnipeg. Bishop Budka took under his control over eighty parishes, all of them being in Western Canada, with the exception of those that were in Fort William, Toronto, Montreal, Ottawa and Sydney. Bishop Budka also incorporated the Church as "Ruthenian Greek Catholic Church". All churches that had been incorporated with Basilian Fathers, Redemptorist Fathers, Bishop S. Ortynsky of U.S.A. or Roman Catholic bishops in Canada, were now re-incorporated in the care of the Ukrainian Bishop Budka. Outside this last mentioned incorporation there were only a few churches remaining—the ones that defended their political independence and refused to submit to any church authority. Their idea was being nourished by some of the leaders of cultural-educational organizations, as well as by the tenacious influences of the Presbyterian Church.

Bishop Budka expanded his visitatorial and organizing activities. In a very short time new churches were being built in Eastern Canada—Montreal, Sydney, Toronto, Hamilton, Brantford, Kitchener, Sudbury and Sault Ste. Marie and in the West—Calgary, Saskatoon, Regina, Transcona and other places. The greatest problem was the lack of clergy and to remedy this, Bishop Budka was able to place a few students in the Toronto Roman Catholic Seminary, in charge of Dr. A. Redkevych and in addition to this brought a few more priests from the old country who arrived in Canada in 1913. These were Fathers—R. Krupa, M. Olenchuk, M. Ircha, N. Drohomiretsky, I. Demchuk, Dr. I. Perepylycia, and others. The new Bishop turned his attention toward expanding the school activities and, with this end in view, evening schools were established and a day school—the "Sacred Heart Academy" was built in Yorkton and catechetical courses held. The Bishop also supported the idea of organizing and building bursas in Winnipeg, Edmonton and Saskatoon. In 1919, with the aid of the "Association for the Propagation of Faith", in Toronto, a college (high school) was built in Yorkton under the guidance of the Brothers of Christian Schools. The bishop also initiated a cultural-educational program for the grown-ups, built "National Homes" and "Prosvitas" (Cultural Centres), including the Prosvita Institute in Winnipeg, and brought a few educationalists and learned men to strengthen the teaching forces and raise to a higher level the guiding leadership of Ukrainian settlers in Canada.

Not all the plans ran so smoothly. There were some failures and heartbreaks as well. The successful years were those of 1913 and 1914. In 1913, the first Sobor (convention) of Ukrainian Catholic priests took place in Yorkton and at this meet, under the guidance of Bishop Budka, the rules and regulations of the Ruthenian Catholic Church in Canada were enacted. This same time saw the final liquidation of the Independent Greek Church which had started to dwindle since 1908. Its so-called independence had been shrivelling gradually, from year to year, along with its growing dependence upon the Presbyterian Church, upon whose funds it now depended to pay its ministers. Presbyterian Church was itself in heavy debt. At the 1912 convention of the Presbyterian Church in Ottawa, it was revealed that the expenses of that church had exceeded its profits by more than half a million dollars. The difference had to be made up from voluntary contributions and gifts and these were not to be had. Dr. E. Grant became the new superintendent of the church and he refused to give any aid to the missions of other nationalities. The consistorium of the Independent Greek Church was given an ultimatum to either join fully the Presbyterian Church, and thereby assure itself of its financial help or else detach itself from the Presbyterian Church without any pretensions. The majority in the Independent Greek Church at the Presbyterian sobor held in Toronto, June, 1913, decided to join and twenty-three ministers of the Independent Church declared themselves, without any reservations, to become members of the Presbyterian Church. This was the last public act of the so-called "Independent Greek Church" which had existed ten full years in Canada, all the while passing through a prolonged metamorphosis from the ritualisitc and religious recognition point of view. In its embryonic stage it was called "Ruthenian (Ukrainian) Independent Greek-Orthodox Church", and later it legalized its name to "Independent Greek Church." It was also called "Independent Orthodox Church" or "Self-Reliance Orthodox Church" and in ordinary every day language it was called simply as Independent or "Samostiyna (Self-Reliant) Church". The added adjective of "Independent" or "Self-Reliant" managed to survive to the end of this church movement, although factually speaking independent it never was. From its very beginning it was already "in dependence" upon the leadership of the Presbyterian Church. The spiritual parent of the Independent Greek Church, Ivan Bodrug, would not join with the Presbyterian Church. In his memoirs he explains his reasons thus:

"Every nation", he said, "has its own specific psychology and culture and every national church has to reflect and represent the psychology and culture of its nation (people). And if any steps at reformation, at any given church are to be taken, then this same reformation must be taken gradually, in line with the spiritual growth and respect for the traditions of that nation. Church reformation must proceed from the basic line of thought and the cultural level of any given nation. The forcing of some alien idea upon any nation or compelling some people to accept another's denomination never succeeds" [11]). These summations of I. Bodrug became self-verified. Many supporters of the Greek Independent Church abandoned it. Most of them joined with the Greek Catholic Church and some went with the Russian Orthodox Church that had been under the control of Russian Orthodox Mission in U.S.A.

The Orthodox Church, or as it was called in Canada, the "tsarophile church" expanded its activities with the arrival in Canada of Abbot Arseny Chechovcev, who came to this country from U.S.A. in 1908. Up till then Manitoba, Saskatchewan and Alberta were served by the Russian Mission

---

[11]) Memoirs of pastor Ivan Bodrug are preserved by Dr. M. H. Boykowich in Saskatoon. Some of them have been printed in the "Evangelical Truth", Toronto, year 1957 & 1958, No. 9-12 and No. 1-4.

from Minneapolis although almost from the beginning Alberta was served by the Russian priests from San Francisco. In 1908, Arseny took over under his charge the whole field in Western Canada. Winnipeg, and later Edmonton, became missionary centres of the Russian Orthodox Church. Manitoba alone had 27 congregations. Almost as many were founded in Alberta and a somewhat lesser number in Saskatchewan, perhaps due to the fact that the Greek Independent Church had a great influence there. Membership of the Russian Orthodox Church was composed mostly of Ukrainians from Bukovina and a lesser number of them were Russians and other nationalities, such as Bielo-Russians, Serbians and Romanians. Several Ukrainian Greek Catholic congregations joined with Arseny during those days when that Church was struggling for its independence, but once the conditions there became stabilized and returned to normal, most of them came back into its fold. In 1910, Arseny departed from Canada and the Russian Orthodox Mission was renamed Russian Orthodox Church with its own Canadian bishop as the head.

When the Russian revolution began in 1917, and on the ruins of the tsarist empire new governments of the subjugated nations came to power, the event also brought great changes to the Russian Orthodox Church which had always been a political instrument of the Russian tsars. And along with the political changes in the Russian Orthodox Church, the Orthodox churches of other enslaved nations were also undergoing a great change. In turn, this affected further the management of Russian Orthodox Church in Canada. Already in 1917, a division took place in the Russian Orthodox Church of Holy Trinity in Winnipeg. A large number of Ukrainians from Bukovina refused to give their allegiance to the Russian Orthodox Church and established a separate one of their own. Similar incidents took place in other places. Dissatisfaction with policies and management of Russian Orthodox Church increased daily. During this same time important re-arrangements were also taking place in the Greek Catholic Church and a certain number of pioneer leaders in Ukrainian community work, and who could not see eye-to-eye with Bishop Budka, made plans to form an independent Ukrainian Orthodox Church.

The organizing centre of this group was Saskatoon where there had been in existence for the last two years, the "Bursa of Petro Mohyla", which was renamed to "Institute of Petro Mohyla", in 1917. Students and leaders of this institute took upon themselves the task of organizing the independent Ukrainian Orthodox Church. They first organized an initiative group that called itself "National Committee". This committee sent confidential and informative letters to all the key members of Ukrainian communities in Canada, in which was voiced the dissatisfaction with Bishop Budka's church policies, stressing at the same time that: "lately a fierce struggle has started between the clergy, guided by His Excellency Bishop Nykyta Budka, and the lay intelligentsia, which groups itself around national institutions such as bursas, national homes, cultural centres and others, in which the clergy wants to stamp its clerical control over the national institutions in particular, and national endeavours as a whole" [12]. In this letter it was stated that consultation meeting consisting of "community-conscious intelligentsia" will be called at Saskatoon to which Bishop Budka will also be invited, to

---

[12] Informative letter dated May 27, 1918 and some other correspondence preserved in the archives of the author.

THE RELIGIOUS QUESTION

discuss, mutually, the church-community affairs. Whether this was the intention of all those initiators of this meeting it would be hard to say. From the correspondence relating to this matter, it would appear that voices were heard against having any talks with the bishop.

In July 18 and 19, 1918, on the initiative of the "National Committee" the "first confidential meeting pertaining to church affairs" took place in Saskatoon. In the National Committee were the following representatives from Manitoba, Saskatchewan and Alberta: Manitoba—W. Kudryk, O. H. Hykawy, J. W. Arsenych, T. D. Ferley, D. Yakimischak, I. Petrushevych, W. Mihaychuk, H. Hykawy and D. Romanchych; Saskatoon—F. Havryluk, Y. Bohonos, S. Sawchuk, A. Vorobetz, M. Stechishin, W. Mychaluk, T. Shvydky, B. M. Saviak, D. F. Stratychuk, T. Stadnyk, A. Bodnarchuk, A. Markovsky, P. Mamchur, M. Chorneyko and I. Kulchytsky; Alberta—T. Goshko, I. I. Rudyk, A. T Kibzey, S. W. Mykytiuk, P. Svarich, M. Sutkovych.

The guiding personalities at this discussion-convention were: W. Swystun, M. Stechishin, T. D. Ferley, P. Shvydky, W. Mihaychuk and several others. About 150 people took part in these discussions. They voiced their discontent at the way church property of the Greek Catholic parishes, was being incorporated under Bishop Budka's authority, and were further dissatisfied with the fact that members of other nationalities were in the ranks of priests in Ukrainian churches and that Bishop Budka, supposedly, was trying to take over cultural and educational organizations under his conrol. The last item in their resolutions was the allegation of those present, that the 1596 church union with Rome "was forced upon Ukrainian people". In view of this, all those present at the convention felt amply justified in taking this step of organizing the Ukrainian Greek-Orthodox Church in Canada. They also decided that in this newly organized church, the priests should be married, the bishops should be chosen by the whole sobor (general convention) and that the church congregations were to have the right of hiring and firing the priests, as well as retaining the ownership of the church property. Ideological and organized decisions at this convention had somewhat run away with the original intentions of its initiators and were also basically at variance with the principles of the Catholic Church. At this same meeting the "Ukrainian Greek-Orthodox Brotherhood of Canada" was formalized which was to look after the incorporation of the newly established church.

The head administration of the "Ukrainian Greek-Orthodox Brotherhood" of the Greek Orthodox Church in Canada was composed of both the Orthodox and the former Catholic members. These were: Wasyl Hawrysh, Tymko Goshko, A. Zhylych, M. Stechishin, P. Svarich, P. Shvydky, W. Mihaychuk and A. Shandro. A committee was formed, comprised of sixteen persons. The brotherhood took upon itself the duties to look after the affairs of the planned church, on temporary basis, until such time as bishop and church hierarchy were chosen [13]. The Brotherhood committee enlarged the organizational work in all provinces, with the Institute of Petro Mohyla in Saskatoon as its material and moral bastion. The Syrian Metropolitan Germanos became the first bishop of the Ukrainian Greek-Orthodox Church in Canada. He was under the jurisdiction of the Patriarch of Antioch and living in U.S.A. The Syrian Metropolitan pro-

---

13) "Ukrainian Voice", No. 32, pp. 2 & 3, 1918.

claimed (acknowledged) the Ukrainian Greek Orthodox Church as an independent self-governed church. In 1920 Metropolitan Germanos ordained the first priests of this new church. These were: Rev. S. W. Sawchuk, Rev. Dmytro Stratiychuk and Rev. Petro Sametz. Later Rev. Wasyl Kudryk, the former editor of "Ukrainian Voice" and "Orthodox Messenger" made up the fourth. This clerical quartet organized the first Ukrainian-Orthodox congregations and had them incorporated, thus becoming the first pioneers in the U.G.O.C. work. At the third sobor of the Ukrainian Greek-Orthodox Church Rev. S. W. Sawchuk was chosen as its administrator. With the establishment of the Ukrainian Greek-Orthodox Church, a new page began in the life of Ukrainian Canadians.

To fully encompass the religious and church affairs of the Ukrainians in the pioneer era it will be necessary, from the historical point of view, to make some mention about the work of several Baptist congregations. Such congregations were formed in Winnipeg and at Oleskiw (Overstone-Tolstoi) and two or three other districts. The guiding figures in this movement were —I. Shakotko and M. Kryvetsky. The first Ukrainian Baptist conference was held in Canora, Saskatchewan, in 1909. This conference passed into history as the first such conference of that church in Western Canada in which nine congregations from the prairie provinces took part.

At this conference the first Ukrainian Baptist newspaper was initiated and later in the same year its publication was materialized in Toronto as the first Ukrainian paper in Eastern Canada. [14].

The Ukrainian Canadian settlers passed through some terrible religious and spiritual upheavals. These stemmed, primarily, from the course of outside influences and were specifically conditioned by the settlers' own situation. New church affiliations were formalized. The enormous national energy was used, wastefully, upon a struggle that lasted for a quarter of a century. There were different angles and turning points in this religious struggle but the outcome of this strife revealed that it was mostly confined to the two basic Ukrainian churches in Canada—the Ukrainian Catholic Church and the Ukrainian Greek Orthodox Church—which in turn clearly mirrored, even here on this continent, the religious twin-division of the Ukrainians in the Old Country.

---

[14] See chapter "Press" and especially pp. 283-284.

PUBLIC SCHOOL EDUCATION

Public school education in Ukrainian settlements in Manitoba began at the close of the last century. In the contemporary Ukrainian newspaper "Svoboda" (Liberty) published in Mount Carmel, Pennsylvania, which served the inerests of the Ukrainian immigrants in the U.S.A. and in Canada, we come across numerous letters, lengthy articles and advertisements from Canada concerning the needs of Ukrainian teachers. From this material it becomes clear that in the very beginning the problem of finding teachers for the Ukrainian settlements was much more difficult to solve than that of priests. Each of these settlements required a teacher who had the knowledge of both Ukrainian and English. The settlers and their children could not speak English, therefore it was impossible for a teacher without the knowledge of Ukrainian to carry on his work. Historical research discloses that only four qualified teachers landed in Canada with whole shiploads of Ukrainian settlers before 1900. One of them, Cyril (Kyrylo) Genik, became the first Ukrainian interpreter and civil servant of the Immigration branch in Winnipeg while the other three taught in schools: Ivan Negrych in "Trembowla" school, Valley River, Manitoba; Ivan Bodrug in "Kosiw" school, Dauphin, and Vasyl Cichocky in "Galicia" school. Newly established school districts, such as Stuartburn, remained without teachers.

Although the oldest Ukrainian school district was "Galicia" in Northern Rockwood, teaching began earlier in the districts of "Trembowla" and "Kosiw", under the care of the Presbyterian Church. Only in later years did these schools pass over to provincial administration. Concerning the "Galicia" school we read in the inspector's report as follows: [1])

"I am glad to be able to report the steady introduction of modern ideas in the matter of school buildings. Excellent houses have been erected in Galicia, Pleasant Home, Rossdale and Meadowdale".

With their "Galicia" school the Ukrainians had made a good start in Manitoba, for in 1916 it was noted in "Sessional Papers of Manitoba" that "There are now one hundred and thirty-two Ruthenian and Polish schools in Manitoba" [2]). In 120 of those districts Ukrainians were the predominant majority. This was an impressive achievement for the Ukrainian settlers.

No lesser successes in the field of education were achieved by the Ukrainians in Alberta and Saskatchewan. In 1912 there were 90 Ukrainian school districts established in Alberta and by 1915 this was increased to 130. During the same period of time there were over 200 such districts in Saskatchewan. Some of these were inactive because of a shortage of teachers.

On the whole, over 400 school districts in Western Canada conducted bilingual schools in which children received instruction in both English and Ukrainian. In Manitoba, Ukrainian was the language of instruction, whereas in Alberta and Saskatchewan, the teaching of Ukrainian was permitted in classrooms only between 3:00 and 4:00 in the afternoon each day.

---

[1]) Report of the Department of Education for the Year ending December 31st, 1899.
[2]) Sessional Papers, 1915 (No. 3) 5 Geo. V, p. 218.

The history of these achievements is full of trials and tribulations but regardless of this we often come across remarks that the Ukrainian pioneers were not putting enough effort into the organization of public school education. In 1902, School Inspector Hooper in Manitoba noted in his report that many new school districts had been established among the Ukrainians, but that the difficulties remained in the fact that there were no teachers. For that reason a general public clamor was raised, first in Manitoba and later in Saskatchewan and Alberta, urging the Department of Education to attend to the training of suitable teachers for these schools. Behind these demands for bilingual teachers were practical considerations. A School Inspector at Vegreville explained these demands:

"In the majority of cases the parent desires the best for the children as he realizes the magnitude of his own shortcomings and handicaps" [3]. It is known that a great many of the pioneers were illiterate, especially in the English language. After all, the parents wanted the children to know their native language and thereby possess the key to cultural acquisitions of their own people. Moreover, the religious practices of the Ukrainian people required the knowledge of Ukrainian. On the other hand, teaching the children the English language and objecting to the teaching of the Ukrainian language alarmed the parents and they began to compare the situation of subjection in the Old Country with the situation in Canada. For reasons easy to understand, other national groups raised their voices in support of a bilingual school system for the Ukrainians. In Winnipeg there was formed a separate committee—the Galician Education Committee—which included such notable citizens of Winnipeg and Manitoba as Ven. Archdeacon Fortin, Dr. W. Patrick, Dr. G. Bryce, Wm. Whyte, R. J. Whitla, Thos. Gilroy, Rev. Alfred Andrews, Rev. Fr. S. J. Drummond, Rev. Fr. Cherrier, Rev. Fr. Kulawy, T. D. Deegan, F. W. Russell, Dr. I. T. Reid, known as "Presbyterian Medical Missionary to the Galicians", Rev. C. W. Gordon, Prof. Hart, N. Baw, J. F. Fowler, Chairman of Winnipeg School Board, Prof. J. Stewart, and others. From the press reports preserved to our times we see that members of this committee supported the most progressive ideas with regard to the education of New Canadians. At the same time they supported the need of bilingual teachers for the "Galician" schools, demanded subsidies from the provincial and federal governments for these schools and stressed the necessity of teaching children not only the official language of the country but their own language as well [4]. Members of this committee held several conferences under the chairmanship of Archdeacon Fortin, out of which came unanimously adopted resolutions urging the governments to provide school inspectors and organizers for the "Galicians" in Manitoba. Undoubtedly, the very fact of the committee being made up of prominent educators and representatives of church organizations must have had a great influence in the shaping of general public opinion in favor of a bilingual school system. The endeavors of Roman Catholic Archbishop Langevin also pursued the same line.

The hasty opinion had been expressed that the Ukrainian settlers were opposed to the establishment of schools. This untruth should have been resolutely refuted on the spot. Even if any such incidents had taken place, investigation will show that they occured against a background of deter-

---

[3] Report of Inspector at Vegreville, as quoted in C. H. Young, op. cit., p. 204.
[4] The Winnipeg Tribune, Jan. 17, 1902.

mined demands for instruction in the native language in elementary schools [5]), only because the settlers entertained reasonable fears that in the course of receiving insruction solely in English their children could be alienated from their parents and their cultural heritage. In January 1901 Archbishop Langevin wrote a special letter to the provincial government on this matter. From the reply of the then Premier Rodmond Roblin, one can learn that the provincial Government of Manitoba had no clear-cut solution for this problem [6]). Also special delegations of teachers from Winnipeg appealed to the government of Manitoba to take heed of the need of education for the children of new settlers. Moreover, delegations from the Ukrainian people began to arrive from all quarters at the seat of the government. At the congress of the Independent Greek Orthodox Church one of the most important items on the agenda was the question of public schools and education of children. Behind the demands of the immigrants, some of whom were then naturalized citizens of Canada, stood the School Act, enacted on the basis of "The Laurier-Greenway Agreement" of 1897, which said: "When ten of the pupils speak the French language, or any other language than English as their native language, the teaching for such pupils shall be conducted in French or such other language, and English upon the bilingual system".

As a result of these endeavours and the School Act, the government of Manitoba announced at the end of 1904 that early in 1905 it would open a special school for the training of bilingual school teachers. This school was opened February 16, 1905, in Winnipeg on Minto St. (which explains why this school has been often referred to as the "Minto School".) The official name of the school was the "Ruthenian Training School", although Ukrainians called it the Ukrainian Teachers' Seminary. In the beginning two courses—a higher and a lower—were created in the school, and within a short time 32 students were enrolled. The government decision to establish such a school was received by the Ukrainian population with undisguised enthusiasm. In justification of this it was noted in "The Report of the Department of Education for 1905" that, "the people appreciate the action of the Government in establishing a training school for Ruthenian teachers, and are rejoicing because they will soon be able to get properly qualified bilingual teachers who will have an excellent knowledge of English as well as Ruthenian. When a supply of teachers can be counted upon from this source it will tend to encourage the districts to erect and operate schools".

Apart from the said teachers' seminary, but at the same time, special courses for training teachers had been started in Manitoba College. These courses were conducted by Prof. Michael Sherbinin under the watchful eye of the Presbyterian Church which by then started giving financial assistance to students. In the college, subjects of pedagogic order were supplemented by instruction in the Presbyterian faith. The lecturers were Dr. W. Patrick, Prof. G. Bryce and Dr. J. A. Carmichael.

When Manitoba had the matter of Ukrainian schools in working order, Saskatchewan and Alberta were just then getting ready to organize school districts. Having formulated the provincial statutes, the two provinces pro-

---

[5]) Studies in the History of Ukrainians in Canada, Vol. II, pp. 139-140.
[6]) Letter of Premier Roblin of Manitoba to Archbishop Langevin, No. 193, St. Boniface Archives, dated Jan. 26, 1901.

ceeded slowly with the task of setting in order the matter of education.

The first school organizer appointed in Saskatchewan was Ivan Bodrug, followed later by Osyp Megas. The earliest organizers of schools for the Slavs in Manitoba were J. Baderski in 1903 and M. Rudnicki in 1904. These two organizers did not enjoy the confidence of Ukrainian settlers in Manitoba, so when the demand for organizers who could understand the problems of Ukrainian settlers was eventually heard, the government in 1907 appointed Theodore Stefanyk to the position. Stefanyk was a well-known public worker, and the organization of school districts was carried out with best results in the first year of his work. In the meantime, 15 student teachers completed their studies at the seminary in Winnipeg [7]), and the first graduates emerged from the teachers' course in Manitoba College. The student teachers graduating from Minto were under obligation to teach in Manitoba while those graduating from the Manitoba College were obliged to teach in Saskatchewan. Since the Manitoba government was providing the students in the Ruthenian Training School with financial assistance, the graduated teachers were obliged to repay in due time the amount of $600 which represented a refund of the cost of common board and room in the two courses. With the school walls behind them, and without delay, the graduates proceeded with the work of organization. First of all, they organized themselves. In the summer 1907, they held a teachers' convention where a number of resolutions were adopted regarding the formation of a professional teachers' association. The following teachers were elected to the executive committee: Ivan Kotsan (Kocan), chairman; Yar. Dedelyuk, O. H. Hykawy, O. Klymkiw, V. Saranchuk, P. S. Ogryzlo, T. D. Ferley and M. Drabinyasty, as members.

The teachers present at the convention demanded that the Ruthenian Training School continue its work, for even then rumors circulated that it was to be closed. Participating in the deliberations were leading members of the Ukrainian community in Winnipeg, some of them, such as Theodore Stefanyk, A. Novak and others, being nominated honorary members of the newly formed teachers' organization. The convention also decided to name as honorary members Mykhaylo Hrushevsky and Ivan Franko, both of Lviv, poet Borys Hrinchenko of Kiev, S. Yarychevsky of Chernivtsi, and several other outstanding figures in the cultural and political life of Ukraine. In another resolution attention was called to the pressing need of bilingual textbooks and for this purpose a 5-member commission was elected. Also, it was decided to turn to Dr. Ivan Franko for advice and assistance. It was further resolved to have the School Act translated into Ukrainian so that Ukrainian settlers might have a better comprehension of the school laws. The teachers decided to arrange special lectures for illiterates. Regarding the organization of school districts, the convention resolved to propose to the Department that two Ukrainian organizers be trained and that one of the suggested candidates be eventually accepted by the Department. To characterize the ideological attitude of the teachers it would be relevant to include here the resolution which said that "the teachers' convention does not attach great importance to the question of salaries, leaving this matter to individual teachers and school trustees, and "puts the main em-

---

[7]) V. Karpets, V. Chumer, V. Kolodzinsky, S. Lytwyn, V. Hrushovy, Ivan Kotsan, Ya. Kolltek, O. Klymkiw, Ya. Mayevsky, P. Chaikovsky, D. Vovk and M. Ostapovych.

phasis on the work of the teachers which the people will later evaluate and on the basis of merit know how much they ought to pay". Therefore, neither personal nor occupational interests stood before the eyes of these idealistic teachers who were motivated by a concern for the general well-being and educational development of their own people.

The Ukrainian press in Canada and the U.S.A. published reports on the proceedings of the convention, couched in superlative terms, and the journal "Svoboda" expressed the hope that the teachers will prove to be an important and beneficial factor in the public life of Canada. Indeed, the expectations of "Svoboda" have been fulfilled because pioneer teachers have played a leading and highly useful role in the Ukrainian community of Canada. They were not only teachers in the schools, but were also the cultural and educational workers of the districts in which they worked. They gave the backbone to the social and cultural life of the Ukrainians in Canada and became a driving force which directed the community into the future. In this connection one must note still another detail, namely, that for the first time, it was decided at this convention that the modern appelation "Ukrainian" be used, instead of the archaic "Ruthenian".

This modern and proper name has become a common denominator for all former "Ruthenians", "Galicians", "Bukovinians", "Russians", "Austrians", 'Lemkos", and so on. A highly-principled force was being generated in the teachers' organization which began to influence the entire Ukrainian community in Canada. At the same time these teachers were becoming a kind of bridge, linking the Ukrainian community with the outside world. They were the interpreters of the desires and aspirations of a community which was being progressively integrated into one Canada. Within three days of the convention, June 9, 1907, the teachers forwarded a letter to the Department of Education of the Government of Manitoba in which the situation of Ukrainian schools in the province was presented. According to this document, in 1907 there were only 40 English-Ukrainian schools for a population of 30,000 Ukrainians in the province. The teachers advised the Department on ways to intensify the training of teachers and establish compulsory school attendance. They adopted unanimously a resolution which read:

"This convention declared itself to be strongly in favor of compulsory education and requests the Government of the Province of Manitoba to make legislation to that effect". This and other resolutions and actions of the young teachers could not but impress all others that they had in them good qualities to become better Canadian citizens. In the Ukrainian language the teachers' organization was called the "Ukrainian Teachers' Association" and in English the "Ruthenian Teachers' Association". Its motto was: "Virtue, Industry, Education". This motto was used as letterhead on all stationery of the Association.

In 1908, through the endeavours of Ukrainian teachers, the "first national Ukrainian mass meeting" was held in Winnipeg, at which the teachers, together with the delegates from different organizations discussed the educational problems of the people as well as organizational and school matters. One item of particular importance concerned the organization of new school districts and a second organizer for these schools. In matters of a general educational and organizational nature, it was resolved that reading halls in farm districts and small towns should form an organizational superstructure under the name of "Canadian Prosvita" and it was proposed that a convention of this organization be held within a short time so that all cultural and educational problems of the Ukrainian people in the province and Canada as a whole could be discussed. Those present at the meeting elected a 22-member delegation which was to outline these matters before the provincial government. At the same time the teachers held their own convention at which they discussed their professional problems with great enthusiasm. At this convention the teachers raised for the first time the question of a bursa (a home for students—a semi-educational Ukrainian institution) and the training of both male and female teachers. In support of their point, Miss V. Drelinkevych, a teacher from Stuartburn, was accepted as the first female member of the Ukrainian Teachers' Association. Also brought up for discussion was the matter of self-education of teachers for whom short term courses were to be held in the Normal School in Winnipeg during the summer holidays. It is clear from these resolutions how seriously the teachers pursued the matter of their professional training and what momentous public responsibilities they took upon their shoulders.

The organization of reading rooms and preparations for the first convention were almost exclusively the work of teachers. Thereafter, annual conventions of the Ukrainian Teachers' Association in Manitoba have been held each year, and each subsequent year saw the ranks of this organization augmented with new forces. In the same manner, the number of school districts was constantly increasing, thanks to the persevering efforts of Theodore Stefanyk. In 1908 he reported that 50 schools had been organized and 4 new school buildings erected [8].

Some of the schools had libraries for the general public, as for example, in the "Chervona", "Kosiw", "Shevchenko", "Franko" and "Taras" schools. Despite the numerical increase of teachers, the shortage of them was being felt just the same. Everywhere people demanded bilingual teachers because they could best understand children and their problems. In the report of an organizer of that time we read: "I believe that in schools where the teacher is able to speak the two languages and is using the Ruthenian elementary textbooks, or some Ruthenian-English dictionary, the children are making better progress in all subjects of study than they otherwise would" [9]. The organizer further reported that the teachers' salaries rose from the then prevailing rates of $350 a year to $500, and even $550. There were instances where certain districts were paying their teachers as much as $50 a month. It was noted in the reports of 1909 that there were now 80 school districts and 62 new schools erected [10]. In the newly settled areas, 14 new school districts had been organized. During the same period such schools as "Horod", "Seech", "Zaporozhe", "Zbruch", "Lemberg", "Wisla", and so on, came into being. The schools were being constructed, as the report has it, "according to the plans and specifications authorized by the Advisory Board of Education for the Province". It is also of interest to note the inspector's report on the teaching in the so-called "Galician Schools", written by F. H. Belon just from one district [11].

---

[8] "Dnister" (near Gimli), "Stryj" (near Komarno), "Ivan Ardan" (Lac du Bonnet) and "Mountain Road".
[9] Department Report for 1908, p. 107.
[10] Department Report for 1909, p. 19.
[11] Manitoba Department of Education, Annual Report 1909, North-Western Inspectoral Division F. H. Belton's Report, page 112, Galician Schools.

Erected in 1910, were the following schools: "Gonta", "Franko", "Mohyla", "Mountain Stream", "Kupchenko", "Chmelnycky", "Limna", "Slovo" and "Zoria". Also in the succeeding years more school districts emerged which frequently bore Ukrainian names, such as "Jaroslaw" in the municipality of Bifrost; "Postup" at Gilbert Plains; "Komarno" at Rockwood; "Pawlyk" (S.D. 1715, T. 23. R. 2 West); "Budka" at McCreary; "Zalisia", "Kulish", "Bohdan" and "Doroshenko" in the Ethelbert district; "Zelota" in Franklin; "Tarnow" in Bifrost; "Dehova", Rus "Sniatyn" in Bifrost; "Karpaty" (S.D. 1751), and others.

In 1910, Paul Gigeychuk commenced his work as school organizer. Just like Theo. Stefanyk he proved himself a good organizer. Towards, the end of an era of the existence of bilingual schools, the number of Ukrainian-English school districts came close to 125. Some of the districts merged with others, due to the shifting population.

Excellent work had been done by the Ruthenian Training School which, in 1907, had been transferred from Winnipeg to Brandon where it continued to function until 1916. J. T. Cressy was principal of this school for many years. John Norquay and Major MacLaren were in charge of physical training. The Ukrainian language instructors were: James Makohin, D. Pyrch, W. Kudryk, Petro Karmansky, T. D. Ferley and I. Basarab. At the beginning Chas. Kamienski taught English in the school until the arrival of J. T. Cressy. The name of Principal J. T. Cressy is indelibly imprinted in the memory of some 200 students who went through a course of studies in this English-Ukrainian teachers' school. The teaching in the school was conducted five days and half-day on Saturdays. In addition to this, there was a course in physical education held twice weekly at the Y.M.C.A. in the evenings. "Our school", reported Principal Cressy in 1914, "is for three years, but I am afraid we are trying to crowd into these three years work which should really take four years" [12].

All students resided in the dormitory of the school under supervision of the principal. Upon graduation, the student was given a "Third Class Normal School Diploma". These diplomas were printed on the same forms as those given the graduates of Normal School, save for the inscription over the banner head: "Ruthenian Training School".

Apart from the regular course of studies, the students were gaining a general education in things of intrinsic value, the fundamental principles of life, which had become their life's philosophy. Concerning these ideals, the longtime principal and father of the school, J. T. Cressy, expressed himself thus: "We encourage the student to be a searcher after the truth, to appreciate the beautiful and to do good, so that by standing for high ideals they will enable their people to be true nation builders..." [13]. In the course of his work, J. T. Cressy came to know his students, their values and attitudes, and stressed this, as we see, when he wrote: "I have come to the conclusion that in the years to come the Ruthenian people will do their share in making Canada a great nation" [14]. With each passing year J. T. Cressy became more convinced of the tremendous importance of this teachers' seminary and of the constructive potential of teachers in social life. This is evident from his annual reports, published in the "Department Report"

---

[12] Sessional Papers (No. 2), 1914, 4 Geo. v., p. 278.
[13] Departmental Report for 1919, p. 115.
[14] Ibid.

and in the "Sessional Papers" of Manitoba. In 1914 he adds to the characteristics of the Ukrainians a few fundamental reflections: "As these foreign immigrants are coming into the West in great numbers, the education of these foreign people is going to be a serious proposition in the future. It is a good sign that the Ruthenians are eager to have their children learn English, swift to Canadianize themselves, a people most fervently and touchingly grateful to Canada for boons of freedom and land. There are no more intelligent and laborious immigrants in the Dominion" [15].

The bilingual teachers were teaching the youthful settlers not only the official language of Canada but they also infused into the minds of pupils the Anglo-Saxon principles of democratic forms of government while endeavouring at the same time to contribute the values of their own people: the concepts of freedom and social justice, the subordination of individual interests to the higher ideals of a sociey, an awareness of the need for improvement in the lot of the "little man", the struggle for the progress and happiness of people as a whole. The teachers were doing all this with a sense of responsibility for the destiny of their own people in a new country. Concerning this dedication of bilingual teachers, one of the school organizers wrote: "Each of us realizes that the greater the number of champions of the common people, especially those who are pioneers in the field of popular education and progress, the sooner will our efforts triumph over ignorance. Of course, we have cast a great idea into the maelstrom of work not for the sake of glory, not for personal or political gain, but simply because of the sense of duty which the people's honor imposes upon us" [16]. And these were the sentiments that constantly inspired the teachers in their cultural and educational work from the very beginning.

As if to sum up a program of this work, was the annual commemoration of the birth of the Ukrainian national poet Taras Shevchenko (the first of which was held in Winnipeg, 1906) with the students themselves performing the program artistically. Curiously enough, the proceeds from admission donations to this first program went in aid of the "Action Front" of their compatriots in the Old Country. In the following year 1907, the "students of the English-Ruthenian Teachers Training School in Winnipeg" again invited the general public to pay tribute to poet Shevchenko; however this time the admission donations went in aid of "Ruthenian students" in Lviv who were waging a struggle for the rights of their people and for admission to higher learning in universities. This tradition of the Shevchenko anniversary celebrations has continued year after year and it is impossible to estimate accurately the contribution of these teachers to that event in 1961, when, upon the grounds of the Manitoba Legislature, a monument was erected in memory of the one to whom these teachers paid tribute over the years. These annual commemorations represented a clear program in relation to Canada and the homeland of their parents and grandparents.

On the whole, the students of Brandon Teachers' College advanced in the vanguard of Ukrainian cultural and political thought. In 1908, they addressed an appeal to the Ukrainian community urging them to discontinue the use of all sorts of subordinate names for their nationality and to stick to one alone: "Ukrainian". In later years, with a view to becoming more acquainted with the culture of their people, they proposed bringing over

---

[15] Sessional Papers (No. 2), 1914, p. 279.
[16] "Svoboda", No. 22, 1907.

from Lviv qualified lecturers for a course of advanced lectures in Ukrainian history and literature [17]). As for the dramatic arts activity, which has been not only a culural but also a recreational page in the life of the settlers and in which the teachers participated from the student days, they strove to expand this field to the extent of it becoming a live means of popular teaching art. They used various means to reach the people in order to bring a ray of hope, self-respect and stature into the hearts of those who during their lives went through severe tests. Apart from their work in school, the teachers devoted their energies to the people in the reading rooms. It was said in those times that the school building served children during the daytime and the reading room, usually located on the same premises, was a school for the adults in the evening. In addition to a general course in self-education for the older folks, the teachers arranged in some reading rooms study classes in the English language, provided information about the basic laws of Canada, and so on. But to be able to educate others it was necessary to improve one's own education. This discipline was exercised by way of self-criticism in their own vocational organization. The teachers held their convention each year. During the pioneer era the organization of Ukrainian teachers was headed by Ivan Kotsan, Kornylo Prodan, Theodore J. Marciniw, Ivan Rudachek and M. Stechishin; while O. H. Hykawy and Wm. Mihaychuk were secretaries of long standing.

The Ukrainian Teachers' Organization of Canada, located in Winnipeg, emerged as an institution towards which the eyes of not only the teachers and citizens of Manitoba turned for orientation but of Canada as well. The bilingual school system served as a model for both Saskatchewan and Alberta.

Saskatchewan was first to follow in the footsteps of Manitoba. Early in 1909, official notices appeared in the press to the effect that beginning September of that same year, a teachers' training school would open in Regina for the purpose of training young lads as "Ruthenian-English" teachers in the province of Saskatchewan. In these notices the following information was offered: The candidate must be at least 16 years old and not over 20. He must have at least elementary school education completed and a sufficient knowledge of English. Besides the subjects of a specific course of study, the student was to receive instruction in vocational discipline: class leadership, discipline, rights of school trustees and pupils, school hygiene, and public health. Included in this course was practical teaching in which the student had to have at least four demonstration lessons in a year. The one failing to pass the examination in this subject had to repeat it the following year. The cost of maintenance amounted to $200 per year and the student was required to reimburse the government within three years of his graduation. To this effect each student signed a contract with the Department of Education. The number of candidates for the school was limited to 25 applicants [18]). Only the "Ruthenian boys from Saskatchewan" had the right to apply for admission to this teachers' school, we read in the announcements. The applications were received by I. N. Zaitsev.

At that time Osyp Megas was school organizer in Saskatchewan. Sub-

---

[17]) P. Karmansky and A. Kryzhanovsky arrived from Lviv in 1913. They conducted a course of lectures on Ukrainian history and literature during the summer holidays.
[18]) "The Canadian Farmer", No. 26, July 9, 1909.

124 UKRAINIAN CANADIANS: A HISTORY

C.L. Sifton, minister of Canadian immigration,
who was appreciative of the quality of the Ukrainian settler.

Sifton, Ukrainian settlement in Manitoba, 1905

The first church and belfry in Ukrainian settlement
Dnister (north of Gimli), Manitoba

PIONEER ERA — ILLUSTRATIONS

THE FIRST UKRAINIAN BASILIAN PIONEERS IN CANADA

Rev. Damaskyn Polivka

Rev. Platonid Filas

Rev. Matey Hura

Rev. Navkraty Kryzhanovsky

126 UKRAINIAN CANADIANS: A HISTORY

THE FIRST HIERARCHES OF THE UKRAINIAN CHURCH LIFE IN CANADA

Archbishop A. Langevin

Metropolitan A. Shepticky

The first consistory of the Independent Greek Church with Bishop Serafim, Winnipeg, 1903

PIONEER ERA — ILLUSTRATIONS 127
THE FIRST HIERARCHES OF THE UKRAINIAN CHURCH LIIFE IN CANADA

Bishop Nykyta Budka

Metropolitan Germanos Shegedy

PIONEER PRIESTS

Rev. A. Dalaere, Redemptorist
Founder of the order in Canada
(Ukrainian Branch)

Rev. E. Krasicky
Ardent supporter of the creation of a
Ukrainian Ecclesiastical province in
Canada.

The first Ukrainian Catholic Church in Winnipeg, prototype of the present St. Vladimir's and Olga Cathedral

The first Ukrainian Orthodox Church in Manitoba, St. Michael's in Gardenton

PIONEER ERA — ILLUSTRATIONS 129

Memorials of pioneer church architecture on the prairies

Above: Blessing of the church at Stuartburn, 1900
Below: Ukrainian Church of the Assumption, Jaroslaw, near Yorkton. This is the oldest Ukrainian Catholic Church preserved in Saskatchewan until now. Built in 1902-03, picture taken in 1906

St. Josaphat Church, Edmonton, 1904

Ukrainian Greek Orthodox Church, Arbakka, Man.

PIONEER ERA — ILLUSTRATIONS 131

Ukrainian Catholic Church of Sts. Peter and Paul, Mundare, Alta. Convention of Ukrainian Presbyterian preachers in Toronto (1913), at which unification of Greek Independent Church with the English Presbyterian Church of Canada was consummated

Above: The first Sobor of Ukrainian missionaries of Canada held at the monastery of St. Saviour at Yorkton, Sask., under the leadership of Bishop N. Budka, Nov. 27-29, 1914
Below: The first Ukrainian alumni of the Seminary of St. Augustus with Bishop N. Budka, Toronto, 1914

PIONEER ERA — ILLUSTRATIONS

Rev. I. Malarevsky, the first Ukrainian Orthodox priest in Canada, 1897-1898

Rev. M. Strutynsky, representative of Bishop Soter Ortynsky in USA, who visited Canada in 1907

Rev. M. Olenchuk, the first administrator of the Ukrainian social service in Canada, also known as "Ukrainian War Relief"

Rev. A. Redkevych, D.D., Vicar General of Bishop N. Budka

"Soborchyk"—meeting of Ukrainian Catholic priests in Winnipeg, 1919

134 UKRAINIAN CANADIANS: A HISTORY

The first Ukrainian Catholic church choir of St. Nicholas, Winnipeg, 1910

The first Ukrainian church choir, Calgary, Alta., 1915

PIONEER ERA — ILLUSTRATIONS 135

Above: The first Ukrainian choir under the direction of C. Prochoda, Toronto, 1912
Below: The first Ukrainian choir under the direction of Julian Pieluch,
Montreal, 1916

Members of the congregation of St. John the Baptist with Rev. J. Fylyma, Ottawa, 1914

Sisterhood of the Holy Family with Rev. J. Fylyma, Ottawa, 1914

Members of Young Brotherhood of St. Nicholas Congregation, Winnipeg, 1915

The laying of the cornerstone for the first Ukrainian Catholic Church in Eastern Canada, St. Josaphat's in Toronto

Consecration of the first Ukrainian Church in Fort William by Bishop Budka

UKRAINIAN CANADIANS: A HISTORY

THE ORIGINAL PLANNERS FOR THE ESTABLISHMENT OF THE UKRAINIAN GREEK ORTHODOX CHURCH IN CANADA

Wasyl Swystun

Michael Stechishin

Onufrey H. Hykawy

Wasyl Mihaychuk

PIONEER ERA — ILLUSTRATIONS

THE FIRST UKRAINIAN ORTHODOX PRIESTS:

Rev. S. W. Sawchuk

Rev. D. F. Stratychuk

Rev. P. Sametz

UKRAINIAN CANADIANS: A HISTORY

POST OFFICES WITH UKRAINIAN NAMES

sequent organizers were N. Romaniuk, John Kun and Julian Andrukhovych. Despite the initial notices that only applicants of Ukrainian origin would be accepted into the teachers school, in reality this was not so. The records of this school show that students of other ethnic backgrounds attended. True, this was a very small proportion as, for example, in 1912, only 5 out of a total of 42 students were non-Ukrainian (3 Germans and 2 Poles). Curiously, the official name given this school was "The English School for Foreigners". In the beginning, the school was housed in the old premises of the RCMP in Regina and the students resided and attended class lectures in these barracks. Not much attention was paid to the question of teaching the Ukrainian language in the school. This policy of the administration and the strange name of the school satisfied neither the general public nor the students. After prolonged solicitations on the part of Ukrainian students, the teaching of the Ukrainian language was included in the curriculum, but not until sometime in 1913. The first Ukrainian instructor was H. Platsko and he was succeeded by N. Romaniuk. Principal Greer was responsible for the education of students. Later he was replaced by Principal Jackson. The frequent misunderstandings between these principals and the students indicate now that these men were not up to the mark in their responsibility. The students did not experience either scholastic or constructive atmosphere in this school. The spirit of alienation and hostility emanated from this system of administration. Notwithstanding this, the Ukrainian Canadian press referred to this school as the "Ukrainian-English Teachers' Seminary in Regina". The cultural-educational activity in the school remained at a very low level because of severe government restrictions. Not until 1912 was the first Shevchenko anniversary concert held there.

In the following year, 1913, the first Ukrainian conference of Saskatchewan teachers was held [19]. The conference raised broadly the question of Ukrainian textbooks and the necessity of Ukrainian language instruction in the teachers' school. Perhaps in consequence of these demands, the above-mentioned teachers of Ukrainian were nominated to this post in the school. The leading role at this convention was played by Osyp Megas, a former school organizer and the editor of the newspaper "Novy Kray" (The New Country). The efforts of students and public in general brought good results, because the school was eventually moved into the Normal School building where the classes were conducted. The students resided in private homes. Among the better teachers available in the Normal School was A. Anderson, subsequently the Premier of Saskatchewan.

At the time when the Ukrainian teachers in Saskatchewan were getting ready to launch an intensified program of activity, the situation in Manitoba was confounded by attacks on the bilingual school system. True, the Liberals were in power in Saskatchewan, but in relation to the bilingual school system, they were accepting to a certain degree the "Conservative policy" of Manitoba as their own. The Department of Education of the Saskatchewan Government assisted in improving the qualifications of the teachers following their graduation from Normal School, by arranging courses with the object of raising the standard of teachers' education. Noticeable bene-

---

[19] The more prominent teachers: A. Shtyk, H. Platsko, Illa Pernarowsky, Jos. Bohonis, T. Volsky, Jos. Boychuk, A. T. Kibzey.

fits resulted from this policy. The system of training bilingual teachers in Saskatchewan was becoming similar to that in Manitoba.

The contemporary Liberal government of Alberta followed the matter from an entirely different concept of reasoning. It firmly refused to accept the idea of a public school system as established in Manitoba and Saskatchewan. Only as a result of the public pressure and constant petitions by the Ukrainians did the Department of Education issue the authority to establish the so-called "Foreignorka". This was a contemptuous nickname for the "English School for Foreigners in Vegreville" which was opened February 3, 1913, in that town. The task of this school was not to train teachers but students, who, upon the completion of Grade 9, desired to continue their education in the Normal School. The school also provided short courses in English for students who intended to go into the commercial field. Only students of Ukrainian origin were accepted. There were different students here, some had average education but there were also those who started at the elementary level. This disparity in the education of the students was not conducive to any outstanding success by the school. The very reference to "Foreigners" in the name repelled the students. They simply did not want to be "foreigners", said the Ukrainian Canadian journal "Novyny" (The News) of Edmonton. They wanted to be Canadians and feel on equal footing with the students of Anglo-Saxon origin. Principal of the school was W. A. Stickle and was succeeded by E. S. Farr, just prior to the closing of the school. The former was very stern and lacked understanding of the needs of his pupils who found themselves in a new environment and with a natural desire for learning. As a result of constant disciplinary measures applied to students and finally of an investigation launched by the Department of Education in Edmonton, W. A. Stickle took his departure. Shortly thereafter the school was liquidated, having existed three full years. Notwithstanding the oppressive atmosphere prevailing in this school, it had the enrolment of close to 120 students [20]. Peter Svarich was the real patron of this school. Afer the prescribed class hours he gave the pupils instruction in the Ukrainian language, encouraged and comforted the lads as well as helped them financially. Thanks to a positive attitude on the part of young scholars, the school also had a degree of success to its credit, about which E. S. Farr, Stickle's successor, expressed himself thus:

"The English School for Foreigners has made possible the more ready adaptation of the young foreigner in Alberta to our Canadian citizenship; it has a great moral effect, directly and indirectly, on foreign communities, and thereby has proved its usefulness" [21].

For a long time the Ukrainian public carried on a struggle with the Department of Education of Alberta for bilingual schools and teachers in those settlements where the children of Ukrainian parentage constituted a majority. In support of this action a "Provisional Committee in Aid of Native Schools in Alberta" was set up, which was headed by Roman Kremar, editor of "Novyny." Members of the committee were: W. A. Chumer,

---

[20] From this school came out such cultural workers as Illa Kiriak, O. Hryhorovych, I. Ruryk, I. Shklanka, Jos. Tovpushchak, I. Dalavrak, and many others.
[21] E. S. Farr, "English School for Foreigners", Tenth Annual Report of the Department of Education of the Province of Alberta, 1915, p. 145, J. W., Government Printer, 1916.

Nicholas Andreyiv, Ihnat Kukura, M. Ferbey, Jos. Yasenchuk, V. Kostyk, F. Ferbey, S. Gura, N. Kebych, St. Fodchuk, Yu. Lazaruk, H. Bodnarchuk and D. Yaremko. Roman Kremar, the capable and temperamental editor, wrote in one of his exhortations addressed "To all Ruthenians in Canada":

"They are trying to defeat us on one point... They deny us the constitutional right to teach our children the native language in public schools. The Ukrainian teachers, who alone were capable of giving children at least rudimentary knowledge of Ukrainian literacy, were thrown out of the schools last summer by the Department of Education who then, against the will of taxpayers, imposed upon us Anglo-Saxon teachers who not only do not know the Ukrainian language but are poorly versed in English as well. Tens of thousands of Ukrainian children in Alberta are growing up in illiteracy, thanks to the culture-propaganda efforts on the part of Education Minister Boyle... In order to preserve their racial origin and prevent the youth from going to waste, some farmers are now thinking of building and supporting private schools. The farmers of school district of "Bukovina" have already carried this idea into effect and for several months have been maintaining their own private school with a qualfied Ukrainian teacher".

Such an appeal testifies to the fact that relations in the public school system of Alberta were quite unhealthy. The Ukrainian population had no confidence in Education Minister Boyle. Instead, they evinced confidence in the bilingual teachers who usually came from Manitoba and Saskatchewan and who were graduates of the teachers' training schools in those provinces. In order to deprive these teachers of the right to teach in schools of Alberta, the government enacted an amendment to the "School Ordinance" which was adopted at a session of the Legislature in October 1913. It reads:

"Any person not so qualified, (namely, having a valid certificate of qualification issued under the regulations of the Department) shall not be entitled to recover in any court of law, any remuneration for his services as such teacher.

"Any person other than the holder of such certificates of qualification who undertakes to conduct a school as teacher shall be guilty of an offense and, on summary conviction, liable to penalty not exceeding fifty dollars, and in default to imprisonment for a term not exceeding one month.

"Provided, however, that no prosecution shall be instituted under this section except on the orders of the Minister".

Such government decisions must have had far-reaching consequences. The unreasonable policy promoted by Minister Boyle had very ill effects upon the processes of consolidation of a Canadian community. Qualified bilingual teachers from Manitoba and Saskatchewan were being dismissed from their teaching posts on the pretext that they lacked qualifications. Thus dismissed was William Chumer who had full qualificaions from Manitoba. He was, like many others, one of the better teachers and Canadian citizens of the pioneer era. A glaring anomaly in Alberta was the lack of Ukrainian school organizers who could understand the needs of the settlers and be able to explain to them in their own language school and national affairs. School organizer R. Fletcher, whose designation was "Supervisor of Foreign Schools", travelled about the colonies and in his work of organizing school districts made use of interpreters who quite often did not know what they were translating. Such alienation of people from the government could produce neither good results nor create an atmosphere of trust and wholesome growth. Not infrequently there were incidents of school districts taking court action against the Department of Education and its organizers [22]). Notwithstanding the great pressure put to bear upon the bilingual teachers by the government of Alberta, the teachers were aware of their task and strove to present the needs of their compatriots to the provincial government. In 1915 the bilingual teachers organized themselves and held their first convention in Edmonton. But in the climate of heavy government pressure it was quite difficult for the young idealists to develop their work.

The approach to the public school question taken by Education Minister Boyle had serious consequences not only for matters of public education but also for himself and his government. In his book of reminiscences, William A. Chumer writes about this:

"The Ruthenians, who once fervently supported the Liberal Party candidates in time of election, have since lost confidence in it as a freedom-loving party which before the election boasted about liberalism and friendship for the Ruthenians in Canada" [23]).

If the opinion expressed by W. A. Chumer seems severe, it nevertheless reflects perfectly the views of the Ukrainian settlers in Alberta of that time. This policy of E. R. Boyle also failed to impress many a Liberal politician because of its bigotry and short-sightedness.

The lack of textbooks is a source of frustration in any field of study and this deficiency prevailed in the bilingual schools of Manitoba, Saskatchewan and Alberta. A variety of textbooks was being put to use in these schools. There were cases where the teachers had to use textbooks which had been brought here from the Old Country and were by reason of their scheme and thematical content, wholly unsuitable to the requirements of this environment. The teachers were acutely aware of this and that is why the question of bilingual textbooks was a pressing topic of debates, even at the first teachers' conference in Manitoba. Although their petition to the government of Manitoba had been accepted, the work of preparing such a textbook for publication proceeded in a leisurely manner. In 1913 the Manitoba government finally published the first Ruthenian-English Reader, entitled "The Manitoba Ruthenian-English Readers". It comprised 56 bilingual and 17 exclusively English lessons in a book of 144 pages. Part II of these Readers was made up of 223 pages, 185 of which were bilingual. This volume carried a closing section, entitled "Additional English Lessons". As we see, both these Readers in their contents accented the importance of the official language of the country while their bilingualism lay in the fact that on one page the lessons appeared in English and on the other the Ukrainian translation. Both readers were published in London[24]), approved by the School Board of Manitoba and authorized for use in public schools of the province. There was still another textbook, the so-called Primer, which had been prepared earlier by Paul Gigeychuk, a school organizer, but this was completely withdrawn from use in schools. Two years prior to the appearance of these textbooks in Manioba, Peter Svarich of Vegreville prepared and published in Winnipeg at his own expense a school text-

---

[22]) School districts "Kolomyja", "Stanislaw", "Bukovina", and others.
[23]) W. A. Chumer, Reminiscences, Edmonton, p. 125.
[24]) Thomas Nelson and Sons, London, Edinburgh, Dublin and New York. Format $3\frac{1}{2}$ by $7\frac{1}{2}$.

book, entitled "An Aid to Little Scholars for Use in Elemantary Schools of Alberta and Saskatchewan". This was a literal translation of the English "Primer". There was still another textbook of the Department of Education of Manitoba, only a small quantity of which (169 copies) ever got into the hands of pupils and, for the great shame of it, at the liquidation of the bilingual school system, the remaining stock of this textbook was consigned to flames on the grounds of the Manitoba parliament buildings. This was done on orders of Premier T. C. Norris.

There were great demands for such textbooks because not only school children but also adults wanted to study from them. The bilingual school system was salt in the eyes of the establishment who wanted to see Canada as a homogeneous country, based upon the language and culture of the Anglo-Saxon. That is why voices were constantly raised in the English-language press as well as in the Manitoba Legislature to discontinue the bilingual school system. For this purpose they pursued expedient arguments in order to show that the bilingual school system did not provide sufficient knowledge of English and that the bilingual teachers fell short, so to speak, of the required high standard of teaching. All sorts of missionaries and missionary teachers were in the van of this campaign. Gradually the critics of bilingual schools shifted from the pages of the daily press to the floor of the Manitoba Legislature. This campaign assumed greater intensity, particularly at the time when the Liberal Party of Manitoba, under the leadership of Premier Norris, included in its election platform as one of its objectives the complete liquidation of the bilingual school system. In the election platform, outlined in the 136-page Liberal handbook, the Party attacked the bilingual schools on the alleged charge that the English language was poorly understood and indifferently spoken in these schools. It said:

"In the French, Polish and Ruthenian settlements of Manitoba the English language is but poorly understood and indefferently spoken by the children and by a considerable number of the adult population. The Liberals contend that this condition represents not only a wrong inflicted upon these children individually, but a prejudice to the entire province and to the entire Dominion. For this condition of things means that the French children and the Polish and Ruthenian children are being unprepared not only to make their own way of life, but unprepared also for the responsibilities of Canadian citizenship and the burdens of Canadian nationality" [25].

Undoubtedly, the schools were not without shortcomings, but these problems ensued not entirely from the bilingual system, but were in consequence generally of any number of hardships which confronted the pioneers. It was often pointed out in reports of school inspectors that class attendance in bilingual schools was more highly satisfactory during the winter months, whereas in summer a good number of the children did not attend. This was due to the fact that farm work required many helping hands, with mothers and older children helping in the field while the younger ones were left at home to look after smaller children and infants. This state of affairs could have been prevented only by compulsory school attendance, but at that time no legislation existed compelling parents to send their children to school. As a matter of fact, the Ukrainian teachers, at their first conven-

---

[25] Liberal Handbook, Winnipeg, 1914, p. 16.

tion, fought for the enactment of such legislation. Still, it is questionable whether such an Act would have solved the problem of school attendance. To be sure, the vital interests of pioneering, from sheer necessity, had to take precedence over the matter of education. The altering of priorities in favor of education only took place when the demands of the farms were met and mastered. It seems only reasonable that children who spoke their native language at home and at play, could hardly be expected to promptly acquire an Oxford accent from a bilingual teacher. The settlers required long years of linguistic processes to make the new language an integral part of their daily life. In his report for 1909, School inspector Young had this to say:

"In driving through these districts (Eastern Division—M.H.M.) and coming in contact with the people, it is made very clear that a knowledge of the English language is becoming more general from year to year. The fact that an English teacher was this year engaged to teach in the Bukovina school makes it evident that these people are anxious to acquire a knowledge of the English language" [26]).

Also Robert Fletcher, Deputy Minister of Education of Manitoba, stated clearly in his report for 1912-1913:

"The criticism is also directed upon certain schools in non-English speaking communities, the suggestion being that the English language is slighted or neglected in some districts, particularly where foreigners have settled in blocks. Every effort is being made to maintain the status of the English language in all schools. The Department has no doubt that this purpose is being achieved. There are, as everybody knows, certain difficulties in the way, but these dfficulties are being steadily overcome, and the progress made in this important feature of public instruction is encouraging and satisfactory" [27]).

In the same report R. Fletcher made still another important observation regarding bilingual teachers:

"They are not only able to give efficient instruction in two languages, but to inculcate the true spirit of Canadian patriotism" [28]).

Because intellectual arguments often do not carry weight in political propaganda, these arguments had little effect upon the efforts to save the bilingual school system in Manitoba. Party propaganda of T. C. Norris relentlessly pursued its aim to abolish the bilingual school system. Intellectual arguments were scattered to the winds while emotions gained force. When in 1914-15 certain government abuses in the construction of the Manitoba parliament buildings started to leak out, the Official Opposition to the government of R. Roblin launched a full attack on the bilingual school system. The Winnipeg Free Press, which supported the Liberals and their point of view, came out in 1915 with over 60 editorials and articles against the bilingual school system. The Winnipeg Evening Tribune to a degree supported The Free Press. The Winnipeg Telegram alone defended the bilingual schools. From the numerous articles published in the two organs opposing the bilingual schools we get the impression that the Liberals were counting on Anglo-Saxon patriotism and from a purely emoional level were setting the Anglo-Saxon majority in the province against the French Ca-

---

[26]) Report of the Department of Education for 1909, p. 18.
[27]) Report of the Department of Education for 1912-1913, p. 18.
[28]) Ibid., p. 19.

nadians, German Mennonites, Ukrainians and Poles, and against all those ethnic groups that made use of these schools. These press articles were appearing under such significant and high-flown headings as: "Bilingualism Unfair To Children", "Ruthenian Ideas Retard Teaching of English", "Bilingualism—Unnecessary", "Bilingualism Weapon for Reactionaries", and so on.

As soon as the Liberals came to power with T. C. Norris as premier, the Ukrainians sent a delegation on January 7th, 1916 for the purpose of discussing the matter of bilingual schools. The delegation, which included I. Petrushevych, J. W. Arsenych, A. Malliniuk and Jos. Boyanivsky, was given a cool reception and the government avoided giving a clear-cut answer. Following this representation, the Ukrainians organized the "Ukrainian Central Committee for Defence of Bilingual School System".

This committee was headed by well-known citizens of Winnipeg: J. W. Arsenych, O. Boyanivsky, A. Malliniuk, T. J. Marciniw, I. Negrych, I. Petrushevych, I. Sluzar, S. O. Kharambura. Later this committee carried on its work as an enlarged body which, apart from the above-mentioned, included Rev. M. Olenchuk, W. Kudryk, D. Yakimischak, Dr. I. Pazdriy, V. Kazanivsky, N. Hrechka and M. Pasichnyk. The committee was constituted in such a way that at least one representative came from each constituency of Greater Winnipeg. Thus on March 30, 1916, the Committee called a mass meeting in which more than 1,000 citizens of Winnipeg and the province took part. The resolutions adopted at this meeting defended the bilingual school system and branded the "chauvenistic daily press", "racial bigotry", and so on. The Committee also launched a drive for signatures to a parents' petition in which they demanded retention of the bilingual school system. Over 6,000 signatures were received by the editorial offices of two newspapers, "The Ukrainian Voice" and "The Ruthenian Canadian",

On February 3rd, 1916, the Ukrainian delegation again asked to make presentation to the government of Manitoba, but to no avail. Two days later the Minister of Education, R. C. Thornton, submitted a bill to the Legislature proposing the abolition of the bilingual school system in the province; this bill provoked long and dramatic parliamentary debates. The bilingual school system was defended by the French-speaking members as well as by a Conservative member for Roblin constituency and, of course, by T. D. Ferley, the only member of Ukrainian origin in the Legislature. Following the second reading of this bill, the Ukrainian delegation, headed by I. Petrushevych, again called upon the governmnt. This was on March 7th, 1916. After the spokesman of the delegation presented his case, the government gave the floor to Victor Hladyk, editor of "The Russian People" and a notorius Russophile and Ukrainophobe. In a prepared speech, this "little fellow-countryman" insultingly denounced the Ukrainians as "German agents engaged in bringing discord and disunity into the life of Canadian community" and went on to contend that in reality there were no Ukrainians, only "Russians", who had no desire for bilingual schools for themselves. Thus Victor Hladyk had precisely carried out what his close collaborators M. Chernyak and M. Ostrovsky had accomplished in Alberta for Education Minister Boyle. These were Russophile activists who served the interests of the Russian Empire and organically hated the Ukrainians. Although the delegates promptly refuted Hladyk's "arguments", they were unable to stop the government steamroller, now set in high gear for the task of demolishing the bilingual public school structure.

Thus on March 8th, 1916, the Manitoba parliament finally passed the proposed legislation and that same year the Ukrainian public schools in Manitoba closed their doors. Shortly after this the teaching of Ukrainian, after regular class hours, was excluded from the school program in the two other prairie provinces. The "Ruthenian Training School" in Brandon, the "English School for Foreigners" in Regina and the "English School for Foreigners" in Vegreville were also abolished. Closed in the same manner eventually were the schools of other ethnic groups—the French, German and Polish, but in their case the system survived for a much longer time. In January 1916, Charles K. Newcombe, Superintendent for schools in Manitoba, reported on the state of bilingual schools at the time of their abolition as follows:

"There are altogether 120 French bilingual schools in operation, employing 234 teachers, with an enrolment of 7,393 pupils and an average attendance of 3,456; 27%. Sixty one districts operate German bilingual schools. These employ 73 teachers, with an enrolment of 2,814 and an evarage attendance of 1,840; 61%. One hundred and eleven districts operate Ruthenian, or Polish, bilingual schools, employing 114 teachers, with an enrolment of 6,513 pupils and an average attendance of 3,884; 96%. Thus there are altogether 16,720 pupils in the three groups of bilingual schools" [29].

If we accept the fact that at the termination of the bilingual school system there were, according to the statistics, 1,450 public schools in Manitoba, then more than one-fifth of them must have been bilingual, while out of a total of 2,950 teachers in the province almost one in seven was bilingual or multi-lingual. It would also be relevant to take a note of the fact that the figures used by Chas. K. Newcombe with regard to Ukrainian and Polish schools do not coincide with the same statistical figures from the previous years. As for example, in 1914 there were 132 bilingual districts with bilingual schools in Manitoba, but in 1916 only 111 of these schools were reported. What became of those 21 schools, it is difficult to discover, and it is just as difficult to imagine that within one year all of them could have been liquidated, particularly at a time when this determined contest was drawing to its conclusion. Besides, even these inaccuracies provide the reader with a clear picture of the fate of the bilingual school system.

The entire ethnic press received the news of the abolition of the bilingual school system with an expression of national grief and undisguised and vehement protest. Mass meetings, conferences and discussions had been held in the course of which the political moves of the Norris government were condemned, labelling its action a flagrant violation of rights and its ignorance of the cultural requirements of a minority. The Irish too came out in defence of bilingual schools. At a public meeting in Winnipeg they passed a resolution in which the action of the party in power was condemned. For its own part the government endeavoured to mollify the hostile reaction of the minorities. It increased school grants to certain districts, dispatched its spokesmen into the areas and tried to explain the problem in its own way as if the abolition of bilingual school system was at the same

---

[29] Special Report on Bilingual Schools in Manitoba, Department of Education, 1916, p. 1.

time an effort to raise the standard of teaching in these schools to a higher level, and so on. Also bilingual teachers were being accused of lacking ability to teach and of having insufficient education. This was wholly inconsistent with what was being asserted on the part of the government up to that time. Some of the districts were even criticized for building "ostentatious" schools in their areas while lacking the necessary financial resources for this. In other words, there was a lot of "bad" in what otherwise had been "good". So it is quite evident that the struggle for bilingualism was passing into the sphere of politics, not education. As a sign of protest, some of the bilingual teachers resigned. This created a still greater difficulty in conducting proper teaching in schools. In order to remedy this shortcoming the government assigned to these schools teachers who had no qualifications [30]. It must be kept in mind that the Norris government had enacted compulsory attendance of children up to age 14. There was a serious shortage of teachers and, willing or unwilling, it was necessary for the government to retract all the insults that were being flung in the direction of bilingual teachers. As an example, in a report of the Deputy Minister of Education we read about the progress in the teaching of English language that was being made by the teachers of French and Ukrainian origin:

"The pupils are growing up with our language spoken and written. This applies particularly to the Ruthenians and Poles. The teachers of French and Ruthenian origin teach English in most learned manner" [31].

Notwithstanding that Ukrainian was no longer officially taught in schools, the teaching of this language continued. It was conducted after 4 o'clock, following the regular class hours. In many a case the Ukrainian instruction was given in a surreptitious manner because certain school inspectors looked askance upon this [32]. The bilingual teachers also conducted evening courses for children. But all this was being done for the most part in a most unsystematic manner and for this reason the effort failed to produce the desirable and anticipated results.

In order to fully exhaust the subject of Ukrainian and provincial bilingualism, it is necessary to mention in quite general terms, in passing, the Ukrainian bilingualism of Quebec, most correctly of Montreal, where a Ukrainian colony of several thousand people existed during the same period of time. The school system in Quebec province was divided into two distinct branches—Catholic and Protesant. In 1912 Ukrainian workers in Montreal used their best endeavours before the Catholic School Commission so that their children might receive Ukrainian language instruction in the city schools. These efforts were realized when Rev. T. Dwulit assumed leadership of the Ukrainian parish congregation in Montreal. Upon his renewed solicitations, supported by massive petitions, the school authorities agreed to a formation of four separate classes for the Ukrainian children who henceforth received instruction in the two languages. The language of insruction in the morning was Ukrainian, and in the afternoon the teaching was conducted in French. Thus all school subjects were taught in these two languages. The teachers of this bilingual school system were on the provincial payroll. The first Ukrainian teachers in this system were: P.

---

[30] Departmental Report for 1916, p. 359.
[31] Departmental Report for 1917, p. 25.
[32] Information collected on the basis of interviews with bilingual teachers: T. Marciniw, Y. Koltek and M. Boychuk.

Shymonska, M. Krushelnytska, M. Kryva, M. Pelukh, M. Chypchar and S. Kowbel. These and other teachers of the system were members of the official teachers' union, affiliated with the American Teachers' Federation. There were also children who attended the Protestant public schools; however, they could not receive Ukrainian instruction there. Attending to the needs of this group of children was the "Ridna Shkola" (Native School) in Montreal, functioning within the premises of the M. Drahomaniv Society. M. Chypchar was a teacher of this school of long standing. The great patron of this bilingual school system in Montreal was . Dr. A. Redkevych who through his interventions and memoranda was able to properly explain the indispensability of such a system. This bilingual system produced a good number of useful and public spirited citizens.

PRIVATE SCHOOL SYSTEM OF EDUCATION

The beginning of the private school system of education is closely related to parishes and churches. Rev. P. Tymkevych took initial steps in that direction in 1898. While visitng Star-Edna district he observed that many local girls lived in not too distant Edmonton where they were employed as domestics. He wanted to organize them into a single social group where they would be able to learn to read and write and at the same time receive moral and spiritual guidance in their new environment. With this in mind, Rev. P. Tymkevych ordered, at his own expense, a quantity of textbooks, Primers in particular, with the object of starting a school. Actually, we can learn very little about these "initial steps" towards private schooling from the incidental press reports which have been preserved to our time. We can only surmise that with the departure of Rev. Tymkevych his work fell into oblivion. Nevertheless, a very small beginning had been made.

Three years later the Sisters of the Faithful Companions of Jesus assumed care of these Ukrainian girls in Edmonton. With the support of Roman Catholic Bishop Legal in 1901, they organized night classes for these girls. The classes were conducted twice weekly and the pupils, numbering close to forty, began learning English. As a lasting memorial to this school, there is a stained glass window installed in the Roman Catholic Church of St. James in Edmonton, with the inscription: "Presented by Galician Night School Girls". Subsequently the supervision of this school was taken over by the Sister Servants of Mary Immaculate, the pupils began learning the Ukrainian language, religion, singing and embroidering as well as English. In Winnipeg, the initial steps in this direction were taken by Fr. D. Polivka. In co-operation with the newly established First Ukrainian Church congregation in 1899, he attempted vigorously to acquire the Old Dufferin Public School (South-East corner of Logan and Salter Streets) for the purpose of accommodating therein, in addition to a church, a school and a reading room. A down-payment was made, but the deal did not go through.

The first daily school in which Ukrainian children received instruction was established at Beaver Lake, three miles from what is now Mundare. It was opened in 1905 in a small pioneer church which was built by the Basilian Fathers in 1904. About 60 pupils received instruction in this parochial school. The school was conducted by the order of Sister Servants who also looked after a number of girls who occupied a small residence close to the chapel and school. Under these conditions the school carried on its work until 1914 when a new and modern structure was erected and opened by the Basilian Fathers near the original school and chapel.

The first "Ridna Shkola" (Native School) in Winnipeg commenced its program of teaching in January 1905. It was established in the St. Nicholas Parish through the endeavours of Rev. Matey Hura, V. Kudryk and M. Hladky. The so-called "Little Church" was converted into a school and reading room. About 50 children attended the classes conducted by V. Kudryk [1]).

---

[1]) Studies in the History of Ukrainians in Canada, Vol. 2, p. 25.

The St. Nicholas School in Winnipeg was the first daily school with a full program of public school instruction. The history of this school has all the characteristic flavor of pioneering. In June 1905 two Sister Servants, Athanasia and Alexandra, arrived in Winnipeg. They were brought over by Rev. M. Hura to teach at the school which, for the preceding six months, had been located in the "Little Church". Primarily this was a night school, but Fr. Hura wanted to lay the foundations for an all-day Ukrainian-English school in the Manitoba capital. Thus, after extended efforts, he succeeded in making a start. The two Sister Servants commenced teaching in this school on the 28th of August of that year. The school was located in the Edinger Hall which had been purchased by Fr. Hura. Originally this was a theatrical hall, situated at the South-East corner of Selkirk and McGregor Streets. In the winter of 1905, with an enrolment of 50 pupils, the school moved into the basement of the St. Nicholas church (the so-called "Big Church") at the South-West corner of McGregor and Stella Streets. The school remained in these premises for six full years. In 1906 the school had 160 pupils, with a still larger enrolment in the succeeding years. In addition to regular public school program, the children were instructed in the Ukrainian language, history, religion and such handicrafts as carving, embroidering, and so on. In the basement, which had been converted into classrooms, small pools of water could sometimes be seen on the floor after a heavy rainfall and where rats dropped in as uninvited "guests". But in their devotion to learning and to the culture of their people, both the pupils and the teachers bravely endured these inconveniences and difficulties. At last the happy day arrived for the school. On the 24th of October, 1911, the school moved into a modern structure which had been erected by Bishop Langevin with the aid of the Catholic Mission Fund in Toronto. The bishop turned the building over to Sister Servants for the use of school and a little later to their full ownership. In return for his generosity, the bishop asked nothing more than the gift of a "Ukrainian cake each year at Christmas".

In Edmonton, the Sister Servants made a start in 1905 by opening a school in their own residence at 98th S. and 108th Avenue. This school was later moved into the church premises which was built with the assistance of Catholic organizations in Toronto, under the patronage of Bishop Legal. The Sister Servants also started an all-day school in Sifton, Manitoba, where they conducted classes in the basement of a church for four years. When in 1912 the school for boys was established there through the endeavors of Rev. Josaphat Jean, these Sister Servants made partial use of this school. It was only in 1931 that a school building and residence for the Sister Servants was erected. The school for boys in Sifton continued meanwhile to function well. The initiative for this school (Mission School in Sifon) was officially suggested by the Roman Catholic Church Council in Quebec at its session in 1909. Actually, the recommendation of the council called for the establishment of this school in Winnipeg, not far from the seat of the Basilian Fathers, and under their administration. This recommendation read:

"Commencer au plus vite, pres de l'eglise des Reverends Peres Basiliens, a Winnipeg, un Petit Seminaire pour les enfants ruthenes de tout l'Ouest sous direction d'un Pere Basiliens" [2].

---

[2] Rapport de la Commission chargée par le Premier Concile plenier du Canada

For various reasons the school was established in Sifton. It was probably mainly because the Sifton district had become the base of Russian political and religious propaganda in Canada promoting the interests of the Russian Empire and glorifying the Czar. In order to counteract this movement, Archbishop Langevin assigned several of his priests to Sifton where, in addition to teaching, they were to attend to pastoral duties as well. Teaching in school were such priests of French origin as Joseph Gagnon, Desire Claveloux and A. Sabourin. These priests adopted the Ukrainian Greek Catholic rite and learned the Ukrainian language at a special course in the town of Galicia. The teachers of Ukrainian origin were: Vasyl Bulyk, P. Pasichnyk, I. Koltsun, N. Pelekh, Jos. Tymochko, George Skvarok, A. Zaharychuk, M. Demchuk and Rev. P. Oleksiw. The purpose of this school was to train religious missionaries and to help educate the children of the settlers. The Mission School existed four full years and notwithstanding the fact that it produced a few excellent individuals it failed to survive simply because of the inherent attitude of distrust on the part of fhe Ukrainian public towards the Roman Catholic clergy, even when they changed their rite and could talk to the people in their own language.

Yorkton, in Saskatchewan, is the well-known local of two schools—the women's academy and the men's college. In 1915, with the assistance of Bishop N. Budka, the Sisters of the Immaculate Heart of Mary established a convent there and from the very outset proceeded with the task of establishing a private school. For this purpose they received financial aid from the Sulpician Fathers in Montreal amountng to $25,000 and soon thereafter a splendid structure arose in Yorkton which accommodated an orphanage and an 8-Grade school. This school was named the "Sacred Heart Institute" and teaching began in 1917. The school building included a dormitory for girls coming from distant farms. The initial pioneering work in this school was carried out by Sisters Athanasia and Alexandra who by then possessed a wealth of experience acquired at the St. Nicholas School in Winnipeg.

Through the initiative of Bishop N. Budka and with substantial financial aid from the Catholic Extension Society in Toronto which contributed $100,000, St. Joseph's College came into being in Yorkton. In 1919 a modern structure was erected in which the college commenced its work. The monastic Brothers of Christian Schools assumed direction of this college. The first director was Brother Ansbert, F.S.C. A great deal of help was given by the Redemptorist Fathers: A. Delaere, L. Van de Bosch, N. M. Decamp and others.

In the beginning all these private schools were maintained exclusively by fees paid by parents of students and by financial assistance from the Catholic Church. Some of these schools existed for many years while others had to liquidate themselves. All experienced great hardships and survived the pioneer era only through the great devotion and determination shown by the organizers and the teaching personnel. Also the devotion of the students to everything their parents and educators considered meaningful played more than a small role in this struggle.

---

d'étudier la question des Ruthènes et de soumettre quelques conclusions, p. 7. Quebec, Sept. 28, 1909, Archives of J. Jean O.S.B.M. Basilian Fathers, Mundare, Alta.

BURSAS AND INSTITUTES

With the launching of the attack upon the bilingual schools in the three western provinces, quietly at first and later, more openly, the Ukrainians began to give serious thought to the best ways to pass on to their children the knowledge of their native language and culture. Each article in the English-language press that stressed the need for speedy assimilation of the Ukrainians, or for that matter of other immigrant groups in Canada, aroused in them a disappointing anguish which demanded counteraction to resist any such enforced development. Such articles served only to aggravate the feelings of ethnic groups in Canada and provoke this understandable defensive reaction. When the League for Education was organized in Saskatchewan and set before itself the aim of work for the abolition of the bilingual school system, the first to react were the Ukrainian students. When The Saskatoon Daily Star, or The Winnipeg Free Press, were running a flurry of editorials and letters of Readers calling for the abolition of the Ukrainian language in public schools, the Ukrainian press in Canada—"The Ukrainian Voice", "The Canadian Ruthenian" and "The Canadian Farmer" of Winnipeg, "The News" of Edmonton and "The New Country" of Rosthern — in their rebuttals, spoke of "Anglo-Saxon chauvinism", "Disregard of democratic principles of education", "Violence in cultural activities of citizens", and so on. This somewhat strong reaction by the Ukrainians resulted in the examination of public school instruction in Saskatchewan by Dr. Edmond H. Oliver who published an article in The Missionary Messenger [3]) under the heading of "Ukrainians in Saskatoon" in which he not only criticized the Ukrainians on account of their bilingual schools but also for having found their way into the councils of many school districts and because they "dictate the policy in many municipalities", and have "intruded into the Legislature of Manitoba" and now "are knocking at the door of the Legislatures of other provinces".

All this was true, but Dr. Oliver and his likes reasoned, it appears, that the Ukrainians were not deserving of such recognition and that the first obligation of a "good Canadian" was to renounce altogether the language, culture and traditions of his own people. The Ukrainian press and public leaders saw Canada as a pattern of cultural mosaic in the process of political and economic integration. Seeing that the campaign of assimilation was aimed at their young generation, the Ukrainians raised a cry demanding that their children be taught the native language and culture in private night schools and that for the young people, studying in colleges and universities, a system of bursas and institutes be established in which they might receive not only room and board but also an upbringing in keeping with the traditions of their own people.

When the bilingual school system was in the final stages of abolition, a general public meeting was held in Winnipeg, in the procathedral of Sts. Vladmir and Olga, for the purpose of establishing a Ukrainian bursa, to be named after Adam Kotsko. During this phase of the campaign against the bilingual school system the name of Adam Kotsko had a special appeal and sentiments to the large masses of Ukrainian people, for here was a Ukrainian student who paid with his life in the struggle for the Ukrainian univer-

---

[3]) "The Missionary Messsenger", May 3, 1916.

sity in Lviv. However, a sharp division of opinion developed at this meeting. One group of those present wanted the proposed bursa to have a general national character while the opposing group insisted on Catholic education. Those who supported the national education left the meeting en masse and in a different hall elected the executive board of the Adam Kotsko Bursa. The executive was headed by J. W. Arsenych, who in later years was appointed to the bench and became the first judge of Ukrainian origin in Canada. During the first year, the Bursa was located at 117 Juno Street in Winnipeg and in the following year moved into the Ukrainian National Home, at the South-East corner of McGregor and Burrows Streets. Thus this bursa existed for only two years but during that period 39 students enjoyed its benefits. Their tutors were O. Zadurovych, T. Havryluk, N. Romaniuk and Wm. Baleshta.

The faction at that meeting who supported the Catholic upbringing of students, under the leadership of Bishop N. Budka organized The Metropolitan Andrey Shepticky Ukrainian Bursa which was placed under the care of the Metropolitan Andrey Shepticky Society in Winnipeg. Before being accepted into this Bursa, the student had to make and sign a solemn declaration. The declaration was orthodoxical and its text read:

"I hereby solemnly declare that as a son of the Ukrainian people and our ancestral Greek Catholic Church, I shall work sincerely for the good and glory of the Metropolitan Andrey Shepticky Ukrainian Society and never shall I act either by word or deed to its moral and material detriment" [4].

Emil Orobko [5] headed the first administration of this Bursa. The committee acquired a building in St. Boniface, at the corner of Tissot and Lafleche Streets, for the use of Bursa. In the first year of its existence, close to 60 students lived in this Bursa. This position was sustained during the ten years of the existence of the institution. Directors and educators of the Bursa were: George Skwarok, teacher Nicholas Boychuk, teacher-lawyer Dr. John Kopach and Rev. Michael Pelekh. Apart from their studies in colleges and the university, students were taught the Ukrainian language, history, literature and religion. Since the cost of maintenance paid by the student was very low—$20 a month—the Bursa also received support from general public contributions. A Students' Club existed in the Bursa which offered the students an opportunity to prepare themselves for public life. In addition to this, there was a choir, a drama group, and other similar activities. The students even issued their own newspaper in the Ukrainian language [6].

The P. Mohyla Bursa in Saskatoon had developed to a still greater extent. The initiative in the establishment of this Bursa came from the students themselves; students such as A. Kryzhanovsky, M. Mykhasiv, I. Rybchuk, A. T. Kibzey, O. Megas, W. Swystun, Jos. Vavryniuk, Jos. Bohonos, A. Prystupa, and others. The idea of establishing a bursa was conceived at a meeting of a Ukrainian Students Club, held on March 4, 1916. On the

---

[4] The Canadian Ruthenian, No. Feb. 2, 1916.

[5] The first executive board also included Gregory Skehar, S. V. Kharambura and P. Popil.

[6] Its editor was I. H. Syrnick, eventually editor of The Ukrainian Voice of long standing.

NOTE: From this bursa there came such prominent citizens of Canada as O. Dyk, S. Ozero, Omer Miles Malitsky and Elias Evasiuk, and a number of teachers and other professional men.

following day a general meeting of students and some of the local citizens was held, in the course of which the urgency of establishing a bursa had been made clear by the speakers. The initiative committee was headed by Jos. Bohonos and A. T. Kibzey. Elected to the executive board were for the most part the active students, including Wasyl Swystun who was making his way toward prominence in public life. The action to establish the bursa was given an impetus when the Department of Education refused to grant the bilingual teachers its permission to hold their convention. The teachers, who during the summer holidays usually attended supplementary courses at the university, wanted to discuss at the proposed convention not only the question of public schools but also that of the bursa. The ban on the teachers' convention only intensified the efforts of students who had in June of the current year announced competitions for admission of candidates to the bursa. At the same time the student-teachers were getting ready for another convention, this time not a teachers, but a popular convention for the purpose of vindicating a number of cultural and educational issues. The question of bursas was at the top of the agenda.

The convention was held August 4 and 5, 1916. Nearly 500 participants deliberated over the above-mentioned issues. In addition to representatives from 60 localities in Saskatchewan, there were delegates, and messages of greeting, from Winnipeg, Edmonton, Mundare, Vegreville, Lanuke, Borshchiv and Benito. Taking part in the convention were such prominent guests as Dr. W. E. Murray, President of the University of Saskatchewan; the Mayor of Saskatoon, Dr. Young, and J. S. Woodsworth, who at the time was conducting a study of the Ukrainians in the western provinces. Also attending the convention were Bishop N. Budka, T. D. Ferley, the first Ukrainian elected to the Manitoba Legislature, and many other Ukrainians of note from the three prairie provinces. J. S. Woodsworth's address made a tremendous impression upon the audience. He literally said:

"I am ashamed of the man who is ashamed of his native people. One cannot expect much from the man who so quickly forgets his own ancestry, because he has no stable character. He can at any moment also change his opinion".

The convention was carried through in an exemplary manner and was the first such mass assembly of Ukrainians in Canada. Bishop N. Budka delivered an address in which he stressed the necessity and importance of religion in the education of youth. Wasyl Swystun spoke on the necessity of establishing the bursas, and G. Skwarok spoke on responsibilities of the citizens to Canada. The latter speaker developed the view that loyalty to Canada did not mean the renouncing of the culture of one's own people. At the same time it was resolved at this convention to establish the Petro Mohyla Bursa, and the direction of same was entrusted to such well-known citizens as Osyp Megas, Wasyl Swystun, M. Stechishin, A. T. Kibzey, S. W. Sawchuk, I. Pernarowsky, S. M. Saviak, Jos. Sikorsky and A. Bodnarchuk. Among the 15 resolutions adopted by the convention were those calling for the establishment of a professor's chair of Ukrainian language at the University of Saskatchewan, for Compulsory School Attendance Act, and so on. In the course of the convention, separate conferences of Ukrainian school trustees from the whole province were held, resulting in the formation of the Association of School Trustees in Saskatchewan which set for itself the task of uniting the Ukrainian schools in collaborating with the system of English school trustees.

Thus on the 5th of March, 1917, the bursa in Saskatoon had been incorporated as the Petro Mohyla Ukrainian Institute. Actually, the Institute was already well on its way towards developing successfully, for on the 7th of July of that same year it opened a branch in Canora. For the 1917-1918 academic year the Institute had three buildings ready for students, one of which was for girls. Students jointly set up a students' society, called "Kameniari", which exercised great influence upon the education of youth. In the heat of activity in the Institute a disagreement occurred between the directors and Bishop N. Budka. The latter was upholding the position that the Institute should be conducted in the Catholic spirit because the students were predominantly of Catholic faith while the leadership of the Institute insisted on religious neutrality.

The Second National Convention, which was held in Saskatoon in 1917 and the initiator of which was again the Institute, endorsed the position taken by the Board of Directors. This convention turned into a singular manifestation of concern for the reaction to the events which at the time were developing in the Ukraine as well as in Canada. Taking part in the convention were more than 700 delegates and guests coming not only from the prairie provinces but also from Ontario. The convention expressed regret to the Government of Canada for its action in depriving the Ukrainian Canadians of their citizenship rights and at the same time laying stress on the Ukrainian contribution on the development of Canada and emphasizing Ukrainian support for Canada's war effort, the patriotic drive for funds, the Red Cross, the sale of war bonds and the enlisting of Ukrainian youths for military action overseas. The convention also forwarded a message of greeting to the Ukrainian Central Rada in Kiev which had been set up as the political leadership of the Ukrainian people in their struggle for independence from Russia. The convention appraised the work of the Institute and in appreciation of this those present started a collection of funds in support of its further expansion. At the convention alone nearly $14,000 was collected. Answering the call of Saskatoon, Alberta raised $17,926 within a short time.

Meanwhile in Edmonton, work in connection with the M. Hrushevsky Institute was forging ahead. The initiative came from the Adam Kotsko Students' Club. The same was true also with respect to the Shevchenko Bursa in Vegreville. Later the Hrushevsky Intitute and the Shevchenko Bursa, which filled the place of the liquidated "School for Foreigners" in Vegreville, merged into a single institution.

In 1918 the Institute in Saskatoon acquired its own building in the Nutana district of the city and this strengthened the organizational determination on the part of both the leadership and membership. In the meantime, preparations were made for a new convention to take place in December of 1918. This convention did not, however, come off in the same grand manner, for in the meantime a serious clash occurred between the leadership of the Instiutute in Saskatoon and the Ukrainian Greek Catholic Church. In consequence of this, by the initiative of the Petro Mohyla Institute and its sympathizers, there came into being the Ukrainian Orthodox Brotherhood which set out to organize the Ukrainian Greek Orthodox Church in Canada. Also a widely spread epidemic of Spanish influenza in that same year had a derimental effect upon the convention attendance. But despite all these complications the convention was held after all. Dr. V. Simenovych, of Chicago, president of the Federation of Ukrainians in the United States, participated in the convention and by his presence, to a certain degree, represented the Ukrainian Americans. The Fourth and Fifth popular conventions, sponsored by the Institute, were arranged in such a way that in 1919 and 1920 they were held in the three prairie provinces—in Saskatoon for Saskatchewan, in Winnipeg for Manitoba and in Edmonton for Alberta.

These conventions were comparatively less successful. Prof. I. Boversky was the guest speaker at these conventions. All the same, they made everyone feel that the people were greatly concerned about the native school education. All three conventions had been organized under the slogan of preserving and nurturing the Ukrainian language and culture in Canada, in order to create a highly productive and spiritually enriched citizen of Canada. These principles and these slogans appealed to the broad masses of Ukrainian Canadians, for they were consonant with their own viewpoint and philosophy of life.

At the time when a branch of the Petro Mohyla Institute was being established in Edmonton, the Ukrainian Catholics organized in 1917, in that city, the Taras Shevchenko Institute which was housed in the former Grand Hotel, at the corners of 98th Street and 107th Avenue. At the Catholic convention held in Mundare, in 1919, the main item on the agenda was financial support for the Taras Shevchenko Institute in Edmonton. Taking part in the convention were various government dignitaries, such as the Hon. Frank Oliver and members of the Legislature, H. A. Makie and Jos. McCallum, Dr. Jos. Boulanger, and other guests. When Bishop Budka made an appeal for financial support of the Taras Shevchenko Institute, those present at the convention contributed $6,000. Taking into consideration the still meager financial resources of Ukrainian farmers of that period, the amounts raised at both the convention of the Petro Mohyla Institute and the convention of the Taras Shevchenko Institute served as proof of their remarkable understanding of these matters. The Ukrainian Canadians had been contributing large sums of money in order that their youth might be brought up in the culture of their parents. In spite of these efforts, it was still difficult to maintain these institutes and bursas, which required large sums of money.

In order to exhaust completely the question of bursas, one must mention the institutions conducted by the Presbyterian Church for the young Ukrainians in Canada. The initiative in this instance was given by the Zaporozhian Seech Society in 1910, and The Ukrainian Voice conducted the fund raising. However, in Manitoba and Alberta the initiative was taken over by the Presbyterian Church. When the Ukrainians in Alberta started to organize the "Ruthenian-Ukrainian Bursa" in 1912, the Presbyterian Church gave them solid support. Later the Presbyterians assumed control of the bursa, in spite of the fact that initially the Bursa was established on a non-denominational basis. The Bursa provided an opportunity for 20 students to pursue their higher education. The leading figures in this undertaking were: Paul Rudyk who contributed $1,000 and who supplemented this contribution each subsequent time to match the total amount conributed by all other Ukrainians; Pastor A. Wilchynsky, Pastor M. Zalizniak,

Jos. Danylovych, S. Gura, M. Belegay, V. Ferbey, V. Fedun, V. Rudyk, P. Gonsky and others.

In 1911 through the endeavours of Dr. A. J. Hunter, a Presbyterian philanthropist, work had been started to establish a bursa in Teulon. The funds for this undertaking were provided by the Home Mission of The Presbyterian Church. The bursa was opened in 1912 for boys of intermediate school age. A similar bursa was opened there for girls five years later. Ukrainian boys and girls alone were admitted to these bursas where they received a religious upbringing in the Presbyterian faith. As regards the Ukrainian language and culture, the students sensed a certain degree of assimilatory pressure, which was quite understandable considering the fact that Anglo-Saxon elements had been the exclusive guardians of the two bursas. It is interesting to note, though, that this policy on the part of Directors of these bursas, produced the opposite results. In private, the youths spoke in their native language, read Ukrainian books, and established the Ukrainian students club, "Zoria" [7]. As it finally became apparent that this policy failed to produce the desired results, the administration began accepting only those applicants over whom, in their opinion, it would be easier to exercise their influence. But even this approach failed to alter national and cultural ties of the students because of their inherently unshakable feeling of identity prevailing among them [8]. Similar to the one in Teulon was the bursa in Sifton, maintained by the Presbyterian Mission Home. In addition to the bursa, there was the medical clinic directed in the beginning by Dr. I. Reid and later by Dr. Samuel Eshoo. The immediate superintendent of the bursa was Edith MacEwen. Dr. Eshoo looked after the two buildings in Sifton; however, these establishments did not last long. The best organized and longest lasting was the establishment in Teulon under the administration of Dr. A. Hunter who with true devotion laboured for the education of the youth and provided medical services to the whole district.

In summing up, it needs to be stressed that while the Bursas and the Institutes prior to 1915 and in later years, were a manifestation of concern on the part of the Ukrainian settlers for the education of their children and the preservation of Ukrainian language and culture which in subsequent years adapted a role of filling the vacuum which was created by the abolition of bilingual schools and the banning of Ukrainian language classes in the public school system, the Bursas operated by the Presbyterian Church were designed to provide their pupils with religious education of this faith and in relation to the language, culture and the Ukrainian community, to offer the youth a model of the Anglo-Saxon institutions and thereby the more readily and completely assimilate them, not only at the religious level but cultural as well. But even this tendency failed to produce the desired results after a decade of effort, both in Manitoba and Alberta. As we have already established the case of Teulon, the youth basically did not take to this, although they did to a degree embrace the religious tenets they were exposed to. Research shows that even those—a very small handful—who were assimilated (and the change of their surnames was the first indication of this) did not sever the ties with the cultural roots of their Ukrainian origin.

---

[7] "Dnipro", Almanac, 1917, pp. 217-219.
[8] Studies in the History of Ukrainians in Canada, Vol. II, p. 152.

As regards the educational role played by the Ukrainian bursas and institutes after 1916, they contributed considerably in strengthening the national feelings of the Ukrainians in Canada. They sharpened the sense of responsibility of members of the Ukrainian community with regard to the education of their children, intensified the thoughts and ambitions of parents with the determination that their children must strive towards bettering their education and helped the youth to lose their inferiority complex, which to a certain degree, had been created by chauvinistic attacks from outside. The bursas and institutes also assisted students of limited financial means to complete their studies successfully. These bursas and insitutes were also an excellent stimulant from a social and community viewpoint: they trained the youth to be members of the Canadian community, to take an active part in public life and to bear the responsibility for the progress and development of their community. From these bursas and institutions came hundreds of active Ukrainian Canadians who assumed leading posts in the Ukrainian Canadian community and quite often established the tone of its social activities. Thanks to these institutions Ukrainians got a large number of people who became qualified workers in every field of endeavour. If we look over the past, we see that quite a number of older Ukrainians, members of the educated class, the intelligentsia, are linked with one or another bursa or institute, whether it was in Winnipeg, Saskatoon, Edmonton, Vegreville, Teulon or Canora. There is no doubt that in relation to language and culture these institutions have left an indelible mark on the memory of former pupils. Beginning with 1916, these institutions stood at the height of the task they had been called upon to perform.

In conclusion it is necessary to answer an imporant question: why is it that these bursas and institutes had to end in self-liquidation after a long period of existence? One contrasting exception is the Petro Mohyla Institute, although there are some others.

Rev. J. Skwarok, OSBM., who made a study of this subject, asserts that in many cases this was due to unsuitable preparations and lack of proficiency in the management of these institutions [9]. But the idea of such institutions has been kept alive among the people and the endeavours of Ukrainian community to establish them again in the postwar years, speaks eloquently of their worth and the value placed on them by the people whom they served.

---

[9] J. J. Skwarok: "The Ukrainian Settlers in Canada and their Schools", Edmonton, 1891-1921. p. 85.

CULTURAL-EDUCATIONAL WORK

Ukrainian settlers cared for more than the physical development of their children before whom there blossomed great possibilities of enlightenment and achievement in the new land. Forefathers greatly taxed their own resources. Many of them could neither read nor write. The then exploitive authority in Ukraine cared little for education. Statistics show that in 1908 of the seven and one-half million population in Galicia district over four and one-half million were illiterate. This included 2,459,410 Ukrainians, 2,104,899 Poles, 100,836 Germans. Even those who could read and write had not received any learning in school, since in most villages there were no schools. People learned from each other. As soon as settlers took up homesteads and gradually revived from their troubles, they began to reflect on the setting up of formal schooling.

When people from Western Ukraine left their homeland, there had existed in Lviv, since 1868, an institution known as "Prosvita". Its name implies its aim and so under the influence of its use there sprang throughout urban centres branches of this institution which beckoned the people to learning, to training in and revival of their past, the betterment of their hopes, and to thrift. "Prosvita" organized reading societies, co-operatives and credit unions. Among other things, the Ukrainians transferred to their new homeland fairly exact copies of their customs and traditions. As early as 1900 a "Svoboda" publication reported [1]:

"Ukrainian Brethren! 30,000 of us have arrived in Canada; of this some 12,000 in Alberta, and in such sparsely populated land as Canada there lies strength in such numbers. Let us remember that we must all create one Ukrainian family, help one another and, above all, never forget that we brothers are all sons of the renowned Mother Rus-Ukraine. It is necessary that we immediately acquaint ourselves with the ways of the land in which we live, that we cultivate enlightenment, love one's faith and language and learn the language of the country as well. We must add courage to our morale and show that we are an honourable race which respects human dignity. We are a resolute people, heeding the truth of the statement: "Knock and it shall be opened; search for truth and you shall find it" [2].

Such were the underlying principles of the Ukrainian settlers. To respect the rights of others, to quickly become part of the new way of life, to live in harmony with others who esteem the part played by co-operative effort. Their past seemed unbearable. In the midst of new surroundings they gave vent to their feelings, their hopes and their desires. In order to fully realize their hopes, they began founding cultural centres called "Chytalnia" association, "Chytalnia Prosvita" or National Home. These helped to initiate the continuity of their past ways of life. Usually these were exact copies of what they had left behind them in Ukraine, because their ambition was to build "as it used to be in the old country".

---

[1] In some instances the old name of Ruthenian has been used but we substitute with the modern name of Ukrainian.
[2] "Svoboda", No. 49, 27, 1900.

Referring to the "Chytalnia Prosvita" in Canada, a quote from an almanac published by the central Prosvita in Lviv, in 1913, follows:

"Our brethren whose unforseen lot sent them across the seas in search of better fortunes are not forgetful of their Rus'-Ukrainian origin. In addition to schools, they were forming various organizations, religious, political, social and for the learning of international affairs they set up Prosvita Reading Associations. Of prime importance is the library through which members, dramatic clubs, choirs, orchestras, etc. reap benefits. On the whole, life in these reading halls differs little from life in those of our own. Canadian Reading Association Prosvita exists as a medium of their cultural enlightenment. It strives for the erection of an actual building to accommodate other national organizations whose beginnings are initiated here. It is also here that the initiative to observe national holidays, etc., arises".

It can be readily deduced that these Ukrainian reading associations were in fact "Community Clubs", dotting rural and urban areas and providing cultural possibilities for young and old alike. They, however, had large libraries which, it is regretted, community clubs lack.

FIRST SPROUTS AND MANITOBA

In the history of Canadian Ukrainians there are numerous accounts of cultural-educational life. At times these may appear couched in doubtful authenticity as to form and date. What is given here is an observation by the then contemporary press which, in this instance, is perhaps the most reliable source, since notations appeared rather hastily in the face of existing decisions. The first Ukrainian organization appearing in Canada possessed a rather religio-brotherly objective. It seems that Rev. N. Dmytriw was the first priest who started organizing Ukrainian religious groups. On a wider basis, the language was a separate division dedicated to church organizations. Even before the arrival in Canada of Rev. N. Dmytriw, a Brotherhood organization appeared which had just recently been organized by Anthony Sawka in Edna-Star area. This was the first Brotherhood and on the whole the first organized Ukrainian branch with its objectives centered in Canada. About the genesis of this Brotherhood and its beginnings A. Sawka submitted to the "Svoboda" publication a more detailed account which we quote here as an authentic historical moment in the founding of Ukrainian organizations. Under the heading "News from Canada" we read:

"We Albertan Ukrainians celebrated Christmas on a grand scale, in as much as we can term it without church or priest. All three days of this festivity, in clement weather, there were gatherings of Ukrainian Colonials at the home of J. Halkiw, my neighbour, who had built a large house, and where we sang our beloved "God Is With Us" under my direction. On the second day of Christmas we decided to set up a church Brotherhood. To achieve our aims, we went from house to house, according to our old custom, to sing carols, and in such manner we gathered 31 members who donated $17.00. On New Year's we gathered all the members and initiated a Brotherhood with me, Anton Sawka, as president, Michael Melnyk as vice-president, and Constantine Nemyrsky as treasurer to whom we entrusted the collected funds.

Honourable mention goes to Messrs. John Lakusta, John Halkiw, Theodore Rudyk, Joseph Dzivenka who contributed so much towards the work of organizing the St. Nicholas Brotherhood, the first Ukrainian religious Brotherhood in Canada. With God's help may this serve as an example for numerous Brotherhoods throughout Canada; may God enable us to live the day when we may in this far-off North America thunderously through song acclaim at Easter festivity, "Christ Is Risen". With this I hope that our brethren in Halychyna will be gladdened by the reading that their brethren in far-away Canada, like frozen ants, are beginning to revive"[3]).

Such is the record of this first organization. Four months later when Rev. N. Dmytriw made his tour again he found that every parish had a Brotherhood organization.

The first Ukrainian religious Brotherhood of St. Nicholas was organized by the group through the efforts of Dr. O. Oleskiw, immigrated into Canada in the spring of 1896. Major part of this group settled in Edna-Star, Alberta. Here, also, was organized the first Prosvita with a following notation from "Svoboda":

"Rev. P. Tymkevych started a "Chytalnia" by bringing in some 80 books from the "Prosvita" in Lviv and members are glad to be learning— we shall be writing to the Old Country for more books and papers. The Club is operating at Alexander Karpet's home [4]). This group came into being a year and a half after the existence of St. Nicholas' group.

The first urban reading association came into existence in 1899 in Winnipeg. It was "Multi-National Chytalnia" to which others than Ukrainians could belong. It was named the "Shevchenko Reading Association". The organizers of this group were Sawa Chernecky, Kyrylo Genik, Theodore Stefanyk, John Kuch, George Panischak and others [5]). This group, however, suffered self-liquidation within a year of its operation. It is said that it had socialistic coloring and was renewed as such in December, 1903, when it became known as the "Shevchenko Reading Society".

A few interesting events resulted. On May 14, 1904, a Ukrainian Youth Club presented the so-called "Argonauts" play, the first Ukrainian play ever presented in Canada. Some of the participants were: O. Kosowy, O. Antoniuk, Y. Koltek, Y. Makohin, A. Novak, I. Puhaty, D. Kyrstiuk, Y. Dedeluk, P. Tesluk, and P. Pasichnyk. Chytalnia members even decided to set up an "Ivan Franko National Library" [6]). The library was to have a dominion character and hence the reason for the term "National". Then the appeal went out for donations of books and money to the "Ukrainian National Library" of the "Kanadiyska Rus"[7]). From time to time there was a gathering here of delegates to the Convention of the Independent Greek Church of Canada. In 1904, besides religious matters, discussions took place regarding bilingual schools for Ukranians in Canada. Shevchenko Reading Society members K. Genyk, G. Panischak and T. Stefanyk, and the Independent Greek Church members—I. Bodrug and I. Negrych—went as delegates to Manitoba government in an attempt fo secure recognition for the use of the Ukrainian language in Manitoba's educational

---

[3]) "Svoboda", Feb. 25, 1897.
[4]) "Svoboda", August 4, 1898.
[5]) Studies in the History of Ukrainians in Canada", V. II. p. 345.
[6]) "Svoboda", March, 1904.
[7]) It needs to be explained that Ukrainian Canadians often used the name "Kanadiyska Rus" as a collective for the Ukrainian Canadians. Some chauvinistic newspapers tried to interpret this as though the Ukrainians tried to build a Ukraine in Canada under the name "Kanadiyska Rus".

system. At meetings in this Chytalnia the members were also concerned about the need of a Ukrainian newspaper in Canada, and some of these members later became the initiators of such first publications in Canada.

The year 1905 was of special significance in the field of cultural-educational work in Winnipeg when on January 6 a decision was reached for the setting up of a second cultural-educational centre in Winnipeg. Executive members were Mykola Hladky, president, Dmytro Dushchenko, secretary, Michael Hawryluk, treasurer, and Roman Dudar, librarian. Two years later there were 83 members, 326 books in the library and 6 different newspaper subscriptions [8]. In 1905 the Ukrainians in Winnipeg set up what was a short-lived National Home.

On October 11th of the same year St. Nicholas Brotherhood held its organizational meeting, led by Rev. M. Hura, T. Jastremsky, V. Karpets, M. Lewycky, I. Zubachek, V. Lisowy, V. Sholdra, V. Chornenky, M. Kuziw, Y. Orlowsky, and J. Zakharkiw. On the first day of its operation the association had 76 members. A month later, at a St. Nicholas Brotherhood meeting there came into being a "Kanadiysky Rusky Narodnyj Sojuz" (Canadian Ruthenian National Association). The year 1906 was noteworthy when the cultural-educational work at Taras Shevchenko Reading Society was intensified and its offices were transferred from Euclid Avenue to T. Jastremsky Hall, southeast corner of Stella and McGregor. Included in this transfer was the "Ivan Franko Ukrainian National Library" made up of 450 books and ten newspaper periodicals. This became a gathering place for the then prominent Ukrainian members, such as T. Stefanyk, V. Holowatsky, J. W. Arsenych, K. Kachmarek, A. Novak, D. Ferley, D. Rarahowsky, K. Genyk, T. Jastremsky, G. Panischak, H. Slipchenko.

On Oct. 22, 1906, a Taras Shevchenko Educational Association was organized. It purchased a hall on the north-east corner of Powers and Manitoba, presently 467 Manitoba Ave. This hall embraced both the cultural-educational and political life. Both aspects took firm root. This also gave rise to the Ukrainian Free Thought Federation which ideologically influenced the evolution of Taras Shevchenko Educational Association. Free Thought Federation precluded a socio-liberal-minded organization which opposed clericalism and even religion. Another group that gathered here was the Winnipeg branch of the Ukrainian Socialist Party in Canada. Among the first executives of the Educational Association were: A. Slipchenko, V. Kulka, M. Kolisnyk and D. Rarahowsky. Activities taking place at the Taras Shevchenko Educational Association were lectures, dramatics, the learning of English and Ukrainian languages, recreational undertakings and often assemblies regarding labor matters. "Verchovyntsi" was the first theatrical performance here.

As though in opposition to the first reading centre, there arose in Winnipeg, in 1901, at the St. Nicholas parish, three organizations, viz., St. Nicholas Brotherhood, the Holy Trinity Women's Association, and the St. Olga's Girls Association. These organizations failed to uncover broader ideologies. On the other hand, the Shevchenko Reading Society effectively influenced not only the urban but the rural areas as well.

In 1907 another "Chytalnia", "The Ukrainian Star" in Winnipeg, was organized. Next year it was renamed "The Canadian Star", with its offices at the Independent Greek Church, corner of MacGregor and Prichard. Its

---

[8] Calendar Almanac of Ruthenian National Association, Mount Carmel, 1908, p. 153.

organizers were: Z. Bychynsky, J. Bachynsky, and M. Bachynsky. At this church there also existed the "Brotherhood Benefit of the Feast of Transfiguration", which had come into being in 1904. A similar Brotherhood, that of "Holy Trinity", with a religious and moral aim was organized by the Canadian Orthodox Mission in 1908. With its centre at 598 Manitoba Avenue, it directed religious teaching and cultural enlightenment.

The formation of reading associations (Chytalnias) and brotherhoods in Winnipeg differentiated the religious, political and cultural life of the Ukrainians not only in this city but in the rest of Canada as well. The most independent group was that of Taras Shevchenko. These were composed mostly of the moderate socialist elements who, within the prismatic sphere of this movement, carried on their cultural educational work, including courses in English and Ukrainian language for the benefit not only of their members but also for the masses as well. A second cultural-educational centre was the "Chytalnia Prosvita" which collaborated very closely with the St. Nicholas parish and later with the parish of St. Vladimir and Olga. In very close personal and ideal ties with this centre was the Brotherhood of St. Nicholas. The chytalnia "Ukrainska Zoria" (Ukrainian Star) named later as "Canadian Star", which united together the different elements grouped themselves around the Independent Greek Church. This group followed along the line of greatest integration assimilative tendencies. This was accomplished partially through the medium of the Presbyterian Church which held a financial control over the Independent Greek Church. The mood here was never in the same pattern—it was always in search of new religious and cultural pathways. In addition to these there was, at this time in Winnipeg, the Brotherhood of Holy Trinity backed by the Russian Orthodox Mission in U.S.A. and from 1918 by the Russian Orthodox Church in Canada. Outwardly the Holy Trinity Brotherhood masked its work under the camouflage of the "cultural needs" of the Ukrainian Canadian community but just the same there stood behind it the missionary aims of the Russian Orthodox policy which demanded a total loyalty to the "one and only indivisible Russia". All this one way flowing stream was cleverly directed by the authoratative power of the Archbishop of Aleutian Islands and of North America. Actually this influential stream was not Ukrainian in content but it needs to be mentioned because many Ukrainians supported this work if for no other reason then that they themselves were of the Orthodox faith. This especially holds true for Ukrainian-Bukovinians.

Under the influence of the four aforementioned streams of thought there was being moulded the complete culturally-enlightened life. It need be noted that the course of Greek Catholic Church, in its resulting divergencies with the politics of the Latin hierarchy, split in two: national, which repudiated the primacy of this hierarchy within the Greek Catholic Church in Canada, and the "Basilian" which recognized such primacy. However, with the arrival of the first Greek Catholic hierarch N. Budka in Canada, the said divergencies disappeared.

With regard to the Ukrainian cultural area, except for the tsarophile, all communities found common interests and language in all Ukrainian matters. Of concern to them was the national tongue, that in Winnipeg there be made available the mother tongue for their children; they set up courses in the English language, attended to their cultural undertakings together and concerned themselves with the events that were taking place in their native homelands, such as the struggle for their electoral rights, for a Ukrainian university in Lviv, aid in strikes, politics, etc. Just as the growth of their ideological, political and sanguine connections with Ukraine on the one hand, so on the other hand there was growth of newly-developed social, cultural and political demands. This was no national ghetto that simply seethes within itself. Already through their religious associations they co-worked with the local churches, for example, the French Catholic and the Anglo-Saxon Presbyterian.

The most orthodox and conservative influence was that directed by the Russian Orthodox Mission; the most elastic was the socialistic one to which belonged members of other ethnic groups and which worked very closely with the Socialist Party in Canada. Two other streams of thought supported both parties. The Greek Catholic Church lent support to the Conservatives, whereas the Independent Greek Church sponsored the Liberals. The Russian Orthodox sphere of thought worked at that time closely with the Liberals in all three Prairie provinces. It was instrumental in opposing all Ukrainian endeavours, and especially demanded the liquidation of English-Ukrainian bilingualism in schools and often produced information that added to the misunderstanding of Ukrainian problems and activities of the pioneer era.

Apparently in the process of categorising these influences as cultural, educational and political, some exceptions could have escaped here and there.

Later on Ukrainians in Winnipeg formed a number of organizations, as church groups, dramatic and choral, edited newspapers, and were involved in bilingual schooling. All these activities qualified Winnipeg in the very beginnings as the capital of Ukrainians in Canada. Cultural-educational activities of the Ukrainians in Canada centered themselves in Winnipeg and this city became a pattern in matters cultural and political. Winnipeg became a meeting place for various groups from rural districts which both organized and differentiated the lives of Ukrainians in Manitoba, Alberta and Saskatchewan. Although organizational silver-linings first appeared in Alberta, it was Winnipeg in Manitoba on which fell the primacy for organizing the activities of the pioneer days.

Winnipeg provided leadership for other settlements in Manitoba. Among the first cultural-educational organizations appearing in rural areas were those in Sifton, Brokenhead and Stuartburn. The first chytalnia appeared in Sifton in 1903 and in the fall of the same year the "Chytalnia Prosvita" was organized in Brokenhead. The "Ruska Chytalnia" was organized in Stuartburn in 1904. Two more chytalnias were organized in 1905 as follows: "Taras Shevchenko" in Venlaw; "The Seech Association" and "Chytalnia Prosvita" in Riding Mountain. Six more chytalnias were organized in 1906, namely: the "Prosvita of I. Ardan" in Pleasant Home; "M. Pavlyk" in Shevchenko (now Vita); "Prosvita" in Mink Creek; the "Kanadiyska Rus Prosvita" in Portage La Prairie; the "Taras Shevchenko" in Sifton and the Chytalnia of M. Pavlyk in Oleskiw (Tolstoi).

The year 1907 was fruitful in organizing chytalnias, when the following ones appeared: Progress in Oakburn, "Prosvita" in Stuartburn, "Ruska Slava" in Garland, "Taras Shevchenko" in Rosa, "Prosvita" in Venlaw, "Markian Shashkevych" in Winnipeg Beach, "Narodny Postup" (National

Progress) in Stoney Mountain, the "Rus-Ukrainian Chytalnia" in Stonewall, Labor organization "Freedom" in Portage La Prairie, "Prosvita" in Sarto, "Ivan Franko" in Rossburn, "Morning Star" in Dnister, "K. Trylowsky" in Rossburn, and "Progress" in Oakburn. In 1908 new branches appeared, as "M. Shashkevich" in Trembowla (Valley River), "Taras Shevchenko" in Volkiwci, "M. Drahomaniw" in Oleskiw (Tolstoi), "New Star" in Brokenhead, "Ukrainian Prosvita" in Fishing River, "M. Drahomaniv " in Arbaka, "Prosvita" in Ethelbert, "Our Star" in Loon Lake. Incorporated in 1909 were "Prosvita" in Broad Valley, "Adam Kocko" in rural Roblin area, and a new one, "Taras Shevchenko" in Pleasant Home. In 1910 the "Sichynsky Chytalnia" appeared in Selkirk, followed in 1912 by two more: "Prosvita" in Chmelnytsky (P.O. Mears) and "M. Kahanec" in Roblin. Foremost distinction was gained by "Prosvita I. Ardan" in Pleasant Home when on Oct. 16, 1906, it staged "Courting in Honchariwka" at the "Galicia School" (by then already renamed Plum Ridge). The drama was organized by the bilingual teachers in the district. This was the first theatrical presentation in a rural area.

To this imposing list of chytalnias in Manitoba's Ukrainian settlements may be added a few Winnipeg organizations, as the M. Kropywnytsky Drama Club, started in 1908, the dramatic association "Vidrodzenia" (Rebirth), the "Zaporozhska Seech" in 1910, "Vilna Shkola" (Free School), "Tovarystvo Besida", Benefit Fraternity of John the Merciful, 1911, Students Club of Self-education, Drama Club, "Tovarystvo of M. Sichynsky "Boyan", Dramatic Club of M. Zankovetska, Committee to Aid Ukrainian School (1912), Ukrainian National Home, Educational Association of Ivan Franko, Independent Ukraine, Ukrainian Women's Educational Fraternity (1916), Canadian Ukrainian Institute Prosvita", and a number of other organizations. It is clear that in the field of cultural-educational organizations the Ukrainians were among the best organized groups in Winnipeg as well as in the whole of Manitoba [9]).

ALBERTA

Next to Winnipeg, Edmonton, Alberta, became the most active Ukrainian cultural-educational centre. In 1901 Edmonton had a population of 2,626 and was located close to the areas of Ukrainian resources of Vegreville, Beaver Lake, and surrounding settlements. Peter Svarich succeeded in his experiment to institute the Reading Association of Taras Shevchenko in Beaver Creek and surrounding area, and in 1900, upon his departure for Alaska, he was able to turn over the beginnings of a library to his friends in Edmonton. According to pioneer story, this library gave rise to the first "Chytalnia Taras Shevchenko" in Edmonton, located at 96th Street and 101 A Avenue, at John Kilar's residence. By this time there had already been a few Ukrainian tenant families living in Edmonton and a number of girls employed as domestics. The major part of the organizational work for this chytalnia was done by Michael Gowda who also wrote for the newspapers and composed song verses. The founding members of the "Chy-

---

[9]) The author is aware that the comment of the cultural-educational organizations is not complete. His remarks are based on information gathered from the news then appearing in newspapers which, as usual, never give the full text of organizational life.

talnia" were M. Lytawsky, Paul Rudyk, Toma Tomashev sky and John Kilar [10]).

In the fall of 1902 the Basilian Fathers endeavoured to provide for cultural-educational life in connection with the S. Joachim and Ste. Anne's Roman Catholic Church, where masses were held in Ukrainian language. Lacking their own building facilities, this effort failed to bring the expected results. Success would only come with the building of their own St. Josaphat's Church in 1904, the first Ukrainian church in Edmonton.

At that time a Ukrainian Labour Fraternity "Rivnist" was set up in Edmonton. Its activities helped to revitalize the life of the "Chytalnia Taras Shevchenko", whose work had suffered due to internal dissentions. Yakiv Makohin became the head of this revived organization, who was later the Ukrainian language teacher in a Winnipeg seminary. This same chytalnia was also sometimes known as "Postup", whose members included such well-known figures as P. Rudyk, D. Solanych, T. Tomashev sky, T. Yasenchuk and M. Tychkowska.

The organization "Rivnist" appealed "to the supporters of the working classes for financial assistance" [11]) for in its hopes lay plans for the building of their own National Home. Its headquarters were at the home of P. Rudyk. With the "Rivnist" organization were associated some socialist elements who had a great influence on the Ukrainian community in Edmonton. Through the efforts of Rev. M. Hura "Chytalnia Prosvita" was organized. The meeting took place March 24, 1907, at the home of Luka Yarmoniuk, where Oleksa Karpets was elected president. At the same time there was organized the Brotherhood Benefit Association of Peter and Paul which announced its membership in the Canadian Ukrainian National Association. The founders of these two organizations were: H. Chychka, I. Goleychuk, I. Oliynytsky, S. Holovach, T. Babukh, P. Boychuk, M. Trubchak, T. Tomashewsky, M. Chorney, I. Frishta, and others [12]).

The memorial book of the Ukrainian National Home in Edmonton has this to say about the chytalnia:

"In February, 1906, the first discussions took place at Iliya Kostyk's home, 97th Street and 107 Avenue, regarding the founding of "Chytalnia Prosvita". Following a speech by Rev. M. Hura, about the dire need of such a cultural centre, there was a signing up of membership which left its lasting memory in the hearts of Ukrainians of almost the whole of Alberta. The alphabetically (in Ukrainian alphabet) arranged list of the founding members follows: M. Andreyiw, G. Vitsentylo, I. Holeychuk, Alex Holeychuk, S. Holovach, Alex Kostyk, John Kilar, D. Chorney, I. Chychka, and M. Yakhnitsky. It was moved that the first meeting be held for electing the management but which did not take place until 1907 [13]). In 1908 the annual meeting of "Chytalnia Prosvita" was held in its own quarters beside St. Josaphat church where there were also a residence for the Sisters Servants and a residence for the Basilian Fathers. The purchase of the building was made by I. Kilar and I. Kostyk. Later on "Prosvita" under-

---

[10]) Broader history of this chytalnia: "Ukrainian Pioneer", Edmonton, No. 6, 1955.
[11]) "Svoboda", No. 51, Dec. 22, 1904.
[12]) Remembrance Book of the Ukrainian National Home, Edmonton, 1965.
[13]) Canadian Farmer, No. 52, January 5, 1909.

went some important internal adjustments as well as external undertakings which led to the expansion of its constitution in 1911 [14]).

A third cultural-educational centre in Edmonton came into being, initiated by Paul Rudyk, and located near the Independent Greek Church. In 1904 this group built its own church which had a great influence on the cultural life of its members, and later the "Ivan Franko Tovarystvo" (Association) was organized.

"Chytalnia Prosvita" of M. Shashkevych, founded with the help of St. Josaphat's parish in 1913, was able to undertake heavier obligations. A dramatic-musical "Tovarystvo Boyan" and the "Ukrainian Band" were organized. From 1912 to 1918 there were 85 plays and 6 concerts given which brought in a total of $5,149.39 in proceeds. The total sum was earmarked for the building of a National Home, towards which end the work started in 1919. Purchase of the plot was completed on Feb. 7, 1914, and registered under the name "Ukrainian Greek-Catholic Association". Michael Bilynsky was the first president. The M. Shashkevych "Chytalnia Prosvita" became an active campaigner for the erection of a "National Home" and for raising funds and began to set up affiliate branches in other areas of Alberta. On April 21, 1914, "Chytalnia Prosvita" was incorporated as the "Ukrainian Greek-Catholic Tovarystvo of M. Shashkevych". A National Home under the same name was built in 1917. The constitution required that only a Catholic may become a member. In this way it was hoped to avoid the going back and forth changes that very often took place in the agitated crucible of the pioneers' life.

When the organizational life, on the cultural-educational plane,—in Edmonton and Alberta—had been established, the next obvious step to take would be to raise this life to a higher level, and to find some common denominator that would bring into cohesion the Ukrainian socio-community in Alberta. It was quite a difficult task to find such an equalitarian medium in connection with the various organizational establishments. Despite serious difficulties, in December, 1909, there was launched in the press a communique of Gregory Kraykiwsky and Peter Svarich, in which an appeal was made to the Albertan Ukrainians to hold a "Ukrainian-National Viche" (convention) in Edmonton. This communique was approved by 40 citizens at a meeting held on November 14, 1909. At this "Viche" an organizational committee was chosen which, in addition to the two mentioned above was also composed of the following: Z. Bychynsky, N. Onyshchuk, D. Solanych, M. Yachnitsky, S. Bura and M. Ferley. All core centres were represented. Four topics for discussion were slated, dealing with the following subjects: "Prosvita" by Z. Bychynsky, "Organization" by P. Onyschuk, "Economy" by P. Svarich, and "Politics" by D. Solanych.

The organizers of the convention wrote in their invitation notices:

"Religious matters at the convention shall be avoided... Socialist windbags are asked to hold their peace or better still, not to appear at all. (This last hint referred to the obstructive tactics that were used by the socialists of Manitoba in 1908-M.H.M.). Misguided moscophiles and the newly recruited ones are highly desired guests; loudmouths and rogues should stay home... Time has arrived and the opportunity is here for the Ukrainians in Alberta to awaken, to open their eyes, to make careful scrutiny of conditions around them".

---

[14]) Ibidem, p. 41.

Following the publication of this communication there appeared one longer statement by Zyhmund Bychynsky, entitled, "The Great Bell is pealing loudly, saying: come to the viche! Viche! Viche!" He appealed to all "whether you are Greek Catholic, Orthodox, or Independent—makes no difference, for you are all Ukrainians, and there will be a "Ukrainian Viche" in Edmonton; there will be a place and a welcome for every Ukrainian regardless of his religion... Here in Canada we are divided by the three provincial boundaries of Manitoba, Saskatchewan and Alberta, each province leading its own life. One may say that the lives of Ukrainians in Saskachewan and Alberta are closely united while that of Manitoba is somewhat apart. While the Ukrainian populaion of Manitoba makes up the largest group and their organizational work is varied and numerous, the Ukrainians in Saskatchewan and Alberta are only in their initial stages with their organizational work. We have yet to hear of a "viche" in Saskatchewan or Alberta. The Ukrainians of these provinces are standing with their hands behind their back and warming themselves at the fireside" [15].

This meant that Manitoba even then, though not a wealthy province, provided an inspiration to the wealthy Alberta for organizational work. The "Viche", convention was attended by 200 delegates on December 27, 1909. It was conducted in accordance with its program and resulted in the following motions: "1) That a delegation be sent to the provincial government to ask for the fulfillment of its pre-election promise regarding schools, in Ukrainian language, and the appointment of a school organizer".

"2) That the government place, in Ukrainian schools, Ukrainian teachers only, who would also teach the mother tongue".

"3) That a "National Council" be established consisting of organizers from areas of Ukrainian settlements".

"4) That, should the government refuse to establish a Ukrainian teachers' seminary, a national bursa be established in Edmonton for providing students with an opportunity for higher learning".

"5) That the Ukrainian Viche in Edmonton recognizes the need for a political democratic party in Alberta and that the "National Council" be entrused with instituting it in time".

The National Council was composed of the following members from Edmonton: M. Yachnitsky, S. Gura, H. Kraykiwsky, V. Poleshiy, S. Holowach, I. Letawsky; from Vegreville: A. Svarich, V. Kyryluk, F. Lemishka, P. Svarich; from Mundare: S. Palamarchuk, H. Sawchuk; from Kolomyya: Z. Bychynsky, S. Draganiuk, V. Khlibetsky, H. Vynnychuk; from Borshchiw: T. Hoshka, N. Kalynchuk; from Myrnam: P. Melnyk. P. Fedorkiw, V. Romaniuk; from Andrew: V. Nykyforuk, A. Myroniuk; from Wostock: S. Panych; from Beaver Creek: P. Pasemko, I. Koziar, I. Pylypiw; North Vermillion: Y. Sereda, F. Bencharyk; Chipman: I. Yuzkiw; Rabbit Hill: A. Pidhirny and I. Ivanyshyn [16].

This was the first representative body of Ukrainians from Alberta composed in turn, of those who represented the various Ukrainian colonies in the province. Chairman of this province-wide representation was H. Kraykiwsky.

Exactly one month after this "viche"-convention in Edmonton a public meeting was held in Vegreville dealing with the organization of "Narodna

---
[15] "Canadian Farmer", 49th Issue, Dec. 15, 1909.
[16] "Canadian Farmer", No. 52, Jan. 5, 1909.

Torhovlia" (National Trading Company). About 500 people took part in this gathering who discussed and debated about their economic problems. The meeting was addressed by Rev. N. Kryzhanowsky, who in his well prepared speech encouraged those present to strive for unity and constructive work. Another speaker who was well received by the audience, Petro Svarich, spoke about the farming matters concerning Ukrainian Canadians. Through his initiative the National Trading Company was formed, with P. Rudyk, a well known Ukrainian businessman of Edmonton, elected as a temporary chairman of the board of directors [17].

A great stride in its work was shown by the Ukrainian unit that grouped itself around the "Narodny Dim" (National Home) in Edmonton. Having close ties with the Greek-Catholic parishes and organizations throughout the province, this cultural centre sent out province-wide calls for national public assemblies. In its program this centre confined its activities to the culural field among its own members and to the events that were taking place in Ukraine. The assemblies were held under the patronage of bishop N. Budka. By the combined efforts of the Catholic National Home, the "Boyan" association and the "M. Shashkevych" association a grand assembly, comprising the whole of Alberta, was held in Edmonton on Nov. 30, 1916. P. Kremar, editor of "Novyny" (News) gave a political speech, dealing with the events of the then raging war. Other speakers were: O. Shyba, M. Korchynsky, S. Holowach, T. Tomashevsky and others. One of the speakers brought up the question of giving aid to the Ukrainian Nation in its struggle for freedom while others touched on the subject of preserving traditions in the new country, loyalty to Canada, religious tolerance and other matters. The head of the National Home, M. Bilynsky, spoke about the need of books for the libraries. The assembly also passed several important resolutions, and expressed its loyalty to the Crown of Great Britain and to Canada. The participants appealed to parents to educate their children along the line of age-old faith and national traditions, the expansion of cultural-educational life and the building of national homes. One resolution in particular was in the form of a protest against Austria's and Germany's aggrandizement plans in regard to the Ukrainian lands (territories) in Europe.

The assemblies were held yearly in Edmonton. This gave a certain prestige to that city and qualified it as a leading Ukrainian centre in Alberta. It is worth-while to mention that similar public gatherings were organized by the so-called "Narodovtsi" also known as "Nationalisty" (Nationalists) that grouped themselves around Petro Mohyla Institute in Saskatoon and its branches in Winnipeg, Canora and Vegreville. To arrange for such a gathering there had to be certain preliminary preparations made among the farmers' colonies. This work was cut out for the "chytalnias".

Among the oldest "chytalnias" in Alberta, outside of Edmonton was "Postup" (Progress) in Lethbridge, founded in 1904. Many coal-miners lived in Lethbridge and next to Edmonton and Calgary it was the third city centre where Ukrainians began to organize themselves. The organizers and founders of the cultural centre here were: T. Tomashevsky, D. Solanych and Y. Bubniak. The "Chytalnia" was first located in the

---

[17] On the board of directors were the following: M. Belegay, P. Kolemanytsky, S. Porayko, E. Yanishevsky, Stepan Sawchuk, A. Svarich, P. Zasiybida and Y. Bartman.

home of S. Svider. The labourers were very generous in those days as proved by the fact that at one meeting alone when a collection was taken no less than $400.00 was donated by the 40 people that were present. This sum of money was sent to Lviv to buy a large number of books from the Taras Shevchenko Society and to subscribe to the following papers: the daily "Dilo" (Deed), "Chlopska Pravda" (Man's Truth), "Volia" (Freedom), "Zoria" (Star), 'Literaturny-Naukovy Visnyk" (Literary-Scientific Herald), and several Polish papers like: "Naprzod" (Forward), "Krytyka" (Critic), "Robotnik" (Worker), "Kurier Polski" (Polish Courier) [18]. In July 1910 a branch of the "Ukrainian Socialist-Democratic Party" (USDP) was organized in Lethbridge, under the name of "Borotba za Voliu" (Fight for Freedom). This branch of USDP soon cooled off in its work and did not revive its full activities until 1914.

Calgary did not stay far behind Lethbridge and in the spring of 1905 the "Chytalnia Postup" (Progress) was organized in that city. Among its first founders were: W. Kalytchuk, H. Maryniak, M. Vorobetz, I. Mariyanych, A. Ormak, F. Pylypchuk and Y. D. Kravetz. The last one named could "speak like a Christian to the people in order to encourage them, the older and younger ones, boys and girls, Orthodox, Bukovinians and Ruthenians'[19]. These active citizens also made efforts to organize the "Kanadsko-Rusky Narodny Soyuz" (Canadian Ruthenian National Association), and the "Ko-operatyvna Kramnytsia" (Co-operative Trading Store). We should also mention about the existence of an unorganized pro tempore "chytalnia" with the St. Mary's Roman-Catholic parish in Calgary where Ukrainian Greek-Catholics would gather occasionally to read books and newspapers. At this point we may also mention that during this time (1904-1908) there was not any organized parish in Calgary until 1909 [20].

In 1907 Y. D. Kravetz organized a branch of the "Canadian Ruthenian National Association" in Bankhead, near Banff. This branch was called Brotherhood of St. Vasyliy with Vasyl Toma as its first head. There was a large coal mine at Bankhead at this time where many Ukrainian labourers were at work. Accidents were an every day occurance and this influenced labourers to insure their lives in order to provide security for their families. Brotherhood benefit associations were the best answers to this problem.

One of the leading cultural centres in Alberta was Vegreville. Cultural-educational work began to expand here when in 1908 the "Chytalnia of Myroslav Sichynsky" was organized. The organizers were: M. P. Berezynsky and P. Svarich and the co-founders were: H. Bilash, W. Voyevidka, H. Dikur, A. Gutyk, A. Lakusta, I. Tomashevsky, P. Tymchuk, A. Svarich and V. Vorobetz, with the last one named as its head. Vegreville gained some fame later as the seat of the so-called "Forinorka" School for Ukrainian Students—with the official name: "English School for Foreigners" and the earlier mentioned Bursa of Taras Shevchenko. In 1914, by the united efforts of Foreign School students and the rest of Ukrainian community the "National Home" was built—one of the first in the province of Alberta.

In 1908 at Vostok (formerly Ruska Svoboda), not far from Vegreville, the "Chytalnia of Ivan Franko" was built. It was founded by Pastor M.

---
[18] "Svoboda", No. 9, 1904.
[19] "Svoboda", No. 19, 1905.
[20] Dr. M. Hladyshewskyj, "Yuvileyna pamiatka...", Edmonton, 1962.

Hutnykevych with H. Vorobetz at the head. Near by another "Chytalnia" in honor of Dr. K. Trylovsky was formed by S. Fodchuk, with 15 members at the start but greatly expanded as time went on. S. Svarich was the head with F. S. Kostashchuk as secretary. In addition to its cultural objectives this "chytalnia" also displayed its party politics character with socialist orientation.

On the initiative of P. Melnyk and V. Romaniuk "Chytalnia Prosvita" in honor of M. Shashkevych was established in Myrnam. At the first meeting eleven members were recorded but this number grew to half a hundred in a short while and within three years the "chytalnia" had a library of 262 volumes and subscriptions to every Ukrainian paper that was then published in Canada and U.S.A. Amateur drama group was also located here as well as the choir, a while later. Through the efforts of this "chytalnia" Ukrainian school was organized in Myrnam, lectures on local themes and current events were given especially about the need of participating in the affairs pertaining to Canada and the giving of aid to the kindred souls in Ukraine.

By 1910 almost every district in Alberta had one of these "chytalnias". This included Mundare, Leduc, Krakiw, Two Hills, New Kiev and others. Every colony considered it not only a necessity but also a matter of honor and prestige to have a cultural-educational organization in its district.

SASKATCHEWAN

When Edmonton was striving to outdistance Vegreville, Lethbridge, Calgary and other points, in order to gain the title of being the Ukrainian cultural centre of Alberta, Saskatoon was able to win this prize in Saskatchewan in a short one or two year period. It had its competitors, with Rosthern being one of them where, in 1911-1913 a Ukrainian paper "Novy Kray" (New Land) was published three times per month. Regina too had its claim to qualify it for first place if only with its own "English School for Foreigners". But the national assemblies that were organized in Saskatoon in 1916, 1917, 1918 and later, about which we already spoke in connection with school and religious questions, proved at every point that Saskatoon, and with it the rest of Saskatchewan, had developed a very successful organisational life. From that time on Saskatoon had qualified itself as the Ukrainian centre of Saskatchewan for many years to come. In the beginning fate had placed the Saskatchewan Ukrainians in somewhat the same position as the children with a cruel stepmother—as may be evidenced from the press complaints of those early days. In 1901 "Svoboda" wrote that Yorkton, in Saskatchewan, had 400 Ukrainian families who had not seen a Ukrainian priest for many years.

In the fall of 1901 Rev. I. Zaklynsky came to Saskatchewan and in the winter of the same year Rev. W. Zholdak arrived. They were the first Ukrainian priests to visit the colonies in Saskatchewan, although we have information that in 1898 Rev. N. Dmytriw had been staying in Danville but he was then working as an immigration official and did not perform any special religious duties. We are also informed that about this time Rev. I. Malarevsky, the first Ukrainian Orthodox priest in Canada, made his visitations in Saskatchewan. The first priests to hold regular services in Saskatchewan were Rev. N. Kryzhanovsky and Rev. A. Strotsky, of the Basilian Fathers order. Only the "Independent Greek Church", that was supported by the Presbyterian Church, had turned a great deal of its attention to Saskatchewan. The first organizer of the church in Saskatchewan was I. Bodrug, the founder of the I.G.C. In 1903 he held his religious mission and later was an organizer of schools for a while. Several other energetic Ukrainian Presbyterian pastors worked in Saskatchewan. These were: Y. Sikorsky of Fish Creek, M. Sikora of Saskatoon, N. Zaytsev, Y. Cherniavsky and others. Y. Cherniavsky may have been the one who founded the first chytalnia "Prosvita" in Saskatchewan [21]. It was named in honor if Ivan Sandulak and located in Skalat, with Cherniavsky being at the head of it and other members at large were: V. Ovchar, P. Kudyba and H. Horobetz. In June of 1907 H. Zaytzev organized the "Kanadiyska Rus" (Canadian Rus) chytalnia in Beaver Hills [22]. This community was much larger than the one at Skalat, and it subscribed to nearly all the Ukrainian papers that were published at that time on the North American continent. Its executive members were: I. Chernetsky, H. Kozakevych and I. Martyniuk. About this same time the "Taras Shevchenko Chytalnia" was organized in Bonne Madone with the following executive members: M. Havryluk, T. Prytula and I. Borsa. Another chytalnia was built, in January 1908, in Horodenka district, post office Raddison, through the efforts of M. Sikora. In Menofield work was carried on by the Presbyterian Pastor U. Bohonko and following him, by Pastor W. Pyndykovsky who established the "Chytalnia Prosvita".

From the above mentioned facts it would show that the first "chytalnias" in Saskatchewan districts were organized and remained so under the spiritual influence of the Independent Greek Church. Its leaders, at that time, had enough guiding influence that enabled them to organize regional council-meetings at which were discussed the then existing actualities of Ukrainian life in Canada. One of the first of these assemblies was held in Fish Creek on June 29, 1907. At this gathering a special attention was paid to farmers' needs, particularly with organizing agricultural cooperatives, grain elevators requirements and the establishment of trading centres. A teachers' fund was also established and the problems of "Ruthenian-English teachers of Saskatchewan" was discussed. The assembly especially underlined the great need of "chytalnias" in the whole province as well as the urgent necessity of farmers' federations, for as it was boldly stated in the resolutions: "It is not in the least befitting, nor is it even possible, for our people to join the English organizations—with us knowing neither their language nor the spirit of the English farmer" [23]. The guiding figures at this meeting were: Y. Sikorsky, A. Hrycak, T. Oleskiw and P. Shvydky.

The resolutions passed at this meeting had a great effect on the further establishment of various "chytalnias". In 1908 the following "chytalnias" were built: Buchanan — "Prosvita"; St. Isidore de Bellevue — "Canadian-Ukrainian Rus"; Quill Lake—"Prosvita"; Starlag—"M. Sichynsky"; Dana —"Prosvita", and in other places as well. Later on, in 1914, a branch of the Ukrainian Socialist Democratic Party (USDP), the "Vilna Dumka" (Free Thought) was organized. In 1908 the young people from St. Julien

---

[21] "Canadian Farmer" Dec. 15, 1906.
[22] "Canadian Farmer", No. 24, 1907.
[23] "Canadian Farmer", No. 24, 1907.

district put on a play, the "Bethlehem Night", in Sokal school. This was the first Ukrainian play to be staged in Saskatchewan.

"Chytalnias" showed great activity in every sphere—cultural-educational, communal and political—as may be witnessed by he following notice that appeared in the Ukrainian Canadian press in 1910 under the title: "Honourable kinsmen of the province of Saskatchewan" [24]. The "Temporary Organizational Committee", composed mostly of the representatives of Saskatchewan's "chytalnias", called into assembly at the Rosthern city hall, on March 15-16, 1910, a great "viche-narada" (public gathering) of the Ukrainians from every part of Saskatchewan. At this meeting eight important questions were dealt with. These were: (1) How the farmers may avoid the exploitation of various farm equipment companies. (2) Best way to expand national culture among the people. (3) What attitude should the Ukrainians hold regarding the different political parties during the provincial and dominion elections. (4) The matter of translation of the provincial government's official documents into Ukrainian language. (5) Affairs concerning national press and organizations. (6) The matter of railroad and post office services in Ukrainian colonies. (7) The need of life, fire and hail insurance security. (8) The possibility of establishing a Ukrainian bank. All these issues were of pressing concern to the Ukrainian pioneers.

In the introduction to this eight-point proposition, which was signed by a committee composed of twenty-seven persons, appeared the following declaration: "Our settlements in this province number some 40,000 souls (people) representing nine percent of the total population of the whole province. In the amount of grain produced we stand in second place and the same may be said about the business turn-over. Politically we are numerous enough that, given a fair chance within any political election organization we could elect at least nine of our Ukrainian members to provincial legislatures and one or two to the dominion parliament. Materially we are powerful enough to carry out amongst us financial operations involving hundreds of millions of dollars". These and similar ambitious ideas were running through the minds of Saskatchewan's Ukrainian pioneers who in their open appeal declared candidly their claim for the betterment of their living conditions and for raising to a higher level their educational and political standard of life. They were able to correctly gauge their integrated strength and their potential political power and these they wished to mine and bring out of their own organizations. This was the first general, public appeal to the Ukrainian masses of Saskatchewan. Three fourths of the initiators of this historical meeting were composed of members of the various cultural-educational centres. It will enrich the pages of this history if we present here the names of those who signed this memorable manifesto. These were: O. Megas, P. Shvydky, H. Platsko, Y. Sikorsky, D. Taciuk, O. Syroyizhka, M. Mamchur, H. Vorobetz, I. Dyrbavka, I. Dehid. P. Bodnar, M. Kotelko, M. Bilyk, I. Holinaty, I. Kvasnytsia, I. Magus, I. Kinar, Y. Hrytsak, S. Zhariy, V. Katerynych, I. Boyko, H. Sagansky, I. Kushniryk, I. Borsa, F. Kindrachuk, A. Hrytsak and A. Turta.

The "Viche" took place as planned and was a great success. After a longer discussion the "Association of Ukrainian Farmers of Canada" was formed. This association stated that its objective was to establish "chy-

---

[24] "Canadian Farmer", No. 5 & 9, 1916.

talnias" and educational centres; to cultivate national culture and national pride in the people; to help build co-operative stores; to give material aid to needy families; to stand on guard for the citizenship rights of Ukrainian settlers; to publish a "national farm paper"; to print and publish educational books and so on. At this "viche" a provincial executive leadership was chosen composed of the following persons: I. Kvasnytsia, H. Machniy, I. Holinaty, D. Barabash, P. Shvydky, Rev. A. Maksymchuk, Rev. A. Vilchynsky, P. Mamchur and A. Syroyishka. Osyp Megas was chosen for the head and Hnat Platsko as the secretary-treasurer. Headquarters were at Rosthern. This was the first representative Ukrainian provincial organization with dominion-wide aspirations.

The Ukrainian "viche" (meeting) in Rosthern, in 1910, was an important step forward for the Ukrainians of Saskatchewan. Although not all the proposed plans, presented by the initiators of this meeting, were realized, nevertheless the proposals served as an integrating force for the pioneers. When we take into consideration the fact that some of the leading men from Winnipeg and Edmonton — such as T. D. Ferley, D. Solanych and H. Kraykivsky, in the role of representatives from Manitoba and Alberta, — were present at this meeting then we can boldly state that the Rosthern "viche" was more in the form of a parliament for the Ukrainians living in the prairie provinces. As we can see the process of national integration of Ukrainian Canadians was gathering in strength. The cultural-educational organizations were beginning to show the first fruits of their labour. According to statistics there were 20 "chytalnias" actively engaged in Saskatchewan at the time of Rosthern meet.

In 1917 near Dana, Saskatchewan, the first Ukrainian women's organization was formed in the farming area. It was called "Trud" (Toil) and its members sent out an appeal to all women in Canada saying: "Ukrainian Women, organize yourselves". Thus, in addition to men, the women too were being organized.

Most likely they followed the good example set by the Ukrainian Women's Educational Association, with the Ukrainian National Home in Winnipeg, that had been organized on November 16, 1916, and comprising pioneers in the women's movement, headed by M. Boyaniwska, M. Zerebko, E. Demchuk, N. Ferley, E. Hykawa, U. Uhryniuk, O. Arsenych, F. Negrych and others. This was the first Ukrainian women's association in Canada to issue a public announcement to the women in general advising them on matters dealing with voting for the legislature. As we know the women in Manitoba received voting rights at that time.

THE FARAWAY WEST

British Columbia occupied a minor position at the beginning of the Ukrainian Canadian history. If the hypothetical theory of some of our historians—seeing that the first Ukrainian settlers landed in Canada on the Pacific coast and in Alaska, afer fleeing from Siberia to escape from social and political repressions of Russian tsars—could have been somehow realized, then the history of Ukrainian Canadians would have taken on a reversed form and British Columbia would have been first in taking the Ukrainian freedom seekers into its fold. The father of this theory must be considered no other than Rev. Ahapy Honcharenko of Kiev, who came to U.S.A. in 1865 and at one time edited the "Alaska Herald" newspaper for the settlers in Alaska. In his writings he often speaks of the "Kozak people" that moved up and down along the Pacific coast. Even his travelling card with "Pacific Ukraine" printed on it has somehow escaped the ravages of time. Whether the "facts" about which Honcharenko spoke are historically correct or are merely the romantic dreams of a fervid patriot it is difficult to confirm.

Among the many Ukrainians who came to Western Canada, to settle on homesteads, some travelled still farther to work in coal mines of British Columbia. But when Yurko Syrotiuk, a member of the "Ukrainian Brotherhood of California", arrived in B.C., in 1904, he already found some Ukrainians that were working on land. In his column, "Colonization of British Columbia" he writes:

"I have been living two years in B.C. There is one man here who came from Winnipeg 12 years ago and bought 10 acres of land, cleared it of brush and cultivated most of it. Last year he made $2,000.00 from the sale of his orchard products... Eight to ten years ago this was a wild jungle. ... British Columbia is an ideal place for organizational work as the people who own small pieces of land do not live very far apart and getting together is much easier than on large farms. Almost half of the Ukrainian people living in British Columbia come from Manitoba" [25].

These observations, by Yurko Syrotiuk, are most interesting. He was a land agent for many years and knew the territory well and so his comments should be accepted as being authentic. His brother, Wasyl, who lived in Vancouver and often sent his articles to "Svoboda", mentions that there were some Ukrainians living around Vancouver, though none in the city itself but that there were some Russians living in that city. Whether these were actually Russians or perhaps more likely Ukrainians, from the eastern parts of Ukraine, is hard to say. Nevertheless the fact remains that most of the Ukrainian settlers in B.C. worked in coal mines and lumber camps. Who was the first to work, and where, in B.C., is almost impossible to verify as we have not here the benefit of such given information as that appearing in "Land Titles Office" in which names, places and dates of homestead settlements are clearly shown. The only possibility of verification, of the early history of Ukrainian settlers in B.C. that is at our disposal, are the memoirs of the labourers themselves and the write-ups in the temporary press about the cultural-educational work of these same labourers. Ivan Nimchuk, in his memoirs [26] recalls the year of 1898 when he and about 30 other Ukrainian labourers worked in the mines of British Columbia. To these could also be added the reminiscences of Vasyl and Ivan Romaniuk of Myrnam.

When it comes to the cultural-educational work of the Ukrainian labourers in B.C. the newspaper year books attest to the fact that it began quite early. It could be even stated that the labouring class of B. C. kept in step with their fellow-homesteaders of the three western prairie provinces. Our earliest information about this work comes from Fernie, B.C. We are informed that Rev. A. Strocky made his visitation to this community from 17 to 23rd of March, 1904, being one of the first Basilian priests to visit

---
[25] "Svoboda", No. 19, 1906.
[26] "Ukrainian News", Edmonton, 1966.

Fernie. He was also the first Ukrainian priest to make his visitations among Ukrainians throughout British Columbia. With his help the labourers of Fernie formed the initiative committee whose task it was to organize a brotherhood organization which in turn was to join as a member of the "'Ukrainian National Association" [27]). The head of this initiative committee was S. Dragan, with Petro Cherevaniak as treasurer and Pavlo Onyshchuk its secretary. The last one named sent a news item to the newspaper in which, among other things, he said: "From the 17 to 23 of this month (March, 1904, MHM) Rev. A. Strocky, the missionary priest from Beaver Lake, Alberta, was making his visitation call to our community. Many people came to confession. Taking advantage of his short stay here a meeting was called, on the 23rd, concerning the establishment of a branch of the brotherhood and joining it with the "Ukrainian National Association", as well as discussing the possibility of building a Greek-Catholic Church in Fernie... The difficulty lies in the fact that there are only a few of us Galician Ukrainians here while the bulk of the Hungarian Ukrainians belong to foreign, Slavic organizations. The church's need here is of the vital concern as the number of us Galician Ukrainians is not so small, by any means, and Fernie could become the Ukrainian centre of Southern British Columbia" [28]).

P. Onyschuk's article clearly shows that the initiative for organizing a brotherhood association in British Columbia was far ahead of any other branch of the Ukrainian National Association on Canada's territory. The Fernie initial start beats by a year and a half the "Ukrainian Mutual Benefit Association of St. Nicholas" which is the oldest Ukrainian benefit (insurance) association in Canada. The British Columbia branch was probably the first one in Canada to join the now "Ukrainian (formerly Ruthenian) National Association Corp. of U.S.A." As early as 1907 the "Chytalnia of St. Vladimir and Olga" was organized in Fernie [29]). It was founded by Y. Kravetz who had also founded about the same time, a branch of the Canadian Ukrainian National Association (Ukrainian Mutual Benefit Association of St. Nicholas) [30]) whch had 36 members in its first year of operation. From newspaper articles we can see that Y. Kravetz was an excellent organizer, who in addition to the above mentioned activities also helped to organize labourers in Hosmer, Fernie and Frank, as is evidenced from further newspaper items.

The first items about the attempts of Ukrainian labouring class towards organizational efforts in Vancouver bear the date of 1906. On the 9th of September of that year the "Ukrainian Club" was organized, being located in room 17, at 472 Alexandria Street, with H. Begar at the head and Myroslav Stechishin as its secretary. The secretary sent his report to "Svoboda" in which he stated that the Ukrainians of Vancouver may not be able to meet in their own "Ukrainian Club" to read books, newspapers and to carry on friendly discussions. The club subscribed to a long line of Ukrainian periodicals, including such noted journals as the "Literary-Scientific Herald", the "Ukrainian Herald" and others. Of the English language

---

[27]) "Svoboda", No. 14, 1904.
[28]) "Svoboda", April 14, 1904.
[29]) "Svoboda", No. 19, May 9, 1907.
[30]) The "Canadian Ukrainian National Association" was organized in 1905, with headquarters in Winnipeg.

press the club subscribed to the "Western Clarion" and the Vancouver daily "The World" [31]). Regular official club discussions were held on the first Sunday of the month [32]). The Ukrainian Club of Vancouver was an unusually active institution which worked diligently on behalf of its own members as well as the good of Ukrainian national cause. Although its activities were mostly under the aspect of socialistic ideas still its members were able to appreciate the value of other political trends, as may be evidenced by the fact that when funds were being collected for national-political objectives in the old country it was specified that "the sum was to be divided into three equal parts for the benefit of the three political parties in Galicia", as the whole three of them have their worth although each one travels a different road" [33]). A year later the "Borot'ba" (Struggle) Association was formed, whose members were mostly the same people that belong to the Ukrainian Club. These were: Myroslav and Mykhaylo Stechishin, P. Tzymbal, Mykola and Wasyl Kamenetsky, Yurko and Wasyl Syrotiuk, H. Slipchenko, I. Dalavrak and others. This group was very active. It arranged for meetings and discussions on political and cultural-educational themes. The ornament of this organization was its choir, composed mostly of "Pokutian" (Pokutia: district of Galicia) from the village of Balyntsi with I. Dalavrak as the conductor. It also had a theatrical group under direction of I. Karalash.

In June of 1907 a socialist "Volia" (Liberty) association was formed in Nanaimo, B.C., with Petro Tsymbal at the head, M. Stechishin as secretary and Mykola Kamenetsky as cashier. In its first year of existence it had 27 members and a 70 book library, donated by the members. Later more books were brought from Lviv [34]).

A small organization existed in Michelle, B.C. In June 1908 the "Brotherhood Benefit" association and a branch of Ukrainian National Association were formed [35]). Hosmer had its "Ukrainian Educational-Labour Association of M. Sichynsky". This last mentioned organization was the most active of all. A large number of labourers were concentrated here who took a lively interest in community affairs and worked in unison. Illa Kyriak, well known Ukrainian novelist in Canada, was, for a while, a secretary of this active group and writes, in his biography, about his stay in Hosmer as being his unique "school of life". Hosmer was the labourers' centre between Fernie and Cranbrook.

Undoubtedly there were other organizations in existence elsewhere but all those that we have mentioned so far point to this one salient fact that the Ukrainian labourer knew the value of organized strength and was seeking his own identity in the midst of the alien miners' world. At the same time he took good care to utilize the spare time for his own education and cultural development. Both of these movements draw our attention to the above average intelligence of the people and their sense of responsibility on their own behalf as well as on behalf of their national identity and the over-all Canadian entity.

---

[31]) "Svoboda", No. 33, Sept. 20, 1906.
[32]) "Svoboda", No. 19, May 9, 1907.
[33]) "Svoboda", No. 19, 1906.
[34]) Calendar Almanac of Ruthenian (Ukrainian) National Association 1908, Moant Carmel (USA), p. 153.
[35]) "Svoboda", No. 28, 1908.

As an expression of the consummation of the organizational strength of the Ukrainian labourers in B.C. the play "Vechernytsi" (Evening Revelry) honoring the poet Taras Shevchenko, was presented on Feb. 28, 1909, by the combined efforts of all the Ukrainians living in that part of B.C. Although the "Ukrainian Educational-Labour Association" of Hosmer initiated this celebration, others had come from Hosmer, Fernie, Michelle, Coleman and Lily to pay their homage to the memory of the great Ukrainian poet. Toma Tomashevsky of Edmonton made his introductory remarks at this concert, and the performers were mosly Hosmer and Fernie citizens. The committee in charge of the concert truthfully remarked that this was the first time, on the B.C. territory, that such an imposing celebration was being held in honour of the unforgettable poet [3]).

EASTERN CANADA

When the life of Ukrainians, in Western Canada, was seething with activities, where the parishes had been well established and bilingual schools were opened and cultural-educational organizations were flourishing in profusion—in Eastern Canada only here and there were to be noticed the embryonic sprouts of Ukrainian culture and community identity. These communities differed basically from the western ones. Where in the west they had been almost exclusively of the farming nature, with the probable exception of British Columbia, those in the east were, with but a very minute exception, exclusively of the labouring variety. These were formed mostly in larger cities and business centres, such as Montreal, Ottawa, Toronto, Fort William and others.

One of the outstanding Ukrainians of Eastern Canada, during the pioneer era, W. Anastazievsky, in his newspaper articles, stated very aptly that eastern Canada was merely a stopping place—a temporary way-station—for the Ukrainians who only stayed here long enough to earn sufficient money to take them "farther into Canada", to settle firmly on the farms. There were some of them who, having made enough money, would go back to Ukraine, gather up their family and return again to Western Canada, to settle on the farms—to be their own "hospodar" (landlord). The soil was always like a magnet to the land-loving Ukrainian villager.

But there were many others who would become accustomed to their work in cities or coal mines. Those working in the cities were toiling mostly at such heavy occupations as digging ditches, building roads, doing hard labor in mills, foundries, and meat-packing houses. The above mentioned W. Anastazievsky wrote that "There is not any problem of getting a job here as the "bosses" are very pleased with the way our people work" [37]). It would appear that Ukrainians were fond of work and the work was fond of them. And so they stayed at their work, from year to year, while allied closely with their manual labour there grew in time the set pattern of their national and community life.

QUEBEC — MONTREAL

As shown by the yearly chronicles, Ukrainian communities in Montreal area began to show their organizational activities as early as the year 1903

---
[36]) "Canadian Farmer", No. 6, Feb. 19, 1909.
[37]) "Canadian Farmer", No. 33, 1906.

PIONEER ERA — ILLUSTRATIONS   181

TEACHER PIONEERS AND ORGANIZERS
IN UKRAINIAN SETTLEMENTS IN CANADA

Ivan Kotsan, (Kocan),
The first chairman of the "Ukrainian
Teachers' Association"

W. A. Chumer

T. J. Marciniw

Ivan Rudachek

A committee of Ukrainian leaders and teachers in Edmonton who promoted Ukrainian language in public schools in Alberta

Participants in the first Ukrainian Teachers' Convention, Winnipeg, 1907

PIONEER ERA — ILLUSTRATIONS

The first students of the Ukrainian Teachers' College, named the Ruthenian Training School, Winnipeg, 1905

The first Ukrainian Teachers' Convention in Alberta, Edmonton, 1917.

The first Ukrainian Teachers' Convention in Saskatchewan, Rosthern, 1914

PIONEER ERA — ILLUSTRATIONS 185

Above: Students of bilingual (French-Ukrainian) school with their teacher
M. Chypchar, Montreal, 1913
Below: Students of bilingual school (French-Ukrainian) with Rev. A. Redkevych
and teacher S. Kovbel, St. Charles, Montreal, 1913-1914

Ukrainian Teachers' Football Team of which John Diefenbaker was a member, Wakaw, Sask., 1919

The first football club of Ukrainian students of the Normal School in Brandon, 1910. This club was the first of its kind in Canada

PIONEER ERA — ILLUSTRATIONS

The first Ukrainian students of the University of Manitoba, 1912

The Ukrainian class of the School for Foreigners, Vegreville, Alta., 1913-1914

Students of the Apostolic School with Rev. A. Sabourin in Sifton, 1914

A. V. Kotsko Students Organization, Edmonton, 1917

PIONEER ERA — ILLUSTRATIONS

Brandon Seminary students (known as "Ruthenian Training School"), 1913

Participants of the first educational courses at Winnipeg under the direction of poet Petro Karmansky, 1913

Above: Ruthenian (Ukrainian) English Reader for beginners
Below: Ruthenian (Ukrainian) English Reader—advanced

Bilingual texts for the students of Ukrainian extraction, published under the authority of Manitoba government, 1914

PIONEER ERA — ILLUSTRATIONS

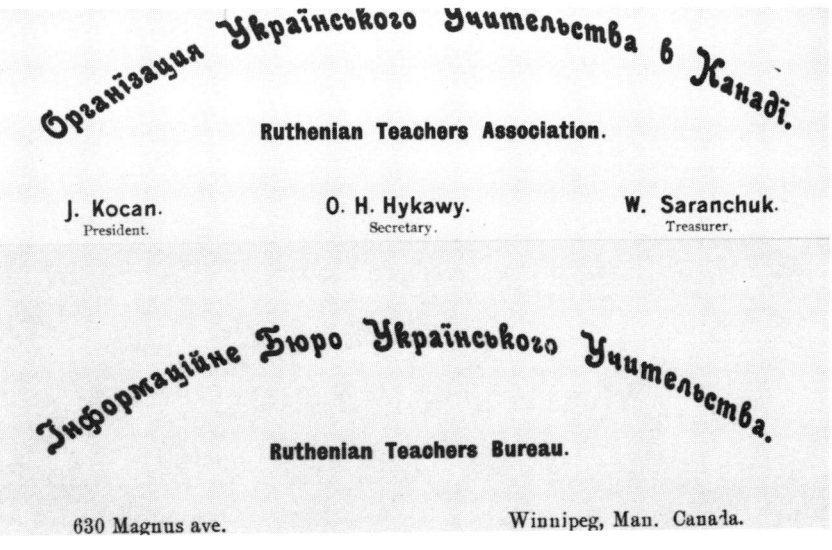

Third class diploma—Ruthenian Training School

Letterheads of the Ruthenian (Ukrainian) Teachers Association and Ruthenian (Ukrainian) Teachers Bureau, Winnipeg, 1907

Residence and College of Taras Shevchenko, Edmonton, 1912

The first headquarters of "Ukrainian Bursa" of Petro Mohyla in Saskatoon, later renamed the Petro Mohyla Ukrainian Institute

PIONEER ERA — ILLUSTRATIONS 193

Charter membership form of the Ukrainian Greek Catholic Bursa of
Metropolitan Shepticky, St. Boniface, Man., 1918

Delegates of the II Congress of the Ukrainian National Rada, photographed
in front of Shepticky Bursa, 1920

Boyan Association, Winnipeg, 1912

Members of Mariya Zankovecka Association, Winnipeg, 1913

PIONEER ERA — ILLUSTRATIONS 195

Ivan Kotlarevsky Dramatic Society, Winnipeg, 1912

Association "Self-Help" of the village Lysovci Zalishchyky Rayon, Winnipeg, 1914

Above: Members of Chytalnia (Reading Association) of M. Drahomaniv, Montreal, 1910
Below: "Dzvin" (Bell), Montreal Brass Band, 1919

PIONEER ERA — ILLUSTRATIONS

Above: Members of Chytalnia "Prosvita" of Markian Shashkevych, Myrnam, Alta., 1909
Below: Actors of the Drama Group of Vegreville after staging "Natalka Poltavka" in Edmonton, 1909

Above: Consecration of the Ukrainian National Home with Bishop Budka, Edmonton, 1917
Below: Drama group in Vegreville, Alta., staging "Oy ne khody Hryciu", 1917

PIONEER ERA — ILLUSTRATIONS

Above: The Board of "Prosvita" in Montreal with M. Poremsky in the centre, 1916
Below: Members of Chytalnia of Taras Shevchenko on the "suburb of Montreal", Point St. Charles

Members of "Chytalnia" and Ukrainian Catholic Parish, Ukraina, Man., 1910

Members of the Ukrainian National Home, Winnipeg, 1914

Ukrainian National Home of Taras Shevchenko in West Fort William, 1914

PIONEER ERA — ILLUSTRATIONS 201

Members of Vegreville Dramatic Society visiting Mundare, Alta., 1916

Brotherhood of St. John the Baptist, Brantford, 1914

Students Drama Group of Shepticky Bursa in costumes for "Julius Caesar", St. Boniface, 1916

Boyan Choir under the direction of T. Panchyshyn, Edmonton, 1911-1914

Members of "Chytalnia Prosvity", Melville, Sask., 1914

PIONEER ERA — ILLUSTRATIONS 203

Above: Taras Shevchenko Institute, Vegreville, Alta., 1914
Below: Bishop Budka visiting parish in Borschiw, Alta., 1916

Above: Study group ("Samo-obrazovannia"), Edmonton, 1917
Below: "School of higher learning" under the direction of P. Krat, affiliated with U.S.D. Party, Toronto, 1919

PIONEER ERA — ILLUSTRATIONS   205

Above: Members of Markian Shashkevych Chytalnia, Toronto, 1916
Below: The first Ukrainian brass band "Bandurist" in Winnipeg

Above: Delegates to the Ukrainian Socialist Congress, Edmonton, 1910

Foremost Socialist Quintet of "The Executive of Seven", 1911

PIONEER ERA — ILLUSTRATIONS

Ukrainian National Home, Winnipeg, acquired 1916

Delegates of the Second Congress of U.S.D. Party and members of Winnipeg Branch of U.S.D.P., Winnipeg, 1917

Ukrainian Labour Temple, Winnipeg, erected 1918

The first Ukrainian newspaper on the American continent "America", Shenandoah, U.S.A., 1886

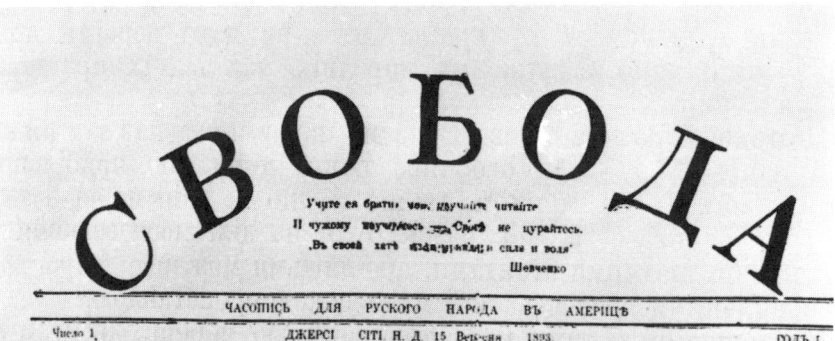

"Svoboda" (Freedom), Jersey City, U.S.A., 1893

when there was already in existence the "Association in Care of Settlers" which must be regarded as the first Ukrainian organization in Eastern Canada. This was a cultural centre whose duty, among other things, was to look after the needs of labourers arriving in Montreal, in particular, and take care of the new settlers in general. First meeting of this organization took place September 17, 1903, with Volodymyr Anastazievsky as its head. Among the founders of this organization we see such names as: Yakiw Sysak, S. Horak, S. Kostyrsky, O. Didych, J. Sozansky, S. Drohobytsky, N. Kalyniuk, I. Stelmach, Y. Vypruk and others. The oldest pioneers, in this Montreal organization, in terms of residence, were brothers Ivan and Stepan Tuchtie who came to this city before 1900.

From the start of its work the association could show four main aspects of its activities: helping their own members, acquiring better education, assisting the new settlers and sending aid to their families in Ukraine. From these four main activities followed even the extension of the association's name with "Aid to the Old Counry" being added to it and now its full name was: "Association in Care of Settlers and Aid to the Old Country". An amateur group of young people was organized in time, connected with this association, being the first such in eastern Canada. The association was far ahead of others of this kind in the national-political sphere, as may be seen from the ties it had with progressive elements and movements in the old homeland. It sent aid to the Ukrainian Revolutionary party and under the influence of this movement it had started to use the newly emerging name of "Ukrainian" as early as 1907, re-naming itself as "Association of Ukrainians". Its hall was on 481 Wellington Street.

In 1906 the "Youth Association", affiliated with "Association of Ukrainians" presented its stage-play "Who is with God, the God will be with him", and later another play, a comedy called "Mr. Secretary". Steps were taken to build a "National Home". At the height of these activities a cultural centre called "Drahomaniv Society" was organized, which within its own sphere provided strong influence on the ideal plane. The initiators and founders of this active national center were: J. Sozansky, I. Zabroda, P. Makohon, P. Olovetz, S. Kostyrsky, K. Krasutsky, V. Hobovych and others. Women were also members of this association, with Claudia Vypruk as secretary.

One of the oldest Ukrainian organizations in Montreal was the "Self-Help", formed on February 3rd, 1907, which had an exclusively brotherhood-benefit character. Pioneers of this organization were: Y. Vypruk, W. Hudyma, M. Spodarek-Petrovych, S. Kostyrsky, S. Drohobytsky, I. Vypruk, M. Krayevsky, W. Suryn, H. Moch, M. Bochkovsky and others. The association was fast growing and the following year it already had over a hundred members, holding its meetings in Richmond Hall at 280 Richmond Street. In that year the Ukrainian population of Montreal numbered about 3,000 families. This was a large community. Its greatest shortcoming was the lack of church and clergy which led some Ukrainians to change over to the Latin rite. "Self Help Association" and "Ukrainian Association" were much alarmed by this move and in an open letter addressed to Ukrainian Canadian priests, they stressed the urgency of giving spiritual care and looking after this community in Monrteal [38].

The first priest to answer this plea was Rev. N. Kryzhanowsky, OSBM.,

---

[38] "Canadian Farmer", No. 41, 1907.

who arrived from western Canada and conducted holy liturgy in the church of Redemptorist Fathers on MacDonald Street. This was a great historical event in the life of Ukrainians in Montreal. In its own way and time this was a veritable national manifestation which was repeated again the following year when Rev. N. Kryzhanowsky made his second visit to Montreal and celebrated High Mass at the church of St. Eusebius. To the more characteristic moments in the life of Montreal community belong its efforts to organize national schools, and courses for the teaching of reading and writing in Ukrainian and acquisition of English. These courses were the urgent need of the time. Settlers exerted themselves greatly so that they could in this land of freedom prepare themselves to be worthy of becoming citizens of this new country, in every meaning of this context.

A separate page, in the history of Ukrainians in Montreal, could be considered the organizing of the first parish in this city. Solid foundation for this community work was laid in 1910, when during Eucharistic Congress Metropolitan Shepticky of Lviv and Bishop Soter Ortynsky of U.S.A. were visiting in Montreal. The first church committee, formed July 16, 1911, was comprised of: I. Ziolkowsky, M. Nahirny, I. Stelmach, T. Zyla, T. Humenny, Hr. Zelenetsky, D. Parchin, I. Telenko, W. Hoshko, P. Kunytsky, H. Sydorenko and S. Pavlyshyn. In the beginning the congregation availed itself of the church of the Franciscan Fathers on Placier Street which was served by the French and Belgian priests—Rev. A. Delaere, Rev. M. Decamp and Rev. A. Sabourin. The first steady Ukrainian parish priest was Rev. Karlo Yermiy, followed by Rev. T. Dvulit who took in charge the congregation in the suburb of St. Charles. Their successors were: Dr. A. Redkevych and Dr. I. Perepylycia. The last one mentioned founded the cultural centre "Prosvita of Taras Shevchenko", on December 13, 1913—one of the oldest Ukrainian organizations in Montreal and continuing its cultural activities to this day. In its earlier days it was located in the home of I. Hanovsky and later moved to 594 St. Patrick's Street. Ivan Telenko was its first head. Through its efforts the operetta, "Natalka Poltavka", by Ivan Kotlarevsky, was the first presented in eastern Canada.

During pioneer days Montreal had two other associations: the "Prosvita Centre of Markian Shashkevych, organized by Rev. A. Redkevych in the centre of the city and the "Ivan Franko Prosvita Centre", in Frontenac district of Montreal. Both organizations were very active in the beginning but later went into decline and ceased to exist. Much activity was shown by the choral group, the "Boyan", that was organized in October 1914. Its leading members were: W. Kobitovych, W. Maydansky, M. Chypchar, E. Yakubovych, M. Tkachuk, M. Yuriychuk, S. Zuzenkiv, P. Kovalyshyn and W. Shukh.

Through the efforts of Rev. A. Redkevych a church was being built on Iberville Street and on the initiative of his predecessor, Rev. T. Dvulit, courses in Ukrainian language were inaugurated in the public schools at the so-called Point where there was a large concentration of the Ukrainian labouring class in the city of Montreal. Rev. A. Redkevych, with assiduous care, looked after this school project.

Still another dynamic organization existed in Montreal in those days of old, which was more of a political than educational character. This was an offshoot of USDP and headed by I. Hnyda, who was an inimitable, regional cultural organizer of labour elements in the province of Quebec and

Ontario. And finally, near the bottom of the list, was the Ukrainian Workers' Club organized in 1909 at Montreal, through the initiative efforts of A. Naydevych, N. Mech, M. Nedilsky and M. Bechak.

A special mention must be made about the city of Lachine, Quebec, where the Ukrainians began their cultural activities in 1905. When their frame church burned down in 1911 they built one of brick, dedicated to St. John of Suchava, but later when religious animosities flared up the parish was split into Catholic and Orthodox groups.

During the First World War, when Ukrainian Canadians as the former citizens of Austria were feeling the stress of living under political pressure coming from the government side of Canada, their various organizations and cultural centres got together and formed the "Committee of Ukrainians of Eastern Canada" in the name of which a delegation, composed of Rev. Dr. A. Redkevych, S. Kostyrsky, Pastor I. Bodrug and A. Pysarsky was sent to Ottawa. Subsequently these same organizations formed the Ukrainian National League, which collaborated very closely with the Ukrainian Canadian Citizenship Committee, as well as with the Ukrainian Red Cross, throughout the 1920-ies.

ONTARIO

The second Ukrainian colony to be formed in eastern Canada was the one organized in Fort William. Here was a large concentration of labouring forces, at work on port and shipping industry, with Ukrainian labourers doing their share. Many of them toiled in the huge grain elevators. Working conditions could not have been very congenial, especially for the foreigners, when we read the following press report: "Fifty men were working in the elevators, including ten "Slovaks" and five "Rusyns" (Ukrainians). In order to receive a better treatment they all wanted to strike. When the dispute was over all the foreigners were fired and only the Anglo-Saxons remained at work [39].

In "Svoboda" we also read the following: "Some blood was spilled in this struggle for their daily bread... On the first of October of this year (1906—M.H.M.) C.P.R. labourers went on strike in the elevators and on shiploading docks in Fort William and likewise the C.N.R. workers in Port Arthur. Huge demonstrations were put on by Italians and Greeks, with Rusyny (Ukrainians) and later on the Slovaks, solidly supporting the first group. Fort William lists 700 labourers and Port Arthur 400. The companies attempted to smash the strike, by bringing in outside workers comprised of illiterate Ruthenians and Englishmen [40].

Those very same labourers who strove so valiantly for their human rights were the ones who established the first cultural centre in Fort William. Mykola Babyn, one of those diligent toilers, wrote in the press about the gathering of the labourers before Christmas of 1905 and organizing Ruthenian cultural centre and a sick benefit association. They also voiced their hope to form a "Brotherhood Association" (Ruthenian National Association —M.H.M.). During this pre-Christmas meet a committee was picked composed of: Semko Sas, A. Boyko, I. Ostap, T. Lysowych, M. Sviy, M. Brygadyr, M. Ladunetz and I. Kustiak. In a prepared statement the follow-

---

[39] "Svoboda", No. 35, 1906.
[40] "Svoboda", No. 44, 1906.

ing principles were enunciated: "None of those who had been "chruni" (unprincipled, self-seeking nit wits—M.H.M.) or betrayers of the "Ruthenian Party" could belong to it. Only Ruthenians, of both sexes, who held radical convictions could be members of this party. The aim of the party was—the future betterment of the Ruthenian (Ukrainian) people, to support the cultural centre, library, sick benefit fund, to establish brotherhoods and credit unions, and to present amateur plays and hold socials" [41]. As we can see the first cultural centre in Fort William assumed some very biased principles and was largely politically oriented and had less of the educational proclivities, generally speaking. In time it re-organized itself and took on a more positive stand to show its over-all Ukrainian character. Such is the story of the Fort William Prosvita which is still in existence today.

An early cultural-educational organization in Port Arthur was the "Prosvita Association", formed on the initiative of Ivan Ukrainetz, who was one of the first Ukrainian businessmen in this city. On the 10th of April, 1909, the first meeting of the Prosvita Association was held in the home of Ivan Ukrainetz at which a committee of the following persons was selected: I. Ukrainetz, I. Horbovy, S. Pochynok, W. Koziy, I. Slobodian, I. Polansky, W. Shevchuk, H. Horbovy and S. Bluta. At this centre an amateur group was formed and the first productions in its repertoire were a comedy, "Corporal Tymko", and a Christmas play, the "Bethlehem Night". The centre was first located in the home of I. Ukrainetz and later moved to the home of I. Horbovy and in 1918 it was finally moved to the "National Home". About the same time the Association of Ivan Franko was organized and "National School" was established and located in the National Home. In the course of time, when political differences came to the fore, the leftist elements in the Ivan Franko Association took possession of the National Home and the nationally oriented Ukrainians renewed the activities of the cultural centre and built their own hall.

The normalized church-life, in Fort William, appeared very late on the scene, and it was not until 1909 that a piece of land was acquired on Pacific Street, for the building of the church. The cornerstone was laid and blessed churchground by Metropolitan Shepticky but the church itself was built later in a new place on McIntosh Street. Prior to Rev. T. Dvulit's visit— who established conditions for a steady parish—Fort William was served by Basilian Fathers from Winnipeg. The resident parish priests in Fort William, in the course of time were: E. Andruchovych, Dr. K. Yermiy, M. Ircha, M. Kinash and M. Shumsky. The Church of Assumption parish in Fort William was organized in 1916.

The cultural-educational awakening of the Ukrainians living in Ottawa arrived quite early in the pioneer era when, on the 12th of July, 1908, the "Prosvita Cultural Centre" was founded. "Only a few members have joined so far" wrote a correspondent of that period, "but hopes are held that our founding brethren will make special efforts that the centre may expand its field of activities and then more people will join". Unfortunately this correspodent did not give his name (only his initials I.P.) nor the names of founders. Neither did he state where the centre was located. But reading further in this same report we come to an interesting passage where he says: "I take this opportunity to call on you, my Ukrainian brethren,

---

[41] "Svoboda", No. 3, 1905.

who are conscious of your national obligations, that you should strive diligently wherever possible to establish cultural centres with mutual understanding as to the rules and statutues so that Prosvita would become one strong national organization to bring the much desired success". We gladly record this echoing of the distant past for it is the oldest voice we have that tells us about the first organizational efforts in the life of Ukrainians in the capital city of Canada [42]).

On the 25th of February, 1912 another Ukrainian Association was organized in Ottawa, called the "New Life", a branch of the USDP. Its founders were: W. Holowacky, M. Chopovyk, P. Yakubovsky, F. Morak, W. Prestay, Y. Chopovyk, I. Sahaydak, and G. Bobinsky. This association was re-organized in 1913, with the aid of I. Hnyda of Montreal, and it had its amateur group and choir under the direction of F. Morak. In the "New Life" hall the convention of the USDP branches of Eastern Canada was held.

The socio-religious life of the Ukrainians in Ottawa was finally formalized in 1911 in the home of Petro Diak. The elected church committee went to work at once and the Association of St. Cyril and Methodius was organized. The first parish priest in Ottawa was Rev. Y. Fylyma who came to the capital in 1914 and celebrated the first High Mass in the Roman Catholic Church on Murray St. When his church was destroyed by fire the Ukrainians transferred to St. Anthony's and still later to the Franciscan Fathers' church on Wellington St. In 1916 Rev. M. Kuzmiak took charge of the parish and during his stay bought several lots at Balsam and Rochester streets where in 1918-1919 the Church of the Nativity was built—the first Ukrainian church in Ottawa. In 1909 Rev. W. Gigeychuk arrived in Ottawa where he served as parish priest for nineteen years. Prior to 1914, the Redemptorist Fathers, Rev. A. Delaere and Rev. M. De Camp, carried on their religious work here.

In the pioneer era Ukrainian settlers in Toronto had to undergo a long struggle before they could become a strong and single monolith.

"Nine years ago there were no more than 20 Ruthenian (Ukrainian) families living in Toronto and no more than 80 Ruthenians in all" [43]) wrote Rev. Boyarchuk in 1915. Only once a year, at Easter time would a Ukrainian priest pay a visit here, from U.S.A. In 1907 Ukrainians of Toronto asked Bishop S. Ortynsky of U.S.A. to provide them with regular services of the clergy. Shortly after Rev. I. Slyvynsky came to Toronto who, due to the inimical attitude of the Roman Catholics, only stayed here for half a year and returned to U.S.A. In response to the many requests, appearing in the press, Rev. Ivan Zaklynsky, who at the time was in Western Canada, answered to this clarion call. As soon as he arrived he went to work to strengthen further the organized community and even persuaded the little parish of St. Josaphat to buy a piece of land on which to build their own chapel. It was at this crucial point that some differences arose and the discontented priest departed for the west. In 1910 Rev. K. Yermiy came to Toronto, remaining here for a year but once again there was a conflict between the parish and Roman Catholic hierarchy, on the church ritual level, and so Rev. Yermiy left Toronto. After this the parish was looked afer by Rev. L. Sembratovych, of Buffalo, U.S.A., who was instrumental

---
[42]) "Canadian Farmer", No. 30, Aug. 7, 1908.
[43]) Canadian Ruthenian Almanac, 1916, page 111.

in buying a piece of land on Franklin Street where a church was built in 1910. This church of St. Josaphat was not only the first brick-built church in Toronto but in the whole of Canada as well. Rev. Y. Boyarchuk was in charge of its construction and he saw to it that it should have solid foundation—to carry the heavy weight of his parish activities. He organized "Prosvita" centre, amateur drama group, courses in Ukrainian language, literature and choral singing, the "Brotherhood of St. John the Bapist" and "Fraternal Benefit Association" [44]). During its first two years of existence the amateur drama group presented fourteen plays. Pioneers of this parish and drama league were: H. Sukota, I. Kupnytsky, I. Dydiuk, D. Panovyk, K. Troyan, I. Zvarich, S. Prychoda (Toronto's first Ukrainian choir director), S. Hilius, P. Woloshynsky, M. Oliynyk, T. Yurechkiv, M. Panovyk, M. Kondrat, M. Zroyko, N. Panovyk, A. Kryva, Z. Wolodyshynska, M. Vovk, V. Siomra, I. Soyka, O. Shafranska, A. Babiy, H. Danyluk. Later on the Brotherhood of St. Michael the Archangel and the Sisterhood of Virgin Mary were formed. St. Josaphat parish was the only Ukrainian parish in Toronto during the pioneer era.

Hamilton belongs to the newer ranks in regard to Ukrainian cultural centres in Canada. At the beginning, starting from 1911, Ukrainians of this city were members of the Polish Roman Catholic parish. Not until 1916 did they organize their own parochial committee headed by S. Stoykevych, and Rev. Y. Boyarchuk took over, under his personal care, the guiding of the first steps, leading to the progressive growth of this new born community. Once the building plans were announced the Polish parish of the Holy Ghost Church refused to allow any further use of their premises. The only move left was to arrange for co-habitation with the Italian community and the use of their church of St. Anthony. The initiative act, once begun, was not abandoned nor even slackened and so in 1918, Christmas day, the first High Mass was celebrated in their own church. The first priests who served this parish were: Y. Fylyma, M. Shumsky and A. Sarmatiuk. Under their vigilant care the "M. Shashkevych Cultural Centre" was established. Even prior to the building of the above centre, an earlier one, the "Prosvita of Taras Shevchenko" was organized by the socialists in 1910. On October 22, 1915, a labour organization, actually a branch of the Ukrainian Socialist-Democratic Party (USDP), was formed in Hamilton. This work was first begun by I. Stefanicky and later continued by U. Demidiuk, W. Maydansky, P. Kovalyshyn, M. Kaminsky and others. In 1916 this branch had 125 members. In addition to party-political work among the labouring class this organization was also engaged in cultural-educational activities, had a small amateur drama group and even its own choir under direction of I. Kvasniak.

An event that deserves a special mention was the first visit of Bishop Budka to Hamilton in 1916. A contemporary chronicler describes this occasion in the following article:

"During the Whitsunday holidays the then Bishop of Canada Nykyta Budka paid his visit to the pioneers of Hamilton and celebrated High Mass in the Polish St. Stanislaw's Church. Wih his inspiring sermon he strengthened the faith of the citizens and uplifted them spiritually. After dinner a meeting was held in the Polish hall concerning the building of a church during which time His Excellency donated $500 towards this purpose. From

---

[44]) In 1926 the name was changed to: The League—"Soyuz Ukrainskych Bratstv".

the previously collected fund the building committee was able to buy a piece of land on Gray Street, from the Latin Church authorities for the sum of $3,800. The construction of the building was started in the spring of 1917 and as the idea had been originated on the Holy Ghost day it was called the Holy Ghost Church. The blessing of the cornerstone was performed by Bishop N. Budka in October, 1917. The first service was held on Christmas day in 1918. After ten years of wandering from one church to another the Ukrainians had finally arrived at their own house of God" [46].

Oshawa is a close neighbor of Toronto. Organizational life and cultural work began with the existence of the parish of St. George the Martyr that had been established in 1912. Those in charge were: I. Hryciw, P. Sobol, P. Markiv, S. Shyan, K. Baran and I. Chovhaniuk. The parish was served by Rev. Y. Boyarchuk and during his stay here, 1914-1916, a church was built. Later on Rev. M. Ircha used to commute to this city from Brantford. Quite an active part in community activities was shown by a branch of USDP which had been organized here as late as 1917.

A group of Ukrainian immigrants, originally from Lemkivshchyna (part of Western Ukraine) and later settled in U.S.A., arrived in Brantford in 1911. As soon as they had settled themselves comfortably here they went ahead and in that same year organized the "Brotherhood of St. John the Baptist". Its founders were: S. Murayka, M. Madarash, M. Pontus, M. Seredynsky, S. Syvyk, I. Yurchak and D. Cherevaty. The association could boast of 32 members in the first year. This group supplied both the name and the incentive for the "St. John the Bapist" parish that was organized here. The congregation was served by priests who came from Buffalo and Detroit, in U.S.A. When in 1917 Rev. M. Ircha became the resident priest in Brantford the activities increased rapidly and land was bought for the building of the church. The socialist group formed a branch of the USDP which steadily expanded its work in this locality. The well known by now I. Hnyda had tried to organize the labourers on the basis of political party orientation as long ago as 1914 but had not found a fertile ground for this proletarian movement.

Only seventy miles south of Toronto lies the city of Kitchener (called Berlin, until the First World War). In 1910 the "Prosvita" cultural centre was established here and in 1916 the "Parish of Transfiguration". The leading pioneers here were: M. Kovpak, I. Maga, M. Stadnyk, P. Kobiluch. First High Mass was celebrated here by Rev. Y. Fylyma in the Prosvita Hall.

In Copper Cliff, near Sudbury, the organizational life began as early as 1908. It was then that a church committee was formed, composed of A. Ostapovych, D. Halushchak and I. Shlemkevych [46]. Early beginnings were difficult here but a strong determination achieved its own objective. On Feb. 12, 1909 the church was finished and blessed by Rev. T. Vasylevych. A. Ostrovsky was the head of the church committee. Copper Cliff Church served also as a mother church for the neighboring mining town of Sudbury and the following priests had, in turn, served these two communities: K. Yermiy, W. Gigeychuk and W. Vyniarsky. When the economic crisis hit Canada in 1919 Copper Cliff became almost a ghost

---

[45] Stepan Hewak: "A short sketch of the past", page 2, manuscript copy, preserved in the archives of the author.
[46] "Canadian Farmer", No. 24, 1908.

town, with no work for the labourers. The pioneer church became somewhat of a ghost church also and the community life began to formalize itself in Sudbury.

The summer-resort town of Kenora, Ontario, proved to be a veritable foster-mother to the Ukrainian settlers in the second decade of our century. By 1915 there was a fairly large group of labourers who decided to form a Ukrainian association. The first discussions took place in the home of Mr. and Mrs. A. M. Tzurkan and the founding meeting was held in the home of Stepan Rapinda. The organizers were: P. Plishka, D. Virun and M. Derenetsky, with the last named as the head, and the executive composed of K. Zulkovsky, O. Permsky, M. Franchuk, D. Pasichniak, Y. Zarsky and D. Virun. The "Taras Shevchenko Cultural Association" expanded its educational activities and made great efforts to acquire its own premises. This ambition was realized when in 1918 the "National School" was organized with O. Permsky as its first teacher. In its first year it already had 43 children in attendance. The Ukrainian parish in Kenora dates from 1917. Shortly after the church of St. Nicholas was built with Rev. E. Andruchovych as its first parish priest.

In London, Onario, the social-religious life of the Ukrainian people began in 1911 and 1912. First priest to visit here was Rev. Y.. Boyarchuk. For a long time the parish of the Christ the King held its services in the Roman Catholic Church of Blessed Virgin Mary, but finally the Ukrainian parish built its own community centre and the church services were held there.

Both Vancouver in the west and Sydney in the east received the Ukrainian immigrants with open arms in the first decade of our century. The first of the "first ones" to arrive in Sydney was Mykola Fedora (Fedoriv) who played a very important role in the life of Ukrainian community in this coal mining city. When in 1904 larger groups of labourers started to arrive in Sydney most of them were Ukrainians from Besarabia and Podila (Husiatyn county) but in 1907 others arrived from Bukovina and other parts of Western Ukraine to join them. It was with these two groups of settlers that M. Fedora went to work to organize and formalize a church-conscious and cultural community. Confidential talks were held on May 12, 1912. The Association of the Holy Ghost was founded at this time with the aim of building a church and carry on a cultural and educational work among the labourers. The association was located in the home of Mykhaylo Fedora at 110 Ferris Street. Pioneers in this organization were Mykola Fedora, S. Pavluk, Mykhaylo Fedora, O. Ivaniuk, I. Nalepa and M. Svystun. In the same year land property was bought with the intention of building a church and community centre. A few months after the land was purchased a national home was built which was used for carrying on cultural work. To obtain the services of a priest a call was made to Montreal and on Nov. 17, 1912, Rev. K. Yermiy, came to Sydney and later Rev. W. Vyniarky as well. The visits of these two clergy animated the organizing enthusiasm and helped to harness the community element to work with a still greater degree of concerted effort. By 1913 a completed church was standing as a symbol of diligence and devotion. This noble deed was accomplished by Rev. E. Krasitsky and his dedicated parishioners. The above referred to pioneer priest who had a rich experience from his work with the St. Vladimir and Olga's Parish in Winnipeg organized amateur drama group, "National School" and cultural centre, under the direction of Illa Nahorniak. Up to 1916 all Ukrainians grouped themselves around the parish. In the year an Orthodox parish was formed that was served by Rev. I. Tertychny, Rev. K. Bodnarchuk and Rev. A. Dutko This parish kept going until 1923 when it became liquidated. During the First World War the Ukrainian colony in Sydney rendered great help to those Ukranians who were interned during the war and who were put to work in iron ore mines and iron foundries. In 1916 some 100 prisoners from Bukovina and later about 200 more from Galicia and Bukovina were brought to Sydney. The prisoners were given the so-called "Release of Imprisonment" paper and by their presence increased the size of Sydney colony. The Ukrainians of Sydney were of great help in the release of the prisoners but a special credit belonged to M. Fedora who whole-heartedly worked on behalf of his fellow countrymen.

Among other Ukrainian labourers' colonies that were organized in eastern Canada at the end of the first pioneer era that deserves our mention was the one that was established in Sault Ste. Marie. To be exact, the Ukrainians began to settle here as early as 1907 but the cultural-educational life did not formulate itself here until 1916, while the Ukrainian church was not built until one year later.

The "Workers' Organization" began its activity in Timmins, Ontario, in January of 1913, as a branch of U.S.D.P. It was organized by W. Holowacky and concerts, plays and meetings were held in their own hall. Similar activities were carried on by the "Fighters for Freedom" association of Porcupine, which was also a branch of U.S.D.P. Actually an earlier association had been organized here in 1912 but when the labourers were transferred to Timmins the organization followed them as a matter of course.

One of the more active branches of U.S.D.P. along the cultural-educational line was established by I. Hnyda in Welland, Ontario, on May 25, 1913. In 1917 the "Labour Temple" was built here and the cultural work was expanded further. This so-called "Labour Temple" was one of the first to be established in Eastern Canada.

All these mentioned activities were but mere sprouts of the Ukrainian life in Eastern Canada. As with all beginnings these were meagre in extent and wrought with difficulty in their execution. In many instances long were the waiting periods and much nurturing was required before any harvesting could be done. But the creative spirit of the Ukrainian pioneers would not be dampened nor held back. Often they had to humbly tread their steps from one rented hall to another, from this free-offer church to that, before they built their own national homes, cultural centres and places of worship. These humble beginnings of integrated activities in the sphere of religion, education, culture and labor relationship, on the part of the Ukrainian immigrant-labourer—who had found himself surrounded by a sea of alien culture—was his documentary proof as well as a desire to reveal to the rest of the world his very own national values. These first efforts at the manifestation of his Ego we can discern especially in the later and truly imposing cultural development: the unpretentious given facts about different parishes, cultural centres, amateur groups, labourers' organizations, etc.,— all these are but the beginnings of the cultural birth-proof of the Ukrainians in this part of Canada, in general.

In 1917 a cycle of reportorial articles appeared in "Canadian Ruthenian" written by Rev. M. Olenchuk [47]) and titled: "Life of Ukrainians in Eastern Canada", in which, this diligent community worker, faithfully mirrors the dynamic activities of the Ukrainians in the eastern part of Canada.

"About this time the Ukrainians of Toronto showed their advancement to the extent that they started competing with their brethren in Montreal although the last ones named had a head-start, having had much earlier opportunity to organize themselves along cultural, educational and religious aspects. In this respect Toronto was favored by a steady flow of labourers who were attracted by the city's wage-earning opportunities where, in 1917, an average labourer could count on making five dollars per day.

Hamilton also provided extensive employment for Ukrainians through its many plants and factories. The Ukrainian labourers helped to augment the size of the pioneer Ukrainian community. Two cultural centres were already very active and a preparation was being made for the building of a church. Along with the "Shevchenko Association" a "Women's Educational Organization" was affiliated, showing much activity and was perhaps the first such group in Eastern Canada.

Brantford, at this time, could be proud of its well-disciplined church organization while in Sudbury, Copper Cliff and Commingston a national cultural consciousness could be clearly perceived. Of course here and there one could still detect that "I am my own boss" attitude but the bulk of Ukrainian labourers were fighting it with zeal and vigor. Fort William was still minus its own church but it had an excellent and well-run "Ridna Shkola" (National School), unequalled anywhere in the east. The "Prosvita" too was one of the best organized cultural centres in Eastern Canada. A similarly good reputation belonged to the small "Ivan Franko" centre in West Fort William which town could also proudly show its first Ukrainian Church".

According to the given statistics that we find in the "Trans-Oceanic Herald", [48]) there were close to 40,000 Ukrainians at the end of the First World War. Toronto led with 9,000, Windsor next with 8,000 followed by Sudbury's 6,000, Montreal had 5,000, Hamilton 3,000, Sault Ste. Marie 2,000, Ottawa 1,000, Oshawa 500, and such places as St. Catherines, Thorold, Welland, Niagara Falls, Guelph and other having 200 to 300 each.

In spite of this remarkable growth of the Ukrainian settlers of Eastern Canada, in the sphere of national consciousness and organizational endeavours, they were still far behind the Western Canada's fellow brethren. Proof of this may be easily found in the later contemporary press out of which we select this one example: "The life of Ukrainians, in the East, has not, as yet, made such a great stride as the one shown in the West. Different conditions prevailed here. In most cases Ukrainian labourers in Eastern Canada did not have the benefit of a steady abode and so were not interested in building houses or acquiring farms and had not much to show, otherwise, for their efforts. However, the war and the unrelenting fate's blow that was dealt to them in the old country combined to raise the national and communal consciousnes of Eastern Canada's Ukrainians to the same measure as that of the rest of our people in America. The old country serf, along with the foreman, disappeared. The people revolutionized their way

---

[47]) "Canadian Ruthenian", November, 1917.
[48]) "Trans-Oceanic Herald", Nov. 1, 1920, page 22.

of thinking, albeit, in two different directions, the national and the international".

It could be said that such evaluation of the Ukrainians, in Eastern Canada, presaged a new era in which there was an expansion and development of the national organizations on the one side while on the other side was the formation of the socialist oriented organizations, of which an important segment allied itself with the international labour movement. This growth and differentiation reached its massive dimension only in the wake of the First World War. All this took place during the second era of our history.

PARTICIPATION IN MUNICIPAL AND POLITICAL LIFE

The gradation of interest, on the part of the settlers, into social-communal affairs proceeded step by step. Once they had solved the problem of church and school, the next in line was that of the cultural-educational organization and coupled along with this arose also the interest in municipal and political affairs of their district, province and the rest of the country. In order to have a voice in municipality or settlement, it was necessary to be the owner of a homestead. The ownership of a homestead bestowed upon its owner certain rights and responsibilities, with the latter in much greater predominance over the former. The settlements' beginnings were based upon the commandment: "Work hard in order to contribute the most toward the community storehouse", but they received very few dividends in return. It was, strictly speaking, a one way contract. This onesided contraction was prolonged over a period of years, until such times when suitable roads were built, schools organized, post offices established and some form of communication with the rest of the world was achieved. In any district that had been settled by other nationalities, prior to the coming of the Ukrainians, it was only natural that these same nationalities should be at the helm of the local government. In most instances, they were the ones who acted as mediators between the powers that were and the new settlers and, very often, were the first ones in business circles which in turn placed them favourably in social standing. It came to pass that in some districts the offices of reeves were held by local merchants and this gave them additional dividends. When these positions were filled by the public-minded individuals, they then would be re-elected to the same offices, over a long period of years, as for example, in Ethelbert, Manitoba. But quite a different lot fell upon those who abused their given trust of power, as happened in Stuartburn, Manitoba. This created dissatisfaction and consequently the discontented ones bethought themselves to take matters into their own hands. At last, when the settlers had somewhat rid themselves of their first and most pressing personal and homestead-living needs, they then began to take a deeper and wider interest in municipal affairs.

The need of roads and schools was a prime concern; the A.B.C., for the first settlers, the foundation on which to build the system of municipal life. Sooner or later, within the ever-growing Ukrainian settlements, the municipal affairs were coming closer into the sphere of their interest—and thus into their hands.

The first all-Ukrainian municipality in Manitoba was Stuartburn, which prior to that, had been a part of Franklin municipality. The citizens of Stuartburn complained about the lack of roads, bridges and schools as well as the unjust division of taxes. When the municipal council of Franklin paid little heed to this complaint, a mass petition was sent to the provincial government of Manitoba which agreed upon the formation of a separate municipality. Thus, in 1902, the new, and the first all-Ukrainian municipality came into being *[49]).

Similar history, as above, was repeated with the municipality of Gimli, Manitoba; but in this case, the Provincial Government did not bend itself in favor of those who made their claim. Not always did the Ukrainian settlers take such "revolutionary action". Most often such affairs were settled by the democratic method of vote. In due course of time, the Ukrainian majority administered such municipalities at Ethelbert, Mossey River, Gimli, Dauphin, Broken Head and Kreuzberg; Rosthern, Hafford and Yorkton in Saskatchewan, and Vegreville, Myrnam and others in Alberta, all of them being in the Western Provinces.

The "palm of glory" for having been the first Ukrainian to triumph in municipal affairs belongs to John Storozuk, who became reeve and to Theodoseus Wachna, first Ukrainian secretary—both in the municipality of Stuartburn. Apart from the above, a whole line of municipalities were bilingual; that is, Anglo-Ukrainian and in some of them, as in Ethelbert, Stuartburn, Rossburn, Vegreville, Hafford and others, the more important notices were printed in both languages. In actual practice the following method was used: All correspondence between municipal and provincial government was in English while that between municipality and tax payers was in Ukrainian.

Such a satisfactory system and politics could not help but evoke among the settlers genuine confidence toward the country of their adoption. In this process they became aware of a personal as well as national dignity and when any mention of it was voiced in the press it was mostly by way of comparison of benefits derived from the democratic system as practiced in Canada, in contrast to the one they left behind in the old country, which had been founded on undemocratic principles, wherein one nation exploits another and where some, who are on higher social levels, hold privileges that are denied to all the rest.

The success of the Ukrainians on the municipal level encouraged them to play a still greater part, first in provincial and later on, in the dominion affairs. The strength of the Ukrainian votes in the three Western Prairie Provinces of Manitoba, Saskatchewan, and Alberta became very attractive to the candidates during the provincial and dominion elections. But the potential power of these same votes acted at times as a detriment for the Ukrainian settlers in as much as the two political parties in Canada, both the Conservative and the Liberal, used them merely as a weapon in their fight with each other. While the election fever was still in its infancy, already thousands upon thousands of letters, posters, briefs and cirulars were spread and scattered throughout the Ukrainian settlements "explaining" of how one or the other party either tried to prevent Ukrainians from coming to Canada, ignored them politically or exploited them economically, while it (the good party) itself was ready to bestow all of its blessings upon the poor settlers as soon as it came to power. Sometimes members of one party would engage in shady deals, abuse their privileges or resort to bribery and then the other side would stoop low enough to exploit these evil doings

---

[49]) Studies in the History of Ukrainians in Canada, page 41.

for their own selfish ends "making", so to speak,"mountains out of molehills" and blowing up in size minute matters to unheard of proportions. Small incidents of such trivia as mentioned above took place even in the dominion parliament. For instance: On the 15th of May, 1905, Mr. A. B. Ingraham, M.P., ridiculed Ukrainian names by saying that they looked like montrosities to him. He took time off in the House of Commons to spell out 109 surnames from one of the electoral districts in Alberta—all this because most of those whose names he spelled voted for the opposite side [50].

Similar acts of discrimination, emanating from one or the other party or members of parliament registered themselves very deeply upon the souls of those against whom these were aimed, and bred in them the feeling of resentment toward the outer world and a strong desire to oppose such indignities. This induced the settlers all the more to depend upon themselves and to take greater interest in electoral affairs.

It was not easy for the Ukrainians, especialy those who came from Austria and Russia, to reach the voting booth during provincial or dominion elections. Ownership of land property alone, was not sufficient. One had to become a citizen of Canada in order to have the right to vote. In accordance with Canadian law as interpreted through the "Naturalization Act", an immigrant could only be naturalized after three years' sojourn in Canada. By the Act of 1809, the administration of naturalization was transferred to the Department of State in Ottawa. In 1914 this Act was changed and required five years' residence in Canada and finally, as a result of events during the First World War, by order of Canadian Law, the Ukrainians could not be naturalized. As a matter of fact the right to be naturalized was withheld from all foreigners during the war years. Undoubtedly, the best years for obtaining citizenship rights were those prior to 1914. Only three years' living in Canada was required by the immigrants to "obtain papers", as was then popularly called, and on the basis of these papers one could become a full-fledged citizen. Alas, these rights did not altogether pertain to the former citizens of Austria and Russia—and thus to Ukrainians who came from these countries.

In 1897, the government of Manitoba through its "Order-in-Council" required from each applicant who was requesting citizenship papers, that he must be able to prove that he possesses sufficient knowledge of either English, French or German language. Of course, none of the above mentioned was a mother tongue of the Ukrainians. The three years sojourn, and most of it spent in the bush or on the prairies, left but little time in which to master the English or the French tongue. Only a few among the settlers knew the German language. The hardest hit were those who came from Russia, for there they never had any possibility to acquaint themselves with the German language. The "Order-in-Council" dealt a grievous blow to Ukrainians, for by its action not only were they deprived of the right to vote but it also prevented them from obtaining legal ownership of their farms. Lacking citizenship rights, they were obliged to remain as mere homesteaders.

Usually before the elections, not only would there be intensification of interest about the electors, but also about "potential electors". Therefore, the electoral committees would strive to help in the process of obtaining

---

[50] "Canadian Farmer", No. 38, October 2, 1908.

citizenship documents. In every electoral committee there would be an official to examine the applicant regarding his knowledge of language. If the examination proved to be successful, the applications would then go through the bureau of Attorney General, who in turn, delivered it to the court house. The applications were then posted in the court house and the post office for public inspection. In this way over 1,500 Ukrainians in Winnipeg alone obtained their citizenship papers at the beginning of 1903, during the preparations for provincial election in Manitoba [51]).

According to summaries which have survived until our times, the year of 1903, in Manitoba and even more so in Winnipeg, was for the Ukrainians, a break-through in interest, pertaining to political matters. The passive state had ended and with "the first Ukrainian political gathering" in Winnipeg a new era had arrived. The meeting was arranged by Toma Jastremsky on behalf of the Conservative Party. Those who took an active part were Andrew Norquay, Samson Walker, and Sir Hugh McDonald, the son of the first Prime Minister of Canada. Invitations were printed in Ukrainian, with the help of Latin alphabet, as there was no Ukrainian press available in Winnipeg at the time. The meeting took place in a hall on Henry Avenue between Main Street and King Street. Over 1,000 Ukrainians were present and the hall was too small to hold them all. The previously mentioned attendant of this gathering, Sir Hugh MacDonald, on seeing such a huge crowd of Ukrainians was quoted as having said, with great emotion: "And I was told that you were all Austrian Indians. What a great mistake I made in my believing it". The speakers at this meeting, especially C. Walker, assured those present that they would make strong efforts in support of bilingual schools for the Ukrainians in Manitoba. Perhaps it was thanks to this promise that S. Walker was easily elected.

It is worth our attention to note that this first political gathering of the Ukrainians in Winnipeg gave them a certain prestige and underlined the fact that they were a separate race apart from the Poles. Up till then the Polish parish of Holy Ghost tried continuously, to monopolize the contention that it was a true representative of the Slavic group, not only in Winnipeg, but in Manitoba as well [52]).

An interesting trend may be observed among Ukrainians when one stops to consider the political mood of that time. In provincial elections, they voted Conservative, perhaps because this party promised to extend further the building of schools, which promise was fulfilled later, and in federal elections they tended to support Liberals because these in turn favoured immigration from Eastern Europe. In actual practice, it worked out something like this: For the Province of Manitoba the Ukrainian settlers supported Rodmond P. Roblin, but for Ottawa they gave all their support to Sir Wilfred Laurier. These two politicians had a strong influence on the political thinking of the first pioneers.

It was not only in cities that our first pioneers began to concern themselves with political matters. On farms also a gradual interest in "bigger politics" was taking roots. At the Liberal convention in Stonewall in 1906, four Ukrainian delegates took part [53]). Similar activities were taking place in other parts of the province—Sifton, Ethelbert and Dauphin.

---

[51]) T. A. Jastremsky in "Canadianization", Winnipeg 1946, page 49.
[52]) Ibid, pp. 50-52.
[53]) "Svoboda", No. 30, 1906.

Having become interested in political affairs, the Ukrainian citizens not only took a sporadic participation in election propaganda and in elections as well, but they also started to organize political clubs. On May 6, 1908, there was organized "The Ruthenian Liberal Club" (Rusky Liberalny Klub) in Winnipeg [54]. It was headed by Z. Bychynsky and its founders were: M. Hladky, M. Humilowych, W. Novak, W. Chornenky, W. Rudko, I. Slobodian, A. Novak and A. Pyniansky. The leadership of the club was composed mostly of sympathizers of the Independent Greek Church, Presbyterian and of other religious denominations. The Ruthenian Liberal Club was an "answer" to the existence of the Ruthenian Conservative Club that had been active in Winnipeg since 1907, under the alert leadership of Toma Jastremsky. His close co-workers were: N. Kotlaryk, W. Karchut, M. Makarsky, T. Stefanyk and others. The head of the Club (Toma Jastremsky) even tried his own luck as a candidate in ward 6 in Winnipeg City election 1907. His lack of success did not prevent him from trying again the following year, this time for the position of city controller. He ran as a representative of "Ruthenians and Germans". "Canadian Farmer", whose orientation at that time was in favour of the Liberal party, had this to say about T. Jastremsky's second unsuccessful attempt at city politics: "We are, indeed, too weak to elect from among ourselves, a city controller, but we are sufficiently strong enough to have our own city alderman, and this should be our concern, ahead of us, for any future elections" [55].

The expectations of the "Canadian Farmer" were fully realized, three years later, when Theodore Stefanyk was elected in 1911, as the first Ukrainian alderman, in the city of Winnipeg. During the same time Wasyl Holowacky, a socialist, was a candidate in the dominion elections from the district of Selkirk, Manitoba. This was the first and unsuccessful attempt. The first Ukrainian MLA of Manitoba Provincial Legislature to be elected was T. D. Ferley, in 1915, when he ran as an independent candidate in the Manitoba Provincial elections, and remained in provincial parliament till 1920. He was born in Ukraine in 1882 and came to Canada in 1903, and had the distinction of being the sole Ukrainian member of the Manitoba Legislature during the pioneer era.

Ukrainian settlers in Alberta and Saskatchewan also were not indifferent in matters of politics. A the first provincial convention of Ukrainians of Alberta at Edmonton in 1909, its organizers solved the political question in a somewhat revolutionary way: They elected the so-called "National Council" (Narodna Rada) and empowered it to organize a political democratic party in Alberta. The first Ukrainian provincial convention of Saskatchewan even went so far as to mention the possibilities of electing as many as nine members to Provincial Legislature and one or two to the Dominion Parliament in Ottawa. Albeit, it was only political wishful thinking on the part of the pioneers, but it throws some light upon their great ambitions and their sense of responsibilities in public affairs. How seriously the Ukrainian settlers of Alberta applied themselves in this matter may be seen by the fact that in the provincial election of 1913, they fielded no less than eight candidates. These were: H. Kraykiwsky, M. Gowda, P. Rudyk, A. Shandro, P. Svarich, M. Fuyarchuk, P. Kulmatycky, and M. Semeniuk. Although almost all of them fell through, still it was not, in the least, an

---

[54] "Canadian Farmer", No. 17, May 8, 1908.
[55] "Canadian Farmer", No. 48, 1908.

insignificant expression of the great political stride of the pioneer spirit. Anly Andrew Shandro alone (1886-1942) was elected and thus he was the first Ukrainian in Canada to sit in Provincial Legislature. At the same time, he was the sole representative from among Ukrainians of Alberta during the pioneer era. A. Shandro was re-elected again in 1915 and 1917. He came from Bukowina, while T. D. Ferley came from Galicia. Both were Liberals.

Naturally, the beginnings were harsh and difficult but never again did the Ukrainians abandon the idea of their political co-responsibility for the good of the country in which they had settled. Therefore, Dr. E. H. Oliver was amply justified when in his article entitled, "Ukrainians from Saskatchewan" and printed in "The Missionary Messenger" [56]), had this to say: "The Ukrainians have come into power not only in this province (Saskatchewan—M.H.M.) but also in all the other western provinces. Today (1916—M.H.M.) they control many school districts, dictate the future trend in many municipalities, have entered into the parliament of Manitoba and even now, they are knocking on the doors of other provincial parliament buildings".

When we add to these collective efforts the fact that, as early as 1904, Michael Gabora was already campaigning as an independent candidate for Ottawa from the McKenzie district of Saskatchewan it is then possible to form a bold conclusion that the Ukrainian settlers acquired, very rapidly, the feeling and the understanding of their responsibility for the fate and the guidance of the country of their newly-found settlement.

A different type of attention among Ukrainian settlers deserves a political grouping known in general as "socialists". The socialistic movement was not foreign to Ukrainians. Socialists in Western Ukraine grouped themselves around "Ukrainian Socialist Radical Party" in the cities, although in much smaller numbers, and around Ukrainian Socialist Democratic Party. Both of these parties were oriented toward the "Second International" and strove to improve the social system through evolutionary means. At the same time they were also a national party, for they aimed toward the regaining of freedom for the Ukrainian nation on its ethnographic territories. The social-radicalism was widely spread in Western Ukraine, in such regions as Stanislaviv, Ivano-Frankivsk and Tarnopol and to a lesser degree in Chernivtsi. When the first settlers to Canada were coming from Pokutia and Tarnopol regions, they also brought with them socialistic ideas. Such leading active figures of the pioneering era as Kyrylo Genik, Ivan Bodrug, I. Negrych, M. Stechishin, Y. Syrotiuk, T. D. Ferley and many others were all socialists. They were the leading lights in public affairs and it is not to be wondered at that, having come here, they began to seek similarly associated elements somewhat after the fashion of "birds of a feather flock together". Moreover, a group of Ukrainian socialists from Manitoba decided to organize a so-called "Ukrainian Brotherhood" (Ukrainske Bratstvo), based on socialistic principles, and in 1902 rented a farm in Hayward, California and even declared their wish to have it operated on a communal basis—without any personal ownership—something like a modern communist collective farm. The father of this idea and adventure was K. Genik and its protector was Rev. Ahapey Honcharenko, on whose farm was to be realized this experimental community that attracted to it over

---

[56]) Missionary Messenger, Vol. III, No. 5, May 1916.

twenty members. The experiment failed and all members of this community, including Syrotiuk brothers, M. Stechishin, T. D. Ferley family and others, found themselves again back in Canada—in search, once more, of kindred souls.

The first united socialist groups in Canada were also members of American Socialist Workers Party. In 1899 came a break-up of this party, which led to the formation of a separate "Canadian Socialist League", and two years later to the creation of the "Socialist Party of British Columbia". In 1905, all these socialist groups formed the "Socialist Party of Canada", but even this was split up. By this means there came into being the "Canadian Socialist Federation", in the east, and the "Socialist-Democratic Party of Canada in Winnipeg which, in 1911 united all socialists and took them under its fold.

As early as 1899, Rev. D. Polivka, in his correspondence, mentions about a "socialist hall" which also at times was known as "International Reading Association. It was, probably, the first organized cell of Ukrainian socialists in Winnipeg territory, but according to the memoirs of some of its members, its role was exclusively of a cultural-educational nature. When in the fall of 1906, there had been organized the "Shevchenko Reading Society" in Winnipeg the socialist movement, among Ukrainians, started to gain in strength. In the hall of this society, which was also in the hands of the socialists, a yet another socialist organization was formed, which began to publish its own newspaper a year later. At the same time, in Nanaimo, B.C., a different socialist organization came into being, and in Portage la Prairie, Manitoba, a separate labor-socialist branch of this group was established. These three organizations joined together in 1907 into "Ukrainian Socialist Union. All these three cells were quite active, although the bulk of the settlers were not socialistically inclined and did not support them too actively. The newspaper "Red Flag", did not receive sufficient financial support and with its 18th edition, ceased to exist. In 1909 this same group, headed by P. Krat, M. Stechishin, W. Holowacky, H. Slipchenko and T. D. Ferley, and in Edmonton headed by T. Tomashevsky and R. Kremar-Soloducha, started to publish a paper "Robochy Narod" (Working People). In between these times several other branches were formed which in February 1910 shaped themselves into the "Federation of Ukrainian Socialist Democrats of Canada". To this federation belonged branches in such localities as Winnipeg, Brandon, Edmonton, Calgary, Cardiff, Vostok, Hosmer, Phoenin and Canmore in the west and Montreal in the east. This federation was headed by M. Stechishin, T. Tomashevsky, I. Bohonos, I. Boychuk, M. Gowda, Ann Stechishin and A. Pawchuk. In the meantime a difference of opinion crept into the socialist party of Canada which finally ended in the division of it. The Ukrainian Socialists supported a branch of Canadian Socialist-Democratic Party and, together with Jewish, German and Lettish branches in Winnipeg organized Canadian Socialist-Democratic Party. With this began the so-called "course to the left".

In August of 1910 the first convention of the Federation of Ukrainian Socialist-Democrats was held in Edmonton with its helm falling into the hands of a committee composed of moderate elements, including among them: R. Kremar, M. Ferbey, H. Kraykivsky, Y. Seniuk, I. Humen, I. A. Pawchuk and I. Boychuk. The leading members of this federation lived mostly in Edmonton and strove to take over all matters into their own hands, and when they failed in their effort to transfer the newspaper "Working People" to Edmonton, they then started to publish their own paper "Nova Hromada" (New Community). Between these two papers there began a bitter fight and along with it those elements in the party who placed their national principles ahead of socialist interests began to pull out of the socialist movement. At the party conference in Winnipeg, in 1911, the left wing took over the leadership of a party being joined by the following persons: W. Holowacky, E. Basisty, M. Stechishin, I. Boychuk, N. Panteliuk, Ivan Kowalsky, I. A. Panteliuk, I. A. Pawchuk, and K. Dzvidzinsky.

Within the electoral committee itself, contradictory opinions arose and as result two of the leading activists, M. Stechishin and later Pavlo Krat, left the party. In vain were all the efforts and resolutions of the court of arbitration composed of such well known public figures as Dr. W. Starosolsky and Dr. M. Hankewych of Lviv, Western Ukraine. R. Kremar-Soloducka and late M. Stechishin, after the demise of "Nova Hromada", began to publish "Novyny" (News) in Edmonton. Still later, such individuals as I. Stefanicky, who edited "Svidoma Syla" (Knowing Strength) and "Robitnyche Slovo" (Worker's Word) in Toronto as well as M. Yeremiychuk and others parted company with the socialist centers. However, in spite of continuous ferments in the party, the socialist group managed to gather more sympathizers. In January 1914 the Federation of Ukrainian Socialist-Democrats re-named itself to "Ukrainian Socialist-Democratic Party" and I. Hnyda became its organizer who was replaced later by W. N. Kolisnyk. The party was able to keep alive "Robochy Narod" newspaper and gain further adherents by means of its propaganda. During the second convention of "The Ukrainian Socialist-Democratic Party" which took place in Winnipeg, it was announced that there were 25 branches consisting of more than 600 active members. With the beginning of 1918, the number had risen to 1500 members. The helm of the party passed into the hands of such active leaders as W. N. Kolisnyk, D. Lobay, S. Chwaliboga, M. Popowych, I. Navizivsky, L. Nykoriak. These continued to wind up the spring in the direction of the leftist orientation—drawing ever nearer toward communist doctrine.

Complete re-orientation from socialism to communism in the above mentioned party did not come until 1918-1919. From that time on a steady and bitter struggle in the history of Ukrainians in Canada, ensued between this group and those Ukrainians who were nationally oriented and who in their political work supported fully the traditional Ukrainian parties—an unvaried and uninterrupted struggle that has never let up to this day.

There were times when socialist centres held much power and influence, especially during the First World War. In this, they were even aided by outside factors. Persecution of Ukrainians by government actions on the pretense that they held sympathies with Austria aroused in them antagonistic mood against both the government and the social set-up, and this in turn increased the rows of the "malcontents".

It is worthwhile to note that Ukrainian socialists in Canada were capable, to a great degree, to capitalize on the affair in connection with the gaining of freedom for Myroslav Sichynsky from the "Dibrova" penitentiary in Stanislaviv, Western Ukraine. M. Sichynsky, at that time, was hailed as a

PIONEER ERA — ILLUSTRATIONS

THE FIRST:

Ivan Negrich,
editor of the "Canadian Farmer',
Winnipeg

Roman Kremar,
editor of "News", Edmonton

J. A. Kolesnikow,
editor of "Witness of the Truth",
Toronto

Toma Tomashewsky,
editor of several publications

Osyp Megas, one of the first Ukrainian-Canadian editors

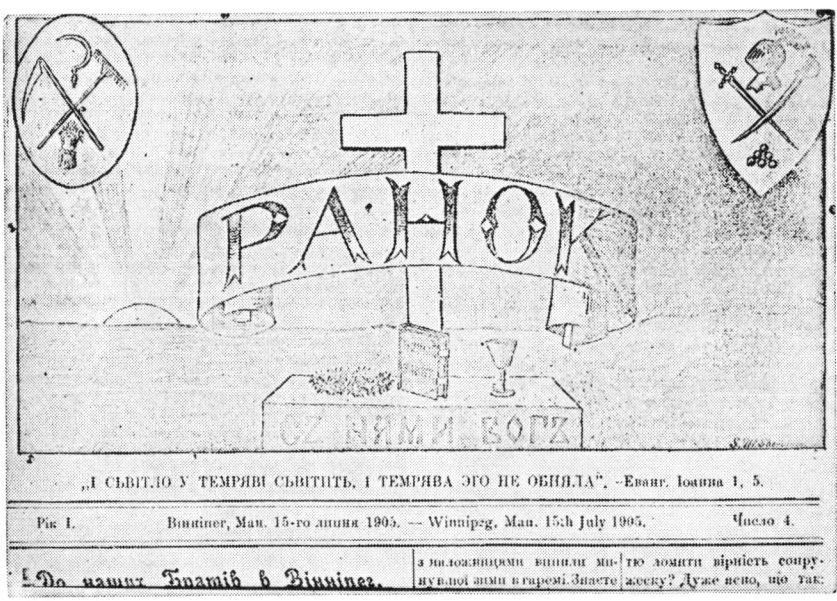

"Ranok"

PIONEER ERA — ILLUSTRATIONS

I. K. Pazdriy
The first Doctor in Canada

T. D. Ferley
The first MLA, Manitoba

Ivan Bodrug,
preacher and editor of "Ranok"

Mykola Syroidiw,
editor of "Canadian Ruthenian"

J. N. Krett,
publisher and editor

F. Dojacek,
publisher

PIONEER ERA — ILLUSTRATIONS

FIRST AUTHORS IN UKRAINIAN-CANADIAN LITERATURE:

Sawa Chernecky

Theodore Fedyk

Wasyl Kudryk

Appolinariy Novak (sitting) with his guest from Motherland, Dr. Julian Bachynsky

LEADING PERSONALITIES IN THE PIONEER ERA:

J. W. Arsenych

Petro Svarich

Myroslaw Stechishin

Pawlo Krat

national avenger, whose bold act had made amends for all the wrongs suffered by his people. In 1908 and the years following, in Ukrainian lands as well as among Ukrainian emigrated settlers, the name M. Sichynsky never left the pages of Ukrainian press. His successful assassination attack upon Andrew Potocki, the governor of the Province of Galicia in Austria, qualified him as a national hero. In all Ukrainian corners of Canada, the Ukrainians held gatherings and signed petitions to the governments of Canada and Austria asking the Austrian government to grant an amnesty for M. Sichynsky. Ukrainian socialists in Canada led a campaign to collect funds which they hoped would help to gain freedom for M. Sichynsky. For this same purpose they organized a "Council of Seven" composed of P. Krat, M. Stechishin, T. Tomashevsky, W. Kotelak, W. Kulka, N. Kochanowsky and E. Wolodin. This committee collected a large sum of money, by means of which they brought over from Europe Irene, the sister of M. Sichynsky, who was a teacher of "Ridna Shkola" which was named "B. Hrinchenko", in the city of Lviv, Western Ukraine. In October 1910, she arrived in Winnipeg from whence she departed for Alberta and B.C. Accompanied by P. Kremar and later by T. Tomashevsky, she visited such places as Calgary, Lethbridge, Frank, Coleman, Banff and Canmore in Alberta, and Hosmer, Vancouver and Nanaimo in B.C. As in Winnipeg so in other places the Ukrainians, with elated spirits welcomed her heartily, and donated generously toward the fund for the purpose of obtaining freedom for the avenger of national wrongs. It is easy to imagine what a great joy it was for all, when in November, 1911, a news flash reached Canada that M. Sichynsky escaped from jail and still later, when it was announced that he had arrived on the American soil. The socialists were able in a capable manner, to apply to their own credit this successful political action. And it may also not be amiss to note that this event had a great influence in cementing together the mass of Ukrainian socialists in Canada, although in the flow of time there had cropped up temporary sharp incidents, especially during inventories of collected party funds.

It is understood, of course, that strong anti-socialist forces were also active in their effort to crumble the socialist movement. Still, in this political struggle there was a hardening process working on both, the individual and the collective will of the people, and the gradual evolution of their political thinking. Rugged individualities were forged in the heat of this same struggle, and strong characters were formed.

THE FIRST BUSINESSMEN AND PROFESSIONALS

In religious and organized church life, and in cultural-educational work, as well as in participating in political life among Ukrainian settlers in Canada, there grew up a group of community-minded people, scattered over the wide territory, who, by their innate abilities, qualified themselves as natural leaders of the people. True enough, they were in no way different from their farm-and-labor surroundings, but when they took part in local meetings or provincial gatherings, they instantly took on a different stature. This was the inborn selective element at work among the people that in the beginning was comprised only of homesteader and the hard working laborer. Out of this dull, grey mass, figuratively speaking, there grew up, in time, individualities that led and guided community life. To their aid came graduates from Ukrainian-English seminaries in Winnipeg, Brandon, Regina, Vegreville and Manitoba College. Already in 1907 there were 36 registered teachers who, in a very short time, made a name for themselves through their school and community work and by devotion in serving the peoples' needs, thereby winning the confidence of their countrymen and, starting with the First Teachers' Convention, 1907, each one became a unique core of separate community cells. Each year registered new teacher forces who, in the eyes of the people, were not only "teachers of schools", but they were also teachers of "a way of life" and its guiding lights. Here was a brand new young strata flourishing in a pioneer jungle who, very often had their first introduction to hard work on a homestead or "extra-gang", and who not only had the knowledge of the teaching theory, but a practical taste of life as well. In one word: from within the sphere of natural emanation and out of the heart of its being, there was evolved the most perfect product, rewarding both the Ukrainian homesteader and the worker, by giving them their own sanguine intelligentsia—the third social class—hereby filling in and eliminating the gap in the social structure of Ukrainian community in Canada.

According to general summaries the bilingual seminaries, up to their liquidation in 1916, graduated more than three hundred Ukrainian-Canadian teachers who played an important role, quite often a leading role, in different communities during the pioneer era. Together, with a great number of priests, they became the basic foundation in the building of the third stage which grew step by step and flourished in time. With the help of the teachers, along with their conventions, there began a series of regional, provincial and even national meets. This was a great step ahead in the growth of Ukrainian community life in the course of which the selected national leaders, in their community work received great support as well as the injection of fresh blood.

The Ukrainian teachers, as we have already stated many times, never confined themselves strictly to their teaching alone. Many of them were not totally satisfied with their qualifications as teachers. The liberal atmosphere of the settled country, sound ambition and a strong wish to lift themselves to a higher living standard as well as a burning desire to help their fellow countrymen in difficulties made their mark.

In 1913, we have the first graduate of Canada, Orest Zerebko, a teacher by profession, with a B.A. university standing. In 1917-1918, we see teachers of the leaders-in-community caliber in the universities of Manitoba, Saskatchewan and Alberta, such as Stechishin and Yakimischak brothers as well as Prodan, Kibzey, Mihaychuk, Bodnar, Basarab and others. In addition to the teachers, and by natural process, students of younger generations—some thirty of them at the time—found their way to universities to take up studies in arts, philosophy, medicine, law and agriculture, with a few of them even obtaining scholarships, including the Governor General's gold medal [1].

To round off this picture we must also mention that there were tens of theological students studying for priesthood in the Catholic seminaries in Toronto and Montreal and as many others attending Presbyterian and Methodist Colleges. All of these were potential material and qualified candidates for the "Third Stage". Toward the end of the pioneer era, in addition to the teachers, several other Ukrainian professional classes worked as diligently in the same field: The lawyers, among them J. W. Arsenych being the first; doctors, of whom Dr. Ivan Kost Pazdriy was the first, followed by other doctors—Hryhoriy Nowak, B. Dyma, I. Orobko, A. T. Kibzey and I. Yakimishchak; agronomists, with K. C. Prodan being first, and dentists, with the honor of being the first in this profession, going to Dr. E. Mihaychuk, and others.

In mentioning professionalists, we must not omit the fact that Ukrainian students, though few in numbers in those days, still managed to form small student's clubs at different universities. The Students' Club (Studentsky Kruzhok) was organized in Winnipeg in December, 1916, and even collected funds for the purpose of editing students' journal called "Plowed Field" (Nyva). Simultaneously successful was the students' club called "Kameniari" (The Stone Cutters) at the Institute of Petro Mohyla in Saskatoon which not only collected funds but also began to publish a students' journal in Canada which carried the same name. About the same time there also was founded a students' organization at the University of Alberta, but it never showed any outstanding activity. During these same pioneering days of student life, other Ukrainians were scooping up their knowledge from the universities in Montreal and Toronto, and some even went beyond Canada's borders, to U.S.A. to pursue their studies. One of the first of these was M. Hrushka (M. Harris), who devoted himself to journalism.

Somewhat less qualified professionals of the pioneer era were notaries and municipal secretaries. The first Ukrainian notary in Canada was D. M. Svoboda, owner of "Ruthenian Bureau", who received his nomination in March, 1909. In his footsteps followed several other notaries and Justices of Peace (J. P.s) such as Hr. Machula in Winnipeg Ivan Puhaty and Wasyl Piniansky in Yorkton, Petro Svarich in Vegreville, Wasyl Kolodzinsky in Tolstoi, Hryhoriy Mech in Saskatoon, Ivan Hrushowy in Sifton, and a few others in different districts. In municipal districts, the following Ukrainians held offices as secretaries: In Stuartburn, J. M. Mysyk and Joseph Kulachkowsky; in Sliding Hills, S. W. Sawchuk; in Ethelbert, K. F. Slipetz; in Fish Creek, A. Syroishka; in Kreuzberg, B. I. Marek; in Russia (Prince Albert) T. Drabyniasty; in Berry (Hafford), B. H. Hryvnak and others.

Ukrainians were also engaged in running and managing employment offices. The first of these was established by Antin Karakotiuk in Winnipeg

---

[1] K. C. Prodan, in Agriculture.

in March, 1907. Both, the public notary's bureaus and the employment offices were of immense help to the first settlers who were, to say the least, somewhat hindered and restricted in language communication.

In the contemporary Ukrainian press, we meet up with many advertisements such as "Rusky Likar" (Ruthenian doctor), "Ruska Aptica" (Ruthenian Drug Store), "Rusky Advocat" (Ruthenian lawyer). But these were mostly professionals of other nationalities who used liberally the name "Ruthenian" (Rusky) as a camouflage, in order to acquire a larger clientele from among Ukrainian settlers. In answer to these so-called "Ukrainian professionals and businessmen" in North Winnipeg, the publicist, Petro Karmansky, devoted a separate satire in the newspaper "Kanada" (Canada) which was then reprinted in every Ukrainian paper of those days. In 1912, there already existed in Winnipeg a "Rusky Shpytal" (Ruthenian Hospital) that was established by Dr. B. Gerzabek at 415-417 Pritchard Avenue. At first it only contained two beds but in 1917, it could boast of having a sixteen bed capacity. Every year saw more new names added to the professional list but among them all, when judged by the most stringent appraisal, the teachers led the way.

Not an inconsiderable number of professionals on the American continent were businessmen. The Ukrainian businesmen, in time, far outdistanced the professionals, perhaps mainly because in this active field, the required qualifications must submit themselves to life's skill, the risk of commerce and the desire to get rich.

Even toward the end of last century we find small trading stores throughout Ukrainian settlements. Among the first Ukrainian businessmen, we must list the name of Yurko Panishchak, who came to Canada in 1892. A year later he was already in business. When Ukrainians started to arrive in Canada en masse, Yurko was well established in his store on Higgins Avenue in Winnipeg, opposite the C.P.R. Railway station. Those who followed in his footsteps were: Theodosius Wachna, in Stuartburn who came to Canada from U.S.A., M. Fekula in Dauphin; H. Hupalo in Trembowla (Terebowla)—Valley River, all in Manitoba. In Alberta, Pavlo Rudyk in Edmonton and Petro Svarich in Vegreville were first in the business field, while in Saskatchewan, Petro Shwydky was the first storekeeper in that province. In addition to single individual stores, there were also collective business establishments or company stores. First among these was the "Ruthenian Trading Company" (Ruska Torhovelna Spilka) in Sifton and other trading stores with similar names, in Ethelbert, Manitoba and in Rosthern, Saskatchewan. Down the list we also find the Austro-Canadian Co. in Winnipeg; Ruthenian Trading Co. in Calgary; Ruthenian Merchants in Winnipeg and such others. In the course of time we meet with various efforts to establish credit companies (kasy) in Edmonton and Winnipeg as well as a Ukrainian Bank in Edmonton.

All this is a sure witness to the fact that Ukrainian pioneers, from the first beginnings, strove to send down deep roots into Canada's business world. True enough, it was at first mostly all starts and trials. Lack of experience and small capital investment held no prophesy of long existence of this or other individual or company business establishment. But this was nothing new on the American territory. Freedom ensured the means to grow for all who wanted to grow. If the first one or two went down, others came up to take their place. The stream of life does not end with the first.

In press advertisements of the war years, we note a considerable number of Ukrainian businesses in almost every town and settlement in Western Canada. The majority of them limited themselves in their trading to a mixed variety of goods, especially to food products among which the Ukrainian brand of different choices of meats became very popular. There were many so-called "boarding-houses" which were easy to manage as they required only a small capital investment. Many single men availed themselves of the opportunity in running such eating places, which were also of great benefit to the newcomers who were not acquainted with the language and the customs of this country. In cities we also observe numerous shoe repair shops, various stores, hotels, restaurants and small apartment blocks. Most popular of all were the real estate dealers. House and land values rose from year to year. Many of these dealers made small fortunes, especially in rapidly growing cities and towns, such as Winnipeg, Brandon, Portage la Prairie, Rosthern, Saskatoon, Vegreville, Edmonton.

With the growth of the Ukrainian printed word, Ukrainian bookstores came into being. There were already eight of them in 1916. M. Ferbey established his "Ukrainian Book Store" in Edmonton which was later enlarged by his brother D. S. Ferbey; P. Hawryliw opened his "Ukrainian Book Store" in Saskatoon and a similar one, with the same name, was also opened by H. Mech in Montreal. N. Shydlowsky started his "Ukrainian Worker's Bookstore" in Winnipeg; O. Ornarovsky opened his "Ruthenian Bookstore" in Fort William and A. M. Pasichniak ventured forth with his special "Musical Supplies" in Winnipeg. In Toronto, there was organized "The Ukrainian Workers' Educational Bookstore Prosvita". But the oldest of them all was the Ruthenian Bookstore (Ruska Knyharnia) established by F. Dojachek in Winnipeg in 1905. Some of these bookstores, like the Ukrainian Bookstore in Edmonton and the Ukrainian Bookstore in Montreal, were also engaged in reprints of popular Ukrainian editions. The largest of these, again, was "Ruska Knyharnia" in Winnipeg, which later changed its name to "Ukrainian Bookstore" (Ukrainska Knyharnia).

Among the special Ukrainian trading establishments, the following are worthy of mention: The lumber store of P. Svarich and P. Melnyk in Vegreville; the first market of C. T. Lytwyn, Winnipegosis; the farm machinery sales outlet in Vonda; the hardware store in Wakaw, M. Venger's bakery shop in Fort William. In the realm of larger establishments, of those days, belong such "giants" as: Ruthenian National Trading Store (Ukrainska Narodna Torhovla) in Alberta with branches in Vegreville, Chipman and Innisfree and the Ukrainian Farmers' Elevator Company (Ukrainska Farmerska Elevatorska Spilka) with its main office in Winnipeg and several branches in Western Canada. It also boasted of a popular euphonic name of "Ukrainian Grain Company". In addition to these, The Farmers' Loan Co. (Farmerska Pozychkowa Kasa) was organized in Edmonton and a similar one in Winnipeg.

The Professionals and businessmen showed a steady growth in the pioneer era. At the end of this period you could find them in every branch of active life. True enough, in proportion to the number of Ukrainian population, they represented but a small percentage; but when we stop to consider its steady, unbroken progress, we cannot help but perceive its onward stride from year to year. Coupled with this energetic stride, the Ukrainian community in Canada, with each passing year, expressed its own unique identity through ever richer forms. Farmers and laborers alike, along with businessmen and professionals, forged their inborn characters and strengthened their rugged backbones during this epochal era.

THE PRESS

It is quite possible that a person never feels the need of a printed word more than when he finds himself isolated from the rest of the world. The press and the printed word becomes for him a medium of communication that puts him in touch with the outer world and reassures him that he is still a part of it. And this is the way the Ukrainian pioneers felt when they found themselves stranded on the wide Canadian prairies, in the depths of the coal mines or working in the lumber camps of primeval forests. Wherever they found themselves their life was still isolated from the surrounding world. Lacking in knowledge of the country's language and faced with the new and alien social-conventional terms they were forced to seek a human bond with their own kind. In the early beginning not only colonies but even the farms were separated from each other with wide open spaces in between. Communication facilities were not built as yet and the so-called mass media of transmission, like radio and television, were unheard of. It is therefore understood that press was the only basic means of transmitting information for the news-hungry settler-pioneers. The kind of press that Ukrainian pioneers were longing for was not to be had in Canada during that early period. As is well known the first Ukrainian newspaper did not appear until the end of 1903. The distance between Canada and Ukraine was very great, to say the least, and one had to wait at least a month or more before a paper from the homeland found itself in the hands of a settler.

"Svoboda"

To find their way out of the lack of the printed word, the Ukrainian pioneers turned their attention to the only Ukrainian newspaper that was being published on the American continent, namely the weekly paper "Svoboda". True enough, prior to Svoboda's appearance, there had been in circulation another Ukrainian paper, the "America", that was edited by Rev. I. Voliansky and later by Rev. K. Andrukhovych in Shenandoah, in 1886 but it did not last very long as its editors themselves were obliged to depart from U.S.A. Three years after "America's" demise the "Svoboda" came into life. Its first issue saw the light of day in Jersey City on the 15th of September 1893. It was at first a private enterprise under the total ownership of one person. Father H. Hrushka, at its first beginning, was the whole establishment by himself, even to the menial post of type-setter. He perceived the great need of Ukrainian settlers, both in U.S.A. and Canada—to have their own national newspaper. These people were living in a new world where there was a great deal of the unknown to contend with and he had to find an explanation for these things. In addition to this need a new life was coming into its own in these new settlements, composed of the integrated creative spirit that would blossom in time into churches, schools, cultural-educational organizations, political clubs, business establishments and others of their kind. All this was searching for a tribune from which all these questions could be answered or posed—a medium on whose pages human thoughts and opinions could be registered, stimulated and exposed.

The very name of the paper "Svoboda" (Freedom) appealed to its readers. The name stood for the exact opposite, the enslavement of national and social life, against which they had been so bravely fighting and fleeing in the end. For this reason alone, if for no other, "Svoboda" became very quickly the national tribune filled not only with sketches and pictures of the life of Ukrainians living in U.S.A., but also of those living in Canada.

Already in Svoboda year-book for 1894 we come across bits of news depicting interesting moments in the life of Ukrainian settlers in Canada. Starting with 1896 "Svoboda" printed a regular column the "Kanadiyska Rus" (Canadian Rus) in which were recorded absorbing incidents from the life of Ukrainian Canadians. The inestimable value of this paper lies in its yearly records of Ukrainian immigration to Canada. These consisted, in large measure, of the articles written by Kyrylo (Cyril) Genik who, as an immigration official in its Winnipeg bureau had official statistics on which to base his reports. Of an immense value to the history of Ukrainian Canadians are the articles written by the first Ukrainian priests in Canada who came here from U.S.A., such as—Rev. N. Dmytriw, Rev. P. Tymkevych, Rev. D. Polivka and Rev. I. Zaklynsky—who considered it as a part of their duty to send to the press accurate reports about their organizational visitations across Canada. We also find in "Svoboda" official reports of the Canadian Immigration authorities as well as their official advertising notices. On the pages of "Svoboda" could also be found many polemic articles sent from different Ukrainian communities regarding the conditions in Canada and from these the readers could also guage the many-sided development of the pioneer era. For nearly twenty years "Svoboda" was a unique official oracle of the Ukrainian national thought in Canada. This function was diligently performed by "Svoboda" until such time as Canada was able to produce its own Ukrainian press which was independent outside influences and interests.

"Svoboda" transferred its offices in 1895-1896 to Shamokin and later to Mount Carmel. From here it was moved again to Olyphant in 1900 and then to Scranton. In 1907 it was moved to New York and from here to Jersey City in 1911. Its editors in turn have been: H. Hrushka, I. Konstankevych, N. Dmytriw, S. Makar, I. Ardan, M. Strutynsky, A. Curkovsky and O. Stetkevych. With the exception of the last two all the others were priests who had come to America from Western Ukraine. All the above mentioned were nationally oriented and so they naturally fought against the russophile tendencies that were being spread widely, across U.S.A. and Canada, by the Russian Orthodox Mission and other political agents. The clarion call of these editor-priests had been clearly defined as: "enlightment for the people", "orientation on one's own strength" and "the building of religious-cultural-educational life within the scope of one's own organizational system". They very often appealed to Ukrainians to settle in Canada on homesteads and establish their own distinctive Ukrainian colonies. They considered the wage-earnings in factories and coal mines of U.S.A. as a temporary transition period for those who wished to settle down on farms and lead the pastoral life of agriculturalists. By this "prompting aid" from "Svoboda" a large number of families moved from U.S.A. to Canada. In 1897 alone tens of families, mostly from the "Lemkivshchyna" district of Western Ukraine, and who had been living for several years in U.S.A., came to settle in western Canada. Usually they had already mastered the English language and this enabled them to take a leading place in the cultural-educational and community activities, among the new Ukrainian immigrants in Canada.

In 1908 the publishing house of "Svoboda" was bought by the "Rusky Narodn y Soyuz" (Ruthenian—now Ukrainian—National Association, Inc.) publication retaining its ownership until the present time. The size of "Svoboda" was very small at first consisting of four pages only. With the growth of immigrant community life, in U.S.A. and Canada, the size and volume of the paper also grew in proportion. Finally it transformed itself from a weekly to a daily status, but this change was gradual and was realized somewhat later. The early yearbook volumes of "Svoboda" are the best chronicles of Ukrainian Canadian life.

Newspapers of a different type also came from U.S.A. to Canada during the early times. These were the russophile oriented publications that were financed and propagandized by the Russian Orthodox Mission in America and there was even some support that came direct from Moscow. Such Russophile papers were: "Svit" (World) of Old Forge, Pennsylvania, in 1897 and "Pravda" (Truth) of New York, in 1900. The first named paper also supported "Pravoslavne Obshchestvo Vzaymopomoshche" (Orthodox Mutual Benefit Association) while the latter one supported "Obshchestvo Ruskykh Bratstv" (Federation of Russian Brotherhood). Both papers carried on exclusively the all-Russian policy and tried with all the powers at their command to destroy everything that contained even a small kernel of Ukrainian ideology or was in any way connected with it. A steady battle was always in progress between "Svoboda" on one side and "Svit" and "Pravda" on the opposite side. A great deal of help was rendered to the Ukrainian press, in this verbal battle, by "Chaly", whose real name was Sava Chernetsky who through the medium of his humorous and biting satire ridiculed the paid mercenary servility of "Svit" and "Pravda".

Manitoba

The continuous flow of Ukrainian immigration into Canada and the gradual growth of its cultural-educational life in the new country prevailed upon the leading figures of that period to consider the idea of having their own Ukrainian newspapers in Canada. Such an idea was first presented on the pages of "Svoboda", in 1902, by Kyrylo Genik-Berezowsky who was, in his time, an official in the Winnipeg immigration bureau and who had a steady contact with Ukrainian immigrants, travelled widely and knew the basic needs of the settlers. A discussion was started in "Svoboda" at the beginning of 1902, concerning the Ukrainian Canadian press. K. Genik wrote that the planned paper should: "stand on guard for our rights and for the interests of Canada" [1].

"Canadian Farmer"

Public gatherings were held concerning the need of a local press and so after two years of preparations the first Ukrainian paper in Canada under the name of "Kanadiysky Farmer" (Canadian Farmer) [2] and dated November 5, 1903 — published by "The North West Publishing Company"— made its first appearance. The directors of this first publishing company

---

[1] "Svoboda" No. 12, March 29, 1902.

[2] M. H. Marunchak: "Who organized the publishing establishment and the newspaper—"Canadian Farmer", page 28-34 in "Canadian Farmer Almanac for 1966".

PIONEER ERA — ILLUSTRATIONS

Socialist Press of the Pioneer Era: Above—"The Red Flag" and "The Working People", below: "New Society" and "The Workers' Word"

Above: Process of change—from "Canadian Ruthenian" to "Canadian Ukrainian"
Below: Printing shop "Narodna Knyharnia", Winnipeg, 1916

PIONEER ERA — ILLUSTRATIONS

Press in Alberta and Saskatchewan

Above: "Canadian News", Edmonton and "Progress", Mundare, Alta.
Below: "New Country", Rosthern, Sask.

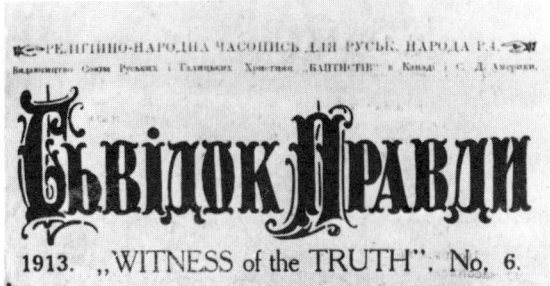

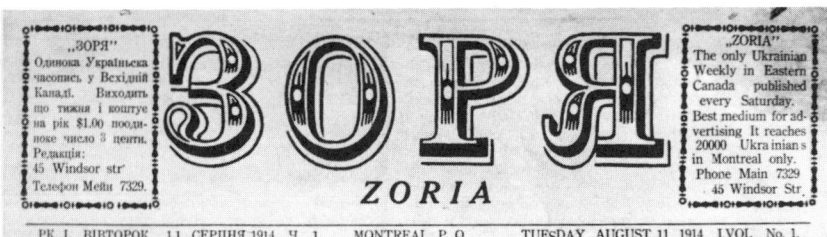

Press with special features:

Above: "Witness of the Truth", Toronto, "Zoria", Montreal
Below: "Canada"—conservative paper and "Ukrainian Labour News", first Ukrainian pro-communist paper in Canada

PIONEER ERA — ILLUSTRATIONS

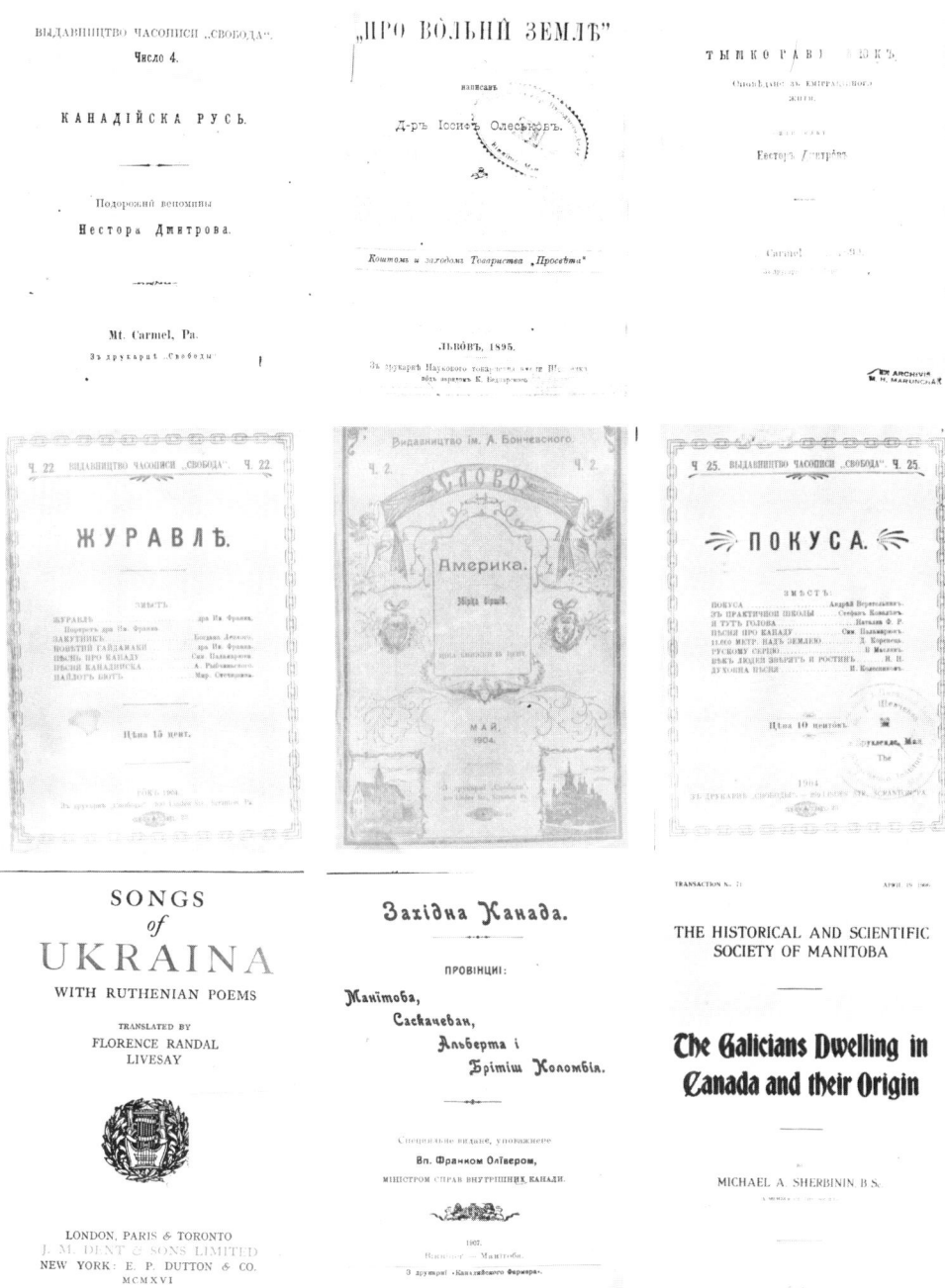

Issues of historical significance in the formation of Ukrainian ethnicity in Canada

Middle: Samples of Ukrainian Canadian writing outside Canada
Bottom: "Songs of Ukraina" and "The Galicians Dwelling in Canada and their Origin"—the first publications about the Ukrainians in Canada in the English language

"Western Canada" (bottom in the middle)—first historical account

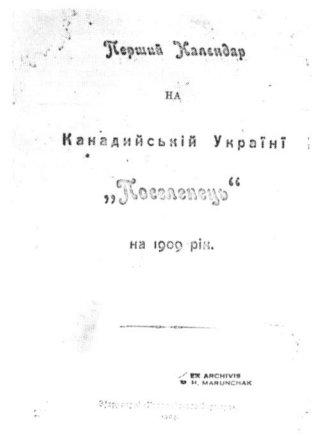

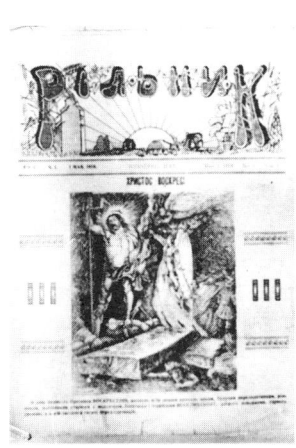
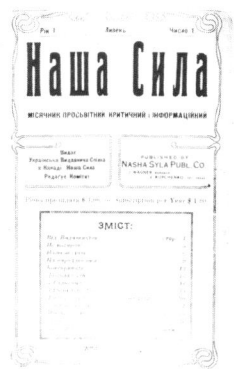

Top: First published books in Ukrainian in Canada
Middle: First Ukrainian journals in Canada: Home (Khata), Ukraina (Ukraine), Agriculturist (Rilnyk)
Bottom: Our Strength (Nasha Syla), Bell (Dzvinok), Incense (Kadylo), Uncle (Vuyko), Field (Nyva)

PIONEER ERA — ILLUSTRATIONS

Bilingual respectively multilingual paper—a segment of "The Farmers Weekly Telegram"—Ukrainian section under the name "Worldwide News For Ukrainian Readers", 1910

Bilingual poets and prosaics: M. Gowda, Florence R. Livesay, Fred Nex

Editorial staff of "The Stone Breakers" journal

248 UKRAINIAN CANADIANS: A HISTORY

Northern section of military "Camp Hughes", where Ukrainian volunteers were trained during the First World War

Ukrainians in Canadian Army leaving for training camps, Canora, Sask.

Ukrainian platoon in the Canadian Army at "Camp Hughes", consisting of 34 Ukrainians and 8 Anglosaxons, 1915

PIONEER ERA — ILLUSTRATIONS

"190 Overseas Battalion Little Black Devils" in which were many Ukrainians from Winnipeg, 1916

Ukrainian Canadians of 184th Battalion under the command of Lieut. R. M. MacTaggent, Winnipeg, 1916

War documents—Identification card for foreigners to be submitted once a month for inspection

UKRAINIAN CANADIANS: A HISTORY

Letter from "Detention Camp" in Brandon to the parish of the Ukrainian Catholic Church in Winnipeg pleading for books for the detainees

Ukrainian pioneers in "Detention Camp" in Brandon, 1915

Evidence of the cultural ties with the motherland:

Letter from the historian Mykhaylo Hrushevsky to the Ukrainian Teachers' Association in Canada, Lviv, 1907

До "Організації Українського Учительства в Канаді."

Дуже дякую Організації за ту честь, яку мені зроблено, вибравши мене почесним членом. Щирим серцем радію, що і в Далекій од Київа Канаді все організувалося українське просвітнє війство, щоб залогти ся в темряві. Що в трийцятий день свого ювилейного організаційного життя виявило Товариство своє прихильність до мене, — се мені велика честь. Приймаю-чи її в подякою, бажаю Організації як найширо-шого і найкращого розвитку і участи на доброї своєї праці над справою рідньої просвіти.

З великого шанування
Б. Грінченко

1907. IX. 11.
З Київа

P. S. Разом з цим посилаю до бібліотеки Організації деякі свої книжки. Дуже дякував-би, коли б мені прислано статут Організації.

Адреса: Київ, Маріїнсько-Благовіщенська, 67, кв. 8 і б. д.
Грінченко.

Writer Borys Hrinchenko welcomes Ukrainian Teachers in Canada as their honorary member, Kiev, 1907

Intellectuals from Lviv and Chernivtsi extending greetings to the Ukrainian Teachers in Canada: M. Lozynsky, M. Spynul, and Konstantyna Malycka

Dr. Kyrylo Trylowsky in constant contact with Ukrainians in Canada—above: his letter to teachers

Visit of Dr. S. Demydchuk, representative of "Ridna Shkola" in Lviv, Vegreville, 1913

PIONEER ERA — ILLUSTRATIONS

Outstanding women in various social aspects of the pioneer era:

A. Budnyk-Stechishin

M. Boyanivska

D. Pavlukevych

P. Boykowich-Korchynska

A. Yonker

R. Sozanska

A. Arabska

C. Vepruk

N. Rurak-Ferley

UKRAINIAN CANADIANS: A HISTORY

Pioneer teachers with the oldest teacher Sister Athanasia:

V. Karpetz   Sister Athanasia   S. Lytvyn

M. Boychuk   M. Mihaychuk (teacher & dentist)   P. Humeniuk

A. Malliniuk   A. Skorobohach   J. Havirko

PIONEER ERA — ILLUSTRATIONS

Prominent community workers, businessmen, professionals:

M. M. Gabora   J. Sozansky & J. Vepruk   T. Tuchtie

M. Lazechko (first druggist)   P. Rudyk   I. Semeniuk

P. Gigeychuk (school organizer)   T. Panchyshyn   D. Romanchych

258　UKRAINIAN CANADIANS: A HISTORY

Members of the Board of the Ukrainian Canadian Citizenship League:

PIONEER ERA — ILLUSTRATIONS

Poets, writers, editors, scholars:

P. Karmansky · M. Shcherbinin · Dr. O. Sushko

D. Rarahowsky ький · S. Kovbel · I. Kovalsky

S. Fodchuk · G. Skvarok · M. P. Berezynsky

260   UKRAINIAN CANADIANS: A HISTORY

Outstanding Canadian statesmen, scholars and intellectuals who constantly entertained a high esteem of the Ukrainian settlers and defended their good name:

Charles Tupper

Sir Wilfred Laurier

T. Mayne Daly

Dr. A. J. Hunter

Sir Rodmond Roblin

Prof. G. Bryce

S. J. Doherty

Arthur Meighen

H. A. MacKie

were: K. Genik (Genyk), I. Negrich, I. Bodrug, T. Stefanyk and J. Dyma. The first three named were then known as "Berezivska Triytsia" (the Bereziv Trio) from the name of the Bereziv village in Western Ukraine where the three of them came from. This quintet belonged to the top level pioneer leadership of those, now distant, days. Their names are often found in connection with many important church and community activities.

Ivan Negrich was the first editor of the "Kanadiysky Farmer". The first printer and type-setter was Osyp Kosovy, brought by the firm from U.S.A., and who was a professional printer from the city of Lviv. His assistant was the young college student, Oleksa Antoniuk, who hailed from Trofanivka-Balynci, district of Kolomyja, Western Ukraine. This trio from distant lands essembled brought out the first issue of the first Ukrainian "gazeta" (newspaper) in Canada. In its sub-title could be seen the assuring script which said that this was "A paper for the Ruthenian (Ukrainian) people in Canada", and that it will be published every week on Thursday and subscription to Canada and U.S.A. will be a dollar per year and to Austria a dollar and a half." In the English language it was printed thus: "Canadian Farmer", The Ruthenian Weekly published every Thursday, corner McDermot and Arthur St., Winnipeg, P.O. Box 82.

Unfortunately, neither the first issue nor the first year-book of this first Ukrainian paper has been found in Canada. On account of this we haven't any samples to show what were the guiding editorials of the "Canadian Farmer" during its formative, first-step period. But this lack of information is somewhat compensated for by the ebullient greetings sent by "Svoboda" to "Canadian Farmer" on the occasion of the first appearance of this new Canadian journal, saying: "Canadian Farmer stands on a solid national foundation and desires strongly to serve, first of all, the interests of Ruthenian-Canadians although the Ruthenians of U.S.A. will also find on its pages much that will be of interest to them [3]).

The Canadian Ruthenians had need of such a newspaper for quite some time, so for that reason we are delighted with this progressive step of our Canadian kinfolk and we greet them with open arms. We wish it every success in its growth and development, and that it will ever bear in mind the welfare of its readers, be it moral, spiritual or material".

There were occasional deviations of the "Canadian Farmer" from the guide lines suggested by "Svoboda". The first four editors were members of the Independent (Ukrainian) Greek (Orthodox) Church whose policies and material support stemmed from the Presbyterian Church. It was said that one section of the "Canadian Farmer" was devoted to espousing the cause of this church, while people of other church affiliations were supposedly without access to this press. Another anomaly arose out of the financial weakness of the "Canadian Farmer" and its sponsors who found it necessary to seek financial aid elsewhere. Help came from the Liberal Party and notably from the Winnipeg Free Press. He who pays the piper, calls the tunes. The "Canadian Farmer" took on the flavor and philosophy of the Liberal Party and championed that point of view in all succeeding elections and spoke out against conservatives and socialists.

A temporary reversal of the fortunes of the Independent Greek Church caused a similar decline of the press—but this situation did not last long. During this period the Greek Catholics began to seek fulfillment of their

---

[3]) "Svoboda", No. 48, 1903.

desires and aspirations and so began to demand of the press recognition of and tolerance for their point of view. The build-up of this pressure contributed towards a change of editors. John Negrich was succeeded by Joseph Megas as chief editor and reversed the editorial policies on the religious front. This change in policy received inadvertent assistance from the fact that the Independent Greek (Orthodox) Church in 1905 launched its own church paper, thus enabling the "Canadian Farmer" to disengage itself from the religious question and to assume the role of being truly secular in character.

Succeeding editors pursued similar policies—albeit Zyhmont Bychynsky, finding himself in the midst of Presbyterian subscribers, could not maintain complete neutrality. In this Appolinary Nowak was more successful. Most successful was Onufriy Hykawy who became editor in 1912—when the "Canadian Farmer", a four page edition, numbering some 2000 copies per issue, found itself in dire straits, and at which time full ownership was acquired by Frank Dojacek. Hykawy served long and well. During this pioneering era the editors were ably assisted by Hnat Platsko, Julian Sytnyk and M. Syroidiw who later became the first editor of the Ukrainian Catholic press in Canada. In 1908 "Canadian Farmer" had 3000 subscribers distributed as follows: Manitoba—818, Ontario—327, Nova Scotia—1, Saskatchewan—612, British Columbia—142, Quebec—69, Alberta—564, Yukon—1, U.S.A.—125, Europe—100, and the city of Winnipeg—300. In 1911 the "Canadian Farmer" numbered 4000 subscribers. By 1915 the subscription list reached 7000 and remained at this number to the end of World War I.

"The Word"

In September of 1904 [4]) there was organized in Winnipeg another Ukrainian newspaper appearing as a four-page format. Like the "Canadian Farmer", "The Word" accepted financial backing of a political party—the Conservative—and it adopted the conservative point of view and supported both the Greek Catholic and Greek Orthodox Church groups. Unfortunately no copies of "The Word" came to hand, but one gathers from other contemporary journals that O. Kosowy was the editor-in-chief and his assistant P. Sniezek. Administrative assistants were M. Hedinger, M. Rudnicky, J. W. Arsenych and Y. Koltek, the latter two doubling as typesetters, having learned the trade at the "Canadian Farmer". Other co-workers were O. Hykawy, Y. Sichynsky and W. Fekula who, under the pseudonym of Shpekula, wrote folksy verses and conducted a vigorous campaign against seraphimism. One such versification was dedicated to Seraphim and Genik. Both newspapers conducted a polemic contest against each other which at times was rather rough and ready, punctuated by bursts of name-calling and mud-slinging. The "Canadian Farmer" dubbed "The Word" as the "Polish rag" for employing some workers of Polish origin Sniezek, Rudnicki and in turn "The Word" called the "Canadian Farmer" the "Seraphim rag" for espousing Seraphim's political philosophy. Ultimately "The Word" withdrew from this sniping contest probably due to the fact that Rudnicki and Sniezek transgressed the criminal code by virtue of having become involved in some questionable real estate transactions which carried for some a cooling-off period in the local "cooler". This episode cast a pall of doubt upon "The Word". In May 1905, "The

---

[4]) Surmised data.

Word" ceased to appear. Attempts were made to resurrect it, but to no avail. At the time that "The Word" fell into difficulties, the "Canadian Farmer" "stole a march" by reversing its stand pertaining to seraphi mism, thus removing the principal "raison d'etre" for "The Word".

"Morning"

The third newspaper to be launched by Canadian Ukrainians was "Ranok" (Morning). The first issue appeared June 15, 1905, as the monthly organ of the Independent Greek Church of Canada"—a four-page tabloid costing 50 cents a year. It was anti-Catholic from its inception, a role which was pursued with vigor. It was supported financially and religiously by the Presbyterian Church and its political orientation was liberal. It was cleverly edited by Ivan Bodrug, founder and leader of the seraphim-presbyterian movement. Although the editorial board included J. Bachynsky, M. Bachynsky, and I. Danylchuk, nevertheless Bodrug played a dominating leadership role. Technical difficulties in 1906 curtailed the press momentarily. By 1907, "Ranok" had grown to an eight-page, semi-monthly paper. Bodrug acquired ownership of the publication, located at 477-479 Stella Avenue, Winnipeg. In 1908 Ranok was printed in New York to which city I. Bodrug had moved. Here also appeared another Presbyterian newspaper called "Union", intended primarily for the U.S.A. The editor was O. Kosowy, formerly compositor and typesetter at the "Canadian Farmer" and editor of "The Word". Bodrug's influence was clearly evident. Ambrose Karchut continued as editor of "Ranok" for many years. Ranok had a complement of reporters throughout the country, among which were M. P. Berezynsky, W. Wiwchar, J. Sytnyk, Z. Bychynsky, P. Svarich—a satirist, and P. Bozyk—poet and writer of anecdotes. In 1911, "Ranok" format changed from tabloid to newspaper and was reorganized under corporate ownership headed by J. Bodrug, J. M. Glowa, J. Bachynsky, M. Bachynsky and I. Danylchuk—with Glowa as president and editor. "Ranok" became a popular newspaper which, in addition to its publicity, contained many interesting stories, (serialized) novels and satire about life in Canada. In 1916-17 "Ranok" reached new heights under the influence of Paul Krat and Dr. Alexander Sushko—both outstanding editors —the former had been editor of the "Red Banner" and co-worker of the "Working People", and the latter editor of the "Canadian Ruthenian", 1914-1915. Another talented associate of "Ranok" was A. Maksymchuk who was a pastor, first in Eastern Canada and later in Western Canada and who penned courageous editorials on community affairs. On occasion his incisive, analytical, critical and satirical articles stung the high and mighty. It is worthy to note that Maksymchuk spoke out strongly against the rescinding of statutes (laws) during World War I pertaining to Canadian Ukrainian privileges and practices. In his editorial entitled "In Defence of Canadian Ukrainians" he wrote: "We conquered the wilderness, and transformed it into agricultural domains where the English failed. The Ukrainians, too, like other Canadians contributed wholeheartedly to the successful prosecution of the war effort against the common enemy. Britain's enemy is Ukraine's enemy". This was a most courageous editorial which was supported by other newspapers. "Ranok" was among the first to publish grievances wrought upon the Canadian Ukrainians and addressed to the Canadian nation under the heading "An Address to the Canadian Nation" in which was elaborately delineated the national stand of Canadian

Ukrainians and their relationship to the so-called Austrophilism. Maksymchuk wrote under the pseudonym of "O. Kyryliw". P. Krat and O. Sushko contributed to the literary section their own creations and they frequently returned to religious polemics. In "Ranok" there appeared continuous historical exploration of Dr. G. Bryce, Canadian historian, who had written a review study of the Ukrainian Presbyterian movement in Canada in which he gave vivid character portrayals of outstanding Presbyterians such as Y. A. Carmichael, R. P. McKay, C. W. Gordon, A. B. Bird, who had close contacts with the Presbyterian movement amongst the Ukrainians. "Ranok" initiated the Christian-farmer convention held in Saskatoon December 26 and 27, 1916, attended by some 200 delegates from all across Canada but with the majority coming from Saskatchewan. This was one of the most important conventions to take place in this pioneering era. At this convention there was passed unanimously a resolution requesting the teaching of Ukrainian at the University of Saskatchewan. A most vigorous protest was voiced against the rescinding of certain legislation once extended to Canadian Ukrainians. Representatives from the University of Saskatchewan as well as local elected representatives participated at the convention. "Ranok" was also instrumental in the organizing of bursa at Canora, February 17 and March 16, 1917, and at Wakaw convention held on February 11th, 1917, it was resolved to organize a Saskatchewan Ukrainian Pedagogical Society and a Ukrainian Museum at the University of Saskatchewan. "Ranok" was also in the vanguard in advocating the formation of the "Ivan Franko Educational Society", the principal champions being Dr. O. Sushko and A. Maksymchuk-Kyryliw. "Ranok" carried translations of D. F. B. Livesay's poetry. In the religious field "Ranok" ran "Sunday School" lessons, featured for a long time Christian songs gleaned from the collections of the Christian world, translated into Ukrainian by Ivan Bodrug and later appearing as an anthology under the editorship of Dr. O. Sushko. "Ranok" also devoted a section to "Canadian Agriculture and Home Economics".

In general, "Ranok" was interestingly edited and its annuals preserve much valuable and durable material. "Ranok" was issued as 4 and 6 page editions; the subscription rate was one dollar per year, making it the least expensive of comparable papers, perhaps because it was subsidized by the Presbyterian Church. When publication management of "Ranok" passed into the hands of a business group it was converted into the so-called "Union Press" located at Pritchard Avenue and McGregor Street and its Post Office box was for a long time No. 3596. Ranok also published popular religious booklets and pamphlets designed to spread protestantism amongst the populace.

In 1906 an attempt was made to organize a new Ukrainian newspaper. Concern arose over the fact that existing papers were completely immersed in party or religious politics. Editorials began to appear in "Svoboda" calling for an independent new paper unencumbered by political affiliations. M. Gowda of Edmonton wrote a lengthy editorial entitled "We Need a Good Ruthenian Newspaper in Canada", saying:

"We cannot spend our hard-earned money on decrepit political cliques which does not provide the reader with worthwhile intelligent, educational material but rather continues to rehash election after election. They do not understand the role of national life—Ukrainian—here in a new country... We need a Ruthenian (Ukrainian) newspaper which would defend our interests courageously, confidently... Let us build our society on the broad, free prairies of Canada where a harvest is assured once the seed is planted in the fertile soil. Let us build an enduring society upon sound foundations and not on quicksand" [5]). Gregory Bagger wrote from Vancouver that Ukrainians need a newspaper, progressive, independent of all party affiilations, basing itself upon membership dues. There were many such expressions which, no doubt, encouraged T. Jastremsky of Winnipeg to organize the "Canadian Star" [6]). But in view of the fact that T. Jastremsky himself was an active Conservative, it seemed doubtful that the publication would be idependent. Nevertheless, some one hundred individuals each purchased twenty-five dollar shares in the new venture. The organizers had hoped to receive Catholic support. For this support the Catholics wanted the paper to be solely Catholic in nature. The venture collapsed.

"The Red Banner"

In 1907, the T. Shevchenko Educational Society—a socialistic group—organized the "Ukrainian Free Thinkers Federation" "of socialists and anarchists". As the title suggests the federation served as the rallying point for diverse opinions disregarding personal political affiliations. This subsequently had reverberations when in this setting the hour of reckoning struck. In a provocative article one of the leaders of this federation, Myroslaw Stechishin stated that "The Ukrainian Free Thinkers Federation" is giving serious thought to publishing its own paper [7]). Such a journal appeared November 15, 1907, under the title of "Chervony Prapor" (Red Banner), at whose masthead appeared this bilingual inscription in English "Socialist Party of Canada", with a sub-title "The Red Flag Socialist Weekly for Ukrainian Proletariat". Exhortations were featured such as: "Proletariats of All Countries Unite", and "In this battle workers will lose only their chains and gain the whole world". The editorial and administrative board had its quarters at 467 Manitoba Avenue, that is, with the T. Shevchenko Educational Society. The editor was Paul Krat—who had participated in the revolutionary movement in Ukraine—a giant of a man, with strong political beliefs. Although there appeared on page 4, the last page, in English "Issued by Ukrainian-Ruthenian Local—Winnipeg—Socialist Party of Canada"—the three most active Ukrainian socialist groups were located in Winnipeg, Portage la Prairie, in Manitoba, and at Nanaimo, B.C. The "Red Banner" castigated the exploitation of the working man and urged workers to organize for social improvement and it led the anti-clerical movement. For these reasons, The Red Banner won to its cause faithful followers, but on the other hand, it alienated itself from the conservative masses. Although registered as a weekly, with a circulation of 2000, at its height, it dwindled into a bi-weekly, then into a monthly and following its 18th edition, August 8, 1908, it folded up. The last editor was Wasyl Holowacky, a person not widely popular. His co-worker was Myroslaw Stechishin who ran articles contributed by laborers who bemoaned their

---

[5]) "Svoboda", No. 3, 1906.
[6]) T. Jastremsky—"Canadianization", section on "Organization of a Publishing Firm", pp. 72, 73.
[7]) "Svoboda" — No. 5, January, 1907.

hardships in Canada. "Red Banner" was the first to use the modern term "Ukrainian", then spelled, "Ookrainian" as a synonym for Ruthenian.

"The Working People"

With the collapse of "The Red Banner", the active socialists headed by Myroslaw Stechishin organized in 1909 "The Working People", with headquarters located at 135 Stevens Avenue. This 4-page publication appeared as a monthly, under the sponsorship of the Ukrainian Socialist Publishing Company with M. Stechishin as editor-in-chief. The introductory issue stated that "'The Working People" goes out into the world as an organ of Ukrainian Socialists of Canada and the United States, and that one of its objectives is the formation of a "Ukrainian Socialist League" whose purpose is "to propagate socialistic ideas amongst Ukrainian citizens of this country and to organize our working masses for battle against our exploiters, for a socialist Canada". The name Ukrainian Socialist League did not last long. On August 15, 1910, there appeared the "Manifesto of the newly-created Social-Democratic Party of Canada". At the first convention of the Federation of Ukrainian Social-Democrats held in Edmonton, from August 22 to 27, 1910, among the resolutions adopted was one "to publish "The Working People" as a weekly". This took some time to realize. One mitigating factor was the appearance in Edmonton of a paper entitled "The New Society" also sponsored and supported by the Federation of Ukrainian Socialists from Western Canada. "The New Society" under the resolute leadership of Roman Kremar, entered into polemic controversy with "The Working People" which had developed more leftist tendencies. In 1911 "The Working People" became a weekly under the direction of C. Kotylak, D. Rarahowsky and M. Stechishin as general secretary; Ivan Nawiziwsky succeeded Stechishin as editor. The paper flourished because it had fairly good reporters from the old country and from Canada. For a while the editorship was assumed by E. Hucaylo, a delegated representative of the Ukrainian Social Democratic Party of Halychyna and Bukowyna. In January, 1914, "the Federation of Ukrainian Social Democrats" changed its name to "Ukrainian Social Democrats of Canada".

I. Stefanicky succeeded E. Hucaylo as editor for a brief period, but soon departed for Toronto where he published a semimonthly paper called "Conscious Force", later renamed "The Workers' Voice". Paul Krat followed next as editor of "The Working People" until 1916 at which time he severed his relations with the Social Democrats. He, in turn, was followed by Danylo Lobay and Matwiy Popowych who frequently travelled across the country soliciting financial support for the press. In this role he was assisted by both W. H. Kolisnyk and I. Nawiziwsky who were considered the heart and soul of the socialist movement in Canada. Events in Russia and Ukraine strengthened the position of "The Working People" so that by 1917 it had 3000 subscribers. By 1918 the Ukrainian Social Democratic Party of Canada numbered over 20 branches with a membership of 1500. When the struggle for independence broke out in Ukraine in 1918, "The Working People" assumed a most positive attitude towards the bolsheviks.

In Montreal, Ivan Hnyda organized his own publishing enterprise, "The New World" where he published numerous socialistic brochures and a journal called "New World".

Both "The Working People" in Winnipeg and the "Workers' Voice" in

Toronto were padlocked in September of 1918 by the Federal Government. The same fate befell all other Canadian Ukrainian newspapers.

In 1907, in Winnipeg, there appeared "The Orthodox Newspaper" published at irregular intervals by Bishop Seraphim who initially co-operated with the Independent Greek Church, but following his break with the Consistory of the Independent Greek Church, he attempted to organize an Orthodox Church independent of the Russian Synod. It was to this end that he organized "The Orthodox Newspaper". The second edition carried the date line October 26, 1907, and stated that it was the "first all-Russian church gazette for the whole of America" devoted to the dissemination of American Metropolitan Seraphim's ukases and directives".

It is unknown how many issues of this organ were published. Perhaps a few at most during 1907 and 1908. At best very little was to be found in the archives, but for the sake of gleaning a general impression it is worthy to cite "Svoboda", which wrote:

"Certainly from his exploits 'Bishop' Seraphim of Winnipeg, Canada, embarked upon the publication of a weekly paper "The Orthodox Newspaper". From the beginning of printing, such phenomenal originality as "The Orthodox", no one has ever seen. The one page newspaper with letters of various sizes and characters, gives evidence that the "bishop" himself is playing at type-setting. Where he lacks Russian characters, he substitutes Latin or Greek, or even such as do not appear in any orthography.

The orthography, the language and style appear in sharp conflict with all the languages of the whole world" [8].

Ordinarily such a publication could not survive long even in a pioneering era. Nevertheless, Seraphim had principles in certain respects when he noted that "neither fool nor traitor accept these articles".

The early Ukrainian press in Canada was replete with polemic editorials on religious or political themes, often embellished with personal opinions which displeased many citizens. This state of affairs was most displeasing especially to teachers and like-minded citizens who desired to have a press dedicated solely to cultural needs, growth and development of Ukrainian Canadians. At this time there was a sizable number of public-spirited leaders who desired to have a press which would orientate the people to develop their own resources and to become self-reliant and not remain beholden for favors and help from this or that party or religious groups.

"The Ukrainian Voice"

At the first conference of Ukrainian teachers held in Winnipeg in 1907 leading personalities such as O. Zerebko, T. D. Ferley, J. W. Arsenych, I. Kocan and others voiced the need for establishing an "all-national newspaper". This matter was raised and discussed at succeeding teachers' conferences, and was debated editorially by "Svoboda" and at various other conferences and conventions. This question received closest attention from those who stood four-square on the principle of providing a favorable cultural atmosphere and religious independence. The fruition of these numerous deliberations and yearnings appeared in 1909 in the formation of "The Ukrainian Publishing Company, Ltd." To the Board of Directors were elected T. Stefanyk, J. N. Krett, W. Chumer, W. Piniansky, T. D. Ferley, O. Charambura, W. Karpetz. The first general meeting was held Aug-

---

[8] "Svoboda", No. 21, November, 1907.

ust 21, 1909 in the parochial school of Sts. Vladimir and Olga. The membership of the board and the place of meeting speak convincingly and auspiciously. The advance notices announcing the calling of the first general meeting bore the signatures of 31 idealistic and prominent leaders such as Paul Gigeychuk, Thomas Jastremsky, Wasyl Kudryk, B. W. Smook, I. Puhaty, A. Slipchenko, M. W. Sloboda, P. Chaykowsky, and others. Among these was a goodly number of teachers, Catholics, Independent Catholics, and Presbyterians. There were supporters of various political convictions —Liberal, Conservatives and Democratic Socialists. This kaleidoscopic profile unanimously endorsed the principle that the proposed newspaper give national leadership, maintain equilibrium and espouse and support the aspirations of the Ukrainian citizenry. The "Canadian Farmer" took an antagonistic stand against the formation of such a new paper and refused to run any advertisements, notices and even news items concerning it. "Ranok" was equally cool. Both of these newspapers at that time were "opinion moulders". It was precisely because of that, that "The Ukrainian Voice" arose and acquired a "revolutionary name" whose very form and content bespoke its progressive and national flavor and philosophy. During this era newspapers rarely used the word "Ukrainian" either as noun or adjective. Common press usage treated as synonyms the old terminology Ruthenian, Rus (or Russ). The founders and publishers of "The Ukrainian Voice" adhered to the recommendations and declared principles of the Teachers' Conference in using the modern terminology—"Ukrainian". "The Ukrainian Voice" editorialized that it was a progressive paper in the fields of education, economics and politics dedicated to serve the needs of Ukrainian Canadian citizens for the common welfare". The first issue of "The Ukrainian Voic e" appeared March 14, 1910 under the press of J. N. Krett with headquarters at 292 Selkirk Avenue. It was an 8-page paper, hand-set. The editor was Wasyl Kudryk and the directors were T. D. Ferley, W. Chumer, W. Kudryk, W. Karpetz, A. Zylych, H. Slipchenko and J. W. Arsenych—all bilingual teachers. The clarion call of the paper was: "Education (enlightenment) for the Masses" and in the initial editorial the statement:

"We emigrated in great numbers to a country beyond the sea where now other people (ethnic groups) are beginning to pay closer attention to us, albeit, in a condescending manner, nevertheless, each (group) would like to absorb us. Therefore, we should cherish our self-respect and not become slaves to others but show that we have national dignity, and deserve and are entitled to the same rights and privileges accorded to others. To enable us to defend ourselves we must know how this is done—which comes with education and more education. It would be an everlasting disgrace not to acquire enlightenment because only through knowledge we will develop our full potential. Only through knowledge can we attain a good life to which all nations are entitled. Ignorance is crippling, enslaving, dehumanizing... We believe we can rely upon our national strength for it is only through our own efforts and resourcefulness that we can improve our welfare—never through the generosity of others, nor through begging...".

Succeeding editorials expanded and complemented the general enunciations by giving specific illustrations to serve as guidelines towards the attainment of these lofty goals. The publishers discerned clearly that the circumstances of the Ukrainian settlers in Canada were entirely different from those confronting Ukrainian settlers elsewhere, whence came reports that Ukrainians "fell into totally different environment—climatic, economic, political and cultural". These reports served to confirm that Ukrainians in Canada "have not as yet succeeded in benefiting from the opportunities open to them for full cultural growth". Exhortations went out to the people to rectify the situations and to fall in step with other Canadian citizens. Drawing attention to certain objectives, the publishers deemed it essential to single out a typical episode of that period, saying: "Although the written law is the same for all, nevertheless we have been short-changed almost every step of the way".

Wherein lay (did they see) the grievances? Apropos group alienation "The Ukrainian Voice" underscored in its first issue and subsequently, that the Federal Government aggrieved Ukrainian settlers by settling them on submarginal and unproductive land. It was also noted that employers classified employees according to ethnic origin, favoring some, while discriminating and aggrieving others whereto fell the lot of Ukrainians. To rectify this unfortunate situation, "The Ukrainian Voice" emphasized that its readers seek full benefit from the laws of Canada and especially to participate fully under the aegis of the Canada Election Act—through which medium future legislation can be effected for the common well-being. In addition, "The Ukrainian Voice" advocated "entry into higher educational spheres, organizations and the professions, the cultivation of one's own spiritual and moral strength so as to be qualified to discharge with competence one's responsibilities of citizenship as well as to participate in federal affairs". The ideological-political section of "The Ukrainian Voice" was emblazoned with the rising sun whose spreading rays attracted from the dark a maiden bearing a burning torch over whose flickering flame appeared the motto: "In knowledge and union lies our strength".

"The Ukrainian Voice" was edited during the pioneering era by Wasyl Kudryk who in 1921 entered pastoral service, and T. D. Ferley, who for many years was administrator. A stable administrative staff enabled "The Ukrainian Voice" to adhere to its major objectives, namely, faith in one's own strength, the cultivation of respect for self and others, preservation of language and culture, bilingual competence (English and Ukrainian), formation of cultural societies, continuous exhortation for education and world enlightenment, self-defence against unfriendly environment, and active participation in municipal, provincial and federal elections.

"The Ukrainian Voice" provided leadership for Ukrainians in their social and political battles. It assisted in raising funds for "Ridna Shkola"—"Ukrainian School",—supported various community projects in wholly Ukrainian centers, called Ukrainian students to petition for a Ukrainian University in Lviv, supported the Ukrainian cause on diplomatic levels, and supported the Ukrainian-Canadian delegation to the Paris Peace Conference. In retrospect, one can certainly affirm that the principles espoused by "The Ukrainian Voice" were in harmony with the aspirations of the general public. In essence, the "Ukrainian Voice" became the spokesman of a broad national movement, thus acquiring a mandate to speak authoritatively on each issue, unfettered by political or religious pressures. "The Ukrainian Voice" derived its strength from donations and subscription dues. Having general public support from the Teachers' Society, National Home Associations, Reading and Cultural Societies, "The Ukrainian Voice" continued to expand to become a popular Ukrainian news media, educator and mentor. In the religious arena it enjoyed a carte blanche, having the support of Catholics, Independent Catholics and Orthodox, thus being the fountainhead of the religious current amongst Ukrainian Canadians, a role and status enjoyed to about 1916-18, at which time it committed itself to the cause of organizing The Ukrainian Greek Orthodox Church. Participation in this venture seems to have circumscribed its horizon and subsequently projected it into a religious controversy of varying dimensions.

In passing it needs to be mentioned that as far as Canadian policy and loyalty to Canada is concerned, "The Ukrainian Voice" remained true to its principles.

"Canadian Ruthenian"

The last publication to appear was sponsored by Ukrainian Catholics who accepted the jurisdiction of Archbishop Langevin [9]. Archbishop Langevin, together with his advisers, Basilian and Redemptorist Fathers, realized the need for a separate paper for Ukrainian Catholics—and after lengthy stallings—finally such a paper appeared May 27, 1911, under the name of "Canadian Ruthenian". It was a large 8-page weekly, 16x22 inches, issued every Saturday. Its headquarters were located at 619 McDermot Avenue—the home of "West Canada Publishing Co.".

The yearly subscription in Canada was one dollar; abroad, $1.50, single issues, 5 cents. The paper carried an announcement that all business communications pertaining to itself be addressed to "West Canada Publishing Co.".

The first editor was Mykola Syroidiw who wrote in his editorial, "The editor and publishers enunciate the following principles of this publication: the preservation of the Greek Catholic (Ukrainian) faith, the propagation of our language and literature, the founding of our churches, schools and societies... Our paper, based upon a national-religious foundation will consider its first duty to propagate and defend the foundations of the Greek Catholic (Ukrainian) faith—the faith of our fathers, grandfathers and great-grandfathers. The same applies to the aspirations of our people: that is, to nurture our language, songs, literature, the needs of political and economic life—all this will have our support. In subsequent editorials "that above and beyond the foregoing aspirations and endeavours (undertakings) we must learn the language of our adopted country". Learning the English language and becoming familiar with customs and traditions of Canada will not interfere with preserving our own, for in the words of our famous poet, Taras Shevchenko, "Learn the language of others, but do not forget your own". In the first editorial there were already underscored three problems on which "Canadian Ruthenian" declared war. There was talk about those "who believe in the white or good czar", i.e., the Russian Mission (Russian Orthodox Mission). Another issue was "those who seek to spread a new progressive religion"—an attack directed at the Independent Greek Church and "Ranok". The third target was "those who would like to mislead the people into irreligion"—i.e. the socialist group under the leadership of "The Working People". In its first issues "Canadian Ruthenian" directed most of its attention, editorially and in letters to the editor, to the Presbyterian stream. There appeared editorials addressed to

---

[9] A similar paper for Polish Catholics titled "The Canadian Voice" was financed by Archbishop Langevin in 1904—and edited by Adelbert Kulawy.

the Russian Mission. Much less attention was directed at the socialists. Editorials upbraided those ministers who would not accept the jurisdiction of the Roman Catholic hierarchy. For two years a violent campaign was conducted against such ministers as T. Wasylewych, I. Krochmalny, I. Zaklynsky and E. Krasicky. The latter bore the brunt of these attacks because he advocated establishing a Greek Catholic (Ukrainian) Church in Canada with its own bishop. The "Canadian Ruthenian" also featured editorials on such weighty issues as bilingual schools in Manitoba and correspondence concerning cultural work at rural points. In 1911 this weekly published "Epistles to Canadian Ruthenians" written by Metropolitan A. Shepticky.

On the whole, the paper was edited interestingly and popularly. Numerous contributions, mostly religious, bore testimony to the contacts the editor enjoyed with his readers. Although the weekly bore the name "Canadian Ruthenian", nevertheless in its texts the term Ukrainian was generally used in lieu of the older term "Ruthenian" or "Rus". How to explain the retention of the old name "Ruthenian" for this weekly newspaper to April, 1919, when it was renamed "The Canadian Ukrainian"? Who knows? Perhaps out of deference to the conservatism of its readers. And yet as early as April 1914, in the 17th issue, the publishers stated the paper is published by the "Ukrainian Publishing Company". As a result of political interference on the part of some members of the Roman Catholic consistory the editor-in-chief, M. Syroidiw resigned. He was succeeded by Dr. O. Sushko who was sponsored to Canada from Europe by Bishop Budka specifically for this purpose. Differences deepened due to the fact that Dr. Sushko was even more pro-liberal and progressive, whereas the publishers were staunch supporters of the Conservative Party.

In January, 1916, the publishers became independent and moved, lock, stock and barrel, to new quarters located at 590 Pritchard Avenue. This independence move cost Bishop Budka $5,000.00 to pay off old publishing debts. With the move there was formed a separate group of directors who came under the complete control of the "Ruthenian Greek Catholic Church". With this step Bishop Budka once and for ever disarmed his critics who maintained that the "Canadian Ruthenian" was an exploitive tool of the Roman Catholic hierarchy.

Dr. O. Sushko was succeeded into the editorship by A. Sarmatiuk, Peter Oleskiw and I. Petrushevych. All these performed other duties as well. Petrushevych also served as an administrator. Bishop Budka from time to time would "pitch in" at critical moments, and commented in a church circular to his clerics: "To maintain our "Canadian Ruthenian" on a high plane is rather taxing—the most difficult responsibility of your bishop, who at times fatigued to exhaustion still must contribute to the gazette" [10].

Bishop Budka was relieved of these responsibilities when Roman Kremar, formerly of "The News", Edmonton, assumed the editorship in 1918. The newspaper immediately gained momentum and aroused interest in the readers. He renamed the paper "'The Canadian Ukrainian" and gave whole-hearted editorial endorsation of the policies pursued by the Ukrainian National Rada (Parliament) in the revolutionary struggle for independence in Ukraine.

---

[10] Bishop Budka's letter entitled "Most Reverend Pastors of Our Eparchiate", No. 110, November 16, 1915, from the author's archives.

At the beginning of the second decade of this century there were in Winnipeg five impressive weekly newspapers which fully mirrored the moods and aspirations of Ukrainian communities in Canada. "The Ukrainian Voice", "The Canadian (Ruthenian) Ukrainian", "The Canadian Farmer", "Ranok" and "The Working People" supplied the keynotes to all Ukrainian political questions in Canada. To these keynote publications in Edmonton, Toronto and Montreal paid close attention and used them for purposes of orientation. When one takes into account attempt at publishing monthly journals—concerning which discourse will appear elsewhere—Winnipeg certainly qualified as a trail blazing, pace-setting publishing centre for Ukrainians of the pioneering era.

Alberta

"The New Society"

The first newspaper in Western Canada, was "The New Society" which appeared in Edmonton on February 4, 1911, as an organ of the "Federation of Ukrainian Socialists in Canada". As we already know this weekly paper took a critical stand in opposition to "The Working People", a Winnipeg-based socialist paper with strong leaning towards the Internationale. "The New Society" a small 4-page gazette had a subscription fee of two dollars. Its business address was 443 Kinistino Avenue, Edmonton. Its slogan was "Proletarians of all countries unite". The first editor was Roman Kremar who was followed by Toma Tomashevsky. Next came Ivan Semeniuk and finally Illa Kyriak, formerly a type-setter. To prevent the paper from folding Kyriak doubled as editor and printer—a task beyond his capacity. The paper folded up in September of 1912. It maintained itself by subscription and dues from chapters of the Federation of Ukrainian Socialists located in Edmonton, Hillcrest, Lily, Lany, Lethbridge, Coleman, Cardin, Canmore, Calgary—in Alberta—and a unit "Thunder" in Nanaimo, B.C. Similar units in Saskatchewan, Manitoba nd Eastern Canada were mostly under the influence of "The Working People". All Canadian units interlocked through the Central Executive Committee of the Federation organized by M. C. Ferbey of Hillcrest, J. Seniuk of Edmonton, J. Humen of Edmonton, W. Skoreyko of Coleman, N. D. Tkachuk of Canmore and S. Fodchuk of Edmonton. The party conference of the Federation of Ukrainian Socialists and the Federation of Ukrainian Socialist-Democrats held in February, 1912, was not successful in mending the differences existing between the two Federations of "The Working People" and "The New Society". Basic ideological disagreements and financial difficulties forced closure of "The New Society" whose combined issues totalled 67.

"News"

Within a few months of the collapse of "The New Society" there appeared in Edmonton in January, 1913, another weekly entitled "The News" (Novyny) whose editor was Roman Kremar (Soloducha), the same person who earlier founded "The New Society". "The News" was non-political—without party flavor, the editor having re-orientated his thinking concerning party affiliation. He continued to stray ever farther from socialist slogans until he finally arrived in his thinking to give support to espouse the worth of Canadian Ukrainian culture, to champion national unity, and to encourage full participation in the development of Canada through political action. "The News" became the organ of the "National Organization of Alberta", sired by Kremar, nurtured by his "News" and born in Vegreville on January 14, 1914.

"The National Organization" manifested political curiosity and awareness and urged Ukrainians to become active in the political life of Canada at all levels. These ideas were fostered by "The News" published every Wednesday and cost two dollars in Canada, 12 crowns in Austria, and 5 rubles in Russia. "The News" appeared as a 4-page medium-sized paper —15x21 inches. By June 1st it became a semi-weekly—publishing days being Tuesdays and Fridays. This was the first semiweekly Ukrainian newspaper in Canada. Four months later its format was enlarged to 18x24 and it began to appear Mondays, Wednesdays and Saturdays. This was a great stride forward in the field of publishing. The press was housed at the rear of "Ferbey's "Ukrainian Book Store" at 536 Kinistino Avenue. There was a close liaison between the bookstore and "The News". Stephen Fodchuk was an early associate of the publishing firm. In 1914 Myroslaw Stechishin, a capable, prolific writer, joined the publication. "The News" won great popularity—but to publish three times per week required finances. Dynamic Kremar in 1913 became associated with "The Great Athabasca Land Co.", an urban land-developing firm based in Edmonton, which was instrumental in promoting such developments as Royal Park, Central Park and Industrial Park. The land company prospered—and Kremar, a substantial partner, contributed his share of the earnings to "The News" enabling it to operate comfortably for almost two years on a three issues per week basis. Kremar's editorials were serious and weighty in nature which pleased his readers. As additional inducements to cultivate and maintain quality readership he awarded good books and musical instruments from the Ferbey's "Ukrainian Book Store". He called for and announced in "The News" the first Literary Competition in Canada, concerning which he wrote: [11])

"Having in mind the unenviable status of Ukrainian literature in Canada and the United States and wishing to encourage the cultivation of talents, we announce herewith a competition on literary topics listed below which will be rewarded by six prizes".

What sort of topics and prizes?

(1) For a story of the Ukrainian people in Canada—fifty dollars award prize;
(2) Research to take into account geographic distribution of the settlements, economic and cultural status, disadvantages of dispersion and advantages of concentration of settlements;
(3) "Ukrainian Schools in Canada"—$25.00 award.
(4) Domestic themes selected specifically for "Ukrainian Farmers In Canada"—with three awards at $10.00 each.

Unique requirements Kremar sought of the writers—namely, they had to contribute at least two pages. "The principal characters of the story", he wrote, "must be strong, healthy and energetic, who do not whine and grumble at their fate but on the contrary, who grit their teeth, redouble their

---

[11]) "The News" No. 12, March, 1913.

determination and forge ahead even against adversity to gain a better life for themselves and others".

Such a determined person was Kremar himself. His "News" conducted a continuous advocacy for Ukrainian schools in Alberta—a struggle for basic democratic principles that knows no discrimination irrespective of station, privileges or responsibilities. When his critics took objection to his views, and in particular Mr. Boyle, the Minister of Education, on grounds that he, Kremar, wished "to build a Ukraine in Canada", Kremar replied by citing his first editorial entitled "Equal Laws" in which he wrote: "No, we do not intend to establish a Ukraine in Canada. Canada is Canada. All that we seek is equal laws for all and abolition of privileges... In view of the numbers of Ukrainians in Canada, they are entitled to much more than they have... The ethnic origins of Canadians are numerous—English, Ukrainian, French, German, etc. According to one liberal principle, the law applies equally to all with no special privileges to any. Equal laws means the same for the rich and poor, the strong and weak—equal laws for all people who are citizens of this country" [12].

Kremar probed deeply into the fundamental base of Canada's laws and legislative machinery. In his pronouncements he was discerning, in his thrusts—courageous, his dynamic personality was reflected in his editorials —his succulent utterances at times castigating. Furthermore, he always had the courage to admit being severely critical [13]. He strove always to attract sincere friends for Ukrainians in Canada and never permitted chauvinistic or inimical criticism to sneak by unchallenged. On the contrary, he would rebuke severely native traitors, corrupt or venal men and Judases.

In July, 1915, "The News" discontinued coming out three times a week. A few issues appeared on a weekly basis. Shortly after, financial difficulties coupled with war circumstances, dealt "The News" a heavy blow. Political sniping and attacks on Ukrainians on pretext of their being "Austrians", alluding to former citizenship, resulted in curtailment and abrogation of their rights as Canadian citizens, dismissal from jobs—these acts had far-reaching concomitant effects. Indefatigable, invincible Kremar, "caught his second breath" and by January, 1917, took up once more publishing "The News" as a semi-weekly through the "Commercial Printers Ltd." of 10317—101 Avenue, which also served as headquarters for "The News". Once again financial stringency caused "The News" to go into a weekly basis, considerably reduced in its dynamism as a result of war-time restrictions. In format it consisted of four large pages. The last issue carried the date line of October 10, 1918. On this day the Royal Canadian Mounted Police, under instructions of the Federal Minister of Internal Affairs, Censorship Department, padlocked "The News". That same month "The News" passed into the ownership of the Edmonton Ukrainian National Home. A month later Kremar departed for Winnipeg to assume editorship of the "Canadian Ruthenian" at which time it was renamed the "Canadian Ukrainian". Fast on the heels of the rescinding of censorship in April, 1919, "The News" was published at intervals by the Edmonton National Home from then until 1922, when the quality of the staff declined considerably. The personnel of "The News" consisted of Andrew Zaharychak, John Basarab, Stephen Sawula and Peter Lepinsky as illustrator.

[12] "The News" No. 51, September 23, 1913.
[13] "The News", No. 1, 1914—Editorial—"To Work, to Work".

"The Canadian"

On January 1, 1913, the bi-weekly "Canadian" saw the light of day at Edmonton, published by the Methodist Church, while "Ranok" was published by the Presbyterian Church in Winnipeg. The main difference between these two organs was perhaps in the areas of national and political interest. "Ranok" concerned itself mainly with Ukrainian National problems while "The Canadian" deemed them of little interest and no account. "The Canadian" was a four page gazette issued on the first and fifteenth of each month, costing one dollar per year, and had its headquarters at 10336—96th Street. The front page carried Canadian and world-wide news items; pages two and three dealt with religious themes (and Bible lessons) as well as instructions on domestic science and husbandry; the last page consisted of advertising and announcements. Two years later (1915) it became an 8-10 page tabloid, edited with discernment and more heterogenity. Nevertheless "The Canadian" never became a popular paper. It ran a lengthy serial entitled "Frightful Secrets Behind Monastery Walls" and, in general, pointed news items and various stories were directed against the Catholic clergy. The paper engaged in a controversy with R. Kremar and "The News" and propagated Methodism and staunchly supported the Alberta Liberal Party. It was edited by Pastor Johnson with full support of Michael Belegay. At the 1918 Methodist congress union of "The Canadian" with "Ranok" was discussed and rejected on grounds that "Ranok" was too much a Ukrainian nationalist paper. However, union did come in 1919 and with it an amalgamation of names to that of "The Canadian Ranok" with headquarters in Winnipeg.

"The Ukrainian Evangelist"

This paper appeared in Edmonton in 1917 with John Kocan, formerly a teacher, as editor, and later a Presbyterian minister. Subsequently he moved to Philadelphia and Pittsburgh and ultimately entered the ministry of the Ukrainian Orthodox Church. Announcement of the appearance of the "Evangelist" was made in both "The Canadian" in Edmonton and "Ranok" in Winnipeg. Very little has been uncovered to date as to the size, form and number of issues of the "Ukrainian Evangelist". Sufficient is it to note that it was the first children's publication in Ukrainian in Canada.

"Progress"

Another weekly paper appearing in Alberta during the pioneering era was "Progress" (Postup). In 1915 with the approach of provincial elections a Liberal candidate by name of Joe McCallum, who learned Ukrainian flawlessly, decided to give assistance to some Ukrainians in their attempt to found a Ukrainian Liberal paper. The first editor was Dmytro Yaremko, a young college student recently emigrated from Ukraine. His assistant, and compositor and type-setter, was Illa Kyriak who had press experience at "The New Society" and "The News". John Ruryk, a student, became Kyriak's assistant and later an administrator. The first issue of "Postup" was date-lined July 10, 1915. This event drew forth yearly celebrations at Mundare each July 12, the day of Saints Peter and Paul. The paper became widely regarded [14] as one dedicated to the "Ukrainian

---

[14] Some 8 to 10 thousand people participated in the yearly celebration.

People of Canada". The English version had it as the "Ruthenian Paper published every Thursday" by the "Mundare Publishing Company". The paper without attendant idealistic direction, showed the influence of its initiators both in the editing and in format. The objective of the paper was couched in this sentence: "The goal of this paper is the elevation of our people in Canada in the realms of the spiritual and material, and we anticipate that our people will support us in our good endeavours".

The first issue of "Postup" consisted of 8 large pages, whereas succeeding ones just 4. Subscription rates were $1.50 per year in Canada and $2.00 elsewhere. Disregarding many shortcomings, the appearance of "Postup" evoked much interest and sympathetic support. Among the supporters were G. Nowak, W. Kurietz, I. Genik, H. Kuziw who contributed much to its expansion and readership growth.

It was not an easy task to blaze a trail for the new paper. The second issue, printed on blue paper, appeared August 26, on Postup's own press. It was the first Ukrainian paper to appear in color. By next spring it began to appear more regularly. When the fall school term rolled around many of the staff went teaching on permits. Editorial responsibilities were assumed by Myroslaw Stechishin who had just left "The News". During his period of editorship the paper prospered—but not for long, because M. Stechishin in 1916 left for Washington to join the "Ukrainian Diplomatic Mission" headed by Dr. Julian Bachynsky. The Mundare "Postup" then engaged Toma Tomashevsky as editor, and who one and a half years later purchased the press and moved it to Edmonton to publish a second "News". T. Tomashevsky also served as printer during this period. "Postup" appeared irregularly for a while as a tabloid and later reverted to its original format. At this time "Postup" became the official organ of the Union of Canadian Ukrainian Farmers (Ruthenian Farmers Organization of Canada). This served as a "blood transfusion" and prolonged the life of "Postup", but not for long. He published one more yearly almanac (calendar) in 1917 under the title of "The Star". Near the end of 1917 "Postup" ceased to appear. Tomashevsky joined the staff of "The News" as typesetter for a brief period. From there he went to Winnipeg to serve on the "Canadian Ruthenian".

Saskatchewan

"The New Country"

The Association of Canadian Ruthenian Farmers was organized at Rosthern, Saskatchewan March 15 and 16, 1910. Very quickly the Association effected "Clause Four" of its constitution, i.e. the founding of its own organ. Accordingly, on August 9, 1910, the first issue of "The New Country" was released to the world from Rosthern, Saskatchewan. It measured 15 by 12 inches and consisted of six pages with publication dates on the 10th, 20th, and 30th of each month. Subscription cost was one and a half dollars which was raised subsequently to two dollars. The organ was considered as the only Ukrainian farmers' publication in Canada and was also the farmers' teacher. With the sixth issue "The New Country" became an 8-page paper whose central theme was to call to the readers continuously to form strong associations and rural co-operatives and to re-kindle national consciousness. In this aspect "The New Country" adhered closely to clause 23 of the Association of Ruthenian Farmers, which stipulated that the "Association does not tie in with any political party, but must remain strictly unbiased and neutral and serve the needs of the people".

From the beginning of its career "The New Country" took on the task of preparing the farmers for the second Congress of Saskatchewan Farmers which was held December 27-28, 1910, at Canora, Saskatchewan. The tenor of this convention is evident from the titles of the talks (papers) given by the principal participants as listed: O. Megas—"Our National-Political Stance in Canada", W. Steshyn—"The Struggle for Our National Rights", P. Shvydkyj—"Our Ruthenian Farmers' Association", H. Platsko—"National Renaissance", G. Machnij—"National Enlightenment and Education" and A. Wilchynsky—"Our Economic Situation". The organizers of this encompassing convention delved deeply into fundamental problems and met them head-on in search of national solutions.

With a similar agenda on February 2, 1911, at Rosthern, Saskatchewan, a "General Meeting" was held which culminated in the formation of a new chapter of "The Ruthenian Farmers' Association with the following persons elected to the executive: P. Shvydkyj, T. Oleskiw, J. Nowalkowsky, P. Mamchur, T. Bilinsky, M. Korpan, M. Wizniuk and W. Holiuk. The leading role was played by P. Shvydkyj who contributed a substantial sum of money for the expansion of "The New Country". Shvydkyj was chosen president of the Association. The retiring president was relieved of the editorship of "The New Country" to devote full time to the organization of bilingual schools in Saskatchewan. Victor Steshyn succeeded to the editorship. According to the minutes carried in "The New Country" the new executive of the Ruthenian Farmers' Association introduced strict discipline. For the purpose of organizing the farmers throughout Saskatchewan and the rest of Canada some 23 field men were employed. In addition to strong support given in the realm of cultural growth and general enlightenment, the Ruthenian Farmers' Association exhorted and encouraged Ukrainians to participate in municipal-provincial and federal affairs. In keeping with the 23rd clause of the Constitution which read "that in event of elections, the Association must call a special meeting of all delegates to discuss the political issues and to sponsor Ruthenian candidates in Ruthenian districts". When federal elections were called in 1911, "The New Country" urged its readers to become involved in the campaign. "The Ruthenian Farmers' Association" released for its part this point of view [15]), namely, "that Ruthenians in Canada must organize public political meetings and discussions with respect to sponsoring Ruthenians as candidates for office". The advocates of such action were very ambitious and most optimistic when they wrote concerning Ukrainian farmers "being sufficiently mature and conscientious to be able to elect a number of parliamentary representatives to provincial assemblies".

Following a publicity campaign political meetings and conferences were held, resulting in the formation of the first Ruthenian political Association of Saskatchewan, called "Farmers' Will" [16]), with headquarters at Fish Creek near Rosthern. Delegates from Vonda, Duck Lake and Saskatoon, Humboldt, et al, took part in launching the "Farmers' Will". Chosen president was J. Sikorsky; members at large were Theodore Oleskiw, A. Hrytsak and J. Kuryliw. With the advent of provincial elections in Saskat-

---

[15]) "New Country", Nos. 14 and 15, 1911.
[16]) "New Country", Nos. 22 and 23, 1911.

chewan in 1912, the Association was cautious about nominating candidates and in "The New Country", generally speaking, there were timely voices urging that first things come first; namely, to conduct sound, political orientation and not to nominate candidates at this juncture. Of a different opinion was M. Gabora who permitted his name to be submitted for candidacy in the Canora electoral district. His candidature was not successful, but he set a historic precedent in Saskatchewan as being the first Ukrainian candidate in Saskatchewan provincial elections. A non-commital gain of his (Gabora's) electioneering was the crystallization of political consciousness of Saskatchewan Ukrainians. Within two years "The New Country" changed its views concerning Ukrainian political activity on a separate ethnic basis and in 1912 began to speak out forcefully against the impropriety of Ukrainians in shunning and down-grading Canadian political parties and in wanting to be a political force under the banner of "Independents". This point of view was so sufficiently convincing that at the next provincial elections "The New Country" favored the Liberal Party under the leadership of W. Scott and specifically actively supported the candidacy of Dr. Al. Calder, Deputy Minister of Education, supporter of bilingual schools in Saskatchewan, who ran in the electoral constituency of Saltcoats inhabited most by Ukrainians. Calder received whole hearted and solid support from the Ukrainians in recognition of his sympathetic understanding and loyalty to their needs and aspirations.

"The New Country" not only evoked the interest in political matters but also influenced thinking [17] along economic lines. Specifically, it propagated the idea of creation of co-operatives. In due course the co-operative movement took root in Saskatchewan and flourished vigorously. A shining example for a while was the "Ruthenian National Co-op" at Rosthern under the leadership of Peter Shvydkyj with branches in Vonda and Cudworth. "The New Country" was published for almost four years. It is uncertain when the last issue appeared [18].

The editor of "The New Country" was very objective in his research to authenticate its articles for publication—and supplied these figures concerning the Ukrainian press in Canada for the year 1912. Circulation of Ukrainian publications is listed as follows: "Canadian Farmer"—4,000, "Ukrainian Voice"—3,000, "Ranok"—1,000, "New Society"—1,000, "The Witness for Truth"—600, "New Country"—3,000, "The Working People" —2,500, "The Canadian"—1,000, "Canadian Ruthenian"—2,000.

Winnipeg Again

On the second of September, 1913, appeared in Winnipeg a newspaper entitled "Canada", published by the Ruthenian (Ukrainian) Publishing Co., 261 Fort Street, Winnipeg, Manitoba. This 8-page weekly, published every Tuesday, was 22 by 16 inches. Its principal themes were broadly educational, economic and political. Nevertheless the gazette dealt, on the surface, with the political issues. According to the introductory issue the editor and publishers stated: "We in Canada "politicked" up till now in fits and starts or withdrew from political life completely. Such participation will not ensure us our future, but, on the contrary, will lead to oblivion.

---

[17] "New Country" No. 18, 1912.
[18] A copy of the last issue dated Feb. 1, 1913, is located in the author's archives.

We cannot, we dare not continue thus. We must choose another course which will lead us to our goals, profitable for our people". It editorialized on the need of political integration in these words: "To conduct our own, separated political action in Canada, measured by any guage, we are too weak, and wishing to achieve anything whatsoever for ourselves, we must comprise with those who are strong". Who possessed this strength was amplified by "Canada" in its first issue on the front page, featuring a full-page picture of the leader of Manitoba's Conservatives and Premier of the Province of Manitoba, Sir Rodmond Roblin. It is reported that the Conservatives gave substantial financial support to "Canada". R. Roblin was criticized by the Liberals on grounds that he supported "Canada" from public funds and that the newspaper "Canada" was housed in the same building (The Charles H. Forrester Block) wherein were headquarters of the Provincial Police and other provincial agencies. This criticism and allegations appeared in the "Liberal Handbook, 1914". It is an indisputable fact that "Canada" was privately published by a dedicated group of Conservatives headed by Theodore Stefanyk. He also headed "The Ruthenian Publishing Co." The vice-president was Paul Gigeychuk and the secretary, Gregory Bodnar. The editor-in-chief was John Sluzar, former editor of "The Man's Paragraph" [15]) of Salem, Mass., U.S.A. In 1910, when the latter ceased to appear, J. Sluzar migrated to Canada and was employed for a while as a linotype operator at the "Ukrainian Voice". Following his arrival to this country he reorientated his ideology towards conservatism. Quite naturally he joined forces with Stefanyk to publish "Canada". Individualism which left an imprint on the newspaper "Canada", was not Sluzar's, but that of Petro Karmansky, professor of Ukrainian grammar and literature at Brandon College. In the third issue of "Canada" Karmansky contributed articles and feuilletons under the heading of "Monkey Mirror". The feuilletons were written in the form of letters, hence the subtitle, "Letters from Canada and about Canada to "Canada". In these letters Karmansky fought mercilessly all and sundry. In the realm of Canadian politics he lambasted the Liberals who mounted a campaign against bilingualism in schools. In the Ukrainian sector he criticized unsparingly Ukrainian community leaders who surrounded themselves by such newspapers as "The Ukrainian Voice", "The Working People" and "Ranok". This he did, disregarding that such criticism by general consent became indecorous, unseemly invective on both sides so that ultimately all this indecent controversy became known as "Karmanism". After a lengthy series of "Monkey Mirrors" there was a brief respite followed by a "Second Edition of "Monkey Mirrors". Karmansky also wrote other articles under the cryptonym of "K" or under "Dispatched". This did not differ in context from former invectives. In short, "Canada", thanks to Karmansky waged a running battle with all, excepting Bishop Budka and Kremar's "News". The aftermath of this "Bellum contra omnes" was the resignation of the editor-in-chief, J. Sluzar. Early in 1914 the editorial duties were assumed by Mykola W. Bachynski who became subsequently a member of the Manitoba Legislature and Speaker of the House. "Canada" was closely edited, and its permanent correspondents, W. P. Hrushowy, J. K. Slipetz, T. J. Marciniw, M. Ogryzlo and J. Basarab—staffed the paper with the assistance of local correspondents. On the pages of "Canada" there appear-

---

[15]) "The Man's Paragraph" first appeared in January, 1906.

ed literary articles such as "Captive in the Caucasus" by L. Tolstoy, "Zaporozhian Seech" by P. Kulish, "Ruined Baturyn" by O. Ostrowsky, "Teacher's Fortunes" by D. Mackohon, anecdotes and stories by Chaykowsky, Les' Martowych and others. Without doubt that in this field P. Karmansky, as a literary man, left his imprint on "Canada". Karmansky's worst enemies were Liberals headed by T. C. Norris who did not forgive him for his criticism of their handling of the issue of bilingualism in schools. In this respect Karmansky had the support of almost the entire Ukrainian community, including his avowed opponents in other matters. Prior to "Canada" ceasing, appearing in 1915, Karmansky said his "adieu" to "Canada" and to Canada and departed for Europe, mesmerized by European war events.

"Canadian News"

This publication was an organ of the "Ruthenian Book Store" in Winnipeg owned by Frank Dojacek (Dojack). The first issue appeared in December, 1913, with an announcement that it was intended to be a monthly tabloid. However, in early March, 1914, the editor announced plans to make it a weekly paper. In April, the paper had its format enlarged. At this time there was a change of editors because D. Demchuk retired and was succeeded by M. Pasichniak, who remained at that post until the termination of publication in February, 1915. "Canadian News" was pro-Liberal and avoided involvement in religious questions. In its early issues it devoted much attention to the preparation of celebrating the centennial of Taras Shevchenko's birth, and discussed problems arising from World War I. Literary questions were also discussed. Stories by Borys Hrinchenko were published as well as narratives, such as "For Sister's Sake" by A. Chaykowsky, "Martians" by W. Herinowich, and "Amalunga" or "Daughter of the Jungle" which related battles of Europeans with North American Indians". The author of this tale is not given [16]). The whole publishing facilities and personnel had accommodation at 901 Main Street, in the "Ruthenian Book Store" of F. Dojacek and printing was done by "National Press".

MAGAZINES

There were also in pioneer days attempts to publish magazines. The first of these was "The Khata" (The Home)—an illustrated magazine of literary works, politics and contemporary life, that was published in Winnipeg on the first of each month by J. N. Krett. James Krett had his own printing-press and besides "The Khata" (Home) edited small popular pamphlets. His publishing firm was called "The Ruthenian Press, James N. Krett, Proprietor", and was situated at 850 Main Street in Winnipeg. It was in this printing-shop that the first edition of the "Ukrainian Voice" was published. The appearance of the magazine "The Home" was quite an event in those times and J. N. Krett earned a well-deserved priority for himself in this field. More about the magazine "The Home" and its contents is given in the chapter "Literature". Unfortunately, the magazine, "The Home" did not last long perhaps only because, at the time, the intel-

---

[16]) T. J. Marciniw, a teacher, wrote this story. It was not published in toto, and remains as a manuscript.

lectual class, for which this magazine was destined, was not large and therefor it was difficult to maintain the planned periodical [17].

Two years after the publication of "The Home", a monthly periodical, dedicated to education, criticism and information and called "Nasha Syla" (Our Strength), was edited. The first edition of this monthly periodical was published on the first of July, 1913, at 901 Main Street in Winnipeg in the "National Press". In the introductory article of the publication we notice that "The Canadian Ukrainians have no reason to complain about the scarcity of their newspaper, but on the contrary they may boast about the number of the later ones. Almost every party, sect or group had its own printed newspaper. To date, in Canada, there existed nine of these publications and this one made it ten". As we mentioned, in this first editorial, "Our Strength" desired to elevate one constructive idea which was to create one denominator of understanding-tolerance and immediately following this, a mutual fraternal social interaction among all groups. Although "Our Strength" set forth for itself such high and noble objectives, little success was realized in all that was planned. Its publication was terminated the same year that it first appeared. The magazine was in the form of a book, with 28 pages in one edition, edited by a committee. J. Wegner was the director of the publication and V. Kupchenko, the secretary. The latter was also editor-in-chief of "Our Strength".

Ukrainians in pioneer times attempted also to publish an agricultural newspaper called "The Rilnyk" (The Agriculturist). The editor-in-chief responsible for publishing "The Agriculturist" was Walter Pyndykowsky, who had a higher education and was interested in the economic life of the farmers. "The Agriculturist" had as its task, and as it stated, "to lead farmers unto the prairie overgrown with brush and to show them how to clear it to make it into productive fields, how to destroy wild oats, how to clear away the stones so as not to break the ploughshares, how to drain the lakes so that grain crops or at least hay could be grown, to raise a better breed of horses, cattle, hogs, poultry, ducks and dogs"... Several numbers, probably four, which were published, gave replies to questions sent in by readers. The newspaper, in tabloid format and 16 pages of content, with a pleasing vignette, although it had interesting advice and articles, did not gain many readers. The first edition of "The Agriculturist", which was thought of as a fort-nightly periodical, appeared in May, 1918. Publication was done by the Agricultural Publishing Company in Winnipeg, which was sponsored by the editor himself. The publishing firm was situated at 507 Union Tract Building.

To the exceptional publication of pioneer times in Winnipeg belongs the journal "Ukraina" (Ukraine), of which the first edition appeared in January 1918. It was published by a firm with the same name. The aim of the publication "Ukraina" was, as was claimed by the editors, "to offer the Ukrainian settlers in America, in generally accessible form, the acquisition of contemporary science, literature, art and technology, and to acquaint them with an inexhaustible storehouse of native culture". Only two issues of this well illustrated magazine appeared; each copy contained more than

---

17) D. Lobay in his article in "The Ukrainian Voice Almanac" 1910-1960 mentions also a weekly publication "The House" that was to have made an appearance in Winnipeg in 1912. Its editor was supposed to be Eugene Koslowski. The author of this volume did not discover any other data to corroborate this statement.

100 pages. Besides educational articles there were works of such literary lights as Ivan Franko, M. Pavlyk, O. Hrycay and others. At the "Ukraine" publishing place was also printed the "A Scientific Library". The publication lasted two years, 1918 and 1919. Besides Dr. O. Sushko, I. Turkevych and N. Lewycky also worked at publishing it. The magazine appeared in book form on good paper. In content and form "Ukraine" outgrew all other publications of its time and became a representative magazine [18]).

It is difficult to determine the number of all the issues of the monthly periodical "Nyva" (The Field) that began its publication in December, 1919. This was a religious national journal of 32 printed pages. The editor's office and administration was situated at 115 McGregor Avenue in Winnipeg, which is the parochial office of the Cathedral of St. Volodymyr and Olha. The editor of this unpretentious little magazine was Father Oleksiw, the parish priest of this cathedral who not only attempted to be a journalist but a poet as well. "The Field" established its own unique record—it was the first religious monthly periodical printed in Canada for the Greek Catholics on the North American continent. The magazine published a great deal of fine literature and excerpts from the history of the Church, had light material for school children, and also engaged in polemics with its enemies. It co-operated partly with "The Canadian Ukrainian" and was printed in the latter's printing office. Its subscription fee was one dollar annually. This periodical struggled for its existence not fully a year.

Publications for Children

It is with much pleasure that we mention about the publications for young people. Besides children's corners in various weeklies, a small periodical, "Dzvinochok" (The Little Bell) began to be published in 1918. Its editor was Father P. Oleksiw. In its subtitle it was noted that this was "an organ of Ukrainian youth in Canada". It was published monthly in book form of 32 pages with large print. It was produced by "The Canadian Ukrainian Publishing Association in Canada" and the editor's office and administration was located at "The Canadian Ukrainian" press building. The small periodical was financially tied up with the aforementioned newspaper, as in "The Invitation for Subscriptions" it was stated that its annual subscription fee was one dollar, but for the subscribers of "The Canadian Ukrainian" it would only be 50 cents per year. The credo of the editors was also expressed there with these words: "With this publication we are sending out into the wide spaces of Canada the first issue of "The Little Bell", a periodical dedicated to our youth which, until now, was deprived of its own reading, was growing up totally estranged from us, not understanding our aims and endeavours. The need for such a publication was clear to us for a long time, but no one had the courage to set to work and begin such an essential, worthwhile, and beneficial assignment for our youth". From this it can be noticed that some publishers and editors desired to incline the youth to the source of Ukrainian culture, family ties, churches and institutions, to the entire Ukrainian community life in Canada. It is difficult to determine the number of issues of this first periodical for Ukrainian youth, which appeared in Canada. At the publication pre-

---

[18]) More about the magazine "Ukraine" and "A Scientific Library" is given in the chapter "Pioneer Literature".

mises of "The Little Bell", a great activity was shown by "The Children's Society"—a constitutional association—organized at the church of St. Vladimir and Olha, where Father Shumsky, Father M. Zalitach and T. J. Marciniw, worked together—the last one named having organized a similar society at Mink Creek, Manitoba, called "Zirka" (Starlet).

In December, 1917, a students' circle, "Kameniari" (The Stone-cutters), was established at the Institute of Petro Mohyla in Saskatoon. Its first head was Ivan Danylchuk and its first secretary S. M. Doroschuk, who later became well known writers. These two first began to sharpen their pens while still sitting at the students' desks. Through the endeavours of this circle a magazine in book form, "The Stone-cutters" began to be published. It was issued on the first and fifteenth of each month and regularly, from the 15th of January, 1919 and on. Until that time there were only sporadic attempts. In the first year, six issues appeared, comprising a total of 208 pages. The collection was edited by the collegium, which was composed of A. Arabska, H. Evach, S. B. Mykytiuk, J. Stechishin, A. Wawryniuk, M. Chorneyko. The editor-in-chief was S. W. Sawchuk. The magazine was printed at the "Ukrainian Voice" in Winnipeg. "The purpose of the magazine" as was stated by the editor-in-chief, in the epilogue to the collection, "is to increase among the students a love for their own literature, to encourage them to literary endeavours as well as to outline the development of the more important events, in the Institute, of the student circles". These three objectives ran like a golden thread through the pages of the journal. Besides articles from Ukrainian literature in it, there was a lot of literary and publicity material, written by the students themselves.

EASTERN CANADA

Pioneer times were rich in religious papers. In 1909, a religious journal "Svidok Pravdy" (Witness of the Truth) with the explanation in its subtitle that this was a religious, national paper for the Ruthenian people in Canada, began to be published in Toronto. This journal was edited by "The Alliance of Ruthenian and Galician Christian Baptists in Canada and United States of America". The editor-in-chief of the journal was J. A. Kolesnikow, and the assistant editor was M. Androw. "The Alliance of Ruthenian and Galician Christian Baptits in Canada" had several of its centers, of which the larger ones were in Toronto, Hamilton, Winnipeg, Montreal, Edmonton, and in Petrowka in Saskatchewan. The Alliance collaborated closely with the Mennonite Brethren of Canada. "The Witness of the Truth" appeared at the beginning as a weekly but in a short while it became a monthly publication. It had 15 pages, book-size, and its annual subscription fee was $1.00 in Canada and $1.50 in U.S.A. and Europe. With its circulation of 1,000 copies the publication of "The Witness of the Truth" weathered through the pioneer era with little interruption. At the printing establishment of "The Witness of the Truth", a spiritual, moralistic, and political Bulgarian gazette, "Novy Zhyvot" (The New Life) was edited for some time and was widely spread around among Bulgarians and Macedonians. It is worth mentioning that prior to the appearance of "Witness of the Truth", also appeared a magazine "Dobry Pryatel" (The Good Friend) of which, unfortunately, no trace remains. Because we have no first issue of "Witness of the Truth" we wish to refer to the news item in "The Canadian Farmer" called "A New Paper" in which we read, among other things, "In Toronto, Ontario, a new Ukrainian religious national newspaper, "Witness of the Truth" began its publication. The newspaper promises to please every Christian and to teach, with words of truth, how to love one's fellowman and perform good deeds" [19]. This memo must serve as the original birth-certificate of the above mentioned newspaper because, after all, the appearance of "Witness of the Truth" did not have a great influence on the formation of religious thought of Ukrainian pioneers. All the same this little newspaper was also an original borderline marker-post of the Ukrainian printed word in Canada. Just as "The Canadian Farmer" was the first Ukrainian newspaper in Western Canada, so "Witness of the Truth" was the first Ukrainian newspaper in Eastern Canada.

"The Star"

The second newspaper in Eastern Canada was "The Star" (Zoria) in Montreal, which first saw daylight August 2, 1914 and announced that it was "The only Ukrainian weekly in Eastern Canada published every Saturday". According to the summations of "The Star" in Montreal alone there were at that time more than 20,000 Ukrainians. "The Star" had 8 pages, tabloid in form and its editorial office was situated at 45 Windsor Avenue. The address for subscriptions was 385 Frontenac—which was also the address of "The General Bookstore". The initiative spirit for the publication of the paper came from the cultural centre, "Chytalnia" (Reading Room) of M. Drahomaniv. At the meeting in this hall on August 2, 1914, a publishing committee was elected, which included Hryhoriy Mostovy, who was the proprietor of the bookstore and printing office in Montreal, and furthermore Yakiw Vepruk, Savaryn Kostyrsky, Ivan Vepruk, Mykola Kolpetsky, Dmytro Voloschuk and Ivan Bodrug. The latter was the editor of the paper. The newspaper was to be generally informative; it was even the resolution of the organizers beforehand "not to publish political opinions, or religious disputes or personal quarrels". The newspaper began publication right at the beginning of the First World War and it is no wonder that the royal imperial consul-general of Austria called upon all Austro-Hungarian citizens and begged them to reside quietly in their settlements, to behave calmly and with dignity, not to take any part in any demostrations and to comply with all the regulations of the local authorities pertaining to the maintenance of law and order. In this same spirit, "The Star" addressed itself to its readers. It is difficult to establish the length of time during which "The Star" was published. For certainty, at least five issues appeared. This was the first general non-religious, non-political Ukrainian newspaper in Eastern Canada, edited by the M. Drahomaniv Publishing Co. In the statute of this institution it was insisted that "the objective of this company is the publication of progressive newspapers, pamphlets, and books consisting of political, literary and educational material not only in Ukrainian but also in other languages according to necessity ("First Statute of the M. Drahomaniv Publishing Co.").

Thus it will be seen that the publishers had broad and far-reaching plans but World War I prevented their realization.

---

[19] "Canadian Farmer" 50th edition, December 22, 1909.

THE PRESS

"The Workers' Word"

In 1915 a fortnightly periodical "Svidoma Syla" (Conscious Strength) began to be published in Toronto, in Eastern Canada. The periodical was edited by the socialist fraction U.S.D.P., which was in opposition to "Robochy Narod" (The Working People), published in Winnipeg. The former editor of "Working People", Ivan Stefanicky, dissatisfied with the more leftist course of U.S.D.P. in Winnipeg became a publisher of "Conscious Strength" [20]. There are some who regard "Conscious Strength" as being the first Ukrainian paper in Eastern Canada. From our research it follows that this was in turn the third periodical in the East, where the first was "The Witness of the Truth" in Toronto and second "The Star" in Montreal.

"Conscious Strength" advertised itself as an "enlightening, educational and progressive periodical for the working masses". It was issued monthly; the annual subscription in Canada was 75 cents and in U.S.A. one dollar.

At the end of 1916 "Conscious Strength" was renamed "The Workers' Word" (Robitnyche Slovo) with a note in the subtitle that this was the former "Conscious Strength" with "a progressive trend for the working masses". The periodical was printed at 405 Queen Street, in Toronto; subscription rate was $1.50 per annum; a single copy cost three cents. It was published by the Workers' Publishing Co-operative Association. "The Workers' Word" was issued up to September, 1918—that is, for a period of four years. And, though during those years it changed its vignettes, it retained the same large format. It also did not change its credo, expressed in the April 30th issue, 1916, and continued to disseminate class enlightenment and socialist doctrine among the workers, in order to create one large family, well-informed of their own strong interests and whose aim was to strive for a finer social order. "The Workers' Word" printed labour-political reading material which would give its readers an ideological foundation for political thought and deed. Almost all of them were published as separate reprints for distribution among the labourers. "The Workers' Word" conducted a political and ideological struggle with "The Working People" in Winnipeg, which was gradually turning to a socialist-communist position. "The Workers' Word" supported socialist independent parties in Ukraine and had even published the candid letter of Serhiy Yefremov to Yuriy Kotsiubynsky, Commander of the Communist Army and the National Commissar, about the domination of the Communists in the Ukraine, in which S. Yefremov accused Y. Kotsiubynsky of betraying his people. "Conscious Strength" and "The Workers' Word" was edited by Ivan Stefanicky who had the experience of editing a newspaper from "The Working People" days. His assistant was H. Mak, who translated quite a few selections from the Russian language, particularly political literature. J. Stefanicky's close collaborators were D. Borysko and Paul Krat, who in 1918 transferred the humorous publication "Kadylo" to Toronto and came into a closer contact with "The Workers' Word"—both periodicals being printed in the same printing shop. In time "The Workers' Word" began to advertise itself as a "culturally-scientific" newspaper, for the Ukrainian labourers and farmers in North America. The newspaper gradually passed from doctrinaire to

---

[20] "Fifty years of Ukrainian Press in Eastern Canada" an article in "Homin Ukrainy", No. 825, 1965.

the practical problems of farmers and labourers but it never stopped being socialist .

HUMOROUS NEWSPAPERS

"Kadylo" was the first humorous newspaper in Canada. This was a monthly periodical, of which the first issue was published in May, 1913 in Winnipeg. Its editor was Paul Krat, known for his rigorous leftist views and, naturally he considered all the problems of community life from the angle of his own viewpoint. The spearhead of the paper was directed, first of all, against the clergy, and the editor, who was also his own publisher, wrote his political articles, under the pseydonym of "O. Prokolupiy". The newspaper was of a tabloid format, consisting of eight pages. In November, 1913, "Kadylo", with its editor, moved to Vancouver, and from that time on it was published twice a month. Its annual subscription fee also increased from one to two dollars. Under the sub-title of "The Canadian-Ruthenian Humoristic Gazette", "Kadylo" was located at 650 Richards Street and was printed by the Linguistic Printing and Publishing Company. The same company also published "Vancouver German Press", "Svenska Vancouver Posten" and "L'Italia del Canada". We mention this particularly because a rumor was spread against P. Krat that "Kadylo" was printed by the Russian Consulate. With the transfer of "Kadylo" to Vancouver the newspaper began publishing a longer satirical novel by O. Prokolupiy called "God's Last Walk on Earth" or "God in Revolution" in which was depicted the social mutual relations of Czarist Russia [21]. In June, 1914, "Kadylo" was again transferred to Winnipeg where it was published by "The Ukrainian Free Thinkers Association" but behind that very loquacious firm stood no other but the editor of "Kadylo" himself, who was supported by a Ukrainian Social-Democratic group. However, its assistance was not great as the newspaper stopped publication from November, 1914, but appeared again in October 1915, but this time as a monthly periodical. The one year's silence of the chief editor was instrumental in an important change in his perception of the world outlook because he discontinued to lead the struggle against religion and his anticlerical caricatures disappeared from the "Kadylo". In the editorial P. Krat stated distinctly that the objective of "Kadylo" will be general and that its password from now on, will be: "Correct errors through ridicule", but inconsistent with its alterations and declarations, "Kadylo" still waged war against the Catholic clergy. But after all this war did not last long because finances were no longer available and the newspaper again disappeared in April 1916. P. Krat restored "Kadylo" only on the first of January, 1918, but this time in Toronto and again as a fortnightly periodical. In the introduction P. Krat once more declared that in the future he would remain an international socialist, but this time independent of any political party. But just the same, in the third issue of the new "Kadylo", P. Krat united the interests of his paper with "The Workers' Word", which, as we know, was the organ of the opposition in the Socialist Democratic Organization.

After this "Kadylo" struggled for half a year yet and was published mainly thanks to the so-called "Kadylo Publishing Synod", in other words

---

[21] This satirical story saw the light of day as a separate book, published by "The Working People".
[22] "Canadian Farmer", No. 9, 1908.

the lovers of party humor who financed it with their five-dollar donations for the publication of the newspaper. When the funds were finished, Kadylo was finished also.

"Uncle"

"Uncle" (Vuyko) was another humorous Ukrainian newspaper in Canada. It was published by Yakiw Maydanyk with the help of "The Canadian Ruthenian". The format of "Uncle" was the same as that of "Kadylo" but the humor and satire, all the same, were directed towards actual daily affairs. "Uncle" which was published once a month became a reality in February, 1918 and stipulated that "it does not believe in bothering either the intelligentsia, or the Catholics or the "Reshbeteriany" (the Presbyterians—M.H.M.), or the dependent or the independent, or the totalitarians or anyone", but it did publish happy tales, verses, novels, jokes, witticisms and cartoons. "Uncle" was shaped up by Y. Maydanyk who, with his illustrations, added to the outer appearance of the periodical. His collaborator was Ivan Novosad, who contributed humorous verses. The humour and satire of "Uncle" were not exceedingly choice but its vocabulary differed somewhat from the language used in "Kadylo" with a plentiful mixture of Ukrainian Canadianisms. Although popular among a large multitude "Uncle" existed not quite a full year and came to an end. Publishers returned to using the title "Uncle" even in times after the war, for example "The Canadian Farmer" and "The Canadian Ukrainian" published their humorous supplements to the newspapers under the title of "Uncle".

THE BILINGUAL PRESS

Besides the voluminous press output in the Ukrainian language, that appeared in Canada, there was also a so-called bilingual press, in early pioneer times. Priority in this category goes to "The Sifton News" (Syftonski Novyny), which was published by Fred E. Nex, the local printer of the English paper in Dauphin called "Dauphin Herald". In 1897 he married a Ukrainian girl, C. Zarowny, began to learn the Ukrainian language and in 1901 was already a bilingual teacher in the school "Ukraina" near Sifton. The need for the printed word at that time was great and Nex began publishing "The Sifton News" in tabloid format but not periodically. The newspaper was printed on a manual printing press but it is difficult to establish when the first issue was published and how many issues appeared. F. Nex acquired great popularity with his "Sifton News" and, from 1905 to 1908, was a councillor in the Dauphin Municipality which was inhabited almost exclusively by Ukrainians. Probably teaching and editing did not pay in those times because near the end of 1908 we see F. Nex in real estate in the vicinity of St. Andrew and still later as secretary of the Whitemouth Municipality.

In Canada, there was also a compulsory bilingualism for periodicals. In September 1918, government agents from Ottawa demanded from the Ukrainian Press in Canada that beside the Ukrainian text there should be an exact duplicate in the English language. This compulsory bilingualism did not last quite half a year.

There were also separate Ukrainian sections in English newspapers in

Winnipeg, particularly in "The Farmers' Weekly Telegram" in 1909 and in 1910. This section was called "Universal News for Ruthenian Readers" [23]. It is worthwhile to mention that "The Canadian Farmers" was published, in 1918, two of its issues, No. 43 and 44, in the Polish language when it was impossible to publish them in Ukrainian.

THE RUSSOPHILE PRESS

When the Ukrainian Press—"Ukrainian Voice", "New Country", "News" and others, oriented the reader toward Ukrainian culture, his past and future in the new country, it strengthened, at the same time, his spiritual attitude and desire to feel himself at home in it. The Russophile Press, which in the majority was published with the aid of funds from the Russian Orthodox Mission in U.S.A. and later a similar mission and Church in Canada, exhorted its readers to orient themselves towards Russia, its national, imperial indivisibility and its czarist regime (Tsareetslavism). The Russophile Press was devised, first of all, for the purpose of preventing the rebirth of Ukrainian epoch and in all sectors strove to stifle the national impetus to rebirth, and to direct public sympathies towards Moscow and the czar. The theorists of this propaganda maintained that there is one great "Russian Nation" with different racial and tribal origins and cultures. In the religious field they acknowledged the one and only unique Orthodox religion, at the head of which was the czar. Whoever proved it differently was the enemy of the Russian people and their country. The Russophile press considered the national Ukrainian press as its number one enemy and all its efforts were directed towards liquidating this press. For this they used unrestricted slander, defamation, underestimation of progress and denial of any kind of respect and so forth. Similar beginnings of the struggle of the press took place in U.S.A. at the turn of the century when "Svoboda" (Freedom), the only Ukrainian newspaper on the American continent at that time, was under slanderous attacks of such Russophile papers in U.S.A. as "Truth", "World" and others, a classical example of an indiscriminate press warfare.

As soon as the culturally-enlightened life of the Ukrainians began to form in Canada and the first Ukrainian newspapers began their work, the propagators of the Russophile ideology and the representatives of czarism began to assemble their publications in Canada. It would be worthwhile to recall that the Russophile press, as well as all of Russophile literature was spread around at the same time along with the religious stream—and even contrariwise—to the popularly called tsaroslavism (czarism), at that time. When Abbot Arseny, who came to Canada in 1908, began to build up the Russian Orthodox Church, he immediately began to publish his own newspaper called "Kanadiyskaya Nyva" (The Canadian Field). The first issue of this organ appeared in September, 1908 and its subtitle underlined that this was "a religious-political paper for the Russian People in Canada and America". This was a fortnightly periodical of tabloid format with six pages; its editor and publisher was I. Arseny [24], the paper was printed

---

[23] Besides Ukrainian sections there were also similar ones for Dutch, Germans, Poles. All of them were under the same title: "News of the week for our foreign-born readers".

[24] Abbot Arseny signed his name in English as Rev. Arseny Chahovzov; in Russian as Chechowtsev and in Ukrainian, Chahovets.

at 242 McGregor Avenue, and its annual subscription fee was one dollar. The newspaper was printed in Ukrainian with Russian transliteration. In his introductory editorial Abbot Arseny summarized the task of the newspaper which had to "enlighten our people (that is the Ukrainians—M.H. M.) in a foreign land".

The first editions of "Kanadiyskaya Nyva" (Canadian Field) were filled with religious information , appeals, reports of organizational-parish meetings and others. When readers became accustomed to the paper's routine then the editors, or publishers, brought up political and national questions. Arseny was a good organizer and speaker and with his capabilities knew how to gain sympathies, not only of Orthodox Ukrainians, but even of some of the Ukrainian Catholics. He founded "Bratstwo Sviatoyi Troyci" (Brotherhood of Holy Trinity) which became the battering ram of "tsaroslavia" and in this brotherhood organization worked for a while such well known figures of those days as Josyf Dyma, Ivan Negrich, Theodore Kochan and others. The brotherhood was engaged in the spreading of the "Rosiyska Pravoslavna Misia" (Russian Orthodox Mission) throughout Canada, and built schools and reading rooms. The statutes of this brotherhood were under the control of the Russian Orthodox Mission in U.S.A. and of its mouthpiece in Canada, the Abbot in Winnipeg, who in 1909 transferred his office to Edmonton and took with him the "Canadian Field". Along with this, the paper increased its format. Mykhaylo Gowda, a prominent Ukrainian, became his co-worker in Edmonton. In 1910 Arseny departed from Canada and his spiritual child "Canadian Field" ceased to exist.

But although Arseny was no more, he left behind him his followers, who continued to carry on his work. In Vostok, Alberta, in 1912, the priest, Dmytro Yarema, started to publish, at his own expense, a four-page tabloid newspaper "Warning" (Ostoroha). Its front page editorial stated that "the paper will be distributed free" and that the editor will publish his paper at irregular intervals [25]. Only two numbers of this paper were issued.

With the first of November, 1911, a tsarophile monthly, "Pravoslavny Rusyn" (Orthodox Ruthenian) was started in Mundare. Its editor and publisher was a priest—Rev. Panteleymon Bozyk. Its policy programme was revealed in this sentence: "Pravoslavny Rusyn"—a religious national newspaper for the Ruthenian People in Canada and it stands for the dignity of "Pravoslavna Vira Rusy Sviatoyi" (The Orthodox Faith of Holy Russia). But only a few editions of this magazine were seen.

In 1913, Victor P. Hladyk, the former editor of Russophile gazette "Postup" and "Pravda" (Progress and Truth) published in U.S.A., came from that country to Canada. Having been in conflict with his surroundings in U.S.A.—and with the blessing of Russian political circles in U.S.A. and Canada—Hladyk began to publish a weekly paper "Russkiy Holos" (Russian Voice) at 100 Grierson Street, in Edmonton. The paper was organized by Wasyl Cherniak who came from the village of Chechy, district Brody, and who was a rabid Russophile. He had made his fortune in the gold mines of Alaska and now was trying to invest his money in editorial enterprise. In this he received substantial aid from the two brothers—Ivan and Kindrat Sheremeta. Financial funds were adequate enough to begin the work of publishing the above mentioned paper which was printed for

---

[25] "New Country" No. 29, Nov. 20, 1912.

over three years. In all, 158 editions saw the light of day. The first issue to appear had a double date—17 and 4 April, 1913, and the last issue was dated June 20, 1916. It was published by Russian Publishing Co. with W. S. Cherniak as chairman who, in 1914—when W. Hladyk moved to Winnipeg to start a new paper—took over the ownership of "Russkiy Holos". M. Ostrovsky became the manager, at the same time retaining his position as the Slavic organizer of the Liberals in Western Canada. A group of these Russophiles had managed to make a strongly binding contact with the provincial liberal government of Alberta—then under the premiership of A. L. Sifton—who morally and financially supported their publishing venture. On the question of schools the Rossophiles from "Russian Voice" and the minister of education, George P. Boyle stronly opposed the teaching of the Ukrainian language in schools.

Minister Boyle did not wish to see bilingual schools in Alberta and the "Russian Voice" fought bitterly against Ukrainian language, at every step. A special weight was added to the Russophile community when A. S. Shandro, on April 17, 1913, was elected a member of provincial legislature for Alberta from the district of Whitford, and who was at the time board member of "Russian Voice" publishing establishment. A. S. Shandro came to Canada, as a thirteen year old boy, in 1899, and had very little knowhow as to what was the national politics of "Russian Voice". The Russophiles, seeing his organizational and oratorical abilities lost no time in harnessing him to pull their wagon. Against A. S. Shandro, and in the same district, ran Pavlo Rudyk, one of the top Ukrainian leaders in Alberta. This sharpened so much more Shandro's attitude toward Ukrainians. Only somewhat later, when A. S. Shandro saw his error, did he rid himself of his Russophile allegiance and in a public announcement, which he signed on Dec. 28, 1916—and which was printed widely in Ukrainian press—in Vegreville, in the presence of leading figures of Ukrainian National entity. His announcement exposes the political characteristics of Russophile press and its ilk and so we take the liberty to quote from it somewhat extensively.

"From the very beginning of the recently departed years there had begun to spread, in Alberta, the Russophile propaganda, into the maelstrom of which it was my lot to fall. I noticed that the work, carried on by the leaders of this group, was always harmful to the Ukrainian people... During the last year I edged myself as much as I could, away from these groups of people, not wanting to have on my conscience all those abuses, mudslinging and false accusations which they, in their blindness and stubborn hatred created among Ukrainian citizens of Canada. As prior to 1913, so even now, I declare myself to be a Ukrainian, acknowledge the Orthodox religion—like all our people from Bukovyna.

I publicly protest against the Russophile press and its malicious attack upon Ukrainian citizens of Canada, who, in my view, are loyal British subjects and honest citizens.

My conscience was weighted heavily with grief and bitterness while tolerating this abysmal work that was spread by these people among Ukrainian settlers, thereby doing much damage not only to the Ukrainian nation overseas, but also to the Orthodox Church and the liberal party... It led to misunderstanding in Orthodox Church affairs and in electoral districts, settled by Ukrainians. I need not present any specific proofs for the events of the last four years are only too well known to all".

The condemnation of the Russophiles by A. Shandro—the first Ukrainian M.L.A. in Canada—made its own strong political impression with an invaluable meaning, not only in his immediate district, but also among the whole Ukrainian community in Canada.

What the attitude of "Russian Voice" was toward Ukrainians may be gathered from the paper's headlines such as: "Ukraine and the association of bandits", "Banditism of Uniate Bishops", "Galician Ukraine is the work of Bismark" [26]. "Death Throes of Bishop Budka" [27]) and ad inifinitum. This was a thoroughly through and through Ukrainophobe paper, in spite of the fact that in the establishment's directory could be found such Ukrainian names as: T. Shevchuk, I. Sheremeta, T. A. Fiarchuk, and others. Puffing himself up, the "Russkiy Holos", Russian Voice wrote: "We are not a step-mother, like some Galicians, Ruthenians or Ukrainians—as we have been, up till now, mistakenly called by the English... We are sons and daughter of the great "Russky nation" which in English is called Russians" [28]). But just the same the Russian Voice was published only as long as it was being helped by the Liberal government of Alberta. Printed in both, Russian and Ukrainian, in etymological spelling, the paper was able to revive, to some degree, the russophilism in Alberta, which, after Arseny's departure had started to dwindle. Under the influence of "Russkiy Holos" the Russohpiles began to organize their school in Edmonton, while in Mundare, under the leadership of Rev. P. Bozyk, a separate school was being organized which did not last very long. They also built a large co-operative store, to which many nationally conscious Ukrainians belonged, as the Russophiles maintained that political convictions have nothing in common with the business world.

The one single barrier, opposing this advancing attack on Ukrainians in Alberta, was the newspaper "Novyny" (News) and around it were grouped nationally conscious elements who were strongly supported by the priests of the Greek-Catholic parishes. The leading figures in this camp were— Roman Kremar, Stepan Fodchuk, Pavlo Rudyk and others. The last one named even made sworn accusations against A. Shandro's legal right to sit in provincial legislature and so the elections were held the second time. And although Shandro again won the elections, still this political fight with Rudyk helped to transform his thinking processes, in the field of Ukrainian national affairs. A. Shandro was strongly supported by his Bukovinian compatriots, who very often did not have any ties with Moscophiles. Still, the Edmonton Moscophiles managed to harvest some benefits even from this situation and used it to forward their politics by falsely informing the Liberal government of Alberta that all the thirty-six Bukovinian parishes in that province support the Rusophiles and thus, consequently the Liberals. Thanks to this kind of "information" the Russophiles even succeeded in having copies of Alberta acts printed in Russian language.

Similar politics as those of "Russkiy Holos" were also attempted by "Russian People" (Russkiy Narod) in Winnipeg, being aided in its initial start by the previously mentioned V. P. Hladyk who, with the Nov. 18, 1914 dated issue began to publish the second Russophile weekly paper consisting of four pages. These were war times and V. Hladyk had this to say

---

[26] "Russkiy Holos" No. 6, 1913.
[27] "Russkiy Holos" No. 1, 1913.
[28] "Russkiy Holos", No. 1, 1913.

about the appearance of his paper: "In view of the fact that a large number of Russian immigrants from Russia as well as from Austria, Galicia and Bukovyna, and also because the so-called Ruthenian (Ukrainian—M.H.M.) press shows an unfriendly attitude toward the Russians in general, especially during the present war, and stands clearly on the side of the Germans while at the same time accusing the Russians as being an enemy of the triple alliance of England, France and Russia, it therefore behooves us to publish such a gazette [29]). Such printed dribble, during the war, was an open show of derision against Ukrainians in Canada and of their patriotic loyalty and dignity. This same political wood-hewing method was used by "Russian People" for a period of five years, up to the end of its last issue, which came out on June 1, 1919. Finally "Russian People" found itself in the same "favourable" position as its sister paper, "Russian Voice", in Edmonton. When the Liberal government of T. C. Norris came to power in Manitoba it utilized Hladyk as its tool to bear testimony against the Anglo-Ukrainian bilingual schools in Manitoba. March 7, 1916, was the "black day" for the representatives of Ukrainian communities in the Manitoba legislature. When the spokesman for Ukrainians, headed by I. Petrushevych, clarified the need for retaining the bilingual system of teaching in Manitoba schools, the minister of education, Thornton, called upon V. Hladyk, editor of "Russian Voice" to say a word on behalf of "the second portion (section) of Ukrainians", who then spoke about or rather smeared, Ukrainians as being German war sympathizers. It was said that for a long time "Russian People" was greatly favored, morally and materially, by Premier Norris for its help in liquidating bilingualism. During 1918 and 1919 "Russian People" appeared only at irregular times. Even before that its readers were getting fewer in number and the government aid was shrinking. The Russian czar was gone and Russian Orthodox Mission in U.S.A. and Canada, lost its main source of finances. National revolutions by the subjugated countries under Russia, strengthened national consciouness, and their national obligations, in the hearts of their fellow countrymen in Canada. All this had such a great influence upon Ukrainian settlers in Canada, especially on those who had been less nationally oriented and thus had allowed themselves to be snared by the gold-plated and far reaching tsarophile calls. Towards the end of World War I, V. P. Hladyk left for England and Europe and although he was still a figurehead with the paper, it was edited by P. H. Samilo. The new editor of "Russian People" had been, for a long time, a co-worker of V. Hladyk and so he followed stubbornly in the footsteps of his predecessor—and thoroughly hated Ukrainians and ardently defended the "indivisibility of Russia". He also introduced a minor news sensation. When the question of Carpatho-Ukraine was first beginning to take shape—as to the political-historical belonging of this land—at the International Peace Conference in Paris, P. H. Samilo, with others such as himself, conceived "The League for the Liberation of Carpatho-Russia" in the city of Winnipeg, and in "Russian People", in a subtitle, declared that it is the official organ of the newly created organization in Canada. The paper was printed in Russo-Ukrainian jargon (gibberish) which the editors called "Rusko-Halyckoe narechiye" (Russian-Galician dialect). When the source of material and political outlook was dried up, the "Russian People", on June 1, 1919, became

---

[29]) "Russian People", No. 1, 1914.

silent for evermore. But near the end of its infamous existence, an enmity ensued between a group of Russophiles in Alberta, headed by Cherniak, and the other group-centre of the newly-created League in Winnipeg.

V . Hladyk proved himself to be not only a clever organizer but an astute editor as well. He was able to attract to himself willing co-workers and even to hitch to his Russophile wagon, such well known leaders of Ukrainian life in Canada as—Kyrylo Genik, Rev. Panteleymon Bozyk, Theodore Kokhan, a teacher, and others. All of them were finally able to free themselves from this "anti-national" action. Some of them had their articles printed in the official organs of Russophile press, as for instance, Rev. P. Bozyk who wrote sharp and smearing editorials in which he belabored, unmercifully, "Ukrainianism", "Uniates" and Ukrainian political Independents. After the First World War he not only cured himself of Russophilism but even broke away completely from tsarophilism and was accepted as a priest by the Ukrainian Catholic Church. A grievous undercut was administered to Russophiles, in this country, by the creation of the Ukrainian Greek-Orthodox Church in Canada, which gradually attracted to its organizational system, not only members of Russian Orthodox Church — those who were of Ukrainian origin—but also individual parishes of this same Church, and all these actions were helping to pull the rug from under the feet of the Russophile movement.

The war times produced a prolific crop of Russophile press. On Sept. 28, 1916 was spawned "Kanadiyskaya Pravoslavnaya Rus" (Canadian Orthodox Rus) the official organ of Russian Orthodox Mission in Canada. It was an eight-page tabloid, printed mostly in Russian, with a smattering of Ukrainian, and planned as an official religious information medium. In its appeal for subscription was this inscription: "Kanadiyskaya Pravoslavnaya Rus" is a "religious-national newspaper". But in this same semi-monthly, outside of church chronicles, very little was written about religion. On the other hand, the pages were filled with information about the Orthodoxism being an expression of Russian patriotism while Ukrainianism was criticized as being nothing more than a political invention, and that Ukraine itself was only a figment of geographical imagination. For the purpose of confusing and bamboozling its readers even Taras Shevchenko's works were twisted out of context and cited [30].

The base of operation for newspaper "Canadian Orthodox Rus" was the Trinity Sobor in Winnipeg at 643 Manitoba Avenue. Political editorials and polemical articles were written by V. P. Hladyk, who signed himself by the cryptogram VPH, and by archimandrite Adam Fylypowsky who also signed his articles cryptographically, as A.A.F. The appearance of "Canadian Orthodox Rus" supplied the beginning for the independent era of Russian Orthodox Church in Canada. From this time on the Russian Church in Canada had its own bishop-administrator, stationed in Montreal. The first such bishop was Alexander Nemylowsky, from Volyn [31]. With its anti-Ukrainian platform "Canadian Orthodox Rus" was unable to find a sufficient number of readers among Ukrainians and so in less than one year of its existence it suffered its demise. Still not paying too much attention

---

[30] "Canadian Orthodox Rus", No. 2, 1916.
[31] Born in 1876. Carried on his work as a priest in U.S.A. and for a while edited a paper "Svyet" (World). In 1909 he was called to Moscow by the Synod and was nominated a bishop. He was a quiet sympathizer of Ukrainianism.

to such a state of affairs the Russophiles—or as they were popularly called in Canada, the Moscophiles—organized on the 10th of July, 1917, a so-called "Russkiy Kongres" (Russian Congress) which was held in Winnipeg. The congress was projected to receive delegates from all across Canada, but, outside of Winnipeg, only a small group from Edmonton and a few delegates representing a few districts in Manitoba, came to attend. The basic core of Congress was from Winnipeg which was coached by Hladyk and Fylypowsky. Those two prepared the resolutions for Congress, written in very poor Russian, as they had but a meagre knowledge of Russian language—both of them being of Ukrainian descent. These ill-phrased resolutions became the butt of long discussions and obstructions, on the part of the Ukrainian group, which prevented the rest of the delegates from holding meetings or forming any resolutions—and at one time transforming the whole Congress into a regular "free for all" fight. At this Congress the Russophile group proposed to choose a delegation, composed of "three representatives from Canada" to be sent to Paris, with a demand that all the western Ukrainian lands—meaning Galicia and Bukovyna—be joined to Russia. There were not any funds to send this delegation to Paris, as the income of Russian Orthodox Mission was very meagre and so Hladyk alone was sent—and came back with nothing to show. Nor were the Russophiles any more successful with organizing their "M. Gogol Bursa" (M. Hohol), in Winnipeg. The funds for this latest venture had been collected a long way back but of students and candidates there were but very few. This was perhaps the truest measure in showing that the Russophile sympathies in the masses were dying and that the movement, which during the years 1908-1910 and 1913-1916 had such far-reaching influences, was now disappearing from view—and all because the external forces that had been supporting this movement, both morally and financially, had ceased to exist. In this way was dying the political ideology, which had cost Ukrainian settlers an enormous amount of national energy and which had been a great road block in Ukrainian-Canadian development. Into this whirlpool of Russophile stream even some leading individuals of national movement, were sucked in, but who were men enough to admit their error and made an effort to redress their mistakes. This ill-conceived ideology spumed a singularly devastating whirlwind which wrought so much damage amidst Ukrainian national entity in Canada, and which had tried so hard to undermine the solid ground in which this same Ukrainian entity was endeavouring to plant its national-cultural roots.

The most infamous work, of this Russophile press—and the one which harmed Ukrainians the most—was accomplished during the First World War. With the help of its whispering and open propaganda it tagged all Ukrainian settlers with the political and unfriendly seal of "Austrophiles", which accusation was easily believed by some non-discerning elements of Canadian community. The fruits of this propaganda were terribly bitter. The sufferings of innocent people knew no end. This slyly conceived, and cleverly manipulated, maneuver weighed down heavily on any further course in the integration of Ukrainian people in Canada. We will have more to say about this matter in other chapters of our history.

THE NEW MOVEMENT

When the Ukrainian Canadian community, during the First World War, was engaged in a hard struggle with imperialistic Russophilism in Canada, vital changes were taking place in the realm of national-political and social-economic structure of Eastern Europe. National revolutions in these subjugated countries, under the rule of Russia, and the liberation struggle of these same enslaved nations for self-rule, had a considerable influence on those immigrants in Canada whose national-cultural roots had been cultivated in those now rebelling countries. On the background screen of these events two extreme currents were deeply etched. On the one side stood the national liberation movement of these countries—who strongly desired to see their people living in independent nationally democratic countries on their own ethnographic territories—while on the other side stood the likewise extremely active international force, centered in Moscow, whose single political idea was the world-wide spread of international communism. Socialist movement, which had been the god-father of this current, began to differentiate itself. This same process became noticeable in Ukrainian socialist movement in Canada.

The Ukrainian Labor News

In September of 1918 the "Ukrainian Socialist-Democratic Party of Canada" and its paper "Robochy Narod" (Working People) was, by a government decree declared to be illegal and by this same action the socialist centres were deprived of their organizational framework and their official press organ. The eyes of all such centres throughout Canada, were now turned toward the Ukrainian Labor Temple in Winnipeg, which was the headquarters of the chartered organization bearing the same name. This organization carried on a propaganda campaign to gain more members and, as a result, branches were being hatched all over Canada. Towards the end of February, 1919, when the building of the Ukrainian Labor Temple had been completed—which, by the way, had been built at the expense of Ukrainian community in general—the organizational nucleus of the Labor Temple printed, on the twenty-second of March, 1919, its first issue of the weekly newspaper the "Ukrainian Labor News", and backed by the firm of: "The Winnipeg Trades and Labour Council". Editorial and administrative offices were in the Ukrainian Labour Temple, corner of Pritchard and McGregor. Those who worked with Ukrainian Labor News were the same who were also working with "Working People", but between those two organs there was this noticeable difference: Whereas "Working People" stood at the crossroads of the Second and the Third International, the Ukrainian Labour News, on the other hand, most decisively took the side of the international communism. In the beginning the new weekly was printed bilingually—as was required by war censorship—but starting with its sixth issue, dated May 2*, 1919, it was then printed, exclusively in Ukrainian. Such easing off conveniences were granted to all Ukrainian press. "The Ukrainian Labour News" was printed regularly in large (17.5x24 inch) format, and consisted of eight pages. Danylo Lobay was the editor and Ivan Navizivsky its administrator. The paper worked hand-in-hand with Ukrainian Labour Temple, which shortly after became the core of numerous branches, clustering around it. Soon after this the weekly paper changed to a twice-weekly and later on to a thrice-weekly project, under the firm name of: The

Ukrainian Labour News Association. The policy line of this official organ was a decidedly communist one. The Ukrainian Labour Theatre, which was opened in conjunction with Ukrainian Labour Temple, also peddled this same ideology. Similar work was carried on by the Drama League of Vynnychenko, which was later renamed to: The Educational and Dramatic League of Vynnychenko and still later it was named the Dramatic Choral Association and finally—at last—to Dramatic Choral Group. The Winnipeg Centre led the way and supplied the guiding tone to the rest of the branches beyond Winnipeg. We will have more to say about this press in the second part of our history between the two World Wars.

LITERATURE OF THE PIONEERS

The press records facts and events. Poetry reflects human feelings—emotions, thoughts, dreams and desires. In other words, it speaks of a person's fullness of life and environment, as well as reactions to the outside world.

It is interesting to study the psychology of the Ukrainian pioneer, to understand him and his powers and weaknesses, his longings and pains, his hatred and love towards the old and the new worlds.

The social exploitation and the national oppression of the Ukrainian people at the end of the nineteenth century created in the people a slogan: "Into the world beyond". It was a slogan of some hopelessness and resignation. Such was its evaluation at first. But the slogan was followed by action, recorded by Ukrainian annalists in their annals. Hundreds, then thousands of people left their native land for the "world beyond". Some left in search of work in Prussia, some to Hungary, and a large percentage of them beyond the sea, to America—to the United States, to Canada, to Brazil. The slogan of searching for a new fate is expressed in verse form by Bohdan Lepky in his words.

> So into the world beyond,
> If our native land will not feed us.

That necessity of life was expressed in stronger words by another poet, Alexander Kolessa-Khodovitsky, as follows:

> Perhaps a river deep
> We shall cross,
> But in our native land
> We shall perish.

These poetic words were not fantasy, bound with poetic freedom. It was reality, and the world full of great realism.

The exodus of masses of Ukrainians was accompanied by Ukrainian writers, who, by their writing, dedicated to their pains and humility, love of their own people and the teaching of the foreign language and customs, craved new life. Let us recall the words of Ivan Franko's poem "To Brazil", the stories of Tymko Borduliak under the same title, the novel of Wasyl Stefanyk "The Stone Cross" and many others, who worried about the fate of Ukrainian immigrants in the new countries of settlement.

They came by the thousands, in whole families, often broken families, father and son, sometimes only the father, and sometimes only the son, leaving the rest of the family behind. They really went "far beyond the horizon, into the world beyond". They knew not what awaited them in new lands.

They left the native land with a hopeless determination, and they found hopeless eagerness in the new land. What thoughts and emotions did they bring with them here? In one song we find the following words:

> "Neither a path, nor a road,
> Only forest and water,
> Wherever we look, we see
> Not our own, but foreign land".

In another song an anonymous writer says:

> "Oh, do not whisper, my grove,
> You green grove,
> Do not give my heart more pain
> Because I am in a foreign land".

Finding oneself within a foreign environment, unexpected situations, uncertainties of tomorrow, one always turns his thoughts to his past, to find a rest at least for a moment, for the suffering soul. It flies to the beauty of youth, to dear ones left behind, to the nearest ones. One thinks about the memorable moments of one's life. No wonder, then, that one newcomer to the Canadian West describes his first Easter here in these words:

> Our Easter is so beautiful,
> As the green grove,
> While here in Canada—snow and ice,
> And cold winds blow.

From the depths of life's adventures came various thoughts and feelings. They were painful, sacred and unforgettable. One wishes to put them into the best poetic form, not to hoard them, but to convey them to one's closest people. These poems were passed on from people to people. Some were put into songs. Some remained only in memories. But all these memories were of the inhospitable, cold western prairies.

"The kolomayka" form of verse was most suitable for those who wished to express in song their own and the people's suffering. Thus gradually the Ukrainian folklore of Canada began to take shape. It was being created on the basis of the contrasts of life in the past and the present, on the contrast between nature, a way of life, culture and an ideal acceptance of the world.

At the same time a new philosophy of life was being created. One had to find himself in new situations. In other words—one had to live, and through life to create new values in this new land. It was necessary to preserve and to convey these new values to share them with others, the same type of people, and then to pass them on to younger generations.

In the pioneer press of the times of the beginnings of a mass immigration of the Ukrainians to Canada, and especially in the first Ukrainian newspaper on the North American continent, "Svoboda", which, as we know, served the Ukrainian immigrants in the United States and in Canada, were published the first verses of our pioneers. In them we may see not only the way of life of the Ukrainian pioneer in this new country, but also to come to know the psychology of his everyday trials and tribulations, his pains, as well as his elations through obtaining work and a livelihood for himself and his children.

The first of these verses appeared in print in the "Svoboda", 1898-99. It was quite characteristic that the author, M. Gowda, of Edmonton, Alberta, in his verses entitled "To the People of Rus" was the first one to turn to his people in Ukraine and to refute his hardships in the new land, as if forgetting his fate and emphasizing his ties with his own people in their native land in Europe. This verse reveals a certain symbolism, which permeates throughout the entire history of the Ukrainians in Canada during the past 90 years. The Ukrainian community in Canada was concerned with their people in their native land in Europe. The poetic form and the phraseology in Gowda's verses are not very polished, but the thought content is worthy of note [1].

Another writer depicting Ukrainian-Canadian fate, Ivan Drohomeretsky, from Pleasant Home in Manitoba writes about his own life's adventures as well as about those of his brothers-in-fate in Canada. His "kolomayka"-style verse radiates goodnaturedness and optimism. In his poem "Exodus From the Old Country", dated September 14, 1899, he says:

> "I once was in my native land,
> And I often think:
> Why should I be suffering
> In unhappiness?
> I shall go into the wide world,
> Where there's neither oppression nor lord,
> Where there are no masters,
> In the field an overlord.
> But where to go? I think —
> Where else but to Canada,
> Where there's land and steppe
> From the east to west.
> Oh, to Canada I'll go,
> To the new land,
> And where, as they say,
> It is a free country".

Here again is an interesting thing. M. Gowda, in his poem, worries about the fate of his relatives and countrymen back home, and Drohomeretsky speaks of another ideal, an ideal of universal values—the freedom of men. For the sake of a life of freedom, human dignity, he and his kin leave their fatherland and go into a land of freedom, where one may live a free life, where there are no lords, overlords and overseers in the fields. Drohomeretsky's poem wafts a breeze of level-mindedness, happiness, confidence. It is obvious that he, like others, have regained their self-confidence when they came to live here in this new land.

Only after these two poems were published in the "Svoboda" other poems appeared—poems of a lyrical style. Ivan Drohomeretsky and M. Gowda appeal to the readers of the "Svoboda" in Canada. They call for education, knowledge, enlightenment. These two were followed by others. Their number increased yearly, and the subject matter or topics became more and more diversified.

The Ukrainian newspapers in Canada, which appeared at the beginning of the twentieth century, preserve in their pages many poems and songs written by the first immigrants. In them we read of the longing for the old country, of the dreams of the future here, and of a deep relief in the happiness for all in this new land. Besides lyrics, one may find very often many verses of life's hardships and tribulations.

More prominent among the poets of those days were: Dmytro Rarahowsky (1878-1957), Pawlo Krat (1882-1952), Wasyl Holowatsky. These

---

[1] For this reason perhaps some of them were translated into English. One of them was printed in The Boston Evening Transcript of October 17, 1905. The translator was E. W. Thompson, a friend of Gowda. Gowda came to Canada in 1898. He was born in 1874 and died in 1953.

men wrote mostly about social problems, social injustices, and injustices done to the average human being. It is noteworthy that all three of them had an education above the average high school. They had been community leaders in the old country, and they felt social injustices done to their people very deeply.

A prominent place amongst these early writers belongs to Theodore Fedyk (1873-1941) [2]. In 1908 he published a collection of poems in the "kolomayka" style under the title "Songs of Canada and Austria". The appearance of this booklet, containing over thirty poems of various writers, amongst them nineteen of his own, was for those times a pioneers' anthology in itself, which attracted the attention not only of the reading community, but also of the critics. The poems were about the worries, misfortunes, and hardships of the early immigrants, about the hard labor of the immigrants on Canada's virgin lands, about the longing for the native land and village, about the past, and about the youthful and happy years in the homeland.

They glorified and adored the mother and the father, idealized the betrothed. These writers loved the freedom in this land, dreamed of wealth, and felt anguish in disappointments. They rebelled at national insults and social exploitation. Quite often in one song we read about suffering and about happiness, about tears and laughter. Theodore Fedyk and others did not subdue their emotions. They made up by frequent changes of topic rather than by the intensity of emotions. The rhythm and the rhyme were not always very good. For this they were criticized by their contemporaries. Yet, in spite of that, their verses were very popular and had much success amongst the readers. They felt what the poets felt and expressed in their verses. The style was simple enough for everyone.

The large number of poems written by pioneer writers of those times serves as evidence that the average pioneer felt what he read in them. These poets touched their heart strings. The verses deepened their emotions and emphasized them to the core. If only these pioneer poets had had the education and had mastered the art of writing poetry—what they could have contributed to our Canadian literature!

Prof. Watson Kirkconnell became interested in these poetical expressions. He took deep interest in the amateur poetry of all ethnic pioneer peoples. In 1935 he published a few translations of these poems under the title "Canadian Overtones". He emphasized the high level of thinking and the intelligence of the writers.

In 1908 another collection of songs was published under the title "Songs of the Laborers", written by D. Rarahowsky. This, together with Fedyk's collection, comprised a good collection of poems in the "kolomayka" style.

In this prolific production of pioneer poetry grew and flourished a political individualism. The most prominent of the poets of this category was Sawa Chernetsky-Chaly, also written Czernecky (1873-1934).

His verses appeared in "Svoboda" as far back as the year 1900. Beside his name appears the word "Winnipeg, Canada". The subject matter of his poems was exclusively life in Canada. As an example, one of them is entitled "From Canada's Garden", another one—"Canada's Laborers", "Two Pictures", "The One Lone Cranberry". He produced a collection

---

[2] Fedyk's collection of poems were republished six times, outnumbering the editions of all other publications even in later days.

under the name of "Ruthenians in Canada", with the following preface: "This verse is only an introduction to more verses, which I plan to write and send to "Svoboda" for publication. I intend to portray as truly as possible the life of the Ruthenians in Canada".

To his collection belong the verses entitled "New Emigrants", "In a Canadian City", "I Want to Return Home", "This Is What It Is", and others. We could include here his later poem "The Present Soldiers", which could serve as a background to the whole series. In them Sawa Chernetsky-Chaly describes the immigrants as soldiers, who go to struggle with poverty and lead an open battle against adverse conditions.

It seems that the most bitter adversity of the times was the longing for the native land, Ukraine, for the native thatched roof, and the dear ones left behind. Very often it brought about serious depressions of spirits. The very memories of the old land was something that caused pain and brought about tears. These emotions are described in Chernetsky-Chaly's verses which appeared in "Svoboda" in April 1900 under the heading "Spring in a Foreign Land" [3].

A pioneer in a new environment seeks identities with his former environment. The more contrasts there are, the more psychological reactions. For this reason it was difficult for a pioneer from one country with beautiful fields and groves to become accustomed to Canada's monotonous prairies. Sawa, who spent his youth on the scenic banks of the river Dnister and Pokutia region, pours out his longing for the beauty of his native land in his poem "The One Lone Cranberry":

The One Lone Cranberry

All is different in you, Canada!
The plants, the birds and all the animals—
Sadness and dreariness, like in a grave.
Nothing to see in here that's dear to me
Save the lone cranberry, the only plant
That took our roots—beloved cranberry!

The Ukrainian immigrant in Canada had not only a yearning for his dear native country. He also had his moments of happiness and recreation. Sometimes they went to extremes and contradicted his longing. Sometimes there were repressions of the soul. With this background a new category of pioneers emerged, contemptibly called the "Jacks". This slang name originated in the lumber camps where there were lumber-jacks, who made good money. They lived in isolation in the forests, and there developed a free way of living, unrestrained by any customs prevalent in good society. They came into cities occasionally and there made up for the privations of the lumber camps. They spent their money on liquor. They did not usually have a good reputation. Sawa Chernetsky-Chaly described them in his "Two Pictures", where he contrasts the two ways of living.

This poem is not the only one in its category. The newspapers of those times often carried advertising material of wives searching for their lost husbands.

Sawa also wrote about this life in his "Canadian Laborers", and "In a

---
[3] "Svoboda", No. 13, 1900.

Factory". In the latter he ponders on the social problems of exploitation of the laborer by the employer. But Sawa was always an optimist and believed that these conditions will pass in time, that truth and righteousness will prevail. The problem of truth and righteousness is his subject matter in the poem "Love of Neighbor". The Truth, which was trampled on in Europe, "came here to America, to the new world".

He gives a fuller description of the fate of the whole family that is faced with starvation in the forest during a long and cold Canadian winter. He writes about this in his story "From the Depths of Despair". He added a subtitle "The Life of the Canadian Pioneers". With this he commenced a new series of poems and stories, published not only in newspapers, but also in almanacs. To this series belong such of his works as "One of the Many", "Horrors of America", "The Tail of the Devil", "The Sea Bandits", "A Woman's Tongue", "American Wit", "The Adventures of a Bum", "High Prices", "Worries of the Devil", "The Dog in a Bag", "A Gypsy's Guest", "Terrible Cooks", and others. These were published in "Svoboda", "Iskra", "Osa", "Lys Mykyta" and other periodicals [4]. Some of Sawa's stories were published in small booklets.

In both poetry and prose Sawa proved that he had an above average talent in the pioneer days. His power of life's experiences and poetical expression put him into the leading ranks of poets of his time. He left for us splendid descriptions of the life of the Ukrainian settlers in Canada. He distinguished himself in his creativeness in another way—in satirical expressions. In the middle of 1900 S. Chernetsky went to the United States, where his literary interests changed as well as his style of writing. In the second half of that year he wrote satires and feuilletons, and he illustrated them himself. His satire is witty and biting, and often sharp. He did not spare any traitors of various sorts, especially Russophiles and the Latin clergy, which in those days worked against the Ukrainian Catholic Church in the U.S.A. Sawa also attacked all types of self-styled lords, especially the rotten nobility of the olden days. He always defended the poor, the under-privileged, the exploited; proclaimed faith in truth and in people; provided humor for the Ukrainian immigrants at a time when humor and satire were medicine for all the ills of immigrant life. In his poetry he immortalized for all time, in poetical form, the anguish in the soul of the mother, father, child, and the whole community when they had to build their homes and hearthstones in the unfriendly wilderness of Canada.

Another poet-bard of these early times in Canada was Wasyl Kudryk (1880-1963). His first poems appeared also in the "Svoboda". There is another similarity between him and Sawa Chernetsky—they were both teachers. Sawa often used the pen-name Daleshiwsky, because he had been born in the village of Daleshewa, in the district of Horodenka, and Kudryk in the village of Cebriw, in the Tarnopol district — using the pen-name Cebriwsky. Kudryk was not as prolific in his writing, and was younger than Chernetsky, and emerged later. In 1911 a collection of Kudryk's poems appeared under the title of "Vesna" (Spring)' and another one under the title "The First Adventure of Nechypir Dowhoch'ghun". In the same year he published in booklet form his story "The Laborer's Revenge", in which he described the exploitation of a laborer, especially that of an immigrant. This story brought out misery, hatred and revenge. Kudryk

---

[4] "Svoboda", No. 18, 1900.

tied his life with Canada. He worked as a common laborer on a farm at Oleskiw (later named Tolstoi, Manitoba), taught school, and when the weekly newspaper "Ukrainian Voice" was established, he was one of the organizers. He was also one of its first editors (1910-1921). Journalism became his main concern over his literary creations. He never abandoned it for the rest of his life, maintaining his philosophical and contemplative spirit. Under the influence of this same contemplative spirit he left journalism and went into theology. After having been ordained, he wrote less. Some of his best creations are such as "Flowers by the Roadside"—poetry in the form of prose. His best literary works are similar to Lev Tolstoi's. This is especially borne out in his collection of poems "Vesna" (Spring), which are historical because they were the first collection of poems written by an early immigrant in Canada.

A talented writer was Semen Kowbel (1877-1965), who emerged in the period between the two world wars, but who had his roots in the pioneer days. He came to Canada from the Borschiw district in 1909, and threw himself into community life, never relinquishing it to almost his last days. He wrote, besides poetry, also much prose. But he gained recognition mainly for his dramatic works and for his amateur acting on the stage. During the pioneer times he wrote "The New Christmas Scene", a tragicomedy, "A Girl's Dreams", which gained a wide recognition, a drama "Liakhty-Tatary" (Confidantes), and a few one-act plays. Many of them were staged from the manuscript. All of them had a moral in them and were of the character-building type. They portrayed characters acting in their environments. Kowbel was also a good caster. In 1917 he prepared for the first time in Canada the Ukrainian opera "The Cossack Beyond the Danube", which was played in Queens Theatre in Winnipeg.

Of his poems the best known are "The Longing", "Blossoms and Needles", and "The Birds' Revolution".

At the end of the pioneer period there were also such talented writers as Ivan Nowosad, Petro Chaykowsky, Petro Oleksiw, T. J. Marciniw, Anna Pruska (Podolanka), Panteleymon Bozyk, Joseph Yasenchuk. The latter published his collection of verses under the title "The Canadian Kobzar". Amongst the average talents, who rose to heights after the first world war constitute a separate group, young students in Saskatoon, who were publishing a students' journal "Kameniari" (The Stone Breakers): Onufry (Honore) Ewach, Semen Doroschuk, Ivan Danylchuk, and Semen Sawchuk.

Onufry Ewach and Semen Doroschuk rose highest on wings of song, poetically speaking. Some of the above mentioned writers are dealt with in another part of this history.

PROSE

As we tie in the pioneer Ukrainian Canadian poetry with the appearance of M. Gowda and I. Drohomyretsky, and above all with Sawa Chernetsky-Daleshiwsky, who in 1900 with a wide diapason of his verse portrayed the fate of the Ukrainian settler in Canada, so do we likewise connect the beginning of the pioneer prose with the name of Rev. Nestor Dmytriw, the first Ukrainian priest in Canada. During 1896 and 1897 he worked in U.S.A. as an editor of "Svoboda" and from the letters and articles of his readers he got to know about the life, troubles and miseries of the settlers in Canada. When in May of 1897 he arrived in Canada and met with settlers' problems face to face he wrote, under the influence of these concrete realities, several absorbing stories without which it would be difficult to fathom the psychology of the immigrant-pioneer. After his visit to Calgary he wrote a satire "Ruthenian Paska" (Easter bread) and the French Priest". While travelling between Winnipeg and Halifax in 1898, as an immigration official he originated a cycle of stories under a collective title of "Pictures of Canada". These stories were based on the contrast of the two, the Ukrainian and non-Ukrainian, cultures. For example: in the "Ukrainian paska and the French priest" the author portrays the clash between the Ukrainian and French cultures, and in "Assimilation" a similar clash between Ukrainian and Anglo-Saxon cultures. For the material in his story N. Dmytriw took the life experiences of the immigrants and these were nothing more than repetitions of similar events that could have happened in Calgary, Stuartburn or Terebovla. In these stories the author always defends traditions and cultural attainments of his people although he never preaches them, leaving the final choice with the reader. In "Assimilation" the author pictured the first Ukrainian-English marriage in Canada that took place in Dauphin in 1897 between Frank (Nex—M.H.M.) of London, a printer in Dauphin, and Caroline (Zarowny—M.H.M.) from Halychyna. Similar event took place in Stuartburn in 1897, where a Mennonite was married to a Ukrainian girl. N. Dmytriw dramatized it in his story "Married to a Mennonite". Another one of his pioneer stories is "Tymko Havryluk" (1897), a kind of an original Ukrainian Odyssey through Scylla and Charybdis to final destination—a homestead in Canada. His cycle of "Pictures of Canada" includes a story entitled "Sunday in Ottawa". Although Rev. N. Dmytriw lived less than two years in this country his literary work is bound much closer with Canada than with the country where he lived, the U.S.A.

Like Sawa Chernetsky who came from the Horodenka district in Halychyna and was the first in the poetic sphere of the pioneer era, so did another son of the same soil from the village of Serafynci, Appolinariy Novak (1888-1961) distinguished himself with his brilliant talent in prose and fiction. Apollinariy came to Canada as a young student and his education and knowledge he attributed to the incessant effort at self-improvement. At that time he cooperated with "Svoboda" in U.S.A. and took an active part in cultural-educational work of Winnipeg and was a close observer of life. He wrote his first story in 1906 entitled "First pay-day in Canada". The heroes of the story are killed by a rock-slide, during the building of the first transcontinental railroad, and are buried by their comrades alongside the track. The author finishes his story by describing how "the labourers chewed their way further and further into the rocks. They were penetrating through the wild jungles of Ontario and fell as the first victims for the benefit of Canada's development". A. Novak printed his stories in various papers and in them he described social inequality, injustice, exploitation, lack of employment, uncertainty of life and what tomorrow may bring. All these human interests supplied the material for his stories. His heroes do not bend nor stray from their path and only fall when struck down by the forces of nature. Among his first stories belong: "He worked Faihtfully", "Unemployment", "Funeral", "Laugh" (taken from the life of iron-workers in Canada), "Shekey" and others. The first collection of stories written by A. Novak, and other contemporary writers, appeared in 1910 under the title "Canadian Stories".

A somewhat different writer's talent from the pioneer era was shown by Zyhmont Bychynsky (1880-1947). He came to America already with his name established as a budding writer having some of his material printed in the "Literaturno-Naukowyj Wisnyk" ("Literary-Educational Herald") including one of his first stories, "Daughter of Stundisty", under the pseudonym of "Anyn" and another story, printed in the same journal, "The Army of Salvation" written under the pseudonym of "'Hanyn". Themes for those two stories were partly taken from American life, as well as the other two "The Pedlars" and "'March of Doukhobors". Z. Bychynsky took up law at the Lviv University but never finished his studies and came to New York in 1904 and from there to Canada, where he pursued further his education at the Manitoba College in Winnipeg. In 1908 he took over the editorship of the "Canadian Farmer" from Osyp Megas at which post he stayed for one year, moving to Alberta to take up teacher's position. In 1910 he moved to U.S.A. where he wholly devoted himself to the Presbyterian movement as pastor and editor of the newspaper "Soyuz" (Union). During the years that Bychynsky worked with "Svoboda" and "Canadian Farmer", as well as during his teaching days, he wrote a series of stories about the life of Ukrainian pioneers that were printed in the two above mentioned papers. Among them are "He Became Rich", "Strikers", "Parents and Children", and others. He wrote a four-act drama "In the Old and New Country" that was printed by the A. Bonchevsky Association, and published a novel "Emigrants" and a series of stories. He also prepared and edited the first Ukrainian calendar in Canada "Poselenec" (Settler) and helped with the publication of collected writing by T. Fedyk and D. Rarahovsky. Not only was he a writer, but also the first Ukrainian literary critic in Canada.

Onufry Hykawy (1886-1945) made his debut in poetry and prose al though it was the latter which revealed him as being the qualified master of that medium. His poems and stories were printed in various papers but mostly in "Canadian Farmer" of which he became the editor in 1913, holding this post for 20 years. He wrote a 70-page book "Stories for Children" that was published by "Ruska Knyharnia" (Ukrainian Bookstore) in J. Krett's printing shop in 1910 and with it he initiated the start of children's literature which was further developed in the post-war period. O. Hykawy made translations from English and Russian that were financed and published by "Pravda" (Truth) of New York and in 1904 his "National Fables" were printed. He also had several educational books to his name, such as "Basic Laws of Canada", "Short History of Canada" and a series of lesser works.

Myroslav Stechishin (1883-1947) deserves a special niche in the realm of the Ukrainian pioneer literature, who, through the use of his pen placed himself in the ranks of belletristic connoisseurs and publicists. The latter profession was by far his strongest medium of expression and to it he fully submitted himself during his later years. He made translations and wrote original stories, among which may be included the following: "Bum", "Meat Only", "The Labourer in the Gentlemen's Court", "Pilot Butte", and others. In his translations, such as the "Night of Ernest Poll", and in his original writings the author dwelt on the social injustices and voiced his anger against those who exploited their fellowmen. As we already know he edited "Robochy Narod" (Working People) and "Postup" (Progress), "Novyny" (News). The author was a fanatical believer in his own credo, passionately conducted his polemics, and loved and hated with equal measure—everything was black or white, no middle road for him. Undoubtedly M. Stechishin's writing greatly influenced the formation of political problems in the minds of Ukrainian pioneers. During the first World War the writer completely broke his connection with the socialist circles and after the war took over the editorship of "Ukrainian Voice", formulating that paper's policy for the period of twenty years, during which time he also matured as an ideological exponent of the Ukrainian National concept in Canada. It could be said, in truth, that the author's total engrossment in publicity and journalistic work, to the complete exclusion of other things in life dulled to some extent his writing interests and literary abilities.

Paul Krat was another talented author who not only wrote verses (his collection of poetry titled "For Land and Freedom" was published in 1914), but also stories, educational articles, critical reviews and translations as well. Some of his first stories were "The Visit of the Red Friend", "The Pilgrim Lady", "The Victim", "Children", "When Will It Get Better?". He also wrote a humorous novel titled "'God's Last Walk on Earth" or "God at the Revolution", which appeared in 1915. In addition he wrote political satires under the pseudonym of "P. Ternenko". As was mentioned, P. Krat was the editor of the first Ukrainian socialist paper in Canada, the "Red Flag", cooperated closely with "Working People" and also edited the humorous journal "Kadylo". After he broke away from the socialist circles he wrote religious articles for the "Ranok" (Morning).

In 1915 there appeared an English translation of the "Ukrainian National Songs" that was done by Florence Randall Livesay, with the aid of Paul Krat. The latter also wrote the introduction to this song collection which heralded the beginnings of translation work in the field of Ukrainian-Canadian literature. Soon after this, in 1922, Dr. A. J. Hunter translated Shevchenko's "Kobzar" into English.

The starting point of the English-Ukrainian translated literature actually began in 1910 when Ivan Bodrug translated into Ukrainian John Bunyan's "Pilgrim's Progress". The book was published in New York although the translation work itself was done in Canada. The author also translated religious songs from the English hymn books that were printed by the publishers of the "Ranok" (Morning). Another pastor, the Presbyterian church minister Z. Bychynsky, translated from the English the great historical novel of L. Wallace, "Ben Hur". Also Maksym Pasichniak translated from the Polish language the long novel titled "The Tattered Child". There also were writers of a different genre than the ones mentioned above. Among them may be found such individualities as Stephen Fodchuk (1888-1967) and Yakiw Maydanyk (1891), who distinguished themselves by their satire. In a separate category appears the thematical legend of "Shteef (Steve) Tabachniuk", the brain-child of Maydanyk and fostered by S. Fodchuk and others. "Shteef Tabachniuk" stands as a typical prototype of an unsocial non-constructive character that could be found among the pioneer immigrants in general and whom the writers ridiculed by means of humorous cartoons and satire.

A much more prominent poet and satirist was Petro Karmansky (1878-1956) who created a whole cycle of political satire in Canada under the name of "The Monkey's Mirror" which was systematically serialized in the newspaper "Canada" (1913-1914).

The first literary steps in Social Science were made by O. Zerebko and Mykhaylo Shcherbinin. The latter, with the aid of Manitoba Free Press, published the first book in English about the Ukrainians in Canada entitled "The Galicians Dwelling in Canada and Their Origin". To the group of educationists must be added the name of Dr. O. Sushko, who published the first educational journal in Canada "The Ukraine", in two volumes, and in addition wrote several works about the Ukrainian church life in Canada. He also composed verses and wrote satirical articles.

In viewing the early poetry and prose of the pioneer era we could very conveniently, divide it into two periods. The first period began with the appearance of "Khata" (Home) and the second with the formation of the "Association of Writers and Journalists". In the first period the chief role was played by J. N. Krett (1883-1964) who, in addition to his writing and educational talents, also showed business and organizational abilities. He loved books and held close affinity for its print and this induced him to open a print shop. Having a printing press at his disposal brought J. N. Krett into close relationship with the contemporary Ukrainian literators of that time, namely: A. Novak, M. Stechishin, W. Kudryk, O. Hykawy and others. Being acquainted with literature, led him to try his hand at writing. All these men of letters greatly felt the need of a literary journal as the newspaper pages became too crowded for the wider expression of the writers' activities. After long discussions and final counsel it was decided to publish an "Illustrated journal" of literature, politics and contemporary life, which was aptly christened "Khata" (The Home) and edited by J. N. Krett.

The first issue of "Home" appeared in Winnipeg in 1911, printed by the "Ruthenian Press" of J. N. Krett. The "Home" was published through the combined cooperative efforts of the following individuals: P. Krat-Ternenko, who wrote under P.K.T. initials, W. Cebriwsky (W. Kudryk), A. Novak, M. Stechishin, O. Zerebko (who wrote scientific columns), Osyp Boyan, P. Kazan and others. In one word, around the "Home" were grouped all the active wielders of pen, joined by the elite of the literary world. The aim of the journal was made very clear in one of its editorials which stated that "it is the wish of the editors to make the "Home" a place where the literary forces shall find the means of developing themselves on this, the overseas Rus (Ukraine)". The journal had a 8.5 x 12 format consisting of 32 pages. Its full name, in English, was: "Home" (Monthly Magazine for Ruthenian People in North America). In spite of all these promising auguries the "Home" did not last very long as only six issues of it saw the light of day. Still the journal helped to identify a specific historical process and with it came to a conclusion the first stage in the advance and development of the Ukrainian literary form in Canada.

At the close of the decade from the first appearance of the "Home" the Ukrainian literature in Canada had come to the second stage that was concluded with the organization of the "Association of Writers and Journalists of Canada". In the formation of this association the chief role was played by A. Novak and I. Danylchuk. The first one, to a certain extent, represented the pioneer group and I. Danylchuk reflected the image of the younger talents that were brought up in Canada. After much preparation an organizing meeting was held in Winnipeg on April 30, 1923, in connection with the proposed writers' association which at the same time became the first covention of the Ukrainian writers in Canada. A survey was made among those present to find out how many writers there were in Canada, and A. Novak, the organizing secretary of this meeting, submitted a list of 110 persons who in one way or another "gave evidence of their writing talents".

The written word of the group of young poet-folklorists and prose writers of the early pioneer era also had an additional strong influence on the formulation of the Ukrainian spiritual life in Canada. And not alone in Canada; this influence, to a certain extent reflected itself in the life of the Ukrainians in U.S.A. partly due to the fact that nearly all of the Canadian journalistic elite, at some time or another, had been previously connected with the Ukrainian-American newspapers.

The first three collections of poetry that appeared in U.S.A., namely: "America", "Cranes" (Zhurawli), and "Temptations" were predominantly the work of Canadian authors. About their influence on the formulation of the world's outlook among the Ukrainian citizens Omelian Reviuk has this to say: "In the beginning the Canadian writers wrote in the American papers about the life of the immigrants in Canada... but with the development of Canadian press these writers ceased to send their material to the American press and thereby lost their influence on the fellow-Americans" [5]. That group of literators of the pioneer era were all youthful enthusiasts and almost all of them were of the same age. Like birds, they flocked together in their youth, in preparation for their fancy's flight into the poetic realms and when they had passed their twenties they all matured to take on the responsibilities of leadership in the social and cultural life of their times. They became the pioneers of the Ukrainian press in the new country, most of them spending ten or more years behind the editors' desks. To accept this honoured position of an editor with its entailed duties during the pioneer era also meant the dedication of oneself to continuous toil. In addition to the editor's duties one had to take on the extra work of reporting, expediting and a whole series of various functions. These overworked editors could hardly find the time to court the gentle Muse of poetry. Their heavy editorial duties would quickly bring down to earth their poetical flights of fancy. They, instead, became the stone builders, the sculptors and the carvers of the printed word among the Ukrainian entity during its early period of development in Canada.

---

[5] O. Reviuk in "Our Literary and Artistic Achievements in America" from the Memorial Book of Ukrainian National Association (UNS), Jersey City, 1936, page 349.

THE FIRST BOOK EDITIONS, BOOK-STORES AND PUBLISHING ESTABLISHMENTS

It is very difficult to correctly establish the fact as to which were the first Ukrainian books to appear in Canada. However, we do know for a certainty that the first printing establishment that began to publish the first Ukrainian newspaper in Canada was "The Canada North-West Company" that was organized in September 1903. In November of the same year the company received Ukrainian print from New York and on November 5, 1903 sent into the world the first Ukrainian newspaper in Canada. We also know that until then anyone wishing to print anything in Ukrainian had to use the Latin type. During 1903 and the first half of 1904 "The Canada North West Company" was the only one in business. In the latter part of 1904 the "Publishing Company" was organized that edited the weekly paper "Slovo" (Word) and by 1905 a third printing establishment was formed and began to publish the paper "Ranok" (Morning). Still later, in 1907, the "Red Flag Publishing" firm was organized. In the beginning all of these printing establishments limited their work almost exclusively to the publishing of newspapers only, which often proved to be a difficult undertaking in putting out regular editions on time. The firmest footing was held by "The Canada North West Company", publishers of the newspaper "Canadian Farmer". It fell to the lot of this company to arrange for the publication of the first Ukrainian book in Canada in 1904 [1]. This was the Ukrainian-English dictionary, compiled in that same year by I. Bodrug and M. Shcherbinin, entitled: "Ruthenian-English Glossary or Dictionary as English Manual for Ruthenians". This was, as stated in its introduction, "a universal handbook for learning the English language" which saw the light of day at the end of 1904 with the 1905 date imprint.

The first Ukrainian book appearing under the date of 1904 was the 40-page edition of the "Christian Catechism" published by the Independent Greek Church. In 1904 appeared a political brochure under the title "Take It, Read It, and Judge It", containing propaganda material and was issued prior to the federal elections on Oct. 3, 1904. Another party propaganda brochure appeared in the same year titled: "For the Good Ruthenian (Ukrainian) Electors". The first brochure was prepared by the Liberals and printed by "The Canada North West Company", while the second, prepared by the Conservatives, was printed by the "Slovo (Word) Publishers". These, like the legendary swallows, were the first harbingers of the Ukrainian book-world that was to flourish later so abundantly on Canadian soil.

"The Ukrainian Free Thought Federation" in Winnipeg made a press announcement in 1907 that it had printed, in November of that same year, "First booklet in Ukrainian language in Canada". This little book consisted of two separate productions: "The Biography of M. Drahomaniv" by M. Lozynsky and "Nationalism and the National Hallowed Treasures", written by M. Drahomaniv. Both of these two separate works appeared under one cover and had a mutual title, "The Free World". This gave rise to a mistaken belief that it was only the beginning, with more books to follow

---

[1] The contract was signed April 10, 1904 a copy of which is preserved in the archives of the author.

—especially when one considers the allusion made in its introduction as being "The first Ukrainian book in Canada".

To the earlier publications among the first books in Canada belongs the previously mentioned "The Galicians Dwelling in Canada and Their Origin" which was printed in English as the 71st Edition in the series published by "The Historical and Scientific Society of Manitoba".

Among the early publishers whom we previously mentioned belongs the "Ruthenian Press" which was established in Winnipeg in 1908. It differed from others that we have listed before in that it devoted itself exclusively to the publishing of books, while most of the rest were interested in paper-editing only. J. N. Krett was both the organizer and the owner of this project. From the printing press of this publishing establishment came numerous editions, including the first Ukrainian literary journal, the "Home", and a handbook of the Ukrainian language that was financed by Petro Svarich and titled "The Helper for Small Pupils". Both editions first appeared in 1911, the same year that initiated the advance of Ukrainian publishing houses, newspapers and popular books.

A large measure of success in the spreading and popularizing of Ukrainian books belonged to the existence of the "Ruthenian Book Store" (later changed to Ukrainian Book Store) which opened for business at the end of 1905. It was owned by Frank Dojacek and at its earliest beginning consisted of one bag and a suitcase filled with books—a truly mobile bookstore—and with this equipment he travelled from farm to farm, from house to house, selling books. By 1906 he was advertising his own book store at 435 Selkirk Avenue in Winnipeg. Hundreds of various publications and around 50 almanacs and calendars under such names as "Canadian Farmer", "Canadian Ruthenian", "Soldier", "General Calendar", "Vuyko" (Uncle) and others were printed by the "Ruthenian Book Store".

The first mail order book store in the pioneer era was the "Ukrainska Knyharnia" (Ukrainian Bookstore) organized by A. Novak at the begining of 1909, who brought books from Kiev, Lviv, Chernivtsi and other publishing centres in Ukraine, arranged them in sets and advertised them in the newspapers. "The Ukrainian Bookstore" endeavoured to handle books of higher quality, and higher price, mostly of educational nature, and perhaps for that very reason did not stay in business very long.

The publishers of "Ranok" (Morning) put a series of religious and political works. Although it began its printing jobs in 1905 it did not edit any books until 1908.

Among the more active and qualified printing establishments was the "Ukrainian Publishing Company", organized in 1910, which started to publish books in 1911, the first of these consisting of W. Kudryk's books of verses, "Spring", "The Worker's Revenge", as well as some stories from Canadian life. At least half a hundred of small but choice books went out into the world from these publishers and some four calendar-almanacs that contained valuable material for the history of the Ukrainians in Canada.

The various publications that were put out by "Canadian Ukrainian" (formerly Canadian Ruthenian) were advertised under the firm name of "Providence". To the larger edited work of this firm belong the "Kobzar of Taras Shevchenko" which was printed in large number . The publishers always stressed the need of good books and also printed some valuable calendar-almanacs.

All the above mentioned publishing establishments were located in Winnipeg which had become an important centre of the Ukrainian printed word in Canada. About this same time the "Ukrainian Publishing Company" in Edmonton began to operate, but on a smaller scale.

A separate, ideologically allied, group was represented by the socialist publishing houses. Winnipeg was the first centre for the organized publishing firms of "The Red Flag" and the "Working People", that also included bookstores under the same two names. In Toronto, along with the editing of the "Workers' Voice" there came into existence a very active "Workers' Bookstore and Publishing Company", while in Montreal, I. Hnyda organized his publishing company, the "New World Library". All these socialist publishers put out a hundred or so editions which amounted to what may be termed as being well prepared ideological-political school lectures. They also included educational and historical publications. "The Working People" publishers edited in 1918 a calendar-almanac that was formulated by the Ukrainian Socialist-Democratic Party which was a veritable exposition of the history of the workers' movement in Canada.

A great role in the spreading of Ukrainian reading material was played by the book stores that became the communication medium between the publishers and the readers. These bookstores came into existence with the expansion of newspaper and book publication. The oldest of them was the "Ruthenian Book Store" in Winnipeg. After it, others came, such as: "Ukrainian Book Store", "Ukrainian Workers' Book Store", "The Accord Book Company" under the direction of M. Pasichniak and the Catholic book store "Providence". In Saskatoon there were the "Ukrainian Book Store" and the "Ukrainian Trading and Bookstore", organized by F. Sochynsky. In Edmonton there was the well established "Ukrainian Book Store" under the management of the M. & D. Ferbey brothers, while in Fort William O. Ornarovsky opened his bookstore in that city. Toronto had its "Ukrainian Workers' Prosvita Book Store". Montreal had two— the "Ukrainian Book Store" and the "General Book Store" while in Hamilton, during the war, there was the "Ukrainian Book Store". Toward the end of the pioneer era there were several Ukrainian book stores in operation in Canada.

THREE BASIC CHARACTERISTICS OF THE UKRAINIAN CANADIAN ENTITY IN THE PIONEER ERA AND THE ROLE OF THE PRESS

When we stop to examine the development of the Ukrainian community, its press and literature, in which was mirrored the life of this community, it then will be seen that there were three factors at work.

The first and the basic one was the desire of the society to mold itself by means of its own innate values as a separate cultural-national entity possessing its individual cultural characteristics and along with it its own national aims. This society differed basically from other societies in Canada. This factor was dominantly revealed in the literature and such press organs as "Canadian Farmer", "Red Flag", Working People", "Truth and Freedom", and was especially noted in "Ukrainian Voice", "New Country" and "News". The three last mentioned papers observed the highest principles in the preservation of Ukrainian culture in Canada, its development and expansion. They strove to orient the people about the need of depending on their own strength and underlined the feeling of pride in the effort that the Ukrainian people had put into the development of Canada. That they should consider themselves as being the responsible citizens of this country and in return as payment for their material hard work invested into the economic build-up of Canada, they wished to be sufficiently recompensed in terms of civic rights and privileges, especially in the church, cultural, social and educational areas. Some of these objectives were difficult to be put into effect and so several of the mentioned organizations stressed the need of forming political bodies and by this means attain the desired aims. This tendency revealed itself especially in Saskatchewan and Alberta. Three newspapers, "Ukrainian Voice", "New Country" and "News" very strongly supported this creative line and judged on the basis of this action, and the enunciation of these principles on the pages of the three papers, it truly could be stated that these tree press organs were, for all purposes, the backbone in the national structure of the Ukrainians in Canada. In this recpect the Canadian Ruthenian (known later as Canadian Ukrainian) also supported the policy of the other three papers, although its dominant concern was with the religious question, which at times overshadowed the problems of national entity in the ethnic sense.

The religious question in those days was most acute, especially when we consider the fact that a strong attack was in progress against the Ukrainian Catholic Church by the Methodists, Presbyterians, the so-called Independent Greek Church and the Russian Orthodox Mission.

"Canadian Ruthenian" took the middle line between the purely national and the religious papers. "Ranok" (Morning), "Canadian" and the Russophile press stressed the religious question but back of them was a huge arsenal of arguments to show why this or that culture was superior to the culture of the Ukrainian people—for whom these very same press organs were planned. This press received its information and support primarily from non-Ukrainian sources and basically was financed by various religious and political associations and congregations.

The most extreme in this respect was the Russophile press which fundamentally opposed Canadian aims and very often worked for the imperialistic interests that were outside of Canada and thereby was harmful, from every point of view, to the people for whom it was printed and to the country in which it was doing its work. It tried to orientate its readers not toward the strength of its people and the values of the country of adoption, but rather led their gaze away from these, in the opposite direction— in summary, this press was a decentralizing alien force in every respect.

A different matter was presented by such press organs as "Morning" and "Canadian". When, from the religious point of view, they brought in some new elements that very often did not harmonize with national traditions of Ukrainian people, then even more detrimental conditions were created in the cultural relationship which often developed conflicting situations. By force of continuous pressure they tried to graft the first seedlings of the so-called "assimilation" and known in their own lexicon as "Canadianization". The greater and longer became this pressure, the more traces of its work it left behind. Canadianization, according to them, consisted of erasing any traces of national identity, the changing or shortening of names, replacing traditions with new customs and other adaptations. In the political matters this press was strongly oriented in favor of the state active element of the country and therein lay its positive inclination toward that state.

A different factor was at work in the formation and edition of such press as "Canadian Farmer", "Word", "Canadian News", "Progress", "Canada" and the earlier "Red Flag" and "Working People". These were mostly influenced by party-politics motives and at rare times even by business matters. Every existing party in Canada wanted to have in their political echelons appropriate loud voices by means of which they could communicate their ideas and appeals. When the Liberals saw that the initiators of "Canadian Farmer" needed financial aid they were glad to oblige. The same treatment was given by the Conservatives to "Word" and "Canada", and the socialists, although they themselves were in financial straits, tried to at least give some moral support to such press as "Red Flag", "Working People", "New Community" and the "Workers' Word". The last group, the so-called socialist press, began to sharpen its teeth for joining in with the general socialist world movement, which partly resulted in its losing its orientation and influence on the integrating elements in Canada. One thing must be stressed, namely, that this press never broke the cultural ties with its people—for whose benefit it was published. On the contrary, it even helped in smaller or larger measures to strengthen and deepen these cultural connections.

The intensity of this question was often based on the individual approach of each editor or the direct influence of the publishers. The socialist press almost exclusively built with their own financial means, stood very close to the so-called purely national press like "Ukrainian Voice", "Native Country" and "News" in all matters relating to the national question. Towards the end of the pioneer era this question of national orientation underwent a drastic change when the "Working People" took on the mantle of the extreme international communism.

The large number and multiform nature of the press organs proves that Ukrainian settlers in Canada knew their own worth, on the one hand, and on the other, they expressed in this press the specific burden of the community although there were incidents when one could discern lack of appreciation of their own cultural heritage on the part of the settlers.

The large volume of Ukrainian periodicals even disturbed the next-door neighbor "Svoboda" of Jersey City, U.S.A. which in 1911 wrote this comment: "There was a time when Canadian Ruthenians (Ukrainians) complained that there was no one to plow the native field (alluding to the lack of printed word) but now it is hard to avoid running into one of these workers on the native land. Each one plows as he deems fit on this overgrown with weeds national field... This is quite a phenomenon: that among the Canadian Ruthenians there is such a prolific output of newspapers which may be interpreted by the circumstances that the Canadian Ruthenians were destined to be that happy flock over whom not only were the political parties fighting, but even more so, the multidenominational churches as well" [1]. This same paper casually mentioned that the Ruthenian-Latins were reading "Gazeta Katolicka" (Catholic Gazette) that was printed in the Polish language.

Svoboda's observations were only partly correct. The Ukrainian settlers in Canada from the very beginning felt themselves to be regular citizens of Canada. Possession of the 160 acre homestead and the hope that in three year's time the farm will be his own property converted him from the start into a full-fledged farmer and citizen of the country and upon these psychological foundations there grew a whole series of cares and anxieties about his cultural and political side of life. From this rose the critical thought of self-examination which led him to seek the way of solving the daily problems of life under one common denominator. This thinking, in time, brought the first newspaper into existence and others followed. The surroundings produced additional problems that evolved out of mutual growth of the community with some of these problems being dealt with on the experimental basis.

In this process of growth some opposition movement would arise to interfere with the over-all progress. The action brought reaction. In this struggle new forces were mobilized leading in time to a well integrated community based on the quality of the sub-conscious and fully conscious gravitation to its national ethnic root and national identity.

Despite the decentralizing forces, the integration grew stronger with each year even though Ukrainians came from different cultural and political occupied territories and belonged to several religious denominations. They found mutual ground on which to meet in the sphere of their historical past and national culture, church life, self-education and schooling. This common denominator to a greater or lesser degree we find in almost every contemporary press organ of the Ukrainian settlers of those times—even in the least sensitive about such matters, the Methodist "Canadian".

Responsibility for the well-being of Canada, its development and future, comprised the second component part which, subconsciously or consciously broke through with a greater or lesser effort, depending on the basic aim of every press organ. The least of this responsibility is seen in the Russophile press which should be examined rather as an ephemeral conjunctional appearance that had nothing in common with the organic growth in society. This feature we strongly underlined in one of our previous chapters "Participation in municipal and political life". Responsibility for the well being of Canada will be seen in greater detail in the subsequent chapter "Ukrainian participation in military formations of the First World War".

---

[1] "Svoboda", No. 50, 1911.

In addition to those two factors there was a third element that entered into the general human sphere namely, the inborn desire for freedom, to feel like a human being, to be oneself. This was revealed in the beginning, started with the pioneer development of community life. In evidence of these factors speak the names of the places, schools, post offices and other institutions in the settlements. The first group settlement established by the Ukrainians in Canada was called "Ruska Svoboda" (Ruthenian-Ukrainian Freedom), uniting the general human element with the national. The first cross erected to commemorate the first Liturgy in Canada was called the "Cross of Freedom" and almost in every colony where these crosses were erected, they invariably were called "Crosses of Freedom". All the settlers worshipped the names of "Svoboda" (Freedom") "Pravda" (Truth) and "Volia" (Liberty). Even today we find post offices with the names "Pravda" (Truth) and "Zhoda" (Harmony) and at one time there were chytalnias—cultural centres—and other establishments bearing the name of "Volia" "Yednist" (Unity) or "'Pracia" (Work). Until recent times there were schools named "Seech" and "Zaporozhe", that were historical Ukrainian symbols that stood for freedom and independent spirit of the individual and the nation.

Among the numerous Ukrainian names of places, and there are over 130 of them still in existence, a large percentage is composed of those names that identify them with the historical-geographical heritage of the people. The first Ukrainian settlement in Manitoba got the name of "Rus" (ancient name for Ukraine) and the "Halychyna" school, one of the oldest in Manitoba was named after that part of Ukraine whence the greatest number of the settlers came. The "Bukovyna" school brought to mind another part of Ukraine. Other names of school such as "Terebovla" (Trembovla), "Kosiw", "Kolomyya", "Stryj", "Dnipro", "Dnister", "Prut", "Yaroslav", "Volodymyr", "Shevchenko", "Doroshenko", "Taras", "Kulish", "Olha", "Petlura", "Khmelnytsky", represented the names of famous persons from the past history as well as the names of rivers and cities in Ukraine.

When we consider the general Canadian integration, then we meet such names as Sifton, Roblin, Beckett, Laurier, King Edward, and others. This integration in the general Canadian sense also may be noticed in the cultural sphere of individual settlements and organizations. In many of these the immigrants organized courses of Ukrainian and English language not only for the younger, but also for the older ones in order to fit oneself into the new environment. The feeling of responsible citizenship led some Ukrainians to consider even prior to the first World War the organizing of a Ukrainian Canadian battalion. This expression of patriotism was not actually realized but the very idea of forming such a battalion speaks for itself. This same idea was clearly revealed when the war broke out and thousands of volunteers joined the military ranks to fight for Canada.

If we speak of integration of Ukrainians in the realm of general Canadian community affairs, then we may deal with it along the business and political line. However, the ethnic integration developed strongly in the psychological sphere, especially in the religious, cultural-educational and social-welfare field. In this last mentioned activity we have many classical examples where the pioneers publicly encouraged their neighbors to help each other in times of disasters as shown by the following appeal made by I. Drohomyretsky when he wrote: "Let us show our sympathy not only by words but also by deeds and then it will look better before all that we did not let our countrymen to perish" [2]). We find hundreds of these appeals in the press. Along with this, when life became more stabilized, there came into existence many social mutual benefit organizations. The oldest among them was the Ruthenian (Ukrainian) National Association in U.S.A. and in Canada with "Ukrainian Mutual Benefit Association of St. Nicholas", the "Brotherhood of St. John the Merciful" and similar benefit associations in Edmonton, Brantford and other places. When the economic depression came the Ukrainian pioneers mutually helped themselves and each other with food and life's necessities.

It is worth mentioning here about the work carried on by the "Canadian Ruthenian (Ukrainian) Aid Committee" in Winnipeg under the direction of Rev. M. Olenchuk which, in 1915, had around 200 families under its care, with 150 of these receiving regular aid. In a single month in the spring 800 persons were receiving aid from this committee [3]). Many more of these committees were active throughout Canada.

The feeling of social unity not only was the expression of cultural and national values of the community. It also showed itself strongly, when the need arose, to defend oneself against the attacks of the various chauvinistic elements. In the beginning there were hardly any means or time to deal with this matter where some political party agencies took a negative and unfriendly stand toward the Ukrainian immigration settlements. But toward the end of the pioneer era and especially during the war when some irresponsible citizens brought to the pages of the press the political scarecrow of the Austrophile bogey and tried to fasten it to the Ukrainian settlers who basically were opposed to every form of enslavement of the land of their fathers. The pioneers solidly reacted to these unwarranted attacks and false accusations.

A whole community would be aroused in self-defence especially where the cultural heritage of its members was concerned. This particularly was noticeable in matters pertaining to schools. When in Alberta the provincial agencies in one way or another were trying to limit the teaching of the Ukrainian language in schools, then the local and provincial committees were formed in defence of their rights. The native-school question was the sensitive item in the sphere of the ethnic-national integration and to this all-burning question there was no exception whatsoever. The community and its press were totally against any restrictions to the native-language teaching rights.

Another important area of the pioneer life was the one that was manifested in the field of church and religious traditions. Any attempt to introduce here some changes along the line of Latin and Presbyterian churches were met by a strong reaction from the whole community. Often this reaction arose from the subconscious inclination and only after some time had elapsed would it bring a rational realization leading to an active opposition—but it would surely come and just as surely act. In general the feeling of national belonging, on the part of the Ukrainian pioneers was very deep both in the subconscious realms and on the rational plane. This had its beneficial results revealed in the organizational sphere of the

---

[2] "Svoboda", No. 13, 1899.
[3] "Canadian Ruthenian", May 12, 1915.

community life in all of its various branches including the formation of its own press, books and publishing establishments.

It would be quite to the point to comment about the multi-form genre of the newspapers. Among the series of purely political press organs there were attempts made to produce a strictly farm paper such as the "Rilnyk" (Agriculturist) and a humorous one like "Vuyko" (Uncle) or a purely educational journal like "Ukraine". Basically the bulk of the papers devoted themselves to politics, either national or general, and along with it the strengthening of the religious positions. Later on the religious traditionalism and conservatism met and collided in the newly formed settlements with the democratic and liberal movement and its interpreted credo. This was the time of reappraisal that used up such a great amount of national energy. Very often the religious elements took precedence over the political and general national matters. These in turn led to violent upheavals that harmfully affected the monolithic social structure. But in spite of all this we still can note that the pioneer era, which had distinguished itself in the religious-missionary field, fully succeeded in differentiating church denominations and indicating further paths along which the religious life could proceed — in summary, we must admit that the press was that very medium which paid the maximum attention to this diversification.

By 1912 already there were four religious channels that had a great influence upon the formation of homogenous society. The first, strongest and the most active was centered around the independent group that belonged to the so-called "Little Church" and later the St. Vladimir and Olga Church, in Winnipeg. This church was supported by prominent individuals and several communities of the three western provinces. The second Catholic channel was under the Roman Catholic jurisdiction and was supported by the Basilian and the Redemptorist Fathers. In 1911 it obtained its press organ, the Canadian Ruthenian. The third channel, very strong at the beginning, was centered around the Independent Greek Church, with its organ the "Ranok" (Morning) and which, at least on the material plane, was dependent upon the Presbyterian Church for its funds but in the traditional sphere followed the practice of the Greek Catholic and the Orthodox Church. The fourth channel was formed around the Russian Orthodox Church to which were drawn by the force of circumstance Ukrainian Orthodox who were obliged to be under the jurisdiction of the Russian Orthodox Mission in Canada. The mouthpiece of this fourth church division channel was the Russophile press. Such a four-way church division existed till 1912 or to be more exact, until 1913.

With the arrival of the first Ukrainian Catholic Bishop Nykyta Budka to Canada, the first and second channels started to unite. The third channel, the Independent Greek Church, liquidated itself by uniting with the English Presbyterian Church. In the last channel tied with the Russian Orthodox Church there came, a few years later, a diversification of the Ukrainian elements who, along with others formed in 1918 the Ukrainian Greek-Orthodox Church. In this last process a very active part was played by the press organs namely: "Ukrainian Voice" and "Canadian Farmer".

It would not be amiss to make a brief comment about the role of the press and its publishers and editors. These were the amateurs, but they also were idealists who not only sacrificed their money and labour, but even life itself. It is due to this high idealism that the Ukrainians attribute the prolific number of the then existent press and the long-term survivors among them that have been edited continuously without a break, such as "Ukrainian Voice" and "Canadian Farmer". The quality of printed word and the editing skill was variously presented, starting with an amateur attempt and ending with highly qualified product. Time and practice brought experience and qualifications. It is to the credit and compliment of the pioneer settlers that they were able to produce, out of their own element, qualified editors and publishers—for they had none of these to start with.

During the pioneer era another function was allotted to the press. Its editors and publishers not only were the informers for the people, but they also were their leaders and guides. After a long day's work, during which time the expediting of editorials would absorb their thoughts and energy, they would become in the long evening hours the reporters or the exponents of national questions who would sit at the meetings of various organizations and take part in discussions about the daily problems and general affairs. The editors of those pioneer days were the most competent authorities and their words were highly respected.

When this universal function of the editor-leader fell into the hands of an honest man, it then became a blessing for that paper and the community. But there were times, though not too often, when this condition was reversed. On the whole, it truly can be said that the press of the pioneer era gave sufficient evidence of socially conscious responsibility and in a great measure aided the Ukrainian entity in Canada to cement its national forces and reach its full maturity. Thanks to the Ukrainian press the various regional names of "Bukovinian", "Halychanyn", "Volyniak", "Karpatoros" and the outgrown names of "Ruthenian"', "Rusyn", "Maloros", and other given foreign names, that trailed back to the former country's origin —all these had finally disappeared. The Ukrainian press in Canada had created, out of the dispersed and widely scattered Ukrainian families and communities, one national, cultural monolith.

Still another very important function was performed by the press—the implantation in its readers of the understanding of problems arising in the new country and interpreting them in the spirit of the tradition and laws of the Anglo-Saxon democracy rule. When the democratism "wronged" the Ukrainian settlers, then the Ukrainian press of Canada had the courage to defend the mistreated ones and appeal to the traditional sense of justice of the British Empire. Such moments became frequent during the first War when the government of Canada, under the weight of over-worked feeling toward its enemy, Austria, and not taking time to figure out the difference between the national origin and the citizenship belonging, classified all Ukrainians as "Austrians" and deprived them of Canadian citizenship rights—and treated them as enemy aliens. This was a gross misunderstanding for which, in a large measure, the Moscowphile press was to blame by branding Ukrainians as Austrians and German agents. To explain and clarify the state and national position of the Ukrainian settlers in Canada and to present a general picture of the political struggle of the Ukrainian people in Ukraine, six Ukrainian press editors held councils and public meetings at which a national announcement was formed and signed by the following editors: O. H. Hykawy—"Canadian Farmer", A. Dziola—"Robochy Narod" (Working People), I. M. Glowa—"Ranok" (Morning), P. T. Krat—"Kadylo", all from Winnipeg, M. Belegay—"Canadian" in Edmonton, and I. Stefanicky,—"Robitnyche Slovo" in Toronto. Although the editors of "Ukrainian Voice", "Canadian Ruthenian" and "Progress" did not sign this announcement, they agreed with the principle of it and only objected to the form of the memorial appeal which contained awkward invectives directed against some groups in Canada and individual leaders (like bishop N. Budka).

Although the "Appeal" had some important shortcomings, nevertheless, the reaction toward it of the English press was very positive. The first reply came from the Free Press (Winnipeg) which among other things said: "The more the Ukrainian question is studied by the Canadians the clearer it becomes that these people deserve sympathy and the same kind of respect as all other nationalities have" [4]. Other papers followed in Free Press' footsteps. This greatly helped to dissipate the ill opinion held against Ukrainian settlers during the war and shortly after this publicity the government began to release the internees from the concentration camps. A positive opinion about the Ukrainians began to shape up and this in turn evoked new confidence on the part of the Ukrainians toward the country of their adoption.

Every war brings many surprises and in this one the Ukrainians and their press organs found no exceptions. When the problem of the concentration camps had been solved and almost forgotten the federal government, only six weeks before the end of war, banned all the newspapers published by those ethnic groups in Canada that came from the countries at war with the Allies. This was another hard blow for Ukrainians as the majority of them came from the lands that were under Austrian rule. Delegates from the Ukrainian papers went to Ottawa to again clarify the political situation of the Ukrainians in their former homeland and beyond the seas. The result was that the government authorities altered their decision to the extent that would allow the publishing of the papers on the condition that these be printed bilingually (outside of advertisements) with both texts alongside (English and Ukrainian) and complementing each other. This was a heavy burden that entailed much extra work and made the content less interesting as well. An additional headache for the editors was the difficulty of obtaining sufficient number of qualified printers and translators. All this raised the publishing costs. Every paper published in this form had to have a special permission from Ottawa which was printed on the first page under the paper's name and was headlined as follows: "Published under special licence of the Secretary of State—Mailed under Authority of the Post Master General". This stage lasted for five months, from November of 1918 to May 1919.

With the war's ending all these difficulties disappeared and a new era began, not only for the press but also for the whole community as well. In spite of all the difficulties—material, political and moral—the Ukrainian press in Canada faithfully mirrored the ethnically-national and Canadian state attitude of the Ukrainian people. It resolutely intervened on behalf of the mistreated and oppressed, and regularly revealed its loyalty to the country for which it was doing its work. By this means it greatly helped in the integration of the Ukrainians as a national community with its cultural values and assignments on the one hand, and on the other hand, its inclusion into the general Canadian unity and state responsibility.

---

[4] "Free Press", Winnipeg, June 17, 1916.

CULTURAL TIES WITH MOTHERLAND

A separate chapter in our history should be devoted to cultural ties of the Ukrainian Canadian community with its motherland. A steady contact of the Ukrainian Canadians with their homeland brought them constant vitality and nourishment for their cultural life, traditions and aspirations. It also helped to keep this community in close identification with their cultural traditions of the country of their origin.

True enough, some of these cultural values the settlers had brought with them to start with. This is clearly reflected in their daily living, in farm-economy, world outlook, building of churches, desire to have married priests and the use of their own language facilities. About the cultural identification we have reserved a special chapter in the second era of our history. We only pause here to say that the wealth of Ukrainian tradition and culture enabled the settlers to remain steadfast in the pursuit of their life's aims against which all the efforts of various reformers and modernizers were broken up.

In the cultural bond with their motherland there was also the consciousness of political ties. The press would often draw attention to this fact and with the greatest sympathy refer to the political struggle of its countrymen in their homeland. It was quite obvious and easily understood that those who, under the weight of social and political pressure, were forced to roam beyond the seas would want to help their kinsmen that still were living under hardships and in bondage. On this one account there always had been a full and mutual accord among the Ukrainian immigrants in Canada. Should any centre, group or press organ show its indifference towards the fate of the homeland, it instantly would have been degraded in the eyes of the whole community. It was considered to be a great honor and national duty to help, either individually or collectively, the relatives and kindred souls in the old country. Thousands of letters from Ukrainian settlers in Canada that were sent "to our own kinsmen" (as popularly worded) in the old country carried with them—in addition to the conversational content—some measure of material aid to the relatives and close friends. Thousands of dollars were sent through the banks and even more through ordinary letters and unregistered mail. These transactions lent a certain amount of prestige, not only to those sending the contributions, but also to the country from which they were sent. In this respect the Ukrainian settlers were in no way different from the settlers of other nationalities.

In the history of this patriotic generosity it will be to the interest of the readers to reveal a few incidents that took place. As early as 1897 the "Svoboda" of Mount Carmel in Pennsylvania that catered, at that time, to the Ukrainians in U.S.A. and Canada printed appeals to the settlers to help establish Ukrainian gymnasiums (secondary schools) in Rohatyn and Zbaraz, cities in Halychyna. These were Ukrainian high schools that did not receive any government aid. In the same year the settlers sent aid to the bursas in Nadvirna, Sianok and Horlytzi (cities in Halychyna, Western Ukraine). In the wake of the bloody Baden elections that left behind them widows and orphans, there came an appeal for aid which was promptly supplied. The Radical Party and the Socialist-Democratic Party also appealed for help in their political work, to which the settlers generously contributed. In 1902 Ukrainians in Canada and U.S.A. rushed their aid to the students of Lviv university to enable them to finish their studies there. In 1906 a wide campaign was carried on, for elections reforms, to the Austrian parliament. Funds were needed and these were collected among the settlers. Two funds were organized—the "Front Fund" and the "Peasant Fund". In 1907 a mass collection campaign was carried on to raise funds for the imprisoned students of Lviv University. In the following year funds were collected to aid the widow and orphans left as the result of Marko Kahanetz's murder. In 1909 a special "Myroslav Sichynsky Fund" (already mentioned in another chapter) was formed and in 1910 "Adam Kotzko Fund" was organized. In 1912 "Sokil-Bat'ko" (name of scout organization) appealed for funds and shortly after another appeal was made for a "Jubilee Gift" for the poet Ivan Franko.

There were funds that brought in thousands of dollars. Not only were they of great help to the countrymen in the homeland, but they also had their good influence in developing moral strength and character on the part of the donors. This amounted to a plebiscite in manifestation, showing the feelings of the settlers for their brethren in Ukraine. Later on the press printed the donors' lists and these were the valid documents of national and political maturity of the generous settlers.

In addition to these general national collection funds that were so widely mentioned in the press, there were other local collections made on a smaller scale. Quite often the former denizens of some particular village in the old country would gather together in their farming district or in the city and make a donation to help build a church, a school or a "chytalnia" (community centre) in their former place of habitation. These, and others like them, fund-raising campaigns and aid donations helped to maintain the close relationship between the settlers and the political and cultural heritage of their homeland.

Even greater influence in cementing closer ties with their native land came from the direct visits of cultural and religious representatives from the old country. When Dr. Julian Bachynsky, who previously had visited U.S.A. to gather material for the first history of Ukrainians overseas, landed on Canadian soil in the middle of June, 1906, he was greeted with great ovations and showered with high honours. He visited many cultural-educational centres, schools and even churches. Everywhere he went he was treated as the father of their country, their guardian and the counselor of the problems arising in the life of the settlers. Poems were written in his honour. After his two-month stay in Canada Dr. J. Bachynsky was able to correctly evaluate the cultural and economic situation of Ukrainian Canadians and was the first to publicly announce that his countrymen primarily should settle on land in Alberta and Saskatchewan in view of the fact that the soil in the province of Manitoba had a low production value. Dr. J. Bachynsky encouraged his countrymen to devote their attention to schools, self-enlightenment and self-organizing efforts. He was able to infuse into the life of the settlers, the spirit of national unity, having covered every province in Canada and at each stopover he preached and underlined the same cohesive principles. As the author of "Ukraine Irredenta" he was able to influence the settlers into choosing for themselves a modern name for their national identity and shortly after Dr. J. Bachynsky's departure a national "Viche" (mass gathering) took place in Winnipeg at which the following resolution was passed:

"We, the Rus-Ukrainians of the city of Winnipeg, partly Austrian and party English subjects, representing all political parties and also as the representatives of all the political classes of Rus-Ukrainian nation, gathered to the number of 500 on March 10, 1907, do unanimously make a request to the Austrian government for a Ruthenian (Ukrainian) University in the city of Lviv, in Halychyna. To implement, as soon as possible, impressive culture and political justice as well as the granting of a full national autonomy" [1]. Such candid expression of political will of the settlers helped to strengthen the attitude of their countrymen in the native land. But Dr. J. Bachynsky spent his two-month visit in Canada not under the aegis of any political party. Primarily, he came to Canada to gather the material for his history of the Ukrainians in Canada. This was the first effort, by anyone, to compile such a history in this country.

While in Canada Dr. J. Bachynsky endeavoured to acquaint the Anglo-Saxon citizens of Canada with the problems of the Ukrainian nation in Europe, especially with its political struggles [2]. Because of his acquaintance with the life of the Ukrainians in U.S.A. and Canada, Dr. J. Bachynsky became the diplomatic representative of the "Ukrainian National Republic", for U.S.A. and Canada, from 1918 to 1922.

About the visit of Irene Sichynsky to Canada and the action on the part of the Ukrainians to aid in the release of her brother Myroslav Sichynsky from Austrian prison we already have made comments earlier. In this action, that was under the care of the "Council of Seven", were included secular and church notables. From the narrow circle of a few like-minded individuals the action soon developed into a nation-wide movement that electrified the whole Ukrainian community in Canada. Pleas and telegrams were sent to the Canadian government requesting its intervention, to the Austria government, on behalf of M. Sichynsky and also that Canada should draw the attention of the Austrian authorities to the injustices that were meted out to the Ukrainians on their own soil under the Austrian occupational rule.

Much light was shed upon the religious problems of the Ukrainians in Canada by Metropolitan Andrey Shepticky when he paid a visit to this country in the fall of 1910. This noted authority of the Ukrainian Greek-Catholic Church in the old country basically helped to solve the problem of the independence of the Ukrainian Catholic Church in Canada. Metropolitan A. Shepticky's letter of appeal under the title: "The Address on the Ruthenian Question to Their Lordships the Archbishops and Bishops of Canada", had in it a high significance toward the history of Ukrainian Canadians, especially in its relationship to the church-religion question. Of a similar value was his popular pastoral letter, written in the same year, entitled "To the Canadian Ruthenians".

The Metropolitan visited all the larger Ukrainian centres in Canada such as Montreal, Winnipeg, Yorkton, Sifton, Calgary, Mundare, Edmonton, Vancouver and other places. This highly respected church dignitary not only strengthened the sentimental attachment of the settlers to their former homeland, but also helped to solve the local church problems that had remained unsettled for years. With his distinguished personality he raised the prestige of the Ukrainians in the eyes of their fellow-Canadians and

---

[1] "Canadian Farmer", No. 9, 1907.
[2] Interview in the Vancouver paper "The World", Aug. 10, 1906.

left unforgettable impression in the hearts and minds of his faithful followers. The numerous receptions that were made in his honour by lieutenant-governors, ministers, archbishops and bishops served as evidence of the great respect that was shown to the Prince of the Church. The name of Metropolitan A. Shepticky is closely bound with the history of the Ukrainian Catholic Church in Canada in the same way as the name of Dr. O. Oleskiw is tied with the Ukrainian immigration to Canada.

Ukrainian Canadians were honored with the visit of Dr. Semen Demydchuk who was a representative of the "Ridna Shkola" (Native School) in Ukraine. He arrived in Canada in the middle of 1912 and visited all the more important settlers' centres with a series of lectures on the meaning of school education for the nation and about the effort of the Ukrainians in the old country to enable them to free themselves from the political and economic slavery by means of private schools. Dr. Demydchuk also informed Ukrainian Canadians about the political struggle in Ukraine, particularly the Western Ukraine. The problem of schools was the most burning question for all—irrespective of church denomination or political belief. Ukrainians in Canada wholly supported the ideas of their guest from overseas and in their whole-hearted response helped to strengthen the sentiment for what was fondly referred to as "the old country". The donation fund for the benefit of schools in the old country that was initiated in Canada by Dr. S. Demydchuk surpassed all other funds that were ever collected in Canada or U.S.A. In the city of Edmonton alone over $5000.00 was collected. Some larger individual donors came to the front, such as Hryhory Kraykivsky and Pavlo Rudyk. Scholarships were established for teacher's candidates and for students of business schools, giving proof of the understanding of the national needs and showing sympathy towards the cultural matrix. Although Dr. S. Demydchuk departed for Lviv in January 1913, the school fund continued to operate in the form of Christmas Carols fund in 1913 and 1914.

The school fund campaign was conducted by the "Central Committee of Native Schools" in Winnipeg with the aid of various local committees. The Winnipeg committee sent an "Appeal" on October 8, 1912, to the Ukrainian people in Canada, signed by such leading Ukrainian figures as: T. D. Ferley, O. Hykawy, O. Zerebko, M. Hladky, T. Stefanyk, M. Glowa, I. Nawiziwsky, E. Kozlowsky, Y. Chorney, Y. Sytnyk, M. Stechishin, B. Kudryk, J. W. Arsenych, and J. A. Dyma. All of them represented various organizations and centres. Among the visitors to Canada in the pioneer era could also be included Roman Sirecky (1911) who was a representative of the C.P.R. Steamship Co. in Chernivtsi, Bukovyna, and who later held a post of the Director of the Ukrainian Theatre in Lviv. He was the only Bukovinian notable to visit Canada. Another visitor to this country was Petro Karmansky who decided to stay here for a longer period of time. Although the last two mentioned visitors came to Canada as private guests, still the engagement of Prof. Petro Karmansky as lecturer at the "Courses of Higher Education", in Winnipeg, was in the nature of an authorized courtesy visit from the Ukrainian National School Board in Lviv, which had delegated him to give a series of lectures as an expression of gratitude to the Ukrainian Canadians for their aid toward the native schools in the old country. Such visits and friendly gestures helped to strengthen cultural ties of unity between the Ukrainian nation and its immigrants in Canada.

UKRAINIAN PARTICIPATION IN MILITARY FORMATIONS OF THE FIRST WORLD WAR

A few years before World War I some Ukrainians in Alberta conceived the idea of organizing a "Ukrainian infantry regiment" as a unit of Canada's military forces. Michael Gowda was the initiator of this action. A man of broad outlook, he contributed articles to Ukrainian newspapers. In April 1909, he published a press appeal, addressed "To the Ruthenians of Alberta and Canada as a whole" in which he said, in part: "We are recruiting our own regiment of the Canadian army, therefore we invoke you, the youth of our nationality in this new strange land, with these words: To whom the honour of his people lies at heart; to whom it is pleasant to recall the glorious ancestors, the Zaporozhian Cossacks of the times gone by; to whom it matters much that other people here hold us in greater esteem and all those who wish to create a mark of distinction as good citizens of this new country and a good name for their children—join our regiment!" At the same time, M. Gowda published a sample of the petition to the "War Department in Ottawa" which was to be signed by those willing to enlist in the proposed new regiment. The signers of the petition requested the approval of the military authorities for the projected organization of an Ukrainian infantry regiment, "inasmuch as it were convenient to military districts command in the various areas in which the undersigned reside". The petition also defined the purpose explaining the motivation in organizing such a regiment. The organizers of the regiment clearly emphasized that "as a people" the undersigned wish to actively participate in the defence of the sovereignty of this empire, mainly because as foreigners and former subjects of the contries overseas, we have been given the privilege of becoming loyal citizens of this country and at the same time of the British Empire, of which Canada is a part" [1].

As we see, organizers of the regiment wanted, above all, to demonstrate their loyalty to Canada and willingness to defend it. Apparently their action was gaining ground, because on May 1, 1910, the first mass meeting regarding the formation of the "Ruthenian infantry regiment" was held in Edmonton. The speakers included two military men, Capt. W. Kriesbach of the cavalry regiment and Pte. I. Litovsky, a Ukrainian member of the 101st Infantry Regiment in Edmonton. Also well-known citizens of Edmonton, such as Paul Rudyk, H. Kraykivsky and M. Gowda himself, took active part in this meeting. The action to organize the proposed regiment was also supported by Peter Svarich, a respected man of authority in Alberta. In a prominent article to the press on this subject, he said, among other things, that "All speak of peace, but at the same time they are preparing for war" [2].

Nevertheless, the campaign to organize such a Ukrainian regiment encountered certain opposition from the side of Ukrainian Social Democrats who proclaimed loyalty to Canada but at the same time expressed doubts as to "whether armed forces bring nations glory" [3].

---

[1] "Canadian Farmer", No. 16, Oct. 30, 1909.
[2] "Canadian Farmer", No. 19, May 21, 1909.
[3] Quoted from the text of a protest resolution, passed by the "M. Sichynsky Society" in Gosmere.

This attitude towards the proposed regiment resulted in a polemical discussion between the Socialists and supporters of the regiment, which filled the columns of the press for some time. Unfortunately, we have no data as to the number of volunteers who applied for enlistment. We know, however, that apart from the military circles, this action was also supported by The Edmonton Journal. This initiative action has strongly underlined the loyalty of Ukrainian settlers to the government and country, Canada.

When war broke out between Austria and Serbia in 1914, the question arose among certain Ukrainians as to where they, former subjects of Austria stood in this situation. These doubts grew and deepened when the Austro-Hungarian consulates in Canada proceeded with the mobilization of Austrian subjects for military duty and emphasis was placed on the consequences of desertion. A great many of the Ukrainian Canadians had left behind kinfolk, wives and children, in the Old Country, whom they intended to bring to Canada eventually. The pressure of Austro-Hungarian consulate and the existing family ties of Ukrainian settlers with the old country prompted Bishop Nykyta Budka to issue a "Pastoral letter" in which he underlines that the citizens of Austria but not those of Canada, as he was later accused of doing, would carry out their citizenship duty towards their country which had become involved in war. At the same time the Bishop stressed the duty of his faithful towards their families in the old country and the Ukrainian people who had found themselves in an unenviable war situation [4]. Soon after the publication of this "Pastoral letter" on August 5, 1914, England declared war on Germany which had gone to the Austrian side. Thus Britain and Canada found themselves in an open war with Austria. Therefore, all Austrian subjects in Canada, who initially declared their willingness to answer the call to duty, now had to decide where their first loyalty lay. Consequently Bishop Budka promptly issued the second Pastoral letter in which he urged his faithful to prove their complete loyalty to Canada and Britain [5].

In addition to these declarations on the part of the Ukrainian Catholic hierarchy, the Ukrainians held mass meetings throughout Canada at which they pledged their loyalty to Canada and Britain. One such meeting was held in Winnipeg, at the Industrial Bureau auditorium, with nearly 3,000 Ukrainians in attendance. Following the speeches made by representatives of the community (I. Pertushevych, T. D. Ferley, T. Stefanyk and Father A. Redkevych, general vicar of Bishop Budka), those present adopted the following unanimous resolution: "Whereas the welfare of the British Empire being imperiled, we Ukrainians, the citizens of Canada, assembled at this meeting, hereby pledge our loyalty to the British flag and declare our readiness to stand up in its defense whenever occasion arises" [6].

Such declarations of loyalty and Bishop Budka's second Pastoral Letter fully clarified the situation of the Ukrainians in Canada. Deeds followed the declarations. There is no accurate statistical data to show the number of Ukrainians who served in Canada's armed forces in the First World War. The number is roughly estimated as being between 10,000 to 15,000 [7].

The great majority of enlisted Ukrainians came from urban localities,

---
[4] "Canadian Ruthenian, No. 31, Aug. 1, 1914.
[5] "Canadian Ruthenian", No. 32, Aug. 8, 1914.
[6] "Ukrainian Voice", August 9, 1914.
[7] Wm. Burianyk: "Ukrainian Canadians in the First World War", in the "Jubilee Almanac" of the Ukrainian Voice, 1960, pp. 114-117.

however, when it comes to territorial origin, most of them came from the Ukrainian territory which remained under the Russian domination. The Ukrainians who came from Austria were distinguished by those who possessed Canadian citizenship and those who did not. The former had the right to do military service, the latter had to register as enemy aliens. The consequences of such registration regulations were somewhat ill-fated. Many did not wish to be registered as enemy aliens because to a large degree this offended their sense of loyalty to Canada and simply contradicted their integrity. But wartime regulations were rigid and those who failed to register were sent to concentration camps. Large internment camps were located in Kapuskasing, Brandon, Lethbridge, Vernon. Those who registered as Austrian subjects remained under police surveillance and were obliged to report periodically at the nearest police station. Usually there was no work for these people and if some of them held a job, they were dismissed, as suspicion of hostility to Canada weighed heavily upon all of them. These were the tragic days for the Ukrainians who had the misfortune of having been under Austrian domination and at the outbreak of hostilities had still not been granted Canadian citizenship. Not only men but wives and children also suffered. To illustrate these complicated and wrongful conditions we are quoting a few passages from a protest of Ukrainian women in Calgary. In their appeal to Anglo-Saxon women of Calgary, they said: "We came to this country in order to make Canada our future home. We are no spies. Thousands of our men are now fighting at the front under the British and Russian colours. We are dismissed from jobs because we happen to be foreigners. But we are loyal to Canada. What can we do if jobs are denied to us? Are we to perish from starvation, or fall upon the road to evil?..." [8].

This was a voice of despair from innocent people who found themselves in a very critical situation as a consequence of war. Notwithstanding this, a large number of Ukrainians enlisted with Canada's armed forces. It also happened that Imperial Russia, an ally of Britain, published an order three times in succession requiring all its subjects of military age living in Canada and other countries abroad, to register at the Russian consulates. Since none of the called up men, by and large of Ukrainian origin, could be sent to Europe, the volunteers enlisted with the various Canadian military units. There were even some Ukrainian Americans who crossed the border to join the army as the United States favoured such action. Of course, the enlisted Ukrainians served in different branches of the Canadian army having been distributed among the various service units. There were no special Ukrainian formations, although there were several battalions in which Ukrainians were numerically predominant, as for example, the 218th Battalion of Northern Alberta, of which A. Shandro was a lieutenant. When these battalions were shipped to Britain, the men of the 218th Battalion were assigned to various technical branches of the army.

We learned from accounts of World War I veterans that the combat prowess of Ukrainian servicemen has been more than satisfactory. They were fighting for their new homeland with real courage and self-sacrifice. Philip Konoval was a symbol of this dedication. He was the first Ukrainian in history to be awarded the Victoria Cross, the highest distinction of the Bri-

---

[8] "The Golden Jubilee of the Ukrainian Catholic Parish in Calgary, 1912-1962", Dr. M. Hladyshevsky, P. 48-49.

tish Empire. Only 66 such awards have been bestowed upon the heroes of that war.

The women of the auxiliary units of Canada's armed forces also played a distinguished role in World War I. Eva Bohun of Edmonton was the first Ukrainian Canadian girl to enlist with the Women's Army Auxiliary force.

Briefly, the Ukrainian Canadians did their part in all areas of Canada's war effort. The contemporary press carried frequent appeals for contributions to the Red Cross and the "Canadian Patriotic Fund". The Ukrainian bilingual teachers, who as ever set a good example for their people to follow in all public matters, led the way in this national drive for funds. At their convention, held in Winnipeg, in July 1915, the teachers stated the matter quite clearly: "When Britain is at war, so is Canada. We live in this country and call it our new homeland, therefore it is our duty to defend it as we would our own home" [9]. The Ukrainian press published articles and appeals in support of Canada's war effort in the same spirit. In addition to this, these bilingual teachers voluntarily assessed themselves for regular monthly contributions to the Patriotic Fund. The Ukrainian farmers, too, were doing their best in support of the war effort. Exerting their energies, they produced and provided the necessary foodstuffs not only for home consumption but also for Canadian boys at the battlefront and their allies as well. Whenever the question of Canada's war effort was touched upon in the contemporary Ukrainian press, the editors, and for that matter the leaders of the Ukrainian community, stressed the fact that the agricultural sector was the second front line of battle for all those who were not fighting on the first line in the battlefields. They urged that farmers must work harder and more efficiently than ever in support of the fighting front and that Ukrainians must prove themselves to the limits of their ability.

In spite of such a patriotic stand on the part of the leadership of the Canadian community and the rest of the settlers towards the war efforts, some sinister atmosphere produced in the suspicious surroundings of war psychosis seemed to be hovering over the Ukrainian society and preventing the Ukrainian soldiers from being sure of themselves—even when they were in the front lines fighting for the freedom of Canada, forcing them to change their family names. It was not unusual at that time to read in the press something in the nature of the following example: "Yakiw (Jacob) Marchuk, a Ukrainian born in Halychyna (Galicia) changed his name to John Marshall and joined the 90th Regiment of the Canadian army. During one of the hottest battles at Ypres on the 30th of April, he died a hero's death in the defense of this new fatherland. The deceased left his parents in East Selkirk, Manitoba." The first such notice was printed in the "Canadian Ruthenian" in 1915, under the title: "The death of a Ukrainian on the battlefield, for Canada" [10]. Many other similar notices were to be found on the pages of the newspapers in the latter stages of the war. Still, in spite of these circumstances, the optimistic spirit prevailed. The idea of a just Canada lighted the course for them and for this kind of Canada they were willing to sacrifice their blood even under an adopted foreign name.

---

[9] Quoted from "An Appeal of the teachers, united in the Ukrainian Teachers' Association", published in all Ukrainian newspapers at that time.
[10] "Canadian Ruthenian", No. 20, 1915.

AID TO THE CAUSE OF UKRAINE'S LIBERATION

When ominous war clouds darken the world horizons the hopes of the enslaved peoples for their national liberation often glow brighter and with deeper significance. Thus it was in the case of the many enslaved people of the Imperial Austria and Czarist Russia—the Poles, Chechs, Byelorussians, Slovaks, Serbs, Croats, Slovenes, Georgians, Letts, Esthonians, Lituanians, and others. The very same hopes were nurtured by the Ukrainian people who had long been under the two imperial powers, Russia and Austria. It so happened that these two powers were waging war against each other and the chances for a complete liberation did not appear favourable. Nevertheless, the policy of the Ukrainian leaders in Ukraine under both occupations was first of all to win reforms for their people at all political and social levels. When the peoples of Russia suddenly erupted in an all-engulfing revolution and while the Austrian empire was on the verge of collapse, the Ukrainians took the advantage of the situation and proclaimed independence for their nation in the form of Ukrainian National Republic.

The succession of war and political events in Ukraine could not be watched without concern by the Ukrainian Canadians who not so long ago had themselves gone through the mill of political and social iniquities under the Russian and Austrian domination. Now, as free citizens of the British Empire, more precisely of Canada, and enjoying the benefits and democratic liberties of their new homeland, they naturally wanted to see their fellow-countrymen overseas achieve a similar state of existence. At least they sought reasonable alleviation of the oppression endured by the people, among whom were their parents, sisters, brothers, and other kin. Not only blood relationship but also national and cultural obligation called most of them to help their compatriots achieve better life in this cataclysm of war and revolution which however did raise hopes for a liberation of Ukraine.

In the previous chapter we examined the cultural relations established by the Ukrainian Canadians with their fellow-countrymen in Ukraine, especially those under Austrian occupation. As a matter of fact, the spiritual ties had been maintained with the cultural and often with the political life of the Ukrainians under the Austrian and Russian occupations. The Ukrainian scholars and political leaders contributed articles to the Ukrainian Canadian press. A lively exchange of correspondence was carried on, so the Ukrainians in Canada knew exactly what was going on in Europe and in Ukraine. They were wide awake to the events developing in their homeland and to the heart-beats of their people. This is also evident from their organizational gestures just before the outbreak of the war.

At the close of July 1914 the Ukrainian press carried an announcement that a big mass meeting would be held in Winnipeg on August 2nd to establish "the Sitch Organization". The organizers of this meeting made it known that the proposed organization "is designed to awaken the people's consciousness and take up the struggle for a free and independent Ukraine" [1]). The organization emerged from the milieu of "The Ukrainian Voice" and Catholic circles.

A similar action was projected by another group which was being established in Edmonton at about the same time. The organizing work in this direction was conducted by Paul Krat who inspired the idea of aid to the homeland among Ukrainian Socialists and circles clustered around the Presbyterian Church.

The association organized in Edmonton gained greater momentum and more publicity. Its character was wholly political, as implied by its name, "Independent Ukraine". Similar societies were organized in Toronto and Montreal.

Somewhat later the "Committee for Aid to Ukraine Immigrants" was organized in Toronto. In other words, the whole Ukrainian community in Canada demonstrated its readiness of extend their helping hand to the homeland at a crucial moment in history.

All these endeavours, designed to bring aid of the Ukrainian people at home, proceeded under such meaningful names from the history of Ukraine as mentioned above, "Sitch Organization", "Independent Ukraine", and so on. One often comes across the names of 'Sitch' and 'Zaporozhe' in dealing with the history of Ukrainian Canadian organizations.

The "Independent Ukraine Association "Sitch" was organized at a general public meeting in Edmonton, July 30, 1914. The principal objective of this group was to aid the "liberation movement in Ukraine" with this in mind, to conduct educational and economic work among the Ukrainian Canadians. It was a non-partisan and non-confessional organization permitting its members to belong to any political party or religious denomination. A member was required only "to be of republican views in regard to a prospective state system within Ukraine", to recognize the separation of Church from State, the religious tolerance and the right of all peoples to an independent existence". Elected at this meeting, was a "Hetmanite Council" to direct the affairs of the association and its branches in other localities.

At the very beginning, branches of this association were established in Vegreville, Cardiff and Calgary. A branch of the association was organized in Winnipeg on September 3rd of that same year. It was headed by O. Boyanivsky, M. Syroidiv and H. Skehar. Chief organizer of the Independent Ukraine Association was P. Krat.

The Manifesto addressed to the "Ukrainian people in Canada" and published by the Hetmanite Council after the outbreak of World War I called upon the Ukrainian Canadians to struggle against the "brutal Russian Czarism and the Austrian grasping of the heritage of our Ukrainian ancestors". The Association set before itself as its ultimate aim the "emergence of an independent Ukrainian republic". It became incumbent upon the Association by reason of Canadian circumstance, which the Manifesto explains thus: "Here in a free country we became free, we fraternize with freedom, and now this freedom takes us by the hand and tells us: Let us go and drive the enslavement out of the land of our ancestors" [2]).

The organizers of the Association for an Independent Ukraine placed

---

[1]) "Ukrainian Voice", No. 30, 1914.
[2]) The Manifesto was published in the "Ranok" and "The Canadian Farmer". A copy of same is preserved in the archives of the author.

great hopes upon their work, but quite often life runs contrary to expectations. This was true in the case of the "Sitch" Organization and the "Independent Ukraine Association". Several reasons contributed to the fact that these organizations had to suspend their activity. The most important of these was the position of Britain, and automatically of Canada, in the war. Any activity directed against any one of their allies was in conflict with the Canadian interests. Coupled with this was the phantasm of Austrianism produced and spread abroad by the Russophile propagandists which weighed heavily on the activity of these organizations. It was an exceedingly complicated question to understand at any public level, and more so for the contemporary government of Canada. In order not to delve into details of the problem, the Canadian government simply applied the principle of homogeneity to Austrian citizenship, without bothering to examine the racial origin concealed under the surface of this citizenship.

Stirred up through the influence of the Russophile press, the spectre of Austrianism raised its ugly head at the very outset of the war, haunting the Ukrainian community until the war ended. In 1916 the Winnipeg Telegram came out with a front page editorial in which the government was urged to disenfranchise all naturalized citizens who emigrated to Canada from Germany, Austria, Bulgaria and Turkey. The editorial laid particular stress on the Austrians. In 1917 the war veterans in Winnipeg adopted a resolution, couched in similar terms, for publication in the daily press with a specific demand addressed to the federal government in Ottawa. About the same time The Winnipeg Tribune published a news report about the alleged existence of a "secret organization" among the local "Austrians", although this was later admitted as having been the exclusive hoax of the Russophile newspaper. Nevertheless, several months later, there followed mass arrests of Ukrainians.

To express more explicitly what was going on in Ukrainian communities in Canada at that time it will be worthwhile to cite the following notation which is preserved in St. Michael's Parish records at Montreal. Under the year 1916 the parish priest Dr. A. Redkevych wrote:

"False information by the enemy (Moscophiles—M.H.M.) resulted in 60 families, along with women and children, being taken from Montreal and placed in detention at Spirit Lake. In addition to these some 1500 men also were taken from Montreal and incarcerated in Spirit Lake, Quebec, Kapuskasing, Ontario, and Petawawa, Ontario. The general condition of the Ukrainian colony in Montreal is onerous" [3]. This was a very high price for the aid to the cause of the "Ukraine's liberation" which was paid by the Ukrainian Canadians across the country. It required time and much suffering to rectify the condition of the innocent people and even then the ideal situation was short-lived.

Disregarding the unjustified pressures and undeserved teasing and hissing, detention or concentration camps, the Ukrainians of Canada did not fall short of their loyalty to Canada and the Dominion government. When the final $150 million Victory Loan bond issue was announced in November 1917, the entire Ukrainian press called for all-out support. This was not a hollow-sounding gesture, as shortly after, there followed long lists of Ukrainian subscribers to this loan.

---

[3] "St. Michael's Ukrainian Catholic Parish Jubilee Book 1915-1966", Montreal, 1966, p. 12.

RELATIONS WITH FEDERAL GOVERNMENT AND UKRAINIAN CANADIAN CITIZENS COMMITTEE

The Ukrainian public leaders saw, on the one hand, sincere devotion of their people to the new homeland and the wrongful actions of the Canadian government, on the other. The situation made it necessary to clarify the problems directly before the federal authorities in Ottawa. Thus in February 1918, the first Ukrainian delegation left for Ottawa. It consisted of A. Shandro, Peter Svarich and I. Petrushevych. The delegation was received by Prime Minister Borden and the delegates explained to him all the injustices. They also raised the matter of the interned Ukrainians in Canada, their citizenship rights and documents, and the need for changes in the Naturalization Act.

The positive reception of the Ukrainian delegation in Ottawa is evident not only from the comments of the press, but also from further actions of the Ukrainian Canadians. Several months later the second Ukrainian delegation went to Ottawa for consultation with the government. This delegation included T. Stefanyk and J. W. Arsenych. Among other things, the delegates discussed the question of Ukrainian Canadian soldiers at the war fronts, particularly those who had no citizenship rights in Canada, suggesting that they be utilized in auxiliary capacity.

These two delegations succeeded in clarifying the atmosphere surrounding the Ukrainians in Canada and identifying the position of their compatriots. In addition to this, the posibility was created for further organizational activity in aid of Ukraine's liberation. For up to now, under the pressure resulting from the spectre of "Austrianism", the "Sitch Organization" and "Ind. Ukraine" Association were obliged to suspend their activity. Moreover, even the organizations without any political tendencies voluntarily restricted their normal activity in order to avoid suspicion or harassment. These were the times when the use of other than the English language was forbidden at public gatherings. The use of "other languages" was permitted only for purposes of interpretation in case of those who could not express themselves in the official language of the country. Still, in spite of all the restrictions—often disregarded—the mainstream of life continued to flow along its old, determined course, but at a retarded pace.

When the situation began to clear up a little for the Ukrainians in Canada close to the end of 1917, there emerged in Winnipeg a central Ukrainian body which adopted the name of "Ukrainian Canadian Citizens Committee". The Committee was headed by J. W. Arsenych, O. Boyanivsky and P. H. Woycenko. The executive also included I. Sluzar, T. Stefanyk, I. Petrushevych, D. Yakimischak and P. Ruta. This was a representative body of various lay and parish organizations. At the outset the Committee confined itself to community problems of their fellow-countrymen, but after a while the scope of its work was extended to other problems, especially at the time when the political situation in Canada and in Ukraine began to crystallize.

As it were, the Committee developed energetic activity from the very beginning. It possessed experience and tradition in this line of work carried on formerly in Winnipeg where similar committees existed in the past.

Almost the same leading public men were repeatedly elected to the executive. We have already dealt with their work and in passing we recall the fact that the earliest such committee in Winnipeg was the Committee in Aid of Native School which was organized in 1912 when Dr. S. Demydchuk visited Canada. At a later date, the Ukrainian Central Committee for Defense of Native Language was formed which struggled with the Manitoba government for a bilingual (English-Ukrainian) school system.

After a while the work of the Ukrainian Canadian Citizens Committee also embraced the problems connected with efforts to preserve the independence of Ukraine, which was stated in one of the appeals of the Committee. In that same appeal the Committee discussed Ukrainian matters in Canada which, in its estimation, were "in a pitiful state of affairs", because "all sorts of uninvited guardians", the executive continued, "muddle up the public opinion of English-speaking masses about our people". Undoubtedly, the Committee had in mind the Russophile propagandists from "The Russian Voice" and "The Russian People" already mentioned in another chapter, who openly and blatantly incited the Anglo-Saxons against the Ukrainian settlers. To clarify the Ukrainian situation in Canada more fundamentally, the executive announced the intention of publishig a serious book on Ukraine in English, written from the standpoint of Ukrainian Canadians. For this purpose they invited prominent Anglo-Canadian publicists who possessed the necessary grasp of and sympathy for the struggle for liberation of Ukraine, to collaborate on the publication.

Thus the Ukrainian Canadian Citizens Committee developed its work in two basic directions — rendering aid to compatriots in Ukraine and to those in Canada. Despite its local origin and composition, in a short time and on the merit of its work, the Committee achieved prestige in other provinces and by silent agreement became a natural representative of the entire Ukrainian community in Canada. Eventually provincial committees were instituted which recognized the Ukrainian Canadian Citizens Committee as their central committee. The Committee received general approbation for sending two prominent Ukrainian Canadians, Osyp Megas and Ivan Petrushevych as a delegation to the Peace Conference in Paris. Their mission was to assist the official delegation of the Ukrainian National Republic which was engaged in a diplomatic and legitimate struggle with big powers for the status of Ukraine and representatives at the Peace Conference. They were also to act as first hand advisers to Canada's delegation.

In March 1919, the Ukrainian Canadian delegates participated at a session of the delegates of the Ukrainian National Republic in Paris, then headed by H. Sydorenko. After a short time, Osyp Megas left Paris for Ukraine and was received by Symon Petlura, Commander-in-chief of the armies of the Ukrainian National Republic. Megas also made a tour of Western Ukraine and from there dispatched to the Ukrainian press in Canada news reports of historical value, which later became the basis of his book, "Tragedy of Galician Ukraine", published in Canada after the war.

The sending of two delegates to the Paris Peace Conference had the effect of mobilizing thousands of Ukrainians in Canada for active work in their community. Local branches of the Ukrainian Canadian Citizens Committee sprung up in various areas with Ukrainian population. These accepted the jurisdiction of the provincial committees and the latter, of the Central Committee in Winnipeg.

Coupled with the UCCC, the Ukrainian Red Cross Society in Canada commenced its work in 1919. At a convention, held in Winnipeg, November 25-27, 1919, the Ukrainian Relief Committee of the Red Cross Society was established and charged with the task of conducting relief work as a central body in Canada. This convention was sponsored by the UCCC and about 500 delegates from Manitoba, Saskatchewan and Ontario attended. Premier T. Norris of Manitoba and Ald. MacLean of Winnipeg extended greetings. Prof. Osborne, speaking on behalf of the University of Manitoba, assured the delegates of his support with the following words: "Do not think that foreigners are hated in Canada, or that some of the Canadians consider them as a burden to this country... Throw this out of your head. This is the notion of a small number of our extremists... There is no scarcity of good and fine people in Canada of whom this country might be proud if everything had been done the way it should have been done..." The principal address was made by Dr. V. Simenovych on behalf of the Ukrainian Americans, who represented the Central Committee in Aid of Ukraine in Chicago. On the opening day of the convention the delegates resolved to establish a Ukrainian Red Cross Society in Canada. There and then, the first successful collection was carried out for the new organization with Anna Yonker, the well-known patriot and philanthropist heading the list of contributors. It should be stressed that close co-operation existed between the Red Cross and all Ukrainian central organizations.

A similar organization under the same name was organized by Paul Krat in Toronto. It was a chartered organization, registered on Dec. 10, 1919. The petition for a Charter was signed by Mary Demydiuk, Olga Dmytriw, Mary Wicinski, Julian Konikewich and Michael Petrowsky.

At the Ukrainian provincial conventions in Saskatoon and Edmonton the Winnipeg Committee was recognized as the national body. Toronto cooperated with Winnipeg very closely and finally accepted Winnipeg's leadership. In a short time local chapters of the Red Cross Society were organized in Fisher Branch, Vita, Krydor, Canora, Hafford, Redberry, Hamilton, Montreal, and in other parts of Canada. The English version of the name adopted for this Society was: "Ukrainian Red Cross Society in Canada".

The executive of the Relief Committee of the Ukrainian Red Cross was headed by such women pioneers as Anna Yonker, Emilia Hykawa, O. Arsenych, Jos. Kovbel, N. Ferley, M. Romanovych, M. Boyanivska and A. Pankiv. Executive officers were: O. Boyanivsky, secretary; P. H. Woycenko, treasurer; and N. V. Bachynsky, organizer. The presidium also included J. W. Arsenych, W. Kudryk and V. Babienko. As we see the posts of secretary and treasurer were occupied by the same men who were engaged in the same capacity in the Ukrainian Canadian Citizens Committee. This personal and functional unity provided efficient planning and insight into the financial prospects of the community.

At the close of 1920 the Committee was reorganized and at a conference of all organizations in the city of Winnipeg there was elected a new All-Ukrainian committee of the Ukrainian Red Cross, but we shall deal with these basic changes with greater detail in the chapter covering the second period of our history.

The Ukrainian Canadian Citizens Committee efficiently illuminated the sequence of political events evolving in Ukraine. At a most crucial moment for the Ukrainians of Galicia, when the Polish army of Gen. Haller occupied the Eastern Galicia in 1919, Gen. Sam Hughes, Canada's former Minister of Defense, appealed to the Prime Minister of Great Britain, Lloyd George, on behalf of the Ukrainian Canadians many of whom served in the Canadian Army, not to surrender Galicia to Poland [1]. There were other historic actions of this kind.

An address made by S. J. Doherty, Justice Minister in the government of Arthur Meighen and later Canada's delegate to the League of Nations, during the debate over the fate of Eastern Galicia in Geneva, represented a measure of real appreciation for the Ukrainians of Canada. In the course of his speech, he uttered the following remarks about his Ukrainian fellow-citizens: "I feel impelled hereby to raise the matter (of Eastern Galicia—M.H.M.) by reason of the fact that in our Canadian land we have a large number of the Ukrainians among our population who together with other citizens built the Canadian nation and whom we respect as full-fledged citizens who hold out their promise of further co-operation to this country".

Another delegate of Canada to the League of Nations, Sir George Perley, spoke in the same spirit during that debate. These actions of the Canadian representatives before the political representatives of the nations of the world have been not only an act of recognition of the labours of the Ukrainian individual in Canada, but these actions were a nullification of the spectre of Austrianism that scourged the country in wartime inflicting a lot of damage to those who detested with their whole being everything that was imperial Austrian.

Of course, a great deal of work in this respect was done by the Ukrainian Citizenship Committee (which was know to the general public as the Ukrainian Canadian Citizenship League) and its branches across Canada. A considerable part of this clarification should be credited to the Ukrainian National Council which came into being at the end of the war.

---

[1] Sir Sam Hughes' telegram of June 25, 1919, "The Ukrainian matter in Ottawa, 1921".

UKRAINIAN NATIONAL COUNCIL

Even at the time of intensified activity of the Ukrainian Canadian Citizens Committee in 1918, certain problems of a religious nature within the Ukrainian community had become so involved that they began to weigh upon the work of the Committee. Tempers ran high, particularly when it came to the final assignation of delegates to the Peace Conference in Paris. A candidate of the Catholic camp, George Skvarok, was not accepted by a majority vote and the Committee decided to send O. Megas and I. Petrushevych, leading public workers and closely linked with a new religious movement. Thereupon three members of the Committee demonstratively walked out of the meeting in order to mark their opposition to a policy of balloting because up to now the principle of compromise has been maintained. After Theodore Stefanyk, Roman Kremar and John Sluzar bolted the Committee, the executive was complemented with such citizens as T. D. Ferley, M. Bahriychuk, S. Basisty, O. H. Hykawy, P. Popil and Illa Slobodian. Simultaneously with the w i t h d r a w al of the three members and the reorganization of the Committee, the Catholic press organ, "The Canadian Ruthenian", raised the question of control of the Committee's funds. It announced that the collected funds, hitherto remitted to the Committee through the offices of other Ukrainian newspapers, should be sent directly to "The Canadian Ruthenian", where already plans were made to launch the "Quarter Million Dollar Fund" for political aid to Ukraine and a charitable fund, "For the Galician Orphan Johnny". At the same time preparations were made for setting up an institution parallel to the UCCC.

The preliminary discussion resolved to call the church-people's convention which was held in Winnipeg, January 29-30, 1919. The convention proceeded under the personal patronage of Bishop N. Budka. On the eve of the convention Bishop Budka published in his press organ, "The Canadian Ruthenian", an article, headed "The Church-People's Convention", [1]), in which he pointed out that church matters are fundamental and that they will have a serious effect upon the course of further society work. He expressed the hope for settlement of the issue and, addressing himself to the initiators of a "dissident church convention" in Saskatoon, he added: "You have not yet burned all the bridges behind you" [2]). But there came to the convention in Winnipeg exclusively those who completely supported Bishop Budka, chiefly from Manitoba and adjacent provinces. After two days of deliberations, the several hundred delegates and guests finally resolved to consider the assembly as the constituent body to assume the direction of Ukrainian affairs in Canada. Thus the convention set up a "Ukrainian National Council" consisting of Central Executive and an Enlarged Council. Elected to the latter body, were: Bishop N. Budka, Rev. A. Sarmatiuk, R. Kremar, A. Havrylechko (East Selkirk), Greg. Bodnar, Jos. Dyk (a lawyer from Dauphin), S. Repinda (Kenora), Ya. Knysh, V. Onyshko (Cooks Creek), T. Ivanyshyn (Foaming River), I. Zawidowsky, P. Gigeychuk, G. S kvarok, I. Sluzar, D. Luhovy (Olga), S. Fodchuk, P. Ruta (Winnipeg),

---
[1]) "Canadian Ruthenian", Jan. 29, 1919.
[2]) "Canadian Ruthenian", Jan. 29, 1919.

I. Boychuk (Cooks Creek), Ya. Chorneyko (Ethelbert), Greg. Dutchak (Angusville), J. Gilewich (Janow), N. Bodnarchuk (Vita), D. Rostotsky, S. Paley (Rosa), Rev. M. Olenchuk, M. Havrysh, M. Medvid (Portage la Prairie), S. Kisil, A. Smaha (East Kildonan), P. Kindzersky, Father R. Krupa (Ft. William), Ya. Nachulak (Canora), T. Farion (Sifton), I. Nykyforchuk (Komarno), I. Zbitnyuk (Roblin), I. Mimka (Sarto), S. Kryshtolavych (Sandy Lake), E. Bilynska and M. Koreska (Winnipeg). In addition to this 42-member Council there was a 15-member Central Committee of Ukrainian National Council, presided over by Fr. A. Sarmatiuk, consisting of R. Kremar, P. Ruta, T. Stefanyk, Greg. Bodnar, G. Skvarok, I. Sluzar, I. Zawidowsky, Fr. P. Oleksiw, St. Fodchuk, I. Boychuk, D. Luhovy, Jos. Dyk, T. Probizansky and I. Semeniuk.

The Winnipeg convention stirred up great enthusiasm in the life of Ukrainian Catholics. Among other things, the Edmonton weekly, "The News", characterized the convention thus: "The fact that attending the convention were delegates from certain areas of Saskatchewan and Ontario while eastern Canada was represented by Father A. Redkevych, who came with the mandate from the Ukrainian delegation in the East, gives this convention the character of a wholly Catholic assembly" [3]. Another significant outcome of the convention was the adoption of a resolution to establish a Ukrainian organization, Dominion-wide in its scope. "In spite of the fact that the newly established Ukrainian National Council considered itself an All-Ukrainian representative body in accordance with its avowed principles, in reality it did not become an All-Ukrainian national organization in the full meaning of the term, simply, because the Catholics alone included themselves in its work. Nevertheless, considering the fact that the great majority of the settlers belong to the Ukrainian Catholic Church, the Ukrainian National Council did become an important political factor in its time. Without delay, it assumed control of the so-called "Quarter Million Dollar Fund" as well as of the "Fund for the Galician Orphan Johnny". In order to establish connections with Ottawa, the Council authorized federal member of parliament, H. A. Mackie of Edmonton, to act on its behalf before the government authorities in Ottawa in all matters, particularly to look after the matter of sending parcels to the Ukrainian war prisoners in Italy, financial aid to Ukrainian Canadian mission in Paris, and so on.

The Ukrainian National Council extended its work to other provinces. A month after the Winnipeg convention, the so-called Church-People's convention was held in Saskatoon on February 26 and 27, and in Edmonton on March 2 and 3. Both were successful. The Edmonton convention represented nearly 1,000 participants from Alberta. Both of these conventions recognized the Central Committee of Ukrainian National Council in Winnipeg as the directing organ of the UNC, and intensified its work in extending individual membership. Besides declarations of loyalty to the Crown and Canada, it was resolved at all these conventions to aid the cause of Ukraine's liberation. Demands were put forward that the Canadian government undertake a revision of its position on the matter of the so-called "Austrianism of Ukrainians in Canada". In this and similar other matters the Central Committee prepared several petitions to the government in Ottawa which were submitted by H. A. Mackie, M.P. These were courageous and determined steps taken by the Central Committee,

---

[3] "The News", Edmonton, Feb. 14, 1919.

particularly at this period of time when all Ukrainian newspapers appeared in two languages because of the sharpened censorship. We learned from later reports of the UNC Central Committee, that it has co-operated with the Ukrainian National Council in Paris, France, which was headed by Prof. Sawchenko. The UNC supported it with funds, continued to send parcels to war prisoners, etc. The soul of the Ukrainian National Council in Canada was Roman Kremar while Bishop Nykyta Budka was its official head.

The emergence of the two dominant Ukrainian bodies in Canada, the Ukrainian Canadian Citizens Committee and the Ukrainian National Council, conducting work along parallel lines within the internal and external sectors of Ukrainian society, were positive forces. Particularly evident was the motivation of popular masses to greater effort in public activity and of pointing out to the government agencies, the injustices done in relation to the Ukrainian Canadians. In the negative sense however, each of these central bodies laid claims to exclusive representation, although of course, neither of them could exert complete dominance. Still the appearance of two rival representations has not been a blunder but rather an epilogue of those events that were ripening and reached the point of culmination in 1918 [4]. They were closely related to religious life and church politics which seriously complicated the public life of the Ukrainians in Canada in years to follow. Both these representations competed with each other, above all, in the collection of funds; while attacking and publicly discrediting each other, only served to undermine their prestige and the respect of the majority of the Ukrainian community. This rivalry did, however, produce some positive results, especially during the Meighen term of office. It was at that time that Ottawa raised the unfamiliar Ukrainian question at the International Forum in Paris and Geneva. This action can be credited to them both, the U.C.C.C. and the U.N.C., who rarely failed to raise the Ukrainian Question in Ottawa. They provided the Government with the objective interpretation of the problem as it related to the Canadian interests generally. This and similar actions of these official agencies of Canada aided other nations in respecting Canada as a nation maturing into a democratic and progressive force at the form of world diplomacy.

---

[4] Creation of the Ukrainian Greek-Orthodox Church.

STRUGGLE FOR CONSUMMATION OF UKRAINIAN ENTITY

In one of the preceding chapters of this history we had occasion to underline the basic trends in development of Ukrainian Canadians; that is, toward general integration, on the one hand, and the struggle of the Ukrainian ethnic element to retain a distinctive cultural identity within a Canadian mosaic. The desire for a complete community, which we observe even at the very beginning of pioneer days, played an important role in the process of this integration. The drift of Ukrainian settlers toward unity did not end with local organizations of a parochial, private school, or cultural-educational character. A strong need was soon felt for closer co-operation between the various localities in order to jointly solve the common problems affecting the life of the broad community. These contacts proceeded at a local provincial and generally, at the national level.

First such endeavours to merge into a more complete community can be observed as early as 1902, when in October, by the initiative of such pioneers as A. Zailo, T. Stefanyk, I. Chorniy, G. Panischak and J. Orlowsky, the first Ukrainian general mass meeting in Canada was held in Winnipeg for the purpose of discussing church matters [1]. For purpose of clarity it should be noted that in the pioneer days the concept of "mass meeting" was synonymous with today's "convention". Whereas the first mass meeting, or convention, of 1902 confined itself almost exclusively to church affairs, the Ukrainian convention convened 16 months later by the (Ukrainian) Independent Greek Orthodox Church, discussed not only church matters but also those of general public interest, and above all, the question of Ukrainian schools in Canada. About 60 delegates participated in the convention, chiefly from Manitoba, although there were representatives from Alberta and Saskatchewan. A large convention was convened in 1907; although this was primarily a teachers' convention sufficient other members of the community attended in an advisory capacity that it could be considered a general convention. The Ukrainian Teachers' Association was established at this meeting and they delved into matters far beyond the local order of things. Although from the organizational viewpoint the Association was confined to Manitoba, at the ideological-political level this organization already illuminated the way towards the completeness of Ukrainian community in Canada. The Ukrainian Teachers' Association, located in Winnipeg, was emerging as a natural provisional leader of the Ukrainian community in Canada. Subsequently the Ukrainian Canadians as well as many in Ukraine proper turned to the teachers for orientation. The prestige of the organized teachers was greatly enhanced in that among the honorary members of the Association were several leading figures of the Ukrainian community in Europe. Thanks to the Ukrainian Teachers' Association the "First General Convention of Ukrainians in Canada", which was simply called "a three-day delegates' public meeting" was held in the following year. A considerable number of delegates and teachers came to the convention, and not just from Manitoba. The convention adopted a series of resolutions dealing with further cultural and

---

[1] "Studies in the History of Ukrainians in Canada", Vol. 2, p. 347.

organizational growth of the Ukrainian community, particularly in Manitoba.

Thus Manitoba led the way in its capacity to organize.

Right after the delegates' meeting the Ukrainian Canadian press raised the necessity of convening a "national general meeting" and of organizing "all Ukrainians in Canada". Taking part in the discussions on this subject, were more prominent figures of the Ukrainian community, such as P. Svarich, T. D. Ferley, Z. Bychynsky, who initiated the discussion, T. Wachna, W. Vivchar, Al. Wilchynsky, J. W. Arsenych, O. Zerebko. A prominent pioneer farmer of the Ethelbert district, O. V. Magis, clearly wrote in the press that at such a "national general meeting" there should be established "an organization that would lay strong foundations at the very beginning and all the Canadian Ukrainians should be duty-bound to join it and support it morally and materially... in the economic, educational and political fields of endeavour" [2].

It took quite a while before this popular desire was fulfilled. First it was necessary to consolidate community life in the provinces, to start building everything from the very bottom, to organize municipal and school districts, social and cultural life of the settlers. Under the existing conditions it was difficult to talk about a Dominion-wide Ukrainian organization, still the idea of it remained in the minds of the pioneer public leaders.

In 1912, the newspaper "New Country", commenting on the unsuccessful bid of W. Holowacky (1912) and M. Gabora (1904) for election to Ottawa and of M. Gabora to the Saskatchewan Legislature, raised the question of urgent need for organized power. It literally said: "Until Canadian Ruthenians achieve their own powerful organization for popular-political purposes, there is no use to dream of any successes whatsoever" [3].

Curiously, the writer of this comment made it crystal-clear that the proposed organization must not be utilized solely for election campaign purposes but that it had to provide leadership in cultural matters of the community. At the political level the writer suggested that the Ukrainian Canadians support the existing Canadian political parties. The "New Country" even proposed the setting up of an organizing committee which quite naturally embraced the outstanding lay representatives of contemporary Ukrainian community in Canada [4]. Although these discussions and proposals of "The New Country" had not been realized, they did influence the thinking of the people in that direction.

In the meantime the Ukrainian Teachers' Association and the Federation of Ukrainian School Trustees were organized in Saskatchewan according to the pattern set in Manitoba. A. T. Kibzey was the guiding spirit. In Alberta P. Svarich was making similar preparations. It was exactly these organizations, particularly in Manitoba and Saskatchewan, that were the guiding force in presenting the demands of the community to the provincial government authorities. They were becoming also the core of organized life in each province.

To what degree the name of Ukrainian teacher was held in esteem at that time, can be judged from the authoritative opinion expressed by Dr. O. Sushko in the "Canadian Ruthenian". According to him, "the teachers

---

[2] "Canadian Farmer", No. 5, Feb. 1, 1909.
[3] "New Country", Nos. 18 and 19, 1912.
[4] "New Country", June 20, 1912.

and clergymen should hold joint consultations in these matters with the enlightened members of their community. Then in the near future the eagerly and hopefully anticipated teachers' conventions in Manitoba, Saskatchewan and Alberta should transform, after the convention agenda is exhausted, into Ukrainian provincial parliaments. The participation of the representatives of all Ukrainian associations and organizations for the common and concordant discussion of the Ukrainian situation in Canada should be encouraged. The object of these discussions should be the adoption of a series of common and mutual goals which could then become the Ukrainian socio-political ideals for our ethnic populace. These goals could become a popular platform, popular in the fullest sense, having been adopted by the true representatives of the Ukrainian element in this country" [5]. O. Zerebko expressed similar opinion in his article published in the "Dilo" of Lviv, two years earlier.

The question of achieving general representation for the Ukrainian settlers in Canada stirred up the interest not only of the compatriots in their new land but also in Europe. That the glowing reports on the Ukrainian teachers' conventions had not been just hollow-sounding phrases is shown in the article entitled "A Survey of the Life of Ukrainian Settlers in Canada". This was published in one of the early Ukrainian Canadian Almanacs where we find the following passage on this subject: "The annual convention of Ukrainian teachers in Alberta, Saskatchewan and Manitoba were preceded by lively discussions in nearly all Ukrainian newspapers in Canada on the following topics: 1) Introduction of lectures on Ukrainian history and literature at the universites; 2) Confederation of Ukrainian teachers associations; 3) Confederation of Ukrainian school trustees in Canada; 4) Confederation of Ukrainian schools in Canada; 5) Publication of a teachers' periodical; 6) Establishing a Ukrainian college; 7) A students' fraternity and 8) A children's newspaper" [6].

The above-enumerated problems that troubled the minds of the community remained exclusively in the domain of cultural growth, expanding with fruition. From this it becomes evident that the teachers influenced the attitudes of the Ukrainian people in Canada; not being content with just a one-room school in a rural district, they strove towards accomplishment in many other areas. This was no longer a current of the subconsciousness but a positive action. This was evident from the official appeal of the teachers, issued in 1915 and adressed "To Ukrainian Teachers in Manitoba", in which we find the following passage: "Are we to be or not to be—this is the big question. This means, are we to be Ukrainians, live the life we know best and naturally which suits us best, or are we to be unworthy of a man's name—the hewers of wood and drawers of water for the ruling elements? Two pathways lie open before us. We stand at the very crossroads of these pathways. One of these leads towards the natural growth of the people, the other to assimilation. It is possible to put our foot forward without stepping upon one of the roads. The road leading towards the growth of our people is a thorny one, but it opens the vista into a bright future. We must have strong belief in a bright future. In

---

[5] "Canadian Ruthenian", May 26, 1915.
[6] Almanac of The Canadian Ruthenian for 1916, p. 161-62.

order to attain this bright future we must resolutely proceed along this true road" [7]).

That the Ukrainian settlers had chosen the natural course of development stressed in the teachers' appeal is evident from the very beginning. As we see these problems today, the stand taken by the teachers is considered as obvious and compatible with the law of development. But half a century ago the people held a different opinion of these problems. In the eyes of many a Canadian this was a peculiar revolution which had to be curbed. In other words, to oppose cultural assimilation meant to oppose the established custom of a decent citizen. In addition, these were the wars when rigid wartime measures regulations, quite often unjust from the objective viewpoint, held sway. Frequently war does not know where objectivism and where subjectiveness lie. But in spite of this, the masses of Ukrainian settlers of the pioneer era viewed the so-called assimilation as outright denial of their cultural birthright, and a "degeneration". A slogan was raised that "assimilation was demoralization and degeneration". From the standpoint of their natural rights, the Ukrainians set out to build their life in Canada. The internal and external stimuli of the community interests strove towards building natural defenses, giving it a rudder (direction) and a push towards completion. From this standpoint proceeded lengthy discussions, frequent provincial and even national conventions. For all that, the teachers and university students, for the most part, recruited from the ranks of teachers, provided leadership. Thus an elite of the community was emerging before the eyes of all, reared upon the principles of Anglo-Saxon law and democratic system of government. It was precisely to these principles that this elite subordinated the "natural" growth and development of the community. No doubt, the teachers had been in close contact with the population of the settlements and by reason of this they were like seismographs of the feelings and aspirations of the broad masses who lived by the cultural traditions of their ancestors. Aware of the reactions of their environment, the teachers had the opportunity to give their people a timely call and urge them on to determined work. The proposal to hold joint conventions of teachers and general public found frequent application.

The first larger gathering of this kind in the second period of the pioneer era took place in Winnipeg, 1915, and passed into history as the "first large gathering of Ukrainian delegates in the province of Manitoba". As a forerunner of this first convention was the three-day conference of bilingual schoolteachers that took place July 14-16, and on the 17th active discussions were held by the 156 delegates. The discussions were centered around the four basic questions that were covered by such papers as: "The duties of Ukrainian settlers pertaining to Canada" and "The duties of Ukrainian settlers toward the old Fatherland". Among the more practical problems dealt with was a paper entitled: "The stand of Ukrainian Canadians toward the two political parties and to the eventual provincial and dominion elections" as well as the establishment of the Department of the Ukrainian language and literature in the University of Manitoba.

The resolutions that were prepared and passed during these discussions all led to the following fundamental principles: "The declaration of com-

---

[7] "An Appeal to Ukrainian Teachers in Manitoba", 1915, signed by I. Rudachek, chairman of the Association, and W. Mihaychuk, secretary.

plete loyalty towards Canada"; "support for the war efforts of the Old Fatherland"; "substantial aid" for the "Ukrainian veteran fund" that would entail cash collection to be put into use after the war; the "desire for a rapid healing of grievous wounds" and the "fulfillment of national aspirations in the sacred freedom endeavours". In this way basically, were the political and ideological positions clarified. From the practical considerations it was decided to "adopt in politics the free hand policy" towards the political parties in Canada and to support the party that aided the cultural growth of the Ukrainian community in Canada. Those present also made their intentions known of demanding from the University of Manitoba the establishment of the Ukrainian language and literature Department.

On the organizational level the gathering voiced the need for creating a Ukrainian National Council in the province of Manitoba, composed of 66 members and recognizing it as "the representative body of all the Ukrainian citizens in Manitoba having the power to decide in Canadian affairs on behalf of all the Ukrainians—groups, organizations, associations and newspapers (political centres—M.H.M.) of Manitoba, all of them responsible before the delegates of the convention" [8].

Such a formula dealing with the organizational question of the community was a further attempt at the formation of Ukrainian national representation in the province which was to be responsible before the widely acclaimed delegates of the national convention. And what was even more, during this "national gathering" in Manitoba a desire was voiced that the newly elected Ukrainian National Council of Manitoba which in reality was the emanation of "chytalnias", national homes, parishes and different organizations, should make "all possible efforts with the aim of forming analogous national organizations in Saskatchewan and Alberta". The principle of the Ukrainian National Council was again renewed, following 1918 when the Ukrainian Canadian Citizens Committee was divided and the Ukrainian National Council was formed for the second time, as we have mentioned in a previous chapter.

Truthfully said this was not the first such show of unity but it was the first among the largest and best organized ones since the formation of the representation. Among the ranks of the Ukrainian National Council of Manitoba we find such leading figures in the community life of those days as: T. Stefanyk, J. W. Arsenych, N. Hladky, T. D. Ferley, H. Woycenko, T. J. Marciniw, Charambura, I. Rychliwsky, I. Zarowsky, H. Bodnar, S. Nychyk, T. Jastremsky, P. E. Orobko, M. Lewycky, J. Dyma, Zubachek and others. Among the speakers and presidium council were the following: Dr. O. Sushko (the head organizer of the convention). O. H. Hykawy, W. Mihaychuk, W. Smuk, H. Skehar, I. Besarab, M. Mihaychuk. All those mentioned above were either teachers or university students [9]. Although the then head of the Catholic Church, Bishop N. Budka, did not take part in any of these gatherings as he was attending the Eucharistic Congress in Montreal, still he sent his personal greetings in the form of an address and fully supported the idea of this national convention. This was substantiated by further announcements appearing in the "Canadian Ruthenian" the official press organ of the Bishop.

During both of these conventions—the teachers' and the general—the

---
[8] "Canadian Ruthenian", July 21, 1915.
[9] "Canadian Ruthenian", No. 30, 1915.

representatives of the city of Winnipeg and provincial government took part. At the teachers' convention the provincial educational institutions were represented by the following persons: R. Fletcher, Superintendent of Education, Dr. W. J. McIntyre, J. B. Hales and J. T. Cressey, the principals of the teachers' colleges, as well as several school inspectors. J. P. Folley, the M.L.A. for North Winnipeg represented the political world at the general convention and mayor R. D. Waugh civic authorities.

Even in the midst of the hammering blows of war the Ukrainian community of Manitoba was not confused as to the direction it should follow and took the unifying and mature stand that would bring it in step with the integrated life of the rest of Canada. This was an important beginning of the great provincial gathering that later took place in the three prairie provinces and these helped to forge the chain in furthering the co-operative work of the Ukrainian community in Canada.

In this regard Saskatchewan recorded numerically the largest conventions which were held in Saskatoon during that period. First such convention was held August 4 and 5, 1916, with more than 500 delegates and guests taking part. Although most of them came from Saskatchewan, by its composition and character the convention was to all intents and purposes the first natural parliament of Ukrainian Canadian community which strove for its national and cultural "emancipation". Taking part in the convention were the clergymen with Bishop N. Budka at the head, lay representatives of municipalities, school districts, cultural-educational organizations, parishes, and so on. The wartime required certain platitudinous declarations which were made by the chairman of the convention and Bishop N. Budka, who addressed the convention and spoke of Canada as "our adopted homeland".

The tenor of addresses stressed "respect for everything Canadian" but at the same time those present also called for respect for their own people.

Notwithstanding its concrete and practical objectives the Saskatoon convention became at its ideological level a pronunciamento, both before its own community and their fellow-citizens. At no other convention up to that time were the basic principles and position of the Ukrainians in Canada so precisely outlined as at this convention. The next convention in Saskatoon, held December 27-29, 1917, was a continuation and an endorsement of proposals adopted at the first convention.

One of the salient deliberations concerned the defense of Canadian citizenship which was revoked for all foreigners several months before the convention and which was applied to the Election Act for the duration of war. [10]. In view of the fact that at that moment a struggle was going on in Ukraine for self-determination, those present manifested the warmest sentiment for the land of their ancestors. About 800 participants attended this convention.

Almost at the same time, just three days earlier, a similar convention was held in Edmonton, however, with a smaller number of participants, but with more or less similar political and ideological proposals. The organizer of the Saskatoon convention was the Petro Mohyla Institute, and of the Edmonton convention—head of the Ukrainian Catholic Church, Bishop N.

---

[10] As a matter of record it should be noted that out of 210 MP's present in the House of Commons, 85 members had voted on the Election Act amendment—53 in favour and 32 against.

Budka. There were certain divergencies at these conventions, but not with regard to the relationship of the Ukrainians to Canada. These related to certain religious issues, particularly the relation of religion to education and vice-versa. But in spite of this nonconformity both conventions were an expression of a common desideratum by the Ukrainian community in Canada. They gave Ukrainian community its natural roundness, which already exceeded the boundaries of municipalities, districts and even provinces. Perhaps the above-mentioned conventions, and a series of provincial conventions before this, finally united the Ukrainian colonies in Canada into one great community which had its own purposes, tasks, cultural needs, ambitions and common anxieties related to wartime.

Neither of these two conventions succeeded in creating any permanent representation, although both of them affirmed the need for such a representation. Very likely it was not created because the conventions were held outside Manitoba which had usually been regarded as the leading province relative to general affairs of Ukrainians in Canada. The polarization of the forces of Petro Mohyla Institute and Bishop N. Budka was a negative reason of no mean importance. These obstacles did not deter the Ukrainian leadership in Manitoba, and particularly in Winnipeg, where in the earlier years the "Central Committee of 'Native School' " came into existence. There its work was continued by the "Committee for Defense of Bilingual Schools" and a little later the "Ukrainian Canadian Citizens Commitee" developed intensive work, having already established relations with Ottawa. This was a big step forward in the process of completing the organizational structure of the Ukrainians in Canada.

True, all this has been built up on a kind of provisional basis, but at the same time it was the fulfilment of the desires of many individuals and the entire mass of people was constantly stressing the necessity of achieving one leadership for the community. The Ukrainian Canadian Citizens Committee did in fact assume such leadership in 1918. This Committee applied itself not only to the welfare of the Ukrainians in Canada, but also it succeeded in representing Ukrainism outside Canada—in London, Paris and in Ukraine. There were various reasons for the short existence of the Ukrainian Canadian Citizens Committee, notwithstanding this it was the first voluntary step of the Ukrainian community in Canada toward fulfilment.

When we speak of the fulfilment of the community at a public level, we must mention also the long struggle of the Ukrainians at the religious level. Specifically this relates to the endeavours of Ukrainian Catholics for their own hierarchy, that is, a separate ecclesiastical province independent from others and directly responsible to the Vatican [11]. These endeavours had been crowned with complete success in 1912. Six years later the Ukrainian Greek Orthodox Church was established which set before itself the task of uniting all Orthodox Ukrainians under one national leadership. The struggle for cultural fulfilment and independence of their life, lasted nearly a quarter of the century. It continued nearly throughout the entire pioneer period in order to finally succeed in form and completion.

This instinct for national identity indicates the great vitality and power-

---

[11] See a separate work of the author, entitled "Struggle for independence of Ukrainian Church in Canada".

ful cultural cohesion of the Ukrainian community. There were many moments when the settlers saw before them the situations as they were in the Old Country when even there they were obliged to fight for their national-cultural identity. This instinct asserted itself particularly at a time when the settlers faced a series of injustices that the turmoil of world war hopelessly brought upon them. Therefore it is possible to maintain that internal and external factors have had tremendous effect upon the processes of moulding the national-cultural cohesion of the Ukrainians in Canada. Each heedless action of the English-language press, which seldom understood the problems of Ukrainian settlers, aroused spontaneous and often an organized reaction from the community, always prepared to defend its natural rights toward full development in this new land. In fact, the entire liberation process taking place in Ukraine at the close of World War I also had a powerful influence on the course of integration and fulfilment of the Ukrainian community in Canada. The eruption of the people for the independent and sovereign Ukrainian nation in 1917 broke the chains of foreign bondage and lifted the people of dismembered Ukraine to constructive nation-building endeavours. The events of January 22nd, 1918, in Kiev and those of November 1st, 1918, in Lviv (Lvov) and in other parts of Ukraine, electrified the Ukrainians in every part of the world, seeing their homeland rising to statehood. When in addition to this, the Allies recognized the sovereignty of the Ukrainian State and when the unification of all Ukrainian lands was proclaimed in Kiev on January 22, 1919, the resulting situation in Ukraine not only raised the spirits of Ukrainians everywhere but their prestige as well.

The Ukrainian conventions that were held in Winnipeg, Saskatoon and Edmonton as well as in other centres of western Canada brought together large numbers of delegates from cities and rural areas. Sympathy and support for the liberation processes in the Ukraine was voiced by hundreds and thousands at public meetings. The Ukrainian workers in eastern Canada also reacted to the events in Ukraine and began to unite. The dimensions of these demonstrations and sentiments can best be illustrated by the mass meeting of Montreal Ukrainians, held in March 1919 and attended by three thousand enthusiastic participants. Mayor Marte was the guest of honor. In the same manner other ethnic groups in Canada—Poles, Czechs, Serbs, Slovaks, and so on—manifested their enthusiasm over the liberation of their homelands. Canada had become a symbol of freedom not only in the hearts of her citizens but also in her international relations. The Canadian delegates to Peace Conferences in Paris and Geneva emerged as the bearers and champions of the ideals of liberation of enslaved peoples. This can be adduced even from the document received by the Ukrainian Canadians, but with a specific reference to the Canadian government. In October 1921 Evhen Petrushevych, President of the Ukrainian National Council of the Western Region of the Ukrainian National Republic, made public a letter of appreciation entitled "To the Ukrainians of Canada". It read in part: "When you, dear brothers and sisters, were leaving your Fatherland on a long journey into the then unknown open spaces of Canada, a great many of us thought that you would be lost to your people and the land of your ancestors... For even the most fervent supporters of emigration never hoped to see the day when your former homeland would turn to you for support at a crucial moment... Your former Fatherland sends you its greetings and profound thanks for presenting a united front and through the voice of your External Affairs Minister

Doherty have called the representatives of many nations assembled in Geneva for help in delivering your cherished Galician homeland from enslavement by foreign invaders".

Such political gestures and declarations never completely pass into oblivion. The course of political events in Ukraine had still another effect upon the development of Ukrainian community in Canada. This came about with the differentiation of political moods and the program of the liberation struggle by the Ukrainian people. The events related to this process were evolving into the next era of the Ukrainians in Canada which opened a new page of history after the World War I. One of the more glowing pages in the first year of that new era concerns the participation of the broad masses in the work of the Ukrainian Red Cross Society in Canada. This aid to the war prisoners, widows, orphans, the disabled and such other victims of the war, who in their need were turning their eyes towards Canada, was greatly appreciated from a free and prosperous land where so many of their fellow-countrymen lived.

In its turn Canada never denied aid to those in need—and this was the moment when the factors of ethnic unity of the Ukrainian Canadians and the national prestige of Canada, already visible upon the international horizon, began to form a pattern.

The relief work carried on by the Ukrainian community in aid of their compatriots in Europe was but a single flower of their work in the external field of activity in relation to their enduring work carried out within Canada in the organizational, cultural-educational, religious, political and economic sectors. These were their long years of struggle that they might finally behold the ripening fruit of their labour. The pioneer era of the Ukrainians in Canada was closing with a colorful canvas, a positive balance of achievements and new horizons for the future.

Although the pioneer era did not bring into existence a complete national consummation still some very strong foundations were built during this period that were found to be so essential in the second era which brought this consummation into reality. The Ukrainian Canadian Citizens Committee and the Ukrainian National Council were the evidential expressions of the persevering stride of the wide masses that were demanding further development from their leadership. In this there may well be seen the great constructive ability of the Ukrainian pioneer in Canada who desired to see himself identified in his own national-cultural community as well as in the overall structural development of the general Canadian statehood.

THE SECOND ERA

EXPANSION, DISINTEGRATION AND INTEGRATION

INTRODUCTION

The second era of Ukrainian Canadians closes with the two World Wars. This is the period of development in every branch of the community activity in the life of the Ukrainians in Canada whose work takes in the wider dominion scope, encompassing the whole country. Upon the foundations laid by the local, regional and provincial formations built mostly during the pioneer era, we can see the rising, dominion-shaped, superstructures of the second era that became the fitting monument-towers for each individual establishment. Thus was provided an impetus for a further implementation of national integration, albeit only in the religious ideological and political sphere. Dominion organizations seek the pathways of their self-expression though not always along parallel lines. Very often they become criss-crossed and this in turn leads to divergencies and conflicts. Most often this happens in the sphere of mutually exclusive opinions and ideas such as in religion and ideology. But even here the process of sound and natural integration did not cease to perform. In the face of outer events that could have possibly had some effect upon the future course of the whole community, this process continued to grow in strength and the Ukrainian entity was able to finish the forging of the protective ring of its national defensive apparatus. This conscious and subconscious self-preservation intelligence was most in evidence during the period of the two World Wars. As a result of the inner development processes and the outer dangers the course of national integration was finally consummated with an all-inclusive national unity.

The uniting processes were not only following the line of national integration. Augmented integration was also taking place in the general Canadian sphere. Branches of husbandry and political life in Canada—these were very wide fields on which Ukrainian Canadians could well express themselves and add their building blocks to the grand structure of the Canadian state. In this same sphere great changes had taken place. During this whole era a continuous migration from farms to cities is markedly revealed. In cities too the Ukrainian element gradually acquires a respectable and lawful claim to citizenship. This element is primarily strengthened by the second generation that had been brought up and educated in Canada and emerged into its own in every segment of life, but most of all in the political and professional sphere. This city-bred element is noticeably enhanced by the post-war Ukrainian immigration from Europe which flowed in thousands to Canada. This augmented still further—from the economical and political aspect—these unfolding social processes, thus strengthening and revitalizing the cultural community branch of Ukrainian life.

Ukrainian Canadian entity bases its life on the belief that Canada is not just a transitory corridor for the thousands of pioneers and immigrants. On the contrary, to them it is their adopted fatherland for centuries to come. They feel themselves to bear integral part of their new homeland. With this deep feeling is intertwined their sense of responsibility towards this country, its development and its future destiny. From this rich source of their characteristic being there grows a patriotism that embraces the land, its people and everything that this country stands for—and this they amply prove by their full participation in municipal affairs, provincial and dominion government administration and at the helm of various community undertakings in Canada. Each year the contemporary press and the growing volumes of literature give their attestation as evidence of the gigantic stride ahead. The crowning point of this responsibility and patriotism was the part played by the 35,000 Ukrainian Canadians in Canadian army units during the Second World War.

Toil, blood and the sacrifice of life—these were all interwined together to form an integral Canadian entity and within its enfolding sphere the Ukrainian Canadian community manifested a strong and undeniable desire to live its life according to the cultural acquirement of its own people and yet feel itself to be an indivisible part of Canada.

From these sanguine feelings flowed the justifiable obligations toward their people in moments when moral and political stimuli and arguments spoke to their hearts.

It is exactly these same social processes, in their historical aspect, that we are trying to examine in this second era.

MIGRATION AND IMMIGRATION

Statistics of the year 1911 show that 85 percent of the Ukrainian settlers were engaged in agriculture and lived on farms, but 1921 data shows that fully 20 percent of them lived in cities. Ten years later, according to 1931 census, 30 percent lived in cities and by 1941 this increased to 34 percent. These statistical figures prove that the social structure of Ukrainian settlers during the second era of their history in Canada—which includes the time between the two World Wars—underwent a gradual change. It would look, then, that almost 20 percent of the farming population had moved to the cities during this second era. However, there were several factors that contributed to this migration of the settlers.

It had been possible to record with more details Ukrainian settlements during the first era—the era of the pioneers. A greater number found themselves living on sub-marginal lands, especially so when we consider the province of Manitoba. There were farms on which their owners struggled for years only to surrender them without any remuneration to the government, or to offer them gratis to their neighbors. Some of the farms had to be turned into communal pastures, as their crop-growing usefulness was less than minimal. "Very often we have to admire the tenacity of these people", wrote R. W. Murchie and H. C. Grant, "on being able to survive for years on their bare existence, depriving their families of the most meagre necessities of life." But there came a time when a decision had to be made—whether to seek a better homestead or move to the city and look for work there. Coefficient growth of Ukrainian population in cities was also, in part, the resulting effect of the young generation that grew up in Canada and could see but very little benefit derived from staying on the unproductive and barren prairies. A portion of this young generation, travelling along the road that would lead them to the source of educational opportunities and higher living standards, found their way into the cities. Modern, technical methods of farming also favored the larger migration from the farm to the city, especially when we take into consideration the more prolific increase of Ukrainian families. The primal and immemorial sickle was replaced with the mower (binder), the spade with the plow and tractor, and the flail surrendered to the threshing machine. Still later, even the powerful threshing machines were finally replaced by a much more economically useful combine. The gradual evolution in the perfection of agricultural implements helped, at the same time, to evolve a new social structure. The great factor in accounting for the large growth of Ukrainian population in the cities may be attributed to the new immigration which began again after the Second World War. The outlook of this latest immigration differed somewhat from the previous one in the first era but we will have more to say about it later.

Migration of Ukrainian population to the cities was not the only one. At the turning point of the two eras we also see a noticeable shift of the population on the farms proper. A move to—or rather the appropriation of—new rich fields surrounding the Ukrainian settlement blocks of land was now progressing rapidly at the expense, primarily, of Anglo-Saxon settlers. These were glad to sell some of their farms to the land-hungry Ukrainians for a good—at times even an exhorbitant—price. The war helped to speed up these transactions. In 1919 farm products constituted 134 percent of pre-war prices. In cities, too, the earning potential was very good. Those whose farms were poor made up for it by gardening. Gardening, especially, was flourishing around the cities. The work- and save nature of pioneer settlers enabled them to lay aside a small amount of cash as a down payment on a better farm. In this way the settlements were spread out as, for example, south of the Riding Mountains in such municipalities as Harrison, Strathclair, Rossburn, and particularly south of Oakburn—in the locality of Shoal Lake. Likewise in the Gilbert Plains district and around Dauphin as well as in the vicinity of Emerson and Dufrost—all of them in Manitoba. The same kind of process was going on in the province of Saskatchewan, in the Rhein, Hamiota, Calder, Canora, Wroxton districts and all around Yorkton and at a later time, near Melville and Balcarres. In the twenties, when the Indian reserve of "Small Black Bear" was parcelled out, almost the whole tract of land came into Ukrainian hands. Similar tendencies of Ukrainian expansion may be noted in the province of Alberta, which, taking into consideration the rich quality of its soil, enabled the more enterprising farmers to add new sections of land to their possessions. The most outstanding evidence of this progress may be seen in Shandro, Andrew, Willingdon districts, as well as in the south of Renfurly, Lavoy, Innisfree and other centres. This expansion was often the result of some farmers acquiring several farms. Of course, more often this acquisition of farms was handled on the set-payment plan. The aftermath of war brings along many changes in economy, basic changes and quite often even depressions. Such a depression was experienced by Canadians after the First World War. It reached its summit—or rather its depth—in 1923 when farm products fell down in prices seven percent lower than the pre-war prices. Many farmers lost their deposits on the purchased farms. Some of them had to make great withdrawals upon their savings in order to rid themselves of heavy debts. Still the process of expansion of Ukrainians to better land was not seriously curtailed. In the course of this expansion the value of land played an important role. Where the land was good the farmers were able to acquire another section or more. To be sure even where the land was less productive it was still in demand, but this only happened when the pioneers turned to the so-called mixed farming, consisting of the cultivation of land plus the raising of cattle, feeding of pigs and poultry and, above all, being engaged in dairy industry. This mixed farming idea was most suited to Manitoba where the soil compared with that of other western provinces, was poorest of all. The change in farming methods was trailing behind it other eventualities. Grain elevators that had carried themselves so proudly in their vertical form,—that could be spied afar at almost every railway point—were now forced into liquidation, for soon enough from handling tens of thousands of bushels they were receiving only a few thousand. The change in the system of farming operations in Manitoba brought along with it the liquidation of the "Ukrainian Elevator Co.", which had in its possession several elevators and substantial funds. Both, the cultivation of the soil and the raising of cattle required a great amout of land and all soundly-ambitious owners endeavored to expand their holdings.

How this same expansion appeared in different provinces, and in figures may best be shown by the results of researches of the Department of Immigration that were carried on in 1929 [1]).

Average Land Holding and Clearings in Ukrainian Settlements in the Prairie Provinces

District	Farmers Visited	Average Years Here	Average Holdings Quarter	Clearing Per Farm Acres	Clearing Per Quarter Acres
MANITOBA:					
Kreuzberg	16	28	1	18.1	18.1
Stuartburn	18	26.5	1	50	50
Ethelbert	15	28	1.2	70	58.33
Sandy Lake	16	25	2.2	155	70.45
SASKATCHEWAN:					
Canora	14	25.4	2.0	133	68.50
St. Julian	12	28.8	2.35	185	78.82
Hafford	10	24	2.8	250	89.29
ALBERTA:					
Shandro	11	27	2.6	248	95.39

The above statistics clearly show that the better the land the more cultivated acres it will process. The poorer the land, the smaller are the farms. The quality of the land provides its own farming exigency (demands). In this Alberta and Saskatchewan lead the way.

What was presented in figures may serve as a further explanation taken from the so-called divisional census in Alberta No. 10 1925, that embraces to a greater extent the Ukrainian district of Vegreville. This district was producing: Grain production $14,901,855; garden products $287,668; lumbering $220,359; cattle sold $2,384,812; butchered stock $544,087; dairy and other products (milk, hides, feathers etc.) $1,591,913. This shows very plainly what great farming force was represented by the new settlers of the Canadian prairies.

The settlement, or rather the dis-settlement, took place not only on those lands where the settlers or their descendants were. Many families also moved to altogether new regions and especially to those terrains that were opened up for colonization between the two war periods. To such new terrains belonged first of all Peace River. Here they settled in the region of Rycroft, Grand Prairie, Sexsmith, Peace River Crossing and other places. Many others settled around Slave Lake, Father Buller River, Athabasca, Cunnington and Dorchester. A few had settled north of the Saskatchewan River near Coal Lake, St. Paul, Bonnyville, Lac Labiche and De Shay, and some in the districts of Samburg, north of Prince Albert and still others around the so-called wedge of the Hudson

---

[1]) "The Ukrainian Canadians", by Paul Yuzyk, Toronto, 1967, p. 98.

Bay. Much denser settlements were in evidence at St. Walburg and Meadow Lake in Saskatchewan and around Wabamun in Alberta. Considerable numbers of Ukrainian families moved to U.S.A. The ones who made these moves were mostly those that were living along the Canadian-American border. From the district of Stuartburn—the first Ukrainian group-colony in Manitoba—several families left for U.S.A. in the twenties, while a much greater number, a hundred families or more, left for Prince Albert and Peace River. These displaced settlers left behind them, in the hands of their neighbors, or just simply abandoned some 58 thousand of these unusable acres which very often—in addition to their poor condition—were also subject to flooding from Roseau river. Likewise from Sifton-Ethelbert region, a large percentage of settlers left for U.S.A. —mostly from those stretches of land which today constitute large public pastures stretching for tens of miles. On these same abandoned lands there once had been whole settlements, like Volkivci, Mink River and districts around Taras [2]) and others. Most of those who left, or re-settled somewhere else, came from the so-called Interlake District. A considerable number of these departing settlers left this district in the middle twenties. About these migrating settlers R. W. Murchy and H. S. Grant have this to say:

"In the last five years the population of Lakeview, Glenella, St. Rose, Lawrence and the unorganized territory has decreased considerably due to the abandonment of homesteads and the Soldier's Settlement grants in this area [3]).

According to the statistics given by the above authors, population in Kreuzberg municipality had declined from 3,987 in 1921 to 3,607 in 1926, and in Glenella from 2,501 in 1921 to 1,897 in 1926. The history of this stretch of land could not record a single increase in population. A similar transmigration process continued also after the Second World War.

Quality of land, farming and climatic conditions, as well as the technical advances in the methods of farming did much to influence the switching movement of the Ukrainian population in Canada, especially in regard to the three prairie provinces—Manitoba, Saskatchewan and Alberta. The first of these saw the most changes, followed by Saskatchewan; but the one which proved to be the most attractive and stabilized was Alberta. A further influx of immigration was an added factor that had a decisive influence upon the social structure of Ukrainian settlement-life. But in contrast to these different factors and changes, as well as the resulting conditions therefrom, the settlement motif which had been implemented during the first era had not been changed in its basic form. The territory of block settlements that spread itself from south of Winnipeg to the American border continued its farther spread in the north-westerly direction across Saskatchewan and Alberta, toward the farthest expanded prairie land of Athabasca. This territory was comprised of 200 to 300-mile wide stretch of land and nearly 1800 miles in length. During the second era this territory widened and lengthened

---

[2]) M. H. Marunchak: Studies in the History of Ukrainians in Canada—Vol. II, 1966, p. 112-116.
[3]) R. W. Murchie & H. C. Grant, "Unused Lands of Manitoba", 1926, page 173.

to take in Peace River, Athabasca and Prince Albert regions. This huge territory encompasses 250,000 square miles and at least twenty-five percent of those living on these lands were of Ukrainian descent. In this expansive territory were to be found three of the largest Ukrainian cultural centres, namely: Winnipeg, Saskatoon and Edmonton and these three centres, during the first and second era, played a very prominent role in cultural and political fields. On the peripheries of these big three, two others but smaller centres, Regina and Calgary, were located, with a fair number of Ukrainian settlers.

During the second era the settlements were spread to B.C. About the same time, city settlements were also growing in cities of Eastern Canada, such as Toronto, Montreal, Hamilton, Oshawa, Ottawa, Windsor, Sudbury and others. These city settlement enlargements were greatly helped by the arrival of the new immigration and the gradual flow of youth from prairie lands in their cityward moves.

This transposition and relocation of Ukrainian settlements in the second era can best be appreciated from the two statistical lists shown below. For the basis of their reliability we take the official government data which grew more accurate every year in respect of the Ukrainian settlers in Canada. Of course, the 1921 census does not clearly mirror the actual state, but for the later continuity and statistical uniformity we are inclined to lean upon the solid ground of this, and the follow-up censuses. To help us better understand the given facts concerning the national identity, we present for a more accurate orientation the language statistics as well—the nearest truth as to the number of Ukrainian settlers in Canada, covering the period between the two world wars. As shown by these language statistics, the following facts were revealed: In 1921 there were 204,000 Ukrainians living in Canada; in 1931 — 286,000, in 1941 — 322,000. These furnished language statistics will help us understand more clearly the represented charts depicting different degrees of settlement and the social structure [4].

PROVINCES

	1921 1000	%	1931 1000	%	1941 1000	%
Prairie	96.0	90.1	192.8	85.7	241.4	79.0
Alberta	38.8	22.3	55.8	24.8	71.8	23.5
Manitoba	44.1	41.4	73.6	32.7	89.8	29.4
Saskatchewan	28.1	26.4	63.4	28.2	79.8	26.1
Ontario	8.3	7.8	24.4	10.9	48.2	15.7
British Columbia	0.8	0.7	2.6	1.1	7.6	2.5
Quebec	1.2	1.1	4.3	1.9	8.0	2.6
Others	0.4	0.3	1.0	0.4	0.7	0.2
Canada	106.7	100.0	225.1	100.0	305.9	100.0
Of Canada's Total population		1.2		2.2		2.7

---

[4] We make use of the charts prepared by Prof. I. Tesla, see "Ukraine: A Concise Encyclopedia", edited by V. Kubijovych, Vol. I. University of Toronto Press, 1963.

This provincial change in settlement is shown further by a different chart which lists the settlers in units of one thousand and how these units were placed on farms and in cities. The chart shows clearly the shifting of movement of the settlers from the farm to the city.

	Cities		Farms		Together	
Years	1000	%	1000	%	1000	%
1921	21.1	19.8	85.6	80.2	106.7	100
1931	66.3	29.5	158.8	70.5	223.1	100
1941	103.5	33.9	202.4	66.1	305.9	100

When we consider the urbanization tendencies of the Ukrainian settlers it may be worth to underline another social phenomenon which must be looked for in the relationship between the city and the village, or rather between city and farm. This is the so-called rural-urban settlement which contained both, the city and country elements. Urbanized centres have come into being in the larger and more densely populated Ukrainian settlements. These were helped by the handy railroad lines and, later on, by well built highways. Beside each railroad station, elevators were built, a store or two opened for business and the inevitable restaurant-hotel establishment as a matter of course. Following these closely would be the notary public and lawyer's bureau and doctor's office. In turn, would come ministers and missionaries to carry on their religious work, and still later recreational and entertainment facilities, like cinema, theatres, billiard-rooms and others. All these together formed a singular city-like complex for the far-scattered farms from which one had to travel one or two hundred miles to reach a city. Such rural-urban centres were of immense help to the settlers on Canadian prairies in meeting social needs. The rural-urban centres were formed among Ukrainian colonies throughout the west. As example we refer to a few of them such as: Sifton, Tolstoi, Oleskiw, Gardenton, Canora, Rosthern, Mundare, Myrnam and others. Some of them even rivaled with larger organizational centres, such as—Rosthern versus Saskatoon; Sifton versus Dauphin or Vegreville versus Edmonton. The larger towns in many instances were, and still are, a good base for the future development of farm service centres. And, indeed, history does prove that centres of this type become cities in due time.

POLITICAL SITUATION IN UKRAINE AND THE INFLOW OF THE NEW IMMIGRATION

The First World War disrupted the immigration wave of the Ukrainians but with the ending of the turbulent events in Europe and Ukraine the wave was continued. However, in its social background and political atmosphere, it differed from the one prior to the First World War. Before we begin to speak precisely about the second immigration wave of Ukrainians to Canada we would need to—in a general outline, at least —say a few words about the post-war situation on Ukrainian land in Europe, which continued to be a prolific source of new immigrants to Canada.

For six full years Ukraine was the terrain for war operations. In the beginning the front battles were waged between Russia on one side and Austria and Germany on the other to see which side would have the right to control Europe. Ukrainian patriots were waiting for the moment when these two contending sides—both occupying Ukrainian lands —would weaken themselves enough for the rightful owners of their respective territories to raise their voice and take possession of their lands. Such a long-awaited moment arrived with the downfall of the Russian empire in March of 1917. A constitutional assembly gathered in Kiev which called into being the political leadership which became "the Ukrainska Centralna Rada"—Ukrainian Central Council—with Prof. Mykhaylo Hrushevsky as its head. This move called upon the Ukrainian National Congress then allocated to the Ukrainian National Council a wide-ranging authority "to take the national affairs into their own hands", and in the month of November, 1917, the Council proclaimed the Ukrainian National Republic, on ethnographic Ukrainian lands (territories). On January 22nd, 1918, the Ukrainian National Council proclaimed in Kiev the full independence for the Republic of Ukraine. Red Russia, which had strengthened its position in the north, was not at all pleased with the creation of the Ukrainian National Republic that had always, both politically and militarily, weighted the scales of its interests toward the West. The ink was barely dry on the proclamation form of the "Chetvert y Universal" (Fourth Universal) when a sudden need arose to defend the capital of Ukraine, Kiev, from the advancing Bolshevik army. The Brest-Litovsk peace treaty of February, 1918, signed by the Central Powers, Germany, Austro-Hungary, Bulgaria and Turkey, strengthened the powers of the young republic. But the new allies abused the confidence of the young partner and with the aid of military force established in Ukraine a system of government with Hetman Pavlo Skoropadsky at its head. There were great sympathies, among the village masses, toward "Hetmanism" as this was the lawful system of government in Ukraine during the cossack period of rule. The First World War, in annihilating the different monarchies also brought down the Hetmanate state. In the meantime, with the fall of Austria, Galicia and Bukovina—which had been under Austrian rule—joined to form in November 1918 the Western Ukrainian National Republic, which, in January 1919 in Kiev proclaimed the union of all Ukrainian lands as an independent state under the rule of the Ukrainian, so-called Directoria, headed by Symon Petlura. Poland, reborn during the First World War—and strengthened militarily by France—went to war with Western Ukrainian National Republic at the same time as the Red Russian army attacked Ukraine from the east. The old story was repeated. Russia and Poland "shook hands" in Riga in 1921 and parcelled out Ukrainian lands between themselves, setting up the common border at the river Zbruch, Romania, which had been helping Poland in its war with Ukraine, annexed Bukovina, while the remaining part, known in olden days as "Karpatska Rus" (Carpathian Rus) and by its modern political name of Carpatho-Ukraine, went to Czechoslovakia. Long and bitter was the battle carried on by the insurgent squads against their new invaders but all their efforts and sacrifices could not turn back the politically wrought state of affairs. Instead of two pre-First World War occupants there were now four of them. True enough, on territories under Bolshevik rule had been created "Ukrainian Socialist Soviet Republic", in union with Russian Socialist Soviet Republic, along with other "Soviet people" of Russia, that formed together the U.S.S.R.; but these were only bare state forms, without any true content. The central government in Moscow treated Ukraine as its colony. Considerably more freedom was allowed to Ukrainians living in Czechoslovakia. Unenviable were the living conditions of the half million Ukrainians living under Romanian rule and likewise of the seven million under the heel of Poland, who carried on their incessant struggle for political independence and self-rule.

On the western and eastern parts of Ukrainian territory several war fronts marched across, ruining and destroying what was still left of the accumulated prosperity of the Ukrainian people. Not only were whole villages going up in smoke but even large regions with towns and cities were being totally demolished and destroyed. Both direct and indirect war losses undermined severely the national economy. Statistics show that during the war, over twenty percent of the farm buildings were destroyed. This would mean that every fifth farmer was left without a roof over his head. Livestock, working and earning inventory, declined much more proportionally—78 percent of horses, 36 percent of cattle, 77 percent of hogs were lost, not to mention other livestock and fowl, and farm equipment. Farmers (villagers) who made up 86 percent of the population found themselves in a difficult situation.

It is worth mentioning that of quite a different category was the lot of those who found themselves living under the communist rule where national, political and social life was differently structured and where the borders were almost totally closed for any emigration. A somewhat different condition prevailed under the other three occupants—Poland, Romania and Czechoslovakia. Undoubtedly the regime in each of those three countries was much more liberal and people had a greater opportunity to emigrate. The Ukrainians were forced to emigrate by a still another set of circumstances. The Polish government took rapid steps to settle the newly parcelled-out estates with settlers from Eastern Poland whom Ukrainians called the "Mazury". With the parcellation of these large private estates there also disappeared the means of earning a livelihood by the local inhabitants. To prevent devaluation of currency the Polish government tightened the tax screw. This led to a further depletion of Ukrainian farmers' strength. Seasonal emigration in search of work to other countries of Western Europe—which in the past had been accepted as a mode of life by many Ukrainians—and which provided an extra economic lift, was now denied. Emigration to U.S.A. was closed. Only Canada and South America were left, and so quite naturally the eyes of the Ukrainians were turned in that direction. Canada proved to be more attractive not only because of its being well stabilized in the political and the governing sphere, but also because of the higher employment opportunities. Many of the would-be immigrants still retained the memories of the pre-war ten-dollar homesteads. In Canada there were already large numbers of Ukrainian population who considered Canada to be their country. Ukrainian Canadians had given a substantial material and political aid to their national homeland during its liberation struggles. Canada had also been looked upon by many of those living in Ukraine as a symbol of what a democratic country should be like. In the minds of many were the etched memories of the active part played by Canada's representatives during the Paris and Geneva Conferences, in support of Ukraine's freedom. Canada also held wide stretches of prairies to be settled by those who dreamed of coming here to live in peace after their turbulent war days. The need for the settlement of the prairies was debated and planned in the immigration bureaus of Ottawa. Desires and possibilities had to be directed into a single stream. This same question was also considered by the Ukrainian leaders in Canada and the old country. As a result of these discussions an idea was formed about the necessity of creating a social organization that would take care of immigrants' and settlers' problems.

The year of 1924 was the boundary mark in the crystallization of this idea. During this same year, in the city of Lviv, there came into being "The Ukrainian Emigrants Aid Committee" and in Winnipeg: "The St. Raphael's Ukrainian Immigrants Welfare Association of Canada was formed. It so happened that in the fall of the above mentioned year, Osyp Dyck, a lawyer—who was empowered by Canadian Government to deal with emigration and re-emigration matters—arrived in Lviv. It was not by chance that the government-entrusted envoy was a Ukrainian by birth and educated in Canada. From the correspondence that took place between the St. Raphael's Association and the Ministry of Immigration in Ottawa during Jos. Dyck's stay in Lviv—we learn that the Canadian Government was strongly interested in the renewal of Ukrainian emigration to Canada. Mykola Zayachkivsky, head of the Ukrainian Emigrants' Aid Committee, writing in his letter to Ottawa—about Jos. Dyck's stay in Lviv—has this to say:

"I am instructed by the Executive of the "Ukrainian Emigrants Aid Committee" in Lemberg, Europe, to communicate with you regarding emigration matters generally, and particularly to congratulate and thank your Department for its renewed interest in the movement of desirable settlers from our country to Canada, as shown by the arrival of Mr. Joseph Dyck as your representative to investigate and report on these matters.

We are assisting his work as far as possible, and hope that as a result of his report you will see fit to admit to your country a number of our good farmers who desire to find new homes under better conditions.

Our Committee is established for the information and assistance of Ukrainian emigrants, and has connections in all important centres among a population of over seven million people within the republic of Poland. These people, as you probably know already, are almost entirely agriculturalists, and your experience with those who have already come to Canada must have convinced you that it is their main object to own for themselves a farm home and live peacefully with their families under a stable government. Our work naturally became completely disorganized during the war, but now that it is over, especially in view of the many hardships our people have endured, and the difficult living conditions now encountered by our local farmers, the time has arrived when more of this work can be done to the great advantages of all concerned. We are therefore reorganizing our work among the Ukrainian people now in the Polish republic, and have the active support of the leaders of political and religious thought among our people" [1].

From this letter we learn that, supporting the work of the "Ukrainian Emigrants Aid Committee" were such leading authorities as the Metropolitan Andrey Shepticky from Lviv, Bishop Nykyta Budka from Canada, the head of the Founding Association of "Prosvita", Mychaylo Halushchynsky, director (manager) of the co-operative bank 'Dnister", Dr. Stephan Fedak and the director of the State Credit Union, Omelian Sayevych. In its initial piloting stage, and in its later founding and managing period, some noted individuals and leaders in public affairs of Lviv played their role. There were: Dr. Volodymyr Bachynsky, Rev. W. Tomowych, Dr. A. Howykowych, Dr. W. Decykewych, Dr. I. Krypiakewych, Dr. L. Kulchycky, Dr. I. Kurovets, Dr. M. Korduba, Dr. D. Lewycky, Dr. W. Ochrymowych, R. Sosnowsky, J. Pawlykowsky, Rev. W. Laba, Dr. S. Baran, Y. Koltuniuk, O. Pashchak, S. Magalas, S. Ferencewych and many others. The names of these leaders of the economic, political, and national life speak for themselves. They point out that an important part of Ukrainian society stood solidly behind the work of the Ukrainian Emigrants Aid Committee. True enough, there were to be heard voices of dissenters who looked upon this latest emigration policy as a betrayal of national interests for it was at this time that the ancient history of age-old struggle between Ukrainians and Poles for the ownership of Galicia, Volyn, Polisia and Pidliasia provinces was in progress. All the same, in comparing the consultations and decisions—on the part of Ukrainians—pertaining to emigration matters, in 1924, with those others taking place in 1895, under the inspiration and direction of Dr. O. Oleskiw, we then see that the almost one hundred percent agreed-on-decision of 1924 was initiated not only by the difficult material and political national conditions, but also by the great wealth of Ukrainian settlers in Canada. Having such strong moral background for their work, the initiators of the new emigration to Canada could well afford to take their time in assaying the settlers' situation for the Canadian government and be, at the same time an unconfirmed, unique partner in longer discussions that were begun, with the earlier quoted letter of Mykola Zayachkivsky, and even more accurately with Joseph Dyck's visit. As in the pioneer era so even now the need arose for

---

[1] The Hon. Minister of Immigration, Parliament Building, Ottawa, Canada, dated October 20, 1924.

financial aid to those wishing to come to Canada. About this matter we make a longer quotation from the above mentioned letter:

"We recognize fully that at this time your country requires only those who are able and willing to devote themselves to agricultural work, and on our part we intend to assist only emigrants who belong to this class. It is almost impossible, however, for these people to get permission to enter Canada, unless they already have friends or relatives there who will make the required application, guaranteeing them employment for at least a year. There are here many good agricultural workers who are able and willing to come to Canada to work on land and later take land for themselves if permission is given them to enter, and we suggest that your Department consider the possibility of finding the desired employment for them through Labor bureaus, or with the assistance of your Provincial Governments and other employment agencies. There are also here many small families with some financial resources who could be settled on land at once if properly instructed and given a reasonable amount of assistance during their first year in Canada" [2]).

These and similar problems were touched upon in the above quoted letter.

In view of the various restrictions for emigration to Canada the St. Raphael's Association had to consider other possibilities of earning a living on the part of the needy families. A separate department was formed in connection with the committee to take care of those who went to France for seasonal work and even more so of those who were going to Argentina. In the meantime, in order to find closest co-operation with Canadian government, the committee's secretary—who was also the heart and soul of all the committee's work—Dr. Volodymyr Bachynsky, went to Canada to study first hand the immigration possibilities and to discuss directly the question of new settlement work in Canada with the immigration authorities in Ottawa. He arrived in Canada in April of 1925, accompanied by Rev. J. Jean, the latter having a specially entrusted mission from Metropolitan Andrey Shepticky, to find out about the possibility of bringing some Ukrainian families living in Yugoslavia to be settled in Canada.

The journey of the new emissaries of Ukrainian emigrants to Canada took place exactly thirty years after Dr. O. Oleskiw's and I. Dorundiak's visit in Canada, when they initiated their first tour of this country on behalf of the future Ukrainian settlers. These new emissaries had a somewhat easier task to fulfill. They had Prof. I. Bobersky to greet them in Ottawa who, at that time, was the official representative in Canada of the as yet unliquidated government of Western Ukraine National Republic. The envoys, accompanied by Prof. I. Bobersky, held prolonged consultations with the deputy minister of immigration, W. J. Eggan and discussed mutually the Ukrainian emigration possibilities to Canada. Following these consultations Dr. V. Bachynsky and Rev. J. Jean made tours of Canada to see first hand amid what conditions the Ukrainian settlers were making their living and to what extent they could be helped from across the sea—from Europe. The result of this tour in June of that same year was a well prepared memorandum by Dr. V. Bachynsky,

---

[2]) Ibidem.

to the ministry of immigration in Ottawa [3]. This memorandum reminds one in some ways of Dr. O. Oleskiw's memorandum in its composition and the propositional form. But there were other new additional pages in this document, which in view of their historical value are worth our mentioning them. First of all Dr. V Bachynsky in co-operation with Ukrainian Canadians formulated or rather re-organized the St. Raphael's Association in Canada. About the similar committee in Lviv, of which Dr. V. Bachynsky was the secretary, the memorandum refers to it as "the parent society". During their travels the emissaries were able to organize branches of the St. Raphael's Association in such places, as mentioned in this memorandum: Manitoba—Sifton, Valley River, Halych, Bohdan, Gilbert Plains, Keld, Dauphin, Lemieux and Brandon; Saskatchewan—Canora, Saskatoon, Hafford and Yorkton. The greatest number of branches of this committee were organized in Alberta—probably in view of the fact that the settlement possibilities were most favorable in that province. Branches were opened in these places: Myrnam, Mundare, Rycroft, High Prairie, Angel Lake, Northern Valley, Slava, Monckman, Vegreville and Lethbridge.

Appraising the political situation on Ukrainian lands Dr. V. Bachynsky expressed, in the name of Ukrainian people, his thanks to the government of Canada, and also full acknowledgement for the government empowered representative minister, in the person of S. Doherty, for his manly stand in defending the Ukrainian cause at the international forum in Paris and Geneva. In summing up his own and Rev. J. Jean's tour of Canada Dr. V. Bachynsky wrote:

"That there is scope for the placement of a large number of Ukrainian farm labourers, on farms of their fellow nationals.

That there are opportunities for the placing of Ukrainian families, provided the conditions of entry could be modified.

That your esteemed Government should be invited to permit of the taking up of Homestead lands, when such lands are in the immediate vicinity of Canadian Ukrainian farmers, and that a certain number of Ukrainian families be admitted for this purpose.

That consideration might be given to the possibility of admitting Ukrainian settlers to take up Government lands in smaller sections of from 40 to 100 acres, thus necessitating a smaller capital requirement, but of course room should be left for expansion, which will be possible when the proceeds of the sale of the land at home is effected.

That Ukrainian farmers are the best type for Canadian conditions, as they can stand a hard winter, apply themselves to mixed farming and the rearing of stock, and do not bankrupt themselves at the commencement by requiring complicated machinery.

That a strong enough organization now exists for the care of Ukrainian immigrants to protect the interests of the Canadian Government. The European society has the ability to direct to Canada only suitable settlers and the Canadian branch has the full confidence of the Canadian Ukrainians thus ensuring the after care of the newcomers.

---

[3] The memorandum was dated June 25, 1925, and addressed to: "W. J. Eggan, Esq., Deputy Minister, Department of Immigration and Colonization, Ottawa, Ontario."

That the two organizations are now strong enough to ask the privilege of their endorsement being accepted as sufficient value to ensure the grant of letter or permit without the usual investigation.

And finally the issue of any permit is recommended, should be made much earlier, that is that a longer time be given to recruit and select the immigrants, this being especially important because of the passport formalities" [4].

Four days following the composition of the main memorandum two other memorandums were introduced by Dr. V. Bachynsky and Rev. J. Jean. One of them dealt with the miserable living conditions of Ukrainian settlers in Cuba—whose bad luck it was to fall into its orbit—with the request to allow their entrance into Canada. The second memorandum dealt with Ukrainians living in Bosnia (Yugoslavia), where Father J. Jean carried on his religious duties among some 15,000 Ukrainians living there since 1899.

In the resultant course of discussions and memoranda the representatives received a written agreement that was prepared by the ministry of immigration and signed by the deputy minister, W. J. Eggan. In this letter-agreement, dated July 2, 1925, among other things—and addressed to Dr. V. Bachynsky personally, who was then living in Montreal—was written the following evaluation of his and his colleague's work. For the benefit of our readers we make our own brief summary, from that government letter, regarding the terms under which the immigrants could come from Western Ukraine or other parts of Ukraine to Canada, preferably to Western Canada, to be settled on farms.

Strong, healthy men were wanted, with bona fide agricultural experience. Applications were to come from Canada cleared through the local Ukrainian association and central bureau in Winnipeg, guaranteeing work for the applicant as well as giving the assurance that the said applicant shall not become a burden to this country. These bona fide applications in turn were to be sent to the association's headquarters as well as to the Canadian Government's representative in the old country for processing.

It was stressed that whole families should be encouraged to come with the menfolk coming first and sending for their families later when a suitable place had been found here, and after the families had made suitable arrangements to dispose of their property in the homeland. It was also stressed that these families coming to Canada should bring with them "a substantial quota in cash" [5].

As this document so amply shows, Dr. V. Bachynsky's stay in Canada was a great success. He not only succeeded well in his dealings with ministry of immigration of Canada but he was also capable of harmonizing into co-ordination work the different elements of Ukrainian colonial leadership on Canadian soil in the sphere of organizational-immigration matters. Returning to Lviv Dr. V. Bachynsky expanded the work of the Ukrainian Emigrants Aid Committee with the added incentive that, starting with April 1927, the informative semi-monthly journal "Ukrainian Emigrant" made its appearance. At the same time the committee acquired its own bureau at 95 Horodetsky Street and opened its branches in the larger cities of Galicia, Western Ukraine—Tarnopol

---

[4] Archives of Prof. I. Bobersky, Author's Collection.
[5] Ibidem.

and Stanislaviv (now Ivan-Frankivsk). In addition to this the committee had its so-called "circles"—organizational-type cells that concerned themselves with emigrational questions. Such "circles" were in existence in Sambir, Peremyshl, Zolochiv, Chortkiv, Rohatyn and Berezany. Effective public relations work was carried on by the "Ukrainian Emigrant" which was a natural successor to the "Emigrant" [6]) an official organ of "Association of St. Raphael—for the protection of Ruthenian emigrants from Galicia and Bukovina" that was published in the years 1911 to 1914. True, in 1923 there had been another "Ukrainian Emigrant" in circulation—"a semi-monthly publication devoted to matters pertaining to Ukrainian emigration and re-emigration", and edited by Klym Polishchuk in Lviv, but this "Literary-social semi-monthly" did not function for very long. Therefore the "Ukrainian Emigrant" in its new edition was the only paper that was fully devoted to emigration. The St. Raphael's Association and the above-mentioned journal carried on their work very cautiously, advising people not to abandon their lands but if the circumstances necessitated such move then the St. Raphael's Association was the one to guide those wishing to leave on the right path. This caution on the part of the Association was necessary in view of pronounced opposition coming from some of the political ranks toward emigration in general—which had developed in due course—and also by the fact that it was difficult for Canada, on the farm-economical side to absorb all those who wished to settle on its territory. Already in 1926 about 8,000 farmers arrived without any affidavits. When it was revealed that people wanted to emigrate to Canada in large numbers (en masse), the Canadian Government made a move that would require the use of affidavits, the documental proofs, that upon immigrants's arrival in Canada he will be assured of work by some firm or taken care of by friends or relatives and not become a burden to the government.

The Ukrainian Emigrants Aid Committee of Lviv also carried on its work and made connections with other countries especially with those in South America as well as Europe, particularly France. When Dr. V. Bachynsky died in 1927, [7]) the full burden of work in this committee was heaped upon the head of the committee, Mykola Zayachkivsky, who possessed a great amount of experience from the days when he studied emigration to Brazil in 1911. His close co-workers were H. Rohozhynsky and Dr. A. Howykowych, who at the same time were responsible for publishing "Ukrainian Emigrant".

The Ukrainian Emigrants Aid Committee of Lviv enjoyed great respect in government circles and was an approved member of Conference Internationale des Organizations pour la protection des Migrants.

But the greatest co-operative work by the committee was carried on with its similar sister committee in Canada, the St. Raphael's Ukrainian Immigrants Welfare Association of Canada, at whose premises was also housed the separate reference department dealing with old country affairs under the direction of Prof. I. Bobersky in its earlier days, and later, from 1933, under Kornylo Prodan's direction.

---

[6]) The monthly magazine "Emigrant" was published by Rev. Nykyta Budka who later became the Ukrainian Bishop of Canada. Rev. M. Shchepaniuk took over the editorship from Rev. Budka.

[7]) Dr. V. Bachynsky died tragically in 1927.

ST. RAPHAEL'S UKRAINIAN IMMIGRANTS WELFARE ASSOCIATION OF CANADA

The question of organizing a Ukrainian Immigrants Aid Committee to look after the settlers that came to Canada after the First World War was brought to public attention by Bishop N. Budka who while still living in Lviv before the war, organized in 1907 the Austrian branch of the "Association of St. Raphael for the protection of Ruthenian Emigrants from Galicia and Bukovina". While still a priest Rev. N. Budka worked for five years in this organization and could see clearly the needs of emigrants and immigrants. Basing his observation on actual practice in connection with the existing pre-war St. Raphael's Association, the prelate, beginning in 1924, organized the association to which also belonged in addition to Ukrainian members, French and English representatives. This association proved itself to be unsuitable for every-day living because of the conflicting cross-currents of various national interests. The idea that only Ukrainian immigrants finally triumphed and took root in the convictions of the church and community leaders.

In 1924, two educational-farmers' conventions were held; the first on the 18th of November in Saskatoon and the other on 9th to 11th of December in Winnipeg in the newly built Prosvita hall. At both these conventions a resolution was passed and accepted about the need of founding the St. Raphael's Ukrainian Immigrants Welfare Association of Canada. At both these meetings it was also resolved that this association should be of a charitable nature and its duty would be to have a working understanding with a responsible association in Europe to give protection and aid to those would-be Ukrainian immigrants who wish to come or have already come to Canada both during their departure, arrival, and final settlement in Canada [1].

At the Winnipeg convention, an initiative committee was chosen whose duty it was to organize the proposed association. This committee was composed of: K. S. Prodan, D. M. Elcheshen and A. Zaharychuk. In less than a month later, on the 4th of January 1925, the first meeting of the planned organization was held. Although St. Raphael's Association was originally initiated by Catholic circles it had full support from different religious adherents. Its first chairman was Rev. Prof. Eugene Turula who later relinquished his post in favor of Stepan Sawula, a lawyer who in turn was succeeded by Kornylo Prodan. The latter remained as chairman of this institution for fifteen years—that is, for the remainder of its existence. A secretary of many years service in this association was Dmytro Elcheshen who for over ten years was the soul of this immigration. Around this organization were grouped the leading community-minded notables such as Prof. V. Biberovych, Dr. M. Mihaychuk, Rev. M. Hryhoriychuk, I. Zarovsky and Prof. I. Bobersky and later on—Rev. P.

---

[1] The Association was incorporated Sept. 23, 1925, Dept. Registrar General of Canada, Lib. 260, Fol. 550, under the name of "St. Raphael's Ukrainian Immigrants Welfare Association of Canada".

Bozyk, V. H. Koman, E. Wasylyshyn, W. Dyky, H. Juba, T. Melnychuk, M. Koreska, I. Rudachek, J. Pecheniuk, Rev. A. Luhowy and others.

The St. Raphael's Association began its work without any material funds [2]). All they had at their disposal was the good will and word of sound advice which proved to be the grandest capital of this institution during the long years of its existence. The bureau of the association which was housed in the Confederation Life Building soon became a post office clearing house for temporary contacts of separated families, friends and acquaintances not only in Canada but in all the other countries throughout the world. Many immigrants were constantly on the move in search of relative or work. The war separated thousands of families. Just how wide-spread were these lost and separated souls may be gauged by the fact that the association had to employ an extra secretary-referee to take care of this pressing matter.

The archives of this organization reveal that it had a lot to worry about. It received a continuous stream of appeals from those eager to emigrate not only from Galicia, Volyn and Polisia—the territories under Polish rule—but also from Bukovina and Carpatho-Ukraine.

The Welfare Association's call was also answered by Ukrainian political emigration that was, at that time, scattered throughout the different countries of the world. A spokesman for such emigrants in Paris who was dealing with the Association was one Colonel Fylypowych, according to the correspondence that took place between the Association and the General Emigration Council in Paris. From Prague over 1,500 expressed their wish to emigrate; from Podiebrady about 600 and around 400 from Brno. Letters came from Germany, Bulgaria, Ro mania and Yugoslavia. Ukrainian political emigration endeavored to get out of Europe and find a steady habitation in countries overseas, many of whom had fond dreams about Canada. Among the emigrants were those who held the so-called Nansen passports that were issued by international agencies but of those last few who lacked such passports were the Ukrainians from Western Ukraine lands assigned to Poland. But the lack of these passports was not the only bar to emigration. There were financial problems as well—how to pay for transportation. All those with their particular troubles turned for advice to the Association which found itself in a difficult situation. This called for wise counsel and realistic plans.

These matters were not easy to deal with. Canada was admitting, first of all, agricultural workers and relatives of those at work in Canada. Permits and affidavits were a "must". The Association expanded its work among Ukrainian farmers, requesting them to help their brethren in moving to, and settling in, Canada. To be sure, not all of people's needs were processed through the association but the positive action employed by the association in regard to immigration matters achieved splendid results not only in immigrational but also in psychological spheres. Between the settlers in Canada and political emigrants a continuous emotional contact was being evolved. It became a natural patriotic duty of every farmer to aid in bringing over his own countryman from

---

[2]) From the archives of Welfare Association.

across the ocean and giving him work. Although the association was organized solely for giving aid to Ukrainians, it did not refuse to help anybody who asked for its assistance. There are interesting notations recorded on files regarding such matters. In one of these we read: "Two Slovaks ask to find them work. Give them your help" writes Prof. I. Bobersky.—"I know it lies in the best interest of all of us in that line." When the author of the above quoted memo made his tour of Europe he found that in addition to Ukrainian emigrants who wished to come to Canada there were other nationals as well wanting to make this move and so he wrote a separate letter to the association in which we read: "Bulgarians, Serbians and Czechs take very friendly attitude towards our immigrants and it would appear that we Ukrainians in Canada should come to their aid in this way—that we can help their emigrants to come to Canada by providing them with applications from our farmers" [3]. The atmosphere of mutual aid was strongly in evidence among the new and the old settlers.

In reminiscing about the emigration from Europe we cannot leave unrecorded the help that was provided by the St. Raphael's Association to the Ukrainians from South America, especially those from Parana, Brazil and Cuba. The association also made efforts to help even those whom the war's turbulence carried to China and the Far East.

To fulfill even the minimum requirements of the charter and to satisfy all the crying needs of the times called for almost super-human strength. In addition to the concerted work with farmers and whole colonies among whom 23 committees and 88 intermediaries were active, the association also made efforts to acquire tracts of land in British Columbia and Quebec to open up new group settlements. The work in Quebec was progressing successfully under the guidance of Rev. J. Jean, who had special authorization and recommendation from Metropolitan A. Shepticky and the Abbot of the Studite Order, K. Shepticky.

In 1926 Father J. Jean set up in Landrien, Quebec, a settler's committee to which, in addition to the organizer himself, belonged the local priest, Father M. Chappleau and M. R. Lambert. Father J. Jean obtained 300 square miles of land in the vicinity of Abitibi for a settlement. The plans were made for the establishment of a colony and the building of a monastery which were to serve the needs primarily of those who were to come from Bosnia. The actual start was made and even a few families were brought and settled on land, each family receiving 100 acres apiece, putting down ten dollars as the first payment and the rest to be paid up in the consecutive six years at the rate of ten dollars per year. In these regions were deposits of gold, silver and copper and the outlook was favorable for the settlers to make good on wage earnings. Before any of these proposed plans could be formalized an economic crisis hit Canada and along with it came even harsher restrictions on immigration, and what is more, a deportation order was issued to many of those who were without work or funds. In all such cases the St. Raphael's Association came speedily with its aid.

In addition to contacts and counsels the Association put into the press

---

[3] Archives of St. Raphael's Ukrainian Immigrants Welfare Association of Canada.

various informative articles dealing with immigration and during its existence published some ten almanac-calendars which were full of valuable material and statistics in regard to the past history of Ukrainians in Canada. Editors of these information-packed journals were: Prof. I. Bobersky, Father P. Bozyk and D. M. Elcheshen [4].

The St. Raphael's Association made every effort to work hand in hand with the entire Ukrainian community in Canada and with the representatives of its maternal organization in Lviv. Not always did the succeed for there were often political and sometimes religious differences and other drawbacks. When we take into consideration the railway companies, the association worked closest with the Canadian National Railway, although regular contacts were also kept with the Canadian Pacific Railway and Steamship lines. The question of this co-operation was very important because the railway companies had authority from the government to deal with immigration matters, including the disposition of immigrants to various settlements. There were cases on record where C.N.R. placed the settlers on poor lands in such districts as Sifton, Pine River, Slater and others in Manitoba and C.P.R. did likewise in other places. Intervention was in order along with information about the good quality of soil and where it could be found.

The work of St. Raphael's Association may be divided into two stages with the dividing line between these two periods being dictated by the economic situation in Canada. To be more precise the year, 1930 was known as the year of severe economic crisis and a sharp restriction of immigration. Any possibilities of expanded immigration in that first period slid almost down to zero in the second period. It was during this time that the Association turned its attention to the cultural field and later on to ideological and political matters. By then the scope of the association's activities began to be limited. Its closest co-operation at that time was with the organization known as Kanadiyska Sitch (Canadian Seech). One of the more commendable initiative deeds was the founding of Canadian Library of Ivan Bobersky, and shortened to, "Canadiana", whose objective was: "To collect, continuously, proofs and reports about ideas, thoughts, and works of Canadians of Ukrainian descent, in order to preserve the memory of their past and give a set direction for the work in the future" [5]. The said library soon became a veritable Ukrainian Canadian documentary centre in which were collected thousands of valuable exhibits, but during the Second World War, due to various moving changes a considerable number of them were destroyed, resulting in a regrettable loss to the Canadian community. The library listed several thousands of unique documents, over 6000 pictures and sketches, over 4000 slides and around one hundred newspaper annuals and others. All these and more were given to the library by Prof. I. Bobersky who was the first Ukrainian in Canada to study assiduously the part played by Ukrainians in the development of this country.

---

[4] The association published such almanacs as: 1927, Nove Pole (New Field); 1928, Preria (Prairie); 1929, Klenovy Lystok (Maple Leaf); 1930, Farma. From 1931 to 1936 inclusive, they published each year a "Calendar of Canadian Ukrainians" (The Providnyk—Leader).

[5] Basic Documents of the founding of Canadian Library of Ivan Bobersky, dated April 6, 1932. Copy in the archives of I. Bobersky.

UKRAINIAN IMMIGRATION AND COLONIZATION BUREAU, AND OTHER IMMIGRATION FOUNDATIONS

The "St. Raphael's Ukrainian Immigrant Welfare Association of Canada" that we spoke about in our previous chapter was not the only institution that engaged in dealing with immigration matters among Ukrainians between the two wars. As far back as December 1923, during the session of the First Educational-Economic Congress of Ukrainians in Canada, the following resolution was announced:

"The future of Canada depends upon the amount of immigration composed of agricultural element. In view of this the First Ukrainian Educational-Economic Congress decided to appoint, and forthwith appoints, an immigrational committee to aid the government or any other organization in bringing Ukrainian settlers from Europe *).

In the outcome of these consultations and discussions about immigration of the above mentioned Congress, a committee was called into being whose duty it was to formulate plans in advancing further immigration matters. This committee consisted of some of the most prominent men in national life from different parts of Canada, including: Mychaylo Stechishin—who later became a judge in Saskatchewan—M. Hryhorczuk, MLA, N. V. Bachynsky, MLA, editor O. Hykawy, Rev. S. W. Sawchuk, editor Z. Bychynsky, M. Luchkowich—who became M.P. later—A. Wawryniuk, a lawyer, W. Swystun, a lawyer, the former M.L.A. — T. D. Ferley, editor T. Tomashevsky and I. Humeniuk. Some time later this committee, under the chairmanship of N. V. Bachynsky and T. D. Ferley, brought into existence the "Ukrainian Immigration and Colonization Bureau". One of the drawbacks of this bureau was the fact that its executive members were scattered all over Canada and also because the bureau from its beginning, co-operated with only one railroad company, namely the C.P.R. It lasted for a while and later liquidated itself and some of its members joined the "Ukrainian Settlers Aid Association". In this enterprise worked such immigration experts as H. Kurdydyk, I. Rudachek, V. Biberovych, T. Dackiw, Rev. N. Bartman and P. Gigeychuk. The enterprise which was at the same time used as an advisory bureau for C.P.R. had the lawyer W. Baleshta in charge. A similar bureau existed in Edmonton under the name of "Ukrainian Immigration and Colonization Bureau" and its executives were Y. Kuzyk, Y. Bohonis, Y. Hawrylak, A. Kuprovsky, W. Pylypivsky, M. Korchynsky and I. Ruryk. One of the more talented organizers of immigration matters was Ivan Ruryk, who later founded the "Ukrainian Colonization Bureau" in Saskatoon and who was for a while, responsible for immigration and colonization affairs with the C.P.R. company in the provinces of Saskatchewan and Manitoba. It should be mentioned that during this time there was also in existence in Edmonton a branch of the St. Raphael's Association of which the following were in charge: I. Pasnak, I. Isaiw, I. Basarab, Father S. Dydyk and Father U. Zydan.

---

*) "Memorial Book" of Ukrainian National Home, Winnipeg, page 171.

Although the interests of colonization bureaus under the patronage of C.P.R., and the St. Raphael's Association which stood closer to C.N.R. were at times somewhat at loggerheads, still, in the actual field of work, there did exist quite often on the part of these two bureaus a close co-operation. This was true especially during such times as when the representatives of both these bureaus returned from their visits to the old country and considered it to be a fit occasion to share their newly acquired information with all those who were interested in the immigration problems of their people. The list of those who travelled to Lviv in Europe in the interest of immigration includes such well known public figures as: W. Baleshta, I. Rudachek, I. Bobersky, K. S. Prodan, V. Biberovych and others. In turn, from Europe came in addition to the previously mentioned Dr. V. Bachynsky and Father J. Jean also Mychalyna Hovykovycheva, Dr. M. Konstantynovych and others.

TO THE CHARACTERISTICS OF SECOND IMMIGRATION

The arrival of the new immigration to Canada in the second era differed greatly from the arrival of the pioneer-immigrants of the first era. First of all it took place in an atmosphere of organized life and had moral, and in many cases, material help. The material aid was received by these immigrants from local inhabitants in places where they were being settled, which was usually near the pioneer communities. Homogeneous character of the immigrants had its own reward. The newly arrived settlers to Canada found themselves more like visiting guests. In addition to the Ukrainian officials connected with CPR and CNR, there was the St. Raphael's Association and other organizations to give advice and moral aid. In the port cities of Quebec, Halifax and Montreal the immigrants were greeted by the representatives of parishes and other organizations. The mere knowledge of the fact that the immigrant could count on finding—in this new promised land—his own well-organized countrymen, gave him a certain sense of security. The settlers' agencies drew attention to the wise scheme of having the immigrants come in family groups, which proved to be the best stabilizing element in every settlement. The immigrant who left his family beyond the seas remained undecided for a long time as to what he should do and thus, living in this disorganized family atmosphere, he was not able to enter into the scheme of things nor to make any plans for the future. The settled family group was able, from the very beginning, and for the time being, to lead a self-sufficient social and economic life. When we take into account that in the traditional Ukrainian family every member—father, mother and children—was usefully employed, there was no wonder then that such families were encouraged and welcomed to come to Canada. Many families had the rare opportunity after not seeing each other for many years to be finally reunited. These family re-unions had a great moral influence on the lives of the settlers and the total community.

Although the Canadian government continued to stress the accent on its requirement of agricultural settlers, still the immigration interests did not interpret this government wish too literally and so we have, during this second era of immigration, a marked percentage of intelligentsia and professionals who—having put in the required time as farm workers—settled down in the cities and there opened up their business or professional establishments and in this way they strengthened the Ukrainian element and influence in the cities. As was stated earlier, during this second phase of immigration many veterans of the Ukrainian liberation wars came to Canada from Europe. These had in their hearts, a great love for the land of their fathers and a deep respect for the principles of freedom. These in turn strengthened the morale of the new community —both in respect to the individual and the collective concept of freedom —and thus were formed the first connecting bridges leading toward the national and cultural integration in the new country.

The World War and national revolution of the Ukrainian people gave birth to a new human being endowed with dignity and higher consciousness. The new immigrant showed a higher degree of progress with more general knowledge and with greater immunity to the surrounding world around him. This enabled him to find more convenient roads to integration and to the conquest of the new world.

One other characteristic adjunct could be traced to the new immigrants: materially they were much better off situated than their predecessors. They were better endowed financially—having received aid from co-operative institutions and the so-called land-banks. The financial security enabled them to settle themselves more comfortably, acquire better land or set up their workshops or places of business. Of course this was not the general rule as there were many among the new settlers who had only bare hands and an iron will to work with in order to earn and win a better tomorrow.

The new immigration not only settled in the prairie provinces among which Alberta and Saskatchewan were first, with the result that in these two provinces the Ukrainian population almost doubled itself between the two war periods. The new immigrants also took to settling in British Columbia and Ontario. Ukrainian population, in the last mentioned province, tripled itself during the twenties—from 8,000 in 1921 to 24,000 in 1931. What percentage of this could be claimed by the new immigrants and what could be attributed to those who came from other provinces is hard to determine. Taking into consideration the educational-cultural life in Eastern Canada during the second era, we could make certain conclusions that the new immigrants outnumbered the settlers from the Western provinces by a ratio of four to one. Already in the first year after the war a mass immigration from Europe to Canada took place, that is, in 1926 about 10,000 Ukrainians arrived in Canada [1]. The general summation is that during the nineteen twenties, 49,000 Ukrainians came to Canada. The world's economic crisis that was triggered by the New York stock-market crash on that memorable black Friday, in the fall of 1929 froze up the fresh new stream of Ukrainian immigration to Canada. In accordance with government statistics for the years 1924-1934, some 59,895 Ukrainian immigrants came to Canada. All in all, even during the thirties, when the influx of Ukrainian immigration is compared with the wide stream of other immigrating nationals from Europe, the Ukrainians still represented an imposing figure on the immigration balance sheet of those years.

Generally speaking, we could state that during the second era, that is between the two World Wars, over 70,000 Ukrainians came to Canada. The majority of them came from western Ukrainian lands as was the case during the pioneer era. Not all of the above given number remained in Canada. A certain number of these immigrants re-emigrated again, as the so-called "dirty thirties" years in Canada's history did not provide them with any hope for a quick improvement in the economic sphere. Those who left Canada first were the seasonal workers who during the twenties had settled down for a steady living in Canada. A different story can be told about those who came toward the end of the twenties. During the thirties there too was a forced re-emigration. Something like 15,368 persons, of various nationalities, were deported from Canada

---

[1] Ukrainian Emigrant, No. 3, 1927.

during the thirty months—from 1930 to 1932 [2]). Over 60 percent of them were deported for constituting a burden to the state for they were not able to find work. What percentage of this amount was represented by Ukrainians is hard to say. The serious economic situation of the thirties period not only was oppressive to the new immigrant, but also reflected itself as being equally oppressive to those who lived in Canada over a long period of years.

When we evaluate the inflow and the outflow of Ukrainian immigrants and re-emigrants to Canada and from Canada, we could then with certainty accept the fact that between the two World Wars about 70,000 Ukrainians came to settle down permanently in Canada.

Ukrainians in Canada entered into the new mid-wars period with a conspicuous educational-cultural achievement and a whole string of local and provincial organizations. What is more, great steps had been taken to go beyond the provincial boundaries as was evidenced by the dominion-wide build-up of religious and organizational life. Two separate churches had their own organizations of dominion standing—the Ruthenian Greek-Catholic Church had its own bishop, while the Ukrainian Greek-Orthodox Church was represented by a consistorium, headed by an administrator and a bishop. The Protestant churches worked in cooperation with the same existing Canadian organizations. In schools and universities, with each passing year, more and more students were finishing their courses. Clearly for all to see a new level of Ukrainian Canadian intelligentsia was being formed. In cities a greater amount of the Ukrainian element was grouping itself and reaching out for trading and commercial enterprises. Both the World War and their own wars of liberation gave Ukrainians a great amount of political experience. In general terms these were prime positives in the achievement field of Ukrainians in Canada. But there were negatives to contend with as well. These grew first of all out of heated passions engendered by religious strife that fanned themselves out between the two traditional Ukrainian churches, the Catholic and the Orthodox, at the end of the pioneer era. Also in the organizational life of Ukrainians in Canada there were felt some elements of political struggle that very often had their roots growing out of the differences of opinions held by the various groups in Ukraine, and who came to live in Canada following their unsuccessful attempts to gain freedom for their homeland. Those last mentioned cast a strong reflection on the life of the Ukrainian community of the mid-wars period.

However, the balance of values was incomparably much heavier on the plus side, as may be proved so convincingly by the historically depicted development of Ukrainian community life. In every instance it was shown that the new immigration spread its influence far and wide and that it gradually projected itself onto the screen of organized activities and adapted itself fully to the ways of Canadian community life.

---

[2]) *Winnipeg Tribune*, Dec. 13, 1932.

AID TO THE HOMELAND
UNITES UKRAINIANS RELIGIOUSLY AND POLITICALLY

As we already know, at the end of the First World War, two dominion-wide organizations were hard at work in bringing aid to the Ukrainian struggle for freedom in Europe. These were the Ukrainian Canadian Citizens' Committee and the Ukrainian National Council. The Committee collaborated closely with the newly founded Orthodox Church and with the Protestant adherents. The Council was under the influence of the Greek-Catholic Church. In this work, whose aim had the same objective, much energy was wasted on mutual polemics and negative criticisms. Sometimes it was difficult to pierce through the mist of polemical articles and editorials to see the basic aims and final objectives of the above mentioned organizations, but in spite of these verbal wranglings they still received full measure of support from the Ukrainian community in Canada. This state of affairs lasted for two full years.

At the end of 1920, in the month of November, Prof. Ivan Bobersky —a leading public figure from Western Ukraine, and a noted pedagogue and organizer of Sokil groups—arrived in Canada. He came to this country as plenipotentiary of the Western Ukraine (Galicia) National Republic. His first task was not only to request the Canadian Government for the recognition of the legal right of action on the part of the Western Ukraine National Republic, for political endeavours and self-rule by Ukrainian people on their own territory, but also to obtain from the Ukrainians in Canada material aid for these struggles and especially for the Ukrainian Red Cross. True enough, even before Prof. I. Bobersky's coming to Canada there had been in existence a Ukrainian Red Cross but it, too, had its own peculiar double-deal because at this time the Ukrainian Red Cross (URC) worked very closely with (UCCC) Ukrainian Canadian Citizens' Committee known also as Ukrainian Canadian Citizens' League. Prof. I. Bobersky who had good contacts with both these organizations—the UCCC and UNC—was able to arrange the matters so that in a short while the Executive of the Red Cross was formed and named as the Central Committee. This re-organization took place in January, 1921. The Executive consisted of 15 members, who were elected during the National Convention at Winnipeg in 1920, at which time Prof. I. Bobersky made his first appearance, and also of the 15 members, delegated from UNC. To this group of 30 members were added an additional 2 members from each of the 30 Ukrainian organizations then in existence in Winnipeg. This meant that the Central Committee had an executive consisting of 120 members. The five member presidium of this committee composed of A. Yonker, J. A. Arsenych, Rev. P. Oleksiw, S. Kovbel and N. V. Bachynsky ruled on all current affairs connected with the work of URC. Members of the Executive were also chosen from leading figures of other nationalities. such as Dr. Henry Yonker, Dr. M. Blake and from the Ukrainian side such figures as Dr. Hryhory Novak and M. Yacyk. The controlling committee consisted of T. Jastremsky, O. Babinec, S. Fodchuk, O. Boyanivsky, O. Bohonos and P. Barycky. The formation of the Central

Committee led to a gradual liquidation of the two other mentioned representative bodies—the UCCC and UNC. The Central Committee worked with redoubled energy and in two years raised over $50,000 for the URC. The whole of Canada was divided into 36 districts, each one having its own separate command, but responsible to the Central Committee. It is interesting to note that every district had its own special Ukrainian historical name as for instance: Winnipeg—Taras Shevchenko; Edmonton—Wolodymyr the Great; Toronto—Oleksa Dovbush; Quebec—Peremyshl; Fort William—Maksym Zalizniak; British Columbia—Ivan Gonta; Nova Scotia—Zaporozhe; Prince Edward Island—Khortytsia, etc.

The Central Committee also publicized a protesting action on behalf of justice for the Ukrainian nation, registering its strongest protest against the terroristic politics of Polish government on western Ukrainian territory. Such demonstrations were started by Edmonton in 1921, to become an accomplished fact in Winnipeg where, on the 22nd of April, 1922, around 10,000 citizens took part in a massive manifestation. The march stretching for over two miles was punctuated by such distinguished persons as Charles W. Gordon, Dr. A. J. Hunter, Capt. Geo. Wilton, Pastor G. Shaver, W. R. Wood, Prof. I. Bobersky, J. Arsenych and others, who by their presence drew public attention to Ukrainian demands. This was by far the largest manifestation of Ukrainians in Canada up till that time. This revealed the organized strength of Ukrainian community. At more or less the same time a delegation of leading Ukrainians—A. S. Shandro, Edmonton, the first Ukrainian MLA in Canada; Dr. A. T. Kibzey and M. Sytnyk, Montreal, and Dr. M. Mihaychuk and others, called upon Dominion government in Ottawa. Prime Minister McKenzie King expressed his sympathies for the Ukrainian demands.

The successful Ukrainian manifestations throughout Canada and the sympathetic response of the Canadian Government reinforced the general desire to have a single representative body that would speak on behalf of all Ukrainians. Following this line of thought the Central Committee, on May 7, 1922, called into being, a national convention at which all the organizers of the various manifestations were able to present some truly impressive reports. Those present expressed their complete faith in the work of the Central Committee of the URC and renamed it the "Ukrainian Central Committee" (UCC) with powers to represent all Ukrainians living in Canada. To the Ukrainian Central Committee belonged in addition to the elected members such members as held titles in their professions, which took in—by a popular approval—all priests, ministers and editors of national newspapers. The UCC was headed by—T. D. Ferley, J. W. Arsenych, I. Slusar, M. Zalozecky, P. Dral, M. Turchyn and I. Punak.

At the same time and connected with UCC The Ukrainian Press Bureau of Canada was formed. A separate committee was at work compiling a statute which would enable the formation of a single, binding and all-enfolding organization that could stand guard and protect all those interests that are "dear and common to all Ukrainians" [1]. In accordance with the planned statute every district in Canada formulated a local committee and all these local committees were to work according

---

[1] Ukrainian Voice, No. 35, Aug. 30, 1922.

to the instructions given by Ukrainian Central Committee. The UCC was empowered to call upon all Canadians to attend the gathering of national councils, popularly known as "soyms".

Perhaps it was under the influence of the prevalent idea that was being echoed from sea to sea—the need for concentrated efforts to bring about the union of the drama and singing leagues with Ukrainian National Home. Three organizations, viz. Association Boyan, Association M. Zankovetska and Association I. Kotlarevsky that had behind them a long record of stage performances—as every one of them had presented, both in Winnipeg and surrounding districts, numerous theatrical plays—decided to join their forces into one theatrical organization and work in unison for the good of Ukrainian stage art. Their theatrical libraries provided a start for a large joint-library in connection with the Ukrainian National Home in Winnipeg which became in a short while not only one of the largest private libraries in the city but in the whole of Canada as well. With these united groups, of gifted artistic talents, major theatrical performances were an every-day occurrence—including operettas and operas. Even more was expected both on the part of the spectators and the players. On the heel of these concentrations of forces came certain disadvantages as well. First of all was the absence of competition—as there was no one left to compete with. Then again quantity was not a valid substitute for quality.

Along the line of this same union of forces and ideas went the preparation for the "First Educational-Economic Congress of Ukrainians in Canada." The initial move for the preparation, and the holding of this Congress, came from the Ukrainian National Home in Winnipeg. The Congress was held in the middle of December 1923 and for a three-day period dealt with such diverse matters as: the future of the young Ukrainian generation in Canada; the aim and task of national schools and bursas; professional training for youth; obligations of National Homes, Chytalnia Prosvita , amateur theatre groups and social clubs; the organization of farmers for "higher economic standard and the increase in the knowledge of farming in its practical adaptation"; the question of trade and commerce and fuller participation of Ukrainians in the life of Canada. There was also talk about organizing aid associations and the need of women's organizations. Many of these had been discussed at other conferences or gatherings of Ukrainian Canadians but these had been primarily of a provincial scope. At the First Educational-Economic Congress these same problems were dealt with on the dominion-wide basis.

In addition to the resolutions that were approved at this Congress a separate resolution was passed which stated that the First Congress brings into existence "a representative body of the Ukrainian people living in Canada to be known as: Ukrainian Central Committee". The committee was to be composed of heads and secretaries of the various Ukrainian national organizations at work in educational, youth training, charitable, benefit-aid and economic fields. Why did this Congress bring out a different resolution, about the formation of Ukrainian Central Committe, than the one that was passed in 1922 is hard to say. What is more, the Congress gave full power to the Ukrainian National Home

SECOND ERA — ILLUSTRATIONS

Appeal of the Ukrainian Red Cross Society in Canada to aid the thousands of flood victims in Western Ukraine.

Osyp Nazaruk

Ivan Bobersky

Representatives of the Western Ukrainian National Republic for Canada.

378 UKRAINIAN CANADIANS: A HISTORY

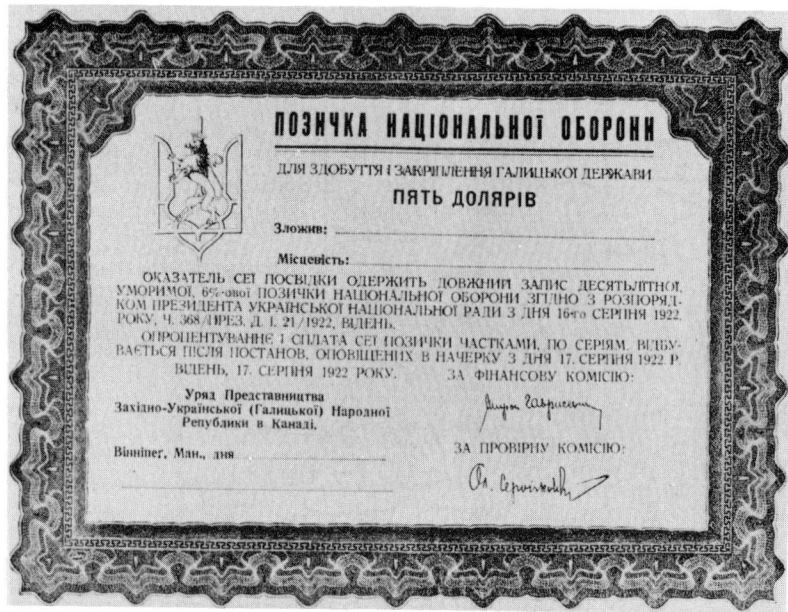

Facsimile of the documents on National Loan, issued by the government of the Western Ukrainian National Republic.

SECOND ERA — ILLUSTRATIONS 379

Metropolitan A. Shepticky in Sandy Lake, Man., 1921. Above a richly worded sign: "Welcome Prince of the Church, Father, Leader and Defender of the Faith and Freedom of the Ukrainian People".

Metropolitan A. Shepticky with clergy paying a visit to Sister Servants. Winnipeg, 1921.

380 UKRAINIAN CANADIANS: A HISTORY

Mykola Zayachkivsky, Lviv,
President of the Ukrainian Emigration Welfare
Association.

Planning immigration of Ukrainians to Canada: Rev. J. Jean, OSBM
(Yugoslavia), I. Bobersky (Canada), Dr. V. Bachynsky (Lviv), 1926.

SECOND ERA — ILLUSTRATIONS 381

The first Executive Committee of the St. Raphael's Ukrainian Immigration Association of Canada, Winnipeg, 1924.

Dr. V. Bachynsky, guest of the St. Raphael's Ukrainian Immigration Welfare Association of Canada. Sitting (from l. to. r.): D. M. Elcheshen, Rev. M. Hryhoriychuk, Dr. V. Bachynsky, St. Sawala, Dr. M. M:haychuk, M. Koreska. Standing: A. Zaharychuk, K. S. Prodan, V. Biberovych, Rev. P. Oleksiw, I. Zarowsky, I. Bobersky.

**Alexander Koshetz (1926),
composer and conductor.**

**Eugene Turula (1928),
composer-conductor.**

**Vasile (Vasyl) Avramenko (1928),
balletmaster.**

SECOND ERA — ILLUSTRATIONS 383

Vasile Avramenko's first School of Ukrainian National Dances, Toronto, 1926.

The Ukrainian National Chorus with conductor Prof. Alexander Koshetz, known throughout Europe as "The Human Symphony Orchestra".

Choir and Symphony Orchestra "Ukraine", affiliated with Institute "Prosvita", conductor E. Turula, Winnipeg, 1925.

Choir of the Ukrainian National Home, Winnipeg, 1927, conductor E. Turula.

Choir "Boyan" of the Ukrainian National Home in Edmonton, G. Cukornyk, conductor.

Choir of the M. Drahomaniv Association, Montreal, 1922, I. Vypruk, conductor.

"Samopomich" Association, Montreal, 1927.

Mandolin Orchestra of the Ukrainian Labour Temple, conducted by P. Uhryniuk, Winnipeg, 1926.

SECOND ERA — ILLUSTRATIONS 387

Mandolin Orchestra of the Ukrainian National Home, Winnipeg, V. Parasiuk, conductor, 1927.

Ukrainian Sports Organization "Sitch", Montreal, 1925.

Ballet School of Ukrainian National Dances, conducted by Michael and Alexander Darkovych, Dauphin, Man., 1928.

"Evening of the Meadow" — Dancers of the Ukrainian National Home in Toronto with their instructor I. Levko.

SECOND ERA — ILLUSTRATIONS 389

Ukrainian Community in Regina commemorating "The First Lystopad", 1929.

"Boyan" Choral Society, Winnipeg, 1930. In the middle H. Block, president (left) and M. Pasichniak, choirmaster.

Ukrainian Students Association of A. Kocko, affiliated with M. Hrushevsky Institute in Edmonton, 1921.

Metropolitan A. Shepticky Bursa in St. Boniface, Man. In the first row in the middle M. Boychuk, rector, and his wife Maria.

SECOND ERA — ILLUSTRATIONS

Ukrainian Students Association in Winnipeg, 1927, organized in 1916. In the front (l.—r.): E. Kanchir, M. Batenchuk, N. Budnyk; first row (sitting): M. Zalozetsky, H. Hawryluk, W. Yaremiy, N. Bunka, I. R. Kovalevich, L. Taciuk, I. Ovshanek.

Ukrainian Students Association of M. Shashkevych in Edmonton, 1932.

Delegates of Ukrainian Women Organizations with Senator Olena Kysilewska (first row, fifth from the left), Winnipeg, 1929.

Pedagogical course of Ukrainian teachers in 1924, Winnipeg. First row (l.—r.): J. H. Syrnick, P. Humeniuk, N. Bilash, A. Mykutiuk, I. Bobersky, M. Mihaychuk.

in Winnipeg to convene this very same committee. The last resolution of the Congress was also the least successful, for it crossed out all the previously approved resolutions, thereby bringing dissention and disorganization into the very existence of the Ukrainian Central Committee. The second anomaly of the Congress was the total absence of Catholic priests and laymen. All this taken together showed very clearly that the three year period in the co-operation of Ukrainian organizations in Canada with U.C.C. under the fold of Ukrainian Red Cross ended in disunity that lasted for many years.

The natural reaction to the First Educational-Economic Congress was the holding in the following year of two educational-farmer conventions under the sponsorship of the Ukrainian Catholics with Bishop N. Budka, in charge. These conventions, with their limited scope in reaching the many problems, were reminiscent of the previously mentioned Educational-Economic Congress. The shortcomings of these conventions lay in the fact that the Greek Orthodox wing was missing.

But although between these two main streams representing the faithful of the two dominant Ukrainian churches, Catholic and Orthodox, were revealed further differences and disagreements, still these were not serious enough to prevent marked progress of the uniting process that was by now dominion-wide—this time not along the line of exclusive national association but along a different line that took into consideration the national-religious and national-political affiliations. In other words, religious and ideological-political affiliations were the deciding factors that gave the dominant tone to the community work in the second era. If we should try to analyze this further it would then be revealed that religious dissentions were typical to the pioneer immigration. Ideological-political disagreements were brought in by the immigration of the second era and are, perhaps, the natural result of the unsuccessful efforts to gain national freedom in Europe—and along this line flowed the stream which helped to integrate and differentiate Ukrainian life in the midwars period in Canada.

CANADIAN SITCH ORGANIZATION

Canadian Sitch Organization came into being in Toronto on May 25, 1924. On that day the Convention of the Ukrainians of Eastern Canada took place and it then decided to organize a single Sitch organization that would become a confederative centre of all Ukrainians from Eastern Canada. As is well known the Sitch organization existed in Western Ukraine before the First World War and their objective was not only ideological-political but consisted primarily of propagation of physical training.

Organizers of "Sitch Organization"—for such was its name in the beginning—proclaimed that in every Ukrainian organization there should exist a Sitch branch. Where there were not any other organizations, the Sitch organization came into being as a natural outcome. The organizer of these individual cells as well as of the overall Sitch movement was Wolodymyr Bossy, a new imigrant, who made his home in Canada. At the end of 1924 the Sitch Organization had its branches in Toronto,

Oshawa, Hamilton, Windsor and Preston and started to publish its own organ the "Kanadiyska Sitch" which was of great help in the organization work that went rapidly ahead from day to day. Such well organized group activity made a great impression on the total community, and similar organizations in U.S.A. proposed to the Canadian leaders of the Sitch movement to unite. The result of this was that Canadian Sitch organizations declared themselves in favor of the Hetman movement which, in addition to the previously mentioned W. Bossy, was headed by such leading Ukrainian easterners as Rev. A. Sarmatiuk, M. Wozny, S. Yarema, Rev. N. Drohomyrecky, I. Skalecky, S. Mozevsky and many others. The Catholic organ "Canadian Ukrainian", supported this movement and W. Bossy had an opportunity to deliver his speech— on how to organize Sitch branches—during the Greek Catholic convention in Winnipeg. When in the course of time W. Bossy was given the position of a school teacher in the St. Joseph's Catholic College in Yorkton, he had ample opportunity to spread the Sitch movement in Western Canada. At the end of 1926, Sitch centres were organized in Saskatchewan in such places as: Yorkton, Wroxton, Modelfarm, Ituna, Wishart, Hubbard, Melville, Krasne, Saskatoon, Lanigan, Dysart, Bedfordville, Veregin, Regina, Goodeve, Holer, Buchanan, Willow Creek, Arran and later in other places as well.

In 1927 the Supreme Command of the Sitch Organization was stationed in Winnipeg and consisted of well-known community leaders such as —I. Isaiw, A. Zaharychuk, Rev. N. Bartman, N. Danylchenko, W. Dyky, D. M. Elcheshen, Dr. V. Kysilewsky, M. Hetman, Dr. D. Stasiuk and others. The Catholic paper, "Canadian Ukrainian" was the main source of information for the Sitch movement whose editor during this period was none other than W. Bossy. When disagreement arose between the new publisher of the Canadian Ukrainian and its editor the Sitch organization began to publish its own organ, the "Canadian Sitch". The year 1928 was an exceptionally active one in Sitch organizing endeavours and the following year the organization was renamed Canadian Sitch Organization (CSO). At this same time the Sitch provincial conventions were held in almost all provinces—the larger ones taking place in Toronto, Yorkton and Mundare. It is interesting to note that it was also at this time that Canadian Sitch severed its connection with its prototype in U.S.A. When in 1930 a re-union, with Chicago centre, took place the "Canadian Sitch" organ ceased to exist. Soon after that Stanislav Mozevsky took over the leadership of Canadian Sitch Organization (CSO) and in 1932 Mychaylo Hetman became its head, at which post he stayed for a good many years. His co-workers were: S. Mozevsky, W. Duzy, I. Skaletsky, D. M. Elcheshen, I. M. Korchynsky, M. Lapka, S. Babiy and others. M. Hetman proved himself to be a good organizer and community leader, and was able to form additional Sitch branches in western and eastern Canada.

The Sitch movement, which in 1934 took on a new name—from "Sitch Organization" to United Hetman Organization (UHO)—developed finally into an important organized movement. It could boast of over fifty branches, its own Sitch or Hetman halls, and last but not least, its own weekly newspaper the "Ukrainian Toiler". Great credit for the strengthening of Hetman idea in Canada must be given to Hetmanych

Danylo Skoropadsky who made a cross-country tour of Canada in 1937 and 1938 when he visited all the larger Ukrainian centres in this country. As a lawful pretender to the throne of Ukrainian monarchy he was cordially received by government ministers, bishops, generals, university professors and other high dignitaries. Even the Ukrainian republicans showed respect to the honored guest and a noticeable sentiment toward the Hetman movement.

If we take time to trace the Sitch-Hetman movement of the second era we may come to a false conclusion that this movement was far removed from the question of the growth of Canada. But in reality such is not the fact. In political affiliation this organization stood closest to the conservative party with which it was closely allied because of its monarchical-conservative ideology. The organization laid stress on the development of a dignified character in their members as well as physical and military discipline. The members of Sitch organizations worked hand in hand with the Canadian military agencies. All Sitch members had their own distinctive uniforms and were subject to systematic military rules and some detachments of this organization even took part in the regular manoeuvers of the Canadian Military Districts—for example, the 10th Canadian Military District of Camp Hughes [2]). The Sitch organizations even had their own aeroplanes and air-force detachments. While the male members of the Sitch organizations were receiving their military training, the women's detachments of this organization also took their training as Red Cross nurses. The organization very often paid considerable attention to the role the women should play in all phases of organized life. In 1925 the Women's Sitch Committee sent out a proclamation: "To the Ukrainian Women of Canada" with the appeal to organize branches of one large Sitch Organization" [3]).

UKRAINIAN SELF-RELIANCE LEAGUE

The second dominion-wide organization formed in the post-pioneer era was the Ukrainian Self-Reliance League (U.S.R.L.), in Ukrainian S.U.S. and just like the former nation-wide organization the Canadian Sitch Organization recruited its members for the most part from the second immigration, so in like manner the U.S.R.L. was the emanation of the original immigration. The rudiments of these organizations reach much more deeply into an earlier period than its formation in December of 1927. They could already be noticed, in part, in 1916 during the National Convention which took place in Saskatoon and in the formation of the P. Mohyla Institute. Much more resemblance could be noticed between U.S.R.L. and the National Conventions of later years. The centres of attention of these conventions were the P. Mohyla Institute, the M. Hrushevsky Institute and newly-formed Ukrainian Greek Orthodox Church. It was then not an accident that during two such conventions in both Edmonton and Saskatoon a resolution was formulated to organize a general alliance under the name of the Ukrainian Self-Reliance League. This was the singular consummation of the organizational process which

---

[2]) "Ten years of war with chaos", a historical sketch by D. M. Elcheshen, printed in "The Leader" Winnipeg, 1935, page 38.
[3]) "Canadian Farmer", May 30, 1925.

had behind it a history of ten years. The definition of U.S.R.L. given by the organizer and ideologist of this organization, Myroslaw Stechishin was expressed most ably in the following words: "The U.S.R.L. is the concentration and consummation of our entire organizational and national life in Canada. This is the body which binds together our Institutes, our People's Homes, united in the Union of Ukrainian Community Centres, our womanhood under the name of the Ukrainian Womens' Association of Canada (S.U.K.) and our youth, the Ukrainian-Canadian Youth Association (S.U.M.K.)" [4].

In other words around the U.S.R.L. were formed other organizations and institutions which in a religious attitude were associated with the Ukrainian Greek-Orthodox Church (U.G.O.C.). The organizers of U.S.R.L. were for the greater part those who organized the U.G.O.C. The first president of the Ukrainian Self-Reliance League was Wasyl Swystun, the most active members were the lawyer Julian Stechishin, Rev. S. W. Sawchuk, Rev. Wasyl Kudryk, the lawyers T. Humeniuk, Jaroslaw Arsenych, and also W. Burianyk, as well as many others.

The U.S.R.L. accounted for its name in this manner: There must be independence of the individual, of an organization, and of a nation, with self-reliance in matters concerning politics, economics, and religion, but above all independence of thought and action.

The initial programme of U.S.R.L. clarified its stand upon these political, economic, and religious matters. Regarding its relationship toward Canada, the constitution of the Ukrainian Self-Reliance League stated: "bearing in mind that Canada is the new and adopted homeland of the Ukrainians, the USRL appeals strongly to the Ukrainians that as citizens of this country they take a most active part in all matters concerning this state, at the same time benefiting from their rights and privileges as citizens, but at the same time carrying out their obligations as such" [5].

As to its relationship to both Ukraine and Canada, U.S.R.L. did not express its sympathies with any one political party, but placed the welfare of the nation above all such parties. The members of USRL had at all times a free hand in their choice of supporting any political party. In matters of religion USRL believed that any display of differences is disruptive. The striking motto of the Ukrainian Self-Reliance League was: "Self-respect, self-reliance, and independence".

The executive of the Ukrainian Self-Reliance League (S.U.S.) consisted of its own elected members and of delegates which entered this council as accredited from Ukrainian Self-Reliance Association (T.U.S.), Ukrainian Women's Association of Canada, the Canadian Youth Association (S.U.M.K.), and the Union of Ukrainian Community Centres (S.U.N.D.). The Ukrainian Voice was declared to be the official organ of U.S.R.L. With the formation of the U.S.R.L. the central group which was closely associated with the Ukrainian Voice and the Ukrainian Greek Orthodox Church was considerably strengthened. Every year there were held conventions which represented not only the men, but women as well, along with representatives from the People's Homes, both provincial

---

[4] M. Stechishin, USRL in Canada, Winnipeg, page 7.
[5] USRL in Canada, its principles and programme—Winnipeg, 1928 p. 3.

and dominion-wide. Such conventions were actually held systematically resulting in a great regularity in the work of the above-mentioned organizations.

In its history the U.S.R.L. was always governed by democratic principles. It suppressed both the left and the right-wing totalitarianism and worked hand in hand especially with the central Ukrainian executive, and always upheld the representatives of the government of the Ukrainian People's Republic in exile. As regards Canadian politics the predominant sympathies of the U.S.R.L. lay close to the Liberal Party.

Besides educating the rank and file of its members the U.S.R.L. led an active part in bringing to light the Ukrainian Question in Europe. This League also brought from Europe prominent Ukrainians who travelled through the U.S.R.L. branches with educational lectures. Such were W. Kedrowsky, formerly an army inspector in the Ukrainian People's Republic, Prof. O. I. Bochkovsky, a specialist in the liberation movement of submerged nations, Gen. V. Sikevich, and many others. Prof. Dmytro Doroshenko deserves special mention for, thanks to the efforts of this noted exponent of Ukrainian history, the U.S.R.L. was able to publish the first history of the Ukraine in the English language.

An interesting characterization of this period was given by Dr. Osyp Nazaruk in his lengthy observations concerning the united action of the Ukrainians in Canada in 1923. He regarded the Ukrainian Voice as an organ of the Ukrainian Nationalists also known as the Orthodox group because of their faith. Dr. O. Nazaruk wrote: "The Ukrainian Voice is the organ of those who emigrated from Galicia (the Western Ukraine) during the so-called "spring storms" and who were captivated by the ideological radicalism in their homeland. Here after a period of time they became engaged in a fierce struggle with Ukrainian Catholic clergy which ended with the ogranization of the Ukrainian Greek Orthodox Church. This dissention arose because of the struggle for influence in churches, schools, and other educational institutions. The appearance of this organization is most characteristic yet very interesting for many reasons..."

Among the most outstanding aspects of this movement is the fact that the Bukovinians of the Orthodox faith often do not co-operate with those of the same faith from Galicia, especially those groups in which the Russian priests have become deeply rooted ever since the days of czarism. The group of Ukrainian Nationalists has among its ranks the majority of the Ukrainian intelligentsia, almost all of them lay—not of the clergy. Besides, this group is quite young. They organized two educational institutes patterned after the European bursa. The senior leader of this group was T. D. Ferley. Other leaders were: Petro Svarich, Wasyl Kudryk—the Canadian Tolstoi, three Stechishin brothers —an editor, a lawyer, a director of the Institute in Saskatoon, two Swystun brothers, lawyer J. Arsenych of Winnipeg, J. Pasnak, editor T. Tomashevsky, the young M. Luchkovich of Edmonton, H. Slipchenko from Dnieper, and many others. The Ukrainian Greek Orthodox Church has 8 married priests; their administrator is the Rev. S. Sawchuk. This most active group has also its own library. It has also organized a grain buying company in 1916. To this group belong, or are favorably inclined, members of the legislature of Ukrainian origin: N. V. Bachynsky, Dm. Yakimischak, Mykola Hryhorczuk, and even the Latinized M. Rojecki has leanings toward it. In all fairness let me admit that not one of these members of the legislature was elected upon the platforms of this group. All this makes their attitude all the more typical" [6]).

From this evaluation by Dr. O. Nazaruk it is evident that this "cluster" which later assumed the name of the Ukrainian Self-Reliance League was an influential communal force which through its activity generated a large dose of dynamism and was a kind of a landmark that provided the magnetic force for a large part of the Ukrainian-Canadian unity during the mid-war period.

UKRAINIAN WAR VETERANS' ASSOCIATION
UKRAINIAN NATIONAL FEDERATION

Two months after the formation of the Ukrainian Self-Reliance League there was formed the nucleus of the Ukrainian War Veterans' Association (U.W.V.A.-U.S.H.) which resulted in an imposing growth of a medium finally culminated in the organization of the Ukrainian National Federation (UNF-UNO), which also played a leading part in the reorganization and led to the development of Ukrainian unity in Canada.

The groundwork for this union lay entirely in the hands of the Freedom Fighters of Ukraine. This was a distinct category of men who having lost their fight against foreign oppression found themselves in concentration camps in several European countries. When after a period of years these camps were liquidated many of the Freedom Fighters expressed the desire to emigrate to Canada and since in 1925 through the efforts of the Canadian-Ukrainian citizens the doors of immigration were thrown open, it was not long before these new arrivals settled in many localities with an earnest desire to lead a peaceful life. However, they did not give up hope that even in times of peace they could work devotedly for the freedom of their own occupied land. Led by such dreams the first groups of the Ukrainian War Veterans' Association were formed throughout Canada in 1928. Following the formation of the one in Winnipeg some of the outstanding memebers of which were: E. Wasylyshyn, Dr. I. Gulay, D. Gerych, J. Pecheniuk, W. Kossar, I. Chayka, and others; similar groups were formed in Yorkton, Edmonton, and Montreal, and later in Toronto, Saskatoon, Sudbury, Moose Jaw, Windsor, and elsewhere. These organizations grew in size and number each year since this immigration continued and there arrived more and more former combatants, especially from the territories occupied by the Poles. They brought with them news of the humiliation and oppression of their countrymen by governments which had occupied Ukraine. This strengthened the desire of former soldiers to help their native land.

Due to the creative initiative of the Ukrainian War Veterans' Association there appeared a committee for the protection of the Ukrainian political prisoners called Ukrainian Defence Committee. This was a representative organization whose program was concerned with the fate

---

[6]) What is Canada? How Do We Appear in It? — Ukrainian Banner, Vienna, No. 9, 1923.

of thousands of Ukrainian political prisoners in Polish prisons. This committee collected funds to send to the Old Country for the legal and political aid of these prisoners. It also drew up memorandums to be placed before governments of democratic nations, thus striving to obtain an intervention in matters pertaining to the inhumane treatment of these prisoners of war.

In Ukraine there were impressive numbers of Ukrainian invalids who did not receive any pension, for the occupying regimes regarded these as their former enemies. The local Ukrainian population despite its straitened means gave what help it could to these and appealed to their compatriots overseas for financial aid. The Ukrainian War Veterans' Association was the first one to devote itself to this cause, as most of these invalids requiring help were their former battle-front comrades. Due to these efforts a representative Home for Ukrainian Invalids was constructed in Lviv.

The work of the Veterans was greatly strengthened by the visit of Col. Ewhen (Eugene) Konovalets who in 1928 toured such organizations, the more so since the Colonel was regarded as the original symbol of the revolutionary struggle for freedom by the Ukrainian people. At that time Col. Konovalets headed the Ukrainian Army Organization which led under-ground movement, and later renamed as the Organization of Ukrainian Nationalists, an organization which became an importnat factor in its drive for political freedom of the Ukrainians. In 1931 Omelian Senyk-Hrybivsky, a close co-worker of Colonel Konovalets visited Canada, and a year later it was Col. Roman Sushko (M. Melnychuk).

This placing of the so-called Old Country matters in the first place raised serious discussions between the Ukrainian Self-Reliance League and the Ukrainian War Veterans' Association for the former believed that the budget of the Ukrainian community in Canada should be divided equally between the cultural needs of the local Ukrainian unity and the struggle for freedom of the Ukrainian people in Europe. This discussion intensified into a hot controversy and even in animosity, but this fight ended in a draw for while some members supported the Ukrainian War Veterans' Association, others gave their support to the Ukrainian Self-Reliance League. However, this heated argumentation brought forth even good results, for both organizations could once more assess their position regarding their attitude toward the Ukrainian-Canadian unity and toward the country of their choice, Canada, and also toward the events taking place on the Ukrainian soil. It was not so easy to demand from those who had behind them only a two or three-year stay in this new country the same sort of reasoning as from those who had been rooted here for two or three decades. The same could be said regarding the attitude of both of these organizations toward the Ukraine and her needs.

The strength of this new organization grew to such an extent that in 1930 there arose a need for the publication of the monthly "Veterans' News" (Striletski Visti) which in 1932 was replaced by the weekly 'New Pathway'. During that same year there appeared important changes in the organization. The third convention of the delegates of Ukrainian War Veterans' Association gave its approval for the formation of general nationalistic organization to which would belong not only the former veterans of the front, but also the general public. It is worth noticing that the UWVA made special concessions to the women in 1931 and began the organization of the Olha Basarab Branch of the UWVA. Such branches arose in Canora, Toronto, Windsor, Sudbury and Saskatoon. In 1932, through the united efforts of the members of the UWVA, there arose a new organization which adopted the name of the Ukrainian National Federation (UNF-UNO) and its first branches which organized the general public were formed in Edmonton and Saskatoon. Two years later there were already 45 such branches, not including those of the women and the youth, the latter becoming known as the Young Ukrainian Nationalists. In 1934 there was held the First Nationwide Conference of the Ukrainian National Federation, in which all the branches of this organization took part, that is to say, the Women's Section of Olha Basarab which in due time adopted the name of the Women's Organization of Canada, the Ukrainian National Youth Federation, the Ukrainian National Federation, and the creator of all these, the Ukrainian War Veterans' Association. The convention was held in Saskatoon to which city just a year previously had been transferred from Edmonton the weekly "New Pathway" and Saskatoon became the main centre of the Ukrainian National Federation for many years.

The central executive of the UWVA was also transferred to this place from Winnipeg where it had functioned for six years. The first president of this unification, under the name of the Ukrainian National Federation became A. Gregorovich, who had arrived in Canada before the First World War, and whose personality together with that of the others of the executive represented the pioneer element in this organization. By stages, the Ukrainian National Federation was becoming the connecting link between the two generations of the immigration. The new element exerted a noticeable influence upon the further growth of this organization which became more deeply ingrained into the land of its settlement, Canada. This gave rise to the building of their own centres—people's homes—the members of which played a more important part in the life of the local communities, not forgetting at the same time their obligations which had been set before them ever since the formation of this union. For many years Wolodymyr Kossar, who because of his idealism had resigned his post as lecturer at the university accepted the duties of a community leader.

The Ukrainian National Federation held close ties with parallel organizations outside Canada, with the O.D.V.U. in the United States, the Organizations of Ukrainian Soldiers in Brussels, the Ukrainian National Union in Paris, and others. Above all there was always an active and friendly contact with the executives of the Ukrainian National Union in Europe. Among those executives already mentioned, Gen. W. Kurmanovych and Gen. Mykola Kapustiansky also visited Canada.

The idealistic aims of this medium were characterized by Prof. I. Bobersky in his work "Ukrainians in Canada" [7] as follows: "In matters pertaining to Canada the Ukrainian National Federation directs itself toward a firm understanding of its privileges and its duties. In matters concerning Ukraine it adopted as its basis the re-education of the

---

[7] "Providnyk" Almanac of the Canadian-Ukrainian, 1938, p. 32.

masses, and a close, active struggle for the restoration of the united independent Ukraine through the fortitude of our own Ukrainian people. The close collaboration of the church is essential."

Before the outbreak of the Second World War the Ukrainian National Federation had 50 branches in Canada, the Ukrainian War Veterans' Association 19, the Organization of the Ukrainian Women's Organization of Canada 33, the Ukrainian National Youth Federation 38, and the Ukrainian Students' National Organization had 5. The last of these upheld its connections with the Central Union of the Ukrainian Students in Europe. The spokesman of this union in both ideological and political matters of this environment was the weekly "New Pathway" edited by Michael Pohorecky. Among the leading promoters who spent many years working in the Ukrainian National Federation, and who at various times held executive posts are—besides those already mentioned—P. Shtepa, W. Hultay, W. Topolnycky, D. Gerych, E. Tarnawecky, W. Ruryk, T. K. Pavlychenko, Hnat Poworoznyk, B. Zeleny, P. Shulha, and many others.

UKRAINIAN CATHOLIC BROTHERHOOD

The last to be organized was the Ukrainian Catholic Brotherhood (U.C.B.) which had the greatest accessible organizational basis among the Catholic parishes and its membership, for according to statistics they numbered 186,587 in 1931 and the Catholic Official Directory recorded as many as 350,000. There is no doubt that the need of a lay organization was replaced to a certain extent by the parishes. However, there was a pressing need of an organizational system and of solid ideological foundations which would harmonize with the wholeness of the Catholic creed. Such ideas were discussed in the group of ideologists which met for consultation in July, 1932, in Regina. The initiators of this meeting were three teachers: M. Hrynevych, M. Hrynevych (husband and wife), and Fred Mamchur, and three farmers: Mykhaylo Bilynsky, Dmytro Bayda, and Hryhoriy Dubyk took part, with Father Stepan Semczuk being present. This was that lucky seven which met several times and finally drew up plans for a general convention which was held on December 28 and 29 of the same year in Saskatoon.

Perhaps there was a real need for such an organization for during the first year there were 20 centres organized across Canada. Saskatchewan was in the lead. Besides the organization of the men there were organizations formed of both the women and the youth. There were branches of the Ukrainian Catholic Fraternity in Saskatchewan, Manitoba and Alberta. The latter two provinces held their conventions in October, 1933. Besides these provincial gatherings there were also local meetings at which, besides organizational matters, three basic questions dealing with the Catholic religion, the Ukrainian culture, and the Canadian state were discussed. These problems were clearly grasped by the idealist and organizer of Ukrainian Catholic Brotherhood, Father S. Semczuk, who wrote that for the members of the U.C.B. the Catholic religion was the guide and helm of life from which there emerged cultural and spiritual values of the nation not to be destroyed even by the passage of time. Among these cultural values, according to the U.C.B., were the language, the songs, the music, the paintings, sculptures, dances, the architecture, the embroidery and needle-work, national food, and customs of our forefathers. This ideologist wrote, "We understand differently, and feel different toward the world surrounding us and so have re-created it as seen through the prism of our spirits, into indestructible and unchangeable values of our culture."

Exceedingly clearly was examined from the ideological standpoint the problem of Canadian nationalism. "Canada is our country, and all that this entails is also ours," wrote these ideologists. "We are not exiles here, nor seasonal laborers whom fate has forced to seek employment here in order to make a living, but masters and owners of this land. Therefore the army is our army, her laws are our laws, her government is our government. We wish to exercise a most active part in all matters of state concerning Canada, being not only an active force as co-workers but also as "co-rulers"...Our religion, our culture must live in Canada where we have come to stay...We can never forget the land of our fathers and forefathers. We owe her our respect and our help. We owe her our love" [8].

Such and similar goals began to form the Ukrainian Catholic action in Canada.

In order to unite the scattered branches of the organization across Canada the members of which numbered in thousands, the Brotherhood began to publish the Bulletin of the Ukrainian Catholic Brotherhood. Special attention was paid to the youth which was grouped in numerous youth organizations, and with various contests their work was strengthened.

The executive also made provision for a seminary which would aid those who wished to continue their studies and yet lacked sufficient means to be able to do so. The organizers wished to provide the youth with a healthy environment in which they would be able to find all those educational principles which are embraced by the creed of the U.C.B. This seminary was founded in Saskatoon in 1935. It was organized by Father P. Suliatytsky and a teacher Osyp Pryma. Later it was renamed as the Institute of Metropolitan A. Shepticky.

Besides the Bulletin the U.C.B. printed popular publications under the name of "the Literature of U.B.C." which dealt with the basic aims of the organization, that is, the Catholic religion, the Ukrainian culture, and the Canadian nation.

Of great help in the work of the Ukrainian Catholic Brotherhood was the weekly "Ukrainian News" which had been published in Edmonton since 1930, and which became its official organ, more so since the former "Canadian-Ukrainian" ceased its publication in 1931. Besides this weekly there appeared two monthly publications: the "Redeemer's Voice", and later, "The Voice."

More than 60 branches of the U.C.B. were already at work before the Second World War. There was also a large membership of women and of the youth. Together with the parishes, these formed quite a large and active medium in which a considerable number of the intelligentsia, which was growing up during the period between the two World Wars

---

[8] Father S. Semczuk: "Ukrainian Catholic Brotherhood". Edmonton, 1958.

was also included. This medium, this group of the intelligentsia, appeared without any doubt to be quite different from the one immediately following the First World War, and it was concerning this latter group that Dr. Osyp Nazaruk, in the already quoted study, expressed himself thus in connection with the "Canadian-Ukrainian" and the Ukrainian-Catholic centres: "This is the organ of Bishop N. Budka. Here the stream of Catholicism is stressed much more vividly than in the Old Country. This force, great in numbers, is quite naturally the most powerful one. But there is hardly any of the lay intelligentsia in it. It consists of the clergy which is composed of three distinct groups: (a) about 20 married priests, (b) 7 celibates of the Basilian Order, and (c) 70 nuns. These nuns are engaged in important cultural work, and I have heard even from the lips of those who were avowed enemies of Catholicism, how they have been credited for their work. The celibates are for the greater part Belgian priests who have embraced our faith and whose Superior is Father Delaere. Besides these there are working among our people the "Christian Brothers" under the leadership of Brother Ansbert, who are conducting a school in Yorkton. This is not a religious order. Among the Catholics there are now 7 members of the lay intelligentsia at work ...The work of this group is not easy to assess, nor to compare with that of other groups. This would necessitate a thorough analysis beginning with its foundation. But this work continues for it can be seen from the mathematical computation of the sermons if you take into account only the Sundays and the 30 priests (30 lessons each Sunday. M.H.M.) This work may be evaluated from various viewpoints, but their work continues to act upon the masses, slowly yet systematically, beginning with the bringing up of 4-year old orphans in their six orphanages" [9].

The prognoses of the quoted author were extraordinarily factual when we take into consideration that toward the end of the second period there were hundreds of the intelligentsia in the Ukrainian Catholic Brotherhood and in the related organizations. Just as an example, it is worth mentioning those who were in the lead of this medium in the period under discussion. Some of these were: G. Skwarok, a lawyer; J. Stratichuk, a banker; the teachers Orest Zerebko, J. Topushchak, Bohdan Korchynsky, Wolodymyr Fylypovych, and Franko Mazurkevych; Stepan Meush, and Ivan Isaiw, both architects.

A separate category is occupied by the women of the Ukrainian Catholic Brotherhood, but mention of these will be made in another chapter.

UKRAINIAN LABOUR AND FARMER'S TEMPLE ASSOCIATION

The formation of this dominion-wide organization, the Ukrainian Labour and Farmers' Temple Association (U.L.F.T.A.), is closely tied in with the organization and expansion of the Ukrainian Labour Temple in Winnipeg and with the appearance and publication of the "Ukrainian Labour News", the ideological organ of the Ukrainian Labour Temple, or according to its constitutional name the Ukrainian Labour Temple Association. This was a cultural and educational association which intended to give moral and material aid to the Ukrainian workers and farmers. With the liquidation of the Ukrainian Social-Democratic Party in 1918

---

[9] What is Canada Like and Our Place There: a characterization of Ukrainian groups in Canada. Essays in the "Ukrainian Banner", Vienna, 1923.

the Ukrainian Labour Temple (U.L.T.) not only took over all the locals of that party, but became also the axis of the new organization which was formed around it under the name, the Ukrainian Labour Temple Association.

The first convention of the Ukrainian Labour Temple Association was held in Winnipeg, January 16 — 18, in 1920. Already during that year there had been organized close to twenty locals of this organization most of which were in Welland, Ontario; Edmonton and Regina. The second convention held in 1921 was attended by representatives from Montreal, Toronto, Sudbury, Hamilton, West Fort William, Saskatoon, and many others from larger and smaller centres. In the fourth convention held in 1923 there were already delegates representing 54 branches scattered across Canada. By now the organization had also 17 of the Women Workers' Association with a total membership of 450. It was from these locals that there was formed the Women Workers' Section, at this fourth annual convention. A year later this "Section" already consisted of 27 locals. At that same time there was formed, in connection with the U.L.T. organization, the "Ukrainian Workers' Youth Association". Then, too, it was decided to publish the "Woman Worker's Voice", a separate journal for the womenfolk. After a year's work, in 1925, there were already organized 12 youth locals with a combined membership of 445 members, 25 women's locals with 807 members, and 68 branches of U.L.F.T.A. conducted 38 classes in the native Ukrainian language with an aggregate enrollment of 1719.

In pursuance of the summary drawn up by the eighth convention there were already, in 1927, 71 general locals with 2,223 members, 41 branches of the Women's section with 993 members, and 30 locals of the Youth with a membership of 1,142. Besides these there were as well four organizations affiliated with the U.L.F.T.A. Altogether there were 146 locals with a combined membership of 4,723.

The peak of the organizational work of this organization was reached in the 1930's. In 1933 the total membership had passed the 6,000 mark united by 116 general locals with 3563 members, 50 Women's Sections with 1,438 members, and 55 Youth locals with a membership of 1,640. Among the cultural and educational achievements of this organization were the formation of 75 mandolin orchestras, choral, and dramatic clubs. More than 2,000 children were taking Ukrainian lessons and the 60 libraries contained about 25,000 volumes worth $15,000.00. The 75 buildings themselves were worth approximately three-quarters of a million [10]. To this great expansion of the organization there must also be added the press that was formed in connection with it. Besides the previously mentioned weekly "Ukrainian Labour News", which before long came to be published tri-weekly, there also appeared the following journals: the monthly "Woman Workers' Voice" published for the women which later changed its name to the "Woman Worker" and became a bi-monthly publication, the weekly "Farmers' Life" intended for the farmers, and the monthly "Youths' World."

In 1929 the U.L.F.T.A. carried out its resolution that the students be

---

[10] M. Wolynec: Fifteen Years of the Association of "Ukrainian Labour and Farmers' Temple Association"—Winnipeg, 1918, p. 133.

provided with an accommodation in which they would be brought up according to the beliefs of the organization. A building was bought in Edmonton for this purpose, which came to be known as the Students' Institute of the U.L.F.T.A., which could accommodate 50 students.

Upon the initiative of the U.L.F.T.A. there was organized "Working Men's Benefit Association" (W.M.B.A.) a life insurance association which was to give financial aid to its members in case of sickness and death. The first branch was formed in Winnipeg in 1922, and the first convention of the W.M.B.A. was held there in 1925. After two years and four months of organizational work the W.M.B.A. boasted of 20 branches; in 1928 it had 101, and a year later 111. During its marked growth the W.M.B.A. bought two large buildings along with 74 acres of Parkland near Winnipeg, and organized a home for the aged and an orphanage. By 1933 the W.M.B.A. could count over 6,000 members. The W.M.B.A. co-operated closely with the Association of Ukrainian Workers & Farmers Home.

How can we account for this imposing growth of this organization? What was the stimulus in its organizational work? How did it differ, in its methods and its aims, from the other organizations of which we had spoken in the previous sub-heading?

The U.L.F.T.A. was not only a Canadian cultural and educational association. As already had been mentioned it took upon itself the tradition of political action of the dissolved Ukrainian Social-Democratic Party. But while the above-mentioned party oriented itself upon the socialism of the Second International the U.L.F.T.A. turned more to the left and adopted as its principles the Marx-Lenin teachings. In other words the staunch supporters of this movement in Canada began to orient themselves upon what was happening in the U.S.S.R. In particular they were interested in the Ukrainian national processes which were reaching their peak under the leadership of Mykola Skrypnyk, the minister of Education of the Ukrainian Soviet Socialist Republic. In the existence of this Republic they saw the ultimate resolution of the Ukrainian question, while the other organizations in Canada not only rejected the materialistic outlook of the Marxist communism, but foresaw in the structure of the U.S.S.R. further enslavement of the Ukrainian people. It was along these lines that there arose a grim cleavage between such Ukrainian nationalistic organizations as the Ukrainian War Veterans' Association, the Ukrainian Self-Reliance League, the Ukrainian National Federation, and the Ukrainian Catholic Brotherhood. More so since a large part of the active membership of the above mentioned organizations were recruited from the second immigration which had come face to face with communism in practice, and which, in the ranks of the Ukrainian army, had fought against communism and the Soviet regime. It is to be understood that the feelings and experiences of these new arrivals were too fresh to challenge the U.L.F.T.A. centre exclusively on a rational political plane. Then the other Ukrainian-Canadian organizations were hostile toward each other and wasted their energy by quarrelling among themselves instead of presenting a solid front. Furthermore the U.L.F.T.A. was in a better position inasmuch as it already had strong cells of organizational work, while the S.U.S., the U.N.F. and the U.C.B. were just beginning to be organized. Finally the leaders of the U.L.F.T.A. had already obtained the confidence of the masses, for several of these had led the Social-Democratic Party, and to a certain extent had defended the rights of both the workers and the farmers. Such were W. N. Kolisnyk, I. Nawiziwsky, T. Kulchycky, D. Lobay, M. Shatulsky, M. Popowych, T. Kobzey, and others. Besides, there came from the U.S.S.R. others, along with a mass of political literature all of which spoke of the social and cultural advances. There were also many films shown portraying the contentment of large masses with the existing conditions. A large proportion of the members took the leaders at their word. More often than not they were not interested in politics, but were satisfied to have their children take the evening classes in Ukrainian, read Ukrainian books and newspapers, sing their songs, and learn about the history of the nation (*which, in the case of history, was badly perverted*). In all, the parents carried out their duties and obligations toward Canada and looked forward toward a better future for their children.

The economic crisis in Canada resulted in an impressive strengthening of the U.L.F.T.A. Many of the unemployed trying to find a solution to their economic problems, cast their eyes toward Eastern Europe where not only political but economic experiments were being carried out, and quite naturally these discontented ones found those who capitalized upon their feelings to their own advantage.

Both the organizers and the leaders of the U.L.F.T.A. tried to attach to their organization the aureole of freedom, underscoring, on every public occasion, that the Association demanded the liberation of the Ukrainian people in the territories held by Poland, Czecho-Slovakia, and Romania. Usually this organization helped the Communist movement demanding the annexation of those regions to the Ukrainian Socialist Soviet Republic (U.S.S.R.) which had been engulfed by the Russian Soviet Socialist Republic. In support of this propaganda came the material aid. In 1923 alone the U.L.F.T.A. sent $15,000 to help the political prisoners and to strengthen the work of the Communist Party in the Western Ukraine. From the above-mentioned territories there often came terrifying news about the nationalistic, political, and economic persecution. Besides arrests there were hangings, and finally the so-called pacification, all of which the U.L.F.T.A. took to advantage for their own political purposes. In fact it was the nationalistic groups, crystallized into a solid block, that raised the first protest against these acts of violence and gave a strong support to the movement for freedom, but this was done with the firm belief that the whole of Ukraine should be liberated. This block, too, gave financial aid to the Freedom Movement. The U.L.F.T.A. connected their liberation movement with some of the arrests which continued to be carried out in the Western Ukraine and even formed a separate "Association in Aid of the Freedom Movement in the Western Ukraine". In all this lay both the strength and weakness of this movement. If we add to this the special attention and the dynamism of this organizational movement it is no surprise that the masses heeded the call of the U.L.F.T.A. In short, the objective tendencies which had their origin both in Canada and in Ukraine after the First World War were to a great extent capitalized upon by the U.L.F.T.A. for its own growth and expansion.

Then, when the U.L.F.T.A. was reaching the peak of its greatness, from the Western Ukraine and the U.S.S.R. came more and more alarming news of a famine, deportations to Siberia, and massive murders of the Ukrainian intelligentsia, and even of farmers and peasants, allegedly for the "kurkul" [11]) propaganda and for separatist movement of the Ukrainian masses. At first the executive of the U.L.F.T.A. would not give any credence to what was repeatedly printed and spoken by the Ukrainian nationalist block: S.U.S., U.C.B., U.N.F., U.H.O. and others in various press publications. But it happened that at that time there were deported from Canada to Ukraine, among others, the teacher Ivan Sembay, from Edmonton, D. Chomicky from Winnipeg, and others who were very active members of the U.L.F.T.A. Also, previous to this, in 1929, Andrey Babiuk, a well-known writer and active member of the same organization, who wrote under the pseudonym "Myroslaw Irchan", had emigrated from Canada to the Soviet Ukraine. These were tragic moments for many members of the U.L.F.T.A. when before long, news reached them that all of these had either been liquidated or deported to Siberia. This is what one of the top leaders of that association wrote about these developments in his documented material [12]): "A group of us leading members of the U.L.F.T.A. met in 1932 to discuss what was happening in Ukraine and consult with each other what stand we should take." This group consisted of D. Lobay, T. Kulchycky, O. Chomicky, M. Smith, N. Handziuk, M. Kashchak, later there were drawn to our group: M. Smiyowsky, S. Chwaliboga, M. Brychka, I. Gybowsky, and T. Pylypas.

Finally in 1933 news arrived that the Minister of Education, in Ukraine, Mykola Skrypnyk had committed suicide in protest against the reign of terror. Shortly after that Mykola Khvylovy and Panas Lubchenko also committed suicide. Then again in 1934 M. Irchan and I. Sembay were arrested and in due time executed. That, as one would say, "was enough for us".

UKRAINIAN WORKERS' LEAGUE (U.W.L.)

The reign of terror in the Ukraine in the 1930's, the famine, the murders, the arrests, and the deportations to Siberia of even idealistic Communists led to a crisis in the U.L.F.T.A. The executive became sharply divided. The leading Stalinist faction supported and exonerated the regime saying that all this resulted in the political successes for the good of the world-wide Communist Revolution, but the opposition, headed by the "Twelve" mentioned in the previous chapter, evaluated the terror as the liquidation of the Ukrainian activity in order to subordinate the Ukrainian masses to the all-Russian Kremlin, and to destroy the struggle for Ukrainian independence. It was not until 1935, during the party caucus just before the General Convention, that this duel became apparent. Danylo Lobay, who headed the opposition, condemned the political situation and the terror in Ukraine. He was supported by the following members of the central executive committee of the U.L.F.T.A.: T. Kulchycky, the president; T. Kobzey, the financial secretary; and the controllers S. Chwaliboga and M. Smiyowsky. Therefore of the eight members

---

11) "Kurkul". Derogatory term for well-to-do peasant in communist terminology.
12) Memoirs and Testimony of Toma Kobzey, preserved in the archives of the author of this history, under the name of: "How and Why in 1935 the Communist Party U.L.F.T.A. came to be split".

of the committee five were in opposition. Nonetheless, there was no formal condemnation of the Stalinist policies in Ukraine and those who supported these actions were able to manipulate the elections in such a way that only the Stalinists were elected, all except T. Kobzey. After this rigged election the energetic D. Lobay led an open attack upon the Communist Party. Together with his friend I. Zeles prepared a pamphlet entitled "The True Conditions in the Soviet Ukraine." Besides this, the opposition printed "To All Those Who Want the Truth". All this mobilized the masses. From among those who were so strongly condemning the reign of terror in Ukraine there was formed the Ukrainian Worker-Farmer Educational Society with locals in Winnipeg and Transcona, and later in Portage la Prairie, Edmonton and Calgary. In the east, in Montreal, it was the Ukrainian Educational Society, and in Toronto the Stone-Cutters were active. All these organizations held a convention in Toronto on the 30th of July, and the 1st and 2nd of August in 1936. There it was decided to amalgamate into one organization known as the Federation of Ukrainian Worker-Farmer Organizations.

In the following nation-wide conference held in Toronto, December 27 and 28th of the same year, the name was changed to the Alliance of Ukrainian Organizations. Those participating in this conference were planning to unite, under this organization, all anti-Communist Ukrainian organizations. Therefore it was resolved to continue the publication of the official organ formerly known as "The Truth" under the new name "Forward".

A.U.O. was never able to unite all the Ukrainian organizations because of the political activities of its leaders in the past, and because there never was a strong enough mandate, a desire on the part of its members, for the formation of such a union. It required much time and even more labor to correct the past political activities of many of its leaders. In the meantime the newly formed organization adopted the name of the Ukrainian Workers' Union which became a component of the Ukrainian-Canadian Centre which began its formation in 1940. The newly-formed organization, in its several forms, was headed by such well-known figures in the labor movement as S. Chwaliboga, T. Kulchycky, Y. Elendiuk, D. Lobay, T. Kobzey, T. Pylypas, M. Kashchak, and others.

With the formation of dominion-wide workers' organizations in the form of: Federation of Ukrainian Worker-Farmer Organization, Alliance of Ukrainian Organizations, and/or Ukrainian Workers' League, the highly monopolizing U.L.F.T.A. began to lose its aura as the representative of the laboring class. A certain number of its members joined the new organizations, and some others left all forms of organizations. Such was the position of the U.L.F.T.A. until June, 1940 during the Second World War when the Canadian Government banned any further activities of the Canadian Communist Party, the League of the Communist Youth, the Canadian Workers' Defensive League, the Russian Worker-Farmer Club, the Finnish Club, the Federation of the Canadian-Ukrainian Youth, and along with these organizations also the U.L.F.T.A. and its affiliated organizations at the head of which stood such promoters as: I. Nawiziwsky, M. Shatulsky, P. Lysec (formerly Lysecky), I. Boychuk, I. Stefanicky, M. Sawiak, P. Prokopchuk, P. Krawchuk, M. Lenartovych, I. Horbatiuk, and others.

THE UKRAINIAN LABOUR ASSOCIATION

There were other dominion-wide organizations during the period between the two World Wars, but none of these lasted long. To such belonged the Ukrainian Labour Association (U.L.A.) which devolved from the Ukrainian National Home in Winnipeg toward the end of the 1920's. Its spiritual leader was M. I. Mandryka who, at that time was the chief editor of the newspaper "Truth and Liberty". The convention of this Association was held in Toronto from August 29 to September 1, 1930. A partial preparation for this was the "All-Ukrainian Educational-Economic Convention" which began in the Ukrainian National Home in Winnipeg. At this convention the representatives of a score of various local organizations in Canada conferred upon means of enlivening and strengthening the ties with the other Canadian organizations.

It is worth noting that acting upon the initiative of the National Home in Winnipeg there was already formed in 1929 the Union of the Ukrainian National Homes which set for itself as a goal the unification of the National Homes in Canada into one chartered organization, to give a planned character of action to the activities, and to raise the cultural work to a higher standard. At that time the All-Ukrainian Educational-Economic convention, too, was conferring upon such problems. The work of this Ukrainian National Home upon such matters met to a certain extent with obstacles since there already had been in existence another Union of Ukrainian Community Centres founded on the principles advocated by the Ukrainian Self-Reliance League. This led not only to enmity but to an open court action as well. The Ukrainian National Home in Winnipeg which had the sympathy of over 20 of the parent organizations in the area strove to form an organization which would give to these cells their own peculiar organizational and ideological omophor but at the same time under a different name. In such a manner there came into existence the Ukrainian Labour Association which beyond its cultural and educational work regarded itself as the ideal of the social structure with the purpose of "uniting the labor element with the principles of Freedom, Equality, and Fraternity, and a sensible division of work in such a way that nature and capital—the material resources—and learning would serve mankind to improve its welfare and standard of living, to shorten its hours of toil, for the cultural advancement so that there would be no exploitation of man by man" [13]. The U.L.A. built its constitution upon the principles of Canadian citizenship and also upon the closest and most amicable co-operation of the Ukrainian people for the development of prosperity and of culture of 'our new fatherland'. The U.L.A. specified that "the Canadian working class is to conduct its so-called total class policy through the general Canadian organizations so that these organizations of Ukrainian-Canadian workers would bear not only a political character, but an ideological, economic, cultural, and educational one as well" [14].

The ideological aims of the Ukrainian Labor Union proved that this

---

[13] Truth and Liberty, No. 31 of 1930, page 2. The program of this U.L.A. was based upon the scientific work of Dr. M. Mandryka, entitled "Theory of Social Democracy".
[14] Truth and Liberty, No. 2, 1930.

was a socialist organization. In several instances it resembled the high principles of the Ukrainian Social-Democratic Party of the pioneer era in that it did not accept the Marxist theory as its basis. The Ukrainian Labor Association strove to unite the socialists in Canada, and the very cells of this organization were formed from the former socialist Organization for the Defence of Ukraine. At the time of the formation of the U.L.A., that is in 1930, upon the invitation of the above-mentioned Ukrainian National Home, Dr. Mykyta Shapoval, a noted and active Ukrainian socialist and scholar from Prague, toured Canada. It was his lectures that helped greatly in the ideological formation of the Ukrainian Labour Association. The convention of the U.L.A. drew up a declaration that there should be a connection both in its action and ideals with the Ukrainian Social Revolutionary Party in Prague, and with the Ukrainian Socialist-Radical Party in Lviv. This convention also resolved to give aid to the Ukrainian Workers' Home in Lviv, and the Ukrainian Workers' University in Prague.

The Ukrainian Labour Association which operated for almost ten years was headed by such citizens as: the above mentioned M. Mandryka, W. Baran, W. Brylynsky, D. M. Hunkevych, S. Kotyk, W. Lewycky, P. Pawlukevych, O. Bassowa, S. Yemchuk, S. Zadorozny, N. Liber, I. Palka, and others.

LEAGUE OF BRITISH UKRAINIANS

When the Polish Government sent into the territories of the Western Ukraine its punitive expeditions to terrorize the Ukrainian population and to demolish its cultural and educational institutions, and Stalin in the Eastern Ukraine caused a mass famine thus crushing what vestiges there still existed for the establishment of the Ukrainian Republic, a group of Ukrainian-Canadians and many of those in Great Britain began to propagate a British Protectorate of the Ukrainian land under Poland and under the U.S.S.R. There was formed in Canada the initiative committee which centred around the National Press in Winnipeg, and whose noted leaders were: V. Biberovych, H. I. Kurdydyk, T. C. Dickinson, Dr. Mykola Bodrug, Hryhory Kuz, and others.

The League of British Ukrainians was entirely a political movement, the cells of which were to influence its environment concerning the idea of the British Protectorate over Ukraine, which country would then have the same rights and privileges as did the members of the British Dominion at the time. The constitution of this League referred to this planned protectorate in the following manner:

"In its relation toward the Western Ukraine, and later when the time was ripe, to the Greater Ukraine, an appeal was to be made to the British Crown to take under its protection those Ukrainian territories which are under the Polish and especially under the Soviet rule. This protectorate would be based upon the same system of self-government as that enjoyed by the British Dominions overseas, with all the rights and national ties in the framework of the British Empire" [15]).

---

15) The Constitution of the League of British Ukrainians, Winnipeg, 1930 — page 7.

The spokesman for this League of British Ukrainians were the Canadian Farmer, and the New Canadian, both of which were published under the aegis of the National Press. In Manitoba and in the East there were formed locals of the League. In Manitoba these were organized by the teacher, Hryhory Kuz. All this movement, with its local cells lasted several years. In practice this movement did not display any great accomplishment and during its existence demonstrated only the wishes of its members. With the passing of the National Press into private hands, there was no official spokesman for this movement.

WOMEN'S ORGANIZATIONS

A separate and grand part in the social life is recorded to the credit of women in Canada. For the very beginning of the organization of women we must look in the first place into the parishes. It is certain that in conjunction with each parish there were formed the so-called "Sisterhoods".

There are also reasons to believe that besides these "Sisterhoods" which had a purely religious character there existed other women's organizations. Two of the oldest of these were the Women's Society of the Holy Trinity and the St. Olga Girls' Association, both of which were organized in 1901 by the members of the first Ukrainian congregation of the Church of St. Nicholas, in Winnipeg [16]. Just like "Sisterhoods", these women's organizations of the parishes had a predominantly or an entirely religious character.

Much later we meet with women's organizations which had different and more general aims. To the oldest of these belonged the Ukrainian Women's Educational Society which arose in Winnipeg in 1916 from among the members of the Ukrainian National Home. This Society came into being at the time the women obtained equal rights and with them equal duties in the province of Manitoba. Under the auspices of the Ukrainian Women's Educational Society there was printed "An Appeal to the Ukrainian Women of Winnipeg" which asked the women to register for the elections, and for the purpose of performing their duties as citizens. This, most likely, was the first official printed document pertaining to the work of the Ukrainian women in Canada. The most active members of this organization, which lasted 10 years, were: M. Boyaniwska, M. Lipinska, E. Hykawa, M. Zerebko, O. Arsenych, F. Negrych, N. Ferley, J. Uhryniuk, E. Demchuk, and others [17].

One year after the formation of the above-mentioned Society there appeared the women's organization known as "Trud" (Toil) in the rural area of Dana, Saskatchewan. In Ethelbert, Manitoba, there was organized also the Women's Educational Society in 1919, and a similar one affiliated with the T. Shevchenko Society, in Hamilton in 1920.

The Women's Association of Winnipeg organized in 1922 was of much greater importance. The ultimate reason for such an organization was ably expressed by the secretary of this organization, Zenovia Uhryn,

---
[16] The Chronicle of Winnipeg and Its Neighborhood, in the chapter entitled "A Study of the History of the Ukrainian-Canadians" 1966-67, page 346.
[17] Canadian Morning, No. 100, October 26, 1922.

who wrote: "For a long time the Ukrainian women of Winnipeg have felt the need of a solidarity in the cultural-educational field and the conclusion has been reached that this can be obtained by the unification of women into one association in which all of them would co-operate for the good of all the Ukrainian women in Canada, at the same time not forgetting the needs of our Ukrainian people in the Old country" [18].

According to the press notices it would appear that the Women's Association of Winnipeg was striving to unite the local women's organizations with its own organizational system by establishing locals of the Women's Association, making it the parent organization. In this organization there worked such noted members of the women's movement in Canada as: Anna Yonker, Anna Bychynska, Maria Korecka, Olena Sushko, Euhenia Uhryniwna, E. Hykawa, A. Stechishin, N. Rykhliwska, and others.

It is quite apparent that there were great inclinations toward the organization and the unification of the various women's organizations when in the spring of 1925 there appeared the already mentioned "Appeal" from the Women's Sitch Committee which was signed by: Anna Arabska of Stony Mountain, Katerina Okhitva of Yorkton, and O. Arabska of Bedfordville, which stated: "Let us remember that we, women, comprise fully not only one half of our nation, but in our hands lies the bringing up of all the children." This was a most realistic approach to the problems of women and with it the role and importance of the women in the society.

UKRAINIAN WOMEN'S ASSOCIATION OF CANADA

As it would appear, the women of Saskatoon adopted a more purposeful and systematic approach to their work. In 1923 there was organized, in conjunction with the National Home, the Olga Kobylanska Women's Society which was headed by Charytia Kononenko. A group of the female students of the P. Mohyla Institute formed a group called "Mohylanky". Some of these students, were also members of the Olga Kobylanska Women's Society. They, along with other interested members, began to confer upon the formation of more local organizations, but above all upon the need for a unification of all such organizations into a "chain system" with a central executive at its head.

After numerous discussions a Temporary Committee of the Women's Section was formed which consisted of Savella Stechishin, Maria Madiuk, Tetiana Kroitor, M. Hryniuk, Dorothy Yanda and others. It was the Committee that carried on a correspondence with the various women's organizations scattered throughout Canada, and taking advantage of the P. Mohyla Convention which was celebrating its first decade of activity, it prepared the groundwork for the first women's convention in Saskatoon, where there was formed the first dominion-wide organization of the women in Canada—the Ukrainian Women's Association of Canada (S.U.K.). Already at that time many organizations of women took an active part in this first, memorable gathering. There besides representatives from the Olga Kobylanska Society were delegates from the Societies of the same

---

[18] Memorial Book of the Ukrainian National Home in Winnipeg, 1949, pages 227-228.

name in Meacham, Whitkow, Goodeve; the Daughters of Ukraine from Regina; Lesia Ukrainka Society from Canmore in Alberta, and the Hanna Barwinok Society in Vonda, Saskatchewan.

At the second convention of this new organization there were already represented the following localities: from Saskatchewan: Goodeve, Meacham, Skoon, Yorkton, Canora, Stornoway, Mikado, Glasslyn, Foam Lake, Wakaw, Vonda, Prudhomme, Regina, Borden, Lauverna, Rosthern, Willowbrook, Colonsay, St. Julien, Numera, Krydor, Saskatoon, Hafford; from Manitoba: Winnipeg; from Alberta: Edmonton, Vegreville; from Ontario: Fort William. It is quite evident that this first executive of the S.U.K. consisting of Olga Swystun, Savella Stechishin, Hanka Romanchych, M. Madiuk, O. Sawchuk, D. Yanda, and others worked successfully since in one year more than 20 women's locals were organized. In 1928 the chief executive of this organization had its headquarters in Saskatoon and its president until 1934 was Savela Stechishin for she had been the foremost organizer and builder of this organization since its very beginning. In 1934 the head office was moved to Edmonton.

In a very short time the S.U.K. had developed a wide-spread action in the raising of the young generation, the nurture of the cult of womanhood and the conducting of the Ukrainian language classes. It also gave financial aid to the public institutions, published a separate Women's Section in the "Ukrainian Voice" in conjunction with such international organizations as the Women's International Council, the *Associated Country Women of the World,* etc. Great attention was also paid to the fostering of the national art and craft through the organization of the S.U.K. Museum in Saskatoon with branches in Winnipeg, Edmonton, Vancouver and Toronto.

During its second period of existence, besides O. Swystun, S. Stechishin, and Dorothy Yanda, the S.U.K. was headed by Maria Tkachuk, Anastasia Ruryk, N. Kohuska, O. Woycenko, K. Miskew, S. Wasylyshyn, S. Paush, A. Tokarek, L. Khorosh-Gregory. To commemorate the 25th anniversary of its activities N. Kohuska wrote a book in 1951 under the title of "Twenty Five Years of the Ukrainian Women's Association of Canada". The same author wrote a brochure in 1967 entitled: "Forty Years in Retrospect".

THE UKRAINIAN WOMEN'S ORGANIZATION OF CANADA

The Ukrainian Women's Organization of Canada, in its history is closely tied in with the very beginnings of the Ukrainian War Veterans' Association (U.W.V.A.), and the Ukrainian National Federation (U.N.F.) beginning with the girls and women's branches of the Ukrainian War Veterans' Association and the Olga Basarab Women's Associations. Concerning the beginning of these organizations we have the following information: "In proportion as the membership and the number of supporters of the U.W.V.A. increased, and when the girls and women's organizations began to be formed from these, and more so, later, when alongside the newly-formed organization—the Ukrainian National Federation—came to be grouped the O. Basarab Societies, there arose an acute need for the formation of an ideological superstructure for organizational initiatives..." In the middle of 1934 it was felt that this matter could no longer be put off and under the influence of the First Country-wide Conference of the Ukrainian National Federation, held in Saskatoon in July 28, 1934, the womenfolk passed a number of resolutions which became the clear-cut guide for further organizational activity of our women" [19]).

In a similar manner just as the Ukrainian Women's Association of Canada evolved from the P. Mohyla Institute so the Ukrainian Women's Organization of Canada sprang from the U.W.V.A. — U.N.F. This resulted in further historical connections with the above-mentioned organizations. As with the formation of the Ukrainian Self-Reliance League, which in itself developed from the P. Mohyla Institute, with the S.U.K. becoming an integral part of the Ukrainian Self-Reliance, so likewise with O.U.K., when it had fully established its independence, it became an integral part of the Ukrainian National Federation.

If we wish to consider the membership of these organizations it is quite evident that around the S.U.K. was grouped the generation which had grown up in Canada. Again the membership of the O.U.K. consisted mostly of those who had arrived in Canada after the First World War. This, of course, applied only to the period when these were organized. There were many similarities in the programs of both of these organizations. There were also differences which affected the basic principles of each.

The newly-formed section of the women's organization in its early years had at its head both men and women. Among such women were Stefania Bubniuk, Kateryna Krouse, Anastasia Pavlychenko, and Sofia Romaniuk. Among the men there were I. Gulay and M. Pohorecky. The latter two were the temporary representatives of the Ukrainian National Federation as the Women's Section did not yet have its own constitution and it depended upon the National Executive of the U.N.F.

The first executive of the Organization of O.U.K. was headed, among others, by such prominent promoters as Anastasia Pavlychenko, Anastasia Ukrainec, Stefania Bubniuk, Anna Romaniw and F. Kossar. At the Convention there were called into life the provincial organizers. These were: for Alberta—S. Romaniuk; for Saskatchewan—A. Basaraba; for Manitoba—E. Sytnyk; for Ontario—S. Sawchuk; and for Quebec—P. Drewniak-Kowalska, who quite often toured the whole of Canada.

The first women executive of the O.U.K. strove for its independence and in the fall of 1934 renamed itself the Central Executive of the Olga Basarab Organization of the Ukrainian Women in Canada, and plunged into an intensive activity. In five years' time it could boast of 33 locals in six provinces. The Second World War placed new duties upon the O.U.K. Apart from its cultural work among its own members, and the required co-operation with the organizations of its system, there arose the need for appreciating more fully the Canadian unity. Its full load of work the O.U.K. directed toward co-operation with the Canadian Red Cross, and the war effort of Canada. The Organization co-operated also

---

[19] Iryna Knysh—"In the Service of Our Homeland"—Winnipeg, 1955, page 44. This book commemorates 25 years of activities of the Ukrainian Women's Organization.

with the Ukrainian Golden Cross in the United States. When it came to cooperation with other women's organizations in Canada the O.U.K. worked with the Canadian Women's Council.

In the post-war period the O.U.K. became a member of the world Federation of Organizations of Ukrainian Women and took upon itself the task of organizing youth sections of those who had grown up in Canada. The lecturer upon such matters was for a long time Anna Wach. A. Pavlychenko was the president of O.U.K. during most of the pre-war period, while during the Second World War Maria Gulay and Evhenia Sytnyk were in charge. In post-war times the organization was headed by A. Tarnovecka, Olha Stebnitska and since 1954 by Stefania Sawchuk. Headquarters of this organization were Saskatoon, Winnipeg and lately Toronto.

THE UKRAINIAN CATHOLIC WOMEN'S LEAGUE

The unifying processes of the Ukrainian Catholic women acted much more slowly. There was already a number of women's organizations in the parishes at the beginning of our era but because of the parochial discipline their interests were directed toward matters which concerned their individual congregations. But as soon as the Ukrainian Catholic Brotherhood was formed in 1932 the organizers began to give serious thought to the formation of similar organizational structure for the women. The initiators of this movement, directed toward the organization, were the women themselves, from Winnipeg and Yorkton. Acting upon the consideration of the inter-provincial conferences in those two places there was constituted in April 1944, the first dominion-wide council of the Ukrainian Catholic women, which later adopted the name of the Ukrainian Catholic Women's League (U.C.W.L.). The first executive of this League, which in a short time became very active, consisted of Maria Dyma, A. Semotiuk, P. Kuzenko, I. Nazar, A. Yakimischak, N. Shun, L. Wall, M. Lazechko, M. Hawryluk, E. Kaluzhniacka, and Olha Lewycka. The executive enlisted the services of several local departments, namely: the Committee of War Efforts, Committee of Citizenship and Immigration, Cultural and Training Matters and Press Information. There was also an Advisory Council led by Mary Wawrykow.

The Ukrainian Catholic Women's League, in a very short time developed very thoroughly its activities among the women of the Ukrainian Catholic parishes. Without hardly any delay its branches were formed in all larger parishes throughout the country. At the end of the 40'ies this organization had over 200 branches, in every part of Canada. The headquarters were in Winnipeg, but with the division of the Ukrainian Catholic Church into several eparchies, divisional eparchial offices were formed to oversee the local women's leagues. Such offices, in addition to that in Winnipeg, were installed in Edmonton, Toronto and Saskatoon. All the eparchial councils of the Ukrainian Catholic Women's League formed a central body which in its existent history has been headed by the following leaders: Maria Dyma, Kateryna Krouse, Luba Wall, Anna Pryma Dr. Stefania Potosky, Iryna Pawlykowska. The dominion congresses of the Ukrainian Catholic Women's League normalized its affairs in such a way that its central office was subject to a three-year rotating system divided between the eparchies. Due to the lack of a stabilized steady location the main work of the Ukrainian Catholic Women's League was done by its eparchial representatives on whose dedication and energy depended most of its activities. At the head of these provincial executives were such activists as Anastasia Semotiuk, Anna Yakimischak, Mary Wawrykow, Vera Buchynska, Anna Baran, Isobel Sudol, Anna Petriv, Kateryna Harasevych, Anastasia Kozoriz, Emilia Kanchier and others. With these should be included a few other active workers like Maria Hawryluk, Anastasia Zuck, Kateryna Hnatiuk, Paraskevia Kuzenko, Maria Homyk, Kateryna Woytkiw and many more.

The Ukrainian Catholic Women's League organized in Canada three national art museums in Edmonton, Saskatoon and Toronto. It also takes care of the newly formed eparchial museum in Winnipeg. The League developed close co-operation with other women's organizations in Canada and beyond. We mention only a few of these, such as the World's Federation of Catholic Organizations, the World's Federation of Ukrainian Women's Organizations and others. A great deal of effort is devoted to social care and the cultural life of the community.

In its work the Ukrainian Catholic Women's League is fortunate to have the co-operation of the Catholic press organs that often devote separate pages to women's activities. Anna Petriv had her column for a long time in "Nasha Meta" (Our Aim), and Vera Buchynska had a similar one in "Postup" (Progress). The Edmonton Diocese prepared a special edition of its work, entitled "For God, Church and Nation", written by one of the leading women's workers, Iryna Pawlykowska.

WOMEN'S COUNCIL

The organization of the League of Ukrainian Catholic Women helped in the formation, in 1944, of the Ukrainian Canadian Women's Council Committee, which consisted of three dominion organizations of women, that is, the Ukrainian Women's Association of Canada, the Ukrainian Women's Organization of Canada, and the Ukrainian Catholic Women's League, as well as Women's Division of the United Hetman Organization. The first chairman of this council was M. Dyma, head of U.C.W.L. The Council accepted at the very beginning the principle of a rotating chairman from the several organizations and of the other functions of the Ukrainian Canadian Committee. In such a manner there was formed a centre for the co-ordinating of one work of Ukrainian women in Canada, which, in their programs, had many similarities, as well as numerous specific aims, depending upon the goals set forth in their constitutions.

The first executive of the Ukrainian Canadian Committee Women's Council also included the following: Maria Gulay, Olha Woycenko, Anna Wasylyshyn, Maria Symchych, Maria Lazechko, Anna Yakimischak, Maria Pecheniuk, Hanna Mandryka, Pelagia Genik.

In its first circular the Ukrainian Committee Women's Council called upon all Ukrainian Canadian women to consolidate their forces in carrying out the planned activities. In the beginning all attention was concentrated toward the war effort and the Red Cross work, but when the war was over their energy was turned to a peaceful development of the country. The women, united in the Ukrainian Canadian Committee, took upon themselves the great responsibility of organizing social work in aid of the Ukrainians that were stranded in Europe after the Second World War. Thanks to this effort a special fund was started into action to collect and send food and clothing to the displaced persons camps overseas. On Canadian soil the Women's Council of the Ukrainian Canadian Committee joined in the work of the National Women's Council, the Save the Children Fund, Community Chest campaigns and other charitable organizations.

The Ukrainian Canadian Committee Women's Council worked with a dedicated zeal and so the first executive head of this organization was amply justified when during the Second Congress of the Ukrainian Canadian Committee in Toronto she stated that "the Ukrainian women in Canada stood like a granite wall, an invincible strength on the home front in all of its various efforts to speed the day of victory" and that they "took full participation in the unrelenting labor for the building up of the country." New times brought new challenging tasks for this institution.

The year 1944 saw the completion of the organizational system among the Ukrainian women in Canada and united all women under one disposing and co-ordinating centre. In all larger centres there were formed local branches of the Ukrainian Canadian Women's Councils to which belonged women organizations which had not branched out.

It is worth mentioning that in larger separate centres before the locals of dominion organizations of women were formed, there already existed various local organizations. One such association, the Council of Ukrainian Women in Winnipeg organized in 1936, had united 12 other organizations. All such associations were replaced by the Ukrainian Canadian Committee Women's Council. During its nearly twenty five years of existence the Ukrainian Canadian Committee Women's Council has been headed, in addition to Maria Dyma, by such prominent leading women as Natalia Kohuska, Evhenia Sytnyk, Olha Woycenko, Anna Tarnovecka, N. Bashuk. More about the UCCWC in the "Decade of Multiculturalism".

YOUTH ORGANIZATIONS

As has already been partially mentioned in our history of the pioneer era we meet with the first attempts at the organization of the Ukrainian youth in 1904. In conjunction with the "T. Shevchenko Chytalnia" in Winnipeg there was formed a group which called itself the "Ruthenian-Ukrainian Youth" (RUM). It was this group that in that same year produced the first theatrical play in Canada entitled the "Argonauts". This group is mentioned again in the news in 1905, but it was in that same year that the group became inactive as "its members had spread out looking for work" according to the words of the press. In connection with this youth association we meet such names as: A. Novak, A. Antoniuk, J. Koltek, I. Puhaty, D. Krystiuk, J. Arsenych and others. All of these, in later years, played a prominent part in the Ukrainian communities in Canada. In the East the first group of Ukrainian youth, under the name of Ukrainian Youth Association, was organized in connection with the Association in Care of Settlers in Montreal, some time in 1906. At that time this Montreal group presented a drama entitled "If You Are with God, God Is with You" [20].

In later years, with the development of local societies, there began to be formed youth organizations in the cities, in towns, in rural areas, and quite often in the parishes of the various denominations. But all of these organizations worked on the individual basis, only from time to time did they speak a common language when it came to some group activities in a certain region.

Canadian Ukrainian Youth Association

It was not until the period between the Wars that the organizers of youth abandoned their narrow municipal boundaries and upon a provincial and later national basis began to build its superstructure. One of the first organizations to turn its attention to this problem of youth organization was the Ukrainian Women's Association of Canada (SUK). In 1927 during the second convention of the organization there were delivered two talks dealing with the subject of Youth and the need of a permanent organization. It was then that the SUK resolved that "the locals of this Association are to organize youth branches under the guidance of the women's organizations". Along these lines the action took place, and there was work on both a constitution and a program to guide the youth. In certain areas of the SUK locals only the girls belonged while in others there were both boys and girls. When in 1931 the network of Youth Organizations began to spread, the Ukrainian Self-Reliance League took over the guidance of Youth locals in 1931, and helped to form the Canadian Ukrainian Youth Association (SUMK).

This work went well particularly when the SUMK was able to engage the services of H. Tyzuk. About 200 youth branches were put to work in the various centres in Canada. These youth locals made arrangements for the putting on of concerts, consisting both of choral and instrumental music, put on plays, organized national dances, and even sports days. This was a great training for the youth, for future community activity. At first in the ranks of the SUMK there were members of various religious denominations but later this Union took on solely an Orthodox character and the members of other denominations dropped out. Even so, as many as 170 locals of SUMK were registered and thousands of the youth took part in conventions. In this Saskatchewan took the lead. The SUMK also made use of the page allotted to it in the "Ukrainian Voice."

A source of great inspiration to the Youth in their activities were the "Supervising Councils" which consisted of older people experienced in all types of community work. Important helpers of this were the teachers who understood the youth from their school days, and the activities of the SUMK was like a continuation of their school training. The leaders of the Ukrainian Self-Reliance League always tried to provide upright individuals who would oversee the training of the youth. For example, in 1927-1928 Illa Kiriak was the general secretary of the SUMK, and Ivan Danylchuk its general leader. Both were very active in their communities and both were pedagogues.

---

[20]) Studies in the History of Ukrainians in Canada, Vol. IV, p. 92.

Ukrainian National Youth Federation

The Ukrainian Students' Nationalist Organization founded in 1933 requires a separate section and separate treatment in our work. This Organization consisting of five branches at the university centres did not last long because of the limited number of its members. These were in the first place college students who sympathized very strongly with the program of the Ukrainian National Federation. There appeared an urgent need to organize the non-students who had gravitated toward this organization. Therefore in 1934 there was formed a general organization of the youth known as the Young Ukrainian Nationalists (MUN) which in its program stressed the need of helping the Ukrainian freedom movement in Europe. Besides the cultural and educational aims, the Nationalists operated for its members a radio and telegraph school in Toronto and a flying school in Oshawa. During the Second World War many of the students and instructors from these two schools joined the Canadian army units. Almost 40 locals were active before the outbreak of the Second World War. The weekly "New Pathway", which helped to formulate the aims and ideals of the Youth, dedicated a page to the activities of this organization. The first organizer of this Youth Movement was Paul Yuzyk, later a university professor and a senator. During its early stages A. Hlynka and A. Holowach, who became later members of Parliament, and K. Magera who became a lawyer, played an important part in the organization of the MUN. Some of the members of the first executive were P. Sawchuk, I. Kishynsky, A. Mysyk, A. Wach, and others. As we can well appreciate the Ukrainian National Youth Federation gave Canada a number of leading citizens.

Ukrainian Catholic Youth

The third dominion-wide organization of the youth which became active before the Second World War was the Ukrainian Catholic Youth (U.C.Y.) organized in 1938. Locals of this youth movement had already existed at a much earlier date as part of the Ukrainian Catholic Brotherhood. All this was carried on, on a local, sometimes regional and at times even a provincial basis. However, all their activities were carried on in a haphazard manner. When Father Horoshko, who had arrived in Canada in 1937, was appointed chaplain, he expanded the Ukrainian Catholic Youth into a federal organization. The second convention for the purpose of organizing the U.C.Y. was held in Winnipeg for it was there that the executive had its headquarters. Spurred into action were other chaplains as well as local priests for upon them depended the activity of the various locals.

The Ukrainian Catholic Youth had its own page in the "Future of the Nation", which was printed in English. In its activities this organization in no way differed from the other similar youth movements. There were concerts, theatrical productions, debates, contests, sports activities, etc. Special attention was paid to religious practices. The Ukrainian Catholic Youth tried to publish its own weekly, the "Youth Messenger", "Y.C.Y. Lore" and others.

Student Organizations

In order to complete this picture, portraying the various youth organizations, it is well worth adding some information about the students' organizations which existed at the universities. It appears that the group of students at the Manitoba University in Winnipeg was quite active. Such a group was already mentioned toward the end of our history dealing with the pioneer era. This group was so active and patriotic that in 1921 it arranged for donations to give financial aid to the students in Europe. The appeal was signed by: M. Sawczak-Dyma, N. Bilash, M. Lazechko, I. Symchych, M. Zalozecky. All these, later prominent citizens took an active part in unifying the Ukrainian communities.

There was also another students' society at that time in Winnipeg. The students of the A. Shepticky Institute in St. Boniface formed their own Students' Union. They also published a periodical the "Precious Diamond".

The students' group at the University of Manitoba continued its activities for many years, and among its most active members who even in later years continued to serve their communities in public work were: Doctor of Law J. Yatchew, D. Yakimischak, J. Solomon, J. Hawryluk, S. Krawchyk, M.L.A.'s in Manitoba; Wasyl Wall, senator; M. Ewanchuk, inspector of schools; H. Hawryluk, teacher; Rev. J. Robert Kovalevich, and many others.

In Saskatoon the Ukrainian Students' Union entitled the "Kameniari" (Stone Cutters) carried on its community work. It continued the traditions of the earliest pioneers, already mentioned. This organization of the Saskatoon students showed a great deal of life in its organizational work for it was able to establish connections with other students' unions, of a similar nature, in Canada. Together these Unions formed the Centralia of Ukrainian Students which co-operated with the Ukrainian Students' Central Federation in Europe (CESUS) [21].

There was also, in Saskatoon, a Section of the female students which had adopted the name of "Mohylianky" [22]. Working together, the students edited a mimeographed periodical, the "Stone Cutters".

In 1930, at the University of Saskatoon there was organized the first local of "Alpha Omega"—a students' organization. At that same time there appeared in Winnipeg, the "Prometey" (Prometheus)—a students' club which had very close connections with the branch of the P. Mohyla Institute in Winnipeg that existed there from 1927 to 1934. Somewhat later there were organized locals of the Ukrainians Students' National Organization (U.S.N.O.), which have already been mentioned.

In Edmonton there was a very active "A. Kotsko Students' Group" in the Hrushevsky Institute. Between the years 1917 and 1943 the Kotsko Group had a membership of 741 students, both boys and girls, most of them resident students. They were brought up in a spirit of patriotism toward the Ukrainian people and to Canada. When Canada joined the War a large number of these, mostly first year students, volunteered for military service: 52 joined the R.C.A.F., 32 the R.C.A., and 5 the R.C.N. Thus the ideals for which they had stood were upheld both by their actions and their sacrifice [23]. In Edmonton there was

---

21) Julian Stechishin: P. Mohyla Institute—Past & Future, Winnipeg, 1966; page 12.
22) Two of the deans of these were Petrunia Boykovich and Savela Stechishin. They and the others put in a great deal of effort to bring up these students.
23) The Twenty-Fifth Jubilee of the M. Hrushevsky Ukrainian Institute in Edmonton, 1945. See the chapter entitled "Members and Resident Students of the M. Hrushevsky Institute in the Canadian Services in 1943"—page 122.

also an energetic Markian Shashkevych Students' Union organized in 1930. There was also in operation a separate group of students from the Ukrainian Catholic Brotherhood Bursa in Saskatoon, which even published one edition of its periodical "The Bell".

In 1940 in Toronto there was organized the Ukrainian Students' Club. There were also students' sections which were a part of the larger local organizations such as the Ukrainian National Home in Winnipeg, in Edmonton, and other institutions.

The programs of these students were directed toward the following objectives:

"To provide the University students with a forum for the discussion of the problems concerning the Ukrainian culture in Canada; to foster the inlaying of the Ukrainian cultural patterns into the total Canadian mosaic; and, to encourage the students in their efforts for self-improvement and to work for Ukrainian Canadian organizations and other worthwhile causes. More about youth in chapter "UCC and its organizations".

MUTUAL BENEFIT ASSOCIATIONS

To a special category belong the mutual benefit associations whose purpose it was to help its members and their families in case of unemployment, sickness, or death. As we are aware the oldest organization of such a nature was the Ukrainian National Association (UNS), New Jersey, U.S.A., the first branch of which was formed in Fernie, B.C. in 1904. Powerful competitor of the Ukrainian National Association in the U.S.A. was the Ruthenian National Association in Canada which later changed its name to the Ruthenian-Canadian Association and the Mutual Benefit Association of St. Nicholas which began to operate in 1905.

The Ruthenian-Canadian National Association did not last very long and in the meantime the St. Nicholas Association from a local provincial organization became a dominion organization in 1930.

During the period between the World Wars it boasted of 30 branches with a membership of over 5,000. The Organization paid out over a million dollars for funeral expenses and over a quarter million for sickness. The Mutual Benefit Association of St. Nicholas supports with its donations cultural and educational community institutions, and by 1967 has donated $40,000. The property of the St. Nicholas Association is valued at one and a quarter million. For 50 years the St. Nicholas Association was under the management of I. Zarowsky, I. Nowosad, I. Zborowsky, S. Romaniw, I. Parkasewych, J. Kozoriz and others.

In Eastern Canada, in Toronto there was organized in 1910 the Ruthenian National Benefit Society which continued its mutual aid for 16 years. There also were organized several other Ukrainian Catholic mutual benefit associations which later formed the Union of Ukrainian Benefit Societies that had its headquarters in Toronto.

In 1921 there was formed still another benefit organization under the name of the Ukrainian Fraternal Society (U.F.S.). The initiators and the first members of the executive were I. Trach, S. Basisty, H. I. Block, W. Bilenky, P. Popel. This organization grew steadily.

In 1967 the U.F.S. was worth $2,000,000 with a membership of 6,000. In the cases of sickness $250,000 have been paid out and over a half a million for funeral expenses. The Ukrainian Fraternal Society has laid aside special funds for the support of the Ukrainian culture in Canada. The leading promoters of this organization were: M. Stechishin, T. D. Ferley, O. Babynec, W. Kazaniwsky, I. Trach, I. H. Syrnick.

The youngest dominion insurance organization in Canada is the Ukrainian Workingmen's Association (U.R.S.) whose head office is located in Scranton, Pennsylvania. This Union began its work upon the Canadian terrain in the period during the World Wars, but a much stronger organizational activity began in 1936 when the opposition to the U.L.F.T.A. sought membership in the U.R.S. At the beginning of the Second World War there were already 15 branches. At present this organization numbers 2,000 members in 30 branches with a value of a million dollars. However, the property of the Ukrainian National Association (UNS) in Canada is valued at $2,500,000 with a membership of almost 8,000. Figures correct as of 1967.

Each of the four benefit organizations, just discussed, has its own ideological and political affiliations. The Mutual Benefit Association of St. Nicholas is closely connected with the Catholics. The Ukrainian Fraternal Society is mostly Orthodox, while the Ukrainian National Association and the Ukrainian Workingmen's Association do not take into consideration religious denominational elements, but are connected with national organizations. The Ukrainian National Association is more closely allied with nationalistic organizations while the Ukrainian Workingmen's Association, with the organizations which in their programs pay more attention to the social question. Headquarters of the first two benefit associations are in Winnipeg, while the last two are in Toronto.

The work of the Workers Benevolent Association (RZT) has already been mentioned in another place. This is the association which both ideologically and politically was tied in with the Ukrainian Labor and Farmers' Temple Association, respectively with the Association of United Ukrainian-Canadians (TOUK). It is valued at $4,000,000 with a membership of 17,000.

It was after the Second World War that another Ukrainian insurance and benefit company from the United States became active in Canada. This is the Ukrainian National Aid which is centered in Toronto.

LOCAL ORGANIZATIONS

By listing the dominion-wide organizations we are not exhausting the organizational life of the Ukrainian people in Canada during the period between the World Wars. Both in smaller and in larger centres where the Ukrainians had settled there was always a number of organizations of a local character which did not belong to any dominion-wide organization. Quite often these numbered hundreds of members who, in broader organizational structure of the community, took an important lead. Only as an example we can point out here such organizations in Winnipeg as the Ukrainian National Home [24] the Ukrainian-Canadian Educational

---

[24] The Memorial Book of the Ukrainian People's Home in Winnipeg, in 1949, page 863.

Institute Prosvita, [25] "Ridna Shkola" Association, [26] and others. All of these obtained spacious buildings for the purpose of carrying on their cultural activities. Each of these has a long list of accomplishments in the field of Ukrainian schools, theatrical and choral art, popular and educational lectures, etc. The same can be said of such institutions as the Prosvita Association in Fort William and Port Arthur, [27] Ukrainian National Home and the Chytalnia Prosvita in Toronto, the T. Shevchenko Association, [28] and the M. Drahomaniv in Montreal, the Ukrainian National Home in Edmonton, [79] the Prosvita Association in Kenora, [30] and in other localities in Canada.

According to the statistics in 1936 there were 227 such educational organizations under various names, but mostly such as "Prosvita", "Prosvita Associations", or "National Homes". They were divided among the provinces as follows: 1 in British Columbia, 1 in Nova Scotia, 5 in Quebec, 27 in Ontario, 37 in Alberta, 64 in Saskatchewan, and 92 in Manitoba [31].

According to the regulations of its constitution each had a library for the use of its members, and subscribed to newspapers published in Canada and elsewhere. Every organization had its dramatic group, and quite often choral ensembles. There was also carried a varied cultural work with occasional lectures dealing with various topics, depending upon the interests of its members. Above all each organization tried to hold evening, Saturday, or vacational classes where the children learned their heritage language. On the whole, in all of its activities, each organization strove to uphold and spread its national and cultural values among which the native language was the basic element.

As many as 1,200 parishes, cultural and educational institutions, four sports clubs, [32] and 14 students' clubs were at work in the Ukrainian communities in the period between the two World Wars.

All of these, if consolidated, are expressions of the vitality and the aspirations of the Ukrainian communities as a separate cultural entity in the Canadian mosaic. All of these organizations were helped by various benefit societies numbering more than 200 which, besides the material aid, gave its members encouragement for national and cultural growth.

---

[25] Half a Century of Activity of the Ukrainian Association of the Chytalnia Prosvita in Winnipeg, 1958, page 224.

[26] Studies to the History of Ukrainians in Canada, Vol. I, Winnipeg, 1964-1965, page 255.

[27] "The Golden Gate", the Jubilee Book of "Prosvita" in Port Arthur 1909-1969, Port Arthur—Winnipeg 1960, page 328.

[28] The Golden Jubilee of the T. Shevchenko Enlightenment Society in Montreal —1913-1965, "Torch of Enlightenment & Life" p. 296.

[29] Memorial Book of the Ukrainian National Home in Edmonton, 1966, page 542.

[30] Jubilee Book of the Prosvita Association in Kenora 1915-1965, Winnipeg, page 296.

[31] "The Guide", Winnipeg, 1936, page 36.

[32] One such club "The Canadian Ukrainian Athletic Club" was organized in 1923 and has an extraordinary history of its great successes.

Its annual yearbook was not merely a record of its achievements, but also the history of the great concern of the older citizens managing this club. During the first 25 years of its existence its presidents were: M. Shaley, John Moroz, V. H. Koman, W. Lewicky, S. Rebchuk, S. Mykytyn, I. Shaley, I. Mirus.

THIRD STAGE

We have already made some references to Ukrainian professionals when we outlined the pioneer decade, but they really became noticeable at the break of the second decade. In 1923, 25 Ukrainian Canadians completed university education and received diplomas. This was an initial group of highly qualified Ukrainian professionals even though it was a very small percentage in proportion to the Ukrainian population at the time. But it was only a beginning.

In 1925, Petro Mohyla Institute reported that in this single institution between the years of 1916-1925, 470 students were receiving higher education, of whom 117 became teachers, 10 physicians, 5 lawyers, several priests, engineers, mechanics, etc [1].

In the reports of other institutions, such as Bursa of Metropolitan Shepticky in Winnipeg, and of Michael Hrushevsky in Edmonton, we find that these institutes had an overwhelming influx of students from farming areas who wanted to attend urban schools and higher education institutions.

Dr. H. G. Skehar, who maintained a register of Ukrainian professionals in Canada and the U.S.A. in 1931, listed over 250 lawyers, physicians and engineers, and admitted in his report that this roster was not complete [2]. In any event, even that figure had a positive effect on the emancipation of the Ukrainians in Canada.

More accurate data in relation to Ukrainian professionals was prepared and published in 1935, by F. T. Hawryluk [3]. In accordance with his assertions, in Western Canada alone, during that year, 164 Ukrainian students graduated from universities.

In the three prairie provinces there were 727 teachers of Ukrainian descent who practiced their profession while in the same period of time around 60 teachers were unemployed. During the same period there were 160 university students in the said provinces registered in various faculties and 144 attended teachers' institutes. The same author also disclosed that during that period there were in the prairie provinces over 2500 Ukrainians who graduated from high schools. In his remarks and explanations to these statistical figures, F. T. Hawryluk stated: "All this consists of only one percent of our population which is far below the level of the proportional distribution among English people, but we must consider the fact that we had no ready means to start with" [4].

This honest statement needs no further explanation, but we would like to further clarify some of these statistics. In the first place, the author in his compiled data did not include the Ukrainian clergy, which at that time in all Catholic, Orthodox and Protestant churches numbered more than 150 ordained clerics. Moreover, he took into consideration only those persons who graduated from Canadian schools and colleges but did not include the intellectuals who came to Canada from Europe after

---

[1] Official Communication to the members of Petro Mohyla Institute, dated 17/10/25, in author's archives.
[2] "Canadian Farmer", 11/9/31.
[3] "Our Cultural Development in Canada", Winnipeg, 1936, p. 8.
[4] "Ukrainians in Canada, Business Year Book", 1949-50, Winnipeg, p. 4.

the First World War and who, as we have stated earlier, constituted a fairly high percentage of new immigration; a few even succeeded to important posts in State Universities [5]). None the less it is an indisputable fact that in the second decade the Ukrainians of Canada laid a cornerstone in the formation of the third dimension. It is, therefore, understandable that the early Ukrainian farm and urban communities welcomed with great enthusiasm the appearance of every new professional man and woman as evidenced by the warm announcements in press, random discussions, and many statistical reports.

Accounts of accomplishments of the second decade are recorded in minute details in the statistical annuals of F. Macrouch, designated as "Ukrainians in Canada, Business Year Book" [6]). These accounts were prepared on the basis of Dominion Census Reports and, therefore, reflect more accurate professional standing of the Ukrainians prior to the year 1941. It was evident from these reports that teachers comprised the main category among the professionals and numbered 1213; next came the clergy 208, followed by nurses, who were listed as 108 registered and 126 non-registered. Musicians and teachers of music also comprised a significant portion as there were 116 of them. There were 89 engineers including architectural, mining and electrical, 59 physicians, 49 chemists and metalurgists, 38 lawyers and notaries and 26 journalists, as well as 5 college professors. Added together, there were 2383 professionals, including special practitioners and experts. Surprisingly, no judges or magistrates of Ukrainian origin are listed in those reports at the time, though it is shown that in the "public service" there were 9 firemen, 59 police officers and 36 held various post office positions. The latter category chiefly consisted of rural post office managers, and not clerks, who were separately listed as 32 persons. Thus, the total number of civil service workers was only 202.

From the foregoing figures, it can be assumed that the Ukrainians preferred free professions rather than public service. Undoubtedly, besides their own preference there have been other determining factors; it was easier for a Ukrainian at that time to become a dentist (there were 32) than to become a post office manager, of whom, as shown above, there were also 32, as compared to only 9 firemen. Seemingly, the same trend can be noticed in other divisions of public service which was considered a privilege reserved for certain nationalities, and the access to which for the Ukrainians was only accidental.

In the early thirties, the Ukrainian professionals of Canada and U.S.A. considered themselves sufficiently important and possessing the necessary stamina to have their own organization which they named "the Ukrainian Professional Association." The first convention of this association was held in Chicago in 1933. The program speeches were delivered by I. Bobersky, V. Biberovych, T. Humeniuk, H. Hawryluk, J. Yatchew and H. G. Skehar. There were four speakers from Canada and 2 from the U.S.A. The Canadians spoke in Ukrainian and the Americans in English. This reflected the political symbolism of the American melting pot and the Canadian multicultural process. The first president of this

---

[5]) Professors at Saskatchewan University—T. K. Pavlychenko and W. Kossar.
[6]) F. Macrouch (Macrovich) published 10 such yearly reports between 1944-1955, which contained very valuable statistical data about the Ukrainians in Canada.

organization was attorney O. E. Miles-Malycky of Cleveland, Ohio, who was born in Canada and received his early training in Canadian schools. Other first officers included: Dr. H. G. Skehar, Dr. John Yatchew, Prof. A. A. Granovsky and Attorney Stephen Shumeyko.

The main purpose of the organization was: "To encourage the Ukrainian Youth to devote itself to knowledge and to attain the highest ranks in the realm of education" [7]. The young professionals deemed themselves duty-bound to continue the tasks of their parents. This was stressed in the speech by Attorney John Yatchew of Windsor, when he said: "Our pioneer fathers did their share. They carried on with integrity as best they could, and left us their unblemished name. Now it is our turn!" [8].

The Ukrainian Professional Association with headquarters in Chicago continued its existence until the Second World War. It was presided over for several years by Attorney O. E. Miles-Malycky of Cleveland. After the Second World War, new professional organizations have arisen in Canada with headquarters in Winnipeg and branches in other major cities. We will come to this subject again in later chapters.

In conjunction with the reports as to various professions, it would be of definite interest to present some facts as regards other trades and occupations, chiefly sales and exchanges of real estate, construction in all its forms, commerce, transportation, etc. This is also of major significance since it demonstrates that out of purely farm communities in the pioneer decade new generation was born with special talents leading into industrial, commercial and professional activities. In 1941, it was determined that 13,148 persons were engaged in industry and related fields, in construction and building 3,303; in commercial enterprises 4,463; in lumber projects 1,526; and in mining 2,904. In fact, out of 113,931 persons, excluding active military service, only 54,972 persons were engaged in agriculture; all others were already occupied in other activities, only slightly related to agriculture [9].

One enterprise that appealed to the Ukrainians between the two World Wars was business. A reference has already been made in another chapter about the First Informative Economic Congress held in Winnipeg in 1923, and about the Educational Farmers Conference of the same time and place. Eventually, when Dominion organizations — SUS, UNO, BUK and others came into existence, they all, within the scope of their activities and statutory authority, turned their serious consideration towards economic problems. One of the more important econo-informative conferences at a later period was held in Winnipeg (towards the end of 1929 and the beginning of 1930) which was prepared by the League of the Ukrainian National Homes in Canada with the cooperation of the Ukrainian National Home of Winnipeg. During that conference separate permanent committees were created for business, cooperative, labor and farming affairs, which were to examine and consider all questions and problems affecting economic standing of any and every community.

---

[7] "The Ukrainian Professionals in U.S.A. and Canada", Winnipeg, p. 9.
[8] Same reference, page 45.
[9] Ukrainians in Canada, Business Year Book, 1949-50, Winnipeg, p. 4.

Winnipeg, and Manitoba generally, were the initiators of these conferences, but other provinces kept their own pace also. In December 1928 one such significant conference was held in Edmonton, known in history as the First Ukrainian Business Conference of Alberta, wherein a considerable number of business-minded Ukrainians exchanged their views and judgments relative to business affairs. Economic matters of Saskatchewan were frequently discussed at conferences held at the Institute of Petro Mohyla in Saskatoon.

Competent knowledge and experience assumed greater perseverance not only among business people and professionals, but also among the farmers. Their conferences, among others, have been good examples of this trend. One of them was held in Dauphin, Manitoba, in 1928. In Alberta, the Ukrainian farmers were united with the "United Farmers of Alberta" (UFA).

Exceptional initiative in particular was revealed by the Ukrainian business men of Winnipeg in 1934, when through their efforts a Journal called the "Business-Industrial Guide" was initiated and began to popularize the benefits derived from business ventures. After the appearance of several issues of this popular economic journal, there also was organized the "Ukrainian Economic Society—Chain," an original ideological society with the purpose to encourage and support business enterprise among Ukrainians. This society was organized by the Ukrainian professionals and businessmen, under the initiative of persons like D. Yakimischak, D. Gerych, K. S. Prodan, W. A. Krysky and others. The "Chain" henceforth, conducted an extensive campaign to bring together the Ukrainian business, industry, and professional men, not only in Winnipeg and Manitoba, but even sent organizers into Saskatchewan to strengthen the "Chain".

As a result of this campaign, an "Economic Convention" was held in Winnipeg late September, 1935, in which several hundred business and professional men took part and which issued a summons to create new enterprises and to include the already existing ones into the system of the "Chain."

Because of the "Chain" an additional unit was created known as "Standard Wholesale," which assisted its members in buying merchandise at wholesale prices, not only in Manitoba but also in other provinces. The central figure of the business organization in Winnipeg was attorney D. Yakimischak, who was the head of the "Chain" as well as of the wholesale unit and the association of merchants and retailers for a long time.

As this "Chain" complex also included some professionals, it can be assumed that this complex was the forerunner of the "Ukrainian Business and Professional Club" in Winnipeg, which came into being shortly after the Second World War.

Somewhat similar circumstances surrounded the creation of the Business and Professional Club of Toronto. It began its activities in 1934, headed by Mykola Paraschuk. These circumstances are outlined by one of the organizers of that group who also became its president for a number of years, I. Ilaschuk, who wrote:

---

[10]) In this initial group were also included: C. H. Andrusyshen, V. H. Koman, N. Halas, N. Fedyk, D. Rostocky, T. D. Ferley, I. Wachniak, A. Malofie, I. Wachna, J. Kulachkowsky, I. Probizansky, I. Dolynchuk, K. Pidlubny, I. Hawryluk.

"One Sunday, during the course of 1934, several store-keepers met in a store room to discuss their mutual problems—business difficulties, etc. It was not a very prosperous year at that time, and we had no organization or a meeting place to get advice or encouragement. That Sunday we exchanged our views and ideas for improvement, and came upon an idea of forming our own business association. A year later, 1935, we enlisted 240 members" [11].

Summing up the beginnings of the development of the third stage — professionals and businessmen — in the Ukrainian Canadian community, it is necessary to note that during the period between the two World Wars this third stage began to expand, to consolidate and search for new avenues of expression. Professionals and businessmen became aware of the role in the community may be played by them due to their organized strength. This awareness was transferred from Winnipeg and Toronto to other Ukrainian centres in Canada. Tiny rivulets needed time to develop into a strong current. This process developed fully after the Second World War mainly to the fact — increased number of professionals and businessmen. Development of these events will be discussed in subsequent chapters: "Achievements and Integration" — "Ukrainian Professional and Businessmen's Club". We record increased awareness of the importance of the role played by professional and businessmen's organizations in the seventies in chapters of our history as "Development of Ukrainian Studies Courses", "Ukrainian Canadian Committee and Its Organizations" and others.

The latest economic activity in which the Canadian Ukrainian entered into was industry which required considerable capital, but even in this enterprise considerable progress has been achieved. The leaders in this venture were the following: P. Rudyk, F. D. Sicinsky, I. Kowal, I. Markiw, and others.

---

[11] Ukrainian Canadian Business Almanac, Toronto, 1955, p. 17.

COOPERATIVE MOVEMENT

Cooperative movement plays an important part in the economic world. It brings into business that reinforcing element which creates potential mutual assistance in undertaking a business proposition where individual attempts would be impractical or impossible. Mutual assistance has a long standing tradition among Ukrainian people. In villages, soil was tilled with mutual cooperation, most important activity was performed together such as cultivation of fields, transportation of grain, threshing, etc.

It is not surprising therefore, that during early settlements, as we have already pointed out, the Ukrainians pooled their resources at work and established cooperative stores, although at that time there was no co-operative law or regulation to control them. It may be one of the reasons why these stores did not last too long.

Vegreville Co-operative in Alberta and Fisher Branch Co-operative in Manitoba, both established in 1929, have the distinction of being the oldest co-operatives under the management of Ukrainian Canadians. But expanded co-operative movement on sound ideological base began in 1930 with the founding of "Kalyna" Co-operative in Winnipeg by the members of the Ukrainian War Veterans Association "Striltsi", who were then organizing their chapters in Canada. Thus was the idea of the co-operative movement simultaneously dessiminated among Ukrainians living in other centres.

Another significant factor in the extension of the cooperative movement among the Ukrainians in Canada was the impressive cooperative movement itself that was going on in Western Ukraine. Taking into consideration the fact that consumer cooperatives in Western Ukraine were in the lead at that time, it is presumable that the Ukrainians in Canada were prompted by the fact and showed such an intense interest in that branch of the cooperative life.

The years 1930 and 1940 marked the epoch of the Ukrainian co-operative movement in Canada. In Alberta alone 10 consumers cooperatives were organized. Besides the aforementioned Vegreville Co-operative others were formed in the areas: Smoky Lake, in 1934, Willingdon in 1938, Myrnam in 1938, Derwent in 1940, Cherhill in 1941, Mundare in 1942, Thorold in 1944, Boyle in 1945. The movement in those areas was guided by pioneer workers such as: T. Tomashev sky, Romaniuk brothers—Bill, John and Nick, M. Gawinchuk and others.

In Saskatchewan, three energetic cooperators were in full swing—M. Babey, P. Ivanycky, and O. Topolnycky. They first organized a consumers cooperative in Regina in 1932, and later on, a credit union. After Regina, came Ituna in 1937, Smuts in 1938, followed in 1940 by Alvena, Arran and Wishart.

The most active cooperative movement took place in Manitoba. In addition to the two already mentioned, there came into existence two fuel cooperatives, namely, North Winnipeg Cooperative 1931, Cooperative Union of St. Boniface 1936; National Consumers Cooperative of Winnipeg 1937 and then later in Sandy Lake 1935, Broad-Valley 1936, Britestone 1938, Dauphin 1945, Gilbert Plains 1947, Ethelbert 1949.

Aside from the aforementioned consumers cooperatives there were in operation also manufacturing cooperatives in Manitoba such as Western Cooperative which made gloves in Winnipeg. There also functioned in Winnipeg a "Cooperative of Manitoba Producers of Grain and Vegetables." There was still another very active "Cooperative of National Dairies", which afforded employment to around 100 workers. Another dairy cooperative was formed in Vita 1939, and the "Cooperative Bakery" in Winnipeg was organized in 1945.

The most prominent leaders in Cooperative Movement in Manitoba were William Topolnycky, a highly qualified cooperator, ideologist and an author of many articles on cooperative topics, Danylo Budka, I. Hrushowy, I. Ferentz, M. Brelis, S. Skoblak and others.

In Eastern Canada, the nucleus of the movement originated in Toronto. Consumers Cooperative "The Future" 1933, had two branches in Thorold (1935) with two retail stores: one in Sudbury (1941) and another in 1945, named "Progress."

Over 10,000 families were members of these cooperatives. Cooperative movement strove hard, but not all the results that were achieved during that decade in the economy movement had a long-lasting existence. Consumers Cooperatives experienced the hardest conditions, having to compete with flexible processes of the "chain-stores." The fuel cooperatives could not withstand the improvement brought about by gas and electric appliances. The most promising and successful enterprises were the credit cooperatives or "credit unions" which as the years went by grew from thousand dollar institutions to million dollar institutions.

The credit union movement among the Ukrainians began about ten years later than the consumers cooperatives. "The New Community" in Saskatoon was the first "star" so to speak on the Canadian horizon (1939). It was organized by William Topolnycky, to whom a reference was made earlier. A year later, in Winnipeg, credit union "Carpathia" was organized, and still later, credit unions were formed in Regina (1941), Arran (1942), Smuts (1943), Wishart and Redberry (1944), all in Saskatchewan. In Alberta, credit unions began to operate in Smoky Lake and Andrew (1943). In 1943 "North Winnipeg Credit Union" and "Ukrainian National Credit Union of Hamilton" commenced their operations. The latter was organized by M. Babey, who, during the war, also organized "Ukrainian National Credit Union of Toronto," and one in Sudbury (1944). During this time a credit union was established in Montreal, also named "the Ukrainian National Credit Union."

Nearly all of these credit unions, especially in the East, were originally organized members of the Ukrainian National Federation and in connection with their chapters. With the influx of membership from various environments, the organizational influence of individual initiators noticeably diminished, but not the idea of credit union philosophy itself, which significantly increased in its scope, importance and necessity. During the war period there were 14 credit unions organized, 10 in the West and 4 in the East. In general, this was a good beginning of credit union cooperative movement, which in the third decade of our history, has attained such vast proportions.

AGRICULTURAL ACHIEVEMENT

In discussing the progress made by the Ukrainians in the spheres of various professions, industry, business and cooperative movement, it would be an omission not to review at least cursorily the achievements made by them in the argricultural sector of our economy.

We have already pointed out that the percentage of farm labor has been going down not only as a result of undesirable or unprofitable farmland, but also because of the change in farming techniques. Tractors and combines have taken over the work of thousands of employees. With modern machinery one family could complete not only its own chores, but also give assistance to its neighbors. It also became too costly and unpractical to operate small farms with great amount of expensive machinery, and so it became a natural tendency to acquire additional acreage in order to make farming a profitable enterprise. Mechanization and proper effort usually brought successful results. Senator Paul Yuzyk who was making a research as to the contributions made by Ukrainians in the development of Canada, declared that the Ukrainian settlers tilled more than 19 million acres of farm land [1].

The efforts of the Ukrainian settlers were not aimed only at expansion of their economy, but also at getting out the maximum returns on their labor. This fact was well demonstrated, particularly when in 1930, through the initiative of Henry Thornton, president of the Canadian National Railways, a so-called "Competition of Community Progress" in the prairie provinces was inaugurated.

The judges evaluated this progress in various rural municipalities, took into consideration only three aspects: progress in farming, in community life and in cultural development. In 1930 the first prize in Manitoba was awarded to the Municipality of Rossburn which is 75 percent Ukrainian. The 4th prize was won by the Ukrainians in the Municipality of Ethelbert. In Saskatchewan, the Ukrainians of Yorkton won 3rd prize and 4th prize went to the Ukrainians of Redberry.

Similar results were observed in Alberta where Ukrainians were awarded first rank in Norma and a 3rd place in Pine. Approximately the same results were obtained in the ensuing years. Judicial praises were bestowed not only for economic gains, but also for Ukrainian cultural attainments. In his remarks, the chairman of the judging committee Dr. John McKay stated: "The judges were deeply impressed with the wealth and variety of this inheritance that Canada so badly needs" [2].

There is no doubt in the least that this great progress of the Ukrainian farmers, apart from their hard work and experience, was also due to the valuable help and advice received by them from the Ukrainian agronomists who were operating in Western provinces as farm experts or advisors by appointment of the federal governments. Among them was K. S. Prodan, the first Ukrainian agronomist in Canada, who served as

---

[1] "Ukrainian Canadians: Their Place and Role in Canadian Life", by Senator Paul Yuzyk, Toronto, 1967.
[2] The Colonization of Western Canada, by Robert England, pp. 175-225.

instructor of the division of agriculture in Manitoba for over 15 years and 25 years as a district representative. During his long years of service he delivered and published thousands of lectures on farm and agricultural topics in general. Long years of services were also rendered by Theodore Bodnar as representative of the Dominion Government in agricultural department specializing in the cattle breeding industry. D. M. Elcheshen was also active in this line for some time. In Alberta, William Pidruchney devoted most of his life to these agricultural activities as government appointee.

Remarkable success in husbandry was accomplished by the so-called Junior Clubs. Among these clubs the province of Alberta units received most of the valuable awards at various farm produce exhibits. The greatest honor was bestowed on grain-producing groups in Chicago at the World's Grain Exhibit. William Skladan, of Andrew, Alberta, became the Oats King in 1939. Paul F. Pawlowsky of Vilna, Alberta, received First Award for best oats in 1940, while I. Lastiwka of Andrew was awarded First Prize and Championship for the quality of his barley and oats. Meanwhile E. Kowalsky of Fernview, Saskatchewan was the First Award receiver in alfalfa exhibit. At "Manitoba's Seed Fair" in 1938, Pushka brothers in Angusville, Manitoba, received most of the awards in Manitoba for best seed, and a year later the Ukrainians of Stuartburn were recipients of most of the awards for poultry where John A. Negrych was the agricultural representative (agronomist).

In the orchard industry the leading personalities were William Salamandyk, William Zazula, and William Fedun. The leaders in the honey producing sector and bee-raising were Nicholas Pankiw of Dufrost, Manitoba, and Peter Kowalsky of Bon Accord, Alberta.

The Canadian winners of awards highly distinguished themselves again in Chicago in 1941 when the aforementioned W. Skladan became the champion in the production of oats and P. Pawlowsky in barley. Within the three years, 1938-1941, the Ukrainians in Canada received 12 awards at the Chicago Exposition and 24 out of 54 provincial awards in various exhibits in Alberta [3]. Much of this accomplishment should be attributed to the efforts of the aforesaid William Pidruchney, who as a journeyman in farming from department of agriculture has contributed many and valuable services to the farmers of his district. Similar services were also credited to Theodore Magera and John Charnetski who were active as government advisors.

In the province of Saskatchewan this function was performed by Ivan H. Maduke and S. O. Hrycak who acted as cattle inspectors for the province. Also in Saskatchewan, as a soil expert, was Dr. W. Chepil who conducted an experimental farm in Swift Current. W. M. Blahy was head of experimental substation in Regina, and in Edmonton, William Odynsky supervised the soil research division of the Dominion Government Department of Agriculture. Positions as Dominion land inspectors were held by N. J. Strynadka in Alberta, W. Shewkenyk in Saskatchewan and M. Chepesiuk in Ontario.

There were agronomists of Ukrainian descent teaching in Canadian Universities. Among the most authoritative in this position was Dr. T. K.

---

[3] Contribution of Ukrainian Agronomists in the Agriculture of Canada, "The Ukrainian News", Edmonton, 1942, Nos. 12-13.

Pavlychenko, researcher in the applied economy of plants at the University of Saskatchewan. Others actively engaged therein were W. Kossar and W. Mysak. At the University of Manitoba a highly recognized instructor of Pomology was Dr. W. J. Cherewick who later after the Second World War was a director of agricultural division for "Colombo Plan" on Malay Islands in Asia, and lately a supervisor of dominion establishments of pathology research. Dr. P. Kondra was specializing in poultry science at the same university. P. Nikolaychuk held an important post at the University of McGill. A number of other agronomists specialized in their particular fields.

In recent years Dr. Isydore Hlynka, engaged by the Department of Agriculture at Ottawa as wheat chemist since 1939, has shown considerable prominence and has been elevated to an important position with the Board of Grain Commission.

A number of these are engaged as agronomy professors outside of Canada. Among them are: Dr. G. Semeniuk, Dr. N. Holowaychuk, Dr. M. Peech and others. They were all brought up and reared on Canadian farms as sons of Ukrainian pioneers. In 1941 statistical reports showed that 46 qualified agronomists who graduated from agricultural departments of various universities in Western Canada were engaged as experts in agricultural divisions in farming areas.

The progress in agricultural undertakings is closely related to the progress the Ukrainians made in business, industry, cooperative enterprises and professional life. If comparisons were to be made between the years 1920 and 1930, definite advancement can be observed among Ukrainians in every line of endeavor. This marked and rapid advance can be easily explained when first we consider the fact that every sector of economy was enlarged by the new force of the second generation of Canadian Ukrainians who did not hesitate to try their skills and talents at every given opportunity in the economy of life, and secondly, the immigration of the second era had sufficient qualifications and experience to be able to compete in their new invironment. The first factor was aptly emphasized by P. Yuzyk in his history . He wrote:

"The second generation of Ukrainian Canadians upon reaching adulthood, was quick to see the advantages in the economic sphere as in personal service. The year 1930 is approximately the turning point which marks the beginning of the entry of a large number of Canadian-born into other than agricultural pursuits" [4].

The above conclusions with reference to Manitoba may be fully applied to two other provinces, namely Alberta and Saskatchewan. The same processes of growth were taking place in these three provinces, where Ukrainians settled in compact mass. The Ukrainian urban colonies in Eastern Canada followed the same pattern as they did in the Western section. An active process of integration between the second generation of Canadians and the second immigration to Canada had to be realized. This positive and creative process involved not only the professional and economic life, but it resulted in the subsequent political integration and cultural identity which will be discussed more fully in subsequent chapters.

---

[4] Paul Yuzyk: The Ukrainians in Manitoba, p. 55.

INTEGRATION IN THE POLITICAL SPHERE

The First World War rendered a great blow to Ukrainian Canadians with respect to politics. Legislative enactments, promulgated at that time, treated them as a hostile element. In addition, the antagonism which appeared earlier on the premise of racial superiority on the part of the ruling class, instead of diminishing, became more prominent due to these legislative acts. In short, the unfriendly environment which confronted the Ukrainians in the early stages of their life in Canada reappeared once again almost with the same degree of intensity.

Only the typical stoicism and their aptitude to be able to withstand the blows of fate have enabled the Ukrainian community to honorably withstand injustices of the moment. This attitude convinced even the most skeptical about the civic loyalty of the Ukrainian Canadians. Concerning this loyal attitude of the Ukrainians, Dr. W. Anderson, one of the government leaders in 1922, made this remark in a speech at a Canadian Club: "When with the outburst of war, the country found itself before the extreme scrutiny of its entire existence the Ukrainians, at the critical period, responded magnificently. About 20,000 Ukrainians joined the army services. This twenty thousand volunteers did not include the additional ten thousand Ukrainian woodsmen who volunteered to cut lumber in England which was needed for trenches at the Western Front and to construct and maintain railroads in France. This remarkable contribution of human force in time of war was gratefully received by the English people" [1].

This response to the war needs and to the country's call basically changed the sympathies of the fellow citizens towards the Ukrainians. Everything that was decreed or imposed by the exigencies of war began to disappear under normal conditions after the war which was evidenced to a degree, by the provincial and federal elections in the years 1920-1921. Having received harsh treatment during the period of war, the Ukrainians came out of it much more consolidated.

During the first post war elections in 1921, they elected four members to provincial legislatures: N. V. Bachynsky and Dmytro Yakimischak in Manitoba, and William Fedun and Andrew Shandro in Alberta. The latter's election was annulled and in his place Michael Chornohuz was chosen. The Ukrainian candidates in the Saskatchewan elections, namely Gregory Slipchenko from Pelly district and Michael Saviak in Canora Constituency, did not have much success. Unsuccessful was also Wasyl Swystun who was a candidate from the Canora district as a member to the Parliament at Ottawa.

During the ensuing elections in Manitoba the following year the Ukrainians already were able to elect four legislators; in addition to the two that were elected in 1921, there was Nicholas Hryhorczuk of Ethelbert and Michael Royetsky of Gimli. During the Dominion elections in 1926 Michael Luchkovich of the Vegreville district in Alberta emerged as the

---
[1] Paraphrased from editorial "Ukrainian Pioneers in the Decisive Decade of Canada", "The New Pathway", No. 26, 1967.

first Ukrainian who had the honor to represent this electoral district and to some degree become a spokesman for the Ukrainians in Ottawa. This political course of the Ukrainians continued and somewhat increased in the post war years. It would be of interest to analyze this growing tendency from the standpoint of party affiliations, professional and religious connections, and other social aspects.

Provincially, most of the Ukrainian legislators were elected in Manitoba. Up to the year 1941, there were 10 representatives of Ukrainian descent: D. Yakimischak, N. V. Bachynsky, M. Royetsky, N. Hryhorczuk, W. Lisowsky, J. Wawrykow, W. Kardash, S. M. Krawchyk, M. Stryk and J. Solomon.

Dmytro Yakimischak (1882-1958) born in Western Ukraine, Catholic by religion, came to Canada in 1898, was a public school teacher, later became lawyer; elected in 1922 and continued as legislator for 7 years; was an independent Liberal representing Emerson district.

Nicholas V. Bachynsky (1887-1969) born in Western Ukraine of Orthodox religion, came to Canada in 1906; became a public school teacher and taught school for six years; was reelected 1922, 1927, 1932, 1936, 1941, 1945, 1949 and 1953. Was a member of provincial parliament for 36 years and speaker of the house since 1949 to the end of his legislative career 1958; he was elected as a Liberal from Fisher Branch district.

Michael Royetsky [2]) (   ), born in Western Ukraine, Roman Catholic by religion; was a farmer in Gimli and became elected from that district as a Liberal, served only one term.

William Lisowsky (1892-   ), came from Ukraine, Catholic by religion, and a teacher by occupation; was elected from the district of Ethelbert in 1936, as a Social Credit Party candidate.

Joseph Wawrykow (1908-1979) Catholic Religion, born in Gimli; completed agronomical studies and a teacher's seminar, taught school and conducted farm experiments; ran as a CCF candidate and was elected from Gimli district in 1936 and 1941.

William Arthur Kardash (1912-   ) born in Hafford, Saskatchewan, no religious affiliation, mechanic; served for two years in the Spanish war on the side of Republicans; was head of the provincial executive committee of the so-called Progressive Labor Party (Communist) and was elected and reelected from Winnipeg in 1941, 1945, 1949, and 1953.

Stephen M. Krawchyk (1903-1943), born in Garland, Manitoba. Ukrainian Catholic teacher by occupation; was also for some time on the staff of the Board of Education in Brooklands; was an independent candidate from North Winnipeg and was elected in 1941, but died two years after being elected.

Nicholas Hryhorczuk (1888-1979) born in Western Ukraine, Orthodox by religion, came to Canada in 1897; was a farmer and conducted his own hardware store. He was Mayor of Ethelbert 1917-1919. Ran on a Liberal Progressive ticket in 1922 and reelected again in 1927, 1932, and 1941, acted for some time as vice-speaker of the Legislature.

---

[2]) We are giving his surname as Royetsky in accordance with the present historical material and the press. In "Canadian Parliamentary Guide 1923-1927" this surname is given as "Rogeski" without any other data as to religion or national identity.

Nicholas Stryk (1896-1950) born in Western Ukraine, Ukrainian Catholic religion, came to Canada as a two-year old infant; completed a teacher's seminar and taught school in Winnipeg area; was a Liberal candidate and was elected in 1941 and in 1949.

John Solomon (1910-   ) born in Halicz, Manitoba, Orthodox by religion; he was a lawyer by profession with offices in Selkirk and Winnipeg; was a Liberal candidate from Emerson district, elected in 1941, and reelected in 1945, 1949 and 1953. In 1957 he was appointed as a provincial judge.

From this short review it is apparent that out of these ten members of parliament, four were already born in Canada and the remaining majority of them were born in Ukraine. Two of them were lawyers, five were teachers, one was a farmer and a businessman, and one a skilled laborer. Four members had a University education, four completed high school, and two had partial high school education. Five of them belonged to the Ukrainian Catholic Church, one was a Roman Catholic, three had Orthodox affiliations and one belonged to no religious denomination. The average of the members when they began their career was around thirty.

Somewhat different political results can be observed in Saskatchewan. The Ukrainians of this province, whose political ambitions in the pioneer era were far advanced, produced only two members of parliament during the pioneer decade and during the mid-war period. They were Dr. G. Dragan and O. Zerebko; both were raised in Manitoba.

Orest Zerebko (1887-1941) born in Horodenka, Western Ukraine and came to Canada when he was thirteen. He set a record as being the first Ukrainian in Canada to receive University education. He taught school for a long time and was on the staff of various newspapers. Although he supported monarchical ideas among Ukrainians, he ran as a Liberal Party Candidate, and was elected from the Redberry district in 1938. He died during his first term of office in 1944.

George Ernest Dragan (1898-1965) born in Pleasant Home, Canada, he completed his medical studies and was the first Ukrainian legislator in Saskatchewan running on Liberal Party ticket in Kelvington district. He was elected in 1934, and served his 4 year term. Both these legislators started on their political careers at the age of 40. Dr. Dragan professed Orthodox religion, and Zerebko was a Catholic. Both served only one term each.

The electoral mosaic of Alberta possessed its own original design and, in some instances, resembled that of Manitoba. Alberta, it is true, provided only seven parliamentarians, but she was specially privileged to send to the Dominion Parliament at Ottawa the first Ukrainian member and thereby, in a way, enhanced or equalized her position with that of Manitoba. Alberta in fact was the first province where a Ukrainian was elected to Ottawa parliament. Electoral districts such as Victoria, Witford and Vegreville where Ukrainian legislators were elected, and their counterparts in Manitoba are Gimli, Ethelbert, Emerson or Fisher Branch.

The first Ukrainian legislator in Alberta, following Shandro whose election was annulled, was *William Fedun* (1879-   ) a Presbyterian, born in Western Ukraine, came to Canada in 1898. Aside from being a farmer he also conducted a general merchandise business. The Union of Alberta Farmers nominated him as its candidate and he was elected in 1921, and served in office until 1925.

Michael Chornohuz (1888-   ) born in Bukovina, Ukraine; also was a candidate of Union of Alberta Farmers in a supplemental election in 1923 at Witford. He likewise operated a farming enterprise in Witford, and as member of Ukrainian Orthodox Church was very active in religious affairs.

Isidore Goresky an Orthodox, was born in Bukovina, Ukraine in 1902; came to Canada in 1906; later, after completing his teacher's training, he taught school and for a long period of time was engaged as an inspector of schools for Alberta; became a candidate for the Union of Alberta Farmers in Witford district and was elected in 1930; he finished his term in 1935.

P. A. Myskew (1899-   ) born in Western Ukraine, Ukrainian Catholic; had a college education and was a lawyer by profession with offices in Edmonton; he was elected in 1930 from Victoria district as Union of Alberta Farmers Candidate.

Three Ukrainians were elected as members of the Social Credit Party —all three were Catholics and were born in Canada—J. Popil, J. Woytkiw, and W. Tomyn.

James M. Popil (1909-   ), teacher by profession, was elected from the Redwater district in 1935, then reelected in 1940 and in 1944.

George Woytkiw (1909-   ) Government worker, became a victim of party politics; elected in 1935 had to resign in order to secure a place for his political chief Solon Low.

William Tomyn (1905-1972) had the most illustrious career of all of the Social Credit partisans. Teacher by profession, he became a legislator in 1935 from the Vegreville district, was reelected there in 1940, 1944, and 1948; although he was defeated in 1952, he emerged successful in the ensuing elections, and his career can be easily compared with that of Nicholas Bachynsky from Manitoba. In short, the legislators of Ukrainian descent in Alberta can be grouped as follows: There were four representing the Union of Alberta Farmers, and three were affiliated with the Social Credit. All in the former group were born in Ukraine ,two of them were of Orthodox Faith, one was a Catholic and one a Presbyterian. Teachers were leading first of the list—three in total, farmers two, one lawyer and one government employee. Two had university education; others had a high school or partial high school training. Their average age was approximately thirty years.

From the results noted in the three prairie provinces, where the Ukrainians formed a basic force and a cultural reservoir, we perceive that the political integration of the Ukrainian Community was deeply rooted. The Ukrainians have merged into the political life of the country and have made their presence visible not only in the two traditional Canadian Parties, but also in such new political creations as CCF, Social Credit and Union of Alberta Farmers which, after the Second World War became important political forces. In other words, the Ukrainian Canadians became sensitive and responsive to the national needs of the country.

In that political complex they not only became perceptive of their own particular environment but also that of their neighbors, and the entire Canadian community. This is further evidenced by the political platforms which the candidates accepted and pledged to support.

There is no doubt that during election campaigns certain candidates were more favored because of their national origin, as was evident from their sources of publicity, and from editorials about them. But basically, the decisive point was the platform, the platform he supported, and not the candidate himself. There was marked improvement in this respect. When comparisons are made between the first political attempts and the winning candidates in the pioneer decade, great emphasis indeed was laid on the political platform as to how it evaluated the national problems of Canada and its citizens and not how these problems were resolved by the candidate himself. The Progressive Parties received more votes and sympathies from the Ukrainians due perhaps to the hostile legislative enactments of the Conservatives during the First World War which were not advantageous to the Ukrainians, and which were the real cause of why the sympathies of the Ukrainians were tipped in the direction of the Progressive Liberals or other forward moving forces which were being formulated at the time. It took long years of political persuasion and the change of platforms before these sympathies were equalized.

Another significant fact was observed relating to the integration of political life of the Ukrainian Canadians. All vulgar propaganda and political tricks disappeared from political campaigns during that decade and became a part of history of that era.

In many electoral districts Ukrainian candidates opposed each other frequently and that in itself contradicts the impulsive assertions on the part of some historians or sociologists who claimed narrow nationalism of Ukrainians precedes the political wisdom or the political platform. For documentation purposes we may refer to the provincial election of Manitoba in 1927 where among the 153 candidates there were 14 of Ukrainian descent. In such districts as Ethelbert there were two Ukrainian candidates opposing each other; in Emerson there were three, in Gimli three, in Fisher Branch two, in Roblin, Russell, Springfield and Rockwood one each. We present this established pattern also for another reason, because it depicts the originality of the Ukrainians of the province as relates to candidates for election which, compared with other nationalities of the province, is fully balanced. This same pattern existed in Alberta, but it showed some weakness in Saskatchewan.

In our survey of candidates it is clear that the integral-political processes in various provinces were accompanied by relative tensions. The mid-war decade was marked by another remarkable feature. Political integration during this period made another forward step from the provincial horizons to the Dominion parliament at Ottawa. The successful and in fact the historical election of *Michael Luchkovich* (1893-1973) [3] native of Shamokin, Pa., U.S.A., but reared and educated in Canada, in 1926, from Vegreville district, gave a new incentive to the Ukrainians in the arena of politics. It is true, as we are informed, there were other attempts of the Ukrainians in that direction, but they failed. The election of M. Luchkovich to Ottawa was received by the Ukrainians with un-

---

[3] "A Ukrainian Canadian in Parliament", edited by J. Gregorovich, Toronto, 1965, foreword by A. Gregorovich, p. 15.

concealed satisfaction. Primarily it appeared as a unique symbol of deepened integration, but on the other hand it gave the masses a feeling of equality, certain definite prestige and at the same time a sense of civic responsibility. This was the first Ukrainian representative in the British Commonwealth of Nations and placed the Ukrainians on the same level with others. Henceforth, political democracy for them was not merely an empty phrase. One of the contemporaries of that event writes:

"Luchkovich's election contributed significantly to the higher self-esteem of the Ukrainian community... Ukrainian Canadians gained confidence from his example and went into politics in a big way to serve Canada in Parliament" [4].

Michael Luchkovich served in Parliament for nine years, his appearance in defense of civic equality and against discrimination of minorities are praiseworthy contributions to the political history of Canada.

When great injustice befell the Ukrainians on their own homeland in Europe in 1931, M. Luchkovich took a firm and decisive stand in their defense in the sessions of the Canadian Parliament. He was actively supported by over 50 of the Canadian Parliamentarians. The strong stand made by M. Luchkovich and his parliamentary colleagues had a wide repercussion beyond the boundaries of Canada, especially among those who were the victims of these injustices. Rightfully did the Canadian press comment at the time that the speeches uttered by the Canadian Parliamentarists made it appear like it was a "Ukrainian Day" in the Parliament at Ottawa.

M. Luchkovich added another important contribution to the history of the Parliament of Canada and of the entire British Commonwealth. In 1931 he was extended the privilege to represent Canada at the International Congress of the League of Parliaments held in Bucharest, Romania. Members of the London Parliament were busy with important internal matters and authorized M. Luchkovich to represent in Bucharest all the Parliamentarists of Great Britain. It can be imagined how much influence this representation had on the sentiments of the Ukrainians in Canada, and how many sympathies it raised for Canada among the Ukrainians of Europe.

In 1940 representation of Vegreville in Ottawa was taken over from Luchkovich by another Ukrainian who was nominated and elected as an exponent of the Social Credit Party.

Anthony Hlynka (1907-1957) was the second Ukrainian parliamentary member at Ottawa. He came to Canada from Western Ukraine at the age of three and was raised and educated in Alberta where he received recognition through his public appearances and because of his enthusiasm for Social Credit theories. In this spirit for several years he edited a journal named "Call" and later "Social Credit." A. Hlynka was reelected in 1945, and his representation in Parliament was an example of dignity worthy of emulation by his and Mr. Luchkovich's successors. After the war he rendered strong political assistance to the masses of displaced Ukrainian immigrants in Europe who later decided to settle permanently in Canada. This historical accomplishment of his vast undertakings re-

---

[4] Ibidem.

quires further clarification and his activities will be further discussed in another chapter.

M. Luchkovich and A. Hlynka, the first Ukrainian members in the Dominion Parliament had certain similarities. Both of them set upon their political careers when they were 33 years old and both had good writing talent and were excellent speakers. They were also mutual political competitors and leading figures in community life.

In fact, almost all above mentioned provincial legislators also highly distinguished themselves in various community activities. Each of them, while representing his own electoral district, also acted as semi-official representative in the efforts and endeavors of the entire Ukrainian-Canadian community[5]. The community heeded their sound advice and considered them their spokesmen.

Twenty one elective representatives elected mostly by Ukrainian votes and in districts with Ukrainian majority have shown through their many-sided activities that in the political sphere the Ukrainian Community in Canada has increasingly integrated itself with the general Canadian thinking, which was further reinforced to a marked degree by keen cooperation of Ukrainians in the municipal sphere of politics as well. All of this is self-evident and due to lack of space we will not go into it further.

If we should assume the correctness of the statements of Premier Bracken of Manitoba who, after the war, headed the Farmers Progressive Party—that the Ukrainians in Manitoba alone controlled 17 electoral districts—then the Ukrainian nationality group, integrating itself with the Canadian community in general, has also become an imposing political force in the domain of Western Canada [6].

---

[5] To illustrate the attitude of the two above mentioned Ukrainian representatives in Ottawa we might quote the following expression of Anthony Hlynka at the convention of S.U.S. in 1940 where he said: "In Ottawa I represent my electors of my riding but in Ukrainian matters I feel that it is my duty to represent the whole Ukrainian community in Canada". (Ukrainian Voice, March 12, 1941).

[6] An interview with Nicholas V. Bachynsky, close co-worker with Bracken, Author's Archives.

SCHOOLS AND THE TEACHING STAFF

If a gradation of cultural value were to be set up to which the Ukrainians of Canada in the past have devoted their attention, especially in the era between the two wars, the teaching of one's mother tongue would be foremost. To impart knowledge of native language to the coming generation was the concern of the family, religious congregations and educational establishment. It is hard to believe that there might be a religious congregation or a parish of one or another denomination, which would not be concerned with its native educational problems. It is, therefore, with deep admiration that we do note some congregations and establishments which conducted native schools for several years under strenuous circumstances. Without doubt it created a great burden upon the communities, the parents, and the children. Religious or educational institutions had to provide for accommodations and the teaching staff. The parents were obliged to pay salaries of the teachers, and the students had to attend their classes while their public school classmates played and took it easy.

It is a known fact that after the bi-lingual system was abolished, the teaching of native languages was conducted in private schools and after the regular public school hours. Very often these classes were held during evening hours and on Saturdays. The teaching usually was carried on in library rooms, national homes or parish halls. If comparisons were to be made between the two school facilities, the private schools were deficient in many respects, and especially as to hygiene, and the teaching itself was conducted under somewhat more primitive conditions than in public schools. There might have been exceptional cases in favor of private schools but they were rare instances. We emphasize this situation, as it indicates the sacrifices that were made in order to preserve one's native language.

It is also a fact that this interest in preserving one's own language was lacking in many quarters for various reasons and motives. Ordinarily those that failed to send their children to private or native schools thought it was useless because of "Canadiazation." Those that were in favor of the private schools usually criticized such indifferences as being unpatriotic or even as traitorous.

If one should consider the interest shown in native schools from the standpoint of immigrants, then it was more intense among the first generation in Canada and somewhat weaker among the generation already born here. All this was conditioned by various circumstances. Nevertheless, the drive towards native schooling was very pronounced.

Very often it proved impractical to carry on this kind of schooling in localities where there was insufficient number of children. Here and there some families were not in a position to support a teacher; then again, long distances and scattered communities prevented a teacher from serving additional schools and finally there became a shortage of qualified personnel. Briefly, very many factors were at work against private schools where Ukrainian language could be taught.

Bilingual teachers, who exhibited such shining progress in the pioneer era, continued as spokesmen for national consciousness among ethnic communities during the mid-war era, although they were no longer responsible for the rise of problems among communities as they were in the pioneer times. The circle of spiritual and intellectual leadership which carried certain responsibilities for national affairs has now been greatly extended. But the fact is that the bilingual and native school teachers still comprised an important category of citizens, who by virtue of their position were expected to be in the center of and in guiding posts of national and cultural life of the locality where they were teaching and occasionally, even of the entire district.

Outstanding cultural work was performed by teachers who possessed musical talents and were able to direct choirs and amateur theatricals. This kind of teacher was greatly in demand and were sought for by most communities who desired to have in their midst a full cultural life. Where there were no such teachers available, then the priest who had comparable qualifications, had to act in both capacities—as a priest and as a teacher. These priests and teachers enhanced the cultural standing in their church and in the school community.

As regards the history of organizations of Ukrainian teachers in Canada in the second era, it is necessary to classify them into two categories. The first group will comprise the teachers of public schools who were versed in the Ukrainian language and who, in addition to their daily duties in public schools, also taught children the Ukrainian language after regular school sessions or in the evening.

The second category includes those teachers who were engaged to teach Ukrainian language exclusively and besides teaching also conducted other cultural activities in the community or in their church congregations. The first category of teachers continued to perform the services rendered by the bilingual teachers of the pioneer era. They had behind them a cherished tradition of community work, and their duties as teachers were to add to the effectiveness of the accomplishments of their predecessors. Furthermore, at the beginning of the second era they still used the original organizational name as in the pioneer period. They continued to hold annual conventions, in which the Manitoba teachers were in the fore—front. The first such annual convention after the war was held in Winnipeg on July 22-23, 1921. About 50 teachers participated—they convened during summer vacation period and discussed their specific problems. As to the general procedure of these conventions and the problems constituting the agenda for the discussion, one of the pioneer-teachers in his memoirs said this:

"When a teacher was being hired as such, the school trustees, as one of the conditions, required that he teach children the Ukrainian grammar after the regular school hours. Ordinarily all Ukrainian teachers who attended the conventions, knowingly and willingly accepted those additional duties and strongly disapproved those who shirked them. It is taken for granted that a teacher who performs additional duties is entitled to additional remuneration, but how much more? This question was much discussed as were also the questions of school books and where they could be obtained. The usual duties of teacher in a community, etc were determined on a local basis.

Every day they listened to four lectures, which were subsequently discussed; the convention usually ended on the third day with a dinner or banquet to which outside guests were invited. The conventions as a rule proceeded in an orderly manner. The participants always departed with fresh ideas and plenty of encouragement for the work ahead" [1].

From the foregoing quotation we can infer that the bilingual Ukrainian teachers had plenty of problems for discussion and debate at their conventions.

The convention of the Ukrainian teachers of Manitoba which was held on July 12-20, 1923, initiated two very important matters: First to organize a Dominion Federation of Teachers, and second to create a national committee for Native Schools, "which would have as its task, to coordinate the teaching of the native language."

As a general rule and a matter of practice all plans and methods of teaching the native language were promulgated in the provincial sphere. This followed, perhaps, the established constitutional practice of public schools, that each province resolve its own problems. The convention of the Ukrainian teachers in 1923, in this respect, went beyond the provincial boundaries, and created a "General Committee for Native Schools" which two months later issued official announcement to the Ukrainian community in Canada, proclaiming its aims and purposes, which narrowed down to the following main guides:

1. To coordinate all efforts in the direction of teaching Ukrainian language to the young generation.

2. To take necessary steps to effect the establishment of "Native Schools" in every locality in a manner that is best therein.

3. To maintain a record of such schools.

4. To inaugurate an informative section in connection therewith, providing for a teacher, etc.

5. To make available a sufficient number of teachers for such schools, by conducting special courses in Ukrainian even through correspondence if necessary.

6. To keep proper statistics of these schools, their teachers and children, etc.

In the membership of the General Committee for Native Schools at the time we note such individuals as: J. W. Arsenych, Myroslaw Stechishin, J. Rudachek, J. Dyck, Z. Bychynsky, N. Bilash, Dmytro Rostocky, Maria Korecka, Peter Humeniuk, W. Swystun, Dr. M. Mihaychuk, Dr. H. Novak, P. Woycenko, Rev. M. Olenchuk, O. H. Hykawy, Dr. O. Nazaruk, Prof. I. Bobersky, Dr. I. Karach, T. D. Ferley. The membership of the committee reveals a unification of social and educational groupings. Here we find qualified teachers and other professionals who in their own period of time have been pedagogues and now, with contemporary teachers, comprised a very important center of social and educational thought in the affairs of native teaching. From the rank of members of this committee it is apparent that there were included all active religious denominations and political affiliations. Among the resolutions that were adopted at the 1923 convention the following are worthy of special notice:

---

[1] M. Kumka: "Portrayal of My Life and Work in the Centennial of Canada and 60 Years of My Life Therein" (in manuscript), pp. 19 and 20, Author's Collection.

The old name of the organization was replaced by a new one and instead of the Ukrainian Teachers Organization it became "The Association of the Ukrainian Teachers of Canada". The Maple Leaf, with appropriate arrangement of the initials of the new name (AUTC), was chosen as the official emblem of the teachers and as official ensignia on documents.

Another significant resolution was a unanimous decision, that in the ensuing year, i.e. 1924, during the summer vacation period, a course of Ukrainianization be conducted. Such a course did take place in one of the old university buildings on Broadway at Winnipeg.

The responsibility for the course rested with the executive committee of the A.U.T.C. and Prof. I. Bobersky was not only its director, but also a vital force in its entire program. The instructors and lecturers of the course, besides the aforementioned Prof. Bobersky, were such pedagogues as V. Biberovych, E. Turula, M. Mihaychuk and M. Kumka. They lectured on the history and geography of Ukraine, on the Ukrainian language and literature, and on the theory of music and physical education. Such courses and the yearly conventions of the teachers aided and augmented their qualifications and minimized their problems which were mushrooming in conjunction with the teaching of the Ukrainian language and other social and civic activities within their localities.

Among distinctive figures of the teachers' conventions in early years we note these well-known popular names: I Bobersky, Dr. M. Mihaychuk, N. Bilash, J. Yatchew, J. & M. Stechishin, P. Humeniuk, A. Danyleyko, A. Chorneyko and P. Nykorchuk.

At the turn of the 1930's some decline could be detected in the work and activities of the A.U.T.C. organization. It was due perhaps to economic crisis which afflicted Canada at the time. But again in the spring of 1932 a group of teachers held a conference in Winnipeg in order to reactivate their organization and in the following year through the efforts of the teachers a seminar is being conducted in Winnipeg at which Ukrainian disciplines are taught, as well as pedagogy, music and dancing which became part of the teaching program along with other subjects in all the succeeding courses of Ukrainization [2]).

The teachers' convention of 1934 assumed a character that was reminiscent of the vigorous post-war period. M. Ewanchuk who in time became an inspector of schools in Manitoba, was made head of the association and continued in that position for several succeeding terms. Among the leading teachers of that era we also recognize Stephen Krawchyk, M. Wawrykow, W. Kostiuk, Halia Hawryluk, W. Wall, W. Sarchuk, M. H. Hykawy and others. Up to the time of the second world war there appeared to be very intensive activity even beyond the province of Manitoba. A.U.T.C. was in close cooperation with similar teachers organizations in Saskatchewan and Alberta, but the teachers' activities in latter provinces took a somewhat different turn. In Saskatchewan the teachers at first centered their activities around the yearly conventions of the Institute; they also held their own conferences. It was only in 1929 that a separate "Association of Ukrainian Teachers of Saskatchewan" was formed [3]). The organizational congress, aside from other resolutions

---

[2]) "Canadian Farmer", April 6, 1932.
[3]) I. Shklanka prepared a school guide for teaching Ukrainian language.

exclusively of professional character, also decreed "that the teachers and their education should undertake to impart qualified knowledge and training to their younger colleagues." The leading principals of this association were: I. Shklanka, I. Danylchuk, S. B. Mykytiuk, Anna Chepesiuk and others.

In Alberta, the teachers formulated their activities around the Institute of Mykhaylo Hrushevsky, but also had their own separate organization in which active leadership was given by M. Sheveluk, M. Lemishka, Nadia Svarich, P. J. Woroboc and others.

Individual provincial educational systems, in many instances, showed negative attitude towards centralization of Ukrainian teachers in the West and from that aspect they experienced difficulties in realizing the plans and purposes of the General Committee for Native Schools as envisaged in 1923. Nevertheless, autonomous bodies of teachers did exist in the Provinces of Manitoba, Saskatchewan and Alberta throughout the entire period of the second era and utilized every possible means in order to give the Ukrainian children, after the regular school hours, the knowledge of Ukrainian language in the most effective and efficient form.

Between the two wars another category of teachers was in action whom we will truly classify as native teachers, as the ones just discussed rather belonged to the bilingual class. These native teachers did not teach in public schools. They taught in native schools only, ordinarily in urban localities and mostly in parochial communities or cultural organizations. Such teachers conducted evening and Saturday schools and were financed exclusively by the organizations and parishes. They, in most cases, possessed European qualifications and were recruited primarily from the second immigration. The bilinguals frequently taught after four in the afternoon outside of official hours prescribed by the school boards. They were on the payrolls of the public school systems and basically were graduates of Canadian Institutes. Even though the bilingual and the native teachers had identical occupations, i.e. the teaching of the Ukrainian language, but because of circumstances they were employees of two different systems. This created certain adverse situations requiring more planned coordination, and in 1932 a separate organization was formed: "Society of Ukrainian Native School Teachers in Canada". The initiative in this respect was provided by teachers of Winnipeg native schools which were connected with such cultural institutions as Ukrainian National Home, "Prosvita" Library, Institute "Prosvita", Institute of Shevchenko of Brooklands, "Kobzar" Society of Fort Rouge, Shevchenko Society of St. Boniface, "Ridna Shkola" of M. Shashkevych and others. In their utterances and discussions they came to the conclusion that "Ridna Shkola" (native school) in Canada is in need of one direction, uniform planning in studies and hourly sessions. It requires uniform text books and one definite method of teaching [4].

On the basis of such results the by-laws of the Society were prepared which had for its aims: "To unite the Ukrainians in Canada, who are affiliated with teaching professions and are now teaching in the native schools, in order that they may expand among the teaching elements, the knowledge of the present and of the past of the Ukrainian people,

---

[4] Dr. M. I. Mandryka: "Half a Century of Activity of "Prosvita" Library in Winnipeg", Winnipeg, 1958, p. 147.

its language and literature and to consider the various methods of teaching in order to successfully carry on the educational work among the Ukrainian settlers in Canada" [5]).

The Society of the Ukrainian Teachers of Native Schools of Canada included other aims in its by-laws. It made it a mandatory duty "to acquaint the Ukrainian people in Canada and Europe with the English art, literature, economy, social and political processes, and conversely, to acquaint the English community with the Ukrainian literature, art and culture" [6]).

It is obvious from the by-laws and the activity of the Society, that its member-teachers did not confine themselves exclusively to their own environment, but also directed their attention towards cooperation with other ethnic groups.

The Society in 1933 compiled and published statistics of the Native Schools, which were operating in Manitoba in conjunction with parochial and other cultural organizations, as well as those of Saskatchewan, like Moose Jaw and Bienfait, and of Calgary in Alberta, and in such locations in Ontario as Kenora, Thorold, West Fort, Fort William and Fort Frances. Altogether, there were 29 teachers in native schools attended by 1419 students [7]).

On the average, there were about 49 students assigned to each teacher. The Society continued its activities until the second world war, but contrary to its best intentions, it was unable to unify all Ukrainian Native Schools in Canada. The initiators of the concept of the Society (UTNS) were: A. Zaharychuk a long-time school board member in Winnipeg, and such other teachers as G. Cukornyk, A. Gospodyn, M. Kumka, Euhenia Sytnyk, S. Shkromeda, I. Sawchuk, M. Borysyk, T. Kuz and others.

Holidays and celebrations in native schools usually featured school concerts and theatrical presentations and in many instances they were combined productions of two or more schools. Too often they turned out to be a manifestation of national feeling, presented in speech, song, music and dance. This gave immense satisfaction to both, teachers and parents as well as the youngsters.

The great impediment in teaching the Ukrainian language was the lack of proper textbooks. The bilingual and native teachers were making use of European text-books, but they were impractical for students in Canada. The Canadian method of teaching requires textbooks that are applicable to the new conditions. In order to publish a well illustrated textbook required a substantial amount of money which no institution at that time could very well afford on its own. Finally an agreement was reached with the publishing establishment of M. Matwiychuk in Lviv, Western Ukraine, whereby it was agreed that the Society (UTNS) in Winnipeg would reissue the textbooks of M. Matwiychuk, adapting them

---

[5]) Statute of the Society of Teachers of the Ukrainian Native Schools in Canada, Winnipeg, 1933, p. 7.
[6]) Same, page 4, article 2.
[7]) Refer to article "Ridna Shkola" by A. Gospodyn in the book "Half a Century of Service of the Society of Library "Prosvita" in Winnipeg", pp. 148-149, also "Ridna Shkola Canadian Almanac", Winnipeg, 1934, articles: "Ridna Shkola" and "Report of Ridna Shkola", p. 29-30.

to the Canadian requirements. The Second World War, however, interfered in the realization of this project. Up to the war period, the Society recommended the use of M. Matwiychuk's primer in the first four grades, and for the grades 5 to 8, the "reader" of Anthony Krushelnytsky was to be used, also the latter author's primer book and his first reader.

From the reference books recommended by the Society for the use in native schools it could be assumed that the teaching was conducted in accordance with the advanced methods and with the use of modern literary language. Through the efforts of the Society, there also appeared "An Aid to Learn Ukrainian Language for Beginners", authored by A. Zaharychuk.

Furthermore, in order to complete the portrayal of the affairs surrounding the development of native Ukrainian schools during the second era let us briefly review the work carried on in this respect by the institutes, student halls known as "Bursa" and the separate Catholic schools. The most active was the Institute of Peter Mohyla in Saskatoon, which in time also opened a temporary branch in Winnipeg.

In Edmonton this movement was continued by the Institute of Michael Hrushevsky and the Bursa of A. Shepticky, the former under the direction of the Orthodox faith and the latter under the direction of the Catholics. This latter, at the end of the third year of its existence ceased its operations, but reorganized them in 1925 under the name of "Ukrainian Catholic Institute" which lasted until 1931.

More successful was the Bursa of the Brotherhood of the Ukrainian Catholics in Saskatoon, which commenced its operations after the third yearly convention of the Brotherhood in 1934 at Saskatoon. The enthusiasts of this endeavor were: Rev. Paul Sulatycky, Osyp Pryma and Joseph Topuschak. The latter two together with O. Zerebko, W. Charko, B. L. Korchynsky and Rev. P. Kryworuchka, were directors of this institution for many years and laid a solid foundation under this new educational center. As in the aforementioned institutes and "bursas", the students of the higher education, besides the room and board, had been offered nightly classes in Ukrainian language, history and literature, as well as in singing and music, and at intervals in religion. In each of the institutes and bursas there arose spontaneous groups who prepared themselves for general community activities.

The Ukrainian Catholic schools comprise a separate category, which, basically began to organize in the pioneer era, but in the second period have broadened their activities to a great extent. In this category we can include the Sacred Heart School in Edmonton, the St. Nicholas School in Winnipeg, and two schools in Yorkton, Saskatchewan—the Sacred Heart Academy for girls and the St. Joseph's for boys. Both have High School accreditation. The former is conducted by the Servant Sisters, and the latter by the Christian Brothers. The schools conducted regular high school courses prescribed by the Public Board of Education and in addition included courses in Ukrainian language and religion.

All these schools were highly regarded by their respective School Boards and the Ukrainian communities willingly provided them with necessary material support as these schools did not receive any aid from the regular provincial educational budgets [8]).

In order to provide higher educational facilities for students who have completed the primary evening courses the Executive Board of the Ukrainian National League of Canada resolved to organize courses of higher education during summer holidays and the first such session was held in the summer of 1940 continuing to the present.

During these summer courses a special emphasis was laid on the Ukrainian language, grammar, literature, popular arts, and how to conduct the native schools; music, singing and directing of choruses or choirs, were also on the program. These summer sessions also serve another valuable and important purpose. They bring the youth together from various parts of Canada who acquire lasting acquaintances. They broaden their knowledge of Ukrainian culture and intensify their desires and ambitions to become future leaders in their own respective communities. During the first decade of these higher educational courses over 600 students participated in and completed them with additional honors. Some attempts at organizing similar summer courses were made by the Institute of Petro Mohyla at Saskatoon, but it was not successful in developing them into a strong and prevalent system.

Therefore, it is more than evident that the Ukrainians of Canada have made extensive and undiminishing efforts in trying to impart to their children the knowledge of the Ukrainian language and culture so that the upcoming generation might reveal in some degree a cultural heritage and identity of their forefathers.

---

[8]) It is generally known that all private schools in Manitoba receive no financial support from public funds.

CULTURAL IDENTIFICATION

Cultural identification of the Ukrainians was manifest not only in the great struggle to retain their mother tongue in the family, but also by input of the evening schools and the church. As part of their cultural values the Ukrainians included also their traditions, customs, arts, drama, press and literature. In this field of cultural identification and activities they found themselves and this was the framework in which they displayed their national genius. This, as a last resort, gave them the strength to safeguard their national indentity. Without these inner forms which provide rational and determinant stimuli, the Ukrainian ethnic group in Canada would cease to exist.

One of the pioneers of the Ukrainian cultural life in Canada provides a suitable characteristic of those cultural and historical values. He maintains that "if the Ukrainians did not have their own characteristics and were unable to evaluate them, if they had not brought them into the new world, if they had not resolved to retain and develop them in the new country, not only as their sole means of consolation in the struggle for existence, but also as a bulwark against assimilation, which binds us as a strong chain with our abandoned fatherland, and if we did not have sufficient courage to compete with other cultures, then who knows whether the Ukrainians in Canada would have attracted the attention of others to their existence here" [1].

The Ukrainians in Canada developed their life on the knowledge of their national identity and their culture. They valued their cultural and historical facts as their heritage and the community as a living organism, as a unit with a definite dynamic purpose. In view of such a concept the full man would be only he who grew up on the traditions of his predecessors. This philosophical-political foundation we regularly discern in all cultural manifestations of initial development; it becomes more evident especially in the second stage of the development.

The tenacity to tradition and customs was evidenced during the pioneering times by the fact that the wives threatened to divorce their husbands if they ventured to change their external appearance in any form [2]. If such trivial matters were adhered to with such force, then how much stronger were the national values as tradition and customs, which were fostered for centuries and some of them reached as far back as the pre-Christian era in Ukraine, such as those connected with Ivan Kupalo, the spring and harvest songs, and others [3].

To the most widely observed holy-days belong the family and religious customs which pertain mainly to the observance of Christmas, New Year, Resurrection, Whitsunday, etc. Christmas is especially known by its charming Christmas Eve ceremonials and its carols. The supper on Christ-

---

[1] S. Kowbel: Memorial Book of the Ukrainian National Home Association, in Winnipeg, p. 208.
[2] Nestor Dmytriw: "Canadian Ruthenia".
[3] Officially the Ukrainians accepted Christianity in 988 A.D.

mas Eve must have 12 meatless dishes in honour of the 12 Apostles. Heads of the family lead the prayer for all present, while vacant covered places are reserved for the departed ones. The Christmas tree, a sheaf of grain and hay are also essential items. According to a well-established custom the supper begins with the appearance of the first star; all members are dressed in their best attire and no alcoholic drinks are served. "Kutia" is the main dish. Prayers, greetings and carols follow the supper. After the supper, the young people and sometimes also the older ones, go out carolling to their neighbors and friends. The carols glorify the birth of Christ and the greetings and best wishes for the household are usually expressed in the versified form. In the past, the carollers were given land products, while in recent times, cash is the usual reward. Formerly, the young people carolled for themselves, but later the proceeds went for community needs such as schools, cultural activities, charitable institutions, etc. Traditionally, the custom of carolling begins on Christmas Eve and continues to New Year, which for Ukrainians is January 14th. New Year's day is the time of "sowing" by the teen-agers—for their parents, relatives and neighbors. Wheat, as a symbol of wealth, is usually used for "sowing". The younger the sowers, the more blessings they bring to the household.

The Epiphany and the Epiphany Eve (Schedryj Vechir) is observed two weeks after Christmas and it is the time for blessing of waters in the church, more appropriately in the wells or rivers, where ice crosses are erected. The Epiphany holiday is the time for further carolling, which are called "schedrivky". The difference, however, between the carols and the "schedrivky" is in the content of the songs. The motif of the carol is religious, while that of the "schedrivky" is not.

A very solemn holiday for the Ukrainians is Easter; that is, the Feast of Resurrection, which inspires in them the hope of the resurrection of Ukraine. Greetings and best wishes are conveyed to relatives and friends now as on Christmas. These greetings are imbued not only with personal but also with religious and national feelings. One of the customs of Easter is preserved in the blessing of "Paska", Easter eggs and other food products. Easter without the blessed "Paska" is no Easter. Easter joy is expressed by the church bells which ring throughout the day. The youth, especially the girls, play and sing special Easter songs, the "Hayilky", around the church. There are special verbal greetings for Christmas and Easter, namely "Christ is Born" and Christ has Risen", to which the reply is "Glory be to Him" and "He has Risen".

Another solemn religious holiday is Whitsunday which falls on the seventh Sunday after Easter. According to tradition, families visit the graves of their departed members and the whole community pays tribute to the fallen war victims at the grave or a monument of the Unknown Soldier. All this is performed with the participation of the clergy and lay members and is usually headed by the war veterans.

Besides these holidays, every family has also its own important days such as birthdays, baptism, matrimony and death. Special traditions and customs are observed on these days: namely, on weddings and funerals, which are accompanied by many songs and the latter by lamentations. Some of the above mentioned songs are now presented on the stage, e.g. the "Hayilky". Many of those songs have been forgotten, while others are passed from one generation to the next.

Besides the family and religious holidays, the Ukrainian community also has its national holidays. These are: January 22nd, which marks two important days in modern Ukrainian history, namely, the Declaration of Independence in 1918 and the Union of all Ukrainian Territories into one Ukrainian National State in 1919; January 29th in commemoration of 300 students who fell in the struggle with the Bolsheviks, in defence of their country in 1918; March days to mark the birthday of the Ukrainian poet, Taras Shevchenko. During the month of May the Ukrainians commemorate several of their leaders, namely: Symon Petlura, Evhen Konovalets, and later Stepan Bandera and Lev Rebet who were assassinated by Bolshevik agents. These dates are observed by specially arranged concerts, academies and lectures. Some Ukrainians who are internationally oriented, observe the May Day and the October Bolshevik Revolution of 1917.

It is interesting to note that the Ukrainians observe their national holidays according to the Gregorian calendar while the religious holidays they celebrate according to the Julian calendar. The calendar question has become a serious problem among the Ukrainians. Prior to the First World War Ukrainians everywhere retained the Julian calendar which is 13 days behind the Gregorian calendar, namely Christmas and New Year are 13 days behind the official calculation. Other holidays, especially Easter, fall on different dates. In the intervals between the wars and especially during the Second World War, the question was raised in favor of adopting the Gregorian calendar in the Ukrainian church. The special war conditions were used as an argument. Church authorities granted permission to individual parishes to celebrate Christmas and the New Year according to the Gregorian calendar—the "new style". This innovation was introduced in the Ukrainian Catholic Church. The Ukrainian Greek Orthodox Church, after a prolonged debate in the press, refrained from making any changes. After the war, the Catholics went further and some of the parishes obtained permission to adopt the new calendar in toto. This process is still being continued. In practice the Ukrainians still retain two calendars, the Julian and the Gregorian, and this sometimes leads to some confusion. If a parish wishes to change the calendar the members vote on it and usually they are equally divided in favor of one and the other. The defenders of the Julian calendar argue that the Julian calendar is considered as a tradition in the Ukrainian Church and if it is removed it will lead to other changes which will end up in the obliteration of cultural identity.

Besides their traditions and customs the Ukrainians have a rich folklore, which may be subdivided into two principal groups. To the first group belongs the folklore brought in from Ukraine, and to the other the stories, novels, anecdotes, proverbs, wedding and cradle songs collected and composed in Canada. The first group might be called genuine Ukrainian folklore, and the other Ukrainian-Canadian folklore. The tendencies to conservatism and traditionalism among the Ukrainian settlers reacted favorably in the development of this national culture.

The first person interested in the Ukrainian folklore in Canada was Mrs. Tetiana Koshetz (1892-1966), but she was mostly interested in the songs. More serious researchers in this respect were Onufrey Ewach and Jaroslaw Rudnyc'kyj. The latter compiled a considerable number of songs, stories, anecdotes etc. which the Ukrainian Free Academy of Sciences published in three volumes [4]. One volume was translated by O. Ewach and published in the English language.

Of special interest is the collection of proverbs, compiled and published by Volodymyr Plaviuk [5]. This is very valuable material, because it expresses the Ukrainian national philosophy. In his review of this work Prof. Watson Kirkconnell noted:

"From the point of view of scholarship quite the most interesting book of the year is Volodymyr S. Plaviuk's monumental collection of Ukrainian proverbs dedicated to the Ukrainian pioneers in Canada. Here are recorded some six thousand proverbs, methodically arranged according to an alphabetical list of subjects and supplied in each case with an explanatory paraphrase... If this treasure of Ukrainian popular wisdom could be translated into a world-language such as English or French, it would arouse great enthusiasm among the folklorists on this continent."

However, the Ukrainians by their folklore did not attract the interest of their fellow Canadians. The customs, traditions, proverbs, stories, and legends were only of passing value in the community. They were a valuable asset in the community only, but not outside. To other fellow-Canadians it was essential to speak the language of beauty, harmony, aesthetics and feelings. And in this aspect the Canadian Ukrainians had a rich treasurechest. The principal item in this treasury was the Ukrainian song, folk and classical music, dances, theatrical plays, operas, ballets, and also ceramics, wood carvings, handicraft etc. Of special significance in this activity is church architecture.

From our history we know that churches were the first community buildings on the Canadian prairies, but their structure and architecture due to shortage of capital were very primitive. Only the small cupola with a cross indicated its ethnic origin. It was only in later days when money was easier to get that church architecture flourished and beautiful, massive buildings were erected which attracted the attention of many visitors. Interior of the church is rich in paintings, artistic icons, carvings etc. Not only the cathedrals and sobors in such cities as Winnipeg, Edmonton, Saskatoon and Toronto are central churches richly decorated by the Ukrainian-Byzantine art, but also churches in provincial centres are noted for their artistic decorations and architecture. For instance, such churches are at Mountain Road [6] and the Cathedral of the Prairies at Cooks Creek, Manitoba, and others. An outstanding architect-builder was Rev. Philip Ruh, OMI, who designed and built many churches several provinces in Canada, and Stephen Meush, and in the pioneer days H. Hykawy, and in recent days Radoslaw Zuk and Victor Deneka. In interior church decorations there have been such talented artists as Sviatoslaw Hordynsky, J. Bucmaniuk, M. Dmytrenko, I. Kubarsky, Roman Kowal, Theodore Baran, Leo Molodozanin (Mol) and others. These are only a few outstanding names. In the past, the Ukrainians always

---

[4] Materials to Ukrainian Canadian Folklore, V. I, 1956, V. 2, 1958, V. 3, 1960, V. 4, 1962-3, compiled by Prof. J. B. Rudnyc'kyj.
[5] "Proverbs, or Ukrainian national philosophy", Edmonton, 1947.
[6] The building was 96 by 120 feet, 9 doors, 5 altars, 135 windows and seating accommodation for 3,000. Burnt down in 1966.

devoted their best efforts to church architecture, and as a sample of this effort they have such historical buildings as Sobor of St. Sophia (1037) and St. Michael Sobor (1070-1088) in Kiev, Uspenskyj Sobor in Kanev (1144), Illinska and Piatnycka Churches in Chernyhiv (XII century), Uspenska Church in Halych (1157) and St. George's Cathedral in Lviv.

But the best mirror that reflects the soul and beauty of the Ukrainians in Canada is their song. The treasure of the Ukrainian song encompasses all aspects of life of an individual and the group so that the Ukrainians are known generally as a nation of singers. Whenever two or three of them get together they sing in as many voices. A Ukrainian sings and consoles himself in solitude. In the pioneering days they sang at work and at construction projects. The Ukrainian "kolomyyka" expresses universal feeling and yet it breathes joy and humour. Actually "kolomyyka" verse was used to describe the "new life in the new country". The wedding songs describe a wide variety of feeling from laughter to tears. There are songs describing the seasons of the year and individual experiences, family and clannish unity, cradle songs and other varieties.

Of another category are the historical songs, among which the principal ones are the "dumy" which, besides historical events contain also a deep philosophy of life. The "dumy" are the product of the Cossack era. During the First World War the songs of the Sichovi Striltsi were developed. In the process of the struggle for freedom another category of songs was produced, namely the songs of the insurgents, and later the songs of the UPA (Ukrainian Insurgent Army). Although these songs originated in Ukraine they were brought to Canada by the immigrants and thus became part of the Ukrainian-Canadian repertoire. Besides these so-called folk songs, the Ukrainians brought to Canada also the works of such composers as Bortniansky, Lysenko, Ludkevich, Hayworonsky, Bezkorowayny, Stecenko, Barwinsky and others. The compositions were of popular and religious themes.

References to the carols and "schedrivky" were made previously. The solemnity of Ukrainian religious services is bound with the art of choral music. Even at the beginning of Christianity in Ukraine the whole congregation sang in chorus. The so-called "samoyilka" gradually assumed the artistically-musical style of separate choirs, solos, duets, trios, etc. The more important religious ceremonies are rich in their choral music, and during the Way of the Cross and the Resurrection Service and Lytanies are known for their highly inspirational values.

The Ukrainians were conscious of the beauty of their song and whenever an occasion presented itself they participated in various festivals together with their fellow-citizens. Their first such appearance took place in 1897 when they participated in the Dominion Day festival on the Saskatchewan prairies. The Ukrainian choral participation on a larger scale began in 1914, when the entire Ukrainian community celebrated the 100th birthday of their poet Taras Shevchenko. Long and elaborate preparations had to be made to meet this epoch-making occasion. It is true, that prior to this in 1906 and later, the students from the teacher's college performed on the stage in Winnipeg, but all that was only of local character. The year 1914 provided an impetus for greater actions. Musical and choral activity was revived soon after the war. A choral society

"Boyan" was organized in Edmonton, in 1911-14 with Mr. T. Panchyshyn as choir conductor. In Saskatoon there was a choir directed by Y. Bubniuk. In Toronto, members of the Prosvita society organized a choir in 1924, conducted by G. Hassan, member of the Ukrainian Republican Chorus directed by Alexander Koshetz. After that, the choir was conducted by D. Burtnyk, P. Yundak, H. Holynska. In Montreal there was a well-known Drahomaniv Choir under the leadership of Y. Vepruk, and the St. Michael Choir with P. Pieluch as conductor, and later on there was a Dramatic Society headed by Zenon Telishevsky, and the Prosvita Choir with J. Marcyniuk and later M. Petrashyk as conductors.

The choral and musical activities were more developed in Winnipeg. The first choral unit here was the church choir organized by the Ukrainian Catholic parish of St. Nicholas, directed by George Magalas (1910). Also the association of I. Kotlarevsky, of M. Zankovetska, as well as "Boyan" had their choral groups whose activities were noted for developing drama and vocal music. Theatrical and musical life was greatly enhanced when the above mentioned three organizations united into one group in 1922, and under the leadership of W. Kazanivsky and Semen Kowbel succeeded in organizing and staging genuine theatrical plays and highly disciplined choirs. There was also a semi-professional theatrical and musical ensemble "Rusalka". In the intervals between the first and second periods there functioned the choir of the Ukrainian National Home Association, at first conducted by M. Pasichniak, and later it was greatly improved by such conductors as Prof. Eugene Turula, P. Yundak, G. Cukornyk and Dr. P. Macenko.

Special significance in the field of choral art in Canada must be attributed to the Choir "Canada", organized by Prof. E. Turula in the Institute Prosvita in 1924. Up to that time there was a choral group "Banduryst", which originally was located in the parish of St. Vladimir and Olga and later in the Institute Prosvita. It is worth mentioning that this choir had its first grand concert in the Board of Trade building in 1924. During the Jubilee celebrations of the City of Winnipeg this choir was awarded first prize both for its singing and for its float, the "Ukrainian Music", which was designed by Prof. E. Turula. When the Choir "Canada" ceased to exist Prof. Turula organized a new one in the Ukrainian National Home. There were also smaller choirs in Winnipeg, such as in the Ukrainian Reading Hall Association, conducted by C. Andrusyshen and by T. Hubicky. Also there were choirs in the Ukrainian Catholic parish in Elmwood, in the Ukrainian Literary Society of M. Shashkevych, a male quartet conducted by J. Samotilka, which regularly appeared on radio, and others.

Special opportunity for the Ukrainian choirs in Winnipeg presented itself in 1923 when Mr. Lloyd George, the Prime Minister of Great Britain paid an official visit to the city. The Ukrainians had a special sentiment to that statesman for his defence of the Ukrainian question in Europe. These choirs also participated in the celebration of the diamond jubilee of the confederation of the Canadian provinces. The choir of the Ukrainian National Home accompanied by Army orchestra performed during the Convention of the British Empire Medical Association in Winnipeg, 1929. In the choral competition in 1930 the Ukrainian choir won first prize. The Ukrainian choirs participated in the celebrations marking the coronation of King George VI, as well as in the La Verendrye celebration, and during the Musical Festival of Manitoba in 1939, the Ukrainian National Home Choir was awarded the J. J. McLean Trophy.

The Ukrainian National Home choir in Toronto was also very active. It annually participated in the Canadian National Exhibition and frequently was invited to perform in English-speaking societies, clubs and church affairs. During 25 years of activities of this choir its repertoire consisted of 290 songs by 36 composers. The choir had 402 members and besides concerts it also presented operas (Zaporozets za Dunayem, Kateryna, Chornomortsi, Sorochynsky Yarmarok, Zaporozsky Klad) and operettas (The Gypsy Baron and Sharika) [7]. Many plays, concerts, operattas, were staged at the Ukrainian Canadian Institute "Prosvita".

The MUN choir was organized in Winnipeg in 1941 and it deserves special mention for its contribution to the musical and choral art. Musical foundation for this choir was laid by Alexander Koshetz, the world-famous conductor, who from 1940-1944 lectured at the Summer Courses arranged by UNO in Winnipeg. He organized and originally directed a choir consisting of the students who attended his Summer Courses. Later on Dr. P. Macenko conducted this choir, since 1950 W. Klymkiw and it participated in many musical and choral festivals in Manitoba.

The Ukrainian Men's Choir in Winnipeg was organized and conducted by Walter Bohonos during the Second World War and won highest awards during the Manitoba Musical Festivals. They sang on radio and appeared on television. Many of its songs as well as of other choirs were recorded. All told, Ukrainian choirs in Canada produced thousands of records. The following individual musicians greatly contributed to these recods— J. Zukowsky, the brothers J. and M. Humeniuk, W. Gregorash. Severyn Vindyk of Toronto has a great collection of these musical and song records. Choral groups and musical ensembles closely cooperate with one another.

In Winnipeg the pioneer musician was Peter Uhryniuk, student from the Teacher's College on Minto Street (1907). His principal work was to conduct a mandolin orchestra which at first he did at his home and later, after the First World War, he moved to the Ukrainian Labor Temple. M. Huculak was another pioneer in this field. In 1926 this orchestra toured Canada and was enthusiastically received in all cities. It was generally admitted that this mandolin orchestra enhanced the popularity of the Ukrainian Farmer-Labor Temple. That orchestra laid the foundation for further development of mandolin music to the extent that mandolin orchestras were organized practically in every Ukrainian Farmer-Labor Temple across Canada. M. Borysyk had also organized and conducted a mandolin orchestra in Winnipeg. In all between the wars over 80 mandolin orchestras functioned in Canada.

The association known as "Sitch" in the period between the two wars, had organized a number of bands, one of the best such bands was in Montreal. In the west, Osyp Pryma was active in promoting instrumental music and conducted such an orchestra first in Saskatoon and later

---

[7] Dm. A. Nykolak: "Brief Historical Resume of the Ukrainian National Home in Toronto", 1953, page 16.

in Edmonton. He was also interested in theatricals and in 1929 produced the opera "Zaporozets za Dunayem" in Edmonton. P. Ostapchuk had organized and directed vocal-theatrical ensembles in Winnipeg and Edmonton. Prof. Eugene Turula also conducted a school of music and a violin orchestra in Winnipeg. The Worker's Benevolent Association financially assisted the orchestra known as the "North Star". H. Storozuk had organized the Prosvita choir in Kenora. Well equipped choirs were organized by one UNF organization and in the parish of St. Sophia in Montreal.

As proof of how well coordinated was the work in the field of music, drama and songs we have the fact that each Ukrainian hall had a stage, costumes and decorations the cost of which usually amounted to around one thousand dollars. On Sundays and holidays the stage was used for concerts, dramas, comedies and even light operettas. Now and then there were vaudevilles, lectures, songs, comedies, etc. These were known as variety concerts. In these evening performances the young people participated, where they sang, recited, played games and danced. This was the family and community atmosphere in which the youth of the first and second periods was brought up.

One of Ukrainian educationists who himself grew up in that atmosphere, wrote thus: "The whole life of my youth was centered within the cultural and educational work... Every young person who participated in such organization, spiritually benefited from it and became imbued with the love of Ukrainian art, drama and song. The influence of the Reading Hall was extraordinary and left indelible impressions on those who participated in its cultural treasury" [8].

Besides those above mentioned there were other artistic groups in several other localities, but we do not mention them either for lack of space or because of their short duration. It is worth-while mentioning that practically in all the larger parishes there were church choirs conducted either by the church cantors or the clergy. Their repertoire in most cases consisted of religious content.

Winnipeg also produced several talented individuals. These were, to mention only a few—John Melnyk, pianist; John Kuchmy and Cornelia Gayowska, violinists; Luba and Nadia Novak, cellists, and others. An exceptionally talented violinist was Donna Grescoe, whom musical adjudicators called "The child prodigy". During her musical career Donna Grescoe, among other places appeared in the Town Hall and Carnegie Hall in New York. High musical recognition was attained by the Hubicky brothers, Taras and then Bohdan, who as a student of his older brother every year received medals, cash awards and scholarships. During the Second World War, Bohdan studied music in the Royal Academy in London, where he was killed during one of the air raids. In Edmonton, Sonia Lazarovich attained high recognition in the musical world. All those talented individuals were born and educated in Canada. Their work was strengthened by the arrival in Canada of such renowned conductors and composers as Eugene Turula and Pavlo Macenko; conductor and violinist

---

[8] Prof. C. Andrusyshen: "Cultural and educational work of the Ukrainian Reading Hall Prosvita—see "Fifty years of work of the Ukrainian Reading Association" in Winnipeg.

Bohdan Kowalsky, conductor and cellist Jacob Kozaruk, pianist Lubka Kolessa, opera singer Michael Holynsky and some students of Alexander Koshetz, and especially his wife Tetiana who continued the work of her husband for a while as a conductor, as well as George Hassan, Lev Sorochynsky and others.

All the above-mentioned individuals and choral and musical ensembles principally cultivated and propagated the Ukrainian song, so that it is no surprise that the Ukrainian song gained for them general recognition of all co-citizens in Canada [9]).

A crowning point of this process was the staging of the better known Ukrainian operas, such as "Taras Bulba", "Zaporozetz za Dunayem", "Chornomortsi" and "Kateryna" in such cities as Winnipeg, Toronto and Edmonton. The operettas "Natalka Poltawka" and "Zaporozetz za Dunayem" were filmed, and the director Vasil Awramenko planned to produce them on a large scale. However it was hard to compete against million-dollar industries in Hollywood. Prior to this, a play "The Star of Bethlehem", produced by Prof. E. Turula, was filmed in Winnipeg.

The folk dancing was also an interesting feature, which was duly appreciated by the audiences. The Ukrainians cherish their national dances as well as their songs. The national dances usually portray deep meaning as well as historical motifs. The dance "Chumak" reminds one of the chumak caravans winding across the steppes of Ukraine. The sole chumak drives his oxen, meets various problems on the way and finally returns home safely. The Zaporogian Dance—is a sword dance, and the "Arkan" of Hutsuls is an elegant male dance, showing respect to their fathers. "Metelytzia" portrays a winter snowstorm. "The Harvesters" shows appreciation of the produce of the fields. "The Romance" expresses the feeling of love between two young persons. Besides various other dances, such as "Kateryna", "Hopak", or "Podilsky Kozachok", the most popular dance is the "Kolomyyka", which has many variations. National dances usually are included in the programs of festivals and especially in the youth festivals.

A real and lasting contribution to the appreciation of the Ukrainian Folk Dancing was made by Vasyl Avramenko, who came to the American continent as a political immigrant following the First World War. He is the author of many popular handbooks on national dances, which had been widely distributed both in Europe and in America [10]). His triumphant achievement was revealed in 1926, when nearly 200 of his students, for two weeks performed at the Canadian National Exhibition in Toronto, and in 1933 at the World Fair in Chicago. Here his dancing group was a genuine sensation for all who saw it at that fair. It is worth mentioning that at the World Fair in Chicago, the Ukrainians of the United States and Canada had erected a "Ukrainian Pavilion" at which there was abundant collection of Ukrainian art which attracted the attention of the visitors from all continents.

The Ukrainians also brought with them to Canada other artistic works such as embroidery, wood carving, ceramics and Easter egg decorations.

---

[9]) "Music and song among Ukrainians in Canada", Canadian Farmer Almanac, 1929, pp. 119-124.
[10]) V. Avramenko: "Ukrainian National Dances, Costumes and Music", Winnipeg, 1936.

Embroidery has its usefulness not only in wearing apparel, but also in home decoration. Embroidery in Ukraine is very widely used and it has its own style and variations in different districts or provinces. Embroidery is done by cross-stitching and all its beauty depends on the choice of colors and the symmetry of the pattern. There are embroidered shirts, pillow slips, kerchiefs, scarfs, table cloths, bedspreads, towels, skirts and blouses. Embroidery is also used in the decoration of icons in homes and in the churches. There are also embroidered church vestments, banners and altar covers. Embroidery is a very exacting work and consumes much time but its lasting beauty is a reward for the person doing it.

Wood carving and incrustation have their own beauty. The most popular carving is the so-called Hutzul carving which is done by bead imprinting; this type of carving is applied particularly to tables, picture frames, crosses, plates, boxes, tomahawks and other small articles.

Still more complicated is the art of egg decoration which is usually associated with Easter. People who know estimate that it takes from five to eight hours of work to decorate one egg. In spite of that this art flourishes extensively among Ukrainian women in Canada.

Decorative pottery which originally was done by many craft experts, in later date became converted into the rare art of ceramics, which now is the field of art work-shops.

The art of making "kylyms" is highly developed in Ukraine, but it did not take root in Canada. It was replaced by factory product. Similar fate overcame other textiles, which in Ukraine were part of domestic and artistic industry.

The Ukrainian national handicraft by its workmanship and beauty satisfied the most exacting tastes. The Ukrainian handicraft was first successfully exhibited at the Canadian National Exhibition in Toronto in 1921. Ever since those exhibits were shown practically at all local, provincial, or national fairs and exhibitions. The Ukrainian Women's organizations are constantly working to maintain and improve this handicraft. In Winnipeg, in 1932 a Ukrainian Handicraft Society was organized whose object it was to collect and teach the art of embroidery, collect descriptive literature and inform others about the Ukrainian handicraft art. It became affiliated with the Canadian Handicraft Guild. In the history of this society it is recorded that its members were invited by other women's organizations to exhibit their handicraft or to speak at their fairs or exhibitions. Ukrainian handicraft societies were organized in several Ukrainian rural and urban settlements. Embroidery, tapestries, wood-carving, wicker work, Easter eggs are very characteristic to Ukrainian folk culture as far as customs are concerned. There is a great deal of symbolism especially evidenced in religious celebrations, funerals, weddings and christenings.

In this deep interlocking aspect of the national spirit and culture we find the answer to the question why the Ukrainian community in Canada cherishes its cultural values and since the beginning of its life in the new land does its best to preserve those values and transmit them to the new generation and to the general treasury of Canadian culture.

We may also discuss the indentification in the field of material culture. Here we have all the plants that were brought to Canada by the pioneers.

According to one agronomist there are at least fifty such plants [11]). These are such plants as flowers, greeneries and shrubs which are cultivated by every house, such as "malvy", "lubystock", "maruna", "rumianok", "vasylok", "blavatky-voloshky", "hrycyky", "miatka" and others; and in the gardens, sunflowers and garlic. And on the prairies we have the Red Fife wheat which was brought to Canada from Ukraine fifty years prior to the arrival of the first Ukrainian immigrants, W. Eleniak and Iwan Pylypiw. To this material aspect also belongs the fact that practically every family coming to Canada brought with it a handful of soil as a memento. That handful of soil contained all cultural and national symbolism. An icon, the handful of soil and Shevchenko's Kobzar were the most treasured possessions of the pioneer family.

What psychological effect had this on the immigrants is revealed in a poem "Kalyna" (Cranberry) by the first Ukrainian pioneer writer, Sava Chernecky. In his poem he draws a parallel between a strange country and the cranberry which was the same in Canada as in Ukraine. It alone soothed his lonely soul. Thus the imported material culture had a very positive additional influence on the psychology of the new settler. This material culture was a reminder to him of his former homeland. The settlers erected their dwellings with thatched roofs consisting of two rooms and surrounded them by gardens; they made their own kitchenware and farm implements; they produced their own textiles and prepared the old-Ukrainian dishes [12]). This was at the beginning. This self-sufficiency in agriculture preserved the first pioneers from extinction on the Canadian prairies and it provided a stimulus for progress in the new country. We have discussed this aspect more extensively in the previous period of our history.

New material conditions resulted in the development of new products. In the material sense the settlers had to adapt themselves to new conditions and this adaptations lasted for years. Many of the above-mentioned products had to be abandoned so that now they remain only as antiques; the same goes for the buildings. Nevertheless, similar process was experienced by other nationalities, namely French, English, German, etc. This process of adaptation was forced on them not only by material circumstances, but also by the technological progress—everything that had exclusively utilitarian value had to submit to better methods and technical improvements. Integration in the economic field was directed into faster and wider ways and means. Markedly different were the conditions in the sphere of spiritual culture. Fundamentally the Ukrainian culture took a firm root in Canada not only because of its instrinsic high quality, but also because of the compact settlements, long tradition of that culture and the desire to retain and develop that culture in the new land. A sector of spiritual culture is also exposed to the influence of other cultures. It is evident that mutual processes take place also in this sector, but this is a matter of long years and even centuries. We will have more to say about this aspect in the third period and in the resume of the new tendencies in the Ukrainian community in Canada.

---

11) M. L. Borowsky: "Flora transplanted from Ukraine to Canada", Winnipeg, 1967.
12) "Traditional Ukrainian Cookery", by Savella Stechishin, Winnipeg, Trident Press, 1959.

RELIGIOUS MATTERS

In classifying cultural identity traditional church and religious practices stand very high. In many instances they are to a certain degree connected with national traditions of the people. At the same time they hold an important position in the field of culture psychology of the nation.

The end of pioneer period piloted the road to the development of church life among the Ukrainians in Canada. This road proceeded in four parallel lines: Ukrainian Catholic Church (at that time known as Ruthenian Greek-Catholic Church), headed by Bishop Nykyta Budka, which was responsible to Vatican in Rome; newly created Ukrainian Greek-Orthodox Church, which was under the guidance of Greek Metropolitan Germanos; Ukrainian Presbyterian Church (formerly Ukrainian Greek Independent Church) and exclusively under the leadership of English Presbyterian or United Church; and a separate insignificant group formed the Baptist, wholly responsible to Ruthenian-Ukrainian Conferences, separately as the East and the West. In all these religious groupings relative developing processes were taking place which had important influence upon the aims of Ukrainian life in Canada, but only those churches developed in prominence that were traditional in respect of Ukrainian people, namely: the Orthodox and the Catholic Churches. These two churches claimed in the second decade of our Ukrainian life in Canada approximately 90 percent of all Ukrainian settlers; the balance fell to the Protestants of various sectors.

With the development of Ukrainian Greek Orthodox Church, religious relationship among the Ukrainians became notably complicated. In the newly formed Ukrainian Orthodox Church was to be found a group of former Greek Catholics who began to carry on action in its locals for new members. It is understood that such and similar actions created animosity among church congregations at local points. Political affairs in Ukraine, which at that time had reached the highest point of tension (the years 1918 to 1920) were pacifying to some degree, to enemy feelings among the worshippers of both churches. Action of relief towards liberation of Ukrainian National cause directed the national energy into unified national spirit under the influence of which the hostile feeling among the two groups was dying out. As matters on native lands gradually became stabilized, although not in favor of Ukrainian people, the matter of action of relief even in Canada had slowed down. Central Committee ceased to be central and the responsibility of leadership towards national unity fell more and more upon the two main Churches. In its turn each church aimed at deciding such matters in its own way and through lack of central co-ordinating committee and lack of united national responsibility, deepened the tension of public relations between the Churches. Out of such conditions came the unusually difficult times in the religious life of Ukrainians in Canada, which lasted some fifteen years. In many districts the two factions resorted to lawsuits concerning ownership of church property and moving of church buildings from place to place, because some group or other was intent upon gaining possession of a church and its land. There had even been tragic instances of burning a church, as an example in Tolstoi, Manitoba, etc. etc. In this enmity began to ripen controversies concerning church rituals and calendar changes, which matters in their turn further divided the two Churches of the same order. Only the threat of Second World War and the war itself brought the tension down in these problems, but of this we will speak later

UKRAINIAN CATHOLIC CHURCH
(RUTHENIAN GREEK CATHOLIC CHURCH)

The Ukrainian Catholic Church underwent important changes in the face of new social and political upheavals. We have already mentioned this in the first decade when an intensive struggle took place with the Protestant Mission. In the second decade a similar struggle repeated itself with the Orthodox. Both latter Churches were supported by the better educated class of Ukrainian Canadians which demanded from the Catholic bishop the right to have its influence concerning management of church matters. This did not agree with the spirit of the Catholic Church and Bishop Nykyta Budka, who in private life was a liberal and even relatively speaking a great humanist, was unyielding in church matters. In his attitude he was supported by his clergy of both orders, the Basilian and the Redemptorist. There were successes but there were also failures. The greatest blow that came to Bishop Budka was the loss of his newspaper "Canadian Ukrainian", which passed in 1927 to the hands of National Press in Winnipeg. Lack of lay organization which would give necessary aid to the Catholic Church was also felt badly. Political alliance of the Bishop with one political group also limited the church supporters. All this led to a number of changes but these changes were brought into effect by his successor Bishop W. Ladyka.

In 1927 Bishop Budka was called to Rome to report on his work in Canada and from there to Lviv, Halychyna, from where he did not return to Canada. In his absence the Diocese was managed by General-Vicar Father P. Oleksiw. In 1929 Vatican Rome appointed the new Bishop W. Ladyka of the Basilian Order, who came to Canada in 1909 and finished his studies in Montreal Seminary. He was ordained as Bishop on the 14th of July, 1929 and from that time took over the control of the whole Ukrainian Catholic Church in Canada. The new Bishop had great support from the priests of Basilian Order, from which he himself had come. With the aid of this Order and a few better educated laymen the Bishop organized the publishing of the newspaper "Ukrainian News" by the end of 1929. He also turned his attention to increasing the number of priests in Canada and in the meantime was receiving support from Basilian and Redemptorist Fathers overseas. On the occasion of the twenty-fifth Anniversary of his Diocese he brought to Canada six new priests, while earlier newcomers were Father S. Semczuk and Father W. Kushnir who in a short while became his right-hand men in church work. The latter became General Vicar and tactfully created in his own surroundings a feeling of peaceful co-existence and co-operation with other churches and lay groups. The new Bishop made constant visits to his parishes from ocean to ocean.—New training institutions and residential schools gave him important assistance in his work. A newly-formed organization, known as Brotherhood of Ukrainian Catholics, greatly re-inforced the work of Church. Dominion census of 1931 showed the number of Ukrainian Catholics as 186,587. This was also the result of his intensive church work. At that time in the Diocese there were 100 priests, of whom fifty-eight were secular priests. Bishop Basil Ladyka diligently and sincerely worked his field which was begun by Bishop Nykyta Budka.

The Church counted 350 parishes; of this number British Columbia had three, Alberta one hundred and two, Saskatchewan one hundred and eight, Manitoba one hundred and ten, Ontario twenty-one, Quebec five, Nova Scotia one. Three Monastic Orders worked in this large Catholic Diocese, namely: Basilian Fathers, Redemptorist Fathers and Sister Servants. There was also hope of getting new help from Oblate Fathers.

The Basilian Order

As we mentioned earlier, Basilian Order dedicated itself to the building of Ukrainian churches in Canada. In the second decade this Order turned its attention to the education of youth in general, and particularly to monastic vocations. The town of Mundare, Alberta, served this purpose in particular, where a Novitiate was opened in 1922 for young students who wished to dedicate their lives to monastic life. At that time, the head of the Basilian Mission, Father N. Kryzanowsky received support from the Old Country and the following pedagogues, successive priests of the Basilian Order came to Canada: P. Bodnar, E. Teodorovych, J. Zhydan, S. Diakovych and others. This had further results. The completion of courses in Mundare were: two year course in philosophy and conclusively theological studies after which came ordination into priesthood. In other words, out of the pioneer thickets emerged a new generation of priests. In the beginning of the thirties, to aid in theological studies and missionary work, came new priests who remained in Canada to work in missionary field as well as in community work. Some of these were: P. Olinsky, N. Horechko (1930), K. Woytowych, N. Savaryn(who became a Bishop of Edmonton in 1932), A. Truch, a talented sermon speaker, M. Romanowych and W. Baranyk (1933). The peak of the development of the monastic order of Basilian came when in 1932 there was created an American-Canadian (religious) Province, thereby receiving complete separation from old country factors and becoming directly responsible to Basilian Curia in Rome. In the second period Basilians expanded their stations and besides Winnipeg, Mundare and Edmonton, they organized Basilian homes in Montreal (1932) Rycroft (1937) and Redway (1939). A notable achievement was made in favor of the Order when the Basilians installed their own printing press in Mundare, Alberta, and began editing a bi-weekly paper "Svitlo" (Light). By the end of our period Basilian Fathers had 32 priests, 47 students and 29 Brothers. Mundare at this period was regarded as a native Ukrainian-Canadian Rome.

Sister Servants

In close co-operation with the Basilian Order were Sister Servants. The toil of both these Orders began together dating back to their arrival in Canada in 1902. Mundare, Edmonton, and Winnipeg were the first stations of these Orders. In all these three locations they opened bilingual schools, evening language courses, singing, handicrafts, etc. The opening centre of the work of Sister Servants was Mundare where a Novitiate was inaugurated and regular teaching conducted. When in 1926 Sister Servants built suitable quarters they opened in them, besides a novitiate and school, an Orphanage. Two years later they opened a 30-bed hospital in Mundare and in 1935 another such hospital at Willingdon.

Another larger centre of the Sister Servants in Alberta, besides Mundare, was Edmonton, where there was a St. Josaphat's Monastery and an all-day school.

In the province of Saskatchewan Sister Servants opened their work with the help of Redemptorist Fathers and particularly Father A. Delaere. Their first station in this province was Yorkton and here a school was built, which in a short time had a high school program. Besides Yorkton, which became a Catholic centre for Saskatchewan, there was a Home for Sister Servants in Ituna where they organized an Orphanage. Further, they had a Home in Saskatoon where they opened a small residential school for girls, also a Holy Family Home in Regina with a school that was conducted by Sister Servants.

Manitoba, especially Winnipeg, belonged to earlier territories of labor of the latter Order of Sister Servants. Their work in Winnipeg began, as we know, in 1905 with the help of Basilian Fathers. Sifton became their second centre to which Sister Servants came in 1935, where, besides conducting a school, they administered medical aid in emergency cases. In Dauphin, the work of Sister Servants dates back to 1928. In the neighboring Ukrainian districts they were conducting schools and teaching Ukrainian language and catechism during summer holidays. In Komarno the Sister Servants opened an Old Folks Home in 1937. In the same year they opened a St. Anthony Home in Portage la Prairie. Manitoba.

In Eastern Canada Sister Servants began their initial work in Montreal in 1925, where besides teaching in schools they also had quarters for girl students and for homeless girls. In Toronto they opened a St. Rita Home in 1937, where they taught school in native tongue and assisted in teaching catechism. The same type of work they carried on in Windsor, Ontario, where they opened their own Home in 1939.

Just as the Basilian Fathers, the Sister Servants created in Canada and the United States one religious Province and only after the second World War were they divided into two separate Provinces. By the end of our period there worked in both countries 150 Ukrainian Sister Servants, 19 Novitiates and 10 postulants. In Canada they had 14 Homes and 15 in U.S.A. In the beginning there worked only a small number of the "first" Sisters under the leadership of Mother-Superior A. Lenkewych; later when the number of Sisters increased, leadership was taken over by Atanasia Melnyk, 1926-1934, and Elizabeth Kassian, 1934-1949. During the whole time the aim of the Sisters was to help the needy. Besides schools—daily, evening, Saturday and vacational, in which they taught native language and catechism—Sisters looked after orphans, visited and took care of the sick, established Homes for the aged, gave first aid to the needy, organized and managed hospitals. In religious matters they acted as right hand to the work of the priests. They took care of decoration of churches and conducted church singing, thereby maintaining the traditions of the Church and the Ukrainian people.

Redemptorist Fathers

The beginning of this Order, or rather the branch of this Order in Canada, was introduced by a Flemmish priest, Rev. A. Delaere, who is already known to us, played an important role in evaluating the true need of schools, seminaries and the establishment of hierarchy for Ukrainian settlers in Canada. His information helped Vatican to understand the aims and needs of pioneer-immigrants. In 1906 this eminent missionary accepted Eastern Rite and began to call for more Belgian missionaries to assist him in serving the Ukrainian pioneers. The willing priests adopted the Eastern Rite, but found that their greatest handicap was lack of knowledge of Ukrainian tongue. It was necessary to have great devotion to missionary idea to overcome all difficulties.

What Mundare was to the Basilian Fathers, Yorkton was to the Redemptorist Fathers. The latter location was selected by Father A. Delaere as a centre for his Order and from there he was serving the great prairies of Saskatchewan. On the threshold of our time Redemptorist Fathers built another missionary centre, this time in Manitoba, at Komarno, from where they served some 40 districts. Those who worked here and in Yorkton were the following missionaries: Redemptorists, such as Ludwig and Franz Bosky, Richard Kostenobl, Joseph Ghiekiere, A. J. Van Bisen, N. N. De-Camp, A. Delforge. The latter in his loyalty gave his life for his missionary work in Saskatchewan. Their third great centre became Ituna, from where they served some 14 districts in the province of Saskatchewan. After the first World War the following Redemptorist priests served the Ukrainian settlers: J. Bala, S. Bachtalowsky, H. Shyshkowych, N. Kopiakiwsky, D. Hawryluk, R. Chomiak, W. and J. Korba, W. Krayewsky, S. H. and S. S. Shavel. This was not only an addition of new blood but also a new spirit. They gave their Order a complete Ukrainian character, and although Belgian Missionaries, they sincerely sacrificed themselves even if their Order was regarded by the masses as foreign. To the religious pathos it was necessary to add national-cultural color and this was brought by the missionaries from Ukraine. In the meantime on the Canadian scene began to grow young priests—monks out of pioneer throng. In 1920 began to toil in Yorkton Juvenite (C.S.S.R. Order) and in 1941 a large seminary was built, offering classes in theology. At the same time great plans and efforts were made to transfer these training institutions to Roblin, Manitoba, where they had new and more modern quarters. At the end of our period this Order already had 16 priests, 8 deacons, 5 Brothers and 4 Novices. This was already an outstanding achievement of Father A. Delaere, the first founder of the Ukrainian branch of the Redemptorist Fathers in Canada and Ukraine. At the time of his death, in 1939, there were some 150 active priests and Brothers.

Order of Oblate Fathers

The first Oblate priest of Ukrainian Rite in Canada was Father Phillip Ruh, who came in 1913. In this Order, for some time, served two other priests, namely: J. Lopushansky and J. Sluha, but through lack of addition of new blood, the Order did not increase in number. Father Ruh has gone down in the history of Ukrainians in Canada as an architect and builder of several large, mostly wooden Ukrainian churches in Canada, and as creator of the Holy Grotto in Cook's Creek, Manitoba, where also stands the large Prairie Cathedral built by Father Ruh.

UKRAINIAN GREEK ORTHODOX CHURCH

The Ukrainian Greek-Orthodox Church is the youngest Ukrainian Church in Canada as compared to others, primarily the Ukrainian Catholic Church which correlates its existence in this country with events of the early Canadian history. This church, nevertheless, ties its origin to the historical tradition of the church in Ukraine and relies on such authorities as Metropolitan Ilarion of the 11th Century, Metropolitan Klym Smolatych and Metropolitan Petro Mohyla, as well as the Ukrainian Brotherhoods of the 16th to 18th Centuries, which played such an important part in the growth of the church in Ukraine.

The Ukrainian Greek-Orthodox Church appealed likewise to popular emotions and national ambitions and strongly opposed any foreign control or supervision in the church. But even in this respect the beginnings of this church were paradoxical, and as we have expressed earlier, the church organizers were compelled of necessity to submit to the jurisdiction of the Syrian Metropolitan Germanos. The rector of the Saskatoon religious seminary of this church and the Head of its consistory, Rev. Dr. Lazar German, was likewise not a Ukrainian. It is true that the leadership of the Ukrainian Greek-Orthodox Church earnestly strove to find contacts with the Autocephalous Church in Ukraine and Rev. S. W. Sawchuk, Administrator of the Church, even went to Europe in search of a bishop but due to political situation in Ukraine, all these endeavors were in vain.

That state of affairs continued to the Fourth Council (Sobor) of the Ukrainian Greek-Orthodox Church which took place in Yorkton, on 16-17 July, 1924 [1]).

This Council was attended by Archbishop Ivan Teodorovich of U.S.A., one of the bishops of the Ukrainian Autocephalous Church in Ukraine who came to U.S.A. early in 1924 and was made Head of the Ukrainian Orthodox Church in that country. He was unanimously elected bishop of the Ukrainian Greek-Orthodox Church of Canada and its initial "national" crisis was thus resolved. The organizers promptly set to Ukrainize all divine services of the church, using Ukrainian language instead of Church-Slavonic. The first divine liturgy in the Ukrainian language in Canada was conducted by Rev. S. W. Sawchuk on June 18, 1920 in Saskatoon. Thereafter, this process continued systematically and with acceleration.

With the arrival of Archbishop I. Teodorovich, the organizational work of the church committees went on more smoothly. Since his seat of office remained in U.S.A. the organizational affairs were carried on by the Consistory of the Ukrainian Greek-Orthodox Church with Rev. S. W. Sawchuk in the vanguard. Number of priests in 1925 increased to 14, and

---

[1]) The First Council took place on December 28, 1918, attended only by four priests from Russian Orthodox Church. Bishop Alexander who was invited, failed to come. The Second Council took place in Winnipeg in 1919, wherein Metropolitan Germanos participated. The Third Council also took place in Winnipeg in 1920. The latter Councils continued their sessions in Saskatoon and Edmonton.

in addition to the pioneer clergy already mentioned, included the following: Peter Bilon, C. Hrebeniuk, M. Kucher, W. Sluzar, W. Novosad, P. Melnyk, D. Kirstiuk, D. Seneta, I. Kusy and K. Kirstiuk.

This was an enlarged group of pioneer priests of the church and in time new names were added as trainees were being released from special courses held at the seminary in Winnipeg.

Later Councils were not held as often as at first. The Fifth Council for instance, was held in 1927 at Saskatoon, the Sixth 3 years later at Yorkton, the Seventh in 1935 five years later, and the Eighth in 1940 also in Saskatoon. At the Ninth Council held in 1946 the Archbishop Ivan Teodorovich resigned as Head of the Church but continued his service as such until a new bishop, Mstyslaw Skrypnyk, was appointed in 1947. He was the first bishop with headquarters in Canada and with his appointment the organizational status was concluded and a new stabilized era of the church began. One of the first acts of this era was the establishment of Saint Andrew's College in 1946, with the faculty of theology where new priests receive their education and training. Up to that time this training and education was carried on in a seminary which began its existence and operation in 1932.

The early progress and development of the Ukrainian Greek-Orthodox Church were greatly aided by two popular newspapers "The Ukrainian Voice" and "The Canadian Farmer" whose editor, O. H. Hykawy, was one of the initiators of the church organization. From April, 1924, the church also published its own organ, "The Orthodox Herald" appearing monthly until 1928 at which time it shortened its name to "Herald" and became a bi-monthly publication.

At first the attitude of the Russian Orthodox Church toward its younger sister Ukrainian Greek-Orthodox Church was somewhat restrained but gradually became hostile. This hostility advanced as more Russian Orthodox Congregations comprising Ukrainian faithful as well as individual worshippers turned over to the jurisdiction of the Ukrainian Greek-Orthodox Church. This naturally resulted in the decrease and decline in the membership of the Russian Church. Statistical reports of 1935 showed the Russian Church with only 68 communities, whereas in the peak of its growth it boasted over 100 congregations [2]. This regressive process did not diminish as later statistics indicated that in the Western Provinces only 39 congregations still remained with the Russian Church, but most of them with depleted membership [3]. At the same time there was an aggressive and steady growth in the membership of the Ukrainian Greek-Orthodox Church to such a marked degree that in 1935 it listed 180 congregations scattered in various provinces as follows: Quebec 1, Ontario 7, Manitoba 43, Alberta 53 and Saskatchewan 76.

These statistical results clearly demonstrated that the activities and accomplishments of the Ukrainian Greek-Orthodox Church were timely and badly needed to change certain stagnant situations and undesirable conditions that existed at the time.

Although this growth and progress was achieved largely by and through

---

[2] Professor Ivan Bobersky, "Ukrainians in Canada", A Guide, p. 36, Winnipeg, 1936.

[3] M. H. Marunchak, Studies in the History of Ukrainians in Canada, Winnipeg, vol. II, p. 480.

the enlightenment of Russophile congregations, the initial action, however, was started in the peripheries of the Greek-Catholic parishes which often aroused serious disturbances within the Canadian-Ukrainian communities but which finally resulted in their mutual benefit.

Leaving Russian Church and joining a Ukrainian one was an act of national pride and not a mere revolution of dogmas and canons which were the same in both churches. Fundamentally, the problem revolved around national identity rather than religion. This was taken advantage of by the Ukrainian Greek-Orthodox Church and no stones were left unturned to strengthen and expand the Ukrainian consciousness among its converts.

The activities and the aims of the Ukrainian Greek-Orthodox Church were keenly encouraged and supported by two educational institutes— The Peter Mohyla Institute of Saskatoon and Michael Hrushevsky Institute of Edmonton. When in 1927 the Ukrainian Self Reliance League (Samostiynyky) was formed, which also included women's and youth's chapters, they likewise inserted a provision in their bylaws affording support and allegiance to the Ukrainian Greek-Orthodox Church. The church thereby was further reinforced in its moral and material structure, and added many new followers and cohorts to its ranks.

In the second decade the Ukrainian Greek-Orthodox Church was not the only Ukrainian Orthodox Church in Canada. In 1932 another "Ukrainian Orthodox Church" came into being. It was formalized by Rev. Dr. Joseph Zuk of U.S.A. upon an unfounded premise that the Ukrainian Greek-Orthodox Church is Protestant in character because it has no apostolic succession. Towards the end of our decade this church numbered 31 congregations and 6 priests who were subordinate to the jurisdiction of the Greek hierarchy of the U.S.A. This new church also became recipient of some congregations of the Russian Orthodox Church. Its official organ was "The Ukrainian Herald", published in Carteret, New Jersey, U.S.A. With the death of its organizer, Rev. Dr. J. Zuk, in 1934, the initial organizing enthusiasm began to decline but the organizational structure continued its activity even in later era though some of its membership became affiliated with the Ukrainian Greek-Orthodox Church. Its spiritual head for a long period of time was Bishop Bohdan Shpylka whose official see was also in U.S.A.

PROTESTANT CHURCHES

This chapter deals with such churches as Presbyterian, Methodist, Baptist, which were better known and more active of the Protestant Churches among the Canadian Ukrainians. When the Presbyterian and Methodist Churches merged into one, known as the "United Church", the movement of both denominations centered around this church. For the Ukrainian group of the church there was published a bi-monthly newspaper in Winnipeg known as "Canadian Morning" which in reality was a successor to the "Canadian" of Edmonton and to the "Morning" of Winnipeg. There also existed Ukrainian congregations within the United Church, but for practical purposes they had their own leadership and their own pastors. Among the most aggressive individuals of that church within the Ukrainian group were: P. Krat, O. Maksymchuk, M. P. Berezynsky,

M. Glowa, J. R. Kovalevich and a number of others. Its outstanding leader, however, was Dr. J. Hunter who conducted an Institute in Teulon for young people of both sexes. For some time another Institute or "Bursa" operated in Sifton. At Teulon, Sifton and Ethelbert there were medical hospitals under the direction of that church. About 30 Ukrainian preachers of the United Church received their education at Blumfield and in colleges of Winnipeg and Saskatoon, but its Ukrainian assemblies were included under the general name "United Church" and as a result the denomination lost its significance as a Ukrainian Church both in its expansion and new congregations.

In order to preserve the indentity of the Ukrainian Reformed Church, the Protestant leaders of Canada and the United States held a Ukrainian Evangelical Conference at Rochester, N.Y. in 1922, in which pastors and delegates of almost all Protestant Communities participated.

"Among the topics discussed at this Conference, writes one of its participants, Rev. J. R. Kovalevich, "and the definite conclusion reached by everyone, was the fact that in order to make any further and substantial progress in this church movement it is necessary to have one's own organization." Thus it was resolved by the Conference to create 'Ukrainian Evangelical Alliance (U.E.A.)'.

The main purpose of the Ukrainian Evangelical Alliance was to further unify and bring together all the Ukrainians of the Evangelical Reformed Religion" [4].

The Ukrainian Evangelical Alliance held its Conferences almost every year in Canada or in the United States. In 1925 the Conference adopted the resolution to send to Western Ukraine, then under Poland, three clergymen who were to head the Protestant congregations wherever they were active. The first of these missionaries was Paul Krat, later followed by Lewko Buchak and Wasyl Kuziw. The latter was consecrated there as bishop and became the spiritual head of the entire religious movement which was financed partially by the United Church. Through the efforts of the Ukrainian Evangelical Alliance there appeared a translation of the Bible which was prepared by Professor I. Ohienko, who later became Metropolitan of the Ukrainian Greek-Orthodox Church. The Ukrainian Evangelical Alliance comprised in its fold not only the Presbyterians who belonged to the United Church, but also the Presbyterians who were non-participating, i.e. Preacher M. Fesenko, the editor and publisher of the "Evangelical Truth", and others. The Ukrainian Evangelical Alliance was directed for a long period of time by Pastor W. Kuziw, then came M. Fesenko, L. Standret, J. R. Kovalevich, I. Yacenty and others.

The Ukrainian Baptists had a somewhat longer history because they carried their missions under two separate federations in Eastern and Western Canada. In both federations linguistic and traditional Russian influences were noticeably in vogue. When Pastor Peter Kindrat took the helm in 1921, a Ukrainization in the Western faction of the federation began to appear in formal religious services. This process was accelerated when Dr. Ivan Kmeta-Ichniansky established his prestige on Canadian soil, not only as a talented spiritual leader but also as a poet and educator.

---

[4] I. Robert Kovalevich, Ukrainian Evangelical Alliance, a historical treatise, page 2, Author's Collection.

The candidates for ministers or preachers received their training at the Bible College in Saskatoon in which, after the Second World War, a special wing was established for Ukrainian students. The Baptists also issued their publications which will be reviewed in a separate chapter.

In accordance with the official records of 1935, there were 28 Ukrainian Presbyterian and Baptist communities. These congregations were the strongest in Saskatchewan and Manitoba with eleven churches each; there were 3 congregations in Alberta, 2 in Ontario and 1 in Quebec. Denominationally, they were divided into the following memberships, i.e.: United Church 3,667 members, Presbyterians 1,823, Baptists 1,262, Lutherans 1,180, Bible Students 1,003, Adventists 769, Anglicans 755, Menonites 385, Protestants 369, Evangelical Society 344, Seventh Day Adventist 105, Salvation Army 44, Church of Christ 24, Mormons 20, "Christians" 23, Christian Science 6, United Brotherhood 2, Confucians 1, Miscellaneous 350. It was interesting to note that 1,215 Ukrainians classed themselves as non-denominational, and 56 declined to be classified at all.

THE PRESS

Winnipeg

In the mid-war era even as in the pioneer times, Winnipeg remained as the Ukrainian publishing centre. Here, such pioneer papers as "Canadian Farmer", "Ranok" (Morning), that had acquired the new name of "Canadian Morning", "Ukrainian Voice", "Canadian Ruthenian" with the new name of "Canadian Ukrainian", continued their publications. The very appearance of these four organs in Winnipeg gave that city a leading place in the history of the Ukrainian press in Canada. But the publishing activity in Winnipeg was not limited to those four weeklies, to which was added in 1919 a fifth and very powerful political competitor, the "Ukrainian Labour News".

During the First World War there was a whole line of various smaller and larger publications in Winnipeg that gave specific features to the life and development of the Ukrainians during the second era. But leaving aside all these new publications and journal productions, the undeniably leading place was held strongly by the formerly mentioned weeklies, which not only were the informers of social-cultural and political life of the Ukrainians of that era throughout the whole of Canada, but they also were the stimulators of that same life as well, and their editors very often worked in the midst of those who were responsible for the moral and political side of that life.

Along with the march of time the role of these organs began to change and into the leading place moved "Ukrainian Voice" and "Canadian Ukrainian"—the two papers that constantly competed with each other if only for the reason that they were the expression of two different religious and political worlds.

As we have mentioned in the first era of our history, the "Ukrainian Voice" expressed itself religiously. It took the side of the Ukrainian Greek-Orthodox Church at the same time as the "Canadian Ukrainian" continued to faithfully support the Ukrainian Catholic Church. The political sympathies of these two papers ran along the line of the two traditional Canadian parties—"Canadian Ukrainian" sympathized with the Conservatives, and "Ukrainian Voice" went with the Liberals. Interestingly enough, along similar lines were their sympathies toward the Ukrainian state politics also. "Ukrainian Voice" developed its contacts with the republican centre, particularly with the representatives of the Ukrainian National Republic, while "Canadian Ukrainian" co-operated very closely with Hetman-state movement which began its work in Canada by organizing a system of "Canadian Sitch" formations. In addition, members of the Hetman movement, at various times, were prominent editors of "Canadian Ukrainian" as for instance Wolodymyr Bossy, Andrew Zaharychuk and others. Bishop Nykyta Budka played his wholehearted sympathies toward the monarchial movement. This fact somewhat complicated the matters as not all Ukrainian Catholics were of the monarchical-conservative belief.

The religious and political differences of the two press organs often led to sharp polemics and even bitter enmity. When the "Ukrainian Central Committee" came into existence in 1920-1923, these two centres worked together in harmony. However, this cooperation was terminated when during the "Educational-Economic Congress of Ukrainian Canadians", which was held without the official representation from the Catholic centre, resolutions were adopted to make some changes in the method of operation of the "Ukrainian Central Committee". From that moment on, the committee ceased to be the central body and the two centres launched their long years of mutual silence, negative relationship and at times even open warfare. It was only the serious political situation in Ukraine under Poland and USSR in the thirties that brought these two warring camps into closer cooperation.

During these times the fate of the "Canadian Ukrainian" was also somewhat complicated, a situation that brought to mind similar stories from pioneer days. The fact that the paper in the short period of a few years had no less than nine editors amply shows that there was a great lack of stability in this establishment. Only the authority of Bishop N. Budka, who at one particular time almost himself had to play the role of the editor, was able to bring to this periodical some semblance of purposiveness and religious-political direction to guide the footsteps of over 200 thousand Ukrainian Catholics. Other Catholic publications came to the aid of "Canadian Ukrainian", but more will be said about them later on.

Among the editors of "Canadian Ukrainian" of that period were: the formerly mentioned Roman Kremar, Ivan Rudachek, Dr. Alexander Sushko (1923 — second time), Volodyslaw Biberovych, Andrew Zaharychuk, Rev. Petro Oleksiw, Wolodymyr Bossy, Wasyl Dyky and Danylo Budka. During the time of W. Bossy's editorship a court action, the so-called "libel" case took place. The court decreed that the publishers must pay the costs, which amounted to quite a large sum, and this basically resulted in the financial shake-up of the paper. It lost its offices and had to move to the previously held premises, "The West Canada Publishing Co." on McDermot Avenue. From there it moved to the National Press and in 1932 it ceased its publication. Weakened by the financial losses due to the court action, the final blow came from the economic crisis—the great depression had set in.

When we stop to consider the stability factor of the various newspapers then we must admit that the paper which most revealed the steady purpose was the "Ukrainian Voice", edited by Myroslav Stechishin from 1921 to 1946, who not only was its editor, but also the ideologist of this organ as well as of all the elements that grouped themselves around this journal. It was through the initiative effort of M. Stechishin, as we already have mentioned, that the Ukrainian Self-Reliance League along with its youth organization, the SUMK, and the women's organization, the SUK, was formed. All these organizations very actively supported the paper. The editorial stability and the capable organizational formation greatly influenced the growth and development of the "Ukrainian Voice". The work of the Orthodox centre received still greater impetus with the appearance of the second organ, the religious bi-weekly "Orthodox Herald" later shortened to "Herald" which became, from 1924 (year of its origin) the official organ of the Ukrainian Greek-Orthodox Church in Canada. The "Herald" was printed by the "Ukrainian Publishing Co." and its editors were Rev. S. W. Sawchuk (1924-1941) and Rev. W. Kudryk. Both "Ukrainian Voice" and "Herald" were printed regularly and in their particular formats. The "Herald" became a rich source for the study of the Ukrainian Greek-Orthodox Church history while the "Ukrainian Voice" had always been a suitable forum for the young talents and creative writers. To complete the total picture in this one segment of our history we also may add that during 1926-1927 Rev. S. Sawchuk edited the "Sunday School" circular for the Orthodox children.

Canadian Farmer

In the twenties, the 'Canadian Farmer' weekly paper continued its publication under the management of Frank Dojacek, with O. Hykawy as editor. Although the paper considered itself to be neutral in matters of politics and religion, still the sympathies of its editor leaned towards the Liberals which practically had become a tradition in the history of "Canadian Farmer". On the religious plane the paper supported the Ukrainian Greek-Orthodox Church—its editor, O. Hykawy, being one of the initiators of this church and therefore understandably enough supported its growth. At the same time "Canadian Farmer" never denied the right to any other denominational adherents to express their opinions, religious or otherwise, on its pages. The paper faithfully supported the national aspirations of the Ukrainians in Canada and in Ukraine and very strongly fought against all international trends.

Toward the end of 1927 the publishing firm of the "Canadian Farmer" was bought over by the newly created National Press under the management of H. Kurdydyk, but less than four years later it was brought back by F. Dojacek who continued to publish it under the firm name of National Publishers. In 1932, after spending nineteen years (1913-1932) as its editor, O. Hykawy left the paper. Being an experienced editor he had brought to the paper a strong measure of stability and succeeded in attracting the direct cooperation of the noted publicists from Europe—Dr. K. Trylowsky, Dr. E. Levytsky, Dr. O. Nazaruk, Dr. Kedryn-Rudnytsky and others. After O. H. Hykawy's departure V. Biberovych, Dr. T. Dackiw and Dr. C. Andrusyshen took, in turn, the editor's position. In December, 1944, Onufry Hykawy came back to his old post to finish the mid-war period of the "Canadian Farmer's" existence, but only for a short while as death came to claim this veteran editor in May 1945.

"Canadian Farmer" which held the favorite place as the first Ukrainian paper, also was best situated, financially speaking. Its source of income was the publishing activity plus its so-called neutrality, although in truth it was a private enterprise since 1912. Thanks to its open-to-all pages for expressing various opinions the periodical won the sympathy of a wide circle of readers.

Canadian Morning

In 1920 the "Morning" of Winnipeg and the "Canadian" of Edmonton joined together to form a new periodical called the "Canadian Morning", published at 146 Logan Avenue, with the subtitle "a newspaper for the

Ukrainian family". The union of these two papers came as the result of a religious process that had been going on in the Presbyterian and Methodist Churches which ended in the formation of the United Church. Through the union of two churches there also came the union of two papers. But even this fusion of the two weeklies into one periodical failed to bring any noticeable strength to the "Canadian Morning" as the former Methodist organ, the "Canadian" was in full decline and the newly-formed paper had to depend almost exclusively upon the resources of the former Presbyterian organ, the "Morning". The new periodical was published regularly every Tuesday and consisted of eight pages (58 X 38). After the war, Dennis Perch, a teacher by profession who took a theological course in Saskatchewan to become a pastor, took on the duties of editor. Prior to that, at one time, Z. Bychynsky had been the editor. For a longer period of time M. Karabut, a new arrival from Europe and who was the right-hand man to Dr. J. D. Hunter, took on the full duty of editing the paper. M. P. Berezynsky spent nearly ten years as editor of this journal. In the mid-war period the popularity of this paper had diminished, compared with its prestige in the earlier pioneer days. The liquidation of the Independent Greek Church, or to be exact, with its absorption into the purely Presbyterian sphere, brought disillusionment on the part of its adherents and some of them turned away from Presbyterianism to join the traditional Ukrainian churches. Along with this deteriorating condition, the paper's authority began to diminish and so did the ranks of its readers. In spite of these circumstances "Canadian Morning" still remained an important representative of the Ukrainian Protestant movement and opened its pages equally to the Ukrainians of Presbyterian, Methodist and Baptist faiths.

"Canadian Morning" stood closer to the "Ukrainian Voice" than to the "Canadian Ukrainian" in the general Ukrainian community field and supported the centre for whom the "Ukrainian Voice" was the official organ although it very often engaged in polemics with it. On the whole, the "Canadian Morning" always stood on solid ground in regard to the national-cultural position of the Ukrainian settlers in Canada.

National Press

In July 1927 a new printing and publishing company was formed under the name of National Press. The owners of this new company did not try to edit some new periodical. They merely bought the whole publishing concern from F. Dojacek. In this way the young company not only became the new owners of the "Canadian Farmer" but also of three other papers: "Czas" in Polish language, "Nordwesten" in German and "Kanadsky Hlas" in Croatian. To these four were added, at the end of 1927, the "Canadian Ukrainian" and in 1929 a monthly magazine "The New Canadian" printed in English.

The National Press soon became the most prominent publishing company of the so-called third power in Canada during that particular period of our history. Over thirty persons in editorial, administrative and technical capacity worked in this private publishing enterprise. Hryhor (Ivaniv) Kurdydyk became the general manager and Volodyslav Biberovych the editor-in-chief of publications of this huge publishing complex. On the editorial board were Dr. Danylo Lalkiv of Saskatoon, Andrew

Hawrylak of Edmonton, Thomas K. Dickson, publisher of the Journal of Commerce of Montreal and Ivan Beda, of The Pas, with George Hyde as secretary of the company. It generally was believed at the time, that National Press was receiving financial support from the Conservative Party but the publishing company soon denied these allegations with the following announcement in "Canadian Farmer":

"There are different nameless and subvertive politicians who spread false news among the people implying that National Press has a clandestine connection with the various so-called political clubs of the Conservative, Liberal or some other political party. In view of this we wish to make an announcement, right here and now, that our press is completely independent of any political party. The Ukrainian (that is the National— M.H.M.) Press works and will work exclusively for the good of Ukrainian immigration" [1].

The National Press during the period of its existence truly endeavoured to live up to its professed policy. This undoubtedly was the reason for the differences that arose between the editor of the Polish "Czas" and the publishers. About these complications V. Turek has this to say in his work:

"In 1927 the control of the company (National Press Company) passed into the hands of a Ukrainian group. Since that time the relations between the publishers and the newspaper "Czas" deteriorated. The editors lost their former freedom in commenting on Polish-Ukrainian relations, while other periodicals published by the same firm started attacking the Polish Government's Ukrainian policy" [2].

As a result of these and other differences the National Press sold its interest in the newspaper "Czas" to Polish organizations in Winnipeg It is worth adding this one point of interest to our history at this time, that the first editor of "Czas" was a Ukrainian Pasnych, who had been working in the publishing firm of F. Dojacek [3].

National Press under the management of H. I. Kurdydyk began its operation at the time when the serious economic crisis first appeared on the world's horizon. The stock market crash at the end of 1929 dealt a heavy blow to the publishing firm. The business world had to struggle through the most difficult times in the first years of the so-called "dirty thirties". The mortgage payments forced the company to sell the whole concern back to its former owner, F. Dojacek, with great losses.

Among the interesting events in the life of the above mentioned publishing concern was the one where the "Canadian Farmer" had, at this particular time, humorous-satirical supplement and that from this press concern came the idea of the League of British Ukrainians. Considering the fact that the Company edited the paper the "Canadian Ukrainian" it then will be seen that over a period of four full years the National Press played a very important role in promoting, among the Ukrainians in Canada, the idea of good citizenship.

---

[1] "Canadian Farmer", No. 17, 1929.
[2] "The Polish Language Press in Canada", Its history and bibliographical list, Toronto, 1962, p. 108.
[3] "Gazeta Katolicka", Aug. 188, 1915.

The Canadian Sitch

When Wolodymyr Bossy parted from "Canadian Ukrainian" as the paper wanted to take a neutral stand towards all political trends, he began to publish a semi-monthly journal the "Canadian Sitch", the first issue of which appeared on May 15, 1928. It became the official organ of the Hetman movement which began to set deep roots among many Ukrainian settlers. The best ground for its growth was found among the second immigration although some of the elements of the first immigration were not altogether deaf to the clarion call of the "Canadian Sitch" which proclaimed in the Ukrainian language their motto: "One path, one Hetman, one flag, work and order". In the English language this motto was somewhat altered and read: One God, one King, one flag, one Empire.

This 8-page weekly was published by the "Head Command of Canadian Sitch" and edited by the "Press and Propaganda Section" under the direction of D. M. Elcheshen. W. Bossy was the "Obozny" (head) of the movement, and editor-in-chief of the "Canadian Sitch". In the head office of the executive board as well as on the editorial board were the following persons: V. Duzhy, A. Zaharychuk, V. Kysilewsky, I. Esaiw, M. Hetman, Dr. V. Stasiuk, N. Yatsyk and M. Lapka. The paper continued its publication until 1930. In the last few issues of this ideological-political organ appeared a notice stating that the full responsibility for publishing this paper rested with the Ukrainian Sitch Organization of Canada with the Main Council of Scout Organization of Canada.

"Truth and Liberty"

Almost at the same time and only eight months after the first appearance of the conservative periodical the "Canadian Sitch" there came into existence a weekly paper, the "Truth and Liberty", with a very strong national-socialist trend. It called itself as being "an independent organ of Ukrainian labourers, farmers and working intelligentsia in the new country". Its first task was to "uplift culture, strengthen the unity and material well-being of the Ukrainian settlers in Canada and America and to aid the Ukrainian nation in its struggle for freedom." The paper stood on the outside of the religious controversies and preached "respect for the honest opinion of others" [4]. "Truth and Liberty" was published by a cooperative association with its executive board consisting of: D. M. Hunkevych, N. Baran, S. Kowbel, M. Onofreiv, P. Pavlukevych and M. Mandryka. The last one mentioned was the editor and the paper consisted of 8 pages in a 12 X 18 format.

"Truth and Liberty" considered itself as the press organ of the "Ukrainian National Home" in Winnipeg and of the other national organizations in Canada that were allied with the Home, as well as being the official spokesman for the "Ukrainian Labour Association" that only recently had been formed during the convention in Toronto on August 30, 1930. The paper was published for a period of two years and represented, on the ideological plane, the ideas of the Ukrainian socialist-revolutionaries, who carried on a continuous and bitter warfare with the marxist socialist-democrats. Mykyta Shapoval was the European leader

---

[4] Quotations from the first editorial of "Truth and Liberty", January, 1929.

of the Ukrainian socialist-revolutionaries and "Truth and Liberty" invited him, in 1930, to visit Canada and give a series of political lectures. Directly cooperating with the paper and contributing their articles to it were such well known publicists and men of learning as: S. Borodayevsky, S. Zhuk, S. Shelukhyn, N. Hryhoriyiv, S. Dovhal and others. In addition to the valuable articles of the above mentioned authors, "Truth and Liberty" also printed a whole cycle of articles about the labour movement in Canada, as well as a fairly long sketch by S. Kowbel entitled "Ukrainians in Canada, their development and steps forward and backward".

"Truth and Liberty", as well as the earlier mentioned "Canadian Sitch", both fell, under the relentless blows of the economic crisis.

"Veterans News"

This paper mirrored a different trend of the Ukrainian political orientation than the other two that were mentioned previously—the "Canadian Sitch" and "Truth and Liberty"—but it still was the product of the postwar immigration. It became the press organ of the "Ukrainian War Veterans Association" in Canada and was oriented toward the nationalist movement in Europe and the Organization of Ukrainian Nationalists that propagated the idea of creating the Independent Ukrainian State by revolutionary means and which was headed by Col. Evhen Konovalets. Members of the "Ukrainian War Veterans' Association" considered themselves to be part of this movement.

The first issue of "Veterans News", a monthly magazine, came out in November 1930, consisting of 16 pages in 7½ X 10 tabloid size and it was published in this form for two years and then was absorbed by its sister publication, the "New Pathway", but still continued to appear on the pages of this paper under its old name "Veterans News", published by an editorial board under the direction of Pavlo Shulha. It first was initiated by the Ukrainian War Veterans Association in Winnipeg that came into existence in 1928. Branches of this organization were formed in 1930 in Toronto, Edmonton, Montreal, Saskatoon, Regina, Sudbury, Windsor, Calgary and other places, and these provided the basis for the regular appearance of this press organ.

"The Truth"

Another and a somewhat different type of newspaper which brought to the Ukrainian community in Canada a new moment of interest was "The Truth" with the following sub-title" "for the Ukrainian farmers in Canada and U.S.A.". This paper reflected the thought of those labourers and farmers in the Ukrainian Labour and Farmers' Temple Association (ULFTA) who were disillusioned with the organization, especially with its faithful-subjection line toward the Stalin's terroristic and exterminating policy in Ukraine, and which the newly formed journal very strongly condemned on its printed pages [5]. The first issue of "Truth" appeared on February 15, 1936, and with its third edition it became

---

[5] The later history revealed that this Ukrainian Canadian organ was the first among the Communists that in a most decisive manner condemned the terror of the dictator Stalin and that its condemnation was correct. The same condemnation was made by the Communist Party during its 20th Congress in Moscow.

a semi-monthly of 4 pages and 17½ X 22½ format. Its initiators were the labourers from Winnipeg and Transcona supported by many labour centres in Canada such as Toronto, Montreal, Windsor and others. Its editor was Danylo Lobay who previously had been, for many years, the editor of the Ukrainian Labour News." The impetus toward the creation of this new periodical was given by a brochure entitled: "The National Question and the Chauvinism of the Great Russian Empire" that was written by D. Lobay. In view of the leading ideological and political role that had been played by D. Lobay in the leftist labour movement the paper was referred to as the "Lobayite Paper" and those grouped around it were called the "Lobayivtsi". The "Truth" was published by the Ukrainian Workers' and Farmers Educational Association with its editorial board consisting of, in addition to D. Lobay—T. Kobzey, N. Handziuk, S. Chwaliboga, M. Smith, I. Slobodian and V. Kulchytska. "The Truth" was edited for two years. Those who broke away from their orientation toward Bolshevism were not satisfied with the name of the paper that reminded them of the same name official Communist organ in Moscow, and so during a convention in Toronto the name was changed from "Truth" to "Forward", and the paper was edited not in Winnipeg but in Toronto, where there was a great reserve of labour forces.

Specific Publications

In Winnipeg, during the mid-war era, there was a whole string of specific publications that served different purposes. The greatest number of them consisted of monthly magazines and non-periodicals or those that appeared as a result of some bigger event or historical dates. For a closer examination of the press section we divide them into different categories: political and literary, economic, children's, humorous, Anglo-Ukrainian and others.

Political and Literary Publications

To this class, first of all, belong the four publications that are closely tied with the "Chytalnia (cultural centre) Prosvita" in Winnipeg, corner McKenzie and Flora. In this chytalnia, and on its initiative, there was organized, in 1933 "The Ukrainian National Council" which endeavoured to unite the Ukrainian organizations not only in the city of Winnipeg but also those in the rest of Canada in order to achieve the political aims of the Ukrainian community in this country and in Europe. To let the general public know about its work the new organization began to publish in 1933 a non-periodical publication called "The Herald of the Ukrainian National Council".

This was a 24-page, bilingual tabloid whose first issue appeared in August 1933. It changed its format with the third edition to a book-size and a new name, the "Ukrainian Herald", with a sub-title "Organ of the Ukrainian National Council of Canada". It was printed by a mimeograph method during the years 1934 and 1935, at the address of "Chytalnia Prosvita," 667 Flora, and prepared by the editorial board consisting of: M. Mandryka, C. Andrusyshen, V. Biberovych, A. Gospodyn and D. Budka. Only ten issues in all made their appearance.

In the same "Chytalnia Prosvita" in Winnipeg a war veteran journal "Struggle for Freedom" was published by the "Association of Sitch War Veterans of D. Vitovsky", and under the direction of the head of this organization, S. Syvak, with A. Gospodyn as its editor. The first issue of this book-size 48 to 60 page journal appeared in January 1940 and only ten issues in all were put out. One year later, in January 1941, a change took place and the "Struggle for Freedom" was renamed to "Echo". This change, as the editors explained, was motivated by technical and business reasons in the wake of the war. "Echo" was a popular literary-bent journal that contained a variety of interests, including poetry, stories and literary sketches in its 32-page edition, but only three issues of it saw the light of day.

About the same time as the "Echo" came into existence, another publication appeared on the horizon, "Our Life", a monthly journal dealing with the culture and social life, whose content was similar to that of Echo." It printed the works of such well-known literati as S. Kovbel, S. M. Doroshchuk, Myra Lazechko, Rev. S. Semczuk, A. Gospodyn, K. Novosad, Tetiana Kroitor and other. The magazine was in a book format of 64 pages and edited by the editorial board with M. Mandryka at the head. It was published by the "Association of Ukrainian Culture" [6]) that had its office in the "Chytalnia Prosvita" and which had set for itself the task of publishing an "Anthology of Ukrainian Literature in Canada" and also Ukrainian-English text books for the teaching of the two languages. War times hampered the cultural work and the initiators of this plan only succeeded in publishing an Anthology [7]) in Ukrainian language and another work "Ukrainian Question"—both of them written by M. Mandryka.

Economic Publications

The first issue of the illustrated journal titled "Apiary", dealing with bee-keeping, and prepared by M. Pankiw and D. M. Elcheshen was printed in 1924. The publication was intended for the apiarists in Canada and U.S.A. as the sub-title explained but perhaps due to the scarcity of bee-keepers in this country to support a specific journal dealing with this trade, only two issues of the 48-page book format magazine was ever published under that name. The third issue came out under a new name, the "Agriculturist". The thematical content of the journal was altered, or rather expanded, and in its first introduction the editors and publishers emphasized that "the farm, garden, orchard and apiary" form the foundation of economic life and that the journal will devote its services to these four branches. Although the periodical was professionally edited, for in addition to the other experienced editor-agronomists already mentioned, the well-known agricultural authority K. S. Prodan also joined the editorial ranks, still the journal was unable to survive and was discontinued after its fourth issue. In addition to the informative articles, dealing with the represented trade matters the journal also encouraged the farmers to create their own organizations.

The "Trade and Commercial Guide" journal first appeared in Winnipeg in November 1934. In its self-introduction we read: "We wish to give a start to a serious work of lifting up and rebuilding our nearly destroyed and almost totally neglected class of intelligent and materially independent businessmen, tradesmen and professional men". It was edited by V. A.

---

[6]) The Executive Board also included: A. Gospodyn, M. Ivanyshyn, S. Skoblak.
[7]) "Anthology of Ukrainian Literature in Canada".

Krysky with six issues of it appearing in the first year. Its next six issues (7 to 12) appeared in one volume in December 1935 under the title "National Economy" and represents the best compiled statistical information about the Ukrainian business establishments in Canada during the mid-war period. In the second half of 1936 "National Economy" changed its form from tabloid to a book-size and by the end of 1936 it ceased its publication. "National Economy" had a terse business motto: "Sviy do Svoho" (freely interpreted it means—"support your own") and with its articles greatly influenced the Ukrainian people in Winnipeg and the rest of Canada to take more interest in business matters. "Trade and Commercial Guide" and "National Economy" were financed by an organization called "Lanciuh" (Chain) and later on, in 1936, when a club of Ukrainian businessmen and the so-called "General Wholesale" were formed in Winnipeg, they both provided funds for the upkeep of the two journals.

Through V. A. Krysky's endeavours another publication came into existence entitled the "Summary of Our Work". This was a statistically compiled historical outline of cultural-educational organizations in Winnipeg. The editorial committee consisted of H. Mudry, D. Yakimischak, I. Moroz and Y. Shcherbanievych.

Winnipeg had a political, economic and cooperative paper, the "Co-operative Community" with its first issue appearing in June 1935. In its introductive editorial it said that the Canadian ideal should be not so much integral mechanical uniformity but rather unity in diversity. The 8-page tabloid that expired the same year it started, was supported by a group from the Co-operative Commonwealth headed by G. S. Woodsworth.

Youth Publications

The weakest representation among Ukrainian publications was to be found in the field of children's literature, but even here Winnipeg led the way. The first children's monthly magazine after the First World War was the "Children's World" consisting of 32 pages in 6 X 9 format, richly illustrated and well edited. The moving spirit back of this journal was Stepan M. Doroshchuk, a teacher by profession and educated in Canada. This was the only illustrated journal for the Ukrainian children in Canada and U.S.A. and came into existence in May 1924. S. M. Doroshchuk was not satisfied to publish a journal for children only. He wanted to have something for young people as well and so in January 1925 he put out the illustrated monthly journal for children and youth titled the "Sunbeam", consisting of 32 pages in book-size, that was published for a period of three and a half years. Those who first took part in formulating this journal were: S. M. Doroshchuk and O. T. Darkovych, to be joined later by D. Hunkevych and I. H. Syrnick. Its chief illustrator was O. T. Darkovych with Anna Moroz and Anna Pushchak contributing their share. M. Petrowsky, O. Ewach and I. Danylchuk frequently sent their articles to the journal. The publishers of "Sunbeam" also put out children's editions that were of great help in the bringing up of children. The journal had a motto taken from the verse written by S. M. Doroshchuk which we present in free translation: "He who believes in his own strength (self-reliance) shall gain very very much".

Two years after "Sunbeam" ceased to exist two teachers, M. I. Borysyk and I. Biletsky, began to publish a monthly journal for the young people called "Yahidka" (the Berry) and illustrated by O. T. Darkovych. Several issues of this journal appeared in 1931, consisting of 16 pages in book format and only fifty cents for a year's subscription, whereas the "Sunbeam" cost one dollar and fifty, but even the low price failed to save the life of "Yahidka".

The Catholic young people of Winnipeg printed, in 1940, their "Youth Herald" in English, size 9 X 12, but only three issues of it appeared [8].

Humour and Satire

In 1922 "Vuyko" (Uncle)—the Canadian Ukrainian humorous monthly paper (for old and young) in Canada and United States, came back to life. It first appeared in 1918 as a brain child of J. Maydanyk and it was he who resurrected it again in 1922. The first issue of the new "Uncle" had four pages, in a tabloid form of double columns and only several editions of it appeared. It was printed more regularly in 1925 and 1926 and published by "Canadian Ukrainian" with J. Maydanyk as editor. Uncle's motto was: "Correct the bad habits through humour" and its objective was "to be the means of bringing amusement and entertainment for the Ukrainian people in Canada, irrespective of opinions, cultural pursuits, beliefs or anything else."

In 1927 "Uncle" was printed as an eight page supplement to "Canadian Ukrainian" and "Canadian Farmer". Both supplements had the same content, the only difference was in the titles of these two editions. J. Maydanyk, who often used the signature of "Vuyko Shteef" (Uncle Steve) was the editor of these supplements that were printed for three more years.

There also were "Uncle" calendars. One was printed in 1925 and edited by J. Maydanyk. A year prior to that a re-print of the 1918 issue of "Shteef Tabachniuk Calendar", which at that time had been prepared by J. Maydanyk and S. Fodchuk, was published. Both authors used the humoristic pseudonym of "Shteef Tabachniuk" for their signature, while J. Maydanyk provided the caricature drawings for the comical looking figure "Shteef Tabachniuk".

The year 1930 brought the "Tochylo" (Grindstone) Ukrainian illustrated monthly, a journal of humor and satire whose editor was S. M. Doroshchuk. Having suffered a financial failure with his youth magazine the "Sunbeam", he began to publish the tabloid monthly "Grindstone", consisting of 12, 24 and even more pages, which lasted for thirteen years. The magazine was well illustrated and somewhat anti-clerical. From time to time English pages were included. M. Zaokipny, of Moose Jaw and E. Berezynsky and M. Horishny, of New York, contributed their material to it. In the beginning S. M. Doroshchuk was the sole owner of this publication which also put out a yearly calendar by the same name. Later Ivan Andrusiak became part owner of "Grindstone". During the Second World War he took over the full ownership of the publication and continued with it until 1947. There were 60 issues altogether published under his management—when it expired. In all the "Grindstone" existed for 18 years.

---

[8] Rev. N. Savaryn, The Ukrainian Catholic Press in Canada, see: "Memorial Book of the Settlement of Ukrainian People in Canada", Yorkton, 1941.

The Anglo-Ukrainian Press

Winnipeg was the first Ukrainian centre in Canada to publish a Ukrainian-English journal. In 1929 the first issue of "The New Canadian" came out, as previously mentioned, published by the National Press. The need of information in the English language about the life, struggles and achievements of other national societies that already had the papers in their own language, was felt very strongly at this time and so the National Press, which by now was publishing in four different languages, considered itself duty-bound to speak on behalf of all of them through the medium that was general to all Canada. Therefore, the president of the National Press was justified when in the introduction to the new magazine he stated:

"We trust that 'The New Canadian' will be the medium towards a better understanding of the ambitions of the near-million citizens."

"The New Canadian" also had this sub-title: "A reflection of the great Foreign-Language News Papers published in Canada" and endeavoured to mirror the life of Canadian community especially of such national groups as German, Hungarians, Slovaks, Poles—but most of all the Ukrainians. It had a series of articles about the history of Ukrainians in Europe and Canada. Of some interest to our readers may be the fact that the journal advocated the idea of the League of British Ukrainians about which a mention is made in another part of our history. T. Kelly Dickinson was the chief spokesman for "The Canadian" which consisted of 12 and 24 pages in newspaper format, 11 X 16½. During the second half of 1931 the journal, while still retaining its name, changed to a 32-page tabloid. V. Biberovych was its chief editor and among the better known co-workers were A. Zaharychuk, who wrote reviews from Ukrainian history, T. Kelly Dickinson, writing on economic subjects and H. I. Kurdydyk who wrote on political themes. Undoubtedly, the many issues of this reliable monthly publication threw much light on the problem of the so-called third element in Canada, particularly on the question of Ukrainian Canadian community. The advance of the economic crisis in Canada no doubt prevented any further publication of this journal.

Following the demise of "The New Canadian" there was not a periodical in the English language until 1936 when a new monthly magazine, the "Ukrainian Review", appeared with the sub-title "A Periodical devoted to Ukrainian Interests". As may be seen from its sub-title, the magazine was exclusively limited to the Ukrainian community in Canada. It was edited by Wasyl Scraba, a community leader who had developed his citizen's career starting with the school board and graduating to an alderman and finally reaching the Legislature of Manitoba as M.L.A. The "Ukrainian Review" drew together a group of noted citizens and was in existence for six full years. In a large tabloid 10½ X 14 format, consisting of from 8 to 32 pages, it dealt with various themes but gave special attention to the affairs connected with the Ukrainian community. Among those who made it possible for the journal to be in circulation were the following contributors: V. Biberovych, M. Mandryka, Halia Hawryluk, V. Paliuk, A. Zaharychuk, T. Hubicky, Maria Dyma, S. Derzhko, Olha Livak, John Slym, S. Rebchuk, W. Burianyk, Myra Lazechko and others. On the whole, the Ukrainian Review was a reliable and objective informer to all Canadian citizens about the achievements of the Ukrainians in their new country.

In 1942 the "Ukrainian Review" changed its name to "Canadian Ukrainian Review" and took on the more distinctive appearance of a representative cultural-artistic journal. Wasyl Scraba remained as its editor but Ivan Danylchuk, who was called from Saskatchewan, became the manager in charge of the publication. I. Danylchuk already was known in the literary world and was able to attract the cooperation of such talented journalists as Savella Stechishin, O. Ewach, S. N. Krawchyk, K. Ketchen, M. Zubrycky and others. The complete volume of the luxurious editions of the "Canadian Ukrainian Review" consists of ten issues of the same format with some containing as many as 64 pages. Subscription was very low, only one dollar per year. The sudden death of the editor-in-chief, I. Danylchuk, erased all further future hopes of this truly original and valuable representative publication.

After I. Danylchuk's death his co-workers formed a publishing company under the name of "The Canadian Ukrainian Review Company" and it continued with the journal's publication, which by now had become somewhat less glamorous in appearance—a triple column tabloid consisting, on an average, of 22 pages. Although the new journal, under the editorship of Volodymyr Levytsky, had a somewhat lesser pretension to fame than its predecessor, still it justified its appearance and among the better pages of this journal was the "Our Teachers' Page", regularly edited by Halia Hawryluk. Among the contributors are to be found such well known public figures as William Wall, later a senator in Ottawa, Dr. J. Yatchew and others. Unfortunately, due to financial difficulties the journal was discontinued.

Prior to the time when I. Danylchuk, with the aid of W. Scraba, began to publish the "Canadian Ukrainian Review" he had put out two issues of the "Ukrainian Tribune and Review" in Edmonton during May and October 1939.

Other Publications

Winnipeg was a prolific publishing centre and even had many publications that make it difficult to list them under any category. Some of them fail to provide us with the vital statistics of their origin, while others only are mentioned on the pages of contemporary press or their names by chance discovered in information registers. To such category belonged "Bukovina", the "educational, economic, religious and political paper" published by Rev. P. Bozyk. The first issue appeared on August 15, 1920 and the following editions of it came out on the first and fifteenth of every month, during the years 1920-1921, and was the official organ of the "Association of the Ukrainian Bukovinians in Canada and United States". As underlined on one of its pages, "Bukovina's" objective was to bring national-political consciousness to its contrymen on the North American continent and to give material aid to "the brethren in Bukovina". Although the paper was edited in the spirit of Orthodox belief it failed to receive any support from the Russian Orthodox Mission. Being a thoroughly Ukrainian periodical it supported the representative body of the Ukrainian National Republic of Western Ukraine (ZOUNR) and the liberation of Halychyna and Northern Bukovina. The publication office of "Bukovina" was located in the basement of the Ukrainian Orthodox Church of St. Michael on Disraeli Street, and in addition to Rev. P. Bozyk, had T. Sobal, I. Biletsky, I. Petrashchuk and I. Hnatysh on its executive board.

Rev. P. Bozyk edited another paper, at Point Douglas in Winnipeg, called "Church Life" which was an official organ of the Ukrainian Catholic Parish of St. Andrew. The paper had a very modest beginning. Rev. P. Bozyk wanted to have a paper to help him in the organization work of his parish. Originally planned as a quarterly, the "Church Life" drew to itself the attention of other Catholic parishes in the city and shortly after that it was changed into a monthly 8-page tabloid that was printed, starting with August 1938 to the end of 1940. The journal not only supplied valuable spiritual-religious material but also was a rich source of information about the cultural-educational life in Winnipeg during those years. Rev. P. Bozyk was both the editor and administrator of the publication that was located on his premises at 73 Disraeli Street.

Another religious paper the "Sunday" was published in Winnipeg by the Russo-Greek Orthodox Brotherhood of St. Yov of Pochayev, which identified itself as being "the church-national paper for the Ruthenians in Canada". The first issue of this 16-page tabloid appeared in April 1932. Both names—that of the paper as well as of its publishers reveal the fact that this was a strongly conservative paper, in the national political sense, which continued its existence for a year. Following on the heels of the expired "Sunday" another monthly tabloid "The Faith" made its short-lived appearance. Both of these small journals were edited by Rev. S. D. Verbovy.

Still another, but this time non-religious and only dealing with insurance benefits, the "Brotherhood Herald", was started in 1927 as a several-page tabloid and edited by the Ukrainian Catholic Brotherhood of St. John the Merciful.

Among the religious papers must be included the "Voice of Truth", a Protestant organ that was started in 1924 as a 4-page tabloid but only a few issues of it appeared. In 1929 the Association of Ukrainian and Russian Baptists of Western Canada put out its 8-page tabloid, the "Evangelical Herald" which was edited by the Pastor Ivan Kmeta. Only four issues of it were printed. And finally, in this same category, was the "Voice of Truth" printed in 1931 and "The Light and the Voice of Truth" published by the Dawn Bible Student Association in 1939, a tabloid in different numbers and sizes sent free to any one enclosing a two cent postage.

In the spring of 1932 a four page tabloid "The Monitor" was printed in Winnipeg, that gave information about the Ukrainian organizations in that city. It was edited by A. Zaharychuk and D. M. Elcheshen with only six issues appearing altogether.

Very similar, in form, to "Monitor" was the "Winnipeg News" printed in the fall of 1932 that proved to be a good information medium about the activities of Ukrainian organizations, not only for the city but the countryside as well. It carried a head-line in English saying, "Review of the activities of Ukrainian Organizations in Greater Winnipeg—Comments on Local Happenings and Public Affairs." The first issue of it appeared in October 1932 and several other editions were put out during that fall and winter season. It would appear that its editors were the same ones who published the earlier "Monitor".

"The Canadian News" printed in 1930 was not more than a pre-election bulletin. This bi-lingual 4-page tabloid was edited by The Assiniboia Publishing Company with the first two pages printed in Ukrainian and the last two in English. Only a few issues of it appeared although the publishers quoted the subscription at one dollar per year.

In the thirties "The Voice of Truth" an "educational-enlightenment" monthly journal was printed in the Nokomis Building without mentioning the names of editors or publishers. Several issues of this large size, 8-page tabloid made its appearance.

In 1932-1933 a four-page non-periodical tabloid, "The Herald of Health" was edited by Dr. I. P. Oshanek. Also two or three editions of the beautifully illustrated "Zaporozhets za Dunayem" (Kossack Beyond the Danube) was printed in English as an organ of the Ukrainian film studio of Vasyl Avramenko with the sub-title: "Herald of the V. Avramenko-Ukrainian Film Studio".

On the basis of information gained from different almanacs we can also mention such ephemeral publications in Winnipeg, during the mid-war period as: "Prosvita" (1929), "Farmers' Herald" (1932, "Thought" (1932), "Ukrainian Gazette" (1933), "Surma" (1934), "Native Church" (1936), "Reform" (1937), "Canadian Eparchical Herald" (1940), that made its appearance from time to time and "Our Life" (1941). Deserving a special attention is the organizational bulletin of the St. Vladimir and Olga Cathedral in Winnipeg titled "Church in Our Nation" which has been published regularly until our times.

WESTERN CANADA

The development of the Ukrainian press in Western Canada, during the second era, is to a large degree tied in with the name of Toma Tomashevsky, a well known individual from pioneer days when for a while he had edited the "New Community" paper in Edmonton and later on the weekly paper "Progress" in Mundare, and who in his life's career had been all three—printer, editor and publisher. After the liquidation of "Progress" and following his two year stay in Winnipeg, T. Tomashevsky made his appearance in Vancouver where he made plans to publish a party paper for the labouring class.

The first Ukrainian weekly paper in Vancouver was "The Truth and Freedom" which began its existence on May 22, 1920. Officially the paper was financed and published by a company of sharcholders, at ten dollars a share, but in reality the initiator and the editor of it was none other than T. Tomashevsky who already had professional experience from his former editorial days in Edmonton and Mundare. The Ukrainian press was brought in from Seattle and the paper was printed by the Broadway Printers where T. Tomashevsky was working as a linotype operator. The new periodical had a socialist political-party platform but at the same time was a bitter enemy of communism. "The Ukrainian Labour News" having claimed for itself the monopoly as the protector of the worker used every means at its command to fight "The Truth and Freedom" which by now had become an eight-page edition of 500 copies per issue. Only eighteen issues in all were put out. Vancouver was no place for his weekly paper venture, as T. Tomashevsky soon realized, and at the end of 1920 he returned to Edmonton, the place that brought to memory his former publishing days.

In Edmonton T. Tomashevsky began to organize the publishing of a new weekly paper resulting in the appearance in 1921 of several issues of the "Farmers' Voice". It was a somewhat hasty, rather amateurish, and temporary product of the editor-publisher which was followed sometime later, in November 1922, by the eight-page bi-monthly "Our Progress" with the announcement that in the following year it will be published every week. T. Tomashevsky kept his word and the paper came out as a four-page of six columns each, weekly journal devoted to the "educational, cultural and economic matters of the Ukrainian people in Alberta", published under the firm name of Canadian-Ukrainian Printing Co. and a $2.00 per year subscription or 3 cents each copy. "Our Progress" was printed on the same printing press as the "Canadian" which was owned by T. Tomashevsky and D. Solanych. To ensure for itself a steady flow of fresh support the paper started to organize the farmers of Alberta. T. Dackiw was for a while the editor of "Our Progress" but later the post was taken over by J. N. Krett who edited the paper, with a few breaks, for several years until 1929 when the publication went out of existence. All together about 200 issues of "Our Progress" appeared. The paper played a very important role in the life of the farmers and helped them to organize in June 1923 the Ukrainian Farmers' Convention in Edmonton during which a separate Ukrainian branch of the United Farmers of Alberta (U.F.A.) was formed. A strong opinion prevailed that "Our Progress", as the only weekly in Alberta, was greatly instrumental in the election of M. Luchkovich, the first Ukrainian parliamentarian in Ottawa. The paper's Christmas issue of December 29, 1926, in two colors, made the Ukrainian press history as being the first such edition of its kind in Canada.

In 1921 and 1922 T. Tomashevsky put out several issues of a humorous eight-page monthly tabloid, the "Whip", but when our busy editor-publisher in one person became totally immersed in "Our Progress" the "Whip" was silenced. But as soon as "Our Progress" expired T. Tomashevsky brought the "Whip" back, this time enlarged to 16 pages. A. Gregorovich not only wrote articles for this paper but also drew cartoons for it, and so did the already known to us, J. Maydanyk. Others also contributed their material, among them being—L. Snaychuk, Y. Syrotiuk, H. Shevchyshyn, A. I. Pavchuk, I. Letavsky and others. The "Whip" had a circulation of 1000 and was printed in I. Solanych's printing shop and at the Western News publishing place, comprising 18 issues altogether.

In 1932 and 1933 T. Tomashevsky and I. Solanych published a bi-monthly, the "Farmers Voice" devoted to farmers' interests. T. Tomashevsky was its editor and I. Solanych, who was the owner of The Alberta Printing, set the type and did the printing of this eight-page periodical, of newspaper format. After several scores of issues the paper went out of existence and its editor having bought a printing press in Andrew, Alberta, began to publish, in 1936, the English newspaper "Andrew News—District Press" that continued its publication for nearly ten years. It was an independent local weekly periodical of an average newspaper size whose subscription rate was $1.50 per year.

The name of the indomitable Toma Tomashevsky is connected with other publications of the mid-war era namely, the "Western News". This monthly journal was first published by S. Fodchuk in January 1928, when he started his real estate business, and it was edited by Y. N. Krett. The paper was devoted to cultural and economical affairs of Canada and was printed irregularly. S. Fodchuk's business enterprise failed and when he left Edmonton, at the end of 1928, T. Tomashevsky took over the paper's management—changing it to an eight-page weekly of large format and had it published by the Alberta Herald with which firm the new editor made arrangements for part ownership of the "Western News". At first the paper was edited by Michael Pohorecky, M. Koziak, I. Esaiw and V. J. Kaye and later by M. Pohorecky again, and M. Stus, and from 1930, by Wasyl Dyky. In 1929 the Ukrainian Catholics bought the publication from T. Tomashevsky and on December 13, 1929, the first issue of the new press organ of the Catholic Eparchy made its appearance which later, in 1931, was renamed as "Ukrainian News" with a sub-title saying that this was: "The only Ukrainian Catholic weekly in Canada". It was printed regularly every Wednesday consisting of eight pages in large format with the subscription rate of two dollars and published by the "Ukrainian News Publishers".

Following the transfer of the "Canadian Ukrainian" to the National Press concern, the "Western News" and later the "Ukrainian News" truly became the only Ukrainian Catholic press organ in Canada. This condition lasted until 1948. The publication in Edmonton of the only Catholic paper in Canada gave that city a measure of prestige all the more so since it attracted the cooperation of the better known talents in the Catholic world. The purchase and further upkeep of this publication over a period of years was the work and care of the new Bishop Wasyl Ladyka [10].

Edmonton gave the origin to another Ukrainian weekly that played an important role in the formation of the Ukrainian society in Canada. This was the "New Pathway" that primarily had been developed by the leading figures of the second immigration. The first issue of this periodical appeared in October 1930.

The "New Pathway" made its appearance at the same time as its ideological counterpart, the "War Veterans' News" came into existence and both of these papers propagated the same ideas and politics in the sphere of Ukrainian affairs in Europe. In the internal Canadian politics they also oriented themselves to the traditional conservative parties. "The New Pathway" was one step ahead of the "War Veterans' News" in that it was a general national paper whereas the latter was more restricted in its stand and therefore had a narrower circle of readers. This was a main reason for the gradual expansion of the "New Pathway" which, in a short while became the forum for the war veterans in general. The first pioneers connected with the "New Pathway" were M. Pohorecky, who was its editor, I. Solanych, owner of Alberta Printing, P. Kuzyk and W. Hryvnak. In the beginning, the "New Pathway" consisted of four pages in large 15 X 22 format with the subscription rate of $2.00 a year. In

---

[10] Memorial Book of National Home in Edmonton, 1906-1965, page 98.

1931 the original company reorganized itself to form "The New Pathway Publishing Co." and shortly after the journal became the official organ of the Ukrainian National Federation of Canada. At all times M. Pohorecky was the soul of the "New Pathway" and the moving spirit of this new press establishment. The board of directors included A. H. Hlynka, W. Hawrysh, and S. Waskan. Roman Kremar, an editor from the pioneer days; A. Hlynka and A. Gregorovich were on the editorial board, with the last named holding the office of general manager, which position later was taken over by W. Ruryk. The publishers had to struggle with great financial difficulties as the serious economic crisis still was in full sway. In 1933 the publication was moved to Saskatoon where the ownership of a building was acquired along with a printing press. In rapid time the newspaper became a spokeman, not only for the Ukrainian National Federation and the Ukrainian War Veterans Association, but also for the Ukrainian Women's Organization and the Ukrainian National Youth Federation. These four organizations provided a close support for the weekly periodical which became an accepted organ of the Ukrainian political guidepost with the following motto: "Our strength is in ourselves". The paper, as well as the organizations, were fully in agreement with the ideas proclaimed by the Ukrainian revolutionary nationalism in Europe that was under the spiritual helm of the "Organization of Ukrainian Nationalists" (OUN) and headed by Col. Evhen Konovalets. In Saskatoon the "New Pathway" was supported by such well known Ukrainians as Prof. T. Pavlychenko and W. Kossar and earlier by W. Hultay, and others. In the course of time the periodical increased the size of its format and the number of pages while the organizations that were supporting it received their individual branch allocations. The periodical introduced as a novelty an illustrated page and provided for its readers a great variety of interests in printing articles by various correspondents from different countries and continents, gaining thereby for itself a wide popularity. As the core of the Ukrainian life always had been in Winnipeg, the board of directors decided in 1941 to transfer its publishing enterprise to that city. With its 91st issue in November of 1941 the "New Pathway" began its publication in the Ukrainian capital of Canada.

Other Alberta Publications

Edmonton also had its sporadic publications of lesser meaning to community, but which still reflected its moods and interests.

In February 1930 the "Renaissance", an official organ of "The Ukrainian Temperance Society" made its appearance. Edited by W. Hryvnak it only lasted through several issues.

During the years 1935-1937 Anthony Hlynka published a political-economic monthly journal "Klych" (The Call) and in January 1937 he edited a non-periodical of the Social Credit Party "The Social Credit". Both of these organs were of the party-politics type intended to bring more sympathizers to the Social Credit Party but it is difficult to give the exact dates of their appearance and circulation scope.

The Seventh Day Adventist sect printed in 1930, in College Height, Alberta, a twenty-page bi-monthly publication called "On Guard of Truth—The Star of Truth", published by The Western Canadian Union

Conference and edited by M. H. Filbrick and Rossequier, that only lasted for a very short time.

Mundare, the close neighbor of Edmonton, published its periodical "The Light" in the mid-war period, that was prepared by the Basilian Fathers. The first issue of this bi-monthly, consisting of four pages, came out in June of 1937. Later it increased to eight pages and in this form was edited for many years. The first editor of "The Light" was Rev. M. Romanovych and later Rev. A. Truch and still later Rev. I. Nazarko. When the journal was transferred to Toronto, in 1949, it was changed to a monthly periodical and increased to 32 pages. "The Light" diligently applied itself toward the crystallization of beliefs, defended and propagated Catholic world outlook and stressed the need of Catholic organizations.

Prior to the Second World War a small 22-page, book-size, journal, the "Voice of Truth" was printed on a mimeograph by M. N. Cependa with the first issue appearing in 1937. Even Smoky Lake came into the publishing limelight with the appearance of a several-page issue of the Orthodox "Informer".

SASKATCHEWAN

The oldest publication in Saskatchewan, and the one with which we have been acquainted in the pioneer era, was the "Kameniari" (Stonebreakers).

The second press organ in that province that already had a history back of it and a wide circle of readers, was the "New Pathway" which spent eight years of its existence in Saskatoon before moving to Winnipeg.

The "Christian Herald", organ of the Russo-Ukrainian Evangelical Baptists of Western Canada, edited by Ivan Shakotko and managed by P. Kundy of Winnipeg, was also published for a while in Saskatoon. Its first issue appeared in 1923 but the publication was discontinued shortly after that. It was renewed in Winnipeg in 1929 by I. Kmeta-Ichniansky under the title: "Evangelical Herald".

Roman Kremar made an effort to publish his "Canadian News" with the first issue dated October 14, 1932. With the transfer of "New Pathway" to Saskatoon there was not any room left for two weekly papers and a few issues later the "Canadian News" ceased to exist.

Yorkton

With the passage of time Yorkton became the publishing centre of Saskatchewan, where the Redemptorist Fathers established their printing press and began their publication work. The first periodical entitled the "Voice of the Saviour" came out in May 1923, at first consisting of 15 and later raised to 24 and 32 pages, and continuing in this form until 1928 when it was discontinued for a period of five years. In November 1933 the publication was renewed under the new name of "Redeemer's Voice", and has been published regularly ever since. Voice of the Saviour was edited by the two brother monks, Joseph Bala, 1923-1926 and John Bala, 1926-1928, with the latter renewing the publication in 1933 under its present name of the "Redeemer's Voice". Following him, Fathers Mykola Kopiakiwsky and Stepan Bachtalowsky held the editorial positions and after them Rev. John Bala came back to his old post.

From the printing workshop of the Redemptorist Fathers in Yorkton there also came into existence the "Eparchial Herald" for the whole diocese in Canada, whose first issue saw the light of day in 1924, and with this city also was connected the "Bulletin of the Ukrainian Catholic Brotherhood" and the semi-monthly "Future of the Nation".

The "Bulletin of the Ukrainian Catholic Brotherhood" began its existence on the heels of the formation of this organization and the first issue carries the date of January 1933. At its beginning the Bulletin was a 24-page monthly edition printed on a mimeograph in Alvena, but in September of the same year it was printed by the press of the Redemptorist Fathers in Yorkton, with Rev. John Bala as editor and Rev. S. Semczuk as the assistant. A short while after Rev. S. Semczuk took over the editorship of the Bulletin and was the heart and soul of this publication until 1943. Of a tabloid format, the publication had artistic covers and was wholly dedicated to the organizational interests of the "Ukrainian Catholic Brotherhood" and its component formations, namely the "Ukrainian Catholic Youth" and the "Ukrainian Catholic Women", the latter taking on the more popular name of "League of Ukrainian Catholic Women". The Bulletin had specially allocated pages devoted to organization, ideology, history and literature and carried on a wide correspondence with other branches of the "Ukrainian Catholic Brotherhood". With the expansion work of the above organization the framework of the Bulletin became too narrow in scope and in 1937 it was replaced by an 8-page, of small format semi-monthly journal, the "Future of the Nation" and published by the editorial board with most of its printed material coming from the pen of Rev. W. Kushnir and from Rev. S. Semczuk, its editor. The children's page was edited by Ivan Nowosad. With his transfer from Saskatchewan to Winnipeg, Rev. Semczuk also brought over the editorial function of the paper with him, but the administration office under the direction of Dmytro Kobrynsky remained in Saskatchewan. In 1943 the administration also was transferred to Winnipeg, bringing the complete publication to one central location although the printing of it was done in Yorkton up to the end.

Canora

Canora too had its publications. In October 1931, an 8-page "illustrated self-enlightenment and educational journal", "The New Era Magazine" came into existence. It was a book-size format, filled with social news and business advertisements, but hardly any educational or self-enlightenment material was to be found. It was printed from 1931 to 1936 and edited by P. Levchuk.

In June 1937 I. D. Stratychuk began the publication of his economic-cooperative paper, the "Ukrainian Co-operator," that was printed once a month. It was financed by the Saskatchewan Wheat Pool.

EASTERN CANADA

Toronto

Toward the end of the pioneer era, and as if to herald the dawn of the post-war times in Canada, a semi-monthly journal "The Trans-Oceanic

Herald" came into being with its first issue dated January 1920. It was a 32-page tabloid, dedicated to the different branches of knowledge—astronomy, geology, geography, hygiene, history of social problems and even such dry and drab subjects as arithmetic, algebra, geometry and mechanics. In other words, the journal was planned to provide, in accessible form, the means of gaining knowledge for "those who had no opportunity of receiving school education and now are making an effort at self-enlightenment".

The initiator of this publication was Paul Krat and the owner was M. Yaremiychuk; I. Stefanicky, N. Kolisnyk and W. Pyndykovsky were on the editorial board. In the first year 17 issues appeared with 368 pages in all. In addition to educational articles and lessons there also were excerpts from finer literature, but mostly articles and reviews written by Dr. Z. Kuzela, Dr. I. Rakovsky, Dr. I. Kurovec, G. H. Laurendeau, F. Shindler and others. "The Trans-Oceanic Herald" lasted less than two years.

Paul Krat brought another publication into existence in Eastern Canada when in June of 1923 he began to edit, in Toronto, the "newspaper of Evangelical Christianity" under the title of "Faith and Knowledge". This was a monthly journal of book format consisting of 18 pages and financed by the Canadian Women's Protestant Federation. The paper was published for five years but nothing much of interest can be said about it. It was religious through and through.

June of 1924 saw the appearance, in Toronto, of the weekly periodical the "Probee" but only eight issues of it were printed. This was the organ of the "Federation of the Ukrainians of Eastern Canada" that was prepared by Rev. A. Sarmatiuk and W. Bossy, especially the latter who had just arrived from Europe. The paper was the first publication in Canada supporting the Hetman movement as well as being the first periodical to appear in Eastern Canada. The editorial office of the "Probee" was located at 135½ King Street. In these same premises also were the offices of the "Central Committee of the Federation of Ukrainians of Eastern Canada" and of the "Sitch War Veterans Organization" as well as the bureau of the representative of the Ukrainian Free Secret University of Lviv. However, the national ramification of the Ukrainian life in Eastern Canada was not developed strong enough to support a weekly neswpaper and so the "Probee" was discontinued.

To provide at least a small information medium about the Ukrainian organization in Eastern Canada, Rev. A. Sarmatiuk began to print his four-page semi-monthly tabloid "The Eastern News". The first issue came out in May 1927 published by the parish of St. Josaphat at 143 Franklin Street. It was more in the nature of a chronicle of the community life in Eastern Canada and only nine issues were printed.

Several issues of the so-called "independent gazette of enlightenment in Canada" named "New Paper" appeared in Toronto in 1934.

A much longer existence was recorded by the "Ukrainian Bazaar", the "literary journal of the Trans-Oceanic Ukraine", that was printed in Ukrainian and English. The Ukrainian section was formulated by M. Petrowsky, who also was the editor of the paper, and the English section was prepared by John Rae Parigo. The first three issues were printed bi-lingually, the next three in Ukrainian—six issues in all. It was printed on a mimeograph with the exception of the first number and had some variations in its format. Its content consisted of stories, novels, sketches and other material. The very name of the paper "Ukrainian Bazaar" suggested that it was "the journal of the Ukrainian fiction stories". The periodical was printed by the "Ukrainian Publishing House" at 331 Bay Street, Toronto.

The only Ukrainian national weekly in Eastern Canada that managed to stay in existence for many years even after the Second World War, was the "Ukrainian Toiler" and which was continuing the work started by "Zveno" that had been edited by I. N. Korchynsky in 1934. On the initiative of I. N. Korchynsky, M. Hetman, O. Luhovy and others the "Ukrainian Publishing Co." was organized, which had set for its objective the publication of the above-mentioned political organ, whose mottos were: "God and the Fatherland" and "Work and Order". "Ukrainian Toiler" became the official organ of the Hetman movement that showed increased activities in Canada in the mid-war period. The movement received great impetus from the visit of the Hetmanych, Danylo Skoropadsky, in 1937. The Ukrainian Canadians welcomed him as a symbol of Ukrainian statehood in Europe and as the standard-bearer of the Hetman idea. Even the republicans who, in principle, opposed the traditional Hetman form of government, reacted sympathetically towards his visit.

For many years Mykhaylo Hetman, a leading figure in the Hetman movement, was the editor of the "Ukrainian Toiler". The paper was published regularly, in 15 X 22 format, consisting of eight pages, until 1953.

In September, 1938 the weekly periodical "The Forward" reached its 100th issue and folded up. It had been printed by "The Forward Publishing Co.", and was continuing the political and ideological work of the Winnipeg paper "The Truth". It reflected the beliefs of those Ukrainians who broke their connection with the "Ukrainian Labour and Farmers' Temple Association" and had the same format as the "Truth" and was edited by Danylo Lobay and Ivan Lilicak. Politically, this paper not only was anti-Stalinist, but it also was anti-Soviet and continuously propagated socialism of a non-Marxist type.

Similar ideas also were propagated by the weekly four-page tabloid "The Bell" that first appeared in November 1941 under the editorship of Ivan Lilicak. The periodical lasted less than a year and although a private enterprise, still it was closely allied with "The Forward" and "The Truth". Together they formed an unbroken chain that made the dividing line between the group that finally was formulated into the "Ukrainian Workers' League", becoming a co-equal creator of the organized Ukrainian national force in Canada—on the one side, and the "Ukrainian Labour and Farmers' Temple Association" that oriented itself toward the Soviet Union, on the other side.

Among the press organs of the second era must be included the "Evangelical Truth", a contemporary religious journal of small format that started as a four-page tabloid and later enlarged to eight pages, and which was edited by M. Fesenko in 1940.

Toronto also had an English newspaper that was started by Ivan Korchynsky in 1937 entitled "The New Canadians". M. Petrowsky was the editor and J. Grudeff, a Macedonian, who later became the judge of the "Family Court" in Toronto, worked on the paper along with the other two. The journal was a weekly edition consisting of four pages in large newspaper format but only lasted for a short while in this form, changing to a monthly periodical and shortened in name to "The New Canadian". The outer change brought a variation in personel with J. Grudeff in charge and I. Korchynsky as the new editor. H. G. Wilson and V. E. Burda supplied the financial means—the latter becoming the general manager. The publication lasted for a period of four years and since it was comprised of different nationalities it thus became a central medium of information about the so-called "New Canadians" not only in the city of Toronto but also the whole of Canada as well. Among its promoters we find such well known names as Prof. W. Kirkconnell, the lawyer J. Yatchew, Florence Randall Livesay, Robert Thompson, Myra Lazechko, Honore Ewach and others.

Ottawa, Montreal and Oshawa

The eastern cities of Canada also had their publications. In 1922 a bilingual political-economic and immigration weekly periodical, "The Friend of Ukraine", made its appearance in Ottawa. It consisted of 8 pages in 12 X 18 newspaper format with pages 1, 4, 5 and 8 in Ukrainian and 2, 3, 6 and 7 in English. The paper was edited by Ivan Bodrug and only nine or ten issues of it appeared.

In one of its appeals to the readers "The Friend of Ukraine" had this to say about itself: "The newspaper has an opportunity to provide a colossal service toward the Ukrainian affairs not only through the use of the printed English word, but also by the fact that the members of its editorial board have a splendid chance to aid Ukranian cause by means of spoken word at political clubs, banquets and public gatherings here in Ottawa, as well as in other cities of Western Canada" [10]. It will be seen from this statement that "The Friend of Ukraine" had a specific objective in its relationship to the Ukrainian cause in Europe, which clearly is shown by the articles and notices, especially the information regarding the loan of the Ukrainian National Republic of Western Ukraine (ZOUNR) and the work of its representatives. The weekly paper was financed by the publishing company of "The Friend of Ukraine" and its editorial and administration offices were in The National Bank Building. The publication cooperated very closely with the Central Committee of the Ukrainians of Eastern Canada, composed of M. Ruzhytsky, M. Yurechkiv, T. Humeniuk, P. Krat and A. Sarmatiuk.

In 1939 a group of sport minded enthusiasts in Montreal endeavoured to publish a fortnightly organ dealing with physical culture and "Sitch" movement among the Ukrainians in Canada and U.S.A. The publication was called "Sitch" ("Siege" also "Seech") and the first edition appeared in March, in newspaper format, but changed later to an eight page tabloid and instead of being printed on the 1st and 15th of each month as was announced in its first issue, it was published irregularly. The edition of "Sitch" was prepared by W. Bossy in Montreal while the printing of it was done in Toronto. The editors of "Sitch" tied, ideologically, the

---

[10] "The Friend of Ukraine", Montreal, 1914.

Canadian "Sitch" to the historical "Sitch" in Ukraine—the "Zaporozhian Sitch", to the "radical" (Sitch of Dr. K. Trylowsky), the "striletska" (Sitch of 1914) and the "Hetmanska" (in Canada and U.S.A. after the First World War). With the outbreak of the Second World War the publication of "Sitch" came to an end.

A much earlier publication was the 18-page tabloid "Our Word" that was published in Oshawa in 1939 by the "Taras Shevchenko Prosvita Association" in connection with the Ukrainian Presbyterian Church of that city and edited by the pastor, Luka Standret. This periodical not only was devoted to cultural-educational needs but also to the interests of the church matters, particularly those of the Presbyterian Church. It was published regularly during 1934 but in the middle of 1935 went out of existence. The monthly magazine provided interesting reading material as it contained numerous chronicles of the Oshawa community life during the period of the journal's existence.

MOSCOPHILE PRESS

In the era between the two World Wars there were several publications of the Mosco-phile or the Russo-phile press. Among them was the "Will of the People" (1921) about which a mention has been made in the first pioneer era. It introduced itself as "the organ of the Association for the Liberation of the Carpatho-Ukraine in Canada" and died the same year it was born.

"The Canadian Life", a semi-monthly publication that stood close to the Russian Orthodox Church and in its time was the official organ of that church, had a somewhat longer existence. We might have ignored it except for the fact that it was printed in Ukrainian language and was aided in its publication partly by the material support of the Ukrainian settlers. It was initiated by the Abbot Benjamin Basalyga in 1921 and published by the "Russian Orthodox Enlightenment Association". On the letter-head of this publishing firm could be seen such Ukrainian names as M. Mandziuk, H. Dutchak, M. Karpenko, I. Bilecky (its later editor) and Deacon W. Kachurovsky. Among the co-editors of this semi-monthly were P. Bozyk (Ukrainian language) and C. D. Verbovy (Russian language). The paper was printed by the "Canadian Ukrainian" press and was of the larger tabloid format consisting of four pages. Toward the end of the 20-ies its life also came to an end.

Edmonton also had its Russo-phile publication, the "People's Friend". It was bilingual (in Ukrainian and Russian languages) monthly journal of the large gazette format. P. N. Samilo, already known to us from his former connection with the Russo-phile press, was both its editor and publisher for four years, starting in 1926. "People's Friend" was a factional paper and combatted Abbot Arseny and Bishop Platon, whom it accused of being Ukraino-philes.

Regina

The humorous little journal, the "Sprinkle", appeared in Regina in 1934. It advertised itself as being a "Russian Illustrated Monthly Journal of Humor and Satire".

A year later another small journal, the "Russia", boastfully announced itself as: "The only Russian instructive Political Journal published monthly by the Russia Publishing Co." Both of these tabloid papers were mimeographed copies, printed in Ukrainian language but basically anti-Ukrainian in content and constantly propagated Russophile ideas. Most likely the editors themselves did not believe in what they preached for neither they nor the publishers signed their names.

When we compare the Russophile press of this era with the one that existed in the pioneer days it will be seen that it now represented only a minor portion of its previous strength in Canada. The great decline in the Russophile trend may be attributed to two basic reasons: the great national consciousness of the Ukrainian people in general, which enabled them to differentiate between their own national interests and those of the alien element on the one side, and on the other, lack of material resources on the part of the Russophile forces. As the result of these depressive conditions the Russophile ideology was unable to muster enough strength for the publishing of a single weekly paper while the semi-monthly "Canadian Field" that had been able to survive the longest, now was obliged to retreat from the political Russophile field and devote its pages to the question of the Russian Orthodox Church in Canada,—to which Church belonged a large number of Ukrainian adherents prior to the Second World War.

THE COMMUNIST PRESS

In reality there was no press under this name but we must qualify it not by its outer form but by its content. More often this press identified itself as being labour or farmers' and most often, since 1935, as people's.

The origin of the communist press starts with the "Ukrainian Labour News" that began its publication at the turning point of the first and second era in 1919. The organizers for this periodical were Danylo Lobay, Ivan Navizivsky, Ivan Zelez and others. The paper started as a weekly in 1919 and in 1920 it changed over to a semi-weekly. At this time Matviy Shatulsky (M. Volynets) joined the editorial staff and a while later M. Popowych also came on the staff. On the paper's fifth anniversary the editors decided to publish it three times a week. In addition to recording Canadian and world events, the periodical contained a great amount of material from Soviet Ukraine. Among them were literary works of such known writers as V. Sosiura, V. Blakytny (Valerian Pronoza), O. Vyshnia, V. Chumak and Ivan Kulyk. The last one named held the post of a Soviet consul in Canada and cooperated very closely with "Ukrainian Labour News" (U.L.N.). Very often the paper published the works of Myroslav Irchan who came to Canada from Czechoslovakia. "U.L.N." expanded from year to year and in 1924 a publishing company was formed under the name of "The Labour-Farmer's Publishing Co." which not only took over the printing of "U.L.N." but it also started to publish a semi-monthly women's journal "Robitnytsia" (Working Woman) and later on two more weekly papers "Farmers' Life" and "Youth's World". In 1929 the circulation of the "Ukrainian Labour News" reached 10,000, "Farmers' Life"—6,000, "Working Woman"—6,800 and "Youth's

World" — 3,700[11]). On the occasion of the 15th anniversary of "U.L.N." the editors organized a wide campaign to gain material support and due to its success the paper changed to a daily, starting from the first of January 1935. When the split came to the "Ukrainian Labour and Farmers' Temple Association" (U.L.F.T.A.) the 16th party convention of this organization in 1937 decided to change the name of the paper. The highly verbose decision of this convention gave the following reasons for changing the name:

"In order to move successfully popularize and bring to the wider masses the daily paper it becomes advisable to the organizers to change the name of the "Ukrainian Labour News" to such other name as not to show any sectarianism but that it would appeal generally to all the Ukrainian people in Canada. It is advisable to name it "Narodna Gazeta" (People's Gazette) [12]. September 1937 saw the first issue of this periodical with the new name which continued its publication until July 1940 when it was banned by the government order in the early stage of the Second World War, during the time of USSR'S close cooperation with Hitler's Germany.

The "Ukrainian Labour News" later "People's Gazette" was printed daily for five and a half years. To publish a press organ of this magnitude was not easy, especially when the organizational form of the "Ukrainian Labour and Farmers' Temple Association" began to show some cracks and its leaders were struggling desperately to keep alive. The publishers tried to remain solvent with the aid of the aforementioned Labour Temple centre by organizing press committees in all the branches of this organization and these conducted special campaigns to collect funds and news subscriptions. The committees brought thousands of dollars into the coffers of the publishing establishment. It truly was an exhibition of generosity and united effort.

I. Navizivsky was at this time not only the publishing manager, but he was also the top-most party chief of the whole system of the "Ukrainian Labour and Farmers' Temple Association".

On the editorial board, in addition to those already mentioned, were I. Stefanicky, M. Mykhayliuk, P. Kravchuk, M. Hrynchyshyn, M. Yukas, Maria Kostaniuk and S. Zeniuk.

When the government banned "People's Gazette" in 1940, another paper with the same name but different in content came into existence. It was edited by M. Mandryka, A. Zaharychuk, O. Hykawy, editor of Canadian Farmer, T. Dackiw—all of Winnipeg and W. Bossy of Montreal, who became the chief editor of the new periodical. The paper was anti-Communist and was sent to all the subscribers of the former publication. It continued its existence for nearly a year.

Three years after the appearance of the "Ukrainian Labour News" another paper, "The Voice of Labour" dedicated "to the labouring people" came into existence in 1922 in Winnipeg, published by the "Prolet-cult Publishing Association". Edited by M. Popowych, this 32-page tabloid contained articles about labour movement, popular reviews from different branches of education and science, stories from the life of the working

---

11) M. Volynets: "Fifteen Years of Ukrainian Labour and Farmers' Temple Association" (U.L.F.T.A.), Winnipeg, 1933.
12) P. Kravchuk: "Fifty Years in Serving People", Toronto, 1957, page 127.

people, verses and reviews of world events. In the two annuals of this journal, the last of which appeared in 1924, are preserved the works of some of the writers who later were placed on the USSR Prohibitory Index, such as: Ivan Kulyk, Hryhoriy Epik, Wasyl Blakytny, Ostap Vyshnia and others. It also printed works by Myroslav Irchan who was condemned to death and shot in USSR, in the thirties.

In 1921, when the women's branches of the "Ukrainian Labour and Farmers' Temple Association" (U.L.F.T.A.) began to grow in numbers the need arose of having their own press organ and so the "Working Woman's Voice", a 24-page tabloid, came into being in January 1923. In addition to articles dealing with the general women's themes, the journal printed different material about the work of women in the U.L.F.T.A. organization, informed about women's activities in USSR and reprinted writings from the Ukrainian classics. On its pages were to be found names of the leading figures in the women's "labour-farmers" movement such as: Olena Skehar, Anna Babiy, Maria Kucherian, Maria Vynohradova, Maria Navizivska, Olena Shmon, Kateryna Ambrosiak and Anna Moysiuk.

In place of "The Voice of Labour" and the "Working Woman's Voice" a new paper, the "Working Woman" appeared in 1924. M. Irchan (Andriy Babiuk) became the editor of this newly formed journal, which post was held by him until he left for Ukraine in 1929. After him came the following editors: M. Lenartovich, (1929-1933), Petro Prokopchak (1933-1936), P. Chaykivsky and P. Lysets. In 1937 the journal went out of existence and a separate page was reserved in the daily "People's Gazette" to serve the women's interests. It may be of some interest to note that during its fifteen years of existence the "Working Woman" did not have a single woman editor. It also was the first women's journal printed in Ukrainian language in Canada.

When in 1924 the "Ukrainian Young Labour League" (SURM) was formed in connection with the U.L.F.T.A. organized system it was decided that instead of having a separate section for the newly formed youth organization, to start a new publication, which was began in April 1927 as a 24-page tabloid journal called the "Youth's World". M. Irchan was the editor during its first two years of existence and after he left, M. Lenartowich took his place. The journal was a training base for a line of leaders who later filled the ranks in this communist centre among them being the following individuals: M. Hrychyshyn, M. Kardash, A. Larchuk, A. Bilecki, M. Korol, I. Boyd, M. Mokriy, A. Melenko, M. Seychuk and others.

In 1930 the "Youth's World" was replaced by the "Militant Youth" which was edited by M. Lenartovich and later by Ivan Boychuk (Ivan Boyd). "Militant Youth's" struggle for existence only lasted two years. It had to be liquidated to save the life of some other journal in the leftist movement.

All the ideological and political work of the "Ukrainian Labour and Farmer's Temple Association" and its sister-organizations was based on the teaching of the class-struggle theory. If you have "the labour news" then you also must have "the farmers' news". For this reason the above mentioned centre, U.L.F.T.A., began to publish, in 1925, "The Farmers' Life", consisting of four and later six and eight pages in large format. At the beginning the paper did not propagate any political ideas along the line of its ideological parent body but merely announced, in its first editorial, that its prime objective was "to spread, among the Ukrainian farmers, enlightenment and culture and to help farmers to organize beneficial clubs and social groups" [13]). When the paper had expanded its work it then began to funnel all of its information material through the propaganda mill of the U.L.F.T.A. centre and was constantly engaged in battles with the Ukrainian papers of national trend such as "Canadian Ukrainian", "Ukrainian Voice" and others, that took the opposite and anti-communist stand. "The Farmers' Life" managed to keep itself alive for fifteeen years until it was suppressed by the government in September 1940, along with the daily "People's Gazette". "The Farmers' Life" at first was edited by D. Prystash and from 1929 to 1940 by M. Saviak and Stepan Pura.

When "The Farmers' Life" and "People's Gazette" were suppressed the U.L.F.T.A. centre was able to find and revive the barely known little paper, the "Voice of Truth" that, irregularly, was published in Smoky Lake. M. Hıynchyshyn became its editor and succeeded in increasing the circulation and printing it every week. "The Voice of Truth" continued its existence until August 1941 when a new weekly, the "Ukrainian Life" was started in Toronto to serve the communist' interests. This paper and the one similar to it, in Winnipeg, the "Ukrainian Word", continued their existence into the third era of our history.

An eight-page semi-monthly tabloid, "The Labour News", began its existence in Toronto in November, 1933. Anti- Stalinist in content, it supported the Trotskyite communist group. Leon Trotsky himself had sent his congratulations to this paper which printed some of his speeches, especially those parts that referred to Ukraine and the Ukrainian question in USSR. It is hard to ascertain who was the chief editor of the "Labour News" but the names most often appearing on the signed editorial articles were those of H. Gurov and W. Bosowych, the latter along with M. Oleniuk being the publishers. At the end of its fourth year of existence the paper became self-liquidated.

A few issues of the "Bulletin" of the "Association for the aid of the Liberation Movement (evidently communist) in Western Ukraine" (TODOWYRNAZU—short in Ukrainian) were printed in Montreal, starting in January 1933. This mimeographed, eight-page tabloid fought a hard battle with the national organizations, such as the "Committee of Political Prisoners", "Ukrainian War Veterans Association" and others that were collecting funds for Ukraine's liberation from soviet domination.

"The Voice of the Carpathians"—"a monthly gazette devoted to the interests of the labourers that came from Lemkivshchyna, Boykivshychna and Huculshchyna"—originated in Toronto in 1932. At the same time it also was the official organ of the "Labour Enlightenment Carpathian Association" from which it got its name. The editorial committee was composed of all those who had broken away from the "Ukrainian Labour and Farmers' Temple Association" centre in Toronto. The mottos of this periodical were: "Workers of the world, unite" and "Class above nation".

Among the publications that reflected international thinking was the cultural-educational illustrated monthly periodical, "New World", which

---

[13] "Farmers' Life", May 1, 1925.

was printed in Montreal and edited by Iwan Hnyda. This little journal came out irregularly during 1928-1930 and was officially published by "The New World Library and Printing Co."

Several mimeographed issues of the "Canadian Proletarian" and the "Proletarian News" appeared on the scene and all of them strongly reviled the leading figures in the Ukrainian Labour and Farmers' Temple Association organization.

To present a complete mosaic picture of the Ukrainian press it would be advisable to mention some publications that went out of existence after their first few issues. Among them could be listed: "Truth of the People" (1929), "The Widest Road to Complete Life" (1934), "Progress" (1936), "Our Age" (1936) published by the Bible Students in Toronto, "New Life" (1940), "Canadian Orthodox Missionary" (1929), "Dawn of the New Era" (1936), "Bell" (1940).

To this group may be added publications that appeared during election campaigns such as Ukrainian Labourer in Winnipeg (1930), and Canadian News, printed bilingually (1930). There were others that belonged rather to the pamphlet printed material than to the press section. According to our summary there were over 110 names of newspapers and journals that were being published during the mid-war period. All of them, taken together, bear witness to the tremendous life forces of the Ukrainian entity that sought many diverse paths to express its social interests. The network of this press is multifarious but its backbone has always been national in scope, including the religious sphere, and basically built on the traditions of the Ukrainian culture. They all have worked together to preserve this Ukrainian culture in Canada. The Anglo-Ukrainian press also has played its useful role in interpreting this culture to all other fellow Canadians. The second important task of the Ukrainian press is the interpretation and integration of the social, political and economic life of Canada. These two positive trends constantly reveal themselves in the rich composition of the press mosaic. In other words they continued to uphold the tradition that already was established by the dedicated press disciples of the pioneer era.

When the question comes on to the material side of the press, it then will be seen that they managed to exist by the support through subscriptions and by the dedication of its editors. The work of editor devoted to the life of the Ukrainian Canadian newspaper always had been considered as a mark of honour and patriotism. This high distinction was bestowed upon the editors who steadfastly served the various needs of their community. Among those who have set an example of editorial idealism are such well known wielders of the pen in our era as O. H. Hykawy and M. Stechishin, both of them veterans in this field of work, and among the younger set were: D. Lobay, M. Pohorecky, T. Dackiw, M. Hetman, I. Dyky, Rev. S. Semczuk, and others.

LITERATURE

Between the two World Wars a number of talented writers came into being who, though they followed in the footsteps of the pioneers, began to implant themselves deeper and deeper in the Canadian soil. When during the first period of literary creations the writers and poets were far removed from the threshold of the Muse, the second period produced talented writers who attained the heights of poetry and prose and created a bridge for the settlers to acclimatize themselves into the new surroundings. The writers gradually moved to the second step of interest. The pioneer era was fading out and, even as some settlers were coming in, they found themselves not among strangers, but in their own community. Thus a new community was being developed among material attributes of the new land and with new spiritual and cultural forms derived from the culture of their parents and grandparents. And these were only the general trends of influence on the settlers and their progeny. It is understood that to these two general factors there were additional aspects and influences. Cultural trends of other nationalities, especially the English and the French, greatly contributed to the development of cultural values within the Ukrainian community. The school and general education also played an important part and gradually became the third factor, which in many instances on many occasions decided the formation of further progressive tendencies in Canadian integration, in general. Those three factors have left their imprint on the development of new literary talents which the Ukrainian Canadians produced in the period between the two wars.

On the basis of these factors we can also divide those individuals, who to a great extent influenced the formation of a Ukrainian-Canadian. To the first group belong those who came here in their early youth and grew up under the dominating cultural influence of their parents and the immediate surroundings; in the second group are those who were educated in a wider sphere, by means of formal schooling or by self-education; in the third group are those who came in the period between the two wars, with an already formulated outlook on life; they were exclusively under the cultural influence of their own people and the new surrounding had little influence on them. Along these cultural lines and influences we wish to discuss a number of literary individuals who left their imprint on the Ukrainian-Canadian community and made considerable contribution to the Canadian cultural treasury as a whole. The cultural contribution to Canadian life cannot be described as purely Ukrainian, nor, as someone might wish—purely Canadian. Both designations would be incomplete. The most suitable description would be Ukrainian-Canadian, as it conveys the idea of the component parts of this cultural process and contribution.

To the first group of Ukrainian writers in Canada in the second period who grew up on the culture of their own people and in the surrounding atmosphere, belong the following individuals: J. Pawchuk, J. Nowosad, Catherine Nowosad, Anna Pruska, Anna Adamowska, D. Hunkewych, M. Kumka, D. Solanych, Peter Chaykowsky, P. Bozyk and I. Kiriak.

In some respects it was a continuous line of writers from the pioneering era and of the type of Sava Chernecky, Appolinary Novak, Wasyl Kudryk and others. Practically all of them began their writings in the first era, but their full development came to fruition in the second period of integration. Their work clearly shows the growth of the community; they grew with the development of their community in its political and literary sense.

One of the oldest in this group is John Pawchuk, 1884-1966. He was born in Vilchiwchyk, West Ukraine, and came to Canada with his parents as a young boy in 1900. He worked on farms and in factories and later had his own business. He wrote poetry and short stories, usually sprinkled with healthy humor. They were published in a weekly "Narodna Vola" in Scranton (1908), and later in Canadian papers, mainly in "Ukrainian Voice". More outstanding of his satires were the "Soap Bubble", "By Devious Ways" and others.

A neighbor of John Pawchuk from the old country was John Novosad (1886-1956), who was born at Ilavche, West Ukraine. He settled at Oakburn and sent his literary contributions to several papers, mostly to the satirical papers "Vuyko" and "Osa", and closely cooperated with the weeklies "Canadian Ukrainian", "Ukrainian Voice" and "Ranok". Although he was a prolific writer, he did not publish anything in a book form. He knew the life of the settler-farmer as well as that of the laborer, because he himself worked at different jobs in British Columbia, Alberta and Saskatchewan, and because of that, the subject matter of his writings, mostly poems of four lines, is very rich. He died at Homefield, Manitoba, and left many poems still unpublished.

Of special literary merit are three women—Mary Adamowska, Anna Pruska and Catherine Novosad.

Mary Adamowska (1890-1963) was born in the village of Mychalkiw, West Ukraine. She came to Canada with her parents as a nine year old girl and they settled in Saskatchewan. For some time she lived in Canora and later in Melville. Her poems are noted for their depth of feeling and the memories of her youth. She published her poems mostly in the "Ukrainian Voice".

Anna Pruska (1895-1947) was also born in the village of Mychalkiw in the district of Podillia from which she assumed her pen-name of "Podolanka". She came to Canada when she was seven years old, and lived with her parents on a farm where there was no school. She learned to read and write from her father. She liked books which were her consolation in her difficult family life. Despite serious chest illness, she became very active in community life — she was a good actress, an effective speaker and wrote poetry which was published in "Ukrainian Voice", "Canadian Farmer" and in "Pravda and Vola", with the political policy of which she sympathized. Her verses are light, deeply sentimental and colored by the linguistic dialects spoken in the districts from which her parents came.

The youngest of these three is Catherine, married to John Novosad (1900-1975), who came to Canada from Dawydkiwtsi, West Ukraine. She also suffered from a chest illness. The melancholy feeling and long illness left their mark on her poetic works. She wrote selected verses, among which were "To the Spring", "The Wide Field" and "From Sorrow". Regrettably her poems were not published in a book form.

The rich Podillia district, which gave three Ukrainian-Canadian women folk-song writers, gave also a talented poet—Michael Kumka (1893-1967), who was born in Hovyliv Velyky, West Ukraine. He came to Canada as a 16-year old youth and worked as a laborer, but at the same time he did not forget that by means of education he could "pull himself up", as he notes in his writings [1]. He attended evening and then teachers' courses and later taught evening schools in Ukrainian institutions in Winnipeg and in Toronto. He was fond of children and gained their attention and respect. He wrote poetry and stories for children and published them in the Canadian papers as well as in the children's Magazine "Svit Dytyny" in Lviv. For a considerable period he worked for the "Ukrainian Voice" weekly and during that period he published the following works: "School Songs with Music and Physical Exercises" (1926), "The Riddles for Young and Old" (1931), "Ukrainian Schools in Canada" (1931), "Monologues and Dialogues" for children and teenagers (1934), and four books called "Snip" (1939). He edited interesting almanacs for the "Ukrainian Voice" in which he published many valuable articles describing the cultural and community life of the Ukrainians in Canada. During the Second World War he left Winnipeg for Toronto and discontinued his literary works.

Dmytro Hunkewych (1893-1958) was a noted community worker in Winnipeg. He was born in Lysovychi, West Ukraine. He came to Canada by way of the United States, where he stayed for the first three years. He revealed his unusual talent in dramatic works and children's stories. He published his first dramatic work "W Halyckij Nevoli" in 1921. In 1924 he published a drama "Victims of Darkness" in Lviv, and "Christmas Night" in Winnipeg. In Lviv he published a play "The Suffragette Club", "Bloody Pearls" and a tragi-comedy "Maniwciamy" and others, and in Canada "On the Waves of Love", "The League of Nations", and a play for children entitled "Herioc Descendants", and a vaudeville play "Slavko in Troubles", as well as versification "Welcome Spring". In all he published over twenty plays for adults and children. He also wrote a number of articles under the pen-name of "Dmytrowych" and "Bursak". Up to 1934 he worked in a foundry in Winnipeg and it was during that period that he produced all his literary works. In that year he moved to Toronto where he died prematurely.

Dmytro Solanych (1876-1941) was born in the village of Ustia, by the Prut River, West Ukraine. He closely cooperated with Kyrylo Trylowsky and Ivan Sandulak in organizing gymnastic societies 'Sich' (Seech). To Canada he came in 1903 and tried to organize "National Home Association" in Winnipeg. Later he moved to British Columbia and thence to Alberta where he was engaged in community work, mainly in Edmonton. He was a good organizer and assisted the new settlers in many ways. During that period he wrote newspaper articles and short novels, modelled on the famous Ukrainian novelist Wasyl Stefanyk, his former friend and neighbor. The most marked feature in the works of D. Solanych is the vernacular dialect from Pokuttia which he used freely.

Panteleymon Bozyk (1879-1944) belongs to the generation of early

---

[1] "Pictures from My Life and Work".

pioneers who suffered many hardships. He came to Canada in 1900 from the village Onut in Bukovina. He began his first literary work by writing short stories and publishing them in the paper "Ranok". His first publication "In Defence of Faith" appeared in 1909, and was printed in New York. Later he published his poetry and stories in various papers. He developed his literary activities in the period between the two wars and for that reason he is considered as a representative of that period. He came to Canada with well defined outlook on life, but he searched for creative means, especially in the sphere of religion. In 1935 he published his poems in a book form "The Canadian Muse". His more important work is the "Ukrainian Church in Canada" (1927), and a selection of prose writings entitled "Canadian Stories" (1933). He also wrote some propaganda pamphlets advocating conservative ideas. His work is marked by extremes—likes or dislikes.

Peter Chaykowsky (1888-1938) also belongs to the first pioneer period. He came to Canada in 1897 from the village Hryciwka and received his education in the Ukrainian-English Seminary and for a long time he taught in the bilingual schools. His poems were published in several newspapers of that period. He published a one-act play entitled "A Cup of Coffee".

Wasyl Chumer (1882-1963) from Drohoyeva, West Ukraine, came to Canada in 1904 and was one of the first pioneer teachers. In 1942 he published his "Memoirs", a documentary of the pioneers attempting to preserve their language in the schools at that time. He also wrote a historical outline of cultural development of the Ukrainian pioneers in Western Canada.

The most successful of the pioneer writers was Illia Kiriak (1888-1955) who came to Canada from the village Kniaze, Pokuttia district, in 1906. Elementary education he obtained in his native village and the rest by his own efforts while working in Canadian forests, saw mills, mines and in the normal school. In his own biography, called "Confessions" [2] he describes his work with other men at Hosmer, where he received an ideological outlook for the rest of his life. When he was 24 years of age he enrolled for formal education in the School for Foreigners in Vegreville, but, as he writes himself—"having gone through all the troubles in the old country and then again in the new world, my head was full of past experiences, which always were fresh in my memory". Under the influence of these experiences his imagination was reborn and he began to write poetry and short stories. He did not publish much of his material, but his large collection of writings fully qualifies him as a pioneer writer and poet. Nevertheless Illia Kiriak produced more than others. Between the two wars, and understanding the life of the new settlers, due to the fact that he lived among them as a writer, teacher and organizer [3], he wrote a novel in three volumes entitled "The Sons of the Soil". This is a grand canvass upon which I. Kiriak depicted three Ukrainian generations in Canada showing the process of their integration in the new land with all their joys and sufferings from day to

---

[2] Letters to his close friends, Mr. and Mrs. John Ruryk, Vancouver, also to Mr. and Mrs. P. J. Lazarowich, Edmonton.

[3] For a time he was the organizer and secretary of the Ukrainian Self-Reliance League and promoter of the Peter Mohyla Institute.

day. This novel was not only the highest achievement of his literary efforts, but also it provided a symbolic crown to all pioneer writers of the first and second periods as well as to their followers. For his writings I. Kiriak attained recognition in Canada as no one did before or after him. In his poetic works he combined the periods of pioneer development and indicated the perspective for future progress. It suffices to mention only such poems as "Our Field", "The Dream", "In the Quiet Summer Night", "Life, Life", or "The Only Flower": and from his prose "The Betrothal", "The Friends" and "The Humoresques". His extensive heritage awaits the attention of a researcher and a compiler. His monumental work "The Sons of the Soil" was translated into English by Michael Luchkovich and published by the Ryerson Press in 1959.

From the literary activities of I. Kiriak we may now proceed to another group of talented writers who were already educated in Canada and were fully bilingual—Ukrainian and English, and who wrote in both languages, although the dominant language was still the mother tongue. Among them there are those who write exclusively in the official language of the country. To this group of writers who grew up in Canada from their childhood belong the four who were mentioned previously in "Kameniari"—a magazine published in Saskatoon: O. Ewach, S. W. Sawchuk, S. M. Doroschuk and J. Danylchuk. In this category we also include Michael Krepiakevich, Harry Skehar, Tatiana Kroitor, Michael Petrowsky, William Paluk, Myra Lazechko-Haas, Vera Lesyk-Lysenko and some others. Most of these wrote in the atmosphere and cultural influence of the Peter Mohyla Institute in Saskatoon.

Onufriy Iwach (Honore Ewach — 1900-1964) was born in the village of Pidpylypia, District Borshchiv. Elementary education he received at Garland, Manitoba, and secondary at the University of Saskatchewan in Saskatoon. His education in the Ukrainian language he received at home and later at the Peter Mohyla Institute in Saskatoon, where he lectured on Ukrainian history and literature. For a few years he taught public school in various districts. His home and community environment inspired him to write poetry which he published in the "Ukrainian Voice", the "Canadian Farmers", and "The New Pathway". He also wrote some in English and published in the U.S. daily "Svoboda". His first collection of poems appeared in print in 1931 called "Boyova Surma Ukrainy", and two years later, in 1933, he published another poem called "One Whom the World Wanted to Catch but Failed", and about the same time another collection "Ukrainian Songs and Lyrics" which in English translation was called "Songs and Lyrics". He tried his hand at writing dramatic work as "The Flight of the Crane" (1923), and "The Golgotha of Ukraine" (1924), and some novels, e.g. "The Voice of the Soil". He wrote a few educational articles, viz. "Short History of Canada", "Historical Outline of Great Britain" (1939-1940), and in the English language "Ukraine's Call to America". He was a diligent writer and an outstanding poetic individual of the second period. He devoted much of his time as an editorial writer first for the "New Pathway", and for a longer period for the "Ukrainian Voice".

Of unusual ability was Stepan M. Doroschuk (1894-1945), who came to Canada with his parents from the village Baryshkivci in 1897 and settled in the Fishing River district. After teaching for twelve years in the country he came to Winnipeg and organized the publication of a magazine for children, "Promin". At the same time he published popular booklets for children and adults and during these few years of activity published nearly two hundred some of which were in English. He also published a comic journal "Tochylo" which we have mentioned previously. Publishing activity consumed his energy and this detracted him from his literary work. Following the Second World War he moved to the United States and continued his publishing activity in Detroit.

Semen W. Sawchuk (1898-   ), who showed his original talent for poetry and satire, did not develop his talent along these lines, and only now and then published some of his work in the newspapers. He became fully engaged in church and community work. He signed his articles by pen-names — "Semen Kremen", "Semen Mateiw" "Tadey Yestyk".

John Danylchuk (1900-1942), the youngest of the Saskatoon quartet in 1929 published a small book of poems "The Dawn", most of the poems were published in the "Ukrainian Voice", Canadian Farmer" and other papers. Although born in Canada he cherished the memory of the land of his parents when he wrote:

"Remember that your brother is enslaved, and you will not be his brother if you do not assist him".

He also wrote in the English language and even published two journals dedicated to the Ukrainian culture in Canada. Premature death put an end to the work of that productive and talented individual.

Joseph Wizniuk (1900-1975), United Church Minister, born in Canada, tried his skills in poetry and especially sharpened his pen in translation from Ukrainian authors and poets, like T. Shevchenko, I. Franko, I. Vorobkevych and others. He translated a major part of Vasyl Stefanyk's novels, which were published in 1971.

Michael Krepiakevych (1897-   ) was educated at Hampton and at the Peter Mohyla Institute in Saskatoon where he completed his Normal School and studied pharmacy. He wrote humorous dialogues and monologues and published a few comedies such as "On Vacations", "The Magic Flute", "Three Engagements", "A Hero in the Bag", and others. Most of his work are written in Ukrainian. He came to Canada with his parents from the village Verbova, West Ukraine.

Hryhoriy Skehar (1891-1957) came to Canada as a youngster from Bukovina in 1908. During his hard physical work he decided to acquire education, in which he succeeded and soon became a school teacher. After teaching in public schools during the summer for a number of years he enrolled at the University of Chicago where he graduated in dentistry. He wrote in prose and his best known descriptive and critical articles about pioneer community life were published in several Ukrainian Canadian weeklies. His articles were also published in Ukrainian papers in the United States as well as in Lviv and Chernivci. In the English language he cooperated with educational publications and especially with the "BOOKS ABROAD". He also revealed his ability as a critic and published a number of reviews of Ukrainian literary publications.

Michael Petrowsky (1897-   ), has much in common with the characteristics of H. Skehar. He came to Canada in 1912 and immediately decided that he must acquire an education. Elementary education he received in his native village, Rozubowychi, but it was not easy to

SECOND ERA — ILLUSTRATIONS

Archbishop Basil V. Ladyka

"Soborchyk" of Ukrainian Catholic Priests in Winnipeg, 1923. In front (middle) Rev. P. Oleksiw, administrator.

Metropolitan Ivan Teodorovich

Archbishop and priests of Ukrainian Greek Orthodox Church of Canada, 1925. First row (l.—r.): P. Bilon, S. W. Sawchuk, Archbishop I. Teodorovich, W. Kudryk, S. Hrebeniuk; Second row: M. Kucher, W. Sluzar, V. Novosad, D. F. Stratychuk, P. Sametz, P. Melnychuk, D. Kyrstiuk, D. Seneta, I. Kussy.

SECOND ERA — ILLUSTRATIONS 507

Central Committee of the Self-Reliance League in 1936-1942. In the middle P. J. Lazarowich and around him, clockwise: D. Yanda, Dr. I. Verchomin, Rev. E. Hrycyna, O. Lukianchuk, I. Kiriak, P. Wasylyshyn, I. Danylchuk, 1937.

"Committee in Aid of Ukrainian Political Prisoners in Motherland", existed in 1928-1940. Sitting (l.—r.): A. Gospodyn, I. Baydak, P. Matwiychyna; behind: S. Makitra, M. Kowal, S. Bilinsky, M. Meleshchuk, A. Hyndra, Winnipeg, 1935.

Dominion Executive of the Canadian Sitch Organization (l.—r.): I. Esaiw, Rev. N. J. Bartman, M. Hethman, N. Danylchenko, W. Dyky, W. Bossy, D. M. Elcheshen.

"Sitch" members from Winnipeg at physical training, headed by I. Esaiw (far left) and behind (second row) D. M. Elcheshen.

SECOND ERA — ILLUSTRATIONS

Col. E. Konovalets in Winnipeg, 1929. Sitting (l.—r.): P. Shtepa, Col. E. Konovalets, E. Wasylyshyn; second row: D. Gerych, W. Topolnycky, V. Demianchuk, V. Semets.

Members of U.S.H. with their guest from Europe, O. Senyk-Hrybiwsky. Second row from front: D. Gerych, I. Dutkewych, B. Zeleny, W. Kossar, O. S. Hrybiwsky, I. Gulay, P. Shulha, M. Seniuk, S. Cybulski, Winnipeg, 1931.

Hetmanych D. Skoropadsky

Lord Tweedsmuir

D. Doroshenko

George Simpson

Senator
Olena Kysilewska

W. Kirkconnell

O. I. Bochkovsky

E. Konovaletz

M. Shapoval

SECOND ERA — ILLUSTRATIONS

Gen. V. Sikevich with Toronto community representatives. Sitting (l.—r.): Dr. W. J. Yaremiy, Gen. V. Sikevich, T. Humenniuk; behind: W. Hultay, J. Korchinsky, Rev. I. R. Kovalevich.

Members of U.S.H. with their guest General Mykola Kapustiansky, Winnipeg, 1935.

Memorandum from the representatives of Ukrainian churches and lay organization to Rt. Hon. David Lloyd George of Great Britain, regarding the Ukrainian question in Europe.

Interorganizational Committee commemorating 70th Jubilee (1868-1938) of the "Prosvita" in Lviv, Winnipeg, 1938. Sitting (l.—r.): Dr. P. Macenko, T. D. Ferley, Rev. W. Kushnir, H. Mudry, I. Baydak, A. Gospodyn; second row: K. Hrycyshyn, S. Motalo, P. Kalyniuk, T. Melnychuk, P. Siry, A. Zaharychuk.

SECOND ERA — ILLUSTRATIONS

"Mohylanky" of the Petro Mohyla Institute, Saskatoon, 1928-29. In the second row in the middle Savella Stechishin, dean.

"Markian Shashkevych Bursa" of the Ukrainian Catholic Brotherhood, Saskatoon, 1936.

Students of Higher Education Courses with the folk dancing instructor Petro Hladun (in the middle), Winnipeg, 1942.

Ukrainska Striletska Hromada No. 3, Montreal, 1939.

SECOND ERA — ILLUSTRATIONS

Ukrainian Institute of M. Hrushevsky, Edmonton, 1928-29. In the middle P. J. Lazarowich, rector.

Second annual Choir-Masters Course of U.N.F. Winnipeg, 1941. In the middle teaching staff: T. Koshetz, Dr. P. Macenko, Prof. A. Koshetz and Dr. J. Kozaruk.

Weeklies of the Inter-Wars

Ukrainian News

New Pathway

The New Pathway

The Canadian Sitch

Ukrainian Toiler

Siege (Sitch)

SECOND ERA — ILLUSTRATIONS

Newspaper and Journals in the Inter-Wars

Bukowina

Labor News

Canadian Ukrainian Citizen

The Forward

The Bell

The New Canadian

518 UKRAINIAN CANADIANS: A HISTORY

Magazines of the Inter-Wars

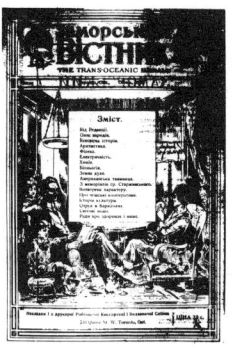
Trans-Oceanic Herald

Western News

Children's World

Leader of National Economy

The Ukrainian Review

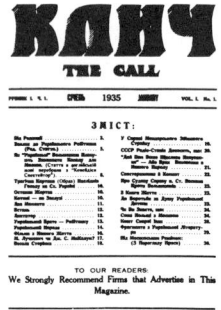
The Call

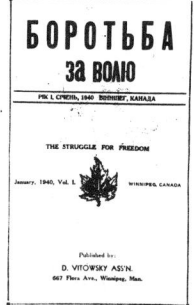
The Struggle for Freedom

Future of the Nation

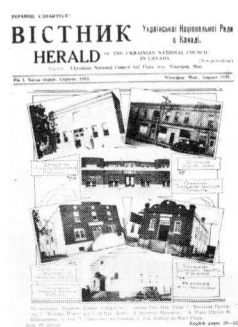
The Herald of the Ukrainian National Council in Canada

SECOND ERA — ILLUSTRATIONS

Editors during the Second Era

W. Bossy (left) and W. Dyky

I. Danylchuk

S. Doroshchuk

Rev. P. Oleksiw

V. Biberovych

Rev. P. Bozyk

T. Datzkiw

H. Kurdydyk

M. Hethman

520 UKRAINIAN CANADIANS: A HISTORY

Pro-communist Press between the two World-Wars

"Zaokeansky Hart" Literary Association, sitting: M. Irchan, Lucylia Piontek, I. Kulyk; standing: M. Shatulsky, M. Smith, M. Popowych.

SECOND ERA — ILLUSTRATIONS 521

Members of Legislatures and House of Commons

N. Hryhorczuk

N. V. Bachynsky

G. E. Dragan

I. Goresky

M. Luchkovich

Wm. Tomyn

J. Wawrykow

A. Hlynka

Wm. Fedun

522 UKRAINIAN CANADIANS: A HISTORY

Leaders in Church and Community Life

Rev. S. Semczuk

Rev. E. D. Hrycyna

Rev. J. Pulak

Rev. Ph. Ruh

Rev. T. Kovalyshyn

Rev. P. Kryworuchka

Rev. J. R. Kovalevich

Rev. D. Popovych

Rev. P. Kindrat

SECOND ERA — ILLUSTRATIONS 523

Professionals and Community Leaders

T. Bodnar

K. S. Prodan

T. K. Pavlychenko

P. J. Lazarowich, Q.C.

Dr. J. Yatchew

D. Lobay

John Panchuk

Roman Gonset

O. E. Miles-Malycky

524   UKRAINIAN CANADIANS: A HISTORY

Leaders in Woman's World

M. Dyma

S. Stechishin

E. Sytnyk

M. Hawryluk

H. Mandryka

A. Pryma

P. Kuzenko

A. R. Ruryk

T. Skremetka

SECOND ERA — ILLUSTRATIONS

Writers

M. Petrowsky

I. Kiriak

I. Kmeta-Ichniansky

D. M. Hunkevych

M. I. Mandryka

C. H. Andrusyshen

J. Stechishin

V. J. Kaye-Kysilewsky

H. Ewach

526 UKRAINIAN CANADIANS: A HISTORY

Community Leaders and Inspirers

A. Gregorovich

T. Humeniuk

J. Pryma

T. Kobzey

W. Hultay

A. Zaharychuk

S. Korban

J. J. Ruryk

M. Chypchar

SECOND ERA — ILLUSTRATIONS

Community Leaders and Inspirers

B. Zeleny

M. Pohorecky

M. Sharik

I. Gulay

W. Kossar

E. Wasylyshyn

V. H. Koman

N. Chabal

D. Gerych

The first Executive of the Ukrainian Canadian Committee: Front (l.—r.): S. Chwaliboga, J. W. Arsenych, Rev. S. W. Sawchuk, Rev. W. Kushnir, W. Kossar, A. Malofie, A. J. Yaremowich. Standing: M. Pohorecky, M. Stechishin, S. Skoblak, Rev. S. Semczuk, T. D. Ferley, P. Barycky, A. Zaharychuk; third row: I. Gulay, W. Sarchuk, Dr. B. Dyma, E. Wasylyshyn, Dr. C. Andrusyshen, T. Melnychuk.

continue education in Canada at the time. Only in 1921 he began his formal education at Bloomfield in the U.S. and later continued at the University of Iowa and Ottawa. At the same time he tried his luck writing poetry and prose which the Ukrainian press accepted and published. He wrote stories for children and short articles and also did some translations. He contributed articles to the "Ukrainian Voice", "Svoboda", "Overseas Herald", "Promin" and the "Ukrainian Worker". The last named, published his novel "Secret of the Silver Island". In 1928 he published a novel "The Magic City", a comedy "The Canadian Groom" (1921), and a drama "Assassins of the White Eagle" (1922); still in manuscripts are the novels "The Millions", "The Eternal Students", and others. His short stories in the English language were published in the "Canadian Forum", "Svoboda" (U.S.A.) and the "Oshawa Daily Times" published his novel "The Flames of Hate". By his own efforts he organized the "Ukrainian Bazaar Publishing Co." and was an editor of "The New Canadian" in Toronto.

Tetiana Shevchuk-Kroitor-Bishop (1904-   ) came from Sushno, District Radekhiw, West Ukraine, and was educated in the Peter Mohyla Institute in Saskatoon. She was a teacher and during that time she completed a correspondence course at the Queen's University. She published her poems in Ukrainian papers in Canada beginning in 1922, and also in Ukrainian magazines in Lviv and Kolomya. She published her English contributions in the "Winnipeg Free Press Farmer" and in the "Youth of Today", "The McFayden Publications" and the "American Foreigner". Her last collection differs fundamentally from her first compositions as to her sentiments to the country of her parents and her feelings for the new land. Her verses are imbued with theosophical outlook. In 1964 she published a collection of poems in Ukrainian and English, "An Overture to Future Days". Her latest published work is a travelogue —"Pilgrimage to Kiev". Although T. Shevchuk lives in the United States she frequently refers in her works to the land of her youth—Canada. Her poetry constitutes the transition from pioneer to modern writings.

Maara Lazechko-Haas (1920-   ) was born and educated in Winnipeg. She studied journalism at the University of California, but her poetic talent took precedence over journalism. She wrote verses and longer poems in the English language and published them in the Winnipeg Free Press as early as 1934. Some of her poems were published in the "Pebar Anthology", in the "Important American Poets" and in the "Spring Anthology" in London. The poems—"Vision", "Loss" and "Spirit of Love" were published in the "Anthology of Ukrainian Writers in Canada". Her poetical paraphrase of T. Shevchenko is ready for publication. She writes selectively with deep modern methods.

Vera Lysenko (Lesyk) was born and educated in Winnipeg and wrote stories in the English language. She wrote two books—"Men in Sheepskin Coats" (1947) and "The Yellow Boots" (1954). The theme of both these books is the early pioneer life of the Ukrainian settlers, with slightly left political coloring. Both these books were favorably received by the literary critics.

William Paluk (1914-   ), born and educated in Winnipeg. His parents came to Canada from Bratkovets, West Ukraine, in 1907. He tried his writing skill while still in public school. In 1943 he published his first collection of stories "The Canadian Cossacks". Prior to that he translated into English "A Short History of Ukrainian Music", written by Alexander Koshetz. He also likes drama and his "The Kidnapping at Scratching River" and "Taken at the Flood" were televised, and a number of others were broadcast by the CBC.

To the Canadian born writers also belongs Constantine H. Andrusyshen (1907-   ), who was educated in Winnipeg at the University of Manitoba, Paris and Harvard. He was keenly interested in Slavic literatures and during the university studies found time and translated into English many Ukrainian poems, which, with the assistance of Prof. W. Kirkconnell, were published in one volume "The Ukrainian Poets" containing poems of many Ukrainian authors, including a number of Canadians. He and Prof. W. Kirkconnell translated and published "The Poems of Taras Shevchenko KOBZAR" [4].   Dr. C. H. Andrusyshen headed the Slavic Department at the University of Saskatchewan. His English articles were published by the "Ukrainian Quarterly", (New York), "The Slavonic Review" and others. Together with J. N. Krett he edited and published "A Complete Ukrainian-English Dictionary".

To a separate group in our evaluation belong the people who came to Canada between the two World Wars. They are—A. Gospodyn, T. Volokhatiuk, V. Tulevitriw, I. Kmeta Ichniansky, O. Luhowy, Rev. S. Semczuk, Natalia Kohuska, H. Mazuryk, M. I. Mandryka and others. All of them came here either direct from Ukraine, or as war refugees from various European countries. Majority of them are political immigrants who participated in the struggle for Ukrainian independence. This political and patriotic episode left a deep imprint on their literary works. Both in poetry and prose they dwell on the beauty and greatness of the past; they mention the tragic days and sufferings of their people, they foresee the future strength of Ukraine. They compare their past experiences with those found here and this is the reason for their warm appreciation for Canada.

Andrew Gospodyn (1900-   ), former member of the Ukrainian Army of West Ukraine, teacher by profession, came to Canada in 1923, directly from refugee camps in Czechoslovakia. In Winnipeg he taught evening schools and was active in community work. He wrote poetry and short sketches and published them in local papers and journals. His compositions "The Sun Woke Up", "To the Ukrainian Pioneers" and "On the Dnister's Whirlpool" were published in the "Anthology of Ukrainian Poets in Canada".

Victor (Lysenko) Tulevitriw (1886-   ), as captain in the First World War he first came to the United States and then to Canada. For a considerable time he worked physically and wrote poetry and anecdotes and published them in various papers and journals. His first book of poems "Thoughts and Songs" was published in 1938, and in 1940 he published a drama "Such Is Her Destiny".

Taras D. Volokhatiuk (1898-   ). After arriving in Canada in 1923, he finished his theological course and became a priest of the Ukrainian Greek-Orthodox Church. Most of his poetry is based on Biblical subjects. He translated the Canadian Anthem "O, Canada" and has published

---

[4] Both those monumental works were published by the Ukrainian Canadian Committee.

collection of his poems and stories. He also wrote a number of comedies and one-act plays.

I. E. Kmeta (Myroslav Ichniansky) came to Canada in 1929 from the village Ichnia, near Kharkiv, Ukraine, hence his pen-name "Ichniansky". He belongs to the more productive class of writers, as he had some of his works published in Ukraine before coming to Canada, e.g. "Arfa" (Kiev 1924), "National Melodies" (Kharkiv, 1927), and his novels "The Night" and "Hurricane" were published in Poland. In Canada he published a collection of poems "Fragments" (Winnipeg, 1929), and "The Immigrant's Muse" (1936). Many of his poems were published in Evangelical press in Canada and the U.S.A. Up till 1945 he worked as a Baptist minister in Canada and the close contact with the people inspired him to literary activity in which he frequently referred to his native fields and cities. In Ukraine he was on intimate terms with V. Sosiura who had a marked influence on his writings. He belonged to the impressionistic group and his poetic works were translated into the English, Russian and Latin languages. He has also translated some works of R. Kipling, Charles Robertson, Henry Longfellow, Watson Kirkconnell, Isabella Crawford and others [5]).

Volodymyr Kupchenko (1897-1966) came to Canada from Bukovina in 1921, as a member of the West Ukrainian Army. In Canada he finished Normal School and taught school for 44 years. His first poetic work was published in a pedagogical journal "Promin" in Chernivci (1920-1923).

In Canada his contributions were published in the "Ukrainian Voice", "The New Pathway" and other papers. His first writings were based on the themes of the old country, but later they assumed a Canadian background to the extent that he even wrote poetry in the English language and published them in the Edmonton papers.

Alexander Luhowy, real name Alexander W. Owrucky-Schwabe, (1904-1962), came from the East Ukraine, and revealed his literary talent as a novelist, although he began as a dramatist. His first dramatic work "Vera Babenko" was published in Canada in 1936, and "The November Night" and "In the Days of Glory" in 5 acts (1938), based on the revolution in East Ukraine. One of his more important novels is the "Black Clouds from the Prypiat River", depicting the Cossack living conditions after the war of Bohdan Khemlnycky. He prepared a trilogy based on the First World War entitled "By Fire and Blood". He also worked on exclusively Canadian themes. In 1946 he published his first novel, describing the life of Ukrainian settlers in Canada—"Bezkhatnyj". He also made a detailed outline of a new novel based on life in Canada —"In Search of Fate in the World". His great interest was education and journalism. In 1942 he wrote and published historical biographies— "Outstanding Women of Ukraine", and in 1947-49 he published and edited a popular literary and historical journal "The Ukrainian Family" (A Journal of Popular Literature and History), in which he recorded historical events in different countries, and devoted considerable space to the events in Canada and the Ukrainian community here.

Hryhory Mazuryk (1898-1963), also a member of the West Ukrainian Army came to Canada in 1926. A teacher by profession, he taught in evening schools and contributed articles to several papers. He wrote short

---

[5]) Real name of M. Ichniansky is Ivan Efymovych Kmeta.

stories and poetry which were printed in the "Canadian Farmer", during the last thirty years, and he published a book "100th Anniversary of Shevchenko's Testament", many satires in the Ukrainian papers and almanacs under a pen-name Hryc'Otruta, and for a few years he edited a monthly "News-Letter of the Ukrainian Workingmen's Union", which organization he represented in Eastern Canada. He was co-organizer and secretary of the Ukrainian Writer's Union in Toronto.

Stephan Semczuk (1899-   ), came to Canada in 1928 from West Ukraine, as a Catholic priest and a recognized writer; a very enthusiastic missionary of the church and community worker. He organized the Ukrainian Catholic Brotherhood and edited its many publications, Bulletin," Buduchnist Natziyi—Future of the Nation, etc. Originally he worked in Saskatchewan and later came to Winnipeg. In 1924 he published his collection of poems "The Meteors", in Lviv, and in 1927 a song book "Resurrection", in Zowkva, which was confiscated by the Polish government. In the same year he published a collection of stories "The Prophets". On the American continent he published "The Fanfares" in Chicago, 1931, and a few years later, a collection of prose and poetry "The Canadian Rhapsody", based entirely on Canadian themes. In 1965 he published "Reflections" and in 1967 "Poems". The longest poem in this collection is the poem about Canada, describing and glorifying the Spring, Eastern Canada, Saskatchewan, Red River, Lake Erie, Lake Waskesieu, Niagara Falls and Canadian farmers. This work was dedicated as a Centennial project. S. Semczuk is the most talented poet, firmly entrenched in Canadian soil. Among his historical works is his "Outline of Ukrainian Literature" (1948) and a manuscript ready for printing, a biography, "Metropolitan Joseph Benjamin Rutsky" etc.

Natalia Kohuska (1905-   ), came to Canada in 1928 from Wyshnivets, West Ukraine. She revealed her aptitude as a prose writer. She has published a novel "Mother", a historical novel "In Flight to Freedom" describing the struggle for independence in 1918, and an educational essay "Religious Motifs in the Works of Lessia Ukrainka". She edited the history of the Ukrainian Women's Association, which was published on its 25th anniversary, and a history of the Ukrainian Youth Association (SUMK). She is the Editor-in-Chief of the monthly, "Promin", an organ of the Ukrainian Women's Association, in Winnipeg.

Mykyta Mandryka (1886-1979), with extraordinary attributes in Ukrainian-Canadian literature, came to Canada from Prague where he lectured at the university, in law and political science. As a former member of the Ukrainian Central Rada he was active in political life. In Winnipeg he was fully occupied with political and educational work. He edited a paper in Winnipeg and was engaged in purely research work, and wrote "A Theory of Agriculture Democracy", History of Ukrainian Cooperatives", "History of Consular Institutions", and others. Besides that he wrote poetry in which he achieved considerable success. His first literary work "Radomysl" appeared in 1916. This was followed by the "Book of Vengeance" (1917) and "The Songs of Anemona" (1917). Most of his poems were published in the papers in Ukraine, "Rada", "The Native Country", "Ukrainian Home", "The Kuban Star", "The New Ukraine" as well as in a number of periodicals in Europe and in Canada. The best known of his translations is "The Hiawatha" of

Longfellow. In 1940 he organized "The Ukrainian Cultural Society" and published the first "Anthology of Ukrainian Literature in Canada". After a short lapse in his work, he returned again to his poetic Muse and in 1958 he published his collection "The Golden Autumn", in 1959 "The Joy", in 1961 "Symphony of the Ages", and in 1965 "The Sunflower". Four individual poems were published separately: "Mazeppa" (1960), "Canada" (1961), "The Wanderer" (1965), and "The Age of Petlura". All his publications were warmly received by the critics. On his 80th birthday he compiled a "History of the Ukrainian Literature in Canada", in English [6]), and previous to that, also in the English language, he published several brochures, such as "The Ukrainian Question" and "The Ukrainian Refugees".

Although M. I. Mandryka was educated in Ukraine, he devoted his sympathies both to Ukraine and Canada. He harmonized his feelings in that direction and transmitted them to other writers and poets. He wrote critical articles and book reviews. By his writings he influenced the older generation as well as the younger one; those who came here between the two wars and those who came after the Second World War.

Besides the above named writers there are several others who have contributed their share of work in the Ukrainian-Canadian mosaic. Here we wish to mention at least the following: Dorothy Yanda who graduated from the Peter Mohyla Institute and writes in both Ukrainian and English, for which she received literary awards; Andrew Truch, Joseph Saik, John Yatchew, Victor Kupchenko, John Korchynsky, Vasyl Kazaniwsky, O. Darkovych, P. Ostapchuk [7]), P. Hnatiw, M. Darkovych, M. Romanowa, T. K. Pavlychenko who published a separate book of poems, "The Spirit of a Nation", W. S. Sklepowych, W. Babienko, S. Kuryliw [8]), M. Stechishin [9]), Dmytro Zakharuk, P. Kivshenko (who wrote Bezbatchenko), and others.

The Marxist Group

In the twenties there was an active group of writers in Canada, about which we briefly referred in the first chapter and which was known as "The Overseas Hart". This group was organized by Myroslav Irchan (1896-1937), a talented writer, who came to Canada in 1923 with a group of emigrants from Czechoslovakia. His political conviction was diametrically opposed to the other political emigrant-writers whom we mentioned previously. He himself participated in the struggle for Ukrainian liberation, but later reorientated himself to the Marxist line. In Canada, as we have mentioned before, he became an editor of a semi-monthly journal "Robitnycia", ("The Working Woman"), and through his writings he spread his influence to his surroundings. We might as well mention, that, before his coming to Canada he was closely connected with the Marxist press, so that due to his talent, he soon became a leader among the writers who held the same political view.

---

[6]) Subsidized by the Canada Council as a Centennial project.

[7]) Director, actor and organizer of theatrical plays. He wrote several stage plays that were shown in Ukrainian organizations, e.g., "In the Claws of CHEKA" and others.

[8]) He wrote a novel "The Mother's Curse".

[9]) He wrote and published "Fairy Tales" which, in their content may be compared to those of S. Rudansky.

Another active leader of this group was John Kulyk (1896-1941), who was an official in the Soviet consulate in Ottawa. In Ukraine he was a member of a writers called "Hart". The ideological aims of this group he published and explained in "The Ukrainian Labor News". He also wrote and published other articles, which he signed "Wasyl Ronenko". In 1924 M. Irchan and John Kulyk organized a branch of "The Overseas Hart". The group was not strong numerically, but was very vocal and active. At the head of this group, besides those mentioned, were also the following — Lucylia Piontek (wife of J. Kulyk), M. Popowych, M. Shatulsky, who signed his articles M. Wolynec, and M. Semanciw (M. Synio-Verholec). All of them decided to adopt unconditionally the ideological platform and constitution of the revolutionary proletarian writers group in Soviet Ukraine [10]). As is known, the "Hart" in Kharkiw was under the influence of Mykola Khwylovy, who in 1925 organized "Waplite" (Free Academy of Proletarian Literature). When the "Hart" in Kharkiw terminated its activity, the Canadian group changed its name to "Overseas Hart" and remained active until J. Kulyk left his post at the soviet consulate, and M. Irchan left for Ukraine in 1929. Both of them in the thirties were accused of "bourgeois nationalism" and later on were liquidated.

While in Canada M. Irchan published a novel "Carpathian Night" (1924), and "Against Death" (1927), based on Canadian theme, especially in the collection of stories "Among the People", but most noted were his dramatic works: "The Unemployed". "The Revolutionary", "The Unwelcome Guest", "The Twelve", "The Family of Brush Makers", "The Underground Halychyna", and "In the Brushwoods", which were frequently staged in Ukrainian Labor-Farmer Temples. He also wrote articles against the nationally oriented Ukrainian settlers, signing them by various pen-names, such as I. Syvulsky, M. Lelyk, George Ropsha, Ivan Nezamozny and others.

John Kulyk knew the conditions of the immigrants in the United States and Canada, as he was in the U.S.A. from 1914 to 1917. During the war he returned to Europe and there, in Ukraine, he joined the Communist Party and this gave him the opportunity to get the appointment as a USSR consul in Canada. While here he wrote and published his memoirs and stories "The Consular Diary", containing many Canadian themes. The fate of an immigrant he described in "The Adventures of Wasyl Rolenko". He also wrote a number of poems e.g. "Canada", and in his collection "The Surroundings", among others there are poems "The Niagara" and the "Prairies". In the latter poem he described the struggle of the Indians and the Metis under the leadership of Louis Riel. During his stay in Canada he made some translations which later were published under the title "Anthology of American Poetry".

Within the Marxist group there are the following more or less talented writers: Andrew Ponur, Michael Harasymchuk, John Mykytyn, Wasyl Bosowych, Semko Podilsky, O. Zwonets, Jacob Manchurak, and others. Most of them wrote poetry, essays, stories and novels, all of which were colored by special political tendencies, or direct Marxist propaganda. There were some works that have permanent value. All of them were

---

[10]) One of the eight resolutions adopted at a meeting in Winnipeg, August 24.

active in the Marxist movement in Canada, about which there are references elsewhere.

The Anglo-Saxon Group

In the history of the Ukrainian Canadian literature of the second period there were a few Anglo-Saxon individuals who greatly contributed to the better understanding of that literature among the Canadians as a whole. Among them are Dr. A. J. Hunter, Percival Cundy, Dr. Watson Kirkconnell, Edward W. Thompson, and Florence Randal Livesay.

Dr. A. J. Hunter (1868-1940) belongs to those non-Ukrainian individuals who spent many years of his life among the Ukrainian pioneers. Recognizing the positive qualities of his co-citizens, he respected them and tried his best to convince the Anglo-Saxon world to see and judge the Ukrainian community in its true light. His work "A Friendly Adventure" discusses many aspects of Ukrainian life and shows much sympathy for the spirit and work of the Ukrainian pioneers in Canada. In cooperation with Zygmunt Bychynsky he translated some of Shevchenko's poems and published them in a book "The Kobzar of Ukraine" (1922). Later he published in the Ukrainian language an educational essay "The Study of Philosophy", "Life Principles of Evangelism" and "A History of the Prophets" (1927). For a longer period he assisted in editing a religious paper "The Canadian Ranok". He also delivered hundreds of addresses for English audiences about the Ukrainians, their history and literature, which he knew quite well. He was in charge of a hospital in Teulon, Manitoba, and supervised two "Bursas"—boarding houses for Ukrainian students. After he passed away the hospital was named "The Hunter Memorial Hospital", in appreciation of his work for the people of Teulon and the district.

When Dr. A. J. Hunter took keen interest in the works of Shevchenko, another Presbyterian missionary, Percival Cundy (died in 1949), took similar interest in the writings of Ivan Franko. He was in charge of a mission among the New Canadians in 1932, in the town of Roland, Manitoba. He translated and published some literary works of Ivan Franko—"A Voice from Ukraina", with suitable biography and the works of the author and their influence on the Ukrainian people. Later he translated the works of Lesia Ukrainka, another important figure in Ukrainian literature. Besides these he contributed many educational and informative articles in "The Ukrainian Quarterly" in New York, where he lived the rest of his life. It was only after his death that his translations were published—"Ivan Franko, the Poet of Western Ukraine" (New York, 1949), and "Spirit of Flame" (New York, 1950).

There were other Presbyterian missionaries who were interested in Ukrainian literature, such as J. A. Carmichael, Prof. G. Bryce, Dr. C. W. Gordon (Ralph Connor), and others. As early as 1910 Ralph Connor wrote a longer treatise entitled "The Foreigner", in which he devoted much space to the Ukrainian immigrants. His errors in this work he attempted to rectify in his later publications [11]).

The most authoritative observer of the Ukrainian literature in Canada among the Anglo-Saxon citizens is Dr. Watson Kirkconnell (1895-1977),

---

[11]) Review "Ruthenians defended by a Ruthenian", by W. J. M. (W. J. Mihaychuk—M.H.M.), Manitoba Free Press, Jan. 25, 1910.

former Professor at Manitoba College in Winnipeg and later President of Acadia University in Wolfville, N.S. He wrote many articles and critical essays and reviews on the subject of the literature of the East-European peoples in Canada and among them he devoted considerable portion of his attention to the Ukrainian and Ukrainian-Canadian literature. Dr. Kirkconnell was the first in Canada who, in his "Canadian Overtones", highly evaluated the Ukrainian pioneer literature.

In his "Twilight of Liberty" (1946) he evaluates the third element in Canada. About the Slavic literature he wrote articles to the "Slavonic Review" in London, and to the "University of Toronto Quarterly" and others. Besides his literary contributions and more important works Dr. Kirkconnell published several researches about various aspects of Ukrainian life in Canada, such as: "The Ukrainian Canadians and the War" (1940), "Our Ukrainian Loyalists" (1943), "The Ukrainian Agony" (1943), "Seven Pillars of Freedom" (1944), and others.

Dr. W. Kirkconnell's most important contribution to Ukrainian literature is his translation of the poems of Taras Shevchenko "The Kobzar" and "The Ukrainian Poets", which were completed in collaboration with Dr. C. Andrusyshen in 1963. There is no doubt that Dr. Kirkconnell's works greatly contributed to familiarize all Canadian citizens with the history, literature and community life of the Ukrainian Canadians. From this point of view Dr. Kirkconnell is one of the outstanding personalities in the realm of Canadian identity.

In concluding the second period of Ukrainian literary development in Canada we must emphasize that it is a rich and promising period during which there was full-blossoming and fruition of the expression of the hopes and feelings of a new community in the integrative process in both languages—Ukrainian and English. In the vanguard of this bilingual group are to be found graduates of the Petro Mohyla Institute in Saskatoon. From the Anglo-Saxon group the major interest and activity was shown by members of the Presbyterian Church, later the United Church, who early sought to proselytize, established mission homes for school children and hospitals. Their initial subjective curiously soon gave rise to an acquaintance with appreciation of the objective works. How better to become acquainted with the Ukrainian culture than to read the original? Accordingly, they acquired competence in Ukrainian and being humanists and humanitarians, they sought to share their new understandings and appreciations with their contemporaries through the media of the English press, thus making known to the Canadian community the riches and contributions of the so-called third element to the emerging Canadian mosaic. To the younger generation of Ukrainian Canadians growing up in Canada this served as a catalyst to augment their interest in their culture and to quicken the growth of Ukrainian ethnicity in Canada.

As to the quality of the poetical productions, we note great forward strides. In place of the pioneer verse which was a pure folklore, we perceive deep feelings with national and general humanitarian motifs reflecting variety of interests, literary schools and influences. Another interesting effect in the writings of this period is the aura of confidence permitting the patriotic poetry while the prose was pragmatic and deeply rooted in Canadian soil.

THE LIVING TIES WITH THE LAND OF THEIR FATHERS

The cultural identity of the Ukrainians also flowed along the line of living ties. Ukrainians of Canada kept their close ties with the land of their fathers not only by means of correspondence with their kinsmen, but they also received many Ukrainian newspapers and journals from the former overseas homes of their occupied lands. Most of this warmly welcomed reading material came from Lviv. Books and journals from the "Prosvita Association", the publisher of "Chervona Kalyna" (Red Cranberry); the edited material by Ivan Tyktor and "The Fatherland", helped to fill the shelves of Ukrainian book stores, libraries and reading rooms in Canada. A somewhat lesser amount of printed word found its way to Canada from Bukovina and Carpatho-Ukraine. Members and fellow-sympathizers of "Ukrainian National Federation" disseminated printed material expounding their own organization, such as "The Bugle" (Surma), "The Building of a Nation", "Hucul Kurin", and others that had been banned in Western Ukraine but were printed by emigrants in other countries of Europe. The Ukrainian Labour and Farmers' Temple Association distributed printed material from the eastern regions of Europe. The press and books from homelands brought news about the current life of Ukrainian people. All printed matter arriving from Poland and USSR had to pass through a strict censorship and one could gain but very little of worthwhile news—especially in the sphere of politics. Best and most authentic information was that which came "live"— from living people.

Already on the morn of the mid-two-war era, as is well known, there arrived in Canada Ivan Bobersky, one of the leading pedagogues and public-minded figures of Western Ukraine. He came to this country as a representative of the Ukrainian organized life in Lviv, with an ardent appeal to help in the liberation movement and to give aid to the thousands of political emigrants scattered throughout Europe. He worked diligently in cooperation with the National Republic of Western Ukraine and when in 1922 a representative body of this administration was formed in Canada, with Dr. Osyp Nazaruk as its head, I. Bobersky filled the post as its secretary. Being a man of great stature he exerted a positive influence over the extremist elements and was capable of uniting together the whole national element around the activities of Ukrainian Red Cross and Ukrainian Central Committee. After the dissolution of this representation of government in exile, I. Bobersky went to work for the Cunard Line and devoted much time and energy to St. Raphael's Ukrainian Immigrants' Welfare Association of Canada (St. Raphael's Association). He was the first among Ukrainians who worked earnestly to compile Ukrainian statistics in this country and to prepare material for the history of Ukrainians in Canada. He travelled throughout Canada, gave speeches, collected various mementos and held interviews. He was the first to prepare the Chronicle of Ukrainians in Canada, as well as statistics of Ukrainian churches, national homes and cultural centres, and had a large collection of rare pioneer pictures. He also prepared a map of Canada, showing where Ukrainians settled during the first and second era. Much of his material was printed in different almanac-calendars. In 1931 he went back to Europe and from there sent further valuable materials about Ukrainians in Canada and revisited this country during 1932 and 1937, died in Yugoslavia during the Second World War. It may truly be said that Professor I. Bobersky was the first devoted researcher of the Ukrainian past in Canada.

Metropolitan Andrey Shepticky visited Ukrainians in Canada for the second time in 1921. He showed lively interest and was thoroughly acquainted with the history of his fellow-countrymen living in this country, and especially with their religious complications. In addition to his inspection of the diocese he also paid visits to other hierarchs and statesmen of Canada. He also sought to organize help for the Ukrainian orphans in Western Ukraine. Some districts, such as Edmonton city for instance, granted him permission to collect funds in public for this noble purpose. In his sermons and speeches at banquets in his honor this eminent hierarch informed Canadians about the multi-sided situation and Ukrainian immigrants in Ukraine.

In 1922 Dr. Osyp Nazaruk, minister of foreign affairs for the National Republic of Western Ukraine, paid a visit to Canada. He criss-crossed the whole country to inform his own countrymen about the pressing needs of the National Republic and the government of Evhen Petrushevych in exile, and at the same time transacted his national defence loan. He also collected material for the history of Ukrainians in Canada and wrote a separate study of their life, about which mention is made elsewhere. In addition he took part in the forming of the Association of Ukrainian Writers and Journalists in Canada.

The post-war years were not only rich in the numerous visits of leading Ukrainian political figures and church dignitaries, alone. In December, 1923, Winnipeg played host to the famous Ukrainian National Choir of Europe, under the baton of Prof. Oleksander Koshetz. Prof. Koshetz continued the good work of the renowned "Respublikanska Kapelia" (Republican Kapella), which at that time played the role of what may be fondly called as the "Cultural Ambassador" of the Ukrainian National Republic on the European and American continents. The choir charmed, with songs and music, not only its own countrymen, but also those of their North-American compatriots. The press reviews about these concerts were praised in highest superlatives, and Ukrainians of Winnipeg feasted the choir at no fewer than three banquets. Similar outstanding successes were repeated in other parts of Canada. Prof. O. Koshetz visited Canada with his choir for the second time in 1926, and once again elicited genuine interest and a feeling of awe toward Ukrainian vocal art in the highest musical circles of Canada.

Concerning the visit of Dr. V. Bachynsky, Rev. J. Jean and Dr. V. Konstantynowych, previous mention has been made in a separate chapter on this era, in connection with the problems of the so-called "Second immigration" to Canada [1].

Two years following the first visit of Ukrainian National Choir, Canada was favored by a visit of artist-choreographer of Ukrainian National dances, Vasyl Avramenko. His public appearances, speeches and teach-

---

[1] See the separate chapter: "Migration and Emigration between Two World Wars".

ing of the art of national dancing he began in Eastern Canada, organizing schools of dancing in every Ukrainian community across the whole country. Avramenko's brilliant dance courses and his widely organized schools of dancing brought him much public acclaim and laudable press reviews which gave him great encouragement to go ahead in his artistic field. He spent three full years, with the youthful elements, systematically teaching courses in dancing. In time he promoted the more promising students into qualified dance instructors who continued to teach the art of folk dancing in locally provided schools that were usually operated in connection with various reading rooms, national homes and church parishes. In 1928 Vasyl Avramenko moved to the United States of America leaving behind in Canada many dedicated neophyte folk dance instructors. From time to time he returned to Canada for renewed visits with his pupils. Later on, a few years prior to the Second World War he produced two Ukrainian films "Natalka Poltavka" and "Zaporogian Beyond the Danube".

Further popularization of Ukrainian song came from the concerts of the Ukrainian opera singer, Solomia Krushelnytska, who was invited, by her countrymen, to come to Canada, taking advantage of her tour of U.S.A. She performed at two concerts only, in Winnipeg and Toronto, in 1928. The whole Canadian press in its reviews acclaimed with superlatives, both her brilliant singing talent and the charming beauty of Ukrainian songs.

The second woman to visit Canada, after the First World War, was senator Olena Kysilewska, the foremost leader of women's movement and editor of the newspaper "Zhinocha Dolia" (Women's Fate), in Western Ukraine. She came to Canada primarily to visit women's organizations and spent the summer of 1929 in this country. In her talks she gave out information about women's movement in Europe and at the same time she wove stronger ties between Canadian and European woman's world. About her impressions of Canada she wrote valuable reviews in her "Women's Fate" journal and in other publications associated with it.

In 1928-29 Lev Yasinchuk toured Canada lecturing on the role of "Ridna Shkola" (National School) in Western Ukraine. He also spear-headed a fund-raising campaign in support of these schools. A compilation of these lectures and his writings on the problems confronting Ukrainians in Canada appeared in print under the title "Beyond the Ocean" which contained much valuable material to the history of Ukrainians in Canada.

To a special category of prominent visitors to Canada belong the political leaders who were engaged in political and diplomatic work in Europe and on the American continent for the liberation of Ukraine, with a special degree of activities being evinced by the former army veterans who were destined to be the head of "Organization of Ukrainian Nationalists". Sponsored by this organization there came to Canada, in 1929, a man who was at the head of this national movement, Colonel Evhen Konovalets. He did not make any public appearances, confining himself to a series of talks with the leading members of Ukrainian War Veterans' Association and Ukrainian Self-Reliance League.

The action aiming at the cooperation between the Ukrainian War Veterans' Association and the Ukrainian Self-Reliance League that had been started by Col. E. Konovalets was continued by Omelan Senyk-Hrybivsky who was also a prominent member in the leadership group of those who were at the head of Ukrainian Nationalists in Europe [2]). He came to Canada in 1931, made public appearances before the chapters of the U k r a i n i a n War Veterans' Association and engaged in a series of basic talks with the leadership of the Ukrainian Self-Reliance League. Support of the Ukrainian Self - Reliance League was sought by another member of the Executive of Ukrainian Nationalists, Col. R. Sushko, also known as M. Melnychuk, who stayed in Canada for a year in 1932. Thanks to his active support there came into being the "Ukrainian National Federation (U.N.F.—U.N.O.) [3]). All these leaders informed their countrymen in Canada about the underground activities of the Organization of Ukrainian Nationalists which had widely spread its political work throughout Western Ukraine in the 30's, and was badly in need of financial support—to which appeal the Ukrainian Canadian fellowmen responded with most generous donations.

The ties of the Organization of Ukrainian Nationalists with the Ukrainians in Canada that were first started by Col. Evhen Konovalets were continued throughout the whole period between the two wars. In 1935 General Mykola Kapustiansky came to Canada where he spent ten full months, visiting larger Ukrainian communities and making closer contacts with Canadian military leaders. Both the English and French wrote extensively about the "First Ukrainian General" in Canada, who spoke about the Ukrainian freedom movement which sought to establish independent Ukraine. General Kapustiansky's tour was sponsored by the Ukrainian War Veteran's Association and the Ukrainian National Federation. Two years later, in 1937, another Ukrainian military leader, General W. Kurmanowych, the former minister of war in the government of the National Republic of Western Ukraine arrived in Canada to attend the jubilee convention of Ukrainian War Veterans' Association at Saskatoon.

One of the outstanding personalities who visited Ukrainians in Canada between two Wars was General Vladimir Sikevich. In 1917-1919 he served with Ukrainian diplomatic corps. He was head of the Repatriation Commission after World War I in Hungary and Austria and from there he arrived to Canada. After his visit here, in 1930 he became a naturalized Canadian. He cooperated very closely with the Ukrainian Self-Reliance League, toured Canada and visited Ukrainian centres with lectures and memoirs. His memoirs under the title "From My Notebook" were published in five volumes.

There were other such visitors to Canada in due time. All of them, through the medium of their information and action, were able to infuse, into Ukrainian settlers in Canada, a deep psychological consciousness of cultural and political ties that were binding them to their fellow brethren in their former homeland.

When all those mentioned continued their ties, first with Ukrainian War Veterans' Association, and later with Ukrainian National Federation, yet another link was added to this "the tie that binds" communication with the old country, with the arrival in Canada of the young Hetmanych Danylo Skoropadsky, the son and successor to Pavlo Skoropadsky,

---

[2]) Michael Stechishin: "The Ukrainian Self-Reliance League and Unification of Ukrainian Nation", Winnipeg, 1933, p. 22 and following.
[3]) Almanac "Ukrainian War Veterans' Association", 1928-1938, Saskatoon 1938 —p. 31.

as the future Hetman of the whole Ukraine. His visit sponsored by the United Hetman Organization (S.H.D.) at the end of 1937 and the beginning of 1938, proved to be a veritable way for revitalizing and infusing new life into that organization. About the visit to Canada of this representative of Ukrainian monarchy, there appeared a special book "For Ukraine" which remains as a useful and valuable contibution to the history of Ukrainians in Canada.

Among the visitors to Canada must also be included the representatives of the socialist movement. Most prominent among them were Nykyfor Hryhoriyiv and Mykyta Shapoval, both of them considered as being the authorities in the realm of national and anti-marxist socialism and members of the Socialist Revolutionary Party, centred in Prague, Chechoslovakia. Both of the above mentioned politicians were noted scholars and so were able to make contacts with higher Canadian educational circles. H. Hryhoriyiv wrote under the pseudonym of "Hryhoriy Nash", and had a whole string of lecture-type material on political and sociological themes. He first visited Canada in 1927 and again in 1939, on the heels of his American tour. About Mykyta Shapoval's lecturing tours and of his being the founder of the Ukrainian Sociological Institute in Prague, has been reviewed by us before, in connection with the formation of the "Ukrainian Labor Association". The socialist anti-marxist movement was sometimes referred to as "Shapovalystic" movement in honor of this well kown socialist leader.

A separate category of Ukrainian visitors to Canada, in the nineteen-thirties, is composed of leading figures in the field of arts and science.

In another chapter we mentioned the name of a well-known sociologist and an expert student of nationalism, O. I. Bochkovsky, who came to Canada in 1936 as a delegate from the Friends of the Ukrainian Economic Academy in Podiebrady, Szechoslovakia. He informed Ukrainian Canadians about the work of this educational and training institution and at the same time he himself studied the social prolems of Ukrainian settlers in Canada, visiting over a hundred communities and giving as many lectures. His valuable observations about life of his countrymen in Canada were transformed into interesting, valuable and well-written articles that were eagerly sought for and printed in all local Ukrainian journals. Following along this line was his literary output, called: "Through United Forces—for Ukrainian Politechnics", in which he elucidated the prominent part played by the Ukrainians in the development of this institution.

Ukrainians played host to a noted historian of their own origin, Dmytro Doroshenko, who, during the First World War, was the minister of foreign affairs of the government of Ukraine, as well as a professor in Prague and Warsaw universities. The Institute of Petro Mohyla, in Saskatoon, invited him in 1937 to give a series of lectures there. The same year he held a five-week course in Ukrainian history for Ukrainian students in Edmonton which was organized by the leaders of the Institute of Mykhaylo Hrushevsky. In addition to this he gave lectures in Regina, Saskatoon, Winnipeg, Toronto and Montreal. In 1938 Dmytro Doroshenko, in answer to a second invitation, again came to Canada and this time he taught history of Ukrainian literature in Edmonton.

In the last few years, preceding the Second World War, the following distinguished Ukrainians came from Europe to visit Canada: Wasyl

Yemets, Mykhaylo Holynskyj, Antin Rudnycky, Maria Sokil and Olha Lepkova [4]).

Kobzar-bandurist Vasyl Yemets made his first tour through Canada in 1936 and repeated it again in 1939—revealing before his countrymen and their fellow Canadians the haunting charm of the unique ancient instruments, the kobza and the bandura.

Mykhaylo Holynskyj, operatic tenor of European concert stages captivated thousands of Ukrainians with his melodious voice and songs. Arriving in Winnipeg from Western Ukraine in 1938, he soon departed for U.S.A. but returned again to Canada in 1940. Later he made a second visit to U.S.A. for an extended concert tour and settled finally in Canada, to live peacefully, amongst his many friends.

Maria Sokil and Antin Rudnycky—the husband and wife duo—were guest-visitors of Canada in 1938 and remained here until the spring of 1939. Maria Sokil, an operatic soprano, staged several of her concerts, accompanied by her husband, A. Rudnycky. Both artists worked earlier with the Kharkiv State Opera, where A. Rudnycky—who is also a composer—held the position of a conductor. During their American concert tour they both collected funds for the Ukrainian National Hospital in Lviv.

Still other visitors to this continent were the representatives of the erstwhile rulers of the Ukrainian SSR, whose visits were reserved exclusively for inspecting the working system of the Ukrainian Labor and Farmers' Temple Association.

In our summaries, dealing with the living ties with the old country, we spoke about the visits of the leading figures from Ukraine, and diaspora, who came as representatives of political, cultural-artistic and educational life. Some of them made strong appeals for political or financial help, others informed about the Ukrainian life in Europe and sought in turn, for themselves, information about Canada and what its living conditions may be—especially those conditions that pertained to the life of their countrymen. Still others came here to bring the magic charm of lilting music, lively national dances and the beautiful, haunting melodies of Ukrainian songs. In the mutual contact with them all, there came into being the gradually evolved and strongly binding, spiritual ties between Ukrainian Canadians and the rich, cultural storehouse of their fatherland.

Magnificent exertion was singularly evinced by those artists who, in addition to the above mentioned psychological period of time, presented Canada with the priceless treasure of Ukrainian culture. About this same cultural inlay into Canada's national mosaic one of the Ukrainian papers in Canada had this to say: "It has been our good fortune that in the last ten years we have been able to play host to our most eminent conductor-composers, pianists and national-dance artists. And when, today, our people in Canada are well known to other nationals, which is primarily due, in the first measure, to the popularity of our dance, music and songs, then undoubtedly a great measure of credit for this must be given to those creative artists who were capable of presenting to the

---

[4]) "What European Ukrainians Visited Canada" in "Ukrainian News", Edmonton, No. 14, 1941.

people of other nationalities the rare beauty of our national art, expressed in its most perfect form" [5]).

There is no doubt that the art presentation of the honored guests also had an added influence on raising to a higher level Ukrainian art and culture in Canada through the working medium of numerous amateur singing and theatrical groups.

Of a singularly expressed equilibrium—as a sort of friendly answer to the many famous visiting individuals who came from Ukraine and Europe to America — were the revisits of the somewhat equally noted public leaders of Ukrainian Canadians, to Europe. These included the clergymen and community leaders as well as many others who went back to see their loved ones and their numerous friends. All of them helped to strengthen the psychological, cultural and political ties in the realm of national entity, and through the revitalizing medium of fresh culture they kept constantly alive the identification of Ukrainian Canadians with the land whence they, and their fathers, came.

---

[5]) "Ukrainian News", April 8, 1941, No. 14, p. 5.

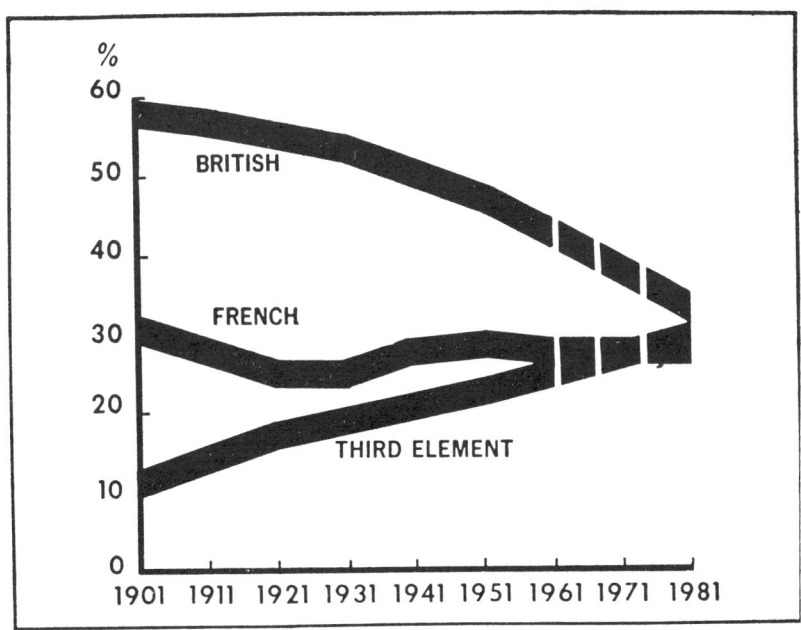

Canadian Population Trends (percentagewise)
(Chart courtesy of Prof. P. Yuzyk)

THE DEVELOPMENTAL PROCESSES OF NATIONAL CONSUMMATION

When, at the end of 1923, the Ukrainian Central Committee ceased to be active and the Ukrainian National Home in Winnipeg was unsuccessful in carrying out its entrusted mission from Ukrainian Educational-Economic Congress of 1923, to form a similar committee, there then had not been any close ties between Ukrainian churches and Ukrainian organizations in Canada. But in spite of this, life flowed in its regular stream and some measure of cooperation was maintained among the single and separate local organizations. Only a lack of more widely active platforms was felt—otherwise all were busy with their local private affairs. About this same time a germinating idea shaped itself about the possible formation of a dominion-wide organization in religious, ideological and political field. Step by step there grew a strong conviction about the need of such organization, followed, in turn, by actual deeds.

In previous chapters of this history we spoke about these processes in connection with the formation of such first organizations as Ukrainian Sitch Organization, Ukrainian Self-Reliance League, and even prior to that, of leftist-communist elements in Ukrainian Labour and Farmers' Temple Association (U.L.F.T.A.). In addition to the above mentioned organizations there were also the Ukrainian churches—Catholic, Orthodox and Evangelical—that had their dominion-wide ties. Only the Ukrainian Red Cross, alone—which left such a shining memory of its work in the years 1919 to 1923—ceased its useful operation as there were no more objective aims for its activities.

Then there came the summer of 1927 when unexpected floods on Western Ukraine lands, especially in Galicia and Bukovina, inundated the widely stretched fields, destroying the products of the soil and the accumulated possessions that took many long years and much hard labor to acquire. Ukrainians from Lviv and Chernivci appealed to their countrymen in Canada and U.S.A. for help. Without any delay, two committees were formed in Canada. One of them, "Help for the Old Country" was formed by Hetman's Sitch Centre (Centralia Hetmanskych Seechey), which, working in cooperation with the hierarchy of Ukrainian Catholic Church, held a fund-raising campaign among Ukrainian Catholics, relying partly on the aid of its official organ—the "Canadian Ukrainian" journal; and the other, the "Committee in Aid of the Ukrainian Flood Victims in Galicia and Bukovina", carried on its work through Ukrainian Greek-Orthodox Church and its official church organs, the "Ukrainian Voice" and the "Orthodox Herald". When it was realized that all these efforts would be more effective if both committees would work jointly, they formed the "General Committee of the Association of the Ukrainian Red Cross", whose executive was comprised of the representatives of the two, above mentioned, former committees. And with this came a new opportunity for a platform on whose stage the now disunited organizations and the churches could play their part, in unison again. This joint committee was headed by such pioneer community leaders as: Jos. Dyck, J. W. Arsenych, I. Pidlubny, O. H. Hykawy, W. Baleshta, A. Yonker, S. Kowbel, W. Bossy, Z. Bychynsky, and M. Stechishin. Truly enough the work went rapidly ahead and the General Committee of the Association of the Ukrainian Red Cross collected thousands of dollars in aid of the flood victims. This work, for a worthwhile cause, lasted for nearly a year. In every province there were branches of this committee, subject to the head administration in Winnipeg. This aid may be described as being one of the brightest periods in the Ukrainian Canadian history between the two World Wars.

As soon as the relief work of the Ukrainian Red Cross subsided, the Ukrainian Canadians, once again, lost the incentive for closer cooperation. To a certain extent, at a later time, some activation was shown in the formation of the committee to aid Ukrainian political prisoners, which began its work in 1930 [1]), but as a result of differences of single isolated organizations all of the committee's former activities passed mostly into the hands of the new immigration, centred around Ukrainian War Veterans' Association. A somewhat long and lively discussion took place between "Ukrainian Voice", the official organ of the Ukrainian Self-Reliance League, and the "New Pathway", organ of the Ukrainian National Federation. A very heated discussion was carried on, in print, between the "Orthodox Herald" and the "Canadian Ukrainian", pertaining to religious matters. "The Ukrainian Toiler", organ of monarchical orientation, maintained its lively debate with the "New Pathway" and the "Ukrainian Voice", the last two defending the republican form of government ideology. But all of these journals carried on jointly, a sharp and most bitter campaign against the communist press, which included "Ukrainian Labour News", "Farmer's Life" and others. On this attitude all of the national press and national organizations found a joint tongue and came out, very strongly and severely, against the Ukrainian Labour and Farmers' Temple Association, and all the other organizations allied with it. To be exact, and to the point, these last arguments mentioned above, rose to such a high peak that in the nineteen-thirties physical violence and force were employed during the public gatherings. The hatred between the national and the communist camps grew even stronger when from the bolshevism-ravaged Ukraine, in 1933, came the terrible news about the artificially produced famine, the shooting orgies, the massive exile of Ukrainian intelligentsia to Siberia, the total liquidation of autonomic rights in Ukraine, and other acts of terror. The news from Ukraine became so alarming that once again the national camp was compelled to seek joint pathways for a common cause. In many larger centres talks were going on about a unified national action. To such inceptive moves belonged the formation of Ukrainian National Council, in Winnipeg, by the initiative action of the leading public figures. Thanks to their efforts several confidential conferences were held, in the spring of 1933, that led, finally, to the above mentioned central federation, the Ukrainian National Council.

Ukrainian National Council

The Ukrainian National Council (U.N.C.) sent out a proclamation "To the organized Ukrainian community in Canada", in which it spoke

---

[1]) Its first chairman was the lawyer, Dmytro Yakimischak.

about the need of a Ukrainian central representation in this country. In its introductory remarks we read: "From the time the National Committee—(Ukrainian Canadian Citizen's Committee and later Ukrainian Central Committee—M.H.M.)—ceased to exist, that is, during the past ten years, there has been, among the thinking, community-minded Ukrainians, a conscious feeling of the existing lack of national representation, at the highest level of national entity, that would provide us with a directive in the various activities of our life and, in decisive moments, could speak on behalf of our overall Ukrainian community in Canada, or at least a salient portion of it."

In addition to the above general appeal the Ukrainian National Council sent out two other declarations, one, the "Declaration of Ukrainian National Council about the defense of Ukrainian lands, unlawfully seized by Poland, Ro mania and Czechoslovakia", and the other, the "Declaration of Ukrainian National Council, about the communist propaganda that was being spread among Ukrainian Canadians". Both of these declarations were political acts, par excellence, to aid the liberating processes of Ukrainian nation in Europe, and to make an impression on Canada. The Ukrainian National Council edited its material bilingually, in its own official organ "The Herald of the Ukrainian National Council".

In forming this institutional body the following Winnipeg organizations took part: Chytalnia Prosvita, Ukrainian Canadian Institute Prosvita, Kobzar Association, Taras Shevchenko Association of St. Boniface, Association Taras Shevchenko in Elmwood, St. Nicholas Mutual Benefit Brotherhood, M. Shashkevych "Ridna Shkola", T. Shevchenko Institute in Brooklands, Mutual Benefit Association, Ukrainian Sitch Veterans' Association, Ukrainian Canadian Women's Association, Ukrainian Labour Association, and others. Each organization was allotted five representatives but only one voice from each quintet.

Ukrainian National Council was recognized as being the official representation of Ukrainian people in Canada and only those organizations could belong to it that stood on solid principles for the independence of Ukrainian territories and defended the concept of a corporate state, and were desirous of bringing to it material and political assistance. Such formulative aims on the part of the organization tended to direct, clearly, the work of Ukrainian National Council against the communist core which was strongly oriented toward U.S.S.R. The resulting effect was evident soon enough when, during the political public meeting of the U.N.C., in Winnipeg, July 16, 1933, an open and violent hand-to-hand fight enveloped the two opposite sides.

Ukrainian National Council endeavoured to extend its influence to other cities in Canada, but in spite of its concerted efforts was not able to achieve its objective because, at that time, there were already in existence the following dominion-wide organizations: Ukrainian Self-Reliance League, Ukrainian National Federation, Ukrainian Catholic Brotherhood and United Hetman Organization, that did not wish to recognize this body as their overall political authority. But still, this same somewhat rejected body, through its repetetive efforts, was able to strengthen—within the sphere of the local cultural-educational organizations—the desire to have an all-inclusive Ukrainian federation in Canada.

At the head of U.N.C. for many years, was S. Skoblak, and its collegiate consortium included: V. Biberovych, C. Andrusyshen, H. Kozmuk, H. Kuz, A. Pruska, E. Sytnyk, A. Gospodyn, M. Mandryka, D. Budka, K. Hrycyshyn, T. Hubicky, H. Mudry, D. Ravlyk, W. Lach; and in the presidium there were: I. Baydak, P. Matwiychyna, I. Cymbalisty, W. Kohut, I. Kowal, W. Koshovsky, Y. Lyhach, D. Ptashnyk, H. Klymkiw, D. Mykytiuk, and H. Baran. With this, more or less, above mentioned composition the U.N.C. carried on its task for several years.

With every passing year the press would quote the remarks of the individual leaders as well as of various members of community centres, expressing their conviction for a need of a coordinating agency which would, in the sphere of public affairs, act as a clearing centre in the over-all community life. Nevertheless, the disparity between the individual dominion organizations—on different matters—was so great, and the discussions about them so passionate, that through the thick atmosphere of these much lesser affairs, it was difficult to see the long range goals. These transients, and very often trifling matters were, to a large extent, a reflection of "the general run of the mill" Ukrainian politics and their existence should only be considered as a connective evidence. As for the specific tasks and objectives of Ukrainians in Canada, a special attention was given to it by the noted Ukrainian sociologist, Professor O. I. Bochkovsky of Prague, who, at the end of his tour of Canada, announced: "Ukrainians should all meet 'at the round table'. They have, in Canada, a specific assignment. They should unite in all matters pertaining to the general Ukrainian affairs. Before their own countrymen they should come out as Ukrainians and not as members of single separate groups. They should give special attention to the propagation of Ukrainian cause among other Canadians" [1].

O. I. Bochkovsky's ideas were an expression of the historical past of the Ukrainians in Canada, in which their external performance — in both the pioneer and the mid-wars eras — was an accurate and exemplary proof of what the European guest was telling them. In the perspective run of time, it may be truly said that Professor O. I. Bochkovsky was only trying to revive, in the minds of his countrymen, the memories of their years-old accumulated philosophy.

Events in Europe Lead to United Action

When, in the spring of 1938, the Ukrainians in Canada learned about a concentrated advance on the Kholm region—by the then Polish government in power—and its destruction of Ukrainian Orthodox churches, the liquidation of "Chytalnias-Prosvita," as well as of other cultural organizations; then, throughout the larger Ukrainian communities in Canada, public meetings of protest were held, at which memoranda were formed and telegrams sent to the dominion government in Ottawa with a plea for intervention.

The most resolute protest came from Winnipeg. By combined action of all organizations and parishes, with emphatic participation of all denominations, conferences were held concerning a mass demonstration. At these conferences discussions were also going on about the possibility of forming a Congress of Canadian Ukrainians—a question which, due

---

[1] "Canadian Farmer", Oct. 4, 1936 and June 2nd, 1937.

to the complicated organizational situation and the need of psychological moment was, for the time being, postponed. A public demonstration took place on June 18, 1938. Over three thousand Ukrainians, from every walk of life, with the war veterans in the forefront, took part in this manifestation. We could perhaps leave out the mention of this event because many similar demonstrations were going on, at different times and in many places, but the Winnipeg demonstration deserves our attention in that it was a prelude—following years of mutual talks—which finally led to the unity of all nationally-minded Ukrainians in Canada. The subject of persecution of Ukrainian Orthodox church was discussed in the city auditorium, by the protestant minister MacLean and the Ukrainian Catholic priest, Rev. Wasyl Kushnir, as well as by others. In the period of strong religious hostilities this was a bold step in the direction of closer ties in the field of religion. Following this came other new stirring events.

When, in 1938, the case of Carpatho-Ukraine—which, between the two World Wars, had been a component part of Czechoslovakia and had, during the re-construction of that republic received the status of an autonomous country within the composition of the above mentioned republic—came into prominence, a new burning need arose to give moral and material aid to their countrymen. Above the newly-formed, autonomous fledgling, the dark clouds of invasion hung, from the direction of Hungary in the south, aided by Poland from the north. In this critical situation Carpatho-Ukrainians sent urgent appeals to their fellow-brethren, scattered through the various continents. The response was instantaneous. In Canada, editor O. Hykawy appealed to Ukrainians to convoke a special congress that would deal with this issue, but the events in Europe took such a rapid course that time would not permit the necessary preparation for such a meet [2]). In October of 1938, a council of the leadership of Ukrainian dominion organizations was held in Winnipeg, at which the helm, in the guiding of this council, was taken over by the Ukrainian Self-Reliance League and the United Hetman Organization.

Meanwhile the leaders of the Ukrainian National Federation were already in action and formed local committees which looked after the collection of funds, clothing and medical supplies for Carpatho-Ukraine. To the side of the Ukrainian National Federation, in regard to this matter, also came—if only partially—the Ukrainian Catholic Brotherhood and so, politically, there came into being two different blocks—Ukrainian National Federation and Ukrainian Catholic Brotherhood on the one side and Ukrainian Self-Reliance League and United Hetman Organization on the other side. It may be of interest to note that in this second block close cooperation was secured between the republicans and the monarchists, whereas the first block was considered to be of more egalitarian nature and in which the main role was played by the war veterans. But although in the fall of 1938 there had not been achieved any united action in giving aid to Carpatho-Ukraine; still the talks in regard to a full federation of Ukrainians in Canada, never wavered and two years later finally led to a complete national unity and organizational consummation.

---

[2]) "Canadian Farmer", Sept. 7, 1938.

When, in the spring of 1939, discussions between the single dominion organizations became bogged over a dead issue, and the situation in Europe required that it be thoroughly clarified in Ottawa, it was then agreed upon, in further talks, that a memorandum from the consistories of the two largest Ukrainian churches in Canada—the Ukrainian Catholic and Ukrainian Orthodox — be sent to the Federal Government in Ottawa. The memorandum was signed by the two chancellors, Dr. Wasyl Kushnir and Dr. S. Sawchuk.

The final discussions on this subject were held in June and on the 5th of July the head of the delegation was already in consultation with the Prime Minister Mackenzie King. The following day a delegation, composed of Rev. Wasyl Gigeychuk of Montreal, Theodore Humeniuk, a lawyer from Toronto and Wasyl Burianyk from Saskatoon [3]) held a discussion with O. D. Skelton, Minister of External Affairs, and Norman Robertson—who later became Canada's ambassador to Washington—informing them about the events in Europe and in Ukraine, especially in Carpatho-Ukraine. The delegation voiced its opinion that the democratic world was in danger and that Ukrainians aligned themselves, basically, with the Western democracies. Those present at these talks felt that the time and the need had arrived for closer cooperation on the part of the government with the citizens and representatives of the various single groups [4]). The visit of the Ukrainian delegation to Ottawa was the culmination of the long discussions that took place among the individual dominion organizations and at the same time brought to a successful completion of a definite phase of long extended debate.

In the fall of 1939 the Ukrainian National Federation expressed its desire to work in closer cooperation with other dominion organizations, but especially with Ukrainian Catholic Brotherhood. The Ukrainian Self-Reliance League and the United Hetman Organization, in their relationship with the Ukrainian National Federation had made specific political demands but this attitude served only to solidify still more strongly the ties between the Ukrainian National Federation and the Ukrainian Catholic Brotherhood, and as the result there appeared, under the date of Feb. 3, 1940, a mutual proclamation of the two last mentioned organizations announcing, that with that day began the existence of the Representative Committee of Ukrainians in Canada, with Dr. W. Kushnir as its head. To the presidium of this newly-formed committee belonged O. Zerebko and T. Melnychuk from the Ukrainian Catholic Brotherhood, and W. Kossar, Prof. T. K. Pavlychenko and W. Swystun a lawyer, from the Ukrainian National Federation. Places were reserved in this presidium for the Ukrainian Self-Reliance League and the United Hetman Organization.

This Representative Committee placed Ukrainian Self-Reliance League and the United Hetman Organization in an awkward position. They had visiualized a somewhat different picture of what the representation of Ukrainianism in Canada should be. They did not approve major decisions being made almost unilaterally.

Furthermore there was another organization which, from the

---
[3]) The fourth delegate, Rev. Mykhaylo Olenchuk, of Hamilton, was unable to attend.
[4]) Interview with W. Burianyk, head of delegation—author's archive.

title of its organizational and national position, deserved a place in this representative body, namely, the Ukrainian Workers' League that first came into being as the result of its strong opposition to the Ukrainian Labour and Farmers' Temple Association, and which stood on solid national ground and the Ukrainian Self-Reliance League and United Hetman Organization wished to have included in this united leadership. The "Representative Committee" had behind it a positive force that went straight into action and was able to loosen this pressing matter from its dead-centre logged position of multiform discourses. By action it also helped the onward move of those three other above mentioned organizations that had grouped themselves and made their stand be known, by their mutual public announcement dated February 7, 1940, and signed by: M. Stechishin for Ukrainian Self-Reliance League, T. Dackiw for United Hetman Organization, and M. Kashchak, for the United Workers' League. The positive result of this action lay in the fact that the situation was finally clarified. All three organizations declared themselves in favor of the formation, in Canada, of a representative Ukrainian centre, built on party foundation for the coordination of cooperative work of all Ukrainian organizations in Canada on the basis of full loyalty of all those represented organizations. Accordingly, these three united formed the Ukrainian Canadian Central Committee.

By this means two separate representative committees came into being: The "Ukrainian Canadian Representative Committee" and the "Ukrainian Canadian Central Committee". This state of indecision lasted for half a year; and though both committees regarded themselves as being central and representative, they, in reality, were nothing of the sort—notwithstanding the fact that, in their long discussions and platform-policy formation, they had achieved the basic principles of mutual discourse. There still was a lack of the final step that would lead to the crowning of the deed, which did not come about until the seventh of November, 1940. For this final step that led to the summit Ukrainians are partly indebted to Prof. George Simpson and Tracy Phillips—when the latter was touring Canada, on behalf of Federal Government, delivering speeches pertaining to war efforts. At their urgings, talks were renewed and meetings held in Saskatoon and Winnipeg, resulting in the creation of the Ukrainian Canadian Committee (U.C.C.). The discussed about ideas and problems became, after long intermission, the property of all. It may be even said that these same problems and ideas, that were so difficult to solve—after being so much discussed at the closed meetings and in the pages of the press—could be compared to the dry goods that become well packed and set after their long laying on the shelves. The protracted controversies over philosophical, theological and political theories and issues that had for too long sapped sorely needed energies and resources were at long last dissipated. All efforts were now directed in pursuit of the two major objectives.

1. Consolidation of Ukrainian opinion and coordination of the work of Ukrainians in Canada so as to provide help for Canada and Great Britain for the successful ending of war.

2. Presentation of the consolidated opinion and the carrying on of the coordinated work in general [5].

---

[5] Rev. Dr. W. Kushnir: "Ukrainian Canadian Committee as an exponent of the

Ukrainians in Canada with great yearning awaited the final centralization of their forces and efforts and so they welcomed the formation of the central body with great enthusiasm. Along with his expression of feeling came the evident proof of the reward of their concerted labor about which one of the leaders of this achievement wrote:

"That through the creation of this Committee our efficiency in aiding Canadian war efforts has been greatly increased, needs no further say-so. This efficiency can be traced at every step: it may be traced in the increased donations to the Red Cross, to the ambulance fund, in the amount of the war certificates being purchased, in the enlistment of the Ukrainian youth in Canadian army and generally speaking in all the various activities of local war committees" [5].

Participation in war efforts and the vigorous display of patriotism, on the part of Ukrainian community, toward their country, Canada, was only one aspect of the work of the Ukrainian Canadian Committee. About another such work-depicting page the above mentioned author wrote: "The Ukrainian Canadian Committee's task, for today, is to gather together all the scattered forces of the Ukrainian community in Canada and to create out of it a dignified united entity—organically cohesive and built on strong moral foundations of thought and action, an entity that would not only have the strength to solve its internal difficulties, but that it should also be capable of realizing its God-given right to exist" [7].

The above voiced thoughts were now the property of the five dominion organizations that had created a guiding apparatus—the Ukrainian Canadian Committee. Into the composition of its presidium the following leading figures were chosen: president— Dr. W. Kushnir of Ukrainian Catholic Brotherhood; 1st vice-president—Rev. S. W. Sawchuk, the then army chaplain, from Ukrainian Self-Reliance League; 2nd vice-president—engineer W. Kossar, Ukrainian National Federation; general secretary — J. W. Arsenych, Ukrainian Self-Reliance League; treasurer—A. Malofie, United Hetman Organization; financial secretary — S. Chwaliboga, Ukrainian Workers' League.

As we can see, the U.C.C. presidium was composed of the delegates from the five organizations that were chosen on the basis of parity. The U.C.C. encompassed only the nationally oriented organizations, leaving outside of its organizational frame U.L.F.T.A. and all those other organizations that recognized the principles of marxist communism.

For the wider scope of history it is worth our while to record the names of those who also played their part in the pre-parliament days of U.C.C. and who debated on matters concerning its formation. To this group belonged the oft mentioned Dr. W. Kushnir, Myroslav Stechishin, Dr. T. Dackiw, engineer W. Kossar and Dr. T. K. Pavlychenko and close behind came—W. Swystun, J. Stechishin, Rev. S. W. Sawchuk, M. Stechishin, Rev. S. Semczuk, T. D. Ferley, N. V. Bachynsky, MLA, T. Melnychuk, T. Kobzey, S. Chwaliboga, Dr. M. Mandryka.

The full scope of the Ukrainian Canadian Committee's declarations

---

national-political conscious responsibility of Ukrainian people". "Ukrainian News", No. 14, 1941.
[7] Ibid.

was not revealed until the First Congress of Ukrainians, which took place during the three days, June 22-24, in 1943. Over 600 delegates, from all parts of Canada, were in attendance, as well as a great multitude of other guests. It was conducted in an atmosphere of exuberant enthusiasm and exceeded even the fondest expectations of its organizers. It was here that the yearning desire for unity was fully revealed [8]. Rev. Dr. W. Kushnir, president of the Ukrainian Catholic Brotherhood, in his introductory speech remarked that: "This great event will surely leave its impression upon the future course of Canadian nation in its specific social, political and cultural tendencies... Today we are guiding our people, in Canada,"—spoke this authoritative source—"toward the social efforts of the whole Canada and of its citizens and not in the direction of our narrow tribal interests. We have set the course of our people in Canada toward reaching the heights of an active, responsible community and so we have full rights to see that our investment of spiritual culture, physical labor and the sacrifice of wealth and blood should be received with equal measure and appropriation on the part of the responsible authorities... We stretch our hands to our fellow-Canadians for mutual cooperation and equal share in all public activities on the Canadian soil and among its people".

The political thinking of U.C.C. president was actually paved with the help of a long range of co-creators of the Ukrainian Canadian Committee: J. W. Arsenych, Dr. T. K. Pavlychenko, engineer W. Kossar, Dr. T. Dackiw, M. Stechishin and others. Anthony H. Hlynka, M.P., in his speech, "Some Problems of Canadian Nationality", had this to say: "Our multi-national cultures may be flowing from many different streams and so they have to be directed and guided in such a way that they may, at the end, find their expression in the composite mosaic of an all-inclusive and cohesive Canadian culture" [9].

The request for the teaching of Ukrainian language in high schools and universities was stressed very strongly at this Congress. The spokesman on behalf of this problem was W. J. Sarchuk, a representative of the younger generation.

This was the common front approach of the five founding organizations representing 1249 separate associations located throughout seven provinces. The voiced opinion of the 405 National Homes and 705 parishes and mission stations, with 13 educational institutions; schools, colleges, 12 weekly newspapers and 10 monthly [10] magazines. This was an impressive organized strength — not to be easily ignored.

Ideas and problems that were brought into form, with the first founding of U.C.C. and the holding of the First Congress of Ukrainians in Canada, not only brought the second era to its summit, but they also were like an all-enclosing "omophor" (haven) for the fifty year-old group settlements of the Ukrainians and their processes, along with the history of these same processes and their future course for many years to come. The validity of these processes began with the first erection of the

---

[8] M. Marunchak: Twenty Years of Work of the Ukrainian Canadian Committee in Canada—"Ukrainsky Samostiynyk" (Ukrainian Independent) No. 49, 1961.
[9] First All-Canadian Ukrainian Congress in Canada, Winnipeg, 1943, p. 9.
[10] W. Kossar: "Sixty Years in Canada", see the "Calendar-Almanac of New Pathway" 1951.

"crosses of freedom" that were set up by the pioneers on the wide steppes of Canada and which were a symbol of liberty and a desire for the national-cultural development in a democratic self-ruling state. True enough, there were fears that the Ukrainian entity, having once lost its right to the teaching of Ukrainian language in prairie provinces—during the First World War—will, sooner or later, dissolve itself in the yet unformed—from cultural point of view—mass but thanks to the influence of the home, the church, and the private school, as well as of bursas and institutes, the older generation was able to transmit the language to the younger one. In this same mother tongue were preserved cultural achievements of the young generation that was brought up in Canada and which, although it had—in many instances—lost the knowledge of Ukrainian language, felt itself to be a member of its organized entity. In the daily struggle for their existence and preservation of cultural and ideal values this national entity did not weaken even though it had its separate individual, religious and ideological compositions. A great stimulus, in this work, came from the close ties with the cultural matrix of their ancestors. The greater were the struggles and repressions of their brethren in Ukraine, the more were the hearts and minds, of the Ukrainian entity in Canada, moved. This prompted them, en masse, to stop and think about their present lot and their future. But among these greater or lesser efforts the greatest sacrifice of all was the one the Ukrainian Canadians made in their loyal service to their country, Canada. This was not just a mere gesture for expressing their sentimental feelings. With it, also, was bound the working of a political expedience and of a healthy political mind behind which there followed a genuine Canadian patriotism. And if the true worth of the metal is proved through its being tempered by fire, then the test of gauging the patriotic feeling of its citizens can best be found when the country is at war with its enemy, or enemies, then Ukrainian Canadians have successfully passed this rigid test—as a shining example of national patriotism. This same patriotism helped to create new and longer roads to progress that are so prominently outlined in the third era of our history. In this way, too, they will continue to draw our attention in the oncoming pages of our work.

From the soul-tempering events the Ukrainians of Canada came out united and with an undeniable will to live the life of their cultural entity in the Canadian national mosaic.

The half-century period of travail, growth and development of Ukrainians in Canada attained full bloom and came to fruition.

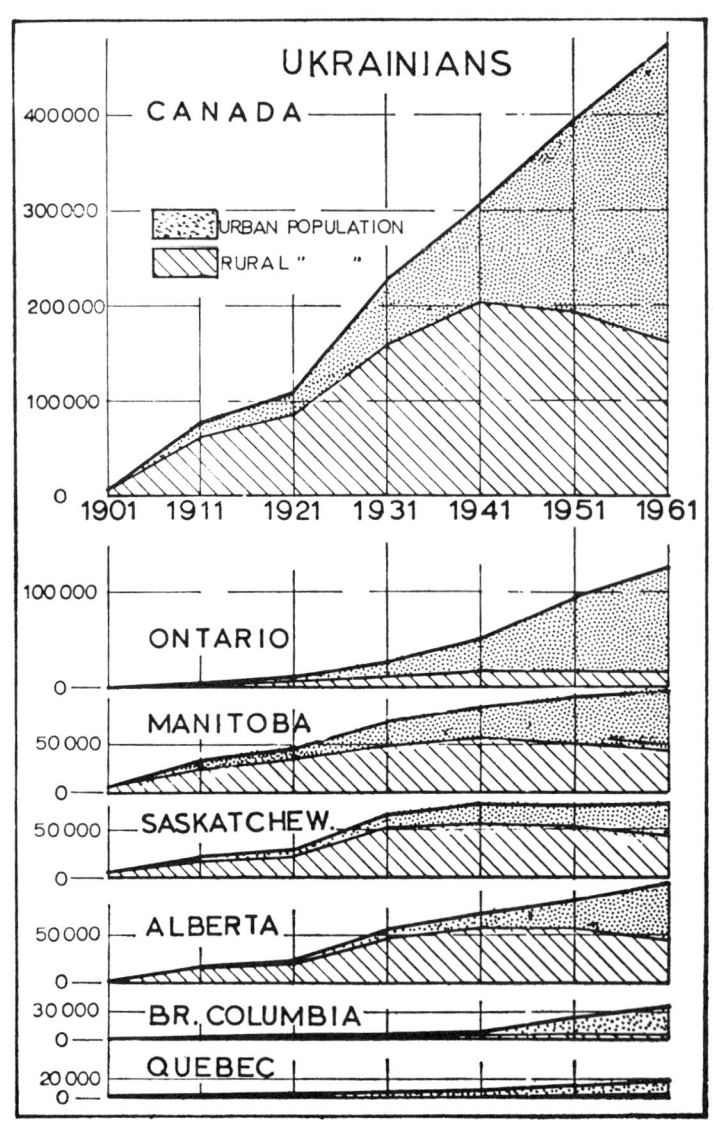

Rural and urban settlement and its changes in 1901-1961
(Chart courtesy of Prof. I. Tesla)

THE THIRD ERA

ERA OF CONSUMMATION

INTRODUCTION

Second World War created a fairly noticeable division between the second and third period of history of Ukrainian Canadians. This division is particularly noticeable in the organizational structure, psychological attitude and the consequences of the war, namely: in the new immigration as well as the further development of cultural life of Ukrainians in Canada.

The crowning of Ukrainian organizational life and the creation of Ukrainian representative body in Canada has been defined earlier. It unlocked a 50-year page of longing and struggle for the crystallization of united leadership for Ukrainians in Canada. The very fact of the formation of this representative body, in itself, creates a separate period in the Ukrainian community. In the wake of the outward form of the new creation, was also created a new psychology of Ukrainian Canadians, a renewed patriotism which became apparent both in regards to Canada and its war effort and to the country of origin—Ukraine.

War effort of every nation deepens its sentiments, clarifies its identification, removes secondary problems and brings to the forefront the ultimate aim of the citizens—self-preservation. It was no different with Canadian citizens.

The members of Canadian Parliament in session, September 9, 1939 voted overwhelmingly in favour of declaring war against Nazi Germany in order to halt further aggression and to guarantee peace in the world. Ukrainian Canadians adopted a positive attitude towards this historic decision of Canadian Parliament. This positive stand was a result of two principles—firstly, Canadian patriotism and, secondly, political as affecting the conditions in Europe. It was no secret that Ukrainians were not satisfied with the results of the First World War, whereby in the aftermath it was impossible to establish an independent and sovereign Ukrainian state. Generally, Ukrainians belonged to European revisionist group which hoped, as a consequence of war to change its fate. On the other hand, they were aware that the power which endeavoured to change the Versailles Treaties, was Hitler's Germany, which in "Mein Kampf" of its Fuehrer called the Slavs, including Ukrainians, inferior nations who were to become the slaves in the so-called New Europe under the leadership of Adolf Hitler. Therefore, patriotic and political considerations compelled the Ukrainian Canadians to embrace absolutely the war efforts on the basis of the democratic Western World.

UKRAINIAN EFFORTS IN THE SECOND WORLD WAR

The Ukrainian Canadian Committee marked a clear and definite course for the Ukrainian people to follow in regard to the war effort on behalf of their country. With its influential authority it saw to it that the declaration by the Ukrainians of their unconditional support towards the Canadian government's total war effort was not just a mere empty phrase. The outward documentation of this patriotic action was primarily to be seen in the enlistment of Ukrainian volunteers in Canadian armed forces. The most conservative figure as to the number of these volunteers in the Canadian army exceeds 35,000. There are some sources that raise this figure to 50,000 or more. Even if we take the lowest figure it will show that 14.4% of Ukrainian population were in uniform. These figures included both soldiers and officers. They served in Canada, overseas, in Hong Kong, [1]) Dieppe and other theatres of war. Everywhere was manifest a live Canadian patriotism for which the servicemen —Ukrainians shed their blood and paid with their lives. It is interesting to note that some provinces gave percentage wise, more than other ethnic groups—this was clearly stated by W. Wright, in "Geographical Journal" that, "More Ukrainians from Saskatchewan in proportion to population have joined up than any other nationality" [2]).

Jointly with the supreme sacrifices of the war effort activities were spurred in the civilian areas. In the four "Victory Loans" and in the purchase of "War Savings Certificates", Ukrainian-Canadians were taking more than merely an active part. In 15 districts in Alberta with predominantly Ukrainian population the loan quota was oversubscribed by 20.9%. In these districts the Fourth Victory Loan reached a million dollars. One district subscribed 198.6% of its quota. In Manitoba, in like districts with Ukrainian majority, 112% of the quota was reached. The same results obtained in Saskatchewan and Eastern Provinces. In Winnipeg itself, Ukrainians working in co-operation with Ukrainian Canadian Committee, during a 30-month period subscribed one-half million dollars in bonds and nearly another one-half million dollars in "War Savings Certificates" [3]).

Innumerable other cases could be cited. However, it must be borne in mind that the earnings of Ukrainian Canadians were average and below average while financial contributions were above average.

Included in the important page of the Canadian war effort during the Second World War is the war effort of Ukrainian women in the Canadian Red Cross and "War Service Clubs". Sewing, knitting, mending, collecting, and packing clothing for overseas shipment was practically a daily occupation during the long months of the war. These women took active part in the Canadian Red Cross campaigns and held teas with

---

[1]) It is known that the losses of servicemen Ukrainians in Hong Kong reached 34% of their total.
[2]) Proceedings of the Standing Committee on Immigration and Labour", The Senate of Canada, May 29th, 1946, p. 76.
[3]) "First Ukrainian Congress", Winnipeg, 1943, p. 47.

proceeds for the same purpose. They sold "War Saving Stamps and Certificates". They held special receptions for service personnel particularly those connected with Ukrainian religious holy days. They organized "Salvage Collections", assisted with the distribution of "Ration Coupon Books", etc. This devotion to the cause was recognized by an executive member of Canadian Red Cross in the statement, "Proportionately, the Ukrainians are contributing to Canada's war effort as well as people of British origin and decidedly more than any of the non-British groups" [4].

Toil, money and recruitment were the results of the intensified patriotism of Ukrainian-Canadians. This was apparent in every endeavour of Canadian war effort. This was a result of the regard for the country which during the two or three quarters of a century became the undisputed adopted fatherland. The second and third generation Ukrainian Canadians felt that they were a part of Canada.

The concern of Ukrainians in Canada during the Second World War was the concern of the war effort of the whole nation. It was radically different from that of the First World War when due to czarist inspired propaganda Ukrainians were accused of Austrianism and many innocent people suffered.

True, even during the Second World War, efforts were made to undermine the confidence of the government in so far as the Ukrainian Canadians were concerned. The lead was taken in this respect by "Pravda" when steps were taken to form a representative body—Ukrainian Canadian Committee. By now Ukrainian Canadians had many friends among the various ethnic groups as well as among the well informed people in government administrative circles who were well versed in Canadian and European political problems and who immediately recognized the calumnious writings of "Pravda". Besides articles in the English press there appeared a pamphlet written by Watson Kirkconnell, in which he also presented the aspirations of European Ukrainians to an independent and sovereign Ukraine [5]. Prof. G. W. Simpson prepared "Atlas of Ukraine" a historical presentation. Anti-Ukrainian propaganda was thus discouraged only to be renewed in 1943. At this time there appeared two pamphlets: Ukrainian—"Canada and Ukraine Have a Common Enemy" [6] and English—"This Is Our Land" [7]. It was also futile to try to accuse Ukrainian Canadians of pro Nazi sympathies. Events in Ukraine were proving to be best antidote to this. It is necessary to pay attention to these events in order to be able to better evaluate the political activities of Ukrainian Canadians as well as evaluate the third immigration of Ukrainians to Canada after the Second World War.

German conquest of Ukraine was felt with unprecedented terror. As soon as the border was crossed, a network of SD police stations were organized which, in fact, created the first concentration camps.

---

[4] Ibidem.
[5] "The Ukrainian Canadians and the War", Watson Kirkconnell, Oxford University Press, Toronto, 1940.
[6] By Association of United Ukrainian Canadians, Dominion Executive, Toronto, 1943, p. 158.

First mass arrests were begun in September, 1941. By now, executive members of the created government under the leadership of J. Stetsko in Lviv were arrested and their representatives in Cracow and Berlin interned. Among the first to be arrested were those who were suspected of being members of Ukrainian Nationalist Organization—so-called "Revolutionaries", underground movement, commonly known as "Banderivtsi". They were now under the active leadership of Mykola Lebed; actual leader, Stepan Bandera, was earlier interned by the Germans. Similar fate was met by the other wing of Ukrainian Nationalist Organization under the leadership of col. Andriy Melnyk when six months later near Kiev in February 1942, editors, journalists, writers and poets faced the firing squads without being charged for any crimes. This wanton destruction of leadership convinced the more "cautious" nationalists that Nazi policy was directed toward making Ukraine a colony and liquidating all vestiges of Ukrainian national life. This Nazi political extremism surprised many of the active Ukrainian optimists who were now seeing the change of Stalinism for equally cool destruction of all those who stood in the way of German imperial march eastward. The Nazi barbarism compelled the Ukrainians to organize defensive units. As we already mentioned the leading part was played by Ukrainian Nationalist Organization under the leadership of M. Lebed-Ruban, who constantly maintained that the political underground resistance should rely upon its own organized forces. About this time Polissia Sitch, under the leader Taras Bulba-Borovetz went underground. The Ukrainian Nationalist Organization (OUN) under col. A. Melnyk also took to underground activity. Basically, this is how Ukrainian Underground Army (UPA) was created which with OUN defended the civilian population against German plunder, deportation and executions, and led the liberation movement among the Ukrainian masses. Final agreement was reached between UPA and OUN in 1944 when liberation center was created—Ukrainian Supreme Liberation Council, in short UHVR. With the defense of civilian population the Germans increased the mass terror as well as physical liquidation of the masses. Barbarian crimes reached their peak in 1943, and continued until the end of the war.

To these events in Ukraine must also be added that the Ukrainian Government-in-exile, Ukrainian National Republic, in 1939-40 made the official unequivocal declaration of its support of western democracies in their fight against the German aggression. At this time Germany concluded the Non-Agression Pact with the Soviet Union. The above gives a brief resume of the reasons for the sympathies of Ukrainian political circles in Canada and Europe during the Second World War.

To complete the picture of the events of this period it is necessary to state the fact that millions of Ukrainian servicemen served in the Red Army and a few thousands in the Polish Army under General Anders. Both those armies were thrown into the fight against Nazi-Germany as a result of the conflict between Soviet Union and Germany. In sum total this was a gigantic contribution by the Ukrainians in Europe to the war effort in the Second World War, which without doubt had positive effects upon the patriotic feelings of Ukrainian Canadians.

---

[7]) "This is our Land"—Raymond Arthur Davis, Progress Books, Toronto, 1943.

ACTIVITIES OF UKRAINIAN-CANADIANS IN THE IMMIGRATION OF DISPLACED PERSONS TO CANADA

Long before the end of the war western nations, particularly Canada and United States of America, were concerned with the new problem which was created in consequence of the Second World War in Europe. In the history of mankind, no other war had created such a displacement of civilian population and war refugees as the Second World War. It is estimated that by the end of the war about 40 millions were uprooted from their homes. A great number of these were deported by the warring nations into different areas, while perhaps an equal number fled before the occupation by totalitarian regimes in fear of political oppression. In German captivity and in slave labour camps were thousands upon thousands of men and women. In the Nazi concentration camps were additional thousands. They were scattered all over occupied Europe with the majority being in German territories. This was the result of the imperial ambitions of Nazi-Germany and her allies.

Among the millions of homeless in Germany and Austria were about 5 million Ukrainians among whom were mostly the youth, both boys and girls. They were deported by the German administration as slave labour to work on the farms but primarily in the war industries. They all were compelled to carry their identification as "Ost" which signified the lowest category of humanity in the social status scale.

A great percentage of the displaced persons were former inmates of Nazi concentration camps. According to statistics, in the death-camps: Auschwitz, Mauthausen, Flossenburg, Gross-Rossen, Majdanek, Ukrainians comprised between 10% to 28% of inmates [1]. Among them were political-prisoners, captured underground workers, and those who were connected with sabotage activities. In the prisoner of war camps—stalags—were thousands of prisoners-of-war. Thousands of families tried to get into the displaced persons camps organized by United Nations Relief and Rehabilitation Administration (UNRRA). These were organized by the western nations with the aim of providing temporary physical amenities for the homeless and without means of subsistence. It soon became apparent that about 800,000 in the category of displaced persons refused to return to their countries of origin. Over one-half of these were Ukrainians. In 1945, the Canadian member of parliament, Anthony Hlynka, officially visited the displaced persons' camps and made an analysis of why this category of people refused to return to their native lands. He found that there were five principle reasons which he stated as follows:

"First, because they are democratically oriented people in the western sense and wish to lead a free life of a free person. They detest dictatorship in all its forms.

Second, because they are deeply religious people and within the communist controlled territories there is no freedom of religion,...

---

[1] M. H. Marunchak: "System of Nazi Concentration Camps and the Extermination Policy in Ukraine", Winnipeg, 1963, p. 89.

Third, because under communist dictatorship there is no personal, national, economic, nor political freedom.

Fourth, because there is the perpetual danger from NKVD (secret police).

Fifth, because those who were forcibly repatriated were not returned to their homes but were transported directly to Eastern USSR places like Siberia" [2]).

When in the process of forced repatriation, the displaced persons began to commit suicide rather than face new persecutions and tortures, the public opinion in the West began to recognize the logic of A. Hlynka's, M.P. reasoning. In principle, forced repartriation was stopped. The displaced persons were given the right to choose the country of their resettlement. Many of them turned their hopes of resettlement to Canada where many of them had relatives and friends, and knew people who immigrated there. Among the Ukrainians in Europe, Canada was the land of freedom and plenty. For this reason many of the displaced persons wished to emigrate there. Between the Ukrainian Canadians and their compatriots in Europe there was immediately established a live as well as psychological contact.

Immediately the Ukrainian Canadians took concrete steps to assist their fellow countrymen. In order that the relief to the displaced persons, in fact political refugees, be effectively administered Ukrainian Canadian Committee organized a truly charitable organization—Ukrainian Canadian Relief Fund. When the Senate Standing Committee on Labour and Immigration held its hearing in 1946, the Ukrainian Canadian Committee prepared a special brief [3]) dealing with the displaced persons. When the hearings [4]) were held on May 29th, 1946, the delegation from the Ukrainian Canadian Committee consisted of Rev. W. Kushnir, D.D., President; Rev. S. W. Sawchuk, Vice-president; Anthony Hlynka, M.P.,; J. R. Solomon, Manitoba M.L.A.; Flight Lietanant G.R.B. Panchuk, M.B.E.; and Eugene Dowhan, business man, Montreal, visited Ottawa. Extensive presentation of the brief was made by J. R. Solomon, followed by a lengthy statement by G.R.B. Panchuk. Further hearing of the Ukrainian Canadian Committee delegation was interrupted to hear another Ukrainian delegation from the pro-communist Association of Ukrainian Canadians, [5]) etc. These gentlemen appeared before the Senate Committee with one specific purpose in mind, namely; "...That the plea that Ukrainian "displaced persons" be admitted to Canada as "political refugees" be totally rejected,...". The Senate Standing Committee then continued to question the delegation headed by Rev. W. Kushnir. It should be emphasized that some members of this delegation visited Europe prior to this and had first hand knowledge about the situation.

The result was that on the same date, May 29th, 1946, when the Senate Standing Committee on Labour and Immigration was holding its hearings, under the chairmanship of Hon. James Murdock, P.C., the

---

[2]) Second All-Canadian Congress of Ukrainian Canadians, Toronto, 1946, p. 122-123.
[3]) Standing Committee of Immigration and Labour. The Senate of Canada, No. 2, Wednesday, 29th May, 1946, p. 57.
[4]) Ibid., p. 27.
[5]) Ibid., pp. 41-44.

Minister of Mines and Resources, Hon. J. A. Glen, whose department included immigration, made the announcement in Parliament that the following categories of immigrants will be admitted to Canada; "Father or mother, unmarried son or daughter age 18 or over, unmarried brother or sister, orphaned male or female cousin under the age of 16 years of a resident of Canada who was legally admitted and who is financially able to accept and take care of such a relative" [6].

This Order-in-Council was the first breakthrough in the change of Canadian immigration policy after the Second World War. Ukrainian Canadians were making representations to the government that this policy should be broadened. In September, 1946, the Ukrainian Canadian Committee sent another memorandum to the Canadian Government, under the heading, "Resettlement of Displaced Persons". This memorandum underlined the need to assist UNRRA in the resettlement of some 800,000 displaced persons found in the camps in Europe:

"As far as Canada is concerned,... we read in this memorandum, 300,000 of Ukrainians displaced persons could be easily absorbed by Canada, resulting in a wise and sound economic venture. We strongly feel that a substantial number of the prospective immigrants on their arrival in Canada will be taken care of by the Canadians of Ukrainian origin, because of friendship and family relations" [8].

The organization comprising the Ukrainian Canadian Committee to impress the importance of the resettlement of displaced persons in Europe made representations individually. Ukrainian Catholic Council of Canada presented a separate brief to the Minister of Mines and Natural Resources, which read, in part, as follows:

"We cannot permit hundreds of thousands of refugees in Europe to find themselves virtually on an empty crossroad, with no assistance and deprived of all essential resources of life. To these people who have been driven out of their native villages and towns and who are to be stranded without the primary necessities of life, must be given food and assistance, in the name of Christian charity and pure humanity" [9].

Just as the Ukrainian Canadian Committee persevered in presenting to the Canadian Government the need to resettle the new immigrants, the Ukrainian Canadian Relief Fund was engaged in Europe with immediate material and moral assistance to the people in the camps.

---

[6] Order-in-Council No. 2071, 28th May, 1946.

[7] Memorandum by Ukrainian Canadian Committee Representing Canadian Citizens of Ukrainian Origin to The Right Honourable W. L. MacKenzie King, Prime Minister, and to the Government of Canada, September, 1946.

[8] The same memorandum was mailed to: "The Economic and Social Council and General Assembly of United Nations, also to those who by the Grace of God or by the will of the people have the destiny of mankind in their hands". September, 1946.

[9] "Memorandum by the Ukrainian Catholic Council of Canada to Honourable J. L. Glen, Minister of Mines and Natural Resources in the Canadian Government", October, 1946.

UKRAINIAN CANADIAN RELIEF FUND

In the fall of 1944 the Ukrainian Canadian Relief Fund was organized. Although information about the displaced persons and refugees was scarce the Relief Fund was making its preparations. The main liaison was maintained through Ukrainian Canadian Servicemen's Association, 218 Sussex Garden, London, Eng. This was a service center for Ukrainian Canadian service personnel. Those, who served on the continent in their off duty hours tried to make contacts with displaced persons and refugees in Western Europe. Usually, they either informed the Ukrainian Canadian Committee directly or through the Ukrainian Servicemens' Association when on leave in England. As the Allied Forces moved eastward liberating occupied countries it was possible for the Ukrainian Canadian servicemen to locate Ukrainians who were brought to those countries as "forced labour", as well as meet some Ukrainians who resided in these countries prior to the outbreak of World War II. The Ukrainian Canadian servicemen thus provided information about Ukrainians in Western Europe not only to the Ukrainian Canadian Committee but also to Ukrainian Congress Committee of America.

The main aim of the Fund was the preparation of plans for money raising campaigns. There was intense interest on the part of Ukrainian Canadians to help their countrymen. Although the Fund was registered under The War Charities Act, the only charitable organizations which were permitted on the continent were those which provided amenities to the service personnel. Their movements were controlled by the military. There was no room for the civilian organizations. Thus historically the work of Ukrainian Canadian Relief Fund may be divided into two periods: 1945-1951 and then 1951-1962.

The first public appeal by the Ukrainian Canadian Relief Fund was made in February, 1945. Due to the fact that the war was far from being won it was impossible to make any direct references to sufferings of the people due to maltreatment by the Soviet regime of the Ukrainians. The Soviets were allies yet it was becoming evident that there will be thousands upon thousands of "forced labour, refugees, political prisoners etc., of all ethnic groups who will refuse to return, after the war's end, to live under the Soviet regime as they were already emerging and greatly extended to what they were before the war. The campaign was conducted primarily by Women's Section of Ukrainian Canadian Committee. By October 18, 1945 the campaign reached the sum of $45,447.62 and by January 31, $62,210.71. With the end of the war in Europe, it was possible to assess the atrocities perpetrated by the Germans during their occupation and exploitation of Western Europe but at the same time, Western Allies in particular, began to realize the scope of the task which faced them with the problem of at first repatriating and then resettling all the displaced persons from Eastern Europe who refused to live under Communist regime. At first these refusals were treated with suspicion. But once the Western Allies realized the consequences of repatriation this was stopped despite the protests from the Soviet Union. In Canada it became obviously clear to Ukrainian Canadians that they will be able to use all monies collected in order to assist in temporary needs and the resettlement of all possible fellow countrymen who were now in the free part of Europe. At Christmas the slogan was, "Let us carol for refugee Ukraine".

With the end of the war in Europe, in June, 1945 the executive of Ukrainian Canadian Relief Fund decided to take over the Ukrainian Canadian Servicemen's Association Club, which was financed by the Ukrainian Canadian Committee, and convert it into Central Ukrainian Relief Bureau. In September-October all the formalities were completed and the bureau began to function with the assistance of the Ukrainian Canadian service personnel who were waiting for repatriation. At the same time there was full agreement for joint co-operation between The Ukrainian Canadian Relief Fund and the United Ukrainian American Relief Committee Inc. The Bureau was to be financed by both organizations. For the time being it was to be the office in Great Britain with its activities extending into the various occupation zones of Germany and Austria. Full co-operation was extended by the Canadian Red Cross and CARE (Cooperative for American Relief Everywhere Inc.). The activities of the Fund became: direct aid in form of food, location of relations of refugees, personal protection against deportations, supplied newspapers and books, assisting in immigration particularly securing sponsors for families wishing to immigrate to Canada.

In this respect a great contribution was made by Anthony Hlynka, M.P., who after his trip to Europe, never failed to stress the position of refugees [1] and the help they needed. He initiated a special resettlement fund for which he devoted a great deal of time in collecting money for it. This fund was to be used for people who did not come within the scope of care provided by UNRRA and later PC/IRO (Preparatory Commission for International Refugee Organization). For his interest in the plight of the refugees, A. Hlynka soon gained the recognition as being the "guardian of third immigration to Canada".

---

[1] During 1946 and 1947 he spoke seven times in the House of Commons in defence of displaced persons and the urgency to have them admitted to Canada. See: "Speeches of Mr. Anthony Hlynka, member for Vegreville on Immigration, House of Commons Debates", Official Report, delivered in the House of Commons on Friday, July 11, 1947.

MISSION OF UKRAINIAN CANADIAN RELIEF FUND IN THE BRITISH ZONE OF GERMANY

Central Ukrainian Relief Bureau which had its office in London, during 1947 turned most of its activities towards the occupied zones of Germany. In the British Zone the office was first located at Lemgo, the head office of British PW/DP Division for the British Zone; later, when a relief organization was formed, the office was located at Bielefeld. The Canadian Relief Mission to Ukrainian Refugees was formed in 1936 and functioned until 1951, when IRO was liquidated. An office was still maintained in London to act as liaison between Canadian and British offices.

By 1948 the Fund collected over $200,000.00 into which sum is included the $30,000.00 resettlement fund collected by A. Hlynka, M.P. Besides extending material aid in food, clothing, and money, legal and moral aid was given. Ukrainian immigrant, away from his native land, without legal aid was helpless. Therefore, in Europe, the appearance of representatives of Ukrainian Canadians was greatly welcomed. They were able to assist in solving the problems facing the people in camps, UNRRA abuses, and protection from Communist efforts for repatriation.

The Fund Mission in the British Zone of Germany carried a very extensive welfare programme taking advantage of funds offered by IRO and some facilities offered by German economy. The value of food, clothing and medical supplies amounted to $145,000.00 while over $13,000.00 was distributed in cash, and books and newspapers to the value of $6,000.00, a grand total of $165,198.01.

The relief and welfare work of the Fund, to the end of 1951, amounted to $386,116,27. If one is to take into consideration the direct private shipments of parcels made to families in Europe by relatives, and branches of Ukrainian Canadian Committee, the sum total of the value of assistance given will be over one-half million dollars.

By 1950 the Ukrainians in Europe after Second World War were 90% resettled through the effort of IRO, and other international and national organizations. They were sent to all countries accepting immigrants, including Canada. The care and welfare of those who could not qualify for immigration (due to physical qualifications) was left in the hands of the German government. The "hard core" as these people were usually referred to, lost all legal protection and material assistance not only from the IRO but also from other transoceanic charitable organizations. The Ukrainian Canadian Relief Fund was also compelled to change the form and manner of its work. The European mission was liquidated. Instead, it started to organize the "patron" activity. The Fund arranged in Canada with individual branches of organizations and separate families undertook to care for the sick in hospitals, kindergartens and schools as well as individual needy families. The patron activity was successful both morally and materially. On the one hand there was the constant assurance of aid and security while on the other hand there was a rise in the morale. In 1954 and 1955 the Ukrainian Canadian Relief Fund had patrons for 30 kindergartens and schools in the British Zone of Germany.

There was another consequence of activity of the Relief Fund. The Fund did not assist only the "hard core" of refugees in Europe but, in accordance with the constitution, it began to organize and co-ordinate welfare work among Ukrainians in Canada. In larger centers of Ukrainian population of Canada—Fort William, Montreal, Edmonton, Toronto there were organized branches of the Relief Fund. Through its search for missing persons, the Relief Fund reunited about 20,000 families. The Fund co-operated with Ukrainian churches and Canadian welfare organizations. With the 1960's modern American-Canadian methods were adopted such as "social work" and "group work". There now is in existence Social Welfare Service of Ukrainian Canadians with its office in Winnipeg. The Sixth Ukrainian Congress of the Ukrainian Canadian Committee approved this constitutional change. Despite the activities of the Fund in Canada, its greatest contribution remains the welfare and the resettlement of tens of thousands of post World War II Ukrainians to Canada who enriched the Ukrainian Canadian life in Canada.

The direction of activities of the mission in Europe was under the guidance of the executive of Ukrainian Canadian Relief Fund. They set the policy for the mission in so far as welfare and resettlement opportunities were concerned. The executive of Ukrainian Canadian Relief Fund consisted of members who also were members of the executive of Ukrainian Canadian Committee. The members of the executive of the Fund were: Dr. W. Kushnir, W. Kossar, J. W. Arsenych, A. Malofie, S. Chwaliboga, Maria Dyma, Olha Woycenko, J. Gulay, Rev. S. W. Sawchuk, Rev. I. Shpytkowsky, A. Zaharychuk, E. Tarnowecky, and M. Lazechko. Executive secretary of the Fund was Anna Mandryka, who was equally responsible for the many detailed and extensive reports of the activities of the Fund. In London and later, on the continent, the following were associated with the Bureau. In the first place it must not be overlooked that the initial efforts were made voluntarily by Ukrainian Canadian service personnel under G.R.B. Panchuk. When the Canadians were being returned to Canada for discharge the office was left under S. Frolick with local London people assisting, in particular, Danylo Skoropadsky and V. Korostovets. The original mission organized in Canada which went as such overseas in August 1947 was composed of Mr. and Mrs. G.R.B. Panchuk, Ann Crapleve and A. J. Yaremovich. At first Mr. and Mrs. G.R.B. Panchuk were in London, while Ann Crapleve was in the American Zone, Germany and A. J. Yaremovich went to British Zone, Germany. When the United Ukrainian American Relief Committee Inc. under direction of Walter Galan became active in the American Zone, Germany, the activities of the mission were confined to the British Zone, Germany. In 1949 Mr. and Mrs. S. Wasylyshyn and Ann Crapleve remained the three members of the mission until it was withdrawn. Of all the members of the mission Ann Crapleve was the sole member who continued with the mission from the start of its activities in Europe.

If one is to be permitted to compare the greater with the lesser, the work of the Fund after Second World War may be compared with the settlement activities of the Welfare Organization of St. Rafael which assisted the second immigration to Canada. Both organizations had as their aim to assist the Ukrainians to immigrate to Canada and assist in their establishment. There are, however, differences in their organization-structure, initiative and the scope of activities. The Fund was organized on the same principle as the Ukrainian Canadian Committee whereby it became the organization of all Ukrainian Canadians. It enjoyed the full support of Ukrainian churches and lay organizations of Canada with the exception of those which were communist oriented. The Fund was organized exclusively by Ukrainian Canadians without any assistance from the European Ukrainian leaders. The same was the case after the First World War. The Fund also shows the fact that Ukrainian Canadians were already solidly established in Canada and were doing their work as Canadian citizens. Furthermore, the activities of Ukrainian Canadians are not limited to "local" matters exclusively, but are transferred to European continent, where the authority of Ukrainian Canadians initiates and inspires the activities they undertake and which in the past would have been the prerogative of the leaders of "Old Country". True, this change in the activities may be explained as due to the exceptional political situation in Ukraine. Be as it may, the historical paradox is that, temporarily, the Ukrainian immigration became the spokesman for the whole Ukrainian nation.

Through a long process the Ukrainians in Canada advanced slowly from the lowly steps of the social and political ladder; at first lacking in knowledge of the English language, they were unable to converse with their non-Ukrainian neighbours, nor deal with government representatives. However, the next 50 years of freedom and democratic rule in Canada gave the Ukrainian settlers an opportunity to achieve the maximum: they spoke in the name of freedom and democracy; they rose in defence of their fellow countrymen in Europe; they strongly defended the rights of their kinsmen and this was recorded in history not only as a defence by an ethnic group in Canada but they spoke on behalf of all those who sought freedom in this country.

SOCIAL STRUCTURE OF THIRD IMMIGRATION

The third immigration to Canada, after the end of Second World War, was composed primarily of displaced persons who considered themselves to be political emigrees. There is no detailed analysis of the social composition of the immigration. But according to the information based on the results given by those who studied the question, the following may be stated: about 50%, in some cases more, stated that they were farmers (in fact this percentage was much smaller—many immigrants gave their occupation as farmers because this type of immigrant was in greatest demand on the American continent); about 25% were craftsmen; 6% were engineers, mechanics, and technicians; 6% were teachers; 2% were artists, musicians, and singers; about 300 were doctors and dentists; about 300 were university professors, about 600 were clergymen among those, a few bishops [1].

As we stated before, all of them refused to return to the territories from which they came because of the occupation of those territories by the Soviet armies and the political situation thus created there. Besides the displaced persons, that is political prisoners, prisoners of war and "forced" labour, there were many refugees who fled their native land which was occupied by the Soviet regime. The composition of the third immigration differed greatly from that of the first and second immigration to Canada. There is an additional difference between the third immigration and the first and second immigration of Ukrainians to Canada. The first immigration to Canada was mainly of people from Galicia and Bukovina. The second immigration was exclusively from these territories. The third immigration is composed of people from all the territories of Ukraine—western, central and eastern. For this reason some term the third immigration as united Ukrainian immigration. Within the ranks of third immigration are also those who left their native land during or after the First World War and between the wars lived in Central Europe. Their inclusion made the third immigration more politically conscious. The political consciousness lies in the fact that generally the third immigration did not recognize the political regime in Ukraine and regarded it as an occupational regime. Furthermore, many of the members fought against the regime as they fought against the Nazi-German occupation. Sections of already mentioned Ukrainian Underground Army, with the withdrawal of Germany armed forces from Ukraine, began fighting the bolshevik regime. They sent their representatives out of the country with the hope that they would popularize their struggle and enlist the support of western European nations. In fact, the third immigration felt more like political army created by the uprising and liberation processes in Ukraine. Some members of this immigration for a time felt it politically inadvisable to emigrate from Europe to the American continent, believing in the inevitability of political conflict between the West and East. However, the gradual stabilization of political relations in Europe convinced the most determined revisionists of the necessity of resettlement and normali-

---

[1] "Ukrainian Refugees" by M. I. Mandryka, Winnipeg, Man., 1946.

zation of family life. In 1947 IRO began its resettlement programme. In the succeeding years thousands of new immigrants came to Canada.

Accordinng to the statistics released by Department of Citizenship and Immigration in the period from 1940 to 1946 only 315 persons arrived in Canada as immigrants. The statistics for subsequent years are as follows: [2])

1947	2,081	1957	530
1948	10,041	1958	405
1949	6,602	1959	346
1950	3,815	1960	349
1951	6,949	1961	165
1952	2,859	1962	170
1953	987	1963	215
1954	724	1964	202
1955	560	1965	283
1956	578		

From the above statistics it is obvious that the greatest numbers of Ukrainian immigrants came to Canada in the years 1948 and 1949. With the liquidation of the immigration activities of IRO in 1951-1952 there was an increase in Ukrainian immigration but it soon dropped very rapidly and continued to decline. This may be explained by the fact that the reserve of the displaced persons was exhausted. Many of them emigrated to U.S.A. and other countries while the borders of Ukrainian territories were hermetically sealed against any emigration. Only in the 1960's, as a result of relaxation of immigration laws of U.S.S.R., was it possible to emigrate to Canada, for mothers advanced in years and under age children of parents who were in Canada. Nevertheless, these are rare cases. The immigration laws of Poland are more favorable. Since the Second World War, there remain in Poland about 300,000 Ukrainians. It is possible for some of them to come to settle in Canada, occasionally whole families. There has been resettlement of Ukrainians from Great Britain, Brazil, Venezuela and even Australia.

Official statistics show that immigration of Ukrainians to Canada in the post-war years, 1946 to 1961 numbered 37,132 persons. In fact this figure is much below the actual number of Ukrainians who immigrated to Canada. The discrepancy lies in the fact that IRO and other immigration authorities did not recognize the ethnic origin of the immigrants but classified them according to their citizenship. Thus many Ukrainians who were Polish citizens prior to 1939 were classified as Poles. The same applied to Ukrainians from Carpathian Ukraine. Since this part of Czecho-Slovakia prior to 1939, the Ukrainians were classified as Czechs. The Ukrainians from Bukovina were classified as Ro manians, since Bukovina was under Ro manian regime. Then there is the position of those Ukrainians who claimed that they were "stateless". Here, the procedures of recording varied. Where the person demanded that his ethnic origin be given, some IRO officials were willing to record them as "Ukrainians" in their documents. In fact as far as records of Ukrainian immigrants to Canada during the period after the Second World War is very much the same as that applied to the earlier immigrations.

---

[2]) Annual Reports, Department of Citizenship and Immigration, Ottawa.

They came to Canada under various national citizenships, which ignored their ethnic origin. Taking into consideration the official statistics and the discrepancies it is estimated that the third immigration to Canada of Ukrainians was over 40,000 persons.

A greater number of these immigrants settled in the cities. A great many of them had to complete their one year of employment in the field for which they were brought to Canada, as farm, sugarbeet, pulp and paper labour before they were able to emigrate to the cities. Most of them, as already mentioned, were skilled craftsmen from home, while others had retraining in the camps in Europe. Among the immigrants there was a reasonable number of intellectuals with average and advanced education. There were also among them many highly qualified professional men—teachers, doctors, economists, engineers, lawyers, university lecturers, etc. Some of these were eligible for immediate employment in their professions while others had to take refresher courses in order to qualify. Within the ranks of the third immigration was the actual cultural elite—poets, writers, painters and journalists. If one is to take into consideration that there were qualified farmers and craftsmen the professional level of the third immigration was equal in scope. In a majority of cases besides their known trades, crafts and professions the third immigration generally had a knowledge of the language of the countries in which they settled. It was much easier for them to integrate into the life of the community.Here was another great difference between the third immigration and the previous two earlier immigrations. This immigration also brought a deep and abiding love for Ukraine, in many instances as a result of actual opposition to the various occupational regimes in Ukraine.

The political economic attitudes of the three immigrations may be briefly stated as follows: the leaders of the first immigration were socialistically inclined while the masses were intensely individualistic; the second immigration's attitude was national-revisionist with very limited socialistic views; the third immigration was completely anticommunist.

If one was to compare the third immigration with the other two, occupationally, then the first was totally of rural origin, the second was composed of various origins but the rural predominated, whereas the third immigration was by far mostly of urban origin.

These various features of the new immigration had their effects on religious, cultural, economic, professional and political life of Ukrainians in Canada. The results of these influences will be taken up in the succeeding chapters of this work.

DISTRIBUTION OF UKRAINIANS IN THIRD ERA

In preparation of demographic studies of Ukrainians in Canada in the third period use is being made of the statistics prepared by Dominion Bureau of Statistics for the years 1941, 1951, and 1961.

The 1961 census shows that there were in Canada, 473,337 persons of Ukrainian origin. This figure is not necessarily authentic as there were 13,000 persons who stated that their mother tongue was Ukrainian but were included under Russians, Austrians etc. It is evident that they gave their ethnic origin, the country from which they came to Canada originally. However, in 1971 Canadian census indicated that the actual number of Canadians of Ukrainian descent numbered at 580,660. 1981 census will enhance this number close to 600,000.

In the second period of Ukrainian history in Canada it was pointed out that there was a tendency to move from the farms to the cities. This tendency, started during the second period, and continues even in the present time, having become more obvious with the third immigration than the second one. With this trend growing, the Ukrainian Canadian population in the Prairie Provinces is declining. This is most noticeable in Saskatchewan, where in 1941 there were 79.8 thousand while in 1961 this figure was 78.9 thousand. There is a smaller decline in Manitoba although, seemingly, there is an increase from 89.8 thousand in 1941 to 105.4 thousand in 1961 but in proportion to the total Ukrainian Canadian population in Canada there is a loss. In 1941 Manitoba population was 29.4% of total while in 1961, 22.3%. Even Alberta, which among the prairie provinces, shows the greatest increase in Ukrainian Canadian population, is on the decline when taken in proportion to the total Ukrainian Canadian population. Despite the decrease in the Ukrainian Canadian population in the three prairie provinces, still over 60% of Ukrainian Canadians live in the Prairie provinces. Out of 473.3 thousand Ukrainians, in 1961, 290.2 thousand lived in the provinces in question. When the Ukrainian Canadian population is decreasing in the agricultural provinces there is an increase in the industrial provinces such as Ontario, British Columbia, and even Quebec. The greatest rate of growth is shown by Ontario where in 1941 the percentage of total population was 17.7% and in 1961 this rose to 27.2%. This increase in the growth of Ukrainian Canadian population in Ontario becomes more noteworthy when one takes into consideration the growth of general population of Ontario in percent as compared with the total Canadian growth during the last 40 years. The Ontario population was 33% of the total; in 1971 it was 34% whereas the Ukrainian population was only 7.8% of total while Ukrainian Canadian population in 1961 was 27.2%.

At the same time, it must be admitted that there is a constant drift of Canadian population from the rural to urban centres. If comparison is to be made with the Ukrainian Canadian shift of population from rural to urban centres this percentage will compare unfavorably with the

DISTRIBUTION OF UKRAINIANS IN THIRD ERA

Canadian average. This view is confirmed by W. E. Kalbach, who in his research states: [1]

"By comparing changes in the distribution of Ukrainians with corresponding changes in distribution of total population it can be seen that the Ukrainians have been affected to a greater degree by these regional shifts than the general population."

The demographic changes may be best illustrated by the tables given below based upon government statistics as given by Dominion Bureau of Statistics for the years 1941, 1951 and 1961:

Percentage to total Ukrainian population in Canada

	1941		1951		1961	
		1,000		1,000		1,000
West:						
Manitoba	89.8	29.4	98.7	25.0	105.4	22.3
Alberta	71.8	23.5	87.0	22.1	105.9	22.4
Saskatchewan	79.8	26.1	78.4	19.6	78.9	16.6
East:						
Ontario	48.2	17.7	93.6	23.6	127.9	27.2
British Col.	7.6	2.5	22.6	5.7	35.6	7.5
Quebec	8.0	2.6	12.9	3.3	16.6	3.4
Others	.7	.2	1.5	.5	3.0	.6
	305.9	100.0	395.1	100.0	473.3	100.0

It is interesting to note some statistics dealing with the population of Ukrainian men and women. From beginning of Ukrainian immigration to Canada there were more men than women. This is frequently defined that men are more aggressive and emigrated first to settle in the colony before the women followed. In 1961 for every 1,000 Ukrainian women there were 1087 men—the Canadian proportion was 1,000 to 1,022; In 1911 the Ukrainian ratio was 1,000 : 1,349 (Canadian—1,000 : 1,129). In this respect among the Ukrainians there is a reduction of the ratio. One of the reasons for the disparity is that for some of the families it has been impossible to reunite since immigration from Ukraine is rigidly controlled. However, in some instances families are reunited after a 20 year separation. Also contributing to this ratio are the veterans who came to Canada as single men.

In the employable age of Canadians the Ukrainians in the ages 25 to 44 years have higher percentage then the general Canadian ratio, being 29.9 to 26.7. In the 45 to 64 years category the proportion is 18.9 to 17.4 general Canadian. Also the employable coefficient for Ukrainians is higher then the general Canadian. This is confirmed by W. E. Kalbach, who on the basis of his research states:

"In comparing Ukrainians with total Canadians over 15 years of age

---

[1] Some Demographic Aspects of Ukrainian Population in Canada by Warren E. Kalbach, "Slavs in Canada", vol. 1, Edmonton, 1966.
[2] Ibidem.

both males and females have larger proportions employed in a job week prior to the census (1961-M.H.M.) than do all male and female Canadians" [2]).

In the third period the Ukrainians are already engaged in all occupations of Canadian economy. They, however, predominate in agriculture and labour fields.

There remains to be examined the Ukrainian urban population and its proportion to the total poulation. For better illustration statistics are given for major urban centres, some for 1951 and all for 1961. 1961 ratios are given as compared with Ukrainian population.

City	1951	1961	% Ukrainian population	Total population
Manitoba:				
Winnipeg		36,000	13.6	
Metropolitan Win.	41,437	53,918	11.3	475,989
Brandon	1,573	2,119	7.5	28,166
Dauphin		2,232	30.3	7,374
Portage la Prairie		1,238	10.0	12,388
Selkirk		1,227	14.3	8,576
Flin Flon		1,104	9.9	11,104
Saskatchewan				
Saskatoon	4,116	9,072	9.5	95,526
Regina	2,702	5,741	5.1	112,141
Yorkton		2,820	28.2	9,995
Prince Albert		2,260	9.4	24,168
Moose Jaw		1,797	5.4	33,206
Canora		1,236	58.4	2,117
Alberta				
Edmonton		32,500	7.5	
Metro. Edmonton		38,164	11.3	337,568
Calgary	3,302	8,033	2.9	279,062
Vegreville		1,518	52.2	2,908
Lethbridge		1,358	3.8	35,454
Red Deer		634	3.2	19,612
British Columbia				
Metro. Vancouver		18,712	2.3	790,165
Vernon		835	8.1	10,250
EASTERN PROVINCES:				
Ontario				
Metro. Toronto		46,650	2.6	1,824,481
Metro. Hamilton	7,088	10,931	2.8	395,184
Metro. Windsor	5,019	5,508	2.8	193,365
St. Catherines	1,599	4,742	5.0	95,577
Sudbury		4,942	4.5	110,694
Kitchner-Waterloo	1,616	2,163	1.4	154,864
Oshawa		3,982	4.9	80,918
Ottawa	1,722	2,985	.7	429,750
Pt. Arthur-Ft. Wm.	7,760	9,609	10.3	93,251
London		1,834	1.1	181,283
Welland		1,693	4.7	36,079
Sault Ste. Marie		1,661	2.8	58,460

DISTRIBUTION OF UKRAINIANS IN THIRD ERA

Brantford		1,295	2.3	56,741
Kenora		1,198	11.0	10,904
Fort Frances		1,171	12.4	9,481
Niagara Falls		1,079	2.0	54,649
Timmins		911	2.3	40,121
Sarnia		782	1.3	61,293
Quebec				
Metro. Montreal	11,154	14,519	0.7	2,109,509
Nova Scotia				
Sydney-Glace Bay		847	0.8	106,144

From the above statistics it is evident that Winnipeg and Metropolitan Winnipeg still remains the most heavily Ukrainian populated urban centre. The nearest competitor in Western Canada is Edmonton and in Eastern Canada Toronto. But both have a large gap to overcome. The youngest competitor is Toronto, which came upon the scene only during the second period but its growth has been so rapid that in the organizational and cultural aspects it is competing seriously with Winnipeg. There are two factors which determine Toronto's dynamism. In the first place about 80% of the third immigration settled in Toronto and the immediate area. With the new arrivals the local population was stimulated to activity and encouraged the other urban centres like Hamilton, Oshawa, St. Catherines to become active. Even Montreal was affected by this. On the other hand Winnipeg is a large Ukrainian island with no competition in the immediate vicinity. Outside Winnipeg, the two largest centres Brandon and Dauphin each have a Ukrainian population barely exceeding 2000. But the strength of Winnipeg lies in the fact that it is in the heart of Ukrainian agricultural community which forms a stable base as well as that it has a historical meaning to all Ukrainians in Canada.

Edmonton has made noteworthy progress but in the cultural field it has been moderately conservative in its aspirations. There have been no sudden spurts but neither has there been any recession. The history of Saskatoon has been varied. Earlier, it played an important role in the Ukrainian Canadian cultural life but since the Second World War its part has been strictly local although progressive. There is no doubt that with the movement of population from Saskatchewan both east and west affected the cultural activities of Saskatoon. Both Port Arthur and Fort William maintain their cultural status and still serve as a gateway from East to West and vice versa. In eastern Canada, Sudbury and Windsor are competing for recognition, while in western Canada, Metropolitan Vancouver is growing in importance with a population of 20,000 Ukrainians. Singular role is played by the Ukrainians in Montreal who form the only major Ukrainian community in French environment. The biggest problem in this respect is that its percentage population to the total is only .8% and in Metropolitan Montreal only .7%. The same problem is faced in Ottawa where the Ukrainians comprise only .9% in respect to the total population. There are excellent opportunities for progress in Calgary and Regina; both of these compete on friendly bases with the Ukrainians in their respective capitals,—Edmonton and Saskatoon.

Brandon, Manitoba, was already a well established Ukrainian community. Kitchener, Ontario, is making every effort to establish a viable centre. Perhaps, the youngest among these is Jasper Place, a suburb of Edmonton which has been booming, (1951—726 Ukrainians and in 1961 —2,437.

In general, the 18 urban centres, already mentioned, and each having at least 2,110 population are assured of further Ukrainian cultural development. Among them the major positions are occupied by Winnipeg, Toronto, Edmonton, Vancouver and Montreal. In the 10,000 population class is Hamilton, followed by Fort William-Port Arthur, Saskatoon, and Calgary. The cities which are in process of expanding are Regina, Windsor, Sudbury, St. Catherines. In the two-thousand class in the first place is Oshawa, followed by Ottawa, Yorkton, Prince Albert, Dauphin, Kitchener-Waterloo and Brandon. Among these is Canora, Saskatchewan, in which the population of Ukrainian community is 58.4% of the total population.

Although over one-half of the urban centres are in Eastern Canada; however, regardless whether they are in Eastern or Western Canada, every centre has active Ukrainian cultural and religious organizations which have a direct influence on the community generally.

In the civic field they take an active part as Canadian citizens. It is no surprise to meet in these centres mayors, aldermen and school trustees who are of Ukrainian descent. They also play an active part in the provincial and federal fields.

Out of the 290,000 Ukrainians in the prairie provinces 52% live in urban centres, that is 151,000, while on the farms are 48% or 139,000. Of the Ukrainian population in Ontario, Nova Scotia and British Columbia almost 80% live in urban centres. The highest percentage of Ukrainians in Manitoba, 11.4 % live in cities, in the second place is Saskatchewan with 8.5% and Alberta third with 7.9%. In proportion to the total population Ukrainians comprise 2.6%, this coefficient when compared with the previous census fell by 2/10%. This can be explained by the fact that there was very little immigration from other countries. Increase in Ukrainian population in Canada is now dependent exclusively upon natural growth. This may be seen from the following data: in 1951 69.5% of Ukrainian population were Canadian born, in 1961, 76.9% and in 1967 about 80%. When comparison is made with other ethnic groups then in the first place are the French with 98% Canadian born, the Anglo-Saxons with 86% and the Ukrainians third. During the last decades Ukrainians were in the fourth place as to total population only to be exceeded by the Anglo-Saxons, French and Germans. Since there are no prospects for any major Ukrainian immigration to Canada there is little doubt that the Ukrainians will lose their fourth place to some other ethnic group. The nearest in numbers of population to the Ukrainians are the Italians and Dutch who have been arriving in Canada in ever increasing numbers.

ACHIEVEMENTS AND INTEGRATION

In the history of second period emphasis was placed on the achievements of Ukrainians in the agricultural field as well as the contribution made by Ukrainian agronomists provincially and federally. The farmers continue with their achievements in the third period as well. In Manitoba itself there were two champions; John Palidvor, Hazelridge, was Canadian barley champion in 1949, and William Disiatnyk, Sandy Lake, won the barley championship in 1951. There were grain champions in other provinces as well.

It is interesting to emphasize that on the less productive lands, Ukrainians are turning to mixed farming, raising beef cattle and carrying on dairying. This gives rise in particular to the dairy industry in Manitoba. Mixed farming offers an opportunity to make better living on the submarginal lands. With the acquisition of more land, land estates are being created.

One more observation may be made; with the mechanization of farming, the farmers are able to live in the neighboring cities or towns and drive out to the farm to work during the seasons.

Due to increase in the size of farm land holdings, the numbers of Ukrainian farmers on the farms have been decreasing. In 1951 there were 34,000 farmers but in 1961 there were only 25,000. On the other hand the average size of the farm is now about 300 acres but 500-600 acre farms are becoming more common.

There is an increased interest in fruit-culture. In Manitoba, among the leading research agronomists in the field of fruit-culture are: Myhkaylo Borowsky, Winnipeg, Mykola Pankiw, Dufrost. Some of them have highly developed apiaries.

There is a constant improvement in the farming methods in Canada. The Ukrainians have no difficulty in adapting themselves to the changing conditions. Because of the general integration it is impossible to single any particular method used exclusively by the Ukrainians.

Just like the agricultural data produced here, detailed statistics about Ukrainians in business have been compiled in Winnipeg by F. Macrouch in his yearbooks which were published annually after the Second World War. From these diligently compiled statistics it becomes apparent that the Ukrainians were in the lead in this field. In 1948, in Winnipeg Ukrainians were engaged in the following commercial enterprises: 125 food stores, 192 shoestores, 40 barbershops, 33 restaurants, 23 women's beauty parlors, 22 tailor shops, 13 pharmacies, 11 hardware stores, 10 hotels, 10 service stations, 10 transfer companies, 10 watchmakers, 10 photo studios, 8 women's tailor shops, 8 radio repair shops, 6 fuel companies, 6 printing shops, 6 clothing stores, 6 electrical contractors, 6 billiard parlours, 5 butcher shops, 5 laundries, and cleaners, 5 confectionery stores, 5 auto parts stores, 5 book stores, 4 lumber yards, 3 furniture stores, 1 luggage wholesale, 1 dry goods wholesale, 1 confectionery wholesale, etc. There were those who were engaged in other industries: 13 building contractors, 9 furniture manufacturers, 6 bakeries, 5 soft drink manufacturers, 4 medicine manufacturers, 3 sash and door plants, 2 bus factories, 1 boat factory, 1 dairy, etc. In all there were over 500 business establishments employing thousands of labourers and craftsmen. This was the part played by Ukrainians in the cities creating means of employment. Similar statistics for Toronto, 1966, show the following: 31 construction companies, each with over a million dollars turnover, 49 restaurants, 18 hotels, 15 motels, 98 dry goods stores, 20 tailor shops, 25 beauty parlours, 20 barber shops, 15 gift shops, 12 billiard parlours, 10 photo studios, 10 furniture stores, 10 dry cleaners, 9 meat and butcher shops, 7 printing shops, 7 fuel oil firms, 7 shoe shops, 6 insurance agencies, 6 hardware stores, 9 jewellers and watchmakers, 6 book stores, 6 shoe stores, 5 clothing stores, 5 florists, 6 export firms, 5 paint shops, 4 bakeries, 3 dairies, 3 funeral firms, 2 transport firms, 2 arts & crafts shops, 2 aluminum window firms, 1 travel bureau, 1 tire store, 1 ceramics store, 1 sash and door plant, 1 shoe factory, 1 soft drink plant. Of the 416 stores in Toronto, 248 had annual business volume of from 25,000 to 50,000 dollars annually, 96 had over $50,000.00 annual business volume, 47 had over $150,000.00 turnover and 25 had over $250,000.00. The wholesale, "UBA" had $5,000,000.00 annual business [1]. Ukrainians in Toronto own real estate firms. Firms like R. Cholkan & Co. Ltd., J. J. Ellis, J. Boyko, have annual business in the millions of dollars.

In Toronto, in particular the Ukrainian businesses were developed in the post war period. Consequently about 50% of the businesses are owned by people who belong to the third immigration. Similar conditions exist in other major cities of Eastern Canada.

Ukrainians are engaged not only in small and average sized industries. They are becoming more and more engaged in industries which require capital in millions of dollars. In Eastern Canada, "Essex Packers" (meat packers) was started by Harry Poworoznyk. The head office of the firm is in Hamilton. In the same category are builders, Henry Winton, Toronto, and William Teron, Ottawa. Among the large companies in Toronto, the following may be included: Dempster's Bread, Future Bakery, Polyethelene Co., Safeway Construction Co., Horizon Wood Mfg., Rogers Dairy Ltd., Alpha Furniture, Dnipro Fuel Oil, Rochester Furniture, etc.

In Winnipeg, Mark G. Smerchanski is engaged in mining and manufacturing. He is connected with Border Chemicals in Manitoba and another factory in Moncton, New Brunswick. Firms whose business run into millions of dollars are Central Products and Foods, the president of which is S. Jankowsky and Foodland Wholesale whose president is J. J. Novosad. Settlers Savings and Mortgage Corporation Winnipeg and Titanium Continental Corp., Montreal are worthy of note. There are large companies managed and owned by Ukrainians in Edmonton and Saskatoon.

The promoters and owners of these companies are Canadians of Ukrainian descent as well as the new immigrants to Canada. There are several contributing factors for the success of these companies. Generally, the economic condition in Canada encourages the organizations of large companies. There is the experienced management personnel who acquired

---

[1] "Ukrainian Canadians", by Paul Yuzyk, Toronto, 1967.

their training in smaller establishments and the natural desire to succeed and to contribute to the general well-being of the community.

According to the Dominion Bureau of Statistics, Ukrainian-Canadians are engaged in the following branches of Canadian economy [2]:

Main Occupations of Ukrainians, 1961.

Percentage of Labour Force

	Numbers	Ukrainians	Total Population
Farmers and farm workers	40,439	21.1	10.0
Loggers, fishermen, hunters, trappers	1,034	0.5	1.8
Labourer	10,150	5.3	4.9
Mining	2,399	1.3	1.0
Janitors, waitresses, barbers, kitchen help, others	16,851	8.8	6.9
Armed forces, all ranks	1,640	0.9	1.8
Artists, athletes, entertainers, guides, others	276	0.1	0.2
Firemen, policemen, guards, other services	5,397	2.8	3.4
Total services and recreation	24,164	12.6	12.3
Railroad sectionmen, trackmen, repairmen	3,083	1.6	0.5
Carpenters, butchers, tailors, others	7,886	4.1	4.0
Mechanics, machinists, plumbers, others	9,904	5.1	4.8
Electricians, bricklayers, longshoremen, others	5,359	2.8	3.5
Craftsmen and tradesmen, others	19,846	10.4	11.3
Total craftsmen and tradesmen	46,078	24.0	24.1
Railway engineers, firemen, signalmen others	1,195	0.6	0.4
Water, road transport communications	8,555	4.3	5.6
Total transportation and communication	9,550	4.9	6.0
Sales clerks	5,848	3.1	3.6
Commercial travellers, salesmen, other sales	3,097	1.6	2.8
Total sales occupations	8,945	4.7	6.4
Stenographers, typists	5,783	3.0	3.3
Bookkeepers and cashiers	4,028	2.1	2.4
Clerical, other	11,412	6.0	7.2
Total clerical occupations	21,223	11.1	12.9
Managers: advertising, credit, sales, office	937	0.5	1.0
Proprietors, retail, trade, personal services	5,879	3.1	3.0
Proprietors, manufacturing, other business	4,371	2.3	4.3
Total managers and proprietors	11,187	5.9	8.3
School teachers	4,025	2.1	2.6
Engineers, scientists, doctors, lawyers, others	2,542	1.3	2.1
Nurses, accountants, auditors, social workers	1,748	0.9	1.8
Artists, musicians, clergymen, others	4,259	2.2	3.2
Total professional and technical	12,574	6.5	9.7
Occupation not stated	3,937	2.1	2.6
Labour force	191,680	100.0	100.0

From the above statistical data is apparent that the Ukrainians are to be found engaged in every occupation in the Canadian economy. The data also shows that by far the largest number of Ukrainians are still engaged in farming. In the field of crafts and trades their percent is

---

[2] Source: 1961 Census, Dominion Bureau of Statistics, Catologue No. 94-515.

practically equal to the Canadian average 24.0 : 24.1. On the other hand in the fields of management, proprietorship and professions the Ukrainian are below the Canadian average. It must not be overlooked that 50 years ago Ukrainians were not to be found in any of the higher responsible positions. The strides made in this respect are gigantic.

To illustrtate the growth of the numbers of Ukrainians in the professions, the following statistics from Winnipeg and Toronto will be of interest: in Winnipeg in 1949 there were 11 doctors, in 1956 17 and in 1966 there were 40. For the same years in Toronto the numbers were 10, 25 and 70 respectively. The same applies to the lawyers: in Winnipeg, in 1949 there were 11, in 1956, 22 and in 1966, 45. In Toronto the number of lawyers for 1949 and 1956 was the same as Winnipeg but in 1966 there were 50. There is a notable growth of dentists: in all Canada there were 34 Ukrainian dentists in 1949. In 1967 there were 26 in Winnipeg and 45 in Toronto. There was a similar growth in other professions.

If comparison is to be made, for 1951 and 1961, as to the numbers of Ukrainians in "higher professions" with the general Canadian coefficient among the Ukrainians it is considerably higher. When the Canadian coefficient for professions is 66% then for the Ukrainians it is 126%; for clerical workers the Canadian coefficient is 47% and for Ukrainians it is 89%, the same applies to proprietors and managers—32% and 53%.

According to the 1961 census, the statistics for the following professions were: (Ukrainians) teachers—4,025; engineers—870; clergymen—430; doctors—349; pharmacists—252: lawyers—196; editors and journalists—165; dentists—147; professors—82; agronomists—59; architects—52; judges—12.

It is to be expected that Ukrainians in Canada will maintain their aggressiveness and ambition to succeed and their numbers will continue to increase in higher professions and responsible positions generally. During 1966/67 at the University of Manitoba there were about 900 students of Ukrainian descent. There were equal numbers at the universities of the prairie provinces with a somewhat higher number at the University of Toronto. If one was to compare the present enrollment figures of Ukrainian students at the universities with those of 1949, the present number would be more than doubled. Yet despite the large increase the Ukrainian coefficient in comparison with the Canadian average is still behind.

Ukrainian Professional and Businessmen's Clubs

In order to stimulate the interest and maintain momentum in professions and business Ukrainian Professional and Businessmen's Clubs were formed across Canada. They are not strictly service and social clubs but encourage interest in professions and businesses through the press, public lectures and special publications. Ukrainian Professional and Businessmen's Club, Toronto, publishes regularly "Addresses of Ukrainian Businessmen and Professionals in Toronto". Earlier it was known as "Almanac of Ukrainian Businessmen and Professionals". The Winnipeg Club, in 1966 began publishing a bilingual journal "Ukrainian Canadian Review" which is also the official organ of Federation of the Ukrainian Professional and Businessmen's Club of Canada. The Clubs hold their conventions in the various Canadian cities as well as "Get-Togethers" and conferences usually during the Congress of Ukrainian Canadian Committee.

ACHIEVEMENTS AND INTEGRATION

The most active clubs are in Edmonton, Toronto, Winnipeg. Some members of these clubs have a quite impressive record in service to their communities, e.g. J. M. Hawryluk, Mark G. Smerchanski, D. Zaharia, Dr. V. F. Bachynski, Dr. J. Boyko, M. Kepron, G. Ratuski, S. Radchuk, J. G. Karasevich, M. A. Negrich, J. Shanski, Dr. D. J. Charney, J. Huyda, M. Chernecky, J. Ellis, V. H. Koman, S. Pulak, P. I. Michalishin, M. Bihus, M. Iwasykiw, M. Shafraniuk, Dr. S. Klimashko, Dr. S. Dershko, S. W. Frolick, R. J. Ostashewsky and others.

There were also professional and businessmen's clubs organized according to religious affiliation. In Saskatoon there was the Ukrainian Catholic Professional and Businessmen's Club. In Winnipeg there is the Professional Section of Ukrainian Catholic Women's League.

Professional and businessmen's clubs assume a responsible part of the cultural and charitable activities in their communities. The Winnipeg Professional and Businessmen's Club was financially responsible for the institution of Ukrainian language at the University of Manitoba and made a substantial contribution to the development of Ukrainian library. It also actively supported the Holy Family Home for the Aged. The Saskatoon Club assisted in the establishment of the Diocese. The Yorkton Club assisted in raising funds for the establishment of Ukrainian Studies at the University of Ottawa.

From the above it is obvious that the Ukrainian professionals and businessmen are interested not only in enhancing their prestige in their fields of endeavour but are a part and parcel of their respective communities in cultural and charitable fields. Their moral and material help is usually most generous.

Summing up organizational life of Ukrainian professionals it would be worthwhile to mention the most famous professional Ukrainian hockey and football players like Johnny Bower, Terry Sawchuk, Terry Evanshen, E. Nesterenko, Bill Mosienko, Joe Cooper (Krupiak), Bill Juzda, Bill Barylko, D. Lewicki, Joe Klukay, Nick Mikoski, Bronko Nagurski.

To this old guard we may add more new names like Montreal-born Mike Bossy and some other Ukrainian Canadians from the National Hockey League: Wayne Babych and Bernie Federko of St. Louis Blues, Dennis Maruk of Washington Capitals, Tom Lysiak of Chicago Blackhawks, Dale Haverchuk, Moris Lukowich and Dave Babych of the Winnipeg Jets and others. With these famous names in sport we include John Jaremy the first man who swam Lake Ontario after Marilyn Bell. Deserved mentioning Jennifer Diachun of Ontario, winner of the Canadian Female Gymnastic Championship 1969-1972.

Activities of Ukrainian Professional and Businessmen's Clubs were intensified at the end of the sixties, when the Federation of these clubs was organized but the ultimate results of their activities was reached in the seventies. The development of this period is presented in detail in the chapter "Role of the Federation of Ukrainian Professional and Businessmen's Clubs in the Development of Ukrainian Studies".

COOPERATIVE CREDIT MOVEMENT

Ukrainian Canadians made great progress on the cooperative credit field. This is shown by the fact that at the end of the Second World War there were only 14 such cooperatives but in 1967 the number had risen to 70. The beginnings were very modest and only here and there could we find one that would have the investment capital counted in thousands. Within the short period of twenty years several Ukrainian credit unions counted their assets in the millions of dollars. Outstanding successes were recorded by credit unions in towns and cities, thanks to the gradual appreciation of the credit unions' services, as well as the availability of experienced individuals in the cooperative field, who arrived in this country with the third immigration stage. These men were able to graft unto the Canadian business tree the methods that they learned and mastered in their homeland. On Canada's soil we find such able cooperative experts as A. Paliy. W. Kochan, J. Temnyk, W. Yashan, O. Stanimir, Vasyl Kucyj, A. Mudryk, A. Kachor, D. Mychayluk, J. Skwarchuk, T. Melnychuk, K. Myhal, S. Charchalis, I. Tatomyr, M. Andruchiw, and others. In addition to the professional cooperative experts there were others who had a great deal of experience in the cooperative field. There is no doubt that the gradual development of the credit union system was due to the great improvement in Canadian economy sphere. The rapid growth of the credit unions may be gauged by the following figures of the 16 credit unions in Manitoba, taken for the years 1959-1965. In 1959 their balance stood at $3,000,000 while in 1965 it had risen to $5,000,000. The membership, during that time, had increased by 3,000. Even greater progress was recorded by the credit unions in Ontario, especially in Toronto, where the "Ukrainian Toronto Credit Union" had a working capital of $5,000,000 while "Buduchnist" credit union had nearly as much to show for its 15 years of operation, the same can be said about "SO-USE". Similar prosperity gauges may be registered by the credit unions existing in connection with Toronto parishes such as "St. Nicholas", "St. Mary's", "Holy Eucharist", St. Josaphat's Cathedral" and others. In Montreal the Ukrainian National Credit Union leads the way with two other branches in large organizations, as well as the "Ukrainian Savings and Credit Union", organized in 1952. There is the "Hetman Mazeppa Credit Union" (renewed in 1955) and the "Kiev Credit Union", established in 1963.

A somewhat slower growth is shown by the credit unions in Saskatchewan and Alberta that number 20 branches. The leading one here is the "Nova Hromada" (New Community) in Saskatoon, which finds itself in the "Millionaire" class, with the "Ukrainian Credit Union of Calgary" as its nearest competitor.

When it comes to the number of credit unions, Manitoba and Ontario are competing with each other. In 1961 Ontario had 22 branches and Manitoba could boast of 26 [1]), but lately Ontario has led the way with

---

[1]) Statistics for this and other chapters are taken from the "Chronicles of Ukrainian life in Canada in the new era" that was extensively prepared by the editor, Anatole Kurdydyk.

30 credit unions in all. Seen from the invested capital point of view Toronto is in first place. Of course not all of the credit unions are singularly successful. Some of them have undergone setbacks, while others that were organized in the last few years, having made a good start, are only recently getting up on their feet, proving at the same time that the credit union movement has a strong tendency to grow. In 1966 according the the latest summaries the Ukrainian Credit Unions had a membership of 34,000 and over $40,000,000 invested capital. Here again Toronto was in the lead, with its 10 branches and over $10,000,000 worth of investment, while Winnipeg came second with 9 branches and $7,000,000 in capital and Montreal occupying third place in this cooperative growth.

These three cities top all other Ukrainian credit union centres, not only with the amount of money invested, but also in the membership count which is in excess of 25,000.

To give a more detailed picture of the growth and strength of the cooperative credit movement among Ukrainians in recent years we present a chart of Ukrainian credit Unions in Canada based on the yearly financial statement of 1968.

City	Number of Credit Unions	Number of members	Total of Assets
Winnipeg	9	6,659	8,524,724
Toronto	10	16,698	23,414,471
Saskatoon	1	912	1,628,772
Edmonton	2	500	400,000 [2]
Calgary	1	300	250,000 [2]
Wishart	1	1,000	1,200,000 [2]
Montreal	4	3,600	6,000,000 [2]
Hamilton	4	1,000	1,000,000 [2]
Windsor	1	552	503,702
Fort William	1	529	386,860
St. Catherines	1	581	481,129
Sudbury	1	275	229,862
Total	36	32,606	43,595,520*

The credit unions also deserve our special attention due to the fact that the majority of them donate, out of their yearly profits, generous amounts of money toward the community's cultural activities. An example of this generosity, on the part of the credit unions, may be shown by the action of the "Ukrainian Credit Union of Montreal" which from 1944 to 1965 donated $21,700 for community's cultural work. This same cooperative designated $3,825 in 1965 and $4,000 in 1966 for community needs. Important roles played in this same field may be shown by another Montrealer—the Ukrainian Savings and Credit Union and such credit unions in the West as the "Credit Union of North Winnipeg", "Carpathia", "Postup" (Progress), "Dnipro" and "Vera" of Winnipeg; as well as the "Ukrainian Savings and Credit Union "Nova Hromada" in Saska-

---

[2] Rounded figure.
[3] A. Kachor, Ukrainian Credit Movement in Canada and USA, presented at the National Convention of Ukrainian Cooperators, New York, 1969.

toon, "Ukrainian Credit Union" in Calgary, and in the East the "Ukrainian Credit Union in Sudbury, Ukrainian Windsor Credit Union" and others. In all Ukrainian cooperatives and credit unions have donated around a quarter million dollars towards the publication of cultural-literary works, maintenance of kindergartens, national schools, and support to universities, the "Taras Shevchenko Foundation" and other worthwhile causes.

The more active credit unions publish their own monthly bulletins, for the members, and by this means propagate the cooperative ideas. In addition there are ideologically federated groups such as the "Kooperatyvna Hromada" (Cooperative Community in Winnipeg) and the "Coordinating Committee of Credit Cooperatives" of Toronto. The leading cooperative centres perceive the need of an over-all connective central office regarding these Ukrainian financial cooperative branches scattered throughout Canada. This idea was presented in Toronto, in 1959, during the convention of the Ukrainian credit unions' representatives from the above mentioned Co-ordinating Committee of Credit Cooperatives of Toronto, the Co-operative Community of Winnipeg and the Associations of Ukrainian Cooperators of New York.

When we speak about the Ukrainian credit unions in Canada it does not mean that their existence represents some kind of ghetto establishments or exclusive enterprises reserved for the Ukrainians only. All of Ukrainian credit union branches are members of the central credit union offices in Canada and U.S.A., and have people of other nationalities belonging to their branches as well as the reverse of this set-up where many Ukrainians are members of credit unions that are in the hands of the people of other nationalities.

If it may be said that the Ukrainian credit unions have made a milestone in their rapid progress, while their sister-establishments — the consumer and manufacturing cooperatives — have not lived up to their mark in the trials of life of Canada. The rapidly extending lines of cooperatives in this category that had shown a steady growth in the thirties, ceased to make any progress after the last war and some of them had even undergone self-liquidation. The business elasticity of private enterprise triumphs sometimes over the co-operative methods. Still in spite of these retarding circumstances, around 20 cooperatives are active in this field and struggle for survival and their place in the business world. This goes to show that the cooperative idea, among Ukrainians, has always been alive and active. This is proven in the next decade of our history in the chapter "Progress in Co-operative Movement".

THE CHURCH LIFE

The gradual growth of the church life, which we have noted in the second era, continued its development in the third era of our history. This process of expansion was noticed particularly in the two traditional Ukrainian churches, the Catholic and the Orthodox. Progress was also recorded in Protestant and Evangelical churches. Much of this growth could be credited to the new organizational structure of the churches themselves that had been adopted after the Second World War, as well as to the arrival, in Canada, of the great number of clergy after the war. It is to these two factors that we can attribute the accelaration of the church life in Canada.

The Ukrainian Catholic Church

In 1947 Cardinal Eugene Tisserant, head of the Eastern Congregation in Vatican, made his visitation of the Ukrainian Catholic Church in Canada, confirming the impressive achievement of this church in the organizational sphere. As a result of these visitations, the Vatican made some changes in 1948, in the organizational structure of this church by dividing the single diocese into three eparchies located in Winnipeg, Edmonton and Toronto. The centre eparchy (Winnipeg) was headed by Bishop Wasyliy Ladyka, the western eparchy (Edmonton) was taken over by Bishop Neil Savaryn, who since 1943 had been an assistant to the only Ukrainian Bishop in Canada, W. Ladyka. The Eastern Exarchate (Toronto) received the newly consecrated Bishop Isidore Borecky as the head of this eparchy. Three years later the central Exarchate (Winnipeg) was divided once more to form the Winnipeg and the Saskatoon eparchies. The last one named became the seat of Bishop Andrew Roborecky. In this way the Ukrainian Catholic Church received four bishops with Bishop Wasyl Ladyka, raised to the rank of archbishop becoming the head of the Ukrainian Catholic Church in Canada.

Eastern and western exarchates became the largest, in territorial scope. The last one named comprised Alberta, British Columbia, the Yukon Territory and a portion of North-West-Territories. This huge terrain was served by 66 priests, including 25 monks from the Basilian Fathers' order who had four monasteries on this territory, one Novitiate and two institutes for university students. As is well known the Sister Servants were doing their share of educational work by establishing educational and training institutions while the Missionary Sisters were also engaged in similar work in their St. Josaphat's Institute in Edmonton. In all there were 149 parishes, missionary establishments and mission stations, serving some 40,000 faithful Ukrainian Catholics.

The Eastern Exarchate was composed of Ontario, Quebec, New Brunswick, Nova Scotia, New Foundland and Prince Edward Island. On this far extended territory 50 priests were carrying on their religious work along with 22 monks, comprising the following religious orders: Basilian Fathers, with three monasteries (Toronto, Montreal and Grimsby), Redemptorist Fathers with two monasteries (Toronto and Waterville) and Studites—a new religious order organized after the Second World War (1951) in Woodstock, Ontario. This new order took its name from an older one that had been active long ago in Ukraine. In addition to the religious orders—the now well-known Sister Servants with six monasteries and one Novitiate. There were also Sister Missionaries with a monastery in Grimsby. Altogether, there were 71 parishes, missionary establishments and mission stations, with 50,000 faithful in the Eastern Exarchate.

The smallest exarchates, speaking in terms of territory, were the Winnipeg and Saskatoon eparchies being limited to their Manitoba and Saskatchewan areas respectively. In spite of that the Manitoba exarchate, with the small addition of a northern territory surpassed all others in the number of its adherents amounting to about 58,000 faithful followers and served by some 60 priests in 59 parishes, missionary establishments and mission stations. Among the religious orders working in this exarchate were Basilian Fathers (one institution), Redemptorist Fathers (one institution), and Sister Servants (four institutions), who also ran two day schools and three senior citizen homes (Dauphin, Sifton and Komarno).

The Saskatoon Exarchate had the least number of priests, thirty seven in all, serving some 35,000 faithful souls in 157 parishes, missionary institutions and mission stations. This exarchate had an advantage over all the other in this one respect: it had several Catholic educational institutions. The Sister Servants had established their Academy in Yorkton and institutes for girls in Saskatoon and Regina. The Brothers of Christian Schools had their St. Joseph's College in Yorkton and the Redemptorist Fathers built their Novitiate in Roblin [2]). In addition to these the Shashkevych Institute (formerly the Brotherhood of Ukrainian Catholics Bursa) and lately the Shepticky Institute was actively engaged in educational and cultural work in Saskatoon.

According to general summaries of 1951 the Ukrainian Catholic Church in Canada had, at that time, 229 priests including 63 monks, 14 male monasteries and 23 monasteries for women, with over 200 sisters and novices. Altogether they conducted two high schools (a Collegiate and an Academy), three novitiates, 13 day schools, 2 hospitals, 3 old folks homes and 3 orphan homes. All these multiform activities were under the direction of five hierarchs, as the Winnipeg Exarchate received, in 1951, an assistant-bishop in the person of a well known educator and theologian, Rev. Maxim Hermaniuk of the Redemptorist order.

This tremendous growth of the Ukrainian Catholic Church deserved a higher recognition which was realized in 1956 when shortly after Archbishop W. Ladyka's death. Pope Pius XII, by a special Papal Bull, established in that same year, the Metropolia of the Ukrainian Catholic Church in Canada. Winnipeg was designated as the Metropolitan seat and shortly thereafter the abbotships of Basilian and Redemptorist Fathers were also transferred to this central city. In this way Winnipeg became not only the church metropolis but also the headquarters of the two religious orders that have played such an important role in the life of the Ukrainian Catholic Church in Canada.

---

[2]) Actually Roblin belongs to U. C. Archeparchy of Winnipeg, but its location is very close to Yorkton, one of very important centres of U. C. Eparchy of Saskatoon.

As we already know, the Basilian Fathers appeared early on the scene in the history of Ukrainians. Starting with the year 1948, they established the religious province that was in charge of well known figures who were following in the footsteps of their distinguished predecessors, Platonid Filas and Navkratiy Kryzhanovsky. These were: Veniamyn Baranyk, Theodosius Dobko, Volodymyr Shevchuk, Bonifatiy Sloboda and Myron Daciuk. With the exception of the first one named all the others were Canadian born. In 1967 the Basilian order had nine monasteries and institutions with a total membership of 109, including 50 monastic priests. Mundare had been considered as an ideal seat of this monastic order due to the fact that the novitiate was here, as well as a large library and archives. In the east the Basilian Fathers have the St. Basil's College in Toronto, monasteries in Ottawa, Montreal and Grimsby, as well as in Edmonton and Vancouver in the west.

After the war a tiny branch of the Ukrainian Redemptorist order came into life and in 1945 Rev. J. Bala was named as the vice-provincial head of this order in Canada, although he was under the jurisdiction of the Redemptorist Fathers of Brussels, Belgium. His provincial successors in turn were: Rev. M. Hermaniuk, who later became a Metropolitan, and Rev. V. Malanchuk, who in time became the Bishop of France, both of them being under the jurisdiction of the Belgian order, but from 1961 were responsible directly to Rome. The Yorkton province (territorial name for the order) has now eight institutions in Canada—one in Meadowvale, two in Toronto, three in Saskatchewan (Saskatoon, Yorkton and Ituna) and one in Newark, U.S.A. In the above mentioned ecclesiastical province of this order there are 65 monastic priests at work. In recent times the order had been, in turn, headed by Rev. Volodymyr Krayewsky and Rev. Paul Maluga. The main base of operation, of this order, is in Yorkton, Saskatchewan, with Roblin, Manitoba, and its St. Vladimir's College as a prominent and close-running competitor.

The Studite Brothers, domiciled in Woodstock, Ontario, are registering their gradual growth, with 14 monks. The Brothers of Christian Schools have not branched out beyond their St. Joseph's College in Yorkton.

Among the women's religious orders the first place belongs to the Sisters Servants who have 22 monasteries and over 250 nuns. They manage two academies, one in Yorkton and the other in Ancaster, Ontario, the latter including the novitiate that was transferred from Mundare. The provincial seat is located in Toronto headed by such noted nuns, of this order, as, Bernadeta Vavryk (1949-1959), Bonifatia Sloboda (1959-1965), and Frances Byblow (1965-70). Among the lesser orders are: Sisters of St. Joseph (known as Josefitky), who work in Saskatchewan and have one institution with five nuns; Missionary Sisters of Christian Charities, 2 monasteries and 13 members, and Oblate Missionaries, 1 monastery and 3 members (organized in 1962) [3]. In all there were, in 1967, 26 institutions comprising women's monastic orders with 300 nuns and novices in attendance. During the same time there were 17 monasteries for men, with 200 members including about a hundred monastic priests. When we stop to consider that the Ukrainian Catholic Church has its own press (three weeklies, six monthly journals, one quarterly,

---

[3] B. Kazymyra in "Development of the Ukrainian Catholic Group in Canada", and "Eastern Catholic Life", April 23, 1963.

seven publishing houses and five printing establishments), and a separate branch of lay organizations of the Catholic Action type, about which we have more to say in another chapter, then it is quite obvious that the Ukrainian Catholic Church has at its disposition a great organizational machine. Material on UCC development in this chapter ends in sixties. Additional information on growth of this and other churches in chapter titled "Ukrainian Churches Symbol of Cultural and Religious Identification".

It will also be of some interest to note that within the Ukrainian Catholic Church circles in Canada there is a continuous action at work to unite all Ukrainian (also known as Ruthenian, Greek-Catholic or Byzantine Rite) Catholic Churches that have their hierarchs in U.S.A., Argentina, Brazil, France, England, Yugoslavia and Australia, under one Ukrainian Patriarchate. The institution of patriarchate has been a traditionally historical supremacy of every eastern church. These same objective aims are the prime religious issues in every country where the Ukrainians had settled. This goal is backed by a logical argument in favour of united action on the part of these churches in the sphere of ritual, tradition and historical entity. This need was especially intensified from the time the Ukrainian Catholic Church was liquidated, by force, in Ukraine, in 1945.

Ukrainian Catholics on all continents, including the Underground Catholic Church in Ukraine, consider Cardinal Josyf Slipyj as the uncrowned Patriarch of the Ukrainian Catholic Church in communion with Rome. Cardinal Josyf Slipyj had been imprisoned for eighteen years in the USSR concentration camp in Siberia but was finally freed in 1963, through the intervention of the Vatican. As the Primate of the Ukrainian Catholic Church, the Cardinal is making every effort to gain freedom for this church in Ukraine. Along with the Metropolitan and the hierarchs in Canada, Cardinal Josyf Slipyj is the highest moral authority for the Ukrainian Catholics in Canada and his name is cited in all the holy liturgies celebrated in every Ukrainian Catholic church.

Although the Ukrainian Catholic Church in Canada has made great strides in its organizational work (increased membership, expansion of missionary establishments, formation of new parishes), still its hierarchs have two serious problems to contend with. The first and most important of these is the need for new applicants from the young generation to take up theological studies with priesthood in view. Out of the 268 priests in the Ukrainian Catholic Church, only one third are Canadian born, the other two-thirds have come to this country either prior to or since the war, and 80% of all the priests are over forty years of age. To enable the youth to take up theological studies a so-called million dollar fund was established in 1966, by the Redemptorist Fathers order, to aid those who wish to devote themselves to the life of service as priests.

The second, and by no means less important question, is the one posed by the census statistics showing that Ukrainian Catholics are gradually losing their faithful members, mostly in favour of Roman-Catholics. When 1951 census showed 165,000 Ukrainian Catholics, 42% out of the total Ukrainian Canadians, the 1961 census recorded only 158,000 as Ukrainian Catholics, just a little over 33% out of the total. During this same period of time the number of Ukrainian Roman-Catholics rose from 57,000 (14.3%) to 80,000 (16.8%). These given figures brought some alarm to those whose interest was aroused while further investigations revealed that not only did these figures show how many Ukrainians had changed their allegiance, but also the fact that in many cases the census takers, unable to differentiate between Ukrainian Catholics and Roman Catholics, had erroneously put down the former as the latter. These transfers in religious allegiance are credited to the fact that many settlers who are leaving the western prairies to seek employment in the larger cities of Eastern Canada, where there is a lack of Ukrainian parishes, finding themselves in the Roman Catholic surroundings, choose that church as their own. Mixed marriages and the narrowing of distances between the two Catholic rites, brought on by the ecumenical councils, also contributed their share to this switch-over in church allegiance. To all these harmful tendencies the Ukrainian Catholic Church, along with its priesthood, is putting up a strong defensive front. The above mentioned problems—the ever present themes of theological conferences—of those who strive for unity, have also been debated at the First Provincial Synod of the Ukrainian Catholic Metropolia in Canada, which was held in Winnipeg in 1962.

The Ukrainian Greek Orthodox Church (U.G.O.C.)

The Ukrainian Greek-Orthodox Church (U.G.O.C.) also showed a remarkable growth after the Second World War, especially from September 1951, when the extra-ordinary U.G.O.C. Sobor was held that year. At the 9th Sobor of this church held in Saskatoon in 1953, Archbishop Mstyslav Skrypnyk, head of U.G.O.C. since 1947, placed his resignation. The resignation was accepted but at the same time a question was posed as to who would be his successor. It so happened that Metropolitan Ilarion (lay name—Ivan Ohienko), the former Archbishop of Kholm and Pidliasha, was staying in Winnipeg at the time. Here was a man who had a doctor's degree in philological and theological studies and was a recognized authority of higher learning, an author of many books and other published works, and who had also been the minister of education during the existence of the Ukrainian National Republic. Not being under U.G.O.C. jurisdiction he headed the Ukrainian Orthodox Sobor in Winnipeg. The extra-ordinary U.G.O.C. Sobor in Saskatoon, by a unanimous acclamation invited him to be the head of that church. At the same Sobor important resolutions were passed and accepted, dealing with organizational system and at the same time the U.G.O.C. was proclaimed a Metropolia, divided into three eparchies; the Eastern, with its seat in Toronto and with Archbishop Mykhail Khoroshy in charge; the Western, in Edmonton, with Archbishop Andrey Metiuk being in charge from 1959, and the Central Manitoba Eparchy, which takes in the province of Saskatchewan, under the jurisdiction of Metropolitan Ilarion. In 1963 a fourth eparchy, outlined by the border of Saskatchewan was formed with Bishop Borys Yakovkevych in charge. As we can see the territorial division of U.G.O.C. corresponds with the Ukrainian Catholic Church set-up. The resulting effect presented the accomplished fact of four eparchies comprised of three bishops with Metropolitan Ilarion at the head. The last one named received the title of "Blazhennishy" (Independent)—from 1963—which designates him as an independent hierarch.

At the extraordinary Sobor of U.G.O.C. in Winnipeg it was proclaimed once more that U.G.O.C. is the self-ruled church by Sobor. The hierarchy, clergy and parish delegates hold periodical Sobors for resolving important church matters, elect or approve bishops' appointments and leaders of the Church-Consistorium comprised of bishops, nine clergy men and nine lay-men, chosen by the Sobor to serve a six year period. The Consistorium, better known as the Presidial Consistorium, rules on all administration matters concerning U.G.O.C. The head of the Consistorium had always been some well known and leading personality and this office had been held for a long time by Rev. S. W. Sawchuk. But when the last one mentioned took over the duties as principal of St. Andrew's College, he was succeeded by Rev. T. Kovalyshyn who stayed at this post until his death. Subsequently Rev. F. Kernicky assumed the chairmanship. There were further changes in this office in the seventies.

The division of Ukrainian Greek-Orthodox Church into separate eparchies resulted in rapid growth of the church. A prominent part in this was played by the fifteen years of stability that the church has experienced under the guidance of Metropolitan Ilarion. When in 1951 the U.G.O.C. had over 200 parishes, missionary institutions and mission stations, in 1967 this number had risen to 300. The number of its clergy also increased from 70, in 1951, to around 100 in 1967.

A great achievement in the life of U.G.O.C. has been the expansion of St. Andrew's College which, in 1965, was moved to its own large and newly built structure on the campus of the University of Manitoba. The college provides two Departments, Philosophical and Theological, and prepares students for advance studies in theology with priesthood in view. This is the only Ukrainian Orthodox theological college on the North American continent and accepts applicants for priesthood studies not only from the U.G.O.C. in Canada, but also from the same church in U.S.A.—both churches are united in prayer communion. At the College they have the Theological Association which publishes "Faith and Culture", whose editor was Metropolitan Ilarion. A large library is included in this educational institution and a separate students' dormitory with 100 capacity.

The Ukrainian Orthodox Church that had been organized by Rev. Dr. Y. Zhuk, and headed for a while by Bishop Bohdan Shpylka, did not show any significant growth in Canada but on the contrary some of its parishes even had joined with the U.G.O.C. With Bishop Shpylka's death the hierarchy of that church in U.S.A. appointed, as its bishop, the Rev. Andrey Kushchak, whose ordination took place in 1967, and who then became in charge of this church, not only in U.S.A., but also in Canada as well. The "Sobor of Ivan Suchavsky" church in Winnipeg is the Canadian cathedral of the Ukrainian Orthodox Church. There are also several Orthodox parishes under the jurisdiction of the Russian Orthodox Church but this breed of "orthodox" variety is becoming sterile and may soon be extinct.

The 1951 census revealed that there were 111,000 Orthodox adherents on that date and 119,000 at the 1961 census. Broken into percentage according to the total number of Ukrainians in Canada will give us 28% for 1951 and only 24% for 1961. Thus it will be seen that the Ukrainian Orthodox believers also are on the diminishing scale. This would be perhaps even more sharply revealed if we were to differentiate very carefully between the Ukrainian Greek Orthodox proper and the Greek Orthodox adherents of other nationalities.

The statistics of the the Evangelical or the so-called protestant churches reveal a significant growth in Ukrainian membership. In 1951 the Ukrainian Evangelical churches had some 50 thousand members while by 1961 the number had risen to over 100 thousand. The largest percentage in growth is shown by the United Church of Canada, from 28 to 59 thousand, and the Anglican Church from 10 thousand to 19 thousand. The Lutherans too doubled their ranks (from 3.4 to 6.6), and so did the Baptists (from 3.7 to 6.1). Much lesser gains were recorded by the Presbyterians—from 4½ thousand to 5 thousand. A new position has been taken by the Pentecostals who, according to the latest census, number some 3 thousand and more, whereas they were not even listed in 1951. In general it will be seen that the significant growth of the protestant churches has been mostly at the expense of the two traditional Ukrainian Churches—Catholic and Orthodox—and mainly due to the large Ukrainian migration into cities, towns and industrial centres where they join with the organized church life that happens to be accessible to them.

Migrations and mixed marriages also brought some noticeable gains for the Ukrainian Catholic Church as well. According to 1961 statistics there were 10,681 Polish, 3,549 British, 1,615 French, 1,361 Hungarian, 1,193 German and some others, forming about 17% of the total Ukrainian Catholics in Canada. Similar gains can be credited to the Ukrainian Greek-Orthodox Church.

The Ukrainian Evangelical Alliance

As we have already stated, in the second era of our history, the Ukrainian Evangelical Alliance was intended to be an outward expression of the organized Presbyterian strength within the organizational scheme of the Presbyterian Church, which later merged together with the Methodists to form a single United Church of Canada. The Ukrainian Evangelical Alliance was formed primarily to carry on missionary and community work but it never gained any influence in the administration sphere of the Reformed Church nor did it even have any influence over the Ukrainians that were included in its system. It is relevant therefore to say that as the time went on the Ukrainian communities that had been organized during the pioneer or at the beginning of the second era began to lose gradually their national character. The leadership of the United Church of Canada has always strived to avoid in having any national categorizing and as a result of this there are no statistics surviving to show the ethnic composition of those congregations that were predominantly Ukrainian. Neither are there any statistics to show how many Ukrainian pastors are in that church although during the mid-war period there were over 20 qualified pastors of Ukrainian origin. Not all the Presbyterians were in favour of this plan. A separate group was formed that published a monthly journal called "Slovo" (The Word) which propagated the idea of an Independent Ukrainian Evangelical Church. This group which included the following pastors: I. Bodrug, P. Krat, L. Standret and W. Borovsky—strove to regain the position held prior to 1913 and although "Slovo" failed to organize any large numbers of independent congregations still its efforts were not altogether in vain. When the United Church of Canada refused to give any further subsidies to "Kanadiysky Ranok" (Canadian Morning) the successors to "Slovo's" idealistic policy took over the publishing of "Canadian Morning" at their own expense after renaming it to "Evanhelsky Ranok" (Evangelical Morning), which is still being published in Winnipeg with W. Borovsky as editor, who is also in charge of an independent congregation in Toronto

There is also a branch of the Presbyterian Church that does not belong to the United Church of Canada, with Pastor M. Fesenko in charge and their own official newspaper, the "Evanhelska Pravda" (Evangelical Truth). Two other congregations of this church work directly with the Presbyterian Church.

The Ukrainian Evangelical Baptist Alliance

The Ukrainian Baptists in Canada passed through a long evolutionary stage. In the beginning they had a joint organization with the Russians but—as we have mentioned in the second era in our history—gradually they began to carry on the work that would lead to a total Ukrainization of this church and to the merging of the two, the Eastern and the Western ecclesiastical Conferences, into a single church union. This was not realized until 1959, followed by its incorporation in 1961. The Ukrainian Evangelical Baptist Convention of Canada, has now over 7 thousand adherents and more than 20 church congregations and mission stations. Their official church organ is the Christian Herald and the affairs of the church are administrated by the Council and the Executive bodies elected from among members at the general conventions whose terms of office last for five years. The leading persons in this church are such pastors and deacons as: P. Kindrat, L. Tarasiuk, S. Skovorodko, Z. Rechun-Panko, M. Podworniak, A. Tkachenko, J. Iwasykiw and others. The Ukrainian Evangelical Baptist Convention of Canada is a member of the All-Ukrainian Evangelical Baptist World Alliance, headed by Zhabko Potapovych and lately by Alexander Harbuziuk, V. Domashovec.

The Pentecostals can also show traces of their success. They have several congregations, including two larger ones in Toronto where they publish their organ the "Evangelist" and have regular radio programs. They are members of the Canadian Pentecostal Church and form the Eastern Slavic Division which is also the financial source for carrying on the missionary work. The more prominent missionaries of this church are pastors—H. B. Derkach, V. M. Kuziv, V. Melnychuk, P. Horban, P. Shelestovsky and P. Kerychuk.

Ukrainian Seventh Day Adventists also have their congregations in Winnipeg, Toronto and other places and are members of the Seventh Day Adventists of Canada.

Ukrainian Lutherans, who number around 7 thousand, are dispersed throughout the different national Lutheran churches.

RAMIFICATION AND CO-ORDINATION OF COMMUNITY LIFE

As we have already broadly portrayed and strongly emphasized, at the end of the second era, the creation of the Ukrainian Canadian Committee, as the highest co-ordinating centre of the Ukrainian community in Canada, was the valid natural process and the organic consummation of the national entity. The culminating point in this process and the obvious expression of its mood was the First Ukrainian Canadian Congress in 1943 which in its comprehensive activity displayed all the signs of a mighty demonstration of a nationally-oriented Ukrainianism in Canada.

True enough it would be possible to evaluate this outward manifestation as being a natural reaction, on the part of the community, towards the events of war that was then raging in the world and the stand of the Ukrainian Canadians as evidence of their Canadian patriotism which, once the danger of war was over would, as a matter of course, find itself diluted and diminished. Even some of the closest architects of this project held this same opinion. In the meantime, in accordance with the resolution of the First Congress preparations were in full swing for the Second Ukrainian Congress which finally took place in Toronto on the 4, 5 and 6 of June, 1946. The presidium of the Ukrainian Canadian Committee, in arranging this Second Congress in Toronto, did it as though it wanted to single out as a symbol of the important social processes that had been taking place during the last several decades in the midst of Ukrainian community and to show to the rest of the world that the Ukrainians not only are the citizens of Canada, but that they also possess their own valuable national resources to give as their contribution toward the development of this country. The great Massey Hall in Toronto was a witness to the three-day councils, proclamations and sound resolutions, and a proof that the Ukrainian Canadian Committee was not only the manifestation and the answer to the war times, but that it also possessed the creative and guiding wisdom to direct the future growth and development of the Ukrainian community life. This feeling and understanding was further strengthened by the Ukrainian Canadian war veterans who had just returned from overseas and who had lent their helping hand by joining in with the Ukrainian Canadian Committee to contribute their share in the building up of Canada.

The Ukrainian Canadian Veterans' Association

The Ukrainian Canadian Veterans' Association was formed overseas, in England, during the Second World War. It began with the traditional religious-cultural gatherings of the Ukrainian Canadian war personnel. Memoirs of those days were vouched in the following sincere statements:

"It seems like only yesterday when a small group of Ukrainian Canadian soldiers were guests at the traditional Christmas Eve feast prepared by the Ukrainian citizens of Manchester, England, during the war in 1942. Out of this small group of soldiers, with G.R.B. Panchuk at the head, the Ukrainian Canadian Veterans' Association (U.C.V.A.) came into being" [1].

The U.C.V.A. grew with a rapid tempo when the Ukrainian Canadian Veterans' Club (U.C.V.C.) was organized at 218 Sussex Street in London. In two years time club membership had grown to over 5,000 (men and women) including not only the Ukrainian veterans from Canada, but also those from U.S.A., England and other allied countries. The so-called Christmas convention of the Ukrainian War Veterans' Association during 6, 7, 8 and 9th of January 1944 provided this organization with a genuine growth.

The Veterans' club premises received a generous moral and material aid from the Ukrainians in Canada and U.S.A., particularly from the Ukrainian Canadian Committee. The club was like a home for the veterans. In it they met, for friendly gatherings and discussions, with their friends, clergymen and army chaplains, which added to a high morale among the personnel. The association edited its own veterans' bulletin which helped to gain them new friends, not only back home, but at the front as well. Club's atmosphere was healthy and active. When the war was drawing to a close both the veterans and the executive of the club and the association voiced their hopes that with their coming home they may be able to form a Ukrainian Canadian war veterans' organization in Canada. This hope was realized as soon as the first ranks became demobilized and reached the shores of their homeland, when a Winnipeg group of veterans supplied the initiative steps and on June 14, 1945, the Ukrainian Canadian Veterans' Association became an accomplished fact. After this the events took their own course. J. Yuzyk became an active organizer and in a short period of time twenty-six branches and committees of former veterans were formed throughout eastern and western Canada. J. G. Karasevich the newly appointed head of this organization announced, at the Second Ukrainian Canadian Congress, that all Ukrainian veterans, irrespective of their political or r - ligious belonging "have a right to be members of this organization as long as they stand united in Canada's defense...and are ready to raise their voice on behalf of freedom and rights of all the (oppressed) enslaved (peoples) nations of this world" [2].

Canada's welfare and aid to the enslaved nations, particularly the Ukrainians in Europe, became the ideal directive of this the second large constituent part of the U.C.C. With the above idea in mind, during the Second Congress, the following well known friends of the Ukrainians spoke at this gathering: Prof. G. W. Simpson, S. H. Y. Snyder, and Prof. Watson Kirkconnell, as well as Hon. Paul Martin, Secretary of State and Col. George Drew, premier of Ontario. In this same aspect were the discussions of the possibliity of having the Ukrainian Canadian Aid Fund help the displaced persons in Europe, popularly called "skytaltsi" about whom mention had been made in another section of this history. In addition to these key questions other subjects concerning the future of the Ukrainian Canadian community were also discussed. The significance of the Second Congress not only lay in its mass attendance, but

---

[1] John Yuzyk, "The Development of the Ukrainian Canadian Veteran's Association", Nov. 11, 1950 from U.C.C.'s archives.
[2] "Second All-Canadian Congress of Ukrainian Canadians", Toronto 1946, p. 44.

primarily in the integration of the new creative forces, the unanimous resolutions and the people's loyalty to its leaders.

The Ukrainian Canadian Veterans' Association, whose branches joined with Canadian Legion, gave its full moral and material support to the central organized body, the Ukrainian Canadian Committee, and was included as the co-founding member in its composition. The U.C.V.A. printed its own bulletin and later the journal "Opinion". Its office, up to 1950, was located in Winnipeg and later transferred to Eastern Canada with the following persons as its executive heads, at different times: G. R. B. Panchuk, J. G. Karasevich, Dr. P. T. Smylski, S. Pawluk, T. Hevus, Dr. S. P. Klimashko, Dr. F. Martyniuk, S. Frolick, lawyer, J. Pohorecky, and others. The work of U.C.V.A. was directed into various channels. For example, the Ukrainian branch of Canadian Legion No. 141, in Winnipeg, had for many years, looked after Air Cadet Squadron and the Toronto branch had a similar unit under its wing and supported cadets' visits, organized a publishing foundation for printing various materials about Ukrainian settlers in Canada, arranged for a music festival and showed other activities. In later period there were two executive branches of Ukrainian Canadian Veterans' Association, the East and the West, and they held their conventions every three years. In the west there were such active members as Dr. W. Grenkow, J. Yuzyk, R. Bryk, A. J. Yaremovich, P. Wach, P. Okrainec, N. Malanchuk and M. Kepron. The organization prepared material about the participation of the Ukrainians in Canada's war efforts in the two world conflicts, the history of the two Edmonton battalions whose personnel consisted of from 68 to 73% of Ukrainians, and other matters.

New immigration merges with community life

As we have already noted it was in a great measure due to the initiative of the Ukrainian Canadian Committee that a large number of the so-called D.P.'s (Displaced Persons) had arrived in Canada during the end of the forties and the beginning of the fifties. At the Third All-Canadian Congress of Ukrainian Canadians there were already several individuals of the new immigration taking part in the general three-day discussions. During these discussions there were differences of opinion on political matters in which the members of the new immigration showed the least measure of orientation in the Canadian political sphere. This was due, to a great degree, to the fact that among those present at the congress were people of diverse social and political ideas, as well as the lack of first-hand acquaintance, on the part of the new arrivals, with the local Ukrainian affairs that had already behind them fifty-year old history of adaptation to the demands of this country. But in spite of some of these dissonant notes the Congress, comprised of the six dominion-wide organizations—Ukrainian Catholic Brotherhood (B.U.K.), Ukrainian Self-Reliance League (S.U.S.), Ukrainian National Federation (U.N.O.), Ukrainian Canadian Veterans' Association (U.C.V.A.), United Hetman Organization (U.H.O.) and Ukrainian Workers' League (U.W.L.) and other local organizations—was able to carry out its appointed task in no less creative atmosphere than the two previous ones. From the first organizational beginnings of the new immigration, as well as from the stand taken by its leaders, it was shown that the organized sector of the Ukrainian life in Canada would be expanded in every one of its branches —educational, cultural and professional. All signs auspiciously were pointing to the future creation and development of new youth and women's organizations and especially the diversification in the social-political sector of life.

Learned societies support the cause of U.C.C.

The Fourth Ukrainian Canadian Committee Congress that took place on the 8-10 of July, 1953, was able to record a long row of organizations created by the new immigration. Among these we must first name the learned societies—Ukrainian Free Academy of Sciences (U.V.A.N.) and the Shevchenko Scientific Society, and following them, the veterans' and the community organizations. We will proceed to write about their work in the same given order. Some of them had been organized after the Fourth Congress but all of them, sooner or later, included themselves into the co-ordinating system of the Ukrainian Canadian Committee thereby leading to a still greater unification in the life of Ukrainian entity in the sphere of organizational system and basic principles.

The Ukrainian Free Academy of Sciences was organized in Canada in 1949 and was a natural continuation of the work of the Ukrainian Academy of Sciences that had been organized in Ukraine in 1918 and which, as a result of political events, was unable to become the forum of promoting a free science, for under the communist regime all teaching had to be filtered through the prism of Marx-Lenin ideology, especially in the sphere of humanities. U.V.A.N. was organized by the scholars and men of higher learning from the third immigration period, as well as by those who had lived in Canada for many years, including some who were native born Canadians. Among the noted leaders and distinguished men of letters who organized the U.V.A.N. were: the historian, Dmytro Doroshenko; the literateur Leonid Biletsky; the onomastic authority and Slavic linguist, J. B. Rudnyckyj, the agriculturist M. Borowsky, author of text books on bee-keeping and orchard cultivation, the archeologist Jaroslav Pasternak, and the well known figures Dr. T. K. Pavlychenko, Dr. P. Yuzyk, Dr. I. Hlynka, Dr. M. I. Mandryka, Dr. P. Macenko, and others. U.V.A.N. publishes a series of educational and research periodicals such as "Slavistica", "Onomastica", "Ukrainica Canadiana", Literature", "Ukrainian Scholars", "Ukrainica Occidentalia", "U.V.A.N. Chronicle" and others, and has its headquarters in Winnipeg.

Another institution, N.T.S. similar to U.V.A.N. is the T. Shevchenko Scientific Society that came into being at the end of the forties and which orientates itself to the traditions of the parent organizations in Ukraine and has its headquarters in Toronto. This institution has behind it, to its credit, notable literary achievements in Western Ukraine where it was first organized in 1873 and later in Eastern Ukraine as well. Some of the most illustrious literary lights, such as historian Mykhaylo Hrushevsky, the poet and man of letters Ivan Franko, Prof. O. Ohonovsky, Prof. Dr. I. Rakovsky and others, have honored the Shevchenko Scientific Society with their prestige as its executive heads. Eugene Wertyporoch, who has expanded its branches to Edmonton, Ottawa, Montreal and

Vancouver, is the head of the N.T.S. in Canada for years. Some of its most active members have been: Ivan Welyhorsky (1889-1955), a linguist and a pedagogue; Stepan Kylymnyk (1890-1966), author of studies in history and ethnography, Prof. V. Ivanys, Dr. V. J. Kaye, Prof. I. Tesla, Prof. B. R. Bociurkiw, Vladimir Mackiw, Bohdan Stebelsky, and others. N.T.S. has published a whole string of scientific works and every year arranges scientific conferences and edits its papers and chronicles. Both of these institutions are affiliated with U.C.C.

When we discuss educational-cultural life mention should be made of such an organization as Ukrainian Cultural and Educational Centre of Winnipeg that was organized in 1944 prior to U.V.A.N. and Shevchenko Scientific Society, and which devotes itself to the propagation of Ukrainian culture. This centre has built up and widely extended what is undoubtedly the largest Ukrainian library, archives and museum in Canada, has edited several publications dealing with the inception of cultural projects and created the system of the higher courses of studies in Ukrainiana. With this institution are connected such well known and distinguished names as: Olexander and Tetiana Koshetz, W. Kossar, Dr. T. K. Pavlychenko, Dr. I. Hlynka, Dr. M. Mandryka, A. Kachor, W. Klymkiw, and others. Over a period of years Sen. P. Yuzyk was at the head of it.

The new immigration noticeably augmented the higher scientific research life of Ukrainian Canadians and diversified its many branches of activities. The Research Institute of Wolyn was established in 1951 which did research study in the sociological life of the Wolyn territory in Ukraine and in addition to publishing several books, it also edited its own twice-yearly Wolyn Chronicles. By 1966 there were nine volumes of these collected works.

The Ukrainian Historical War Institute continued its publishing activity along with its museum-archives expansion that had been first started in Warsaw during the migration period.

The Ukrainian Teachers' Association was organized, whose foremost task had always been the creation and implementation of native school programs and teaching methods.

The Association of Writers of Children's Literature endeavoured to prepare and provide choice reading and teaching material for school children. Bohdan Hoshovsky compiled, for this purpose, the children's encyclopedia in Ukrainian language.

The Research Institute "Studium" of "LVU" formulated the anglo-printed publications dealing with Ukrainian affairs in Europe.

The Association of Friends of the U.V.A.N. engaged in developing further its own objectives. Similar work was carried on by the supporters of the Ukrainian Free University, in Europe.

In more recent times the Markian Shashkevych Centre was organized in Winnipeg, whose dedicated aim had the fervent ardor of a cult to popularize the name and memory of Markian Shashkevych, the great awakener of national life in the Ukrainian people and his influence on Ukrainians in the Old Country and abroad.

For the purpose of discussing the mutual educational problems and representation of Ukrainian scientific endeavours there was formed the

Ukrainian-Canadian Council of Learned Societies (Ukrainska Naukova Rada—U.N.R.), mostly from the leading ranks of U.V.A.N. and Shevchenko Scientific Society.

In formal ties with the world of scholars were the professional associations such as Ukrainian Medical Association of North America with branches in Canada, the Association of Engineers and Technicians of Canada, Association of Ukrainian Librarians in Canada, Association of Ukrainian-Canadian Veterinary Doctors, Association of Ukrainian Social Workers of Canada, Association of Ukrainian Jurists, Association of Ukrainian Journalists of Canada. This well balanced echelon of organizations spoke volumes for the vitality of Ukrainian entity, which had found its expansion in various directions of educational knowledge and professional life. All of them whole-heartedly supported the work of the Ukrainian Canadian Committee.

War Veterans' Organizations

Several war veterans' organizations were formed during the third era and all of them were included into the framework of the U.C.C. We already know about the work of the Ukrainian War Veterans' Association (U.C.V.A.). Prior to this, in 1937 the Ukrainian War Veterans' Inc. was organized and extended its work in later period. The Winnipeg branch was headed by I. Baydak, D. Mykytiuk, S. Bilinsky and D. Budka. The headquarters of this organization, that primarily was composed of the former members of the Ukrainian National Republic Army, was in Montreal with Col. S. Waldstein at the head. With the arrival of the new immigration the headquarters were transferred to Toronto in 1952, and the organization then was headed by: General M. Sadowsky and later by Capt. I. Yanishevsky and Major I. Lypovetsky. The association had 19 branches with General M. Sadowsky in charge and formed the Historical Museum of National Liberation, which in turn was a branch of the afore-mentioned Ukrainian Historical War Institute. One of the chief aims of the association was the "Propagation of Ukrainian national and military virtues" [3]), and all its publications were printed with that object in view.

Another group of veterans were organized in the Ukrainian Sitch War Veterans, with four branches in Canada under the leadership of Dr. Y. Soltykevych, Dr. A. Mospaniuk, Major O. Nawrocky, I. Tyktor, S. Wolynec, J. Bucmaniuk, Rev. M. Markiv and Dr. I. Fediw.

The Brotherhood of Carpathian Sitch was composed of the former veterans of Carpathian Sitch formed in 1939 and headed by Dr. S. Rossocha, G. Hwozdulych, J. Shanta, M. Shiposh, and T. Sydor.

Veterans of the Ukrainian Insurgent Army of the Second World War were united with the Society of Veterans of Ukrainian Insurgent Army (U.P.A.). The veterans of the Ukrainian Division were organized in the Brotherhood of former War Veterans of 1st Ukrainian Division (U.N.A.). The last named organization was much larger than the two previously mentioned and had several strongly active branches. It was headed by Dr. M. Malecky, W. Huzar, O. Zahoroda, R. Turko, J. Cviklevych, M.

---

[3]) Statute of Ukrainian War Veterans Inc.

Bihus, W. Weryha, B. Pidhayny, W. Yavorsky, S. Gulak and others. The "U.P.A." veterans' organizations strove for unity as they were only divided by temporary political sympathies and not by any permanent past associations. The leaders in these formations were: Evhen Shtendera, Mykola Koshyk, Bohdan Chubenko, I. Eliashewsky, M. Fedak, M. Kulyk, E. Shakhay, S. Pasichnyk and others.

The primary task of all these mentioned organizations was the yearly fund-raising campaign in the month of November which was carried out under the motto: "Donation Gift for the Ukrainian Invalids" and had its objective the supplying of material and moral aid to the invalid brethren in Canada and those in Europe who due to the lack of physical health conditions were unable to leave for overseas. These fund collections, with the cooperation of the above mentioned organizations, were carried under the auspices of the Ukrainian Canadian Relief Fund of Canada with a total sum of well over $100,000.

Ukrainian Canadian Youth Council

As we have already seen the combatants' organizations were formed according to their former military associations or even individual unit formations. Somewhat in a similar fashion, along the line of church or ideological-political affiliations, the youth organizations were formed. We have mentioned earlier, in the mid-war era, such youth organizations as: Canadian Ukrainian Youth Association of Canada (S.U.M.K.) closely connected with the Ukrainian Greek-Orthodox Church; Ukrainian Catholic Youth (U.K.U.) affiliated with Ukrainian Catholic Church, and the Ukrainian National Youth Federation (M.U.N.) whose parent organization was the Ukrainian National Federation. The third immigration created three other very active youth organizations, namely: Ukrainian Youth Association—Plast (Scouts), Ukrainian Youth Association of Canada (S.U.M.), and the Ukrainian Democratic Youth Association (O.D.U.M.). All of them have their chartered statutes, uniforms, flags and insignias.

"Plast" (Scouts) relates its work to the traditions of the parent organization that was once in existence on western Ukrainian lands and is now continuing this project by expanding its organizational work in this country. To aid further in this task the so-called "Plast-Friends", was formed composed of parents of the youthful members who give material aid to this branch of work. Plast has erected a chain of recreation buildings across Canada, and issued a series of publications devoted to the bringing up of youth, organized camping trips, arranged conventions and took active part in celebrating traditional national holidays. Although it is true that even prior to "Plast's" formation in 1948 there had been some scattered scout units, but these had not been on a wide organized scale. "Plast" developed itself into a dominion-wide organization, entered into the realm of U.C.C. and revealed itself as a dynamic institution. In 1967 it counted its members at one and a half thousand with ten branches in all.

There is much in common between the work done by "Plast" and that of the Ukrainian Youth Association of Canada (S.U.M.) which was organized at the same time and from the same immigration as "Plast". "S.U.M." also uses similar methods in its work. It formed spiritual ties with the Ukrainian Youth Association that was very active against the Bolshevik regime, which had organized itself on the eastern Ukrainian lands following the First World War. From this original source "S.U.M." was able to derive a more pungent type of political patriotism than the other youth organizations. "S.U.M." works hand in hand with the Canadian League for Ukraine's Liberation and embraces a large number of the Ukrainian youth in Canada. There were 25 "S.U.M." centres or branches in 1963 and by 1967 this number had jumped to 40 with around 3,000 members and over 200 educators. "S.U.M." had also a chain of its own buildings and summer camps, press organ and conducted its own network of native schools.

Ukrainian National Democratic League (O.D.U.M.) was formed mostly from the immigration that arrived from the eastern Ukrainian lands. This organization devotes its time to formulate political thinking within the ranks of the growing-up young people. Politically it stands close to Ukrainian Association of Victims of Russian Communist Terror (S.U.Z.E.R.O.) and its organ in Canada is the monthly journal "Young Ukraine".

All three of the above mentioned organizations formed their educative ideals based on the world-wide accepted ideological and democratic principles and strongly fought against the political Marxist materialism of the prevailing system in Ukraine. In this respect they stood close to the three other organizationally older, youthful sisters namely "S.U.M.K.", "M.U.N." and "U.K.U." All these, mutually allied, youth establishments combined together to form the Ukrainian Canadian Youth Council (R.U.M.K.) in 1953. Facing the youth was the task of working in unison for the future good of Canada, which in turn required united aims and efforts that were so well stated in the Council's constitution-rules: "To strive for the fullest participation of Ukrainian Canadian youth in the general Canadian social, educational, economical and cultural life" [4]. Along with this objective the "R.U.M.K." was to cultivate among the Ukrainian youth in Canada a sound idea of good citizenship and prepare it for the responsibility of preserving the unity of the Ukrainian community life in this country [5]. In toto this was the organic growth of youth which expressed itself through the coordination medium of national up-bringing in the field of culture, education, outdoor camping and sport life. "R.U.M.K." was also a constituent part of the Ukrainian Canadian Committee for in its work it contained many elements for the good of which this Ukrainian centre was originally created.

The Ukrainian Canadian University Students Union (S.U.S.K.) worked very closely with "R.U.M.K." It was formed in 1953 from the following student organizations: "Alpha-Omega" (1930), "Gamma Rho Kappa-Obnova" of the Canadian Ukrainian Catholic Student Organizations; the Ukrainian Greek-Orthodox Students' organization, the "Ilarion"; the Ukrainian Students' Association of Mikhnowsky (T.U.S.M.), and the Ukrainian Academic Association of "Zarevo". There also were some of students' clubs at such Universities as McGill, McMaster, Montreal University, Sir George Williams College and other colleges and universities.

---

[4] Book of Regulations, Ukrainian Canadian Youth Council, paragraph 111, Item D.
[5] Same as above—Item B.

Both "R.U.M.K." and "S.U.S.K." had their representatives in the General Council and the Presidium of the Ukrainian Canadian Committee.

Even if the cohesiveness of "R.U.M.K." was weakened to a certain extent in the last few years, still the spokesmen for these organizations performed their tasks in unison and the evidence of this is preserved in the memorial book in the National Library in Ottawa on the occasion of Canada's Centennial.

"S.U.S.K." collaborated with other Ukrainian students' organizations which existed beyond Canadian borders such as Association of Ukrainian Students' Organization of U.S.A. (S.U.S.T.A.) and the central students' association in the free world, so-called "CESUS".

Ukrainian Canadian Committee—Women's Council

Starting with the year 1944 there had been in existence the Women's Council as a constituent part of the Ukrainian Canadian Committee (U.C.C.) composed of Ukrainian Women's Association of Canada (S.U.K.), Ukrainian Women's Organization (O.U.K.) and the Ukrainian Catholic Women's League (L.U.K.Z.). With a single organized front the women had taken an active part in the Second Ukrainian Congress with the following representatives from the three main organizations: M. Dyma, N. Kohuska and E. Sytnyk, who on behalf of all the women declared their full support for the presidium of the U.C.C. This support was later revealed in the Red Cross work and the aid for the displaced persons in Europe that were under the care of the Ukrainian Canadian Relief Fund.

To this grand trio of women's organizations, each comprising tens of branches in different provinces, was also joined the Women's Association of Canadian League for Ukraine's Liberation (O.Z.-L.V.U.). First branches of this organization were formed in 1951 from the newly arrived immigration. From 1955 O.Z.-L.V.U. has become a separate statutory organization. Among the first branches were those in Winnipeg, Oshawa and Toronto. When the O.Z.-L.V.U. celebrated their tenth anniversary in 1961 it had 22 branches, but by 1967 it had grown to 44. The organization carried on multi-sided activities and considered itself to be a very important adjunct in the front line activities in the work of the Canadian League for Ukraine's Liberation (L.V.U.) [6]. The greatest amount of work done by O.Z.-L.V.U. has been devoted to the bringing up of youth in the S.U.M. organization and, in addition, in the various charitable activities as well as taking part in political and cultural affairs connected with the parent organization of the L.V.U. Although the above named quartet of women's organizations had been like a main motor in the promotion of the organized life of Ukrainian women, it was not able to bring all women into its fold. Outside its frame there was a whole string of small organizations that were included in the local committees of the Ukrainian Women's Council. Of course in this way they were able to influence indirectly the course of community affairs.

The chairmanship of the big four group was held on rotation basis.

---

[6] Maria Solonynka, "Aims and Tasks of O.Z.—L.V.U.", Almanac "Homin Ukrainy", 1962, p. 177.

The style of their activities was similar to and allied with the work of the kindred men's organizations: S.U.S.—S.U.K; B.U.K.—L.U.K.Z.; U.N.O.—O.U.K.; and L.V.U.—O.Z.-L.V.U. All of these organizations together, on the occasion of the 50-year commemoration of the death of Lesia Ukrainka, published a collection of her literary works in the English language. Also in the general presentation of Ukrainian Canadian culture the women's organizations work in unison. In this category of united women's action may be cited the Ukrainian Day at Expo 1967 in Montreal, and similar days of distinction of local and provincial scope.

On the external plane each organization cooperates with the general Canadian and international women's organizations and all of them are members of the World Federation of the Ukrainian Women's Associations (S.F.U.Z.O.) that came into existence in 1948 during a convention in Philadelphia and which is the central federation of all Ukrainian women beyond the native homeland.

Dominion-wide Community Organizations

During the third era of our history a whole network of local community organizations were formed and fanned out, which, in addition to their ideological credos were also concerned with political and local community affairs. We are already acquainted with such organizations as S.U.S., U.N.O., B.U.K., S.H.D. and U.R.O. This category of community's organizations is popularly called the "Founders of the Ukrainian Canadian Committee (U.C.C.)" Some of them had a noticeable political tint, while others a more religious hue. Such typical organizations began to form following the Second World War. The Ukrainian Evangelical Alliance (U.E.O.) already known to us from the second era, joined with U.C.C. after the war and was the only organization in this central institution that had been formed prior to the war out of the Ukrainians from the first and second immigration. All the other organizations comprising U.C.C. were formed from the third immigration. These included S.U.N.D. —U.N.D.S., S.U.Z.E.R.O., U.K.T. and L.V.U.

The Ukrainian National Democratic League had its objective to unite the democratically thinking and socio-community active people and work in unison to develop a universal politically conscious Ukrainian Canadian and to give support to those national organizations that were striving to rebuild the Ukrainian state and were also fighting the extreme leftist and rightist movements. S.U.N.D. was organized in 1950 and later renamed to Ukrainian National Democratic League (U.N.D.S.). It originators in Winnipeg were: W. Kochan, S. Wolynec and S. Radchuk.

The ideology of the Ukrainian National Democratic League stood very closely to that of Ukrainian Association of Victims of Russian Communist Terror (S.U.Z.E.R.O.). This organization was composed mostly of those who had suffered from the communist terror in Ukraine. The very name itself clearly denoted its political character. S.U.Z.E.R.O. stood on the principles of Christianity and democracy and directed its activities towards the strengthening of the constitutional rights, and the propagation of peace among Ukrainian Canadians, condemning especially at every step, the terrible crimes committed by the Stalinist regime against the Ukrainian people in the occupied territories. By the efforts of this organization there appeared in the English language the monumental "White Book" about the black deeds of the Kremlin, in two volumes, the "Islands of Death" and a whole series of other publications. In its statute book the S.U.Z.E.R.O. explains that all its anti-communist struggle is also of great service to the new fatherland of Canada, so that it will not suffer the same fate, a victim to the communist experiment. The foundation work for this organization was laid by the following political idealists: S. Pidhainy, P. Volyniak, M. Prychodko, W. Shelest, M. Shklar and others. U.N.D.S. and S.U.Z.E.R.O. supported the government in exile of the Ukrainian National Republic as well as aided the work of Ukrainian National Council, the latter having been formed from the immigration element to help the former and to propagate the ideals of the Ukrainian National Republic.

The Canadian Friends for Liberation of Ukraine (U.K.T.) began its work at the end of 1951 and its founders endeavoured "to carry on, within the constituent Canadian way of life, moral and material aid to the liberation forces in Ukraine—the Organization of Ukrainian Nationalists (O.U.N.), Ukrainian Insurgent Army (U.P.A.) and the Ukrainian Supreme Liberation Council (U.H.V.R.)". In its relationship to Canada the U.K.T. declared itself to stand for the following principles: "to work for the inception of morality and ethics into the social and political life of Ukrainian Canadians, to cultivate the spirit of friendship, tolerance and self-respect and to fight against fanaticism and intolerance". Founders of U.K.T. were: R. Rakhmanny, A. Iwachniuk, I. Eliashewsky, O. Zhyhar, I. Mishchyna, K. Mykytchuk, M. Fedak and others.

The last socio-community organization on the list and which also joined the ranks of U.C.C. in 1956, was the Canadian League for Ukraine's Liberation (L.V.U.). Even as the other formerly mentioned organizations, the L.V.U. was organized in 1949 and selected two main principles for the foundation of its work. They are: "To unite and enlist the Ukrainian citizens of Canada, as well as Canadians of other nationalities, around the battlefield arena of struggle to liberate Ukraine from the Russian-communist enslavement and to uphold the spirit of loyalty to Canada, defend its independence and its democratic way of life from the direct and indirect attack of Russian imperialism and communist totalitarianism" [7].

L.V.U. expanded its work with much more intensity and energy than the three other previously mentioned organizations and within a short period of time they had a large network of branches and allied women's groups as well as having initiated the active young people's organization, the mentioned S.U.M. to which the parent-body devoted a great deal of time and care. The generosity of the membership enabled them to engage expert organizers, build institutions, arrange for special funds and carry on other types of activities. Of inestimable help in the work of L.V.U. became the weekly newspaper "Homin Ukrainy" and the radio programs presented by the various branches. Following are the founders of the L.V.U.: Dr. R. Malashchuk, W. Makar, M. Krawciw, W. Bezchlibnyk, Dr. O. Kushnir, O. Matla, M. Sosnowsky, W. Klish, W. Boro-

---

[7] Statute "Canadian League for Ukraine's Liberation", Toronto, 1951, p. 4.

dach, J. Spolsky, B. Stebelsky, W. Hyrak, I. Boyko, P. Bashuk, I. Varanycia, W. Solonynka, W. Sagash, and others, and in women's organization there are: M. Solonynka, L. Vertyporoch, J. Iwanchuk, N. Varanycia, S. Sagash, M. Malashchuk, N. Bashuk. In 1967 L.V.U. had 55 branches and around 3,000 members. It has become the owner, or part owner, of establishments and possesses many libraries, inventory etc. L.V.U. has published some 26 larger book editions and hundreds of mimeographed pamphlets and booklets. Every year, it has taken part in the preparation of large national gatherings of the Ukrainians in Canada and United States to honor the great events in Ukrainian history.

Originally L.V.U. declared its support for O.U.N., U.P.A. and U.H.V.R., but later when complications arose in the Foreign Representation of U.H.V.R., it drew its support mostly to the Anti-Bolshevik Bloc of Nations (A.B.N.) and other formations that were in accord with this centre. In line with the spirit of the A.B.N. front, the Union for the Liberation of Ukraine (S.V.U.) was formed with a few of its branches cooperating with the local units of U.C.C.

We mention these political organizations because they had wielded a great amount of influence on the formation of Ukrainian community life in Canada, which at times was perhaps even too new, and incepted their characteristic quality into the vital problems of Ukrainian Canadian entity. Many long years of cooperative work within the leavening atmosphere of U.C.C. helped to smooth out the sharp corners and rough edges and at the same time transformed people's political passions into a mature life.

From the very names themselves and from the objectives of the above mentioned organizations one can judge that their aims were mostly of a political nature, directed toward the combatting of communist theory and politics and the renewal of independent statehood for the Ukrainian nation on its own territories. Such political formations had a great influence on the wholly concerted work of the Ukrainian Canadian Committee, which had, up to the time of receiving these political groups into its central formation, led a wise national policy in exposing the political pace of the Bolshevik doctrine and Kremlin's hideous practice. In this way the Ukrainian Canadian Committee became a coordinator of work in the cultural field, as well as a political information medium for the general Canadian community, about Eastern Europe, as may be attested by the numerous memoranda sent by this central institution to the Canadian government, the United Nations and to the governments of various other countries. This kind of work on the part of U.C.C. harmonized with the action of the Ukrainian centres in exile and these two activities of the various representations led them to a mutual self-fulfillment.

Be it to the credit of the Ukrainian Canadian Committee that in all of its many activities it never went beyond the measure of its competence—the competence of a responsible Ukrainian institution based on the principles of Canadian citizenship. In spite of the fact that the problems of Eastern Europe held much interest for U.C.C. it still considered as its first duty, the good of the Ukrainian community in Canada, its cultural aspects and above all, the future welfare of this community— and thus, the well-being of the whole of Canada. The balancing of these problems helped the steady growth of U.C.C. which in turn gained the confidence and support of all—the Canadian-born and the new immigrants, the pioneer element and those who came after. This brought additional strength to this Ukrainian Canadian co-ordinating centre which became a genuine and official spokesman of freedom and aspiration of the whole Ukrainian Canadian entity and the central powerhouse for balancing and reconciling religious, political and organizational differences. This also had a psychological effect on the total social community about which one of the long-time leaders of this institution had this to say at the Slavic Convention in Ottawa:

"It has given Canadian citizens of Ukrainian origin a feeling of greater security and worth, and paradoxically, a sense of greater interdependence, so vital in this modern and complex age. It has given them a sense of greater usefulness not only in regard to their own group, but also in the wider Canadian sphere, in the field of communication with other groups of citizens" [8].

In 1967 Ukrainian Canadian Committee consisted of 31 different organizations. In addition to these it had 30 branches in Alberta, 36 in Saskatchewan, 21 in Manitoba, 22 in Ontario, 1 in Quebec and 1 in B.C.—111 branches and 28 representations in various parts of Canada. The headquarters of U.C.C. have been located in Winnipeg, which has always been considered as the historical capital of the Ukrainians in Canada, all the more so since the Metropolitan seats of the two largest Ukrainian churches, the Ukrainian Catholic and the Ukrainian Greek-Orthodox, are located here, as well as the abbotships of the two great religious orders, the Basilian and the Redemptorist. During some period of time the headquarters of S.U.S., B.U.K. and U.N.O and the allied women's organizations, were situated here. But coupled with the people's increased movement eastward and the influx of the new immigration, along with the religious divisions into separate eparchies, such dominion organizations as B.U.K and S.U.S. decided to rotate their headquarters between Toronto, Saskatoon and Edmonton, while U.N.O. and L.V.U. always had their headquarters in Toronto. The headquarters of the veterans, youth, and of all those other organizations that were formed after the Second World War—like U.N.D.S., S.U.Z.E.R.O. and U.K.T.—were also moved eastward. As a result of this, Toronto became like a second Ukrainian capital alongside Winnipeg.

The Ukrainian Canadian Committee for a full 25 years has been under the presidency of Rev. Dr. Wasyl Kushnir, with the exception of 1953 and 1955, when this honor was bestowed upon Anthony J. Yaremovich —a lawyer, and in 1956 on the vice-president, Rev. S. W. Sawchuk. The greatest events in the life of U.C.C. have been the triennial Congresses of the Ukrainian Canadians that took place in the years: 1943, 1946, 1950, 1953, 1956, 1959, 1962 and 1965. In between the Congress periods the General Council of the U.C.C. would meet to make a ruling on some exceptionally important affairs, otherwise the presidium itself, comprised of the various organizations' representatives, would handle

---

[8] From J. H. Syrnick's speech during the Slavic Conference in Ottawa in 1967, entitled: "The Ukrainian Canadian Committee: Its Significance in the Canadian Society", Slavs in Canada, Vol. II. Inter-University Committee on Canadian Slavs, Ottawa, 1968.

the matters that would arise from day to day. In the Presidium of U.C.C. which, at the beginning, was also known as the Executive, were the following representatives of various organizations: C. H. Andrusyshen, P. Barytsky, P. and N. Bashuk, M. Borowsky, L. Biletsky, E. Wasylyshyn, O. Woycenko, Pastor A. Vyniavsky, M. Hnatiw, I. Hlynka, M. Hykawy, I. Gulay, B. and M. Dyma, Rev. M. Dyrda, A. Zaharychuk, Rev. S. Izyk, Pastor J. R. Kovalevich, J. Kozoriz, H. Kuksa, N. Kohuska, M. Mandryka, M. Marunchak, T. Melnychuk, T. Mychayliwsky, P. Oliynycky, S. Radchuk, S. Romaniw, Rev. S. Semczuk, M. Seleshko, S. Skoblak, E. Sytnyk, Pastor L. Standred, O. Tarnovecka, Rev. I. Shpytkowsky, A. Figus, T. Cirka, To these we add from the pioneer era: T. D. Ferley, M. Stechishin, K. S. Prodan, J. W. Arsenych and from the younger generation of this same category—D. Lobay, G. Elendiuk, S. Chavaliboga, T. Kobzey, W. Swystun and I. Rudachek. From the leaders of the second era we have: W. Kossar, J. Syrnick—who was for many years a general secretary and the first vice-president, W. Sarchuk, T. Dackiw, Sen. P. Yuzyk, J. R. Solomon, MLA, A. Malofie, M. Poherecky and from the newer period: V. Martynec, G. Hwozdulych, P. Wach, I. Iwanchuk, J. Karasevich, R. Bryk, pastor I. Jatcenty, V. Klymkiw, S. Pulak, V. Sagash, M. Worobec, I. Pavluk, W. Korytowsky, M. Plawiuk, M. Sosnowsky and J. Yuzyk. A principle was established that every component organization was to have its representative included in the General Council of the U.C.C. Some of the aforementioned individuals were also members of the General Council which later was changed to Presidium Council. Other members of the Presidium Council were: O. Gudziak, A. Kachor, P. A. Kondra, P. Krypiakevych, M. Marko, B. Martynowych, S. Mokriy, R. Romanowych, I. Onyfriychuk, M. Boyaniwska, J. B. Rudnyckyj, R. Senchuk, M. Wawrykow, M. Baryluk, M. Spiwak, M. Nowycky and others. From the above list we can well see that both the Presidium itself and the Presidial Council of the U.C.C. had some distinguished representatives of the organized life of the Ukrainians in this country. The right-hand man of the Presidium and of the Presidial Council is the executive director. This function was first performed by I. Ruryk and for long period of 18 years by Volodymyr Kochan (born 1898, died 1966), a well known organizer and the architect of great projects in the life of Ukrainian Canadians. Recently this important post was taken over by Dr. S. Kalba. Among those who have devoted long years of service to this representative organization are—Andrew Zaharychuk, Ivan Pankiw, Osyp Nawrocky, Anna Wach and Dr. Bohdan Martynowych.

During its 28 years of devoted service the U.C.C. has proved itself to be a dynamic institution representing in a dignified manner the Ukrainian Canadians[9]). More on this, see "Decade of Multiculturalism".

---

[9]) This dynamic life is shown by the data of the component organizations. Here we only refer to the given figures of the so-called "Big Four" in the composition of Ukrainian Canadian Committee. The B.U.K.-System of the Ukrainian Catholic Council: B.U.K. branches—56, L.U.K.Z.—172, U.K.U.—71, T.U.S.K.—"Obnova" —5, Knights of Columbus—5. ("Development of the Ukrainian Catholic Group in Canada", 1966) The S.U.S.—System of the Ukrainian Self-Reliance League: S.U.S.—T.U.S.—around 50 branches, SUK.—150, SUMK—about 50 branches. ("Forty Years in Retrospect" by Natalia Levenec-Kohuska, Hamilton—Toronto—Winnipeg, 1967).

The U.N.O.-System of the Ukrainian National Federation: 34 branches plus 12

The strength of the UCC lies not only in the Dominion wide organizations but also in its local branches. All local community organizations consider it their duty to be a member of the local UCC. There are branches of the UCC whose membership numbers in excess of 50 community organizations (Winnipeg, Toronto, Montreal, Edmonton).

First local branches of UCC were organized in Western Canada, Saskatoon, Regina, Vegreville (1940); Calgary, Edmonton, Vancouver (1941). Montreal was the first in Eastern Canada to organize a local branch in 1940, followed by Toronto, Windsor, St. Catherines, and Hamilton in 1941. Recently branches were formed in London and Ottawa. The founding members of the local UCC were organizations such as S.U.S., B.U.K., U.N.O., U.S.H., U.R.O. and Ukrainian Veterans' Association. Frequently the officers of these organizations held table offices in the local UCC.

It has now become traditional for the various community organizations to celebrate national historical commemorations jointly under the auspices of local UCC, e.g. Ukrainian Settlement in Canada, January 22, November 1st, Shevchenko Anniversary, etc.

At the beginning a dynamic branch of the UCC existed in Saskatoon but recently it has been outstripped by Edmonton and Vancouver. In Edmonton the UCC branch was led by such individuals as P. J. Lazarowich, QC, Dr. L. Faryna, D. Yanda, J. Esaiw, I. Verchomin, J. Pryma, Dr. C. N. Suchowersky, Dr. M. Snihurowych, P. Savaryn, R. L. Dzenick, R. Ostashewsky. In Vancouver among the more prominent were Rev. D. Kirstiuk, Rev. T. Dobko, J. Yasenchuk, M. Homola, T. Kuzyk, M. Pukish, in recent years Agnes Cripps and Emily Ostapchuk. Of special note is the longstanding contribution of Paul Bayrak and John P. Svityk in Calgary. More recent prominent leaders were W. Nazarevych, V. Riznyk, M. Masiuk, Lubomyr Hladyshevsky.

The most dynamic branches of the UCC in the East were located in Toronto and Montreal. Both branches were reinforced by an influx of the third immigration of professional and industrial talents. Among the early leaders were Rev. P. Kamenecky and T. Humeniuk, Q.C., and more recently the lawyers: D. Shtokalo and M. Romaniuk, lately—Dr. M. Mycyk, Dr. M. Kushpeta, Dr. J. Boyko, Dr. P. Hlibowych, Dr. G. Danyliw, Dr. O. Rudzik, while W. Muz served as general secretary for around 20 years.

The Montreal Branch was equally fortunate in having in its leadership prominent personalities such as A. Hukalo. M. Hrab, L. Tomashchuk, O. Kushnir, and T. Cechmistro. In Hamilton UCC movement was given direction by Dr. P. T. Smylski, P. Bozok, Dr. S. Klimashko, J. Boyko, Dr. F. Martyniuk. Recently Branches in St. Catherines, Windsor and London have become rather active. In London Dr. E. Roslycky has given outstanding service.

In western Canada we record active branches of the UCC in Prince

---

branches of Ukrainian War Veterans' Association (U.S.H.), 18 groups affiliated with U.S.H., 22 Women's Organizations (O.U.K.) and 15 youth branches (M.U.N.O.). ("Success and Perspectives of U.N.O.", New Pathway, No. 45, 1966). The L.V.U.-System of the Canadian League for Ukraine's Liberation: 52 branches, Women's (O.Z.-L.V.U.)—22 branches. Membership: men 1842, women 607—total 2449. ("Documents of the Tenth Convention of L.V.U. Toronto, April 10 & 11, 1965).

Albert, Regina, Vegreville. Special mention should be made of the Winnipeg Branch which operates in the shadow of the Central UCC. On this sector major contributions were made by such outstanding personages as Dr. V. F. Bachynski, Judge J. R. Soloman, Judge M. Baryluk, J. Kereluk, Dr. I. Hlynka, H. Bryk, S. Radchuk, P. Krypiakevych, M. Spiwak, C. Semchyshyn, M. Skoblak, O. Surasky, I. F. Palamarchuk, and others.

Organization outside the UCC System

For a whole year the pro-communist elements did not have any visible outer forms. The Ukrainian Labor and Farmers' Temple Association, U.L.F.T.A., was by government's order, shut down and its assets went mostly into the hands of Ukrainian national organizations. But within a year the situation was changed in favour of the above mentioned communist centre. As soon as Germany went to war with Soviet Russia the ban was lifted. Already on July 26, 1941, the Ukrainian Association of Aid to the Fatherland (U.A.A.F.) was formed in Toronto headed by the previously mentioned in this history, S. Maciyevych, M. Hrynchyshyn, and others. In less than a year the First Country-wide Convention of U.A.A.F. was called to order and at this gathering the name of the association was changed to: Association of Ukrainian Canadians. All its initial work went in the direction of regaining their expropriated wealth which was finally accomplished by the government's order on Oct. 15, 1943. Soon afterwards the Association of United Ukrainian Canadians (T.O.U.K.) was formed which by 1948 had already held its third convention in a row. During its fourth convention in Toronto in 1950 a resolution was passed to commemorate six decades of Ukrainian activity in Canada and to erect a monument of Taras Shevchenko on Canadian soil. The monument was sent from Kiev and it was unveiled in Palermo, near Toronto. This was the second Ukrainian monument in Canada [10]. T.O.U.K. also celebrated in Winnipeg, in 1956, the 100th anniversary of the birth of Ivan Franko, by the unveiling of museum that had been erected in honor of the poet.

Fanaticism and the work tempo of this erstwhile centre has been greatly diminished lately compared with the thirties, prior to the Second World War. As to its numerical strength, this movement lost its power greatly. This is not only due to political action of the third immigration but also due to intensive Russification in the Old Country by the present Soviet regime. T.O.U.K.'s stand towards russification is portrayed in the chapter "Others Outside the UCC System".

---

[10] The first monument was of Markian Shashkevych in Winnipeg, erected by "Ridna Shkola" of M. Shashkevych and national organizations of Canada in 1943-1944.

THIRD ERA — ILLUSTRATIONS

Rev. Wasyl Kushnir, the First President of: The Ukrainian Canadian Committee, The Pan-American Ukrainian Conference, The World Congress of Free Ukrainians.

Presidium of the Pan-American Ukrainian Conference; Fourth Session, Winnipeg, 1951. (Details—see Supplement).

Hierarchy of the Ukrainian Catholic Church of Canada

Metropolitan Maxim Hermaniuk
Winnipeg

Bishop Neil Savaryn, O.S.B.M.,
Edmonton

Bishop Isidore Borecky, Toronto

Bishop Andrew Roborecky, Saskatoon

THIRD ERA — ILLUSTRATIONS

Hierarchy of the Ukrainian Greek-Orthodox Church of Canada

Metropolitan Ilarion Ohienko,

Metropolitan Mykhail Khoroshy

Metropolitan Andrey Metiuk

Archbishop Boris, Edmonton

Second Grand Convention of the Ukrainian Baptist Brotherhood of North America, Toronto, 1959 (Details—see Supplement).

Executive of the Ukrainian Evangelical Alliance of North America, 1965. (Details—see Supplement)

THIRD ERA — ILLUSTRATIONS

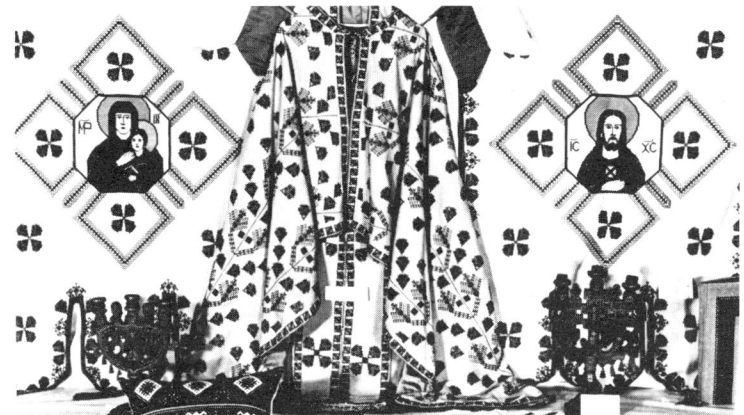

The Adaptation of national art forms for use in Church vestments, holy pictures and candle holders.

The use of carvings and encrustation in the making of crosses, decorative plates, chests, etc.

614 UKRAINIAN CANADIANS: A HISTORY

**Bandura, embroidery, Easter Eggs and the Kobza
provide beauty to the Ukrainian home**

THIRD ERA — ILLUSTRATIONS 615

Beadwork is a popular means of decorating household articles, especially among the Hutsuls.

Courtesy of Michael Dodiak

616   UKRAINIAN CANADIANS: A HISTORY

National Dress of Various Regions of Ukraine

Yavoriv

Kiev

Lemko

Hutsul

Poltava

Borshchiv

Kolomyya

Horodenka

Sniatyn

THIRD ERA — ILLUSTRATIONS

"Dibrova" Women's Choir (in national dress), W. Kardash, conductor, Toronto, 1967. (Details—see Supplement).

Male Choir "Surma" of Winnipeg, conducted by George Hnatiuk, 1955 (Details—see Supplement).

"Prometey" Choir, Toronto, Choirmaster W. Kardash. (Details—see Supplement).

M.U.N.O. Choir and Dance Ensemble "Dunay", St. Catharines, 1967, Choirmaster N. Hladysh.

O. Koshetz Memorial Choir of U.N.F., Winnipeg, 1966, conducted by W. Klymkiw. (Details—see Supplement).

U.N.F. Choir of Fort William, 1952, conducted by O. Cukornyk.

THIRD ERA — ILLUSTRATIONS

S.U.M. Choir of Vancouver, Conductor W. Kardash, 1952.
(Details—see Supplement).

Ladies' Choir "Verchovyna", Choirmaster S. Yaremenko, Edmonton, 1968.
(Details—see Supplement).

S.U.M. Choir of Winnipeg, 1955, conducted by Wasyl Kardash.
(Details—see Supplement).

Participants in the XIV National Convention of the Ukrainian Youth Association (S.U.M.), Toronto, 1967. (Details—see Supplement).

Educational Summer Camp of "O.D.U.M." — "Dnipro", Toronto, 1965.

THIRD ERA — ILLUSTRATIONS 621

Ukrainian Youth Associationn—Past-Scout Organization, Winnipeg Branch, 1961. (Details—see Supplement).

"CYMK" Members and Lecturers during Ukrainian Courses at Summer Camp "Kiev" in 1961. (Details—see Supplement).

All Ukrainians, young or old, feel their national duty to commemorate "Shevchenko Days" in March. Fragment of Edmonton. (Details—see Supplement).

Right Honorable L. B. Pearson, Prime Minister of Canada is delivering his concluding remarks to 1500 participants of "The Ukrainian Youth Day" on the grounds of the House of Commons, Ottawa, July 1967.

Members of the Ukrainian Canadian Servicemen's Association. Active Service Overseas 1939-1945, in front of their club in the Vicarage, 218 Sussex Gardens, London, England (1944).

Royal Canadian Legion delegates to Ukrainian Canadian Veterans' Association of Canada convention held in Winnipeg during the unveiling of Taras Shevchenko Monument, 1961. (Details—see Supplement)

624 UKRAINIAN CANADIANS: A HISTORY

Veterans' Leaders

S. Pawluk

O. Nawrockyj

J. G. Karasevich

M. Seleshko,

G. R. B. Panchuk

St. Rosocha

E. Shtendera

P. T. Smylski

R. Bryk

UKRAINIAN LANGUAGE
IN PUBLIC SCHOOLS AND UNIVERSITIES

From the time the teaching of Ukrainian language in public schools was so drastically eliminated in Manitoba, by Premier T. C. Norris, along with the burning of the Ukrainian school books on the parliament building grounds, the teaching was done only in homes and private schools. Similar situation existed in two other provinces, Saskatchewan and Alberta. All along, Ukrainian Canadians considered such drastic steps, on the part of provincial governments, as a rank injustice to them—as taxpayers and citizens of a free country. Having come to these conclusions they constantly demanded, from the provincial governments, the renewal of their former rights, not only in the teaching of Ukrainian in public schools, but that there should also be courses in Ukrainian instituted in the universities as well. In addition to the formal matter of factual arguments they also, very often, underlined the cultural values of this language not only for the Ukrainians themselves, but even for the good of their fellow citizens as well. In one of the briefs advocating the teaching of the Ukrainian language in schools we read the following:

"The Ukrainian language is recognized by linguists to be in a central position among the Slavic languages. It serves as a bridge between the northern and southern Slavic peoples. Morphologically it has many similarities with Russian language; in the formation of its sounds it is close to the Serbian and Croatian; in the formation of its vocabulary it bears resemblance to the Polish language. Because of these characteristics the Ukrainian language is understood by practically all Slavic groups and for that reason is frequently used as a common medium of communication among them. Historically, Ukrainian is the oldest Slavic language, tracing its history to the ninth century" [1].

But the most obvious argument for the teaching of Ukrainian language in schools was the need of the Ukrainian community itself that strove with dedication and determination to preserve this linguistic key to its national cultural treasures. Towards this very goal the years of effort in the three prairie provinces were directed. There were many combined reasons why all these concerted efforts did not bring immediate results. But time would not stand still and with its onward march it also brought significant changes in the mentality of the Canadian society. The so-called monolithic culture was losing ground, at first to the bi-culturalism and still later to the multi-culturalism. Step by step Canada was abandoning its conviction that there must always be two categories of citizens—the more and less important ones, the better and the lesser class. Thanks to this same evolving process of thinking, the attitude of progressive individuals and the collective efforts of the Ukrainian citizens the Ukrainian language was again repatriated in public schools and introduced into universities. All this, however, did not begin until 1944.

---

[1] Brief to the Royal Commission on Education in Manitoba, by Ukrainian Canadian Committee, November 1957.

Saskatchewan

Although Manitoba was in the lead with Ukrainian language being taught in public schools during the pioneer era and was trying hard to regain its earlier status in the second era, it was left to Saskatchewan to beat her to a draw.

During the Second World War there was, on the teaching staff at the University of Saskatchewan, in Saskatoon, a man of intelligence embracing wide horizons and an expert on Eastern Europe's affairs, Prof. George Simpson. It was mostly due to his influence, as well as to that of such leading Ukrainians of Saskatchewan as Prof. Dr. Toma Pavlychenko, also of the Saskatchewan University, that it was possible to implement the Ukrainian cathedra at the University of Saskatchewan. The professor-founder of this cathedra was the Winnipeg-reared scholar, Dr. C. H. Andrusyshen, although Dr. T. Pavlychenko was the instructor during its first year of existence. Dr. C. H. Andrusyshen, in addition to his knowledge of the "Ukrainiana", also has expanded, at the University of Saskatchewan, the general Slavic philology, Polish and Russian studies and, based on the newest evaluations, the Sovietology. About 4,000 students have taken the Slavic courses at the University of Saskatchewan [2].

In order to have a steady flow of students for the Slavic studies at the university level there had to be a teaching of Ukrainian language in public schools. This was accomplished by the Saskatchewan ministry of education on September 4, 1952, which recognized the Ukrainian language study as an optional subject but as a fully accepted credit. At first this experiment was implemented in the two Catholic institutions— the Sacred Heart Academy and St. Joseph's College in Yorkton. When it was revealed that 116 students from the two above mentioned institutions had successfully completed their Ukrainian language course then the ministry of education extended its ruling to include all high schools in the provinces of Saskatchewan. During the first year of this new implementation there were 1,074 students taking the Ukrainian course and ten years later 1171 students; in the University of Saskatchewan during the academic year of 1966-67, 325 students signed for the Slavic studies courses, 180 of whom were taking the Ukrainian studies. This gives us a picture of an expanding and successful development in the Canadian educational field. In recent times at the Slavic Department of the Saskatchewan University there were four professors and three assistant professors at work. The Department was headed by Dr. C. H. Andrusyshen, V. O. Buyniak, and Roma Franko.

Alberta

The teaching of Ukrainian language in Alberta followed a pattern similar to that of Saskatchewan. In 1957 the Board of Governors of the University of Alberta, along with its president, Dr. A. Stewart, gave their assent for implementing a program of university courses in Ukrainian language. This took place only after a long period of unyielding efforts on the part of Ukrainian citizens and M.L.A. members—William Tomyn, Ambrose Holowach and others. The local U.C.C. branch, to-

---

[2] Slavistica at the University of Saskatchewan, "Vilne Slovo", No. 30-31, 1967.

gether with the U.C.C. Executive president, Dr. W. Kushnir, held a series of interviews with responsible authorities who made a positive evaluation of the need of teaching Ukrainian language at the University of Alberta. Even prior to this, in 1950-51, there were evening non-credit courses in Ukrainian language that had some 130 students five years later, with O. Starchuk, the initiator of these courses, P. J. Lazarowich and Y. Stefanyk as lecturers. The situation improved still further when Ukrainian language became an accredited subject at the university.

When the Royal Commission on Education, under the chairmanship of Sen. D. Cameron, began its work in Alberta in September of 1958, it was inundated with pleas and documented propositions, from Ukrainian organizations to introduce the teaching of the Ukrainian language into the public schools of Alberta. The Alberta University also prepared a brief advising the inception of this language into the framework of public schooling. A short time later, on September 13, 1958, the minister of education for Alberta, A. Aalberg, proclaimed a positive decision in favor of this matter [3]. During 1964-65, 20 high schools in Alberta held courses in Ukrainian language with 554 students in attendance. During this time, in the department of Slavic languages and literature, with nine lecturers, some 76 students completed their course in the Ukrainian language at the University of Alberta. This was another accomplishment in Canadian educational field. In the sixties Prof. O. Starchuk was in charge of the Ukrainian language studies at this university.

Manitoba

It often happens that the first become the last — and so it was with Manitoba. Although the Department of Slavic Studies, headed by Prof. J. B. Rudnyckyj, was inaugurated in July of 1949, the Ukrainian language was not introduced into the public schools until 12 years later. At the Shevchenko's anniversary celebration of 1961, the Premier of Manitoba, Duff Roblin, announced that, beginning with the following year, the Ukrainian language will be introduced as an elective subject into the public schools of Manitoba, starting with the ninth grade. In that year around 300 students took this subject and in 1964-65 it had risen to 402 students in 22 schools. In 1967 the Ukrainian language became fully accredited in public schools and universities, on equal basis with French, Latin and German languages. At the Manitoba University, in 1964-65, 56 students were taking Ukrainian courses, with a total of 340 students at the three western universities. At the same time there were 2,127 students taking Ukrainian courses in the high schools of the three prairie provinces [4]. The Slavic department also has been greatly expanded at the University of Manitoba. In 1980 there were four professors; Dr. J. Rozumnyj (head of the Department since 1976), Dr. H.D. Wiebe, Dr. I. Tarnawecky, Dr. N. Aponiuk and two lecturers: O. Ilnytzkyj and N. Pylypiuk. For a long time, in this same department, Prof. P. Yuzyk, later a senator, carried on his scholastic duties and Metropolitan Ilarion, the world famous linguist, was a guest lecturer. A sincere protector-patron

---

[3] Ukrainian Canadian Review, Winnipeg, 1967, No. 1.
[4] B. Kazymyra, "The Teaching of Ukrainian Language at The Prairie Provinces" in "Light", Toronto, 1966, No. 16.

of this department was Dr. A. H. S. Gilson, while a great amount of work was also expanded by U.C.C. and its integral organizations, toward the implementation of teaching Ukrainian language in public schools and the opening of Slavic Department at the University of Manitoba. The Ukrainian churches, too, supported these efforts very strongly by lending their prestige. For over 40 years the Ukrainian Canadians made the most vigorous efforts to have the Ukrainian language taught in public schools and finally, after such a long period of continuous effort, success was realized. In addition to the Ukrainian triumph in Western universities the Ukrainian language was also introduced at the Montreal University in whose Slavic Department there were five professors and lecturers at work in 1962: Rev. Dr. M. Zalesky, Dr. Y. Lewyckyj, J. V. Bryniawsky, Dr. I Fedoriw and Dr. R. Olynyk. At the University of Ottawa Prof. Constantine Bida introduced post-graduate courses in Slavics. Prof. J. Rozumnyj taught Ukrainian courses at the Laurentian University. Some six Canadian universities had Ukrainian departments of studies. Recently one of these universities had a student exchange program with the Ukrainian University of Kiev. Both the stature of the Ukrainian language and the quality of its lecturers have been raised to a high educational standard.

It should be emphasized that the introduction of a native language into a public school curriculum still poses a number of problems. Due to the selectivity of the matter in a cosmopolitan population, often it is difficult to get enough applications to form a class in one school. This difficulty is resolved by having students from a number of schools travel to a central school for instruction in Ukrainian. The students need the encouragement not only of their parents but also of the teachers and school directors as well. There was also the need of proper school text books and qualified teachers. These were the pressing problems that the ministries of the three western provinces had to solve. Among these hectic conditions there were some lighter moments too—when pupils of other nationalities struggled with Ukrainian pronunciations. There also were instances where the teaching of Ukrainian language became a general necessity. When we stop to consider the fact that the teaching of Ukrainian language in public schools has greatly strengthened the Slavic studies, as well as the studies of Eastern Europe's affairs at the Canadian universities, then we can easily surmise that these same universities, because of such studies could not only become the best on this continent, but could also vie with others abroad. In any case, there are ample grounds for forming these conclusions.

Private Schools

All our contemplations of the previous chapter pointed out the fact that the introduction of Ukrainian language in public school was successful in solving only a part of the problem. In the three western provinces the students, with a few exceptions, do not take up Ukrainian studies until the 9th grade or later. This is most inadequate. Much better results are obtained when a student begins to study a given language in the elementary grades. This question was being resolved by the Ukrainian community through the same methods that were practiced in the second era, about which mention has been made in a separate chapter.

So as not to repeat ourselves unnecessarily, we shall only give a general brief sketch of this problem as a direct continuation of the earlier summary, along the same line.

Vernacular schools, Ukrainian schools, as well as parochial schools had existed, during the third era, in connection with parishes and secular organizations, but with a noticeable tendency to segregate these schools into the so-called elementary classes and courses in Ukrainian culture. Elementary classes were comprised of students up to 14 years of age, and Ukrainian cultural courses were offered to those over 14. The best equipped of these schools are in the larger cities. The Ridna Shkola of St. Nicholas in Toronto has its own large building with enough space for 500 students and many teachers: the S.U.M. school in the same city had over 300; the St. George school in Edmonton, over 200 and the U.N.O. school in Winnipeg around 200. All these schools have their own spacious buildings.

Elementary classes existed in all the Ukrainian centres while the cultural courses were held only in the larger ones. According to the newest statistics for the year 1966 the following numbers of Ukrainian courses on college level were held: Ukrainian Youth Association 13: Ukrainian National Federation 6; Ukrainian Catholic Church 2; and one course given by the already well known school of H. Skovoroda in Toronto headed by Dr. O. Kopach. The Ukrainian Cultural and Educational Centre has, in recent times, renewed its Higher Cultural Courses during the summer vacations, which are usually held either in Winnipeg or Toronto, and similar courses, starting in 1965, have been held during the summer vacations at the St. Andrew's College on the University of Manitoba campus. The latest records showed that around 1,000 students had attended these cultural courses during the year. Some parishes and organizations also endeavor to hold school classes in connection with summer camps, but these provide the least opportunity for learning. Some communities arrange for children's summer schools. We wish to present here a partial list of figures dealing with these different methods of schooling.

The Ukrainian Catholic Church had the highest number of vernacular schools divided between the four eparchies: Winnipeg 45 schools—Saskatoon 88 — Edmonton 92 — and Toronto 104 — 329 in all, and in addition 13 kindergartens with vacation classes being held. Around 5,000 students attended the regular classes with 7,000 taking summer courses, and another 500 in the kindergartens [5].

The Ukrainian Greek-Orthodox Church, at this same time, conducted native schools in 283 church parishes, attended by over 3,000 students with over 1,000 of them in such metropolitan centres as Montreal, Toronto, Winnipeg and Edmonton. In addition to these native schools the Ukrainian Greek Orthodox Church parishes had around 5,000 students in Sunday schools [6]. The Ukrainian National Federation had ten native schools (about 800 students) and four kindergartens [7]. The

---

[5] B. Kazymyra, "Religio-Community Life in Ukrainian Catholic Metropolia in Canada", Toronto, 1965, Chart, No. 4 and 5.

[6] Julian Stechishin, "Our Achievement in Canada and Our Future", Toronto, 1967, p. 17.

[7] The State of Native Schools in Canada", New Pathway, Winnipeg, No. 23, 1967.

Ukrainian Youth Association had nine schools (around 1,000 students) and several kindergartens. When we add to this the 20 or more of such schools that the Association of United Canadians (TOUK) were running, with over 2,000 students, then we will have a grand total of 25,000 students taking courses in native schools at any one time during the recent years. This figure also includes the native schools of local organizations that are not of the dominion-wide scope such as: "Chytalnias" of "Prosvita", National Homes, and others.

The level of education in these schools varies somewhat depending on such things as the time limit, the convenience of system, qualifications and availability of teachers, home preparation—the latter depending on the degree of language proficiency the student is able to bring from home. It is only proper to mention here that the degree of preparation received at home played the greatest role in implementing the correct and systematical teaching in these schools.

In addition to the native schools that were conducted on a large scale, there were others in existence in connection with organizations and parishes. These were private elementary and intermediate schools, with a complete public school program with the additional teaching of Ukrainian language (often referred to as separate schools). We have already dealt with some of these schools of earlier times.

As we already know, the oldest school, the School of St. Nicholas in Winnipeg, was in operation as early as 1905 and was renamed, in later years, to Mary Immaculate School. Another well known school is run by Sister Servants in Yorkton. In 1963 an elementary day school was opened in Toronto in connection with St. Josaphat's Cathedral. Over 700 students were taught in these three schools. Other high schools, named as academies and colleges also were in operation. The oldest of these, were the Sacred Heart Academy in Yorkton and the Immaculate Heart of Mary Academy in Winnipeg, the latter one continuing in the tradition of the St. Nicholas School. A third, the Immaculate Mary Academy, was organized in Ancaster, Ontario, in 1952. All three of them were run by Sister Servants. In 1962 the College of St. Basil the Great was founded in Weston, near Toronto, and prior to that, the Redemptorist Fathers organized the St. Vladimir's College, the so-called Small Seminary, in Roblin, Manitoba. Brothers of Christian Schools carried on with their teaching in the St. Joseph's College in Yorkton. Altogether under the authority of Ukrainian Catholic Church there were six high schools and colleges providing education for 1,200 students.

The St. Andrew's College in Winnipeg deserves special consideration. Established in 1946 it started with two grade 11 and 12, classes and a course in theology. In its twenty years of work it had inaugurated two faculties—philosophical and theological, conducted in the Ukrainian language. The dynamo of this achievement was none other than its long-time principal, the Rev. Dr. S. W. Sawchuk.

For the complete picture of teaching the Ukrainian language we also must mention the educational institutes and boarding-school institutions that had become a tradition from earlier times. The oldest of these were the institutes of Petro Mohyla in Saskatoon and St. John's, formerly known as M. Hrushevsky Institute, in Edmonton. To these two, within the S.U.S. educational system, a third one was added in the third era, the St. Volodymyr's Institute in Toronto. Of the Catholic institutes the foremost was the Institute of Metropolitan A. Shepticky in Saskatoon that took over from B.U.K. Bursa. The resident students conducted their studies under the care of Sister Servants in the following institutions: Mary Immaculate in Saskatoon (1928), in Yorkton and the St. Josaphat's Institute for girls in Edmonton directed by Missionary Sisters of Christian Charities. In 1945-1946 the Institute of St. Basil the Great for boys began its educational work in Edmonton. The Girls' Institute in Winnipeg and the Metropolitan A. Shepticky Institute in Toronto, that were organized by the Ukrainian Catholic Brotherhood after the Second World War, were also carrying on their work for a short while [8].

Statistics show that Ukrainian Canadians reached only 30 percent of the youth with their native school education system and the rest are left to the chances of home training which usually does not go far beyond the elementary conversation level. The greatest weakness that is felt here is the lack of opportunity of an organized system of teaching at country points. The difficulties that are most encountered here are the distances involved and the so-called Consolidated schools that take the children away from under the care of local schools without giving anything in return, in the Ukrainian educational field. This problem is still unresolved. A great anomaly afflicting this work is the lack of uniform programs and adequate text books in this system of teaching. It is encouraging to note that qualified personnel from the School Council of U.C.C. and from the Ukrainian Teachers' Association (Toronto), Saskatchewan Teachers of Ukrainian (Saskatoon), Ukrainian Chapter of the Manitoba Modern Languages' Association (Winnipeg), Ukrainian Langauge Association (Edmonton), are working on drafting and implementations of these programs. The Eparchial School Council of Winnipeg on its directive from the Ukrainian Catholic Church and the General Council of the Ukrainian School of the Ukrainian Greek Orthodox Church are also engaging their qualified educationists to work along the same line [9] giving some hope that these various pressing problems will be solved in time. To encourage students in taking up Ukrainian studies various organizations and private individuals have established scholarships at different high schools, colleges and universities.

The above situation of Ukrainian language existed in public and private schools in the sixties and early seventies. The changes took place in the middle of seventies when in three western provinces the English-Ukrainian Program was officially introduced into the schools. Development and success of this program is fully portrayed in the chapter "School Question in the Period of Multiculturalism".

---

[8] Rev. N. Kushniryk, "From Sea to Sea". Institute of Metropolitan Andrey Shepticky, Toronto.
[9] "The Council of the Ukrainian School", organized and run by the Ukrainian Self-Reliance League.

THE PRESS

The third era of our history was rich in the variety not only of quantity, but quality as well. Next to the pioneer press organs, of the first and second era, the third era produced a multiplicity of weekly, monthly and other publications, some of them publishing for ten and more years without interruption. Although some of them suffered a demise, as had been the case during the first two eras, the majority survived and when compared with the two former periods, these were superior as to quantity, quality and variety. We wish to examine the total scope of this press under the following headings: I. the general community press and II. the religious. A separate group is composed of pro-communist publications that appeared in this era. Due to the recency of this era, we prefer only to record it rather than to comment on it. The wide scope of the material obliges us to list only the most representative elements of it.

THE GENERAL COMMUNITY PRESS

Weeklies

Four general-national weeklies and two religious organs bind together, with their appearance, the second and third era. To this sextet belong the following: "New Pathway", "Ukrainian Toiler", "Ukrainian News", "Canadian Farmer", "Canadian Morning" and "Ukrainian Voice". The last three mentioned weeklies trace their roots to the pioneer era and from it also they derive their greatest prestige. With the exception of "Canadian Morning", both the "Ukrainian Voice" and "Canadian Farmer" are of a general-public nature with this one difference, that Ukrainian Voice has been a spokesman for the Ukrainian Self-Reliance League centre, while the "Canadian Farmer" has been a private enterprise with a history of successful management, first by F. Dojacek and later his son Charles. The common policy of this paper usually has been the personal reflection of its time-interval editors who always had a free hand for the presentation of day to day problems and who usually followed the centre line of the Ukrainian social life in Canada and in the last era orienting itself to the policies of U.C.C. This centre line was loyally followed, for 16 years, by Mykhaylo Hykawy, who took over the editorship of "Canadian Farmer" from his brother Onufry Hykawy after the latter's death. Some changes were introduced when the helmsmanship was taken over by P. Pihichyn and M. R. Shkawrytko. "Canadian Farmer" consistently kept its twelve-page edition limit with four of these devoted to education, literature and art, with a general leniency to free expression of ideas in political sphere and a strong anti-communist view. In this same objective policy a separate edition of "Canadian Farmer", called "Vilny Svit" (Free World) was brought out in February 1966, intended for the U.S.A. readers. The content and the format of both these papers is much the same with the exception of titles and some changes on two or three pages.

"Ukrainian Voice" always had, during its whole existence, propagated the Ukrainian independence movement in Canada, that is, the independence of the Ukrainian entity in Canada, free from all other alien movements or agencies, and maintaining, from the start, its policy of the development of the ideology of Ukrainianism in Canada based on the principles of Canadian citizenship. The preservation of Ukrainian culture in Canada has always been of the utmost concern to the paper and its ideological centre. These principles, as is well known, basically were developed by the long-time editor Myroslav Stechishin and after his death the same philosophy, deepened and widened, has been supported on during the last twenty years by his successor John H. Syrnick. Although the paper cooperates very closely with Ukrainian Greek-Orthodox Church, still the present editor has been able to retain, in recent times, the so-called political "secularity". The "Ukrainian Voice" has been fortunate in having had such durable veterans as the former assistant editors, Danylo Lobay and Stephan Wolynec. Of the other former literary workers with the paper, worthy of our mention, were Leonid Biletsky and the well known literateur Honore Ewach.

The protestant "Canadian Morning" as a religious newspaper has been discussed in another part of this history. We only wish to state here that it had been published under several different cuts of cloth, as well as names, but still tied in with the three eras of Ukrainian development in Canada.

"Ukrainian News" also belongs to a religious category and a leading Catholic organ of those earlier days about which mention has been made in another chapter.

"New Pathway" celebrated, in 1967, its 35 years of work in the field of Ukrainian nationalism and Canadian citizenship. In the early postwar period it had appeared for a while as a twice and thrice weekly paper, but after some experimentation returned again to its weekly form. Its first and longest term editor (1930-1964) was Michael Pohorecky who during its most trying times managed to keep it alive and laid a strong foundation for its growth. The paper always manifested its tendency to centralize divergent problems, avoiding all extremes. For many years it had been printed on twelve pages with four of them devoted to literature and art. Some of the better known editors and assistant editors have been: Wolodymyr Martynec, Makhaylo Seleshko, Zynoviy Knysh, Dmytro Andrievsky, Anatol Kurdydyk, Wasyl Levytsky and lastly Antin Dobriansky as the editor-in-chief. "New Pathway" always had been a tribune in the forum of U.N.O. and the organizations connected with it, though it had been published by a separate firm but personally connected with the U.N.O. leadership. The journal at all times had displayed a great deal of tolerance to other organizations and since its basic philosophy was that of Ukrainian solidarity it cooperated closely with papers of similar outlook in America and Europe.

The "Ukrainian Toiler" reflected the Hetmanite philosophy till 1953 and its long-time editor, Mykhaylo Hetman, belonged to the leading figures of Ukrainian community representation in Canada. Its political sympathies towards other Canadian parties differed from time to time, never showing its policy clearly, but on the whole both, the "Ukrainian Toiler" and the "New Pathway", stood closer to the Conservative politics, while "Ukrainian Voice" was with the Liberals.

Toronto and the East

In 1952 a break came in the organization of the Hetman movement and with it the appearance of two different organs: W. Bossy, I. Korchynsky and J. Tarnowych continued with the "Ukrainian Toiler", while in opposition was the new bi-weekly "Nasha Derzhava" (Our Country) printed at 140 Bathurst Street, with Mykhaylo Hetman as the editor. In this way two press organs claimed their pretense to represent the Ukrainian Hetman movement which even without this competition of its two protectors did not have much to fear from other groups. Both papers could hardly make ends meet: The "Ukrainian Toiler", under W. Bossy's editorship, changed its title to "Ukrainian Catholic Toiler" and then to "Canadian Citizen", in September 1954, but still was unable to continue and so in the fall of 1954, I. Korchynsky changed it to a non-partisan weekly under its old name with A. Kurdydyk as editor till 1956. The same year "Vilne Slovo" publishing establishment took over the "Ukrainian Toiler", changed later to "Batkivschyna" (Our Country) and began to publish its own paper, the "Vilne Slovo" with the explanation in the sub-title that it is continuing the work of the "Ukrainian Toiler".

"Nasha Derzhava" lasted till 1956 and when "Ukrainian Toiler" disappeared, the "Hetmanites" organized a new weekly, "Batkivschyna" (Our Country) with M. Korolyshyn as editor, who struggled hard to keep it going, doing all the work himself including typesetting, and in 1967 he handed over the publishing of it to M. Poroniuk. The paper continued to carry the motto of the Hetman movement—"God, Hetman and Ukraine"—and under M. Poroniuk's editorship became sharp and relentless in tone. Lately editor in chief has been M. Korolyshyn.

"Vilne Slovo" was published by the Association of Free Press in Toronto with Dr. Joseph Boyko at the head. Thanks to the professional editing the paper very soon became known as one of the better independent weeklies in Canada. On the editorial staff have worked the following: A. Kurdydyk (editor-in-chief), W. S. Levytsky, and later Prof. V. Biberovych, Dr. Stepan Rosocha and Ivan Eliashewsky. The paper endeavoured to stay nonpartisan and in the Ukrainian life in general stood in the center line of politics. In latest times it consisted of eight pages and sometimes more and had a special page entitled "Opinion, Official Organ of the Ukrainian Canadian Veterans' Association", edited by Bohdan Panchuk and Lev Cardinal, and another page named, "Detroit Ukrainian News", especially dedicated to the U.S.A. readers and edited by Dr. Oleksander Maritchak.

"Vilne Slovo" and "Batkivschyna" as well as the other publications whose existence was tied in with the single weekly paper in eastern Canada during the second era of our history, formed the new press period in Toronto which flourished in profusion after the Second World War.

One of the very best of these is the social-political weekly "Homin Ukrainy" (Ukrainian Echo). The first issue appeared under the date of December 15, 1948. This was one of the first newspapers organized from the ranks of the third immigration. From this same source came its intimate color-tone, especially when we take into consideration the fact that the paper was started by people without any material funds almost as soon as they opened their immigration suitcases,—with the thoughts of their abandoned homeland still in their hearts. Ideologically, the "Ukrainian Echo" allied itself with the Organization of Ukrainian Nationalists, the Ukrainian Insurgent Army and the Ukrainian Supreme Liberation Council (U.H.V.R.) Here was a huge mobilizing force and so it is easy to understand that the weekly paper received its strong support from the wide ranks of the new immigration and gradually expanded itself, becoming at the same time an interpreter of the needs and desires of its readers in the new country as was soon evident by the self-expression of the large majority. The founders of the journal were: Stanley Frolick, R. Malaschak, A. Iwachniuk, I. Eliashewsky, I. Boyko and H. Dzura. In 1949, a separate firm was organized, namely, The Publishing Association of "Homin Ukrainy" in charge of paper's publication. The editorship was at first headed by Michael Sosnowsky and later by Roman Rakhmanny then back to M. Sosnowsky again. Both editors infused into their periodical a captivating interest and color tone. Since 1954 the editorial college was formalized under the direction of W. Solonynka. Regular associates were O. Matla, I. Waranycia, R. Malaschuk and B. Stebelsky, the latter edited the supplement section, "Literature and Art", from its very beginning. In addition to this the paper carried these other pages: "Woman's Page", "L.V.U." and "S.U.M. Page", "Youth's World". "Students' Thought".

In addition to "Our Aim", about which we remark in connection with the Catholic press, there was an independent weekly, "Nash Vik" (Our Age) devoted to politics, culture, economic and community life printed by the National Publishing. Ivan Hladun started the "Our Age" in 1949 shortly after severing his connections with the so-called progressive-communist movement and later sold it to the National Publishing. "Our Age" was edited by Dmytro Kyslycia, Ulas Samchuk and V. Ivanys. The publication was intended mostly for the new immigration and was printed for a period of three years.

Remarkably successful was the eight-page bi-weekly "Lemkivshchyna-Zakerzonnia" (Lemko Country) which first appeared on September 15, 1949 and, with a few exceptions of interval breaks, lasting till the present days, thanks to its indomitable editor, Julian Tarnowych, and the energetic effort of the Organization for the Defense of Lemkivshchyna which takes advantage of every opportunity to publicize before the whole world that Lemkivshchyna and Zakerzonnia are an integral part of the Ukrainian ethnographic territory. In Toronto there also appeared the "Lemkivski Visti" (Lemko News), a paper "devoted to Lemkian affairs in this country as well as overseas and in the whole world", that was published in Passaic, New Jersey, U.S.A. by the Main Executive of the Organization for the Defense of Lemkivshchyna.

The bi-monthly "Rozbudova" was planned as a press organ of the Association of the Ukrainian Professional and Business Men in Toronto with only a few issues being printed.

There were many monthly magazines in Toronto. The leader among these is "We and the World", a Ukrainian magazine of book-size format containing from 64 to 96 pages, that reminds one of the American style of similar magazines and edited by Mykola Kolankiwsky.

Very popular was the illustrated monthly magazine "Novi Dni" (New Days) edited by Petro Volyniak. The first issue appeared in February

1950 and had a 32-page format with artistic covers. In this same form the magazine has been appearing until the present day. In 1956, P. Volyniak began to publish an illustrated monthly magazine for the children called "The Sun Flower", which lasted for several years.

"Moloda Ukraina" (Young Ukraine) a monthly press organ of the Ukrainian Democratic Youth (ODUM) first appeared in November of 1951 in the eight-page newspaper format and the next year changed to a book-size edition which not only was intended for Canada but U.S.A. as well. It was edited by B. Oleksandriv in cooperation with M. Dalny and I. Dubylko.

There were other journals issued in Toronto during the third era that specialized only in some specific fields. Among these deserving our first attention may be mentioned the bi-monthly "Sportovi Visty" (Sports News) edited in 1954 by Karlo Mulkewych, that received financial support from the Ukraine Sports Association and which lasted over two years. On the occasion of the Artists' Convention two issues of the "Nazustrich" were printed, as well as a few Bulletins of the Association of Business Men and Tradesmen.

There were also several educational journals started in Toronto, the first one being the "Teachers' Word", which later became the organ of the Ukrainian Teachers' Association, then "Ridna Shkola" (Vernacular School) and finally as "Zhyttia and Shkola" (Life and School) as an "independent organ of the Ukrainian teachers and parents in the free world". Part of contents of this book-size journal consisted of methodical teaching material under a separate name of "Teachers' Word". All the above mentioned journals were edited by Dr. Wasyl Luciw, Toronto, later Stamford, U.S.A., but most of the journals themselves originated in Toronto from where they received financial support.

Among the youth magazines published in Toronto that deserve our mention is the quarterly journal "Plastovy Shliakh", organ of the "Plast" (Scout movement). It appeared in 1966 under the editorship of Y. Piasecky, which, in addition to its theoretical-educational articles, printed accurate material relating to the history of Ukrainian "Plast" in Canada and in the old country. This publication was the topmost achievement in the series of earlier attempts along this line in Canada, most of them done by the mimeograph method till finally in 1963 they became centralized in the representative, illustrated monthly journal "Unak", (Youth), which already had several annuals behind it. The National "Plast" Council of Canada edited a non-periodical official bulletin, in 1948, for its members called the "Plast Herald" and devoted exclusively toward the training of new cadres.

The Ukrainian Youth Association (SUM) kept in step with the "Plast" organizations and in 1949 in Toronto it started to publish a book-size monthly magazine "Na Varti" (On Guard) which some time later was merged with a similar S.U.M. publication in U.S.A. and finally changed to an ideological quarterly still retaining the name "On Guard" and dedicated to the S.U.M. organizations throughout the world. This magazine was published in London England.

"Yevshan-Zillia", a bi-monthly journal intended for children, appeared with its few issues in Toronto in cooperation with the Association of Writers of Children's Literature, edited by Bohdan Hoshowsky.

A social-political quarterly journal, the "Kuban Cossack Bulletin", consisting of eight newspaper pages and later changed to a 24-page small book-size format, was published in Toronto and edited by M. Fesenko. The Union for the Liberation of Ukraine (S.V.U.) started to publish its bi-monthly journal, "Mission for Ukraine" in 1951 and although the editorial office was in U.S.A. the magazine itself was published in Canada and disseminated through both countries.

In 1961 Semen Pidhainy organized an English quarterly, "The New Review", a journal of East European history, published by "The World Federation of Ukrainian Former Political Prisoners and Victims of the Soviet Regime" (S.U.Z.E.R.O.) with its editorial staff comprised of: S. Pidhainy, S. Fedorivsky, A. Gudovsky, I. Murha, P. Pavlovych, P. Trepet and its editorial staff consisted of Oleh Pidhainy, M. Mladenovic, Mykola Lypowecky and Martha Skorupska. After the founder's death, his wife Alexandra continued with the publishing of the journal. For a while "Rozbudova Derzhavy" (the Building of a Nation") appeared every second month and was published in this city after its transference from U.S.A.

Another very popular literary-historical monthly journal, "The Ukrainian Family", in a book-size format of 32 pages, was published in Toronto in 1947-1949 under the editorship of Alexander Luhowyj who previously had written several historical novels. This journal contained much historical material under such titles as "History of Ukrainian Orthodox Church", "Chronicles of Historical Events in Canada", "Chronicles of Events from Ukrainian History", and others.

A journal similar to "The Ukrainian Family" was the monthly magazine "The World and Life", printed by "Aritos" publishers and edited by B. Romen-Domazar and J. Beskyd with only three issues of this well-illustrated publication having made an appearance.

The former war veterans of Ukrainian armies published the "Dorohovkaz" (Road-guide), an organ of soldiers' thought and action. It was financed by the general executive of the Association of the Ukrainian War Veterans in Toronto under the editorship of I. Lypovecky. Lately the "War Veterans' News", a military journal that first appeared in New York, is now published in Toronto with the following editorial staff: I. Kedryn-Rudnycky, Wasyl Veryha, A. Valiysky, V. Huzar, G. Lopatynsky, R. Kupchynsky, I. Nosyk. This is the most representative military journal that has the backing of almost every veterans' association in Canada and U.S.A.

There were English journals published in Toronto such as "News Letter", the official organ of Ukrainian War Veterans' Association, that first appeared in 1953, edited by the well known veterans, Bohdan Panchuk and Dr. P. Smylski, in cooperation with V. J. Kaye. "News Letter" did not last very long and in 1955 another journal, the "Opinion" appeared on the scene which was historically tied to the same named veteran journal printed in Winnipeg after the war to be later replaced by the Ukrainian War Veterans Association's News Letter". The "Opinion" of Toronto did not survive very long either and in 1964 the "New Opinion" appeared, a bi-lingual quarterly edited by B. Panchuk. The most consistently appearing of all such publications was the formerly mentioned bi-lingual veterans' "Opinion" that was printed on the pages of "Vilne Slovo" (Free Word) with the first edition dated January 28, 1964.

A yet another 16-page bilingual journal, "MUN-Beams" was published by the Dominion Executive of the Ukrainian National Youth Federation of Canada (MUN) in Winnipeg, in 1954, and later transferred to Toronto. The small illustrated journal was well edited but lasted, with difficulty, for only a few years.

In 1954 an attempt was made to publish a 32-page English monthly, the "Pace". The Pace Publishers Co. was headed by Wasyl Hultay and the magazine was edited by N. Rzepecki and it is to be regretted that this well-edited cultural journal, after some ten issues, ceased to appear. A somewhat brighter side is presented by the English bulletin "Our Viewpoint", a "Commentary on Canadian and World Affairs", of the Studium Research Institute, connected with Canadian League for Ukraine's Liberation, that was transferred to Ottawa and also since January 1967, the English monthly magazine of the Basilian Fathers, "The Life Beacon", allied very closely, as to its format and administrative personnel with the religious monthly journal, the "Light".

"Our Tribune", (Nasha Trybuna), a non-periodical, eight-page bulletin-tabloid, an organ of the Canadian Friends for Liberation of Ukraine (UKT) was published in Toronto in 1953-1954 and edited by Roman Rakhmanny. A social-economic journal, the "Expansion", also was published for a while in 1956.

"Our Contact", intended as an economic cooperative forum, appeared every second month, published in Windsor, but had a short existence and the same fate awaited the journal "Problems", originated by Wasyl Didiuk in connection with Horizon Publishers, in 1965.

Among the many short-lived publications of Toronto belong the following "have-beens": "Sonechko" (the Sun), "Ukrainian Workingmen Association's News", "Arka", "Carpathian Sitch" (from 1950), "Herald", the organ of Ukrainian Revolutionary Democrats, "Nasha Hromada" (Our Community), "Bulletin of the Ukrainian Canadian Veterans' Association", "Bulletin of the Former Ukrainian War Veterans of Canada", Toronto Branch, "Ukrainian Branch Canadian Legion" No. 360, the "Informer" of the Ukrainian War Veterans' Association, the "Bulletin" of the Executive of Ukrainian National Federation, Toronto, the "Bulletin of Canadian League for Ukraine's Liberation", "Bulletin of Ukrainian Social Welfare of Toronto", "League of Ukrainian Engineers", "S.V.U. Bulletin", the Bulletin of the Shevchenko Scientific Society, Canadian Branch" (from 1950), the "Bulletin of the Ukrainian Canadian University Student's Union" (S.U.S.K.) started in 1961 and a similar, "The Information Service of S.U.S.K.", the "Informative Letter of the Executive of "Plast" Centre, "Letters to Our Family of Brethren", "We and Our Children" (1960), "Bulletin of the Workers of Children's Literature, "Toward the Meeting", "Bulletin of the Committee of Artists" (1954), "Bulletin of the Association of Ukrainian Pedagogues in Canada" (1963), "Journal of the Ukrainian Medical Association", The "News Bulletin of Ukrainian Businessmen and Tradesmen", printed in 1966, and the "Bulletin of Ukrainian Professional and Business Men's Club" (1961). There were many more of these bulletins of information dealing with various organizations and their circulation depending on the size and importance of the institution that they represented. Most of these appeared in the fifties when the new immigration revealed its organizing potency in professional activities and organizational establishments. Toronto became the centre of life for the new immigration. True enough not all of it that only belonged to the expediency of day to day existence survived. Life had to be built on strong foundations that not only required planning, but also would take in years and decades to change emigrants into immigrants and those in turn into permanent citizens. Along with this, in place of the mundane matters of yesterday, came the basic long-lasting objectives of the whole community—the small and narrow group interests were dying and their places taken over by the much wider sphere of the national entity. A sound blending process developed instead, without which it would be difficult to visualize a harmoniously adjusted society and the guiding hand in these developing processes was the Ukrainian press in its multiform activities. The branching out and widely spreading social activities needed a creative forum for life's expression and it proved itself capable of creating such a forum. Toronto was the focal point for these processes and the breeding ground for publications in their bid for influence and prestige. It held a dominant position among Ukrainian publishing centers in eastern Canada.

There were other cities in the east that let themselves be heard from in the publishing field during the third era, among them Montreal, Hamilton, Sudbury, as well as other Ukrainian communities. One of the finest publications in Montreal, after the war, was the bulletin of the Federation of the Ukrainian Students' Association of National Solidarity called "Zarevo" that was printed in 1949 (by the multigraph method) by an editorial college with Dr. M. Antonovych as editor. A "Letter of Friendship" was printed in 1950 as a spokesman for the above mentioned students' central organization in Canada, U.S.A. and Europe. Also published in Montreal was the "Eye of the World", an illustrated bi-monthly journal edited by R. Choulguine, I. Vakhnianyn and Roman Ischuk. Much more systematically ordered was the "L'Informateur Montrealais" (Montreal Informer), an economic informative bulletin that appeared in 1958. "The Successor to Zarevo" was the "Smoloskyp" bulletin which was a 20-page bi-monthly journal printed by the "Zarevo" Publishing Committee in cooperation with the Committee of Youth (ISNO). Its editorial staff consisted of B. Hasiuk, M. Carynnyk, P. Bahriy and O. Shevchenko with Osyp Zinkevych as its editor for many years. It is interesting to note that the journal was edited in U.S.A., printed in Winnipeg, and its administrative office was in Montreal, and lately in Toronto.

The monthly "Bulletin of the Ukrainian National Credit Union" appeared quite regularly in Montreal in 1962, and so did the "Bulletin of the Ukrainian Cooperative Savings and Credit". The Ukrainian National Youth Federation of Canada (MUN) published their Montreal Protocol by multigraph process starting in 1955.

The "Federalist-Democrat", a bi-monthly, was published in Ottawa in 1953 by the "Ukrainska Hromada" (Ukrainian Community) with Fedir Bohatyrchuk as editor, who propagated something in the nature of federalism in Eastern Europe although in reality his publication was more like an exposition of policy of the Russian White-guard immigrants.

The Sudbury Branch of the Ukrainian National Federation edited the "News" and the "Bulletin" for the use of its members and the Hamilton branch of the same organization edited its "News"—all three of these bulletins printed by multigraph. Even the Ukrainian Credit Union in Fort William had its multigraph "Bulletin".

Among the many press organs in Toronto, "The Canadian Scene" distinguished itself in that it was a periodical dedicated as a news service medium for the Ukrainian and other ethnic press publications.

Winnipeg and the West

Although Toronto, in the third era, reached a milestone in the publishing field still it may be said that Winnipeg retained its banner of being the first in this sphere considering its trail blazing with such well known press organs as "Ukrainian Voice", "New Pathway" and the much earlier, "Canadian Farmer". To this trio was added later another weekly— the religious bilingual "Postup" (Progress). The "Evangelical Morning", appeared regularly as well as some other religious publications which we mentioned in another chapter. Very prominent places have been earned by the valuable monthly journals, "Woman's World", and "Promin".

There were other publications that in their total number present a favourable balance in competition with their eastern challengers for the publishing crown. The Executive of the Ukrainian Canadian Committee (U.C.C.) starting January 1953, edited their 8-32 page "Bulletin" which appeared as a monthly and at times as a bi-monthly publication in a booklet form with important material about the Ukrainian Canadian Committee and its work. Its editors were the executive directors of the Ukrainian Canadian Committee, Volodymyr Kochan, who spent many years working in this office and, since 1967, Dr. S. J. Kalba. In 1952 and prior to the appearance of U.C.C. "Bulletin", a bilingual monthly bulletin, "Ukrainian Commentary", made its appearance with the following introductory message:

"Canadians of Ukrainian ethnic origin, as a matter of course, associate themselves fully with the policy of their country—Canada. But because of their dual background they have a special, and we believe an important, contribution to make."

The above quotation could have fitted every issue of the "Bulletin" and "Ukrainian Commentary", edited by V. Kochan, A. Zaharychuk and Dr. I. Hlynka, admirably performed its duties for a period of six years. In addition to the two above mentioned publications the U.C.C. also edited, from time to time, a multigraphed "Press News", intended as a press information medium for newspapers in general.

Among the oldest post-war publications appearing regularly in Winnipeg was "My Friend" (1949), a children's journal edited by Rev. Semen Izyk. It originally was planned as "the only journal for Ukrainian children in Canada and U.S.A." but starting with the second edition it was published under the name of the Ukrainian Catholic Center. The 32-page journal was edited with the cooperation of such pedagogues as

J. Nowosad, R. Zavadovych, Ivanka Savycka, M. Michnewych and others, and was illustrated, for a long time, by Myron Levyckyj (Lev).

In 1950, a sixteen-page bilingual monthly journal, "Youth Speaks", began its publication. It was printed by the Ukrainian National Publishers with Taras Cirka as manager and Bohdan R. Bociurkiw and Leo Kossar as the editors. Shortly after being transferred to Toronto the journal ceased its publication.

To the earliest post-war publication belongs the monthly journal, The "Woman's World" (January 1950), published regularly until our times by the Ukrainian Women's Organization of Canada. This journal was initiated by the editorial college consisting of Anna Wach, Maria Magera, Nina Syniawska and Kateryna Lazor, with the last two mentioned as editors-in-chief of this the first women's journal in the third era. Its long-time editor is Stephania Bubniuk. The journal consists of many interesting sections, the most prominent of which is the chronicled history of community life, followed by other also absorbing parts devoted to mothers, the Children's World, and a page for the English readers edited by Halia Hawryluk-Charney.

Ten years after the appearance of the "Woman's World", a second women's journal began its publication in 1960. It was a 32-page tabloid, the "Promin" published by the Ukrainian Women's Association (SUK) with Natalia Kohuska as its first editor, which post she occupies today, with the cooperation of such well known leaders in the field of women's work in Canada as Kateryna Antonovych, Olha Woycenko, Savella Stechishin, Tonia Horochovych, Olenka Negrych and others. The journal has children's and English sections, as well as other interesting variations.

While we are still concerned with journals it may be of interest to mention such publications as the "Wolyn" Chronicles edited twice yearly, starting in 1953, by M. Borowsky and financed by the Research Institute of "Wolyn". Also published yearly, since 1953, was the formerly mentioned "Ukrainica Canadiana", prepared by the Bibliographical Section of the U.V.A.N. and financed by the Ukrainian Canadian Committee for ten years.

To the short-lived publications in the post-war period belonged the "Komar" (Mosquito) (1949-1959) which was a bi-weekly journal of humour and satire, the only one of its kind, at that time, on the American continent. The well known Ivan Tyktor was its publisher with Myron Levyckyj as the editor. In 1950, a few non-periodical issues of "Kultura and Osvita" (Culture and Education) appeared, published by the Ukrainian Cultural and Educational Centre. In 1956 several issues of a mimeographed journal, "Postup" (Progress) "for education and meditation" were edited and published by Petro Pihichyn who later, in 1967, began to publish his bi-monthly paper the "Ukrainian World", printed by the offset method in a 12 X 16 format, with the following mottoes, "Truth against Force", and "Struggle against Evil".

Among the newer editions belongs the semi-yearly publication "Shashkevychiana" which made its first appearance in November, 1963, in the form of onthology devoted to the life and creative work and cult of Markian Shashkevych, published by the Markian Shashkevych Centre and edited by an editorial board with M. H. Marunchak as editor. In

1965 a journal, "Word on Guard", appeared with J. B. Rudnyckyj as editor.

The popular educational journal "Nasha Kultura" (Our Culture) that was first published in 1951 by Metropolitan Ilarion, had a long historical background behind it. This 32-page monthly magazine was tied in with a similar publication that was printed in Warsaw (1937-1939) and edited by Prof. Ivan Ohienko. "Self Help", a non-periodical quarterly, dealing with economic cooperative matters was printed by the "Carpathia" Credit Union in 1956.

Among the newest publications was the bilingual quarterly, the "Ukrainian Canadian Review", begun in the winter of 1966-1967, through the efforts of the Federation of Ukrainian Professional and Business Men's Clubs of Canada, with the following editorial staff: Senator P. Yuzyk, S. Radchuk, G. Lahoda, Dr. I. Hlynka and Dr. R. Laba. The journal differed considerably from the previous publications that primarily stressed the point of economic and professional activity. Thanks to the financial support of the Ukrainian Professional and Business Men's Club the "News Bulletin" appeared monthly (except during the summer) over a long period of time. The Ukrainian Free Academy of Sciences published its UVAN Bulletin in 1952, and the Historical Section of the UVAN printed the "History of Our Days", starting in 1966.

The North Winnipeg Credit Union began printing its "Information Letter" in 1959. Winnipeg had a large number of various regular and irregular bulletins such as the mimeographed "Parents Informat of the Plast", UKT News", published by the Canadian Friends for the Liberation of Ukrane, Winnipeg Branch, the non-periodical students' journal "Alpha Omega Recorder" and "The World of Youth", a mimeographed bulletin of the Ukrainian Youth Association (S.U.M.) and others of greater or lesser scope.

Outside of Winnipeg very little new material was published in the west. Vancouver tried its hand in 1949-1950 with a sixteen-page bi-monthly, "Postup" (Progress) printed by offset method, and in 1960, a few issues of the illustrated monthly journal "Zoria" (Star) appeared, containing much interesting material about the local life of Ukrainians on the west coast. It, too, was printed by the offset method and edited by I. Sorochynsky.

Even prior to "Postup's" appearance the Ukrainian Youth Association made an attempt to print their monthly bulletin, "The Voice of Youth", in 1946-1947 consisting of four pages printed on a multigraph.

In 1957-1958 and later the students of the Petro Mohyla Institute in Saskatoon published their annuals in book-format, called "Kameniari" (Stone-Breakers). In Calgary Volodimir Barabash edited, in 1943-1947, an interesting multigraphed journal in the English language titled, "U.C.Y. Lore", that was financed by the Ukrainian Catholic Youth of Calgary. In Edmonton a few issues of the "Ukrainian Pioneer" appeared in 1955-1956 published and edited by T. Tomashevsky. Ukrainian Youth Association published their quarterly, "The Life of SUM".

That is about all that appeared in the realm of community press activities in the west. However, in contrast to this small output of community-type press, stands the abundant growth of the religious press about which more will be said in the next chapter.

It could be stated that, in general, the community press basically was concentrated in the two centres of Ukrainian life—Winnipeg and Toronto. Winnipeg, primarily, served the West while Toronto dominated the East. Winnipeg became the symbol of the historical, upwardly rising, trend built on traditions. Toronto, on the other hand, was introducing variations and newer streams of thought that did not always harmonize with Winnipeg's ideas. But life equalized these differences in favour of unity—new thoughts and new people strengthened the nerve system of the social organism enabling them all to seek the proper solutions. The total sum of these processes resulted in what is known in sociological thinking as progress.

THE RELIGIOUS PRESS

As the second era of our history was prolific in the output of the general community press, so was the third era notably productive in the field of religious publications. This growth was noted in all of the three branches of this press, which we divide into (a) Catholic, (b) Orthodox and (c) Protestant—the last one named often referred to as Evangelical. We will examine them in this given order.

The Catholic Press

There was a time when the "Ukrainian News" of Edmonton was the sole representative of the Ukrainian Catholic thought. Later, "Buduchnist Naciyi" (The Future of the Nation) of Winnipeg, which we have mentioned before in the second era, came to the aid of the "Ukrainian News". As a bi-monthly the "Future of the Nation", lasted for twelve years under the editorship of Rev. I. Shpytkowsky and J. Nowosad, the latter having formulated and edited a children's page. Before the "Future of the Nation" printed its last issue, there appeared in Toronto, under the date of October 8, 1949, a new Catholic weekly, "Nasha Meta" (Our Aim) published by a firm with the same name. Although the publishers of "Our Aim" wrote in the sub-title that it was a "Ukrainian National Paper", in reality it was a national-religious, eight-page (16 X 22) weekly, which has continued in this form and content till the present time. Its first editor was V. Biberovych and following him, Rev. Petro Chomyn, with H. Chuma, Ivanna Petriw and others as the assistant editors. In a short time "Our Aim" became the official organ of the Eastern Exarchate and later of the Eastern Eparchy, as well as the spokesman of organizations of the Catholic Action type such as Ukrainian Catholic Brotherhood, Ukrainian Catholic Women's League, Ukrainian Catholic Youth, that had their own separate pages. The appearance of "Our Aim" helped tremendously in fortifying the front of the Ukrainian press in Toronto.

Ten years after the first appearance of "Our Aim" another publishing firm was formed in Winnipeg by the name of "Postup" (Progress) publishing company, which began to edit a twelve-page weekly called by the same name as the firm, and which had, since 1963, devoted four pages to the English language. "Progress" helped to fill in the missing link in the journalistic chain and the Metropolitan Arch-Eparchy became the owner of its own organ in which, next to the editors, Metropolitan Hermaniuk expressed his views. The first editor-in-chief, for a short while, was Roman Danylewych and after him the editorship was taken over by Rev. Semen Izyk and its assistant editors were Anatol Kurdydyk and Rev. G. Rudachek, the latter being in charge of the English section. "Progress" was able to satisfy the needs of a wide circle of its readers and became the authoritative organ of the Ukrainian Catholic Church in Canada.

In this way there were in Canada, at the end of the 1950-ies, three Ukrainian Catholic weeklies, namely: "Progress", "Our Aim", and the oldest of the three, "The Ukrainian News", that had among its capable editors W. Dyky, I. Nimchuk, Dr. M. Roslak and Rev. P. Kachur. Along with the "Ukrainian News", beginning with January 1960, an English language, eight-page tabloid, called "The Ukrainian Recorder" was published irregularly with Ronald Zapisocky and Rev. A. Pawliuk as editors, but it finally folded in 1964.

Also published in Edmonton was a non-periodical monthly organ of the Executive of the Ukrainian Catholic Eparchy in Edmonton, entitled "Catholic Action". This tabloid was started in 1950 by Dr. B. Kazymyra and in later years had Rev. J. Fedunyk in charge. The motto of the "Catholic Action was: "For the Social Justice" and "To Renew Everything in Christ". From 1950, for a while, a bi-monthly called, "The Bulletin of the Ukrainian Bureau in Canada", was published in Edmonton.

Two other Ukrainian Catholic monthly journals were printed that made their first appearance during the second era. One of them, "The Redeemer's Voice", was printed by the Redemptorist Fathers in Yorkton, now in a pocket-book size format, that had 64 pages. Its thematical content has been enriched and enlarged and in addition to its Ukrainian language, part of the material appeared in English as well. Its editors have been for many years Rev. J. Korba and Rev. M. Schudlo (1948-1967), ably assisted by the following monastic priests: V. Malanchuk, J. Bala, M. Kopiakiwsky, B. Kurylo, S. Bakhtalowsky, R. Chomiak, and others. With every issue of the "Redeemer's Voice" a special four-page "Supplement" is included, depicting interesting events from the life of its readers.

The Basilian Fathers continued to publish their monthly 32-40 page tabloid "Svitlo" (The Light) in Toronto. Thematical content of the above journal had always been varied and interesting. Its editors have been Rev. W. Dribnenky and Rev. O. Kupranets and the assistants were Fathers—I. Nazarko, V. Wawryk, E. Bilyk, W. Kowalyk, N. Kushniryk, S. Shevchuk, V. Shevchuk, and others, and of laymen, A. Moch and B. Kazymyra. In Ankaster, Sister Servants printed the "Zoria Mariyi" (Star of Mary) journal for the use of their own seminary.

The Redemptorist Fathers edited a theological quarterly, the "Logos" (1950) in Yorkton, in a book-size format. It was originated by a group of professors of the Theological Seminary of the Redemptorist Fathers in Meadowville, headed by Rev. Dr. Maksim Hermaniuk. In time the editorship was taken over by Rev. Dr. V. Malanchuk and following him, Rev. Dr. M. Hrynchyshyn. The quarterly had, in addition to its theological thematics, a great amount of material from the history of the church and a separate "Homiletic Supplement". It is one of the most prominent Ukrainian educational journals on this continent.

Starting with 1944 a bilingual monthly journal, "The Youth", was published in Edmonton in the small book-size format under the direction of the Ukrainian Catholic Youth organization. In 1946 the same youth organization printed a small journal, "Our Future", and another similar one called, "News", had been printed on a mimeograph in Saskatoon in 1958. In addition to these common youth publications there were others of a specific character, such as "The Obnowan" (1955), the non-periodical students' journal "Objective", and another students' journal, "The Correginian", printed in Roblin, as well as the "Acron" edited by the Girls' Academy in Winnipeg. The Students' Association "Gama Rho Kappa—Obnova" had their non-periodical bulletin, and the Obnova Alumni Society published their "Information Bulletin". To complete the list we add that in 1947-1948 there was also in existence the "Herald of the Central Exarchate" and the children's journal "My Friend", about which mention is made in another part of this history.

The Knights of Columbus of St. Josaphat in Winnipeg printed their little journal, "The Scope", and for a short while a supplement called, "The Ukrainian Catholic Front", was issued in connection with the "Ukrainian Toiler" in Toronto. The students in Mundare had their journal, "The Aurora". The Catholic students of the Alberta University edited their monthly magazine, "The Memo", while the Metropolitan A. Shepticky Club published, "The Students' News".

From all these publications it would appear that every age was represented in the publishing world. To this eminent register of Catholic publications may be added the list of parish bulletins, some of which were printed for many years, so that when one considers the size of many of these parishes it qualifies these same bulletins as being their own kind of community weeklies. To this class of parish bulletins belong those already mentioned in the first period of this history and among others we list the following bulletins: "Church in a Nation", published by the Cathedral of St. Vladimir and Olga in Winnipeg; "Cathedral News", St. Josaphat's Cathedral in Toronto; "Cathedral News" St. Josaphat's Cathedral in Edmonton; "Cathedral News", St. George's Cathedral in Saskatoon; "The Parish News" in both the Church of the Blessed Virgin Mary and the Church of Holy Ghost in Winnipeg; "The Weekly", St. Mary's Church in Port Arthur; "Parish Herald", Church of St. Nicholas in Toronto; the mimeographed monthly bulletin, "The Ecclesia", appeared in Montreal, and many others. Deserving special attention was the official bulletin of the Committee for Protection of Rites and Traditions of the Ukrainian Catholic Church in Canada that was irregularly printed in Toronto entitled, "For Native Church". The authors of this bulletin strongly opposed any changes in the traditions of the Ukrainian Catholic Church.

As we can see, the Catholic press was not only prodigious but also heterogeneous as well, covering on the one side the humble every-day information such as would appear in small bulletins, and on the other hand, serving the needs of children, youth, students, academicians and even trying to reach those who only knew the English tongue. The tone of this press was markedly different from the first two periods. Its tolerant attitude toward the stabilization of Ukrainian religious mutual-relationship in Canada showed itself in its step by step progress into the new period of national and international ecumenism.

The Orthodox Press

"The Herald", systematically published twice a month, had at all times stood at the head of the Ukrainian Orthodox press. Rev. S. W. Sawchuk and Rev. W. Kudryk had always devoted their most energetic efforts toward the expansion of this bi-monthly journal. "The Herald" constantly manifested its absolutism in the expressed opinions and never sought any compromising paths with other denominations which was well reflected in its drawback attitude toward the ecumenical movement sponsored under the patronage of Vatican Rome. "The Herald" was the official organ of the Ukrainian Greek Orthodox Church printed by the Ecclesia Publishing Co., and since 1954 it had been published by the editorial board.

In November 1947, in connection with the Ukrainian Metropolitan Sobor in Winnipeg, a sixteen-page Orthodox monthly journal "Slovo Istyny" (The Word of Truth) was edited by Metropolitan Ilarion. After taking over the helm of the Ukrainian Greek-Orthodox Church this same hierarch began to publish, in 1953, the monthly journal of the Ukrainian theological thought and culture, the "Faith and Culture," as the organ of Ukrainian Theological Society. During the time when the Ukrainian Greek-Orthodox Church was under the direction of Bishop Mstyslav Skrypnyk he edited, in Winnipeg, a journal of book-size format called "The Church and the Nation", which was filled with popular religious themes and news connected with the life of the Ukrainian Greek-Orthodox Church.

"The New Chronicle", a quarterly journal dealing with community life, science and art, that first appeared in Winnipeg in 1961, deserves our attention. It was published by the New Chronicle Association and had some well known individuals of the Orthodox faith engaged in its preparation. Dr. G. Mulyk-Lucyk has been its chief editor.

In 1957, "Nasha Hromada" (Our Community), a religious journal, dealing with cultural and community life, was published in Hamilton. It was printed by the "Vera" (Faith) Publishing Brotherhood in connection with St. Vladimir's Greek Orthodox parish, whose editor was M. Pavlyshyn. For a while the "Voice of Truth" was edited in Beverly, Alberta. The students of the St. John's Institute in Edmonton published the Students' Herald, those at the Institute of Petro Mohyla, the "Kameniari" (Stone-Breakers) and the ones in St. Andrew's College, the "Promin".

The Ukrainian Greek-Orthodox parishes also had their local weekly church bulletins as for instance the Holy Trinity Cathedral in Winnipeg, the Sobor Cathedral of St. Vladimir in Toronto, the Ukrainian Orthodox Sobor of Winnipeg, as well as the Ukrainian Orthodox of the Blessed Virgin Mary in Montreal, and others.

When we take into consideration the fact that the Ukrainian Voice had always wholeheartedly supported the Ukrainian Greek-Orthodox Church, then it will be seen that the Ukrainians of Orthodox faith always had a wide opportunity for expressing their views.

The Protestant or Evangelical Press

The oldest organ in this press group is the "Evangelical Morning" which continues the tradition of its predecessors, the "Canadian Morning", the earlier published "Morning", and the "Canadian". "The Canadian Morning", was published quite regularly in Winnipeg during the Second World War as a bi-monthly of 11 X 15 format, consisting of eight pages 4 columns wide. It was edited by such well known leaders of the Protestant Church as D. Pyrch, M. Karabut, Z. Bychynsky, M.P. Berezynsky, John Robert Kovalevich and Luke Standret. In 1961, the United Church of Canada refused to give any further support, being motivated by the assumption that the general majority of the adherents of this church could be easily served by one of the official languages of this country and thus there was not any need of publishing in some other language. Some of the Ukrainian leaders of this church decided to continue the publication at their own expense with the aid of subscriptions and in order to give it something more than an exclusive Canadian tone, they gave it a general name of "Evangelical Morning" published under the name of The Ukrainian Evangelical Alliance of North America. This organ comes out once a month in a sixteen-page tabloid format, edited by well known pastors as W. Borowsky, John Robert Kovalevich, V. Kucher, V. Kustodovych, and others. Although its editorial quarters are in Detroit, the printing and expediting work of this journal is carried out in Winnipeg.

"The Word", an organ of the Independent Ukrainian Evangelical Church was first issued in January of 1950 as a bi-monthly, eight-page tabloid and later changed to a quarterly journal lasting for a full five years in this latter form. Its appearance, as well as that of the "Evangelical Morning" was organized by the already referred to, in another chapter, group of Ukrainian Protestants who had endeavored to form an Independent Ukrainian Evangelical Church—to be more exact, the independent church community in Gorlitz, Saskatchewan with Pastor P. Korsakov at the head. The paper was first printed in Toronto and from 1951 in Saskatoon. Its moral authorities were the pioneers of Ukrainian Protestantism in Canada Ivan Bodrug and Paul Krat. The banner slogans of this journal had been: "Spread the idea of church's independence among our people", and "Join the ranks of the Independent Ukrainian Evangelical Church". "The Word's" slogan was adopted almost ten years later by the "Evangelical Morning" although the latter does not propagate in such an absolute form as its predecessor.

The monthly magazine, "Evangelical Truth", about which we said a few words in the second era, was published by the Ukrainian Presbyterian Church in Toronto and edited by M. Fesenko from its beginning in 1940. At first, it was printed as an 11 X 14½, eight-page monthly tabloid, but in the 60-ies it was changed to a book format of 24 pages. In addition to articles in Ukrainian it also contained religious sermons in English. "Evangelical Truth" supports Ukrainian Evangelical Alliance as the superstructure of the Ukrainian Protestant Evangelical Churches in Canada and U.S.A., as well as of the Ukrainian Presbyterian Church in Canada, which had not included itself into the United Church system although it receives financial aid from it. Pastor V. Kucher is the assistant editor of this journal. The Ukrainian Evangelical Church in Hamilton for a while published its bulletin, "The Church News".

The first edition of "The Christian Herald" was small when it appeared in Winnipeg in October of 1942, under the editorship of P. Kindrat.

The following issues were larger, containing 20-24 pages. It was published by the Ukrainian Baptists who later took on the name of the Ukrainian Evangelical Baptist Alliance of Canada. In 1950 the publication of this tabloid, which by now had become a bi-monthly journal, was taken over by Mykhaylo Podworniak, who has been its editor until recently. P. Kindrat, I. Tarasiuk and I. Iwaskiw have also helped with the editorial work. There also existed, in connection with the Ukrainian Evangelical Baptist Alliance, a book printing establishment called "Doroha Pravdy" (The Road of Truth) under the direction of the formerly mentioned M. Podworniak.

The Baptists also published "The Ukrainian Gospel Field", quarterly of the Ukrainian Missionary and Bible Society which had been printed in Saskatoon for the last twenty years with Yakiv Homeniuk as its first editor. It was started at first as a monthly journal, later changed to a bi-monthly magazine, and finally became a quarterly publication.

For a while the Ukrainian Mission and Bible Society in Saskatoon published an independent monthly journal devoted to the development of chaste spiritual living, under the name of "The Herald of the Lord's Coming".

"The Christian Banner", an educational-theological organ of the Baptist Church, was edited by Pastor V. Kostiw for a short period of time (1955-1965) with only five issues in all.

The Baptists also had a few publications in two languages, the Ukrainian and the Russian. Among these were "The Faith of the Gospel", edited by the All-Canadian Alliance of the Evangelical Christians in Toronto, and "The Life of Faith", an organ of the Alliance of the Slavic Churches of the Evangelical Christian and Baptists in Canada. The first magazine ceased publication after two years. The last one had a twenty-year history behind it. Both of these journals were financed by the Russian Baptists, with the aid of a few Ukrainians and all of them organized under various names in order to entice to their church some of the Ukrainian Baptists who in general had belonged to their own national-religious organization of the Ukrainian Evangelical Baptist Alliance.

"The Evangelist"—the organ of the Christian Missionary Publications is a bi-monthly book-size magazine of 24 pages, which has been published in Toronto without a break since 1957 and propagates the idea of the Ukrainian Pentecostals in Canada. In its editorial office have worked the following persons: M. W. Derkach, W. Kuziw, P. Shelestovsky, H. Derkach, Dr. K. Kostiw and some others. Where all the other previously mentioned journals in this group had also touched upon community affairs, the "Evangelist" has devoted itself exclusively to the spiritual studies.

To complete the list of religious publications it will be necessary to mention the "Dawn of New Era", a mimeographed herald of Christ's presence that was published by the Association of the Bible Students, in Winnipeg.

Association United Sons of Ukraine of Winnipeg published the "World-Outlook News—Native Faith" which has been interpreted by the publishers as "Native Ukrainian National Faith (R.U.N.V.)". The ideologist of this movement was L. Selenko who also edited the above mentioned journal.

THE PRO-COMMUNIST PRESS

As already mentioned, the "Voice of Truth" from Smoky Lake had for a while played the role of a substitute for the pro-communist press that had been banned in 1940, along with the Ukrainian Labour and Farmers' Temple Association (U.L.F.T.A.). The government's act in closing the above organization dealt a sudden blow to this pro-communist centre. However, this condition did not last very long. As soon as Hitler's Germany clashed with U.S.S.R., in June 1941, the situation changed suddenly. The ban was lifted and the U.L.F.T.A. once again resumed its political activities.

September 7, 1941, saw the first issue of the pro-communist "Ukrainian Life" in Toronto under the initiation of Stepan Maciyewych, M. Hrynchyshyn, B. Harmatiuk, A. Holovchak, S. Zeniuk and others. The first one mentioned became its editor at which post he remained until the paper's demise in 1965. "Ukrainian Life", was the official organ of the Ukrainian Association of Aid to Fatherland that had been organized two weeks before the first appearance of that paper. From its very first issue the above mentioned weekly stood uncompromisingly and without any reservation on the side of the U.S.S.R. and supported wholeheartedly its system and national politics in its relationship to the Ukrainian people [1]. This servile attitude on the part of the "Ukrainian Life" was the main reason why the Ukrainian national press about which we have written before, could never find any common ground for meeting, nor a mutual language for expressing their views. The paper consisted of eight and sometimes twelve pages and in 1956 it became a bi-weekly publication. At different times the following persons have worked with the editing of the paper: I. Stefanicky, P. Lysec, M. Kumka, P. Prokopchak, J. Weir, M. Hrynchyshyn, E. Mykhayluk and P. Krawchuk. The last one named had, for many years, supplied the main general tone to this party organ.

It was somewhat awkward for the "Ukrainian Life" to service the far West as the paper would arrive late, with old news. Not satisfied with such conditions, the western "progressives" decided to start their separate organ and so on January 20, 1943, the first issue of a second pro-communist weekly in Canada, the "Ukrainian Word", made its appearance in Winnipeg. It was edited by Mykola Hrynchyshyn with the following editorial staff at work during the period of paper's existence: M. Shatulsky, E. Mykhayliuk, I. Stefanicky, M. Chachkovsky, Maria Kardash who put up the Woman's page and some others. The paper was well edited but its contents were in no way different from its Toronto kinsman, the "Ukrainian Life". Both papers published many reports and articles from Ukraine as well as literary works by Ukrainian soviet poets and writers. From 1950 very often the two weeklies would print memoirs and historical sketches by the Ukrainian pioneers as well as write articles evaluating the social processes from the class struggle point of view. It was exactly in this same sphere of social evaluations that the two pro-communist organs were losing out on their objectivity in the sphere of national values.

For the English speaking reader the pro-communist centre published

---

[1] Ukrainian Life, September 8, 1946.

"The Ukrainian Canadian", of which the first number appeared in September 1947. It was edited by John Weir with the aid of Maria Skrypnyk. Although this paper had strong pro-soviet sympathies it never propagated them clearly, stressing instead the Ukrainian problem in Canada and evaluating it basically in its first issue which said:

"The half-million Ukrainian Canadians have the same loyalty and the same general interests as Canadians of all other national origins. Our loyalty is to Canada. Our aim is to advance the security and well-being of all the Canadian people...We are not a foundling that some unknown hand placed in the dead of night at Canada's doorstep. We are not anonymous. We are Ukrainians, a people with a history, traditions, culture. We are not empty beggars standing hat in hand before our "betters", but an equal among equals in the Canadian family. No democratic Canadian will deny us this right. Our interest in the history, traditions and culture of the Ukrainian people is not something "alien" which we are trying to smuggle" into Canada. It is the special heritage of our section of the Canadian people, which we proudly bring to the common storehouse of Canadian culture. It is our unique contribution and it is good Canadianism.

Our institutions in Canada, the adaption of Ukrainian culture to Canadian conditions and the development of this culture on Canadian soil (we must look to the birth of specifically Ukrainian Canadian literature, history, music) are part of the development of Canadian life and they are good for Canada..." [2])

We purposely quoted the above passage in order to document the fact that even the central core of the "Ukrainian Life" and "Ukrainian Word" found the same solution to the problem of Ukrainian culture in Canada that had been, from the very beginning, avowed and propagated by the national camp. It was only in this sole and single relationship between those two opposite poles that any mention could be made about a common tongue for when it came to the problem of the political situation in Ukraine then, as we have already stated earlier, there was between the pro-communist and national camps a continuous break of communication, bitter enmity and total negation.

Following its basic principles "The Ukrainian Canadian" wrote a great deal about the work of the Ukrainian theatrical groups, choral ensembles and other artistic endeavours. The publication was intended especially for the Ukrainian young generation whose fathers had taken part in the organizational work of the Ukrainian Labour and Farmers' Temple Association and later of the Association of United Ukrainian Canadians. The young generation very often did not quite completely accept the political views of their fathers and for this reason the "New Canadian" was very careful in the way it conducted itself editorially. When John Weir left the paper it then was edited by M. Skrypnyk and later by Mich. Seyho. The co-editors were Rosa Mykhayliuk, Olha Dziatko and Wolodymyr Chernysh.

"Ukrainian Life" and "Ukrainian Word" always wrote with emphasis on how great and mighty and totally infallible they were in the ideological and political spheres. It was therefore a great surprise to the Ukrainian

---

[2]) Ukrainian Canadian, Toronto, No. 1, 1947.

Canadian community when the financial difficulties forced these two organs, in 1965, to merge themselves together and so instead of two, there was now only one "Life and Word", published in Toronto. One assumes the number of subscribers and readers declined yearly. This was the opposite trend in comparison to the other one that was noted, in the mid-war era, of the rapid growth of the Ukrainian Labour and Farmers' Temple Association. The pro-communist center, in Canada no doubt, was paying through its nose, so to speak, for the Russification politics of the Communist Party in Ukraine. A great role in this communist decline was also played by the influx of the new immigration and the inertia and gradual disappearance of the older party members with but very few younger ones replacing them. The same editors that had been with the "Ukrainian Life" and "Ukrainian Word", were now working for the single establishment of "Life and Word", still propagating the same Soviet ideology and practicing the same politics.

CHARACTERISTIC OF THE PRESS

The press quite often plays the part of a reliable barometer by which one may properly guage the life of the community.

From the above observation it could quite properly be stated that the press barometer of the Ukrainian Canadians during the third era rose to its highest peak. The numerical abundance of this press reveals the most diversified interests of its readers starting with religion, politics and education, and ending with the ordinary every-day expression of cooperative or social life. The ramification of the Ukrainian social community life created new forms of press organs, professional bulletins and other printed material. Until the present time the Ukrainian community in Canada has been served by 8 weeklies, 3 semi-monthly, 11 monthly magazines, 2 bi-monthly magazines, 5 quarterly journals and 2 semi-annual publications in addition to a whole array of non-periodcals and bulletins, not to mention the single pro-communist weekly and its bi-monthly cousin 'The Ukrainian Canadian', printed in English. When we compare this newest situation with the previous state before the Second World War, it will be seen that great progress has been made. There were only six weeklies then — and one of these pro-communist. True enough, there was a Ukrainian daily in existence, but that one finally folded up whose loss must be credited to the pro-communist camp which later was not even able to support two weeklies. The pinnacle of growth for the national press was in the 50-ies and since that time the number has been kept at the same level with hardly any room left, as the market demand shows, for another weekly or bi-monthly.

Among the press organs of the third era a prominent place is held by the religious publications. The circulation of periodicals would run from 2,000 to 10,000 while that of bulletins would be from 500 to a 1,000 —a considerably higher number compared with the first or even second era. The third era is also noted for more numerous appearances of bilingual and English publications and the interesting part of it is that not one of them was expanded to any prominent size and all of them disappeared sooner or later. It may be stated that more than 80% of all the publications were printed in the Ukrainian language.

The ethical standard of the press also was raised to a higher level as mud-slinging and bitter accusations disappeared from its pages. This was particularly noticeable in the national press and here a great measure of credit must be given to the Ukrainian Canadian Committee which had been able, through its influence, to untie many political and religious knots. The gradual integration of the new immigration into the life of the Ukrainian Canadian community also played its part in this mellowing process of the press. Undoubtedly the mature age of those editors who guided the politics also had its results. This in turn poses another proposition—the added influx of the new forces. The third generation supplied strong reinforcements to the publishing profession, whereas there is but very little of the natural addition to this calling from those who were born and educated in Canada. The reason may lie in the fact that the young generation, although it speaks in Ukrainian still, forms its thoughts only in the language in which it was educated in schools, and this is hardly enough for the editorship qualification. This would also explain another characteristic actuality that all the high school and university youth publications appeared almost exclusively in the English language. In this era the prestige of the editors had been considerably diminished in comparison with earlier eras, not only because of their pay, which had never been very high, but primarily due to the fact that the editor gradually ceased to be the leader in the life of the community and had only become its commentator. The widening circle of intelligentsia and community leaders have freed him from other duties. Still when we consider the fact that on the whole Canadian press is amicably disposed toward the religious field and represents the views of various organizations and other media, then it will be seen that the editors still possess a wide variety of opportunities to influence the life of society and to direct the course of community affairs. Almost without any exceptions they all are the true living couriers of the Ukrainian culture and the Ukrainian way of life.

There is not any doubt that the ethnic press—the Ukrainian included—had always been the center nerve of its community core, especially when much is being said about the multiform culture of the modern Canadian entity. Very often the weeklies in injecting their color-tone into the religious and community way of life, were cultural reservoirs where each reader could find material for his own education and individual interest. This poses the question of the educational value of the press and how well it performs its allotted task.

To answer the above question the editors of the Ukrainian newspapers held a mutual conference in Winnipeg in 1953 under the initiation and sponsorship of the Ukrainian Canadian Committee. It is interesting to note that several resolutions at this conference appealed for a greater Ukrainian participation in political and social life, including social clubs and other community affairs. The consultation underlined the need of personal contacts on the part of the editors of different views so they "could formulate the Ukrainian public opinion in Canada on different questions" [3].

The conference also brought in the proposition to organize a journalistic association for the purpose of publishing an English edition for those who do not know the Ukrainian language. Such resolutions are additional

---

[3] The Fourth Congress of Ukrainian Canadians, Winnipeg, 1953, p. 119.

proof that Ukrainian editors correctly appraised the press information situation and were not swayed by any narrow group interests.

It was some time before the Association of Journalists was formed, but close ties developed amongst editors had salutary effects on the future events along this line. In 1965 the Ukrainian Canadian journalists held a conference with their colleagues from U.S.A. at the "Souzivka" summer resort near New York. A year later a similar conference was held in Toronto and the Association of Ukrainian Journalists of Canada became an accomplished fact. One of its basic tasks was set to serve the Ukrainian community in Canada and its cultural endeavours, remaining at the same time an integral and fruitful part of the Canadian state. From these resolutions one may clearly perceive that the Ukrainian press, along with its editors and associates, will continue to work in Canada along the prospective line of their professional alliance.

The Ukrainian journalists of Canada did not lock themselves up in their own cultural ghetto. When, during the war period and afterwards, the ethnic press clubs were being formed in Canada, they were the first ones in the ranks to take part in their formation. In this way the Canadian Ethnic Press Club was born in Winnipeg, in 1942, and the Canadian Ethnic Press Association of Ontario in 1945. Similar clubs later were formed in Montreal and Vancouver. The parent body of these organizations came into being in 1958 under the title of the Canadian Ethnic Press Association, comprising over 80 periodicals of the ethnic press in Canada. Among the leading members in these press formations may be found the names of such well known Ukrainian journalists as M. Pohorecky, J. H. Syrnick, Roman Rakhmanny, Stepan Wolynec, Rev. S. Izyk, A. Kurdydyk, W. S. Levytsky, Rev. P. Kachur, Rev. P. Chomyn, M. Sosnowsky, S. Rosocha, A. Iwachniuk, A. Yaworsky, Rev. M. Sopulak, M. Hykawy, W. Solonynka, O. Matla, W. Skorupsky, I. Eliashewsky, Vera Ke and others.

RADIO, TELEVISION AND FILM

Ukrainians, in Canada, also made efforts to have radio, television and film available to be of service in enhancing their culture.

Radio, televesion and film—these are today's modern means of mass communication. Radio and television are first heralds of news in our living rooms. Following them comes the press media which projects the news, brought by the radio or television. Live coverage on television, today is more interesting than arranged scenes. Separated by thousands of miles, onlookers and actors become near and comprehensible. Radio, television and film play an important role in the integration of people, nations and continents. They have great significance even for a country like Canada which is settled by people of different nations with various cultural, political and historical backgrounds. Means of mass communications must stand on such elevation that with their aid it would be possible to integrate society and to find a common denominator for all citizens. This question, by itself, becomes more factual in later period of the history of our country, when, according to the latest statistics of Canadian sociologists and historians, it is evident that Canada in 1967 is quite different from what it was in 1867. From a country of two cultures it has become a country of many cultures. Besides Anglo-Saxon and French elements we have the "third component factor" which is often referred to as a composition of various ethnic groups in Canada which according to 1961 census make up 26% of our total population, besides 30% of French and 44% [1]) composed of English, Scotch. Irish and Welsh.

From such understanding of Canada representatives of various nationalities such as Dutch, Germans, Poles, Finns, Italians, Rumanians, Hungarians and others, including Ukrainians prepared, in 1962 and presented to the Federal Government, a memorandum requesting the establishment of the facilities of radio, television and film for their and general Canadian national benefit, stating that "in the very interests of Canada as well as the ethnic groups, there should be created a system in which they can fully participate in the activities of the public and private organs of Radio, Television and Film..." They also stated: "These Canadians did not come to Canada with empty hands and they have the legitimate desire to share what they have with other fellow Canadians. They wish, indeed, to enrich their country with their own spiritual values, their own precious national traditions, their culture and experiences, which already in the past made for the greatness and glory of old Europe" [2]).

This was not the first appearance of Ukrainians and other ethnic groups requesting the services of mass means of communications for all cultures of this country.

Whereas such and similar attempts resulted in disappointments as confirmed in the quoted brief [3]), since the Canadian Broadcasting Corpora-

---

[1] "Ukrainian Canadians", by Senator Paul Yuzyk, "Three Elements of the Canadian Population", pp. 4-6.
[2] Brief on Radio, Television and Film in Canada, presented by the official representatives of the ethnic groups in Canada, Ottawa, 1962.
[3] Ibidem, p. 3 & 10.

tion ignores the cultural problems of over four million Canadian citizens, therefore, for the Ukrainians there remains only one alternative, namely, to organize short radio broadcasts from different private stations. Some of these radio programs have lasted ten and more years. To such belongs: "The Voice from Native Country" in Winnipeg, under the direction of Rev. S. Izyk. For a long time, also in Winnipeg, there existed a commercial program sponsored by Universal Radio. For three years there was a daily Ukrainian program "Songs of Ukraine", directed by P. Naumchuk in Toronto. There was a Ukrainian daily radio program of Wasyl Sharvan in Niagara Falls. Also a daily radio program of St. Basil the Great College in Toronto, J. Vilk directed a radio program "Surma", "Trembita" of B. Soluk and others. In Edmonton were presented religious radio programs. In Port Arthur and Fort William a branch of the Canadian League for Ukrainian's Liberation, for a few years, had its own weekly programs, etc.

Baptists and various Evangelists have developed a network of radio broadcasts: in Saskatoon "The Hour of God's Word", in Prince Albert and Cameron, "The Voice of Life", also in Vancouver "The Gospel Hour".

The first radio-talks (in Ukrainian) began in Toronto—Hamilton by W. Galan and in Winnipeg even before the Second World War. After the war, in recent period a program known as "Travels in Ukraine" was directed by N. Rzepecki and "The Voice of Ukrainian Insurgent" by B. Chubenko which was sponsored by Ukrainian Veterans of the Ukrainian Insurgent Army (U.P.A.). In Winnipeg, Ukrainians also made steps to obtain a radio-station for the use of ethnic groups, but the committee which was composed of Mrs. S. Juba, M. Smerchansky, J. Shansky and others failed to get a license.

The object of all these broadcasts was to transmit to the listeners the word, vocal music and songs from the treasures of cultural collections of Ukrainians in Canada. Some of these broadcasts were carried out in English and French languages to acquaint the listeners and non-Ukrainians with Ukrainian problems in Canada and beyond. An example of such broadcasts were those given by Jaroslav Schur in Winnipeg in 1966 and 1967.

C.B.C. made no systematic broadcasts for ethnic groups in Canada, but, instead had broadcasts in Ukrainian language overseas. These shortwave broadcasts for Ukrainian listeners in various countries and particularly in Ukraine, were very popular, portraying life, customs and national traditions in Canada, also including description of cultural and political life of Ukrainian Canadians. These radio-talks were started following World War Two under the management of B. Panchuk, later by J. B. Wesolowsky. They contributed much, in eastern Europe, towards understanding Canada in its political field, as a country of freedom and democracy.

Television and film materially and technically are more complicated than radio broadcasting, but even here Ukrainians made important efforts. We have already mentioned, in the second period, production of such films as "Zaporozetz beyond Danube", "Natalka Poltawka" and "Bethlehem Night". After the war, during the third period, in Toronto, Dr. Elias Wachna produced, at his own cost, a colored film: "Treasures of Ukraine". In a similar vein is a list of documentary films of various cultural developments of Ukrainian life; also a film of 60th anniversary of Ukrainian settlement in Canada; the unveiling of the monument of Taras Shevchenko; 50th anniversary of Ukrainian Catholic Church; films of mass meetings of Ukrainians in Canada, the U.S.A. and others.

Attempts were also made, following the initiative of Vasyl Avramenko in the second era, to create, even in the third era, organized production of Ukrainian films. In Beamsville, Ontario, "Trident Studios Ltd" with J. Tomych as producer, was established for the purpose of filming scenes from the life of Ukrainian pioneers in Canada. Following this, there was organized in the earliest part of the third era the "Soluk Productions" in Toronto which made several black and white films: "Ukrainian Displaced Persons in Germany", "Ukrainians of Eastern Canada", "Choir of Bandurists of Taras Shevchenko", "Black Sea Sailors" and "Lviv Catacombs". There was also an extensively planned film company, the Orbit Film Corporation, also from Toronto, whose president was W. Hultay. This Corporation had collected film material covering the life of Ukrainians in the free world and produced a film, in color: "Hutsulka Ksenia". To our regret, "Soluk Productions" and "Orbit" both discontinued their work. The latest of such larger ventures was Ukrainian Film Club in Oshawa Ontario. They made a start by producing a good colored film from the events of the Ukrainian Insurgent Army, "Cruel Dawns", based on the story written by S. Lubomyrsky. This film was produced by a young Ukrainian, Volodymyr Vasik, who had completed extensive studies in Hollywood.

Although some attempts at producing Ukrainian Films were brought to a high level, the industry did not reach the point of mass production. Instead, the National Film Board has tried to make short films with Ukrainian themes. The latest of these films "Kurelek" describes the life of Ukrainian settlers based on pictures and drawings of a gifted Ukrainian Canadian painter, William Kurelek [4]. This film was shown at the International Film Festival in the city of Cork, Ireland.

More about Radio, Television and Film in the seventies can be found in another chapter dealing with "The Decade of Multiculturalism".

---

[4] Based on biography of his father.

SCHOLARS IN VARIOUS FIELDS

With the third immigration of Ukrainians to Canada, there came to Canada a large number of Ukrainian scholars from Europe. They strongly reinforced the first ranks of the intellectuals who arrived after the Second World War and those who completed their studies at the Canadian or American Universities. Some of them filled positions at the Universities, others continued their learning besides their daily tasks. But they all strengthened the humanist and philosophical studies in Canada, because, as it became evident later, most of the educated arrivals belonged to that class. To the outstanding workers in that category belong: Dr. Ivan Ohienko, later Metropolitan Ilarion (Archbishop), U.G.O. Church of Canada; Dmytro Doroshenko, Leonid Biletsky, Jaroslaw Pasternak; Dmytro Donzow, Yuriy Rusow, Maria Pasternak, Natalia Gerken-Rusowa and others.

Dr. Ivan Ohienko-Metropolitan Ilarion (1882-1972), for many years lectured on Slavic philology in Warsaw University and wrote a series of educational books dealing with Ukrainian language and culture. He was also an editor of periodicals "Native Language" and "Our Culture". He wrote a number of books of historical and philosophical content. He showed his talent in poetry in which his favorite form was depicted in "On Golgotha" in which he portrayed the struggle of Ukrainian people, "Unfinished Song" with the theme of the combats of Bohdan Khmelnytsky, "The Birth of a Human Being" with philosophical thoughts on humanity. In Canada, besides journalism, he worked on education, wrote essays and poetry in which the predominant themes dealt with religion. The welfare of people and humanity were always his concern. The leading motto for his writings was: to serve the people and God. He translated the Holy Scriptures and produced such notable works as "Transfer of Ukrainian Church to Moscovite Church", "A Word About Ihor's Campaign", "History of Ukrainian Language", "Three-Armed Crosses", a historical-dogmatic and monographic book "Ikonoborstvo" "Separation of the Only Christ's Church and the First Attempts to Unite It", being a historical and canonical study. In Canada Metropolitan Ilarion identified himself by his ideological graphics under the title: "The Book on our Existence", under the call "Guard Everything that Is Traditional".

A contemporary of Metropolitan Ilarion was his close friend Dr. Leonid Biletsky (1882-1955) for a long period a professor of Literature at the Ukrainian Free University in Prague. He left behind him such works as: "History of Ukrainian Literature", "Bases of Literary-Scientific Criticism" and "Perspectives of Scientific-Literary Criticism". In Canada he worked at the Ukrainian Cultural and Educational Centre, also at the Ukrainian Academy of Sciences (U.V.A.N.) of which for some time he was the president. He also was the president of Shevchenko studies in this Academy and published a four-volume annotated "Kobzar". He prepared also monographs about such educators as Omelian Ohonowsky and Dmytro Doroshenko. On the occasion of the 60th anniversary of Ukrainian settlements in Canada he wrote a short history of Ukrainian cultural life in Canada under the title "Ukrainian Pioneers in Canada" (1891-1951).

Equal in stature to the previous two was Dmytro Doroshenko (1882-1951) a follower of great historian M. Hrushevsky, with whom we became acquainted in the second period of our history. Following his arrival in Canada in 1947, together with others he renewed the work of U.V.A.N. and was its first president. During his three-year stay in Canada he wrote "Memoirs about the recent Past", "A Sketch of the History of Christian Church", and put in much effort in preparing historical material of Ukrainian life in Canada, which was published under the name: "Memorial Book" of Ukrainian National Home in Winnipeg.

All the above three learned men chose Winnipeg as their domicile. The first of them notably influenced the pace of history of the Ukrainian Greek Orthodox Church, as its Metropolitan and leader for many years. The other two left their names with Ukrainian free learning, and in formulating the Ukrainian Free Academy of Sciences.

Another group of Ukrainian intellectuals landed in Toronto and Montreal, in eastern Canada and organized the T. Shevchenko Scientific Society in which the leading role was played by Dr. Evhen Vertyporoch (1898-1973). He was a chemist and college professor in Lviv and Munich, who also wrote in Canada a number of popular educational articles and lectured at the Ryerson Institute of Toronto.

For many years a member of the T. Shevchenko Scientific Society in Lviv and in Canada, was noted archeologist Jaroslaw Pasternak (1892-1969) who also was a professor of archeology at the State University and Academy of Theology in Lviv and later, professor of Ukrainian Free University in Munich, researcher of pre-historic and the Princely Period on Ukrainian lands. His known works comprise "Carpathian Ukraine" in neolite period (1925), "Carpathia in Archeology" (1928) and a monograph "Old Halych" (1944). In Canada he wrote a monumental book "Archeology of Ukraine" which was published in Toronto.

In Toronto, also lived Maria Pasternak (1897-   ) a master and critic of national and ballet dancing and Thadaeus Zalesky (1883-1976) linguist and literary critic. In Montreal Natalia Gerken-Rusova (1902-   ) wrote a series of works on theatrical art, which appeared in English and French languages. In Ukrainian she wrote "Heroic Theatre". In this same field in Vancouver also worked another theatrical writer, Valerian Revutsky (1911-   ), who at one time was lecturer on the History of Ukrainian Theatrical Art in Kiev and Lviv.

In Montreal University lectured Yuriy Rusow (1895-1961), expert on literature and philosophy, author of the books: "The Soul of the People and the Spirit of a Nation", "Mysticism in Shevchenko" and others. In the field of economics and cooperative movement Andriy Kachor (1908-   ) has occupied a leading role. Among his numerous research works the most essential is "Ukrainian Economy in the System of U.S.S.R."

To a special position among the scholars and educators in a broad sense belongs Dmytro Donzow (1883-1973) publisher and literary critic. He was an ideologist of Ukrainian Nationalism on western Ukrainian land, whose writings provided ideological nourishment for the whole generation between the two World Wars. He came to Canada in 1947 and from 1948 to 1953 lectured on literature at Montreal University. In Canada he published the following books: "Spirit of Our Past" (1944), "Poetess of Fiery Horizons" (about Lesia Ukrainka), "Russia or Europe"

(1955) in which he stressed the spiritual bond between Ukraine and the West, "From Mysticism to Politics" in which, again he proclaimed idealistic voluntarism and historical idealism, as important factors of history and also a philosophical political work "With Cross and Sword".

To the younger generation of scholars of broad horizons of the third immigration, who occupied notable positions in the research in the field of humanities belong Dr. J. B. Rudnyckyj, Dr. C. Bida, Dr. B. Bociurkiw, Dr. G. Mulyk-Lucyk, Dr. G. Luckyj, Dr. Yar Slavutych, Dr. Wasyl Luciw, Dr. W. T. Zyla and others.

Jaroslav B. Rudnyckyj (1910-   ), a professor of Slavic Philology in Prague and Munich, became the head, in Canada, of Slavic Studies at Manitoba University and also of the Ukrainian Free Academy of Sciences after the death of L. Biletsky. He is the author of numerous publications in the field of languages and especially of onomastic and Slavic sciences. Of his more important works are: "Ukrainian Orthography", "Canadian local names of Ukrainian Origin" and the most impressive his "Ukrainian Etymological Dictionary". He is one of the founders of the Canadian Linguistic Association of Canada, the Canadian Institute of Onomastic Sciences, the American Name Society and others. He represented Ukrainian and Canadian Learned Societies at various international meetings. In 1963 J. B. Rudnyckyj was called upon by the Prime Minister of Canada to be a member of the Royal Commission on Bi-lingualism and Bi-culturalism. No doubt that he is one of the most active Ukrainian Canadian intellectuals.

Constantine Bida (1916-1979), Doctor of Slavic Philology in Vienna, opened his work in the Slavic Department at the University of Ottawa which he headed for 1957-1979. He was a specialist in Slavic Philology and Comparative Literature. His works "Shakespeare's Entrance in Slavic Literature", "Linguistic Aspect of the Controversy over the Authenticity of the Tale of Ihor's Campaign", "Shakespeare in Polish and Russian Classicism and Romanticism". He also completed a bilingual anthology of French-Canadian poetry and initiated a series of "Etudes Slaves". He represented Canada and the Ukrainian Scholars at international gatherings of Learned Societies.

George S. N. Luckyj (1919-   ) with broad knowledge of Literature, at one time was the head of Slavic Department at the University of Toronto and an author of a series of works in English language: "Literary Politics in the Soviet Ukraine" (1917-1934), "The Battle for Literature in the Soviet Ukraine" and others. He was also an editor of "Canadian Slavonic Papers".

Yar Slavutych (1918-   ) works in Alberta University and is known not only as a linguist of high calibre but also as a poet, writer, and editor. His field of speciality are Slavic languages. George Mulyk-Lucyk (1913-   ) is versed in Slavic philology, psychology and philosophy. He completed his studies at Vilno, Warsaw and Munich Universities and has been with St. Andrew's College in Winnipeg for years. Here he published "Patriotic Elements in the Speech of Ukrainian Pioneers", "Psychological Characteristics of Olha Kobylanska" and others.

Volodymyr T. Zyla (1919-   ), Slavist and linguist, literary critic and writer, studied in Canada and Europe, at present he is at the Texas Technological College. He keeps close ties with Canada and writes on

Canadian topics, both in Ukrainian and English. Among his works: "Contribution to the History of Ukrainian and Slavic Studies in Canada" (Winnipeg, 1961).

As we see, Slavists and linguists of the third immigration have occupied important positions in Canadian Universities. When we add, to the above list the names of such scholars as Dr. C. H. Andrusyshen, whom we have already mentioned, Dr. O. Starchuk, professor of Alberta University and a specialist in Slavic literature, Dr. Victor O. Buyniak, professor of Saskatchewan University, Dr. Jaroslav Rozumnyj of Manitoba University, Dr. Borislav N. Bilash and Brother Methodius Kuziak, F.S.C., authors of articles and short studies on prominent educational themes, and an impressive register of young professors—assistants of Slavic Departments of Canadian Universities, then this list is not only impressive, but also rich in highly qualified talents who are leaders in the department of Slavic languages in Canada.

Allied with knowlege of Slavic Studies is knowledge of Soviet affairs, in which matter one of the leading scholars is Dr. Bohdan Bociurkiw (1925-   ) professor at Alberta University (lately at Ottawa), author of several valuable works on religious and political questions in U.S.S.R.

Another master in Sovietology is Dr. Roman Olynyk (pen-name Rakhmanny, 1918-   ), journalist, political writer, editor and radiobroadcaster, student of Lviv, Toronto and Ottawa Universities. R. Rakhmanny published his research articles in Ukrainian and English in various magazines and papers. Some of them were published in two book collections: "Blood and Ink" and "Along the Fiftieth Parallel". In all his writings and lectures in Canada Dr. Olynyk champions human dignity and liberty for man and nations. Ukrainians also had notable men in other lines of learned fields, particularly those dealing with creative talents. In architecture Radoslav Zuk, professor at Manitoba and Montreal Universities, has won wide acclaim. He adapted Byzantian and Ukrainian church style with modern building trends. He prepared plans for and constructed many modern Ukrainian churches. In 1965 he received first prize in international competition for the best plan for the project of Olympic Games building. Also well known architect of church building is Victor Deneka. Architect Nicholas Flak is known as a historian of architecture. Another Winnipeg-born, Peter Dobush, received gold medals for his work in architecture [1]. In metallurgic chemisty, Vladimir N. Mackiw and Wasyl Kunda received high awards, in petrochemistry Stepan Ilnycky, in microbiology E. B. Roslycky and Roma Havirko of Winnipeg, in genetics M.P. Bachynsky, in electric energetics Michael Tarnawecky, (his plan for the development of Nelson River hydro plant was accepted). Dr. Gregory Messel is widely known as a nuclear physicist (at present in Sidney, Australia) and Dr. Joseph V. Charyk, also a nuclear physicist, son of Lethbridge railwayman, Undersecretary of the U.S. Air Force. A prominent place in inventions occupy Albertans Roman Gonsett and his son Faust (improvement of radio, telephone, photography), who moved to U.S.A.

In this category of scientists we should include Dr. I. Hlynka, recipient of the Brabender Award of the American Association of Cereal Chemists

---

[1] Among others, in 1960 was presented with a gold medal for his work by the Royal Architectural Institute of Canada.

in 1966 for his scientific contributions. He elaborated scores of articles and monographs to leading scientific journals on this continent and in Europe, as well as verses and articles on various topics to the leading Ukrainian publications, published in English and Ukrainian. Since 1947 Dr. I. Hlynka worked with the Grain Research Laboratories of the Board of Grain Commissioners in Winnipeg (1947-1972).

Another Winnipeger, Prof. Mykhaylo Borowsky, contributed a great deal to Canadian and Ukrainian agricultural research having already to his credit over 120 publications and over 100 articles and essays in this field in the Ukrainian Canadian press.

To be able to take a glimpse, at least in a general view, of the part played by Ukrainians in various deparments of studies, we must mention Dr. J. Ruptash, Dean of the Engineering Division in Carleton University, Dr. Peter Smylski, Dean of Dentistry in Toronto University, Prof. W. S. Tarnopolsky, Dean of Law Faculty of Saskatchewan University (lately at Windsor), Dr. M. Pernarowski, Professor of Pharmaceutical Chemistry, University of B.C. and an author of numerous articles in this field plus a list of scientists in the agricultural field whom we have already mentioned in the second era of our history.

The study of theology was notably strengthened after the World War II. There came to Canada the well known theologians, whom we have already mentioned, namely Dr. Ivan Ohienko from Warsaw, Prof. Ivan Wlasowsky and further on the former professors of the Theological Academy in Lviv: Dr. Basil Laba, Dr. Bohdan Lypsky, Dr. M. Sopulak, Dr. Bohdan Kazymyra, and from Western Theology Universities, Dr. Maxim Hermaniuk, Dr. W. Malanchuk, Dr. P. Kachur, Dr. M. Solowiy, Dr. M. Zalesky, Dr. A. Baran, Dr. M. Komar and others.

Enlarged was also the art of history writing of Ukrainians in Canada, the initiative, as mentioned before, was given by Prof. Ivan Bobersky. Dr. V. J. Kaye (1896-1975) notably increased this study and, having access to Federal Archives, put it on a sound basis. Working in the Department of Canadian Citizenship and later, as professor of Ottawa University, he wrote a few basic works not only about Ukrainian emigration to Canada, but also about other ethnic groups: Slovaks, Byelorussians and Poles. Among the larger of his works, as mentioned several times previously, belongs his book "Early Ukrainian Settlement in Canada, 1895 to 1900" and later: "A Dictionary of Ukrainian Canadian Biography", both published through the assistance of "Ukrainian Canadian Research Foundation" in Toronto and sponsored by Ukrainian Branches of Royal Canadian Legion under the direction of S. Pawluk. The above mentioned Foundation also published a monographic story of the first Ukrainian Member of Canadian Parliament in Ottawa, under the title of: "A Ukrainian Canadian in Parliament", from Memoirs of Michael Luchkovich, edited by J. Gregorovich.

On the occasion of the 75th anniversary of Ukrainian settlement in Canada and 100th Anniversary of the birth of Canada, Ukrainian Free Academy of Sciences has printed three volumes of the "Studies in the History of Ukrainians in Canada". These books were prepared by M. H. Marunchak, author of other research publications concerning Ukrainian settlements in Canada. The Ukrainian Self-Reliance League S.U.S., on the occasion of above mentioned important dates concerning Ukrainian settlements in Canada, carried out a campaign for funds to aid in the publication of history of Ukrainians in Canada and to record the role played by S.U.S. in Ukrainian national life, which was prepared by Julian Stechishin, author of a number of larger and smaller publications in connection with Ukrainian historiography. Dr. Bohdan Kazymyra has done much in the development of the history of Ukrainians in Canada, especially along the line of church history and social statistics. Alexander Royick has devoted himself to research on the arrival of Ukrainians to Canada prior to 1891. Dr. Michael Huculak prepared a monographic history of the Ukrainian people in British Columbia. Rev. Josaphat Skvarok published "The Ukrainian Settlers in Canada and Their Schools" and John Panchuk of Detroit, born and educated Canadian, contributed a great deal to the history of the first Ukrainian settlement in Manitoba (Stuartburn-Gardenton).

Ivan Tesla, a specialist in demography, published a valuable research with numerous charts under the title: "Ukrainian Population of Canada: Settlement and Demographic Characteristics". F. Bogdan scored an impressive account in his research: "British Columbia and Ukrainians". His special work is: "Ukrainian Surnames in Canada". P. J. Lazarowich, lawyer and educator added several pages to Ukrainian education in his work "The M. Hrushevsky Ukrainian Institute in Edmonton" and others.

Quite a number of pioneers have sketched interesting memoirs in various Ukrainian Canadian papers. It is worthwhile to mention Rev. P. Kindrat, P. Svarich, K.S. Prodan, S. W. Pernarowski, T. Bodnar, William Mihaychuk, T. Tomashevsky, M. H. Boykowich, A. Bunka, W. Perepeluk, M. Boychuk, P. Humeniuk, N. Chabal, D. Prokop, M. Chypchar, S. J. Porayko, M. Petrowsky, S. Korban, S. Hewak, Rev. M. Olenchuk, A. Kosikowsky and several others.

A somewhat useful place in the historiography of the Ukrainians in Canada has been held by the "Chronicles". These go back to the first Ukrainian Almanacs which recorded each year's important events in Ukrainian social life. In the years 1948 to 1953 Michael Hykawy, at that time the editor of "Canadian Farmer", complied a very effective chronology of events as recorded in his paper, from the beginning of its existence, 1903, until later times, 1945, and these he printed each year in the annual Almanacs, taken from his weekly newspaper. Olha Woycenko had gone farther and on the basis of the weekly newspaper, "Ukrainian Voice", began publishing a similar chronology in separate books (five volumes so far) under the title: "Chronicles of Ukrainian Life in Canada". Although such chronologies do not bring anything new into history, they do refresh the memories of the past and are a valuable source of information concerning those great and small events through which Ukrainian community lived in the past. O. Woycenko has also prepared a lengthy history of the achievements of Ukrainians in Canada under the name of "Ukrainians in Canada", being a component part of "Canada Ethnica". Dr. Paul Yuzyk has prepared a few basic monographic works. Of these we should mention, first of all, his University graduation theses concerning both Ukrainian traditional churches. As professor of history at Manitoba and Ottawa Universities Paul Yuzyk has added many interesting pages to the history of Ukrainians in Canada. He was also, one of the first who named three component elements of Canadian society, stating that besides Anglo-Saxon and French there exists the third element, namely the ethnic groups. As a senator he has also published numerous speeches dealing with the life of the Ukrainians in Canada. Some of his principal writings are: Ukrainian Cultural and Educational Achievements in Canada (1946) "Ukrainian-English Dictionary in Reading in Ukrainian Authors" (1949), "Ukrainian Cultural and Religious Life (for the Encyclopedia of Ukrainian Knowledge, 1952), "The First Ukrainians in Manitoba (1953), "The Ukrainians in Manitoba, A Social History" (1953), "History of the Ukrainian Orthodox Church in Canada" (thesis), History of the Ukrainian Catholic Church in Canada" (thesis), "Ukrainian Canadians, Their Place and Role in Canadian Life", published in English and French" (1967), etc.

The first attempt at making an analysis of the participation of Ukrainian soldiers in the Second World War, was made by Rev. Ihor Shpytkowsky in his comprehensive work "The Almanac of the Ukrainian Canadian Soldiers 1939-1945".

Irena Knysh (1906-   ) devoted her studies to the research of the Ukrainian women's movement not only in Ukraine, but also in the new settlement on Canadian soil. Her published works include "The Patriotism of Anna Yonker", "The Living Spirit of the People", "The Torch in the Darkness", and others are segments of life taken from the history of the Ukrainian people in Canada. She also has written newspaper articles on women's themes. Another writer working in the same field is Stephania Bubniuk whose many articles have appeared in the Woman's World. Stepan Kylymnyk wrote a five-volume work about Ukrainian customs entitled: "Ukrainian Year in People's Customs and in Historic Interpretation". Rev. W. Iwashko prepared and edited, in 1965, his "Schematism of the Saskatoon Eparchy of the Ukrainian Catholic Church", which forms an integral part of the history of the Ukrainians in Saskatchewan. In the same category belongs the "History of the Ukrainian Catholic Parish of Calgary" prepared and published by Dr. M. Hladyshevsky, and a similar work of Joseph Kohut who published his book entitled "The Outline of the History of the Ukrainian Catholic Church of St. Trinity in Stuartburn, Manitoba. Also, F. T. Onufriychuk published his work "The History of the Municipality of Sliding Hills". There were other writers who dealt with similar themes.

There were several separate works published by Toma Kobzey dealing with union movement including, "The Labour Movement and its Problems" written in 1960, "Short History of Trade Union Movement in Canada" (1956) and others. In this same field also were engaged such well known figures in labour movement as Danylo Lobay and G. Elendiuk.

All these publications and researches prove that among the Ukrainians there was awakened a real interest in their past, in Canada. What is more, sociologists and historians of other nationalities have also developed great interest in this vital ethnic community. This also proves that Ukrainians in Canada already have their own rich history in this country and their sociological problems draw the attention of the researchers from the various spheres of interests. The history of this community is colorful, full of aspirations and social impacts which are vital components in a struggle to live and to be one's self.

POETS AND WRITERS

Not only in higher learning, but also in belles-lettres, the influence of the new immigration was felt. There came to Canada a great number of Ukrainian poets and writers, who left behind them, in the old country, or on emigration, great wealth of poetical work. They came from different parts of Ukraine and therefore from various occupied regions and for that reason their word became more synodic-national although it had in itself a variety of poetic and prose reflections. Almost all of them, without any great exceptions, knew how to discern the pathos of the new country and tune it to the pathos of their native homeland. Together with the talented individuals that worked between the two World Wars, and young growing forces that were born in this country, they created a spiritual power which, firmly began to separate itself from its own environment.

Volodymyr Skorupsky (1912-   ) resident of Edmonton and Toronto, was a prolific writer of poetry. He edited five collections of poetry: "My Home" (1954), "On a Journey" (1957), "Without Native Doorstep" (1958), "From a Water Spring" (1961), "Over a Grave" (1963). In his collections, especially in the latter, he showed many philosophical thoughts concerning life and its environment.

To greater heights belongs also Yar Slavutych (1918-   ), poet of patriotic heroism, who is already known to us as a scholar. During his years in Canada (since 1960) he put out several collections of select poetry: "Oasis" (1960), "Majesty" (1962), "Trophies" (1963). In 1966 he published a new collection, "Conquerors of the Prairies", which by its theme is fully dedicated to Ukrainian pioneers of Canada. His verses are full of freshness, good cheer and manliness. By editing his Almanacs "Northern Lights", in Edmonton, he made it possible for various writing talents to publish in them their works. In three of his annuals of "Northern Lights" we find the names of new poets in Canada, such as: "Bohdan Mazepa (1928-   ) who, in 1956 published a collection "Starlit Horizon" with a special cycle of verses "Alberta", with its romantic Banff. Other poets were: Dan Mur, Zenon Harasymovych, Andrew Lehit and Larysa Murovych (Timoshenko), who published a collection of poems "Pioneers of Sacreed Land" which is loaded with Canadian themes, Theodore Matvienko issued his "Collection" (1924) and "Sonnets" (1961). Lev T. Orlyhora published his collection "I Love" (1958) and "Heroes of Our Times" (1959) in Edmonton. He is better known as publisher and editor of a periodic magazine "Our Faith" (Winnipeg).

Volodimir Barabash (1900-   ) another "westerner" drew attention to himself by his verses and aphorisms. He showed his talent in the post-war period, although he had printed some of his works in Calgary Herald back in 1937. His creative works were printed in various papers such as "Calgary Herald", Calgary Albertan", "The Western Farm Leader", "Ukrainian News" and "Progress". Most of his themes are based on love, religion, philosophy, and often cross over into metaphysics.

Danylo Struk (1940-   ) belongs to the young generation which was raised in Canada, and is noted for his modernistic verses in a collection "Gamma Sigma", Winnipeg, 1963. In 1960's Daria Mohylanka, from Edmonton made herself known by her poetry "Thoughts are flying to Ukraine" (1962), and "Songs of My Heart" (1964). With western Canada are also tied the poetic works of a close neighbor of Manitoba, Alexander Neprycky-Hranowsky of Minneapolis, U.S.A. who dedicated a series of verses to Canadian pioneers. Among his poems the "Cross of Freedom" he pays eternal tribute to the first Ukrainian cross of freedom in Canada, that was placed in Terebowla, in Manitoba, in memory of the first Ukrainian church service and the freedom which the Ukrainian settlers found on this soil.

In Eastern Canada Lewko Romen (1891-1981) attracts our attention not only with his interesting poetry but also with his prose and dramatic works (the latest in this genre was his "Zhovtosyl". His collection, "Poems", appeared in Toronto in 1966. He published another collection outside of Canada "Peredpillia", in Philadelphia, in 1953) and is the author of various reviews dealing with literature and linguistic studies.

A separate group of authors is represented by such writers as Borys Oleksandriv (1921-1979) in whose work poetic prose and journalism stand higher than poetry. In addition, he is a good humorist writing under the pseudo-name of "Svyryd Lomachka" and has published a collection of feuilletons "Love your Neighbor", printed in Toronto, 1961.

The journalistic pen has also captivated another poet and writer— Anatol Kurdydyk (1905-   ) who continues to be active in literary and artistic life of Ukrainians in Canada. In Toronto he was the head of the Ukrainian Literary-Art Club and initiated the historic gathering of the Ukrainian Artists of Canada and America with Ukrainian community in Toronto. Earlier, he wrote poetry, novels, and stories that were printed in different anthologies, and he is also an author of several theatre plays. All his literary works portray deep love for his Fatherland and its people. On new soil he wrote satire, edited almanacs, calendars and pathos-laden articles in which he advocated deep national morality. Journalism took the upper hand also in the case of Paul Step (1893-1965), poet and prose writer, who, for some time edited "Young Ukraine" in Toronto.

The youngest of the newly-arrived poets is Ihor Shankowsky, who in recent years worked at the University of Alberta. He occupied himself in translating Japanese poetry and besides his original patriotic lyrics, he also produced a series of other translations.

Ukrainian Canadian prose also has its greatness. The pioneer writer Dmytro Kolisnyk (1883-1958) published in 1950 and 1952 the first and second volume of his novel "My Village", in Saskatoon, and left behind many other stories and sketches. Osyp Kremar wrote his work "Returned" in 1947. After the war Michael Petrowsky, Oleksander Luhowy (O. Ovrutsky-Schwabe), Illia Kiriak and others continued with their creative work and talents, with whom we already have been acquainted during the second era. With them may be associated such rugged individualists as Ulas Samchuk, Wasyl Sofroniv-Levytsky, Fedir Odrach, O. Hay-Holovko, **Mykola Prychodko,** Julian Beskyd-Tarnowych, Petro Volyniak, Ivan Bodnarchuk, Mykhaylo Podworniak, Bohdan Fedchuk, Bohdan Hoshowsky, Wolodymyr Krymsky, Nestor Rzepecki and many others.

Ulas Samchuk (1905-   ) is one of the leading writers of Eastern

Canada who came to this country in 1948 and already has to his literary credit such novels as "Maria", the "Youth of Wasyl Sheremeta", the well known romantic chronicle-novel "Wolyn", two other romantic novels "The Hills Speak", "Kulak", and many others. In addition to these he had a large collection of shorter novels and stories, including a group of revolutionary stories called the "Mesnyky" (Avengers). He belonged to the group of literati that wrote about the "great literature" and about Europe to which theme he dedicated a separate novel entitled "We Discover Europe". In Canada, Ulas Samchuk re-published his "Wolyn" novel and added two more volumes to it, and then, working in seclusion he published, in 1967, a new novel "On Solid Ground" dedicated to the new country in which he and his own countrymen found the freedom of thought and human dignity for themselves and their children.

Wasyl S. Levytsky (1899-1975) is the author of sketches, reviews, novels and stories that were printed in such journals as "Methusa", "Nazustrich", Literary-Scientific Herald, and of translations from western writers as well. He has two volumes of original fiction stories, "Sinner" and "July Poison" and several longer literary reviews. In the old country he edited the Economic-Cooperative Newspaper and the Annals of "Chervona Kalyna". In Canada he also formulated the literary pages of the "Free Word" and the "New Pathway".

Fedir Odrach (1912-1964) died young and left this world in the full bloom of his literary creative power. Born in Polisia, he joined the Ukrainian Insurgent Army to fight against the totalitarian regime that was occupying Ukraine. Out of this struggle he wrote a series of reviews, stories and essays. Among the more prominent of these were "On the Road" (1955), the "Warbler" (1957), "Beyond the Village" (1959), "Abonded Village" (1960), all of them published in Canada—the first one containing much valuable biographical material.

O. Hay-Holovko (1914-   ) is a writer who very accurately grasps and describes the fate of his people under the dictatorial regime of the communist party, especially in his two-volume novel, the "Duel with the Devil" published in 1950. In his "Ochaydushni", a book of collected novels printed in 1951, the writer portrays the struggle of the Ukrainian people against the Russification plan forced upon Ukraine by the Moscow Communist Party. Two different worlds are depicted in these two volumes: truth versus oppression and freedom versus slavery.

Mykola Prychodko, writer and publicist, also lived through the Stalinist-Communist terror and when he found himself on the western continent after arriving in Canada, he published such works as "Moscow's March toward a World Hegemony", "Ukraine and Russia" and "Communism in Reality". These published works represent a kind of a valid introduction to his other literary works such as "At the Crossroads of Death" and "One of 15 Millions"—the latter having been translated into English, Spanish, Arabic and other languages. Mykola Prychodko's works are literary masterpieces of accusations against Kremlin and its destruction of the freedom of thought and the trampling down of human dignity which the writer describes so well in his two-volume work, "Along the Distant Highways".

Petro Volyniak (real name Petro Chechet, 1907-1969) is another writer who lived through Stalinist-Communist terror in Ukraine, and when he was freed from the White Sea—Baltic N.K.V.D. concentration camp, he again began his literary work that had been started in 1932. During his emigration days in Germany he published the monthly "Novi Dni" (New Days) which he continued to edit, under the same name after his arrival in Canada. This edition has been mentioned in another chapter dealing with the press. "Novi Dni" has become a literary tribune to many poets and writers in Canada as well as a literary interpretation of the Canadian day by day life. Above all, P. Volyniak is a master in the field of story writing and reviewing that is so well revealed in the collection "The Land Beckons", "Pid Kizhurtom" and in his narrated stories entitled "Kuban—the Ukrainian Land, the Land of the Cossacks."

Ivan Ireney Bodnarchuk (his pen-names: Chabanruk, Bondarchuk) (1914-   ) has a keen-edged mind that penetrates into the very soul of the human being, especially that of youth, is the author of fine children's stories. He made his debut in the literary world with the "Kameniari" journal of Lviv where he made his first acquaintance with youth whom he never deserted. His collection of stories called "The Lost Flowers" won for him a literary award. Some of his other well known works are: "At the Crossroads", "Footbridge", and Familiar Faces".

Among other writers who are interested in the world of youth and write children's literature are Bohdan Fedchuk and Bohdan Hoshowsky. B. Fedchuk is a pedagogue by profession as may be evident from his poetical works where he not only shows his literary talent but also the pedagogical understanding as well. He has published, in Canada, 20 editions of riddles in versified form, one of which published in 1967, is dedicated to Canada's Centennial and deals exclusively with historical themes.

Bohdan Hoshowsky (1907-   ) writes under the pseudonyms of "Didush" and B. Danylovych and is the author of a collection of children's stories called "A Bouquet of Flowers" and edited such children's journals as "Little Friends", "Young Friends", "For Our Children" (1945), "Evshan Zilia" (1950). He also prepared a history and an anthology of children's literature.

Wolodymyr Krymsky (W. Bilynsky, 1919-   ) is a master in the art of writing stories and novels. He also tried his pen in dramatic work, one of his dramas receiving an award at the literary concourse in 1943. While living as an emigrant in Austria he published there the literary journal "Zveno". He also published a book of collected novels entitled "The Etape" (1953); awaiting publication are several of his novels.

Nestor Rzepecki (V. Lystvych, 1919-1974), originally a writer of verse and story, has gone exclusively for prose since his arrival in Canada. He published his story "Halia" in 1946, the novels "The Waves Seek the Shores" and "The Sun Rises in the West" in 1954, and the satire "Ours are Beyond the Border", in 1955. Among the author's poetical works the best known is his collection of translations from the Japanese poetry entitled "Song of the Distant Shores", (1940). N. Rzepecki's literary works are full of revolutionary scenes.

The creative work of Mykhaylo Podworniak (1908-   ) stands as a singular contrast to the long list of all the other mentioned authors. His stories and essays are distinguished by an unusual display of serenity—

the sufferings of life are for the ennoblement of man. Christian philosophy and evangelism simply exude from such of his stories as: "On the Path of Life" (Vol. I in 1951 and Vol II in 1953), "The Green Grove" (1963), "God's Peace" (1964), and others. "The Unfinished Song" (1967) is the first full-length novel of this talented author.

Mykola Kolankiwsky deserves our special mention as the author of stories and feuilletons such as his collection of "Bombs for Happy Occasions" written under the pseudonym of M. Tochylo. His magazine "We and the World" is a wide revelation of literary talent.

Julian Beskyd-Tarnowych earned his distinction in the literary world with his belletristic and educational works dedicated to Lemkivshchyna, such as the "Illustrated History of Lemkivshchyna" (1938); in addition, he is a well known publicist. He has written around 900 stories and novels many of which are based on Canadian themes. Of a special value for the history of Ukrainian Canadians is his Almanac of the Toronto Eparchy entitled "In Christ's Vineyard" (1964), in which is gathered a voluminous collection of material pertaining to the religious, cultural and educational life of the Ukrainians in Eastern Canada.

Canada became a haven for the noted leader of woman's movement in Ukraine, Olena Kysilewska (1869-1956), who wrote memoirs and reviews of her travels on this continent.

The well known Ukrainian writer Dokia Humenna, (born in 1904) spent a short time in Canada where she wrote her literary work "The Eternal Fires of Alberta". Tied in with the pioneer life in Alberta are the stories and essays by Stefania Paush, written in 1967, under the title of "Let This Be a Lesson". Working in the religious field, but still finding time to write, was the Rev. Andrew Trukh (1894-1959) who, in addition to religious articles, also wrote essays and reviews connected with his religious life in Canada. Archbishop Mykhail Khoroshy (1885-1977) edited his trilogy, "The World's Epopoeia". P. Kowtun (Mykola Samovydets—born in 1901), of Hamilton wrote several dramas and a comedy-satire that was staged by the Ukrainian National Theatre in Canada.

In the field of Ukrainian Canadian literature may be found such individuals as Hanna Mandryka (1894-1957) collected essays—"Selections", literary critics Olexander Moch, Yuriy Stefanyk and Nina Mudryk-Mryc (collection of poems—"Dawn and Twilights" 1958, and "Namystechko"), Petro Pihichyn (lyrical and humorous verses), Ivan Loboda ("They Came Again"), Victor and Volodymyr Kupchenko, Yakiv Bubniuk (lyrics), T. Horokhovych, S. Hurko, O. Chernenko, I. Makaryk and others

There are a dozen or more writers and poets of Ukrainian descent who use their pen in the English language exclusively. Most of them come from the second and third generation in Canada. The leading role in this group has been played by Maara Lazechko-Haas from Manitoba who is known to us from another chapter of our history.

Oleh Kupchenko (1932-   ), educator and writer in Edmonton, has published more than half a dozen of his dramatic works on pages of Edmonton Journal. For his work he was awarded twice. Some of his short dramas were translated into Ukrainian and published in Edmonton "Ukrainian News".

Paul Edward Hapora (1939-   ), a native of Vegreville, Alberta, published a few collections of his dynamic poetry. e.g. "Poems and Passion (1961), "The Crest" (1963), "Hiroshima" (1965), "Auschwitz" (1967), "Death and Belsen" (1967).

George Ryga (1933-   ) showed is talent in short novels where he presents social disparities in this country. Some of his works were translated into Ukrainian and published by the printing house "Dnipro" in Kiev.

The youngest among this group is a Torontonian, Christina Petrowsky, who has won acclaim in musical circles as a distinguished pianist. "Canadian Poetry", quarterly magazine of poetry published by the Canadian Author Association (1968) reveals that Christina Petrowsky has also a brilliant talent for poems and verses.

Many publications of the third era are in the form of narrated travelogues. Among the leading figures in this class is J. B. Rudnyckyj, author of several volumes of his "Travels through Canada and Europe" (1959). Olha Woycenko wrote a collection of travel essays, "A Different World and Our Days" (1959) while Rev. S. Izyk wrote "At the Feet of Cardinal, the Martyr". Rev. P. Chomyn published his separate travelogue articles under the title "In the Eternal City". Wm. Chopek's talented memoirs are printed as a series in "Postup" (Progress), 1967, in which the author portrays the pioneer era as a parallel in comparison with the present day life of the Ukrainian Canadians. Michael Sharik published three volumes of memoirs and a collection "Scattered Pearls".

Kateryna Antonovych wrote a series of her memoirs in the "Woman's World" (1966-1967), Michael Luchkovich printed his memoirs in "Ukrainian News" (1963-1964), while Rev. S. Chabursky wrote his reviews in "Our Aim" (1967), Wasyl Niniowsky published his narrative stories and Gus Romaniuk edited his "Taking Root in Canada" printed in English and published by the Columbia Press in 1954. Ivan Humeniuk wrote his essays "My Memoirs" (1959), while Halyna Kubanska wrote her collection, "Through Thorny Paths". P. W. Kuchta wrote his "Essays from the Road" and Bohdan Zeleny published his memoirs. Michael Hrushka (Harris) prepared a large volume of memoirs dealing with pioneer days, under the title: "Memorable Episodes in My Life", while Rev. Petro Bilon published in 1952 and 1956, his two volumes of "Memoirs" and Alexander Bryk wrote, in 1956, his "My Life Studies" (his scholarly articles on various literary and cultural topics). But even this long line of different memoirs does not complete the list of all the printed material dealing with Ukrainian Canadians. All these memoirs furnish a rich source of studies about the life of Ukrainians in Canada and beyond.

In addition to the long list of individual publications that we have just dealt with, there also appeared, during the third era, collective editions —the almanacs and calendars that played their traditional role in the pioneer period. Finally, such literary journals as "Novi Dni" (New Days) and the "My i Svit" (We and the World) were formed, about which we made some comments earlier. Closely allied with these almanacs and literary periodicals were the women's journals—the "Woman's World" and the "Promin"—that included in their pages fragments and articles of literary nature. A special distinction must be reserved for the long-time editors such as S. Wolynec—"Ukrainian Voice" (his scholarly articles on various literary and cultural topics), W. S. Levytsky—"New Pathway"; B. Stebelsky—"Homin Ukrainy" (Ukrainian Echo) and the several editors of "Canadian Farmer" that printed the literary supplement with the regular editions. The "Ukrainian News" of Edmonton has carried an unspecified page with literary commentaries by Rev. P. Kachur.

To complete this picture in full we take time to mention such translated works as the "Ukrainian Poets" and the "Poetical Works of Taras Shevchenko", both of them published by the University of Toronto Press and sponsored by the Ukrainian Canadian Committee, as well as the Ukrainian National Association sponsored edition of "A Concise Encyclopedia" that was prepared by the scholars of the T. Shevchenko Society and published in Toronto.

One could mention other literary creations and names of authors but the ones mentioned illustrate adequately the rich content of the poetical values and literary forms that the Ukrainians have brought into the treasure house of Canadian literature.

During the third era the sphere of Ukrainian-Canadian literature finds itself under the overwhelming influence of the new immigration and some fifty poets and writers of this new immigration have augmented the ranks of their Canadian colleagues and with their writings have greatly enriched the literary forms and aroused new interest in literature. If we describe the literature of the second era as belonging to the school of realism then it also could be said that the third era brought a new stream of ideas, with modernistic trends and tastes included, that are so dominant in the western world in this our new era. In spite of the different stylized forms there still prevailed, in the poetry and prose of the third era, the innate patriotic pathos, appealing to the freedom of the individual beings, the nations and humanity. When the western literature, in pursuit of new forms, quite often loses the ideal content—that is so noticeable in modern poetry—the Ukrainian poets and writers, on the other hand, had always retained the clearly expressed ideas that flowed from the deep emotional feelings for their own people and the whole of humanity fighting for its freedom and dignity. These feelings were transferred and rooted in the new Canadian soil and from it came the strength for practical action in the new environment. The creative talent of the Ukrainian literati helped to deepen the sound, creative pursuit of other cultures in this country and together, gave to Canada a new modern indentification content and form.

CREATIVE ARTISTS

A most impressive panorama unfolds before our eyes when we take a glance at the array of the Ukrainian creative artists—the painters, sculptors and graphic artists. About thirty of those engaged in this field during the new era had come to this country with the third immigration, although some (like Mykhaylo Hetman) had been active during the second immigration period while still others had risen from the pioneer wilderness. In the last mentioned category the foremost place belongs to such well known artists as William Kurelek and Peter Kuch.

W. Kurelek (1928-1977), son of Alberta and Manitoba pioneers who most keenly fathomed the pioneer era of the Ukrainian settlers and thus inspired its reality, created a whole series of interesting sketches that captivated the eyes of the beholders. Aestheticism is not the final objective of his creativeness. All that he lives for and what intrigues him is the implementation of truth [1]. Who knows if this concept did not come from the principles of the pioneer soul which, for the sake of truth and freedom, went wandering into the far away world. In his short lifetime, he produced over 7,000 paintings, sketches, lithographs, which are represented in numerous major collections in Canada, Great Britain, and the U.S.A. He received the Order of Canada.

Peter Kuch (1917-1980) Manitoban who revealed his unusual creative talents in the field of caricature and works for the daily Winnipeg Free Press. His cartoons not only distinguish themselves in the press galleries, but they also decorate the walls of the most exclusive salons [2]. Other artists who were brought up in Canada and known in the art world are Halia Kohuska (Gomez-Pereles), Stepan Repa, M. Presunka-Harasymchuk, Christine Nawrocka-Kudryk, Bruce Collins, Jerry Humen (landscape painter), Ihor Dmytruk, Ada Lysak, Roman Maraz, Andrij Zadorozny, Ed. Drahanchuk, a well known Calgary artist excelling in pottery and sculpture work, and his brother, Walter Drohan.

A separate group of artists are those who were born in Europe but received their art training in Canada. To this category belong—Daria Krawciw-Yemets, Pavlo Melashchenko, Nina Mudryk-Mryc, Petro Sydorenko, Maria Styranka, Daria Zelska-Darewych, Lida Obroca, and Daria Zalucka and others.

To the older group of Ukrainian artists who came to Canada after the war belong such veterans as Kateryna Antonovych (1884-1975), who conducted a school of painting and drawing in Winnipeg, and Julian Bucmaniuk (1885-1968) who managed a similar school in Edmonton and is well known from his numerous newspaper articles dealing with art. In addition to his pictures he also has decorated several churches, the best known being the Cathedral of St. Josaphat in Edmonton. Petro Sydorenko, representing the younger generation of artists opened his

---

[1] "Interview with W. Kurelek" from "Globe and Mail", Toronto, Aug. 7, 1967.
[2] He published "Five Years Following John", devoted to the Prime Minister John Diefenbaker.

school of painting in Toronto and also painted a whole gallery of portraits and compositions to honour the occasion of Canada's Centennial. Among the older artists belong Nadia Biletska (1898-1963), who exhibited her works in Prague, Munich and Winnipeg. Also from Prague came Mykola Bytynsky (1893-1972), who produced a great number of heraldic-artistic works in Europe and who continued along the same line in Canada, producing, among others, the canvas "The Shooting of 359 Heroes—Martyrs of Bazar". Natalia Gerken-Rusova (1902-   ) is known as a graphic artist and stage decorator who studied at the Sorbonne University and devoted most of her time to the theory of art. Ivan Kubarsky, a product of the Academy of Art in Kiev, specialized chiefly in decorative arts. In Canada he opened his own atelier, formulated a series of stage scenes and decorated several better known churches including the Sobor of St. Volodymyr in Toronto, the latter work being accomplished together with the cooperation of two other artists, M. Dmytrenko and B. Balas.

Mykhaylo Dmytrenko (1908-   ) has distinguished himself in the field of graphic and decorative art. The product of the Kiev Art Institute and co-organizer of the Artists' Association of Western Ukraine, M. Dmytrenko has proved himself to be the master of such large canvases as the "Crucifixion", the "Resurrection", and the "Weeping at the Grave". He is also a co-organizer of the Ukrainian Association of Creative Artists and has arranged several art exhibits and wields a fine pen in writing as a theorist and critic of art.

Besides Ivan Kubarsky (Kurochka-Armashevsky, 1896-1975), in the art of theatre decoration and stage scenery, another artist, Anatol Struver worked in Toronto in the same field. He brought with him experience and innovation from the art schools of Kiev and Kharkiv and has to his credit portrait, scenery and composition paintings. To this group we might include Ivan Belsky who arrived to Toronto via Caracas Venezuela, in both cities he showed his talent in decorative art.

In Eastern Canada Leonid Perfecky also has distinguished himself as a genre painter specializing in battle scene compositions and wall murals. He studied in Cracow and Paris where he decorated the Marie de Luxemburg Church and in addition to the various battle scenes from the wars of liberation, he also decorated the Church of the Holy Ghost and St. Joseph's Oratory in Montreal.

Wolodymyr Balas, a graphic artist and a graduate of the Academy of Arts of Warsaw, decorated several churches in Canada and did some book illustrations prior to leaving for U.S.A. in 1959, where he is now engaged in the film industry. Hlib Radchenko (1914-   ), a graduate of Kharkiv Art Institute is a specialist in psychological portraiture and landscape painting. Stefania Rudakevych-Baziuk, a student of Oleksa Nowakiwsky, continued with her work in Edmonton. Domiciled in Edmonton are painters such as Vadym Dobrolidge, church decorator of Western Canada, Wasyl Zalucky, known for his landscapes, and Julian Kraykiwsky, the well known battle scene painter and muralist, and others.

Stepan Steciw (1905-1964) studied at the Academy Royal de Beau-Arts of Liege, ran art studios in Europe and in Vancouver. P. Dyky painted in Toronto. There are other artists as well. Most of them developed their talents in the seventies.

A large group of younger creative artists are at work in Toronto. Among them is Omelan Telizyn (1930-   ) who received his art training in Western Europe and in Canada and now devotes his time to theatre stage setting and decoration. Working in the same field is Halyna Nowakiwska (1923--   ), a graduate of the Cracow Academy of Arts. Iryna Romana Nosyk, of the younger generation, works in connection with the University of Toronto. Iryna Shumska-Moroz runs a ceramic studio. Mykola Bidniak and Lida Palij have distinguished themselves in graphic art, while Andriy Babych and Petro Magdenko excel equally in composition and landscape painting. Daria Onyshchuk is known for her landscape painting and scenes from nature.

The Ukrainian creative artists of Montreal occupy a prominent place in Ukrainian Canadian life. There work such outstanding painters like Ada Lysak and Luba Genush who displayed their works at various exhibitions in Canada and outside, including Expo. There are also such artists as A. Zadorozny, V. Mazeppa, Ludmyla Temertey, Maria Logush, I. Kolodka, Halyna Kosharych and others.

Roman Ivan Kowal (1922-   ) of Winnipeg devotes his time exclusively to art. In addition to painting, he also turns his talent to sculpture. He was a co-worker in carrying out the sculptural work during the building of Shevchenko's monument in Winnipeg and received third prize for the design of Shevchenko's monument in Washington. He also has had success in the stained-window designing art (Church of the Blessed Virgin Mary, Winnipeg and Holy Ghost Church in Beausejour). In 1967 he held a one-man exhibit of his works in the city of Winnipeg that was received with great enthusiasm. His work, the "Pioneer" is in the Saskatchewan Provincial Museum and another, the "Ukrainian Pioneer —a Commemorative Relief" is in the National Library in Ottawa.

Ivan Keywan (1909-   ) a graduate of the Warsaw Academy of Arts and now continuing his work in Edmonton, has to his credit some fine graphic works and wrote valuable articles, monographs and reviews on creative art. He has published the complete "History of Ukrainian Art" printed in Ukrainian and "Taras Shevchenko—the Creative Artist" edited in the English language. In the field of wood carving the name of Serhiy Lytvynenko (1898-1963) is closely tied with the art world of Canada. As a sculptor and wood carver of wide scope he had distinguished himself as the creator of many beautiful iconostasis including the one at the Metropolitan Cathedral of St. Vladimir and Olga in Winnipeg.

Myron Levyckyj (1913-   ) student of O. Nowakiwsky and graduate of the Cracow Academy of Art is known as one of the finest in the field of graphic arts. He has to his credit a long series of book illustrations, poster displays, portrait and landscape paintings and is widely known as an illustrator and caricaturist having many of his exhibits shown in Europe and America.

Bohdan Stebelsky (1909-   ), a landscape painter, has devoted himself to the studies of Ukrainian art and its history. He has written a series of articles on this theme as well as having published a major work, the "Children's Drawings and Their Gradual Development from One to Sixteen Years of Age".

Leo Molodoshanin (1919-   ) of Winnipeg, popularly known as Leo

Mol, achieved a great measure of success in the field of sculpture and the stained-glass window art. In addition to a series of sculptures for churches, schools, universities and government buildings he also was awarded first prize for his design of Shevchenko's monument that was erected in Washington in 1964. Prior to that he was awarded the Allied Arts Medal of the Royal Architectural Institute of Canada. He has made sculptures of such well known persons as President D. Eisenhower, Prime Minister John Diefenbaker, Cardinal Josyf Slipyj, Pope Paul VI, and others. He was elected a Fellow of the Royal Academy of Arts. Another Winnipeger, Ted Korol, a high school teacher, achieved success in the theatrical decorative art. He works closely with the Manitoba Theatre Centre.

Among Ukrainian creative artists the painters predominated, although wood carving and sculpture also are well represented. All of them cooperate very closely with the Ukrainian artists in U.S.A. and together form the Ukrainian Association of Creative Artists (U.S.O.M.).

Among the U.S.O.M. group who distinguished themselves; Artem Kyryluk (1911-1970) in oil landscapes and urban motifs, Nina Mudryk-Mryc, one of the finest illustrators of children's books as well as the author of children's books, and an unrivalled master in the field of silhouette art. Daria Krawciw-Yemec reveals her artistic talent in colorful still life while Maria Styranka (1922-   ) excells in aquarelles.

A separate group emerged among who were born in Ukraine or other parts of Europe but formulated their artistic features in Canada. In this category are such persons as: Ivan Yaciw of Windsor and already mentioned Luba Genush (1924-   ), a modernist whose elements partake of constructivism and abstractionism; Volodymyr Mazeppa, the painter of Byzantine art; Andrey Zadarozny (1921-   ) the acquarelle painter and a long line of other painters of younger generation who will be discussed in the chapter "New Talents in Creative Arts".

MUSIC AND CHORAL ART

The Ukrainians had already made quite a contribution in the field of music and choral work during the second era. The choral art was a traditional possession of every cultural-educational organization and formed an inseparable part of community life or as was popularly called: "organization's necessity and food for the soul". After the Second World War much musical talent arrived in Canada to increase the ranks of the choir masters that were already engaged in their choral work.

Nestor Horodovenko (1885-1965), the former conductor of the "Dniprosoyuz Kapella" and later of the "Dumka Kapella" in Kiev, who was at one time a Professor of the Kiev Musical Institute, organized the famous choir "Ukraina" in Montreal, while the former choirmaster of the "Donetz Choral Kapella", Yuriy Holovko organized his choir at the St. Volodymyr's Cathedral in Toronto. Also in the city of Toronto Lev Turkewych (1906-1961), the long-time conductor of the "Boyan" and the "Bandurist" choirs in Lviv conducted the "Prometey" (Prometheus) choir and led other separate church choirs.

Ivan Kowaliw (1916-   ), a graduate of the Higher Musical Institute of Lysenko in Lviv, directed the choir at the Church of St. Nicholas in Toronto, where he organized the Musical Institute of M. Lysenko. Winnipeg had such well known conductors as Dr. P. Macenko, T. Koshetz, W. Klymkiw, W. Bohonos, and Rev. B. Sloboda. Their ranks were augmented by George Hnatiuk, the organizer and conductor of the "Surma" choir and Wasyl Kardash conductor of the "S.U.M." choir. The latter took over the directorship of the "Prometey" choir in Toronto while George Hnatiuk took his place as the conductor of S.U.M. choir. R. Soltykevych conducted the "Dnipro Choir" in Edmonton, while S. Yaremenko and M. Ivanyk also directed choirs in the same city. Halyna Holynska conducted choirs in Toronto, while I. Chechowsky did the same in Calgary, S. Huminilovych in Oshawa, H. Myhal in Fort William, and Rev. B. Sloboda in Vancouver, Winnipeg. There are such well known conductors as Evhen Dolny, M. Huculak, M. Shatulsky—all of them graduates of the Kiev Conservatory of Music.

A special chapter was written in the sixties by George Hnatiuk when he organized and conducted a choir of one hundred students of the Association of Ukrainian Students (SUSK) at the University of Manitoba. The choir and the ballet staged a number of concerts in such cities outside of Winnipeg as Edmonton, Toronto and Minneapolis.

In addition to choral art, the instrumental and chamber music as well as solo and orchestration work, also had risen to higher levels. The symphony orchestras of Toronto and Winnipeg, the first under the baton of Walter Suskind and the second under the direction of Lev Turkewych (Shevchenko's celebration in 1961) presented separate concerts devoted to Ukrainian symphonic music. Excelling in musical composition were the previously mentioned — Lev Turkewych, Bohdan Wesolowsky and George Fiala. The latter composed a musical work called the "Canadian Creed", on the occasion of Canada's Centennial. In the soloist class those who rose to the top were: Luba Zuk, the pianist who lectures on music at the University of Montreal, Ireneus Zuk, also a pianist, Chrystia Kolessa, a violin-cellist, Zonia Lazarowich and Irene Bubniuk, pianist and soloists, and others.

On Canada's soil there have appeared such operatic soloists of the European stage as Mykhaylo Holynsky, Wasyl Tysiak, Hryhoriy Yaroshevych, Peter Riabowal-Labinsky, Dometiy Berezynec. Some of them, like P. Riabowal-Labinsky (Winnipeg) and D. Berezynec (Edmonton) also ran studios of vocal training. Others, like H. Yaroshevych, W. Tysiak and M. Holynskyj engaged in pedagogical work as well. Among the younger generation there are to be found such soloists as Eva Stolarchuk, Iris Bala, Osyp Hoshulak, T. Ara Shuflyn, Petro Cherniak, Roksolana Roslak, Joanna Myhal, Sisters Klimashko, N. Bahriy, Mariyka Brezden, Oksana Bryzhun, Luba Hanushchak, Stephania Zhovnir-Klos, Natalia Nestorowska, Oksana Onufriychuk, Stefa Fedchuk, Lisa Ference, and others. Many of them devote their time to pedagogical work and take an active part in Canadian musical life.

Schools of music have been established, already mentioned the Musical Institute of M. Lysenko in Toronto, under the direction of Ivan Kowaliw, in Winnipeg, E. Elcheshen, W. Kysilewska, L. Karpinka-Kushniaryk and John Melnyk have their schools of piano music. Similar schools are run by Valentyna Dobrolidge and Serhiy Yaremenko in Edmonton and by Halyna Holynska, Martha Krawciw-Barabash, Hryhoriy Yaroshevych, Jaroslava Zalucka, O. Floruk, and Stephania Zhownir-Klos in Toronto.

Special mention must be made about the professional artists of radio, television, films, symphony orchestra, ballet and similar other categories where we find such well known names as: Jack Dale (Samotilka), radio singer, Kobzar P. Konoplenko-Zaporozetz, Juliette (Julia Sysak) a talented actress and soloist made famous in her C.B.C. programs, Ivan Romanoff (Pyzhuk), violinist and choir conductor, the artist Joan Karasevich, Olha Kwasniak the cellist, and Lesia Zubrak the singer, Christina Petrowsky, the pianist, Steven Staryk, the violinist. Also the soloist of high calibre like Jaroslav Schur, Cecil Semchyshyn, Edward Evanko, Bill Martin-Viscount, and many others should be mentioned.

THEATRE AND BALLET

In the history of Ukrainian Canadians several attempts were made to establish a Ukrainian theatre that would faithfully represent the national tradition of the stage. Such efforts were made during the second era when the amateur groups strove to turn professional, if only temporarily, when there were no further means to make it lasting. Theatre—this is an expensive affair and coupled with the draw-back of long distances, it tended to dampen the spirits of the most idealistic theatre enthusiasts. But this did not prevent the manifestation, from time to time, of the idea of Ukrainian theatre in Canada and its theme was the subject of hot discussions in the possibility of its realization.

After the Second World War a large number of professional artists, who arrived with the third immigration, settled in Toronto. Among them we find the former members of Lviv and Kiev theatres: Hryhoriy Yaroshevych-Manko, Mykhaylo and Hanna Tahayiw, Ivan and Maria Hirniak, Lavro Kempe, Vera Kempe, V. Dowhaniuk, Yuriy Belsky, M. Lalka, Maria Slusarivna, Yuriy Pochyniuk, and some fine amateur artists, Wasylyna Kozachenko, Stepan Stolarchuk and many others. In the 50-ies, on the initiative of those mentioned above and with the support of organized community, the Ukrainian theatre of Hryhoriy Yaroshevych came into existence in Toronto and staged in that city and other towns near by, the age-old immortal dramas such as: "Oy Ne Khody, Hryciu", "Zaporozhets za Dunayem", "Chornomorci", and a series of new plays. Later on, a theatre ensemble "Zarevo", was formed from among the younger groups under the direction of S. Telizyn who had received his training as drama director in Berlin and Warsaw theatres and who was able to present such important stage plays as the "Advokat Markian" by Lesia Ukrainka, and the d'Anui's tragedy "Joan d'Arc" that had a long run on the stage. Lavro Kempe, who had behind him the experience of actor and director presented a series of operettas such as: "Huculka Ksenia", "Sharika" by J. Barnych, and later the "Zalizna Ostroha" by L. Lisewych and A. Kurdydyk.

Similar steps were made in Winnipeg and Edmonton. In more recent times the graduates of the theatre art in Canada—Cecil Semchyshyn, Roman Michalchyshyn, Joan Karasevich and others—made another attempt to organize the "Ukrainian Theatre". In the years 1964-1967 there were put on the Winnipeg stage and in other nearby centres of Manitoba, the following plays: "Marusia", "Zaporozhets za Dunayem" and "Crucify Him". At the same time the professional drama directors, Iryna Turkewych-Martynec and Daria Nyzankiwska-Snihurowych staged the children's operetta "Koza Dereza" that also was presented during the "Ukrainian Days" at Expo 67. Peter Boretski deserves special mention as an actor, director and a producer of dramas. He is a creator of the faculties of drama at the Canadian universities.

Commendable successes were attained by the dance ensemble groups such as "Evshan" of Saskatoon under the direction of Lesia Pavlychenko-Sotnykiv, the Hamilton group "Chayka" under the direction of Jaroslav

Klun, the "Ukrainian Dance Ensemble Shumka" directed by Yoroslaw Kuc, and the "Dnipro Dance Group" of Vancouver directed by Edward Ciunyk. Of an unusually high degree have been the achievements of the dance ensembles of Petro Marunchak of Montreal, the Toronto ensemble of MUNO, organization under the name of "Kalyna" and the Winnipeg ensemble 'Rusalka'. In Toronto the 'Apollo' school of dancing conducted a successful "Children's Classical Choreography" under the direction of Anna Zawarychin. A stylized form of dancing was introduced and propagated by Olenka Gerdan-Zaklynska in Toronto and by Daria Nyzankiwska-Snihurowych in Winnipeg. Also along the same line has been the work of Betty Pope. It is worthwhile to mention such well known choreographers as Mereos Lechow, Olenka Tkachuk, a choreographer with Ukrainian motifs, the gifted ballerina Halyna Samtsova, and Nadia Pavlychenko, a student of the Royal Academy of Dancing in London who runs her own Art of Movement Studio in Toronto.

Every social activity seeks its own outward manifestation and its representatives try to find a common tongue. This has been true of Ukrainian poets, writers (novelists), journalists, and artists. In the larger Ukrainian centres of Canada the literary-artistic clubs came into being. At the head of this movement was the Ukrainian Literary Club in Toronto (1951), closely followed by other clubs in Winnipeg (1952) and Edmonton (1961). In time some differences arose in this field which led to the formation in Toronto, in addition to the Ukrainian Literary Club, of the Association of Artists the "Kozub", and later on in the same city and alongside the Ukrainian Association of Creative Artists, a separate group was formed under the name of "Palitra", while in Winnipeg in addition to the already existing Ukrainian Literary Club a branch of the New York writers' club, the "Slovo" was formed.

The Ukrainian Association of Creative Artists (USOM) appeared quite early on the scene, having been organized in Toronto in 1951 with branches in Montreal and Edmonton. It showed an unusual degree of activity. It is worthwhile to mention that of all the ethnic groups only Ukrainian Canadians have their own art gallery under the name of "We and the World", headed by M. and M. Kolankiwsky and located on two main thoroughfares, (the Gallery Bloor and the Gallery Yonge) in the city of Toronto. In addition to the Ukrainian art display these galleries also hold numerous exhibits of different Canadian artists and are very well known to all in the East. At these galleries there also is a publishing department that puts out editions of pamphlets and cards dealing with art and special publications ("The Wooden-Built Churches of Ukraine", 1959).

The work of these clubs and associations was divided into common discussions pertaining to matters dealing with literature and art and the appearance of its members before the public on the occasion of celebration of cultural events either from the history of the past or the equally important episodes of present day affairs. Some of these clubs, at different times, revealed an unusual amount of activities that were truly worthy of our admiration. The literati and the artists of Canada cooperate very closely with their colleagues in U.S.A. and other western countries and also are trying to keep in touch with their co-workers of pen and palette in Ukraine. However, due to the political regime and the absolute censorship of everything that enters into that country from overseas it is most difficult to keep this contact alive.

It is only natural that every artist and writer wants to present his creative work before the widest audience of viewers and readers and this in turn creates for them a spiritual atmosphere, for it is to the people and to nature that an artist must go to seek further inspiration for his work. From time to time they also arrange for literary evenings, art exhibits or song recitals. Very often such programs are presented on a high artistic level as for instance the exhibition in Winnipeg of the works of the world famous sculptor A. Archipenko, W. Kurelek's exhibit in Toronto or the exhibition of L. Molodozanin's work in Winnipeg, Toronto and other cities of Canada [1]. In 1954 the Toronto Literary and Art Club went so far as to organize "The Convention of the Ukrainian Artists of America and Canada with the Social Community", that took place during the three days (3-5) in July. At this first convention around 200 creative artists in the field of culture and some 12,000 citizens took part, under the patronage of Canada's high dignitaries, the Ukrainian hierarchies and political figures. This was a great cultural event of large proportions and a lasting monument of this event has been preserved in the almanac that was written about this convention entitled "The Book of Artists and Creators of the Ukrainian Culture" (Toronto, 1954).

Although the core of the Ukrainian culture primarily comes from the work of the painters, the writers, and the poets, still the motifs for their creations are taken from the people's common values and their surroundings. This is clearly shown in the paintings, the buildings and in literature. The creative art fed by the elements of Ukrainian and the surrounding cultures received the highest approbation and also was in the greatest demand and this in turn resulted in the incentive tendency to cooperate with similar associations of other nationalities. It greatly helped to augment the work among its members while from the midst of their own people came the newer and younger reinforcements to enrich the sphere of creative art.

---

[1] L. Mol, A. Archipenko and W. Kurelek exhibits were sponsored in Winnipeg by the Alpha Omega Women's Alumni.

TARAS SHEVCHENKO FOUNDATION

To preserve the Ukrainian culture in Canada and to aid the Ukrainian poets, writers, and artists in their creative work the so-called cultural foundations were formed whose function it was to provide financial resources for the publication of their works or to help them in the furthering of their studies. In this way there came into existence "The Foundation of Olexander Koshetz" in Winnipeg which, after his death, was changed to "The Foundation of Olexander and Tetiana Koshetz", while in Toronto "The Foundation of Yuriy Klen" was formed with the object of publishing the works of one of the more noted Ukrainian classical poets, Yuriy Klen. The "L. Mosends Foundation of Toronto" had similar objectives. After the death of the first Ukrainian senator the "Senator W. Wall Foundation" was formed in 1962, sponsored by the Ukrainian Catholic Brotherhood Council. Mention has been made in another chapter of this history book about the Ukrainian Canadian Research Foundation of Toronto whose aim it was to publish the historical works about the achievement of Ukrainian people in Canada. "The Ukrainian Self-Reliance League Foundation", with much the same aim, was established to provide a solid base for the work of this dominion-wide organization. In 1967 "The Danylo Lobay Foundation" was formed with the object of carrying on research studies on the Ukrainian labour movement in Canada. Of an unusual nature is the foundation of the Markian Shashkevych Centre in Winnipeg which has as its objective the cherishing of the cult of M. Shashkevych (more is written about this in another part of our history). Many other temporary foundations were formed for the purpose of publishing the work of this or that author or to look after his royalty rights, but still the Ukrainian community was constantly striving toward the objective of creating for the benefit of the various Ukrainian cultural activities a single and all-inclusive Ukrainian Canadian foundation which finally became a reality with the formation of the Taras Shevchenko Foundation.

This foundation was planned and realized at the time when the Ukrainians, throughout the whole world, were preparing to commemorate the great anniversary of the birth and death of their greatest poetical genius, Taras Shevchenko. The Year 1961 represented one hundred years from the death of the poet, while 1964 was the 150 anniversary of his birth. On the occasion of these two anniversaries and as a mark of reverence toward their spiritual leader, the Ukrainian Canadian Committee erected a Taras Shevchenko monument on the grounds of the Manitoba Parliament Buildings. On July 22, 1963, the Taras Shevchenko Foundation was incorporated in the Senate and the House of Commons in Ottawa. The foundation was dedicated to the 150th Anniversary of Shevchenko's birth. The charter of Taras Shevchenko Foundation proclaims its aim, namely the fostering, developing and the bringing to perfection of the Ukrainian culture in Canada. The Taras Shevchenko Foundation differs from other above mentioned foundations and associations in that it is concerned with the financial needs of only those organizations and institutions that propagate Ukrainian culture in Canada.

In accordance with its charter the Foundation accepts instalment payments, declarations and donations to invest these, subject to the government laws, in such a way that would correspond with other philanthropic and charitable institutions. The proceeds of these investments are to be used exclusively for the expansion of Ukrainian culture in Canada, such as the printing of school text books, the teaching of the Ukrainian language in schools, the preparation of material dealing with Ukrainian history and literature, giving aid to choirs, orchestras and theatres, collecting books, the production of bibliographical records and microfilms, providing scholarships for students and funds for scientists for the carrying on of research work, and for similar worthy causes.

Although the Foundation began its work in 1964, the banner year of the campaign came in 1967—on the centennial of Canada's Confederation. In this way the organizers of the Foundation, the Ukrainian Canadian Committee, wanted to emphasize the idea and the work of the foundation as being one of the projects that came into being at the beginning of the second century in Canadian statehood, to which the Ukrainian Canadians proudly added their name and worthwhile contribution.

The Taras Shevchenko Foundation differentiates between ordinary members, founders, benefactors and contributors, while the business firms are classified as friends, sponsors and patrons. In its first board of directors and supervisors are to be found such well known names as: Dr. I. Hlynka, Senator P. Yuzyk, Judge J. Solomon, V. Kochan, Judge Mary Wawrykow, T. Chimko, D. Hawrysyshyn, A. Kachor, Dr. R. Romanowych, Dr. B. Martynowych, T. Kobzey.

Ukrainian pioneers and their descendants by the erection of the T. Shevchenko monument on the grounds of the Manitoba Parliament Buildings in 1961 and by the formation of the million-dollar T. Shevchenko Foundation represent a historical landmark for Ukrainian culture in this country. But the creation of this land-mark was not the work of the Ukrainians alone, whose interest in this matter is vital. It was the work of other leading citizens of Canada, consequently the honoring of Shevchenko's anniversary during those memorable days was in truth a celebration for all Canadians.

A few historical facts will help us to understand the symbolism of the events that were taking place before the eyes of our generation. The site for the erection of Shevchenko's monument on the grounds of the Parliament Buildings was approved by the act of the Liberal government of Manitoba under the premiership of the Hon. D. Campbell. A year later this act was approved by the Conservative government of the Hon. D. Roblin, who had succeeded the former premier. The unveiling of the Shevchenko monument in 1961 coincided with the important celebration by Ukrainian Canadians of the 70th Anniversary of their settlement in Canada. On this memorable occasion the then Prime Minister of Canada, John Diefenbaker, in his official unveiling speech had this to say about Shevchenko:

"As a poet he not only enriched the literature of his people but inspired them with new hope for freedom. What he sought for them, he sought no less for the oppressed everywhere in the world.

The seventieth anniversary of the arrival of Ukrainian settlers in Canada is also being celebrated this year. The labour and devotion of these pioneers on the western prairies have meant much to the Canadian epic, and the contribution of them and their descendants to the economic, cultural and public life of Canada, has been a worthy one" [1].

These were not merely the glib words uttered out of respect by a great statesman and a great Canadian addressed toward Ukrainian Canadians on behalf of his country. These words were emphasized again by another statesman, D. Roblin, when during the unveiling of the monument he made an official announcement about the teaching of the Ukrainian language in the public schools [2]. This announcement was a happy contrast to that other dismal date when on these very same parliament building grounds and within a stone's throw from the very spot where the unveiling of the monument and premier Roblin's announcement about the teaching of Ukrainian language in schools were taking place—right here in front of the Parliament Buildings—a tragic drama was enacted some forty-five years earlier when by the act of T. C. Norris' government the Ukrainian language school books were being burnt. This ignoble action on the part of the then existent government was the last episode in the liquidation of bilingual schools in western Canada.

The years of 1961 and 1964, as well as the commemoration of Shevchenko's anniversaries, were in their own intimate ways the rehabilitation of the past. No wonder that the 50,000 audience at the unveiling of the monument was deeply moved while the pioneers even showed a few tears of joy [3]. Here was the birth of a new Canada which had provided a place of merit for the Ukrainian culture in recognition of the worthy contribution made by three generations to Canadian mosaic.

---

[1] "Collection of Documentary Material", compiled on the occasion of 25th Anniversary of the Ukrainian Canadian Committee, 1940-1965, Winnipeg, 1965, p. 57.
[2] More was said about this matter in the chapter dealing with education.
[3] See John Diefenbaker's speech on this occasion, Progress, August, 1964.

HORIZONTAL AND VERTICAL INTEGRATION

When, during the years of the 50-ies and 60-ies the Ukrainian Canadians were reaching a developmental peak of their cultural expression, growth and consummation, they also, at the same time, were undergoing the process of political integration which, as we have mentioned previously, had taken deep roots during the end of the second era of our history. These roots were deeply set in Canadian soil during its newest history and it is these very processes, which we label as horizontal and vertical integration, that we wish to examine here. This integration was taking place in the field of municipal system, provincial administration and federal representation.

When we take a look at the municipal system it will be seen that the Ukrainians have advanced far beyond the local interests. We find them not only at the head of those municipalities where they are in the majority and in positions acquired during the pioneer and mid-war era. In the third era they also hold important posts even in those municipalities where their nationality is in the minority. What is more, we see the Ukrainian Canadians holding the positions of city mayors, whose election to that office is based on the choice of the citizens representing all nationalities. Several examples will serve to illustrate this point. In 1951 William Hawrelak, a son of Ukrainian pioneers, became the Mayor of Edmonton and in 1956 he was elected president of the Canadian Federation of Mayors. Five years later another provincial capital, this time the City of Winnipeg, elected and re-elected several times by acclamation, Stephen Juba, also a son of Ukrainian pioneers. In Eastern Canada, Oshawa also elected a son of Ukrainian pioneers, Michael Starr (Starchevsky) as its mayor, in 1961. Four years later, Michael Patrick was elected as the mayor of Windsor, while in 1957 Peter Ratuski became the mayor of Kenora, chosen by acclamation. A row of smaller cities and towns have chosen, as their representatives, sons of Ukrainian pioneers and their election reveals the fact that the integration of the Ukrainian people in Canada not only is increasing in country municipalities, but also in the cities as well, and that the Canadian community has a set standard of values and seeks, in the field of politics, the best representatives, irrespective of their national origin.

Greater advances have been made by this integration in the provincial and federal representation. This process was aptly underlined by the Winnipeg Free Press when, shorty after the 1953 elections it printed the following editorial concerning Ukrainians:

"It would be difficult to cite a case in any other country in which there has been such a high degree of successful political activity by members of a relatively small minority group, especially one that had to overcome a difficult language barrier. As Canadians, these people have accepted not only the opportunities inherent in a free democracy, but its duties and obligations as well... The manner in which a minority group such as this recognizes itself as an integral—and integrated—part of the Canadian family bodes well for the future of democracy in this country" [1].

---

[1] Winnipeg Free Press, Dec. 21, 1953, "Ukrainian Members".

Let us remember that the Ukrainian Canadians, at that time, had fifteen members in provincial legislatures and four members of parliament in Ottawa. It so happened, by coincidence, that the four federal M.P.'s represented the four different political parties—where, in addition to Liberals and Conservatives, the Social Credit and C.C.F. were also represented [2]. On this occasion the Free Press considered it fitting to make the following statement:

"... But even more remarkable is the degree to which the Ukrainians have merged into the wider Canadian Community. While rightly retaining much of the rich culture of the land of their forebears, the Ukrainian Canadians form no pressure group politically. Their choice of party is dictated by individual preference, the best possible indication that theirs is a Canadian rather than racial outlook."

These, in general, are the objective confirmations of a leading and widely circulated journal and are worthy of our comment if for no other reason, than to expose the faulty conclusions of some sociologists who present controversial information that in turn is used by unscrupulous politicians to deride the Ukrainian Canadian community.

In the year 1957 the Ukrainian Canadians reached the highest point of achievement in the sphere of parliamentary politics. There were six M.P.'s of Ukrainian origin in the Dominion Parliament—three from the Conservative party, two from the Social Credit party and one representative from the C.C.F., while the number of M.L.A.'s increased from 19 to 23 members. What is more, for the first time in the history of Canada a Canadian of Ukrainian origin was made a federal minister, who was given the post of the Minister of Labour. This honor came to Michael Starr of Oshawa, who diligently performed his duties for six years. Along the same line, changes also took place on the provincial government level, when several Ukrainian Canadians received their provincial minister's portfolios. In 1952 the C.C.F. government of Saskatchewan was the first in the provincial field when it appointed Alexander Kuziak to the post of Minister of Telephones and Finance and later as Minister of Natural Resources (1956-1960) and Minister of Mineral Resources (1960-1964). In 1955 the Liberal government of Manitoba called Michael Hryhorczuk to join its cabinet as Attorney-general and he had the honour of performing his duties at this post until the government went out of office in 1958. And finally, the Ontario government took John Yaremko into its cabinet in 1958, at first as the Minister without Portfolio and later as Minister of Transport. In 1960 he became Provincial Secretary and Minister of Citizenship and in 1966, Minister of Public Welfare.

The process of this vertical integration was last to arrive in Alberta, when in 1962 the Social Credit government named Ambrose Holowach as its Provincial Secretary. To this roll of provincial ministers' appointments we add N. V. Bachynsky, who was named the deputy speaker of the House (1950-1956) and later (1956-1958) Speaker of the House in Manitoba Legislature. Duties of the deputy speaker were performed for a number of years by N. Hryhorczuk.

Parallel to the two lines of Ukrainian Canadian representations in the provincial and dominion parliaments, a third line was to be reached as

---

[2] Michael Starr — Conservative, John Decore—Liberal, Ambrose Holowach—Social Credit, Fred Zaplitny—C.C.F.

a matter of course—representation in the Canadian House of Senate. The first nomination was made by the Liberal government under Prime Minister Louis St. Laurent in 1955, and the next in turn by the Conservative government of John Diefenbaker in 1959.

The process of political integration continued to gather strength until in 1966, at the 75th Anniversary of the settlement of Ukrainians in Canada, the total number of representatives in the provincial parliaments, House of Commons and Senate amounted to 83.

The colorful social background of these representatives is interesting enough to be examined on the individual basis, similar to the method used in the two previous eras, and here again Manitoba is in the lead.

Manitoba

In 1945 Manitoba saw its first elections after the war in which three former members—N. V. Bachynsky and J. R. Solomon, both Liberals, and W. Kardash, the so-called progressive—were re-elected. In addition to these three, about whom we remarked in our previous era, W. Danyleyko, M. Sawchuk and B. Scraba also were elected.

Wilbert Danyleyko (1913-   ), born in Rossburn, the son of pioneer parents, and a businessman by profession, tried unsuccessfully, for a dominion seat in 1945; became a member of Manitoba Legislature as C.C.F. representative from the district of St. Clements (1945-1949).

Michael Sawchuk (1911-1969), from Fork River, a teacher by profession and C.C.F. supporter, elected from Ethelbert (1945-1949).

William Scraba (1908-1971), a business man, born in Manitoba, was elected as a Progressive-Liberal from North Winnipeg (1945-1949). He had behind him many years of work as a member of the city school board and put in six years as an alderman in the city of Winnipeg. Well known from his activities in the publishing field, he was among the first of those who published the anglo-tone paper titled "Ukrainian News".

It is interesting to note that none of the three newly elected members mentioned above, put down their religious adherence and all of them lost their legislature seats during the next elections in 1949. However, the three new Ukrainian members—J. M. Hawryluk, W. Lucko and M. N. Hryhorczuk—that were elected at the time, stayed on much longer, to serve their community.

John Martin Hawryluk (1910-1975), school principal by profession, and of Catholic faith, was born in Winnipeg, a son of pioneer parents, who received higher education in pedagogy and had wide experience in community affairs, entered into politics as a representative of the C.C.F. party and was several times re-elected (1949-1953) and 1958-1959) from North Winnipeg.

William Lucko (1911-   ), born in Hazel Glen, a business man of Ukrainian Catholic faith, was elected several times from Springfield (1949-1955) representing the Liberal party.

Michael Nicholas Hryhorczuk (1905-1978), from Ethelbert, of Greek-Orthodox faith, a lawyer by profession, he followed in the footsteps of his father who had represented the same district, in Manitoba Legislature for 22 years. It was in this same district that M. N. Hryhorczuk received his experience of governing when he spent a few years as the Reeve of

Ethelbert Municipality, while his Manitoba Legislature career lasted from 1949-1956 in addition to which he also performed his governmental duties as the Attorney General of Manitoba.

The provincial elections of 1953 added two new figures to Manitoba's Legislature: *Stan Capp* (1953-1958) a Liberal from St. Clement and *Stephen Juba* (1915-   ) from Winnipeg, born and raised in Brookland, Manitoba, and had behind him a long business career as well as the name of a political and community-minded citizen. Having been elected to the Provincial Legislature as an Independent he ran on the same ticket as a candidate for alderman in Winnipeg in 1951, and for the mayor in 1952. Although he was not elected as a mayor on his first try, still his daring plans for bringing reforms into the city's management won for him wide acclaim and for which the Winnipeg Tribune proclaimed him as being one of the most popular citizens in Canada in 1953. With this same high prestige Steve Juba continued his career as the mayor of Winnipeg, transacting into reality such bold projects as the Disraeli Freeway, erection of the new city hall, police station, Pan-American Games, and other accomplishments. His most cherished desire has been to amalgamate the administrative offices of the suburbs with the city of Winnipeg. He spent the years 1953-1959 as member of the Manitoba Legislature.

The elections of 1958 brought *John Tanchak* (1905-   ), a Liberal, to Manitoba's Legislature from the Emerson district, of Greek-Orthodox faith and a teacher by profession. He came with the experience as a community leader and was re-elected in 1959, 1962 and 1966. Two others, both of them from the C.C.F. party, were elected that year—*Peter Wagner* (1916-   ), a Ukrainian Catholic, who sat in the legislature in 1958-1962, and *Stephen Peters* (1916-   ), from Elmwood, Winnipeg.

In 1959 *Fred Theodore Klym* (1917-   ), born in Brokenhead, a Catholic, was elected from Springfield district, representing the Conservative party. He was re-elected in 1962 and 1966.

The 1962 provincial elections saw two Liberals enter the ranks of legislative members. These were: *Mark Gerald Smerchanski* (1914-   ), of Catholic faith and well known industrialist and mining engineer, elected from the Burrows district of Winnipeg (1962-1966), and *Stephen Patrick* (1932-   ), a Catholic and a Liberal elected from the district of Assiniboia (1962-1966). The latter's career was interesting for in addition to his business acumen, he also was a noted football player with the Winnipeg Blue Bombers. He was re-elected in 1966. The same year (1962) brought *Anthony Reed (Rafalsky)* of the N.D.P. party into the ranks of M.L.A.'s, who was elected from the Kildonan constituency (1962-1966).

A few surprises and new individuals appeared during the 1966 elections. *Ben Hanuschak* (1930-   ), a lawyer and a teacher by profession, won the Burrows constituency in Winnipeg for the N.D.P. party, while *Samuel Uskiw* (1933-   ), a farmer of Protestant faith, was elected from East Selkirk and Brokenhead. *Peter Paul Masniuk* (1920-   ), a Ukrainian Catholic, C.N.R. foreman and a war veteran was elected from Fisher-Inwood and *Michael N. Kawchuk* (1931-   ) who also is a Catholic, won for the N.D.P. the Ethelbert-Plains district.

After the war 19 new names of Ukrainian origin appeared on Manitoba's

M.L.A. list, which brings it to a total of 30 members who at one time or another have served in the provincial legislature during its parliamentary history. Classified according to their political adherence we find that out of the 19 M.L.A.'s of Ukrainian origin who were members of Manitoba Legislature after the last war, 9 belonged to the C.C.F. party, 7 were Liberals, 2 Conservatives and 1 Independent. As in the previous era the business men led with 10 representatives, the teachers had 4, the lawyers and the farmers had numbers of two and one from the labour side. According to their religious adherence there were 10 Catholics, 5 non-denominational, 3 Orthodox and 1 Protestant. All of them were sons of pioneers and some of them were third generation Canadians.

Alberta

Literally speaking Alberta's political ambitions paralleled Manitoba's. As we know the traditional political parties were never in the lead here and when the United Farmers of Alberta lost their mandate, the Social Credit party came to power in whose ranks there were three Ukrainian M.L.A.'s namely: W. Tomyn, J. Popel and G. Woitkiw—the last one resigning some time after his election.

At the end of war (1944) provincial elections took place with the result that *Michael Ponich* (1905-   ), Orthodox by faith and a lawyer by profession, was elected from the Vegreville district as a Social Credit member and re-elected in 1948 and 1952. In 1948 two more Social Credit member were added, *Harry Lobay* (1917-   ), a Protestant, teacher and business man, elected from Lac La Biche constituency and re-elected in 1952, and *Peter Chaba* (1903-   ), born in Western Ukraine but brought up in Canada. A Catholic and a business man by profession, he was elected from the Redwater district in 1948 and re-elected in 1952, serving his period as M.L.A. from 1948 to 1955. In the same year *Nick William Duchenski* (1920-   ), belonging to the Orthodox faith, a teacher and a farmer, won the Willingdon constituency for the C.C.F. and retained it during the next election. He was the first Ukrainian of socialist orientation to hold the seat in the Alberta Legislature.

In 1955 *Alfred Macyk* (1924-   ) of Greek-Orthodox faith, a farmer, was the first Ukrainian Liberal to sit in the Alberta Legislature. *Stanley Nicholas Ruzycki* 1916-   ) a Catholic, was elected from Vegreville district on the C.C.F. ticket. Both of the last named served one term only.

In 1959 *William Tomyn,* a teacher, again returned to the Alberta Legislature, having previously served four terms until he was defeated in 1952 and 1955. He was re-elected in 1963 and 1967 and had always been a devoted member of the Social Credit party.

Nicholas A. Melnyk, of Orthodox religion and a teacher by profession, was defeated in 1955 when he ran as a Social Credit from Willingdon, but was successful on his second try in 1959 and re-elected in 1963. At this same time *John Dubetz* (1916--   ), of Orthodox faith, won the Redwater constituency for the Social Credit party.

Ambrose Holowach (1910-   ), a Catholic, was successful in 1959 elections, running on the Social Credit ticket from the Edmonton Centre constituency and re-elected in 1963 and 1967. Prior to that he had been a member of the House of Commons in Ottawa. He has been honored with the post of Provincial Secretary in the Social Credit government of Alberta.

Alexander William Gordey (1912-   ) was another successful Social Credit candidate in the 1959 elections. Born in Western Ukraine and educated in Canada, of Orthodox adherence and a teacher by profession, he was elected in 1959 and re-elected in 1963 from the Vegreville district.

There were two other successful Social Credit candidates in 1963 elections, namely: *Michael Senych* (1926-   ), a teacher, elected from Redwater district and *Albert Ludwig,* a Calgary lawyer who was elected from the Calgary North East constituency and re-elected, with a large majority, from the same district in 1967.

During the May 1967 elections six M.L.A. members of Ukrainian origin were re-elected to the Alberta Legislature. These were: Ambrose Holowach, William Tomyn, Michael Senych, Alexander Gordey, Nicholas Melnyk and already mentioned Albert Ludwig. To the above sextet a newcomer was added in the person of Dr. Walter Buck, elected from the Clover Bar district as a Social Credit representative. This brought the total number to seven members all of them in the Social Credit party, sitting at one time. Altogether the Province of Alberta sent 13 members of Ukrainian origin to its highest legislative body during the newest era. As in Manitoba, where the New Democrats were in the lead, so in Alberta the Social Credit members led the way. There were nine of them. The New Democrats had two, the Liberals one and the Conservatives had none. Judged by religious denominations there were 5 Orthodox, 4 Catholics, 2 non-denomination and 1 Protestant. Teachers and business men were equally divided—five in each profession and only one lawyer and one farmer. During the whole of its parliamentary history Alberta had a total of 20 M.L.A.'s of Ukrainian origin.

Saskatchewan

Saskatchewan came third, after Manitoba and Alberta, in the field of provincial politics and shows the great progress that was made in the newest era compared with its inter-war efforts. Still, in the year 1944 they already had M.L.A.'s, namely: *Dmytro Lazorko* (1908-   ), of Greek-Orthodox religion and a farmer and business man by profession, who was elected from the Redberry constituency, and *Danylo Z. Daniels* (*Zadyrayko,* (1908-   ), a Protestant and farmer, elected from the Pelly district. Both of them were from the C.C.F. party who survived for the one term, 1944-1948. However, Ukrainians in Saskatchewan were the first to have a provincial minister in Canada in the person of *Alexander Gordon Kuziak* (1908-   ), a Protestant, teacher and a business man by profession, who held his cabinet post for twelve years. He was elected from the C.C.F. party in 1948 and re-elected in 1952 from Canora constituency the same district that made several unsuccessful attempts for a House of Commons representation and which had played an important role during the pioneer era.

Bernard Leo Korchinski (1905-   ), of Catholic faith and a teacher by profession, got into the Saskatchewan legislature on a Liberal ticket in 1948, from the Redberry constituency, was defeated during the 1952 elections, but returned again to take his seat in the provincial House in 1956.

THIRD ERA — ILLUSTRATIONS 689

FIRST SENATORS AND MINISTERS

W. Wall

P. Yuzyk

J. Hnatyshyn

M. Starr

M. Hryhorczuk

J. Yaremko

A. G. Kuziak

A. Ho!owach

MEMBERS OF PARLIAMENT

N. J. Mandziuk

W. V. Yacula

F. S. Zaplitny

M. G. Smerchanski

690   UKRAINIAN CANADIANS: A HISTORY

LEGISLATORS

S. M. Krawchyk   J. M. Hawryluk   W. Scraba   B. L. Korchinski

J. Tanchak   B. Hanuschak   A. Ludwig   S. Patrick

S. Uskiw   A. Cripps   M. Ponich   P. Burtniak

THIRD ERA — ILLUSTRATIONS 691

JUDGES AND MAYORS

J. R. Solomon

M. Wawrykow

P. Greshchuk

A. M. Kindred

J. N. Decore

M. Baryluk

M. J. Patrick

S. Juba

W. Hawrelak

692 UKRAINIAN CANADIANS: A HISTORY

LEADERS

S. J. Kalba   W. Kochan   W. J. Sarchuk   T. Mychajliwskyj

E. Mastykash   M. Plawiuk   R. Malashchuk   I. Iwanchuk

T. Cechmistro   M. Sosnowsky   J. Boyko   P. Savaryn

PEOPLE OF THE ARTS

G. Hnatiuk   L. Turkewycz   W. Kardash   W. Bohonos

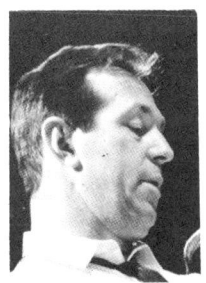   

C. Semchyshyn   P. Macenko   I. Turkewycz-Martynec   R. J. Ostashewsky

O. Rohatyn   I. Romanoff   R. Kroitor   H. Manko-Yaroshevych

PROFESSIONAL ARTISTS

Yosyp Hoshuliak

M. Holynskyj

Jar. Schur

Christina Petrowsky

Julia Sysak-Juliette

Joan Karasevich

Ed Evanko

T. A. Shuflyn

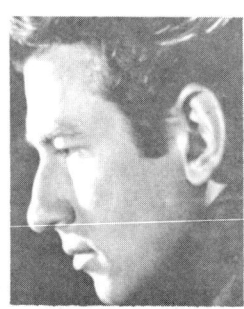
Ireneus Zuk

THIRD ERA — ILLUSTRATIONS

ART AND RESEARCH

W. Kurelek   Leo Molodozanin   J. Bucmaniuk   P. Kuch

R. Kowal   B. Stebelsky   E. Vertyporoch   I. Kubarsky

T. Koshetz   I. Tyktor   I. Keywan   M. Dodiak

UNIVERSITIES AND RESEARCH

C. Bida   J. B. Rudnyckyj   M. Pernarowski   W. Tarnopolsky

P. Woroby   I. Hlynka   B. Kazymyra   B. R. Bociurkiw

E. B. Roslycky   M. L. Borowsky   V. N. Mackiw   J. Rozumnyj

THIRD ERA — ILLUSTRATIONS

WRITERS

I. I. Bodnarchuk   Yar Slavutych   B. Hoshovsky   M. Podworniak

J. Tarnowych   V. Barabash   U. Samchuk   A. M. Mokh

J. Kolasky   N. Mudryk-Mryc   B. Oleksandriv   G. Ryga

698   UKRAINIAN CANADIANS: A HISTORY

SOLOISTS

Luba Zuk   P. Konoplenko   D. Grescoe   S. Staryk

O. Pavlova   S. Zhovnir-Klos   O. Bala   L. Hanushchak

L. Ziubrak   L. Kolessa   R. Roslak   O. Kwasniak

THIRD ERA — ILLUSTRATIONS 699

LEADERS IN WOMAN'S WORLD

E. Ostapchuk   I. Pawlykowska   K. Antonovych   O. Zalizniak

S. Bubniuk   N. Kohuska   O. Woycenko   S. Potoski

I. Knysh   S. Sawchuk   K. Paliyiw   A. Wach

COMMUNITY WORKERS

M. Kushpeta   A. Yaworsky   S. W. Frolick   H. Porochiwnyk

M. Hladyshevsky   M. Bury   D. Prokop   W. Didiuk

Meletiy Snihurowych   A. Petryshyn   M. M. Nebeluk   A. Kosikowsky

THIRD ERA — ILLUSTRATIONS

REPRESENTATIVES OF VARIOUS FIELDS

J. Negrych   N. Zalozetsky   M. F. Szewczyk   J. Slogan

N. Flak   R. Zuk   J. H. Lozinsky   A. S. Bryk

T. Sawchuk   P. Marunczak   C. N. Suchowersky   E. Nesterenko

EDITORS

R. Rakhmanny   Rev. P. Chomyn   J. H. Syrnick   W. Solonynka

Rev. S. Izyk   S. Wolynec   W. Martynec   A. Kurdydyk

W. Levytsky   M. Hrushka   Brother Methodius   P. Volyniak

COOPERATORS

W. Yashan   W. Topolnycky   W. Sytnyk   O. K. Wynnyckyj

M. Andruchiw   J. Skwarchuk   A. Kachor   J. Temnyk

I. Wachniak   A. Topolnycki   A. Gospodyn   P. Kit

704　　　UKRAINIAN CANADIANS: A HISTORY

PATRONS OF NATIONAL CULTURE

F. Bogdan

W. & M. Mihaychuk

W. Perepeluk

W. Duchnij

S. & M. Jankowsky

Domka Babij

Peter Jacyk

I. & W. Paley

Ivan Boruch

Dmytro Zipchen (1905-   ), a Catholic and a farmer, born in Ukraine, but educated in Canada, was elected from the district of Cumberland (1952-1956).

W. J. Berezowsky (1903-   ), of Orthodox faith and a teacher by profession, born in Ukraine, but educated in Winnipeg was elected from the Prince Albert-Cumberland constituency. Both of these two mentioned were well versed in municipal affairs. The last one was re-elected in 1956, 1960 and 1964.

In 1956 there were 4 Ukrainians in the Saskatchewan Legislature, including one woman, *Maria Fodchuk-Batten,* a Catholic and a lawyer by profession, who was elected from Humbolt district on the Liberal ticket and later appointed as a judge. Not only was she the first Ukrainian woman to become an M.L.A. in Canada, but also had the honor of being the first Ukrainian woman to become judge in Canadian history. The quartet pattern was repeated again in 1960 when the following four were elected to the Saskatchewan Legislature: *Dick W. Mychayluk,* from Redberry and *Martin Semchuk* (1914-   ), from Meadowlake, both of them business men of Catholic faith, running on a C.C.F. ticket and who along with A. Kuziak and W. J. Berezowsky formed the Ukrainian C.C.F. quartet in Saskatchewan Parliament.

The 1964 elections brought great changes in the provincial politics when the government of Saskatchewan went in to the hands of the Liberals and only W. J. Berezowsky and D. W. Mychayluk, both of them members of the C.C.F.party, remained in the legislature.

In October 1967, the Saskatchewan elections, in addition to the two above mentioned, brought three more new members to the Legislature, all of them from the N.D.P. party. These were: Miro Kwasnica, B.Ed. (Cutknife), born 1935 at Wakaw, John Kowalchuk (1921-   ) from Melville and Roy John Romanow, LL.B., from the Saskatoon-Riversdale district. In all there were five members of Ukrainian origin elected in 1967, the highest number ever recorded in Saskatchewan Legislature. An interesting sideline to be noted is the fact that all of them were members of the N.D.P. party while the government was Liberal.

In summary, after the Second World War there were 12 M.L.A.'s of Ukrainian origin in Saskatchewan Legislature, comprised of 2 Liberals and 10 New Democratic Party. Professionally classified there were 4 businessmen, 4 teachers, 3 farmers and one lawyer. By religious adherence there were 5 Ukrainian Orthodox, 4 Ukrainian Catholic, and 3 Protestants.

In summarizing, it could be said that Saskatchewan made a milestone in the field of Ukrainian Canadian representation in the provincial legislature. When we consider that there were only two M.L.A.'s of Ukrainian origin in the interwar period in comparison to the 13 since the war, then the number amply speaks for itself. For the first time Saskatchewan was on par with Alberta in the number of members of Ukrainian descent. However, Alberta has this one point to its credit, namely that its representation was more stabilized. This was no doubt tied in with the stability of Alberta's government. Still, Saskatchewan showed a great deal of expansion in the Ukrainian provincial field of politics.

Ontario

Although the number of Ukrainians in Ontario during the third era is greater than in any other province, in the field of provincial politics the Ukrainians are just making a start. The wall was first breached by *John Yaremko* (1918-   ), a lawyer and a war veteran of Orthodox faith and a son of pioneer parents who was elected in 1951 to the provincial parliament from the Bellwood-Toronto constituency running on a Progressive-Conservative ticket and re-elected to the same legislature ever since. As we have already mentioned, he entered the provincial cabinet in 1958 thus becoming not only the first M.L.A. but also the first cabinet minister of Ukrainian origin in that province.

During the last Ontario elections a second Ukrainian entered the provincial parliament, *Bernard Newman (Novoselsky)*, of Protestant denomination and a teacher by profession and who was elected on the Liberal ticket from the Windsor-Walkerville district. In addition to politics he also was a great sports enthusiast.

The 1967 Ontario elections brought a third Ukrainian Canadian to the provincial House, in the person of *Mack Makarchuk* who was elected from Brantford on the N.D.P. ticket. Both, J. Yaremko and B. Newman also were re-elected. Thus there were three Ukrainian Canadian M.L.A.'s in Ontario, one for each political party—Conservative, Liberal and N.D.P. From this we may conclude that in Ontario too, the Ukrainians made a step forward in political integration and representation.

Ontario together with the three western provinces of Manitoba, Saskatchewan and Alberta brought to a grand total of 47 the number of legislators of Ukrainian origin after the Second World War. The Canadian Centennial year saw 21 Ukrainian Canadians sitting in the legislative chambers of the above mentioned provinces. Manitoba was first with 7 members, Alberta 6 and Saskatchewan 5 while Ontario had 3. By 1967 of our history the provincial legislatures in Canada had the following numbers of Ukrainian Canadian descent: Manitoba — 30, Alberta — 20, Saskatchewan — 14, Ontario — 3, 67 M.L.A.'s altogether. They represented all the different political parties in Canada. A majority of them belonged to those group-centers that did not go in step with the traditional political parties of Canada, but sought new means to solve the social problems in favor of the common man caught in the tread-mill of every-day life. The feelings for the down-trodden were deeply rooted in their Ukrainian soul which had, through its long and harried history sought a social and political justice as a natural reaction to the social and political oppression that existed on their ancestral soil. Each human being was trying to find an answer to his quest. This was often worked out on the politically-experimental basis.

Of quite a different nature was the Ukrainian representation in the dominion political field. Here, the supporters of the traditional parties held their sway although the first three representatives in Ottawa came from the ranks of the so-called "political rebels"—the United Farmers of Alberta, the Social Credit party and the C.C.F. party. Only somewhat later the Liberal and Conservative supporters arrived on the scene and took the lead from the "rebels". This transition towards the so-called classic political stability added its outsanding mark to the process of the sum-total of the Ukrainian Canadian integration.

Members of Federal Parliament

Michael Luchkovich and later Anthony Hlynka made a good start in the Dominion Parliament. In 1945 a third Ukrainian was elected namely, *Frederick Samuel Zaplitny* (1913-1964), of Catholic faith and a teacher by profession who ran on the C.C.F. ticket from Dauphin district, was defeated during the 1949 elections but came back in 1953. In the person of F. Zaplitny the Ukrainians of Manitoba had their first representative in the Dominion Parliament. He was a good speaker and wrote pithy satires, which he liked to quote during the session.

In 1949 the Vegreville district of Alberta which had given to the political sector during the inter-war era such parliamentarians as M. Luchkovich and A. Hlynka, had also provided a third representative in the person of *John Decore* (1909-   ), of Orthodox religion and a Liberal, and who was re-elected in 1953. His was the honor of setting a historical record on being the first Ukrainian Canadian to serve as a parliamentary adviser to the United Nations in 1950.

At more or less the same time *Michael Starr* (1910-   ) was making a name for himself in Eastern Canada. On the heels of his three years in office as mayor of Oshawa (1949-1952) he ran on a Conservative ticket and was successful in a by-election in 1952, holding the same seat for the next several terms. He was a Minister of Labour in John Diefenbaker's government for six years and established a record, not only as the first Ukrainian to hold a dominion cabinet post, but also by the fact that there were no major strikes in Canada during his term of office. He also had the honor of being the first of his countrymen to hold the position of the Conservative House Leader in Parliament (1965), and later in the party caucus, and who also was a candidate for the party leadership in 1967. This precedence speaks volumes for the political integration of the Canadian community which had hitherto reserved this unwritten privilege for the Anglo or the Franco candidates.

With the election of M. Starr the Ukrainians had one representative from each political party existing in Canada, in the following order (according to time factor): U.F.A. (United Farmers of Alberta), C.C.F., Social Credit, Liberals and Conservatives.

Ambrose Holowach, of Catholic religion and a business man, was elected to the dominion parliament in 1953 from Edmonton-East constituency on the Social Credit ticket. He was re-elected once and later joined the provincial politics to become the Provincial Secretary.

In 1957 there were six members of parliament of Ukrainian origin in Ottawa. In addition to M. Starr and A. Holowach there were: *Dr. John Kucherepa* (1919-   ), of Catholic faith, a doctor by profession and a Conservative representing the High Park constituency of Toronto; *Peter Stefura* (1923-   ), of Orthodox faith, a teacher by profession and Social Credit supporter representing the Vegreville district in Alberta; *Nick Mandziuk* (1902-1969), of Orthodox faith, a lawyer by profession and a Conservative supporter from the Marquette constituency, and *William Val Yacula* (1907-1957), a business man, representing the Springfield distrist—both of the last two mentioned being from Manitoba. This same six member representation was continued at the next Dominion elections in 1958. In place of the two Social Credit representatives—A. Holowach and P. Stefura—two Progressive Conservative supporters were elected.

These were: *William Skoreyko* (1922-   ), of Orthodox adherence and a business man, born in Ukraine, who was elected from Edmonton-East and re-elected in 1962, 1963 and 1965, and *Stanley J. Korchinski* (1929-   ), a Catholic and a farmer by profession, representing the Mackenzie constituency of Saskatchewan. He had the honor of being the head of the Canadian parliamentarians to the NATO Conference in Paris in 1962 — a further proof that integration was in progress. In addition to these six, the Conservative team was enlarged by one more member when *Dr. Joseph Slogan* (1931-   ) was victorious in the 1958 election in the Springfield district of Manitoba, following the death of W. V. Yacula, and was re-elected in 1962 and 1963. In the 1962 elections there were only five Ukrainian Canadian representatives in the House of Commons, namely: W. Skoreyko, S. Korchinski, M. Mandziuk, Dr. J. Slogan and Michael Starr. The same representation was returned during 1963 elections and again in 1965—but this time without Dr. J. Slogan.

It will be seen, from our summary, that the Conservative representation by the Ukrainians was the last one in arrival but once it got there it increased very rapidly. Classified according to party allegiance there were 7 Conservative, 3 Social Credit, 1 Liberal, 1 Socialist and 1 United Farmers of Alberta members of Ukrainian origin — 13 in all—who not only represented their own fellow countrymen, but also the other citizens of their respective districts. When we take into consideration the fact that many of these districts were comprised of various nationalities, then it will be seen that the integration of Canadian society was progressing very rapidly. Out of the 13 members of parliament, 5 had a high school education and 8 were university graduates.

Still much progress was registered in the seventies. See chapter "Integration in the Political Field."

Senate, Judicial and Other Appointments

Perhaps the clearest evidence of social integration is what we may call the top nominations, the more important amongst them being for the position of senators, judges and on royal commissions. In our conception this vertical integration is, in a way, the consummation of the horizontal integration. Unless these two integrations are bound together, they will be like a structure that is built on solid foundations but with a poor roof over it.

The new era revealed more clearly the first outlines in the sphere of vertical integration. Among these we would name the already mentioned nominations for the senate of those who were of the Ukrainian origin. The first was *William Wall (Wolochatiuk)*, (1911-1964), of Ethelbert, a Catholic and a well known pedagogue and community leader in Winnipeg, a Liberal supporter who was a Lieutenant in the R.C.A.S.C. during the war. He was appointed, as mentioned before, a senator in 1955 by the then Prime Minister Louis St. Laurent. In 1959 Prime Minister John J. Diefenbaker nominated *John Hnatyshyn* to the senate seat, of Orthodox faith and a well known Saskatoon lawyer from the Conservative ranks. John Hnatyshyn, who took an active part in community life and politics, was born in Ukraine and raised and educated in Canada. Both of these, the first Ukrainian Senators in Canada died early—W. Wall in

1964 and J. Hnatyshyn in 1967. In 1963 Prime Minister John Diefenbaker nominated *Paul Yuzyk* to the senate seat that was made vacant by the death of Senator William Wall. Paul Yuzyk, at the time of his appointment was a professor at the University of Manitoba. Of Catholic faith and a Conservative supporter, Prof. P. Yuzyk had made a name for himself as an author of several works dealing with the history of Ukrainian Canadians. In addition to this he had a wide knowledge in the field of community affairs and higher education, having been connected with the Universities in Saskatchewan, Manitoba and Minnesota and was also a member of various learned societies and at one time was the head of the Manitoba Historical Society.

All of the three mentioned senators were highly educated men and leaders in the Ukrainian community life. Two of them were born in Canada and one in Ukraine. One was of Orthodox faith and two were Catholics. All of them together with other selected members of parliament were, from time to time, appointed as delegates to the United Nations or NATO especially on those occasions when the discussions were taking place about East European affairs in which, understandably enough, they were the best experts.

During Canada's Centennial the Ukrainians had only one senator, Paul Yuzyk, in Ottawa although previously they had two. There were five members of the House of Commons. Throughout the whole history (of the Canadian Centenary) there were 3 senators and 13 members of Parliament in Ottawa of Ukrainian origin who, together with the members of provincial legislatures, gave a total of 83 representatives to the Provincial and the Dominion parliaments and the Senate. By provincial designations only Manitoba and Saskatchewan were represented in the Senate. In the House of Commons there were: 1 member from Saskatchewan, 2 from Ontario, 4 from Manitoba and 6 from Alberta. Although Alberta stood first in the House of Commons representation, it had not been able to come up with a representative in the Senate.

Those 83 representatives are listed numerically according to their parties in the following order: C.C.F. and N.D.P.—23 (19 and 4), Liberals —23, Social Credit—17, Progressive Conservative—12, U.F.A.—5, Independent 2 and 1 Labour-Progressive. All of them together represent an interesting political mosaic.

Vertical integration also was noticeable in the appointments of judges. As already known, the first judge appointee was *J. W. Arsenych* (1882-1953) in 1947, who was one of the outstanding leaders in the life of Ukrainian community in Canada. Two years later *Michael Stechishin* (1889-1964), from Saskatchewan was appointed a judge for Wynyard district (1949-1963), and still later *Peter Greshchuk* was appointed Alberta judge. In the 50-ies other appointments were made—John R. Solomon, whom we mentioned previously, Andrew Kindred, John George Roberts (Roborecky), Robert Dnieper, Walter Tuchtie, Orest Bendas, Mary Wawrykow, and others. A larger number of nominations were made for the position of magistrates, the first one of them being Nicholas Bartman (Vancouver) and the youngest the 27-year old lawyer, W. M. Darichuk of Selkirk, Manitoba.

There also were exceptional and short-term appointments such as that of Dr. Stephanie Potoski to the Board of Directors of the Canadian Broadcasting Corporation, and of lawyer Peter J. Lazarowich, Q.C., member of the Board of Directors of the National Film Board. In 1961-1964 Monsignor Dr. Wasyl Kushnir was member of the Board of Directors of the Canada Council and Prof. J. B. Rudnyckyj on the Royal Commission on Bilingualism and Biculturalism, Mark Gerald Smerchanski and Daniel Zaharia were appointed Governors of the University of Manitoba, Bohdan Gulak, Governor of the University of Saskatchewan, Leo Kossar was appointed Executive Director of the Canadian Folk Arts Council, which was associated with the Canadian Centennial Commission. On the provincial level, Mary Wawrykow, M. Posmituck, Cecil Semchyshyn and others were on this Commission.

All these nominations—first for the Ukrainians—are healthy signs showing that the vertical integration encompasses every branch of community life on the higher plane. To complete the roster of the vertical integration it will be necessary to mention the nominations in the government departments. Here, for example, we can name such individuals as S. W. Ozero, assistant to the deputy minister in the Department of Fisheries and Z. W. Sametz, the Director of the Economic and Research Division in the same department. Also, P. J. Sereda in the National Research Council. Dr. V. J. Kaye, a historian and professor in the Department of Slavic Studies in the University of Ottawa, worked as Liaison Officer for the ethnic groups in Canada in the Canadian Citizenship Branch in Ottawa. In the same fields such Ukrainian Canadians as St. Jaworski and W. M. Hlady were employed, as well as Dr. W. Darcovich and W. A. Tuskey, and others in the economic field of Canadian government.

We also find Ukrainians holding higher government positions in the country districts, such individuals as M. Lysack, F. Starchuk, and others. When we add to this list those who hold important posts in the Royal Canadian Mounted Police like Supt. E. R. Lysyk, Supt. P. Bazowski, Supt. Wm. M. Harasym, Insp. H. P. Lessick and the Canadian Military Forces, then it will be seen that there is hardly any branch of social and community life, whether it be in the field of politics, economics, national defense or any other department, without the participation of Ukrainian Canadians. The horizontal integration that planted its roots during the pioneer era, had driven them deeper during the inter-war period of the second era, and grew to its greatest expansion in the vertical integration of the third and newest era. With each year the Canadian society is being transformed into a Canadian nation and taking on the appearance of a clearly defined form in which the solid base for these creative processes has been provided by the political integration in its two chief dimensions—horizontal and vertical. And, although these two integral processes suffer at times from disruptions and delays, still they are progressing along a well defined path. From colonial improvisations to the accomplished fact of a well perfected statehood is a long and winding road that is often strewn with unpredictable shake-ups and surprise-filled dramas.

The Ukrainian Canadians had hard going in the pioneer era, but during the third era their efforts were crowned with outstanding success. It is most gratifying to note that many of those who experienced pogroms, dispossessions and denial of civil and political liberties in their native Ukraine lived to see the day in their adopted Canada when their sons and daughters could aspire to and attain full participation in the democratic processes. Continuation of this discussion will be held in subsequent chapters.

Although the development of social stratification and multicultural policy will be discussed in further chapters and in the seventies it is necessary at this time to point out an important event which took place at the very beginning of the mentioned decade.

The appointment of a Ukrainian for the position of the Lieutenant-Governor of Saskatchewan in January 1970 was a turning point in ethnocultural Canadian policy. This dignity was bestowed on Stephen Worobetz, Medical Doctor of Saskatoon by Prime Minister P. E. Trudeau. Of course, the appointment aroused enthusiasm not only among Ukrainians but also among other ethnocultural groups of Canada. There was a feeling that the social barriers between Anglo-Saxons, French and other ethnocultural groups were falling slowly down. Here we should keep in mind that such appointments until that time were only among Anglo-Saxons and French. Ross Thatcher, premier of the Province of Saskatchewan underlined on this occasion in his speech that the appointment of Dr. S. Worobetz was a visible manifestation to recognize Ukrainian input in the growth and development of "three Ukrainian prairie provinces". P. E. Trudeau also strongly accentuated that there were "no more foreigners among Canadian citizens".

This appointment drew special enthusiasm among Ukrainians due to the fact that the Worobetz pioneer family was very active in the community life.[1] Peter Worobetz, school inspector, was instrumental with Brother Methodius Kuziak, F.S.C., in introducing of Ukrainian language in public schools of Saskatchewan and Dr. S. Worobetz was active in professional and church organizational life. He took over the duties of the Lieutenant-Governor on February 2nd, 1970 and performed with distinction as a worthy representative of the Crown of Canada.

Lieutenant-Governor of Saskatchewan, Dr. S. Worobetz presents a first class medal to R. J. Fedorowich, a commissionaire, veteran of Ukrainian Liberation Movement (1918-1920), and Korean War, 1973.

[1]) Ukrainian News, No. 4, 1970, Our Aim, No. 7, 1970, Vilne Slovo, No. 6, 1970.

710b   UKRAINIAN CANADIANS: A HISTORY
HISTORIC EVENTS

In honoring of 50th Anniversary of Ukrainian Revolution and Canadian Centennial UCC President Dr. W. Kushnir proclaiming decision of Pan-American Ukrainian Conference about convening of the World Congress of Free Ukrainians, Toronto, 1967.

The First Plenary Session of SKVU in Toronto, 1969. Seated (L.-R.): O. Lototska, I. Bilynsky, Metropolitan Mstyslav, J. Lysawyer, Rev. W. Kushnir, Metropolitan Maxim, I. Syrnick, Rev. E. Bachynsky; Standing: Dr. B. Hnatiuk, I. Iwanchuk, Dr. M. Marunchak, Julian Revay, M. Plawiuk, Dr. S. Fostun, Dr. M. Sosnowsky.

PAN-AMERICAN UKRAINIAN CONFERENCE

The organizational successes of Ukrainian Canadians in community life, both on the internal organizing plane and in the general political representation sphere, as well as their achievements in provincial legislatures and dominion parliament, won for them the prestige of their fellow countrymen beyond the borders of Canada. We have already mentioned in another chapter the role of Ukrainian Canadian representation in Europe following the Second World War. The Ukrainian Canadian Committee sent a Ukrainian Canadian delegation to the founding convention of the General Assembly of the United Nations in San Francisco. There were other Ukrainian Canadian representations dealing with external affairs. All these public appearances on wider fields were enacted for the purpose of producing a valid representation and to acquaint the whole outside world with the political situation in Ukraine and Eastern Europe and to point out that the war is not over when so many nations are under the heel of a dictatorship.

The leading figures in the Ukrainian Canadian Committee believed that their voice would be more effective if they formed an organization comprising all Ukrainians of North and South America. As is well known there are over one million Ukrainians living in U.S.A. while another half a million or more live in Brazil, Argentina, Paraguay, Uruguay and other smaller countries of South America. This would bring the total to approximately three million Ukrainians who are citizens of the various American countries. It was on the initiative of the Ukrainian Canadians that a decision was made to have the representatives of Canada, U.S.A., Brazil, Argentina, Paraguay and Uruguay take part in mutual councils to discuss matters pertaining to Ukrainians living in the above mentioned countries and the formation of a cultural and political representation in relation to the Ukrainian world affairs. The conference of these representatives took place in New York in October of 1947 and on the 21st of that month resolutions and appeals were made addressed to: "Ukrainians and citizens of North and South America and to those who were uprooted, by the fierce enemy from their native land and scattered, by cruel fate, all over the world" The resolutions also announced that a permanent organization was formed under the name of Pan-American Conference (P.A.U.K.) and which proclaimed as its chief aims:

1. "To put a lion's share of their efforts into the political, cultural and economic development of their country;

2. To show, through creative work and good conduct the merit of the Ukrainian people and by actively spreading the truth about Ukraine and the Ukrainian efforts, gain the sympathy and support of their American fellow countrymen and of the various state governments;

3. To stand on guard and protect the honour of the Ukrainian nationality, to cultivate Ukrainian culture, customs and traditions believing them to be an integral part of the culture of the American countries;

4. To organize the whole social life on the basis of serving the interests and the well-being of their American countries, to help the Ukrainians

in their strivings and to work for the good of the Ukrainian Nation" [1]).

The First Council of the Pan-American Ukrainian Conference was composed of the following persons: Rev. Dr. Wasyl Kushnir, President of the Ukrainian Canadian Committee, who became the head of the P.A.U.K., (Pan-Amerykanska Ukrainska Konferenciya) Olena Lotocka and Eva Piddubchyshyn representing U.S.A., Illia Morachuk from Brazil, Ivan Hryhorashchuk from Argentina and William Hultay representing Canada. In addition to those mentioned above, some of the leading figures on this continent also took part in these important events. These were: Dr. Lonhyn Cehelsky, Prof. Mykola Chubaty, Dmytro Halychyn, Prof. Alexander A. Granovsky, Prof. Lev Dobriansky, Dr. Luka Myshuga, Stepan Shumeyko, Evhen Rohach, Bohdan Katamay, Rev. Mykola Iwaniw, Andriy Bilopolsky—all from U.S.A. and Rev. Dr. Semen Sawchuk, Wladimir Kossar and Dr. Theodore Datzkiw from Canada. Besides the Ukrainian Canadian Committee, other Ukrainian organizations were represented in the P.A.U.K., as follows: The Ukrainian Congress Committee of America, U.S.A., the Association of the Friends of Ukrainian Culture of Brazil, the Central Representation of the Ukrainian Community in Argentina, Paraguay and Uruguay—a complete national representation. There were only a few extremist left elements that stood on the side and to these the P.A.U.K. addressed itself in the following way:

"Pan-American Ukrainian Conference affirms with regret that there is some portion, though not very large, of the Ukrainians on both American continents which has fallen a victim to the false Communist propaganda, bringing thereby much harm and dishonor upon their chosen American Fatherlands and to their own Ukrainian land and people and who consciously or unconsciously serve the interests of the greatest enemy of mankind, the Bolshevik Moscow imperialism" [2]).

Judging from the widely reaching resolutions of the P.A.U.K. it will be seen that its founders declared full loyalty to the culture of their fathers as well as full loyalty to their adopted lands of America, while in the political and ideological field they took a sharply defined course against the Bolshevik Moscow imperialism. Clearly acknowledging these principles P.A.U.K. declared itself to be not only a cultural, but also a political representation of the Ukrainians upon both American continents.

With such a high resolve the P.A.U.K. organization conducted its sessions and continued in the same tone during their intervals. The last one in line, and the eighth in a row, took place in New York in November 1967 on the eve of the World Congress of Free Ukrainians, and with it the Pan-American Ukrainian Conference crowned its one score of years. The Ukrainian Canadians played an important role in the work of this institution. This is manifested if only by the fact that during its twenty years of existence the P.A.U.K. had been headed by the President of the Ukrainian Canadian Committee, Rev. Dr. Wasyl Kushnir. The office of its secretary also had been in Canada during those years and this function was held for a long time by John H. Syrnick, the editor of "Ukrainian Voice" and one of the leading figures in S.U.S. organization. Other members of P.A.U.K., living on Canadian soil, were—W. Kossar, Rev. S. W. Sawchuk, M. Plawiuk, I. Iwanchuk, and few others.

---

[1] "Resolutions of the First Pan-American Ukrainian Conference" in "Ukrainian Voice", Winnipeg, No. 50, Dec. 10, 1950.
[2] Ibiden

UKRAINIAN CANADIANS INITIATE THE WORLD CONGRESS OF FREE UKRAINIANS

The initiative of the Ukrainian Canadian went further ahead when at the Sixth Congress of the Ukrainian Canadians in 1959, in Winnipeg, the Presidium of the Ukrainian Canadian Committee was given an important task, namely, to call together a Ukrainian World Congress for the purpose of creating the World Federation of Ukrainians [1].

The resolution of the Congress of Ukrainian Canadians in regard to this matter was very clear, and it proclaimed: "The federation association alliance of all Ukrainian national organizations in every country for the purpose of coordination of their work and the preservation of spiritual-cultural and national unity." This resolution compared very favorably with the ideals of the Pan-American Ukrainian Conference and it was, no doubt, for this reason that the Sixth Congress of Ukrainian Canadians prevailed upon the Presidium of the Ukrainian Canadian Committee to present this matter to P.A.U.K. and that the latter organization should call into existence a preparatory committee with the object of calling together the World Congress of Free Ukrainians. The Pan-American Ukrainian Conference accpted this challenge and held two sessions in regard to this matter—the 6th in October 1960 and the 7th in September 1964. During these sessions of the P.A.U.K., plans were made for the calling of the Congress, the inception of its organizational form and the handling of various technical matters. For more practical results, P.A.U.K. named two committees to look after the preparations, the first on Canadian territory under the direction of Dr. Wasyl Kushnir, President of the Ukrainian Canadian Committee, and the other in the U.S.A., under the care of the President of the Ukrainian Congress Committee of U.S.A., Dmytro Halychyn and, following his death, under the direction of Joseph Lesawyer.

In the beginning all the preparatory work for organizing the World Congress of Free Ukrainians and of its Program Committee was done by the Ukrainian Canadian Committee, such as the composition of basic principles, the political platform and the structure of the organizational bureau. Seeing that the Ukrainians living under the Communist dictatorship could not take part in it, the whole action was carried on under the name of the "World Congress of Free Ukrainians".

The preparation work was a long up-hill struggle that required eight full years for the accomplishment of its task (1959-1967). The stumbling blocks came not only from the legal status of various countries, settled by Ukrainians, but also from the political and organizational thinking on the part of the Ukrainian representations from different countries. The coordination of these matters called for much effort and communication, especially with the Organizing Committee of New York, so that it could be approved in time and accepted by the eighth session of the Pan-American Ukrainian Conference in November of 1967 which, together with other leading country-wide organizations of Europe and Australia, led to the formation of the First World Congress of Ukrainians in the free world

---

[1] "Collection of Documentary Material" compiled on the occasion of 25th Anniversary of the Ukrainian Canadian Committee, 1940-1965, Winnipeg, 1965, p. 93.

as the expression of the psychological unity of the Ukrainian people who may freely manifest their own will, their cultural and political creed— placing them in opposition to the regime that denies these principles. Undoubtedly there were millions of Ukrainians who, although dispossessed of their freedom, were able, in the silence of their hearts, to identify themselves with this free world manifestations. Perhaps this primarily was the greatest moral strength of the Congress, into which the Ukrainian Canadians had put so much of their material and moral support. The road that stretched from the homestead to the far away world horizons was long and difficult, but finally it was crowned with success.

The First World Congress of Free Ukrainians (S.K.V.U.) took place in New York, November 16-19, 1967. The General Assembly of the representatives of Ukrainians from all over the world was held and the various conventions of scholars and pedagogues in different fields of cultural, scientific and economic life, as well as journalists and leaders in women's and students' movements, met immediately preceding the November 16th date.

In this impressive and historic gathering there participated such Ukrainian national representations like the Ukrainian Congress Committee of America (U.S.A.), the Representation Central de la Collectividad Ucrania (Argentina), the Comite Ucraino-Brasileiro (Brazil), the Association de Ukrainianos en Venezuela, the Centro Ucraino en el Republica del Paraguay, the Sociadale dos Amigos de la Cultura Ucrania (Argentina), the Federation of Ukrainian Associations in Australia, the Association of Ukrainians in Great Britain, the Coordinating Council of Ukrainian Organizations in Austria, the Central Representation of Ukrainian Emigration in Germany, the Ukrainian National Unity and the Union of Ukrainian Workers in France and others. 1003 delegates representing 227 organizations from 17 countries, attended the Congress.

The First World Congress of Free Ukrainians created a permanent Secretariat with the Executive Board at the head. A statute was passed by the Congress with the provision that these Ukrainian world congresses were to be held every six years. The Executive Board of the Secretariat would change in rotation every two years in the following order: Canada, U.S.A., Europe.

From the great amount of work that was put into the preparation by the Ukrainian Canadians, prior to the formation of the Congress, it was only natural that one of its representatives should have the honor of being the first to head the Secretariat of the World Congress of Free Ukrainians. Over a thousand delegates entrusted the helm of this world organization into the hands of Rev. Dr. Wasyl Kushnir, President of the Ukrainian Canadian Committee. The following Canadians were elected to the executive and the presidial councils: John H. Syrnick, (Acting Vice-President), and editor and the First Vice-president of the Ukrainian Canadian Committee, Mykola Plawiuk (General Secretary), Ivan Iwanchuk (treasurer), the last two also being vice-presidents of the Ukrainian Canadian Committee, and the Most Reverend Archbishop and Metropolitan Maxim Hermaniuk, member of the Secretariat, as well as Pastor John Yacenty and Olena Zalizniak. Michael H. Marunchak (a member of the Presidium—U.C.C.) was appointed to the Board of Auditors [2]). The work cut out for the Secretariat of the World Conference of Free Ukrainians has two objectives: to preserve Ukrainian culture in the free world and to aid the Ukrainian people in their struggle to regain the cultural and political freedom of their country [3]).

The freedom-loving Canada and its citizens spread the ideas of free people among the Ukrainian citizens of all continents. When we take into consideration the fact that among the official representatives at the Congress there were members of Canadian government and parliamentarians, it will be seen that the Canadian image in the eyes of the participants at the World Congress of Free Ukrainians was indeed on a very high idealistic level. Not only did Canada reveal itself as a free country in which all have a right to cultivate their own specific cultures, but it also stood out as a true champion of freedom that has the courage to raise the voice in the political wilderness and demand the realization of the principles of the United Nations Charter [4]).

It should be emphasized that the first executive director of this worldwide national body was a Ukrainian Canadian Dr. M. Sosnowsky.

---

[2]) Other members, outside of Canada, were as follows: On the Secretariat of the World Congress of Free Ukrainians: Joseph Lesawyer (U.S.A.), Anthony Melnyk (Germany), Wasyl Iwanytskyj (Argentina), Stephan Plakhtyn (Brazil), Myroslaw Boluch (Australia), Ignatius Billinsky (U.S.A.), Dr. Sviatomyr Fostun (England), Dr. Bohdan Hnatiuk (U.S.A.), Omelan Kowal (Belgium), Mathew Stachiw (U.S.A.), Right Rev. Ivan Bachynsky (Belgium), The Most Rev. Archbishop Mstyslaw Skrypnyk (U.S.A.). Board of Auditors: Julian Revay (U.S.A.), Dr. Nicholas Iwanowych (Austria), Benedict Wasiuk (Venezuela), Myroslaw Shegedyn (Australia).
[3]) "Ukrainian Voice", Winnipeg, No. 48, 29, 12 — 1967.
[4]) New York Times in its evaluation of John Diefenbaker's speech, 1967.

ASSIMILATING PROCESSES

Although the processes for the preservation of Ukrainian national culture in Canada took place in every branch of national life, still in addition to these integrational processes, there also are constantly at work the assimilating processes as well.

If we look upon integration as a social process, or as the result of social process in which the different parts unite to form a single whole, then assimilation may be described as that process in which persons or groups of people adopt the social-psychological characteristics of other persons and at the same time lose their own specifically inherent values or, in other words, they consciously invalidate their natural traits and adept themselves to other social and psychological patterns. In their political aspects such processes are known as "brain washing" and in the cultural and psychological sphere they are called assimilation. There was a time in the history of the Ukrainian settlers in Canada, when the concept of assimilation was deliberately cultivated in the government circles and even forced upon the minority groups by means of different outside pressures together with "religious salvations", or tempted by political privileges while a row of sociologists spoke with satisfaction about the successful assimilation. But this was mostly the reigning period of the American (U.S.A.) "melting pot", which at times would come blowing over the border, although it never found fertile soil for its roots here. True enough, there were those who tried to lend to this assimilation the noble air of patriotism and Canadianization, but the new Canadians, especially the Ukrainians, who were putting a different content into Canadianization, saw this assimilating process for what it was and called it "degeneration". This perversion of the soul came into evidence among the American youth which, having been brought up on the negation and denial of the cultural values of their fathers and in obedience to the call of this same "melting pot", lost their faith in self-reliance and took the downward path of delinquency and crime [1]. The nihilistic man has now become the real evil of the American society in the period of the cultural melting pot, as has been well substantiated by the newest scientific studies. Psychology and sociology gradually reveal the tragic results of the assimilating processes and steps are being taken to counter-act them. The concept of assimilation which, in the pioneer era, was considered in the official circles to be the quintessence of the so-called progressive processes, has gradually taken on, in the second, inter-war era, connotation of reaction. Ethnical identification in its widest span including the national characteristics such as language, customs, art, literature and history, is now replacing assimilation. These are exactly the same concepts that the Ukrainian Canadian society held to be of prime importance during its 90-year march of progress. A classical definition of this process was voiced by Lord Tweedsmuir, Governor General of Canada, when replying to the welcome address in Fraserwood, Manitoba, in 1936, he made the following statement:

"You have accepted the duties and loyalties of, as you have acquired the privileges of Canadian citizens, but I want you also to remember your

---

[1] John F. Cuber, Sociology: A Synopsis of Principles, New York, 1947.

old Ukrainian traditions—your beautiful handicrafts, your folk songs and dances, and your folk legends. I do not believe that any people can be strong unless they remember and keep in touch with all their past. You will all be better Canadians for being also good Ukrainians..." [2]).

The last idiomatic expression became the banner call of many Ukrainian Canadians but before this definition of ethnical identification was accepted by the official Canadian circles, much harm had already been done by the unwise use of assimilation pressure. This was most evident in the matter of language. We all know about the noble efforts exerted by the pioneers, in cultivating the native tongue in their homes, schools and churches. The year 1916 has been given the name of "the black year of the bi-lingual schools" of the prairie provinces for it was then that the teaching of the Ukrainian language was forbidden in public schools. The result of this ban was soon in evidence. In 1941 only 5.1% of Canadians of Ukrainian origin could not speak their native language; in 1951 the number had risen to 10.6% and in 1961 to 35.6%. This would mean that around 169,000 Canadian citizens of Ukrainian descent had lost the opportunity of learning a second language—in this case their mother tongue.

A question could be posed as to whether the above presented statistics are identical with the concept of full assimilation— in other words, the denial of one's own national (ethnical) origin? The answer is simple: the very fact that 35.6% of Canadians declared themselves to be Ukrainians, although they did not speak Ukrainian at home, is evidence enough that the assimilation of language is not identical with national assimilation— the nullification of the nationality. The author of this book had an opportunity to make his own research among the young people of school age who did not speak their parent tongue and yet 99% of the high school students identified themselves with the nationality of their fathers.

Still, the language assimilation is a serious problem as it takes away the basic key to the rich store-house of national culture. These language assimilation processes, among the Ukrainian Canadians, are shown by the following census statistics for the year 1961:

The Ukrainian Mother Tongue Listed according to Provinces
1961 Census

	Total Ukrainians	Ukrainian	English	French	Others
Alberta	105,923	71,804	33,111	77	931
Manitoba	105,372	73,349	30,894	136	913
Saskatchewan	78,851	57,018	21,152	26	655
Prairie Provinces	290,146	202,171	85,157	239	2,579
Ontario	127,911	74,105	50,575	403	2,828
British Columbia	35,640	15,611	19,321	34	674
Quebec	16,588	11,665	3,527	939	457
Atlantic Provinces	2,349	883	1,429	6	31
North West Territories	703	317	373	4	9

---

[2]) Lord Tweedsmuir's Visit to Ukrainian Canadians. Fraserwood, Manitoba, September 21, 1936. Published by the Ukrainian Self-Reliance League of Canada, Winnipeg, Manitoba. This historical meet was organized by Ukrainian teachers of the district under the leadership of John A. Negrych, who was the principal of the local school.

Canada	473,337	304,752	160,382	1,625	6,578
Manitoba	100.0	69.6	29.3	0.1	1.0
Saskatchewan	100.0	72.3	26.8		0.9
Alberta	100.0	67.8	31.3		0.9
Prairie Provinces	100.0	69.7	29.4		0.9
Ontario	100.0	57.9	39.0	0.3	2.2
British Columbia	100.0	43.8	54.2	0.1	1.9
Quebec	100.0	70.3	21.3	5.7	2.7
Atlantic Provinces	100.0	37.6	60.8	0.3	1.3
N. W. Territories	100.0	45.1	53.0	0.6	1.3
Canada	100.0	64.4	33.9	0.3	1.4

These figures show that Ukrainian Canadians suffer the loss of their mother tongue the most in the Atlantic provices (60.8%) with British Columbia being second (54.2%) and Ontario coming third 39.6%). In the prairie provinces, 30.3% of the Ukrainian population do not speak the language of their parents. The highest score for the preservation of Ukrainian language belongs to Saskatchewan that boasts 72.3%, Quebec second with 70.3%, Manitoba next with 69.6% and Alberta with the lowest score in the prairie provinces of 67.8%.

There are two interesting points about the above statistics. It is quite evident that the preservation of the Ukrainian language in the western provinces is due primarily to the block settlement mode, while in Quebec it is mostly the result of the emancipating processes of that province. But even more interesting than those two is the fact that only 5.7% of Ukrainians in Quebec consider the French language as their mother tongue, although 21.3% of Quebec Ukrainians declare themselves for the English language as their own.

Comparing Ukrainians with other nationalities in Canada, it will show us that the French stand highest in the preservation of their native language (90.0%) and next come Chinese (83.1%), Italians (73.5%), Indians and Eskimos (71.4%), Finlanders (67.8%). Lower than the Ukrainian percentage stand the following nationalities: Hungarians (61.1%) Japanese (60.3%), Slovaks (59.1%), Poles (45.5%), Germans (40.0%), Dutch (37.5%), Jews (33.5%), Russians (30.2%), Scandinavians (28.8%) and Czechs (26.3%).

When we take into account the fact that Italians and Finlanders comprise the new element that came here after the Second World War, then we may say that the Ukrainians, in spite of showing some language losses, preserve the language of their fathers to a high degree in comparison to other nationalities that stand much lower in this respect.

Assimilation in the religious field is also noticeable among Ukrainian Canadians. The traditional Ukrainian churches often referred to as the mother churches, the Ukrainian Catholic Church and the Ukrainian Greek-Orthodox Church, account for only 58.5% of the total Ukrainian Canadian population. More than 164,000 or over 34%, according to 1961 statistics, belong to the Roman Catholic Church, the Anglican and Presbyterian Churches, and over 7% belong to such smaller denominations as Lutheran-Baptist, Pentecostal, Mennonite and others.

A good example of this Ukrainian religious mosaic is Ottawa where out of the total of 2,985 in the 1961 census, the following religious adherences were claimed: Roman Catholic—935, Ukrainian Catholic—658, Greek Orthodox—588, United Church—359, Anglicans—264, Judaists—50, Presbyterians—49, Baptists—31, Lutherans—14, Pentecostal—11, others 56 [3]. Of the last ones named only the Baptist Church (Ukrainian Evangelical Baptist Alliance) is self-contained; all the others are dependent on the central boards of these churches. When we consider that in the beginning only Orthodox, Catholics and a few Baptists, better known as "Shtundisty", were coming to settle in Canada, then the present religious picture, with so many varieties of denominations among Ukrainians, is much different to what it was in the pioneer days. About the reason for these changes and their historical processes we have already informed our readers when we were dealing with the thematical matters of religion, encompassing the three eras. We only wish to underline here the process of religious assimilation and consequently disintegration.

A special category of assimilating processes results from mixed marriages. The 1961 statistics show that over 38% of Ukrainian marriages are of the above stated variety [4]. Out of this total 15% of the Ukrainians were married to Anglo-Saxons, over 3% to the French and over 20% to other nationalities—mostly to the Slavs. The highest number of homogenous marriages in Canada is registered among Indians and Eskimos (91.8%). Next come the Jews (91.1%), French (88.3%), British 81.2%, Asiatics (79.9%), Italians (76.6%). A much higher percentage of mixed marriages, in comparison to Ukrainians, is to be found among the following nationalities in Canada: Dutch (45.1%), Germans (48.0%), Poles (51.0%), Scandinavians (68.8%), etc [5].

When we put on the line the above given statistics, about the use of the native language in the home (64.4%), religious adherence (traditional churches—58.5%, and the homogenous marriages (61.8%), then the relative closeness of these figures will show very clearly that the homogenous marriages and the traditional churches (here we must also include the nationally oriented Evangelical churches) foster the cultivation of the native languages of their fathers, whereas on the other hand, the native language all but disappeared in the mixed marriages in which, for the sake of "matrimonial compromise", one of the official state languages is chosen, usually the English. The coefficient of the homogenous marriage runs parallel to the use of native language among such nationalities as French (88.3% and 90.0%), Poles (49.9% and 45.5%), Scandinavians (31.2% and 27.8%). An interesting observation about these statistics is the great disproportion that is shown in the coefficient relating to the Jews where the figure for homogenous marriage stands, as we have mentioned, at 91.1%, but the use of native language registers a mere 33.5% [6].

The statistical data which we have introduced above reveal that these

---

[3] All figures given according to census.
[4] Statistics takes into consideration the nationality of the father only.
[5] Census, 1961.
[6] This obvious evidence of language nullification among the Jews prompted them to great actions, which they have shown in the field of native schools during the last two decades. At present time we clearly see a great process of regeneration.

processes are taking place, to a greater or lesser degree, among all nationalities (ethnic groups) in Canada and that the Ukrainian group belongs to those nationalities that are the least inclined to assimilation.

In this respect the Ukrainian are second only to such great groups of Canada as French and British and to the original natives—the Indians and Eskimos. The Italian nationality cannot be included here as it represents the newer immigration element (only 41.1% were born in Canada, while the Ukrainian data stands at 76.7% of the Canadian-born). However, in spite of this show of immunity, the assimilating processes among Ukrainian Canadians are gradually graining ground in the sphere of language, church and family life by more than 30.0%. We have already pointed out that although these nullifications did not cross out the conscious awareness of one's own national (ethnic) origin, still in the onward march of history the possibilities may exist that would favor the growth of assimilation if the conscious and subconscious concept of national origin is not supported by word and deed. It is therefore easy to understand and to justify the great efforts that are being made by the Ukrainian society in the sphere of Ukrainian education in public schools, language and culture identification with such mobilizing mottos: "To be one's self in Canada", "The living Ukrainian language in Liturgy", "Native language in every parish", "In every Ukrainian home also a Ukrainian press", "A Ukrainian Patriarchate for the Ukrainian Church", and finally, the desire of the Ukrainian community to participate in the use of the modern communication and information media—radio, television, films— through which the rich culture of their people may be represented. No other era in the history of the Ukrainian Canadians could register such extremes—great cultural and political achievements on the one side, and the loss of mother tongue and denominational identification on the other.

Undoubtedly the Ukrainians will be interested to see the patterns of other ethnic groups of Canada that have lost in the language and religious sphere to a much greater degree than Ukrainians and whose mixed marriages have exceded 50.0%, but who still feel themselves to be a part of their original national group—in spite of these cultural losses in their national identity. We have a good example of this in the Icelandic Canadian community which has almost completely lost its mother tongue but still manages to retain very strong ethnic feelings that are so often manifested on the pages of the Icelandic English press [7]. In view of these and other similar (Jews—for instance) arguments, we must state that the potential power of any community will only last as long as the consciousness of its national identity remains and the backbone of the community is strong.

We are living in an era when the feeling of ethnic or national origin has reached the highest level of esteem on all the continents. This is especially true in the lands of American democracies. Even the most relentless theorists of the American "melting pot" variety are falling back, step by step, judging by the latest printed works, such as Joshua Fishman's "Language Loyalty in the United States" and others. According to Fishman's book over 20 million Americans, in addition to the official country language, speak and want to retain the language of their fathers. Sociolo-

---

[7] "The Icelandic Canadian" published in the English language for the last 25 years, but always showing a high degree of Icelandic patriotism.

gical research studies in U.S.A. reveal that the third generation of settled immigrants are turning their faces toward the past of their national origin. M. L. Hansen gives us hundreds of examples of the idiomatic truth that "what the son wants to forget, the grandson desires to perpetuate (preserve)." In another part of his book he states: "Anyone who has the courage to codify the laws of history must include what can be designated as the principle of the third generation interest" [8]. The ethnic identification is more of a functional type rather than the symbolic kind, which had existed in the second generation, and takes into consideration not only the bare symbolical interpretation, but also its natural value. What the son considered to be an ideology, that was forced upon him by his father, the grandson regards highly as an information medium and a treasured history. We must strongly expect that the same laws of history will apply to the Ukrainian third generation in Canada.

If we take into consideration the conscious striving of the active Ukrainian community to oppose the assimilating processes in the lingual and cultural field, and the honest conviction of the government circles that depriving the national entities of their language and cultural values only acts to the detriment of Canada, making it that much poorer in its spiritual content — gaining instead only groups of "cultured" nihilists - and finally seeing that the natural propelling force of every society renews itself at certain intervals in future generations, as shown by modern sociology, then we may assume that assimilating processes will face in the near future much stronger opposition than they have had before. On the contrary, all arguments point to the fact that in the sphere of language and culture a turn-about-face action, toward the past, is coming into its own. In evidence of this we have numerous publications on the occasion of the 90th Anniversary of the Ukrainian settlement in Canada amply proving that the past not only holds interest for the authors of history books, but also for the whole society, especially the young generation. To illustrate this fact we refer our readers to the mass gathering of youth in Montreal and Ottawa on the occasion of Canada's Centennial anniversary, including the installation of the Ukrainian memorial plaque in the National Library in Ottawa. Very noticeable indeed is the participation of youth in various conventions and anniversary celebrations. About these participations one weekly newspaper made the following remark: "The most pleasing phenomenon to behold was the mass participation of youth. Out of the total of 486 registrations 198, or 40% belonged to the young people. Those who had the occasion to see the youth perform on the stage during the final concert program, must have had their faith renewed and their hopes raised that the Ukrainian culture will live and thrive in Canada for many years to come'"[9].

---

[8] Marcus L. Hansen in "The Immigration in American History", 1952, p. 496.
[9] "Ukrainian Voice" No. 30-32, 1967 — "After the Convention" — thoughts on the occasion of the Jubilee Convention of S.U.S.

Underlining this somewhat over optimistic view, we cannot, at the same time overlook and not be aware of critical and disturbing voices about the state of Ukrainian culture and language in Canada.

In this we include the authoritative voice and stand taken by Prof. Manoly Lupul, Director of Canadian Institute of Ukrainian Studies, University of Alberta, who in his writings and speeches portrays a very critical condition of Ukrainian language and culture in Canada* and Ukraine. This scholar has based his views upon personal observations (his visit to Ukraine) and statistics that reveal the loss of language in Ukraine through forceful russification through deliberate spreading of Russian language in the building up so-called "Soviet Nation". Then, again, in Canada the heritage languages are losing ground due to the process of assimilation, limited usage and indifference towards multiculturalism.** If we balance the optimistic and the alarming voices then we have to assume that the problem lies at least in the centre of contrasting views. In spite of this we must underline the fact that the critical views of this situation prevail over the optimistic ones.

In order to improve the situation in Canada the public opinion the critics feel, that must undergo a change in its outlook towards other languages and assume a more friendly and positive attitude, especially on the part of leaders and members of governments in relation to education. A cooperation is necessary on the part of political and educational leaders in order to change the attitude of citizens towards multilingual studies so they would correspond with the same attitude and fervour which they express in their festive declarations.

Here we have to emphasize that the seventies brought much more light on the discussed situation. Therefore the reader will find more upon this theme in the chapter dealing with Ukrainian studies and the school system in the "Decade of Multiculturalism" (see chapters: "Expansion of Ukrainian Studies Courses" and "School Question in the Period of Multiculturalism").

---

*In 1971 of 580,660 Ukrainians in Canada only 22.8% used Ukrainian as the language of speech in the home, although 48.9% know the mother tongue. See Statistical Compendium, Part II, p. 223.

**"Ukrainian News", Edmonton, Jan. 28, 1971, Manoly Lupul: Critical State of Ukrainianism in Canada.

DECADE OF MULTICULTURALISM

GROWING TOGETHER
ANNIVERSARY

ANNIVERSAIRE
S'ÉPANOUIR ENSEMBLE

Official logo to comemorate the Tenth Anniversary of the
Multiculturalism Program, Government of Canada.

A DECADE OF DEVELOPMENT OF CONSTITUTIONAL GROUNDS FOR MULTICULTURAL CANADA

It must be confirmed that the hearing of the Royal Commission on Bilingualism and Biculturalism under the co-chairmanship of A. Davidson Dunton, and André Laurendeau, created by the Federal Government of Prime Minister Lester B. Pearson in 1963, precipitated and aroused the interest of Canadians in the cultural and political problems of their country, not only of Anglo-Saxons and French, for whom it was basically established. It also brought into the arena the question of the cultural contribution of the ethnic groups in Canada. To be more specific, the ethnocultural groups took advantage of this to show to the public forum with sufficient proof that in Canada, in addition to the historical Anglo-French problems, there also existed the problems of other ethnic groups, who through many decades, were treated as if they were the children of a harsh stepmother.

Numerous briefs and memoranda spilled upon the scene, which claimed that multiculturalism was the basic principle of Canadian identity. The arguments were so convincing that the government had the Royal Commission on Bilingualism and Biculturalism include in its terms of reference "contribution made by other ethnic groups to the cultural enrichment of Canada and the measures that should be taken to safeguard that contribution."

The tabled Book IV of the Royal Commission on Bilingualism and Biculturalism accepted multiculturalism as a national policy within a bicultural framework. "Immigrants, according to Book IV, regardless of ethnic-cultural origin or mother tongue, "should choose to integrate with either of the two societies — English or French. Integration did not force the loss of an individual's identity and original characteristics, or of original language and culture,"[1] the Commissioners stated in their report.

Although this recommendation was not synonymous with assimilation which implied total absorption into another linguistic and cultural group, it did create a middle road for it.

On October 8, 1971, in the House of Commons, Prime Minister Pierre E. Trudeau proclaimed "urbi et orbi" clearly the existence of multicultural Canada and Federal Government Multicultural Policy. A day later, the same was solemnly declared by P. E. Trudeau at the 10th Congress of Ukrainian Canadians in Winnipeg.

Historically, this was the last nail driven into the coffin of colonial Canada. A new epoch was being born which basically was altogether different from the previous one.

Now the subject of multiculturalism within the framework of biculturalism and bilingualism was taken up more and more bravely, and upon a basis of principle by those who held conferences on themes of cultural mosaic and

---

[1] *Multiculturalism and the Government of Canada,* published by Minister of State: 1978, revised 1980. p. 10.

heritage languages in such provinces, as Manitoba, Alberta, Ontario and Quebec. In general, the stream of Canadian political thinking, in Western Canada, went further than the Royal Commission in matters of bilingualism and biculturalism. At the above-mentioned conferences, representatives of ethnic-cultural groups raised their voices not only about the input of ethnic culture in the development of Canada, but they also spoke how this cultural implementation should be preserved and developed on language and cultural basis.

For the historical record and to get a better insight into the cultural situation of Canada which existed prior to Prime Minister Trudeau's parliamentary declaration re: multicultural Canada, which became a new cornerstone of modern Canada, it should be mentioned that many conferences were held at the end of the sixties and the beginning of the seventies at which new progressive ideological propositions were advanced and thoroughly discussed. The most significant would be:

In 1968, December 13-15th, Canadian Cultural Rights Committee of Toronto held 'Thinkers' Conference to study Canada's multicultural patterns. The conference was chaired by Senator Paul Yuzyk, who already in 1964 in his maiden speech in the Senate, spoke emphatically of Canada as a multicultural nation.

In 1970, August 7-8, a public conference was held in Toronto again under the slogan: "Canada Multicultural." This conference was sponsored by the Ukrainian Canadian University Students' Union of the University of Toronto and financially assisted by the provincial and federal governments. In the same year, on August 28-29, a conference was held at the University of Alberta, in Edmonton. The slogan was "Multiculturalism for Canada." This conference, too, was sponsored by the Ukrainian Canadian University Students' Union.

Also in 1970 Manitoba as a whole (government and citizens) was working on another multicultural conference. The theme was "Cultural Mosaic". Over 400 representatives from 28 nationalities including English, French, Irish and Scotch of the Province of Manitoba spent five days in work shops with discussions on a number of papers read at the conference. At the end of the conference, Ed Schreyer, the Premier of Manitoba, concluded his speech with these words: "I would propose, to look at this mosaic congress not as its ending, but rather the beginning. For the Manitobans, as well as for all Canadians, it could be the start of a new era of relationship between many cultures that form our mosaic and our heritage."[2]

The spoken words of the Premier harmonized with the unanimous resolutions of the Mosaic Conference of Manitoba. We might say that the Manitoba multicultural mosaic, in which Ukrainians took an active part (124 out of 400 present), made a first breakthrough in Canadian conservative thinking. For the record, we have to state that in October, 1970, Manitoba as one voice pronounced that Canada is a multicultural and multilingual country, and that all those who work for the government on all levels are duty bound to support this multicultural and multilingual program as a typical trait of Canadian identity. The concept of multiculturalism and multilingualism spread in

---

[2]*Svoboda Daily,* New Jersey, October 21, 1970.

Western Provinces of Canada like a prairie fire fanned by a high wind. Alberta followed in Manitoba's footsteps, whose Premier A. Strom, of the Social Credit Party developed (1971) a plan which was to give material support for the component cultures of the province. Evidently, Alberta took an even further step, declaring its financial aid. The same aid was also offered by the Alberta Conservatives, who under the premiership of Peter Lougheed, came to power in the middle of that year. In 1971 two conferences were held in Ottawa. In May, was organized the International Symposium on Languages and Cultures, sponsored by the Inter-university Committee and Canadian Slavs where the Canadian Ethnic Studies Association was formed, and in September "Policy Conference on the Preservation and Development of Ukrainian Culture in Canada." There were other conferences.

These and similar conferences moved social thinking and consciousness of the nation. They brought to the surface a series of problems from the past, not only cultural discrimination but also cultural nihilism and together with these they brought into full view many long years of struggle for cultural existence of various groups in Canada. In comparison with this, there also arose higher elements of cultural pluralism which in the future history of Canada will play the role of cementing ingredients in the building of the Canadian nation. This cultural pluralism will become the Canadian denominator which would also create a strong force in opposing the extreme right and extreme left elements, who in the name of political doctrines deny the natural democratic process of national development.

A notable input into development of this progressive idea was made by the young generation which shook itself free from all former prejudices and marched bravely towards the prestigious solution for all Canadian-National components. It would be timely to state that Ukrainian Canadian University Students' Union and its clubs played an important role by sponsoring several national conferences.[3]

It took over two years, from the time when the Royal Commission on Bilingualism and Biculturalism presented its report and recommendations, until Prime Minister P. E. Trudeau proclaimed that Canada was a multicultural nation. These were the years when on the scale of history the future of Canada was weighed. Even after the historical declaration of multicultural Canada was accepted by all parties, a creative process of cultural fermentation still continued.

In 1972, a second conference of various nationalities of Alberta took place, known officially as: "Alberta Cultural Heritage Conference." At this conference, the government and people expressed their agreement on the question of Canadian mosaic. The same year the Ontario Heritage Conference approved program topics which were totally in agreement with the resolutions held at the previous Alberta conference.

Almost at the same time the Ukrainians of Quebec, held their conference in Montreal, manifested in their resolutions friendship towards cultural emancipating processes of the French people in Quebec and declared their support for other ethnocultural groups in Canada in their endeavour to achieve their cultural self-existence.

---

[3] *Toronto Telegram,* May 26, 1971. "Students work on ethnic culture."

On the 16th of March, 1972, Joint Parliamentary Commission of the Senate and the House of Commons on Canadian Constitution spoke again that Canada was a country "characterized by rich diversity in linguistic communities, cultural heritage and regional identities; a country where individual fulfillment is the fundamental goal of society." Two more significant conferences were held in 1973; in Toronto "National Conference on Canadian Culture and Ethnic Groups" and in Ottawa where "the First Canadian Conference on Multiculturalism" was held by the Secretary of State with Stanley Haidasz, the first Secretary of State in charge of the multiculturalism policy.

It would seem that all these omens pointed to the principle of a multilingual and a multicultural Canada and should, without any difficulties, be embodied into the new Canadian Constitution.

In the seventies multilingualism and multiculturalism repeatedly became the topic of discussion not only at the meetings of provincial premiers with the federal government, but also by the mass media throughout Canada. When the constitutional battle landed also in the House of Commons and the Senate, the Ukrainian Canadian Committee through its spokesman presented to the Joint Parliamentary Committee of Senate and the House of Commons on Constitution on July 28, 1980 another brief underlining the fact that Canada is a country "where *individual and group* fulfillment is the fundamental goal of society."

Continuing in this same vein the Ukrainian representatives demanded that the Charter of Human Rights should be included in the Constitution as well as the guarantees for the ethnocultural societies, for their development of cultures and languages which would assure individual citizens and ethnocultural groups equal opportunity to participate in all aspects of government and community life. Also the Ukrainian representatives placed an accent on changing "The Official Languages Act" (approved in 1969). They demanded that Canadian Languages Act should recognize all languages rooted in Canada as Canadian languages. This recommendation sounded in full as follows:

"In view of the fact that section 38 of the Official Languages Act provides merely for the toleration of Canadian languages other than English and French, and does not recognize any responsibility of The Government of Canada for the linguistic development of Canadian citizens other than those of the two largest ethnic groups: (1) Therefore we submit that section 38 of the Official Languages Act be amended to recognize all languages of Canada towards these languages, and we further sumbit that the Official Languages Act and the Commissioner of Official Languages be renamed as "Canadian Languages Act" and as "Commissioner of Languages of Canada" respectively.[4]

How did the political activists respond to all these demands that flowed from the direction of Ukrainians and other ethnocultural communities? On the whole, the response was very silent. About this condition a very pointed outlook was expressed by one of the leading Ukrainian activists in this way: "How frightful all this becomes when you start to think that when the time came to write a new Canadian Constitution then the politicans involved with

---

[4]*Progress Weekly*, No. 36 (995), September 21, 1980.

multiculturalism, proclaimed ten years earlier, seemed to have suffered a lapse of memory.[5]

How to explain this silence? In the first place, the provincial premiers were responsible for it. At the debate about the Constitution they always defended the principle that it was their lawful domain to solve the cultural affairs in their provinces, especially regarding education and the teaching of heritage languages. There is still another answer. It is tightly bound with the psychological ballast of the past colonial politics, not yet excluded, and that under the cover of the principle of Canadian multicultural identity the old melting pot was still simmering.

In spite of this stand by politicians, the Ukrainian community cannot indulge in self-reprobation because multicultural Canada together with the multilingual problems as well as the Constitutional questions have not paid sufficient attention. And more so, the Ukrainians of Canada can proudly state that they have contributed their own very heavy input into it. Here we may mention that in addition to the many conferences and number of briefs submitted, very important work was done by Roy Romanow, Attorney General of Saskatchewan, who together with the Federal Minister Jean Chretien, headed the Constitutional Commission of Canada as its co-chairmen; Laverne Lewycky, as a representative of N.D.P., also took part in this Commission. Walter Tarnopolsky, Professor of Political Law, appeared before the Commission with a brief in the name of the Canadian Civil Liberties Association and about a half dozen of his propositions were incorporated into the Constitution. The brief from Canadian Consultative Council on Multiculturalism presented by its chairman Lawrence Decore, contributed to the inclusion of section 27 in the Constitution. On behalf of Ukrainian Canadian Committee, briefs were submitted by UCC president J. Nowosad, Professor Orest Rudzik, A. J. Yaremovich and Professor Manoly Lupul who represented the Canadian Institute of Ukrainian Studies. There were briefs from individual Ukrainian citizens (e.g. Professor J. B. Rudnyckyj). It is timely here to mention a few other individuals who constantly were working on these problems at the UCC constitutional "laboratory" such as Dr. Isidore Hlynka, Dr. Peter Kondra, Dr. Serge Radchuk, Dr. J. S. Kalba and others.

And what has been accomplished so far for the ethnocultural groups in the new Canadian Constitution during all those long years of endeavours? Various answers could be given to this question... from the extremely pessimistic to the extremely optimistic. There are two sections in the Canadian Constitution dealing with some aspects of multiculturalism and multilingualism. Section 27 referring to multiculturalism and section 22 under the heading "Official Languages of Canada" dealing with the Canadian ethnocultural (comprising of sections 16-24) multilingualism. Section 27 reads as follows:

"This chapter shall be interpreted in a manner consistent with the preservation and enhancement of the multicultural heritage of Canadians." Section 22 of "Official Languages of Canada" says: "Nothing in sections 16-20 abrogates or derogates from any legal or customary right of privilege acquired or

---

[5]*New Pathway,* Toronto, No. 47, 1981, Peter Savaryn: Canadian Foundation for Ukrainian Studies.

enjoyed either before or after the coming into force of this charter with respect to any language that is not English or French."

While section 27 is simple and clear, to some degree, section 22 dealing with heritage languages is complicated and imperceptible. No doubt much discussion has been aroused regarding this section among Ukrainian Canadians. Roy Romanow, one of the fathers of the new Constitution, characterized it in Edmonton on the occasion of the 90th Anniversary of the Ukrainian Settlement in Canada as follows: "This is just the beginning statement and that Canada is a country of many cultures."[6]

It is quite obvious that the struggle for ethnocultural organization to assert a dignified position in Canada is still ahead.

In spite of this, the beginnings of great changes have been made. We may assume that they will continue when we take into consideration that when the first constitution of Canada was adopted in 1867 the population of Canada consisted of 60 percent of British descent, 31 percent French decent, and 9 percent of other origins. Today, Canadians of other origins comprise 30 percent (27 percent in 1971), the British stock fluctuated as high as 44 percent, while the French fluctuated to 29 percent.

Here we pose the question what changes took place as a result of aid given by the Federal Government for the benefits of Canadian multiculturalism during the least ten years?

In 1971 the Minister of Multiculturalism was appointed; in 1972 the Canadian Consultative Council on Multiculturalism (CCCM) of 101 members was formed. This is an appointed body, comprised of various leading activists of ethnocultural societies. CCCM consults with and advises Minister for Multiculturalism, the Government on the development of multicultural programs and policies in Canada. CCCM consists of a National Chairman, five National Vice-chairmen, 10 chairmen for the provinces and two representatives for the Yukon Territory and the Northwest Territories. In 1980-1982 the chairman of CCCM was Lawrence Decore, a lawyer of Edmonton, past President of the Ukrainian Professional and Businessmen's Club and a former Secretary of the Ukrainian Canadian Committee in Edmonton. A number of other prominent Ukrainians have served on the CCCM, e.g. Professor M. Lupul (1973-1980), Professor W. Tarnopolsky, Professor P. Kondra, M. Plawiuk, Dr. Stephanie Potoski, Emily Ostapchuk, Dr. R. Olynyk (1974-1979), Patricia Sembaliuk, Ted Glowacki, Q.C., Bill Pidruchney, Ivan Boyko, and others.

The executive of the Minister of Multiculturalism is the Directorate of Multiculturalism which was chaired (taking since the beginning, by Jennifer McQueen, Michael Andrassy) for sometime and lately by Orest Kruhlak, who is credited with the following richly worded expression: "We cannot continue to pretend to be a nation if we deny our contemporary pluralistic character." In 1982 the post was assumed by Kerry Johnston.

The Multiculturalism Directorate is comprised of three larger divisions; literary, educational and historical.

---

[6]*Edmonton Journal,* November 28, 1981, "Romanow: A Father of New Canada" by Mary Trueman.

Beginning in 1980 it published a bi-monthly newsletter (English and French) entitled "Cultures Canada" with the subtitle of "Newsletter of Multiculturalism-Directorate, Department of the Secretary of State."

The resources apportioned for multicultural purposes are important. In 1974-1975 the Directorate had at its disposal $8,1500,000, in 1979-1980 fiscal year, $7,783,000. At the same time $190,179,000 was spent on bilingualism with $175 million for "Official Languages in Education."[7] The designated amount for multiculturalism had to cover the administration, pamphlets, publications and various projects of the three divisions. Undoubtedly, this is a meagre amount of funds for the cultural needs of the one-third of Canadian population, when compared with the amount spent on "Official Languages."

These and other reasons impelled the ethnocultural societies of Canada to unite in the so-called "Council of National Ethnocultural Organizations of Canada." This action started in 1979, in Ottawa, during the meeting of the "initiators of ethnic centres" of Canada. The Ukrainian group was represented by Dr. S. Radchuk, president of the UCC at that time. A Founding Conference was held in Toronto, in April 1980. This founding conference was attended by the presidents and representatives of about 40 national ethnocultural organizations,[8] which publish 200 ethnic newspapers and periodicals in over 30 languages. If united, this could be a powerful voice and force, with clear dynamic goals and visions.

Vegreville Pysanka (Easter Egg). It symbolizes the harmony, vitality and culture of the community. It measures 25'7" x 18.3'

---

[7] *The Political Implementation of Multiculturalism* by Manoly R. Lupul. Paper presented to the 9th Biennial Conference Canadian Ethnic Studies Association, Edmonton, October 17, 1981.

[8] *Council Newsletter:* "The Official Newsletter of the Council of National Ethnocultural Organizations of Canada," Toronto, July, 1981.

EXPANSION OF UKRAINIAN STUDIES COURSES

The First All-Canadian Conference on the Ukrainian Studies Courses.

The last decade of Ukrainian Canadian history shows that a great deal of effort was expended on Ukrainian Studies at the university level. Impetus to this question was given by the first All-Canadian Conference on Ukrainian Studies Courses, which was held in Winnipeg on April 6-7, 1974, under the auspices of the Ukrainian Canadian Committee. Participants consisted of 47 professors of Canadian universities; Edmonton, Calgary, Regina, Saskatoon, Winnipeg, Waterloo, Hamilton, Toronto, Ottawa, Montreal, 15 invited guests, and also five graduate students (aspirants). At the conference a summary of discipline of Ukrainian Studies at the Canadian universities was presented. The leadership in this field was held by the University of Saskatchewan where Professor Kost Andrusyshen already in 1945 established a chair of Ukrainian Language Studies. At that time when Slavic studies had 25 years of accomplished in Winnipeg, Edmonton, Ottawa, and Toronto, the social disciplines like demography, anthropology, economics, geography, sociology and political sciences at some universities were being introduced and treated in a fragmented manner. In 1974 only two universities, Winnipeg and Edmonton were offering courses in Ukrainian history and only University of Alberta established a permanent chair in the studies of History of Ukraine under the direction of Professor Ivan Rudnytsky with the financial support from the Ukrainian Canadian Foundation of Taras Shevchenko. Of the above six mentioned disciplines (aside from history of Ukraine) there were 29 lecturers of Ukrainian descent.[1]

In addition, the conference was concerned with the following questions: problems of teaching Ukrainian languages, literature, history of Ukraine and other Ukrainian social subjects and finally problems of research and publications in the field of Ukrainian Studies and last but not least co-ordination and financing studies in universities in Canada.

Eight speakers and 11 commentators, with Senator P. Yuzyk as Chairman of Conference, created a stimulating atmosphere. St. Andrew's College hosted all participants at the campus with a dinner at which Professor M. Lupul elaborated quite broadly about co-ordination and financing research and studies. In connection with speeches and proposals, a number of resolutions were adopted and among them the proposal of a creation of a Canadian Institute of Ukrainian Studies with aid from the four Western Provincial Governments. They would co-ordinate and support financially Ukrainian and Ukrainian-Canadian studies in Canada. The conference also welcomed the establishment of Ukrainian Studies Centre at the University of Ottawa, which was made possible due to the most generous donations by Nadia Iwachniuk, M.D., and Anton Iwachniuk, Engineer in Toronto.

---

[1] Bohdan Bociurkiw: *"Situation, Problems, and Prospects in the Field of Ukrainian Social Studies at Canadian Universities"*, paper at the conference, Historical Publications Archives.

Although resolutions were approved unanimously there were a few optimists. However, there were pessimists, who questioned the possibility of a breakthrough, among the same unconcerned provincial governments, to obtain financial support for the planned institute on a university level. Primarily, the conference felt that the three Western provinces, Alberta, Manitoba, and Saskatchewan were morally obligated to support the projects financially because this is where Ukrainian pioneers contributed immensely to the opening of the West. They were among the first to break the virgin lands. Also the majority of Ukrainian Canadian population is located here. The conference elected a seven member *ad hoc* committee whose duty was to organize a standing committee on Ukrainian studies which would further the project.

Role of the Federation of Ukrainian Professional and Businessmen's Clubs in the Development of Ukrainian Studies.

Before we arrive at the essence of the topic, it is necessary to picture the process of the Federation and underscore the importance of the above-mentioned organization in the seventies in Ukrainian Canadian life, but first let us say a few words about its organizational background.

The organizational beginnings of the professional and businessmen's clubs date to the 1930's. Some representatives of these clubs participated already in Chicago at the Ukrainian Professional Association Convention. Two clubs were being established at this time in Toronto and Winnipeg.[2]

More intensive work was done in 1934-35. During and after the Second World War more interest was shown among the Professional and Businessmen's Club; subsequently, new clubs were formed. It was finally felt there was a need to unite various clubs into one federation.

The idea for an association or federation can be traced to Winnipeg. In the spring of 1959, in view of the forthcoming Congress of the UCC slated for July 9th-12th, the Executive of the Winnipeg Club under the Chairmanship of M. A. Mitenko decided to extend an invitation to the members of other UP & BCs throughout Canada to attend a special meeting in Winnipeg to discuss UP & BC matters of mutal interest. A special committee to look into that matter was elected and consisted of: V. J. Swystun, John G. Karasevich, Sr., Dr. I. Hlynka, J. Shanski, and F. James. The meeting, at which UP and BC members, guests and delegates to the 6th Congress of the UCC were introduced to the members of the Winnipeg Club, was held on July 10th, 1959, at the Empire Hotel. It is interesting to mention that this first national dinner meeting of the representatives of the UP & B Clubs was addressed by Lester B. Pearson, who was the leader of the Liberal Party of Canada at that time, and later became the Prime Minister of Canada. One of the duties of the proposed new organization was to assist in the formation of new clubs. At the following Executive meeting of the Winnipeg Club a new committee was formed, again under the chairmanship of V. J. Swystun, to investigate the formation of a federation. It consisted of Judge John R. Solomon, J. M. Hawryluk, P. Krepiakevich, F. James, J. Shanski and John Yuzyk, as members. A year

---

[2] More about the topic see chapter "Third Stage (pp. 424-428) and Professional and Businessmen's Clubs" (pp. 580-581).

later, on October 22nd and 23rd, 1960, V. J. Swystun and J. M. Hawryluk, attended an organizational meeting at Toronto, where the idea to organize a federation was approved again, and plans were made for founding a "convention" of the representatives of the Ukrainian Professional and Businessmen's Club in 1962.

The proposed convention of representatives of various Ukrainian Professional and Businessmen's Club indeed was held, on July 7, 1962, with V. J. Swystun as Chairman, S. Radchuk, and W. Ratuski, as Secretaries at Winnipeg. The following clubs were represented: Hamilton, Montreal, Vancouver, Fort William, Ottawa, Toronto, Oshawa, Windsor, Regina, Edmonton, Dauphin and Winnipeg. After the addresses of Honourable J. B. Carroll, Manitoba, Minister of Labour and Monsignor Wasyl Kushnir, President of the UCC, the first executive was elected as follows: V. J. Swystun (chairman), Serge Radchuk, Ewhen Wasylyshyn, and John N. Decore, with presidents of the existing clubs as members. Before the delegates went home, decisions were made that the Edmonton Club would draw up a constitution; Toronto would take care of the resolutions and Winnipeg promote memberships, while Vancouver prepared publications. During the next three years, V. J. Swystun visited a number of clubs, gathering data on form, and aims of the federation, and prepared the first official convention of the Ukrainian Professional and Businessmen's Clubs, slated for October 9-11, 1965 at Winnipeg. Well prepared, this was formally called the first National Convention and was attended by 45 members-representatives of 12 clubs across Canada, who made a formal decision to form a Federation of Ukrainian Professional and Businessmen's Clubs, elected the Federation's Executive and decided to publish the *Ukrainian Canadian Review,* a bilingual publication. Elected were: Senator Paul Yuzyk, Honorary president; V. J. Swystun, president; and Dr. Joseph Boyko, Serge Radchuk, Peter Savaryn, John M. Hawryluk, with all the presidents of the clubs and members of the Executive.[3] The key speaker at this convention was Honorable Paul Martin, Secretary of State for External Affairs.

After the early death of the first president of the Federation, Vsevolod J. Swystun in 1966, Serge Radchuk became acting president and headed the Federation until October 12th, 1968, when the Convention (2nd) elected the Executive, consisting of Mark B. Smerchanski, Dr. Joseph Boyko, Nicholas Kraychy, Gregory J. Ratuski, John M. Hawryluk, Ray Bryk and Walter Hlady. Senator Paul Yuzyk remained as honourary president and all the presidents of the clubs became ex-officio members of the Executive. This was the 2nd National Executive formally elected.

In the twenty years of its existence the Federation has held ten conventions. At first the conventions were not elaborately structured and were not regularly held. From the early seventies there was a significant change in the organization of conventions and in the style of work. Resolutions approved by the September, 1972 Convention at Toronto spoke for a new dynamic approach. Resolutions Committee consisted of I. Bardyn, A. Gregorovich, M. Sorokolit, E. Fedak, Dr. I. Hlynka, B. Doliszny, M. Strokan and S. Shabbitts.

---

[3]*Anniversary Review 1943-1968* published by Ukrainian Professional and Businessmen's Club, Winnipeg, S. Radchuk: Federation of the Ukrainian Professional and Businessmen's Clubs of Canada.

Under the chairmanship of Peter Savaryn, 11 resolutions were presented and several of them are pertinent so as to be quoted here because of their significant value and further action.

The Federation decided "to take steps to strengthen the social economic and cultural life of its members", "to encourage the maintenance of the Ukrainian National identity in Canada and fully support the causes of multiculturalism"; "to encourage the clubs and members to participate actively in Ukrainian Canadian organized life and to support it morally and financially", "to support its members to play an active role in Canadian political life at all levels and also in non-Ukrainian organizations", "to increase the political activities and lines of communications between the Federation and all levels of Government in Canada."

In Toronto the Federation was conducted under the chairmanship of Stanley Frolick with the following members: Michael Starr, Joseph Slogan, Manoly Lupul, Ihor Bardyn, Emil Fedak, Edward Topornicki. Following 1973, the convention main office was transferred to Edmonton and the accepted resolutions at the Toronto convention gave new impetus to the newly elected board under the presidency of Professor Manoly Lupul consisting of Lawrence Decore, Dr. Joseph Slogan, Peter Buyer, Professor Walter Tarnopolsky, Dr. Orest Talpash, Peter Oluk, Edward Kay, Peter Savaryn, William Diachuk, M.L.A., Orest Eveneshen.

Canadian Institute of Ukrainian Studies and Canadian Founation for Ukrainian Studies

The Ukrainian Canadian Professional and Business Federation brought to fruition two important projects which shortly put this Federation at the very front of Ukrainian community life. They were the Canadian Institute of Ukrainian Studies and the Canadian Foundation for Ukrainian Studies.

Following the first all-Canadian Conference on the Ukrainian Studies Courses in Winnipeg previously mentioned, the Ukrainian Canadian Professional and Business Federation in co-operation with the *ad hoc* committee took upon itself the responsibility to accept and bring to realization resolutions of the conference in regards to establishing a Ukrainian Institute. Concrete steps were taken not only before the provincial government of Alberta, but also before the governments of Saskatchewan, Manitoba and Ontario. There were many responses and procrastinations but basically it was difficult for the various governments to establish a financial formula which could be applicable for the respective authorities. There were other reasons, and the most important one was probably due to the fact, the project was promoted in the third year after the establishment of the Federal Government's policy of multiculturalism. The champions of this project, Peter Savaryn and Manoly Lupul, did not bow to these difficulties. Manoly Lupul in his editorial titled "Canadian Institute of Ukrainian Studies" disclosed that political contacts through Ald. L. Decore, W. Diachuk, M. A. and P. Savaryn, member of the University of Alberta, Board of Governors and Senate were of great assistance in the realization of the project. Additional assistance was given by MLAs: Mrs. C. Chichak, Dr. K. Paproski, W. Skoreyko and members of

Cabinet Hon. Julian Koziak, Minister of Education and Hon. Dr. Albert Hohol, Minister of Advanced Education.[4]

Finally in combined efforts in 1976, the Government of Alberta made possible the establishment of the Institute with the funding of $350,000 a year in perpetuity. On June 18, 1976 the Board of Governors of the University of Alberta approved the establishment of the Canadian Institute of Ukrainian Studies (CIUS) on its university campus to serve the academic needs of Ukrainians in all parts of Canada.[5] At that time, CIUS ratified the following objectives:

1. To encourage programme development in Ukrainian studies at the undergraduate and graduate levels in Canadian universities.
2. To encourage research on Ukrainian Canadian and Ukrainian subjects by means of undergraduate scholarships, graduate thesis, fellowships and research grants, university academic staff and to proven scholars under contract.
3. To publish research on Ukrainian-Canadian and Ukrainian subjects and reprints of out-of-print books.
4. To serve as a national interuniversity clearing house for Ukrainian studies in Canada by co-ordinating program development and avoiding duplication in research and publication.
5. To serve as a resource centre for English-Ukrainian bilingual education and Ukrainian-language education in Alberta and elsewhere.
6. To assist in the establishment of creative contacts among professors, scholars, writers, researchers and librarians in Ukrainian studies by promoting and organizing meetings, seminars, lectures, conferences and tours.[6]

In the summer 1976 the Ontario Government also announced assistance for Ukrainian Studies. This happened due to the efforts of the following members living in Ontario, at this time namely S. Frolick, W. Tarnopolsky, I. Bardyn. The Ontario Government assured the interested parties that the grants would be alotted in co-operation with the Government of Alberta, and with the understanding that CIUS is a member of the body of the University of Alberta.

Ukrainian community in Western Canada accepted decisions of Alberta Government with great satisfaction and with much enthusiasm. CIUS is the first Institute on the American continent that established systematic financial assistance and subsidy from the government for Ukrainian Studies. It is self-evident that only in the democratic free world the CIUS can research its objective in promotion and research in the studies of Ukrainian humanities. This is in contrast to the doctrinal approach carried on in Ukraine under Marxist theory. CIUS brings to memory the works of Ukrainian Institute in Berlin till 1933 and Ukrainian Sociological Institute in Prague after the First World War.

---

[4]*Review,* May, 1977, Manoly Lupul; "The Canadian Institute of Ukrainian Studies."

[5]*Panorama,* 1977. Published by the National Executive of the Ukrainian Canadian Professional and Business Federation, edited by John Pankiw, "The Canadian Institute of Ukrainian Studies."

[6]*The Canadian Institute of Ukrainian Studies,* The University of Alberta, p. 5.

Canadian Institute of Ukrainian Studies is headed by Manoly Lupul, Professor of Canadian Education History at the University of Alberta, graduate of Harvard University, assisted by Professors Ivan Rudnytsky (research), and Yuriy Luckyj (publications), Toronto University. Later on Dr. B. Bociurkiw joined CIUS in research (Carleton University). The director of the CIUS is also assisted by an advisory council. The Council of Associates is made up of 40 members (professors of various universities) who work in Ukrainian Studies and related fields. Organizational work and research depends also on the academic staff of CIUS: I. Himka, A. Hornjatkevyč, B. Krawchenko, W. R. Petryshyn, F. Swyripa and others.

Together with the efforts in establishing CIUS, attempts were also made to create a foundation which would be the financial base for various CIUS projects. The idea of such a foundation was approved at an earlier date in the spring of 1975. The Foundation was incorporated under the name Canadian Foundation for Ukrainian Studies.

Since October 1975 the following have served as presidents of the Foundation: Stanley W. Frolick, Toronto (1975-76), Walter S. Tarnopolsky, Toronto (1976-77), Orest H. T. Rudzik, Toronto (1977-79) and Peter Savaryn since 1979. The Foundation is managed by a Board of Directors with executive, based in Edmonton. In 1980-81 it consisted of the following individuals: P. Savaryn in Edmonton, President, O. H. T. Rudzik, Ontario V.P. John Stashuk, B.C., V.P., R. F. Clark, Secretary, Len Kowalchuk, Treasurer. Other members of the Board were: Judge E. Boychuk, L. Decore, S. Frolick, R. Herchak, J. G. Karasevich, Jr., E. Huculak, Valerie Kasiurak, M. R. Lupul, G. R. B. Panchuk, Christine Pasterschank, Judge J. R. Solomon, W. S. Tarnopolsky, W. Werbeniuk, E. Zaraska. Due to P. Savaryn's efforts and his promotional ability, the Canadian Foundation for Ukrainian Studies became known and well established.

Chair of Ukrainian Studies at the University of Toronto

One of the corner stones in the realization of establishing Ukrainian Studies across Canada was the organizing of the chair of Ukrainian Studies at the University of Toronto. Attempts to establish such a chair were made before by the Branch of the Ukrainian Canadian Committee in Toronto. However, the funds did not justify at that time and the project did not materialize.[7] A change of phase takes place when the Ukrainian Canadian Professional and Business Federation and the Canadian Foundation for Ukrainian Studies accepted this program as their full responsibility. In 1975-76, Walter S. Tarnopolsky and S. Frolick again initiated discussions with the Government of Ontario regarding establishing of a chair of Ukrainian Studies. Attempts were made to organize a second centre within the framework of Canadian Institute of Ukrainian Studies in Eastern Canada. In 1977 Premier Davis of Ontario agreed on behalf of the Government of Ontario to grant $100,000.00 and the balance of funds totalling one million dollars was to be raised by the Ukrainian Community in Ontario.

---

[7] *Our Aim,* No. 20, 1981, "The Chair of Ukrainian Studies at the University of Toronto".

In 1978 the Federation made a submission to the Secretary of State, John Roberts, proposing that the Federal Government aid the Ukrainian Canadian Community by contributing one half of the required sum, namely $500,000. The Federation for its part committed itself to match this amount within one year. A team of enthusiastic people was working on the project namely O. H. T. Rudzik, Thos. Bardyn, George Danyliw, George Luckyj, Jurij Darewych and others.

Final arrangements to establish the chair of Ukrainian Studies were realized on March 29, 1979. Contracts were signed between the Corporation of Ukrainian Studies in Toronto and the University of Toronto on one part and the same Corporation signed another contract with the Federal Government. On behalf of the Corporation signatories were chairman George Danyliw and secretary Ewhen Zaraska. On this occasion, president of the University of Toronto, G. M. Ham, stated that the chair will embrace history of Ukraine, history of Ukrainian culture and political economy of Ukraine.[8] On behalf of the Federal Government Hon. N. Cafik, Minister of Multiculturalism signed the document and complimented the Federation for its initiative and financial assistance. He also emphasized that the chair of Ukrainian Studies in Toronto is an expression of principle of equality for all citizens of Canada. "Today, he said, we bring this principle into the field of science and humanities." Hon. Minister Cafik presented a cheque in the sum of $300,000 on behalf of the Federal Government and an equivalent sum was presented by the Canadian Foundation for Ukrainian Studies which due to the efforts mostly of Stan Frolick received from the Government of Ontario (Wintario grant). Dr. Paul R. Magocsi was appointed to the Chair. The Ukrainians were passing through a transition period at this time for which the pessimists, ten years previously, would have had no satisfactory answers. Even if the Federation had not accomplished anything else except these projects, the name of the Federation would still go down in the history of Ukrainian community in Canada as an outstanding achievement. The work of the Federation does not end during the decade of multiculturalism. Future references will be made, namely in connection with organizational life of Ukrainians in Canada, safe-guarding constitutional rights for ethnocultural groups, etc.

St. Andrew's College
The Centre for Ukrainian Canadian Studies at the University of Manitoba

During the time when Edmonton and Toronto were taking definite revolutionary steps to establish Ukrainian Studies at the respective universities, Winnipeg was passing through an evolutionary stage but in no way dragging its feet. St. Andrew's College, which had established itself in the sixties on the campus of the University of Manitoba, continued in its efforts to introduce (aside from existing theological disciplines) a system of complete Ukrainian Studies. This was partially accomplished during the principalship of Lucas Tomaschuk (1969-1974). In 1972, accredited courses by University of Manitoba were offered here in the field of Ukrainian studies, and this was part of a

---
[8] *Panorama*, 1979. "Chair of Ukrainian Studies, University of Toronto".

fulfillment of requirements to affiliate with the University of Manitoba. In due time, additional courses were added not only in the field of theology and language but also in the fields of history, political science, geography and arts.[9] The broadened programs led to final approval by the University for establishment of *The Centre for Ukrainian Canadian Studies* at the University of Manitoba. This act was signed on January 28, 1981. The position of the first director was occupied by Dr. Natalia Aponiuk, assistant professor of Slavic Studies at the University of Manitoba for a term of 4½ years. Although St. Andrew's College is basically a theological institution, the Centre of Ukrainian Studies at this college is to serve all Canadian students.

In 1981 St. Andrew's College celebrated its 35th Anniversary. It reminded everybody of its humble beginning at 259 Church Avenue in Winnipeg, at which time it was necessary to prepare students with Grade XI and XII. During the years the College had to overcome many problems. In spite of this, 115 graduated from the Faculty of Theology of which 92 were advanced as priests in the Ukrainian Orthodox Church (Canada and U.S.A.). Basic income of the St. Andrew's College were donations from the Ukrainian community and lately assistance from the Foundation which was organized in the later part of 1979.[10] Since 1974 the following were the principals of the College: Judge J. R. Solomon, Rev. M. Yurkiwsky, Dr. P. Kondra (1977-1981) and since 1981 Rev. Oleh Krawchenko. St. Andrew's College has a collection of approximately 45,000 volumes of which 24,000 are from the original library of Metropolitan Ilarion among which are some editions on Ukrainian paleography.

*New Establishments and Institutions —
Past and Present*

In 1981, *Ukrainian Catholic Theological Seminary* was established in Ottawa by the bishops of the Ukrainian Catholic Church under the direction of Metropolitan Maxim Hermaniuk. Rector of the Seminary became Rev. Josyf Andrijishyn.

In 1978 the *Ukrainian Mohylo-Mazepian Academy* (UMMAN) was established in Montreal — Philadelphia.. This learned society was headed by J. B. Rudnyckyj, Mykola Stepanenko, Olha Woycenko, Oleh S. Pidhayny and others. At the beginning of 1980, from within the same group, there was incorporated *Symon Petlura Institute* in Toronto, an educational, scientific non-profit corporation which actually started its work in 1977. Within both institutions the management consists (almost) of the same individuals. However UMMAN is limited to 12 members, whereas Symon Petlura Institute to 49. The Institute, headed by O. Pidhayny, was organized on the occasion of the 100th Anniversary of the birth of Symon Petlura, Ukrainian national leader during the First World War.

---

[9] *Report of the Senate Ad Hoc Committee to consider alternatives to creation affiliated college status for St. Andrew's College,* March 19, 1974, Historical Publications Archives.

[10] *St. Andrew's College News,* 1981, P.A. Kondra: Thirty-fifth Anniversary of St. Andrew's College.

During this decade we register further continuation of activities in the field of Ukrainian studies and research by the Ukrainian Academy of Arts and Sciences (UVAN) and Shevchenko Scientific Society (NTSh).

In 1973 *Shevchenko Scientific Society* (N.T.Sh.), Toronto, celebrated 100th Anniversary since its inception 1873 in Lviv, Ukraine. Until the liquidation of Shevchenko Scientific Society by the Communist regime in Ukraine, it fulfilled the historic role of Ukrainian studies and research. In 1979 NTSh celebrated 30th Anniversary of its inception in Canada. Since the demise of Dr. E. Vertyporoch in 1974 the institution has been headed by Dr. B. Stebelsky. There are two branches: Edmonton and Ottawa. Numerous conferences have been held every year within the organization with lectures on various topics. In the seventies NTSh published several larger publications namely "In Defence of Ukrainian Culture and People", "Commemorative Collection -- by Prof. Ewhen Wertyporoch" and others. The latest publication is the collection of essays and memoires under the title "Holocaust of the Ukrainian Nation and Culture." During the last few years at the head of the Shevchenko Scientific Society were: Dr. W. Mackiw, Dr. P. Bilaniuk, W. Weryha, Dr. O. Kopach, Prof. W. Janishewsky, Dr. I. Budurowych, Dr. I. Tesla and others.

Ukrainian Academy of Arts and Sciences in Winnipeg, previously known as Ukrainian Free Academy of Sciences, celebrated its 25th anniversary in 1975 with representatives from United States and from across Canada. On this occasion, there was published a collection of scholarly works which covered not only papers read at the conference on celebration, but also those on general Ukrainian and Canadian themes. During the last decade several other publications were produced such as "Ukrainian Canadians: A History", two volumes "Studies in the History of Ukrainian Canadians", "Series of Ukrainian Scholars", "Sources of Ukrainian Canadian History". On the occasion of the 90th anniversary of Ukrainian settlement in Canada UVAN realized three projects; revised the edition, "The Ukrainian Canadians: A History", "Biographical Dictionary to the History of Ukrainians in Canada" and English collection of essays on the Ukrainian Canadian theme.

During the last ten years UVAN was headed by Dr. Mykyta Mandryka, Dr. Jaroslaw Rozumnyj, Dr. Alexander Baran. Some of those who contributed freely of their time were: A. Kachor, Dr. I. Lubynsky, Dr. I. Tarnawecky, Dr. O. Gerus, S. Muchin, Dr. M. Marunchak. Of great value in UVAN is the *Military Historical Museum.*

The Research Institute of Volyn (Winnipeg) also has grown within the last decade. It expanded its publications to 20 volumes of scientific works in the field of history, ethnography, geography, literature, linguistic field and others. Volyn Research Institute was headed during the last decade by Dr. Serge Radchuk, and an editorial board consisted of Dr. Yuriy Mulyk — Lucyk, Associate members: M. Podworniak, E. Onufrijchuk, Rev. S. Yarmus, Rev. M. S. Kiciuk, Dr. Iraida Tarnawecky. The Research Institute of Volyn cooperates closely with the *Society of Volyn* which finances all publication projects.

Continuing within this decade with their programs were the following: *Markian Shashkevych Centre, The Research Institute "Studium"* of the Canadian League for the Liberation of Ukraine as well as professional associations whose membership was tied in more or less to some measure with scientific world and humanities as *"Ukrainian Teachers' Association"*, *"Association for Writers of Children's Literature"*, *"Ukrainian Medical Association of North America"*, *"Association of Engineers and Technicians in Canada"*, *"Association of Ukrainian Librarians in Canada."* Among professional organizations outstanding in activities is *Association of Ukrainian Canadian Veterinary Doctors* with such social activists like Dr. Myroslaw Nebeluk, author of several publications, Dr. S. Dershko, Dr. M. Hladyshewsky and others.

Big steps in expansion of *The Ukrainian Cultural and Educational Centre in Winnipeg* were made in the last decade, when UCE Centre at the Ukrainian National Federation Home for many years was transferred to more spacious premises at the "Ukrainian Pathway" Weekly Building, 184 Alexander Avenue. The Centre occupied two top stories where it was easy to accommodate at the beginning, the library, archives and museum. In addition to this a permanent gallery was opened. In 1971 during the time of transfer, a general meeting of the Centre was held and a number of young people were brought into the management who applied themselves very enthusiastically to programs of the Centre. This increased memberships, donations and exhibits. In 1971-73, the Centre was headed by Prof. J. Rozumnyj, and members of the Board were: W. Klymkiw, Z. Hayworon, R. Babick, W. Ratusky, W. Kaptiy, B. Klymkiw, C. Semchyshyn, S. Korbutiak, S. Muchin, S. Prystupa. Volunteers were of great help in promotion of various programs of the centre. In 1975 the building was purchased from the "New Pathway Publishers" and then began a second phase of reconstruction and expansion. In 1973-1976, the Centre was under the chairmanship of Wolodymyr Klymkiw. After him followed Dr. A. Baran, Z. Hayworon, S. Korbutiak, Dr. O. Gerus. As of January 1980, the five story building is fully operational. The centre has at its disposition a gallery of 1900 square feet of floor space and 250 running feet of walls.

In evaluating the general achievements of Ukrainian studies, and cultural projects during the last ten years, we have to confirm that this decade was rich and successful. This period crowned Ukrainian efforts similarly as the year 1940 was the climax of achieving the unity of Ukrainian Canadian organizations with the creation of Ukrainian Canadian Committee (U.C.C.). For much of this achievement Ukrainians are indebted to the initiative of U.C.C., as well as to the consistent work of the Federation of Ukrainian Professional and Businessmen. The decade of recognition of multiculturalism became a fertile soil for a healthy seed.

Today the research in the field of Ukrainian studies is carried in two directions. Institutions that have occupied themselves with this task for many long years continue their work, basically in Ukrainian language — UVAN, Shevchenko Scientific Society, while the pedagogues and research studies at the universities including the Canadian Institute of Ukrainian Studies are carried on in English.

Thus we must add the fact that the young generation prefers to use in research the English rather than Ukrainian language, as English is the working language, beginning with the pre-school years. For them heritage language is the second language. In some cases it does not even exist. At times, this may act as a negative factor to a further expansion of Ukrainian studies, especially since the researchers, from the utilitarian point of view have ceased to derive any benefit from the prime sources in their studies which, in the first place, are in Ukrainian language — Ukrainian press in the new and old country. They sooner turn to non-Ukrainian sources which quite often are of the secondary nature and very often biased. But it must be emphasized also, that this younger generation of researchers perform the pioneer work on the basic information about the Ukrainian input. So far, both fields of the Ukrainian studies in Canada, in Ukrainian and English languages, supplement each other and this constitutes a healthy process in reserach work. Members of UVAN and NTSh as well as members of other Ukrainian Canadian learned societies and institutions take also an active part in such all-Canadian institutions as the Canadian Association of Slavists (CAS, organized in 1959), the Conference of Ukrainian Studies (CUS), the Royal Architectural Institute of Canada, the Royal Academy of Arts, Canadian Ethnic Studies Association and others. The multicultural decade of the seventies created a healthy climate for Ukrainian Studies in Canada.

Cairn of the Kosiw and Keld Districts, Manitoba.

SCHOOL QUESTION IN THE PERIOD OF MULTICULTURALISM

The system of teaching the Ukrainian language in public schools during the fifties and sixties worried both the pedagogues and parents who had to deal with this subject in practical form. It was shown that by beginning to teach this language in higher classes and not in the lower, satisfactory results were not achieved. Thus a necessity arose to search for other systems wherein the students, in addition to grammar and writing, would have a greater opportunity to use the conversational aspect of it. It was also revealed that the language must be taught not only as an isolated subject, but also as an integral part of culture, history, literature, art and others. The lack of these and their needs were discussed at teachers' and parents' conferences, as well as in the press.

Alberta

Edmonton, Alberta was the first to take steps in this direction. This was the beginning of a long road when in Edmonton and in the Province of Alberta bi-lingual teaching was inaugurated which, today, has assumed an experimental and practical programming in the three Western Provinces; Alberta, Saskatchewan and Manitoba. Wherein lies this bilingual education? It is valid, in the fact that the school children study for one-half a day in Ukrainian, and one-half day in English; in Ukrainian, music, art, social studies, physical education and Ukrainian, and in English, language arts, science, and arithmetic. In these two languages the students study the prescribed curriculum. To give solid ground to both languages the Ukrainian language is taught also in nurseries and kindergartens.

The beginnings of these experiments were in Edmonton. It may be worthwhile to record some details.[1] In December, 1970, the Professional and Businessmen's Club of Edmonton prepared a brief to the Joint Committee of Senate and House of Commons on Constitution regarding the new Constitution of Canada. In the preparation of this brief it became apparent that the school question, which is a provincial matter, needs an additional brief which should be directed to the Government of Alberta. Such a brief was discussed by a Committee consisting of: H. Barabash, L. Decore, R. Dzenyk, W. Kostash, K. Paproski and Peter Savaryn as the chairman. Manoly Lupul, well known professor in educational history, joined this group at a later date. The very title of this memorandum sounded quite original stating:

A brief submitted to the Government of Alberta on the Ukrainians, the new Canadian Constitution, the Laws of Alberta and the Policies of the Government of Alberta.

With the knowledge and participation of R. Ostashewsky, president, Edmonton branch of U.C.C., this memorial was presented to Premier Harry Strom on April 14, 1971. It would seem that the memorandum was quite

---
[1] A wide description of these events was covered by *Svoboda Daily*, 1978, #197-202, M. Chomiak: "Beginnings of bilingual schools in Alberta."

convincing when the above-mentioned premier, as early as April 24 of that year, at the U.C.C. branch banquet, spoke of the "wider language laws by the province" and simultaneously proclaimed a new cultural policy for Alberta. But fate played her fickle part. A few months later the Social Credit Party of H. Strom was ousted from power.

When Conservatives, under Peter Lougheed, took over the helm of Alberta Government, a new path had to be beaten to the ruling party. The Committee for multi-culturalism at the Ukrainian Professional Businessmen's Club started to formulate a new memorandum and also prepared a research upon the theme of Ukrainian language in the Provincial Schools of Alberta. Finally the memorial was compiled and presented in March 1973 at the meeting with the cabinet committee on education: Louis Hyndman, James Foster and Albert Hohol. Not having received an answer within reasonable time, J. Roslak, UCC chairman, again petitioned with solid arguments about the need of bilingual school education.[2] In the meantime young enthusiastic teachers, Fiona Pelech and Kateryna Cherniavska, started to organize a Ukrainian nursery. Simultaneously two parents' committees were formed, one for Public School and the other for Catholic. The work of those committees under the head of Maria Flak helped a great deal in the realization of bilingual school education in Edmonton. In 1973 the government of Alberta agreed upon a system of two languages of instruction — English and Ukrainian at the beginning on experimental basis, which started in the fall of 1974. Further successes in this line of work helped to obtain permission for a regular system of teaching and its wider spread in the province. In 1975 the parent committees were replaced by Ukrainian Bilingual Association (U.B.A.), which also was composed of parents and educators and received its charter.

Even as the first parents' organizations so did the Ukrainian Bilingual Association (U.B.A.) lead an explanatory campaign amongst the parents of school age children about the value of bilingual schools and the need of supporting this system financially. It was a long wait until the province, at least partially, assumed the cost of teaching, printing of books, other educational material, and co-ordinating and evaluating the system.

During the school year of 1980-81 the Ukrainian bilingual schools were established not only in the Edmonton School Division, but also in Sherwood Park, Vegreville and Lamont. Some 350 children were taught in Edmonton public schools, 481 in Edmonton Catholic schools, 66 in Vegreville, 27 in Sherwood Park and 64 in Lamont — 998 altogether. During the seven years of teaching, statistics bears witness to the good success of the system. At the beginning of each year the number of new students increases and there is not a noticeable degree of dropouts. The number of classes is sustained in proportion to the influx of new students.

To illustrate and substantiate this point we present the statistical data, dated October 15, 1980.

---

[2]*Bulletin of the World Congress of Free Ukrainians 1981,* February, No. 1 (9), Petro Savaryn: Bilingual Public Ukrainian-English Schools.

IMPLEMENTATION OF SECTION 150(1)(B) OF THE SCHOOL ACT: ALBERTA SCHOOL SYSTEMS
TOTAL ENROLLMENTS IN UKRAINIAN LANGUAGE CLASSES

Year	ECS	One	Two	Three	Four	Five	Six	Seven	Eight	Nine	Total
1974	101										101
1974/75	86	120									206
1975/76	152	113	105								370
1976/77	116	135	101	99							451
1977/78	152	148	127	86	93						606
1978/79	125	168	140	126	80	90					729
1979/80	120	144	153	128	107	73	87				812
1980/81	185	159	170	137	112	94	74	67			998

In later years the responsibility for this system has been taken over by the Canadian Institute of Ukrainian Studies. The tight co-operation of pedagogical and community activists led to the formation, in Edmonton, of an original working model of a bilingual system. Its work is topped by the fact that here are printed school textbooks whose benefits are also shared by similar systems in the provinces of Saskatchewan, Manitoba and Ontario. Alberta has managed to out-distance Manitoba, which in the pioneer era led the rest of Canada in bilingual teaching.

There is the Interprovincial Editorial Board for the Revision of Ukrainian Audio-Visual method. The members forming the board are from the provinces of Alberta, Saskatchewan and Manitoba. To date in cooperation with Ukrainian Canadian Committee Level I Ukrainian Lessons have been published. Level II and III are in process of preparation. The texts are used in public schools of the three provinces.

Manitoba

Success of the bilingual school system in Alberta has encouraged Ukrainian parents and educators to endeavour further. The results of these efforts culminated in the fact that in July, 1978, the Government of Manitoba announced the Public School Act to provide for the use of languages other than English or French, to be taught in Manitoba public schools. This provincially founded program opened in September, 1979, with 113 children enrolled.

In the school year 1980/81 the bilingual schools operated in six school divisions: Winnipeg #1, River East #9, Seven Oaks #10, Transcona-Springfield #12, Agassiz #13, Dauphin-Ochre #33.

Teaching took place in eight different schools consisting of 14 classes, including 3 nurseries totalling 275 children, with 11 teachers. Students receive 150 minutes of teaching in Ukrainian language per day, 12½ hours per week and 475 hours a year. In the third year there were already 480 students taking part in the bilingual language program, 23 teachers were occupied with this program in seven school divisions with 26 classes. As in Edmonton, so it was also in Winnipeg during the general parents' meeting (June, 1980), that the Manitoba Parents for Ukrainian Education (M.P.U.E.) was formed, which was incorporated as an educational institution. The primary task of MPUE is to support the bilingual program in public schools. Also deserving of mention is the Canadian Ukrainian Students' Club at the University of Manitoba which did extensive research regarding the need of bilingual programs in public schools. This coincided with the work of Stephania Yurkiwsky who did similar research on behalf of the Education Department of the Provincial Government of Manitoba. The Ukrainian Professional and Businessmen's Club in Winnipeg also participated in this research with such members as E. Cicierski, M. Spolsky, J. Pankiw, Dr. Louis Melosky, J. Petryshyn, Dr. S. Radchuk, Dr. J. Rozumnyj, W. Solypa and others.[3]

To present a full picture of Ukrainian teaching in the public schools of Manitoba we submit statistics for the last ten years of 1969-1979.

COMPARATIVE STATISTICS RE NUMBER OF PUPILS TAKING UKRAINIAN FROM 1968-69 to 1979-80 — Total Enrollment

Year	Total	Kindergarten	Grades 1-3	Grades 4-6	Grades 7-9	Grades 10-12
1968-69	937	—	—	—	674	263
1969-70	1,478	—	—	—	1,263	215
1970-71	No Statistics Available					
1971-72	2,273	17	97	455	1,344	360
1972-73	3,169	—	511	691	1,607	360
1973-74	4,187	25	697	1,123	1,881	461
1974-75	4,159	19	649	1,307	1,887	297
1975-76	4,446	47	832	1,274	1,813	380
1976-77	4,094	15	779	1,188	1,752	360
1977-78	3,610	12	688	1,083	1,499	328
1978-79	3,347	16	632	1,051	1,327	321
1979-80	2,978	25	554	1,059	1,057	283

From the chart we learn that beginning with the school year 1975-1976 the number of students was diminishing, especially in junior and senior grades where Ukrainian had been an optional subject. These statistics are even more alarming when we compare the late figures from 1981/82. At this time there were only 2.331 students who chose Ukrainian language as an optional course. If we add to this number 480 students from the bilingual programs,

---

[3]*Svoboda Daily*, New Jersey, #227-228, 1981, Vasyl Balan and Myron Spolsky: "Bilingual Progress in Public Schools of Manitoba."

then we have 2.755 students studying Ukrainian in public school.[4] This makes 223 students less than in 1979-1980. This, perhaps was most convincing to the school authorities of Manitoba the need for the bilingual system in school work.

Saskatchewan

The Saskatchewan Education Act (1978) which came into force in 1979, clearly provides an opportunity for the expansion of minority language education. Subsection 2 of Section 180 of the Education Act (1978), and the accompanying regulations make it possible for the second language to be used as a language of instruction from Kindergarten to Grade 12 according to the following time allocations: In Kindergarten 100% of Ukrainian and Grade 1-12 up to 50% of instruction time.

In Saskatchewan the legislation seems very progressive and enables bilingual Ukrainian-English programs to exist. In 1979/80, the University of Saskatchewan/Saskatoon conducted its first Ukrainian class into methods of teaching Ukrainian. It has been conducted yearly for the past three years. The Department of Education also created a full-time position for a Multicultural Education Consultant. Since its inception this position has been occupied by George Zerebecky. The whole program is set up as sound system for further development. So far (1981) Ukrainian-English Bilingual Program has been offered at St. Garetti School/Kdg. — grade 1 and at St. James School/Kdg. by the Saskatoon Catholic Board of Education. The combined enrollment was 57 pupils. It is worthwhile to mention that the Department of Education began in 1981 participating in a "joint inter-provincial editorial board" with Alberta and Manitoba Departments of Education to develop programs and supplementary instructional materials for Ukrainian-English Bilingual Education.

To get a complete picture of Ukrainian language taught in Saskatchewan public schools we include below a comparative study chart.

UKRAINIAN LANGUAGE INSTRUCTION IN SASKATCHEWAN
(A Comparative Study)[5]

Year	K	1	2	3	4	5	6	7	8	9	10	11	12	Total
1974-75				40	72	166	189	375	366	451	231	146	124	2,160
1975-76		26		42	48	124	146	411	411	402	259	121	95	2,085
1976-77	10	32	27	57	109	149	190	462	459	433	188	150	88	2,354
1977-78	24	21	25	85	95	160	171	421	406	523	182	119	107	2,442
		40 (combined)				27 (combined)				36 (combined)				
1978-79	30	21	13	85	121	172	178	472	440	453	199	122	83	2,470

---

[4]*Ukrainian Language Classes in Manitoba 1981-82.* Official Statistics of the Education Department of the Province of Manitoba, 1981/82, compiled by Stephania Yurkiwsky, Historical Publications Archives.

[5]Ukrainian Language Instruction in Saskatchewan. Official Statistics of the Education Department of the Province of Saskatchewan, compiled by George Zerebecky, Historical Publications Archives.

Ontario

Towards the end of 1970's a committee was formed in Toronto entitled "The Heritage Language Program" that worked along with Ontario Commission of Education and Provincial Branch of Ukrainian Canadian Committee. Its petition was to demand from the Provincial School authorities an improvement in the school system regarding the teaching of heritage languages in public schools. A conference was held in Toronto in the fall of 1980, prepared by the above-mentioned Committee under the name of: "Ukrainian and Education in the '80's." A fairly large number of teachers and Ukrainian Language experts took part in this conference. For the benefit of history we wish to cite the first three resolutions of this conference, directed towards the Ontario Government, with the request for bilingual teaching; 1) that Ontario adopt the concept of bilingual education (involving instruction in the child's mother tongue and one of the two main languages of Canada, as currently practised in several provinces in Canada) as a practical affirmation of the multicultural and multilingual nature of Ontario; 2) that joint committees — composed of representatives of each ethnocultural group concerned, the Ministry of Education, and the Ontario Institute for Studies in Education — be set up as soon as possible with the aim of implementing the above; 3) and that the Ministry of Education change its guidelines to allow language instruction in languages other than English and French at the elementary level."[6] This proved that over 160,000 Ukrainians in Ontario were demanding the same rights as their blood-brothers in the West already possessed.

We must also underline that the Ontario Education Act of 1974 legislated that only English and French may be used in Ontario schools as the languages of instruction. In 1977 the Ontario Government introduced the so-called Heritage Language Program for elementary students, as a continuing offering but the subject must be taken outside of regular school hours, that is after 4 p.m., on Saturday or during vacations. This program enables pupils from kindergarten to grade 8 to study their mother tongues and cultures 2½ hours per week to a maximum of 70 hours per year.[7]

During the school year 1980/81 20 School Boards of Ontario supported Ukrainian language programs financially. There were 70 classes supported by Public School Boards and 49 by Catholic with 71 and 37 instructors respectively, 2,459 pupils benefitted from this assistance, 1,219 from Public School Boards and 1,240 from Catholic.[8]

The Toronto School Board made some concessions in that direction towards the teaching of Ukrainian language during the school year of 1981-1982, allowing to teach the heritage language during school hours, but only when 25 students had registered in a given area. The program consisted of 2½ hours per week. Financial assistance from Ontario Government for financing of heritage languages strengthened in some ways the teaching of heritage languages as evidenced by statistics and press writeups. For instance, in

---

[6]*New Perspectives,* Toronto, November 29, 1980, "Ukrainian Liaison Committee Resolutions," p. 4.

[7]*Ibidem.* "A Step Toward Heritage Languages" by Yuriy Weretelnyk," p. 7.

[8]Summary of Statistical Data for 1980-1981 School Year on Ukrainian Language Education in Canada by Vasyl Balan (Unpublished Report), Historical Publications Archives.

Thunder Bay in 1976-1977, 34 children were studying these courses, but in 1977-78 this jumped to 46, in 1978-79 to 69 and in 1979-80 it went up to 115.[9] Government aid raised the prestige of heritage language resulting in increased enrollment. Also the schools received the timely possibilities of teaching the children in public school buildings as well as the better renumerations for the teachers attracted higher qualified teachers. Simultaneously a process has been started for consolidation of Ukrainian schools under auspices of the Ukrainian Canadian Committee (e.g. Thunder Bay, Welland, St. Catharines). In enlarging the Heritage Language Program of Ontario "Ukrainian Liaison Committee (ULC) was formed which has become the official coordinating body for Toronto Board of Education and parents' committee in that area, along with other organizations and parishes, who are supporting Ukrainian school activities.

We now come to the conclusion that in the era of multiculturalism a new type of school was formed in which the students, with encouragement from their parents could select an additional language of instruction according to their choice. A new progressive bilingual school system was inaugurated, which in many ways has outgrown the bilingual system of the old pioneer era. In principle, the Ukrainian community, in Canada is reconquering that which was lost in the year 1916 in Manitoba.

The compiled statistics point out that even the non-Ukrainian parents are benefitting in a large measure from the bilingual Ukrainian-English system. This also acknowledges that Canada is abandoning its old tendencies to favour the use of one language. In this regard, it is worthwhile to cite the official view of the Commissioner of Official Languages: "As time goes on, the traditionally more sentimental reasons for keeping up the languages of the old country are being joined by more pragmatic, even commercial, arguments for maintaining the many languages that Canada is blessed with. Indeed, by looking around and keeping our ears open, it is not too hard to realize that Canada is a country of immense linguistic potential. . . ."

"Canadians, we believe, are maturing rapidly in this direction. As a people we are beginning to make sensible distinctions between our opportunities to acquire as many languages as we please, the duty of the state to communicate on whatever languages are necessary, and our inescapable fate as individuals to be part of several evolving, even competing cultures."

"Governments and legislators at all levels should continue to emphasize that an official languages policy does not downgrade the importance of other Canadian communities but rather encourages the development of more tolerant attitudes towards all languages and ethnic groups."[10] Such quoted views open a wide window for new Canadian generations to come.

There is no doubt that the above and similar views enabled the Ukrainian community in the three prairie provinces Alberta, Manitoba, Saskatchewan, to achieve bilingual education in the 1970s. Without the climate of multiculturalism that type of education was impossible in the 50s and 60s. Our findings are supported equally by contemporary history as well as by previous

---

[9]*Ukrainian Voice* of Winnipeg, August 24, 1981, "Centralized School in Thunder Bay" by Y. Moskva. *Northern Mosaic*, Thunder Bay, Dec., 1975. Yaroslav Moskva: "Ukrainian Language Schools in Northern Ontario."

[10]*Ukrainian Voice*, No. 23, 1981, Ivan Harmata: For a Broader Linguistic Tolerance in Canada.

experience in the earlier decades when Ukrainians in these provinces negotiated with the provincial governments about the teaching of Ukrainian as an optional subject. Almost 10 years were spent on attempts to gain these "educational privileges" considering the fact that Saskatchewan adopted this system in 1952 while in Manitoba it occured only in the school year 1961-62. It was a great deal easier to obtain bilingual education in the 1970's.

As a result of 30 years efforts (dating from 1952) there appeared in public school systems of the prairie provinces two programs for teaching of Ukrainian language. The first and least complicated was the program of Ukrainian as an optional credit subject (see chapter "Ukrainian Language in Public Schools, pp. 625-631) and the second program was bilingual instruction in several subjects. In this chapter we have utilized some statistics to show how these two programs have been operating. It is evident that the second program is richer and more effective for retention of Ukrainian language in the younger generation.

While the prairie provinces have a firmly established program for Ukrainian language teaching, Ontario where Ukrainians live in concentrated areas has not such a program to date. Moreover, the ethnocultural groups of Ontario are still struggling for recognition of the right to heritage language teaching in any form. From our study it is clear how difficult it is to obatin these rights. It is noteworthy that this struggle continues on the threshold of the second decade of multiculturalism.

Despite the difficulties there has been progress. What has already been obtained creates some opportunity for language teaching. We hope that sooner or later the principle of bilingual education of heritage languages will be accepted throughout Canada.

The remaining provinces, British Columbia and Quebec, where Ukrainians live in more scattered communities there is no Ukrainian language teaching in the public schools and it is only taught in private schools so called "Ridna Shkola". This system, as we already know, has been operating more or less in some organized fashion since the beginning of Ukrainian settlement in these provinces. This applies to the two Ukrainian "islands" Sidney and Halifax in Nova Scotia.

Considering that "Ridna Shkola" system continues to operate in all provinces even in those where Ukrainian is taught in public schools it would be appropriate to become more familiar with the working of that system and to learn more about its difficulties, weaknesses and strengths.

Ridna Shkola in the Prairie Provinces

The system of "Ridna Shkola" has a long history. Actually it started in 1916 when bilingual schools in the pioneer era were abolished and parents started arranging instructional courses in Ukrainian language for their children. Popularly they have been called the Ukrainian "Ridna Shkola" and in English: "Ukrainian School", "Saturday School", "Evening School", "Heritage Language School", "Heritage Language Instruction" and very often "Native School" "Vernacular School" or "Ridna Shkola."

The present "Ridna Shkola" system is under auspices of the Ukrainian *National Centre of Ukrainian Educational Councils* (NCUEC), which came into existence during the Ninth Congress of Ukrainian Canadians in 1968.

National Centre of Ukrainian Educational Councils announced in 1970/71 that the "Ridna Shkola" system comprised 142 schools with 8,558 students.

Eastern Canada	65 schools and 5,150 students
British Columbia	10 schools and 280 students
Alberta	19 schools and 1,103 students
Saskatchewan	20 schools and 724 students
Manitoba	18 schools and 1,271 students[11]
Total	142 schools 8,558 students

At the same time, in public schools in the prairie provinces, Alberta, Saskatchewan and Manitoba, there were about 5,000 students in Ukrainian language classes. If we compare the situation that existed ten years earlier with present time, "Ridna Shkola" is losing ground. Some evaluate this loss to be 30 or more percent. In 19 schools of "Ridna Shkola" in Manitoba during 1982, there were 966 pupils, although there were 1,221 in 1971. Six schools showed decreased enrollment, eight static and five increased. In some school districts Ukrainian courses were conducted during summer holidays only. The above statistics comprise both full and part-time students. It is interesting to note that within the system of "Ridna Shkola" more attention was given to nursery level pupils. In 1982 the enrollment consisted of 146 pre-schoolers. In the system there were eight Ukrainian Catholic schools, six Ukrainian Orthodox and five non-denominational. In Ontario 3,787 students attended "Ridna Shkola" classes in 1970 but in 1980 only 2,763.[12] Statistics of Ukrainian schools in Edmonton denotes even a higher percentage. In 1975 there were 671 students in these schools and 56 teachers, while in 1980 there were only 254 students and 32 teachers. Many of the potential students of Ukrainian Schools in Alberta went to the bilingual classes. The question which arises is that perhaps the bilingual schooling is endangering the existence of "Ridna Shkola." On first examination we may treat this supposition with suspicion, but when we consider the fact that the use of Ukrainian language in home life of Ukrainian families is losing ground for the children who want to learn Ukrainian language, the Ukrainian schools can provide the facility for increasing their knowledge of language. Timely strong voices were heard that Heritage Language Schools should not be abandoned, the more so since the new system of bilingual teaching has not achieved its full capacity. Full evaluation can only come after the ninth grade, that is after 10 years of teaching in Alberta, including the pre-schooling time and 13 years in Saskatchewan. The need of private heritage language classes is still great. A great estrangement has developed between the students and the language of their fathers. The scattering of the families and lack of block settlements produced a negative influence towards the retention of Ukrainian language. Traditional churches were the main bastion of Ukrainian language. As a result of the assimilating process, some parishes have now taken the line of least resistance

---

[11]*Ukrainian Voice,* Jan. 13, 1971. Ivan Bodnarchuk: National Centre of Ukrainian School Councils.

[12]Report of the Council of Ukrainian Schools of the Provincial Council at the Ukrainian Canadian Committee in Toronto, 1981. Historical Publications Archives.

— some have sermons in English. Estrangement from the Ukrainian language grew stronger in spite of the fact that there have been occasions when the parents often have sent their children tens and even hundreds of kilometers away only to learn their native language. This was, undoubtedly, a great sacrifice on the part of the parents and children. The laws of life often rise above the desires of individuals and groups. From this came the idea to find some other answer that would fit the newer times. To regain what was lost and initiate a change that would reverse the assimilation process, the far seeing educators and parents became interested in preserving both systems. The more so since in many school divisions, with the best will and intentions, it would still be difficult to carry out the bilingual teaching system when taking into consideration the lack of sufficient numbers of students and other matters. Therefore the National Centre of Ukrainian School Councils took upon itself to improve the method of teaching in Ukrainian schools too. It started to organize systematic seminars for parents and teachers, to ensure that the Ukrainian Schools and Courses of Ukrainian Studies are supplied with qualified teachers who use modern methods of teaching and to pay greater attention to nurseries and kindergartens. This means to capture the children's interest during the most receptive age for learning the language. They try with the aid of youth organizations to educate young leaders for enlightening work in the field of youth, to recommend sending out active intelligent groups of young people into various areas utilizing for this purpose the summer school vacations, etc.

In 1979 National Centre of Ukrainian School Councils has started to publish a professional journal, called "The Ukrainian Teacher" which acts as a forum for the exchange of ideas and information for the teachers of Ukrainian language and Ukrainian Studies courses. Its editor is Dr. Boryslaw Bilash, the president of National Centre of Ukrainian School Councils and an adviser for multiculturalism for the Winnipeg School System. A number of educators are involved in this venture at the centre. The first president who pioneered the National Centre of Ukrainian School Councils was Natalia Kohuska, a pedagogue and a long time editor of the "Promin" journal. For many years the secretary was Iwanna Kachor, lately V. Melnyk. "Ridna Shkola" system has lead in a number of schools in Ontario. In 1980 there were 53 schools.

The greatest numbers of Ukrainians who emigrated to Canada after the Second World War settled in Ontario, especially in Toronto. Here the Ukrainian language has been largely used in the home and churches where parents wish to impart to their children the knowledge about their past. In Toronto, there were, in 1980, 18 schools attended by around 2,200 students. Ontario has always led the way in Ukrainian School programs after the Second World War. The system of these schools has been under auspices of the Ukrainian Educational Council at the UCC Provincial Council which publishes quite regularly its monthly journal "Ridnoshkilnyk". Here problems are discussed regarding Ukrainian teaching in private and public schools. Connected with this journal are such well-known names in the educational and pedagogical fields as Dr. E. Roslycky, Dr. O. Kopach, Ivan Bodnarchuk, W. Weryha, Yuriy Dzurawec, Dr. J. W. Darewych, Iroida Wynnycka and others. Almost all are members of the Council of Ukrainian

Schools of the Provincial Council of the Ukrainian Canadian Committee. This council co-operates and benefits in its work from the "Association of Writers of Children's Literature" of Leonid Hlibiw which has its publications in U.S.A., Canada and Australia. School children also reap benefit from the material published in children's and youth journals such as "Veselka", "Yunak", "Krylati", "Young Ukraine", and others. Undoubtedly, the Council of Ukrainian Schools of the Provincial Council of the Ukrainian Canadian Committee in Toronto has played a leading role in "Ridna Shkola" activities in Eastern Canada.

British Columbia

British Columbia Ukrainian Schools have had a long and colorful struggle. Ukrainians in B.C. have problems in forming courses of Ukrainian language because they are sparsely settled throughout the province. However, Vancouver is the stronghold in creating a cultural basis for Ukrainians in B.C. At the end of 1970 they intensified their work. In 1978 at Vancouver a three day school conference was held at which representatives of school systems in Alberta participated and shared their experiences in this type of work. It was a well-attended Conference with representatives from centres not only around Vancouver but also other places as Kelowna, Kamloops, Vernon, Campbell River, Victoria, New Westminister and Surrey. At this conference, headed by L. Slobozan, the Provincial School Council of British Columbia was formed to which representatives were chosen from the entire area of the province. In 1981/82 there were 9 "Ridna Shkola" schools in British Columbia; 3 Catholic, 3 Orthodox and 3 non-denominational. Total enrollment was 257 students in 26 classes, with 27 salaried teachers and 13 volunteers. There were pre-schoolers in nursery and 46 adults working on improvement of their language. Total expenses of these schools estimated $18,962. Parents contributed $6,526, Ukrainian Community $7,799 and Secretary of State funded $4,637.[13]

Quebec

The biggest concentration of Ukrainians in Quebec is in Montreal and its suburbs. Here Ukrainian Schools are well organized. In Montreal there is an active group under the name of the Ukrainian School Council of Quebec, which was organized in the fall of 1975. In Greater Montreal and in surrounding area there are four active Ukrainian schools and three schools of Ukrainian Studies Courses. A tradition has been established that every year in March all the schools organize anniversaries in honor of Taras Shevchenko and every fall they hold a graduation for the students that have finished their Ukrainian Studies Courses. The Quebec Council of Ukrainian Schools is headed by Dr. Yuriy Lewckyj.

Finally, interesting to note that in Sidney, Nova Scotia, a Ukrainian school "Ridna Shkola" has been in operation since 1973, with 31 students in 1981/82. The Canadians of Ukrainian descent in Halifax organized "Ridna Shkola" in 1979 and in 1981/82 there were 48 students in attendance.[14]

---

[13]Vasyl Balan: *Summary of Statistical Data for 1980-1981 School Year on Ukrainian Language Education in Canada* (Unpublished Report). Historical Publications Archives.

[14]*Ibidem.*

In the name of the National Centre of Ukrainian School Councils the Ukrainian Schools are inspected by I. Bodnarchuk, a long time inspector of this system. He is an author of a study about these schools which appeared in 1980, entitled: "To Native Lands". In his last inspection he confirms that Ukrainian schools moved from the basements of "National Homes" transformed into well-lit, spacious classrooms, having qualified teachers, thanks to scholarships and higher pay, and in addition, new talents in the persons of younger teachers arriving to strengthen the sagging forces. This is especially noticable in the increase of nurseries and kindergarten teachers.

"The older ones leave us, he says but, alas, to be replaced with younger ones whose endeavours are strong but with lesser knowledge of Ukrainian language." A great lack of textbooks is much in evidence. Also shortcomings and backward conditions, especially in Eastern Canada may be due to the fact that the Ukrainian language did not gain school status in public schools, (lack of school accreditation). In the last few years a strong accent has been placed upon formation of new bilingual school program in every province. It should also be kept in mind that "Ridna Shkola" system of teaching the Ukrainian language emerged at a time when the overwhelming majority of Ukrainian families used Ukrainian as their language in daily life. In that environment the schools concentrated their efforts in the area of grammatical instruction, considering that the student was already conversant in the language. In the last three decades language fluency of vernacular in Ukrainian families decreased considerably under assimilating pressure. This is why all Ukrainian language programs in private and public schools have undergone a serious decline in enrollment. From this there stems the cry and the pressing need for bilingual program in schools.

The system of Ukrainian Schools "Ridna Shkola" in Canada is tightly bound with the Ukrainian world system through the membership of the National Centre of Ukrainian School Councils in the World Co-ordinative Educational Council of the World Congress of Free Ukrainians (so called SKVOR).

And so in the first decade of multiculturalism in Canada three types of schools were working in which the children were learning Ukrainian language: 1) the northern and most progressive bilingual system; 2) the old system of Ukrainian in public schools as an elective subject; and 3) "Ridna Shkola" — a system of private schools.

As history indicates; these three systems of Ukrainian language teaching will continue in the future; they are not mutually contradictory but rather enhance each other. Actually these systems must continue because of objective realities.

* * * * * *

Studying school problems at various levels and in different localities as well as in provincial aspects, it appears, that in addition to the improvement in methods of teaching as well as introduction of modern textbooks and more suitable facilities, synchronization of pupils school programs in public and private schools, there is still a great need to conduct clarification among young parents about the necessity of bilingual teaching, about the need of knowledge of the native mother tongue and the benefits of lingual enrichments, not only for the ethnocultural values but also for the country as a whole. Wherever such actions were enacted from house to house, there was success. Schools were filled up with students. Where this drive was lacking, very few or none were registered.

The second established truth was where the young parents took upon themselves the implementation of these actions, there was a success. These young parents along with experienced educators brought the school problems to successful fruition. In some centres, where the leading positions are in the hands of indifferent pedagogues and disinterested parents, school system declines.

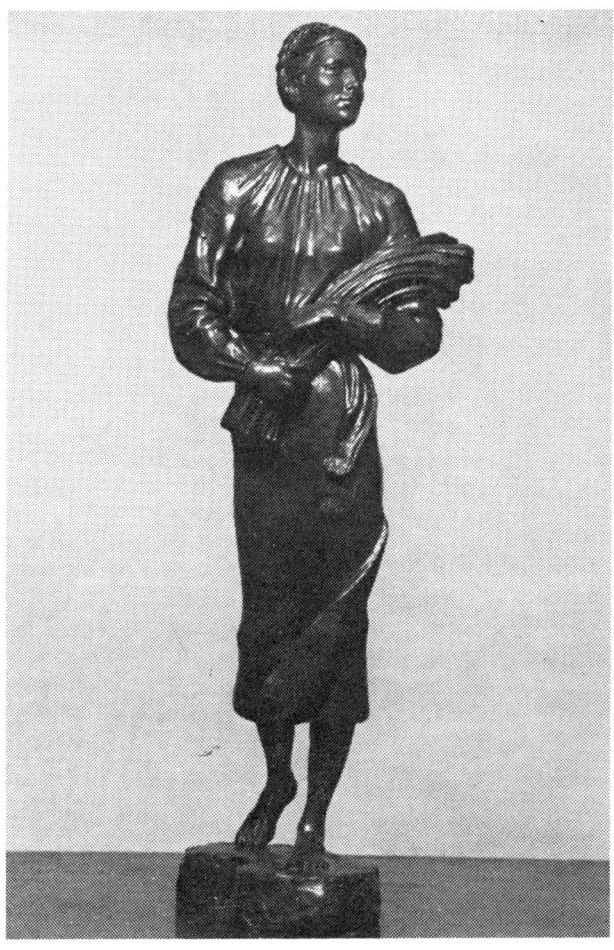

Statue of Pioneer Woman in Edmonton.

NEW TALENTS IN CREATIVE ART

During the last decade in Canada, a new Pleiades of painters, gravurists and graphical artists appeared upon the horizon of Ukrainian creative art. This is a completely new generation that finished its art studies at the universities and colleges of Canada, although there is no lack of middle generation among them. The creative diapason of these artists stretches even further, for, in addition to paintings and graphics they have also mastered the various techniques of gravure work in wood and metal. They have extended their work to include silk-screen art, sculpture and ceramics. Their artistic talents and creative achievements have been seen at Ukrainian Canadian Art Festival, shown in 1971 at Thunder Bay and the All-Canadian exhibit of Ukrainian graphic art at Montreal, in 1973. Likewise the exhibition has been at the Ukrainian Art Foundation in Toronto, the Ukrainian Cultural and Education Centre in Winnipeg and a line of local showings throughout Canada.

The foremost place in gravure art belongs to *Adriana Lysak (1930-)* who began her art education in Gratz, Austria and finished it at the Ecole des Beaux-Arts, in Montreal. She accomplishes her art work through the use of various media: gouache, pastel, casein, acrylic, collage technique, carving in wood by means of hot metal, carvings made on plexi-glass. She is also experimenting in a three-dimensional sculpture construction wherein she uses multi-coloured slates of artificial glass, etc. Adriana's works are distinguished by the flamboyant image expressed through excellent execution, especially their originality.

Among the younger artists of the Montreal group, who were born in the forties, is *Andrey Dutkewych (1944-)* whose works are noted for abstractionism and surrealism. *Mykola Kolodka's (1947-)* works are of similar nature. On the other hand, *Halyna Kosharych,* who began her art studies in Caracas, Venezuela and completed them in Montreal, could be considered as their opposite. Her linecut and blower compositions remind us of the Ukrainian National Art. Two other artists of this group, and the same age, are *Larysa Melnyk and Oksana Serbyn (1945-).* Larysa works in graphics, especially in ink, solving her problems of lines and shadows by semi-abstract forms. Oksana shows her talent through graphics and illustrations. *Larysa Luhovy (1942-)* also of Montreal, excels in etchings and originality of subjects and technical precision. Her works in painting, drawing and engravings have been exhibited in such galleries as Galerie Libre Montreal, I.F.R. Gallery, Washington, Barbara Walters Gallery, New York.

Of all the artists in the Montreal group, born during the fifties, the most noted one is *Ruslan Logush (1950-),* a graphic artist who completed art studies at the Sir George Williams University and who, in his free hours during the university studies brought to masterful perfection the silk-screen art. Logush is exceptionally distinguished by his philosophical treatment of art. This can be easily traced in the rich themes coloured by astrology, a flight into the Cosmos, and especially the conception of the Solar System. He made a debut with his works shown in the Salon of Free Art, in Paris, in 1972, where he received an honour award for his silkscreen called "The Sunflower". Although Logush is a modern artist through and through yet his subjects are realistic and he devotes special attention to Ukrainian themes. In the Montreal area and far beyond, the works of *Ludmyla Temertey* appear in the spirit of realism, the pictures of Ukrainian women in their native costumes from various regions of Ukraine and type of Ukrainian farmer in Canada. She is preparing an album on the occasion of 90th Anniversary of Ukrainian settlement in Canada. *Ludmila Pavliv (1953-)* expresses her artistic talent primarily through graphic sketches in aquarelle and India ink of original stylization. Full of sympathetic feelings are her Christmas cards with the unique signature "Lada".

In Toronto, in the 1960's *Daria Zalucka (1940-)* began to distinguish herself in landscapes and still life paintings that are noted for their gentle and harmonized picturesqueness. She has also made small figurines in ceramic e.g. Shevchenko, Rooster and others.

Christine Welyhorsky-Senkiw (1950-) successfully solves her problem of picturesqueness in paintings and writes articles on art themes, while *Christine Nawrocka-Kudryk* who made her debut at the Ukrainian Association of Creative Artists exhibition in 1965, expressed her views through thematic stylizations colouring and working technique, especially the utilization of geometrical planes in urban landscapes. Her works are denoted by distinctive abstractionism, with some traces of symbolism. *Vera Yacyk* illustrates Ukrainian television programs and projects costumes and marquees for children's stage, especially her valuable projects of costuming for the children's operetta "Koza-Dereza". *Vera Yurchuk's* technique embraces acrylic, monotype and batik. It shows that during the last decade both in Quebec and Ontario women-artists hold primacy in the Ukrainian world of art. We also note that, in Toronto, *Daria Onyshchuk* appears as a talented artist who devotes her studies to ornamental arts and has lately concentrated her interest towards Easter Egg Painting. In the sphere of semi-subjective and abstract art are *Petro Kolisnyk (1934-)* of Toronto and *Vasyl Romanov (1940-)* of Saskatchewan. Many other artists exhibit their works in various parts of Canada, U.S.A. and Europe. The future belongs to them.

With a lively tempo a group of artists from the middle and younger generation appear on the scene in Alberta, especially in the Edmonton area. *Olha Monastyrska,* a former student of Professor J. Bucmaniuk's school, has devoted herself exclusively to ceramics and has organized her workshop on a high level, having already sent a group of qualified students into the world of art. One of the most talented of these is *Iwanna Iwanusiw (1909-)* who excels in the transmission of forms, composition and picturesqueness. A notable position in the field of landscape paintings and architectural designs was achieved in the early 70's by *Parasia Ivanec (1920-).* In the spirit of realism she has around 170 projects of Ukrainian churches in Alberta. Of the younger Alberta artists *Ihor Dmytruk (1938-)* paints and works in graphics. He has already produced a line of portraits and compositions, that express a modernistic trend, especially that of expression. *Ksenia Aronec (1942-)* made a debut of her works at the beginning of 1970. These are noted for their non-subjective modernism, or, to be more specific, uncompromising abstractionism and intellectual movement. *Wasyl Duma, (1936-)* of Calgary, Alberta, expresses his artwork by graphics and India ink etchings that have expressionist character.

An interesting phenomenon in the field of Ukrainian art in Alberta, is that of *Primrose Diakiw (1944-)* (also *Diakow*) of Calgary, who is of Ukrainian-Irish descent but is fanatically absorbed with Ukrainian culture and its spiritual essence. She shows exceptional inventiveness in religious thematics, especially in the Ukrainian Liturgical rites. She works, usually, in acrylics, although etching is the dominant form while the rich, local, colours only appear to crown a given work. Her husband, *Ted Diakiw (Diakow) (1938-)* works as a potter-ceramist, although he is a good India ink etcher and his compositions are imbued with traces of expressionism. *Lena Kostiuk,* nee *Katerynchuk (1930-)* is an example of a "classical" primitive in the field of art. She never attended any art school nor took any lessons or advice from other artists. She developed her style of painting on her own. Not knowing any laws of perspective, anatomy, proportion or any other basic rules of drawing and painting she, nevertheless, works in portraiture, landscape, and still-life, without any models or helps from nature, but depends solely upon her sharp observation and an unusual visual memory. Her works deal mostly with the life of Ukrainian farmers in Canada. Her paintings are closely allied to a group of French primitivist artists of the 19th century.

Some of the younger Ukrainian artists are also working in British Columbia. Amongst the foremost of them is *Petro Shostak (1943-),* a lecturer on creative art, in the Art Department of Victoria University. Farming themes are dominant in his works, especially the life and culture of Ukrainian farms in Alberta, as shown in his paintings and silkscreens. They are very impressive in their excellent drawings and compositional approach, especially the most faithful transmission of given objects which bring to the viewer the illusion of reality. Although in some of his works we may detect traces of naturalism and even primitivism still Shostak remains original and self-reliant who endeavours to reach his aim by planting strongly his footsteps on the pathway of art.

In examining the panorama of Ukrainian visual creative art in Canada, during the period of the last thirty years, we can come to the conclusion that the Ukrainian artists in the various branches of art have reached a great measure of success. They have attained imposing achievements in the graphics paintings, especially the lofty attainments arrived at in the polychromy of Ukrainian churches and the rich carvings wrought upon the Ikonostasis, thanks to the combined efforts of the Ukrainian artists in Canada and U.S.A., such as: *M. Dmytrenko, I. Kubarsky, W. Balas, L. Molodoshanin, R. Kowal, S. Lytwynenko, M. Osinchuk, S. Hordynsky, I. Denysenko* and others. Beautiful examples of this art are: St. Volodymyr and Olha cathedral in Winnipeg, the St. Volodymyr cathedral and St. Nicholas Church in Toronto, the St. Josephat and the St. John Cathedrals in Edmonton and many others that reveal a true synthesis of painting and carving.

A high level of achievement has been reached by the graphics and gravures by *Ivan Keywan* and others, especially the formulations upon the Ukrainian editions by *M. Lewyckyj and B. Stebelsky.* Also in the high artistic level are the monumental sculptures of *Leo Molodoshanin* who in 1972 sculptured the bust of composer Lysenko for the Jubilee Auditorium in Edmonton, in 1980 a monument of the Ukrainian pioneers in Vegreville, Alberta. Among his other achievements are the sculptured busts of Pope John XXIII, Pope Paul VI, A. Y. Jackson, his friend from the famous "Group of Seven" and others.

Roman Kowal has made himself well known in his designs of church mosaics. His fine works may be seen in such churches as the Ukrainian Catholic Church in Russell, in the Orthodox Sobor of St. George in Edmonton and the imposing large scale mosaic in St. Michael Church in Transcona. To his credit is also the Red River Cart, in the Assiniboine Park, Winnipeg (1975).

Other successful artists in their work are *Lydia Palij (1926-)* graphic artist and designer (author of essays on art, literature, short stories, and poetry), *Ivan Belsky, Adriana Stebelsky* (illustrator of book covers), *Nina Mudryk Mryc,* also *Theodore Baran (1911-)* of Saskatoon has been recognized in church polychromy and church decorative art for many years. Of some prominence in the spontaneous talent at the advanced age are such names as the iconographer *Taras Snihurowych* and his sister *Luba Snihurowych,* both of Winnipeg. The latter distinguished herself in sculpture. *Iryna Malycka* began to create her ceramics in Toronto. *M. Gamula* with his oil paintings in Sarnia and *Dmytro Stryjek* with his primitive art in Saskatoon. To this "old guard" belongs also *Igor Gouzenko* who lived and worked under the pseudonym of Peter Brown.[1]

To the names already mentioned we might add names from a younger generation: *Stanley Stech (+1982), Steven B. Repa (1937-), William Harry Lobchuk (1942-), Frank Soprovych, Alexander Saprovych, Olenka Negrych, Halia Arsenych-Stolar, Mariyka Onufriychuk-Sokulska, Jean Bachynsky, B. Achtemichuk (1948-), William Pura (1948-), R. Kostyniuk (1941-), St. Czernecki (1946-), D. Farkavec (1942-), Darka Mudry, Svitlana Muchin, M. Burdeyny, N. Husar, Daria Lusych, Myroslav Sulatycky, M. Kucher,* and others.

They distinguished themselves in all the branches of creative art and various styles, starting from realism and impressionism through expressionism and cubism, up to extreme abstractionism.

Towards the end of this chapter it will be worthwhile to note that in popularizing the Ukrainian art in Canada, in addition to the professional artists and art critics, such as *I. Keywan* and *B. Stebelsky* we also have others: *Volodymyr Hawryluk, Maryna Antonovych-Rudnycka, Wasyl Sofroniw-Levytsky, Anatol Kurdydyk, Stepan Wolynec, Vera Ke* and others. Reviews of their works on the pages of Ukrainian Press are certainly much above the amateur level.

---

[1] Gouzenko defected from the Soviet embassy in Ottawa in September, 1945, and smuggled 109 secret documents which revealed an espionage ring of Soviet spies in Canada, U.S. and Britain. A Royal Commission which investigated the whole affair stated that "Gouzenko has rendered a great public service to the people of this country and thereby has placed Canada in his debt". His autobiography is depicted in the publication "This Was My Choice". He is the author of the novel "Fall of a Titan" which was nominated by a group of Canadian and U.S. professors for a Nobel Prize. Gouzenko died in 1982 at the age of 63.

760   UKRAINIAN CANADIANS: A HISTORY

The seventies also brought us noted loses in artistic talents such as: Ivan Kubarsky, Leonid Perfecky (1900-1977); Volodymyr Balas (1906-1980), who died in San Diego, California, Wasyl Zalucky (1895-1973), Julian Kraykiwsky (1892-1975). Others, too, left this world in the prime of life and creativity: Vadym Dobrolidge (1913-1973) and Peter Kuch, William (Wasyl) Kurelek, mentioned previously.

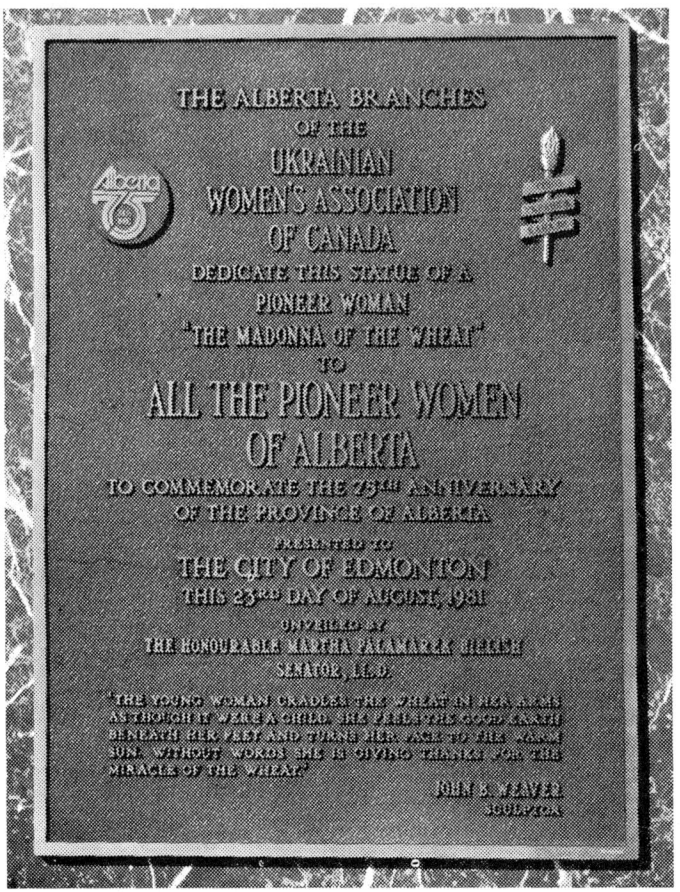

Inscription on the Statue of Pioneer Woman

ASSOCIATION OF ARTISTS
AND
ART GALLERIES

The creative artists, especially those of the older generation are organized, as already mentioned, in the Ukrainian Association of Creative Artists (USOM) in Toronto. This association has a much longer history. Its nucleus was the Literary Art Club of Toronto, which was headed, for sometime, by Mykhaylo Dmyterko. It was he who became the head of this organization. When he left Toronto, the leadership was taken over by Bodhan Stebelsky. The association was headed also by Ivan Keywan of Edmonton and Omelian Telizyn of Toronto.[1]

Lately USOM is comprised of some 30 painters, graphic artists and sculptors. Most of them live in Toronto. The rest are scattered over a wide area, from Edmonton to Montreal.

The younger generation began to organize itself into art groups on the occasion of the Ukrainian Canadian Art Festival which took place in Thunder Bay 1971. At that time the Ukrainian Canadian Art Council was formed, comprised of representatives from various branches of art as well as from the younger members of the literary world. Both, U.S.O.M. and the Council did not show very much organizational activity after 1971. However, we must underline the fact that at the Thunder Bay Festival of Art about 100 members of the new generation participated.[2]

Right now two provincial assocations of artists and adepts of art began their work, namely: The Saskatoon Society of Ukrainian Artists and the much advanced, and well known, Ukrainian Artists Association of Quebec.

A great role in popularizing and spreading the works of creative artists is played by art galleries which truly are the summation of the art world and society. For a long time the place of galleries was represented by the spacious halls of "Reading Associations", "National Homes" and parish halls. But with these half-hearted methods it was not possible to satisfy the desires of those who wanted to add a higher measure of prestige and greater efforts to spread the creative accomplishments and more dignified representation in the world. This state existed until the beginning of the sixties, when a stronger direction started to assert itself. Toronto was the first to answer to this call. In the middle of the sixties the Focus Gallery under the leadership of Iryna Shumska-Moroz came into existence. The already mentioned *Maria Ochrymowych (1927-)* arranged the exhibition.

Mykola and Maria Kolankiwsky opened their M.M. Gallery. But a more imposing moment arrived when they opened their gallery in Niagara Falls as a heritage establishment to look after the art work of the famous artist William (Wasyl) Kurelek. The art council at the St. Volodymyr Institute of Toronto also opened its modern location for exhibits. In 1972 the Winnipeg Ukrainian

---

[1] *Estafeta,* Toronto, 1970, No. 1.
[2] *Svoboda,* New Jersey, Nov. 19, 1971, M. Chomiak: "Ukrainian Canadian Festival of Art in Thunder Bay", Aug. 30 — Sept. 3, 1971.

Cultural and Educational Centre (Oseredok) opened its gallery and art exhibition at its new location at 184 Alexander Avenue, Winnipeg. Prior to that exhibitions were held at various places. This time the gala celebration was opened by Hon. James Richardson, then Federal Minister and Prof. J. Rozumnyj, as host.

After further expansion of Oserodok, the gallery now occupies the whole top floor. During its existence it has held around 70 art exhibitions. The exhibitions are held by advanced artists as well as by beginners. Artists of Central and Western Canada, especially, have taken advantage of the gallery's services. There were no lack of guests from U.S.A. and the East.

In 1975 Toronto moved further ahead. It benefited from the Canadian Ukrainian Foundation (K.U.M.F.) which came into existence at the initiative and funds of Mykhaylo and Yaroslava Szafraniuk, who donated the building and a rich collection of works by Ukrainian creative artists. The "K.U.M.F." foundation is a community establishment whose aim is to enhance and safeguard Ukrainian art and culture in Canada. In its commitments, the Foundation proclaims the need for collecting the finest Ukrainian art works and for holding exhibits to help bring out artistic talents, especially those of the younger generation. It has at its disposal over ten thousand square feet of floor space.[3] Directors of this Foundation are comprised of various active leaders in culture and art work, such as Dr. B. Stebelsky, Dr. P. Hlibowych, L. Kozak, I. Malycka, W. Weryha, S. Pawluk, A. Troyan, R. Wrzesnewskyj, R. Hryshchyn, M. Deynega, Senator Paul Yuzyk, Yaroslava & Mykhaylo Szafraniuk. Because of the Szafraniuk's generous donations and work it is popularly referred to as "The Szafraniuk's Foundation". During its six years of existence it has acquired a high level of recognition.

In 1982 Christine Stodilka and Ksenia Stasiw established in Toronto a new art gallery under the name "Trypilla".[4]

In Edmonton the task of forming an art foundation was undertaken by the Ukrainian Canadian Archives and Museum of Alberta (U.K.A.M.A.). As in the case of Toronto with M. and Y. Szafraniuk, in Edmonton, Hryhory and Stefania Yopyk took on the burden, along with others, not only to start a large Archives-Museum but also to create the possibility of forming an art gallery. Thus the style of work of "U.K.A.M.A." is more like that of the "Oseredok" in Winnipeg. Both places have archives, a museum and a library. U.K.A.M.A. was already available to the artists in 1974. Since then a number of artists have exhibited: V. Dobrolidge, Kateryna Krychewska-Rosanda, J. Kraykiwsky, P. Ivanec, P. Diakiw, A. Krawec as well as showings of rare pictures of such artists as Olena Kulchycka, Lew Gec, B. Lepky and the ceramic works of I. Iwanusiw and others. U.K.A.M.A. Gallery has undertaken an important role in the cultural acquisition of Ukrainians in Western Canada.

---

[3]*Svoboda Daily,* Aug. 24, 1979, A. Kurdydyk: We Shall Grow, We Shall Create.
[4]*Our Aim,* March, 1982, Artgallery "Trypilla" by Volodymyr Barabash.

UKRAINIAN CANADIAN WRITERS' ASSOCIATIONS

In one of the previous chapters — "Poets and Writers" there were presented some silhouettes of the more advanced creators of poetic art. However, in this and the following sections we wish to say something about the organizational work of poets and writers who are grouped within the "Slovo" Association and other associations created during the multicultural decade.

Slovo

The Canadian "Slovo" was founded in Toronto in November 1971, with the agreement and blessing of the Ukrainian Canadian Writers' Association "Slovo" in exile. The president was Hryhory Kostiuk and he took part in that founding meeting. *Yuriy Stefanyk* of Edmonton was elected the first head of the executive in Canada and has continued in that capacity to 1982. The election of an executive in accordance with their constitution takes place every two years, in Toronto.

Its 53 members, as of 1982, live in various provinces of Canada. Actually, the executive of Canadian "Slovo" is composed of two parts: The general administration functions in Edmonton but in addition to it there exists a Toronto branch whose head acts as a liaison officer with the executive in Edmonton. Till 1982 the following have been the heads of the Toronto branch: *Wasyl Sofroniw-Levytsky, Borys Oleksandriv* and *Dr. Oleksandra Kopach.* The general management in Edmonton in addition to its head consists of: *Oleh Zuyewsky, Bohdan Mazepa, Bohdan Medwidsky, Oleksandra Chernenko* and *Yar Slavutych*. The Toronto branch consists of *Ulas Samchuk* as a permanent assistant to the head of the general administration and further *Ivan Bodnarchuk, Maria Holod, Svitlana Hrybinska, Myron Lewyckyj, Lydia Palij, Volodymyr Skorupsky* and others.

When the Toronto branch was preoccupied with activities that are usually undertaken by literary and artist oriented organizations, such as arranging for literary evenings, speeches, concerts, etc., its head worked as a co-editor of the collections of "Slovo", especially of those issues that since 1975 were printed by the publishing establishment "Kiev", in Toronto. The task of the executive in Edmonton was, above all, to raise funds for the purpose of publishing "Slovo", especially in the collective form. Up till now there have been five collections published, plus "Anthology of Ukrainian Poetry in Canada" and some translations including the novel "On Solid Land" by Ulas Samchuk, publication of issues of "Slovo", patronizing the works by its members and so on. The general source of funds for "Slovo" have been Federal grants, Department of Multiculturalism and the Ukrainian Canadian Foundation of Taras Shevchenko, as well as profits from the sales of its publications. In 1981 "Slovo" was preparing to publish its 9th collection of anglophone anthology of Canadian-Ukrainian literature and translation of the first part of "Ost", by Ulas Samchuk. During its ten years of existence "Slovo" has acquired a substantial recognition in the publishing field. The editorial board of "Slovo" consists of: *Sviatoslav Hordynsky* (who edits a branch of poetry in collective forms), *O. Zuyewsky, Yuriy Klynovy, Oleksandra Kopach, Hryhory Kostiuk, U. Samchuk, O. Tarnawsky, Yuriy Shevelov.*[1] Association of Ukrainian Writers "Slovo" is also represented on the presidium of Ukrainian Canadian Committee.

In close cooperation with PEN Club and Amnesty International, the Presidium of "Slovo" conducted a campaign in defence of persecuted and incarcerated Ukrainian writers in Ukraine. Due to the activity of "Slovo" presidium, 10 persecuted Ukrainian writers became members of PEN Clubs in various countries. Canadian PEN honored Evhen Sverstiuk, Ivan Svitlychny and Sviatoslav Karavansky.[2]

Association of the Ukrainian Cultural Workers (A.U.C.W)

A notable number of poets and writers belong to the Association of the Ukrainian Cultural Workers (A.U.C.W.). This is rather an ideological organization. In addition to poets and writers, this organization also includes sculptors, creative artists, painters, musicians, etc. In other words, all those who work in the field of culture. A.U.C.W. encompasses not only the creators of culture in Canada, but also those of other countries, especially the U.S.A. Actually the beginning of this culture establishment took place there. After the Shevchenko Scientific Society conference 1965 held under the slogan: *"For the protection of Ukrainian culture and people"* whose aim was to oppose russification of Ukraine, it was decided to form a new establishment which would have for its objective the development of Ukrainian culture in various countries where Ukrainians settle, as well as to expose the crime of destruction of the Ukrainian culture and people in the native land.

The initiating committee in New York was headed by Dr. M. Kushnir. At the first meeting of A.U.C.W. in New York, the agenda was handed over to the newly elected administration that was headed by *Dr. Bohdan Stebelsky,* of Canada. Thus the seat of A.U.C.W. was transferred to Canada. The second meeting, which took place in 1979, reinforced the position of A.U.C.W. in Canada under B. Stebelsky. On the basis of the report by the head of the executive of A.U.C.W. the organization had really two national administrations, U.S.A. and Canada, 10 branches and 9 representatives, covering Europe, Australia and South America.

During its ten years of work the A.U.C.W. published two collections of "Estafeta", under the editorship of *B. Stebelsky* and seven monographs of "Terem" editd by *Yuriy Tys-Krokhmaluk.* In addition to this, a series of collected poems written by members of A.U.C.W. was also published, such as those by *Volodymyr Hawryluk, Leonid Poltava, Tetiana Shewchuk, Heras Sokolenko* and others. Members of the A.U.C.W., such as *Stefania Hurko, Mira Harmash, Olha Mak, Volodymyr Pasika, Volodymyr Makar, Ivan Kowaliw* and numerous others had their works printed by various publishing houses. In addition to poetry there were novels, memoirs, essays, etc. Dr. B.

---

[1] Yearly Reports of "Slovo", Author's Archives.

[2] *Svoboda Daily,* May 12-14, 1982, "Prior to the Sixth Congress of 'Slovo'" by Ostap Tarnawsky.

Stebelsky, chairman of A.U.C.W., is engaged in the problems of culture and art on a broad scope.

In the sphere of music the following were represented in the Association: *Serhiy Yaremenko, Ivan Kowaliw, Marta Krawciw-Barabash* and *Olena Hlibowych*. Amongst the activists in theatre field that have distinguished themselves are: *Volodymyr Dovhaniuk, Evhen Kurylo, Andriy Ilkiw*.

A struggle on behalf of national culture, its expressions and safeguards are the important aims that A.U.C.W., constantly proclaims in its work. The true tribune for A.U.C.W. are the pages of "Literature and Art", a supplement to the weekly newspaper, "Ukrainian Echo", which appears once a month, in Toronto.

Within each branch of the Association we find groups of art oriented youth who prepare themselves for the work in various realms of culture, but mainly they train themselves to distinguish the true expression of spirituality, which often suffers from deviation under the influence of russification in Ukraine and assimilation in diaspora.[2]

"Kozub" Ukrainian Arts Society

The Ukrainian Arts Society "Kozub" deserves special mention. It is a local Toronto Association which encompasses the workers of arts, stage, and literary world. In December, 1981 it had reached its 25th anniversary of activity which has never slackened. Their work centers on speeches and discussions on cultural themes especially relating to stage, creative art, literature, history and others. According to the archives "Kozub" has held 318 of such evenings, during its 25 years of existence. Lecturers at these evenings were the invited guests from all corners of Canada and U.S.A. On the occasion of this silver jubilee, Kozub decided to prepare an almanac along with an illustrated chronicle. For exemplary purposes only we shall name a few more noted creators of this environment. Stage: *K. Savytsky*, actor, *H. Shvedchenko*, singer, *Petro* and *Iraida Cherniak*, singer and pianist, *Hryhoriy* and *Vera Vasylenko*, actors, *Mykhaylo Gawa*, stage director, *Raisa Sadova*, opera singer, *Valentyna Rodak*, conductor, *Ivan Valko*, actor, *Leonid Skirko*, opera singer, *Valentyna Orlovska*, dramatic actress, *M. Baldetsky*, ballet master, *Yaroslaw Zavarykhin*, choreographer, *O. Hamuliak* and *Leonid Lishchyna*, radio announcers, *Iryna Dolnycka*, singer, *Yaroslav Semyshyn*, pianist. In the creative art field are: *Petro Magdenko* and *Andriy Babych*. Amongst the poets *Vera Vorsklo*, who in 1977 published a collection of poems "Lada", and *Iryna Romaniuk*.

Literary Artists in English and Others

In "Slovo" and other literary associations there are to be found literary persons who use primarily the Ukrainian language in their work. This, however, doesn't mean that there are no Ukrainian writers who do not avail themselves of the English language in their creative work. The more advanced of these are already mentioned *George Ryga, Maara Haas, Paul E. Napora, Andy Suknaski, Oleh Kupchenko, Boris Budny,* and *Volodimir Barabash* whose

---

[2]*Estafeta,* No. 1 & 2, 1971, Toronto.

verses often reflect philosophical themes and who also writes in Ukrainian. There are other writers as well, e.g. *W. Sklepoviych, Motria Farynych,* writers patriotic lyrics mostly in Ukrainian while *Maria Pankiw* and *Frances J. Kasper* write in English only, and *Ivan Dolynsky,* poet of Canadian Prairies, in English and Ukrainian.

In the seventies *Myrna Kostash* appeared upon the scene with her "All of Baba's Children". *Ted (Theodore) Galay,* a son of Manitoba pioneers, professor of the Vancouver College "Langara" wrote a play entitled "After Baba's Funeral", which was awarded first prize for one act play at a festival contest in 1979. In 1981 first prize was also awarded to *Ray Serwylo* in Pulp Press National three day novel writing contest sponsored by Liberation Books. The winner was a research assistant with Manitoba Association of School Trustees. To mark the 90th Anniversary of Ukrainian settlement in Canada a prominent writer *George Ryga* published his new play "Letters to My Son". He is also the author of "Ecstasy and Rita Joe", "Hungry Hills" and others.

Almost in all of the above mentioned poets and writers the dominant theme is Ukrainian, wherein they reveal their quest for the human as well as national values, the people to whom they trace their generation. Often the conflict of cultures and the solving of this problem is the utmost interest in their stories.

Sculpture of Pioneer Family in the Ukrainian Cultural Heritage Village.

PRESS AND ASSOCIATION OF UKRAINIAN JOURNALISTS

The Ukrainian Canadian press achieved its highest expansion after the Second World War in the fifties and the sixties, and was still on a high level, in the seventies, although alarming voices began to be heard about the scarcity of readers. At the same time, news was spreading about the financial difficulties in publishing newspapers and journals, and finally the admission that a crisis existed in the life of Ukrainian press in Canada. The shocking news came when it was announced that the first Ukrainian paper published in Canada, the *"Canadian Farmer"* which had been bought by the Trident Press in 1973 and printed by them for awhile, would finally cease publication. It may be timely to mention that towards its end the paper was well-edited. The editorial work was handled by Dr. Bohdan Martynowych (1973-78), and later on by Dr. Yuriy Mulyk-Lycyk, Nadia Gawrachynska, contributors Dr. I. Ovechko and many others. In spite of this after its long 78 years of life it ceased to exist. The deficit of this weekly paper and discussions clearly revealed that Ukrainian press, without exception, was struggling with financial difficulties. Discussions also brought up the fact that the scarcity of readers was tightly bound with the disappearance of fluency of Ukrainian language amongst the young generation.[1]

To solve the problem Ukrainian newspapers started adding English sections to their editions. The "New Pathway" of Toronto put out a separate anglophone supplement called *"New Perspectives"* and "Homin Ukrainy" began to publish its English section, the *"Ukrainian Echo"*. In Winnipeg "Postup" increased its English section *"The Progress"* whose pages were to equal the Ukrainian section. "Ukrainian Voice" for the last ten years had printed a column in English entitled *"From Behind the Official Language Curtain"* by Ivan Harmata. The weekly *"Ukrainian News"* of Edmonton solved their problem by printing editorials and historical articles in both languages. The above-mentioned practices were similarly adopted by the women's journals, *"Promin"*, *"Woman's World"* and *"Nasha Doroha"*. In general, all Ukrainian Canadian press became bilingual. It was a typical trend of the seventies. What about further prognosis for the future of the Ukrainian press in Canada? Most likely the anglophone pages will be increased. Some even perceive more revolutionary changes in general, especially when we dig deeper into the research work done along the line by Peter Desbarats in USA entitled "Industry in Transition".[2]

It has become public knowledge that Ukrainian publications exist with the support of the organization or churches with which they are affiliated, and donations from the readers. Without these outside aids, publishers would be forced to curtail their publications.[3]

---

[1] *Canadian Farmer,* October 5, 1981, "Instead of Necrologue" by Ivan Ovechko. *Vilne Slovo,* No. 40, 1981, "Why Canadian Farmer was closed?"

[2] *Winnipeg Free Press,* December 24, 1981, "Changes Sweeping Journalism" by Jan Cohen.

[3] *Winnipeg Free Press,* April 7, 1982, "Ethnic papers fight to be heard" by Dave Haynes.

How can one explain the fact that Ukrainian society is carrying on a life and death struggle to maintain its Ukrainian press without a thought of capitulation?[4] This may draw many answers but the most basic answer to it has been provided by the columnist Ivan Harmata in his article: "The Role of the Ukrainian Language Press in Canada." The arguments have been so precisely condensed that we have decided to print the highlights in full, especially since they have been reproduced on the pages of nearly all ethnocultural press in Canada, to convince its readers as to what an important role is played by the ethnocultural press in preserving the culture of a given community.

Here we quote: *Ukrainian Press*

— provides news items about the life of Ukrainian Canadians and their communities in all parts of Canada.
— It interprets general Canadian and world news from the Ukrainian Canadian point of view.
— It contributes, in the print medium, towards retention of the Ukrainian language and its acceptance and recognition within the framework of a multicultural Canada.
— It serves as a social link, joining major centres of Ukrainian population as well as smaller and isolated points.
— It provides a public forum for the interaction of views of individuals, groups and organizations within the Ukrainian Canadian community.
— It serves as a medium to provide direction and an intelligent awareness of the heritage of Ukrainian Canadians.
— It functions as a voice for the legitimate demands of Ukrainian Canadians for equality not only in the responsibilities but also in the privileges of Canadian citizenship.
— It is one of the important attributes of our Ukrainian Canadian identity.
— It is a continuing chronicle and a permanent record of the history of Ukrainian Canadians.
— It is a means of acquainting the Western World with the rich treasure-house of Ukrainian culture.
— It reflects the aspirations of the Ukrainian nation for its rightful place among the free nations of the world".[5]

Evaluating the important meaning of the Ukrainian press, in the development of community, the Ukrainians, despite great difficulties, have even strived to produce new publications. We deem it important enough to note their existence on our pages.

In the middle of 1969, and to be more precise on July 15th, Ukrainian and English bi-weekly appeared in Vancouver entitled: *"The Ukrainian Pacific News."* It was edited by Petro Pihychyn, a former editor of "Ukrainian Thought" in London, who had also been at one time editor of the "Canadian Farmer." Its aim was to serve the Ukrainians of Greater Vancouver, British Columbia and western States of the U.S.A. In less than half a year of its existence it was liquidated.

---

[4]*Our Aim,* No. 3, 1981, Toronto, "Ukrainian Press" by W. Didiuk.

[5]*The Other Canadians* by Isydore Hlynka, Winnipeg, 1981, "Role of Ukrainian Language Press" p. 135, also "Language is the soul of people" p. 129.

In 1975-76 D. Farkavec published *"Canadoon" (Canadian),* a pocketsize monthly of satire, which appeared very irregularly. The same happened to another publication, titled *"Canadian Ukraine",* a sporadic tabloid, under the editorship of Yar Slavutych. More regular in appearance has been: "Lubystok", a magazine of literature, arts and literary critics, published every four months since 1975 with editor Petro Rojenko. *"Bukovina",* Ukrainian quarterly edited by Alexander Kowalsky (since 1974) in Toronto, "Anabasis", a quarterly magazine with nationalistic political and ideological profile, started in Cleveland in 1980 and transferred to Toronto shortly after. It was published by Valentyn Moroz, a former political freedom fighter and prisoner of the USSR, who arrived in the West in 1979. In 1970 the Church of Ukrainian Faith started publishing its quarterly "Novi Skryzhali", a religious magazine with Dr. M. Shkavrytko as editor-in-chief. The World Congress of Free Ukrainians publishes *"Bulletin of the World Congress of Free Ukrainians"* as a semi-yearly tabloid, edited by Bohdan Hoshovsky.

The newspaper *"OKO",* appeared as a bi-weekly in Montreal, in 1979. It is edited regularly by an association: "La Campagne de Publication "OKO" Ltd." Its sub-title states: "OKO" is not affiliated with any political, religious, or cultural organization and open to any opinion that does not contradict objective facts and is expressed in a lucid and rational manner. The Association is comprised of the following directors: W. Hayduk, R. Kosmyra, B. Kerechinski, W. Lewyckyj, Irka Powidajko and B. Tymyc.

"OKO" was edited by Wolodymyr Lewyckyj (1979-1982) and lately by V. Hayduk, A. Lysak, and N. Strilets. Some of the articles also appear in English and French languages. With every year the paper becomes more popular and finds its way even to Western Canada.

The quarterly, entitled the *"Co-ordinator"* appears quite regularly. It is the organ of the Ukrainian Co-operative Council of Canada, in Toronto. The first edition appeared in 1970, dated January - March. The "Co-ordinator" also supports the activities of the Ukrainian World Co-operative Council, created in October 1973. It is edited by Bohdan Hoshowsky with the help of such regular contributors as A. Kachor, W. Sytnyk, W. Kucyj, I. Leshchyshyn.

"Student" first issue appeared in 1968. This is a national monthly newspaper published by the Ukrainian Canadian Students' Union. This is an open forum for facts and opinion reflecting the interests of Ukrainian Canadian students on various topics — social, cultural, political and religious. During the 13 years of its publication there have been 71 issues, edited mostly in English and Ukrainian as well. Editors in chief: Roman Serbyn (1968), Bohdan Krawchenko and Chrystyna Chomiak (1969), Yuriy Boshyk (1970), Zenon Zwarych (70-71), Irka Okipniuk and Andriy Bandera (71-72), Halia Kuchmij (72-73), Myroslaw Shkandrij (73-74), Anhelyna Szuch (74-75), Lubromyr Szuch (75-76), Bohdan Kupych (76-77), Nestor Makuch (77-79). Since 1970 "Student" is administered by a coordinating committee of four people. In this capacity were: Mark Ferbey, Jaroslaw Balan, Sonia Maryn, Bohdan Zajcew, Dave Lupul and others. "Student" receives neither university nor government subsidy. Its revenue is raised through fees, collected by SUSK, private donations, special fundraising events, etc. Since January 1980, "Student" has been a member of the Canadian University Press.

Finally a few words about the anglophone supplements.

"New Perspectives" has been a monthly supplement of the "New Pathway." Since 1977 it has been published in co-operation with the Ukrainian National Youth Federation of Canada. Its editor is Zenon F. Zwarych and his co-workers Sonia Maryn, Myroslava Pastyr, Myron Barycky, Larysa Rohowsky, Ulana Plawuszczak, Yuriy Weretelnyk, Roman Washchuk, Chris Fedyna and others. The supplement is well edited and presents the attitude of the young generation towards the processes of Ukrainian life. It also pays much attention to the past life of Ukrainians in Canada.

"Ukrainian Echo", the monthly supplement to the "Homin Ukrainy" appeared in 1976. It was edited from its beginning by Andriy Bandera, a student activist, in co-operation with the students recruited from the ranks of the Ukrainian Youth Association of Canada such as Yaroslav Zayac, Irene Mohr, Dr. Oleh Romanyshyn and others. "Ukrainian Echo" is well edited, interesting and has numerous readers.

During the last decade the Ukrainian press of Canada lost three of its foremost editors, namely: Ivan Syrnick (1904-1972), Wasyl Sofroniw-Levytsky, and Dr. Bohdan Martynowych (1915-1978). Also the long time editor of the "Ukrainian News" of Edmonton, Dr. Michael Sopulak retired in 1981 and his place was taken over by Michael Chomiak, the former editor of the newspaper "Dilo" of Lviv, in co-operation with Rev. M. Diadio. The "New Pathway" which celebrated its 50th Anniversary in 1980 has undergone great changes. In 1977 its editorial staff and administration were transferred from Winnipeg to Toronto. There were several editors after its transfer and this did not bring any stabilizing atmosphere for the paper. This situation changed considerably when Volodymyr Skorupsky, a well known poet became its editor. Vera Ke with her page, "Joy and Sorrow", had always provided humor and entertainment in this paper.

A characteristic phenomenon of the last decade has been that on the pages of the papers we do not see any more hatred-filled polemics of past years. This, more likely, may be attributed to the existence of the Association of Ukrainian Journalists (A.U.J.) which came into being in 1966 and expanded its activities in the seventies. One of its aims was to safeguard the journalistic ethics.

A.U.J. unites over 80 members-journalists, active editors, writer-correspondents and disc jockeys of radio and television. In 1971-1976 there was a youth section, headed by Iryna Makaryk, which even published a separate collection of its works. The work of A.U.J. carried on the following activities; contests for young writers, awards for finest works, grants for student journalists, panels, orations, press conferences, co-operative work with origanizations of Ukrainian journalists in U.S.A., conventions as well as the publication of "The Ukrainian Journalist". Exceptional and almost annual attraction and popular arrangement of A.U.J. in Canada were the contests of Ukrainian Press and Radio, taking place in Toronto.

A.U.J. has also taken and still is, an active part in the defence of political prisoners in USSR, especially of the journalists, and is a member of the Ukrainian Canadian Committee and the World Congress of Free Ukrainians. At the second W.C.F.U., on the initiative of Canadian A.U.J., a new organization came into existence: "The World Association of Ukrainian Journalists" whose heads, according to the Constitution exchange their duties yearly. The more important task undertaken by A.U.J. is the encouragement given to young Ukrainian journalists.*[6] The heads of A.U.J. through the years have been: Oleksander Matla, (1969); Mykola Lypovetsky (1977-78); Wasyl Didiuk (1975-76) who has been at the helm since 1979.

Editors of Ukrainian papers are also members of Canadian Federation of Ethnic Press, with its executive in Toronto and with branches in almost all provinces. Members of these associations hold their meetings and consultations to deal with financial difficulties and advertising. The latter is the most important source of income to assure their solvency. They also pay a great deal of attention to the problems of ethnocultural journalism, multiculturalism, and multilingualism.

Commemorative Medallion on the occasion of Seventy-fifth Anniversary of Alberta.

[6] *A Collection of Works of the Youth Section of the Association of Journalists of Canada,* Toronto, 1973.

STAGE AND RELATED PROFESSIONS

Winnipeg appears as a capital of Ukrainian Canadian community. The church hierarchy, the Metropolitan seats of both Catholic and Orthodox churches are located here, and Ukrainian Canadian Committee headquarters are situated here. Toronto must be awarded the palm leaf of being the first in the art world, having gained this recognition shortly after the arrival of the so-called third immigration after the Second World War. In Toronto, are grouped not only the leading writers, painters and poets, but also the high-priests of stage art such as the actors, singers, musicians, choreographers, choral and dance ensembles, and others. Here also grew the young art-oriented forces of the newest decade. It is towards this segment of life that we wish to direct our attention.

In the theatrical world special recognition has been given to the *"Zahrava"* group during its thirty years of existence. Since 1972 it has been a member of the *Ontario Multicultural Theatre Association* which, in 1980, counted some 40 theatrical groups. Every year in July a festival is held in which *"Zahrava"* takes part with unequalled success. In 1977 *Yuriy Belsky* was awarded the honor of the best actor at the festival. In 1980 he received the award as the leading actor, while the drama "After Baba's Funeral" received the highest award as the stage drama of the year. In the same year *Volodymyr Dovhaniuk*, a long-time actor and co-founder of the theatre, and lately its head and the very soul of it, was awarded a prize for his brilliant acting in three multi-faceted characters and again in 1981 the award for best leading actor. In 1978, N. Telizhyn distinguished himself as the finest actor of the festival in the drama "The Marriage", and in 1979 *Maria Lucka-Lewycka* received the award for the most beautiful costumes. There were other distinguished events in the life of "Zahrava" at these festivals. Although the actors and actresses of "Zahrava" are on a professional level and garner top awards, they still have to earn their daily bread in various occupations. In addition to those mentioned above it behooves us to mention a few other members of the hard-working ensemble such as *Hanna Tahayiw, A. Ilkiw, Nina Tarnowecka, Maria Sluzarivna, Slav Telizhyn (Tuzhansky), Nina Mykolenko-Telizhyn, Christine Turkewych, Christine Temnyk, Olha Babych, T. Kushnirenko, K. Savytsky, Nadia Kuca, Roma Dolnycka, Taras Parchenko, Valia Orlyk* (Orlovska), *M. Lialka, N. Momotutka* and others.

The theatre locates itself at the Ukrainian Cultural Centre on Christie Street, and presents its stage craft not only in various cities of Canada, such as Montreal and Winnipeg, but it also travels to U.S.A. cities such as New York, Philadelphia, Detroit and others. "Zahrava" belongs to one of the ten best ensembles in the city of Toronto. Its repertoire contains over 20 artistic creations of stage such as "Advocate Markian", "Yevshan Zilla", "Motria" and others.

Since 1979 the theatrical group *"Muse"* has presented its works. These are young students, enthusiasts of theatrical arts. They have been under the art directorship of Mykhaylo Gawa (who at one time was director of S.U.M.K. Ensemble). They have presented two plays from the pen of S. Vasylchenko "Na pershi huli" and "Which Way the Wind Blows" and a comedy by S. Biela, "Oldtimers", and lately "Marusia Churay". Critics have given a positive appraisal of the work of this student ensemble, which is located at St. Volodymyr Institute. The strong supporters of this ensemble are: *Larysa Robovsky, Kateryna Malkovska, Maxym Kolesnyk, Ihor Rohovsky, Lubomyr Khabursky, Olena Bulat, Roman Hurko, Yuriy Horhota, Tetiana Chupryna* and *Andrey Hurko.* The basic aim of the "Muse" is to create interest in the stage by choosing talented and interested young people who would study and learn good literary language, history of native culture and stage play.[1]

Ukrainian artistic forces of Toronto organized, in 1974, the *Canadian Ukrainian Opera Association* which, in 1979, presented the immortal "Cossack Beyond the Danube", that had been staged first in Canada in 1917. In 1979 this Association staged the opera "Kupalo", by A. Vakhnianyn, which was repeated in several cities in Canada. The genre of "Kupalo" consists of a historical, psychological drama intertwined with national folk stories, legends and songs. This is a presentation of high class artistic genre that binds together songs, instrumental music, words, play acting and choreography. The Canadian Ukrainian Opera Association attributes the success of this play to *Volodymyr Kolesnyk*, the former director and artist of National Theatre and Opera of Taras Shevchenko in Kiev, who, in 1972, asked for asylum in Australia along with his family. He was a guest-conductor in Australia (Sydney and Adelaide) and later in Canada. He directed Hamilton Symphony Orchestra and the C.B.C. Orchestra in Vancouver. During the short time of its existence the Canadian Ukrainian Opera Association organized several concerts of operatic music in the cities of Canada, as well as of U.S.A. It united better artistic and operatic forces, such as *Roksolana Roslak, Hanna Kolesnyk* (former Kievan opera singer), *Leonid Skirko, Irena Welhash, Korneliy Optof, Bohdan Chaplynsky, Andrey Soroka, Zenon Lavryshyn* (the composer) and others. A valuable informational service about Ukrainian Canadian stage is rendered by Oksana Bryzhun-Sokolyk and Bohdan Holynsky, authors of numerous musical reviews and essays on musical topics.

Since 1970 a musical association known as "Ukrainian Musical Festival", in Toronto, has set as its goal to organize musical publications and bring into being a specialized musical library, with the aid of music festivals that are held almost every year . . . the tenth one taking place in 1981. Ukrainian Musical Festival has published some compositions of such composers as Z. Lavryshyn, V. Wytwycky, M. Krawciw-Barabash and others. Others who have distinguished themselves in this field were: Rev. B. Malowany, Tetiana Tkachenko, Martha Khomyn.

In the seventies, in Toronto, artistic work was produced by a couple, *Borys Dniprovy* and *Evhenia Chayka*. They arrived in 1968, after being a few years in Paris. They organized a theatrical group that presented stage plays. In 1973-1974 they produced a film for children and young people called: "The Fern Flower." They cut over 30 record albums, seven of them being of their own

---

[1] *Homin Ukrainy*, October 21, 1981. "Young Ukrainians on Stage" by A. Royick.

creation. Borys Dniprovy has also composed songs that have been recorded on albums.[2]

A special place upon the artistic stage belongs to *Taras Shypovyk*. He is an artist in choreography, song, composition, a connoisseur of jazz, ballet, modern dancing, including the artistic modern acrobatics... in one word, the universal artist. With his artistic group "Odessa", he took part in the festivals of Ontario Multicultural Theatrical Association and organized the so-called Ukrainian Cabaret, with the help of *Ted Voloshyn* and *Olha Cholkan*.

For many years Toronto has had artistic vocal ensembles about which we have written before, such as Men's Choir, "Prometheus". Women's Choir "Dibrova", wind-instrument orchestra "Baturyn", all of them conducted under the experienced baton of the conductor *Wasyl Kardash,* who is also a composer. With their appearances, these choirs have made a name for themselves not only in Canada but also in the U.S.A. and Europe. The choir "Vesnivka", under the direction of *Kvitka Zorych-Kondratska* has also brought fame to its name. The quartette "Verkhovyna" under the direction of *Olena Hlibowych* carries on its incessant activity. *The Men's Choir of T. H. Shevchenko* and *The Women's Choir "Hahilka"* have also distinguished themselves. Male Choir "Burlaka" reactivated and strengthened its performances under the energetic conductorship of Oleh Khmil.

Toronto has a greater opportunity than other centres of Canada to host guest artists from various parts of Canada and other countries, such as the famous violinist, *S. Staryk* and *Alec Chorney,* who won the North American fiddling championship for three years in a row, a pianist virtuoso *Christine Petrowsky-Bregend,* the Winnipeg born singer *Edward Evanko, Leo Evanson,* member of Canadian Opera, not to mention the artists who, are part of Toronto community, like Osyp Goshulak, Zenia Kushpeta, Markiana Dublanycia-Huzar, Olenka Hlibowych, Eleonora Berbenec-Bilynska, Stefa Fedchuk, S. Zolkewych-Krekhowec, Joan Karasevich, Roksolana Roslak, Luba Goy, an actress of comedy genre, who appears with the ensemble of Royal Canadian Air Farce. Here also appears on the horizon the new piano star *Olenka Bovkun* and soprano *Jane Kowalchuk*. Artists from U.S.A. often come here, due to the favourable communication with cultural centres of America. We also meet here with guest artists from Europe such as composer *A. Hnatyshyn* from Vienna, *O. Luciv* from London, *Volodymyr Denysenko,* the solo baritone of the Great Theatre of Warsaw, the opera singer *Andriy Dudych,* soloist of the National Opera of Warsaw and others. In 1980 while on a concert tour of Canada the famous Byzantine Choir from Holland under direction of M. Antonovych appeared with its Ukrainian repertoire.

In Toronto there are lesser, but nevertheless popular stage vocal groups that appeared in the seventies, such as the choir *"Boyan",* under the direction of *Zenon Lavryshyn,* the strong orchestra of Professor Ivan Kowaliw, the Hutsul Orchestra *"Dovbush",* the Women's Choir *"Jasmin",* in Mississauga, the *Kohut's Orchestra* at Etobicoke, *the "Yavir" Dance Ensemble* at the church of St. Demetrius. There is a long and rich history behind *the Kapella of Bandurists* under the direction of *Valentyna Rodak*.

---

[2]*Our Aim,* No. 39-40, 1981, "Jubilees".

Toronto was privileged to witness crowning success of Ukrainian Canadian beauty Donna Sawicky, an 18 year old student from Kitchener — Waterloo, winner of the "Miss Canada 1972" title in the 25th annual pageant held in Toronto on November 8, 1971. Donna's successful contest reminded Torontonians of another beauty-queen, Marianne Lenchak, popular "Miss Toronto" of 1958.

In addition to Toronto, Eastern Canada has other cultural centres such as Montreal where the *Men's Choir "Ukraina"* has been active for the past 30 years,[3] and the *Ballet of Petro Marunczak,* the champion of Ukrainian ballet in Eastern Canada.[4] At the Montreal S.U.M. Centre, *The Boyan Choir* under the direction of *Rostyslav Kupish* has been active during the last few years, and so has the *"Trembita" Orchestra* under the artistic directionship of *Yuriy Kulycky.* The *"Zoria"* Ensemble of *Bohdan Tymyc* has also been solidly entrenched and enriched by several record albums. *Anna Chornodolska,* started her career in Montreal and now is a widely acclaimed soloist in Canada and the U.S.A.

Of distinction are choirs *"Young Ukraine"* and Women's Choir *"Ukraine"* at the association "Prosvita" in Verdun under the direction of I. C. Kozachok.

In Sudbury the *"Dnipro Choir"*, under the direction of *Olha Mysyk-Rohatyn* has been in existence for many years and celebrated its 50th Anniversary in 1981. Also the dance group *"Veselka"* is active. Two dance ensembles *"Sokoly"* and *"Kolomya"* are both active in Oshawa, as well as the U.C.C. choir *"Trembita".* Lately the *"Desna"* choir was formed in St. Catherines, but the *Bandurist Ensemble "Kobzari",* under the direction of *Okrsana Metulynska* has been in existence here for many years. She also runs a school for teaching bandura.

Hamilton has several ensembles, the most noted one for its long years of activity, is the singing and dancing ensemble *"Chayka"* under the direction of *Y. Klun* and *M. Kostyk;* Choir *"Homin"* sponsored by *Ukrainian Youth Association* under direction of Natalia Skypas-Prockiw. There is also the Women's Choir *"Berizka".* Ottawa, too, has its bandura and dance ensembles. Other artistic associations exist in Eastern Canada that devote their work to stage craft and strive to develop the Ukrainian art amidst the young generation. On the whole it presents a colorful scene of lively activities.

In Western Canada, Winnipeg and Edmonton are competing with their staging achievements. Winnipeg is enjoying the long lasting life of *"Koshetz's Choir",* while Edmonton is happy with the fruits of labour provided by the mixed *Choir "Dnipro"* and the *Men's Choir "Kashtany".* The dance ensembles *"Rusalka"* and *"Orlan"* of Winnipeg, rival in their work with a similar ensemble in Edmonton, the *"Shumka"* with choreographer Orest Semchuk and E. Zvozdecky, musical director. It has appeared not only in the larger cities of Canada but has also performed in Japan, Tunisia and other parts of the world. "Rusalka" is the only one that was privileged to be hosted with their appearance in Ukraine, but with their program greatly curtailed. During

---

[3]*New Pathway,* #21, 1981, Jubilee Celebrations of 30 Anniversary of the Men's Choir "Ukraina" in Montreal by Maria Davydovych.

[4]*New Pathway,* April 1, 1971, "Montreal is proud of its artists: 25 years of work by the ballet master Petro Marunczak" by Maria Logush.

the last few years it has vied for first place with a somewhat younger group, the *Orlan,* directed by Dr. Taras R. Babick.

As in Winnipeg, so likewise in Edmonton, there are other artistic personalities. Here, among the church choirs the first place belongs to *G. Hnatiuk's* at the Blessed Virgin Mary Parish and St. Nicholas Choir directed by *Rev. B. Sloboda.* The students' choir *"Tyrsa",* at the St. Volodymyr and Olha Cathedral under the baton of *Virlana Kysilewska-Holowka* belongs to a separate category for it has behind it a series of performances in Europe, Australia and even in Japan. At the Canadian Ukrainian Institute of "Prosvita" the *"Dumka"* choir, formerly the S.U.M. choir, has renewed its work under the direction of I. Buyachok. There is also *"Hoosli"* Ensemble (since 1970) under the direction of W. Zulak, lately of Mike Zakaluzny and Tom Sobkow as well as the *"Bandurist"* Choir and the Women's Choir *"Barvinok."* Very active and successful areas are the several students' ensembles of quartets, such as *"Troyanda", "Red Poppies"* and *"Volia",* an instrumental quartet, under the direction of M. Kurievych. Also Winnipeg has the *S.U.M.K. Dancers,* directed by Irka Balan and Ben Vasylyshyn.

Winnipeg has its own well known opera soloists: *Irka Welhash — Spolsky, Jaroslaw Schur* and *Cecil Semchyshyn.* The last one named is a director and producer of dramatic plays. In 1977 he re-activated the work of *Ukrainian Theatre* that first came into existence in the sixties. Although the opera *"Cossack Beyond the Danube"* was a stage success, but not at the box office, C. Semshyshyn stated in his interview with the Free Press correspondent: "It's almost impossible to do these things without outside help, both private and government. It's challenging to our imagination and ingenuity to find ways to do things without financial help from government.[5]

Lubomyr Melnyk, another Winnipeg pianist and composer, is considered by music critics to be one of the most outstanding composers in Canada, at the present time. His performances, in Europe, were sponsored by Canadian Cultural Council. Ukrainian Theatre of Winnipeg sponsored also two productions by Torontonian "Zahrava" for its Winnipeg patrons.

We wish to mention that in 1981 the position of the musical director of the Winnipeg Royal Ballet was held by *Volodymyr Babiak,* a connoisseur of Ukrainian music and dance, and a violinist, well known on Radio and T.V. New stars of stage appeared in the name of *Alexis Kochan-Budyk* and *Kathy Wach.*

In Dauphin, Manitoba, there is the now well known *Canada's National Ukrainian Festival* choir, under the baton of *Helen Lazaruk-Henderson.* The choir has been in existence since the inception of Canada's National Ukrainian Festival, in 1966. In 1972 the Zirka Dance Ensemble was organized and the *National Riding and Dancing Cossacks,* of Dauphin (in 1973) as well.

In Edmonton the following choirs are active: The *"Verkhovyna"* directed previously by S. Yaremenko and after by M. Dytyniak and Irka Tkhoryk. The S.U.M.K. Choir under the direction of M. Hvozdecky, *the Men's Choir of Ivan Franko,* and the *Women's Choir "Vesnianka"* as well as the *S.U.M.K. Dancers "Cheremshyna."* Lately the folk ballet ensemble "Yewshan" started its activi-

---

[5] *Winnipeg Free Press,* Nov. 25, 1977. "Revived Ukrainian Theatre to present "Cossacks in Exile"" by Janice Keys.

ties. In Calgary there is a mixed choir that has existed for a number of years and directed by *Halia Fedkiw*. Vegreville has its dancing group the *"Sopilka."*

In Saskatoon, in addition to the *Catholic Cathedral Choir,* there also exist the *Orthodox Cathedral Choir* (since 1971) under the direction of Lavrenty Klapushchak and *S.U.M.K. Choir* directed by Linda Volion.

In Vancouver the Lysenko Mixed Choir directed by R. Semak has a long history of quality presentations. There are also several other ensembles such as "Homin" directed by Vasyl Shmigel (1973) the women's ensemble *"Voloshky"* (1963) and lately *Women's Bandura Ensemble* (1980). The last two mentioned are directed by Anna Kozak. There we also mention the dance ensemble *"Cheremshyna"* (1969) directed by Nestor Trafenenko and the children's dance ensemble *"Zirka"* trained by M. and Z. Andriashyn and K. and T. Ketura. All these ensembles often perform in urban centres of B.C. and in Spokane, Seattle, Portland and other U.S.A. cities. Kelowna has its mandolin orchestra, directed by Ivan Hnatyshyn.

Thunder Bay, formerly known as Fort William and Port Arthur, is a Ukrainian cultural island and a crossroad between East and West, which always has been in the lead with its organizational and cultural life of Ukrainian Canadians. For years here have been cultural ensembles such as *"Prosvita" Women's Choir, Ivan Franko Men's Choir, the Mixed Choir "Carpaty"*. All three under the direction of conductor *Hryhoriy Myhal*. Rev. *M. Maluzynsky* conducts the vocal ensemble *"Probratymy"* at the local branch of the Brotherhood of Veterans of the 1st Division U.N.A. Here are ensembles: *"S.U.M. Barwinok", Dance Ensemble "Veselka"* and *Vocal and Dance "Vesnivka"*. There are other ensembles, too. Here also exists a radio program under auspices of the Ukrainian Canadian Committee under the direction of Ilko Kozyra. Also from this area is talented cymbalist Ted Harasymchuk. Thunder Bay has a rich heritage of Ukrainian activities.

The above-mentioned ensembles and many others not mentioned present Ukrainian classical, or folk music. There are, however, ensembles of modern music, known as Ukrainian Canadian country music, or the so-called Western music. First step in this direction were made by such musical ensembles as *"Mickey and Bunny", "Kobza", "Armika", "Peter Picklyk"*, the *"Interlake Polka Kings", "Syny Stepiw", "Vizerunky Shlakhiw", "Suzirya and Trio Kalyna", "Nova Hvylia Orchestra"* with *Petro Pyrih* and *the Holubtsi, Les Q,* etc. This type of music is popular among the young but not the old. Gradually a chink has developed between the classical ensembles and the modern music of today. But when we consider the fact that music *not only* preserves the historical traditions and culture of the people, but also it unites the generations together. It will be understood that this kind of music will make some inroads sooner or later. But it doesn't mean that it will outlast the classical. The modern is disseminated in greater measure by record albums. A great deal was contributed to the appreciation of their music by the Ukrainian Canadian recording firms like V-Records (A. Groshak) Winnipeg, Yevshan Records (Bohdan Tymyc) of Montreal, also released album collection of traditional Ukrainian Christmas Carols and others.

Among the vocal and dance ensembles are highly qualified persons who have worked for many years. There are some with high musical qualifications. Here we mention the graduates of the *Institute of Lysenko* in *Lviv* and the *Kiev Conservatory.*

Some musicians are members of the Canadian Music Teachers' Association. In 1972 at Edmonton *The Association of Ukrainian Musicians* was founded by N. Dmytruk, R. Soltykewych, S. Yaremenko, M. Dytyniak, S. Grokh, A. Bayrak, I. Pawlykowska and O. Oliynyk.

Actors of the Ukrainian stage have formed their *Association of the Artists of Ukrainian Stage* (O.M.U.S.). This organization was first founded in Europe. In 1971, it was renewed in U.S.A. and Canada, with headquarters in Philadelphia. Its head, at first, was Yuriy Kononiv who was later succeeded by Volodymyr Shasharowsky and in 1981 by Volodymyr Levytsky. In 1975, O.M.U.S. published "Our Theatre" (1915-1975), a collection of historical essays and memoirs, Volume I. Volume II of memoirs is being prepared. O.M.U.S. is a very active group of professionals.

The Ukrainian stage in Canada suffered great losses in the seventies. The following have departed from the scene: Anna Zavarykhin (1972), Mykhaylo Tahaiw (1972), Hanna Tahaiw (1976), Roman Soltykevych (1976), Mykhaylo Holynsky (1973), Taras Hubicky (1974), K.M. Oleshkevych (1975), Daria Nyzankiwska-Snihurowych (1980), Yuriy Holovko (1980), Lavro Kempe (1981). Also in 1981 Wasyl Avramenko, who had created a new epoch of Ukrainian dancers in Canada and other countries of the Western world, died in U.S.A.

An opportunity for evaluating the work of actors and lovers of stage comes from the yearly Ukrainian festivals and other gatherings of national importance. So far, for historical records we can name the larger festivals that take place during the summer months such as: the *"Vesna"* in Saskatoon, March-June, *"Caravan"* in Toronto, in June, *"Pysanka"* at Vegreville, in July, *"Folklorama"* in Winnipeg in August. Among the most popular ones is the *Canadian National Ukrainian Festival in Dauphin* which always takes place at the end of July and beginning of August. This festival was started in 1965 after the discovery of the place where the first Divine Liturgy in Canada was held in 1897, in the vicinity then called Terebowla (popularly Trembowla), now Valley River, near Dauphin, where the Cross of Freedom was also erected. This historic event contributes to the popularity of the festival.[6]

The date also marks the beginning of organized Ukrainian church life, started by Rev. Nestor Dmytriw, then editor of the newspaper "Svoboda", in U.S.A. This event is celebrated annually by the Ukrainian National Association in U.S.A. and Canada with Church participation. Every year a special Divine Liturgy is held at the "Cross of Freedom", during the Dauphin Festival. Here also is the bust of Rev. N. Dmytriw sculped by the artist Leo Mol and financed by Ukrainian National Association. Here are preserved the cultural memorials of the district, such as the church of St. Michael, the first school building in Terebowla and others. All these are cared for by the Cross of Freedom Corporation headed by John Slobodzian and Michael Szewczyk, the latter one having put in a great amount of labour towards the creation of Dauphin Festival and preservation and further expansion of Terebowla and Dauphin's Ukrainiana.

---

[6] *Winnipeg Tribune,* April 28, 1964, Steve Melnyk: "Ukrainians may enshrine old Dauphin farm house".

There is no doubt that the expression of Ukrainian stage culture is more than an average affair. Numerous song and dance ensembles bring respect for Ukrainians, in general, and help to mobilize the youthful forces to engage in the cultural stream of activities. This sector of work also requires steady guidance and care to direct this stream towards a certain aim and to constantly raise the level of the planned work. A great role in this regard is played by the so-called seminars of choir directors. Every year since 1976 seminars for choir directors are held in Canada. These are experienced music oriented leaders who teach both the theoretic and practical choir directing. Every year dozens of young choir directing enthusiasts take advantage of these courses.

The first three seminars were held in Eastern Canada on the initiative of Provincial Council of U.C.C., under the direction of Olena Hlibowych. The further guidance of these seminars was taken over by the Ukrainian Musical Association of Alberta, under the helm of Serge Yaremenko, Maria Dytyniak and others. By 1981 the sixth such seminar was held in Edmonton. These seminars have been conducted by highly qualified musicologists such as: Dr. P. Macenko, Volodymyr Kolesnyk, Dr. Bohdan Kushnir, Yuriy Oransky, Serhiy Yaremenko, Dr. Myroslav Antonovych. Seminars for choir directing received financial aid from the Directorate of Multiculturalism.

The Ukrainian dance ensembles of Canada strive every year to arrange for seminars of Ukrainian choreography. This undoubtedly would strengthen the work and raise the level of existing dance ensembles, as well as lead to the creation of new dancing units. We must also state that a notable part of song and dance ensembles were formed during the multicultural decade.

Logo of the Ukrainian Music Festival.

RADIO, TELEVISION AND FILM
IN THE ERA OF MULTICULTURALISM

Radio

In the multicultural decade, radio, television and film advanced, but without any noticeable revelations. In the field of radio transmissions many stations had to huddle in close quarters, although four new ethnocultural stations came into existence.

In 1974, after long efforts, Winnipeg, at last, got its first so-called multi-ethnocultural station, C.K.J.S., as a result of efforts of K. Stanchykowski, wherein were centred the programs of various ethnic groups. C.K.J.S. inaugurated its programs in 1975. Mayor Steve Juba, of Winnipeg, warmly welcomed the decision of the C.R.T.C. to grant this type of a station for which long drawn out effort had been made. In 1981, on this station there were over 27 different programs, in as many languages. Here the Ukrainian program runs to 1½ hours daily. Amongst the various programs there are daily news and comments upon Ukrainian themes. Bodhan Zajcew directed the program at the beginning and since 1979 Bohdana Bashuk, Myroslava Stelmach. From the alloted time for the Ukrainians, various religious denominations have their programs such as *The Voice of Orthodoxy* by Rev. T. Slavchenko, the Seventh Day Adventists, Baptist program *"The Voice of Hope"* etc. There were also Ukrainian Catholic programs during the years 1975-1977. Due to the fact that time for broadcasting was limited, the *"Voice of Ukraine"* was transferred to Portage la Prairie station CFRY. From this station Rev. S. Izyk transmits his program since 1978. The CKDM radio of Dauphin transmits some programs in Ukrainian language also.

Several radio programs exist in Edmonton. The French radio station CHFA regularly transmitted (1970-1980) the Catholic program of Basilian Fathers entitled the "Evening Hour" under the direction of Rev. M. Nychka. Since 1980 this program has been continued on CKER.

The Ukrainian Catholic Council of Alberta, with its program on radio station CHFA established in 1963 by Roman Ostashewsky, has quite a history. Hryhor Porochiwnyk was in charge of this program during a ten year period (1967-1976). In 1976-1977 it was conducted by Dr. W. Hyrak and in 1977-1981 by Dr. A. Hornjatkevyč. In 1981, it was taken over by Rev. M. Nychka on the multicultural radio station CKER.

Since the beginning of CKER a new Ukrainian 1½ hour program came into being under the name "In Our Community." This program has attracted a number of young people: Roman Onufrijchuk, Bohdan Chomiak, Myroslav Bodnaruk, Roman Brytan, Bohdan Zajcew, Daria Markevych, Karen Gartner, Yarema Kovalchuk, Irka Onufrijchuk, Anhelyna Shuch and others.

The mission programs of the *Ukrainian Voice of Orthodoxy* are carried regularly since 1977 from station CIOK in St. Paul and the CFOK. These radio stations transmit the religious and lay programs of Rev. T. Slavchenko and K. Telychko. In addition to this, the Ukrainian Greek-Orthodox Church and Self-Reliance League of Alberta avail themselves of the station SKER in their programs "Access". The pioneer path in these radio transmissions has been traced to Kost Telychko since 1952. Similar programs were broadcast in Saskatoon by Rev. Hryhory Udod. Ukrainian Orthodox programs are transmitted by the ethnocultural station CHIN in Toronto. These programs are entitled "Blahovisnyk" of Eastern Eparchy and directed by Petro Rodak and Rev. T. Slavchenko.

Toronto and surrounding area benefited for a long time from the Ukrainian radio broadcasts from Buffalo directed by Wasyl Sharvan which were terminated in 1981. The longest lasting radio broadcasting champion in Toronto was Prokip Naumchuk with his daily one hour program *"The Song of Ukraine"* on waves of station CHWO (1250). *The Song of Ukraine* echoed in Toronto and surrounding areas since March 1959. During this time it acquired a wide circle of listeners and numerous co-workers and friends and thus this station became very popular among Ukrainians in Northern Ontario and Northern America borderlands. Talented announcers were working at this station, Yuriy Pochyniuk and Zina Prusachenko at the beginning and later on Borys Dniprovy, Victoria Naumchuk, Olenka Hlibowych, O. Sahaydakiwsky, Nadia Kuca, Stepan Horlach, Daria Rezchynska and others. The program also includes sport news, children's hour (Yaroslava Lomaga and Myroslav Fotiy) and other items. The director of this program, P. Naumchuk organized a studio and the library of record albums and tape recordings of various engagements, concerts, performances of noted artists . . . in one word, a laboratory of great labor that contains archival values for future researchers of word, music and history.

In Vancouver there is a radio and television program directed by Myroslav Bondaruk, and in Ottawa a half hour radio program on Carleton Radio under direction of Mykhaylo Bociurkiw. Montreal has several programs, among them the one by E. Y. Oryschuk, in St. Leonard, Quebec the "Ukrainian Time" edited by I. Oparick. From time to time there are Ukrainian programs from Windsor, St. Catharines, Kitchener-Waterloo, Prince Albert, Flin Flon and other places.

As P. Namchuk of Toronto has earned Ukrainian gratitude for his many Ukrainian radio programs, so has likewise Rev. S. Izyk in Winnipeg who has become a veteran in that field. His program, "Voice of Ukraine", previously known as *"Voice from the Native Country",* celebrated its 25th Anniversary in 1980. In order to carry on incessantly this type of work required services of several radio stations and he wandered from Dauphin's CKDM to Winnipeg's CKSB and CBC, then on to Portage la Prairie's CFRY, then returned to Winnipeg's CKJS and back again to CFRY in Portage la Prairie. This proves how difficult it is to obtain broadcast time on the radio for Ukrainian programs to serve community needs.

From the observation of the Ukrainian radio programs in Canada it would appear that they may be found in almost every larger Ukrainian community, and in some cities with more than just one. All these programs are bound with the life of local communities primarily in the field of general information, the Ukrainian song, cultural life and historical past. A noticeable group of organizations are involved in religious programs and devote much time to cultural affairs. They all have to struggle with great financial problems for basically these are costly programs. The stations are privately owned, and the programs are only possible through advertising and generous donations of the public.

A separate chapter of Ukrainian radio broadcasting in Canada is represented by the International Service of CBC "Radio Canada" whose beginning dates to July, 1952 when L. B. Pearson, then Minister for External Affairs, officially opened these programs. At that time the CBC broadcasted its new communication in five different languages. Ukrainian was the sixth. In 1982 the CBC marked the 30th Anniversary of this program. Two daily broadcasts are made, one is one-half hour and the other 15 minutes. Programs provide information about the community life in Canada, the role which Canada plays in the world affairs, especially its aid to other countries, and the cultural identity of Ukrainian Canadians and those in diaspora. Several millions of Ukrainians in Ukraine and in the Western world listen to these programs. Dr. Roman Olynyk, well known journalist in the Ukrainian and international world, has been the director of these programs since 1975.

Television

Television may be called the half-sister of radio and its serious competitor, as a mass informer and propagator. However, television is much more intricate and a more costly medium. In spite of this, even here we may boldly record positive accomplishments of Ukrainian enthusiasts. Thus we have in Winnipeg Rev. S. Izyk who, since 1975 broadcasts a Ukrainian television program on cablevision Channel 13. In Edmonton two years earlier such programs were initiated by Dr. Orest Talpash, on behalf of the Ukrainian Canadian Committee on the QCTV station. In 1974 Roman J. Ostashewsky took over the program under his leadership with technical assistance from Taras Ostashewsky and under the name *"Contact"* has been in operation since. In Thunder Bay Rev. Roman Hankevych presented (1979-1981) a similar program on Cable 7 twice a week.

In Toronto the Ukrainian program, under the direction of Yuriy Klufas, made a name for itself when he presented his *"Electronic Rooster"*, a one hour rendition, starting at 7:30 a.m. that awakened listeners, on station City T.V. In 1979 this program was transferred to station MTV with a much more suitable time, around noon. There were other attempts at implementing Ukrainian television programs.

During the last years the CBC television has shown several programs with a Ukrainian Canadian content. The one in the series "A Gift to Last", written and produced by *Gordon Pinsent*.[1] *Ernie Zuk* of Winnipeg, produced and directed a one-hour long, Christmas program for CBC TV in 1978, entitled *"Festival of the Koliada"*. It featured Winnipeg's O. Koshetz Choir, and a background on Ukrainian Christmas traditions. Every year CBC television brings something new but limited in scope. Each program is appreciated by Ukrainian Canadian community and the Ukrainian press reacts very favourably.

Recalling some of the CBC productions it will be appropriate to mention here a few personalities that work at CBC or for CBC. *Roman Melnyk* is head of independent production for CBC. *Ivan Fecan* (pronounced "Fitzan"), a

---

[1] *The Other Canadians* by Isydore Hlynka, Winnipeg 1981, "1978 in Review", p. 232.

former student of York University, has worked in radio and television for many years. He started as a story editor for the radio series *Identities,* later as a producer for *Quirks and Quarks* and *Sunday Morning,* a radio variety program.[2] *Marika Hurko* was story editor on CBC's Quirks and Quarks. Lately she has been with CBC Sunday Morning. *Olha Kuplowska* is chairman of Project Research TV in Ontario.

In mentioning the not so numerous Ukrainian programs on TV and somewhat more of the radio variety we must bear in mind that all these programs, are usually presented once a week, and are of half hour duration. When we consider the fact that certain amount of time is taken up by advertisements then what is left for cultural broadcast is quite limited. Therefore we are justified in saying that in the face of the mass anglophone and francophone CBC broadcasts it then becomes clear that ethnocultural programs are almost non-existent or, at best, they are almost in a complete shadow. Of course, it has a tremendous impact on the development of the minorities' culture. To support our view we will quote an opinion of the Ukrainian Canadian Committee expressed in its brief.

"With the development of mass media, particularly radio and television, French and English programs reduce ethnic groups' cultures by their absence to non-cultures. It would seem that tacit attitude exists that other ethnic cultures will eventually disappear from Canadian scene through attrition and lack of adequate government financial support. There seems to be a great deal of sympathy but very little action to solve the problem. The absolute recognition of the two predominant cultures pressures the other ethnocultural groups into gradual assimilation."[3]

In the end we come to the viewpoint and conclusion held by an average Canadian citizen that the radio and television broadcasts should mirror the cross section of Canadian culture, including the ethnocultural groups of Canada. From these facts flows the conclusion that there stands, before CRTC, a large field wherein to work, in order to satisfy the cultural needs of ethnic groups in Canada. The solving of these problems lies directly on the shoulders of members of CRTC. After John Shansky ended his term in office with CRTC, his place was taken over by Steve Patrick of Winnipeg, a former long time member of Manitoba's Legislature.

Films

To some extent, Ukrainians in Canada relied on Ukrainian films from Ukraine. In Ukraine, even with the existing political restrictions, censorship and total control of the film industry by the government, Ukraine was able to produce such excellent films as "Shadows of Forgotten Ancestors", "Dream", "Stone Cross", "Lisova Pisnia", Dovzhenko's films and others. They were made by highly professional and talented individuals in film-industry — directors, editors, set designers, composers, sound-men, and actors.

---

[2]*Ukrainian Echo,* September 23, 1981, "Ivan Fecan", "CBC Whiz-Kid" by Bill Dunphy.

[3]*Brief of the Ukrainian Canadian Committee submitted to Federal Cultural Policy Review Committee,* dated Winnipeg, March 8, 1981, page 2.

Almost no short, educational films were available from Ukraine on subjects of culture, history, traditions. The onus was on the Ukrainian-Canadian community to produce them.

It has been only relatively recently in the seventies, that young Ukrainian Canadians have been entering film studies as a profession at universities. One of the reasons for the delay in entering film studies, was that film-making is a very expensive art. Shooting a film, even a short, is a laborious process, financing it can be even more so.

Until recently, comparatively limited resources of the Ukrainian community in Canada, a lack of understanding the potential of film, and thus, a hesitation to sponsor or partly sponsor a film on a Ukrainian subject, caused few films to be made in Canada on Ukrainian themes. Yet, there is no question that film is a most effective medium for the transmition of information, values and/or aesthetics.

The following are some of the more recent films produced in Canada on Ukrainian subjects: *Volodymyr (Walter) Wasik* (1930-) produced the 90 mins. Ukrainian-language film "Whispering Highlands". It was filmed on Wasik studio's 170 acre tract of land located some 5 miles from Oshawa, Ontario. The film was directed by Orest Kowalsky, screenplay by Stephen Lubomyrsky, associate producer R. Lytwynchuk and music by Zenon Lawryshyn. "Whispering Highlands" is the studio's sixth film. Among the past 35 mm, features have been mentioned before "Cruel Dawn", "I Shall Never Forget", "Marichka", "Desh-Videsh", and others like his documentary "Shevchenko Centennial in Canada", "Shevchenko in Washington", etc.

A series of films were made on the life of Ukrainian-Canadian artist William Kurelek. Among them were "Pacem in Terris", released in 1972. The 16 mm, 13 min., color, English-language film by John Griffin, depicted the theme of Christmas through William Kurelek's drawing and paintings. In 1973, the National Film Board of Canada released "Kurelek", a 16 mm, 13 mins. color film about the artists' life and work. The NFB made it in English and Ukrainian languages. It was directed and edited by Bill Pettigrew.

Born in Yorkton, Saskatchewan in 1926, *Roman Kroitor,* a highly successful and respected film-maker, joined the National Film Board in 1949, during its very early beginnings. Kroitor has more than 50 films to his credit either as producer and/or director. Most of his films have won numerous awards. Three of his most internationally acclaimed films were *"In the Labyrinth"*, 21 mins., color film which was first released as a multi-screen presentation at Expo '67. These separate images were integrated into a single stand of film, using a "five-on-one" cinematic technique; *"Universe"*, is a 26 mins., black and white film which is called "a triumph of film art." It won 23 awards, including Cannes; "Lonely Boy" is a 26 mins., black and white film made in 1961 concerning the story of popular singer Paul Anka. It won 9 awards including Cannes. Roman Kroiter was executive producer of several NFB Ukrainian-subject films such as "Teach Me To Dance" and "Vignette — The Easter Egg."

Born in Yorkton, Saskatchewan in 1948, *Jerry Krepakevich* works for the National Film Board. He directed the 16 mm, 28 mins., color, English-language film "I've Never Walked the Steppes." The film provides a look into four generations of the Karasevich family of Winnipeg and their feelings on being Ukrainian-Canadians. This film was produced under the auspices of the Government of Canada, Multicultural Program. Krepakevich has made several films on non-Ukrainian subjects.

American producer, director, editor *Slavko Nowytski* (1935-) works primarily as an independent film-producer in the United States. He has made several films in Canada on Ukrainian subjects. His first, "Reflections of the Past", a 16 mm, 38 mins., English-language, color film was commissioned by the Ukrainian Cultural and Education Centre in Winnipeg in 1973. The film deals with immigration of Ukrainians to Canada, specifically to the province of Manitoba. The film was made possible through grants from the Department of the Secretary of State, the Shevchenko Foundation and "Carpathia" Credit Union. Realizing that few films existed concerning Ukrainian-Canadians, the Ukrainian Cultural and Educational Centre was probably the first Ukrainian cultural institution in Canada to begin to sponsor the making of educational films on Ukrainian subjects.

Orysia Tracz of Winnipeg provided the research for the 16 mm, English-language, color, 15 mins., film "Pysanka — The Easter Egg." Made in United State in 1976, this film was produced, directed and edited by Slavko Nowytski and won numerous awards. In Canada, Nowytski also made "Immortal Image" on the Winnipeg sculptor, Leo Mol (Molodoshanin). Made in 1978, this 16 mm, color, 22 mins., English-language film deals with the "lost-wax process" as used by sculptor Leo Mol as he creates a bust in bronze of composer Mykola Lysenko. Piano music for the film was performed by Montreal pianist Ireneus Zuk. The film was made by Nowytski's Minneapolis-based company Filmart Productions with a partial grant from the Secretary of State, Multicultural Directorate.

Robert Klymasz directed the 16 mm, 27 mins., color, English-language film "Luchak's Easter." It was produced by the Visual Anthropology Unit, Canadian Centre for Folk Culture Studies, National Museum of Man, Ottawa.

A pioneer film-maker in Canada, *William Shewchuk*, made several films while living in isolation in Cadomin, Alberta. In 1978, the National Film Board produced and distributed a 16 mm, 20 mins., English-language film on this unique Ukrainian-Canadian entitled "Flash William". This film, directed by Thom Burstyn, reveals some of Shewchuk's stylistic and editing techniques and innovations which William Shewchuk discovered himself, in total isolation, although they may already be used in the industry. Shewchuk became a one man movie industry. In 1950, the mine in Cadomin, where he lived, folded, and the population of the town shrank to a hundred. William continued as a recluse film-maker. His accomplishments were discovered in the late 1970's.

In 1973 and 1975 National Film Board in close co-operation with Ukrainian Canadian Committee dubbed in Ukrainian language commentary to nine of its short films: Already mentioned "Kurelek" and "Teach Me To Dance", also "Paddle To The Sea" (28 min.), "Here is Canada" (10 min.), "Nahani" (18 min.), "The Sea" (29 min.), "Death of Legend" (51 min.), "World In A Marsh" (21 min.), and "Eskimo Artist — Kemjuak" (20 min.).

In 1977 *Halya Kuchmij* directed a 16 mm, 16 mins., color, English-language film entitled "Streetcar" at York University. Born in Toronto in 1951, Halya Kuchmij graduated a bachelor in fine arts in film and English from York

University and in 1978 studied a year at the American Film Institute in Los Angeles. Her second film, made in Manitoba, is the 16 mm, color, 28 mins., English-language film entitled "The Strongest Man in the World". It was released in 1980. She won numerous awards, including the Genie Award (1981).

In 1980 "Paper Wheat" film was produced. The film was to mark 75th Anniversary of Saskatchewan's entry into Confederation, portraying hardships faced by early Saskatchewan settlers, featured the striking performance of *Lubomyr Mykytiuk,* former "Identities" (CBC Radio) host.

Nielsen-Ferns of Toronto was commissioned by Imperial Oil to make a series of films on various cultural-minority groups in Canada for the CBC. The one-hour long, color, English and French language version film entitled "Lypa-1927" concerned with a Ukrainian immigrant's struggle to make a new life for himself and his family in Manitoba. The script was written by Ukrainian-Canadian writer George Ryga and research by Zorianna Hrycenko. The film features actress Joan Karasevich.

"Wood Mountain Poems" is a 16 mm, 25 mins., color, English-language film directed by *Harvey Spak* for the National Film Board. The film depicts the Ukrainian-Canadian poet Andy Suknaski of Saskatchewan as he talks about his home Wood Mountain, of the past and its multicultural background. The film won the Banff Award.

Director producer, *George Mendeluk,* (1947-) has been working in film and television production since his student days at Toronto's York University where he graduated with an honors degree in humanities and English. In 1973, he wrote and directed his first independent film "The Christmas Tree" based on Mykhailo Kotsiubynsky's "Yalynka". The 20-minute, color, English-language film was sold to CBC, and Walt Disney Media Company. George Mendeluk organized his company Ko-Zak Productions Inc. In the Canadian film industry he has worked on many feature films. He was the film director of "The Kidnapping of the President" starring Ava Gardner, William Shatner.

Producer, director, editor *Yurij Luhovy* (1949-) works primarily as an independent film-maker in the Canadian film industry. He obtained his Bachelor of Arts in cinematography and French literature from Montreal's Sir George Williams University in 1973. Luhovy has been editor of numerous Canadian feature films and Canadian-Hollywood co-productions such as "Ups and Downs", "Hot Touch" starring Wayne Rogers, "Tulips" starring Bernadette Peters, Al Waxman and "Death Ship" starring George Kennedy. In 1975, he organized his film company entitled *Les Courts Metrages in Montreal* and produced and directed several short films such as *Sculpteur Social.* In 1978, he worked for the National Film Board directing and editing "Vignette — The Easter Egg." The film's executive producer was Roman Kroitor and narrator was actor Yurij Kelebay. In 1980, Yurij Luhovy released the 16 mm, 28 min., color, English-language film entitled "Ukrainians in Quebec — 1890-1945". It deals with various aspects of the development of the Ukrainian community in the province of Quebec from their arrival to 1945. One of the first films dealing with life of Ukrainians in Eastern Canada. It

---

[4]*New Perspectives,* October 25, 1980, Zonia Keywan: Ukrainians in Quebec: A Film by Yurij Luhovy.

portrays the tragic interning of innocent Ukrainians during World War I as "enemy aliens" at a camp located near Amos, in Northern Quebec.[4] The film directed and edited by Yurij Luhovy, was partially funded by the Multicultural Directorate, Secretary of State, the Shevchenko Foundation, the Montreal community and private funds. It was purchased by the National Film Board of Canada.

In 1981, film-maker *Ariadna Ochrymovych* of Toronto, released the 16 mm, 26 mins., color film entitled "Koza Dereza" based on the composition by Mykola Lysenko which she directed. Choral part was performed by choir "Vesnivka" of Toronto, conducted by Kvitka Zorych - Kondratska.

Among other Ukrainian-Canadian film-makers are *Eugene Fedorenko* who won the Academy Award in 1980 for his "Every Child", a winner of eight awards, *Tom Shandel* of Vancouver who directed a feature entitled "Another Smith For Paradise" about Ukrainians, *John Paskievich* and *Michael Mirus* of Winnipeg (their "Ted Baryluk's Grocery" film, 1981), *Larry Frolick* of Toronto, *Hala Lozinska* of Toronto, *Serhiy Denko* of Montreal, producer, founder of "Dorenko Productions." His film "The Bells" brought him first prize in 1981.

Eugene Boyko is director with the National Film Board of Canada. He has over seven films to his credit including *Helicopter Canada,* a 50 mins., color film which won several awards including an Oscar nomination and a Canadian Film Award.

In summary we must say that the seventies brought positive changes in the field of film production. More professional films appeared on the screen with Ukrainian themes. More professional people of non-Ukrainian descent show interest in Ukrainian culture in Canada. More young Ukrainian Canadians pay tribute to their father's past. More interest and more understanding exists in the circles of the National Film Board for the ethnocultural elements. On the whole, this is a positive step for further development.

**To those who ploughed the virgin prairies.
Monument to Ukrainian Pioneers in Elk Island Park, near Edmonton.**

Ivan Franko Male Choir in Thunder Bay, 1970 — Conductor Hryhoriy Myhal.

Brass Band of SUM "Baturyn" in Toronto, 1970 — Conductor W. Kardash.

DECADE OF MULTICULTURALISM — ILLUSTRATIONS

Mixed Choir of Blessed Virgin Mary of Winnipeg performing Cantata "Rejoice Unploughed Field" on the occasion of 160 Jubilee of the birth of Schevchenko (1814-1974) — Conductor George Hnatiuk.

Girls' Choir "Vesnivka" in Toronto, 1973 — Conductor Kvitka Zorych-Kondratska.

Choir of St. Vladimir's College in Roblin, 1972 — Conductor M. Masniak.

Students' Choir of St. Volodymyr and Olha in Winnipeg, 1972 — Conductor Virlana Holowka.

DECADE OF MULTICULTURALISM — ILLUSTRATIONS

String Orchestra of the Lysenko Musical Institute in Toronto, 1970 — Director and Conductor Ivan Kowaliw.

Choir of Ukrainian Catholic Church in Vancouver, 1972 — Conductor Rev. B. Sloboda and W. L. Smigel.

Dauphin National Festival Choir, 1970 — Conductor H. Lazaruk-Henderson.

Male Choir "Dnipro" in Edmonton — Conductor Roman Soltykewych.

DECADE OF MULTICULTURALISM — ILLUSTRATIONS 793

Ensemble "Mereshi", 1970 in Edmonton — Conductor S. Yaremenko.

Quartet "Verkhovyna" in Toronto, 1973 — Conductor Olena Hlibowych.

Male Choir "Ukraine" in Montreal (on the occasion of 30th Anniversary), 1981 — Conductor I. S. Kozachok.

Ukrainian National Federation "Dnipro" Choir in Sudbury (on the occasion of 50th Anniversary), 1982 — Conductor O. Rohatyn.

DECADE OF MULTICULTURALISM — ILLUSTRATIONS

Dance Ensemble "Ruslan" in Winnipeg, 1977 — Director T. R. Babick.

Theatrical Group "Muse" in Toronto, 1981 — Director M. Gawa.

Monthly, Bi-monthly, Quarterly Periodicals with Religious Content.

DECADE OF MULTICULTURALISM — ILLUSTRATIONS 797

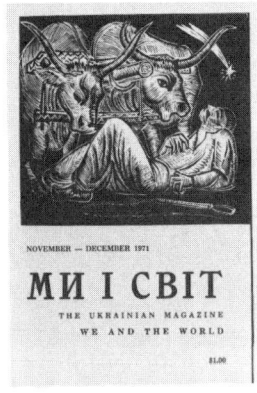

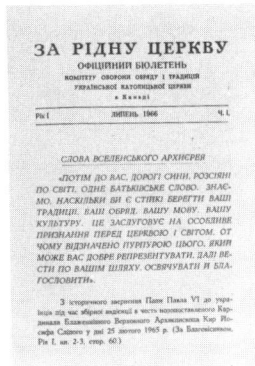

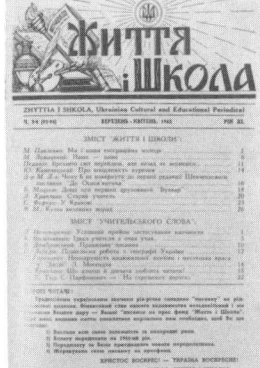
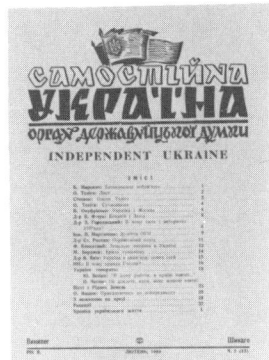

Monthly, Bi-monthly, Quarterly Periodicals with Literary and Community Content.

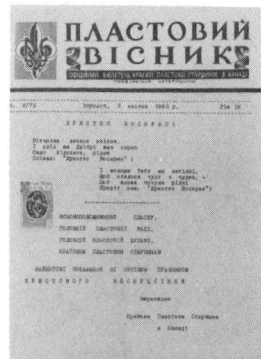  

Publications for Youth.

DECADE OF MULTICULTURALISM — ILLUSTRATIONS 799

Ideological and Political Weeklies established in the Third Era.

Periodicals in the Third Era.

DECADE OF MULTICULTURALISM — ILLUSTRATIONS 801

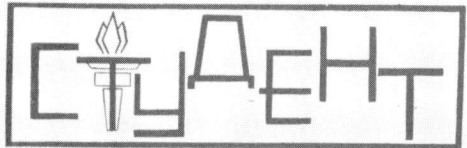

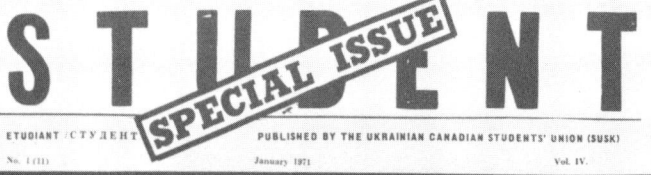

Press of Various Content.

Board of the Association of Ukrainian Journalists, 1975-1976.
From Left Sitting: W. Solonynka, Rev. P. Chomyn, W. Didiuk.
Second Row: M. Figol, M. Hawrysh, M. Seleshko.

802   UKRAINIAN CANADIANS: A HISTORY

EDITORS

M. H. Hykawy   Rev. M. Sopulak   Rev. T. Minenko   M. Chomiak

A. Dobriansky   W. Skorupsky   Rev. Y. Rudachek   W. Lewyckyj

Andrew Gregorovich   Vera Ke   Rev. M. Diadio   Vera Buchynska

PEOPLE IN ARTS

Borys Dniprovy   Wolodymyr Kolesnyk   Hanna Kolesnyk   Oleh Khmil

Taras Shypovyk   Stefa Fedchuk   Evhenia Chayka   V. Dovhaniuk

Leonid Skirko   Irena Welhash   Alexis Kochan-Budyk   Peter Shostak

804 UKRAINIAN CANADIANS: A HISTORY

PEOPLE IN ARTS

 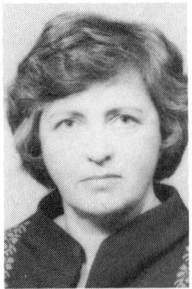  

Orest Semchuk Maria Dytyniak Donna Sawicky E. Zwozdecky

Cathy Wach Luba Goy Markiana Dublanycia-Huzar Helen Lazaruk-Henderson

Yurij Luhovy Halya Kuchmij Virlana Holowka Zenia Kushpeta

UKRAINIAN CANADIAN COMMITTEE AND ITS ORGANIZATIONS

During the years of its existence, Ukrainian Canadian Committee (U.C.C.) has become the symbol of the Ukrainian identity in Canada and a sole representative of the Ukrainian community. In its federated structure, U.C.C. had in 1982 a list of 27 dominion wide organizations. At the same time U.C.C. became not only a visible symbol of Ukrainian Canadians but also the spokesman for the community, working for the preservation and enhancement of Ukrainian culture.

Thus far on the pages of history of the new decade we can observe the role played by U.C.C. in the expansion of Ukrainian studies in the higher educational institutions, in the work of Ukrainian schooling whether it be in the private sector of "Ridna Shkola" or in the development of bilingual systems in public schools. We also note the active role of U.C.C. in presenting Canada as a multicultural country. Great efforts have been made by U.C.C. to promote the basic ideas that Canada's constitution would guarantee the rights of cultural development for all ethnocultural communities in Canada. In line with it, there is a guarantee of the lingual heritage basis for these cultures. During the last decade we can see the great endeavours by U.C.C. and its branches to bring about co-operation and harmony in the Ukrainian community. With its broad-mindedness and progressiveness towards the development of Ukrainian community along with its dynamism the U.C.C. has written its name on the pages of ethnocultural history as being perhaps the leading and the most active among all ethnocultural organizations.

Having in mind a picture of the U.C.C. activities in socio-cultural field of the Ukrainian Canadians, we wish to take a closer look at the structural form of U.C.C. and its organizational process. First of all we must remind ourselves that U.C.C., at the dawn of its history, was a federated structure composed of five Canadian national organizations. A federation which established a rule that in all substantive matters, decision is arrived at by consensus, but in administrative matters, a majority vote. To join the U.C.C. in no way interfered with aims of any given organization as long as it acknowledged the principle of national culture as opposed to internationalism and marxist-communism. Another firm principle was enacted by the founders of U.C.C. Every founding organization had a fixed position on the executive. In the meantime, the expansion of Ukrainian organizational life in Canada brought a variety of changes. New organizations were formed that entered the ranks of U.C.C. while some older ones departed from the scene.[1] All this required structural changes. Some of the founding organizations demanded greater rights in the system. Finally this stability gave way to the so-called rotational system. Under the original constitution each organization had a fixed position. In the rotational system, which was accepted in 1971 at the U.C.C. Tenth

---

[1] "United Hetman Organization", "Ukrainian Workers' League", "Ukrainian Association of Victims of Russian Communist Terror", "Ukrainian Canadian Friends for the Liberation of Ukraine" and others.

Congress, positions on the Executive in the future were to be rotated in sequence among the six big organizations. Under the change, Dr. Peter Kondra, a representative of Ukrainian Self Reliance League (U.S.R.L.) became its president.

In accordance with the new rotational principle, the presidential position at the XI Congress in 1974 was to be assumed by a representative of the Ukrainian National Federation (U.N.F.). But this organization preferred not to use this privilege and proposed that the president be elected by majority vote. The first such elected president was Dr. Serge Radchuk in 1974, and re-elected at the next congress in 1977. The second elected president was Ivan Novosad chosen during the XIII Congress in 1980.

Meanwhile other changes took place in the U.C.C. structure. Youth organizations such as Plast, S.U.M., S.U.M.K., O.D.U.M. and others were permitted to have delegates on U.C.C. executive similarly as was previously achieved by the Women's Council of U.C.C., the Taras Shevchenko Foundation and S.U.S.K. In this way, the rigidity of the U.C.C. structure, which at its beginning was justified one hundred percent, was somewhat eased and adjusted to the present day conditions and life. At the present there is an elected president and rotational system practised by six major organizations. Youth representatives in the Executive body, along with the Shevchenko Foundation and Women's Council, participate in the executive decisions as equal partnership.

Let us take a closer look at the so-called major organizations who benefit from the rotation rule.

Ukrainian Catholic Brotherhood of Canada (U.C.B.)

This organization is celebrating its 50th anniversary in 1982. The strength of this organization lies in the fact that it is a lay organization of the Ukrainian Catholic Church with over 600 parishes and mission stations. Almost in every larger parish there exists a branch of U.C.B. together with the Ukrainian Catholic Women's League (U.C.W.L.) and Ukrainian Catholic Youth (U.C.Y.). All of these have their organizational super-structures in each eparchy. Every two years they hold the provincial conventions and every three years the national conventions of all provincial and local centres. In reality, all these national conventions created a traditional forum for rotation of national executive to one of the eparchies according to established principle. During the last ten years the central executives of the Ukrainian Catholic system were located in Saskatoon, Winnipeg, Edmonton and Toronto. The last national convention was held in 1980, in Edmonton and "Centralia" was transferred to Toronto. The Ukrainian Catholic Brotherhood has been headed by Dr. M. Stadnyk, John Huyda, Marian Prokop and Dr. M. Kushpeta, the Ukrainian Catholic Women's League by Dr. S. Potoski, Vera Buchynsky, Lena Sloboda and Maria Doliszny. The "Centralia" was represented by Volodymyr Podiluk, John Nowosad, Dr. M. Snihurowych and Dr. Julian Pelech. The Ukrainian Catholic organizations benefit from three weeklies: "Ukrainian News", Edmonton, "Our Aim", Toronto, and "Progress", Winnipeg. Since 1970 a women's quarterly journal, "Nasha Doroha" has been published. It was started by Anna Maria Baran, in Saskatoon, as organizer and editor and since 1974 has been edited by Vera Buchynsky. Ukrainian Catholic Brotherhood includes over a hundred branches while Ukrainian Catholic Women's League is much stronger with 136 branches and numbers close to seven thousand active members; the Ukrainian Catholic Youth Organization is more fluid in its structure. Ukrainian Catholic organizations have several credit unions, vocal and dance groups, museums, Ukrainian National Benefit Association of St. Nicholas, insurance organization, St. Josephat's Mission, led by Rev. S. Semczuk and Rev. A. Pakosh since 1972.

Ukrainian Self Reliance League (U.S.R.L.)

While the U.C.B. and its affiliated organizations are bound by spiritual ties to the Ukrainian Catholic Church, Ukrainian Self Reliance League (USRL) is more or less in the same relationship with the Ukrainian Greek Orthodox Church. The organizational scheme of USR League works in four conferences: the West with British Columbia and Alberta, the Central, Manitoba and Saskatchewan separately, and the East with Ontario and Quebec. In each of these four areas mentioned, national conventions are held every year and composed by four conferences every two years. At the 1976 convention in Saskatoon, Ukrainian Self Reliance League celebrated its 50th Anniversary. During the last decade, USRL has been headed by Dr. F. L. Yaremchuk, Dr. Levko Faryna (1980) and since 1981 by Andriy Melnychuk. Along with TUS men's organization of USRL there are also; the Ukrainian Women's Association (U.W.A.) and the Ukrainian Youth Association of Canada (CYMK). All of them during the last few years have realized a need of having strong youth organization and together with co-ordinated forces presented a series of cultural events, especially on the occasions of CYMK's 50th Anniversary, celebrated in 1981. Since 1976 headquarters of USRL have been located in Edmonton and are also the head offices of U.W.A. and CYMK. The system avails itself of the services of the weekly newspaper "Ukrainian Voice", which in 1980 celebrated its 70 years of existence, at present, the oldest Ukrainian paper and bi-monthly, "Herald", official organ of the Ukrainian Greek Orthodox Church. Since 1975 "Ukrainian Voice" has been edited by Mykhaylo Hykawy, the former editor of Canadian Farmer.[2] The official organ of U.W.A., is "Promin" edited by Natalia Kohuska. The USRL has its own credit unions and the following four educational institutes: Petro Mohyla (Saskatoon), St. John's (Edmonton), St. Volodymyr (Toronto) and St. Andrew's College, in Winnipeg. The last one is affiliated with the University of Manitoba and is elevated to the Centre of Ukrainian Studies. There is also USRL foundation organized by lawyer Theodore Humeniuk (1891-1978) of Toronto. USRL conventions take place regularly and show the vitality of this organization e.g. at the Hamilton convention in 1979 there were 275 delegates and guests in attendance.

In Catholic circles, and likewise in Orthodox organizations the women outnumber the men, by a large margin. During the last decade U.W.A. has been headed by: Lesia Vasiuk (1971-74), Stephania Paush (1976-78), Anastasia Shemeliuk-Radomska (1978-79), Nadia Bodnar (1979-81), Anna Zwozdecka (1981-). In 1981 C.Y.M.K. was chaired by Orysia Kryshchuk, TUS — SUND by Otto Yeryniuk, USRL Foundation by W. Kereliuk, Board of

---

[2]In 1982 editor in chief became Vitaly Lekhter.

Directors of St. Andrew's College — by Judge J. R. Solomon and St. Andrew's Order — Dr. P. A. Kondra.

Ukrainian National Federation (U.N.F.)

One of the founders of UCC was non-denominational, the *Ukrainian National Federation,* (U.N.F.) which in 1982 celebrated its Golden Jubilee. It, along with its affiliated organizations Ukrainian Women's Organization of Canada (U.W.O.C.), Ukrainian War Veteran's Association of Canada and Ukrainian National Youth Federation (U.N.Y.F.), comprise one of the central groups of Ukrainian community life in Canada. In their work, they underline the cultural values and the national elements.

Numerous in membership, the branches of UNF and its affiliated organizations reveal their wide cultural activities including the work of choirs and dance ensembles. In both activities are involved not only members of the affiliated organizations, but also the lovers of stage who are not members of any organization. This levity of form or rather the lack of rigidity enables the existence of lavish entertainment in song and dance ensembles of U.N.F. Some of them have many years of work to their credit. The more notable ones are: the U.N.F. choir of O. Koshetz in Winnipeg, Children's choir "Chayka" in Hamilton, the "Dnipro" choir in Sudbury, "Boyan" and "Kalyna" choirs in Toronto and others. Among the dance ensembles that have distinguished themselves are: "Rusalka" and "Orlan" in Winnipeg, "Cheremosh" in Edmonton, "Chayka" in Hamilton, "Kalyna" in Toronto, "Verkhovyna" in Regina, "Veselka" in Sudbury and the P. Marunczak's ensemble connected with the branch of UNF in Montreal and others. Some of the choirs limit their work to only occasional performances. But some of them also engage themselves in devoting the vocal culture by arranging independent concerts of Ukrainian songs dedicated to the famous composers such as Oleksander Koshetz (after whom the Winnipeg Choir is named), D. Bortniansky and others. In 1976 the choir and dance ensemble of U.N.F. and U.N.Y.F. "Kalyna" of Toronto presented their concerts in the Ukrainian settlements in Argentine, Paraguay and Brazil. The Management of UNF branch in Toronto made every effort, in 1975, to organize in Toronto the "Association of Ukrainian Opera", which developed into a high level cultural institution. U.N.F. in Toronto owns one of the finest Ukrainian libraries in Canada.

During the last ten years the following have been at the head of U.N.F. or on its presidium: Dr. Modest Mycyk (1969-74) and Leonid Fil since 1975. In the presidium there were such activists as Yaroslav Bilak, W. Weryha, M. Romakh, E. Mastykash, M. Shebets, Luba Chaykowska, Dr. Myroslaw Nebeluk, Bohdan Holynsky, Julian Temnyk, Y. Zorych, I. Hewryk, M. Rebryk, W. Klymkiw, P. Ostashewsky, Yuriy Hwozdulych, B. Kosharych, D. Ripak, S. Borovets, W. Suknatsky and others. The honorary members were; Senator Paul Yuzyk, Stephania Sawchuk, Mykhaylo Sharik and Dr. M. Suchowersky.

Ukrainian War Veterans Association (U.W.V.A.) along with its branches carried on its work in such cities as Vancouver, Edmonton, Calgary, Saskatoon, Winnipeg, Montreal, Toronto, St. Catherines, Hamilton, Windsor and Sudbury. During the last ten years National Executive of Veterans has been headed by: M. Sharik (1971-72), Julian Temnyk (1972-74) and M. Shebets

(1975-). Great service has been rendered to the organization by Mykhaylo Seleshko (1901-1981), who during many years kept the valuable records for the U.W.V.A. and records of the Ukrainian "One Cent Liberation Fund."

No less active has been the Ukrainian Women's Organization of Canada (U.W.O.C.), which in 1973, transferred its organizational journal "The Woman's World" to Toronto. Here also was located, with some exceptions its national headquarters, headed by Stephania Sawchuk (1969-71), Yaroslava Zorych (1972-74), Luba Chaykowska of Winnipeg (1975-78) and Stephania Prociw (1979-). The UWOC organization has 16 branches and around 2,000 members. In the seventies, the Ukrainian Women's Organization of Canada turned its attention towards the written word and published such works as: "Unforgettable Olha Basarab," "Boyarynia" (Noble Woman) by Lesia Ukrainka, Julian Vassian works and others.

Ukrainian National Youth Federation (UNYF) has several centres. All of its work is mostly devoted to vocal and dance ensembles. Its headquarters are in Toronto and have been headed by: T. Marunczak, Y. Makohon, V. Kish, O. Pidzamecky, R. Farenech, L. Rohatyn, M. Luczkiw, Ulana Plawuszczak. UNYF published the anglophone section of "The New Pathway" entitled "New Perspectives."

The Canadian League for the Liberation of Ukraine (C.L.L.U.)

The Canadian League for the Liberation of Ukraine (CLLU), previously known as Ukrainian Canadian League for Ukraine's Liberation is also non-denominational. Its growth has been accelerated during the seventies. At the 13th Convention that took place in 1975, the organization celebrated its 25th Anniversary. During the 14th Convention in 1978, at Toronto, it was reported that C.L.L.U. had 48 branches; one in Quebec, 2 in British Columbia, 3 in Saskatchewan, 4 each in Alberta and Manitoba and 34 in Ontario. Fifteen branches have their own buildings; Toronto, Etobicoke, Hamilton, St. Catherines, Welland, Oshawa, Windsor, Ottawa, Montreal, Sudbury, Thunder Bay, Winnipeg, Saskatoon, Edmonton and Brantford.[3]

Altogether the Canadian League for the Liberation of Ukraine counts around two and a half thousand members. Till 1975, CLLU was headed by Dr. Roman Malashchuk and later on Wasyl Bezchlibnyk (1975-78), and Theodosy Buyniak since 1978. Those who served for many years on the National Executive: W. Makar, Petro Bashuk for some years National organizer for C.L.L.U., Wasyl Didiuk, its secretary for a period of years, M. Barabash, W. Bezchlibnyk, I. Iwanchuk, W. Hyrak, W. Klish, P. Mykuliak, W. Solonynka, W. Okipniuk, B. Hirnyk, W. Kardash, Y. Choliy, A. Bedriy, B. Lushchyshyn, Yuri Shymko, M. Figol, Yaroslav Kelebay and others.

Women's Association of the Canadian League for the Liberation of Ukraine, women's organization of C.L.L.U. (WACLLU) has been very active in its field and during the 8th National Convention, 1978, their number had grown to 18 branches and over 2,000 members. At its National Conference in 1975, WACLLU declared itself an independent organization. In loyalty to the

---

[3] See the report of the *XIV National Convention of the VIII National Convention of the WA of C.L.L.U.*, edited by V. Didiuk, Toronto, 1978, p. 7-8, 23.

principles adhered to by WACLLU, as well as being loyal to its founding institution, women retained their original name in their new constitution. Maria Solonynka (+1982) has been the head of this organization for many years. After her, this post was taken over by Olha Zaverukha (1974-1980) and Maria Shkambara (1980-). In the front ranks of the organization have been: L. Antonovych, L. Vertyporoch, S. Horlach, O. Romanyshyn, M. Kolodiy, E. Negrych, Y. Iwanchuk, A. Fedak, T. Stachiw, W. Bilyk, S. Savycka, A. Pityk, K. Kobyletska, M. Odnorih, O. Kushnir, A. Shepetyk, L. Shust and others.

Ukrainian Youth Association of Canada (SUM) is a very active organization with ideological ties with the parent organization CLLU. At its 19th National Convention in Toronto, SUM announced that it had 23 branches, 1,581 members, including 713 youngsters. There were also 124 educators and 132 tutors. The work of SUM is aimed in two directions: Ukrainian courses and cultural-educational activity. Ukrainian Saturday and Evening Schools were open in Oshawa, Welland, Thunder Bay and Edmonton and Ukrainian Studies are carried on in such centres as Montreal, Toronto, Hamilton, St. Catherines, Winnipeg. In these centres were located six mixed choirs, three girls' choirs and other ensembles. Altogether, there were over 500 participants engaged in choral singing. All of them perform for their own communities and some organized concert tours in larger cities of Canada and America. SUM has orchestras, "Baturyn" in Toronto and "Trembita" in Montreal and a few mandolin ensembles. In almost every centre there are theatre ensembles, trios and quartets. Ukrainian national dances have become very popular and highly-esteemed. Dances are taught at every centre. They also have schools for teaching wood-cut, ceramics and other arts. Every year SUM holds educational summer courses at its camps. They have such camps in Montreal (Verkhovyna), Sudbury (Bilohorshcha), Thunder Bay (Dibrova) and (Carpaty). SUM's property is worth around $5,000,000. The weekly paper, "Homin Ukrainy", has a regular section "The SUM Tribune", edited by M. Figol.[4]

Like every other youth organization in Canada, SUM strives to get more young people into its ranks. In order to prevent the declining membership the 18th National Convention, held in Montreal in 1977, recommended, among other things, that "the centres take to the streets and seek new candidates; convince the indifferent parents to sign up their children for membership, rather than wait until they come in by themselves." Attention was also given towards the proper schooling that would provide opportunities for leadership and tutoring activities. SUM program is rich and varied in the cultural-educational field. It co-operates with other organizations such as: Plast: "ODUM" and others. They also mingle with groups of various nationalities at the summer camps, and take part in SUM World Congress. In the seventies, SUM was led by Yaroslav Zayats (1974-77), Y. Mlynarsky (1977-80), M. Shepetyk (1980-). At various times the following persons have been involved in working on the National Executive: Dr. M. Huta, P. Bashuk, W. Okipniuk, T. Voloshyn, B. Leshchyshyn, A. Kobyletska, L. Kovalyk, N. Mykhaylytsia, M. Figol, L. Tatryn, A. Bandera, O. Bendiuha,

---

[4]Above information has been gathered from the reports of the SUM National Executive.

M. Zaverukha, P. Mykuliak, Y. Serbyn, T. Buyniak, Luba Kuz, and many others.

With the system of CLLU, WACLLU and SUM is tightly bound the Society of Veterans of Ukrainian Insurgent Army in Canada (UPA) which was founded in Toronto in 1951. The main goal of the organization is to maintain traditions of the liberation struggle of the Ukrainian armed forces. It publishes the periodical page "Voyatska Vatra" in the "Ukrainian Echo" weekly. The Society also plays the role of the joint editor of "Litopys (Chronicles) of UPA." In 1981 the Society had five branches and five stations. During its history it had been headed by: Stepan Kotelec, M. Koshyk, I. Kozak, M. Kulyk, while in the executive division there were Wasyl Didiuk, W. Makar, W. Bamburak, Yurij Husar and I. Waplak.

All the above-named organizations, such as CLLU, WACLLU, SUM and UPA are members of the Organization of Ukrainian Liberation Front (ULF) created from the similar organizations that existed in such countries as England, West Germany, USA, Australia, Argentina and France. During the Second Convention of these organizations at Toronto, 1973, a permanent presidium was formed, with headquarters in Canada. ULF was headed by Dr. P. Malashchuk, a long time leader of CLLU, Dr. Oleh Romanyshyn, Wasyl Bezchlibnyk and some other representatives from other countries. ULF comprises organizations that acknowledge the concept and program of the Ukrainian Nationalist Movement who either identify themselves with it or being an integral part of it.[5]

Organizations belonging to ULF wholeheartedly support the Anti-Bolshevik Block of Nations as well as the World Anti-Communist League and World Youth Anti-Communist League.

Ukrainian Canadian Veteran's Association (U.C.V.A.)

The fifth organization in line of the so-called "major organization" of U.C.C. is the *Ukrainian Canadian Veteran's Association (U.C.V.A.)* which in 1982 comprised six branches and around 2,500 members; Winnipeg Branch alone numbers around 1,100. Its members are also members of Royal Canadian Legions. It also publishes newsletters, which appear regularly every month except during summer vacations. The Bulletin has been edited by collegium under Peter Okrainec. A few branches engaged in cadet training. In Winnipeg alone approximately 1,500 cadets completed their training during 27 years of work. Executive of UCVA has been located in Winnipeg, Toronto and Montreal. UCVA was led during the last decade by John Yuzyk (1974-77), B. Panchuk (1977-80), and by A. J. Yaremovich in 1971-74, and since 1980. To this leading echelon belong such names as Dr. P. Smylski, Dr. F. Martyniuk, Steve Pawluk, Dr. S. Klimashko, Mike Nimchuk, A. Crapleve-Smith, P. Okrainec and a number of others.

Ukrainian Canadian Professional and Business Federation (U.C.P.B.F.)

Ukrainian Canadian Professional and Business Federation (UCPBF) which participates in the rotation system of UCC became active in Ukrainian

---

[5]Dr. Roman Malashchuk, *Ukrainian Liberation Front in Action,* Toronto. Circular #30, (1978-8).

Canadian life only in the seventies. It is the sixth largest organization in U.C.C. Already in one of the previous chapters we observed the role played by the Ukrainian Canadian Professional and Business Federation (UCPBF) in the establishing of Ukrainian studies. We noticed that at the convention of this organization in 1973, the Federation came to some very decisive psychological changes in regard to themselves and its attitude to the community and the role of its membership in the society. With efficient organization the Federation conducted its work at National Conventions which took place in 1975, 1977, 1979, 1981. From the enumerated years we can notice that these conventions were held regularly every two years. The agenda also changed from the style of conventions held before 1973. During the last decade guest speakers were, as a rule, invited to speak on topics of interest to the Federation and the Ukrainian Canadian community. Such speakers were: Minister for Multiculturalism, Norman Cafik, Hon. Peter Lougheed, Premier of Alberta, Hon. William Bennett, Premier of British Columbia, Hon. Roy Romanow, A. G. of Saskatchewan and others.

One of the important topics, still current, that the conventions of P.B. Clubs turned to again and again was multiculturalism. During the 1973 Convention at Edmonton (May 18-21), the delegates heard about multiculturalism from Hon. Robert Stanley Haidasz, Minister of State in charge of multiculturalism and Hon. Robert L. Stanfield, the Leader of the Opposition. Indeed, in 1977, multiculturalism was the topic of a special panel "Multiculturalism: Dead or Alive" by M. Lupul and B. Krawchenko, R. Serbyn, R. Petryshyn, P. Savaryn, as panelists. In 1973 a delegation of the Federation presented its views on multiculturalism to a number of Ministers and officials in Ottawa and discussed also mass media, education and federal-provincial relations.

It can be said with a high degree of accuracy that the biological, linguistic, cultural, national, religious, etc. preservation of Ukrainians in Canada was always a top priority of the Federation. There was hardly a convention that would not discuss some aspect of Ukrainian life in Canada. Frequent speakers on the mentioned topics were: Prof. Manoly Lupul, ("The Unorganized Ukrainians in Canada," "Organizational developments in the Ukrainian Canadian Community and others), Stanley Frolick (Organizational problems in the Ukrainian Canadian Community," "Our Lights and Shadows"), Peter Savaryn, ("The Purpose of Ukrainian Professional and Business Clubs: Language and Culture"), Dr. Joseph Slogan ("Levers of power and the Ukrainian Canadian Community"), Ed Topornicki ("The purpose of Ukrainian Professional and Business Clubs: Social Aspects"), etc. The interest of the Federation in the fate of Ukrainians in Ukraine is evident from the briefs of the delegations to Ottawa, one of March 1976 (W. Tarnopolsky, S. Frolick, I. Bardyn) and of March 1977, jointly with Ukrainian Canadians Immigrant Aid Society. (I. Bardyn, B. Mykytiuk). Ukrainian political involvement in Canada also was of great interest and action and among them the foremost being the Canadian Constitution. Speaking of the new Canadian Constitution the Federation's Prof. Walter Tarnopolsky spoke about it as early as September 3, 1972 at the Convention in Toronto. A number of prominent personalities were involved in different discussions and presentations: Roy Romanow, Lawrence Decore, Prof. Manoly Lupul, Peter Savaryn, Prof. Orest Rudzik, Dr. Geroge Danyliw, Stanley Frolick, Thos. Bardyn and others. Two seminars and conferences should be noted when discussing the Federation, one organized by the Winnipeg club, on Multiculturalism (1974) and the other organized by British Columbia clubs on "Survival of our Identity." In both conferences Peter Savaryn acted as a resource person and delivered the keynote speech under the title: "There are four basic duties that each individual owes" (in Winnipeg) and "An Individual's role in community's affairs" (at Kelowna).

During the last decade the Federation accomplished a great deal and became in the Ukrainian community in Canada an influential organization which began to develop an ideological and political tone. A number of competent personalities arose in organizational and social life in the local clubs and on the national scene. In the last years, the Federation was led by John Karasevich, Jr. (1975-76), Dr. W. George Danyliw (1977-78), Lawrence Decore (1979-80), John Tutecky (1981-). The last convention held in Ottawa and for the first time elected Prof. Walter Tarnopolsky as Honorary President, Senator Paul Yuzyk having served from 1965-81. It should be also noted the retiring presidents are now members of the Executive as past presidents. A wide range of professional activists served on the executive at various times. Because of lack of space we mention only a few; John Staschuk, William Solypa, Walter Hlady, Walter Klymkiw, Bohdan Maksymec, Orest Haras, Dr. Orest Talpash, Dr. L. Melosky, William Ratuski, B. Shulakewych, Peter Monastyrsky, Andrew Gregorowich, Erast E. Huculak, J. W. Darewych, M. Sorokilit, Olha Williams, who represents Nova Scotia and the Maritime Provinces and an extended list of others.

The Conventions' resolutions of the Federation are an excellent witness to the concerns of the organization. The Federations' publications play an important role. It was the Winnipeg club that provided the first editorial board and the first issue of a quarterly bilingual publication *"Ukrainian Canadian Review"* (1965-66). Next issue was sponsored by the Edmonton club (1967). But then, the third issue did not appear until the spring of 1973, published by Toronto club. By that time, in May of 1972 the periodical *"Panorama"* had also appeared in Toronto. Except for one single article in the "Ukrainian Canadian Review" No. 2 (by Peter Savaryn), the "Review" as well as the "Panorama" were always unilingual — English. In 15 years the Federation managed to publish 7 "Reviews", 9 "Panoramas" and 4 "Panorama Newsletters." One must, however, agree that the publications are serious and of better than average quality in every respect. There can also be no better source for studying the work of the Federation and member clubs, and the aspirations of Ukrainian Canadian community in Canada. "Ukrainian Canadian Reviews" and "Panoramas" contain almost all the keynote speeches delivered at conventions, views given at the seminars and panels, resolutions, presidential messages, reports of clubs' activities, submission to various governments, vignettes from and past descriptions of various historical events, etc.

Due to its ideological principles, to its style of work, to its vision the Ukrainian Canadian Professional and Business Federation may become in the course of time the leader in the Ukrainian Canadian Community. As a final touch to this picture we might add a few lines to the first organizational steps in forming it. Nucleus idea of the federation was discussed as early as the late fifties at UCC meetings among such personalities of the UCC as Rev. B. Kushnir, John G. Karasevich, Senior, John Syrnick, Judge J. R. Solomon, Dr. Isidore Hlynka, John Hawryluk, M.L.A., S. Radchuk, W. Kochan, UCC Executive Director and others. They together with John Swystun, the chairman of the Winnipeg club, started rolling the ball of the Federation which after a number of years brought in rich fruits.[6]

Ukrainian Canadian Committee Women's Council (UCCWC)

Ukrainian Canadian Committee Women's Council comprises four nation wide women's organizations; Ukrainian Catholic Women's League (U.C.W.L.), Ukrainian Women's Association (U.W.A.), Ukrainian Women's Organization of Canada (U.W.O.C.) and Women's Association of Canadian League for the Liberation of Ukraine (WACLLU). It has its representatives on the Executive of the UCC. The Women's Council has proved to be a dynamic and a large federation. The executive of the council is rotated over a similar period of years at the National congresses and its presidents rotated as follows: Victoria Symchych (1971-74), Yaroslava Iwanchuk (1974-77), Vera Buchynsky (1977-80), Luba Chaykowska (1980-). On the National executive council served such leaders as Y. Luchak, O. Zawislak, E. Sherman, M. Tomchyshyn, L. Kaptiy, M. Yurkiw, J. Klymkiw and others. UCC Women's Council contributed a great deal in the erection of Lesya Ukrainka Monument in the High Park of Toronto during the International Women's Year in 1975. Federal Minister John Munro and Isydora Kosach-Borysova, sister of Lesya Ukrainka together with UCC Executives unveiled this monument in 1975.

Ukrainian Canadian Foundation of Taras Shevchenko

After the formation of the *Ukrainian Canadian Foundation of Taras Shevchenko,* its chairman became a member of *UCC Executive,* up to 1981— Dr. Isidore Hlynka and Dr. Serge Radchuk since 1981. Growth of this foundation has been encouraging. In 1981 the Foundation has acquired around 1½ million dollars and in that year only alloted for various projects $118,650.00 which together with previous years amounted to $664,108.00. So far the Shevchenko Foundation has made a noticeable input in the development and support of museums, publications, folk ensembles, etc. In 1981 the Board of the Foundation and auditing body were composed of: J. Hwozdulych, Mrs. R. Kondra, Dr. I. Hlynka, J. Nowosad, Dr. J. Barwinsky, P. Bashuk, Luba Chaykowska, Senator Paul Yuzyk, S. Jankowsky, J. Huyda and A. Crapleve-Smith.

Youth Organizations at the Executive of UCC

For some time youth organizations did not have their representatives at the Executive of UCC. Actually, for short periods they were represented by their Youth Council but the mentioned council was short lived. After this a sporadic representation came only from university students who in recent years became quite regular and consistent. At the XIII Congress of Ukrainian Canadians, the *Ukrainian Canadian University Students' Union (SUSK)*

---

[6]*Minutes of the UCC Executive* 1958-1959, and following years.

tackled the question of organizational changes in the structure of UCC and as a result of prolonged debate all nation wide youth organizations — *SUM, Plast, SYMK, ODUM, UCY, MUNO* obtained the right to have their representatives on the Executive of UCC. It brought a great deal of fresh blood to the UCC structure.

As a rule the University students create dynamic organizations. They often bring progressive ideas. The history of students' movement in Ukraine has had rich tradition in such work.

At the beginning of 1970's the Ukrainian Canadian Students' Union raised the question of Canadian multiculturalism — quite fundamentally and discussed it at several meetings and the nation wide conferences. It had quite a positive effect on the course of process of Canadian identity. It would be quite appropriate to mention the names of the leaders of this period such as B. Krawchenko, A. Semotiuk, R. Serbyn, Yuriy Kelebay, R. Petryshyn, V. Balan, M. Pidhirna, M. Kucharyshyn and others. At that time, SUSK arranged continuous demonstrations in defence of Ukrainian dissidents and raised quite vigorously the question of human rights in Soviet Ukraine. During the last few years SUSK started to debate the question of some changes in the constitution of the UCC and to propagate "the need for creating radical movement in the Ukrainian Canadian community."[7] Some of these thoughts were expounded at the XIII Congress of Ukrainian Canadians in Winnipeg but this demonstration did not have support from the delegates present.

Students' congresses are the most visible forum for discussion on current social events. Since the beginning of 1970, such congresses have been held regularly every year during summer holidays. The last students' congress took place in Winnipeg 1982, where leadership of SUSK was elected from the East. In the seventies, SUSK was heded after Bohdan Krawchenko (1969-70) by: Marusia Kucharyshyn (1970-71), Marko Bojcun (1971-72), Andriy Semotiuk (1972-73), Yuri Dashko (1973-74), Myron Spolsky (1974-75), Sheila Slobodzian (1975-76), Marika Hurko (1976-77), Andrij Mukuch (1977-78), Dmytro Jacuta (1978-80), Mykhailo Maryn (1980-81), George Samoil (1981-82), M. Bociurkiw of Ottawa (1982-83).

In 1978 SUSK marked its 25th Anniversary and a special 48 page issue of "Student" appeared at that time with excellent accounts of students' activities during this period.

Plast — is one of the leading educational youth organizations in Canada which has its representative on the Executive of UCC since the XII Congress. Although this organization has been working with Ukrainian Canadian youth since 1948, it obtained its charter only in 1979. In 1981 the whole organization celebrated 50 years of work of the Senior Plast members and in 1982, its 70th Anniversary of Plast movement in Ukraine which started in 1912. The organization paid tribute to the pioneers of the youth movements who were brutally persecuted in Ukraine.

During the several terms the educational leadership was in the hands of Daria Darewych and since 1982 of Iroida Wynnycka and such devoted and experienced youth leaders as A. Kharak, M. Komarnycka, L. Boychuk, R. Wrzesnewskyj, T. Dzulynska, V. Sokolyk, A. Lebid, Wasyl Janishewsky,

---

[7]*New Pathway,* No. 40, 1981, see "XII Congress of UCUSU was held successfully".

O. Kandyba, Sophia Kachor, M. Holowata, A. Hordiyenko, T. Onyshchuk, B. Yaciw, B. Pendsey and others. In 1980 the organization comprised 1,282 members. As a rule the youth of this organization is obliged to attend Ukrainian evening classes, to learn Ukrainian language and during summer holidays to participate in youth summer camps.

The youth, whose parents come from the Western part of Ukraine, is organized mostly in "Plast" and SUM, whose parents come from Eastern Ukraine, is organized in the *Ukrainian Democratic Youth Association (ODUM)*. ODUM celebrated its 30th Anniversary (1950-1980). Its work is concentrated in branches of: London, Oshawa, St. Catherines, Niagara Falls and Toronto. There were around 500 members. Every two years ODUM holds conventions at its summer resort "Ukraine" in Ontario. It has three artistic ensembles; Dance Ensemble "Vesnianka", director M. Baldecky, Bandurist Ensemble "Kobzari", director O. Metelynska, in St. Catherines, and popular Hnat Khotkevych Bandurist Ensemble under Valentyna Rodak in Toronto. ODUM national executive publishes its monthly "Moloda Ukraina". with L. Lishchyna, editor. In 1970's ODUM was headed by L. Lishchyna, V. Pedenko, P. Rodak, O. Kharchenko, V. Tymoshenko. ODUM maintains good relations with other youth organizations in Canada like SUM, Plast, SYMK, etc. All of them have their representatives on the UCC Executive.

Charitable Organizations and Mutual Benefit Associations

At the end of this chapter we would like to make a few comments about charitable organizations and mutual benefit associations. Some of them are formal members of UCC; some are not but support the aims of the UCC. The most popular among charitable organizations is the *Ukrainian Canadian Social Service* which brings aid to the needy in Canada as well as to new immigrants. From time to time the UCSS arranges drives for needy Ukrainians in Argentina, Brazil, Paraguay and behind the Iron Curtain. It also provides direct necessities for political prisoners in Ukraine. The UCSS has eleven branches throughout Canada. Again a number of people are involved in such charitable work. We mention only some of them, mostly heads, national and local: Roman Senchuk, E. Zurawsky, H. Muchin, L. Duda, Ivanka Kushpeta, P. Salyga, O. Piasecka, O. Slywynsky, P. Korbutiak, K. Lazor, B. Mykytyn, M. Spolska, O. Petryshyn, Z. Bryniawsky, O. Babiy, P. Nazarewych, O. Chomiak, Yuriy Salsky and a number of others.

In 1980, the *Canadian Ukrainian Immigrant Aid Society* was organized under the leadership of B. A. Mykytiuk, in Toronto. This organization has been very active in sponsoring refugees and self-exiled Ukrainians from Poland who escaped to Austria and other countries of Western Europe.

Among mutual benefit associations the *Ukrainian National Association* has been in the forefront in membership as well as in assets. In 1980 UNA had 8,361 members with $11,600,538.00 insurance.[8] The oldest Ukrainian mutual benefit association in Canada was organized in 1905, is *Ukrainian Mutual Benefit Assocaition of St. Nicholas,* with, at present, 1,804 members and $2,600,000.00 assets. *Ukrainian Fraternal Society of Canada* made good pro-

---

[8] *Svoboda Daily,* No. 244, 1981, "Report of the Main Director for Canada" by Senator Paul Yuzyk.

gress during the last decade and has 5,649 members with $4,369,172.00 in assets. In 1979, *Ukrainian National Aid of America* was registered in Canada and made some headway in its work, too. There are other mutual benefit associations.[9]

In summary, we must say that the Ukrainian Canadian Committee is well balanced and has a well organized social structure, because it has the support of numerous organizations. It has been enjoying a well deserved prestige of Ukrainian community. It also has been considered to be a very important leading and creating factor of Ukrainian cultural process in Canada.

In 1980 the UCC observed its 40 years of continuous work. A special tribute was paid at the XIII National Ukrainian Canadian Congress.[10] The National Congress of Ukrainian Canadians is a planning body for future activities of the UCC. Decisions of the Presidium (previously known as General Council), where each member organization is represented, are implemented into action by the Executive. The main instrument of the Executive is the Executive Director. He is responsible for the execution of the activities of UCC. Hence his position is very important in the UCC structure.

The UCC has been fortunate enough in having at its services such dedicated executive directors as Wolodymyr Kochan and Dr. S. J. Kalba (1966-1980) both with long standing community experience and visions for the future developments of Ukrainian cultural heritage in Canada. In 1981 duties of the executive director were taken over by A. J. Yaremovich.

Ukrainian Canadian Committee and World Congress of Free Ukrainians

Activity and interests of Ukrainian Canadian Committee is not limited to Canada alone. Due to its membership in the World Congress of Free Ukrainians (WCFU) it might also influence the course of Ukrainian problems and actions in the whole of Ukrainian diaspora. However, if we also take into consideration that the World Congress of Free Ukrainians has obtained the mandate from Ukraine to represent Ukrainian National Liberation Movement on the international forum hence the WCFU and UCC have extremely important tasks before them.

The first World Congress of Free Ukrainians was held in November 1967, in New York and elected the presidium and its secretariat as the executive organ. Rev. Dr. Basil Kushnir of Canada elected president of WCFU for the first six years and at the second Congress he was re-elected for another four years.

During its first term of office (1967-1973) the presidium of the World Congress rotated its headquarters every two years between Canada, the USA and Europe (London). The second congress which was held in Toronto in 1973, abolished the rotation of headquarters of WCFU. It was established in Toronto. The third congress which was held again in New York due to rivalry between some organizations, elected two consecutive presidents, each for 2½ year terms; Mykola Plawiuk and Dr. Ivan Bazarko. For M. Plawiuk, the first term expired on June 30, 1981 and Dr. I. Bazarko took over the position.

---

[9]*Report of Superintendent of Insurance of Canada,* 1979, Vol. III.
[10]See *40 Years of UCC work* by M. H. Marunchak, published by the Ukrainian Canadian Committee, Winnipeg, 1981.

The WCFU works in eight councils and committees whose duty among others is to prepare projects for the congress which is the highest legislative body. Secretariat holds regularly annual plenary sessions to submit reports and to plan current activities. The next Ukrainian World Congress will be held in November 1983 in Toronto.[11]

Others Outside UCC System

There are still two nation wide Ukrainian organizations which do not co-operate with the Ukrainian Canadian Committee. They are: *The Association of United Ukrainian Canadians* and the *Workers Benevolent Association* (WBA). Both organizations are regarded as pro-communist supporting causes promoted by international Communism and with sympathies towards Union of Soviet Socialist Republic. Their delegates participate in such international affairs like World Assembly for Peace (1971), World Assembly for Peace and Independence of People of Indo-China (1972), World Congress of Peace Forces (1973), World Congress for International Women's Year (1975), etc.[12]

Both organizations co-operate closely with each other and have their publications *"Zhyttia and Slovo" (Life and Word Weekly)* in Ukrainian language and the English monthly magazine *"The Ukrainian Canadian"* with the subtitle *"Window on a Cultural Heritage."* Positive attitude towards Ukrainian Culture in Canada enables them also to infiltrate Canadian communities and propagate their leftist political causes. These organizations and especially the *"Association of United Ukrainian Canadians"* maintain choral and dance ensembles like choir "Hahilka" in Toronto, Women's Choir "Barvinok", Men's Choir "Bandurist", Winnipeg and in other cities. In the seventies, these two organizations observed two outstanding jubilees in the Ukrainian literary life, namely 100th Anniversary of the birth of Vasyl Stefanyk, famous Ukrainian novelist and 100th Anniversary of Lesya Ukrainka, the leading Ukrainian poetess. These organizations obtained from the Soviet Union a bust of Vasyl Stefanyk which was unveiled in Edmonton, 1971, and the monument of Lesya Ukrainka which was unveiled on the University campus on 1976, in Saskatoon, Saskatchewan.

A.U.U.C. devoted a great deal of time to celebrating the 90th Anniversary of Ukrainian settlements in Canada. It was marked by special mass gatherings, editorials and publications. Much attention is given to the contacts with Ukraine praising conditions in Soviet Ukraine and denouncing Canada.

In line with this policy it would be worthwhile to record for posterity that these organizations do not protest against the russification policy in Ukraine set up by the Communist Party of the Soviet Union in Moscow.

When during the sixties more and more voices were raised against the russification policy, in Ukraine and abroad, when in the West the smuggled

---

[11] *New Perspectives*, July 4, 1981, "Looking WCFU in the Eye," Interview with outgoing president Mykola Plawiuk by Roman Washchuk.

[12] John Kolasky: *The Shattered Illusion:* The History of Ukrainian Procommunist Organizations in Canada. (PMA Books, Toronto) p. 211.

documents started circulating and finally revealed in publications,[13] A.U.U.C. requested the Communist Party of Canada (CPC) to send a special delegation to Ukrainian SSR to study and verify this problem. The delegation was set up and consisted of Tim Buck, the national leader of CPC, William Ross, the leader of the party in Manitoba and of AUCC members: Anthony Bilecki, George Solomon, William Harasym and Peter Krawchuk. In 1967, the delegation spent 22 days interviewing various officials in Ukraine. Although these interviews were prepared for in advance by the higher officials in Ukraine still the delegation unanimously confirmed the fact of russification policy dictated by Moscow. In the prepared document to the officials in USSR the delegation talked only about "the problems" and "mistakes" emphasizing at the end that if they are overly sensitive to some phenomena in Ukraine it is due to good intentions.[14] Although the wording of the protest was very mild but when the document landed at the Politburo, a strong pressure was applied to the Communist Party of Canada to renounce this document. Tim Buck was in agreement with the order but not the rest of the delegation. The matter was under discussion for two years and finally was disposed of during the plenum party session in 1969 when the report was tabled for final voting. Members of the delegation still supported their view expressed in the report but Tim Buck and the rest of the plenum voted against it. As a result of it the report was withdrawn.[15] Following this event it is necessary to emphasize an interesting expression which was voiced in the report: "Unless this question of the Ukrainian language is resolved there is no future for our organization in Canada.[16] These words became true in the further march of history. In 1970's A.U.U.C. lost a considerable number of members. In spite of this, the leaders of the AUUC have not broken their ties neither with the Communist Party of Canada nor Soviet officials in Ukraine.

In 1981, AUUC which was headed for a long time by Peter Prokopchuk (+1981) and for the last three years by Peter Krawchuk, held its 35th National Convention. For a number of years Anton Bilecki has been chairman of the Workers Benevolent Association whose assets amounted to $5,362,000.00 by 1979.

---

[13]Vyacheslav Chornovil, *Lykho z rozumu* (The Misfortune of Intellect), Paris, 1967, Ivan Dzyuba, *Internationalism chy Rusyfikatsiya?* (Internationalism or Russification?), Munich, 1968, John Kolasky, *Education in Soviet Ukraine: A Study in Discrimination and Russification,* Toronto, 1968. Author of the study, a member of the Ukrainian procommunist organizations and the CPC, for 31 years. Disillusioned with Soviet reality during his studies at the Higher Party School of the Central Committee of the Communist Party of Ukraine from 1963-1965, he had collected valuable materials which revealed the nature of the Soviet national policy.

[14]Cited after John Kolasky *The Shattered Illusion: The History of Ukrainian Pro-communist organizations in Canada,* p. 169.

[15]*Ibidem,* p. 171.

[16]*Ibidem,* p. 163 and p. 238.

UKRAINIAN CHURCHES — SYMBOL OF CULTURAL AND RELIGIOUS IDENTITY

Just as Ukrainian Canadian Committee binds together Ukrainian organizations in the cultural sphere and is a symbol of Ukrainian identity for those who do not even belong to any organization, so likewise Ukrainian churches are a symbol of identity for those who not only practise, but also for those who only formally acknowledge their adherence to a religious denomination. Moreover, churches are also a symbol of cultural affiliation for all Ukrainians.

In the history of Ukrainians in Canada we observe continuous intertwining between community and religious life, which in its historical process is moving closer and closer together. Even the very names of churches contain within their titles national adjective "Ukrainian", e.g. "Ukrainian Catholic", "Ukrainian Orthodox", "Ukrainian Baptist", "Ukrainian Reformist". The national cultural character of this or that church is not of minor importance. This already suggests that church ties are closely bound with cultural heritage of the people and the nation it serves. Precisely on these visual symbols of religious and cultural identity, their environment and further developing processes we would like to shed some light in this chapter.

Ukrainian Catholic Church (UCC)
In some aspects this church has shown further expansion. In 1974 the Ukrainian Catholic Eparchy of New Westminister was created. The Eparchy covers the territory of British Columbia, which formally belonged to Edmonton Eparchy previously. The first eparch of the newly created diocese became Rev. Jerome I. Chimy, OSBM, former rector of the Ukrainian Theological Seminary in Rome. So far the new diocese has 15 priests and over 20 parishes and missionary stations.

Some administrative efforts have been made to create another eparchy on the territory of Quebec. The cost of creating this eparchy would be born by Ukrainian Catholic Eparchy of Toronto which has been expanded into a large administrative body under the leadership of Bishop Isidore Borecky. It should be stated, too, that Toronto Eparchy lost a few parishes which became the basis of the newly created Slovakian Byzantine Rite Eparchy of Saints Cyril and Methodius of Toronto with six parishes and six priests under the leadership of Bishop Michael Rusnak.

The Ukrainian Catholic Church of Canada received in 1974 another bishop in the person of Rev. Demetrius M. Greschuk who became auxiliary bishop to Edmonton Bishop Neil N. Savaryn, OSBM.[1] The Ukrainian Catholic Church celebrated in October, 1981, their 25th Anniversary of erection of the Ukrainian Metropolitan See, the church province, which since 1956 has been occupied by Archbishop Metropolitan Maxim Hermaniuk, C.S.S.R. One of the more notable events for the whole church was the construction of the

---

[1] In 1982 Rev. Myron M. Daciuk was consecrated as auxiliary bishop to the Archbishop, Metropolitan of Winnipeg.

Consistory (1976-1979) in Winnipeg where archives of the whole church, library and other cultural institutions of the church and Eparchy of Winnipeg are suitably housed. Still greater success of the church may be attributed to the establishment of the Ukrainian Catholic Seminary in Ottawa. The need for such an institution was deeply felt by the Ukrainian Catholic Church in Canada for a long time and especially during the last decade when a great lack of young priests became more evident and demanding not only by the Ukrainian Catholic Church but also by other churches[2] and not even necessarily Ukrainian.

We have observed some changes in the leadership of Ukrainian religious orders. Since 1970 Basilian Fathers have been under the guidance of Rev. Vital Pidskalny, Provincial.[3] In 1982 this order celebrated 80 years of its noble work in Canada. Rev. Paul Maluga C.S.S.R. took over the second time the charge of the Order of the Redemptorist Fathers when Rev. M. Hrynchyshyn, C.S.S.R. completed his term in 1980. This order observed its 75th Anniversary in 1981. Sister Servants of Mary Immaculate (SSMI) have also an impressive record of their 80 years of service in Canada. The order was headed by Sister Justine Kowal (1971-81) and Sister Ambrose Stachiw, since 1981.

In addition other orders working in Ukrainian Catholic Church fields are Sisters of St. Joseph, Missionary Sisters of the Mother of God and since 1981 the first cell of Sisters of St. Basil the Great (OSBM) in Toronto. The Ukrainian Catholics in Canada operate a few colleges and Junior High Schools like St. Joseph's College in Yorkton, St. Vladimir College in Roblin, Immaculate Heart of Mary School in Winnipeg, Metropolitan Shepticky Institute in Saskatoon and number of kindergartens, evening and summer courses of vernacular language, Ukrainian culture and history.

A big step ahead in the life of whole Ukrainian Catholic Church in diaspora was the creation in 1980 of Synodical Government of the church, whose sessions (Synods) could be summoned only with approval of the Pope. This was a turning point in resolving the church problems of the Ukrainian Catholic Church by its own bishops who are most competent in appreciating their problems and resolving them. It is ironic that until 1980 Roman Curia with the Congregation of Eastern Churches was sole policy maker for this Church. The creation of the Synodical form of government under the chairmanship of the Ukrainian Catholic Church's Metropolitan and Archbishop Major of Lviv Josyf Cardinal Slipyj is not exactly what the bishops, priests and laymen are demanding. It is the wish that this church be headed by a patriarch, traditional form of government in Eastern churches, but the creation of the Synodical Government is the first step towards the autonomy of the Church in diaspora. We should emphasize here that a substantial party of the church recognizes as patriarch, Metropolitan and Archbishop Major of Lviv Josyf Cardinal Slipyj, now residing in Rome.

In many churches, even in all the dioceses in Canada, Archbishop Major Josyf is regarded and mentioned in the Holy Liturgy as Patriarch of the Ukrainian Catholic Church. Similar practises are also followed in the U.S.A., Australia, France, Argentina. Roman curia neither denies nor approves it.

---

[2]*Herald*, Ukrainian Orthodox organ, No. 10, 1981, se "Nevidkladna Sprava".

[3]The duties of the Provincial office were assumed by Rev. Raphael Melnyk in 1982.

Probably this tactic is due to present ecumenical dialogue between Rome and Russian Orthodox Church.

In the seventies, within the Ukrainian Catholic Church, the patriarchal movement grew rapidly on all continents which in Canada has cristalized in the form of *National Council for the Patriarchate of the Ukrainian Catholic Church.* Members of the local councils were not only religious organizations such as Ukrainian Catholic Brotherhood, Ukrainian Catholic Women's League,[4] Ukrainian Catholic Youth, but also they had sympathy and support from the organizations like Canadian League for the Liberation of Ukraine with all its branches, the organizational system of Ukrainian National Federation, veterans and youth organizations. All of them along with local councils created the *National Council of Ukrainian Organizations for the Patriarchate of Ukrainian Catholic Church.* This organizational structure received blessing for its action from Ukrainian Canadian hierarchy. Headquarters of the National Council were located in the seventies in Winnipeg under the leadership of Dr. M. Marunchak and since 1980 in Edmonton under M. Chomiak. Actively participating in the field were such church and lay leaders as Dr. J. Pelech, Dr. M. Kushpeta, Dr. B. Bilash, Z. Krucko, J. Nowosad, I. Choma, A. Dobriansky, S. Yamniuk, O. Pankiw, Yaroslava Lomaga, Anna Maria Baran, H. Porochiwnyk, Dr. M. Snihurowych, Yaroslav Sywanyk, B. Klymowsky, D. Popadynec, Dr. M. Hladyshevsky, P. Kopachiwsky, M. Tatarniuk, B. Kulycky, Lew Kowalchuk, M. Czujko, R. Ostashewsky, Dr. W. Dacko and numerous others. Special mention of clergy and among them are: P. Chomyn, R. Hankewych, I. Leshchyshyn, I. Syrotynsky, G. Kowalsky, S. Izyk, J. Fedunyk, B. Tarnawsky, M. Sopulak, V. Iwaszko, J. Hajmanowych, J. Hawryluk, R. Naberezny. There is also a list of those who have died leaving behind noble memories of their struggle: R. Brykovych, Dr. H. Chechowsky, W. Klymko, Dr. E. Vertyporoch, I. Stanko, W. Zakharkewych, I. Zelsky, and Dr. O. Metella. The National Council for the Patriarchate in Canada has ideological and organizational ties with the Ukrainian Patriarchal World Organization (UPSO).

Taking into consideration that in 1988 the millenium of Christianity of Kievan Rus' — Ukraine will be celebrated by all Ukrainian people the Ukrainian Catholic hierarchy in the free World has decided to celebrate this historical event under co-ordinated leadership. A special secretariat was organized under the guidance of Rev. M. Hrynchyshyn.

Ukrainian Greek-Orthodox Church (UGOC)

Dynamic activities of the Ukrainian Greek Orthodox Church in no way were weakened in spite of the great losses during the seventies. Undeniable authority of this church was Metropolital Ilarion who passed away in 1972 and his successor Metropolitan Mykhail died in 1977. At the 15th Sobor of UGOC, in 1975 a successor was elected since Metropolitan Mykhail, due to his illness was unable to perform his duties. This responsible position was assumed later on by Archbishop Andrey Metiuk, who at the time was in charge of Edmonton and Western Eparchy. At the same Sobor Rev. Mykolay

---

[4]*35 Anniversary of Ukrainian Catholic Women's League of Canada* by V. Buchynsky, (Winnipeg, 1979), p. 29.

Debryn (1903-1981) was elected as the bishop of Saskatoon. This position was not taken over by him as he became the vicar hierarch of Eastern Eparchy for which he accepted full responsibility after the death of Metropolitan Mykhail.

Extraordinary Sobor was summoned in 1978 and Archimandrite Vasyliy Fedak, (1910-) was elected bishop for the Central Eparchy. Newly elected Bishop Vasyliy at the same time became assistant to Metropolitan Andrey in Winnipeg. Simultaneously Bishop Boris who had been residing in Winnipeg took over the jurisdiction of Western Eparchy in Edmonton.

Language question in Liturgy and sermons of UGOC were always one of the leading issues during the last few Sobors of this Church. At the 15th Sobor, a resolution was accepted stating that official liturgical language is Ukrainian. Only at the 16th Sobor in 1980 the decision was reached that in some cases other languages may be permitted in the liturgical services but with approval of the Presidium of the Consistory and with the final blessing of the resident Metropolitan. This was a first breakthrough in allowing other languages into the Orthodox Liturgy. These changes have been practised in the Ukrainian Catholic Church for almost the last two decades. Among the more important tasks of this 1980 Sobor was of changing the title of the church with the proposition that the adjective "Greek" be omitted and identify the church as being "The Ukrainian Orthodox Church of Canada."

In 1971 UGO Church observed 20 years existence of the Metropolitan See. In 1974 representatives of the whole church participated in the opening of the new imposing building for the Consistory in Winnipeg which is the seat of the ruling Metropolitan as well as location of church offices, library, church archives and a store for liturgical and devotional books, etc. In 1978, UGO Church celebrated its 60th year of Missionary work in Canada. It carries on missionary programs "Voice of Ukrainian Orthodoxy" on radio stations in Winnipeg, Thompson, The Pas, Flin Flon, Dauphin, Saskatoon, Edmonton and Toronto.

The leaders of this church pay a great deal of attention towards the development of theological studies at St. Andrew's College and its affiliation with the University of Manitoba. In one of the previous chapters of our history we devoted some space to this institution. UGO Church was also engaged in the work of the Ukrainian Museum and its branches in Canada.

An important section of this church is its Consistory under the presidency of acting Metropolitan and elected chairman by the Sobor. In 1970-1980, Rev. Dmytro Luchak occupied this responsible position while Rev. Hryhoriy Udod took over the chairmanship after the Sobor in 1980. At that time the following members of the Consistory were elected: Priests: M. Bodnarchuk, I. Kutash, S. Yarmus, W. Wasyliw, S. Zulak, M. Oleksiuk, W. Lakusta, P. Bublyk, and nine laymen: Nadia Bodnar, W. Baziuk, Dr. D. Cipiwnyk, D. Kereluke, Dr. P. Kondra, M. Karpiak, Dr. W. Zmiyiwsky, Halyna Melyk and E. Fedak.

The highest ruling body in the church is the Sobor at which are discussed principal religious matters, decisions have been taken not only upon religious questions but also matters relating to cultural and educational affairs of the church and people. Sobors point in the direction in which the church should proceed. Participation in these Sobors is quite impressive e.g. in the 16th Sobor there were 233 delegates from parishes, 65 priests and over 130 guests.

In Sobor deliberations the whole hierarchy of the church also participate. Official organ of the church has been "Herald", edited in 1960-75 by Rev. St. Yarmus and since 1975 by Rev. T. Minenko. UGO Church is also making preparations for observation of the Ukrainian Millenium of Christianity in Ukraine. In connection with this anniversary an important event took place in Toronto at the plenary session of the World Congress of Free Ukrainians. The representatives of Orthodox and Ukrainian Catholic Churches decided to celebrate the millenium in 1988 jointly. This historical document was signed on June 27, 1981 by three Metropolitans: Mstyslaw, Maxim, Stefan and Arch-priest S. W. Sawchuk, one of the founders of the UGO Church.

Evangelical Churches
There are two protestant churches which closely identify themselves with Ukrainian traditional culture. The oldest is Ukrainian Evangelical Alliance of North America with its organ "Evangelical Morning", and the Ukrainian Evangelical Baptist Conference of Canada. The former is extensively described in one of our chapters.

The Ukrainian Evengelical Baptist Conference of Canada has a colourful history and is still expanding. Alliance has been working into two separate conferences, Eastern and Western which every five years elect the executive for the whole church. In 1972, after the demise of Rev. Petro Kindrat the spiritual leader of this church, it was lead by O. Tkachenko till 1977 and after by Rev. Josaphat Iwaskiw. In the Canadian conference of this church, participated Rev. Ilarion Tarasiuk, Rev. Oleksa Piatocha (Western Conference), Rev. Ivan Dumych (Eastern Conference), Dr. K. Kostiw, Rev. S. Tymciw, D. Mykolaychuk and others. There are 13,000 Ukrainian Baptists in Canada.

Canadian census shows that many Ukrainians are members of other non-Ukrainian churches, e.g. Roman Catholic, United, Lutheran, Pentecostal. This may be due to mixed marriages, and lack of Ukrainian parishes where people live.

It may be mentioned that this contributes to the reasons why Ukrainian churches like Catholic and Orthodox are faced with the use of other than Ukrainian languages in liturgy. The number of faithful of non-Ukrainian descent is gradually growing. Canadian census 1971 shows that Ukrainian Catholic Church itself had among its faithful 41,270 persons of different ethnic origins. In this number were: 7,900 British, 16,485 French and others like Czechs, Slovaks, Polish, Russian, Hungarian, Austrian, German, Netherlands and Asiatic.[5]

To have a complete picture of religious denominations of the Ukrainian community in Canada we include below a table based on Canadian census beginning 1931 to 1971.

---

[5]*Statistical Compendium on the Ukrainians in Canada* by V. Darkovich & P. Yuzyk, University of Alberta Press, Edmonton, 1977. "Ukrainian (Greek-Catholic) Denomination by Ethnic Origin", p. 194.

Religious denominations of the Ukrainian population in Canada, 1931 to 1971. In percentage based on totals.

Religious denomination	1931	1941	1951	1961	1971
Ukrainian Catholic	58.0	50.0	41.7	33.3	32.1
Greek Orthodox	24.6	29.1	28.1	25.2	20.1
Roman Catholic	11.5	12.3	14.3	16.8	15.3
United Church	1.6	3.0	7.1	12.6	13.9
Anglican	0.3	1.0	2.6	4.0	4.6
Presbyterian	0.8	1.0	1.2	1.2	1.3
Lutheran	0.5	0.6	0.9	1.4	1.8
Baptist	0.6	0.8	0.9	1.3	1.4
Other	2.1	2.2	3.2	4.2	1.4
All denominations:					
Number	225,113	305,929	395,043	473,337	580,660
Percentage	100.0	100.0	100.0	100.0	100.0

Source: *Census of Canada,* 1931 to 1951. *Population.*

1961 Census of Canada. Population. Catalogue 92-546 and 92-559. Religions.

1971 Census of Canada. Population. Catalogue 92-724. Religious Denominations.[6]

Canora Welcome Statue "Lesia", erected by the Sasktchewan Council of UCC on the occasion of the 75th Anniversary of the creation of the Province of Saskatchewan (1980).

---

[6] Ivan J. Tesla: The Ukrainian Canadians in 1971, in *The Jubilee Collection of the Ukrainian Free Academy of Sciences,* Winnipeg, 1976. p. 516.

MUSEUMS, MONUMENTS, FOUNDATIONS, FUNDS

In any community cultural institutions such as museums, cultural foundations and monuments play a very important role. About the need of such institutions and symbols, one of the leading personalities of Ukrainian life in Canada expressed himself in the following way:

"We need our community memories as much as we need our personal memories, not only to teach us who we are, but also to comfort, to sustain and to renew us."[1]

In this respect Ukrainian Canadians have made notable progress during the last decade. In another chapter of our history we dealt with the *Ukrainian Cultural and Educational Centre* in Winnipeg emphasizing museum's activities. There was also a reference about the work of the *Ukrainian Archives and Museum of Alberta.*

In 1980 the *Ukrainian Museum of Saskatoon* was opened. Although it had a long history[2], it was incorporated in 1975. The development of this museum was bound somewhat with Linda Lazarovych, co-ordinator and director of the museum, 1973-1980. On the whole, this museum represents the work of the Ukrainian Women's Association which has expanded museums, branches in such cities as Toronto, Winnipeg, Edmonton and Vancouver. For a number of years, the chairman of the board has been Maria Tkachuk.

Of no lesser importance have been the accomplishments of the *Ukrainian Heritage Association* in Toronto which dates its existence from 1968, which arranged exhibitions — "Ukrainians in Canada". There was another initiative in 1973 when "New Horizons" organized "Museum of Canadian Ukrainians in Ontario." In 1977 both organizations were amalgamated and created *"Ukrainian Heritage Association and Museum of Canada."* This museum is housed in Casa Loma, one of the famous landmarks of Toronto. Since the beginning Volodymyra Luchkiw has been its curator. Of special significance is the *UVAN Historical Museum* under the auspices of the Ukrainian Academy of Arts and Sciences where the exhibits of the First and Second World Wars of Ukrainian liberation struggle are stored. In addition to this there is a department with documentation of the Ukrainian settlements in Canada. There are a number of smaller museums such as *St. Vladimir Ukrainian Catholic Museum* in Winnipeg, in Edmonton, Saskatoon, Toronto. All of them were organized by the Ukrainian Catholic Women's League.

The Ukrainian Heritage Village at nearby Elk Island Park in Alberta, maintained by the Government of Alberta is of extraordinary significance. There are 16 restored Ukrainian pioneer buildings. Along with this huge project there is a museum with exhibits of farmers' daily life, etc. Since 1972, all of these projects have been directed by Roman Ostashewsky, C.M.

---

[1]*Ukrainian Voice,* No. 31, 1980. Ivan Harmata: From behind the official Curtain, Saskatchewan's Ukrainian Legacy.

[2]*Ukrainian Voice,* Aug. 13, 1980, "To the History of Ukrainian Museum of Canada" by Savella Stechishin.

Ukrainian Canadians also have made a strong effort to leave a legacy in the form of monuments and parks. In 1980, on the occasion of the 75th Anniversary of the Province of Alberta, a monument was unveiled in the Heritage Village, sculpted by Leo Mol, commemorating Ukrainian pioneer families.

In 1980 a monument in honour of Ukrainian Canadians who died while in the service of the Canadian Armed Forces was unveiled in Etobicoke Park.

In 1973 the Borough of Etobicoke (Toronto area) adopted a resolution to name an area at Eglinton and Scarlet the *Ukrainian Canadian Memorial Park*. In 1981 *Markian Shashkevych Park* was opened in Winnipeg (Point Douglas area) commemorating 170th Anniversary from the birth of Ukrainian poet Markian Shashkevych who revived the Ukrainian nation in Western Ukraine.

Mention was made of *Lesya Ukrainka Monument* in Toronto. The monument was sculpted by Mykhaylo Chereshniowsky, one of the better known sculptors on this continent. In 1980 on the occasion of the 75th anniversary of the province of Saskatchewan Ukrainians of Canora erected a monument of Ukrainian girl who welcomes the visitors to the city with traditional Ukrainian custom of bread and salt.

It should also be mentioned that Ukrainians of Canada built in 1975 a monument honouring *Michael Luchkowych,* the first Ukrainian MP. In 1981 the Ukrainian Women's Association financed the building of a statue representing *Pioneer Woman* of Canada. The statue was unveiled in Edmonton by Martha Bielish, the first Ukrainian woman Senator.

On the occasion of the 100th Anniversary of the Royal Canadian Mounted Police in Canada, the Ukrainians of Vegreville honouring the event erected a monument in the shape of a huge *Easter Egg,* measuring 25.7 feet long, and 18.3 feet wide. This was designed and built by an American architect, Ronald Resh in co-operation with Artist P. Cymbaliuk.

Museums and cultural work, like scientific research, require financial support of the community. Such a support has been given by the community in direct funds or by creating cultural foundations. The most outstanding among them is, as already stated, the *Ukrainian Canadian Foundation of Taras Shevchenko.*

During the last decade a number of foundations have been created. Some of them commemorate prominent personalities of Ukrainian Canadian history, others support cultural causes of the community, and some promote research in cultural fields. It would be quite appropriate to mention some of these.

In 1971, *J. W. Stechishin Foundation* in Saskatoon was established to support studies of the Ukrainian Canadian history; in 1974 *Wasyl Sarchuk Foundation* in Winnipeg, to provide financial help for those who study Ukrainian language. *William Topolnycky Foundation* was organized in 1981, in aid of charitable causes.

The *Leo J. Krysa Family Foundation*[3] has established a fund (1981) in support of the undergraduate scholarship and graduate fellowship programs in Ukrainian and Ukrainian Canadian Studies.

In 1979, *Prometeus Foundation* was created in Toronto by Stephan Onyshchuk and Stefania Shwed in order to promote Ukrainian culture in Canada.

---

[3]Leo J. Krysa is founder and president of the Krysa Construction Machinery Co. Ltd. in Edmonton.

On the occasion of *Bishop A. Roborecki's* 75th birthday, the Foundation of this name was organized to pay for theological studies of Ukrainian students who want to become priests. In 1976, on the occasion of the eightieth birthday of *Rev. Josyf Pulak,* Monseignor of UCC, a similar foundation was established in his honour. The celebrant himself donated substantial sums of money for this purpose. In 1980, two foundations came into being; in Toronto *Saint Sophia Society Foundation* to support religious projects and in Winnipeg *Canadian Foundation for the Ukrainian Free University.*

Regarding foundations we feel the need to mention the names of those who donated larger sums of money to promote worthwhile causes like museums, artworks, historical research, etc. *Ivan Boruch (1897-1980),* of Edmonton donated over one hundred thousand dollars for various projects and causes; Brothers *Osyp and Yosafat Neporany* two hundred thousand dollars to the Canadian Foundation for Ukrainian Studies. Similar benefactors are *Ivan Khrin* of Windsor, (1898-1979), *Stepan* and *Maria Jankowsky* of Winnipeg, *Domka Zelinska-Babij* (1896-) of Toronto, promoter of Ukrainian Canadian history. *Petro Jacyk* (1921-) of Toronto made huge donations to promote Ukrainian studies at the Harvard University as well as toward developing of Ukrainian Studies at the Toronto University. D. Mykytiuk of Winnipeg generously supported W. K. Lypynsky East European Research Institute. There are other founders and benefactors like M. Dedeluk of Winnipeg, A. Kosikowsky of Windsor, H. Yopyk of Edmonton, M. Sokolyk of Dominion City, without whose generous help the development of Ukrainian cultural causes would be hindered. For this reason the Ukrainian communities appreciate very highly the contributions of such promoters. It should be underlined, that this patronage has greatly expanded during the last decade.

Rev. Nestor Dmytriw, First Ukrainian Priest in Canada and First Chronicler of Ukranian Settlements in Canada. Bust in Terebowla — Valley River, Manitoba.

THE LEGACY OF WRITTEN WORDS

In addition to the monuments of the seventies the Ukrainians of Canada during this decade devoted considerable amount of time and effort to the printed word through which they hope to preserve their legacy for the future generations. The series of publications can be divided into several groups.

The most popular of these were "Jubilee Books" which often focused on a certain number of years of various existing organizations. Leading the way among these anniversary books were those that commemorated golden and diamond jubilees. These include the Jubilee Collection of Immaculate Heart of Mary School of Winnipeg, previously known as St. Nicholas School, which in 1980 marked its 75 years as a Ukrainian Catholic day school, the oldest in Canada. In 1980, the Ukrainian Reading Association in Winnipeg celebrated its diamond jubilee (1905-1980) and on this occasion published its collection. The Redemptorist Fathers who began their missionary work in Canada among Ukrainians in 1906 recorded their history in an almanac-calendar "Redeemers' Voice" for 1982. A jubilee collection commemorating the 80 years of service by Basilian Fathers and Sister Servants in 1982 will be published shortly. The dates of these collections, by themselves speak vividly about the long history of dedicated service in community work during the 90 years of Ukrainian settlements in Canada.

Even more numerous are the publications pertaining to jubilees of various community organizations on the occasion of 50th anniversaries. One of the first in that category was the Golden Jubilee of Ukrainian War Veterans Association (1928-1978) by Z. Knysh with a sub-title "For Honour, For Glory, For the Nation," published by the Headquarters in Toronto. Edmonton published its local veterans' story by M. Bayrak. Close behind came jubilee books of local branches. Ukrainian National Federation, too, is preparing a similar jubilee book to celebrate their 50th Anniversary in 1982. The same is the case with Ukrainian Catholic Brotherhood of Canada, Ukrainian Catholic Women's League, and others. All the above mentioned works and others still in preparation, speak convincingly about the continuous growth of organized Ukrainian life in Canada which formed, so to say, the backbone of Ukrainian culture. Without organizations the Ukrainian cultural activities in Canada would have represented nothing more than a heap of shifting sand. Publications of this nature present valuable material, for studying Ukrainian organized life and its social structure in Canada.

A group that stands apart from the rest is represented by writers of memoirs and the community-oriented people who cast their influence upon existing events and social process. A fine example of this would be: "A Pioneer Teacher's Memoirs" (1979) from pioneer era by D. Prokop. Ukrainian Pioneer Association in Edmonton published three volumes of its works under the title "Ukrainians in Alberta" (1970, 1975, 1981). These memoirs and reminicences are among the best sources of information about the pioneer era.

Two volumes of memoirs "50 Year's Perspective" and "Thorny Trails Across Canada," (1971) by Michael Sharik covering the era between two World Wars appear to be not only the memoirs of one person but rather the whole movement of the national stream of life. A somewhat similar evaluation applies to P. Kindrat's memoirs: "Ukrainian Baptist Movement in Canada," (1972). The subject matter for writing memoirs is rich in content and variegated, and serves as good source for studying Ukrainian history of Canada.

In 1978 Hryhory Udod published a major monograph about Julian Stechishin, an outstanding personality between the two World Wars. It is a good beginning for similar publications about those who worked and led the community to social progress. This genre of literature is very much desired because it is not only informative but also educational. We might expect similar publications about such leaders like Jaroslaw W. Arsenych, the first Ukrainian judge in Canada and the leading personality in the pioneer era, T. D. Ferley, the first M.L.A. of Manitoba who influenced his contemporaries, the first Ukrainian bishop in Canada, Rev. Nykyta Budka, Rev. B. Kushnir, whose efforts contributed a great deal to the formation of UCC and WCFU.

Typical of the seventies there is a growth of anglophone literature about Ukrainian Canadians. Between the two World Wars there were a series of non-Ukrainian authors who wrote about Ukrainian community life in Canada, such as Dr. J. Hunter, Robert England, James S. Woodsworth, Ralph Connor, Dr. J. T. M. Anderson, and others. These works represent a rare contribution to Ukrainian Canadian historiography, although they often sin by relying upon anglophone sources which do not always reflect the true picture of the pioneer period. This situation, in some respect, was changed by the English-oriented Ukrainian authors of the seventies. First of all, came the monographs of local type such as M. Ewanchuk's "The History of the Ukrainian Settlement in the Gimli Area" (1975), and "Spruce, Swamp and Stone"; "Hardship and Progress of Ukrainian Pioneers," by P. Humeniuk (1977), etc.

A separate group is represented by those authors who analyse the Canadian situation in the terms of its third element and project the role this element plays in the development of Canada. "For a Better Canada", is by Senator Paul Yuzyk (1973), wherein he expresses his views on multiculturalism in Canada, compositions of national elements, and the direction of Canadian history as influenced by those elements (e.g. his "New Canadian Constitution and the Rights of Ethnic Groups," 1972). Along the same line, but in a different aspect appeared, in 1980, the collection of articles based on solid historical background, by Dr. Isidore Hlynka, entitled "The Other Canadians". It is evident that matters of public policy are receiving more attention. They are often discussed in analytical historical perspective.

From yet another angle the Ukrainian social structure in Canada was examined by such authors as Myrna Kostash in "All of Baba's Children" (1977) and in "The Streets of Gold" (1977), by Helen Potrebenko.

And, finally, a different category is preserved for those who create the basis for further studies. These include such works as "Dictionary of Ukrainian Surnames in Canada" by Forvin Bogdan (1974), "Ukrainian Catholic

Churches in Saskatchewan" by Anna Maria Baran and Christine Pastershank (1980), "Greater Than Kings" by Zonia Keywan and Martin Coles (1977), a well illustrated edition, "Ukrainian Canadian Biography: Pioneer Settlers of Manitoba" (1891-1900) by V. J. Kaye, a publication of the Ukrainian Research Foundation (1975), etc.

Two publications deserve special mention; "Chronology of Ukrainian Canadian History" by Andrew Gregorovich (1974), which provides a selection of over 400 important and interesting dates of Ukrainian history and recorded "firsts" and the "Statistical Compendium on the Ukrainians in Canada (1901-1971)" by V. Darkovich and Paul Yuzyk, published in 1977 by the University of Alberta Press. The compendium contains statistics on a range of topics on the Ukrainian and other ethnic groups obtained from the decennial and quinquennial census of Canada. It is a very useful source in every respect for history, sociology, social history, etc. This is the first work of its kind on any ethnocultural group in Canada. This mimeographed edition was published by University of Ottawa Press in 1980.

A separate category in the anglophone historical literature of the seventies is comprised of young researchers that are grouped at the Canadian Institute of Ukrainian Studies in Edmonton. The Institute, with support of the Canadian Foundation for Ukrainian Studies, publishes "the Alberta Library in Ukrainian Studies", "the Canadian Library in Ukrainian Studies" and a semi-annual "Journal of Ukrainian Studies" under editorship of Professor George Luckyj, Toronto. There are also mimeographed series. So far a number of publications appeared in all mentioned fields and by the end of 1981 it reached over 20 titles. The most impressive project is a four-volume alphabetical "Encyclopedia of Ukraine" in the process of preparation. This project will be published jointly with the Shevchenko Scientific Society in Europe and under direction of Professor Volodymyr Kubijovych. This is a very costly project but the Foundation managed to attract over a million dollars so far and there is no doubt that the project will be successfully completed and is considered the biggest achievement of the Institute and the Foundation.

It will be in order to mention such research works of the Institute as: "Ukrainian Canadians, Multiculturalism and Separation: An Assessment" by M. R. Lupul (1978), "Ukrainian Canadians: A Survey of Their Portrayal in English Language Works" by Frances Swyripa (1978), "Changing Realities: Social Trends Among Ukrainian Canadians" by R. Petryshyn (1980) and some essays printed in "The Journal" by O. Martynowych, N. Kazymyra, A. Makuch and others.

What is noticeable in this group of researchers is the fact that they move further away from the traditional cultural and organic evaluation of the Ukrainian process in Canada. They view the works as being over idealized, and show a lack of analytical and political appraisals. They direct their attention to the field of social stratification, social classes, social rivalry and political squabbling groups, influence of political trends coming from beyond Canada, etc.[1]

---

[1] *Journal*, #4, 1978, "No Gold for Baba's Children," by H. Potrebenko, and M. Kostash, and the "Crises of Ukrainian Canadian Historiography" by A. Makuch.

In the seventies, there were more efforts made to write general histories. The work of J. Kolasky entitled: "The History of Ukrainian Pro-Communist Organizations in Canada" appeared in 1979. Even earlier the "Historical Sketch of the Ukrainian Evangelical-Baptist Church" was written by Rev. G. Domashovetz. A history of the Ukrainian theatre arts in Canada was compiled and edited by P. Krawchuk under the title "Our Stage" (1981). It is a richly documented publication of stories and photos but it does not comprise the whole sector of Ukrainian theatrical life. In 1979, the Ukrainian Evangelical Alliance of North America published its history under the title "Outline of the History of the Ukrainian Evangelical-Reformed Movement" by Alexander Dombrowsky. During these years, both the Catholic and the Orthodox churches are preparing their several volume histories. There are many other sources that will be partly mentioned in our Bibliographical Index.

From what had been written above it appears that Ukrainians in Canada have acquired a great amount of source-oriented literature. Much of it has not been fully developed as of now, but what has been accomplished, or is being prepared, represents vast achievements. When compared with historiographies of Ukrainian settlements in other countries, they are beyond any doubt first in quality and quantity. Many of the mentioned works have benefited from the donations of Taras Shevchenko Foundation or from financial support of the Department of Multiculturalism. The climate of the seventies had a positive effect on the growth of publications in the field of multiculturalism.

Among the achievements of Ukrainian historiography in Canada it would be worthwhile to mention the work of the "Multicultural History Society of Ontario" which was formed in 1976 by a group of academics, civil servants, and librarians who saw a need for a special effort to record the province's ethnic history. The Society is supported by Wintario funds (placed in trust 3,000,000 dollars for 1976-1981),[2] and co-ordinates its program with the Archives of Ontario and the Multicultural Development Branch of the Ministry of Culture and Recreation. Representatives of more than forty different ethnocultural groups have worked with the Society headed by Prof. R. F. Harney as president and Prof. J. M. S. Careless as chairman of the Board of Directors. Ukrainians of Ontario have been represented here by Prof. W. Tarnopolsky, M. Diakowsky, A. Gregorovich, and in the research field have been registered Iroida Wynnycka of Kitchener, M. Stefura of Sudbury, Zoriana Sokolska and Yuriy Weretelnyk of Toronto. The Society carried out its mandate to enhance learning in ethnic studies by a variety of publication programs. "Polyphony," the Society's bulletin, appears twice a year. A separate department is created with so called "Oral History." This a huge and very useful project.

---

[2] *New Pathway,* May 12, 1979. "Documentation of Ukrainian Life in Ontario" by Iroida Wynnycka.

CHURCH ARCHITECTURE

Ukrainian Catholic Cathedral of Sts. Volodymyr and Olha in Winnipeg.

Blessed Virgin Mary Ukrainian Catholic Church, Winnipeg.

Ukrainian Orthodox Holy Trinity Cathedral in Winnipeg.

Ukrainian Orthodox Sobor of St. Mary the Protectress, Winnipeg.

Ukrainian Catholic Cathedral of St. Josaphat in Edmonton.

St. Mary the Protectress Church in Toronto.

Ukrainian Orthodox Church of St. Volodymyr in Hamilton.

Ukrainian Orthodox Church of St. Demetrius in Long Branch, Ontario.

Iconostasis and Interior of Ukrainian Catholic Cathedral of St. Josaphat in Toronto.

St. Cyril and Methodius Church in St. Catherines (Blessing Easter bread).

St. Nicholas Church and Monastery of the Basilian Order in Winnipeg.

St. Demetrius Church in Toronto.

St. George Cathedral in Saskatoon.

St. Joseph Church and Monastery of the Redemptorist Fathers in Winnipeg.

St. Andrew's College on University of Manitoba Campus housing Ukrainian Orthodox Theological Faculty and the Centre for Ukrainian Canadian Studies.

Ukrainian Baptist Chapel on the Summer Campus at Peterborough, Ontario.

DECADE OF MULTICULTURALISM — ILLUSTRATIONS 841

HISTORIC EVENTS

Archibishop Major Patriarch Josyf Cardinal Slipyj with Premier of Manitoba Ed Shreyer (1975), later Governor General of Canada.

Members and guests of the Ukrainian Academy of Arts and Sciences on the occasion of its 25th Anniversary (1975). First Row: P. Woroby, O. Gerus, J. Rozumnyj, A. Baran A. Kachor, Irene Lubynsky, M. Marunchak, M. Mandryka, R. Olynyk.

Board of the Ukrainian Credit Union in Windsor on the occasion of its 30th Anniversary, 1976.

Board of the Ukrainian Credit Union in Montreal on its 35th Anniversary, 1979.

DECADE OF MULTICULTURALISM — ILLUSTRATIONS

The XIII Ukrainian Canadian Congress marking the 40th Anniversary of the Ukrainian Canadian Committee. Front Row, L to R: S. Radchuk, UCC President; M. Marunchak, delivering speech; P. Savaryn, Chairman of the Congress. Second Row: Bishop Wasyliy Fedak, Bishop Neil Savaryn, Rev. S. W. Sawchuk

Photo Courtesy of Globe and Mail

Ontario celebrations of 90th Anniversary of Ukrainian Settlement in Canada L to R: P. Hlibowych, President of the Ontario UCC Council; O. Hlibowych, Conductor of the Ensemble Verkhovyna; Bishop Izidore Borecky: Prof. O. Subtelny.

844 UKRAINIAN CANADIANS: A HISTORY

Edmonton based National Executive of UCPBF (1974). Seated: Orest Talpash, Manoly Lupul, Peter Oluk. Standing: Bill Diachuk, Orest Evenshen, Peter Savaryn, Lawrence Decore, Ed Kay.

Board of the Ukrainian Reading Association "Prosvita" in Winnipeg on the occasion of its 75th Anniversary, 1980. Front Row: P. Mychalishyn, J. Dziurdziewich, M. Chaykowsky, J. Holian, W. Cap, S. Kozelko, M. Worobec, A. Kurdydyk, I. Onufriychuk. Second Row: R. Worobec, S. Karalash, F. Russin, A. Surasky, D. Mazur, W. Panaskewych, A. Shepertycky, I. Pochylchuk, A. Borys.

DECADE OF MULTICULTURALISM — ILLUSTRATIONS 845

Canadian Foundation for Ukrainian Studies, 1976. Seated: I. Bardyn, P. Savaryn, J. Karasevich, St. Frolick, B. Onyshchuk, E. Topornicky, W. S. Tarnopolsky. Second Row: J. Barwinsky, I. Stashuk, Roma Franko, Franko Martyniuk, Manoly Lupul.

Executive of the Society of Ukrainian Engineers and Associates in Canada (1981-1982). Seated: S. Ilnycky, Irena Malashchuk, Y. Sokolyk, W. Yarish, Dr. G. J. Kurys. Second Row: G. A. Senkiw, Dr. G. B. Babiy, K. Brykowych, P. Bubela, N. Chornyj, R. Kowalyk.

Joint meeting of the National Executive of UCPBF and Directors of the University of Toronto Chair of Ukrainian Studies in Ottawa, 1979. Front Row, L to R: Olya Williams, George Danyliw, Maria Barabash, Honorable Norman Cafik. Second Row: Ihor Bardyn, Erast Huculak, Prof. Peter Potichnyj, Steven Howe, Irena Moroz, Prof. Peter Woroby, Bohdan Shulakewych, John Stashuk. Third Row: Michael Wawryshyn, Eugene Zaraska, Bohdan Sirant, Orest Nowakiwsky.

Representatives of the Toronto Chair of Ukrainian Studies Inc. and the University of Toronto signing agreement to establish the Chair of Ukrainian Studies. Sitting, L to R: Irena Moroz, Olya Williams, Frances Danyliw, Lida Palij, Chrystia Isajiw. Second Row: Yurij Boshyk, Jaroslav Moroz, Bohdan Maksymec, Steve Howe, Bohdanna Chuma, W. George Danyliw, Minister Norman Cafik, Ostap Wynnycky, Serge Radchuk, Erast Huculak. Third Row: Wasyl Kereliuk, Bohdan Sirant, Jaroslav Sokolyk, Volodymyr Bolubash, Peter Woroby, Jaroslav Shudrak, Paul Chumak, Edward Topornycki, Leo Cordinal, Eugene Zaraska, Peter Smylsky.

CHURCH HIERARCHY AND CLERGY.

Bishop Demetrius M. Greschuk.

Bishop Jerome I. Chimy, O.S.B.M.

Bishop Myron Daciuk, O.S.B.M.

Rev. Dmytro Luchak

Bishop Mykolay Debryn

Rev. Hryhoriy Udod

Rev. M. Hrynchyshyn C.S.S.R.

Bishop Vasyliy Fedak

Rev. J. Iwaskiw

848   UKRAINIAN CANADIANS: A HISTORY

LEADERS IN VARIOUS FIELDS.

Yuriy Mulyk-Lucyk   Natalia Aponiuk   Wasyl Weryha   M. Ewanchuk

Yaroslav Sokolyk   Yaroslava Sokolyk   Anna Maria Baran   Yaroslav Bilak

P. Salyga   M. Shepetyk   Ulana Plawuszczak   Jaroslav Moskva

DECADE OF MULTICULTURALISM — ILLUSTRATIONS

CHURCH AND COMMUNITY LEADERS.

Serge Radchuk   Peter Kondra   John Nowosad

— UCC PRESIDENTS —

Rev. V. Pidskalny, O.S.B.M.   W. Bezchlibnyk   A. J. Yaremovich   Rev. Paul Maluga, C.S.S.R.

P. Bashuk   Laurence G. Decore   H. A. Yopyk   Leonid Fil

850   UKRAINIAN CANADIANS: A HISTORY

SENATORS, MPs AND MLAs.

Albert Hohol   John Ewasew   Norman A. Cafik   Julian Koziak

Roy Romanow   Roman Hnatyshyn   Steve Paproski   Wilson D. P. Parasiuk

George Topolnisky   Harvie Andre   Laverne Lewycky   Yuri Shymko

INTEGRATION PROCESSES

So far we have been discussing exclusively the cultural aspects of Ukrainians in Canada, or in other words, all the factors which identify the Ukrainian Canadian community as a separate national and cultural entity. This draws the vertical lines that divide to some extent the ethnocultural communities of Canada into separate cultural enclaves.

However, there are other social ties between these enclaves that combine them into one vast unity which we name as a Canadian nation. When these first lines were drawn vertically to denote cultural aspects than the lines follow the horizontal directions bind all ethnocultural groups into one entity. The first lines we call the culturally-vertical while the horizontal would be global integration. These horizontal lines we adapt towards the nation's political process. They include political representation, administration, administrative policies, the administration of justice, legislative work, national self-defense and others. The fundamental horizontal tie also applies to economics in personal and national endeavors. It is along these same vital horizontal lines that we would like to lead the integral prime directions of Ukrainians in Canada.

Let us begin our discussion in this field with Ukrainian co-operative movement with which we have already been partially acquainted in one of our previous chapters. As we have already learned the co-operative movement has two aspects; cultural and economic. In our case it will act as a catalyst between cultural society and the general integral part of the whole national Canadian community. Questions arise, what has been done and what progress has been accomplished in the co-operative movement among Ukrainian Canadians during the last decade.

Co-operative Movement in the Seventies

In 1980 the Ukrainian co-operative movement in Canada celebrated its 50th Anniversary and it was appropriately tied in with the founding of Ukrainian co-operative "Kalyna" in 1930, in Winnipeg. In the beginning "Kalyna" had the task of serving its members through sales of books, journals and other publications.

At the beginning, this proved to be insufficient to cover the cost of administration, and this need was met by adding the sales of wood, coal, and tickets of steam ship agencies. Although the merchandising arrangements changed with times, the co-operative fundamentally retained its loyalty towards the bookstore.

In 1979, the Ukrainian co-operative movement held a different jubilee. It represented 40 years of credit union activities in Western Canada.[1] In this

---

[1] *Svoboda Daily*, November 9, 1979. A. Kachor: 40th Anniversary of the Ukrainian Credit Movement in Canada.

instance the start was made in Saskatoon on February 13, 1939, where the credit union, "Nova Hromada", (New Community Credit Union) was founded. In 1940, a year later, a similar co-operative under the name of "Carpathia" Credit Union, was founded in Winnipeg. Three years later one more co-operative, the North Winnipeg Credit Union was established. These three credit co-operatives, along with "Kalyna", were the result of the activities of Wasyl (William) Topolnycky[2] a devoted co-operator and idealist who, with his professional experience from Europe strove to implant the co-operative values upon the Canadian soil. From these small beginnings, grew the mighty co-operative movement which, in 1980, numbered around 60 co-operatives and around 60,000 members.

Actually in the above cited numbers the credit unions are fundamentally strong. Therefore, for a better insight into this movement and its growth we will deal with statistics for the last decade.

Let us first examine the growth of the credit unions in the Eastern Canada, where this movement now is the strongest. In Toronto alone in 1980, there were 24,530 members and credit union assets amounted to $123,433,027. Below we present the numbers for 1971 and 1980 in membership and assets.

UKRAINIAN CREDIT UNIONS IN EASTERN CANADA
1971 — 1980

	Membership 1971	1980*	Assets 1971	1980
Ukrainian (Toronto) Credit Union	5,039	8,269	$10,602,136	$47,431,293
Buduchnist (Toronto) Credit Union	4,088	5,495	8,571,209	29,146,649
Su-Use (Toronto) Credit Union	3,368	4,675	6,585,213	24,255,695
St. Mary's (Toronto) Credit Union	2,648	2,727	4,986,711	10,860,866
St. Nicholas (Toronto) Parish	779	1,183	1,364,178	7,243,915
St. Josaphat's Parish (Toronto)	625	947	694,974	2,955,918
Ukrainian Veterans' Credit Union (Toronto)	250	—	48,145	—
Free Ukrainian Society (Toronto)	280	—	61,452	—
Plast — Ukrainian Credit Union (Toronto)	209	465	64,650	259,914
Ukrainian People's Home	89	—	27,416	—
Holy Eucharist Parish (Toronto)	86	140	16,143	70,020
St. Demetrius Parish Credit Union	—	629	—	1,208,757

---

[2]*Co-ordinator* "Co-ordinator of Ukrainian Credit Unions in Canada" (No. 23-24), 1978, "Wasyl Topolnycky — Founder of Ukrainian Co-operatives in Canada" by Dmytro Mykytiuk.

	Membership		Assets	
	1971	1980*	1971	1980
Ukrainian (National) Credit Union, Montreal	1,860	1,739	3,337,744	8,256,195
Caisse Populaire Ukrainienne du Montreal	1,536	2,259	3,491,823	9,168,918
Mazeppa Credit Union, Montreal	—	750	—	2,230,734
Ukrainian (Sudbury) Credit Union	265	310	275,098	673,551
Ukrainian Youth Association (Sudbury)	—	126	—	138,161
St. John's Ukrainian Orthodox (Oshawa)	—	230	147,653	429,536
St. George Parish (Oshawa)	—	350	—	779,068
Ukrainian (Hamilton) Credit Union	241	1,365	280,046	5,148,491
"Wira" (Hamilton) Credit Union	—	396	363,457	1,630,149
St. Vladimir's (Hamilton) Credit Union	282	—	344,793	—
Holy Ghost Parish (Hamilton)	496	—	635,795	—
Ukrainian (Fort William) Credit Union, Thunder Bay	626	1,032	504,239	2,203,393
Ukrainian (St. Catherines) Credit Union	617	940	629,620	4,370,075
Ukrainian (London) Credit Union	—	217	—	323,020
Ukrainian (Ottawa) Credit Union	—	140	—	693,813
Ukrainian (Windsor) Credit Union	552	812	503,702	2,173,453

*1971 — Data taken from *"Vilne Slovo"*, Toronto, 14.10.1972; and *"Co-Ordinator"* 1980, also the Ukrainian Credit Unions in Canada, in *"Co-Ordinator"*, No. 1-2(33-34), Toronto, 1981.

UKRAINIAN CREDIT UNIONS IN WESTERN CANADA

	Membership 1977*	Membership 1980*	Assets 1977	Assets 1980
Carpathia Credit Union Winnipeg	6,259	6,992	$24,613,536	$32,701,633
North Winnipeg Credit Union, Winnipeg	1,744	1,948	6,077,645	8,696,777
New Community Credit Union, Saskatoon	1,373	1,675	5,894,675	8,615,137
Ukrainian (Edmonton) Credit Union,	1,066	1,730	4,322,745	16,520,505
Sifton Credit Union, Sifton, Manitoba	—	1,001	—	3,610,784
Vera Credit Union, Winnipeg, Manitoba	981	1,031	2,127,240	2,920,549
Progress Credit Union, Winnipeg	856	959	2,523,385	2,898,000
Vita Credit Union, Vita, Manitoba	1,560	1,657	1,909,437	2,482,947
Oakbank Credit Union, Oakbank, Manitoba	—	598	—	1,794,086
St. Michael's Credit Union	—	250	401,872	1,218,357
Regina Ukrainian Credit Union, Regina, Sask.	174	173	176,500	222,915
Steppe Credit Union, Winnipeg	181	191	141,722	176,000
Dnipro Credit Union, Winnipeg	121	—	188,959	—
Ukrainian Credit Union, Calgary	—	—	1,434,360	—
St. Joseph's Credit Union, Winnipeg	112	—	53,017	—

In summary there were 40 co-operatives with 55 thousand membership and 245 million in assets.

*1977 — Data taken from *"Co-Ordinator"*, 3-4 (23-24), 1978.
*1980 — Data taken from *"Co-Ordinator"*, 1-2 (33-34), Toronto, 1981.

According to the charts there are a few small credit unions that have ceased to exist. All others showed an extraordinary growth in membership and assets. Also a new credit union was created (St. Demetrius, Toronto). Although there have been some financial difficulties for the Credit Unions during the last few years, the numbers presented below regarding the growth of the Ukrainian Credit Unions in the Western Canada for years 1977 and 1981 deny such reports. This chart also indicates that some small credit unions have amalgamated with larger ones, e.g. St. Joseph with "Progress" in Winnipeg, "Dnipro" with "Carpathia", also in Winnipeg. The same happened with "Progress" and "Vera" in 1981. In 1971 three credit unions in Edmonton were amalgamated and created Ukrainian (Edmonton) Credit Union. The amalgamation greatly strengthened this credit union. The same happened in Eastern Canada in Hamilton.

The above two presented charts speak unequivocally about the great progress of credit unions in Eastern and Western Canada.

A somewhat different picture is drawn when we analyze the consumer co-operatives. Reasons for the difficulties are numerous. They were dwelt upon in one of the previous chapters where we discussed the co-operative movement before 1970.

The tendency of all social organisms is to unite with the elements of the same category. Such was the case with Ukrainian co-operatives. At the beginning they carried on their work separately, but mutual problems prompted them to work jointly. In Western Canada, in Winnipeg, "Co-operative Hromada" (Co-operative Association) was formed whose aim was to formulate and instil the community co-operative idea in its environment. In Eastern Canada with a similar idea in mind, the Co-ordinating Committee of Ukrainian Co-operatives was organized in Toronto. In 1971 during the 10th Congress of the Ukrainian Canadians, the economic co-operative session, in reality, turned out to become National Economic Co-operative Convention. After the fundamental speech by A. Kachor, a representative of "Co-operative Hromada", in Winnipeg, leading co-operative ideologist of Canada, the Ukrainian Co-operative Council of Canada (UCCC) was formed and headed by Wasyl Sytnyk, one of the founders of Ukrainian co-operative movement in Eastern Canada. Toronto, being the largest co-operative centre of Eastern Canada, became the headquarters of the UCCC. A similar institution to UCCC was the Association of Ukrainian Co-operatives of U.S.A. In the end, both institutions came to a mutual agreement and created the Ukrainian World Co-operative Council. Such a representative body was formed in 1973, in Toronto, during the Second World Congress of Free Ukrainians (W.C.F.U.) Over 50 co-operative delegates took part in the convention, representing Canada, U.S.A., Australia, Argentina and England. Wasyl Sytnyk of Canada was elected president. The presidium was composed of: A. Kachor, O. Pleshkevych, I. Leshchyshyn, W. Kucyj and five members representing the five countries. Headquarters was located in Toronto.[3]

At the Third Congress of the World Congress of Free Ukrainians in New York, the U.S.A. took over the helm of the Ukrainian World Co-operative

---

[3]*Coordinator* No. 8, 1974, (Toronto). "The turning step in our co-operative work" by Andriy Kachor.

Council with O. Pleshkevych as its president and with headquarters in Chicago.

According to the statistics published by the Ukrainian World Co-operative Council (U.W.C.C.) membership and assets of credit unions in four countries, at the end of 1980, were as follows:

Country	No. of Co-operatives	Membership	Assets
Australia	7	7,122	$ 23,347,540
Argentina	2	8,356	8,340,020
Canada	36	53,391	245,223,129
U.S.A.	34	44,820	164,996,910
Total	79	113,689	$441,907,599

Also very interesting are the statistics of U.W.C.C. on Ukrainian trust companies which have been operating in Canada and U.S.A. The assets of these companies amounted by 1980 to $185,669,000 (Canada $85,000,000, U.S.A. $100,669,000).[4] In this field Canada and U.S.A. are taking first solid steps. From the financial pictures provided it shows that Canada leads the way in credit unions while the U.S.A. in trust companies.

From reports published in Ukrainian papers we may conclude that the Ukrainian Co-operative Council of Canada (U.C.C.C.) has been playing a stimulative role in the development of the co-operative movement in Canada. Without any doubt it has also had a positive impact on its southern neighbours. This is noticeable on the national and international scene of Ukrainian credit movement. In 1980, the board of U.C.C.C. was elected at the national convention in Winnipeg for the period of three years: W. Sytnyk (president) and members: A. Kachor, M. Andruchiw, W. Chyz, V. Kucyj, J. Skwarchuk, Rev. W. Ivashko, O. Chomiak, O. Barwinsky, O. Wynnycky, D. Kowbasiuk, Rev. I. Leshchyshyn, auditors: B. Kalba, P. Kit, A. Gospodyn, L. Fil, V. Antoniw.

Integration in the Economic Field

When on the co-operative plain we can operate with factual statistics with ease and to present the successes of the co-operative movement, even to indicate short-comings of this system, in the economic field of private enterprise it is not possible to make an accurate analysis. Here we cannot take advantage of statistical analysis, neither do we have any specific yearly reports. Private enterprise prefers not to expose its ethnocultural background. The integration here is in the full meaning of the word and it has even a tendency to anihilate the cultural traits of the community. In spite of these difficulties we will try to present at least in general terms some contributions on the basis of Canadian censuses and to indicate some pillars in this field. The years prior to 1961 Census were discussed in the chapter "Achievement

---

[4]Economic News, *Ukrainian Echo*, Toronto: No. 43 (1960), 1981, "Our Economic-Financial Basis" by Omelan Pleshkevych.

and Integration," statistical data was also given referring to occupations on the basis of 1961 Census.

At present when we compare statistics of 1961 with the same of 1971, according to Prof. Ivan Tesla, Ukrainian-Canadian demographer and statistician, who has for years studied this field, then we may arrive at conclusions that the Ukrainians in Canada in the last decade have made substantial progress.[1] In order that we have a better picture for comparison purposes we also take into consideration the average of the statistics of the Canadian economy. Furthermore, in order to delve more fully into development of sectors of occupational economy we take into consideration figures of the statistics of Canadian Census 1951, 1961, and 1971.

The prime occupation among Ukrainians has been agriculture. This field was thoroughly researched by historian Paul Yuzyk who stated that Ukrainians brought under cultivation appoximately 10,100,000 acres (4 million hectares) of land. Thus in 1951 — 30.24% of Ukrainians were engaged in agricultural field while general Canadian representation in this field was 15.70. In 1961 Ukrainian co-efficient was 21.09, while general Canadian was 10.02. This co-efficient changed greatly in 1971. Ukrainian was 11.65, Canadian 5.94%.

How do we explain the change taking place in this social structure? The first answer would be that modern farming does not require as many hands as two or three decades ago. In modern day, farming equipment replaces men. Technical improvement decreased the need of farm laborers. Likewise due to improved technology, small farms are not economical to operate which results in the creation of large farm units. As a result the younger generation is compelled to migrate to towns and cities seeking more profitable employment in industry, retail business, construction, etc. This migration is evident not only in Canada but also in other industrialized western countries. Even in the U.S.S.R. where migration is state controlled there is considerable movement to cities. At the expense of farming population we note the great increase of urban population.

Canadian migration during 1966-1971 years was studied by L. O. Stone who came up with the following statements: "Almost half of the Canadian population changed residence between 1966-1971 and about one-quarter moved to a different municipality. More than one in 10 changed municipality of residence twice in those five years."[2] In another study L. O. Stone comes up with another statement: "When a group of migrants moved between an urban and a rural area in the 1966-71 period, it was the characteristics of the urban area that were most influential in shaping the occupational distribution of the group, regardless of the direction of the migration. This was the result of the dominance of the urban area as a source of higher-education facilities and of varied job opportunities. It was particularly marked when the urban area was a metropolitan area."[3]

---

[1] *Demography of Ukrainian Canadians* by Ivan Tesla, Mimeographed. Author's Archives, also in *The Jubilee Collection of the Ukrainian Free Academy of Sciences,* pp. 481-540.

[2] The Frequency of Geographic Mobility in Population of Canada" by Leroy O. Stone, *Statistics Canada,* 1972.

[3] Occupational Composition of Canadian Migration, by L. O. Stone, *Statistics Canada,* 1972.

This Canadian migration is evident in the Census of 1981, where cities like Calgary, Edmonton and others increased their population greatly due to migrants from rural areas to urban centres.

Now how do we explain that the number of Ukrainians in the agricultural industry is considerably higher than average for Canada? Here the difference is 5.76 where as in professions and other fields the co-efficient is between 0.43 and 1.5. Basically the Ukrainians have traditional love for soil and secondly they have established themselves in the cultivation of prairies in Western Canada and became an important factor in the field of agricultural production.

What is the proportion of Ukrainian labour forces in comparison with overall labour forces in Canada? In the field of construction this co-efficient is quite even. In 1951 this industry occupied 4.53 (Canadian 5.66) but in 1971, 6.48 for Ukrainians when at the same time Canadian average was 6.59. The number of Ukrainians employed in mining industries diminished — 1951 —1.84 (Canadians 1.25), in 1961 — 1.25 (Canadian 1.00) and in 1971 — 0.87 (Canadian 0.69).

In transportation and communication the number of Ukrainians was 3.93 in 1971 (Canadian co-efficient 3.92). Significant increase in number in sales. In 1951 — 4.11 (Canadian — 6) but by 1971 — 8.36 (Canadian 9.46). The greatest progress was made in the clerical field, Professional and Teaching. In clerical there was 6.8% employed in 1951 but in 1971, 14.80 (Canadian average 15.92). Among the professions the co-efficient was 3.37 in 1951, in 1961 increased to 6.55. In 1971 it was 10.44%. Although average Canadian co-efficient was 12.67 in 1971 and there is difference from average Canadian 2% the growth in this field is self-evident.

The lowest progress, indicated by statistical data, is in the managerial field. Here the Ukrainian co-efficient is 2.95 when general Canadian 4.31. In this field human qualifications are not the only factor in final decision. Political, traditional cliques and elites play here a very important role. Wallace Clement who studies this question more thoroughly, stated in his study that in 1972 co-efficient in economic elite among Anglo-Saxons was 86.2, French 8.4 and others 5.4. Of this 5.4, Jewish Canadians lead (4.1), balance 1.3 is spread among other nationalities.[4] Similarly among the media elite: Anglo-Saxons 81.9, French 13.3 and other 4.8, of which Jewish Canadians 2.9.[5] There is the feeling that due to multicultural policy this co-efficient among the various nationalities will find its own level in the satisfactory proportion to any given ethnocultural group. We realize that this situation is a long drawn out process.

In spite of these seen and unseen problems Ukrainian Canadians are advancing to entitled positions in various fields. Here we take advantage of the statistics of Ukrainian engineers — "Society of Ukrainian Engineers and Associates" in Toronto.

---

[4]*The Canadian Corporate Elite* by W. Clement, Toronto, McClelland and Stewart Ltd., 1975, p. 232.

[5]*Ibidem* and W. Roman Petryshyn, "The Ukrainian Canadians in Social Transition" In *Ukrainian Canadians, Multiculturalism & Separatism: An Assessment* by Manoly R. Lupul (ed.), The University of Alberta Press, 1978.

Based on 1980 statistics, Canada had a population of 23,791,000 of which 10,369,000 were employed. Of those employed there were about 110,000 registered Professional Engineers. The estimated number of engineers in Canada of Ukrainian origin is approximately over 2,000. In recent years Ukrainian Canadian engineers, many of whom hold important and responsible positions, have played an important role in the development of Canadian industry.

The Association of Professional Engineers of Ontario has 45,000 members. The President of the Association for 1981-1982 of this prestigious organization is a Ukrainian Canadian born engineer Alexander Kobelak.

The Machinery and Equipment Manufacturer's Association of Canada (M.E.M.A.C.) is a national body which directs the manufacturers' activities. President of this association is a Ukrainian Canadian born engineer — Brigadier General (retired) J. R. Romanow.

Canada is the world's largest producer of nickel. The largest nickel producing company in the world with about 20 plants and 65,000 employees worldwide is Inco Metal Inc. The President and Chief Executive Officer of this company is Dr. W. Curlook (Kuryluk), Professional Engineer, graduate of Toronto University. The Vice-President and Director of R & D is Dr. T. Podolsky. The Sherritt Gordon Mines Limited is the second largest nickel producer. The executive Vice-President of this company is Dr. W. Mackiw. Dr. Mackiw together with other prominent Ukrainian Canadian engineers like W. Kundra, pioneered a new method of extracting nickel from the ore for which Dr. Mackiw received a gold medal from the Chemical Institute of Canada. Their method is known in hydrometallurgy. Canadian nuclear reactor, technologically known as Candu — is perhaps the best in the world. Prominent engineers with the Atomic Energy of Canada Limited are; Dr. O. Trojan and Dr. G. B. Babiy.

A number of Ukrainian Canadian engineers do hold senior positions in various levels of government. Among them are L. Pencak, Assistant deputy Minister; Government Services, Dr. G. Kurys, Senior Scientific Advisor, Ministry of Industry; N. Yurchuk, Executive Director, Ministry of Revenue, Government of Ontario. Professor W. Janishewsky is the Associate Dean, Faculty of Engineering, University of Toronto, while Professor Len Domaschuk is Associate Head of Civil Engineering at the University of Manitoba.

There are a number of Ukrainian Canadian engineers who either own or are partners in Consulting Engineering companies. The following are examples: G. Ochrym, President of Consultec Limited, B. Maksymec, President of Planmac Consultants Limited, J. L. Seychuk, President of Golden Associates, to name a few.

Many Ukrainian Canadian engineers hold corporate positions in the private sector, such as J. Tutecky, Manager of Domtar Limited, in St. Catharines, Y. W. Sokolyk, Manager of Engineering, FMC of Canada Limited, S. Ilnycky, Senior Research Scientist, Imperial Oil Limited, N. Chorny, Manager, Environmental Affairs, Suncor Limited, W. Moroz, Chief Engineer, Steel Company of Canada Limited. S. Michael Tymiak, consultant-project co-ordinator for Dominion Foundries and Steel Limited, Hamilton.

This is not a detailed study of the contribution of Ukrainian Canadian Engineers to the development of Canadian Industry. However, the few names mentioned above reflect some of the achievements of Ukrainian Canadian Engineers.

Ukrainian Canadian Engineers are organized in the *Society of Ukrainian Engineers and Associates in Canada.* This dates back to the post war era of the Second World War. The first Ukrainian Engineering Society in Canada was founded in 1949 and was named The Ukrainian Technical Society. It was established in Toronto with branches in Alberta and Quebec with several chapters in Ontario, Windsor, Ottawa and Sarnia. In 1975 the name of the Ukrainian Technical Society was changed to the present one, the Society of Ukrainian Engineers & Associates to reflect the Canadian Council of Professional Engineers.

The society is very active in Ukrainian and Canadian communities as well as in Canadian societies such as Association of Professional Engineers Chemical Institute of Canada (C.I.C.), Institute of Electrical and Electronic Engineers (I.E.E.E.) and others.

In 1970-76, the Society of Ukrainian Engineers and Associates (at the time still Ukrainian Technical Society) was headed by Yaroslav Sokolyk who edited in 1966-1972 "The News of Ukrainian Engineers." Since 1977 he headed the Toronto Branch of Ukrainian Engineers, which acts as the National Headquarters of the Society of Ukrainian Engineers and Associates in Canada. In the professional work of this ambitious chapter there have been involved such idividuals as Prof. W. Janishewsky, G. A. Senkiw, W. Jarish, N. Chorny, Dr. G. Kurys, S. Ilnycky, K. Brykowych, Dr. G. B. Babiy, P. Bubela, R. Kowalyk, I. Malashchuk, R. Romanchukevych, M. Masley, Dr. O. Trojan, Prof. J. W. Darewych and others.

A special place in the building industry of Eastern Canada is reserved for William Teron, already known to us as a developer of "Canata." Due to his expertise in industrial corporation field he was appointed in 1973 chairman of the Central Mortgage and Housing Corporation. In Toronto, M. Yablonsky made a name for himself in building of skyscrapers. Better known in this field is Peter Jacyk of whom "Mississauga News" in 1979 stated: "P. Jacyk, of the Jacyk Group, an industrial development company responsible for bringing to Mississauga at least a million square feet of industrial space."[6] P. Jacyk corporations; "Prombank Investment," "Accurate Builders," "Askold Association Ltd.," "Upper-Middle Towers." "P. Jacyk Group" and others are well known in Canadian economic circles. P. Jacyk's name is also well known for his generous contributions to cultural and educational projects. E. Huculak, former Vancouverite, acquired wide popularity in Toronto and Sudbury for his developments in the field of pharmaceutical establishments.

There are active leaders/millionaires not only in Toronto but also in Western Canada. Edmonton, Alberta, has special status in this field. One of the activists in Ukrainian community, Rev. S. Semczuk, writes on the occasion of the 75th Anniversary of Alberta and Saskatchewan the following: "In Edmonton alone the people told me and pointed out the names of those whose assets are worth more than one million dollars. They estimated that

---

[6]*The Mississauga News,* May 2, 1979, "Too Many People Getting the Runaround."

there would be one hundred millionaires."[7] In this category of Ukrainian millionaires are such well known pioneer families as Hawrelak, Decore, Shandro, Oluk and others.

In previous chapters we have covered some activities of Ukrainian professionals in Edmonton. At the same time we had mentioned about activities of Ukrainian professionals in other centers. When we take into consideration that in 1982 there were over 300 members in the Ukrainian Professional and Businessmen Club in Edmonton, and when we compare this number of organized professionals (there are many who are not members) with the beginning in Edmonton: J. Orobko, first medical doctor in 1923, Ivan Basarab, first lawyer in 1925, Faust Gowda, first dentist in 1927 and later on Vasyl Sereda, first pharmacist and so on, the achievements of Ukrainian professionals and businessmen are more than impressive. The input of Ukrainian Canadians in the field of economics and professions is noticeable at every step. This is self-evident not only in Western but also in Eastern Canada. This integration is registered in the field of humanities and science are previously mentioned. This input is noted in the field of administration of Canadian universities. It is not by accident that the heads of those Western Canadian universities are Canadians of Ukrainian descent. The Chairman of the Board of Governors of the University of Manitoba is Dr. L. Melosky, son of Ukrainian pioneer bilingual teacher, the Chairman of Saskatchewan University —Board of Governors, Christine Pastershank, whose parents arrived in Canada after the Second World War. In the meantime Peter Savaryn (lawyer) has been appointed for a four year term as chancellor of the University of Alberta. There are more Ukrainians in this field. William Solypa, well known Ukrainian pedagogue, is a member of the Board of Governors of the University of Winnipeg. The same position is held by William Teron of Carleton University in Ottawa. Valerie Kasiurak, citizenship judge for Essex and Kent, was elected to the Board of Governors of the Windsor University.

In Toronto, Andrew Gregorovich, professional librarian, for years headed Historical Council of Toronto which has under its care such landmarks as Fort Garry, Mackenzie House, Colborne Lodge and Marine Museum of Upper Canada. Nela Nakonechny heads Library Council of Metropolitan Toronto Library. Serge Sawchyn, former general manager of Royal Winnipeg Ballet has been known as a "country's premier impressario." In military fields are: Brigadier General Joseph R. Romanow and Brigadier General Steven Andrunyk as well as some inspectors within R.C.M.P. ranks.

All this speaks well for the fact that in most Canadian cities, towns and villages, Ukrainians participate actively in promotion of cultural activities such as education, research, ballet, opera, symphony, orchestra, museums, etc. They participate actively in all professions and other occupations.

However, the political integration speaks fully about mature and complete integration of a cultural community in the national stream of life. Therefore, we finally will take a closer look at this field of integration during the last decade.

---

[7] *Shashkevychiana,* Winnipeg, No. 7 (32-33), 1980, p. 30.

Integration in the Political Field

In this chapter we will deal with provincial legislatures, federal parliament and the senate. It will cover the seventies, including the Manitoba provincial election of 1969, which was not discussed in previous chapters.

Manitoba and Alberta

In 1969, during the Manitoba provincial election 6 M.L.A.s of Ukrainian origin were elected: 5 from N.D.P., one liberal, Steve Patrick. Ben Hanuschak and Sam Uskiw were re-elected. Three new faces appeared on the scene: *Peter Burtniak* (1925-), a farmer and farm implements dealer, from Dauphin constituency, *Bill Uruski* (1942-) born in Poplarfield and elected from St. George riding, and *Harry Shafransky*, a teacher elected from Radisson. The last two named were re-elected again in 1973, and Bill Uruski re-elected in 1977 and 1981. Premier Ed Schreyer appointed P. Burtniak Minister of Tourism and Recreation, S. Uskiw the Minister of Agriculture, and Ben Hanuschak Speaker of Manitoba Legislature. The Ukrainian public recognized this as being one of the highest political achievements of Ukrainians in Manitoba.

Ukrainians living in other provinces who had to look up to Manitoba as being the leader in provincial politics became somewhat envious. This situation lasted until Aug. 30, 1971 when the provincial elections to Alberta's 17th Legislature took place. The unexpected result of these elections not only changed the opinion about Manitoba's prestige but it also altered the whole political map of Alberta. Beginning in 1935, the Social Credit Government under such premiers as Aberhart, Manning and Strom had been successful in winning nine provincial elections, until defeated in 1971, and the Conservative Government, under leadership of Peter Lougheed came into power. Among the 75 members of the Legislature, 11 were of Ukrainian origin.[1] This established a record for any one province. The most interesting part about it was that 8 of those members belonged to the party in power, while the other 3 were from the defeated Social Credit.

Let us examine more closely those 11 representatives as to their social and professional standing, the constituencies from which they were elected, etc.

The Social Creditors previously known to us were: Albert Ludwig, former Minister of Public Works, who served during 1959, 1967 and was re-elected again in 1971. The same record stands for Alexander W. Gordey and Dr. Walter A. Buck, the latter having been re-elected in 1979.

The Progressive Conservatives were as follows: *Edward A. Hohol* (1922-) born at Two Hills, B. Ed., M. Ed., Ph.D., adherent of the United Church, elected in Edmonton-Belmont, re-elected in 1975. Did not run in 1979. Minister of Manpower and Labour (1971-1975) and Minister of Advanced Education and Manpower 1975. *Julian Gregory Josaphat Koziak* (1940-) B.A., L.L.B., Ukrainian Catholic, born in Edmonton and elected in Edmonton-Strathcona, re-elected in 1975 and 1979, and Minister of Education (1971-1975). *Wasyl Diachuk* (1929-) born in Vegreville, general insurance agent, elected in Edmonton-Beverly, re-elected in 1975 and 1979, and Deputy Speaker 1972-1975. *George Topolnisky* (1929-), born in Pakan, Alberta, High

---

[1] Here are included also the names of those who have even one parent of Ukrainian descent. Such names have asterisk (*) beside them (on the left).

School Teacher, elected in Redwater, re-elected in 1975 and 1979, Minister without portfolio, and responsible for Rural Development 1971-1975. *John Batiuk* (1923-) farmer, Catholic, elected in Vegreville, and re-elected in 1975 and 1979. *Catherine Chichak,* Business Executive, Ukrainian Catholic, elected in Edmonton-Norwood, and re-elected in 1975 and 1979. **Kenneth R. H. Paproski* (1931-) B. Sc., M.D., Roman Catholic, elected in Edmonton-Kingsway, and re-elected 1975 and 1979. **William F. Purdy* Power Engineer, Lutheran, elected in Stony Plain, re-elected in 1975 and 1979.

Lougheed's Conservatives were victorious in 1975 and 1979 elections. At that time three more conservatives of Ukrainian descent were elected: *Peter Trynchy Jr.* (1931-) born at Rockfort Bridge, Alberta, member of United Church, businessman and farmer, elected in 1975 at Whitecourt nd re-elected in 1979. *Stanley A. Kushner* (1946-) born at Calgary, businessman, elected in Calgary-Mountain View, 1975, and re-elected in 1979. *John Brian Zaozirny* (1921-) United Church member, barrister and solicitor, elected in Calgary-Forest Lawn in 1979.

In 1982 there were 10 Conservatives and one Social Credit member in the Alberta Legislature. Among them: 2 lawyers, 2 medical doctors, 2 businessmen, 1 businessman and farmer, 1 school teacher, 1 business executive, 1 farmer, 1 insurance agent. Altogether, in the seventies, there were 12 new members of the Legislature and all of them Conservatives. According to religious affiliation they were as follows: 3 United Church, 4 Ukrainian Catholic, 1 Catholic, 1 Roman Catholic, 1 Lutheran and 2 had no religious affiliations.

During the Conservatives' rule in Alberta, Manitoba was for some time under the N.D.P. Government. In the 1973 Manitoba elections, Ed Schreyer was victorious and remained in power. All former members of Ukrainian origin were re-elected, and in addition the party gained one more member, *Steve Derewianchuk* who was elected from the Emerson riding. Thus again there were 7 members of Ukrainian descent: 6 N.D.P.'s and one Liberal. Ministerial portfolios were held by: Ben Hanuschak, Minister of Continuing Education 1973-1976, and Recreation and Cultural Affairs 1966-1977, Samuel Uskiw, Minister of Co-operative Development 1971-1975, Bill Uruski, Minister responsible for Public Insurance Corporation 1975, Minister responsible for Motor Vehicle Branch, Minister of Municipal Affairs 1976, Minister of Civil Service 1976-1977. Peter Burtniak was also Minister of Highways.

In 1977 when the Conservatives, under Sterling Lyon, came into power, not a single Ukrainian member was represented in the government. And even more significant is the fact that fewer cabinet ministers in the former ruling party won their election: Peter Burtniak, Harry Shafransky, Steve Derewianchuk, as well as Steve Patrick, Liberal. Only S. Uskiw, B. Uruski, and B. Hanuschak remained in the Legislature. To this trio another New Democrat was added, *Wilson Dwight Peter Parasiuk* (1943-), born at Stenen, Sask., a former Rhodes Scholar from Oxford, Master of Political Science, and elected from Transcona constituency.

In the elections of 1981 the luck turned in favor of New Democrats, led by Howard Pawley, successor to Ed Schreyer. All four N.D.P.'s from 1977 were re-elected, with two new ones joining them: *John Bucklashchuk,* elected from

Gimli riding and *Harry Harapiak* from The Pas. Cabinet posts, again, were awarded to Bill Uruski and Sam Uskiw and, for the first time, to Wilson Parasiuk and to J. Bucklashchuk in 1982.

In summarizing the political integration of Ukrainians in Manitoba, we find that in spite of upsets that often happen in politics their representation in government kept pace with their colleagues in Alberta. The number of members in Manitoba Legislature is smaller. The total membership in Manitoba is only 57 while it is 75 in Alberta. Since we are on the subject of the Ukrainian penetration into Manitoba's political field we must also take into consideration the fact that during the 1973 election, in addition to those elected there were 20 other candidates in various ridings representing all the existing political parties.[2] In 1977 there were 16 other candidates in addition to those elected and even more in 1981. It is interesting to note that among the victorious ones the total social strata was represented starting with farmers possessing general schooling, teachers with higher education, businessmen, lawyers, medical doctors and Oxford scholars. More noticeable also was the variety of religious denominations although this became somewhat difficult to verify as many candidates did not specify their religious adherence.

It would be worthwhile to mention that Peter Savaryn was president of Provincial Conservatives Party of Alberta and in Manitoba, John Petryshyn, president of Provincial Liberal Party and Dr. Lawrence Reznowksi as president of the National Social Credit Party. In addition W. Sysak, Mayor of Canora, was elected president of the urban municipalities in the Province of Saskatchewan.

Saskatchewan

In 1971, after the Liberal's single term under Thatcher, the New Democrats under Alan Blakeney again came to power. There were seven Ukrainian M.L.A.'s and all of them from the ruling N.D.P. party, which altogether had 45 members in the Legislature. To the Ukrainian group that sat as members on the N.D.P. side in the sixties such as John Kowalchuk, Miros Kwasnica and Roy Romanow a new quartet was added: *Mike Feschuk* (1932-) Ukrainian Catholic, a farmer from Prince Albert, born at Meath Park, Sask., who was re-elected in two consecutive elections in 1975 and 1978. *Dick Michayluk* (1912-) a school teacher from Redberry, who already had the opportunity to represent his constituency when elected for the first time in 1960. *Michael Feduniak,* Greek Orthodox, a merchant from Turtleford. Both D. Michayluk and M. Feduniak did not run for re-election. A different career was followed by the fourth candidate. *Paul Peter Mostoway* (1929-), Ukrainian Catholic, teacher, elected from Saskatoon Centre, and re-elected in 1975 and 1978.

In 1971, Roy Romanow was appointed Attorney General of Saskatchewan and some portfolios were awarded to members of Ukrainian descent — this political gain by Saskatchewan Ukrainians represented the highest achievement so far.

During 1975 elections all the above mentioned members were re-elected again. At the by-election in 1977, one more Ukrainian from N.D.P., *Norman Luzney* (1937-) born in Kamsack, a farmer and adherent of Ukrainian

---

[2]*Statistical Compendium on the Ukrainians in Canada,* Part II, pp. 342-343.

Catholic Church, was elected from Pelly constituency. The 1978 elections brought no changes in Ukrainian representation in the Saskatchewan Legislature. New Democrats stood solidly at the helm. Of the five new faces in the seventies two were farmers, two school teachers and one businessman.

Ontario

Parliamentary record in Ontario was established by John Yaremko, a lawyer, from the Conservative party who sat in the Legislature from 1951 to 1974. During the term he held various ministerial posts. Beginning as a Minister without portfolio with Premier John Robarts, then later, under Premier William Davis, he served as Minister of Transportation, 1958-1960, Provincial Secretary and Minister of Citizenship, 1960-1966, Minister of Public Welfare, 1966-1967, Social and Family Services 1967-1971 & 1971-1972 and Provincial Secretary 1971-1972, Citizenship and Solicitor-General 1972-1974. *Bernard Newman* from Windsor-Walkerville has also a long parliamentary record having sat in the Ontario Legislature from 1959-1974. *Mitro Makarchuk* (1931-) born in Saskatchewan was the third and a long term member of N.D.P. party to sit in Ontario Legislature during the sixties. He was again successful in 1975 and 1977 election but lost his seat in 1981.

To these three political veterans in Ontario during the following years were added: *Nicholas George Leluk* (1935-) Conservative and a Catholic, born at Hillcrest, Alta., B.Sc., M.Sc., elected from York West in 1971 and re-elected in 1975, 1977, and 1981. In 1981 two more Ukrainian Conservative members were added: *Yuri Shymko,* a teacher (M.Ed.) was elected from High Park-Swansea and *Al Kolyn,* a lawyer, also from Toronto. Three members out of a total of 125 in the Legislature is a small number indeed even when compared with Ukrainian population of Ontario. The reason for this may be explained by the fact that the Ukrainian population in Ontario was limited until the second and mostly the third immigrations. In Western Canada Ukrainians are predominantly descendants of the first immigration and form higher percentage of total population.

House of Commons

When in 1968, the 28th federal election was held it brought a noticeable change in the Ukrainian representation in Parliament in Ottawa. Of the previous members only two were left: William Skoreyko, who had been preparing himself for Conservative position since 1958 and Stanley Korchinski also of Progressive Conservative party and the same period of time. Six others joined them, two Conservatives and four Liberals. This was the highest Ukrainian representation in Ottawa of all times. It was also important that in the ruling Liberal party there were four Ukrainians: *Allen B. Sulatycky* (1938-), born at Hafford, Sask., a lawyer, Greek Orthodox, actually elected in a by-election in 1967, but re-elected in 1968 from Rocky Mountain, Alberta. *Mark G. Smerchanski* (1914-), born in Malonton, Manitoba, Mining Engineer, Ukrainian Catholic, elected from Provencher, Manitoba. *Norman A. Cafik* (1928-), Catholic, born in Toronto, Publisher, re-elected in 1972 and 1974. *Walter Cyril Deakon* (1924-), born in Edmonton, professional engineer, elected from High Park, Toronto. In addition to the old guard, the Conservatives were further represented by: *Paul Yewchuk*

(1937-), born at Bonnyville, Alta., a Medical Doctor elected from Athabaska, Alta., a Greek Orthodox, and re-elected in 1972, 1974, and 1979. *Steven Euguene Paproski* (1928-), born in Lviv, a Catholic, business manager, elected from Edmonton-North, and re-elected in 1972-1974, 1979, and 1980.

The eight member representation in Ottawa survived the 1972 elections. However, Liberals suffered a defeat. Mark G. Smerchanski lost his seat in favor of the Conservative J. Epp, a school teacher; W. C. Deakon to Otto Jelinek, a Conservative of Czech descent and A. Sulatycky to Joe Clark the future Prime Minister. Only Norman Cafik remained to become the Parliamentary Secretary of National Health and Welfare and later was appointed Minister of Multiculturalism. The Conservatives were strengthened by two new members: *Peter Paul Masniuk* (1920-), a C.P.R. foreman, born in Norweena and elected again in 1974, and *Harvie Andre* (1940-), Ph.D., a scientist, born in Edmonton and elected from Calgary Centre and re-elected in 1974, 1979 and 1980.

Since the death of F. Zaplitny in 1964, there were no Ukrainian N.D.P.'s in Parliament until 1972 when *Elias Nesdoly* (1931-), a Baptist, born in Blain Lake, Sask., was elected from Meadow Lake, Sask.

Two years later, the 30th federal election was held. The Conservatives kept their posts and even strengthened their position when *Roman J. Hnatyshyn* (1934-), born in Saskatoon, Greek Orthodox, was elected from Saskatchewan West and re-elected in 1979 and 1980. In the group of seven Conservatives, N. Cafik was the lone Liberal, as Elias Nesdoly lost his seat to the Conservative, B. Cadiu, a rancher. Ukrainian Conservatives in Ottawa had a streak of good luck when during a by-election in Parkdale West, Toronto, *Yuri Shymko* (1940-) won the seat without any difficulty.

The 1979 elections resulted in great changes in Ottawa. The Liberals were defeated and Conservatives, under Joe Clark, came into power. Although two Ukrainian Conservatives, P. P. Masniuk and Yuri Shymko lost their seats, their places were taken by two new Conservatives: *John Kushner* (1923-) a hotel proprietor, elected in Calgary East and in Ontario *Gary Gubrin*, M.D., born in Essex was elected from Bruce-Grey and re-elected in 1980. The Conservative group was somewhat whittled down when the ever successful Dr. Paul Yewchuk retired. Still the New Democrats made up for it by electing *Laverne Lewycky* (1946-), a social worker by profession, from the Dauphin constituency.

From 1968 to 1980 there were 14 M.P.'s chosen for the first time. Together with members of previous years this brings the number to 27. Out of this total four held ministerial posts. In addition to the formerly mentioned Michael Starr and Norman Cafik, two others were in Joe Clark's cabinet: Roman Hnatyshyn, Minister of Energy, Mines and Resources and S. Paproski, Minister of State for Fitness and Amateur Sports and Multiculturalism.

All of them represented not only the interests of their constituencies, but also the ethnocultural interests. This revealed political integration when we take into consideration the fact that they were elected by, and enjoyed the confidence of thousands who were of various ethnocultural origins. This represented a great step forward in political orientation and social integration, especially when we consider the fact that the first Ukrainian candidate, in 1904, Michael Gabora running in the McKenzie riding, which at that time was known as North West Territories, received only 6 votes. Six years later Wasyl Holowacky, running as an independent from Selkirk, Man. riding received 234 votes. Later a third candidate Wasyl Swystun, a school teacher who ran in the McKenzie constituency in the province of Saskatchewan in 1921, as a Liberal candidate, received 1,896 votes. It was only the fourth candidate, Michael Luchkowich, who succeeded in being elected in 1926 as U.F.A. member. This shows what a long and difficult road Ukrainians had to travel before achieving valid representation in Ottawa, together with ministerial posts.

Ukrainians have also been represented in the Senate whose members are appointed by the Prime Ministers. Till now there were five such nominations. Three nominated have died in their prime of life. Among them previously known to us: W. Wall and John Hnatyshyn and in the seventies, *John Ewasew* (1921-1978), born in Grenfell, Sask. but lived and carried on his law practice in Montreal. He was appointed by Prime Minister Trudeau in 1976.

Prime Minister Joe Clark appointed *Martha P. Bielish,* a teacher of Warspite, as Senator from Alberta in 1979. Another Senator of long standing is *Paul Yuzyk,* an authority not only on Ukrainian but on international affairs. During the last nine years he has been in Canadian Parliamentary delegation to N.A.T.O. Assembly, Chairman of the Subcommittee for N.A.T.O. publication, etc. He is very active in ethnocultural affairs in Canada — President of Canadian Folk Arts Council and a number of other organizations.

* * * * *

Summing up the political achievements we have to state that on the 90th anniversary of Ukrainian settlement in Canada, the Ukrainians have eight provincial cabinet ministers. In the Alberta Conservative Government: W. Bill Diachuk, Minister responsible for Workers' Health, Safety and Compensation, J. C. Koziak, Minister of Consumer and Corporate Affairs and Peter Trynchy, Minister of Recreation and Parks. In the N.D.P. Government of Saskatchewan: Roy Romanow, Attorney-General and Deputy Premier, and in the N.D.P. Government of Manitoba, three ministers: Sam Uskiw, Minister of Government Services and also Minister of Highways and Transportation, Bill Uruski, Minister of Agriculture, and Wilson Parasiuk, Minister of Energy and Mines. In the Ontario Conservative Government Nick Leluk was appointed Minister of Correctional Services. In summary, so far there have been 21 provincial ministers of Ukrainian descent, 90 Legislators, 27 M.P.'s and 5 Senators. Altogether 122 parliamentarians of Ukrainian ancestry.

SUMMARY OF SOCIAL PROCESSES IN UKRAINIAN COMMUNITY DURING THE DECADE OF MULTICULTURALISM

On our pages of the multicultural decade we emphasized a variety of social processes of the Ukrainian Canadian community. On the whole, we attempted to give a complete picture of the growth and development of this community in the 90th year of its history. We pointed out some shortcomings, too.

The multicultural decade is a decade of realization of some processes in the Ukrainian community and is the first decade which created a new epoch in the general Canadian history. Simultanously new pages in all ethnocultural communities of Canada are being written. This process crowned many years of efforts of ethnocultural communities to achieve recognition of identity in their national and cultural sphere.

The Ukrainian Canadian community has played a great part in the process which led to the entrenchment in the Constitution that Canada is a multicultural nation. When in 1971 the proclamation of multicultural government policy was announced, this was considered more or less as a cultural component but only in 1982 by proclamation of a Canadian Constitution on April 17, 1982 this same cultural component became ingrained also into the entire Canadian political structural sphere.

In previous decades and more so during the first decade of multiculturalism, the Ukrainians in Canada have proven themselves to be not only a "folklore group" but also a "national community." The concept is not only interwoven into dominion wide organizations in Canada, based on the community grassroots level, but also into cultural connections with identical national communities in other countries and with the cultural stream in Ukraine. The Ukrainian Canadian community is vitally interested in cultural processes behind the Iron Curtain and views with concern the Soviet language russification policy. The language problem in Canada remains a cornerstone of cultural existence. It is generally accepted that with the loss of language in a cultural community there follows loss of the entire culture and gradual assimilation of the community itself.

If we are to follow research done by Alan B. Anderson regarding Ukrainian identity in Saskatchewan (his elaborate "Ukrainian Identity Change in Rural Saskatchewan"),[1] in which he proves that eighty percent of Eastern-rite Catholic and Orthodox responded very strongly in favour of preserving their ethnic identity, whereby the Ukrainian Canadian community remains fully in its convictions to be identified as "national community." In this respect, the organizational structure of the community and Ukrainian Churches play a very important role in preservation of Ukrainian identity.

Also a great deal of time was devoted to the school system, teaching and cultivation of the mother tongue, adopting new systems and methods to the new pedagogical and socio-environmental changes.

---

[1] See *Ukrainians in American and Canadian Society*. Contributions to the Sociology of Ethnic Groups, edited by Wsevolod W. Isajiw, Jersey City, 1976.

In the sphere of creative art and stage during the decade of multiculturalism much progress has been made. Some assistance is given here from governmental sources. New talents have appeared in the film industry. These talents will continue to grow, thus bringing to fruition the wishes and aspirations of a multicultural Canadian society. Therefore, justifiably, the Ukrainian Canadians express their desires through the belief of the Ukrainian Canadian Committee "that the broadcasting programming should be a cross-section of Canadian culture that includes ethnocultural groups."[2] At this point the authors of the brief also expressed concern stating that "they watch the erosion of their culture to prominence and the privileged position enjoyed by the English and French cultures."[3] Actually as we mentioned before, some steps have been taken in this direction in order to give multicultural recognition by finance from government sources but this process is moving at a snail's pace. So far this financial assistance in comparison to Ukrainian population is comparatively minimal. According to Multicultural Programs of the State Department in 1980-1981 there was allotted to the Ukrainian projects $249,150 (out of $7,784,907.81). Of this amount $87,087 was given to the school programs.[4] This amount is approximately one-fourth of the annual budget of any rural elementary school. The use of the phrase "where numbers warrant" is the most proper indicator for any policy.

Questions of schools and mother tongue always remain thorny problems for Ukrainians. We might underline again that in 1971 of 580,660 Ukrainians in Canada only 22.8% (132,000) used Ukrainian as the language of speech in the home, although 48.9% know the mother tongue. But it is also necessary to underscore that in 1931, 93% of Ukrainians spoke their mother tongue. From those who were born in Canada, 13% speak Ukrainian at home at present. In spite of these losses, Ukrainian record in retention of mother tongue is higher than those of Polish (38.4%), German (35.9%), Dutch (32.4%), Scandinavians (20%), Jews (16.6%).[5] All these losses are the result of the narrow vision of those who wanted to see Canada as a unilingual nation and vigorously opposed the establishment of teaching of other languages. This attitude reversed itself very strongly in the seventies. However, in order to recapture the losses in the years gone by, it will take many years and perhaps even generations. The future of the Ukrainian community in Canada depends upon the successful solution to this problem.

From our pages of history we have learned that assimilation processes are evident even when there is no political pressure or inspiration. General gravitation of social forces plays an important role. We indicated this in religious field as well as in migration.

Religious and ethnocultural intermarriages are the basis of assimilation processes. Opposition of ethnocultural intermarriages is self-evident in all cultural communities. According to the Canadian census statistics 1971, the Jewish community has the highest homogeneity of marriages. Next in line are

---

[2]*Brief of the Ukrainian Canadian Committee submitted to Federal Cultural Policy Review Committee,* Winnipeg, March 8, 1981.

[3]*Ibidem.*

[4]*Expenditures, Grants, and Contributions 1980-81,* State Department, Directorate of Multiculturalism.

[5]*Statistical Compemdium* by V. Darkovych and P. Yuzyk, part II, p. 223.

Asiatics and Indians. The Ukrainians appear in a halfway strata of these data.

Urbanization also subtracts from the binding cultural forces which are so necessary for the creation of a strong ethnocultural community. Quite often whole rural families perish in metropolitan areas because church association is minimized and traditional values gradually disappear.

Ukrainian churches have suffered some losses. The Ukrainian Catholic Church, which according to 1971 Canadian census, lost 18% mostly to the Roman Catholic Church while at the same time Ukrainian Greek Orthodox Church lost only 2%. Likely the reason for this transition among the Ukrainian Catholics lies in the fact that some consider that there is no difference between Roman and Ukrainian (Byzantine-Rite) Catholic Church. These propagate unification of church calendar, of rites, use of English in church services. Common conferences of hierarchs, clergy and even lay people (Knights of Columbus) create the atmosphere of unity. These tendencies are strongly opposed by administrative conservation forces who closely stick to the traditionl rites and also by those who feel that the future lies in the establishing of the patriarchate which will give due consideration to unification of rites, church discipline and vision for future planning, etc.

Whereas in the field of language, culture and religion there is more concern and controversial discussion but there is less feeling of integration. In economic and political fields, professions, the Ukrainian community achieved much success.

In the field of humanities and sciences, fine arts, the Ukrainians are reaching for the top and the slogan still remains "Let us reach higher".[6] These are healthy indicators for future growth. In their accomplishments the Ukrainians moved from farm and labour communities into a middle level of social strata and even above, as compared with other ethnocultural communities.

During the last decade a tremendous amount of energy was invested in the development of Ukrainian Studies courses at the university level. These efforts were crowned with the establishment of the Canadian Institute of Ukrainian Studies at the Alberta University, Chair of Ukrainian Studies at the University of Toronto, the Centre for Ukrainian Canadian Studies at the University of Manitoba, at St. Andrew's College, Holy Spirit Ukrainian Catholic Seminary in Ottawa. Recently (1982) due to the efforts of the Ontario Provincial Council of the UCC and the Canadian Institute of Ukrainian Studies, Chair of Ukrainian History was established at York University with Professor Orest Subtelny.[7]

Integration on the economic and political field and others indicate the Ukrainian Canadian Community is an organic part of the Canadian nation. 122 parliamentarians during 9 decades of Ukrainian settlement speak for themselves.

Numerous learned societies and professional organizations represent the community's maturity which is also expressed in a number of researches, studies, publications, foundations, monuments, museums, etc. Along with

---

[6]*Ukrainian Voice*, No. 8, 1982, Editorial under the same title.

[7]*The Globe and Mail*, May 12, 1982, Ukrainian settlement remembered by Zena Cherry.

this healthy trend we register insidious assimilation which leaves devastating steps in grassroot organizations.

There is general concern among Ukrainian Canadians that they are entirely dependent numerically upon their natural growth. Lack of new immigration of Ukrainians to Canada from outside and no hope to have it in the near future bothers leaders of the Ukrainian community. Only a change in the political situation in Ukraine can bring some alleviation in severe emigration restrictions. For a long time the Ukrainians were among the top four Canadian ethnocultural communities. Presently they occupy the fifth place after Anglo-Saxons, French, Germans, Italians. Yet they belong to the oldest immigrant groups in Canada.

The decade of the seventies is also noted for the fact that during this time those who have witnessed the very beginnings of Ukrainian settlement in Canada have passed on. To those outstanding pioneers who have departed in this decade belong such names as Anna Wachna (1882-1980), Josyf Sozansky (1880-1970), Mykola Hryhorczuk (1888-1979), Ivan Bzowy (1887-1975), Anastasia Hryhorczuk (1890-1973), Anna Stechishin (1891-1979), Vasylyna Bzowy-Paley (1891-1977), Ivan Paley (1890-1977), Tetiana Skremetka (1891-1981), Anastasia Stechishin (1892-1979), Mykhaylo Kozak (1892-1980), Ivan Rudachek (1886-1979), Hryhoriy Kostash (1896-1970), and others.

In the seventies, Ukrainian Canadian leadership suffered some losses too. Such outstanding leaders departed as Wolodymyr Kossar (1890-1970), Oleksa Gregorovich (1893-1970), Julian Stechishin (1895-1971), Stepan Chwaliboga (1890-1971), Toma Kobzey (1895-1972), Ivan Syrnick (1904-1972), Kornylo Prodan (1888-1973), Rev. Mykhaylo Olenchuk (1886-1973), Mykhaylo Hethman (1893-1973), Wasyl Hultay (1900-1974), E. Wasylyshyn (1897-1974), Mykyta Mandryka (1886-1977), Theodore Humeniuk (1891-1978), Dr. V. I. Kaye-Kysilewsky (1896-1976), H. Tyzuk (-1977), Ivan Robert Kovalevich (1896-1979), Evhenia Sytnyk (1900-1975), Volodymyr Koman (1899-1979), Wasyl Topolnycky (1893-1978), Mykhaylo Sharik (1901-1979). For many years the leadership of Dr. Wasyl (Basil) Kushnir (1893-1979) influenced the Ukrainian Canadian community in growth and achievements. Their place is taken by the "new guard", which follows the path and field of their devoted predecessors.

It is wisely said that everyday is a prologue for tomorrow. This also refers to individual, family and community life. These periods are not measured in years or decades. The period, which we refer to as a decade of multiculturalism, became a prologue to the new era which we would call the Modern Canada. This decade brought to the ethnocultural communities of Canada written laws for their further development including a charter of rights and a protection of civil liberties. This is a beginning of harmonious historical era which delivers to all Canadians a promising and prosperous future. Actually, sociological processes have no definite end. They only continue to exist in other forms. History rather likes milestones. It looks for some definite dates, periods, epochs. Staying between sociology and history it must be concluded with general statements. The living community must remember the past and simultaneously have a vision and build for the future. In this situation the Ukrainian Canadians can look back on their 90 years of settlement in Canada and their achievements with pride. They can now look with confidence to the future.

Places of Ukrainian National Interest. Above: Monument of Taras Shevchenko on the grounds of Manitoba Legislative Building (unveiling by Prime Minister J. Diefenbaker) and right: Monument of Markian Shashkevych, Initiator of Ukrainian National Renaissance in West Ukraine, built in Winnipeg (Point Douglas), 1944.

IDEOLOGICAL PRINCIPLES
IN THE UKRAINIAN-CANADIAN HISTORY

The history of the Ukrainian settlement in Canada is not just merely a few dry summaries of historical events and statistical compilations. This history reveals the rich treasures of the soul of those people who were the main factors as well as of whole generations that created these events and gave them a heroic and an ideal content.

Examining the events of the past, during the 90 years, we come to the conclusion that the Ukrainians from the very beginning had decided on the keeping of three basic loyalties. The first loyalty was to be faithful to the culture of their fathers. This faith was with them as they were leaving their native towns and villages in the old country. With this same faith in their hearts they erected their first homes and the crosses of freedom on the wide stretches of Canada, and continued with that faith to build their religious and social-cultural life. From this loyalty to their culture they organized the press and revealed their soul in the Ukrainian Canadian poetry and prose. On the basis of this loyalty, the pedagogues, scholars and artists created their works. The theme of this loyalty runs like a golden thread through the cultural treasures of the people in every walk of life.

While retaining the loyalty of their culture the Ukrainian pioneers were obligated to a second loyalty almost as soon as they entered the portals of Canada — the loyalty to the new country which they were now adopting as their own. This loyalty was sorely tested when they arrived at the place of their settlement where they had to pass through the front line of fire of racial and political prejudice and even more so during the First World War when they were deprived of their citizenship rights. These were bitter trials and although extremely serious they failed to shake their loyalty to the state. The outer manifestations of this loyalty were the thousands of Ukrainian volunteers during the two World Wars.

In every-day life this loyalty was shown through the participation in the social-political work starting with the municipal affairs and ending in the provincial and the dominion parliaments. Hand in hand with participation goes responsibility. Along with this sense of loyalty was the everyday loyalty shown during the construction of railroads, highways, town and city buildings — wherever strength and fortitude were required.

The third loyalty that was faithfully practiced by the Ukrainian pioneers and later passed on to their descendants was the loyalty to the ideal of holding in high regard the cultural values of other nationalities living in Canada. In the face of this loyalty all the old European disputes and enmities, between the Ukrainian settlers and those of other nationalities, which had been going on for centuries, now disappeared. In declaring their respect toward the culture of other nationalities they had a right to demand the same consideration for their own. The ancient enemies gradually turned into good neighbors and friendly fellow citizens.

These three loyalties became the cornerstone of the Ukrainian history in Canada. Looking from the perspective of these nine decades we may boldly state that this triple loyalty has become the basic thinking among the many thousands of Canadian citizens. The citizenship loyalty of these three dimensions now became like a wide gate through which one may enter into the Canadian cultural mosaic and which today comes into the limelight as the newest trend in Canadian identification that has been the topic of discussion at different times by the leading personalities who are interested in Canada's past and future. One of the greatest exponents of the mosaic pattern in the cultural development of Canada and one of the greatest builders of Canada as well, was Sir Wilfred Laurier under whose government thousands of Ukrainian pioneers took possession of the wide Canadian prairies. In his vision he compared Canada to Gothic architecture in which he visualized the harmony of different elements. About this mosaic he expressed himself in the following words:

"I have visited in England one of those models of Gothic architecture which the hand of genius, guided by an unerring faith, has moulded into a harmonious whole. This cathedral is made of marble, oak and granite. It is the image of the nation I would like to see Canada become. For here, I want the marble to remain marble, the granite to remain the granite, the oak to remain the oak; and out of all these elements I would build a nation, great among the nations of the world."

The far sighted statesman, Sir Wilfred Laurier, brought his visions into actions toward the practical solutions of Canada's future problems and one of them was the Laurier-Greenway Act dealing with the schools of Manitoba, which guaranteed to all nationalities, in that province, the right of teaching in their native language as the basic principle of every culture.

In addition to the great loyalty toward their national origin, the respect for the culture of other nationalities and the patriotic stand in regard to their own country, the Ukrainian pioneers of Canada transmitted to their sons and daughters in Canada a high regard for freedom and justice. Having lived under the forced and alien social and political misrule in their former homeland they could feel in the depths of their souls the meaning of human dignity and its values. For they had fought for the freedom and the dignity of man while living on European soil and when they found themselves on the free terrain of Canada, they considered freedom as one of life's greatest prizes and were ready to defend it at any cost. It is no wonder then that a Ukrainian Canadian was very often seen in the forefront of those who were ready and willing to defend freedom and justice.

The basic traits of loyalty, freedom and justice of the Ukrainian Canadians were aptly portrayed by the Prime Minister of Canada, Lester B. Pearson, in Elk Island Park on the occasion of the 75th Anniversary of Ukrainian settlement in Canada who, while addressing a huge crowd consisting of thousands of Ukrainian youth, pioneers and others, made the following statement:

"You have continued the faith of your forefathers. Through the years you have maintained your own identity, your culture and your institutions, inside the Canadian nation. You have enriched Canada greatly by your contributions to its political, cultural, agricultural, industrial, professional and educational development. Your love of the land, your passion for freedom, personal and national; your belief in democracy — these have been captured and expressed in your poetry, your songs and dances. These are now part of

Canada's heritage. By preserving your own identity, therefore, your own language and traditions, you have added something of value, of strength and colour, to the Canadian character."

Closely allied with the above ideals was the idea of bringing aid to the kinsmen in the old country. This idea arose out of two basic factors, the loyalty to the culture of the fathers and the feeling of human dignity and justice. This unbroken contact with the motherland is justified not only by sanguine considerations, but also by idealistic principles. The more injustices were being perpetrated on their ancestral land, the greater was the intensification of the material and spiritual ties.

Lesya Ukrainka Monument in High Park, Toronto.

In the resulting outcome of these ideal inducements and high principles the Ukrainian Canadians formed their own spiritual citizenship which imposes upon them unwritten laws. These laws were written in their hearts and are the natural reactions of noble minds, which command them to guard the cultural treasures of their people in relation to themselves and to their motherland. With these spiritual values the Ukrainian Canadians enrich the Canadian cultural field that flourishes with the blooms of many other cultures of different continents. The cultivation of these cultures is based on high ideals which in turn provide the energy for the development of immunity towards the nationalistic trends of our era. This is that same high idealism which carries upon its back the heavy burden of healthy growth in the life of our country that reflects itself in the harmonious growth of all the different nationalities. The former Prime Minister, John Diefenbaker, was quite right in his comparison of Canada to a garden.

The Canadian multicultural "garden" became a constitutional reality in the seventies. The Ukrainian Canadians contributed to this reality a great deal. Further growth and development of Canadian multiculturalism depends on devotion and vision of the leaders of the nation, not only leaders of the ethnocultural communities but also everybodys participation in this national process. Such a position is requested from everyone while some patches of this national "garden" are not ploughed at all and some are only scratching the surface.

SUPPLEMENT

Page 609: Presidium of the P.A.U.C.: First Row (left to right): D. Halychyn, Rev. W. Kushnir, S. Shumeyko, W. Dushnyk; Second Row: A. J. Yaremowich, Dr. T. Datzkiw, V. Shandor, J. H. Syrnick, W. Kossar, B. Katamay.

Page 612: Convention of the Ukrainian Baptist Brotherhood: Leaders of the Convention: Seated from left to right: Rev. J. Krystynsky, Rev. A. Piatocha, Rev. S. Nyshchyk, N. Prokopiak, Mrs. H. Domashovetz, H. Domashovetz, Rev. P. Kindrat, Rev. P. Bartkiw, Rev. Z. Rechun-Panko, "guest" (little girl), J. Piatkowsky, Dr. M. Gitlin, A. Mayak, Rev. J. Dumych.

Executive of the Ukrainian Evangelical Alliance: First Row, left to right: Rev. W. Borowsky, M. Kozak, Rev. J. Yatsenty, Rev. J. R. Kovalevich, V. Bahriy, V. Hrysiuk. Behind: P. Honchar, Rev. M. Fesenko, Rev. V. Kucher.

Page 617: "Dibrova" Women's Choir was organized in 1965 from the members of Toronto S.U.M. A young but a very promising and attractive choir under the baton of Wasyl Kardash.

Page 617: Male Choir "Surma" was organized in 1952 by George Hnatiuk at the "Ridna Shkola" of Markian Shashkevych in Winnipeg. The most active years of the choir were 1953-1956. The choir was sponsored by "Ridna Shkola" of M. Shashkevych, "Bratstvo Voyakiv Pershoi DYVIZII U.N.A." and "Stanycia Voyakiv U.P.A.". First Row (left to right): G. Buchynsky, A. Shpytkowsky, I. Shymechko, I. Sawchak, J. Schur, M. Nahorniak, J. Kaban, G. Hnatiuk (conductor), P. Iwanchuk, W. Knysh, W. Rudnyk, M. Kowalyk, M. Terentiak, H. Pona, P. Semenchuk; Second row: P. Korbutiak, M. Knysh, I. Skotnicky, M. Yakymec, W. Kushnir, W. Moroz, R. Musiy, M. Radavec, I. Peniak, L. Nyshta, S. Kuzma, I. Mudry, W. Danyliw, O. Zahoroda; Third Row: W. Korbutiak, R. Baran, B. Matiyciv, W. Hrabyk, S. Pauchok, P. Kralka, S. Trylinsky, B. Balko, R. Kysilewsky, W. Mashchak, M. Kashchiy, W. Lazarewych, J. Nestor, P. Batih.

Page 617: "Prometey" Choir, Toronto. This choral unit was organized in 1948 by Zenon Gnopko. In 1954-1961 the choir was working under the direction of Prof. Lev Turkevych. After the death of the latter the choir was under Yuriy Holovko, and Stephen Huminilovych and since 1965 has been under the baton of Wasyl Kardash. The choir was travelled extensively in Canada and U.S.A. and has won deserved awards for its excellent performance. The 'Prometey" concerted in New York, Philadelphia, Chicago, Detroit, Cleveland, Rochester, Edmonton, Winnipeg, at the Expo, on T.V. and on radio. Its tours were sponsored by the Centennial Commission of Canada and the Canadian Folk Art Council. This is one of the most active and attractive amaeur choirs on the North American Continent.

Page 618: O. Koshetz Memorial Choir of the U.N.F. Winnipeg. This choir has been in existence over 25 years. Some of its original conductors were Tetiana Koshetz and Dr. Pavlo Macenko. It is one of Winnipeg's most active choirs having sung regularly on T.V., on radio, as well as numerous performances on various cultural events. Its Canadian tour was sponsored by the Centennial Commission of Canada in 1967. Walter Klymkiw, conductor, has been with the choir close to 20 years. **Sopranos:** J. Barabash, N. Dobrowolski, D. Hardy, E. Honeybun, V. Hrycenko, Z. Hrycenko, L. Kapty, S. Kereliuk, C. Kosteniuk, K. Kuzyk, D. Mateyko, S. Peters, M. Romanowych, A. Wach, T. Worobec, M. Worobec, O. Zawisliak. **Altos:** O. Babick, O. Beley, H. Goshulak, O. Goshulak, L. Kalyniak, S. Karabin, J. Klymkiw, M. Klymkiw, I. Krawchuk, Z. Negrych, C. Romanyk, A. Ratuski, O. Senchuk, S. Stefanyshyn, I. Stoykewych, D. Ternowetsky. **Tenors:** T. Boyaniwski, G. Buchynsky, J. Dudych, J. Halas, Wm. Kalyniuk, B. Klymkiw, P. Klymkiw, J. Kucher, P. Lucenkiw, T. Perich, B. Seneskiw, J. Sosnoway, I. Tanchuk, O. Wilganowski, S. Zukrowski. **Basses:** B. Bobiski, R. Babick, J. Fedyshyn, B. Hawryliuk, R. Honeybun, G. Hwozdulych, V. Kapty, Wm. Karabin, J. Kereliuk, W. Kuryk, A. Kryschuk, G. Menreck, J. Moskalyk, W. Peters, M. Romaniuk, Dr. R. Romanowych, W. Staciuk, M. Zawisliak, R. Worobec.

Page 619: S.U.M. Choir of Vancouver—the "Famous Choir of the West Coast"—was organized in 1949. The members of Plast, "CYMK" local parishes, as well as the soloists of the "Kozaks' Choir" participated in this choral work. Its creator and choirmaster was Wasyl Kardash. After his departure to Winnipeg, the choir lost its vitality.

Page 619: S.U.M. Choir of Winnipeg. This choir started its performances in 1948, first as a male choir only. Later on it was re-organized into three separate choirs. The first conductor and organizer was Rev. P. Romanyshyn, later on Yosyp Hoshuliak and George Hnatiuk (1950-1951), and since 1952 until 1960 Wasyl Kardash. In last years it was coducted by I. Buyachok and again by G. Hnatiuk. The choir concerted in Winnipeg, in the country and other provinces, having sung on radio and at big cultural events. **Supranos and Altos:** M. Zubata, O. Romaniw, T. Poliksha, O. Nazar, T. Zazula, O. Sheremeta, O. Perih, M. Byckal, A. Solomon, O. Kvasnycia, O. Nykoruk, S. Kinasevych, O. Hoshulak, S. Kowal, L. Kardash, I. Shymkiw, O. Hoshulak, O. Gretchyn, M. Yankiwska, M. Demchyshak, M. Oleshchuk, M. Zurawska. **Tenors and Basses:** S. Zukriwsky, M. Banias, W. Ladashewsky, M. Diakiw, J. Cwyk, S. Lucan, T. Kubas, I. Buyachok, A. Sluzar, T. Humeniuk, I. Hryciw, Y. Luciw, M. Laba, A. Kryskiw, H. Stanowych, W. Lishchynsky, M. Kuryk, I. Klymchak, S. Kozelko, N. Rybchuk, P. Kwasnycia, S. Sheremeta, M. Yarko, P. Segeda, W. Hayowsky, O. Zazula, M. Petryshyn, M. Ference, W. Duduk, M. Haluk, M. May, M. Shawarsky, I. Sobko, W. Hayowsky, A. Bondarchuk, W. Dudar, W. Solomon, S. Kit, M. Romaniuk, M. Pasichny.

Page 620: Participants in the XIV National Convention of the S.U.M. Seated from left to right: I. Korda,—, Dr. M. Ostafiychuk, P. Bashuk, Dr. B. Stebelsky, J. Serbyn, Dr. M. Huta, Dr. W. Hyrak, Dr. R. Malashchuk, Rev. R. Nabereznyj, T. Buyniak, W. Kucy, — , M. Andruchiw, — , M. Bartkiw.

Page 621: Ukrainian Youth Organization—"Plast"—Winnipeg Branch, 1961: Leaders, seated left to right: M. Oboca, Daria Nawrocka, Nadia Gawrachynska, Anna Shkilnyk, Daria Zelska-Darewych, Roman Senchuk, Dr. J. W. Darewych, Zenon Hawryluk, Luba Hnatiuk, Ivanna Kachor, Z. Zalozetska, A. Kachor.
CYMK at Summer Camp "Kiev", in 1961. Seated left to right: Dr. S. Klimashko, Anna Tokarek, G. R. B. Panchuk, Justyna and Petro Hayowsky.

Page 622: Male Choir "Dnipro", Edmonton, commemorating the birthday (150 Anniversary) of the Poet in 1964. In the first row (l. to r.): Ivan Prokop (soloist), Roman Soltykevych (conductor), Orysia Olijnyk (accompanist), Roman Ostashewsky (narrator).

Page 623: Royal Canadian Legion Delegates to Ukrainian Canadian Veterans' Association of Canada Convention held in Winnipeg, during the unveiling of the Taras Shevchenko Monument by Right Honourable John G. Diefenbaker, Prime Minister of Canada, in **1961.** Front Row, left to right: Gordon Panchuk M.B.E., Founding Past President, Ukrainian Canadian Servicemen's Association (Active Service Overseas), Mazeppa Branch No. 183, Montreal; Dr. Peter Smylski, Past National President, Ukrainian Canadian Veterans' Association and past President General Orlick Branch No. 522, Hamilton; John Karasevich, Founding Past President Ukrainian Canadian Veterans' Association and Past President, Ukrainian Canadian Vetermans' Branch No. 141, Winnipeg; Stephan Pawluk, National President, Ukrainian Canadian Veterans' Association and President, Ukrainian Canadian Veterans' Branch No. 360, Toronto; Dr. Monsignor Wasyl Kushnir; President, Ukrainian Canadian Committee; Peter Okrainec, President, Ukrainian Canadian Veterans' Branch No. 141, Winnipeg; J. N. Galonsky, Ukrainian Canadian Veternas' Branch No. 141, Winnipeg; Nick Malanchuk, Ukrainian Canadian Veterans' Branch No. 141, Winnipeg, Peter Wach, Ukrainian Canadian Veterans' Branch No. 141, Winnipeg. Middle Row, left to right: Ray Bryk, Ukrainian Canadian Veterans' Branch No. 141, Winnipeg; George Romanyk, Ukrainian Canadian Veterans' Branch No. 360, Toronto; Jaroslav Pohorecky, Ukrainian Canadian Veterans' Branch No. 360, Toronto; Judge Peter Greschuk, Norwood Branch, Edmonton; Bill Yuzyk, Ukrainian Canadian Veterans' Association Branch, Saskatoon; John Yuzyk, Ukrainian Canadian Veterans' Branch No. 141, Winnipeg; George Tokarek, General Orlick Branch No. 522, Hamilton; Val Eleniak, Ukrainian Canadian Veterans' Association Branch, Vancouver; Peter Karpiuk, Col. Konovaletz Branch No. 502, St. Catharines. Back Row, left to right:Dr. Walter Grenko, Past President Ukrainian Canadian Veterans Branch No. 141, Winnipeg; Anthony Lazarovich, Ukrainian Canadian Veterans' Association Branch, Ottawa; Joe Lemeka and Mike Chelada, Ukrainian Canadian Veterans' Branch No. 141, Winnipeg.

APPENDIX

UKRAINIAN CANADIAN COMMITTEE (CONGRESS) MEMBER ORGANIZATIONS (1982)

Ukrainian Catholic Brotherhood
Ukrainian Self-Reliance League
Ukrainian National Federation
Canadian League for the Liberation of Ukraine
Ukrainian Canadian Veterans' Association
Ukrainian Canadian Professional and Business Federation
Ukrainian Canadian Committee, Women's Council
Ukrainian Canadian Foundation of Taras Shevchenko
Ukrainian Canadian University Students' Union
Ukrainian Evangelical Alliance, Ukrainian National Association
Brotherhood of Former Combatants UD. UNA
Ukrainian Academy of Arts and Sciences, Shevchenko Scientific Society
Ukrainian Cultural and Educational Centre, Research Institute of Volyn,
Association of Ukrainian Journalists in Canada
Ukrainian Canadian Writers' Association "Slovo"
Ukrainian Youth Association "PLAST"
Ukrainian Youth Association of Canada (SUM)
Ukrainian Democratic Youth Association (ODUM)
Ukrainian National Youth Federation (MUNO)
Ukrainian Canadian Social Service
Council of the Ukrainian Credit Unions of Canada
Canadian Ukrainian Immigrant Aid Society
Ukrainian Democratic Republic Auxiliary in Canada
Ukrainian Fraternal Society

UKRAINIAN CANADIAN CONGRESSES
(All-Canada Congresses of Ukrainian Canadians)

First	Winnipeg	June 22-24, 1943
Second	Toronto	June 4-6, 1946
Third	Winnipeg	February 7-9, 1950
Fourth	Winnipeg	July 8-10, 1953
Fifth	Winnipeg	July 5-7, 1956
Sixth	Winnipeg	July 9-12, 1959
Seventh	Winnipeg	July 5-7, 1962
Eighth	Winnipeg	October 9-11, 1965
Ninth	Winnipeg	October 11-14, 1968
Tenth	Winnipeg	October 8-11, 1971
Eleventh	Winnipeg	October 11-13, 1974
Twelfth	Winnipeg	October 7-10, 1980
Thirteenth	Winnipeg	October 11-13, 1980

PAN-AMERICAN UKRAINIAN CONFERENCE
CONFERENCE PAN-AMERICAINE UKRAINIENNE
CONFERENCIA PAN-AMERICANA UCRANIANA

Members:

Ukrainian Canadian Committee
Ukrainian Congress Committee of America
Representacion Central Ucrainiana en Argentina
Comite Ucraino-Brasileiro
Associacion de Ucranianos en Venezuela
Centro Ucraino en la Republica del Paraguay.

First Pan-American Conference New York, November 18-21, 1947
Second	Toronto	October 23-25, 1948
Third	New York	November 8-9, 1949
Fourth	Winnipeg	March 2-5, 1951
Fifth	Toronto	September 24-25, 1955
Sixth	New York	October 29-30, 1960
Seventh	Winnipeg	September 4-5, 1964
Eighth	New York	November 15, 1967

Representatives to P.A.U.C.: Canada: Dr. Basil Kushnir, Dr. S. W. Sawchuk, J. H. Syrnick, Dr. T. Dackiw, W. Kossar, M. Pohorecky, W. Kochan, A. J. Yaremovich, I. Iwanchuk.
U.S.A.: D. Halychyn, A. Batiuk, M. Piznak, S. J. Jarema, W. Shandro, Dr. L. Dobriansky, B. Katamay, J. Lysawyer, I. Bilynsky, W. Mudry.
Brazil: S. Kobylansky, V. Pizar, Rev. M. Ivaniw.
Argentina: E. Onatsky, J. Hrehoraschuk.
Venezuela: W. Wasiuk, B. Wasiuk.
Paraguay: E. Paduchak.

THE WORLD CONGRESS OF FREE UKRAINIANS (W.C.F.U.)
CONGRES MONDIAL DES UKRAINIENS LIBRES
CONGRESO MUNDIAL DE LOS UCRANIOS LIBRES

Members:

The Ukrainian Congress Committee of America
The Ukrainian Canadian Committee
Representacion Central Ucraina en la Republica Argentina
Comite Ucranino-Braziliero
Centro Ucraino en el Republica del Paraguay
Asociacion Prosvita in Uruguay
Asociacion de Ucranianos en Venezuela
The Federation of Ukrainian Associations in Australia
Comite Central des Organisations Ukrainiennes en France

Zentral-Vertretung der Ukrainischen Emigration, Germany
The Association of Ukrainians in Great Britain
The Federation of Ukrainians in Great Britain
The Coordinating Council of Ukrainian Organizations in Austria
Comite Ukrainien de Secours in Brussels and other countries; Italy, Spain, Switzerland, the Netherlands, Luxembourg, Sweden, Demark, Finland.

The First Ukrainian World Congress of Free Ukrainians,
              New York   November 16-19, 1967
Second   Toronto   November 1-4, 1973
Third   New York   November 23-26, 1978
Fourth   Toronto   November, 1983
(in proclamation only)

Presidents of the W.C.F.U.: Dr. Basil Kushir 1967-1978
                             Mykola Plawiuk, 1978-1981
                             Dr. Ivan Bazarko, 1981-1983

PRIME MINISTERS OF CANADA
(Ministries since Confederation)

1. Sir J. A. Macdonald, (Conservative). From July 1, 1867 to Nov. 6, 1873.
2. Hon. A. Mackenzie, (Liberal). From Nov. 7, 1873 to Oct. 16, 1878.
3. Rt. Hon. Sir J. A. Macdonald, (Conservative). From Oct. 17, 1878 to June 6, 1891.
4. Hon. Sir J. J. Abbott, (Conservative). From June 16, 1891 to Dec. 5, 1892.
5. Sir J. Thompson, (Conservative). From Dec. 5, 1892 to Dec. 12, 1894.
6. Hon. Sir M. Bowell, (Conservative). From Dec. 21, 1894 to April 27, 1896.
7. Sir Charles Tupper, Bart, (Conservative). From May 1, 1896 to July 8, 1896.
8. Rt. Hon. Sir W. Laurier, (Liberal). From July 11, 1896 to Oct. 6, 1911.
9. Rt. Hon. Sir Robert Laird Borden, (Conservative). From Oct. 10, 1911 to Oct. 12, 1917.
10. Rt. Hon. Sir Robert Laird Borden, (Unionist). From Oct. 12, 1917 to July 10, 1920.
11. The Rt. Hon. Arthur Meighen, (Unionist — "National Liberal and Conservative Party"). From July 10, 1920 to Dec. 29, 1921.
12. The Rt. Hon. Wm. Lyon Mackenzie King, C.M.G., (Liberal). From Dec. 29, 1921 to June 28, 1926.
13. The Rt. Hon. Arthur Meighen, (Conservative). From June 28, 1926 to Sept. 25, 1926.
14. The Rt. Hon. William Lyon Mackenzie King, C.M.G., (Liberal). From Sept. 25, 1926 to Aug. 7, 1930.
15. The Rt. Hon. R. B. Bennett, (Conservative). From Aug. 7, 1930 to Oct. 23, 1935.
16. The Rt. Hon. W. L. Mackenzie King, (Liberal). From Oct. 23, 1935 to Nov. 15, 1948.
17. The Rt. Hon. Louis Stephen St. Laurent, (Liberal). From Nov. 15, 1948 to June 21, 1957.
18. The Rt. Hon. John Diefenbaker, (Progressive Conservative). From June 21, 1957 to April 22, 1963.
19. The Rt. Hon. Lester B. Pearson, (Liberal). From April 22, 1963 to April 20, 1968.
20. The Rt. Hon. Pierre Elliott Trudeau, (Liberal). From April 20, 1968 to June 4, 1979.
21. The Rt. Hon. Charles Joseph Clark, (Progressive Conservative). From June 4, 1979 to February 18, 1980.
22. The Rt. Hon. Pierre Elliott Trudeau, (Liberal). From February 18, 1980.

GOVERNORS GENERAL OF CANADA

NAME	Date of Appointment	Date of Assumption of Office
The Rt. Hon. The Viscount Monck	June 1, 1867	July 1, 1867
The Rt. Hon. The Lord Lisgar	Nov. 10, 1868	Feb. 2, 1869
The Rt. Hon. The Earl of Dufferin	May 22, 1872	June 25, 1872
The Most Hon. The Marquess of Lorne	Oct. 5, 1878	Nov. 25, 1878
The Most Hon. The Marquess of Lansdowne	Aug. 18, 1883	Oct. 23, 1883
The Rt. Hon. The Lord Stanley of Preston	May 1, 1888	June 11, 1888
The Rt. Hon. The Earl of Aberdeen	May 22, 1893	Sept. 18, 1893
The Rt. Hon. The Earl of Minto	July 30, 1898	Nov. 12, 1898
The Rt. Hon. The Earl of Grey	Sept. 26, 1904	Dec. 10, 1904
Field Marshall H.R.H. The Duke of Connaught and of Strathearn	Mar. 21, 1911	Oct. 13, 1911
The Rt. Hon. The Duke of Devonshire	Aug. 8, 1916	Nov. 11, 1916
General The Rt. Hon. The Lord Byng of Vimy	Aug. 2, 1921	Aug. 11, 1921
The Rt. Hon. The Viscount Willingdon	Aug. 5, 1926	Oct. 2, 1926
The Rt. Hon. The Earl of Bessborough	Mar. 20, 1931	Apr. 4, 1931
The Rt. Hon. Lord Tweedsmuir	Aug. 10, 1935	Nov. 2, 1935
The Rt. Hon. The Earl of Athlone	June 2, 1940	June 21, 1940
Field Marshall The Rt. Hon. The Viscount Alexander of Tunis	Mar. 21, 1946	Apr. 12, 1946
The Rt. Hon. Vincent Massey	Feb. 1, 1952	Feb. 28, 1952
General the Rt. Hon. Georges Philias Vanier	Aug. 1, 1959	Sept. 15, 1959
The Rt. Hon. Roland Michener	Apr. 4, 1967	Apr. 17, 1967
The Rt. Hon. Jules Leger	Oct. 5, 1973	Jan. 14, 1974
The Rt. Hon. Edward Richard Schreyer	Dec. 7, 1978	Jan 22, 1979

INDEX

Subject Index 885
Personal Names 887
Church, Parishes, Church Organizations 920
Lay Organizations and Co-operatives 923
Schools, Education (Institutes, Bursas, Academies, etc.) 934
Printed Word (Print, Bindery, Shops, Publications) 936
Geographic Names of Countries, Places, etc. 943

SUBJECT INDEX

Agriculture, 431
Aid to the Cause of Ukraine's Liberation, 374
Aid to the Homeland, 320, 374
Arrival and Settlement, 78
Artists, 762
Art Galleries, 762
Assimilation, 716, 824, 868
Association of United Ukrainian Canadians, 818
Ballet, 677
Bilingual Classes, 743, 745, 747
Bilingual Press, 287
Bilingual Schools, 115, 441
Bilingual Teachers, 115, 441
Books (First Editions), 309, 829
Book Stores, 309
Bursas, 154
Businessmen and Businessmen's Organization, 234, 811
Canadian Foundation for Ukrainian Studies, 735
Canadian Institute of Ukrainian Studies, 735
Canadian West, 74
Centre for Ukrainian Canadian Studies at the University of Manitoba — St. Andrew's College, 738
Chair of Ukrainian Studies at the University of Toronto, 737
Charitable Organizations and Mutual Benefit Associations, 816

Choral Art, 675, 772
Choirs and Ensembles, 774
Chytalnias — Reading Halls, 161
Constitutional Grounds for Multiculturalism, 725
Cooperative Movement, 429, 582, 851
Creative Artists, 671, 756
Cultural Identification, 320, 328, 338, 449, 537, 544, 820
Cultural — Educational Work, 161, 374
Discrimination, 142, 249, 250, 287, 325
Drama, 677
Economic Field, 856
Emigration, 41, 363
Film, 654, 783
Foundations, 825
Funds, 825
Geographic Distribution of Ukrainian Settlement, 65
Governors General of Canada, 883
Heritage Language Instruction — Ridna Shkola —, 151, 750
Homesteads and Homesteaders, 92
Ideology in Historical Process, 873
Immigration, 17, 23, 351, 357, 561
Institutes, 154, 395
Integration in the Political Sphere, 222, 434, 683, 708
Journalists, 767

Labour Temples (Ukrainian Labour and Farmers' Temple Association), 403
Labourers, 92
Laurier — Greenway Agreement, 117
Literature, 297, 308, 499
Members of Parliament and Legislatures, 434, 683, 862
Migration, 351
Monuments, 825, 872
Multiculturalism, 725
Municipal Organization, 219
Museums, 825
Narodny Dim, 161
Organizational Life, 393, 593
Organizational Structure of Ukrainian Representation, see Ukrainian Canadian Committee
Pan-American Ukrainian Conference, 711
Patriarchate of Ukrainian Catholic Church, 822
Poetic Folklore, 297
Poets and Writers, 664, 763
Political Relations with Federal Government, 331
Prime Ministers of Canada, 882
Press, 238, 470, 632, 767
Professions, Professional Clubs, 234, 733
Prose, 303
Pubishing Establishments, 309
Racial Prejudice, 74
Radio, 654, 780
Role of Ukrainian Press, 768
St. Andrew's College, 738
St. Raphael's Ukrainian Immigrants Welfare Association, 365
Scholars, 657, 739
Senators, 708, 867

Social and Political Factors in Immigration, 17, 23
Socialist Movement, 225, 409
Religious Question and Churches, 99, 460, 582, 820
Taras Shevchenko Foundation, 680, 814
Teachers and Teachers' Organization, 441
Television, 654, 782
Theatre, 677, 772
Third Stage, 424
Ukrainian Canadian Citizens Committee, 331
Ukrainian Canadian Committee, 543, 805
Ukrainian Canadian Congress, 879
Ukrainian Canadian Professional and Business Federation, 733, 811
Ukrainian Canadian Veterans Association, 811
Ukrainian Engineers and Associates, 858
Ukrainian Language in Public Schools and Universities, 625, 631
Ukrainian National Council, 335
Ukrainian Red Cross, 376
Ukrainian Representation, see Ukrainian Canadian Committee
Workers Benevolent Association, 817
Women's Organizations, 411-417, 814
World Congress of Free Ukrainians, 713, 817, 880
World War I, 324
World War II, 558
Writers, 763
Youth Organizations, 417, 814

See separate Personal Index for specific information; on churches, parishes, organizations, schools, academies, institutes, publications, etc. see relevant indexes.

INDEX

Personal Names

Abbott, Sir John, 69
Achtemichuk, B., 759
Adamowska, Anna, 499, 500
Alexander, Bishop, 465
Alexandra, Sister, 152, 153
Ambrosiak, Kateryna, 496
Anders, General, 560
Anderson, A., 141
Anderson, Alan B., 868
Anderson, J. T. M., 830
Anderson, Dr. W., 434
Andre, Harvie, 850, 866
Andreiv, Nicholas, 143, 168
Andrews, Rev. Alfred, 116
Andrey, Metropolitan, 823
Andriashyn, M. Z., 777
Andrievsky, Dmytro, 633
Andrijishyn, Josyf, 739
Androw, M., 283
Andruchiw, M., 582, 703, 783, 856
Andrychowych, Rev. Emilian, 109, 212, 216
Andruchowych, Julian, 141
Andruchowych, Rev. K., 238
Andrunyk, General Steven, 861
Andrusyshen, C. H., 427, 454, 456, 472, 477, 528, 530, 536, 647, 606, 626, 660, 732
Anglo-Saxons, 17, 68, 71, 576, 626, 660, 654, 663, 719, 726
Ansbert, Bro. F.S.C., 153
Antoniuk, O. (Oleksa, Les, Alexander), 163, 261, 417
Antoniw, V., 856
Antonovych, Kateryna, 641, 669, 671, 669
Antonovych, L., 810
Antonovych, Dr. M., 639
Antonovych, Dr. Myroslav, 774, 759
Antonovych-Rudnycka, Maryna, 759
Aponiuk, Natalia, 739, 848
Arabska, Anna, 255, 283, 412
Arabska, O., 412
Archipenko, A., 679
Ardan, Rev. Ivan, 120, 239
Aronec, Ksenia, 757
Arseny, Abbot, 288, 289, 493

Arseny, T., 288
Arsenych, J. A., see Arsenych, Jaroslaw William
Arsenych, Jaroslaw William, 113, 147, 155, 164, 232, 235, 262, 267, 268, 323, 331, 333, 339, 342, 374, 375, 396, 397, 417, 443, 545, 551, 552, 567, 606, 709, 830
Arsenych, Olha, 176, 333, 411
Arsenych-Stolar, Halia, 759
Athanasia, Sister, 152, 153
Avramenko, Vasyl (also Vasile), 382, 383, 457, 484, 538, 656
Babey, M., 428, 430
Babiak, Volodymyr, 776
Babick, R., 741
Babienko, V., 333
Babienko, W., 533
Babij, Domka Zelinska, 704
Babinec, O., see Babynec, O.
Babiuk, Andrey, 407
Babiy, A., 214, 496
Babiy, Dr. G. B., 858, 859, 860
Babiy, O., 816
Babiy, S., 394
Babukh, T., 168
Babych, Andriy, 674, 765
Babych, Olha, 772
Babyn, Nicholas, 211
Bachynski, Dr. V. F., 608
Babynec, O., 379, 422
Bachtalowsky, Rev. S., 464, 488, 644
Bachynsky, J., 106, 165
Bachynsky, Jean, 759
Bachynsky, Dr. Julian, 231, 263, 276, 321, 322
Bachynsky, M., 165, 263
Bachynsky, M. P., 660
Bachynsky, Nicholas V., 15, 279, 333, 369, 374, 398, 434, 435, 440, 521, 684, 685
Bachynsky, O., see Bachynsky, J.
Bachynsky, Dr. Volodymyr, 360, 361, 362, 363, 364, 370, 380, 381, 538, 581, 608
Baderski, J., 118

Bagger, Gregory, 265
Bahriy, N., 676
Bahriy, P., 639
Bahriychuk, M., 335
Bakhtalowsky, S., see Bachtalowsky, Rev. S.
Bala, Iris, 676, 698
Bala, Rev. John (also Rev. I.), 110, 488, 489, 587
Bala, Rev. Joseph, 464, 488, 644
Balan, Irka, 776
Balan, Jaroslaw, 769
Balan, Vasyl, 748, 753, 815
Balas, Wolodymyr, 672
Baleshta, Wm., 155, 370, 545
Baldetsky, M., 765
Bandera, Andriy, 769, 770, 810
Bandera, Stepan, 451, 560
Barabash, D., 176
Barabash, H., 743
Barabash, M., 809
Barabash, Volodimir, 14, 642, 664, 697
Baran, Dr. A., 627, 661, 740, 741, 765
Baran, Anna Maria, 806, 822, 831, 848
Baran, H., 597
Baran, K., 215
Baran, N., 475
Baran, Dr. S., 360
Baran, Theodore, 452, 759
Baran, W., 410
Baranyk, Rev. Veniamyn (also W.), 462, 587
Bardyn, Ihor, 734, 735, 736, 738, 812
Barnych, J., 677
Barsky, Ivan, 34
Bartman, Rev. N. J., (also Bartman, N., Magistrate), 369, 394, 508, 709
Bartman, Y., 171
Barwinsky, Dr. J., 814
Barwinsky, O., 856
Barwinsky, Vasyl, 453
Barycky, M., 770
Barycky, P., 374, 606
Barylko, Bill, 581
Baryluk, Magistrate Michael, 606, 608, 691
Basalyga, Abbot Benj, 493
Basarab, Ivan, 121, 235, 274, 279, 369, 861
Basarab, Olha, 400
Basaraba, A., 414
Bashuk, Bohdana, 780
Bashuk, Natalia, 417, 604
Bashuk, P., 604, 606, 809, 810, 814, 849
Basisty, E., 225

Basisty, S., 335, 421
Bassowa, O., 410
Batenchuk, M., 391
Baw, N., 116
Bayda, Dmytro, 401
Baydak, I., 507, 511, 547, 598
Bayrak, A., 778
Bayrak, Paul, 607
Bazarko, Dr. I., 817
Baziuk, W., 823
Bazowski, P., 710
Bechak, M., 211
Beda, Ivan, 474
Bedriy, A., 809
Begar, Hryhoriy, 178
Belegay, Michael, 159, 171, 275, 318
Belsky, Ivan, 672, 677, 759
Belsky, Yuriy, 772
Bencharyk, F., 170
Bendas, Orest, 709
Bendiuha, O., 810
Bennet, William, 812
Berezowsky, K., see Genik Berezowsky, Cyril (Kyrylo), 709
Berezowsky, W. J., 705
Berezynec, Dometiy, 676
Berezynsky, E., 480
Berezynsky, M. P., 172, 259, 263, 467, 473, 647
Bezchlibnyk, Wasyl, 809, 811
Bida, Prof. Constantine, 628, 659, 696
Bidniak, Mykola, 673
Bielish, Senator Martha, 827, 864, 867
Bielorussians, 112, 328
Bihus, M., 581, 599
Bilak, Yaroslav, 808, 848
Bilan, Ivan, 25
Bilan, P., 506
Bilaniuk, Dr. Petro, 740
Bilash, Boryslaw, 660, 752, 822
Bilash, H., 172
Bilash, Mykola, 392, 420, 443, 444
Bilecki, A., 496, 819
Bilenky, W., 421
Biletska, Nadia, 672
Biletsky, I., 480, 483, 493
Biletsky, Leonid, 596, 606, 633, 657, 659
Bilinsky, S., 507, 598
Bilinsky, T., 277
Bilon, Rev. P., 506
Bilon, Peter, 466, 669
Bilopolsky, Andriy, 712
Bilyk, E., 644
Bilyk, M., 175
Bilyk, W., 810

Bilynska, E., 336
Bilynsky, Michael, 169, 117, 401
Bilynsky, Wolodymyr, 667
  see Wolodymyr Krymsky
Bishop, Tetiana, see Shevchuk-Kroitor, T.
Blahy, W. M., 432
Blake, Dr. M., 374
Blakeney, Alan, 864
Blakytny, V. (also Wasyl), 494, 496
Blok, H. I. (also Block), 389, 421
Bluta, S., 212
Bobersky, Prof. Ivan, 23, 24, 158, 461, 363, 364, 365, 367, 368, 370, 374, 375, 377, 380, 381, 392, 400, 425, 443, 466, 537, 538, 661
Bobinsky, G., 213
Bochkovsky, M., 209
Bochkovsky, Prof. O. I., 397, 510, 541, 547
Bociurkiw, Prof. Bohdan, R., 597, 641, 659, 660, 674, 696, 732, 737, 815
Bociurkiw, Mykhailo, 815
Bodnar, Gregory, 279, 335, 336, 342
Bodnar, Nadia, 807, 823
Bodnar, P., 175
Bodnar, Rev. P., 462
Bodnar, Theodore, 15, 235, 523, 662
Bodnarchuk, A., 113, 156
Bodnarchuk, H., 143
Bodnarchuk, Ivan, Ireney (Chabanruk), 663, 667, 697, 751, 752, 754, 763
Bodnarchuk, Rev. K., 217
Bodnarchuk, Rev. M., 823
Bodnarchuk, N., 336
Bodnaruk, Myroslav, 780, 781
Bodrug, Rev. Ivan, 40, 106, 111, 115, 118, 163, 174, 211, 224, 230, 261, 263, 284, 306, 309, 691, 647
Bodrug, Dr. Mykola, 410
Boels, Rev. H., 107, 108, 109
Bogdan, F., 662, 704, 830
Bohatyrchuk, Fedir, 639
Bohonis, (Bohonos), Y. (or O. or Jos.), 113, 141, 155, 156, 369, 374
Bohonko, Julian, 106
Bohonko, Pastor U., 174
Bohonos, I., 225
Bohonos, O., 374
Bohonos, Walter, 675, 693
Bojcun, Marko, 815
Borden, Sir Robert L., 77
Bordulak, Tymko, 297
Borecky, Bishop Isidore, 456, 610, 820, 843

Borodach, W., 603
Borodayewsky, S., 476
Borovets, S., 808
Borovsky, W., 591, 647
Borowsky, Mykhaylo L., 459, 577, 596, 606, 661, 696
Borsa, I., 174, 175
Boruch, Ivan, 704, 828
Bortniansky, D., 453, 808
Boryska, D., 285
Borysky, Mykhaylo, 446, 455, 479
Borysky, Mykhaylo, 446, 455, 479
Boshyk, Yuriy, 769
Bosky, Rev. Franz, 464
Bosky, Rev. L., 464
Bosovych, Vasyl (also Wasyl), 497, 534
Bossy, Wolodymyr, 393, 394, 470, 471, 475, 490, 492, 493, 508, 519, 545, 634, 751
Bovkun, Olenka, 774
Bowell, Mackenzie, 32, 69, 70
Bowell, T. M., 71
Bower, Johnny, 581
Boulanger, Dr. Jos., 158
Boyan, Osyp, 307
Boyaniwska, M., 176, 255, 333, 411, 606
Boyaniwsky, Osyp, 147, 258, 429, 331, 333, 374
Boyarchuk, Rev. Y., 214, 215, 216
Boychuk, E., 737
Boychuk, I., 336
Boychuk, Ivan, 225, 226, 408, 496
Boychuk, Jos., 141
Boychuk, L., 815
Boychuk, M., 16, 149, 256, 390, 662
Boychuk, Maria, 390
Boychuk, N., 155
Boychuk, P., 168
Boyd, I., see Boychuk, Ivan
Boyko, A., 211
Boyko, Eugene, 787
Boyko, I., 604
Boyko, Ivan, 25, 175, 635
Boyko, Dr. Joseph, 578, 581, 607, 734
Boykowich, Leon, 606
Boykowich, M. H., 16, 111, 662
Boykowich-Korchynska, P., 255, 420
Boyle, Minister, 143, 144, 147, 274, 290
Bozok, Petro, 263, 607
Bozyk (also Bozhyk), Rev. Panteleymon, 106, 289, 291, 293, 303, 366, 368, 483, 493, 499, 519
Bracken, Premier, 440
Brelis, M., 430
Brezden, Mariyka, 676

Bryce, Dr. George, 116, 117, 260, 254, 535
British, 719, 720
Brych, Mykola, 507
Brychka, M., 407
Brygadyr, M., 211
Bryk, Alexander, 669, 701
Bryk, H., 608
Bryk, R., 595, 606
Brykovych, R., 822
Brykowych, K., 860
Brylynsky, W., 410
Bryniawsky, J. V., 628
Bryniawsky, Z., 816
Brytan, Roma, 780
Bryzhun, Oksana, 676, 773
Bubela, P., 850
Bubniuk, Irene, 675
Bubniuk, Stefania, 414, 641, 663, 699
Bubniuk, Y., 171
Bubniuk, Yakiw, 454, 668
Bubnyk, Maria, 26
Buchak, Lewko, 468
Buchynska, Vera, 416, 802, 819
Buck, Tim., 819
Buck, Dr. Walter, 688, 859
Bucklashchuk, John, 863, 864
Bucmaniuk, Julian, 452, 671, 695, 757
Budka, Bishop Nykyta (also Nicetas), 37, 109, 110, 113, 117, 137, 153, 155, 156, 157, 158, 165, 171, 214, 215, 270, 271, 279, 317, 325, 335, 337, 342, 343, 344, 360, 364, 365, 393, 403, 461, 462, 470, 471, 830
Budka, Danylo, 430, 471, 477, 547, 598
Budny, Boris, 765
Budnyk, N., 391
Budnyk-Stechishin, Anna, see Stechishin, Anna
Budurowych, I., 740
Budzynovsky, V., 32, 33
Bulat, Olena, 773
Bulba-Borovetz, Taras, 560
Bulgarians, 367
Bulyk, Wm., 153
Bunka, A., 662
Bunka, N., 391
Bunyan, John, 306
Bura, S., 169
Burda, V. E., 492
Burdeyny, M., 759
Burianyk, Wm., 325
Burke, Rev. A. E., 108
Burtniak, Peter., 690, 862, 863
Burtnyk, D., 454

Bury, Maurice, 700
Buyachok, I., 776
Buyniak, Prof. V. O., 626, 660
Buyniak, Theodosy, 809, 811
Bybliv, Franciska, 587
Bychynska, Anna, 412
Bychynsky, Zyhmont, 165, 169, 170, 223, 262, 263, 305, 306, 339, 369, 443, 473, 647
Bytynsky, Mykola, 672
Bzowa, Maria, 680
Bzowy, Ivan, 871
Cafik, Norman, 738, 812, 865, 866
Calder, Dr. Al., 278
Cameron, Sen. D., 627
Campbell, D., 681
Capp, Stan, 686
Careless, J. M. S., 832
Carmichael, Prof. J. A., 117, 264, 535
Carrick, Stanley,
Carstens, Hugo, 31
Carstiak, Anton, 26
Carstiak, Suzanna, 26
Carstiak, Teresa, 26
Carynnyk, M., 639
Cebriwsky, see Kudryk, W. (also V.)
Cechmistro, T., 607, 692
Cehelsky, Dr. Lonhyn, 712
Cependa, M. N., 488
Chaba, Peter, 687
Chabal, N., 527, 662
Chabanruk, Pseudo of Bodnarchuk, I.
Chabursky, Rev. S., 669
Chachkovsky, M., 649
Chahovzov, Rev. Arseny, also Arseny, Abbot
Chaikovsky, P., 118
Chaly, see Chernecky, Sawa
Chaplynsky, Bohdan, 773
Chappleau, Rev. M., 367
Charak, A., 815
Charchalis, S., 582
Charko, W., 447
Charles, XII, 18
Charnetsky, John, 432
Charney, Dr. D. J., 581
Charyk, Dr. Jos., 660
Chayka, Evhenia, 773, 803
Chayka, I., 398
Chaykowska, Luba, 808, 809, 814
Chechowsky, H., 822
Chechowsky, I., 675
Chekhovtsev (Chohovets), see Arseny, Abbot
Chepesiuk, Anna, 445

Chepesiuk, M., 432
Chepil, Dr. W., 432
Chereshniowsky, Mykhaylo, 827
Cherevaty, D., 215
Cherewaniak, P., 178
Cherewick, Dr. W. J., 433
Chernecky, M., 581
Chernecky, Sawa, 163, 231, 240, 300, 301, 302, 303, 304, 459, 500
Chernenko, Oleksandra, 763
Chernetsky, I., 172
Cherniak, I., 293
Cherniak, M., 147
Cherniak, Petro, 676
Cherniak, Wm., 290
Cherniawsky, Y., 174
Chernysh, Wolodymyr, 650
Cherrier, Rev. Fr., 116
Chichak, Catharine, 863
Chichocky, Vasyl, 715
Chiel, Arthur, 24
Chimko, T., 681
Chimy, Bishop Jerome, 820, 847
Chinese, 781
Chmelyk, pseud. of Volokhatiuk, Taras
Chohovets, see Arseny, Abbot
Cholkan, Olha, 774
Cholkan, R., 578
Choma, I., 822
Chomiak, Bohdan, 780
Chomiak, Chrystyna, 769
Chomiak, M., 743, 761, 77o
Chomiak, R., 464, 644
Chomick, D., 407
Chomicky, O., 407
Chomyn, Rev. Petro, 643, 653, 669, 702, 822
Chopek, Wm., 669
Chopovyk, M., 213
Chopovyk, Y., 213
Chopyk, Anna, 26
Chorna-Semeniuk, Maria
Chornenky, V., 164
Chornenky, W., 223
Chorney, D., 168
Chorney, M., 168
Chorney, N., 859
Chorney, Y., 323
Chorneyko, A., 444
Chorneyko, M., 113, 283
Chorneyko, Ya., 336
Chorniy, I., 338
Chornohuz, Michael, 437
Chornopysky, N.,
Chorny, N., 859, 860

Choulguine, R., 639
Chovhaniuk, I., 215
Chubaty, Prof. Mykola, 712
Chubenko, Bohdan, 599, 655
Chuma, H., 643
Chumak, V., 494
Chumer, William (also V. A.), 118, 142, 143, 144, 181, 267, 268, 502
Chupryna, Tetiana, 773
Chwaliboga, S., 226, 407, 408, 477, 551, 567, 606, 871
Chychak, Stepan, 35
Chychka, H., 168
Chychka, I., 168
Chyz, W., 856
Chypchar, Michael, 16, 150, 210, 185, 526, 662
Cicierski, E., 746
Cipiwnyk, Dr. D., 823
Cirka, T., 606
Ciunyk, Edward, 678
Clark, Joe, 867
Clark, R. F., 737
Claveloux, Rev. D., 110, 153
Clement, W., 858
Coles, Martin, 831
Collins, Bruce, 671
Connor, Ralph, 535, 830
Cooper (Krupiak), Joe, 581
Crapleve-Smith, Ann, 567, 814
Crawford, Isabella, 531
Cressy, J. T., 121, 343
Cripps, Agnes, 607, 690
Croats, 17, 328
Cukornyk, Rev. G., 365, 446, 454
Culbertson, Ely, 89
Cundy, Percival, 535
Curkowsky, A., 239
Curlook, Dr. W., 850
Cviklevych, J., 598
Cybulsky, S., 509
Cymbalisty, I., 547
Cymbaliuk, P., 827
Czechs, 17, 328, 345, 366, 719
Czernecki, St., 759
Czujko, M., 822
Dackiw, Theodor, see Datzkiw, Theodore
Daciuk, Bishop Myron, 587
Dacko, Dr. W., 822
Dafoe, John W., 77
Dalaere, Rev. Achilles, see Delaere, Rev. Achilles
Dalavrak, I. P., 142, 179
Dale (also Samotilka), Jack, 454, 676

Daleshivsky, see Chernecky, Sawa
Dalny, M., 636
Daly, Hon. T. Maine, 31, 32, 69, 70, 73, 260
Danylewych, Roman, 644
Danyleyko, A., 444
Danyliw, Dr. George, 738, 812, 813
Daniels (Zadyrayko), Danylo Z., 688
Danylchenko, N., 394, 508
Danylchuk, Rev. Ivan, 106, 263
Danylchuk, I., (also J.), writer, 283, 303, 307, 418, 445, 479, 482, 503, 507, 519
Danyleyko, W., 685
Danyluk, H., 214
Danylovych, Jos., 159
Darcovich, Dr. V., 710, 831
Darewych, Dr. J. W., 738, 752, 813, 860
Darichuk, W. M., 710
Darkovych, Mykhaylo T., 388, 533
Darkovych, O. T., 388, 479, 480, 533
Dashko, Yuri, 815
Datzkiw, Theodore, 369, 472, 485, 495, 498, 506, 519, 550, 551, 552, 712
Davis, William, 862
Dawydiak, Wasyl, 665
Deakon, Walter C., 865
Debryn, Bishop Mykolay, 823, 847
Decamp, Rev. N. M., 107, 109, 153, 210, 213, 464
Decore, Judge John N., 691, 707
Decore, Lawrence, 729, 730, 735, 737, 743, 812, 813, 849
Decykewych, Dr. W., 360
Dedeluk, M., 828
Dedelyuk, Yar., 118, 163
Deegan, T. D., 116
Dehid, I., 175
Delaere, Rev. Achilles, 107, 108, 109, 127, 153, 210, 213, 463, 464
Delforge, A., 464
Demanchuk, D., 280
Demchuk, E., 176, 411
Demchuk, Rev. I., 110
Demchuk, M., 153
De Meurons, 25
Demianchuk, V., 509
Demidiuk, V., 214
Demydchuk, Dr. Semen, 254, 323, 332
Demydiuk, Mary, 333
Deneka, Victor, 452, 660
Derenetsky, M., 216
Derewianchuk, Steve, 863
Derkach, H. B., 592, 648
Derkach, M. W., 648
Dershko, S., 481, 741

Dershko, Dr. S., 581
De Watteville, 25
Diachuk, William (Wasyl), 735, 862, 867
Diadio, Rev. M., 770, 802
Diak, Petro, 213
Diakiw (also Diakow), Primrose, 758, 762
Diakiw (also Diakow), Ted, 758, 762
Diakovych, S., 462
Diakowsky, M., 832
Diakowsky, Wasyl, 859
Dickenson, Thomas K., (also C.), 410, 474
Dickinson, T. Kelly, 481
Didiuk, Wasyl, 638, 700, 768, 771, 809, 811
Diduch, O.,
Didych, O., 209
Diefenbaker, Prime Minister John G., 186, 674, 681, 708, 709, 722, 724
Dikur, H., 172
Disiatnyk, Wm., 577
Dmytrenko, M., 452, 672, 758
Dmytriw, Rev. Nestor, 37, 39, 40, 41, 59, 75, 100, 101, 102, 103, 162, 163, 173, 239, 303, 304, 449, 778
Dmytriw, Olga, 333
Dmytruk, Ihor, 671, 757
Dmytruk, N., 778
Dmytryshyn, Hnat, 34
Dnieper, Robert, 709
Dniprovy, Borys, 773, 781
Dobko, Rev. Theodosius, 587, 607
Dobriansky, Antin, 633, 822
Dobriansky, Prof. Lev., 712
Dobrolidge, Vadym, 672, 760, 762
Dobrolidge, Valentyna, 676
Doherty, Chas. Jos., 334
Dobush, Peter, 660
Dodiak, Michael, 695, 615
Doherty, S. J., 260
Dojacek, Frank, 230, 237, 262, 280, 310, 472, 473, 474, 632
Doliszny, B., 734
Doliszny, Maria, 806
Dolny, Evhen, 675
Dolnycka, Iryna, 765
Dolnycka, Roma, 772
Dolynchuk, I., 427
Dolynsky, Ivan, 766
Domaschuk, L., 859
Donzow, Dmytro, 657, 658
Doroschuk, Stepan M., 478, 479, 480, 535

Doroschuk, Semen, see Doroschuk, Stepan M.
Doroshenko, Prof. Dmytro, 397, 541, 596, 657, 658
Dorundiak, Ivan, 30, 31, 35, 361
Dovhal, S., 476
Dovhaniuk, V., 677, 765, 772
Dowhan, Eugene, 562
Drabyniasty, M., 118
Drabyniasty, T., 235
Dragan, Dr. George, 436, 521
Dragan, Semen, 178
Draganiuk, S., 170
Drahanchuk, Ed., 671
Drahomaniv, M., 385
Dral, P., 375
Drelinkevych, V., 120
Drew, Col. George, 494
Drewniak-Kowalska, P., 414
Dribnenky, Rev. W., 644
Drohan, Walter, 671
Drohobytsky, S., 209
Drohomiretsky, (also Drohomeretsky), Ivan, 106, 299, 315
Drohomiretsky, (also Drohomyrecky), Rev. N., 110, 394
Drummond, Rev. S. J., 116
Dubetz, John, 687
Dublanycia-Huzar, M., 774, 804
Dubrovsky, Ivan, 35
Dubrovsky, Michael, 35
Dubyk, Hryhoriy, 401
Dubylko, I., 636
Duchenski, Willian, 687
Duchnij, W., 704
Duda, L., 816
Dudar, Roman, 164
Duma, Wasyl, 758
Dumka, Pavlo, 32
Dumych, Rev. Ivan., 824
Dunton, A. Davidson, 725
Duschenko, Dm., 164
Dutch, 79, 576, 654, 719, 726
Dutchak, H., 336, 493
Dutkevych, I., 509
Dutkewych, Andrey, 756
Dutko, Rev. A., 217
Duzy, W., see Duzhy, V.
Duzhy, V., 394, 475
Dvulit, Rev. T., 149, 210, 212
Dydiuk, I., 214
Dydyk, Rev. Sozont, 104, 109, 369
Dyk, (also Dyck) Joseph (Osyp), 155, 335, 336, 359, 443, 545
Dyky, P., 672

Dyky, Wasyl, 471, 486, 508, 644
Dyma, Dr. B., 235, 606
Dyma, Joseph, 261, 289, 323, 342
Dyma, Maria, 415, 416, 420, 481, 524, 567
Dyrbavka, I., 175
Dyrda, Rev. M., 606
Dytyniak, M., 776, 778, 779, 804
Dzenick (also Dzenyk), R. L., 607, 743
Dziatko, Olha, 650
Dziola, A., 318
Dzivenka, Jos., 162
Dzividzinsky, K., 226
Dzulynska, T., 815
Dzura, H., 635
Dzurawec, Yuriy, 752
Eggan, W. J., 361, 362, 363
Eisenhower, D., 674
Elcheshen, D. M., 16, 365, 368, 381, 394, 395, 432, 478, 483, 508
Elcheshen, E., 676
Eleniuk, Y. (George), 408, 606, 663
Eleniak, Michael (Petryshyn), 24
Eliashewsky, I., 599, 603, 634, 635
Ellis (Ilaschuk), J. J., 578, 581
Elyniak, Wasyl (also Vasyl), 23, 24, 25, 26, 27, 28, 35, 57, 459
England, Robert, 830
English, 65, 79, 274, 459, 499, 543, 654
Epic, Hryhoriy, 496
Esaiw, I. (John), 369, 394, 403, 475, 486, 508, 607
Eshoo, Dr. Samuel, 159
Eskimos, 178, 719, 720
Esthonians, 328
Evanko, Edward, 676, 699
Evasiuk, Elias, 155
Ewach, Honore (Onufriy), 283, 303, 451, 479, 482, 492, 503, 525, 633
Evanshen, Terry, 581
Ewanchuk, M., 420, 830, 848
Ewasew, Senator John, 850, 864, 867
Farion, T., 336
Farkavec, D., 759, 769
Farr, E. S., 142
Faryna, Dr. L., 606, 807
Farynych, Motria, 766
Fecan, Ivan, 782
Fedak, A., 810
Fedak, E., 734, 735
Fedak, M., 599, 603
Fedak, Dr. Stephan, 360
Fedak, Bishop Vasyliy, 823, 847
Fedchuk, Bohdan, 665, 667
Fedchuk, Stefa, 676, 774, 803

Fediw, Dr. I., 598
Fedkiw, Halia, 777
Fedora, Mykhaylo, 216
Fedora (Fedoriv), Mykola, 216, 217
Fedorenko, Eugene, 787
Fedorivsky, S., 637
Fedoriw, Dr. I., 628
Fedorkiv, P., 170
Fedoronko, Rev. S., 110
Fedun, W., 432, 434, 436, 521
Feduniak, Michael, 864
Fedunyk, Rev. J., 644, 822
Fedyk, N., 427
Fedyk, Theodore, 231, 300, 305
Fedyna, Chris, 770
Fekula, M., 236
Fekula (pseudo Shpekula), Vasyl, 262
Feniak, Wm., 35
Ferbey, D. S., 237, 311
Ferbey, F., 143
Ferbey, M., 169, 225, 237, 272, 311
Ferbey, Mark, 769
Ferley, O. D., see Ferley, T. D.
Ference, Lisa, 676
Ferley, D., see Ferley, T. D.
Ferley, N., 176, 333, 411
Ferley, Taras D., 113, 118, 121, 147, 156, 164, 176, 223, 224, 225, 229, 267, 268, 269, 323, 325, 339, 342, 369, 375, 397, 422, 427, 443, 511, 551, 606, 830
Feschuk, Mike, 864
Fesenko, M., 468, 491, 592, 637, 647
Fiala, George, 675
Fiarchuk, T. A., 291
Figol, M., 809, 810
Figus, A., 606
Fil, Leonid, 808, 856, 849
Filas, Rev. Platonid, 125, 587
Fibrick, M. H., 488
Finns (Finnlanders), 654, 719
Fishman, Joshua, 720
Flak, Nicholas, 660, 701
Flak, Maria, 740
Fletcher, R., 143, 146, 343
Floruk, O., 676
Fodchuk, D., 16
Fodchuk, Stepan, 143, 173, 259, 272, 273, 291, 306, 335, 336, 374, 480, 486
Fodchuk-Batten, Maria, 705
Folley, Jos. P., 343
Fortin, Archdeacon, 116
Foster, James, 744
Fotiy, G., 626
Fotiy, Myroslav, 781
Fowler, J. F., 116

Franchuk, M., 216
Franko, Ivan, 21, 28, 118, 282, 297, 321, 504, 535, 596, 608
French, 64, 68, 87, 145, 274, 459, 499, 543, 576, 663, 718, 719, 720, 726
Frishta, I., 168
Frolick, Stanley W., Q.C., 567, 581, 595, 635, 700, 735, 736, 737, 738, 812
Fur, Theo., 40
Fuyarchuk, M., 223
Fylyma, Rev. Y., 213, 214, 215
Fylypiw, Rev. A., 105, 108, 109
Fylypowsky, Rev. Adam, 293, 294
Fylypowych, Colonel, 366
Fylypowych, Wolodymyr, 403
Gabora, M., 257, 278, 339, 866
Gagnon, Rev. O. (also Joseph), 110, 153
Galay, Ted, 766
Gamula, M., 759
Gartner, Karen, 780
Gawa, Mykhaylo, 14, 765, 773
Gawinchuk, Nicholas William, 429
Gawrachynska, Nadia, 731
Gayovska, Cornelia, 456
Gec, Lew, 762
Genghis, Chan, 17
Genik, I., 276
Genik, Pelagia, 416
Genik-Berezowsky, Kyrylo (or Kirilo or Cyril), 32, 37, 39, 43, 46, 59, 63, 106, 115, 163, 224, 239, 240, 261, 293
Genush, Luba, 672, 673
Genyk, K., 163, 164
George, Lloyd, 334, 454
Gerdan-Zaklynska, Olenka, 678
Gerken-Rusowa, Natalia, 657, 658, 672
German, Dr. Lazar (Rev.), 465
Germanos, Metropolitan Szegedi (also Shegedy), 114, 465
Germans, 17, 64, 68, 79, 87, 88, 141, 161, 274, 459, 481, 576, 654, 719, 720
Gerus, Oleh, 740, 741
Gerzabek, Dr. B., 236
Gerych, Dmytro, 16, 398, 401, 427, 509, 527
Ghickiere, Josoph, 464
Gigeychuk, Paul, 121, 144, 257, 268, 279, 335, 369
Gigeychuk, Rev. W., 213, 215
Gilewich, J., 336
Gilroy, Thos., 116
Glen, J. A.,
Glova, Rev. I. M., 263, 318, 323, 468
Goleychuk, I., 168
Gonsett, Faust, 660

Gonsett, Roman, 523, 660
Gonsky, P., 159
Gordey, Alexander William, 688, 859
Gordon, Chas. Wm. (Ralph Connor), 116, 254, 375, 535
Goresky, Isidore, 437, 521
Goshko, T., 113
Goshulak, Osyp, 774
Gospodyn, A., 446, 477, 478, 507, 511, 530, 547, 703, 856
Gouzenko, Igor, 759
Gowda, Faust, 861
Gowda, Michael, 167, 223, 225, 247, 264, 298, 299, 324
Goy, Luba, 774, 804
Granovsky, Prof. Alexander A., 426, 712
Grant, Dr. W., 111
Grant, H. C., 354, 531
Greeks, 17, 211
Greer, principal, 141
Gregorash, W., 455
Gregorovich, Alexander, 16, 142, 487, 526, 871
Gregorovich, Andrew, 438, 734, 813, 831, 832, 861
Gregorovich, J., 438, 661
Grenkow, Dr. W., 595
Grescoe, Donna, 456, 698
Greschuk, Bishop Demetrius, 820, 847
Greshchuk, Judge Peter, 691, 709
Grokh, S., 778
Groshak, A., 777
Grudeff, J., 492
Gubrin, John, 866
Gudovsky, A., 637
Gudovsky, A., 637
Gudziak, O., 606
Gulak, Bohdan, 710
Gulak, S., 599
Gulay, Dr. I., 398, 414, 509, 527, 567, 606
Gulay, J., see Gulay, Dr. I.
Gulay, Maria, 415, 416
Gura, Semen, 143, 159, 179
Gutyk, A., 172
Gybowsky, I., 407
Haas, Maara, 765
Haidasz, Stanley, 812
Haiman, Mieczyslaw, 25
Hajmanowych, Rev. J., 822
Halas, N., 427
Hales, J. B., 343
Halkiw, I., 162
Hall, John, 31

Haller, Gen. Joseph, 333
Halushchak, D., 215
Halushchynsky, Mykhaylo, 360
Halychyn, Dmytro, 713
Ham, G. M., 738
Hamulak, O., 765
Handziuk, N., 407, 477
Hungarians, 63, 66, 68, 481, 654, 719
Hankewych, Dr. Mykola, 226
Hankewych, Rev. Roman, 782, 822
Hansen, M. L., 721
Hanuschak, Ben, 686, 690, 852, 863
Hanuschak, Luba, 676, 698
Harapiak, Harry, 864
Haras, Orest, 813
Harasevych, Kateryna, 416
Harasym, Wm. M., 710
Harasymchuk, Mykhaylo, 534
Harasymchuk, Ted, 777
Harasymovych, Zenon, 664
Harmata, Ivan, 749, 767, 826
Harmash, Mira, 764
Harmatiuk, B., 649
Harmatiy, Stephan, 32
Harney, R. I., 832
Hart, Prof., 116
Hasiuk, B., 639
Hassan, G., 454, 457
Havirko, J., 250
Havirko, Roma, 660
Hawrelak, William, 683, 69
Hawrylak, Andrew, 474
Hawrylechko, A., 335
Hawryliuk, F. T., 113, 155, 424
Hwryliw, P., 237
Hawryluk, D., 464
Hawryluk, Rev. Ivan, 822
Hawryluk, H., see Hawryluk-Charney, Halia
Hawryluk, John Martin, 420, 427, 581, 685, 690, 733, 734, 814
Hawryluk, M., 174
Hawryluk, Maria, 415, 416, 524
Hawryluk, Volodymyr, 759, 764
Hawryluk, Zenon, 732
Hawryluk-Charney, Halia, 16, 391, 420, 425, 444, 641
Hawrysh (also Hawrish), M., 336
Hawrysh (also Hawrish), Wasyl, 113
Hawrysyshyn, D., 681, 701
Hawrysyshyn, Petro, 89
Hay-Holovko, Oleksa, 665, 666
Hayduk, W., 769
Hayworon, Z., 741
Hayworonsky, M. O., 453

Hedinger, M., 262
Herchak, R., 737
Herinowich, W., 280
Hermaniuk, Metropolitan Maxim, 586, 610, 643, 644, 661, 714, 739, 820, 822
Hethman, Michael, 394, 475, 491, 498, 508, 519, 633, 634, 871
Hetman, Michael, see Hethman, Michael, 671
Hevus, T., 595
Hewak, Stepan, 215, 662
Hewryk, I., 808
Hilius, S., 214
Himka, I., 737
Hirniak, Ivan, 677
Hirniak, Maria, 677
Hirnyak, Rev. M., 33
Hirnyk, B., 809
Hirsch, Baron, 79
Hitler, Adolf, 557
Hladky, M., 151, 163, 223, 323, 342
Hladun, Ivan, 635
Hladun, Petro, 513
Hladyk, Victor (also W.) P., 147, 289, 290, 291, 292, 293, 294
Hladyshevsky, Lubomyr, 607
Hladyshevsky (also Hladyshewsky), Dr. M., 172, 326, 663, 700, 741, 822
Hlady, Walter, 710, 734, 813
Hlibowych, Olena, 765, 774, 779, 781, 843
Hlibowych, Dr. Petro, 762, 843
Hlynka, Anthony, 419, 439, 440, 487, 521, 552, 562, 565, 566, 707
Hlynka, Isydore, 433, 596, 597, 606, 608, 640, 642, 660, 661, 694, 729, 733, 734, 782, 814, 830
Hnatiuk, George, 675, 693, 776, 877
Hnatiuk, Kateryna, 416
Hnatiuk, Luba, 731
Hnatiw, M., 606
Hnatiw, P., 533
Hnatysh, I., 483
Hnatyshyn, Ivan, 777
Hnatyshyn, Senator John, 689, 708, 709
Hnatyshyn, Roman J., 850, 866
Hnyda, Ivan, 213, 217, 226, 266, 371
Hobovych, V., 209
Hohol, Edward Albert, 736, 744, 850, 862
Holeychuk, Alex., 168
Holeychuk, Illa, 168
Holinaty, I., 175, 176
Holiuk, W., 277
Holod, Maria, 763
Holovchak, A., 649

Holowach, Ambrose, 419, 626, 684, 687, 688, 689, 707
Holowach, S., 168, 170, 171
Holowacky, (Holovatsky) Vasyl (also W.), 164, 213, 217, 223, 225, 226, 299
Holowata, M., 816
Holowaychuk, Dr. N., 433
Holovko, Yuriy, 617, 675, 778
Holynska, H., 454, 675, 676
Holynsky, Bohdan, 773, 808
Holynsky, Mykhaylo, 457, 541, 676, 694, 778
Homeniuk, Yakiv, 648
Homola, M., 607
Homyk, Maria, 416
Honcharenko, Rev. A., 26, 177, 223
Hooper, Inspector, 116
Hotak, S., 209
Horban, P., 592
Horbatiuk, I., 408
Horbovy, H., 212
Horbovy, I., 211
Hordiyeko, A., 816
Hordynsky, Swiatoslaw, 452, 674
Horechko, N., 462
Horhota, Yuriy, 773
Horishny, M., 480
Horlach, Stepan, 781, 810
Horochovych, Tonia, 641, 668
Horodovenko, Nestor, 675
Horoshko, Father M., 419
Hoshka, T., 170
Hoshko, W., 210
Hoshovatiuk, Ivan, 32
Hoshovsky, Bohdan, 597, 636, 665, 667, 697, 769
Hoshuliak (also Hoshulak), Yosyp (also O.), 694
Howykowych, Dr. A., 360, 364
Howykowychewa, Mykhaylyna (also Mychaylyna), 370
Hrab, M., 607
Hrebeniuk, Rev. S., 466, 506
Hrechka, H., see Hrechka, N.
Hrechka, N., 147
Hrinchenko, Borys, 118, 252, 280
Hrushevsky, Mykhaylo, 390, 420, 514, 658
Hrushka, Michael, 669, 702
Hrushovy, I., 15
Hrushovy, V., 118
Hrybinska, Svitlana, 763
Hrycak, S. O., 432
Hrycay, Ostap, 282
Hrycenko, Zorianna, 786

Hrychyshyn, M., 496
Hryciw, I., 215
Hrycyk, Theodore, 16
Hrycyna, Rev. Eronim Dmytro, 507, 522
Hrycyshyn, K., 514, 547
Hryhorashchuk, Ivan, 712
Hryhorczuk, Anastasia, 871
Hryhorczuk, Michael N., 369, 684, 685, 689
Hryhorczuk, Nykola, 398, 434, 435, 521, 684, 871
Hryhorczuk, P., 106
Hryhoriychuk, Rev. M., 365, 381
Hryhoriyiv, Nykyfor, 476, 541
Hryhorovych, O., see Gregorovich Alexander
Hrynchyshyn, Rev. M., 495, 497, 608, 644, 649, 821, 822, 847
Hrynevych, M., 401
Hryniuk, M., 412
Hryshchyn, R., 762
Hrytsak, A., 175, 277
Hryvnak, B. H., 235
Hryvnak, W., 487
Hubicky, Bohdan, 456
Hubicky, T., 454, 456, 481, 547, 778, 814
Hucaylo, Evhen, 266
Huculak, Erast E., 737, 813, 850
Huculak, Dr. Michael, 26, 455, 662, 675
Hudyma, W., 209
Hughes, Gen. Sam, 334
Hukalo, A., 607
Hultay, Wasyl, 401, 487, 511, 526, 638, 712, 871
Humen, I., 225, 272, 369
Humen, Jerry, 671
Humeniuk, Bros. J. and M., 455
Humeniuk, Ivan, 669
Humeniuk, Peter, 256, 392, 443, 444, 662, 830
Humeniuk, Theodore, Q.C., 396, 425, 492, 511, 549, 607, 807, 871
Humenna, Dokia, 668
Humenny, T., 210
Humilovych, M., 223
Hunkevych, D. M., 400, 475, 479, 499, 500, 525
Hunter, Dr. A. J., 86, 87, 88, 159, 260, 306, 375, 468, 473, 535, 830
Hupalo, H., 236
Hura, Rev. M., 104, 105, 109, 125, 157, 152, 164, 168
Hurko, Andrey, 773
Hurko, Marika, 783, 815

Hurko, Roman, 773
Hurko, Stefania, 764
Husar, N., 759
Husar, Yuriy, 811
Huta, Dr. M., 810
Hutterites, 17
Hutnykevych, Rev. M., 173
Huyda, J., 581, 806, 814
Hvozdecky, M., 776
Hwozdulych, Yuriy, 868
Huzar, W., 498, 637
Hyde, George, 474
Hykawa, Emilia, 176, 333, 411, 412
Hykawy, Michael, H., 16, 113, 444, 452, 606, 632, 662, 807
Hykawy, Onufriy, H., 113, 123, 138, 262, 305, 307, 318, 323, 336, 342, 369, 443, 472, 495, 498, 545, 548, 632
Hyndman, Louis, 744
Hyndra, A., 507
Hyrak, W., 604, 780, 809
Icelanders, 76
Ichniansky, Myroslaw, see Kmeta-Ichniansky, I.
Ilarion, Metropolitan Ivan Ohienko, 589, 590, 627, 642, 657, 661
Ilaschuk, I., see Ellis, J. J.
Ililik, W., 427
Ilkiw, Andriy, 765, 772
Ilkiw, F., 35
Ilnycky, Stepan, 660, 858, 859, 860
Indians, 718, 719, 720
Ingram, A. B. (M.P.), 211
Ircha, Rev. M., 110, 212, 215
Irchan, Myroslav, 407, 494, 496, 534, 520
Irish, 17, 148, 654
Irkha, Rev. M., see Ircha, Rev. M.
Isaiw, I., see Esaiw, I.,
Isajiw, Wsevolod W., 868
Ischuk, Roman, 639
Italians, 211, 576, 653, 718, 720
Ivanec, Parasia, 762, 757
Ivanys, Prof. V., 597, 635
Ivanyshyw, M., 478
Iwach, Onufriy, see Ewach, Honare
Iwachniuk, A., 603, 635, 653, 732
Iwachniuk, Dr. Nadia, 732
Iwanchuk, Ivan, 606, 692, 714, 809
Iwanchuk, Yaroslava, 810, 814
Iwaniuk, O., 216
Iwaniw, Rev. Mykola, 712
Iwankiv, P., 592
Iwanusiw, Iwanna, 757, 762
Iwanycky, P., 429

Iwanyk, M., 675
Iwanyshyn, T., 335
Iwashko, (also Iwaszko, V.) Rev. W., 663, 822, 856
Iwaskiw, Rev. J., 648, 847
Izyk, Rev. Semen, 606, 644, 653, 655, 669, 702, 781, 822
Jacenty, J., see Yatsenty, I.
Jaciw, Wasyl, 14, 34
Jackson, Principal, 141
Jacuta, Dmytro, 815
Jacyk, Peter, 704, 828, 860
James, Fred, 733
Janishewsky, Prof. W., 740, 815, 859, 860
Jankowsky, M., 704
Jankowsky, Stephen, 578, 704, 814, 828
Japanese, 719
Jarish, W., 860
Jastremsky, T. A., 164, 222, 265, 168, 342, 374
Jaworski, St., 710
Jean, Rev. Josaphat, A., O.S.B.M., 152, 153, 361, 362, 303, 367, 370, 380, 538
Jews, 17, 18, 24, 33, 68, 87, 88, 718, 719, 720, 726
Johnson, Pastor, 275
Juba, H., 366
Juba, Mayor Stephen, 686, 691, 780
Juba, Mrs. S., 655
Juzda, Bill, 581
Kachala, Rev. M., 33
Kachor, A., 582, 597, 606, 658, 681, 703, 740, 769, 855, 856
Kachor, Ivanna, 732, 752
Kachor, Sophia, 816
Kachur, Rev. P., 644, 653, 661, 670
Kahanec, Marko, 321
Kalba, B., 856
Kalba, Dr. S. J., 606, 640, 692, 729, 817
Kalbach, W. E., 573
Kolyn, Al, 865
Kaluzhniacka, E., 415
Kalynchuk, N., 170
Kalyniuk, N., 209
Kalyniuk, P., 512
Kalytchuk, W., 172
Kamenecky, Rev. P., 607
Kamenetsky, Mykola, 179
Kamenetsky, Wasyl, 179
Kaminski, Czeslaw, 121
Kaminsky, M., 214
Kamyenyew, D., 103
Kanchir, Emilia, 391, 416
Kandyba, O., 816

Kaptiy, L., 814
Kaptiy, W., 741
Kapustiansky, Gen. Mykola, 400, 540
Karabut, M., 647
Karach, Dr. I., 443
Karakotiuk, A., 235
Karasevich, Joan, 676, 677, 694
Karasevich, J. G., 581, 594, 595, 606
Karasevich, J. G., Jr., 737, 813
Karavansky, Sviatoslav, 764
Karchmaryk, K., 164
Karchut, W., 223
Kardash, M., 496, 649
Kardash, Wasyl, 617, 619, 675, 693, 774, 809, 877, 878
Kardash, William Arthur, 435, 685
Karmansky, Prof. P., 121, 122, 189, 236, 259, 279, 280, 306, 323
Karpec, Volodymyr, 118, 163, 256, 267
Karpenko, M., 267
Karpets, Oleksa, 168
Karpets, W., see Karpec Volodymyr
Karpiak, M., 823
Karpinka-Kushniaryk, L., 676
Kashchak, M., 407, 508, 550
Kasiurak, Valerie, 737, 861
Kasper, Frances J., 766
Kassian, Elizabeth, 463
Katamay, Bohdan, 712
Katerynych, V., 175
Kawchuk, Michael N., 686
Kay, Edward, 735
Kaye-Kysilewsky, Dr. V. J., 15, 30, 42, 43, 44, 78, 394, 475, 486, 525, 597, 661, 710, 871
Kazan, P., 307
Kazaniwsky, Vasyl, 147, 422, 454, 533
Kazymyra, Dr. Bohdan, 103, 644, 661, 662, 696
Kazymyra, Nadia, 831
Ke, Vera, 770, 802
Kedryn-Rudnytsky, Ivan, 472, 637
Kelebay, Yaroslav, 809
Kelebay, Yuriy, 786, 815
Kempe, Lavro, 677, 778
Kempe, Vera, 677
Kepron, M., 581, 595
Kereliuk, W., 807
Kereluk, J., 608
Kereluke, D., 823
Kernicky, Rev. F., 590
Kerychuk, D., 592
Ketchen, K., 482
Ketura, K., 777
Ketura, T., 777

Keywan, Ivan, 673, 695
Keywan, Zonia, 786, 831
Khabursky, Lubomyr, 773
Khan, Gengis, 17
Kharambura, S. O. (also S. V.), 147, 155
Kharchenko, O., 816
Khayyam, Omar, 94
Khlibetsky, V., 170
Khmelnycky, Bohdan, 18, 51
Khmil, Oleh, 774, 803
Khomyn, Martha, 773
Khorosh-Gregory, L., 413
Khoroshy, Metropolitan Mykhail, 598, 611, 668, 822
Khrin, Ivan, 828
Khwylowyy, Mykola, 534
Kibzey, Dr. A. T., 113, 141, 155, 156, 157, 235, 339, 375, 523
Kiciuk, Rev. M. S., 740
Kilar, John (Ivan), 167, 168
Kiwar, I., 175
Kinash, Rev. M., 109, 212
Kindrachuk, F., 175
Kindrat, Rev. Peter, 468, 522, 592, 647, 648, 662
Kindred, Judge Andrew M., 691, 709
Kindzersky, P., 336
Kipling, R., 531
Kiriak, Illa, 142, 179, 272, 275, 418, 499, 502, 503, 507, 525, 665
Kirkconnell, Dr. Watson, 300, 452, 492, 518, 530, 531, 535, 536, 594
Kirstiuk, Rev. D., 607
Kirstiuk, K., 466
Kish, V., 809
Kishynsky, I., 419
Kisil, S., 336
Kit, Dr. Paul, 703, 856
Kivshenko, P., 533
Klapaushok, Sister Emilia, 104
Klen, Yuriy, 680
Klimashko, Dr. S., 595, 607, 622, 811
Klimashko, Sisters, 676
Klish, W., 603
Klufas, Yuriy, 782
Klukay, Joe, 581
Klun, Y., 775
Klym, Fred Theodore, 686
Klymasz, Dr. Robert, 785
Klymkiw, H., 547
Klymkiw, J., 814
Klymkiw, O., 118, 813
Klymkiw, W., 597, 606, 618, 675, 877
Klymko, W., 822

Klymowsky, B., 822
Klynovy, Yuriy, 764
Kmeta-Ichniansky, Ivan, 468, 483, 488, 525, 530, 531
Knysh, Irena (Irene), 414, 663, 699
Knysh, Zenon, 633, 828
Knysh, Yuriy, 335
Kobelak, Alexander, 859
Kobeletska, K., 810
Kobiluch, P., 215
Kobitovych, W., 210
Kobrynsky, Dm., 489
Kobylanska, Olha, 659
Kobzey, T., 406, 407, 408, 477, 516, 551, 606, 663, 681, 871
Kocan, Ivan, see Kotsan, Ivan
Kochan, Wooldymyr, 15, 582, 606, 640, 671, 692, 814
Kochan-Budyk, Alexis, 776, 802
Kochanovsky, N., 233
Kocko, A., 390
Kohuska, Halia, 671
Kohuska, Natalia, 413, 417, 530, 532, 601, 606, 699, 752, 807
Kohut, Joseph, 663
Kohut, Mariya, 58
Kohut, W., 547
Kokhan, Theodore, 293
Kolankiwsky, Mykola, 635, 668, 678, 761
Kolesar, M., 26
Kolesnikow, J. A., 227, 283
Kolesnyk, Hanna, 773, 803
Kolesnyk, Maxym, 773
Kolesnyk, Volodymyr, 773, 779, 802
Kolemanytsky, P., 171
Kolasky, John, 697, 818, 819
Kolessa, Chrystia, 675, 832
Kolessa, Lubka, 457
Kolessa-Khodovycky, Alex, 297
Kolishyk, Dmytro, 665
Kolisnyk, M. (also V. N.), 164, 226, 266, 406, 490
Kolodka, I., 673
Kolodka, Mykola, 756
Kolodiy, M., 810
Kolodzinsky, Wm., (also C.), 118, 235
Koloshinski, 25
Kolpetsky, M., 284
Koltek, Yar. (also J.), 118, 149, 163, 262, 417
Koltsun, I., 153
Koltuniuk, Y., 360
Koman, Volodymyr, 323, 366, 427, 581, 527, 871
Komar, Dr. M., 661

Komarnycka, M., 815
Komdowsky, P., 25
Konashevych, Daria, see Yanda, Daria
Kondra, Dr. Peter Alexander, 433, 606, 729, 730, 739, 806
Kondra, R., 814
Konikewich, Julian, 333
Kononiv, Yuriy, 778
Konoplenko-Zaporozetz, P., 676, 698
Konoval, Philip, 326
Konovalets, Ewhen, 399, 451, 476, 487, 509, 510, 539, 540
Konstankevych, Rev. I., 239
Konstantynovych, Dr. M. V., 370, 538
Konstantynovych, Dr. V., see Konstantynovych, Dr. M. V.
Kopach, Dr. Ivan, 155
Kopach, Dr. Oleksandra, 629, 740, 752, 763, 764
Kopachiwsky, P., 822
Kopiakiwsky, N., 388, 464, 644
Kopys, A., 26
Korba, J., 464, 644
Korba, W., 464
Korban, Semen, 526, 662
Korbutiak, S., 741
Korbutiak, P., 816
Korchinski, Bernard, Leo, 688, 690
Korchinsky, John, 394, 491, 492, 511, 533, 634
Korchinsky, Stanley, 708, 865
Korchynsky, Bohdan, 403, 447
Korchynsky, M., 171
Korchynsky, Ivan, see Korchinsky, J. (also I.).
Koreska, Maria, 336, 366, 381, 412, 443
Korol, M., 496
Korol, Ted, 674
Korolyshyn, M., 634
Korostovets, V., 56
Korpan, N., 277
Korsakov, P., 647
Korytowsky, W., 606
Kos, Andrew, 32
Kosach-Borysova, Isydora, 814
Kosharych, B., 808
Kosharych, Halyna, 673, 756
Koshetz, Prof. Alexander, 382, 383, 454, 455, 457, 514, 530, 538, 597, 808
Koshez, Tetiana, 451, 514, 597, 675, 695
Koshorsky, W., 547
Koshyk, Mykola, 599, 811
Kosikowsky, A., 662, 700, 828
Kosmyra, R., 769
Kosowy, O., 163, 261, 262, 263

Kossar, F., 414
Kossar, Leo, 641, 710
Kossar, Wolodymyr, 15, 398, 400, 425, 433, 487, 509, 527, 551, 552, 567, 597, 606, 712
Kostash, Hryhoriy, 871
Kostash, Myrna, 766, 830, 831
Kostash, W., 743
Kostashchuk, F. S., 173
Kostenobl, Richard, 464
Kostiuk, Hryhory, 763, 764
Kostiuk, Lena, 758
Kostiuk, W., 444
Kostiw, Dr. K., 648
Kostiw, V., 648
Kostyk, Illa, 168
Kostyk, M., 775
Kostyk, V., 143
Kostyniuk, R., 759
Kostyrsky, Severyn, 209, 211, 284
Kotelec, Stepan, 811
Kotelko, M., 175
Kotlarevsky, Ivan, 210
Kotlaryk, N., 223
Kotsan, Ivan, 118, 123, 181, 267, 275
Kotsiubynsky, Yuriy, 285
Kotsko, Adam, 157
Kotsur, Wasyl, 125
Kotyk, S., 410
Kotylak, C., 266
Kovalchuk, Yarema, 780
Kowal, I., 428
Kowal, I., 547
Kowal, Sister Justine, 821
Kowal, M., 507
Kowal, Roman, 452, 673, 674, 695, 758, 759, 861
Kowalchuk, Jane, 774
Kowalchuk, John, 705
Kowalchuk, Len, 737
Kowalchuk, Lew, 822
Kowaliw, Ivan, 676, 774
Kowalsky, Alexander, 769
Kowalsky, Bohdan, 457
Kowalsky, Rev. George, 822
Kowalyk, W., 644
Kowbel, Jos., 333
Kovalevich (also Kovalevitch), Rev. Roberts, 391, 420, 511, 522, 606, 647, 871
Kovalsky, I., 226, 259
Kovalsky, Petro, 94, 432
Kovalyk, L., 810
Kovalyshyn, Rev. T., 522, 590
Kovbasiuk, D., 856

Kovbel (also Kowbel), Semen, 150, 185, 259, 303, 374, 448, 454, 475, 476, 477, 545
Kovpak, M., 215
Kowtun, P., 668
Kozachenko, Wasylyna, 677
Kozachok, I. C., 775
Kozak, Anna, 777
Kozak, I., 811
Kozak, L., 762
Kozak, M., 871
Kozakevich, H., 174
Kozarchuk, Jacob, 457
Kozaruk, Dr. J., 514
Koziak, Julian G. J., 736, 850, 862, 867
Koziak, M., 486, 660
Koziar, I., 170
Koziy, W., 212
Kozlowsky, E., 323
Kozmuk, H., 547
Kozoriz, Anastasia, 416
Kozoriz, John, 606
Kozyra, Ilko, 777
Krasicky, Rev. E., 109, 127, 216, 271
Krasucky, K., 209
Krauss, Kateryna, 414, 415
Krat (also Crath), Pavlo (or Paul), 225, 226, 232, 233, 265, 266, 285, 299, 306, 307, 318, 329, 333, 467, 468, 492, 591, 647
Kravchenko, E., 26
Kravchuk, P., see Krawchuk, Petro
Kravetz, J. D., 172, 178
Krawchenko, B., 737, 769, 812, 815
Krawchenko, Oleh, 739, 819, 832
Krawchuk, Petro, 408, 495, 649
Krawchyk, Stephen, 435, 482, 690
Krawec, A., 762
Krawciw, Melania, 603
Krawciw, Mykhaylo, 603
Krawciw-Barabash, Martha, 676, 765, 773
Krawets, Y., see Kravetz, J. D.
Krayevsky, M., 209
Krayewsky, Rev. Volodymyr, 464, 587
Kraychy, Nicholas, 734
Kraykivsky, H. (also Gregory), 169, 170, 176, 223, 225, 323, 324, 762
Kraykiwsky, Julian, 672, 760
Kremar, Osyp, 665
Kremar, P., see Kremar, R.
Kremar, (also Kremar-Solodukha), Roman, 142, 143, 171, 225, 226, 227, 233, 266, 272, 274, 291, 335, 336, 337, 471, 487, 488

Krepakevich, Jerry, 784
Krepiakevich, Peter, 733
Krett, James, N., 230, 267, 280, 305, 307, 310, 485, 486, 530
Krochmalny, Rev. I., 271
Kriesbach, W., 324
Kroitor, Roman, 676, 693
Kroitor, Tetiana, 478, 603
Krucko, Zenon, 822
Krupa, Rev. R., 110, 336
Krushelnycka, M., 150
Krushelnytska, Salomia, 539
Krushelnytsky, A., 447
Krychewska-Rosanda Kateryna, 762
Krymsky, Wooldymyr, 665, 667
Krypiakewych, Dr. I., 360
Krypiakevych, Michael, 503, 504
Krypiakevych, P., 608
Kryshchuk, Orysia, 807
Krystalovych, S., 336
Kryva, A., 214
Kryva, M., 150
Kryvecky, M., 114
Kryworuchka, Rev. P., 447, 522
Kryzhanovsky, A., 123, 155
Kryzhanovsky, Rev. Navkraty, 104, 105, 125, 171, 173, 209, 210, 462, 587
Kryzhanovsky, S., 104
Ksionzyk, Tekla, 60
Ksionzyk, Wm. (also Vasyl), 38, 39
Kubanska, Halyna, 669
Kubarsky, Ivan, 452, 672, 695, 758, 760
Kubijovych, Dr. Volodymyr, 831
Kuc, Jaroslaw, 678
Kuca, Nadia, 772, 781
Kuch, Peter, 671, 695, 760
Kucharyshyn, M., 815
Kucher, M., 759
Kucher, Rev. M., 466, 506,
Kucher, Pastor, V., 612, 647
Kucherepa, Dr. J., 707
Kucherian, Maria, 496
Kuchmij, Halya, 769, 785, 804
Kuchmy, John, 456, 698
Kuchta, P. W., 669
Kucyj, Vasyl, 582, 769, 852, 855, 856
Kudryk, B., see Kudryk, Wasyl
Kudryk, Rev. Wasyl, 113, 114, 147, 151, 231, 268, 269, 302, 307, 310, 313, 396, 397, 472, 500, 505, 646
Kuksa, H., 606
Kukura, Hnat, 143
Kulachkowsky, Jos., 235, 427
Kulawy, Rev. Adalbert, 116, 270

Kulchycka, Olena, 762
Kulchycka, V., 477
Kulchycky, L., 34, 113
Kulchycky, Dr. L., 360
Kulchycky, T., 406, 408, 507
Kulish, P., 280
Kulka, Wm., 164, 233
Kulmatycky, Paul, 223
Kulycky, B., 822
Kulycky, Yuriy, 775
Kulyk, Ivan, 494, 520, 534, 946
Kulyk, Luciana (Piontek)
Kulyk, M., 599
Kumka, M., 443, 444, 446, 499, 501, 649
Kun, Ivan, 141
Kunda, Wasyl, 660, 859
Kunytsky, P., 210
Kupchenko, Oleh, 668, 765
Kupchenko, Victor, 533, 668
Kupchenko, Volodymyr, 281, 668
Kupchynsky, R., 637
Kupish, Rostyslav, 775
Kuplowska, Olha, 783
Kupnytsky, I., 214
Kupranets, Rev. O., 644
Kuprovsky, A., 369
Kupych. Bohdan, 769
Kurdydyk, Anatol, 16, 633, 634, 644, 653, 665, 677, 702, 759, 762
Kurdydyk, H., 369, 410, 472, 473, 474, 481, 519
Kurelek, William, 671, 679, 694, 760, 761, 784
Kuriec, W., 276
Kurievych, M., 776
Kurmanowych, W., 540
Kurovets, Dr. I., 360, 490
Kuryliw, Jos., 277
Kuryliw, S., 533
Kurylo, B., 644
Kurylo, Evhen G., 765
Kurys, Dr. G., 859, 860
Kushner, John, 866
Kushner, Stanley A., 863
Kushnir, Bohdan, 779
Kushnir, M., 764
Kushnir, Dr. O., 603, 607
Kushnir, Rev. Wasyl (also Basil), 461, 489, 548, 511, 549, 551, 552, 562, 567, 605, 626, 710, 712, 713, 714, 734, 817, 830, 871
Kushnirenko, T., 772
Kushniryk, I., 175
Kushniryk, N., 644
Kushpeta, Ivanka, 816

Kushpeta, Dr. M., 607, 700, 806, 822
Kushpeta, Zenia, 774, 804
Kussy, Rev. I., 506
Kustiak, I., 211
Kustodovych, V., 647
Kutash, Rev. I., 823
Kuz, Hryhory, 410, 547
Kuz, Luba, 811
Kuzenko, P., 415, 416, 524
Kuzela, Dr. Z., 490
Kuziak, Alex Gordon, 684, 688, 689, 705
Kuziak, Brother Methodius, 702
Kuziv, V. M., 592
Kuziw, A., 16
Kuziw, M., 164, 276
Kuziw, Wasyl, 468, 648
Kuzmiak, Rev. M., 213
Kuzyk, P., 486
Kuzyk, T., 607
Kvasniak, I., 214
Kwasniak, Olha, 676, 698
Kwasnicia, Miro, 705, 864
Kvasnytsia, I., 175, 176
Kylymnyk, Stepan, 597, 663
Kyriak, Illa, see Kiriak, Illa
Kyrstiuk, Rev. D., 163
Kysilewska, Senator Olena, 392, 510, 539, 668
Kysilewska, W., 676
Kysilewska-Holowka, Virlana, 776, 804
Kysilewsky, Dr. V., see Kaye-Kysilewsky, Dr. V. J.
Kyslycia, Dmytro, 635
Laba, Dr. Russ, 642
Laba, Rev. W., 360, 661
Lacombe, Rev. A., 103
Lach, W., 547
Ladunec, M., 211
Ladyka, Archbishop Basil V., 109, 461, 462, 486, 505, 585, 586
Lahoda, G., 642
Lakusta, A., 172
Lakusta, John, 162
Lakusta, Rev. W., 823
Lalka, M., 677
Lalkiv, Dr. Danylo, 473
Lambert, M. R., 367
Langevin, Archbishop A., 103, 105, 106, 109, 116, 117, 126, 152, 153, 270
Larchuk, A., 496
Lastiwka, I., 432
Laurendeau, Andre, 725
Laurendeau, G. H., 490
Laurier, Sir Wilfred, 32, 70, 222, 260, 723

Lavryshyn, Zenon, 773, 774
Lawryshko, M., 32
Lazarowich, Peter John, Q.C., 16, 502, 507, 513, 514, 607, 627, 662, 710
Lazarowich, Zonia, 675
Lazaruk, D., 106
Lazaruk, Yu., 143
Lazaruk-Henderson, Helen, 776, 804
Lazechko, Maria, 416, 567
Lazechko, Mykhaylo, 257, 420
Lazechko-Haas, Myra (also Maara), 415, 478, 481, 492, 503, 529, 668
Lazor, Kateryna, 641, 816
Lazorko, Dmytro, 688
Lebed, Mykola, 560
Lebid, A., 815
Lechow, Mereas, 678
Legal, Bishop E., 109, 152
Lehid, Andrew, 664
Leluk, Nicholas G., 865, 867
Lelyk, M., 534
Lemishka, F., 170
Lemishka, M., 445
Lenartovych, Mykhaylo, 408, 496
Lenchak, Marianne, 775
Lenkevich, Sister Ambrozia, 104, 463
Lepinsky, Peter, 274
Lepkova, Olha, 542
Lepky, Bohdan, 297, 762
Lesawyer, Joseph, 713
Leschuk, M., 25
Leshchyshyn, Rev. I., 769, 822, 852, 855, 856
Leshchyshyn, T., 810
Lessick, H. P., 710
Lesyk-Lysenko, Vera, 503
Letavsky, I., 170, 485
Letts, 328
Levchuk, P., 489
Levko, I., 388
Levycka, Olha, 415
Levycky, Dr. Kost, 33
Levycky, M., 342, 641
Levycky, N., 282
Levyckyj, Myron, 673, 763
Levytsky, Dr. E., 472
Levytsky, Myron, see Levyckyj, Myron
Levytsky, Volodymyr, 778
Levytsky, Wasyl, 633, 634, 653, 665, 666, 669, 702, 759, 763, 770
Lewicki, D., 581
Lewicky, W., 423
Lewycky, Dr. D., 360
Lewycky, Laverne, 850, 866
Lewycky, M., 164

Lewycky, Volodymyr, 482
Lewycky, W., 410
Lewyckyj, Dr. Yuriy, 628, 753
Lewyckyj, W., 769, 802
Lialka, M., 772
Liber, N., 410
Lilicak, Ivan, 491
Lipinska, M., 411
Lisewych, L., 677
Lisovy, C., 164
Lisowsky, W., 435
Lishchyna, Leonid, 765, 816
Lithuanians, 328
Litovsky, I., 324
Livak, Olha, 481
Livesay, Florence Randall, 247, 264, 306, 492, 535
Lloyd, Bishop, 65
Lobay, Harry, 687
Lobchuk, William H., 759
Loboda, Ivan, 668
Logush, Maria, 673
Logush, Ruslan, 756
Lomachka, Svyryd., Pseud. of Oleksandriw, Borys
Lomaga, Yaroslava, 781, 822
Longfellow, Henry, 531
Lopatynsky, G., 637
Lord Tweedsmuir, 510
Lozinska, Hala, 787
Lozynsky, M., 253, 309
Lubchenko, Panas, 407
Lubomyrsky, S., 656
Lubynsky, Irene, 740
Lougheed, Peter, 784
Luchak, Rev. Dmytro, 823, 847
Luchak, Y., 814
Luchkiw, M., 809
Luchkiw, Volodymyra, 826
Luchkovich, Michael, 16, 369, 397, 434, 438, 439, 440, 485, 503, 521, 660, 661, 707, 827, 867
Luciw, Dr. Vasyl, 636, 659
Lucka-Lewycka, 772
Lucko, W., 685
Luckyj, Dr. G. (also Dr. Yuriy), 659, 737, 738, 831
Ludkevych, Prof. S., 453
Ludwig, Albert, 688, 690
Luhovy, D., 335
Luhovy, Larysa, 756
Luhovy, Yuriy, 786, 804
Luhowy, Rev. A., 366
Luhowy, Oleksander, 491, 530, 531, 665
Lukianchuk, O., 507

Lupul, Dave, 769
Lupul, Manoly, 723, 729, 730, 731, 732, 735, 736, 737, 743, 812, 831, 858
Lusych, Daria, 759
Luzney, Norman, 864
Lyhach, Y., 547
Lypovetsky, Major I., 598, 637
Lypowecky, M., 637, 771
Lypsky, Dr. Bohdan, 661
Lypynsky, W. K., 828
Lysack, M., 710
Lysak, Ada, 671, 673, 769
Lysec, P., 408, 496, 649
Lysenko, Mykola, 453
Lysenko, Vera, 529
Lysenko, Victor, 530
Lysovych, T., 211
Lystvych, Vsevolod, Pseud. of Rzepecki (also Ripecky), Nestor
Lysyk, E. R., 710
Lytawsky, M., 168
Lytvynenko, S., 674, 758
Lytwyn, C. T., 237
Lytwyn, S., 118, 256
Macdonald, Sir Hugh John, 32, 222
Macdonald, Sir John A., 69
Macenko, Dr. Pavlo, 454, 455, 456, 514, 596, 675, 693, 779
Machniy, H., 176, 277
Machula, Greg, 235
Maciyevych (also Macievich), S., 608, 649
Mackenzie King, William L., 549
Mackie, H. A., 158, 260, 336
Mackiw, Volodymyr, 597, 660, 696, 740, 859
Maclean, Alderman, 333
Macrovich, F. A., see Macrouch, F. A.
Macrouch, F. A., 425, 577
Macyk, Alfred, 687
Madarash, M., 215
Madiuk (also Maduke), Maria, 412, 413
Maduke, Ivan H., 432
Maga, I., 215
Magalas, George, 454
Magalas, S., 360
Magdenko, Petro, 673, 765
Magera, K., 419
Magera, Maria, 641
Magera, Theodore, 432
Magis, O. V., 339
Magocsi, Dr. Paul R., 738
Magus, I., 175
Mak, Greg, 285
Mak, Olha, 764

Makar, Rev. S., 239
Makar, W., 603, 764, 809, 811
Makarchuk, Mack (also Mitro), 706, 865
Makarsky, M., 223
Makaryk, Iryna, 770
Makie, H. A., see Mackie, H. A.
Makitra, S., 507
Makohin, Dm., 280
Makohin, J., 121, 163
Makohon, P., 209
Makohon, Y., 809
Maksymec, B., 859
Maksymchuk, Rev. A., 176, 263, 264, 467
Maksymchuk, Oleksa, see Maksymchuk Rev. A.
Makuch, Andriy, 815, 831
Makuch, Nestor, 769
Malanchuk, N., 595
Malanchuk, Rev. V., 587, 644, 661
Malarevsky, Rev. I., 102, 133, 173
Malaschuk, R., see Malashchuk, Dr. Roman
Malashchuk, I., 860
Malashchuk, M., 604
Malashchuk, Dr. Roman, 603, 635, 692, 811
Malecky, Dr. M., 598
Malliniuk, A., 147, 256
Malkovska, Kateryna, 773
Malofie, A., 427, 551, 567, 606
Malowany, B., 773
Maluga, Rev. Paul, 587, 849, 857
Maluzynsky, Rev. M., 777
Malycka, Iryna, 759, 762
Malycka, Konstantyna, 253
Mamchur, F. T., 401
Mamchur, M., 175
Mamchur, P., 113, 176, 277
Manchurak, Jacob, 534
Mandryka, Hanna, 416, 524, 567
Mandryka, Mykyta I., 409, 410, 445, 475, 477, 478, 481, 495, 525, 530, 532, 533, 547, 551, 596, 597, 606, 740, 871
Mandziuk, M., 493
Mandziuk, Nicholas, 689, 707, 708
Maraz, R., 677
Marchuk, Yakiw, 327
Marciniw, Theodore J., 123, 147, 149, 181, 279, 280, 283, 303, 342
Marcyniuk, J., 454
Marcyniuk, J., 454
Marek, B. I., (also V.), 235
Maritchak, Dr. Oleksander, 634
Mariyanych, I., 172

Markevych, Daria, 780
Markiv, Joseph, 33
Markiw, John, 428
Markiw, Rev. M., 598
Markiw, P., 215
Marko, M., 606
Markovsky, A., 113
Marte, Mayor, 345
Martin, Paul, 594
Martin-Viscount, Bill, 678
Martynec, Wolodymyr, 606, 633, 702
Martyniuk, Dr. F., 595, 607
Martyniuk, I., 174
Martynowych, Dr. B., 606, 681, 667, 770
Martynowych, O., 831
Marunchak, M. H., 25, 26, 44, 65, 66, 240, 466, 606, 641, 661, 714, 740, 822
Marunchak, T., 809
Marunczak, (also Marunchak), Peter, 678, 701, 775, 808
Maryn, Mykhaylo, 815
Maryn, Sonia, 769, 770
Maryniak, H., 172
Maschak, Rev. Ivan, 32
Masiuk, M., 607
Masley, M., 860
Masniuk, Peter Paul, 686, 866
Matla, O., 603, 635, 771
Mastykash, E., 692, 808
Matvienko, Theodore, 664
Matwiychuk, M., 446
Matwiychyna, P., 507, 547
Maydansky, W., 210, 214
Maydanyk, Yakiv, 287, 306, 480, 485
Maykovsky, P., 39
Maykovsky, Yaroslav, 118
Mazepa, Bohdan, 664, 763
Mazeppa, Ivan, 18
Mazeppa, V., 673
Mazurkevych, Franko, 403
Mazuryk, Hryhoriy, 530, 531
McCallum, Jos., 158, 275
McCreary, W. F., 43, 73
McEwen, Edith, 519
McIntyre, Dr. W. Jos., 343
McKay, Dr. John, 431
McKay, R. P., 264
McLean, Minister, 548
McTaggent, Lieut. R. M.,
Mech, J., 235
Mech, H., 237
Mech, N., 211
Medwid, M., 336
Medwidsky, Bohdan, 763
Megas, Osyp (also Joseph), 118, 123, 155, 156, 175, 261, 277, 305, 332, 335

Meighen, Rt. Hon. Arthur, 260
Melashchenko, Pavlo, 671
Melenko, A., 496
Meleshchuk, M., 507
Melnychuk, Andriy, 807
Melnychuk, T., 512, 528, 549, 551, 582
Melnychuk, V., 592
Melnyk, Andriy, 560
Melnyk, Atanasia, 463
Melnyk, F., 35
Melnyk, Halyna, 823
Melnyk, John, 456, 676
Melnyk, Larysa, 756
Melnyk, Lubomyr, 776
Melnyk, Mat., 35
Melnyk, Michael, 35, 162
Melnyk, Nicholas, 35, 687, 688
Melnyk, P., 173, 237
Melnyk, Paul, 466
Melnyk, Peter, 35
Melnyk, Rev. Raphael, 821
Melnyk, V., 752
Meloski, Dr. L., 746, 813, 861
Metella, Dr. Osyp, 822
Metelynska, O., 816
Metiuk, Metropolitan Andrey, 611, 822
Messel, Dr. Greg, 660
Meush, Stepan, 403, 452
Michalchyshyn, R., 677
Michalishin, P. I., 581
Michayluk, Dick, 864
Micholski, Nick, 581
Mihaychuk, Dr. E., (also Manoliy), 235, 156, 342, 365, 375, 381, 392, 443, 444
Mihaychuk, Ivan, 58
Mihaychuk (also Mihay), William J., 16, 84, 113, 123, 138, 235, 341, 342, 662, 704
Mihaychuk (also Mihay), Wasylyna, 58, 704
Miles Malycky, O. E., 16, 155, 426, 523
Miles Malitsky, see Miles Malycky, O. E.
Minenko, Rev. T., 14, 802, 824
Mirus, I., 423
Mirus, Michael, 787
Mishchyna, I., 603
Miskew, K., 403
Mladenovic, M., 637
Mlynarsky, Y., 810
Moch, H., 209
Mohr, Irene, 770
Mohyla, Metropolitan Petro, 113, 157, 423, 465, 502, 512
Mohylanka, Daria, 664
Mokh, Oleksander Mykola, 668, 697
Mokriy, M., 496

Mokriy, S., 606
Mol, Leo, A.R.C.A., see
  Molodozanin, Leo
Molodozanin (also Melodoshanin), Leo,
  452, 673, 674, 679, 695, 758, 827
Monastyrska, Olha, 757
Monastyrsky, Peter, 813
Morachuk, Illia, 712
Morak, F., 213
Moroz, Anna, 479
Moroz, I. (also J.), 423, 479
Moroz, Valentyn, 769
Moroz, W., 859
Moscovites, 112
Mosienko, Bill, 581
Moskva, Yaroslav, 749, 848
Mospaniuk, Dr. A., 598
Mostoway, Paul P., 864
Mostowy, Greg, 284
Motalo, S., 512
Moysiuk, Anna, 496
Mozersky, S., 394
Muchin, Halyna, 816
Muchin, S., 740, 741
Muchin, Svitlana, 759
Mudryk, A., 582
Mudyk-Mryc, Nina, 668, 671, 697, 759
Mudry, Daria (Darka), 759
Mudry, H., 479, 511, 547
Mulkewych, Karlo, 635
Mulyk-Lucyk, G. O., 646, 659, 740, 767, 848
Munro, John, 814
Mur, Dan, 663
Murayka, S., 215
Murdock, James, 562
Murchie, R. W., 351
Murha, I., 637
Murovych (Timoshenko), Larysa, 664
Murray, Dr. W. E., 156
Mychaluk, W., 113
Mychajliwskyj (also Mychayliwsky), T., 606, 692
Mychayluk, D., 582, 705
Mycyk, Dr. M., 607, 808
Myhal, H., 675, 777
Myhal, Joanna, 676
Myhal, K., 582
Mykhail, Metropolitan Mykhail
  Khoroshy, 589, 611, 668, 822
Mykhasiv, M., 155
Mykhayliuk, Rosa, 650
Mykhayluk, E., 649
Mykolenko-Telizhyn, Nina, 772
Mykuliak, P., 809, 811

Mykytczuk (also Mykytchuk), K., 603
Mykytiuk, A., 392
Mykytiuk, B. A., 812, 816, 828, 849, 852
Mykytiuk, Dmytro, 547, 598
Mykytiuk, S. B., 283, 445
Mykytiuk, S. W., see Mykytiuk, S. B.
Mykytyn, B., 816
Mykytyn, John, 534
Mykytyn, S., 423
Myroniuk, A., 170
Mysak, W., 433
Myshuga, Dr. Luka, 712
Mysyk, J. M., 235
Muz, W., 607
Nachaluk, Ya., 336
Nahirny, N., 33
Nahirny, M., 210
Nahorniak, Illa, 217
Nakonechny, Nela, 861
Nalepa, I., 216
Napora, Paul Edward, 668
Naumchuk, P., 655, 781
Naumchuk, Victoria, 781
Navalkowsky, J., 277
Navizivsky, J. (also I.), 166, 226, 295,
  323, 406, 408, 494
Nawrocka, Daria, 731
Nawrocka-Kudryk, Christine, 671
Nawrockyj, Major Osyp, 598, 606
Naydevych, A., 211
Nazar, I., 415
Nazarko, Rev. I., 488, 644
Nazarevych, W., 607
Nazarewych, P., 816
Nazaruk, Dr. Osyp (also Joseph), 343,
  377, 397, 398, 472, 537, 538
Nebeluk, Dr. M. M., 700, 741, 808
Nedilsky, M., 211
Negrich, Michael A., 14, 161, 581
Negroes, 28
Negrych, E., 810
Negrych, F., 176, 411
Negrych, Ivan (editor), 106, 115, 147,
  163, 224, 227, 262, 281, 289, 432
Negrych, John (agronomist), 701
Negrych, M. A., see Negrych, Michael A.
Negrych, Olenka, 14, 671, 759
Nelidov, M., 24
Nemylovsky, Bishop Alexander, 293
Nemyrsky (also Nemirsky), Constantine, 162
Neporany, Osyp, 828
Neporany, Yosafat, 828
Nesdoly, Elias, 866
Nesterenko, Eric, 581, 701

Nestorowska, Natalia, 676
Newcombe, Chas. K., 148
Newman (Novoselsky), Bernard, 706, 865
Nex, Fred E., 247, 287, 304
Nikolaychuk, P., 433
Nimchuk, Dr. Ivan, 644
Nimchuk, Mike, 811
Ninowsky, Wasyl, 669
Norris, Hon. T. C., 145, 146, 147, 280, 292, 333, 625
Norquay, Andrew, 222
Norqùay, John T., 121
Norwegians, 79
Nosyk, I., 637, 673
Novak, Appolinariy, 118, 163, 164, 223, 231, 262, 304, 305, 307, 308, 310, 417, 500
Novak, Dr. Gregory (also Hryhoriy), 235, 276, 374, 443
Novak, Luba, 456
Novak, Nadia, 456
Novak, W., 106, 223
Novosad, Ivan (also John), 287, 303, 499, 500
Novosad, Kateryna, 478, 499, 500
Novosad, Rev. V. (also W.), 466, 506
Nowosad, John Joseph (also Ivan), 421, 489, 578, 641, 643, 729, 806, 814, 822, 849, 850
Nowakiwska, Halyna, 673
Nowakiwsky, Oleksa, 672, 673
Nowycky, M., 606
Nychka, M., 780
Nychyk, S., 342
Nykolak, Dm. A., 455
Nykorchuk, P., 444
Nykoriak, L., 226
Nykyforchuk, S., 336
Nykyforchuk, V., 170
Nyzankiwska-Snihurowych, Daria, 677, 678, 778
Nyzhankowsky, Rev. O., 36
Obroca, Lida, 671
Obroca, M., 732
Ochrym, G., 859
Ochrymowych, Adriana, 787
Ochrymowych, Maria, 767
Ochrymowych, Dr. W., 360
Odnorih, M., 810
Odrach, Fedir, 665, 666
Odynsky, William, 432
Ogryzlo, M., 279
Ogryzlo, P. S., 118

Ohienko, Dr. Ivan, see Ilarion, Metropolitan
Ohonovsky, Prof. Omelan, 596, 657
Okhitva, Katerina, 412
Okipniuk, Wolodymyr, 809, 810
Okipniuk, Irka, 769
Okrainec, P., 595
Oleksandriv, Borys, 636, 665, 697
Oleksiuk, Rev. M., 823
Oleksiw, Rev. P., 153, 271, 282, 303, 336, 374, 381, 471, 505, 519
Olenchuk, Rev. M., 110, 133, 147, 218, 316, 336, 443, 497, 662, 871
Oleshkevych, K. M., 778
Oleskiw (also Oleskow), Dr. Osyp (or Joseph), 28, 29, 30, 31, 32, 33, 34, 35, 36, 37, 38, 39, 40, 46, 59, 70, 71, 73, 74, 78, 79, 100, 163, 323, 361, 362, 461
Oleskiw, T., 174, 277
Oleskiw, Vol. 36
Olinsky, P., 462
Oliver, Dr. Edmond H., 154, 224
Oliver, Frank, 158
Olijnyk, Orysia, 732
Oliynycky, P., 606
Oliynytsky, I., 168
Oliynyk, M., 214
Oluk, Peter, 735, 858
Olynyk, Dr. Roman, see Rakhmanny, Roman
Olovetz, P., 209
Olshewski, Rev. F., 104
Onofreiv, M., 475
Onufrijchuk, Irka, 780
Onufrijchuk, Roman, 780
Onufrijchuk-Sokulska, Mariyka, 759
Onufriychuk, F. T., 663
Onufriychuk, I., (also E.), 606, 740
Onufriychuk, Oksana, 676
Onyshchuk, Daria, 673
Onyshchuk, N., 169
Onyshchuk, P., 169, 178
Onyshchuk, T., 816
Onysko, V., 335
Oparick, I., 781
Optof, Korneliy, 773
Oransky, Yuriy, 779
Orlowska, Valentyna, 765, 772
Orlowsky, Jakym, 164, 338
Orlyhora, Lev T., 648, 664
Ormak, A., 172
Ornarowsky, O., 237, 311
Orobko, Emil, 155, 342

Orobko, Dr. I., (also J.), 295, 861
Ortynsky, Bishop Soter, 107, 110, 210, 213
Oryschuk, E. Y., 781
Osborne, Prof., 333
Osinchuk, M., 758
Ostap, I., 211
Ostapchuk, Emily, 607, 699
Ostapchuk, Phillip (also Pylyp), 456
Ostapovych, A., 215
Ostapovych, M., 118
Ostashewsky, R. J., 581, 607, 693, 732, 743, 782, 808, 822, 826
Ostashewsky, Taras, 782
Ostrowsky, A., 72, 215
Ostrowsky, M., 147, 290
Ostrowsky, O., 280
Ovchar, V., 174
Ovechko, I., 767
Ovrutsky-Shvabe, Oleksander Vasyl, see Luhowy, Oleksander
Ovshanek, I., 392
Ozero, S., 155
Ozero, S. W., 710
Paish, Anton, 24, 35, 40
Paish, Jos., 24
Pakosh, Rev. A., 807
Palachek, Sylvester, 41
Palamarek, S., 170
Palance (Palahniuk), Jack, 676
Paley, I., 704, 871
Paley, M., 16
Paley, S., 336
Paley, W., 704, 871
Palidvor, John, 577
Palij, Lida (also Lydia), 673, 759, 763
Paliuk, V., 481
Paliy, A., 582
Paliyiv, Kekelia, 699
Palka, I., 410
Paluk, Wm., 503, 529
Panchuk, B., 637, 655
Panchuk, G. R. B., 561, 567, 593, 595, 623, 737, 811
Panchuk, John (also Ivan), 523
Panchyshyn, T., 257, 454
Panischak, Geo., 34, 163, 164, 236, 338
Pankiw, A., 333
Pankiw, Ivan, 606
Pankiw, J., 736, 746
Pankiw, M., 478, 577
Pankiw, Maria, 766
Pankiw, Osyp, 822
Panovyk, D., 214
Panovyk, M., 214

Panteluk, I. A., 226
Panteluk, N., 226
Panych, S., 170
Paproski, Dr. Kenneth, 735, 743, 863
Paproski, Steven Eugene, 850, 866
Paraschuk, Mykola, 427
Parasiuk, V., 387
Parasiuk, Wilson D. P., 850, 863, 864, 867
Parchenko, Taras, 772
Parchin, D., 210
Parigo, John Rae, 490
Pascal, Bishop Albert, 103, 109
Pasemko, P., 170
Pashchak, O., 360
Pasichniak, D., 216
Pasichniak, M., 237, 280, 306, 311, 389, 454
Pasichnyk, M., 147
Pasichnyk, Rev. P., 153
Pasichnyk, P., 163
Pasichnyk, S., 599
Pasika, Volodymyr, 764
Pasnak, I., 369
Pasnak, J., 397
Pasnych, Editor, 474
Pasternak, Jaroslaw, 657, 658
Pasternak, Maria, 657, 658
Pasterschank, Christine, 737, 831, 861
Patrick, Michael J., 683, 691
Patrick, Stephen, 686, 690, 783, 859
Patrick, Dr. W., 106, 116, 117
Pastyr, Myroslava, 770
Paush, S., 413, 668, 807
Pavlyk, Mykhaylo, 282
Pavliv, Ludmila, 757
Pavlovych, P., 637
Pavluk, I., 606, 722
Pavluk, S., see Pawluk S.
Pavlukevych, Docia, 255
Pavlukevych, P., 410, 474
Pavlychenko, Anastasia, 414
Pavlychenko, Nadia, 678
Pavlychenko, Prof. Thomas K., 401, 425, 433, 487, 523, 549, 551, 552, 596, 597, 626
Pavlychenko-Sotnykiv, Lesia, 677
Pavlyshyn, M., 646
Pawchuk, I. A. (also J.), 225, 226, 485
Pawley, Howard, 863
Pawliuk, Rev. A., 644
Pawluk, S., 16, 595, 623, 661, 762, 811
Pawlowsky, Paul F., 432
Pawlykowska, Iryna, 415, 416, 699
Pawlykowsky, V., 360

Pazdriy, Dr. Ivan K., 147, 229, 235
Pearson, Prime Minister Lester B., 723, 725, 733, 782
Pecheniuk, J., 398
Pecheniuk, Maria, 416
Pecheniuk, Osyp, 366
Pedenko, V., 816
Pech, Dr. M., 433
Pelech, Fiona, 744
Pelech, Dr. Julian, 806, 822
Pelech, Rev. M., 155
Pelech, N., 153
Peluch, M., 150
Pencak, L., 859
Pendsey, B., 816
Perepeluk, W., 662, 704
Perepelycia, Rev. I., 110, 210
Perfecky, Leonid, 672, 760
Perley, Sir G. H., 334
Permsky, O., 216
Pernarowsky, I., 141, 156
Pernarowsky, Dr. M., 661, 696
Pernarowsky, S. W., 662
Peters, Stephen, 686
Petlura, Symon, 451, 739
Petrashchuk, I., 483
Petrashyk, M., 454
Petriv, Anna, 416
Petriw, Ivanna, 643
Petrowsky, Christina, 669, 676, 694, 774
Petrowsky, Michael, 16, 333, 479, 490, 491, 503, 504, 525, 662, 665
Petrushevych, Ivan, 113, 147, 258, 271, 292, 325, 331, 332, 335
Petrushevych, Dr. Evhen, 345, 538
Petryshyn, Alexander, 700, 816
Petryshyn, John, 864
Petryshyn, W. R., 815, 831, 837, 858
Philipps, Tracy, 550
Piasecka, O., 816
Piasecky, Yuriy, 636
Piatocha, Rev. O., 824
Piddubyshyn, Eva, 712
Pidhainy, Oleh, 637, 739
Pidhainy, Semen, 603, 637
Pidhayny, B., 599
Pidhirna, M., 815
Pidhirny, A., 170
Pidlubny, I., 545
Pidlubny, K., 427
Pidruchney, Wm., 432
Pidskalny, Rev. Vital, 821, 849
Pidzamecky, O., 809
Pieluch, P., 454
Pihichyn, Petro, 632, 641, 668

Piliak, Jos., 16
Piniansky, Wasyl, 235, 267
Pinsent, Gordon, 782
Piontek, Lucylia, 534
Placko, H., 141, 176, 262, 277
Platon, Bishop, 493
Platsko, H., see Placko, H.
Plaviuk, V., 452
Plawiuk, Mykola, 606, 692, 714, 817
Plawuszczak, Ulana, 770, 848
Pleshkevych, O., 852, 855
Pochyniuk, Yuriy, 677, 781
Pochynok, S., 212
Podilsky, Semko, 534
Podiluk, Volodymyr, 806
Podolanka, Anna, see Pruska, Anna
Podolsky, Dr. T., 859
Podworniak, Mykhaylo, 592, 648, 665, 667, 697, 740
Pohorecky, J., 595
Pohorecky, Michael, 15, 413, 486, 487, 498, 527, 606, 633, 653
Poles, 17, 19, 25, 63, 64, 68, 97, 104, 141, 145, 147, 161, 222, 328, 360, 481, 654, 718, 719, 726
Poleshiy, V., 170
Poletica, Peter, 15
Polivka, Rev. Damaskyn, 43, 103, 105, 125, 151, 225, 239
Poltava, Leonid, 764
Ponich, Michael, 687, 690
Pontus, M., 215
Ponur, Andriy, 534
Popadynec, Dmytro, 822
Pope, Betty, 678
Popel, J., 687
Popiel (also Popel), P., 155, 355, 421
Popil, M. J., 437
Popovych, Rev. D., 15, 522
Popowych, Matviy, 226, 266, 406, 495, 520, 534
Porayko, S. J., 16, 171, 662
Poroniuk, M., 634
Porochiwnyk, Hryhor, 700, 822
Posmituck, M., 710
Potapovych, Zhabko, 592
Potoski (also Potocki), Dr. Stephanie, 415, 699, 709
Potrebenko, H., 831
Powidajko, Irka, 769
Poworoznyk, Hnat (also Harry), 401, 578
Prestay, W., 213
Preston, V. T. P., 71
Presunka-Harasymchuk, M., 671

Probizansky, I. T., 336, 427
Prochuk, Wm. J., 16
Prociw, Stephania, 809
Prodan, K. (also C.), S., 16, 113, 235, 364, 365, 370, 381, 427, 431, 478, 523, 606, 662, 871
Prokolupiy, O., see Krat, Pavlo
Prokop, D., 662, 700, 829
Prokop, Ivan, 732
Prokop, Marian, 806
Prokopchak, M., 40
Prokopchuk, P., 408, 496, 649
Pronoza, Valerian, see Blakytny V.
Prusachenko, Zina, 781
Pruska, Anna, 303, 499, 500, 547
Prychoda, S., 214
Prychodko, M., 603, 665, 666
Pryma, Anna, 415, 524
Pryma, Osyp (also Joseph), 402, 455, 526, 607
Prystupa, A., 155
Prystupa, St., 741
Prystash, D., 497
Prytula, T., 174
Ptashnyk, D., 547
Puhaty, I., 163, 235, 268, 417
Pukish, M., 607
Pulak, Rev. J., 522, 827
Pulak, S., 581, 606
Pulishiy, M., 35
Punak, I., 375
Pura, Stepan, 497
Pura, William
Purdy, F. William, 863
Pushchak, Anna, 479
Pushka, Bros., 432
Pylypas, T., 407, 408
Pylypenko, P., see Ostapchuk, Pylyp
Pylypiw, Fedir, 40
Pylypiw, Ilko, 35
Pylypiw, Iwan, 16, 23, 24, 25, 27, 28, 35, 57, 170, 459
Pylypiwski, I., see Pylypiw, Iwan
Pylypiwsky, W., 369
Pyndykowsky, Rev. W., 174, 281, 498
Pyniansky, A., 223
Pyrch, Denis, 121, 647
Pysarsky, A., 211
Radchenko, Hlib, 671
Radchuk, Dr. Serge, 581, 606, 608, 642, 729, 731, 734, 740, 746, 782, 806, 814, 843, 849
Radulak, Ivan, 32
Rakhmanny, Roman, 603, 628, 635, 653, 660, 702, 782

Rakovsky, Dr. I., 490, 596
Rarahowsky, Dm., 164, 259, 266, 299, 300, 305
Ratuski, Greg, 581
Ratuski, Peter, 683
Ratuski, W., 734, 813
Ravlyk, D., 547
Rebchuk, Slaw, 423, 481
Rebet, Lev, 451
Rebryk, M., 808
Rechun-Panko, Z., 592
Redkevych, Rev. A., 110, 133, 150, 185, 210, 211, 325, 330, 336
Reed (Rafalsky), Anthony, 686
Reid, Dr. I. T., 116, 159
Rezchynska, Daria, 781
Repa, Stepan, 671, 759
Repinda, S., 335
Resh, Ronald, 827
Reviuk, Omelan, 308
Revutsky, Valerian, 658
Reznowski, Dr. Lawrence, 864
Riabowol-Labinsky, Peter, 676
Riel, Louis, 534
Ripak, D., 808
Riznyk, V., 607
Robarts, John, 865
Roberts (Roborecky), John George, 709
Robertson, Charles, 531
Robertson, Norman, 549
Roblin, Duff, 627, 681, 682
Roblin, Sir R. P., 117, 146, 222, 260, 279
Roborecky, Bishop Andrew J., 585, 611, 828
Rodak, Petro
Rodak, Valentyna
Rogeski, M., 398, 434, 435
Rohach, Evhen, 712
Rohatyn, Olha, 693
Rohowsky, Ihor, 773
Rohowsky, Larysa, 770
Rohozhynsky, H., 364
Rojecki, M., see Rogeski, M.,
Rojenko, Petro, 769
Romanchukevych, R., 860
Romanchych, Dm., 113, 257
Romanchych, Hanka, 413
Romaniuk, Gus, 669
Romaniuk, Ivan, (also John), 177, 429
Romaniuk, Iryna, 765
Romaniuk, Michael, 24
Romaniuk, Nykyta (also Mykyta), 141, 155, 607
Romaniuk, Sofia, 414

Romaniuk, Vasyl (also Bill), 15, 170, 173, 177, 429
Romaniuk, Yavdokha, 24
Romaniw, Anna, 414
Romaniw, Semen, 421, 606
Romanoff, Ivan, 676, 693
Romanovych, M., 333, 462, 488
Romanovych, R., 606, 681
Romanow, J. R., 859, 861
Romanow, Roy, 705, 729, 812, 850, 861, 867
Romanow, Vasyl, 757
Romanowa, M., 533
Romanyshyn, O., 810
Romanyshyn, Oleh, 770, 811
Romen, Levko, 665
Ropsha, George, 534
Roshko, G., 34
Roslak, J., 744
Roslak, Dr. M., 644
Roslak, Roksolana (Roxolana), 676, 698, 773, 774
Roslycky, Dr. E., 607, 660, 695, 752
Ross, William, 819
Rossocha (also Rosocha), Dr. Stepan, 598, 634, 653
Rostocky (also Rostotsky), D., 336, 427, 443
Royetsky, Michael, see Rogeski, M.
Royick, Alexander, 626, 662
Rozdolsky, Rev. K., 109
Rozhankovsky, L., 32, 33
Rozumnyj, Prof. J., 627, 628, 660, 696, 740, 741, 746, 762
Rudachek, I., 123, 181, 341, 366, 369, 370, 471, 606, 871
Rudachek, Rev. G. Y., 644, 802
Rudakevych-Baziuk, Stefania, 672
Rudko, W., 223
Rudnicki, M., 118, 261
Rudnycky, Antin, 542
Rudnycky, Ivan, 732, 737
Rudnyckyj, Prof. Jaroslaw Bohdan, 451, 452, 596, 606, 627, 659, 669, 696, 710, 729, 739
Rudyk, I., 113
Rudyk, Paul, 106, 123, 168, 236, 257, 290, 291, 323, 324, 428
Rudyk, Theo., 162
Rudyk, V., 159
Rudzik, Orest H. T., 729, 737, 738, 812
Ruh, Rev. Philip, O.M.I., 464, 522
Rumanians, 63, 68, 112, 654
Ruptash, Dr. J., 661
Rurak-Ferley, Natalia, 255

Ruryk, Anastasia R., 413, 524
Ruryk, John (also Ivan) J., 16, 142, 175, 369, 502, 526, 606
Ruryk, W., 401, 487
Rusnak, Bishop Michael
Rusow, Yuriy, 657, 658
Russel, F. W., 116
Russians, 17, 18, 19, 25, 63, 66, 87, 88, 147, 719
Ruta, P., 258, 331, 335, 336
Ruzhytsky, M., 492
Ruzycki, Nicholas, 687
Rybchuk, I., 155
Rybitsky, P., 32
Rychliwska, N., 412
Rychliwsky, I., 342
Ryga, George, 669, 697, 765, 766
Rzepecki, N., 638, 655, 665, 667
Sabourin, Rev. A., 107, 108, 110, 153, 188, 210
Sadova, Raisa, 765
Sadowsky, Gen. M., 598
Sagash, S., 604
Sagash, W., 604, 606
Sago, Mitch, 650
Sahansky, H., 175
Sahaydak, I., 213
Saik, Joseph, 533
Salamandyk, William, 432
Salsky, Yuriy, 816
Salyga, Peter, 816, 848
Samchuk, Ulas, 635, 665, 697
Sametz, Rev. P., 114, 139
Sametz, Z. W., 710
Samilo, P. H., 292, 493
Samoil, George, 815
Samotilka, J., see Dale, Jack
Samovydets, Mykola, see P. Kowtun
Samtsova, Halyna, 678
Sandulak, Ivan, 501
Saprovych, Alexander, 759
Saranchuk, V., 118
Sarchuk, W. J., 444, 552, 606, 692
Sarmatiuk, Rev. A., 214, 271, 335, 336, 394, 490, 492
Sas, S., 211
Savaryn, N., see Savaryn, Bishop Neil
Savaryn, Bishop Neil, O.S.B.M., 462, 480, 610, 820, 843
Savaryn, Petro, 581, 607, 692, 734, 735, 737, 743, 744, 812, 813, 843, 855, 884
Saviak, S. M., 156
Savycka, Ivanka, 641
Savycka, S., 810
Savytsky, K., 765

Sawchak-Dyma, M., see Dyma, Maria
Sawchenko, Prof. M., 337
Sawchuk, H., 170
Sawchuk, I., 446
Sawchuk, M., 685
Sawchuk, O., 413
Sawchuk, P., 419
Sawchuk, Rev. S. W., 113, 114, 139, 156, 235, 283, 303, 369, 396, 397, 465, 472, 503, 505, 551, 562, 567, 590, 630, 646, 711, 824, 843
Sawchuk, Stefania, 414, 415, 699, 808, 809
Sawchuk, Stepan, 171
Sawchuk, Terry, 581, 701,
Sawchyn, Serge, 861
Sawiak, B. M., 113
Sawiak, M., 408, 434, 497
Sawicky, Donna, 775
Sawka, A., 37, 40, 162
Sawula, S., 174, 365, 381
Sayevych, Omelan, 360
Sbaretti, Apostolic Delegate S., 108
Scandinavians, 68, 718, 719, 726
Schoenborn, Count, 19, 381, 482, 685, 690
Schreyer, Ed., 859, 860
Schudlo, Rev. M., 644
Schur, Jaroslaw, 655, 676, 694, 776
Scotch, 65, 87, 654
Scraba, Wasyl (also Bill), 481, 482, 685, 690
Seleshko, M., 606, 633, 809
Selkirk, Lord, 25
Semak, R., 777
Semanciw, M., 534
Sembay, Ivan, 407
Sembratovych, Rev. Leo, 213
Sembratovych, Cardinal Sylvester, 100, 102
Semchyshyn, C., 608, 676, 677, 693, 710, 741, 776
Semchuk, Martin, 705
Semchuk, Orest, 775, 804
Semczuk, Rev. Stefan, 401, 402, 461, 478, 489, 498, 530, 531, 551, 606, 807, 850
Semets, V., 509
Semeniuk, Dr. G., 433
Semeniuk, I. V., 257, 336
Semeniuk, M., 223
Semotiuk, A., 415, 416, 815
Semyshyn, Yaroslav, 765
Senchuk, Roman, 606, 732, 816
Seneta, Rev. D., 506

Seniuk, Jos., 125, 272
Seniuk, M., 509
Senkiw, G. A., 860
Senych, Michael, 688
Senyk-Hrybivsky, Omelan, 399, 509, 539
Serafim, Bishop, 105, 106, 126, 266
Sarafin, Antin, 94
Serbs, 17, 318, 345, 396
Serbyn, Roman, 769, 812, 814
Serbyn, Oksana, 756
Serbyn, Y., 811
Sereda, Jos., 170
Sereda, P. J., 710
Sereda, Vasyl, 861
Seredynsky, M., 215
Serwylo, Roy, 760
Seychuk, S. L., 859
Seychuk, M., 496
Seyho, Mich, see Sago, Mitch
Shafraniuk, M., 581
Shafranska, O., 214
Shafransky, Harry, 852, 863
Shakhay, E., 599
Shakotko, I., 114, 488
Shaley, I., 423
Shandel, Tom, 787
Shandro, A. S., 113, 224, 258, 290, 316, 331, 352, 375, 434
Shankowsky, Ihor, 665
Shanski, J., 581, 655, 733, 783
Shanta, J., 598
Shapoval, Dr. Mykyta, 410, 475, 510, 541
Sharik, Michael, 527, 808, 830, 871
Sharvan, Wasyl, 655
Shasharowsky, Volodymyr, 778
Shashkevych, Markian, 512, 513, 597, 641, 680
Shatulsky, M., 406, 494, 508, 520, 534, 649, 675
Shavel, S. H., 364
Shavel, S. S., 464
Shaver, Rev. G., 375
Shchepaniuk, Rev. M., 364
Shcherbanievych, Y., 479
Shcherbinin, M., see Sherbinin, Michael A.
Shebets, M., 808
Shegedy, M., 127
Shelest, W., 603
Shelestovsky, P., 648
Shelukhyn, S., 476
Shemeluk-Radomska, A., 807
Shepetyk, A., 810, 848

Shepticky, Metropolitan Andrey, 104, 108, 109, 126, 155, 210, 212, 271, 322, 323, 361, 367, 379, 390, 538
Shepticky, Rev. K., 367
Sherbinin, Michael A., 117, 259, 307, 309
Sheremeta, I., 289, 291
Sheremeta, K., 289
Sherman, E., 814
Shevchenko, O., 639
Shevchenko, Taras, 122, 141, 180, 270, 280, 293, 375, 453, 459, 504, 529, 536, 598, 608, 680
Shevchuk, Katria, maiden name of Novosad, Katria
Shevchuk-Kroitor-Bishop, Tetiana, 529, 764
Shevchuk, Rev. S., 644
Shevchuk- Tetiana, maiden name of Kroitor-Bishop, Tetiana
Shevchuk, Rev. Volodymyr, 587, 644
Shevchuk, W., 212
Shevchyshyn, H., 485
Shevelov, Yuriy, 764
Sheveluk, M., 445
Shevkenych, W., 432
Shindler, F., 490
Shiposh, M., 598
Shkambara, Maria, 810
Shkandriy, Myroslaw, 769
Shkavrytko, Myroslav, R., 632, 769
Shkilnyk, Anna, 731
Shklanka, Illa, 142, 444, 445
Shklar, M., 603
Shkromeda, S., 446
Shkvarok, J., 303
Shlemkevych, I., 215
Shlepakov, A. M., 22, 25
Shmigel, Vasyl, 777
Shmon, Olena, 496
Sholdra, V., 164
Shostak, Petro, 758, 802
Shpak, Maria, 26
Shpylka, Bishop Bohdan, 590
Shpytkowsky, Rev. Ihor, 567, 606, 643, 663
Shtendera, Evhen, 599, 623
Shtepa, P., 401, 509
Shtyk, A., 141
Shtokalo, D., 607
Shuch, Anhelyna, 780
Shuflyn, T. Ara, 676, 694
Shukh, W., 210
Shulha, P., 401, 509
Shukhevych, Mykola, 32

Shulakewych, Bohdan, 813
Shulhyn, Pavlo, 476
Shumeyko, Stephen, 426, 712, 731
Shumska-Moroz, Iryna, 673, 761
Shumsky, Rev. M., 212, 214, 283
Shust, L., 810
Shvydky, P., 113, 174, 175, 176, 236, 277, 278
Shvydky, T., 113
Shwedchenko, Hryhoriy, 676, 765
Shyan, S., 215
Shydlowsky, N., 237
Shymko, P., 35
Shymko, Yuri, 809, 850, 865, 866
Shymonska, P., 150
Shypowska, Sister Isydora, 104
Shypowyk, Taras, 774, 803
Shyshkovych, Rev. H., 464
Sichynska, Irena, 322
Sichynsky, Myroslav, 226, 233, 322
Sichynsky, Rev. Yaroslav, 262
Sicinski, F. D., 428
Sifton, A. L., 290
Sifton, Sir Clifford, 70, 71, 72, 73, 76, 77, 85, 114
Sikevich, General Vladmir, 397, 511, 540
Sikora, M., 174
Sikorsky, Jos., 156, 174, 277
Simenovych, Dr. Vol., 158, 333
Simpson, Prof. George, 510, 550, 559, 594, 626
Siomra, V., 214
Sirecky, Roman, 323
Siry, P., 512
Skalecky, I., 394
Skehar, H., 329, 342, 424, 425, 426, 503, 504
Skehar, Olena, 496
Skelton, O. D., 549
Skirko, Leonid, 765, 773, 803
Skladan, Wm., 432
Sklepowych, W. S., 533, 766
Skoblak, S., 430, 478, 547, 606
Skoreyko, Wm., 272, 708, 735, 865
Skorobohach, A., 256
Skoropadsky, Hetmanych Danylo, 395, 491, 510
Skoropadsky, Hetman Pavlo, 357, 540, 567
Skorupska, Martha, 637
Skorupsky, Volodymyr, 664, 763, 770, 802
Skovorodko, S., 592
Skremetka, Tatiana, 524, 871
Skrypnyk, Maria, 650

Skrypnyk, Mykola, 405
Skrypnyk, Metropolitan Mstyslaw, 466, 589, 646
Skwarchuk, J., 703, 855, 856
Skwarok, Rev. J. J., 160, 651
Skwarok, Yuriy (also Geo.), 153, 155, 156, 259, 335, 336
Skypas-Prockiw, Natalia, 775
Slavs, 71, 719
Slavchenko, Rev. T., 780, 781
Slavutych, Dr. Yar, 659, 664, 697, 763, 769
Slezin, Roman, 41
Slim, John, 481
Slipchenko, A., 164, 268
Slipchenko, H., 164, 179, 225, 268, 397, 434
Slipetz, Jos., 279
Slipetz, K. F., 235
Slipyj, His Beatitude Patriarch Josyf and Cardinal, 588, 674, 722, 821
Sloboda, Lena, 806
Sloboda, Sister Bonifatia, 587
Sloboda, Rev. Bonifatiy, 587, 675
Sloboda, M. W., 268
Slobodian, Illa, 212, 223, 335, 477
Slobodzian, John, 778
Slobodzian, Sheila, 815
Slogan, Dr. Joseph, 701, 704, 708, 735, 812
Slota, J., 26
Slovaks, 17, 211, 328, 345, 367, 481, 719
Slovenes, 328
Sluha, J., 464
Sluzar, I. (also John), 147, 258, 279, 331, 336, 375
Sluzar, Rev. W., 466, 506
Sluzarivna, Maria, 676, 772
Slyvynsky, Rev. I., 213
Slyvynsky, O., 816
Smaha, A., 336
Smakula, Pseud. of Kudryk, Wasyl
Smart, James, 42, 71
Smerchanski, Mark G., 578, 581, 655, 686, 689, 710, 734, 865
Smith, H. H., 31
Smith, M., 407, 477, 520
Smiyowsky, M., 407
Smolatych, Klym, 465
Smook, B. W., see Smuk, W.
Smuk, W., 342
Smylski, Dr. P. T., 595, 607, 661, 732, 811
Smyt, M., Pseud. of Semanciw, Mykhaylo
Snaychuk, L., 485

Snihurowych, Luba, 759
Snihurowych, Dr. M., 607, 700, 806, 822
Snihurowych, Taras, 759
Snyder, S. H. Y., 594
Sobal, T., 483
Sobol, P., 215
Sochynsky, F., 311
Sofroniw-Levytsky, Wasyl, see Levytsky, Wasyl
Sokil, Maria, 542
Sokolenko, Heras, 764
Sokolyk, Anna, 58
Sokolyk, Ivan, 58
Sokolyk, M., 828
Sokolyk, Yaroslav, 815, 845, 859, 860
Sokolyk, Yaroslava, 848
Solanych, Dmytro, 168, 169, 176, 485, 499, 501
Solanych, I., 485, 486
Solomon, George, 819
Solomon, Judge John R., 420, 435, 436, 562, 606, 608, 675, 681, 691, 709, 733, 737, 739, 808, 814
Solonynka, M., 603, 810
Solonynka, W., 604, 635, 702, 809
Solowiy, Dr. M., 661
Soltykevych, Roman, 675, 732, 778
Soltykevych, Dr. Y., 598
Soluk, B., 655
Solypa, W., 746, 813, 861
Soprovych, Frank, 759
Sopulak, Dr. M., 661, 770, 802, 822
Sorochynsky, I., 642
Sorochynsky, Lev, 457
Soroka, Andrey, 773
Sorokolit, M., 813
Sosnowsky, Dr. Michael, 603, 606, 635, 653, 692, 715
Sosnowsky, R., 360
Sozanska, Rosalia, 255
Sozansky, Joseph, 209, 257, 871
Soyka, I., 214
Speers, C. W., 43, 44, 45
Spiwak, Myroslaw, 606, 608
Spolska, M., 816
Spolsky, J., 604
Spolsky, Myron, 746, 815
Sporadek-Petrovich, M., 209
Spynul, M., 253
St. Laurent, Louis, 685, 708
Stachiw, Sister Ambroze, 821
Stachiw, T., 810
Stadnyk, M., 215
Stadnyk, Dr. M., 806

Stadnyk, T., 113
Standred, Rev. L., 468, 493, 591, 606, 647
Stanczykowski, K., 780
Stanfield, Robert, 812
Stanimir, O., 582
Stanko, I., 822
Starchuk, F., 710
Starosolsky, Dr. Volodymyr, 226
Starr, Michael, 684, 689, 707, 708
Staryk, Steven, 676, 698
Stashuk, John, 737, 813
Stasiuk, Dr. D. V., 394, 475
Stasiuk, Dan, 16
Stebelsky, Adriana, 759
Stebelsky, Dr. Bohdan, 635, 670, 673, 695, 740, 758, 759, 762, 764
Stebnitska, Olha, 415
Stecenko (also Stetsenko), K., 453
Stech, Stanley, 759
Stechishin, Anastasia, 871
Stechishin, Anna, 225, 412, 871
Stechishin, Julian, Q.C., 235, 283, 396, 397, 420, 444, 525, 551, 871
Stechishin, Judge Michael, 138, 179, 224, 235, 307, 368, 397, 709
Stechishin, Myroslaw, 101, 113, 123, 156, 178, 179, 232, 235, 265, 266, 275, 276, 305, 306, 307, 396, 397, 443, 471, 551, 633
Stechishin, Savella, 312, 413, 420, 459, 461, 482, 513, 524, 826
Steciw, Stepan, 672
Stefanicky, John, 214, 226, 285, 319, 408, 490, 495, 649
Stefanovych, Rev. Alex, 33
Stefanyk, Theo., 106, 118, 163, 164, 223, 258, 261, 267, 279, 323, 325, 331, 335, 336, 338, 342
Stefanyk, Wm., 297, 501
Stefanyk, Yuriy, 14, 627, 668, 763
Stefura, M., 832
Stefura, Peter, 707
Stelmach, I., 210
Stelmach, Myroslava, 780
Step, Pavlo, 665
Stepanenko, M., 739
Stetsko (also Stecko), Jaroslav, 560
Steshyn, Victor, 277
Steshyn, W., 277
Stetkevych, O., 239
Stewart, Dr. A., 626
Stewart, Prof. J., 116
Stickle, W. A., 142
Stolarchuk, Eva, 676
Stolarchuk, Stepan, 677
Stone, Leroy O., 857
Storozuk, H., 456
Stoykevych, S., 214
Stratichuk, J., 403
Stratychuk, Rev. Dmytro F., 113, 114, 139, 489, 506
Stratychuk, F. D., see Stratychuk, Rev. D. F.
Strilets, N., 769
Strokan, M., 734
Strom, A., 727
Strotsky (also Strocky), Rev. A., 104, 173, 177
Struk, Danylo, 664
Strutynsky, Rev. M., 107, 133, 239
Strynadka, N. J., 432
Stryjek, Dmytro, 759
Stryk, M., 435, 436
Stus, M., 486
Styranka, Maria, 671
Subtelny, Prof. Orest, 843
Suchowersky, Dr. C. N., 607, 701
Sudol, Isabella, 416
Suknaski, Andy, 765
Suknatsky, W., 808
Sukota, H., 214
Sulatycky, Allen B., 865, 866
Sulatycky, Myroslav, 759
Sulyma, Alex, 94
Suryn, W., 209
Sushko, Dr. Alexander (also O.), 259, 263, 264, 271, 282, 307, 339, 342, 471
Sushko, Olena, 412
Sushko, Col. Roman, 399, 540
Suskind, Walter, 675
Sutkovych, M., 113
Svarich, A., 170, 171, 172
Svarich, Nadia, 445
Svarich, Petro, 15, 106, 113, 142, 144, 167, 169, 170, 171, 172, 223, 235, 136, 237, 263, 310, 324, 331, 339, 397, 662
Svarich, S., 173
Sverstiuk, E., 764
Svitlychny, Ivan, 764
Svityk, John P., 607
Sviy, M., 211
Svoboda, D. M., 235
Swedish, 79
Swyripa, Frances, 737
Swystun, John W. (also V. J.), 581, 733, 734, 814
Swystun, M., 216
Swystun, Olha, 413
Swystun, Walter, see Swystun, Wasyl

Swystun, Wasyl, 138, 155, 156, 157, 369, 396, 397, 443, 606
Sycora, Michael, 26
Sydor, T., 598
Sydorenko, H., 210, 332
Sydorenko, Petro, 671
Sylenko, Lev, see Orlyhora, L.
Symchych, I., 420
Symchych, Maria, 416
Symchych, Victoria, 814
Syniawska, Nina, 641
Synio-Verholec, M., see Semanciw, M.
Syrnick, John H., 392, 422, 479, 606, 633, 653, 702, 714, 770, 814, 871
Syroidiw, Mykola (also N.), 230, 262, 270
Syroishka, A., 176, 235
Syroishka, O., 175
Syrotiuk, John, 177
Syrotiuk, Wasyl, 179
Syrotiuk, Yurko (also F.), 177, 179, 124, 485
Syrotynsky, Rev. I., 822
Sysak, Julia (Juliette), 676, 694
Sysak, W., 864
Sysak, Yakiw, 209
Sytnyk, Evhenia, 414, 415, 417, 446, 524, 547, 601, 606, 871
Sytnyk, Julian (also Yulian), 262, 263, 323
Sytnyk, Wasyl, 703, 769, 855
Syvak, S., 478
Sywanyk, Yaroslav, 822
Szafraniuk, Mykhaylo, 762
Szafraniuk, Yaroslava, 762
Szewczyk, Michael F., 701, 778
Szuch, Anhelyna, 769
Szuch, Lubomyr, 769
Tacher, Rev. K., 107, 109
Taciuk, D., 175
Taciuk, L., 391
Tahayiw, Hanna, 677, 772, 778
Tahayiw, Mykhaylo, 677, 778
Talpash, Orest, 735, 782, 813
Tanchak, J., 686, 690
Tanchak, Maria, 15, 58
Tanchak, Wasyl, 58
Tarasiuk, Rev. I., 648, 824
Tarasiuk, L., 592
Tarnovecka, A. O., 415, 417, 606
Tarnowecka, Nina, 772
Tarnawecky, E., 401, 567
Tarnawecky, Dr. Iraida, 627, 740
Tarnawecky, Prof. Michael, 660
Tarnawsky, Rev. B., 822

Tarnawsky, O., 764
Tarnopolsky, Prof. Walter, 661, 696, 729, 730, 735, 736, 737, 812, 813, 832
Tarnowych, Julian Beskyd, 634, 697
Tatarniuk, M., 753
Tatomyr, I., 582
Tatryn, L., 810
Telenko, I., 210
Telychko, O., 780
Telishevsky, Zenon, 454
Telizyn, Omelian, 673, 761
Temertey, Lydmyla, 673, 757
Temnyk, Christine, 772
Temnyk, J., 582, 703, 808
Ternenko, Pavlo, Pseud. of Krat, Pavlo
Ternopilsky, W., Pseud. of Kudryk, Wasyl
Teodorovich, Metropolitan Ivan, 465, 466, 506
Teodorowycz, E., 462
Teron, William, 860, 861
Tertychny, Rev. I., 217
Tesla, Prof. I., 66, 597, 662, 740, 825, 857
Tesluk, P., 163
Thompson, E. W., 299, 535
Thompson, Sir John, 69
Thompson, Robert, 492
Thornton, Hon. R. G., 147
Tkachenko, A., 592
Tkachenko, Tetiana, 773
Tkachuk, M., 210, 413
Tkachuk, Maria, 826
Tkachuk, N. D., 272
Tkachuk, Olenka, 678
Tokarek, A., 413, 622
Tolstoi, Leo, 280, 303
Tomashchuk, L., 607, 738
Tomashevsky, I., 172
Tomashevsky, Toma, 15, 106, 168, 171, 180, 225, 227, 233, 272, 276, 369, 397, 429, 485, 486, 489, 642, 662
Tomchyshyn, M., 814
Tomowych, Rev. W., 360
Tomych, J., 656
Tomyn, William, 437, 521, 626, 687, 688
Topolnisky, George, 850, 862
Topolnycki, A., 429, 703
Topolnycky, William (also Wasyl), 401, 509, 702, 852, 871
Topornicki, Ed., 735, 812
Topushchak, J. (also Tovpushchak), 142, 403
Trach, I., 421, 422
Trafenenko, Nestor, 777

Trepet, P., 637
Trojan, Dr. O., 858, 859, 860
Trotsky (also Trocky), Leon, 497
Trublak, M., 168
Truch (also Trukh), Rev. A. J., 462, 488, 533, 668
Trudeau, Prime Minister Pierre, E., 725, 867
Troyan, A., 762
Troyan, K., 214
Trylowsky, Dr. Kyrylo, 254, 472, 493, 501
Trynchy, Peter, 863, 867
Tuchtie, Ivan, 209, 257
Tuchtie, St., 209
Tuchtie, Walter, 709
Tulevitriv, Victor, Pseud. of Lysenko, Victor, 530
Tupper, Sir Charles, 30, 32, 69, 70, 71, 260
Turchyn, M., 375
Turek, V., 474
Turkewych, Christine, 772
Turko, R., 598
Turkewycz-Martynec, Iryna, 677, 693
Turkewycz, Lev, 593, 675
Turula, Prof. Eugene, 365, 382, 384, 444, 454, 456, 457
Tuskey, W. A., 710
Tutecky, J., 859
Tychkowska, Maria, 168
Tychkowsky, M., 24, 35, 40
Tyktor, Ivan, 537, 598, 641, 695
Tymciw, S., 824
Tymchuk, H., 106
Tymchuk, P., 172
Tymiak, S. Michael, 850
Tymkevych, Rev. P., 96, 102, 103, 151, 163, 239
Tymochko, Rev. Ivan, 105
Tymochko, Jos., 153
Tymoshenko, V., 816
Tymyc, Bohdan, 769, 775, 777
Tys-Krochmaluk, Yuriy, 764
Tysiak, Wasyl, 676
Tyzuk, H., 418, 871
Tzurkan, A. M., 216
Tzymbal, P., 179
Udod, Rev. Hryhory, 781, 823, 830, 847
Uhryn, Zenovia, 411
Uhryniuk, J., 411
Uhryniuk, Peter, 386, 455
Uhryniuk, U., 176
Uhryniwna, Eugenia, 412
Ukrainec, Anastasia, 414

Ukrainetz, Ivan, 212
Urchak, Stephen, 16
Uruski, Bill, 862, 863, 867
Uskiw, Samuel, 690, 863, 864, 867
Ustvolsky, Stefan, see Bishop Serafim
Vakhnianyn, I., 639
Valiysky, A., 637
Valko, Ivan, 765
Van Bisen, A. J., 464
Van de Bosch, L., 153
Van Horn, W., 76
Varanycia (also Waranycia), I., 604, 635
Varanycia, N., 604
Varkholyk, Alexander, 41
Vasiuk, Lesia, 807
Vasyk, Volodymyr, 656
Vasylenko, Vira, 765
Vasylevych, Rev. T., 215
Vasylyshyn, Ben, 766
Vavryk, Bernardeta, 587
Vavryniuk, Joseph, 155
Venger, M., 237
Vepruk, Claudia, 209
Vepruk (also Vypruk), I., 209, 251, 284, 385
Vepruk (also Vypruk), Yakiw, 209, 284, 385, 454
Verbowy, Rev. S. D., 483, 493
Verchomin, Dr. I., 507, 607
Veretelnyk, Yuriy, 748, 770
Vernyvola, Mstyslav, Pseud. of Luciw, Vasyl
Vertyporoch, Dr. Evhen, 658, 695, 740, 822
Vertyporoch, L., 604
Veryha, Wasyl, see Weryha, Wasyl
Vilchynsky, Rev. A., see Wilchynsky, Rev. A.
Vilk, J., 655
Vindyk, Severyn, 455
Virun, D., 216
Vivchar, Wasyl, 106, 339
Voliansky, Rev. I., 238
Volion, Linda, 777
Volokhatiuk, Taras, 530
Voloshyn, Ted, 774, 810
Voloschuk, Dmytro, 284
Volsky, T., 141
Volynec, M., Pseud. of Shatulsky, Matviy, see Wolynec, M.
Volyniak, Petro, 603, 635, 665, 666, 702
Vorobetz, A., 113
Vorobetz, H., 173, 175
Vorobetz, M., 172
Vorobetz, V., 172

Vorobkevych, I., 504
Voronenko, Pseud. of Babiuk, Andriy
Vorsklo, Vera, 765
Vovk, D., 118
Vovk, M., 214
Voyevidka, W., 172
Vrublevska, Sister Taida, 104
Vydymovych, Dmytro, 34
Vyniavsky, A., 606
Vyniavsky, W., 215
Vynnychuk, H., 170
Vynohradova, Maria, 496
Vyshnia, O., 494, 496
Wach, A., 419, 606, 641, 699
Wach, Cathy, 804
Wach, P., 505, 606
Wachna, Anna, 871
Wachna, Dr. Elias, 655
Wachna, I., 427
Wachna, Theodosius, 41, 236, 339
Wachniak, I., 427, 703
Wagner, Peter, 686
Waldstein, Col. S., 598
Walker, Samson, 222
Wall, L., 415
Wall, Senator William (also Wasyl), 420, 444, 482, 689, 708, 709
Wallace, L., 306
Waplak, I., 811
Washchuk, Roman, 770, 818
Wasik, Volodymyr (also Walter), 784
Waskan, S., 487
Wasylewych, T., see Vasylevych, Rev. T.
Wasyliw, Rev. W., 828
Wasylyshyn, A., 416
Wasylyshyn, E., 366, 398, 509, 527, 567, 597, 606, 734, 871
Wasylyshyn, S., see Wasylyshyn, E.
Wawryk, V., 644
Wawrykow, J., 435, 521
Wawrykow, Judge Mary, 415, 416, 444, 606, 681, 691, 709, 710
Weir, J., 649, 650
Welhash, Irena (Irka), 773, 776, 803
Welyhorsky-Senkiw, 757
Werbeniuk, W., 737
Weretelnyk, Yuriy, 832
Weryha, W., 599, 637, 740, 752, 762, 848
Wesolowsky, J. B. (also Bohdan), 655, 675
Whitlaw, R. J., 116
Whyte, Wm., 116
Wicinski, Mary, 333
Wiebe, H. D., 627
Wilchynsky, Rev. A., 158, 176, 277, 339

Williams, Olha, 813
Wilson, H. G., 492
Wilton, Capt. Geo., 375
Wiwchar, Wm., 263
Wizniuk, Rev. Joseph, 504
Wizniuk, M., 277
Wiznovych, Dm., 24
Wlasowsky, Prof. Ivan, 661
Woitkiw, G., 687
Wolodin, E., 233
Wolodyshynska, Z., 214
Woloshynsky, P., 214
Wolynec (also Volynets), M., 404, 495, 534
Wolynec, S., 15, 598, 633, 653, 669, 674, 702, 759
Wood, W. R. 375
Woodsworth, J. S., 78, 86, 87, 156, 479, 830
Worobec, M., 606
Worobec, P. J., 445
Woroby, Prof. Peter, 696
Woycenko, Olha, 413, 416, 417, 567, 606, 641, 662, 669, 674, 699
Woychenko, P. H., 258, 331, 333, 342, 443
Woytkiw, George, 437
Woytkiw, Kateryna, 416
Woytowych, K., 462
Wozny, M., 384
Wright, W., 558
Wrzesnewskyj, R., 762, 815
Wynarsky, Rev. W., 109
Wynnycka, Iroida, 752, 832
Wynnycky, O. K., 703, 856
Wytwycky, V., 773
Yablonsky, M., 860
Yacenty (also Jatsenty), I., 468, 606, 612, 714
Yachnitsky, M., see Yakhnitsky, M.
Yaciw, B., 816
Yacula, William Val., 689, 707, 708
Yacyk, M., 374
Yacyk, Vera, 757
Yakhnitsky, M., 168, 169, 170
Yakimischak, Anna, 415, 416
Yakimischak, D., 113, 137, 235, 258, 331, 398, 420, 427, 434, 435, 479
Yakimischak, Dr. I., 235
Yakovkevych, Bishop Borys, 589, 611
Yakubovsky, P., 213
Yakubovych, E., 210
Yamniuk, S., 822
Yanda, Daria (also Dorothy), 412, 413, 507, 533, 607

Yanishevsky, E., 171
Yanishevsky, Capt. I., 598
Yankovsky, A., 25
Yarema, Dmytro, 289
Yarema, S., 394
Yaremchuk, Dr. F. L., 807
Yaremenko, S., 619, 675, 676, 765, 776, 778, 779
Yaremiy, D., 106
Yaremiy, Dr. W. J., 391, 511
Yaremiychuk, M., 490
Yaremko, D., 143, 275
Yaremko, John, 684, 689, 706, 865
Yaremovich, A. J., 16, 567, 595, 605, 729, 731, 811, 817, 849
Yarmoniuk, Luka, 168
Yarmus, Rev. S., 740, 823
Yaroshevych-Manko, Hryhoriy, 676, 677, 693
Yarychewsky, S., 118
Yasenchuk, Jos., 143, 303, 607
Yasenchuk, T., 168
Yashan, W., 582, 703
Yatchew, Dr. John (also Ivan), 420, 425, 526, 444, 482, 492, 523, 533
Yatsyk, N., 475
Yavorsky, W., 599
Yaworsky, Alexander, 653, 700
Yefremov, Serhiy, 285
Yereniuk, Otto, 807
Yermiy, Rev. K., 109, 210, 212, 213, 215, 216
Yewchuk, Dr. Paul, 865
Yonker, Anna, 255, 333, 374, 411, 545
Yonker, Dr. Henry, 374
Yopyk, H., 828, 849
Young, Mayor, 156
Young, School Inspector, 146
Young, Charles H., 64, 65, 86, 87, 116
Yukas, M., 495
Yundak, P., 454
Yurchak, I., 215
Yurchuk, N., 859
Yurchuk, Vera, 757
Yurchyk, Andriy, 411
Yurechkiw, M., 492
Yurechkiw, T., 214
Yuremiychuk, J., 226
Urkiwsky, Rev. M., 739
Urkiwsky, Stefania, 747
Yuriychuk, M., 210
Yuzkiw, I., 170
Yuzyk, John (also Ivan), 594, 595, 606, 733, 811

Yuzyk, Senator Paul, 15, 419, 431, 433, 581, 596, 606, 627, 642, 662, 681, 689, 709, 732, 734, 762, 808, 813, 819, 830, 831, 857, 867
Zabroda, I., 209
Zadorozny, Andrij, 671, 673
Zadorozny, S., 410
Zahara, Vasyl (also William), 39, 57
Zahara, Vasylyna, 57
Zaharia, Dan (also Danylo), 581, 710
Zaharychuk, Andrew, 16, 153, 274, 365, 381, 394, 446, 447, 470, 471, 475, 481, 483, 495, 511, 526, 567, 606, 640
Zahoroda, O., 598
Zailo, A., 338
Zaitsew, Rev. N., 123, 174
Zajcew, Bohdan, 769, 780
Zakaluzny, Mike, 776
Zakharkevych, W., 822
Zakharkiw, J., 164
Zakharuk, Dmytro, 533
Zaklynsky, Rev. Ivan, 103, 173, 213, 239, 271
Zalesky, Rev. Dr. M., 628, 661
Zalesky, Thadeus (also Tadij), 657
Zalitach, Rev. Myron, 283
Zalizniak, Rev. M., 158
Zalizniak, Olena, 699, 714
Zalozetska, Z., 731
Zalozetsky, Nicholas, 375, 391, 420, 701
Zalucka, Daria, 671, 757
Zalucka, Jaroslava, 676
Zalucky, Wasyl, 672, 760
Zaokipny, M., 480
Zaozirny, John Brian, 863
Zapisocky, Ronald, 644
Zaplitny, Frederick, Samuel, 689, 707
Zaraska, E., 737, 738
Zarovna, A. (correct name — Caroline), 283, 394
Zarowsky, I., 342, 365, 381, 421
Zarsky, Y., 216
Zasiybida, P., 171
Zavadovych, R., 641
Zaverukha, Olha, 810, 811
Zawarykhin, Anna, 678, 778
Zawarykhin, Yaroslav, 765
Zawidowsky, Ivan, 335, 336
Zawislak, Olha, 814
Zayac, Yaroslav, 770, 810
Zayachkivsky, Mykola, 359, 360, 369, 380
Zazula, Wm., 432
Zbitnyak, I., 336

Zborowsky, Ivan, 421
Zelentsky, H., 210
Zelentsky, I., 106
Zeleny, Bohdan, 401, 509, 527, 669
Zelez (also Zeles), Ivan, 408, 494
Zelinska-Babij, Domka, 828
Zelska-Darewych, Daria, 671, 732
Zelsky, I., 822
Zeniuk, S., 495, 649
Zerebecky, George, 747
Zerebko, M., 176, 411
Zerebko, Orest, 167, 234, 258, 307, 323, 339, 340, 403, 436, 447, 549
Zhan, Father J., see Jean, Rev. Josaphat, O.S.B.M.
Zhariy, S., 175
Zholdak (also Zoldak), Rev. Wasyl, 104, 105
Zhovnir-Klos, Stephania, 676, 698
Zhuk, S., 476
Zhuk, Dr. Y., 590
Zhurawecky, Rev. I., 109
Zhydan, J., 462
Zhyhar, O., 603
Zhylych, A., 113
Zinkevych, Osyp, 639
Zipchen, Dmytro, 705
Ziolkowsky, I., 210
Ziubrak (also Zubrak), Lesia, 676, 698

Zmiyiwsky, Dr. W., 823
Zolkewych-Krekhovec, S., 774
Zorych, Yaroslava, 808, 809
Zorych-Kondratska, Kvitka, 774, 787
Zubachek, M., 342
Zubrycky, M., 482
Zuck, Anastasia, 416
Zuk, Ernie, 782
Zuk, Ireneus, 675, 694
Zuk, Luba, 675, 698
Zuk, Prof. Radoslaw, 452, 704
Zukowsky, J., 455
Zulak, Rev. S., 823
Zulak, W., 776
Zulkowsky, K., 216
Zurawsky, E., 816
Zuyewsky, Oleh, 763, 764
Zuzenkiv, S., 210
Zvarych, I., 214
Zvarych, Peter, see Svarich, Peter
Zwarych, Zenon, 769, 770
Zwonets, O., 534
Zwozdecka, Anna, 807
Zwozdecky, E., 775, 804
Zydan, Rev. V., 369
Zyla, T., 210
Zyla, Dr. W. T., 659
Zylych, A., 41, 268

Churches, Parishes, Church Organizations

Anglican Church, 591, 718, 719
Association for the Propagation of Faith in Toronto, 110
Association of Ruthenian Church Parishes of U.S.A. and Canada, 104
Association of the Bible Students, Winnipeg, 648
Association of Ukrainian and Russian Baptists of Western Canada, 483
Association of United Sons of Ukraine (also Native Ukrainian National Faith or R.U.N.V.), 648
Baptist Congregations, 114, 183, 467, 469, 473, 488, 591, 592, 648, 655, 719
Basilian Fathers, 103, 104, 105, 107, 109, 110, 125, 151, 152, 153, 158, 165, 173, 177, 212, 270, 317, 403, 461, 464, 488, 583, 587 605, 638, 644
Basilian Fathers' Chapel-Church, Mandare, 62
Benefit Fraternity of John the Merciful, 167

Blessed Virgin Mary Parish Choir, 776
Brotherhood Benefit, Michelle, 179
Brotherhood Benefit Association of St. Peter and Paul, 168
Brotherhood Benefit of the Feast of Transfiguration, 165
Brotherhood of Holy Trinity, 289
Brotherhood of St. John the Baptist, Brantford, 215
Brotherhood of St. John the Baptist, Toronto, 214
Brotherhood of St. John the Baptist, Choral Singers, 214
Brotherhood of St. John the Merciful, 316, 483
Brotherhood of St. Michael the Angel, Toronto, 214
Brotherhood of Youth, St. Nicholas Parish, Winnipeg, 136
Canadian Ukrainian Catholic Students' Organization Gamma Rho Kappa "Obnova", 600, 645

Catholic Extension Society, Toronto, 153
Christian Brothers, 110, 153, 403, 447, 586, 597, 630
Church of Holy Ghost, Beausejour, 673
Church of Holy Ghost, Copper Cliff, 215
Church of Holy Ghost, Hamilton, 215
Church of Holy Ghost, Montreal, 672
Church of Holy Ghost, Winnipeg, 645
Church of Holy Ghost (Roman Catholic), Winnipeg, 103, 222
Church of Holy Mother, Jaroslaw, 221
Church of Holy Trinity (Cathedral), Winnipeg, 646
Church of Immaculate Conception, Winnipeg, 26
Church of the Assumption, Fort William, 212
Church of the Assumption, Jaroslaw (near Yorkton), 129
Church of the Blessed Virgin Mary (Greek Orthodox), Montreal, 646
Church of the Blessed Virgin Mary, Winnipeg, 645, 673
Church of St. George (Cathedral), Saskatoon, 645
Church of St. George the Martyr, Oshawa, 115
Church of St. John the Baptist, Brantford, 215
Church of St. Josaphat (Cathedral), Edmonton, 130, 168, 645
Church of St. Josaphat (Cathedral), Toronto, 137, 214, 490, 630, 645
Church of St. Mary, Port Arthur, 645
Church of St. Michael, Gardenton, 128
Church of St. Michael, Montreal, 330
Church of St. Michael, Volkivtsi — Mink River,
Church of St. Nicholas, Toronto, 645
Church of St. Nicholas, Winnipeg, 103, 152, 165, 411, 454
Church of St. Trinity, Stuartburn, 663
Church of St. Vladimir, Hamilton, 646
Church of St. Vladimir (Sobor-Cathedral), Toronto, 646, 672
Church of St. Vladimir and Olga, (Cathedral), Winnipeg, 107, 108, 109, 128, 154, 165, 216, 282, 317, 454, 484, 645, 673, 674
Church of Transfiguration, Kitchener, 215
Chytalnia of Ukrainian Catholic Parish, Ukraina, 200
Chytalnia of St. Vladimir and Olga, Fernie, 178
Committee for the Protection of Rites and Traditions of the Ukrainian Catholic Church in Canada, 645
Congress of Ukrainian Catholic Priests in Yorkton (Soborchyk), 110, 132
Dawn Bible Student Association, 483
Dukhobors, 17, 68, 80, 305
Eastern Congregation, Vatican, 585
Eucharist Congress, 210, 342
First Provincial Synod, Ukrainian Catholic Church, 589
First Convention (formative) of Ukrainian Greek Orthodox Church, 338
Greek Independent Church, see Independent Greek Church
Holy Congregation for the Propagation of Faith, Rome, 99, 104
Holy Family Home, Regina, 463
Holy Trinity Brotherhood, 165
Holy Trinity Women's Organization, 164
Home of Sister Servants, Ituna, 463
Home of Sister Servants, Saskatoon, 463
Hutterites, 17
Immaculate Conception Church, Winnipeg, 26
Ilinska Church, Chernyhiv, 453
Independent Greek Church in Canada, 105, 108, 110, 112, 115, 117, 126, 131, 138, 139, 158, 159, 163, 164, 166, 169, 173, 174, 223, 261, 267, 275, 305, 309, 312, 317, 338, 373, 424, 460, 461, 467, 469, 473, 493, 536, 591, 592, 648
Independent Ukrainian Evangelical Church, 591
Judaists, 719
Knights of Columbus of St. Josaphat, 645
Lutheran Church, 591, 718, 719
Mennonites, 17, 24, 25, 35, 40, 68, 88, 147, 283, 304, 718
Methodist Church, 275, 311, 314, 467, 473, 591
Missionary Sisters, Edmonton, 585, 586
Missionary Sisters of Christian Charity, 587, 631
Mutual Benefit Association of St. Nicholas, 421, 422
National Council for the Patriarchate of the Ukrainian Catholic Church, 822
Oblate Fathers, 103, 104, 462, 464, 587
Orthodox Mutual Benefit Assoction, 240

Orthodox Mutual Benefit Assocation, U.S.A., 240
Pentecostal Church, 591, 592, 718, 719
Piatnycka Church, Chernyhiv, 453
Presbyterian Church, 710, 718
Professional Section of Ukrainian Catholic Women's League, 581
Quakers, 17
Redemptorist Fathers, 107, 110, 127, 153, 210, 270, 317, 461, 464, 488, 489, 586, 587, 588, 605, 630, 644
Roman Catholic Church, 36, 38, 99, 100, 110, 152, 168, 172, 213, 317, 436, 588, 589, 718, 719
Russian Orthodox Church, 99, 111, 288, 293, 317, 466, 467, 493, 494, 590
Russian Orthodox Mission, 102, 103, 106, 111, 112, 165, 166, 240, 270, 271, 288, 289, 292, 293, 294, 312, 317
Russo-Greek Orthodox Brotherhood of St. Yov of Pochayiv, Winnipeg, 483
Russian Orthodox Church of Holy Trinity, Winnipeg, 112, 293
Russian Orthodox Enlightenment Association, 493
Ruthenian Benevolent Brotherhood of St. Nicholas, see Ukrainian Mutual Benefit Association of St. Nicholas
Ruthenian Greek Catholic Church of Canada, see Ukrainian Catholic Church
Ruthenian Church Brotherhood of St. Nicholas of Edna-Star, 162
Seminary of St. Augustine (also St. Augustus), 110, 132
Seventh Day Adventists, 592
Sisterhood of Holy Family in Ottawa, 136
Sisterhood of Virgin Mary, Toronto, 214
Sister Servants, 104, 110, 151-153, 447, 462, 463, 585, 586, 630, 631, 644
Sister Servants Old Folks' Home, Komarno, 463
Sister Servants St. Anthony Home, Portage la Prairie, 463
Sister Servants St. Rita's Home, Toronto, 463
Sisters of the Faithful Companions of Jesus, Edmonton, 151
Sobor of St. John Suchavsky, Winnipeg, 590
Sobor of St. Sophia, Kiev, 453
St. Andrew's College, 738
St. Andrew's Parish, Point Douglas, 483

St. Cyril and Methodius Association, Ottawa, 213
St. George's Cathedral, Lviv, 453
St. Josaphat's Monastery, Edmonton, 463, 585
St. Joseph's Oratory, Montreal, 672
St. Michael's Sobor, 453
St. Nicholas Church (so called "Big Church"), Winnipeg, 152
St. Nicholas Choir, 776
St. Nicholas School, Winnipeg, 153
St. Olga's Girls Association, 164
St. Olga's Girls Society, 411
St. Peter and Paul Mutual Aid Society, 166
St. Raphael's Association, Lviv, 109, 361
St. Sophia Foundation, 828
St. Sophia "Religious Association of Ukrainian Catholics in Canada, see St. Sophia Foundation
St. Vladimir and Olga Reading Hall, Fernie, 178
St. Vladimir Ukrainian Catholic Museum, 826
Students' Dramatic Group of Metropolitan A. Shepticky, 201
Studite Brothers, 587
Ukrainian Catholic Brotherhood (B.U.K.), 401-407, 415, 419, 426, 489, 532, 546, 548, 549, 552, 595, 602, 605, 607, 631, 643, 680, 806
Ukrainian Catholic Church in Canada, 36, 99, 100-114, 126, 127, 153, 155, 158, 165, 166, 171, 172, 193, 261, 262, 270, 271, 302, 312, 317, 322, 323, 336, 342-344, 373, 374, 393, 394, 397, 415, 424, 436, 447, 451, 460, 461, 465, 467, 470, 471, 486, 544, 549, 551, 585-589, 591, 599, 605, 629, 631, 543-645, 656, 718, 719, 727, 820, 821, 822
Ukrainian Catholic Church in Ukraine, 588
Ukrainian Catholic Church of St. Peter and Paul, Mundare, 131
Ukrainian Catholic Council, 563
Ukrainian Catholic Professional and Businessmen's Club, Saskatoon, 581
Ukrainian Catholic Theological Seminary, 739
Ukrainian Catholic Women's League (U.C.W.L.), 415, 416, 419, 489, 601, 602, 643, 806
Ukrainian Catholic Women's League Museums, 416

Ukrainian Catholic Youth (U.C.Y.), 419,
480, 489, 599, 600, 602, 642, 643, 645,
806
Ukrainian Evangelical Alliance, 468, 469,
544, 591, 602, 647, 655, 824
Ukrainian Evangelical Baptist Alliance,
592, 824
Ukrainian Evangelical Church, 591, 824
Ukrainian Greek Catholic Society of M.
Shashkevych, Edmonton, 138
Ukrainian Greek Orthodox Church in
Arbakka, 130
Ukrainian Greek Orthodox Church in
Canada, 99, 101, 103, 108, 112-114,
157, 262, 270, 275, 293, 317, 337, 344,
373, 374, 393, 395, 396, 397, 424, 436,
447, 451, 460, 461, 465, 467, 470, 472,
530, 544, 547-549, 585, 589, 590, 591,
599, 605, 629, 632, 637, 646, 657, 658,
718, 719, 822, 823, 824
Ukrainian Greek Orthodox Brotherhood, 113, 157

Ukrainian Greek Orthodox Students
Organization "Ilarion", 144, 600
Ukrainian Mission and Bible Society,
Saskatoon, 648
Ukrainian Mutual Benefit Association of
St. Nicholas (also called St. Nicholas
Brotherhood) of Canada, 164, 165,
316, 546
Ukrainian Orthodox Church in Ukraine,
464
Ukrainian Orthodox Sobor, 646
United Church, 467, 468, 469, 473, 591,
592, 647, 719
Uspenska Church, Halych, 453
Uspensky Sobor, Kaniv, 453
Vatican, 344, 460, 461, 646
Volkivtsi Church, 49
World's Federation of Catholic
Organizations, 416

Lay Organizations and Co-operatives

Air Cadet Squadron, 595
Alliance of Ukrainian Organizations,
408
Alpha Omega Students Assocation,
Saskatoon, 420
Alpha Omega Women's Alumni, 679
American Association of Cereal
Chemists, 660
Anti-Bolshevik Bloc of Nations A.B.N.,
604, 811
"Apollo" School of Dancing, Toronto,
678
Ardan "Prosvita" Reading Hall,
Pleasant Home, 166, 167, 429
Arran Credit Union, 430
Art Movement Studio, 678
Artists Association of Western Ukraine,
672
Associated Country Women of the
World, 413, 415
Association de Ukrainianos en
Venezuela, 714
Association for the Aid of the Liberation
Movement in Western Ukraine
(TODOWYRNAZU), 497
Association for Writers of Children's
Literature, 741

Association in Aid of the Freedom
Movement in the Western Ukraine,
406
Association in Care of Settlers, 209
Association of Artists of Ukrainian Stage
(O.M.U.S.), 778
Association of Business Men and
Trademen, 636
Association of Canadian Ruthenian
Farmers, also Ruthenian Farmers
Association, 276, 277, 278
Association of Engineers and Technicians of Canada, 598, 741
Association of Free Press, Toronto, 634
Association of Friends of the U.V.A.N.,
597
Association of Friends of Ukrainian
Culture of Brazil, 712
Association of Kozub, 678
Association of Russian Brotherhood, 240
Association of Ruthenian Farmers in
Canada, 175, 276, 277
Association of School Trustees of
Saskatchewan, 156
Association of Ukrainian Bukovinians in
Canada and U.S.A., 482
Association of Ukrainian Business and
Professional Men of Toronto, 428

Association of Ukrainian Canadian Veterinary Doctors, 598, 741
Association of Ukrainian Cooperators of New York, 584
Association of Ukrainian Cultural Workers (A.U.C.W. - ADUK), 764
Association of Ukrainian Engineers and Associates in Canada, 860
Association of Ukrainian Journalists of Canada, 598, 653, 770, 771
Association of Ukrainian Jurists, 598
Association of Ukrainian Librarians in Canada, 598, 741
Association of Ukrainian Musicians, 778
Association of Ukrainian Pedagogues, 638
Association of Ukrainian Social Workers of Canada, 598
Association of Ukrainian Students Organization of U.S.A., 601
Association of Ukrainian Teachers of Canada, 444
Association of Ukrainian Workers and Farmers Home, 405
Association of Ukrainian Writers and Journalists in Canada, 538
Association of Ukrainian Writers "Slovo", 763
Association of Ukrainians in Great Britain, 714
Association of Ukrainians in Montreal, 209
Association of United Ukrainian Canadians (A.U.U.C.), 422, 564, 608, 630, 650
Association of Writers of Children's Literature, 597, 636, 638
Ballet of Petro Manunczak, 775
Banderivtsi (also Revolutionaries), 560
Bandurist Band, Winnipeg, 205
Bandurist Choir, 776
Bandurist Ensemble "Kobzari", 775
Barvinok Choir, 776
Basarab Branch of U.W.V.A., 400, 413
Baturyn, Orchestra
"Besida" Society, 167
Canada Council, 710
Canadian Broadcasting Corporation, 656, 709
National Film Board, 710
"Borot'ba" Society, Vancouver, 179
"Boyan" Choir, 774
"Boyan" Choral Group, Winnipeg, 194, 376, 454

"Boyan" Singing Dramatic Group, Edmonton, 169, 171, 202, 454
"Boyan" Society, Montreal, 210
"Boyan" Society, Winnipeg, 167, 194, 376
Brotherhood of Carpathian Sitch, 598
Brotherhood of Former Combatants U.D. U.N.A., 598
Buduchnist Credit Union, Toronto, 582
Burlaka Choir, 774
Canada Choir of E. Turula, 454
Canada's National Ukrainian Festival Choir, 776
Canadian Authors Association, 669
Canadian Broadcasting Corporation, 530, 654, 655, 727
Canadian Communist Party, 408
Canadian Ethnic Press Club Association, Canada, 653
Canadian Ethnic Press Association, Ontario, 653
Canadian Ethnic Press Club, Winnipeg, 653
Canadian Federation of Mayors, 681
Canadian Folk Arts Council, 710
Canadin Foundation for the Ukrainian Free University, 828
Canadian Foundation for Ukrainian Studies, 735, 736
Canadian Institute of Onomastic Sciences, 659
Canadian Institute of Ukrainian Studies, 735, 736
Canadian League for the Liberation of Ukraine, 809, 810, 811
Canadian Legion, Ukrainian Branch, 595
Canadian Library of Ivan Bobersky, 368
Canadian Linguistic Association of Canada, 659
Canadian National Ukrainian Festival in Dauphin, 778
Canadian Patriotic Fund, 327
Canadian "Prosvita" Reading Room, 120, 162
Canadian Relief Mission to Ukrainian Refugees, 566
Canadian Ruthenian Aid Committee, 316
Canadian Ruthenian National Association, 168, 421
Canadian Ruthenian National Association, Bankhead, 172
Canadian Ruthenian National Association, Calgary, 172

INDEX 925

Canadian Ruthenian National Association, Winnipeg, 164
Canadian Ruthenian Reading Hall, Beaver Hills, 174
Canadian Ruthenian Prosvita Reading Hall, Portage la Prairie, 166
Canadian Sitch Organization, 328, 329, 330, 331, 368, 393, 394, 395, 455, 470, 492, 493, 501, 544, 567, 598
Canadian Socialist Federation, 225
Canadian Star Reading Hall, Winnipeg, 164
Canadian Ukrainian Immigrant Aid Society, 816
Canadian Ukrainian Opera Association, 773
Canadian Ukrainian "Rus" Chytalnia, St. Isidore de Bellevue, 174
Canadian Ukrainian Prosvita Institute, 167, 422, 423, 455
Canadian Ukrainian Youth Association (S.U.M.K.), 396, 418, 471, 532, 599, 600
Canadian Workers' Defensive League, 408
Canadian Library, 368
Caravan Festival, 778
CARE (Cooperative for American Relief Everywhere), 565
Care of Settlers and Aid to Homeland Society, 209
Care of Settlers Society in Montreal, 209, 418
Carpathia Credit Union, Winnipeg, 430, 583, 642
Central Committee for Aid to Ukraine, Chicago, 333
Central Committee of the Federation of Ukrainians of Eastern Canada, 490
Central Committee of Ukrainian National Council, Winnipeg, 336, 337
Central Representation of the Ukrainian Community in Argentina, 712
Central Representation of the Ukrainian Community in Paraguay, 712
Central Representation of the Ukrainian Community in Uruguay, 712
Central Representation of Ukrainian Emigration in Germany, 714
Centre for Ukrainian Canadian Studies, 738
Chayka Dance Ensemble Group, Hamilton, 677, 775
Cheremshyna, SUMK Dancers, 776
Chytalnia of Drahomaniw, 196

Chytalnia Progress, Oakburn, 166, 167
Chytalnia Prosvita, Winnipeg, see Prosvita Reading Hall, Winnipeg
Comite Ucraino Brasileiro, 714
Committee for Aid to Ukrainian Immigrants, Toronto, 329
Committee in Aid of the Ukrainian Flood Victims in Galicia and Bukovina, 544
Committee of Political Prisoners, 497
Committee of Ukrainians of Eastern Canada, 211
Cooperative Community (Kooperatyvna Hromada), 584
Coordinating Committee of Credit Cooperatives, Toronto, 584
Coordinating Council of Ukrainian Organizations in Austria, 714
Council of Seven, 233, 322
Council of Ukrainian Women, Winnipeg, 417
Cross of Freedom Corporation, 778
Danylo Lobay Foundation, 680
Dibrova, Women's Choir, 774
Dnister Cooperative Bank, Lviv, 360
Dnipro Choir, Edmonton, 675
Dnipro Choir, Sudbury, 775
Dnipro Credit Union, Winnipeg, 583
Dnipro, Dance Ensemble Group, 678
Dominion Federation of Teachers, 453
Doughters of Ukraine, 413
Dovbush, Hutsul Orchestra, 774
Drahomaniw Reading Hall, Arbaka, 167
Drahomaniw Reading Hall, Tolstoi, 167
Drahomaniw Society, Montreal, 150, 196, 209, 284, 423, 454
Dramatic Group of M. Zankovetska, also M. Zankovetska Association, 167, 194, 376, 454
Dramatic Group, Vegreville, 197, 201
Dramatic Society of Ivan Kotlarevsky, 195, 454
Dramatic Society of M. Kropywnytsky, 167
Dramatic Society
Dzwin Band, Montreal, 196
Educational Association of Ivan Franko, 167
Educational-Economic Congress of Ukrainian Canadians, 471
Educational Farmers Conference, 426
Emigration Relief Committee, Lviv, 33, 35, 36
"Evshan" Dance Ensemble Group, 677

Farmers Educational Convention of Saskatchewan, 365
Farmers Freedom Society in Saskatchewan, 277
Farmers' Will in Fish Creek, Sask., 277
Federation of Russian Brotherhood, 240
Federation of the Canadian-Ukrainian Youth, 408
Federation of Ukrainian Associations in Australia, 714
Federation of Ukrainian Canadian Farmers, 225
Federation of Ukrainian Professional and Businessmen's Clubs of Canada, 580, 581, 642
Federation of Ukrainian Social Democrats, 225, 226, 266, 272
Federation of Ukrainian Social Democrats of Canada, 225
Federation of Ukrainian Socialists, 272
Federation of Ukrainian Worker-Farmer Organization, 408
Federation of Ukrainians in the U.S.A., 158
First Council of the "P.A.U.K.", 712
First General Convention of Ukrainian Delegates in Manitoba, 341
First General Convention of Ukrainians in Canada, 338
First Informative Economic Congress, 426
First Ukrainian Business Conference of Alberta, 426
First Ukrainian Educational Economic Congress, 369, 376, 393
Fisher Branch Cooperative, 429
Folklorama Festival, 778
Foundation of Alexander and Tetiana Koshetz, 680
Fourth Universal, 357
Franko National Library, 163, 164
Franko Prosvita Reading Hall, Montreal, 210
Franko Prosvita Reading Hall, West Ft. William, 212, 218
Franko Prosvita Society, Portage la Prairie, 167
Franko Reading Hall, Rossburn, 167
Franko Reading Hall, Vostok, 172
Franko Society, Edmonton, 169
Freedom Fighters of Ukraine, 398
"Free School" Society, 167
Friends of the Ukrainian Economic Academy in Podiebrady, 541

"Front Fund" (also called Peasant Fund), 321
Fund for the Galician Orphan Johnny, 335, 336
Fund for Widow and Orphans of Marko Kahanetz (also Kahanec), 321
Gallery Bloor, Toronto, 678
Gallery Young, Toronto, 678
General Assembly of the United Nations (Birth of U.N.), 711
Geneva Conference, 345, 359, 362
Grain Research Laboratories of Grain Commissionary, 661
Hanna Barwinok Society, Vonda, 413
Hart, Literary Organization, 534
Help for the Old Country, 544
Higher Musical Institute of Lysenko, Lviv, 675
Historical and Scientific Society of Manitoba, 310
Historical Museum of National Liberation, 598
Holy Family Home for the Aged, 581
Home for the Ukrainian Invalids, Lviv, 399
Hetman Mazeppa Credit Union, Montreal, 582
Hoosli, Ensemble, 776
Independent Ukraine Association, 330, 331
Independent Ukraine Association "Sitch", 329
Independent Ukraine Organization, 329
Information Bureau of Ukrainian Teachers in Canada, 191
International Congress of the League of Parliaments, 439
International Film Festival, 656
International Peace Conference, 292
I.R.O. (International Refugee Organization), 565, 566, 570
Ivan Franko Men's Choir, 777
Jasmin Women's Choir, 774
Jastremsky Hall, 164
Jubilee Convention of Ukrainian War Veterans Association, Saskatoon, 540
Kahanetz Reading Hall, Roblin, 167
Kapella of Bandurists, 774
Kashtany Choir, 775
Kharkiv State Opera, 542
Kiev Conservatory of Music, 675
Knights of Columbus of St. Josaphat, 645
Kobzar Society of Fort Rouge, 445, 546
Koshetzs Choir, 775

Kotlarevsky Society, 376, 454
Kotsko (Adam) Fund, 321
Kotsko (Adam) Reading Hall, Roblin, 167
"Kozub" Ukrainian Arts Society, 765
Krysa Family, Les J. Foundation, 827
Labour Enlightenment Carpathian Association, 497
Labour Organization "Vola", Portage la Prairie, 167
Labour Temple, Welland, 217
League of British Ukrainians, 410, 411, 481
League of Communist Youth, 408
League of Ukrainian National Homes, 426
Lesia Ukrainka Society, Canmore, 413
Literary Association of Markian Sashkevych, Winnipeg
Mohylanky, Students' Society, Saskatoon, 412, 420
Male Quartet of J. Samotilka, 454
Manitoba Theatre Centre, 674
Marunczak's Dance Ensemble Group, Montreal, 678
Markian Shashkevych Centre, 597, 641, 680
Markian Shashkevych Park, 827
Metropolitan A. Shepticky Club, 645
Metropolitan Andrew Shepticky Society, Winnipeg, 155
Military Historical Museum, 740
Mixed Choir "Carpaty", 777
Morning Star Chytalnia, Dnister, 167
Mosend's Foundation of Toronto, 680
Multi-National Chytalnia, Winnipeg, 163
M.U.N. Choir, Winnipeg, 455
"Muse" Theatrical Group, 772
Musical Institute of M. Lysenko, Toronto, 676
Myroslav Sichynsky Fund, 321
National Convention, 374
National Convention, Saskatoon, 395
National Council, 170, 223
National Council for the Patriarchate, 822
National Home, Lviv, 32
National Home, Montreal, 209
National Home, Port Arthur, 212
National Home, Vegreville, 172
National Organization of Alberta, 273
National Riding and Dancing Cossacks, 776
National Women's Council, 417

New Community Savings and Credit Union (Nova Hromada), Saskatoon, 430, 582, 583
New Star Chytalnia, Brokenhead, 166, 167
North Winnipeg Credit Union, 430, 583, 642
Ontario Multicultural Theatre Association, 772
Organization for the Defence of Lemkiwschyna, 635
Organization for the Defence of Ukraine, 470
Organization of Ukrainian Liberation Front, 811
Organization of Ukrainian Nationalists; see Ukrainian Nationalists Organization
Organization of Ukrainian Teachers, 181
Orlan Ensemble, 775, 776
Our Star Reading Hall, Loon Lake, 167
Overseas Hart, 533, 534
Palitra Group of Creative Artists, 678
Pan-American Ukrainian Conference (P.A.U.K.), 711, 713, 880
Pan-American Games, Winnipeg, 686
Paris Peace Conference, 332, 335, 345, 359, 362
Pavlyk Prosvita Reading Hall, Tolstoi, 166
Pavlyk Prosvita Reading Hall, Vita, 166
People's Progress Reading Hall, Stony Mountain, 166
Plast Friends, 599
Polissia Sitch, 560
Postup (Progress) Credit Union, Winnipeg, 583
Progress Reading Hall, Calgary, 172
Progress Reading Hall, Lethbridge, 171
Progress Reading Hall, Oakburn, 166, 167
"Prometey" Choir, Toronto, 675, 774
Prometheus Foundation, 827
"Prometheus" Students' Club, Winnipeg, 420
Prosvita Association, Kenora, 423
Prosvita Choir of Kenora, 456
Prosvita Library, 445
Prosvita Reading Hall, Brandon, 174
Prosvita Reading Hall, Broad Valley, 167
Prosvita Reading Hall, Buchanan, 174
Prosvita Reading Hall, Dana, 174
Prosvita Reading Hall, Edmonton, 168, 169

Prosvita Reading Hall, Edna-Star, 102, 103
Prosvita Reading Hall, Ethelbert, 167
Prosvita Reading Hall, Fort William, 212, 218
Prosvita Reading Hall, Khmelnytsky, 167
Prosvita Reading Hall, Kitchener, 215
Prosvita Reading Hall, Melville, 202
Prosvita Reading Hall, Menofield, 174
Prosvita Reading Hall, Mink Creek, 166
Prosvita Reading Hall, Montreal, 199
Prosvita Reading Hall, Ottawa, 212
Prosvita Reading Hall, Quill Lake, 174
Prosvita Reading Hall, Riding Mountain, 166
Prosvita Reading Hall, Sarto, 167
Prosvita Reading Hall, Sheho,
Prosvita Reading Hall, Stuartburn, 166
Prosvita Reading Hall, Toronto, 214, 423, 454
Prosvita Reading Hall, Ukraina, 200
Prosvita Reading Hall, Venlaw, 166
Prosvita Reading Hall, Winnipeg (also Ukrainian Association of the "Chytalnia Prosvita"), 423, 454, 456
Prosvita "Ruska Slava", Garland, 166
Prosvita Society, Lviv, 29, 30, 161, 162, 163, 360, 537
Prosvita Society, Fort William, 212, 423
Prosvita Society, Port Arthur, 323
Prosvita Society, Uzhorod, 20, 21
Prosvita Women's Choir, 777
Provincial Organizing Committee, Rosthern, 175
(also Temporary Organizing Committee)
Radical Party, see Ukrainian Socialist Radical Party
Pulak Foundation, Rev. Josyf, 828
Pysanka, Festival, 778
Radio, Television and Film Program, 654, 655, 656
R.C.M.P., 710
Redberry Credit Union, 430
Regina Credit Union, 430
Repatriation Commission, Europe, 540
Representation Central de la Collectividad Ucrania, Argentina, 714
Representative Committee of Ukrainians in Canada (also Ukrainian Canadian Representative Committee), 549, 550
Research Institute Studium of L.V.U., 597, 638, 740

Research Institute of Wolyn (also Volyn), 597, 740
Rivnist, Ukrainian Labour Fraternity, Edmonton, 168
Roborecki Foundation, Bishop Andrew, 828
Royal Academy of Arts, 674
Royal Commision on Bi-lingualism and Bi-culturalism, 659, 710, 726, 727
Rusalka Ensemble, 775
Rusalka Dance Ensemble, Winnipeg, 678
Russian Congress, 294
Russian Worker-Farmer Club, 408
Ruthenian Canadian Aid Committee, Winnipeg, 316
Ruthenian Canadian National Association, 421
Ruthenian Conservative Club, 223
Ruthenian Farmers' Association, Rosthern, 277
"Ruthenian Glory" Reading Hall, Garland, 166
Ruthenian Liberal Club, 223
Ruthenian National Co-op, Rosthern, 278
Ruthenian National Association, Fernie, 178
Ruthenian National Association, Fort William, 211
Ruthenian National Association, Michelle, 179
Ruthenian National Association, U.S.A., 277
Ruthenian National Benefit Association, Toronto, 421
Ruthenian Political Association, 277
Ruthenian Prosvita Reading Hall, Fishing River, 167
Ruthenian Reading Hall, Stuartburn, 166
Ruthenian — Ukrainian Reading Hall, Stonewall, 167
Ruthenian Ukrainian Youth (R.U.M.), 417
Samo-obrazovannia-Study Group, Edmonton, 204
Sandulak "Prosvita" Reading Hall, Skalat, 204
Saskatchewan Ukrainian Pedagogic Association, 264
Save the Children Fund, 417
School of Higher Learning U.S.D.P., Toronto, 204
Scout Organizations of Canada, 475

Secretariat of S.K.V.U., 714, 715
Self-Enlightenment Study Group, Edmonton, 204
Self-Help Lisovets Village, 195
Self-Help, Montreal, 209
Senator William Wall Foundation, 680
Shashkevych "Prosvita" Reading Hall, Edmonton, 169, 171
Shashkevych "Prosvita" Reading Hall, Hamilton, 214, 411
Shashkevych "Prosvita" Reading Hall, Montreal, 199
Shashkevych "Prosvita" Reading Hall, Myrnam, 173, 197
Shashkevych Reading Hall, Terebowla, 167
Shashkevych Reading Hall, Toronto, 205
Shashkevych Reading Hall, Winnipeg, see Literary Association of Markian Shashkevych
Shashkevych Reading Hall, Winnipeg Beach, 166
Shashkevych Students Union, Edmonton 421
Shevchenko Association, Elmwood, 54
Shevchenko Association of St. Boniface, 546
Shevchenko Education Association, Winnipeg, 164, 265
Shevchenko Institute, Brooklands, 445, 546
Shevchenko Monument, Washington, 273, 674
Shevchenko Monument, Winnipeg, 673, 680, 681
Shevchenko Prosvita Association, Oshawa, 493
Shevchenko Prosvita Reading Hall, Hamilton, 214, 218
Shevchenko Prosvita Reading Hall, Kenora, 216
Shevchenko Prosvita Reading Hall, Montreal, 199, 210, 423 (also T. Shevchenko Association)
Shevchenko Prosvita Reading Hall, Sifton, 166
Shevchenko Prosvita Reading Hall, Volkivtsi, 167
Shevchenko Reading Hall, Beaver Creek, 167
Shevchenko Reading Hall, Bonne Madone, 174
Shevchenko Reading Hall, Edmonton, 167, 168

Shevchenko Reading Hall, Pleasant Home, 167
Shevchenko Reading Hall, Rosa, 166
Shevchenko Reading Hall, Venlaw, 164
Shevchenko Reading Society (also Association), Winnipeg, 106, 163, 225, 417
Shevchenko Scientific Society (N.T.Sh.), 172, 596, 597, 598, 638, 658, 740
Shevchenko Society of St. Boniface, 445
Shevchenko Society, Winnipeg, 163, 164
Shumka Ensemble, 775
Sichynsky Reading Hall, Selkirk, 167
Sichynsky Reading Hall, Starlag, 174
Sichynsky Reading Hall, Vegreville, 172
Sichynsky Society, Winnipeg, 167
Sitch Organization, 329, 330, 331
Sitch Organization in Canada; see Canadian Sitch Organization.
"Slovo" Association, 763, 764
Smuts Credit Union, 429, 430
Smoky Lake Credit Union, 430
Sociadale dos Amigos de la Cultura Ucrania, Argentina, 714
Social-Democratic Party of Canada, 225
Social-Democratic Party of Western Ukraine, 320
Social-Democratic Party, Winnipeg, 225, 266
Social Welfare Service of Ukrainian Canadians, 567
Socialist Labour Party of America, 225
Socialist Party of British Columbia, 225
Socialist Party of Canada, 222, 265
Society of Kachkovsky, Lviv, 33
Society of Ukrainian Native School Teachers, Canada, 445, 446, 447 (also Society for the Use of Native Schools)
Society of Ukrainians, Montreal, 209
Society of Wolyn (also Volyn), 740
Sokil "Bat'ko", 374
Songs of Ukraine, 781
SO-USE Credit Union, Toronto, 582
St. Andrew's College, 738
St. Josaphat Cathedral Credit Union, Toronto, 582
St. Mary's Parish Credit Union, Toronto, 582
St. Nicholas Parish Credit Union, Toronto, 582
St. Raphael's Association, (also St. Raphael's Ukrainian Immigrants Welfare Association of Canada), 23, 359, 362, 365, 366, 367, 368, 369, 370, 371, 537, 568

Stechishin Foundation, J. W., 827
"Stone Cutters" Students Association, Saskatoon, 420
Students' Circle, Kameniari, 157, 283
Students' Circle (also Student's Club), Winnipeg, 235
Students' Circle of A. Kotsko, 157, 188, 420
Students' Circle Self Education, 167
Students' Circle "Zoria", 159
Students' Institute of U.L.F.T.A., Edmonton, 405
Students' Dramatic Group of Metropolitan A. Shepticky, 201
S.U.K. Museums, 413
S.U.M. Choir, 675
Supporters of the Ukrainian Free University in Europe, 597
Surma Choir, Calgary, 675
Surma Choir, Winnipeg, 675
Symon Petlura Institute, 739
Toronto Literary and Art Club, 679
Trud, Ukrainian Women's Organization, 176
Trylowsky Chytalnia, Rossburn, 167
Trylowsky Chytalnia, near Vegreville, 173
Trylowsky Prosvita, Rossburn, 167
Tyrsa Choir, 776
"Ukraina" Choir, Montreal, 675, 775
Ukrainian Academic Association "Zarevo", 600, 639
Ukrainian Academy of Arts and Sciences, 826
Ukrainian Academy of Sciences, 22, 596
Ukrainian Aid Society, 422
Ukrainian Archives and Museum of Alberta, 826
Ukrainian Association of Aid to the Fatherland, 608, 649
Ukrainian Association of Creative Artists (USOM), 674, 678, 672, 761, 762
Ukrainian Association of Victims of Russian Communist Terror (SUZERO), 600, 602, 603, 605, 637, 805
Ukrainian Bank, Edmonton, 236
Ukrainian Brass Band, 169
Ukrainian Brotherhood, 177, 224
Ukrainian Bureau in Canada, Edmonton, 644
Ukrainian Business and Professional Club, Edmonton, 581
Ukrainian Business and Professional Club, Toronto, 427, 580, 635, 638

Ukrainian Business and Professional Club, Winnipeg, 427, 580, 581
Ukrainian Businessmen and Tradesmen, 638
Ukrainian Canadian Aid Fund; see Ukrainian Canadian Relief Fund
Ukrainian Canadian Centre, 408
Ukrainian Canadian Citizens League (also Committee), 211, 258, 331, 332, 333, 334, 335, 336, 337, 342, 344, 346, 374, 375, 546, 550
Ukrainian Canadian Committee, 550, 551, 552, 558, 562, 595, 597, 608, 626, 628, 631, 632, 640, 641, 652, 670, 680, 711, 715, 727, 805, 806, 817
Ukrainian Canadian Committee, Women's Division (also Women's Council), 416, 814
Ukrainian Canadian Council of Learned Societies, 598
Ukrainian Canadian Foundation of Taras Shevchenko, 6, 16, 584, 680, 681, 814
Ukrainian Canadian Friends of Liberation of Ukraine (U.K.T.), 603, 605, 638, 642, 805
Ukrainian Canadian Memorial Park
Ukrainian Canadian Mission, 336
Ukrainian Canadian Professional and Business Federation (U.C.P.B.F.), 733, 734, 811, 813
Ukrainian Canadian Research Foundation, Toronto, 661, 680
Ukrainian Canadian Relief Fund, 562, 563, 564, 565, 567, 568, 594, 599, 601
Ukrainian Canadian Servicemen's Association, London, 564, 565
Ukrainian Canadian Social Service, 816
Ukrainian Canadian University Students' Union, (S.U.S.K.), 600, 601, 638, 814, 815
Ukrainian Canadian Veteran's Association (U.C.V.A.), 593, 594, 595, 634, 811
Ukrainian Canadian Veterans Club (U.C.V.C.), London, 594
Ukrainian Canadian Women's Association, 546
Ukrainian Canadian Writers' Association, 763
Ukrainian Canadian Youth Council (R.U.M.K.), 599, 600, 601
Ukrainian Central Committee for Defence of Bilingual School System, 147

INDEX 931

Ukrainian Central Committee for Defence of Native language, 147
Ukrainian Central Rada, Kiev, 157, 357, 532
Ukrainian Chapter of the Manitoba Modern Languages Association, Winnipeg, 631
Ukrainian Colonization Bureau, 369
Ukrainian Congress Committee of America, 564, 712, 713, 714
Ukrainian Credit Union, Calgary, 582, 584
Ukrainian Credit Union, St. Catharines, 584
Ukrainian Credit Union, Sudbury, 430
Ukrainian Cultural and Educational Centre, 597, 629, 641, 657, 741
Ukrainian Dance Ensemble "Shumka", Edmonton, 678
Ukrainian Defence Committee, 398
Ukrainian Democratic Youth Association (O.D.U.M.), 599, 815, 816
Ukrainian Diplomatic Mission, 276
Ukrainian Economic Society "Chain", 408
Ukrainian Educational Economic Congress, 544
Ukrainian Educational Labour Association of M. Sichynsky, Hosmer, 179, 180
Ukrainian Educational Society, 408
Ukrainian Emigrants Aid Committee, Lviv, 359, 360, 363, 364, 365
Ukrainian Fraternal Society of Canada, 816, 817
Ukrainian Free Academy of Sciences (U.V.A.N.), 16, 452, 596, 598, 641, 642, 657, 658, 661
Ukrainian Freethinkers Federation, 164, 265, 309
Ukrainian Golden Cross, 415
Ukrainian Handicraft Society, Winnipeg, 458
Ukrainian Heritage Association and Museum of Canada, 826
Ukrainian Historical War Institute, 597, 598
Ukrainska Hromada, Ottawa, 639
Ukrainian Immigration and Colonization Bureau, 369
Ukrainian Insurgent Army (U.P.A.), also Ukrainian Underground Army, 453, 560, 569, 598, 599, 603, 604, 635, 655
Ukrainian Labour Association, 409, 410, 475, 541, 546

Ukrainian Labour and Farmers' Temple Association, 403, 408, 422, 455, 476, 477, 491, 495, 498, 537, 542, 544, 545, 550, 551, 608, 649, 650, 651
Ukrainian Labour Theatre, 296
Ukrainian Labour Temple, 207, 295, 404, 455, 534
Ukrainian Labour Temple Association, 404
Ukrainian League for Ukraine's Liberation (L.V.U.), 600, 601, 602, 603, 604, 605, 638, 655
Ukrainian Language Association, Edmonton, 631
Ukrainian Literary Art Club, Toronto, 665
Ukrainian Literary Club, Edmonton, 678
Ukrainian Literary Club, Winnipeg, 678
Ukrainian Literary Association of M. Shashkevych, Winnipeg, 454
Ukrainian Medical Association of North America, 598, 638, 741
Ukrainian Men's Choir of Walter Bohonos, 455
Ukrainian Mohylo-Mazepian Academy (UMMAN), 739
Ukrainian National Aid of America, 817
Ukrainian National Association (U.N.S.), 178, 816
  (formerly Ruthenian National Association), 240, 316, 421, 422, 670
Ukrainian National Council, 334, 337, 342, 346, 374, 375, 603
Ukrainian National Council, Manitoba, 335, 336, 342, 477, 544, 545, 546, 547
Ukrainian National Council, Paris, 337
Ukrainian National Council, Western Ukraine, 345
Ukrainian National Credit Union of Toronto, 430, 582, 583
Ukrainian National Credit Union of Montreal, 430, 582, 583
Ukrainian National Democratic League (S.U.N.D.—U.N.D.S.), 602, 603, 605
Ukrainian National Democratic League (O.D.U.M.), 600, 636
Ukrainian National Federation (U.N.O. —U.N.F.), 398, 400, 401, 405, 413, 414, 418, 426, 455, 456, 487, 537, 540, 545, 546, 548, 549, 551, 595, 599, 602, 605, 607, 629, 633, 640, 808, 809
Ukrainian National Home, Edmonton,
Ukrainian National Home, West Fort William, 200

Ukrainian National Home, Saskatoon, 412
Ukrainian National Home, Toronto, 423
Ukrainian National Home, Winnipeg, 155, 167, 178, 200, 207, 376, 409, 411, 422, 426, 445, 448, 454, 475, 544, 658
Ukrainian National Home Association Choir, Winnipeg, 454, 455
Ukrainian National Home Choir, Toronto, 455
Ukrainian National League, 211, 448
Ukrainian National Rada, 371, 357
Ukrainian National Rada (also Congress) 193
Ukrainian National Republic (Z.O.U.N.R.), 322, 328, 332, 345, 357, 358, 410, 470, 482, 492, 537, 538, 589, 603
Ukrainian National Republic Government in Exile, 560
Ukrainian National Theatre in Canada, 668
Ukrainian National Union, 400
Ukrainian National Unity, France, 714
Ukrainian National Viche, Edmonton, 169, 170
Ukrainian National Youth Federation, 400, 401, 407, 419, 455, 487, 499, 600, 638, 639
Ukrainian Nationalists Organization (also Organization of Ukrainian Nationalists), 390, 399, 476, 487, 540, 560, 603, 604, 635
Ukrainian Native Schools of Canada, 446, 447
Ukrainian Pavillion of World's Fair, Chicago, 457
Ukrainian Savings and Credit Union, (Caisse Populaire Ukrainne de Montreal), 582, 583
Ukrainian Secret University, Lviv, 490
Ukrainian Settlers' Aid Association, 369
Ukrainian Students Central Federation (C.E.S.U.S.), also Central Union of Ukrainian Students in Europe, 401, 420, 461
Ukrainian People's Library of I. Franko, 163, 164
Ukrainian Press Bureau of Canada, 375
Ukrainian Professional Association, 425, 426
Ukrainian Prosvita, Fishing River, 167
Ukrainian Reading Hall Association Choir, 454

Ukrainian Red Cross, 211, 333, 346, 374, 393, 414, 537, 544, 545
Ukrainian Red Cross Committee, 333, 374, 375, 376, 537, 544, 545
Ukrainian Red Cross Society, 211, 333, 346, 374, 393, 414, 537, 544, 545
Ukrainian Relief Committee of the Red Cross Society, 333
Ukrainian Republican Chorus (also Republican Kapella), 454, 538
Ukrainian Revolution Democrats, 638
Ukrainian Revolutionary Party, 209
Ukrainian Self-Reliance League (S.U.S.), 395, 399, 405, 407, 409, 414, 418, 426, 467, 471, 502, 539, 540, 544, 545, 546, 549, 550, 551, 595, 602, 605, 607, 630, 661, 662, 712, 717, 807, 808
Ukrainian Self-Reliance League Foundation, 680
Ukrainian Sitch Veterans Association, 546
Ukrainian Social Democratic Party of Western Canada, 164, 166, 226, 266, 295, 403, 405, 406, 410
Ukrainian Social Revolution Party, 410
Ukrainian Social Welfare, Toronto, 638
Ukrainian Socialist Congress, 206
Ukrainian Socialist Democratic Party, 224
Ukrainian Socialist League, 266
Ukrainian Socialist Radical Party (in Ukraine), 224, 320, 410
Ukrainian Socialist Union, 225
Ukrainian Sociological Institute, Prague, 541
Ukrainian Sports Association, 636
Ukrainian Students' Association of Mikhnowsky (T.U.S.M.), 600
Ukrainian Supreme Liberation Council (U.H.V.R.), 560, 603, 604, 635
Ukrainian Teachers' Association of Canada, 119, 181, 191, 251, 338, 443, 444, 597, 636, 741
Ukrainian Teachers' Association of Alberta, 444
Ukrainian Teachers' Association of Manitoba, 120
Ukrainian Teachers' Association of Saskatchewan, 444
Ukrainian Teachers' Association, Toronto, 631
Ukrainian Technical Society, 339
Ukrainian War Veterans Inc., 598

Ukrainian War Veterans' Association (Ukrainska Striletska Hromada (U.S.H.)), 398, 40, 405, 413, 414, 429, 476, 487, 497, 539, 540, 545, 598, 607, 637, 808
Ukrainian Women's Association of Canada (S.U.K.), 396, 412, 413, 414, 416, 418, 471, 532, 601, 602, 644, 807
Ukrainian Women's Educational Association, 176
Ukrainian Women's Organization of Canada (O.U.K.), 400, 413, 415, 487, 601, 602, 641, 808
Ukrainian Worker-Farmer Educational Society, 408
Ukrainian Workers' Club, 211
Ukrainian Workers' League (Ukrainska Robitnycha Organizaciya — U.R.O.), 407, 408, 550, 551, 595, 602, 607
Ukrainian Workers' Youth Association, 404
Ukrainian Workingman's Association, 422
Ukrainian Writers and Journalists' Association, 538
Ukrainian Writers Union, Toronto, 532
Ukrainian Young Labour League (S.U.R.M.), 496
Ukrainian Youth Association in Ukraine, 600
Ukrainian Youth Association of Canada (S.U.M.), 599, 601, 603, 629, 630, 636, 642, 810
Ukrainian Youth Association-Plast, 599, 636, 815, 816
Ukrainian Youth Club, 163
United Hetman Organization (U.H.O.), 329, 394, 541, 544, 546, 548, 549, 550, 551, 595, 602, 805
United Nations Relief and Rehabilitation Administration (U.N.R.R.A.), 561, 563, 566
United Ukrainian American Relief Committee, 565, 567
Union for the Liberation of Ukraine (S.V.U.), 604, 637
Union of the Ukrainian National Homes, 409
Union of Ukrainian Benefit Societies, Toronto, 421
Union of Ukrainian Community Centres, 409
Union of Ukrainian Workers, France, 714
U.S.D.P., Brantford, 215

U.S.D.P., Fighters for Freedom, Porcupine, 217
U.S.D.P., Free Thoughts, Bellevue, 174
U.S.D.P., Hamilton, 214
U.S.D.P., Labour Organization, Timmins, 217
U.S.D.P., Montreal, 210
U.S.D.P., New Life, Ottawa, 213
U.S.D.P., Oshawa, 215
U.S.D.P., Struggle for Freedom, Lethbridge, 172
U.S.D.P., "Thunder", Nanaimo, 272
U.S.D.P., Welland, 217
Vegreville Cooperative, 429
Vera Credit Union, Winnipeg, 583
Verkhovyna Choir, 776
Verkhovyna Ensemble, 776
Vesna Festival, 778
Vesnivka Choir, 774
Vidrodzhennia Association, 167
Vilna Shkola Association, 167
Volia Association, Nanaimo, 179
War Veterans Organizations, 598
Wasyl Sarchuk Foundation, 827
Western Ukraine National Republic, 384
William Topolnycky Foundation, 827
Winnipeg Trades and Labour Council, 295
Wishart Credit Union, 429, 430
Women's Association of Winnipeg, 411, 412
Women's Division of the United Hetman Organizations, 416
Women's Eductional Society, Ethelbert, 411
Women's Educational Society, Hamilton, 411
Women's Educational Society in the National Home, Winnipeg, 411
Women's International Council, 413
Women's Prosvita Organization, Hamilton, 218
Women's Workers Association with Ukrainian Labour Temple, 404
Working Men's Benefit Association, 405
Workingmen's Benevolent Association (R.Z.T.) also Workers Benevolent Association, 422, 456, 818
World Anti-Communist League, 811
World Association of Ukrainian Journalists, 770
World Congress of Free Ukrainians (S.K.V.U.), 712, 713, 714, 715, 816, 817

World Federation of the Ukrainian
  Women's Association (S.F.U.Z.O.),
  602
World Youth Anti-Communist League,
  811
Yavir Dance Ensemble, 774
Youth Association, Montreal, 209
Youth Section of the Association of
  Journalists of Canada, 771
Zahrava, 772
Zirka, Children's Association, Mink
  Creek, 283

SCHOOLS, EDUCATION
Schools, Institutes, Academies, Bursas, etc.

Academy of Art, Kiev, 672
Academy of Art, Krakow, 673
Academy of Art, Warsaw, 672-673
Academy of Sacred Heart of Jesus, 110
Academy of Theology, Lviv, 658, 661
Academy of Royal de Beau-Arts of
  Liege, 672
Adam Kotsko Bursa, see Ukrainian
  Bursa of Adam Kotsko
Apostolic Mission School in Sifton, 110,
  152, 188
B. Hrinchenko Ridna Shkola, Lviv, see
  Hrinchenko Ridna Shkola in Lviv
Beckett School, 315
Bible College, Saskatoon, 469
Bohdan School, 121
Brandon Normal School, see Ruthenian
  Training School in Brandon
Budka School, 121
Bukovina School, 144, 315
Bursa in Teulon, 159, 468
Central Committee for Defence of
  Bilingual Schools, Winnipeg, 344
Central Committee of Native School,
  Winnipeg, 323, 332, 334
Chmelnycky School, (also Khmelnytsky
  School), 121, 315
Committee in Aid of Native School, 167
Committee in Support of Ridna Shkola,
  167
Convention of Ukrainian Teachers of
  Manitoba, 443
Dehova School, 121
Dnipro School, 315
Dnister School, 120, 315
Doroshenko School, 121, 315
Dufferin School, 120 315
English School for Foreigners, Regina,
  141, 148, 173
Federation of Ukrainian School Trustees
  in Saskatchewan, 339

First Convention of Ukrainian Teachers
  in Alberta, 184
First Convention of Ukrainian Teachers
  in Manitoba, 182, 234, 268, 338
First Ukrainian Teachers' Convention in
  Saskatchewan, 184
"Foreinerka", see English School for
  Foreigners in Vegreville
Franko School, 120, 121
Galicia School (renamed Plum Ridge),
  115, 167, 315
General Committee for Native Schools,
  443, 445, 446
General Council of the Ukrainian Schools
  of the Ukrainian Greek-Orthodox
  Church, 631
Girls' Institute of Sister Servants, Regina,
  586
Girls' Institute of Sister Servants,
  Saskatchewan, 586
Gogol Bursa, see Mykola Hohol Bursa
Gonta School, 121
Gymnasium in Rohatyn, 320
Gymnasium in Zbaraz, 320
Horod School, 120
Hrushevsky Institute, see M. Hrushevsky
  Institute in Edmonton
Immaculate Heart of Mary Academy,
  Winnipeg, 630, 645
Immaculate Mary Academy, Ancaster,
  630
Institute of Metropolitan A. Shepticky,
  Saskatoon, 402, 447, 586, 631
Ivan Ardan School, 120
Jaroslav School (also Yaroslaw School),
  121, 315
Karpaty School, 121
Kharkiv Art Institute, 672
King Edward School, 315
Kolomyja School, 144, 315
Komarno School, 121

INDEX

Kosiw School, 115, 120, 315
Kulish School, 121, 315
Kupchenko School, 121
Laurier School, 315
Lemberg School, 120
Limna School, 121
M. Hrushevsky Institute in Edmonton (also St. John's Institute), 157, 395, 420, 424, 444, 447, 467, 541, 630, 646, 662
Manitoba College, 106, 117, 118, 234, 305, 536
Manitoba University, 333, 341, 342, 420, 433, 530, 580, 581, 590, 627, 628, 629
McMaster University, Hamilton, 600
Metropolitan A. Shepticky Bursa (also A. Shepticky Institute), 155, 193, 420
Metropolitan A. Shepticky Institute, Toronto, 631
Minto School, see Ruthenian Training School
Montreal Seminary, 461
Montreal University, 600, 628, 658
Mountain Road School, 120
Mountain Stream School, 121
National Centre of Ukrainian School Councils, also National Centre of Ukrainian Educational Councils, 750
National Committee for Native Schools, 443, 445
Normal School, Winnipeg, 120, 121
Ottawa University, 661
Petlura School, 315
Petro Mohyla Bursa, see Petro Mohyla Institute
Petro Mohyla Institute, Saskatoon, 112, 113, 155, 156, 157, 158, 171, 192, 283, 343, 344, 395, 412, 414, 424, 427, 447, 448, 467, 502, 503, 504, 529, 533, 536, 541, 630, 642, 646
Petro Mohyla Institute, Winnipeg, 412, 447
Plum Ridge, see Galicia School
Provincial Committee in Aid of Native Schools, Alberta, 142
Prut School, 315
Ridna Shkola, Fort William 218
Ridna Shkola, Kenora, 216
Ridna Shkola, Lviv, 233, 254, 269, 323, 639
Ridna Shkola, Montreal, 150
Ridna Shkola of M. Sashkevych, 445, 456, 608
Ridna Shkola, Port Arthur, 151
Ridna Shkola, Sydney, 116

Ridna Shkola, Winnipeg, 151, 423
Roblin School, 315
Roman Catholic Seminary in Toronto, 110
Royal Academy of Arts, Canada, 674
Rus' School, 121
Ruthenian Training School, Winnipeg, Brandon, 117, 118, 121, 122, 148, 183, 189, 191
Ruthenian-Ukrainian Bursa, Edmonton, see Shevchenko Bursa and College
Sacred Heart Academy for Girls, Yorkton, 586, 626, 630, 631
Saskatchewan Teachers of Ukrainian, 631
School Council of U.C.C., 631
School of H. Skovoroda, Toronto, 629
Seech School, 120
Shevchenko Bursa, Vegreville, 157, 172
Shevchenko Bursa and College, Edmonton, 158, 192
Shevchenko School, (also Szewczenko School), 120, 315
Sifton Bursa, 159, 468
Sifton School, 315
Sir George Williams College, Montreal, 600
Slovo School, 121
Sniatyn School, 121
Society of Ukrainian Native School Teachers in Canada, 445, 446
Sokal School, 175
Sorbonne University, 672
St. Andrew's College, 46, 590, 629, 630, 646, 738
St. Basil College, Toronto, 587, 630, 631, 655
St. George School, Edmonton, 629
St. Joseph's College, Yorkton, 153, 394, 586, 587, 626, 630
St. Vladimir and Olga School, 268
St. Vladimir's College, Roblin, 586, 587, 630
St. Volodymyr's Institute, Toronto, 631
Stanislaw School, 144
Stryj School, 120, 315
Tarnow School, 121
Teachers Training School in Regina, see English School for Foreigners, Regina
Teachers' Seminary, Lviv, 29, 30
Trembowla School (also Terebowla School), 115, 315
Ukraina School,
Ukrainian Bursa of Adam Kotsko, 154, 155

936   UKRAINIAN CANADIANS: A HISTORY

Ukrainian Catholic Institute, Edmonton, 447
Ukrainian Catholic Brotherhood Bursa, see Institute of Metropolitan A. Shepticky
Ukrainian Free University, Prague-Munich, 657, 658
Ukrainian Normal School, see Ruthenian Training School
Ukrainian Teachers' Association, 119
Ukrainian Teachers Association of Saskatchewan, 181, 191, 338
Ukrainian Teachers Bureau, 191, 339
Ukrainian Teachers of Saskatchewan, 184
Ukrainian University of Lviv, 269, 321, 322
Ukrainian Workers' University in Prague, 410
University of Alberta, 626, 628, 645
University of British Columbia, 661
University of McGill, 433, 600
University of Ottawa, 629, 581, 628, 659
University of Toronto, 659, 661
University of Saskatchewan, 433, 503, 530, 626
Volkivtsi School, 49
Volodymyr School, 315
Wisla School, 120
Zalissia School, 121
Zaporoze School, 120
Zbruch School, 120
Zolota School, 121
Zoria School, 121

PRINTED WORD
Print, Bindery Shops, Publications, Monuments

Accord Book Company, 311
Address of Ukrainian Business and Professionals in Toronto, 586
Agriculturist, 246, 281, 317, 478
Alaska Herald, 177
Alberta Printing, Edmonton, 485
Almanac of "Homin Ukrainy", 601
Almanac of the Ruthenian National Association, 164
Almanac of the Ukrainian Canadian Soldier, 663
Almanac of Ukrainian War Veteran's Association, 540
Alpha Omega Recorder, 642
America (U.S.A.), 208, 238
Andrew News, District Press, 485
Apiary, 478
Aurora, 645
Bell, Saskatoon, 421, 491
Bell, Toronto, 498
Bell, 246
Book of Artists and Creators of the Ukrainian Culture, Almanac, Toronto, 679
Break-Through, 483
Bukovina, 482
Bukovina, Toronto, 769
Bugle, 537
Building of Nation, 537, 637
Bulletin of Association for the Liberation of Ukraine, Montreal, 497
Bulletin of Canadian League for Ukraine's Liberation, 638
Bulletin of the Association of Businessmen and Tradesmen, 638
Bulletin of the Association of Ukrainian Pedagogues in Canada, 638
Bulletin of the Committee of Artists, 638
Bulletin of the Executive of the Ukrainian National Federation, Toronto, 638
Bulletin, Holy Greek Orthodox Trinity Cathedral, Winnipeg, 646
Bulletin of the Former Ukrainian War Veterans of Canada, 638
Bulletin of the Shevchenko Scientific Society, Toronto, 638
Bulletin of the St. Volodymyr Ukrainian Orthodox Cathedral in Toronto, 646
Bulletin of the Ukrainian-Canadian University Students, 638
Bulletin of the Ukrainian-Canadian University Students' Union, 638
Bulletin of the Ukrainian Canadian Veterans' Association, 638
Bulletin of the Ukrainian Credit Union in Fort William, 640
Bulletin of the Ukrainian Cooperative Savings and Credit, 639
Bulletin of the Ukrainian National Credit Union, 639
Bulletin of the U.N.F., Sudbury, 640
Bulletin of the Workers of Children's Literature, 638
Bulletin of U.C.C., 640
Bulletin of Ukrainian Greek-Orthodox Sobor, Winnipeg, 646

Bulletin of Ukrainian Orthodox Church Blessed Virgin Mary, Montreal, 646
Bulletin of Ukrainian Professional and Business Men's Club, 638
Bulletin of Ukrainian Social Welfare, Toronto, 638
Bulletin of the World Congress of Free Ukrainians, 769
Calendar-Almanac of the New Pathway, 552
Calgary Albertan, 664
Calgary Herald, 664
Call, 487
Canada, 236, 241, 278, 279, 280, 307, 313
Canada North West Company, Winnipeg, 309, 471
Canadian, 243, 275, 278, 312, 313, 314, 318, 467, 472, 485, 647
Canadian Eparchial Herald, 484
Canadian Farmer, 34, 123, 154, 168, 170, 174, 175, 180, 209, 213, 215, 221, 223, 227, 228, 240, 261, 262, 263, 268, 272, 278, 284, 287, 305, 309, 312, 313, 317, 318, 322, 324, 329, 339, 395, 411, 424, 444, 458, 466, 470, 472, 473, 474, 500, 503, 504, 532, 547, 548, 632, 610, 662, 670, 767
Canadian Farmer Almanac, 310
Canadian Farmer Calendar, 23
Canadial Field, 288, 289
Canadian Forum, 529
Canadian Life, 493
Canadian Morning, 274, 275, 411, 470, 472, 592, 632, 633, 646, 647
Canadian News, 243, 313, 484
Canadian News, Winnipeg, 280
Canadian News, Winnipeg, 484, 498
Canadian Orthodox Missionary, 498
Canadian Orthodox Rus', 293
Canadian Poetry, 669
Canadian Proletarian, 498
Canadian Ranok: see Morning (Ranok)
Canadian Rus', pamphlet of Rev. Dmytriw, 39, 40
Canadian Ruthenian, 110, 154, 155, 217, 218, 228, 230, 242, 263, 270, 271, 274, 276, 278, 287, 310, 311, 312, 317, 319, 325, 327, 335, 339, 340, 342, 470
Canadian Ruthenian Almanac, 213, 310, 340
Canadian Sitch, 394, 475, 476
Canadian Slavonic Papers, 659
Canadian Star, 265
Canadian Ukraine, 769

Canadian Ukrainian, 242, 271, 272, 274, 282, 287, 310, 311, 312, 394, 502, 461, 470, 471, 473, 474, 475, 486, 497, 500, 544, 545
Canadian Ukrainian Publishing Association in Canada, 282
Canadian Ukrainian Review, 482
Canadian Voice, 270
Canadoon, 769
Carpathian Sitch, 638
Cathedral News (St. George's Ukrainian Catholic Cathedral), 645
Cathedral News (St. Josaphat's Ukrainian Catholic Cathedral), Edmonton, Toronto, 645
Catholic Action, 644
Catholic Gazette, 314
Censer, 246, 285, 286, 306, 318
"Chervona Kalyna", Annals, 666
Children's World, 479
Christian Banner, 648
Christian Herald, 488, 592, 647
Church and Nation, 646
Church in a Nation, 645
Church Life, 485
Church News, The Ukrainian Evangelical Church, Hamilton, 647
Church of Our Nation, 484
Community Voice, Journal in Western Ukraine, 32
Conscious Force, 226, 266, 285
Cooperative Community, 479
Co-ordinator, 769
Cross of Freedom Monument, 778
Daily Nor-Wester, 74
Dawn of New Era, 498, 648
Dauphin Herald, 287
"Dilo", Lviv, 32, 172, 340
"Dnipro Almanac", 159
Drahomaniw Publishing Company, Montreal, 284
Eastern Egg, 827
Eastern News, 490
Ecclesia, 645
Echo, 478
Economic Cooperative Newspaper, Lviv, 666
Edmonton Journal, 668, 730
Emigrant, 109, 364
Eparchial Herald, 489
Evangelical Herald, 483, 488
Evangelical Morning, 592, 640, 646, 647
Evangelical Truth, 111, 491, 592, 647, 648
Evangelist, 592, 648

"Evshan Zillia", Children's Journal, 667
Eye of the World, 639
Faith and Culture, 590, 646
Faith and Knowledge, 490
Faith of the Gospel, 648
Farm, 368
Farmer's Herald, 484
Farmer's Life, 404, 494, 496, 497, 545
Farmer's Voice, 485
Farmer's Weekly Telegram, 247, 288
Federalist Democrat, 639
Field, 235, 246, 282
For the Native Church, 645
For Our Children, 667
Forum, 12
Forward, 408, 477, 491
Forward (Naprzod), Lviv, 172
Free World, 632
Freedom, Lviv, 172
Friend of Ukraine, 492
Future of the Nation, 419, 489, 532, 643
Gazeta Katolicka, 474
Globe and Mail, 671
Good News, 80
Grindstone, 480, 504
Grindstone Yearly Almanac of Humor and Satire, 480
Halychanyn, 33
Herald, 466, 471, 472, 646
Herald of Health, 484
Herald of the Central Exarchate, 645
Herald of the Lord's Comming, 648
Herald of the Ukrainian National Council in Canada, 477, 546
History of Our Days, 642
Home, 246, 280, 281, 307, 310
Homin Ukrainy: see Ukrainian Echo
House, 281
Icelandic Canadian, 720
In Christ's Vineyard, Almanac of the Toronto Ukrainian Catholic Eparchy, 668
Independent Ukraine, 329
Informer, 638
Information Letter of the North Winnipeg Credit Union, 642
Information Letter of the Executive of Plast Centre, 638
Information Service of the Ukrainian Canadian University Student's Union, 638
Journal of Commerce, Montreal, 474
Journal of the Ukrainian Medical Association, 638
Kadylo; see Censer

Kanadsky Hlas, 473
Khata, see Home, 280
Knowing Strength, see Conscious Force.
Kuban Cossack Bulletin, 637
Labour News, Toronto, 497
Leader (Providnyk), 368, 395
League of Ukrainian Engineers, 638
Lemko Country (also Lemko Land), 635, 640
Lemko News, 635
Lesya Ukrainka Monument, 827
Letters of Friendship, 639
Letters of our Family Brethren, 638
Life and Faith, 648
Life and School, 636
Life and S.U.M., 642
Life and Voice of Truth, 483
Life and Word, 651
Life Beacon, 638
Light, 462, 488, 627, 638, 644
Light and Voice of Truth, 483
Literary Educational Herald, 305
Literary Scientific Herald, Lviv, 172, 178
Literary and Art, 635
Logos, 644
Manitoba Free Press, 307
Man's Paragraph, 279
Man's Truth (Khlopska Pravda), 172
Maple Leaf, 368
Markian Shashkevych Monument, 872
Markian Shashkevych Park, 827
McFayden Publications, 529
Memo, 645
Militant Youth, 496
Missionary Messenger, 154, 224
Mission of Ukraine, 637
Monitor, 483, 484
Montreal Protocol, 639
Morning, 228, 230, 263, 264, 268, 272, 275, 278, 279, 306, 309, 310, 312, 313, 318, 329, 467, 470, 472, 500, 502, 535, 647
Mosquito, 641
M.U.N. Beams, 638
My Friend, 640, 645
Nasha Doroha, 767
National Economy, 479
Native Church, 484
Native Country, 313
National Press, 419, 472, 474
Native Country, European Magazine, 532
National Publishers, 472
National Trading Co., 171

Native Language, 657
Narondna Vola, 500
Nazustrich, 636, 666
New Canadian, Toronto, 491, 529
New Canadian, 473, 481
New Chronical, 646
New Community, 226, 313, 484
New Country, 97, 141, 154, 243, 276, 277, 278, 288, 289, 312, 339
New Days, 635, 667, 669
News Days, Journal in West Ukraine, 667
New Era, 489
New Field, 368
New Land, Rosthern, 173
New Life, 283, 498
New Opinion, 637
New Paper, 490
New Pathway, 379, 400, 401, 419, 476, 486, 487, 488, 503, 531, 545, 629, 632, 633, 640, 670, 767, 770
New Pathway Publishing Co., 487
New Perspectives, 767
New Review, 637
New Society, 266, 272, 275, 278
New Ukraine, 532
New World, 26, 498
New World Library, Montreal, 311, 498
New York Times, 715
News, Edmonton, 142, 154, 171, 226, 227, 271, 272, 273, 274, 275, 276, 279, 288, 291, 306, 312, 313, 336
News, Ukrainian Catholic Youth of Saskatchewan, 645
News, U.N.F. Bulletin, Hamilton, 640
News, U.N.F. Bulletin, Sudbury, 640
News Bulletin, Ukrainian Professional and Business Men's Club, Winnipeg, 642
News Bulletin of Ukrainian Business and Tradesmen, 638
Newsletter, The Ukrainian Canadian Veteran's Association, Toronto, 637
News-Letter of the Ukrainian Workingman's Union, 532
Nor-Wester, 74, 75
Nord Western, 473
Northern Lights, 664
Objective, 645
Obnova Bulletin, 645
Obnovan, 645
Oko, 769
On Guard, 636
On Guard of Truth — The Star of Truth, 487

Onomastica, 586
Opinion, 637, 638
Orthodox Herald, 114, 466, 471, 544, 545
Orthodox Informator, 488
Orthodox Messenger
Orthodox Herald
Orthodox Newspaper, 267
Orthodox Ruthenian, 289
Osa (Wasp), 302, 500
Oshawa Daily Times, 529
Our Age, 498
Our Age (1949), 635
Our Aim, 406, 635, 643, 644, 669
Our Community, 638, 646
Our Contact, 638
Our Country, 634
Our Culture, 642, 657
Our Faith, 664
Our Future, 645
Our Life, 478, 484
Our Progress, 485
Our Strength, 246, 281
Our Tribune, 638
Our Viewpoint, 638
Our Word, 483
Overseas Herald, 529
Panorama, 738, 813
Parents Information of the Plast, 642
Parish Herald of St. Nicholas Church, 645
Parish News, Church of Holy Ghost, Winnipeg, 645
Parish News, Church of the Blessed Virgin Mary, Winnipeg, 645
People's Friend, 493
People's Gazette, 495, 496, 497
Pioneer Woman of Canada, 827
Plast Herald, 636
Plast Road, 636
Plowed Field; see Field
Polish Courier (Kurier Polski), Lviv, 172
Prairie, 638
Pravda (of U.S.S.R.), 559
Pravda and Vola, 500
Problems, 638
Precious Diamond, 420
Press News of the U.C.C., 640
Progress Mundare, 243, 275, 276, 306, 312, 319, 484
Progress, Vancouver, 498, 642
Progress, Winnipeg (1956), 641
Progress, Winnipeg (1959), 416, 643, 644, 664, 669, 682

Proletarian News, 498
Promin, Children's Magazine, 504, 529
Promin, Chernivtsi, 531
Promin, St. Andrew's College, 646
Promin, Women's Magazine, 532, 640, 641, 669, 767
Prosvita, 484
Prosvita Book Store, 237, 311
Providence, 310, 311
Publishing Company, Winnipeg, 309
Rada, European Journal, 532
Redeemer's Voice, 402, 488, 644
Red Banner; see Red Flag
Red Flag, 225, 241, 263, 265, 266
Red Flag Publishing Company, 306, 309, 312, 313
Reform, 484
Renaissance, 487
Ridna Shkola, 636
Ridnoshkilnyk, 752
Road Guide, 637
Rozbudowa, 635
Russia, 494
Russian People, 291, 292, 332
Russian Voice, 289, 290, 291, 332
Ruthenian Book Store (Ruska Knyharnia), Winnipeg, 237, 280, 305, 310, 311
Saskatoon Daily Star, 154
Scientific Library, 282
Scope, 645
Self-Help, 642
Settler, 305
Shashkevychiana, 641
Sifton News, 287
Slavistica, 598
Slavonic Review, London, 536
Slovo; see Word
Smoloskyp, 639
Social Credit, 487
Soldier Aim, 310
Spark, 302
Sprinkle, 493
Sport's News, 636
Star Montreal, 244, 284
Star, Mundare, 276
Star of Mary, 644
Star, Vancouver, 642
Star (Zoria), Lviv, 172
Stone Cutters; see Stone Breakers
Stone Cutters, Lviv, 667
Stone Breakers, 235, 247, 303, 420, 488, 503, 642, 646
Struggle for Freedom, 477
Student, 769

Students' News, 645
Summary of Our Work, 479
Sun, 638
Sunbeam, 479, 480
Sunday, 483
Sun Flower, 636
Sunday School, 472
Surma, 484, also see Bugle
Svit (World), 240, 288, 293
Svit Dytyny, Lviv, 501
Svoboda, 32, 33, 36, 37, 41, 43, 96, 100, 102, 115, 119, 122, 161, 162, 163, 168, 172, 173, 177, 178, 179, 208, 211, 212, 222, 238, 239, 240, 261, 264, 265, 267, 288, 298, 299, 300, 301, 302, 303, 304, 305, 314, 320, 503, 529
S.V.U. Bulletin, 638
Taras Shevchenko Monument, 872
Teacher's Word, 636
Thought, 484
Toward the Meeting, 638
Trans-Oceanic Herald, 218, 489
Truth (Pravda), 240, 288, 289, 305
Truth, 408, 476, 491
Truth and Freedom, 312, 484
Truth and Liberty, 409, 475, 476
Truth of the People, 498
U.C.Y. Lore, 419, 642
Ukraina, 246, 281, 307, 317
Ukrainian Banner, Vienna, 398
Ukrainian Bazaar, 490, 491
Ukrainian Bazaar Publishing Co., Toronto, 529
Ukrainian Canadian, 650
Ukrainian Canadian Memorial Park, 827
Ukrainian Book Store, Edmonton, 237, 311
Ukrainian Book Store, Montreal, 237
Ukrainian Canadian Review, 581, 627, 632
Ukrainian Catholic Center, 640
Ukrainian Catholic Front, 645
Ukrainian Catholic Toiler, 634
Ukrainian Citizen, 634
Ukrainian Commentary, 640
Ukrainian Co-operator, 489
Ukrainian Echo, 285, 603, 635, 636, 670, 767, 783
Ukrainian Emigrant, 363, 364, 372
Ukrainian Evangelist, 275
Ukrainian Family, 484
Ukrainian Flag, Vienna, 403
Ukrainian Gazette, 484
Ukrainian Gospel Field, 648
Ukrainian Herals, 178, 467, 477

INDEX 941

Ukrainian Home, 532
Ukrainian Independent, 552
Ukrainian Journalist, 770
Ukrainian Labour News, 244, 295, 403, 404, 470, 477, 484, 494, 534, 545
Ukrainian Labourer, Winnipeg, 498
Ukrainian Life, 497, 649, 650
Ukrainian News, 177, 402, 432, 461, 486, 542, 543, 551, 632, 633, 643, 644, 664, 669, 670, 767
Ukrainian News (Winnipeg) in English, 685
Ukrainian News Publishers, Edmonton, 486
Ukrainian Pacific News, 768
Ukrainian Publishing Company, Winnipeg, 267, 278, 310
Ukrainian Publishing Company, Edmonton, 311
Ukrainian Publishing House, Toronto, 491
Ukrainian Pioneer, 642
Ukrainian Quarterly, 535
Ukrainian Recorder, 644
Ukrainian Review, 481, 482
Ukrainian Review, 813
Ukrainian Scholars, 596
Ukrainian Teacher, 752
Ukrainian Toiler, 394, 491, 545, 632, 633, 634
Ukrainian Tribune and Review, 482
Ukrainian Voice, 114, 147, 154, 155, 158, 229, 267, 269, 270, 272, 278, 279, 280, 288, 306, 312, 313, 317, 318, 325, 329, 375, 396, 413, 418, 440, 466, 470, 471, 472, 473, 497, 500, 501, 503, 504, 529, 531, 544, 545, 632, 633, 640, 662, 669, 712, 715
Ukrainian Voice Almanac, 281
Ukrainian Word, 497, 649, 650, 651
Ukrainian Worker, 529
Ukrainian Workingmen Associations' News, 638
Ukrainian World, 641
Ukrainica Canadiana, 596, 641
Ukrainica Occidentalia, 596
Uncle, 480
Uncle Alamanac, 310, 480
Union, 263, 305
University of Toronto Quarterly, 536
U.V.A.N. Bulletin, 642
U.V.A.N. Chronicle, 596
Veterans' News, 399, 476
Vilne Slovo, 626, 634, 638

Voice, 402
Voice of the Carpathians, 497
Voice of Labour, 495, 496
Voice of the Saviour, 488
Voice of Truth, 488, 497, 646, 649
Voice of Truth, Winnipeg, 484
Voice of Youth, 642
Vuyko, see Uncle
Warning, 289
War Veterans', News, 486
We and Our Children, 638
We and the World, 635, 668, 669
West Canada Publishing Company, 270
Western Clarion, 179
Western Farm Leader, 664
Western News, 486
Whip, 485
Widest Road to a Complete Life, 498
Will of the People, 493
Winnipeg Free Press, 75, 76, 146, 154, 671, 683, 684
Winnipeg Tribune, 116, 146, 330, 373, 686
Winnipeg Fre Press Farmer, 529
Winnipeg News, 483
Winnipeg Telegram, 146
Witness of the Truth, 114, 227, 244, 278, 283, 284
Wolyn Chronicles, 597, 641
Woman Worker, 404
Woman Workers' Voice, 404
Woman's World, 640, 641, 663, 667, 669, 767
Women's Fate, 539
Wooden-Built Churches of Ukraine, 678
Word, 647
Word, Winnipeg, 262, 263, 309, 313, 591, 592
Word of Truth, 646
Word of Guard, 642
Worker (Robotnik), Lviv, 172
Workers' Book Store Publishing Company, 311
Worker's Voice, 266, 311
Workers' Publishing Cooperative Association, 285
Workers' Word, 226, 240, 285, 286, 313, 319
Working People, 225, 226, 240, 263, 266, 272, 278, 279, 285, 295, 306, 311, 312, 313, 318
Workingwoman, 494, 496, 533
World, Vancouver, 179
World and Life, 637

World-Outlook News — Native Faith, 648
World Red Youth, 642
Yahidka, Children's Magazine, 480
Yevshan-Zilla, Toronto, 636
Young Friends, Children's Journal, 667
Young Ukraine, 600, 636, 665
Youth, 636, 644
Youth Messenger, 416, 480
Youth of Today, 529
Youth Speaks, 641
Youth World, 404, 494, 496
"Zaporozhets za Dunayem", Avramenko's Film Studio Press, 484
Zarevo, 639
Zveno, 691, 667

INDEX

GEOGRAPHIC NAMES OF COUNTRIES, PLACES, ETC.

Acadia 65
Aegean Islands 17
Alaska 26, 167, 176
Alberta 48, 65, 67, 68, 71, 73, 81, 85, 87, 88, 89, 104, 105, 106, 111, 112, 115, 116, 143, 144, 147, 157, 158, 166, 167, 169, 170, 171, 173, 220, 223, 272, 274, 316, 352, 372, 401, 423, 429, 438, 444, 445, 554, 573, 576, 626, 687, 717, 718
Alonsa 44
Altona 25
Alvena 65, 429
Ancaster 587, 655
Andrew 170, 352, 430, 432, 485
Angel Lake 362
Angusville 432
Arbakka 38, 54, 65, 130, 167
Argentine 22, 588, 711
Arran 394, 429, 430
Assiniboia 35
Assiniboine 41
Auschwitz 561
Australia 570, 588
Austria 19, 22, 23, 64, 74, 106, 171, 221, 233, 273, 292, 300, 318, 322, 325, 326, 328, 330, 334, 357, 540, 561, 565
Austro-Hungary 20, 21, 22, 325, 357

Bachka 20
Balcarres 352
Balyntsi 179
Banff 233, 644
Baryshkiwci 503
Beamsville 656
Beausejour 38, 40
Beaver Creek (Edna) 40, 45, 170
Beaver Hills 35, 42
Beaver Lake 151, 167, 178
Beaver Lowland 24
Bedfordville 412
Belgium 103
Belleview 90
Benito 156
Berezhany 32, 364
Berezhsky Komitat 21
Bereziw 32, 65
Berry 235
Besarabia 216
Bielefeld 566
Bienfait
Bifrot 41, 121
Bloomfield 529
Blumfield 468
Bohdan 362
Bon Accord 432
Bonne Maddone 174
Bonnyville 353
Borden 413
Borschiw 39, 40, 156, 170, 203, 303, 503
Bosnia 362, 363
Boston 213
Boykivshchyna 497

Boyle 429
Brandon 39, 69, 70, 88, 107, 121, 189, 225, 234, 237, 250, 326, 362, 574, 575, 576
Brantford 110, 201, 575
Bratkovets 529
Brazil 22, 28, 29, 30, 364, 367, 570, 588, 711
Breton 65
Britestone 429
British Columbia 51, 67, 69, 73, 88, 97, 176, 177, 178, 180, 372, 423, 554, 573, 576, 717, 718
British Empire 41, 292, 325, 334, 326, 327, 328, 410, 550, 565, 570
British Isles 68, 73
Brno 366
Broad Valley 167, 429
Brokenhead 38, 40, 63, 70, 166, 167, 220
Brooklands 435
Bruderheim 25
Brussels 587
Buchach 39
Bucharest 439
Buchanan 174, 394
Budapest 20
Bukovina 19, 20, 21, 22, 28, 29, 30, 39, 41, 46, 53, 64, 71, 101, 112, 216, 266, 290, 292, 294, 315, 323, 357, 358, 364, 366, 437, 564, 531, 537, 544, 569, 570.
Bulgaria 330, 357, 366

Calder 65, 352
Calgary 68, 69, 89, 110, 134, 171, 172, 173, 225, 233, 236, 304, 322, 326, 355, 446, 657, 575, 576, 581, 582, 583, 584, 607, 642
Caliento 38, 65
California 177, 224
Cameron 655
Canadian Rockies 89
Canmore 225, 233, 273, 413
Canora 65, 114, 160, 171, 248, 264, 277, 333, 352, 353, 356, 362, 400, 413, 434, 489, 500, 574, 576,
Caracas 672
Cardiff 225, 329
Cardin 272
Cardston 69
Carpathian Mountains 71
Carpatho-Ukraine 33, 99, 358, 366, 537, 548, 549, 570
Chatfield 41
Cherhill 429
Chernivci 21, 118, 224, 253, 323, 504, 531, 544
Chernyhiv 453
Chicago 158, 394, 425, 426, 432, 457, 532
China 367
Chipman 23, 24, 65, 170, 237
Chmelnytsky 44
Cleveland 426

Chortitz 25, 140
Chortkiw 25, 140
Coal Lake 353
College Height 487
Coleman 180, 233, 272
Colonsay 413
Commingston 218
Cooks Creek 63, 465
Copper Cliff 215
Cranbrook 179
Cromwell 40
Crooked Lake 41, 42
Cuba 363, 367
Cudworth 65, 278
Cunnington 353
Czechoslovakia 358, 406, 494, 530, 533, 541, 546, 548, 570

Dalesheva 302
Dana 174, 176, 411
Dauphin 39, 63, 69, 85, 115, 220, 222, 236, 287, 304, 352, 356, 362, 427, 429, 574, 575, 576, 581
Dauphin Lake 38, 41, 43, 65, 85
Davydkivtsi 500
Derwent 24, 65, 429
De Shay 353
Detroit 504, 647
Dieppe 558
Dnieper, Saskatchewan 397
Dnipro (also Dnieper)—Ukraine 25
Dnipro, Manitoba 38, 65
Dnister 6
Dnister (in Canada) 41, 65, 107, 124
Dolyny 44, 65
Dominion City 38
Dorchester 353
Doroshivtsi 65
Drifting River 38, 49
Drohoyeva 502
Duck Lake 277
Duck Mountains (Forest Reserve) 65
Dufrost 352, 432, 577
Dysart 394

East Selkirk 44
Eastern Galicia 334
Eastern Ukraine 410
Edmonton 63, 67, 68, 69, 89, 91, 102, 110, 112, 130, 142, 144, 151, 152, 157, 158, 167, 169, 170, 171, 73, 223, 225, 237, 272, 323, 375, 413, 416, 567, 574, 575, 576, 578, 583, 677, 678, 683
Egypt 17
Elk Island 62
Elphinstone 44
Emerson 532, 435, 436, 438
Ethelbert 63, 87, 93, 104, 107, 167, 219, 220, 222, 353, 411

Father Buller River 353
Fernie 90, 177, 178, 179, 180
Fernview 432
Fish Creek 42, 43, 63, 174, 235, 277
Fisher Branch 41, 65, 333, 429, 435, 436, 438

Fishers 41
Fishing River 65, 104, 167, 503
Flin Flon 574
Flossenburg 561
Foam Lake 413
Foley 41, 65
Fork River 65
Fort Frances 446, 575
Fort Saskatchewan 40
Fort William 110, 137, 180, 200, 211, 212, 218, 237, 275, 413, 423, 446, 567, 574, 575, 576, 581, 583
France 20, 64, 292, 358, 364, 434, 587, 588, 655
Frank 90, 178, 233
Franklin 121, 219, 220
Fraserwood 65, 711

Galicia 18, 19, 20, 22, 28, 29, 30, 31, 35, 40, 41, 45, 63, 64, 70, 71, 78, 96, 101, 104, 106, 153, 161, 179, 217, 233, 293, 294, 427, 333, 357, 360, 363, 364, 366, 397, 544, 569
Gardenton 38, 65, 102, 128, 356, 662
Garland 65, 166, 435, 503
Geneva 334, 337, 345, 359
Germany 64, 171, 325, 330, 357, 366, 495, 557, 560, 561, 565, 566, 567, 569, 608, 649
Gilbert Plains 121, 352, 362, 429
Gimli 41, 65, 91, 107, 120, 124, 220, 434, 435, 436, 438
Glace Bay 575, 413
Glasslyn 413
Glenella 44, 65, 354
Glengary 65
Gonor 40, 63, 103, 107
Goodeve 394, 413
Grand Prairie 353
Grenfell 35, 36, 40, 41
Gretna 25, 35
Grimsby 585, 586
Gross-Rosen 561
Guelph 218

Hafford 65, 220, 235, 353, 362, 413, 435
Halicz (in Canada) 362, 436
Halifax 34, 80, 371
Halych (in Ukraine) 163, 453
Halychyna 53, 266, 304
Hamburg 23, 72, 80
Hamilton 97, 110, 214, 218, 283, 333, 355, 394, 404, 411, 430, 575, 576, 581
Hamiota 352
Hampton 504
Harrison 352
Hayward 224
Hazelridge 577
High Prairie 362
Hillcrest 272
Hilliard 24, 65
Hleshchawa 65
Hlushkiv 32
Holer 394
Hollywood
Homefield 500
Hong Kong 558

INDEX

Horlytzi 320
Horod 44, 140
Horodenka (in Canada) 174
Horodenka (in Ukraine) 32, 65, 304, 436
Hosmer 90, 178, 179, 180, 225, 233, 502
Hovyliv Velyky 501
Hryciwka 502
Hubbard 394
Huculshchyna 497
Humboldt 277
Hungary 20, 22, 297, 540, 548
Husiatyn 216

Ichnia 531
Ilavche 500
Indian Head
Innisfree 237
Insinger 65
Interlake District 41, 43, 60, 63, 65
Ituna 394, 429, 587

Janow 140
Jaroslaw 41, 65, 129, 140
Jasper Place (suburb of Edmonton) 576
Jersey City 208, 314
Josefberg 35

Kalush 23, 40
Kamchatka 26
Kanev 453
Kapuskasing 326
Keld 38, 51, 65, 66, 362
Kelvington 436
Kelwood 44, 65
Kenora 216, 423, 446, 575
Kharkiv 531, 534, 542
Kholm 547, 589
Kiev 17, 22, 157, 177, 252, 345, 357, 453, 560
Kievan Rus 17, 18
Killarney 69
Kitchener 110, 215, 574, 575, 576
Kniaze 502
Kolomyya (also Kolomya) 30, 39, 65, 261, 529
Kolomyja (in Canada) 38, 65, 170
Komarno 41, 120, 140, 464, 586
Kosiw 38, 65, 66, 115
Krakiw 24, 173
Krasne 394
Kremlin 407, 603, 604, 666
Kreuzberg 41, 220, 353
Krydor 65, 333, 413
Kupchyntsi 32

Lac du Bonnet 120
Lachine 211
Lac Labiche 353
Lacombe 89
Lake Erie 532
Lakeview 354
Lake Waskesieu 532
Lamont 24, 65
Landetz 25

Landrian 367
Lanigan 394
Lanuke 156
Lany 272
Lauverna 413
Lavoy 352
Lawrence 354
Laz 40
Leduc 173
Lemberg 65
Lemgo 566
Lemieux 362
Lemkiwschyna 33, 215, 239, 479, 635, 668
Lethbridge 68, 90, 171, 172, 233, 272, 326, 362, 574
Lily 180
Limestone Lake 45
Liverpool 23, 30
London, England 25, 30, 31, 32, 70, 71, 101, 304, 344, 439, 529, 536, 564, 566, 567, 594
London, Ontario 216, 574, 607
Loon Lake 167
Lviv 29, 30, 31, 32, 33, 38, 49, 103, 104, 105, 107, 109, 118, 123, 161, 162, 163, 25, 253, 269, 321, 322, 340, 345, 359, 363, 364, 368, 370, 410, 453, 537, 542, 544, 560

Mackenzie 67, 224
McCreary 121
Majdanek 561
Malay Islands 433
Manchester 593
Manitoba 23, 24, 36, 38, 40, 43, 44, 48, 63, 65, 67, 68, 70, 73, 75, 85, 87, 88, 89, 94, 96, 97, 103, 107, 111, 112, 115-118, 123, 141, 143-148, 158, 166, 167, 170, 220, 221, 222, 240, 315, 333, 339, 341, 342, 351, 401, 423, 4299, 438, 444, 445, 554, 573, 576, 625, 627, 685, 717, 718, 729
Manitoba Lake 44
Marmarosky Komitat 21
Marquette 67
Meacham 413
Meadow Lake 354
Meadowville 644
Mears 167
Medicine Hat 68
Medika 140
Melville 202, 352, 500
Menofield 174
Menzie 44
Michelle 179, 180
Mikado 413
Mink River 283
Mink River 38, 166, 354
Minneapolis 102, 112
Minnesota 39
Modelfarm 394
Mohyly 44, 65
Monckman 362
Moncton 578
Montreal 23, 31, 91, 97, 110, 135, 149, 150, 180, 185, 209, 210, 218, 272,

284, 330, 355, 567, 575
Moose Jaw 68, 69, 446, 574
Moosomin 69
Moscow 18, 19, 288, 295, 358, 476, 477
Mount Carmel 39, 100, 115, 329, 320, 371
Mountain Road 65
Mukachiv 20
Mundare 24, 62, 110, 131, 151, 153, 156, 158, 170, 173, 201, 243, 275, 291, 322, 356, 394, 429, 462, 463, 464, 484, 488, 587, 645
Mychalkiw 500
Myrnam 24, 65, 170, 173, 177, 197, 220, 356, 362, 429

Nadvirna 320
Nanaimo 90, 233, 265, 272
Nebyliw Colony 40
Nebyliw (in Ukraine) 23, 28, 34, 35, 40
Neepawa 69
Neudorf 35, 36
Newark 587
New Brunswick 67, 585
New Yaroslav 41, 42
New York 75, 89, 105, 263, 305, 309, 372, 456, 502, 530, 535, 583, 584, 653, 711
Niagara Falls 218, 532, 575, 655
North Dakota 39
Northern Valley 362
Northwest Territories 63, 68, 717, 718
Norma 431
Nova Scotia 67, 97, 262, 375, 423, 462, 575, 576, 585

Oakburn 61, 65, 85, 166, 167, 352, 500
Okno 41
Olephant 239
Old Fordge 240
Oleskiw 38, 65, 114, 140, 166, 167, 356
Olha 44, 65
Ontario 67, 97, 157, 211, 216, 221, 262, 284, 304, 330, 355, 372, 404, 413, 446, 462, 463, 466, 469, 554, 572, 573, 574, 581, 582, 585, 594, 605, 653, 706, 709, 717, 718
Onut 502
Oshawa 215, 218, 355, 394, 492, 493, 574, 575, 576, 656, 683
Ottawa 30, 31, 36, 105, 110, 136, 180, 213, 218, 319, 331, 336, 355, 574, 575, 576
Ozerna 44, 65, 140

Paraguay 711
Parana 367
Paris 269, 294, 332, 336, 337, 344, 345, 359, 366
Patterson Lake, 44, 61, 75, 85
Peace River 353, 354, 355
Peace River Crossing 353
Pelly 434
Pennsylvania 100, 115, 320
Perehinsko 35
Peremyshl 364
Pereyaslaw 18

Petawawa 330
Petlura 140
Petrowka 283
Pheasant Forks 41
Phoenix 225
Pieton 65
Pidliasia 360, 589
Pidpylypia 503
Pine River 368
Pittsburgh 275
Pleasant Home 41, 60, 65, 115, 166, 167, 299, 436
Podillia 54, 216, 501
Pohorylivtsi 65
Pokuttia 32, 179, 224, 501, 502
Poland 18, 19, 334, 358, 366, 375, 406, 410, 471, 531, 537, 546, 548, 570
Polisia 360, 366, 560
Poltava 18
Poplar Field 41, 65
Poplar Park 63
Porcupine 217
Portage La Prairie 88, 107, 166, 167, 237, 265, 408, 574
Port Arthur 211, 212, 423, 574, 575, 576, 581, 655
Potutory 32
Prague 366, 410
Pravda 146, 315
Preeceville 65
Preston 394
Prince Albert 65, 67, 89, 103, 353, 354, 355, 574, 576, 607, 655
Prince Edward Island 67, 375
Prudhomme 413
Prussia 20, 297
Prut River 501

Quebec (city) 23, 24, 34, 36, 97, 108, 152, 371
Quebec (province) 67, 97, 149, 180, 210, 423, 554, 573, 717, 718
Quill Lake 174

Rabbit Hills 40, 103, 170
Rabbit Lake 40
Radekhiv 529
Radison 65, 174
Raymond 69
Redberry 65, 333, 430, 436
Red Deer 574
Red River 25, 72, 532
Red River Valley 25
Redwater 437
Redway 462
Regina 68, 69, 110, 123, 141, 234, 394, 404, 413, 429, 430, 432, 476, 493, 541, 574, 575, 576, 581, 586, 607, 608
Rembrandt 41
Renfrew 352
Riding Mountains 43, 63, 65, 67, 74, 166, 352
Roblin 65, 147, 167, 438, 464, 587, 630, 645
Rockwood 41, 115, 121, 438
Rohatyn 320, 364
Roland 535

INDEX

Rome 103, 106, 587
Rome, Vatican City 99, 102, 107, 585
Rosa 38, 65, 140, 166
Rosedale 74, 115
Rossburn 65, 94, 167, 220, 352, 431
Rosthern 40, 63, 65, 69, 173, 175, 176, 184, 220, 237, 276, 278, 413
Roumania 358, 366, 406, 546
Roycroft 353, 362, 462
Rozubowychi 504
Rus 38, 39, 315
Ruska Rava 44
Ruska Svoboda 36, 65, 70, 315
Russell 438
Russia 22, 24, 25, 26, 64, 221, 273, 288, 289, 292, 295, 326, 328, 357, 358, 477
Ruthenia 44, 65

Saltcoats 41, 42, 43, 63, 83, 278
Sambir 35, 364
Samburg 353
Sandy Lake 44, 65, 353, 429, 577
Sandylands 38
San Francisco 112
Sarnia 575
Sarto 167
Saskatchewan 35, 41, 42, 48, 65, 67, 71, 73, 75, 85, 86, 87, 89, 99, 104, 105, 106, 107, 111, 112, 115, 116, 118, 123, 129, 141, 143, 144, 154, 166, 173, 174, 175, 176, 220, 223, 333, 339, 343, 372, 401, 423, 429, 438, 444, 445, 488, 554, 573, 576, 626, 627, 688, 717, 718
Saskatoon 42, 67, 68, 69, 110, 112, 113, 157, 158, 173, 237, 333, 343, 365, 400, 412, 416, 574, 575, 576, 578, 583
Sault St. Marie 110, 217, 218, 574
Scranton 422, 500
Seech 26, 44, 65
Selkirk 44, 67, 69, 167, 223, 327, 436, 574
Senkiw 38, 65, 140
Sexsmith 353
Shamokin 239, 438
Shandro 352, 353
Shenandoah 208
Shevchenko (also Szewczenko) 38, 65, 140, 166
Shoal Lake 43, 44, 63, 352
Shoylyk 44
Sianok 320
Siberia 20, 22, 26, 407, 545, 562, 588
Sidney 660
Sifton 38, 42, 63, 65, 93, 94, 103, 107, 110, 124, 153, 159, 166, 188, 222
Sirko 38, 65, 140
Sitch (in Ukraine) 493
Skalat 174
Skoon 413
Slater 368
Slave Lake 353
Sliding Hills 41, 235
Small Black Bear 352
Smoky Lake 429, 430, 488, 649

Smuts 430
Sokal (in Canada) 65
Sokal (in Ukraine) 38, 65
Souris 69
Souzivka 653
Soviet Union 64, 491, 560, 564
Spirit Lake 330
Springfield 38, 40, 438
St. Albert 101, 107
St. Andrew 38, 41, 287
St. Boniface 104, 105, 117, 193, 201, 420, 429
St. Catharines 218, 574, 575, 576, 583, 607
St. Isadore 174
St. Julien 174, 353, 413
St. Norbert 38, 40, 63
St. Paul 353
St. Rose 354
St. Walburg 354
Stanyslaviv (now Ivano-Frankivsk) 23, 224, 226, 364
Star 40, 65
Starlag 174
Stonewall 167, 222
Stony Mountain 167, 412
Stony Plains 35
Strathclair 75, 352
Strathcona 67, 81
Stuartburn (also Shtombur) 37, 39, 41, 58, 65, 66, 70, 84, 86, 87, 100, 102, 103, 107, 115, 166, 219, 353
Sub-Carpathia 18, 19, 22
Suchno 529
Sudbury 110, 215, 216, 218, 355, 400, 404, 430, 476, 574, 575, 576, 583, 640
Sundown 38, 65
Swift Current 432
Sydney, N.S. 110, 216, 217, 575

Taras 354
Tarnopol (also Tarnopil) 25, 65, 224, 363
Terebovla (also Trembowla) 38, 39, 41, 60, 65, 70, 100, 101, 104, 106, 107, 115, 167, 236, 304, 664
Terebovla (in Ukraine) 65
Teulon 84, 86, 468, 150, 160, 535
Theodore 65
Thorold 218, 429, 430, 446
Timmins 217, 575
Tolstoi 38, 65, 235, 303, 356
Toronto 91, 97, 110, 111, 131, 137, 152, 180, 213, 218, 272, 355, 416, 489, 567, 575, 576, 578, 580, 583, 634, 639, 643, 677, 688
Towmach 39
Transcona 110, 408
Two Hills 24, 65, 173
Turkey 330, 357
Tyndall 40

Uhochansky Komitat 21
Ukraina (in Manitoba) 65, 140, 200
Ukraine 18, 19, 22, 24, 25, 26, 40, 46, 47, 64, 66, 84, 85, 92, 99, 161, 173,

271, 301, 315, 318, 328, 338, 344, 345, 357, 363, 407, 449, 450, 458, 465, 471, 476, 559, 560, 567, 571
Ukrainian Socialist Soviet Republic 358, 406, 407, 494, 534, 542
U.S.S.R. 22, 405, 406, 410, 471, 495, 496, 497, 534, 546, 570, 588, 608
Uzansky Komitat 21
Uzhorod 21

Valley River 38, 60, 65, 100, 104, 115, 167, 236, 362
Vancouver 108, 177, 178, 179, 216, 233, 286, 322, 484, 485, 574, 575, 576, 587, 597, 607, 642, 653, 655
Vasylkivci 91
Vatican 585, 588
Vegreville 24, 65, 85, 156, 157, 167, 170, 172, 173, 187, 197, 198, 201, 203, 220, 237, 254, 353, 413, 438, 574, 607, 608
Venezuela 570
Venlaw 38, 65, 166
Verbova 504
Veregin 394
Vermilion 69, 170
Vernon 326, 574
Vetlyn 40
Vienna 32, 33, 103, 106
Vilna 432
Vilchivchyk 500
Virden 41
Vita 38, 65, 166, 333, 429
Volhynia 18, 360, 366
Volkivtsi (also Wolkiwci) 38, 49, 354
Vonda 65, 277, 278, 413
Vostok (also Wostok) 24, 65, 103, 170, 172, 225, 289
Vysotske (also Wysocke) 40

Wakaw 65, 186, 264, 413
Wabamun Lake 354
Waterloo 574, 576
Waterville 586
Warsaw 541, 642
Washington 276, 549
Welland 217, 218, 404, 574
Western Ukraine 18, 19, 25, 33, 40, 78, 91, 157, 209, 216, 224, 429, 430, 436, 446, 468, 530, 537, 540, 544
West Fort William 404, 446
Wetaskiwin 69, 89
Weyburn 69
Whitemouth 63
Whitkow 413
Willington 352, 429, 463
Willow Brook 413
Willow Creek 394
Windsor 218, 355, 394, 400, 426, 463, 476, 477, 574, 575, 576, 583, 607, 683
Winnipeg 24, 26, 34, 35-42, 67, 69, 72, 81, 82, 100, 103, 105, 106, 108, 110, 112, 116, 117, 133, 136, 147, 148, 152, 154, 158, 164, 166, 167, 182, 222, 223, 235, 237, 272, 278, 321, 333, 335, 365, 375, 444, 453, 470, 482, 574, 575, 576, 577, 580, 583, 640, 643
Winnipeg Beach 41, 65, 66
Winnipegosis 65, 68
Winnipegosis Lake 65
Wishart 394, 429, 430, 583
Wolfville 536
Wroxton 65, 352, 394
Wyshnivets 532

Yaroslav (in Ukraine) 40
Yaroslav (in Canada), see Jaroslaw
Yorkton 41, 43, 63, 69, 110, 132, 153, 173, 220, 413, 463, 488, 574, 576, 587
Yugoslavia 20, 361, 362, 366, 538, 588
Yukon 262, 585

Zakerzonnia 635
Zalishchyky 39
Zaporozhe 44, 315
Zaporozhian Sich 18, 25
Zbaraz (in Canada) 41
Zbaraz (in Ukraine) 320
Zbruch River 358
Zelena 140
Zeleny Klyn 20
Zhoda 140, 315
Zolochiv 32, 364

BIBLIOGRAPHY

to the First Edition

IN ENGLISH:

ADAMS, ARTHUR E., *Bolsheviks in the Ukraine: The Second Campaign,* 1918-1919. New Haven: Yale University Press, 1963.

ANDRUSYSHEN, CONSTANTINE H., *Ukrainian Literature and Its Guiding Light Shevchenko.* Winnipeg: Ukrainian National Youth Federation of Canada, 1949.

—— *The Ukrainian Poets,* 1189-1962, Selected and translated into English verse by C. H. Andrusyshen and Watson Kirkconnell. Toronto, Published for the Ukrainian Canadian Committee by University of Toronto, 1963.

ARCHIPENKO, A., *Fifty Creative Years,* 1908-1958 *and Fifty Art Historians.* New York, Tekhne, 1960.

ARMSTRONG, JOHN A., *Ukrainian Nationalism.* New York and London: Columbia University Press, 1963.

BAYLEY, CHARLIE, *The Social Structure of the Italian and Ukrainian Communities in Montreal* /Manuscript/, 1939.

BORYS, JURIJ, *The Russian Communist Party and the Sovietization of Ukraine: A Study in the Communist Doctrine of the Self-Determination.* Stockholm, 1960.

BROWN, O.E.A., *Settlers of The Gilbert Plains.* Dauphin, Altona, 1953.

BRYCE, PETER, *Continental Europeans in Western Canada.* Winnipeg, 1928.

BURIANYK, W., *S.U.S. Its Meaning and Significance.* Toronto, 1967.

—— *Canadian Ethnic Studies: Bulletin of the Research Centre for Canadian Ethnic Studies.* Vol. I, Edited by Alexander Malycky, Calgary: University of Calgary, 1969.

CENSUS OF PRAIRIE PROVINCES, *Population and Agriculture: Manitoba, Saskatchewan, Alberta,* 1916, Ottawa, 1918.

CHAMBERLIN, W. H., *The Ukraine: A Submerged Nation,* New York, 1944.

CHIROVSKY, N. L. Fr., *Old Ukraine; Its Socio-Economic History Prior to* 1781. Madison, Floorham Park Press, 1963.

CONNOR, RALPH, *The Foreigner: A Tale of Saskatchewan.* New York, 1909.

DAFOE, JOHN W., *Clifford Sifton in Relation to His Times.* Toronto, The MacMillan Company of Canada Ltd., 1931.

DARCOVICH, WILLIAM, Ph.D., *Ukrainians in Canada: The Struggle to Retain Their Identity.* Ottawa: Ukrainian Self-Reliance Association, 1967.

DAVIDSON, GORDON A., *The Ukrainians in Canada: A Study in Canadian Immigration.* Montreal, 1947.

DAVIES, RAYMOND ARTHUR, *This is Our Land: Ukrainian Canadians Against Hitler.* Toronto: Progress Books, 1943.

DMYTRIW, OLYA, *Ukrainian Arts.* New York, Ukrainian Youth League of North America, 1955.

DOROSHENKO DMYTRO, *A Survey of Ukrainian Historiography.* New York: Ukrainian Academy of Arts and Sciences in the U.S.A., 1957.

—— *History of Ukraine.* Edmonton: The Institute Press, 1939.

DZIOBKO, J., *My Songs.* Winnipeg: Ukrainian Pioneer Library, 1958.

ENGLAND, ROBERT, *The Central European Immigrants in Canada,* Toronto: The MacMillan Company of Canada Ltd., 1929.

—— *The Colonization of Western Canada.* London: P. S. King and Sons, 1936.

EWACH, HONORE, *Ukraine's Call to America.* Detroit: Ukrainian Cultural Society, 1947.

—— *Ukrainian Songs and Lyrics: A Short Anthology.* Winnipeg, Ukrainian Publishing Co., 1933.

FEDENHO, PANAS, *Ukraine: Her Struggle for Freedom.* Augsburg: Free Ukraine, 1951.

FIFTH CENSUS OF CANADA, 1911. Ottawa: Government Printing Bureau, 1911.

FIRST UKRAINIAN *Catholic Metropolitan See of Canada.* Winnipeg: Ukrainian Catholic Archdiocese of Winnipeg, 1957.

FIRST ALL-UKRAINIAN *Congress of Ukrainians in Canada.* Winnipeg: Ukrainian Canadian Committee, 1943.

FISHMAN, JOSHUA *and* VLADIMIR C. NAHIRNY, JOHN E. HOFMAN, ROBERT G. HAYDE, *Language Loyalty in the United States: The Maintenance and Perpetuation of Non-English Mother Tongues by American Ethnic and Religious Groups,* New York, 1967.

GIBBON, JOHN MURRAY, *Canadian Mosaic: The Making of a Northern Nation.* Toronto: McClelland & Stewart, 1938.

GREGOROVICH, ANDREW, *Books on Ukraine and the Ukrainians: A Selected Annotated List of 200 Books in English, French, German and Spanish.* Studies in Research Institute, Toronto, 1963.

GREGOROVICH JOHN, *A Ukrainian Canadian in Parliament: Memoirs of Michael Luchkovich,* Toronto: Ukrainian Canadian Research Foundation, 1965.

HALICH, WASYL, *Ukrainians in the United States.* Chicago: University of Chicago Press, 1937.

HERMANIUK, METROPOLITAN MAXIM, *The Manitoba School Question: Pastoral Letter.* Winnipeg: Progress Printing & Publishing, 1964.

HORAK, STEPHAN, *Poland and Her National Minorities, 1919-1939.* New York: Vantage Press, 1961.

HRUSHEVSKY, MICHAEL, *A History of Ukraine.* New Haven: Yale University Press, 1941.

HUNCHAK, N. J., *Canadians of Ukrainian Origin: Population.* Winnipeg: Ukrainian Canadian Committee, 1945.

HUNTER A. J., *A Friendly Adventure: The Story of the United Church Mission Among New Canadians at Teulon, Manitoba.* Toronto: Board of Home Missions of the United Church of Canada, 1929.

KAMENETSKY, IHOR, *Hitler's Occupation of Ukraine (1941-1944): A Study of Totalitarian Imperialism.* Milwaukee: The Marquette University Press, 1956.

—— *Secret Nazi Plans for Eastern Europe.* New York: Bookman Associates, 1961.

KAYE, V. J., *Early Ukrainian Settlement in Canada, 1895-1900.* Toronto: University of Toronto Press, 1964.

—— *Participation of Ukrainians in the Political Life of Canada.* "Almanach Zolotoho Yuvileyu 1905-1955". Winnipeg 1955.

—— *Ukraine, Russia and Other Slavic Countries in English Literature.* Winnipeg: UVAN, 1961.

KAYE-KYSILEVSKYJ, V. J., *Slavic Groups in Canada.* Slavistica No. 12. Winnipeg: Ukrainian Free Academy of Sciences, 1951.

KIRIAK, ILLA, *Sons of the Soil*, Translated by Michael Luchkovich, Toronto: Ryerson Press, 1959.
KIRKCONNELL, WATSON, *Canada, Europe, and Hitler.* Toronto: Oxford University Press, 1939.
—— *Canadian Overtones.* Winnipeg: Columbia Press, 1935.
—— *Our Ukrainian Loyalists.* Winnipeg: Ukrainian Canadian Committee, 1943.
—— *The Ukrainian Canadians and the War.* Toronto: Oxford University Press, 1940.
—— *The Place of Slavic Studies in Canada.* Winnipeg: Ukrainian Free Academy of Sciences, 1958.
—— *Seven Pillars of Freedom.* Toronto: Oxford University Press, 1944.
—— *Twilight of Liberty.* Toronto: Oxford University Press, 1941.
KLYMASH, BOHDAN, *Ukrainian Folk Dance: A Symposium.* Toronto: Ukrainian National Youth Federation of Canada, 1961.
KOHUSKA, NATALIA LEWENEC, *Forty Years in Retrospect.* Hamilton-Toronto-Winnipeg, 1967.
KONONENKO, KONSTANTYN, *Ukraine and Russia: A History of the Economic Relations Between Ukraine and Russia, 1954-1917.* Milwaukee: Marquette University Press, 1958.
KOSTIUK, HRYHORY, *Stalinist Rule in the Ukraine: A Study of the Decade of Mass Terror, 1929-1939.* New York: Praeger, 1960.
KOWALSKY, HUMPHREY, *Ukrainian Folk Songs: A Historical Treatise.* Boston Stratfor Company, 1925.
KUBIJOVYCH, VOLODYMYR, *Atlas of Ukraine and Adjoining Countries.* Lviv, 1937.
LIBERAL HANDBOOK, 1914, Platform of Manitoba Liberals 1914.
LIVESAY, FLORENCE RANDAL, Songs of Ukraina with Ruthenian Poems. London: J. M. Dent, 1916.
LOWER, A., *From Colony to Nation: A History of Canada.* Toronto, 1946.
LUCIW, WASYL, *Ahapius Honcharenko and the Alaska Herald*, by Wasyl Luciw and Theodore Luciw, Toronto: Slavic Library, 1963.
LUPUL, MONOLY R., *Church (Catholic), State Relations in Education in the old North-West Territories, 1880-1905. A Thesis to the Committee on the Ph.D. in Education,* Harvard University, Cambridge, 1963.
LUZNYCKY, GREGORY, *Ukrainian Literature Within the Framework of World Literature.* Philadelphia: America, 1961.
LYSENKO, VERA, *Men in Sheepskin Coats: A Study in Assimilation.* Toronto: The Ryerson Press, 1947.
—— *Westerly Wild.* Toronto: The Ryerson Press, 1956.
—— *Yellow Boots,* Toronto: The Ryerson Press, 1954.
MACKINTOSH, W. A., *Prairie Settlement: The Geographical Setting.* Toronto, 1934.
McWILLIAMS, MARGARET, *Manitoba Milestones.* Toronto & London: J. M. Dent & Sons, 1928.
MANDRYKA, M. I.,*History of Ukrainian Literature in Canada.* Winnipeg: Ukrainian Free Academy of Sciences, 1968.
—— *The Ukrainian Question.* Winnipeg: Canadian Ukrainian Educational Association, 1940.
—— *Ukrainian Refugees.* Winnipeg, 1946.
MANITOBA, DEPARTMENT OF EDUCATION, *Special Report on Bilingual Schools in Manitoba.* Winnipeg, 1916.

MANNING, C. A., *Outline of Ukrainian History.* Winnipeg: Canadian Committee, 1949.
—— *A Ukrainian Liturature: Studies of the Leading Authors.* Jersey City, N.J.: Ukrainian National Association, 1944.
—— *The Story of Ukraine.* New York, Philosophical Library, 1947.
—— *Twentieth Century Ukraine.* New York: Bookman Associates, 1951.
MARTOVYCH, OLEH, *National Problems in the USSR.* Edinburgh: Scottish League for European Freedom, 1953.
—— *Ukrainian Liberation Movement in Modern Times.* Edinburgh: Scottish League for European Freedom, 1951.
MASTERS, D. C., *The Winnipeg General Strike.* Toronto: University of Toronto Press, 1950.
MIRCHUK, IVAN, *Ukraine and Its People: A Handbook with Maps, Statistical Tables and Diagrams.* Munich: Ukrainian Free University, 1949.
MORTON, A. S., *A History of Prairie Settlement.* Toronto: MacMillan Co. of Canada, 1938.
—— *A History of the Canadian West to* 1870-71. Toronto, 1939.
MURCHIE, R. W. and GRANT, H. C., *Unused Lands of Manitoba.* Winnipeg: Department of Agriculture and Immigration, 1926.
MYDLOWKSY, LEV W., *Bolshevist Persecution of Church and Religion in Ukraine,* 1917-1957. London: Ukrainian Publishers, 1958.
NAHAYEWSKY. ISIDORE, *History of Ukraine.* Philadelphia: America Pub. House, 1962.
OHLOBLYN, ALEXANDER, *Treaty of Pereyaslav,* 1654, *translated by B. Budurovych.* Toronto: Canadian League of Ukraine's Liberation, 1954.
OBJECTIVES, RESOLUTIONS, ORGANS. Winnipeg: World Congress of Ukrainians, 1967.
ON LANGUAGE AND CULTURE. Winnipeg: Ukrainian Canadian Committee, 1962.
ONUFRIJCHUK, THEODORE T., *The History of R. M. of Sliding Hills No.* 273. Mikado, Sask. and Their Centennial Park, 1967.
OSTAPCHUK, EMILIE, ed. *Folk Art of Carpatho-Ukraine.* Toronto, 1957.
OUR *Non-English Speaking Canadians,* prepared by: The James Robertson Memorial Fund Committee, 1917.
PALUK, WILLIAM, *Canadian Cossacks.* Winnipeg: Canadian Ukrainian Review Publishing Company, 1943.
PASTERNAK, YAROSLAV, *Archeology of Ukraine.* Toronto: Shevchenko Scientific Society, 1961.
PIDHAINI, OLEG S., *The Ukrainian-Polish Problem in the Dissolution of the Russian Empire,* 1914-1917. Toronto: New Review Books, 1962.
PIDHAINY, S. O., ed. *The Black Deeds of the Kremlin: A White Book,* 2 volumes. Toronto Ukrainian Association of Victims of Russian Communist Terror, 1953-1955.
PIGIDO, F., ed. *Material Concerning Ukrainian-Jewish Relations During the Years of the Revolution* (1917-1921). Munich: Ukrainian Information Bureau, 1956.
PIGIDO, PRAVOBERZNY, F., *The Stalin Famine: Ukraine in the Year* 1933. London: Ukrainian Youth Association in Great Britain, 1953.
PIPES, RICHARD, *The Formation of the Soviet Union, Communism and Nationalism,* 1917-1923. Cambridge, Harvard University Press, 1954.
POLONSKA-VASYLENKO, NATALIA, *Two Conceptions of the History of Ukraine and Russia.* London: The Association of Ukrainians in Great Britain, 1968.

RAFFALOVICH, GEORGE, *The Ukraine* (by Bedwin Sands—pseudonim). London: Francis Griffiths, 1914.
REMINISCENCES *of the Rossburn Pioneers*, Rossburn, Manitoba, 1932.
RESHETAR, J. S., *The Ukrainian Revolution*. Princeton: Princeton University Press, 1952.
ROCKWOOD ECHOES: 90 *Years of Progress* 1870-1960: *A History of Municipality*, 1960.
ROMANIUK, GUS, *Taking Root in Canada: An Autobiography*. Winnipeg: Columbia Press, 1954.
RUDNYCKYJ, J. B., *Ukrainian Canadian Folklore*. Winnipeg, 1960.
RUDNYCKY, STEPHEN, *Ukraine: The Land and Its People, An Introduction to Its Geography*. New York: Rand McNally for the Ukrainian Alliance of America, 1918.
RURYK, NANCY R. ed., *Ukrainian Embroidery Designs and Stitches*. Winnipeg, Ukrainian Women's Asc'n of Canada, 1958.
SCIBORSKY, MYKOLA, *Ukraine and Russia*. Translated by S. Davidovich. New York: Organization for the Rebirth of Ukraine, 1940.
SCOTT, W. L., *Eastern Catholics*. Toronto: Catholic Truth Society, 1927.
SHEPTICKY, ANDREW, ARCHBISHOP. *Address on the Ruthenian Question to Their Lordships The Archbishops and Bishops of Canada*, Leopolis, March, 1911.
SHERBININ, MICHAEL A., *The Galicians Dwelling in Canada and Their Origin*. Winnipeg: The Manitoba Free Press Company, 1906.
SICHYNSKY, V., *Ukraine in Foreign Comments and Descriptions*. New York: UCC of America, 1953.
SIMPSON, G. W.,*The Names "Rus", "Russia", "Ukraine" and Their Historical Background*. Slavistica No. 10. Winnipeg: Ukrainian Free Academy of Sciences, 1951.
—— *Ukraine: An Atlas of Its History and Georgraphy*. Toronto: Oxford University Press, 1941.
—— *The Ukrainian Question and the Present Crisis*. Saskatoon: Ukrainian National Federation of Canada, 1939.
—— *Why Learn Ukrainian*. Winnipeg: U.C.C. 1965.
SISLER, W. J., *Peaceful Invasion*. Winnipeg: Ketchen Printing Co., 1944.
SISSONS, C. B., *Bilingual Schools in Ontario*. Toronto: J. M. Dent & Sons, 1917.
SKELTON, O. D., *The Language Issue in Canada*. Kingston, 1917.
SKWAROK, J. J., *The Ukrainian Settlers in Canada and Their Schools*. Edmonton: Basilian Press, 1958.
SLAVS IN CANADA: *Proceeding of the First National Conference on Canadian Slavs*. Edmonton: Inter-University Committee on Canadian Slavs, Vol. I, 1966.
SLAVS IN CANADA: *Proceedings of the Second National Conference on Canadian Slavs*. Ottawa, Toronto, Inter-University Committee on Canadian Slavs, Vol. II, 1968.
SLAVUTYCH, YAR, — *The Muse in Prison*. Jersey City: Svoboda, 1956.
—— *Ukrainan Literature in Canada*. Edmonton: Slavuta, 1966.
SMAL-STOCKI, ROMAN, *The Captive Nations: Nationalism of the Non-Russian Nations in the Soviet Union*. New York: Bookman Associates, 1960.
—— *The Nationality Problem of the Soviet Union and Russian Communist Imperialism*. Milwaukee: Bruce Publishing Co., 1952.
—— *The Origin of the Word "Rus"*, Winnipeg: Ukrainian Free Academy of Sciences, 1949.

SMITH, W. J., *A Study of Canadian Immigration*. Toronto: The Ryerson Press, 1920.

SNOWYD, D., *Spirit of Ukraine: Ukrainian Contribution to World's Culture*. New York, 1935.

STECHISHIN, SAVELLA, *Traditional Ukrainian Cookery*. Winnipeg: Trident Press, 1959.

STRANGERS *Within Our Gates, or Coming Canadians*. Toronto: Missionary Society of the Methodist Church of Canada, 1909.

SWALLOW, S. J., *Ox Trails to Highways: Yorkton Pioners*. Yorkton, 1955.

SYRNICK, JOHN H., *Community Builders: Early Ukrainian Teachers*, Transactions of the Historical and Scientific Society of Manitoba, Series III, No. 21.

UKRAINIAN-CANADIAN *Business Almanac*, Toronto, 1955.

UKRAINIAN CATHOLIC *Women's League of Canada: Its Origin and Activity*. Toronto, 1957.

UKRAINIANS *in Canada: A Classified Directory of Ukrainian Business and Professional Interests Throughout Canada*. 1945. Editions, Compiled and Published by F. A. Macrouch, Winnipeg, 1945.

UKRAINIANS *in Canada: Business Year Book*, 1949-1950. Compiled and Published by Macrouch, Winnipeg, 1952.

UKRAINIAN *Year Book and Ukrainians of Distinction*. F. A. Macrouch, Compiler and Publisher, 1953-1954, Winnipeg, 1954.

UKRAINIAN *Year Book: The Ukrainian Business Directory*, 1954-1955 Edition. F. A. Macrouch, Compiler and Publisher, Winnipeg, 1955.

UKRAINKA, LESYA, *Spirit of Flame: A Collection of the Works of Lesya Ukrainka*. Translated by Percival Cundy, New York: Bookman Associates, 1950.

VOWLS, HUGH P., *Ukraine and Its People*. London: W & R Chambers, 1939.

WANGENHEIM, ELISABETH, *The Ukrainians: A Case Study of the "Third Force" in "Nationalism in Canada"*, by the University League for Social Reform. Edited by Peter Russell, Toronto: McGraw-Hill Co. Ltd., 1966.

WEIR, T. R., *Rural Population Change: Interlake*, 1951-1961. Winnipeg: Manitoba Department of Agriculture and Conservation.

WERES, ROMAN, *The Ukraine: Selected References in the English Language*. Kalamazoo, Mich., School of Graduate Studies, Western Michigan University, 1961.

WLASOWSKY, IVAN, Outline History of the Ukrainian Orthodox Church. Translated by M. J. Diakowsky, New York: Ukrainian Orthodox Church of the United States, 1956.

WOMAN OF UKRAINE: *Her Part on the Scene of History, in Literature, Arts, and Struggle for Freedom*. Philadelphia: UNWL of America, 1955 .

THE WOMAN'S *Missionary Society in Manitoba*, 1884-1959: The United Church of Canada. Winnipeg, 1959.

WOODSWORTH, S. J., *Strangers Within Our Gates*. Toronto: The Missionary Society of the Methodist Church, Canada, 1908.

—— *My Neighbor: A Study of City Conditions: A Plea for Social Service*. Toronto: Young People's Forward Movement for Missions, 1911.

—— *Rural Communities: Report of Investigation by the Bureau of Social Research*, Governments of Manitoba, Saskatchewan and Alberta. Winnipeg, 1917.

WOYCENKO, OLHA, *Canada's Culture Heritage: Ukrainian Contribution*. Winnipeg: UVAN, 1964.

BIBLIOGRAPHY

—— *The Ukrainians in Canada*, Ottawa-Winnipeg, 1967.
YOUNG, CHARLES H., *The Ukrainian Canadians*. Toronto: Thomas Nelson & Sons, 1931.
YUZYK, PAUL, *The First Ukrainians in Manitoba. Papers Read Before the Historical and Scientific Society of Manitoba.* Series III, No. 8. Winnipeg: Historical and Scientific Society of Manitoba, 1953.
—— *The History of the Ukrainian Greek Catholic (Uniate) Church in Canada.* Master's Thesis. University of Saskatchewan, 1948.
—— *The Ukrainians in Manitoba: A Social History.* Toronto: University of Toronto Press, 1953.
—— *Ukrainian Canadians. Their Place and Role in Canadian Life..* Toronto: Ukrainian Canadian Business and Professional Federation, 1967.

SELECTED BIBLIOGRAPHY

IN UKRAINIAN

ALMANACS AND MEMORIAL BOOKS

Almanakh zolotoho yuvileyu 1905-1955 /"The Golden Jubilee Almanac 1905-1955"/. Winnipeg: Ukrainian Mutual Benefit Association of St. Nicholas, 1957.
British Columbia and Ukrainians. Compiled by F. Bogdan. Published by Ukrainian Fraternal Society, Branch No. 20, Vancouver, 1957.
Calendar of the "Ukrainian Voice" for the Leap Year 1948. Vol. XXXI. Winnipeg, 1948.
Calendar of the "Ukrainian Voice" for the Jubilee Year 1950. Vol. XXXIII. Winnipeg, 1950.
Farma /"The Farm"/: *Canadian Almanac* 1930. Winnipeg: St. Raphael's Ukrainian Immigrant Welfare Association, 1930.
The Golden Gate: A Jubilee Book of Ukrainian Society "Prosvita" in Port Arthur, Ont. — Port Arthur-Winnipeg, 1960.
Half Century of the Activity of the Ukrainian Reading Association Prosvita in Winnipeg, compiled by M. I. Mandryka. Winnipeg: 1958.
In the Vineyard of Christ: A Yearbook of the Eparchy of Toronto. Edited by Julian Beskyd. Toronto, 1964.
In Service of Our Homeland: The Ukrainian Women's Organization of Canada — 25 Anniversary 1930-1955. Edited by I. Knysh. Winnipeg, 1955.
Illustrated Calendar of the "Ukrainian Voice" for the Leap Year 1936. Vol. XIX. Winnipeg, 1936.
Illustrated Calendar of the "Ukrainian Voice" for the Year 1940. Vol. XXIII. Winnipeg, 1940.
Istoria Ukr. Instytutu im. Petra Mohyly v Saskatooni /"Twenty-Five Years of the Petro Mohyla Institute in Saskatoon"/, ed. by Julian Stechishen. Winnipeg, 1945.
Jubilee Book Commemorating 75 Anniversary of Ukrainians in Canada, and Canadian Centennial. Montreal, 1967. (Ukrainian-English).
Klynovy Lystok /The Maple Leaf/: *Canadian Almanac.* Winnipeg: St. Raphael's Ukrainian Immigrant Welfare Association, 1929.
Northern Lights: An Almanac in Ukrainian. Compiled and Edited by Yar Slavutych. Vol. I, II, III, Edmonton, 1964, 1965, 1969.

Nove Pole /New Field/: Canadian Almanac 1927. Winnipeg: St. Raphael's Ukrainian Immigrant Welfare Association, 1927.
Novy Shlakh: Yuveleyna Knyha 1930-1955.| Winnipeg, 1956.
Persha Ukrayinska Katolycka Mytropoliya v Kanadi, Winnipeg, 1957.
Propamiatna Knyha Ukrainskoho Domu 1906-1965. Edmonton, 1966.
Propamiatna Knyha Otciv Wasyliyan v Kanadi. Toronto, 1953.
Propamiatna Knyha Poselennia Ukrainskoho Narodu v Kanadi 1891-1941 /"Jubilee Book of the Settlement of Ukrainians in Canada 1891-1941"/, prepared by the Ukrainian Catholic Clergy. Yorkton, 1941.
Providnyk /The Leader/: Illustrated Calendar for Canadian Ukrainians 1930. Winnipeg: St. Raphael's Ukrainian Immigrant Welfare Association, 1930.
Providnyk /The Leader/: Illustrated Calendar for Canadian Ukrainians 1932. Winnipeg: St. Raphael's Ukrainian Immigrant Welfare Association, 1932.
Providnyk /The Leader/: Illustrated Calendar for Canadian Ukrainians 1933. Winnipeg: St. Raphael's Immigrant Welfare Association, 1933.
Providnyk /The Leader/: Canadian Ukrainian Illustrated Calendar 1934. Winnipeg: St. Raphael's Ukrainian Immigrant Welfare Association. 1935.
Providnyk /The Leader/: Canadian Ukrainian Calendar-Almanac 1936. Winnipeg: St. Raphael's Ukrainian Immigrant Welfare Association. 1936.
Salute to Canada 1867-1967. Hamilton: Ukrainian Canadian Committee. Hamilton Branch, 1967.
Sixty Years in Canada 1891-1951. *Jubilee Celebrations,* Toronto — September, 1951.
Smoloskyp Osvity i Zhyttia, Comp. Maria Davydovych, Montreal: Chytalnia "Prosvita", 1963.
A Souvenir of the First Convention of Ukrainian Artists and Writers from Canada, the United States and Western Europe, who met in Toronto July 3, 4, 5, 1954. Toronto, 1954.
Ukrainians in Kenora 1915-1965: *Prosvita Jubilee Book.* Kenora, 1965.
Ukrainska Strilecka Hromada v Kanadi 1928-1938. Saskatoon, 1938.
Yuvileyna knyha Ukraintsiw Katolykiw Saskatchewanu 1905-1955 */Jubilee Book of the Ukrainian Catholics of Saskatchewan* 1905-1955/). Yorkton: Ukrainan Catholic Council of Saskatchewan, 1955.
Yuvileyna knyha z nahody 30-littia dialnosty Zinochoho Tovarystva pry Katedri sv. Ivana v Edmontoni / Thirtieth Anniversary Jubilee Book of the Ukrainian Ladies' Aid of St. John's Ukrainian Orthodox Cathedral in Edmonton/. Edmonton, 1957.
Yuvileyna Knyha Sester Sluzebnyc Presvyatoyi Neporochnoyi Divy Mariyi. Edmonton, 1942.
Yuvileyny Almanakh 1894-1944 */Jubilee Almanac* 1894-1944/, ed. Luka Myshuha. Jersey City, N.J.: Ukrainian National Association, 1944.
Yuvileyny Almanakh dla Vidmichennia 50-littia Pratsi Ukrainskoho Holosu /Jubilee Almanac to Commemorate the Fiftieth Anniversary of the Ukralian Voice 1910-1960/. Winnipeg, 1961.
Yuveleyny Almanakh Ukrainskoi Hreko-Katolyckoi Cerkvy sv. Wolodymyra i Olhy u Winnipegu 1901-1936.
Yuvilayny Kalendar Ukrainskoi Rodyny na rik 1941: 1891-1941 */Jubilee Calendar of the Ukrainian Family for the Year* 1941: 1891-1941/. Mundare, Alta. Basilian Fathers, 1941.

BIBLIOGRAPHY
to the Second Edition

IN UKRAINIAN:
ANTONOVYCH-RUDNYCKA, M., *Daria Nyzankiwska-Snihurowych.* Montreal: ALU.
BAYRAK, MYKHAILO, *Ukrainian War Veteran's Association in Edmonton.* Edmonton: Ukrainian War Veterans' Association. 1978.
BOROWYK, MICHAEL, *The Ukrainian Canadian Press and Its Significant Role in the Ukrainian Minority in Canada.* Munchen: Ukrainian Free University. 1977.
DAWYDOWYCH, MARIA (Ed.), *The Jubilee Book* commemerating the 85th anniversary of the Ukrainian Settlers in Canada, under the title: *Lest The Toil and The Glory of The Pioneers Be Forgotten*, Montreal: The Ukrainian Golden Age Club "Tryzub" 1979.
DIDIUK, W., *XIV LVU National Convention. VIII OZLVU National Convention.* Toronto: LVU — OZLVU General Secretariat. 1978.
DMYTRIW, NESTOR, *Canadian Ruthenia (Traveler's Memoirs).* Second Edition. Winnipeg: UVAN. 1972.
DOMASHOVETS, REV. G., *Historical Sketch of the Ukrainian Evangelical-Baptist Church.* Irvinington-Toronto. 1967.
DOMBROWSKY, ALEXANDER, *Outline of the History of the Ukrainian Evangelical-Reformed Movement.* New York-Toronto: The Ukrainian Evangelical Alliance of N.A. 1979.
DUVAL, PAUL, *Leo Mol.* Winnipeg: Loch Art Gallery. 1982.
HAWRYSH, WASYL, *My Canada and I. Memoirs and Stories of Canadian Ukrainian Pioneers.* Edmonton: Ukrainian News Publishers. 1974.
HAY-HOLOWKO, OLEKSA, *Ukrainian Writers in Canada. Literary-Critical Sketches.* Vol. I. Winnipeg: Society of Volyn. 1980.
IZYK, S. (Ed.), *Jubilee of the 25th Anniversary of the Ukrainian Catholic Metropolitan See of Canada.* Winnipeg: Jubilee Committee. 1981.
KACHOR, ANDRIY, *Men of Ideas and Work.* Winnipeg-Toronto-Cleveland: Bratstwo Maslosojuznykiw. 1974.
KINDRAT, PETER, *Ukrainian Baptist Movement in Canada.* Winnipeg: Popular Printers. 1972.
KLYNOVY, YURIY, *To My Sons and to My Friends — Articles and Essays,* Edmonton-Toronto: Ukrainian Canadian Writers' Association "Slovo", 1981.
KORBAN, SEMEN, *Na dorohakh i zakrutach moho zyttia.* Toronto: Kiev Printers. 1979.
KRAWCHUK, P., *Ukrainian Socialist Movement in Canada. 1907-1918.* Toronto: Kobzar Publishers. 1976.
KRAWCHUK, P., *Ukrainians in the History of Winnipeg.* Toronto: Kobzar Publishers, 1974.

KURDYDYK, ANATOL, *Nowadays Notes.* Winnipeg: Trident Press. 1977.

MARUNCHAK, M. H. (Ed.), *85th Anniversary of Mykyta I. Mandryka. 1886-1971.* Winnipeg: Published by the Celebration Committee. 1973.

MARUNCHAK, M. H., *History of Ukrainians in Canada.* Volume II. Winnipeg: UVAN. 1974.

MARUNCHAK, M. H., *Illia Kiriak and His Works.* Winnipeg: UVAN. 1973.

MARUNCHAK, M. H., *Metropolitan Andrey Sheptytsky in the West, 1920-1923.* Winnipeg: National Council of Ukrainian Organizations for the Patriarchate of the Ukrainian Catholic Church. 1981.

MARUNCHAK, M. H., *Organizational Beginnings of the Ukrainian Catholic Church in Canada and U.S.A.* Winnipeg: Council of Ukrainian Organizations for the Patriarchate of the Ukrainian Catholic Church. 1978.

MARUNCHAK, M. H., *Studies in the History of Ukrainians in Canada.* v. IV. Winnipeg: UVAN. 1970-1972.

MARUNCHAK, M. H., *Studies in the History of Ukrainians in Canada.* v. V. Winnipeg: UVAN. 1973-1980.

MARUNCHAK, M. H., *Ukrainians in U.S.S.R. Beyond the Borders of Ukrainian SSR.* Winnipeg: UVAN. 1974.

OLESKOW, JOSEPH (OLESKIW, OSYP), *Free Lands* (Second Edition). Winnipeg: UVAN. 1975.

ONUFRIJCHUK, F. F., *A Museum Collection of Ukrainian Treasures.* Yorkton: Redeemers' Voice Press. 1981.

PANCHUK, John, *The First Ukrainian Church in Canada.* Winnipeg: Trident Press, 1974.

PAWLYSHYN, MARIA (Ed.), *Song Book for Schools — For Youth in the Ukrainian Community Schools, For the Purpose of Preserving the Ukrainian Cultural Heritage.* Toronto: Ukrainian Canadian Music Committee. 1977-1979.

PETROWSKY, MICHAEL, *Dreams Sprinkled with Tears. Short Stories of Ukrainian Pioneer and Immigrant Life in Canada.* Winnipeg-Toronto: Published by the Author. 1973.

PROKOP, DMYTRO, *A Pioneer Teachers' Memoirs.* Winnipeg: Trident Press. 1979.

RAKHMANNY, ROMAN, *Self-Determination of Christian Ukraine.* Toronto: New Pathway. 1977.

SAMCHUK, ULAS, *In the Footsteps of the Pioneers. Saga of Ukrainian America.* New Jersey: Svoboda Press. 1978.

SHARIK, MICHAEL, *50 Year's Perspective. Memoirs, Book I.* Toronto: Toronto Free Press Publications. 1969.

SHARIK, MICHAEL, *Thorny Trails across Canada. Memoirs "50 Year's Perspective" Book II.* Toronto: Toronto Free Press Publications. 1971.

SKLEPOWICH, W. T., *The Call of the Mountains, A Memorial to the Ukrainian Pioneers.* Winnipeg: Trident Press. 1975.

SKLEPOWICH, W. T., *The Glowing Embers. (Historical Novel).* Winnipeg: Trident Press Ltd. 1979.

SLAVUTYCH, YAR (Ed.), *An Anthology of Ukrainian Poetry in Canada, 1893-1973.* Edmonton: The Ukrainian Writers' Association in Canada "Slovo". 1975.

SLAVUTYCH, YAR (Ed.), *Collected Papers on Ukrainian Settlers in Western Canada.* Edmonton: The Shevchenko Scientific Society in Canada. 1973.

SLAVUTYCH, YAR (Ed.), *Northern Lights. Vol. V. An Almanac in Ukrainian.* Edmonton: Slavuta Publishers. 1971.
SOSNOWSKY, MICHAEL, *Between Optimism and Pessimism. Selected Articles and Essays 1968-1975.* New York — Toronto: Kiev Printers, Toronto. 1979.
UDOD, HRYHORY, *Julian W. Stechishin — His Life and Work.* Saskatoon: Mohyla Institute. 1978.
WOLYNIAK, PETRO, *Speaking Frankly. A Collection of Essays and Short Stories.* Toronto: Published by "Nowi Dni" Co. Ltd. 1975.
WOYCENKO, OLHA, *The Annals of Ukrainian Life in Canada. Vol. V.* Winnipeg: Trident Press, Ltd. 1973.
WYNNYCKA, JAROSLAWA, *Outline of History of Ukrainian Catholic Women's League of Canada. Eparchy of Toronto. 1945-1975.* Toronto: "New Horizons", Group of W.C.W.L. 1975.
YAREMENKO, SERHIY, *Saskatchewanka and Other Songs.* Edmonton: Slavuta. 1977.
YOPYK, H. A., *Ukrainian Canadian Archives and Museum of Alberta: Artifacts of Ukrainian Pioneers of Alberta.* Edmonton: UCAMA, 1982.
ZELSKA, IVANNA, *Ukrainian "Vyshyvka."* Winnipeg-Toronto. 1978-1981.
_____ *A Collection of Works of the Youth Section of the Association of Ukrainian Journalists of Canada.* Toronto: Association of Ukrainian Journalists of Canada. 1973.
_____ *Eleventh Congress of Ukrainian Canadians.* Winnipeg: Ukrainian Canadian Committee. 1974.
_____ *Funeral Memorial of Metropolitan Ilarion.* Winnipeg: The Consistory of the Ukrainian Greek-Orthodox Church. 1973.
_____ *Golden Jubilee Book. USH — 1938-1978. For Virtue, Glory and Nation 1928-1978.* Toronto: New Pathway & Harmony Printing. 1978.
_____ *Our Theatre, A Collection of Historical Essays and Memoirs. 1915-1975, Vol. I.* New York — Paris — Sidney — Toronto: Association of Ukrainian Theatre — Artists. 1975.
_____ *Tenth Congress of Ukrainian Canadians.* Winnipeg: The Ukrainian Canadian Committee. 1971.
_____ *Twelfth Congress of Ukrainian Canadians.* Winnipeg: Ukrainian Canadian Committee. 1977.
_____ *Twentieth Anniversary of the Canadian League for the Liberation of Ukraine in Saskatoon, 1951-1971.* Saskatoon: 1971.
_____ *Ukrainian Community Library Memory Book of Ukrainians in B.C. — 50th Anniversary — 1928-1978.* Vancouver, B.C.: 1978
_____ *Twenty-Five Years of Devoted Services — An Outline of the Combined Efforts of the Women's Councils of the Ukrainian Canadian Committee for the Years 1944-1969.* Winnipeg: The National Women's Council of UCC. 1971.

IN ENGLISH
BODRUG, JOHN, *Independent Orthodox Church.* Toronto: Ukrainian Canadian Research Foundation. 1980.
BOROWSKY, M. L. *Plants from Ukraine in Canada.* Winnipeg: Ukrainian Free Academy of Sciences. 1975.

BUK, NICHOLAS & URCHAK, STEPHEN, *The History of Two Hills (including Lanuke District).* Edmonton: 1980.

CLEMENT, W., *The Canadian Corporate Elite.* Toronto: McClelland and Stewart Ltd. 1975.

DARCSVICH, WILLIAM, Editor & YUZYK, PAUL, Associate Editor. *A Statistical Compendium on the Ukrainians in Canada 1891-1976.* Edmonton: University of Alberta Press, 1977. (Mimeographed Edition). Second Edition by University of Ottawa Press, Ottawa: 1980.

DOMBROWSKY, ALEXANDER, *Outline of the History of the Ukrainian Evangelical-Reformed Movement.* New York-Toronto: Ukrainian Evangelical Alliance of North America. 1979.

EWANCHUK, MICHAEL, *Pioneer Profiles: Ukrainian Settlers in Manitoba.* Winnipeg-Steinbach: Published by the Author. 1982.

EWANCHUK, MICHAEL, *Spruce, Swamp and Stone: A History of the Pioneer Ukrainian Settlements in the Gimli Area.* Steinbach: Derksen Printers. 1977.

EWANCHUK, MICHAEL, *Vita: A Ukrainian Community — Book One: Its Background and Beginning — Book Two: Making Progress — Book Three: Vita Today.* Vita, Manitoba: 1977. Published by the Boundary School Division under auspices of the Department of Education.

GREGOROVICH, ANDREW, *Chronology of Ukrainian Canadian History.* Toronto: Ukrainian Canadian Committee. 1974.

GULY, CHRIS, *A Living Monument: 75 Year History of Immaculate Heart of Mary. (formerly St. Nicholas School). 1905-1980.* Winnipeg: Jubilee Committee. 1980.

HLYNKA, ISYDORE, *The Other Canadians.* Winnipeg: Trident Press. 1981.

HUMENIUK, PETER, *Hardships and Progress of Ukrainian Pioneers. Memoirs from Stuartburn Colony and other Points.* Published by Peter Humeniuk. Steinbach: Derksen Printers. 1977.

ISAJIW, WSEVOLOD (Ed.), *Identities: The Impact of Ethnicity of Canadian Society.* Toronto: 1977.

ISAJIW, WSEVOLOD (Ed.), *Ukrainians in American and Canadian Society. Contribution to the Sociology of Ethnic Groups.* Jersey City; N.J.: M.P. Kots Publishing. 1976.

JANIS, JOANNA & KOSTASH, WILLIAM (Eds.), *History of Ukrainian Woman's Association of Canada of St. John's Cathedral — 1926-1976.* Winnipeg: 1979.

KAYE, VLADIMR, J., *Dictionary of Ukrainian Canadian Biography Pioneer Settlers of Manitoba, 1891-1900.* Toronto: Ukrainian Canadian Research Foundation. 1975.

KEYWAN, ZONIA & COLES, MARTIN, *Greater than Kings. Ukrainian Pioneer Settlement in Canada.* Montreal: Harvest House. 1977.

KLYMASZ, ROBERT B., *An Introduction to the Ukrainian-Canadian Immigrant Folksong Cycle. The National Museums of Canada.* Bulletin No. 234. 1970.

KOLASKY, JOHN, *The Shattered Illusion. The History of Ukrainian Pro-Communist Organizations in Canada.* Toronto: Peter Martin Associates Limited. 1979.

KOSTASH, MYRNA, *All of Baba's Children.* Edmonton, Alberta: Hurtig Publishers. 1977.

KURELEK, WILLIAM, *The Ukrainian Pioneers.* Published: Niagara Falls Art Gallery. Kurelek Art Collection. 1980.

LOEB, LOUISA (Ed.), *Dawn Singing Centuries: Folk Literature of Ukraine: Translated by Florence Randal Livesay.* Winnipeg: Hyperion Press Ltd. 1981.

LOZINSKY, JOSEPH, *The First Twenty-Five: A History of the Parish of S. S. Peter and Paul Ukrainian Catholic Church, Saskatoon, Saskatchewan. On the Occasion of its Silver Jubilee.* Saskatoon: S. S. Peter and Paul Ukrainian Catholic Church, 1954-1979.

LUCIUK, LUBOMYR, Y., *Ukrainians in the Making: Their Kingston Story.* Kingston, Ontario: Limestone Press. 1980.

LUPUL, MANOLY R. (Ed.), *Ukrainian Canadians, Multiculturalism and Separatism: An Assessment.* Edmonton: The University of Alberta Press. 1978.

MAGOCSI, PAUL R. (Ed.), *The Ukrainian Experience in the United States — A Symposium.* Cambridge, Massachusetts: Harvard Ukrainian Research Institute. 1979.

MALYCKY, ALEXANDER (Ed.), *Canadian Ethnic Studies. Vol. II, No. 1.* Calgary: The University of Calgary. 1970.

MARUNCHAK, M. H. (Ed.), *Two Documents of the Ukrainian Catholic Church, 1911-1976.* Winnipeg: National Council of Ukrainian Organizations for the Patriarchate of the Ukrainian Catholic Church. 1977.

PETRYSHYN, W. R. (Ed.), *Changing Realities: Social Trends Among Ukrainian Canadians.* Edmonton: Canadian Institute of Ukrainian Studies. 1980.

PINIUTA, HARRY, *Land of Pain — Land of Promise. First Personal Accounts by Ukrainian Pioneers, 1891-1914.* Saskatoon: Western Producer Prairie Books, 1978.

POTICHNYJ, PETER J. (Ed.), *Ukraine in the Seventies.* Oakville, Ontario: Mosaic Press. 1975.

POTICHNYJ, PETER J. (Ed.), *Poland and Ukraine, Past and Present.* Edmonton-Toronto: The Canadian Institute of Ukrainian Studies. 1980.

POTREBENKO, HELEN, *No Streets of Gold: A Social History of Ukrainians in Alberta.* Vancouver: New Star Books. 1977.

PRAXIMIDIS, MARY, *Look Who's Coming. The Wachna Story.* Illustrated by William Kurelek. Oshawa: Marcle Press Limited. 1976.

RAKHMANNY, ROMAN, *In Defence of the Ukrainian Cause.* North Quincy, Massachusets: The Christopher Public House. 1979.

SAWYCKY, ROMAN, *Ukrainian Film Guide.* Cranford, New Jersey: "The Keys" Publishing Association. 1980.

STEFANYK, YURIY (Ed.), *Our Heritage.* (Alberta Heritage Learning Resources Project). Edmonton: The Alberta Heritage Savings Trust Fund. 1979.

STONE, LEROY O. *"Occupational Composition of Canadian Migration".* Ottawa: Statistics Canada. 1972.

STONE, LEROY O. *The Frequency of Geographic Mobility in the Population of Canada.* Ottawa: Statistics Canada. 1972.

SWENARCHUK, JANET (GENIA) (Ed.), *From Dreams to Reality: A History of the Ukrainian Senior Citizens of Regina and District, 1896-1976.* Winnipeg: 1977.

SWITUCHA, N. M., *Comecon's Mineral Development Potential and Its Implications for Canada.* Ottawa: Department of Energy, Mines and Resources. 1979.
SWYRIPA, FRANCES, *Ukrainian Canadians. A Survey of their Portrayal in English-Language.* Edmonton: The University of Alberta Press. 1978.
TARNAWECKY, IRAIDA, *East Slavic Cyrillica in Canadian Repositories.* Winnipeg: Volyn Society. 1982.
TRUDEAU, PIERRE ELLIOTT, *A Time for Action toward the Renewal of the Canadian Federation.* Ottawa: Minister of Supply and Services. 1978.
YASEGN, MARIA, *"Education" at the University of British Columbia.* Vancouver: Lithography in Canada. 1977.
YUZYK, PAUL, *For a Better Canada. A Collection of selected speeches delivered in the Senate of Canada, at Banquets and Conferences in various centres across Canada.* Toronto: Ukrainian National Association, Inc. 1973.
YUZYK, PAUL, *The Ukrainian Greek Orthodox Church of Canada.* Ottawa: University of Ottawa Press. 1981.
ZAPORZAN, SHIRLEY and KLYMASH, ROBERT B., *Film and the Ukrainians in Canada 1921-1980,* A Filmography Index of Film Titles and Bibliography with Supplementary Apendices, Edmonton: Canadian Institute of Ukrainian Studies, University of Alberta, 1982.
——— *Emeralds Past in Prose, Poetry and Pictures. A History of Emerald Municipality #277 (including Daystar Reserve . . . Halicz . . . Wishart) and compiled and published by the Wishard-Bankend Historical Society.* Printed by the Inter-Collegiate Press. 1980.
——— *Memorial Souvenir Book. Royal Canadian Legion-Ukrainian Canadian Veterans. Mazeppa Branch — No. 183.* Montreal: 1979.
——— *Multiculturalism and Education in Manitoba.* Winnipeg: The Manitoba Teachers' Society. 1980.
——— *The Multilingual Press in Manitoba.* Winnipeg, Manitoba: Published by Canada Press Club. 1974.
——— *Springfield. 1st Rural Municipality in Manitoba, 1873-1973.* Altona: Dugald Women's Institute, Dugald, Manitoba. 1974.
——— *Ukrainian National Home, Vita, Manitoba. 60th Anniversary Year Book, 1919-1979.* Vita-Winnipeg: Derksen Printers, Steinbach. 1979.
——— *The Ukrainian Pioneers in Alberta, Canada. Vol. I.* Edmonton: Alberta Printing Co. 1975.
——— *Ukrainians in Alberta, Volume II.* Edmonton: Ukrainian Pioneers' Association of Alberta. 1981.
——— *Ukrainian Week in Ottawa. 30.1 — 8.2. 1976.* Ottawa: Ukrainian Canadian Committee. 1976.

IN ENGLISH AND UKRAINIAN
BARAN, ANNA MARIA & PASTERSHANK, CHRISTINE T., *Ukrainian Catholic Churches of Saskatchewan.* Saskatoon: Modern Press. 1977.
BOGDAN, F., *Dictionary of Ukrainian Surnames in Canada.* Winnipeg-Vancouver: Onomastic Commission of UVAN, Canadian Institute of Onomastic Sciences. 1974.
GERUS, O. W., BARAN, A., ROZUMNYJ, J., *The Jubilee Collections of The Ukrainian Free Academy of Sciences in Canada.* Winnipeg: UVAN. 1976.

MARUNCHAK, M. H., *Forty Years of the Ukrainian Canadian Committee, 1940-1980.* Winnipeg: UCC Headquarters. 1981. (Mimiographed).
MARUNCHAK, M. H., *On the 80 Anniversary of Fr. Nestor Dmytriw's Sojourn in Canada.* New Jersey: Ukrainian National Association. 1977.
SKOVORODKO, S. & ULANIUK, P., *History of Ukrainian Evangelical-Baptist Church in Saskatoon on occasion of 50th Anniversary.* Saskatoon: Ukrainian Evangelical-Baptist Church. 1979.
SEVENTEENTH ANNUAL REPORT, Winnipeg: Ukrainian Canadian Foundation of Taras Shevchenko. 1980.

CONTENTS

	Page
Foreword to the First Edition by Dr. V. J. Kaye	7-10
Publisher's Introduction to the Second Edition	11-12
Acknowledgements — to the First Edition	
Acknowledgements — to the Second Edition	13-14

THE FIRST ERA — PIONEER ERA

Social and Political Factors in Ukrainian Immigration to Canada	17
The Beginning of Ukrainian Immigration and the Year 1891	23
Dr. O. Oleskiw, Promoter of Mass Movement of Ukrainian Settlers to Canada	28
The Year 1896	36
The Years of Intensive Immigration (1897-1914)	41
Geographic Distribution of Ukrainian Settlements in Pioneer Days	66
Canadian West at the End of 19th Century	68
Welcome New-Comers and Racial Prejudice	74
First Steps in Homeland and Canada	78
Homesteaders and Labourers	92
The Religious Question	99
Public School Education	114
Private School System of Education	151
Bursas and Institutions	154
Cultural Educational Work	161-218

First Sprouts—Manitoba 162, *Alberta* 167, *Saskatchewan* 173, *The Faraway West* 176, *Eastern Canada* 180, *Ontario* 211

Participation in Municipal and Political Life	219
The First Businessmen and Professionals	234
The Press	238-296

U.S.A.: Svoboda, 238, *Manitoba: Canadian Farmer* 240, *Word* 262, *Morning (Dawn)* 263, *The Red Banner* 265, *The Working People* 266, *The Ukrainian Voice* 267, *Canadian Ruthenian* 270; *Alberta: The New Society* 272, *News* 272, *The Canadian* 275, *The Ukrainian Evangelist* 275, *Progress* 275; *Saskatchewan: The New Country* 276, *Winnipeg: Canada* 278, *Canadian News* 280, *Magazines,* 280, *Publications for Youth* 282; *Eastern Canada: Witness of the Truth* 283, *The Star* 284, *The Workers' Word* 285, *Humorous Newspapers* 286, *The Bilingual Press* 287, *The Russophile Press* 288, *The New Movement* 295, *The Ukrainian Labor News* 295

Literature of the Pioneers	297-308

Poetic Folklore 297, *Prose* 303

The First Book Editions, Book Stores and Publishing Establishments	309
Three Basic Characteristics of the Ukrainian Canadian Entity in the Pioneer Era and the Role of the Press	312
Culture Ties with Motherland	320
Ukrainian Participation in Military Formations of the First World War	324
Aid to the Cause of the Ukraine's Liberation	328

UKRAINIAN CANADIANS: A HISTORY

Relations with Federal Government and Ukrainian Canadian Citizens Committee 331
Ukrainian National Council 335
Struggle for Consummation of Ukrainian Entity 338

II

THE SECOND ERA

ERA OF DEVELOPMENTAL PROCESSES

Introduction 349
Migration and Immigration 351
Political Situation in Ukraine and the Inflow of the New Immigration 357
St. Raphael's Ukrainian Immigrants Welfare Association of Canada 365
Ukrainian Immigration and Colonization Bureau, and Other Immigration Foundations 369
To the Characteristics of Second Immigration 371
Aid to the Homeland Unites Ukrainians Religiously and Politically .. 374
Canadian Sitch Organization 393
Ukrainian Self-Reliance League 395
Ukrainian War Veterans Association—Ukrainian National Federation 398
Ukrainian Catholic Brotherhood 401
Ukrainian Labour and Farmers' Temple Association 403
Ukrainian Workers' League (U.W.L.) 407
The Ukrainian Labour Association 409
League of British Ukrainians 410

Women's Organizations 411-417

Ukrainian Women's Association of Canada 412, *The Ukrainian Women's Organization* 413, *The Ukrainian Catholic Women's League* 415, *Women's Council* 416

Youth Organizations 417-421

Canadian Ukrainian Youth Association 418, *Ukrainian National Youth Federation* 419, *Ukrainian Catholic Youth* 419, *Student Organizations* 419

Mutual Benefit Associations 421
Local Organizations 422
Third Stage 424
Cooperative Movement 429
Agricultural Achievement 431
Integration in the Political Sphere 434
Schools and the Teaching Staff 441
Cultural Identification 448

Religious Matters 460-469

Ukrainian Catholic Church (Ruthenian Greek Catholic Church) 461, *The Basilian Order* 462, *Sister Servants* 462, *Redemptorist Fathers* 464, *Order of Oblate Fathers* 464, *Ukrainian Greek Orthodox Church* 465, *Protestant Churches* 467

CONTENTS

The Press 470-498

> Winnipeg: Canadian Farmer 472, Canadian Morning 472, National Press 473, The Canadian Sitch 475, Truth & Liberty 475, Veterans News 476, The Truth 476, Specific Publications 477, Political & Literary Publications 477, Economic Publications 478, Youth Publications 479, Humour & Satire 480, The Anglo-Ukrainian Press 481, Other Publications 482. Western Canada: 484, Alberta Publications 487, Other Alberta Publications 487, Saskatchewan 488, Yorkton 488, Canora 489. Eastern Canada: 489, Toronto 489, Ottawa, Montreal and Oshawa 492. Moscophile Press 493, The Communist Press 494

Literature 499-536

> Three National Groups in Poetry and Prose 499, The Marxist Group 533, The Anglo-Saxon Group 535

The Living Ties with the Land of Their Fathers 537
The Developmental Processes of National Consummation 544
Ukrainian National Council 545
Events in Europe Lead to United Action 545

III

THE THIRD ERA — ERA OF CONSUMMATION

Introduction 557
Ukrainian Efforts in the Second World War 558
Activities of Ukrainian-Canadians in the Immigration of Displaced Persons to Canada 561
Ukrainian Canadian Relief Fund 564
Mission of Ukrainian Canadian Relief Fund in the British Zone in Germany 566
Social Structure of Third Immigration 568
Distribution of Ukrainians in Third Period 572
Achievements and Integration 577
Cooperative Credit Movement 582

The Church Life 582-592

> Ukrainian Catholic Church (U.C.C.) 585, The Ukrainian Greek Orthodox Church (U.G.O.C.) 589, The Ukrainian Evangelical Alliance (U.E.A.) 591, The Ukrainian Evangelical Baptist Alliance (U.E.B.-A.) 592

Ramification and Co-ordination of Community Life 593-608

> The Ukrainian Canadian Veterans' Association 593, New Immigration merges with Community Life 595, Learned Societies Support the cause of U.C.C. 596, War Veterans' Organization 598, Ukrainian Canadian Youth Council 599, Ukrainian Canadian Committee—Women's Council 601, Dominion-Wide Community Organizations 602, Organizations Outside the System 608

Ukrainian Language in Public Schools and Universities 625-631
> Saskatchewan 626, Alberta 626, Manitoba 627, Private Schools 628

Press 632-653

> *The General Community Press*: *Weeklies* 632, *Toronto and the East* 634, *Winnipeg — and the West* 640. *The Religious Press*: *The Catholic Press* 643, *The Orthodox Press* 646, *The Protestant or Evangelival Press* 646, *The Pro-Communist Press* 649, *Characteristics of the Press* 651

Radio, Television and Film 654
Scholars in Various Fields 657
Poets and Writers 664
Creative Artists 671
Music and Choral Art 675
Theatre and Ballet 677
Taras Shevchenko Foundation 680

Horizontal and Vertical Integration 683-710

> *Manitoba* 685, *Alberta* 687, *Saskatchewan* 688, *Ontario* 706, *Members of Federal Parliament* 707, *Senate, Judicial, and Other Appointments* 708

Pan-American Ukrainian Conference 711
Ukrainian Canadians Initiate the World Congress of Free Ukrainians 713
Assimilating Processes 716

DECADE OF MULTICULTURALISM

A Decade of Development of Constitutional Grounds for Multicultural Canada 725
Expansion of Ukrainian Studies Courses 732-742
> *The First All-Canadian Conference on the Ukrainian Studies Courses, 732; Role of the Federation of Ukrainian Professional and Businessmen's Clubs in the Development of Ukrainian Studies, 733; Canadian Institute of Ukrainian Studies and Canadian Foundation for Ukrainian Studies, 735; Chair of Ukrainian Studies at the University of Toronto, 737; St. Andrew's College: The Centre for Ukrainian Canadian Studies at the University of Manitoba, 738; New Establishments and Institutions — Past and Present, 739.*

School Question in the Period of Multiculturalism 743-754
> *Alberta, 743; Manitoba, 745; Saskatchewan, 747; Ontario, 748; Ridna Shkola in the Prairie Provinces, 750; British Columbia, 753; Quebec, 753.*

New Talents in Creative Arts 756
Association of Artists and Art Galleries 761
Ukrainian Canadian Writers' Association 763-766
> *Slovo, 763; Association of the Ukrainian Cultural Workers (A.U.C.W.), 764; "Kozub" Ukrainian Arts Society, 765; Literary Artists in English and others, 765.*

Press and Association of Ukrainian Journalists 767
Stage and Related Professions 772
Radio, Television and Film in the Era of Multiculturalism 780-787
> *Radio, 780; Television, 782; Films, 783.*

CONTENTS

Ukrainian Canadian Committee and Its Organizations 805-819
  Ukrainian Catholic Brotherhood of Canada, 806; Ukrainian Self-Reliance League (U.S.R.L.), 807; Ukrainian National Federation, 808; The Canadian League for the Liberation of Ukraine (C.L.L.U.), 809; Ukrainian Canadian Veteran's Association (U.C.V.A.), 811; Ukrainian Canadian Professional and Business Federation (U.C.P.B.F.), 811; Ukrainian Canadian Committee Women's Council (U.C.C.W.C.), 814; Ukrainian Canadian Foundation of Taras Shevchenko, 814; Youth Organizations at the Executive of UCC, 814; Ukrainian Canadian University Students' Union (SUSK), 814; Plast, 815; Ukrainian Democratic Youth Association (ODUM), 816; Charitable Organizations and Mutual Benefit Associations, 816; Ukrainian Canadian Committee and World Congress of Free Ukrainians, 817; Others outside UCC Systems, 818.
Ukrainian Churches: Symbol of Cultural and
  Religious Identity 820-825
  Ukrainian Catholic Church (UCC), 820; Ukrainian Greek-Orthodox Church (UGOC), 822; Evangelical Churches, 824.
Museums, Monuments, Foundations, Funds 826
The Legacy of Written Words 829
Integration Processes 851-867
  Co-operative Movement in the Seventies, 851; Integration in the Economic Field, 856; Integration in the Public Field, 862: Manitoba and Alberta, 862; Saskatchewan, 864; Ontario, 865; House of Commons, 865; Senate, 867.
Summary of Social Processes in Ukrainian Community
  during the Decade of Multiculturalism 868
Ideological Principles 873

Supplement 877

Appendix 879

Illustrations: THE FIRST ERA .... Between Pages 47-62
                                                            124-140
                                                            181-208
                                                            241-260
             THE SECOND ERA .... Between Pages 377-392
                                                            505-528
             THE THIRD ERA .... Between Pages 609-624
                                                            689-704
             DECADE OF MULTICULTURALISM
                                           Between Pages 788-804
                                                            833-850

Index on page 970

Index 855

Subject Index 885
Personal Names 887
Church, Parishes, Church Organizations 920
Lay Organizations and Co-operatives 923
Schools, Education (Institutes, Bursas, Academies, etc.) 934
Printed Word (Print, Bindery, Shops, Publications) 936
Geographic Names of Countries, Places, etc. 943
Bibliography to the First Edition 949
Bibliography to the Second Edition 957

40.00